SCHOOL AND SOCIETY

EDITED BY J. McKEEN CATTELL

VOLUME XXVIII
JULY-DECEMBER, 1928

WITH WHICH HAS BEEN COMBINED THE

EDUCATIONAL REVIEW

Edited by WILLIAM McANDREW

NEW YORK
THE SCIENCE PRESS
1929

THE SCIENCE PRESS PRINTING COMPANY
LANCASTER, PA.

CONTENTS AND INDEX

VOLUME XXVIII—JULY-DECEMBER, 1928

NAMES OF CONTRIBUTORS ARE PRINTED IN SMALL CAPITALS

THE PAGE NUMBERS OF ENTRIES FROM JUNE, SEPTEMBER AND OCTOBER NUMBERS OF THE *Educational Review* ARE PRECEDED BY E. R.

Accrediting, Standards of, P. P. BOYD, 414
ADAIR, C. S., Presidential Address, National Education Association, 1
Administration, G. D. STRAYER, 82; School, Chicago's, 794
Administrative Relations in Colleges, F. L. MCVEY, 705
Adult Education, P. N. YOUTZ, 91; in England, 535; The Drama in, 421
Adults, Educated, Education for, 207
Agassiz, Louis, H. A. WARREN, 442
Agricultural Extension Workers, 648
Alaskan Natives, Industrial Training for, 39
Alderman, President, Testimonial to, 753
Algebraization of Mathematics, G. A. MILLER, 363
Alien Schools, Adult, in New York City, 11
Allegany School of Natural History, 106
Almack, J., and A. Lang, "The Beginning Teacher," 563
American Museum of Natural History, Children's Fair, 510
Amherst College, Scholastic Aptitude Tests, C. H. TOLL, 524
ANDREWS, B. R., Art Museum and University, 144
Argentine North American Institute, 291
ARROWOOD, C. F., Teaching Profession, 177; The Backwoods School, 373
Art, Museum and University, B. R. ANDREWS, 144; in Schools, 390; *Digest*, 567; Education, R. F. BACH, 595
Arts, Meaning and Value of, R. M. LOVETT, 16

Baccalaureate, Meaning of, E. O. SISSON, 57
BACH, R. F., Art Education, 595
Bachelor, of Arts, C. H. OLDFATHER, 111; of Citizenship, J. T. WILLIAMS, 383
Backwoods School, C. F. ARROWOOD, 373
BAKER, E. N., "Haint Eney Place," 547
BAKER, F. M., Whither, Busy Teacher?, E. R., 39
BALDWIN, R. D., Rural Schools, 341
BARGER, J. W., The Rural Community Center, 727
Behavior Problem Children, W. C. RYAN, JR., 208
Benet, S. V., John Brown's Body, 568
Bequests of Payne Whitney, 679
Berea College, The Work of, 614
Bibliography, Student, E. P. KIMBALL, 174
Billings, S., Talks to Boys, 697
Binghamton, The Best of, W. MCANDREW, E. R., 91
BLACKIE, J. H., Reviewed by a Briton, E. R., 162
BLOOMFIELD, M., Vocational Guidance, 128
BOARDMAN, M. T., Service of Presidents, 429
Books, Better, W. MCANDREW, E. R., 21; E. R., 69; E. R., 136; 558; 696; Educational, 1928, J. L. WHEELER, 801
Bookstores in College Towns, S. S. SWARTLEY, 314
Boston Public Schools, 201, 326
BOWDEN, A. O., Enlightenment and Emotivation, 435
BOWYER, H., Two Californias Get Together, 453
BOYD, P. P., Standards of Accrediting, 414
British, Educational Matters, W. RICE, E. R., 12; Assoc. for the Advancement of Science, Address of the President of Section L., C. NORWOOD, 281, 317; Committee on School Science, 418; Prime Minister on Progress in Education, 475
Briton, Reviewed by a, J. H. BLACKIE, E. R., 162
BROOKS, R. S., The Perfect Small House, 46
BROOM, M. E., and G. F. FOX, Predicting Success 689
Brown University, Conditions at, 796
Budget of the New York City Schools, 201, 267
Buildings, School, for New York City, 784
Bureau of Education, 750
Burks, Senator, Defection of, L. B. EVERETT, E. R., 62
BURR, A. W., Who's Who in our Classes?, 274
Business, Education, 104; Files Objections, D. H. PIERCE, E. R., 176; Leaders, 649
BYERS, N. E., the American College, 673

California, University of, Summer Session, 41; Museum of Anthropology and the School Children, 447; at Los Angeles, 295; 584; Southern Univ. of, 719
Californias, Two, Get Together, H. BOWYER, 453
Cambridge, University of, Offer to, 492
Canada, Teaching of Modern Languages in, 263
Canadian Traveling School, 292
Carnegie Foundation, Report of President, 752
CARROLL, R. P., What is Intelligence?, 792
CHAMBERS, M. M., The Junior College, 519
CHAMPLIN, C. D., Using What We have, 656
Chapel, Compulsory, W. A. HARPER, 627
CHAPMAN, H. B., Research in Education, 559
Character, Building, H. S. TUTTLE, 300
Chicago, Schools, Superintendency, 231; Appointments in, 327; Finances of, 720; Administration, 794; Growth of Child Welfare in, 419; Univ. of, Dormitories, 782
Child, Exploiting the, H. A. POTAMKIN, E. R., 189; Welfare, Congress, 168, 290; in Chicago, Growth of, 419; Study Assoc. of America, 391; Research Center, Washington, 493; Health Conferences, 507
Children's Bureau, U. S. Dept. of Labor, 781
Chile, Secondary School Reforms, R. S., 361
China, Education in, 430
Chinese, Schools, Financial Difficulties, 323; Exclusion from Mississippi Schools, 388
Citizenship Training, A. G. CRANE, 34
Clark University, The Situation at, 50
CLARK, H. F., The Schools of Russia, E. R., 96

Cobb, S., The New Leaven, 702
Coffman, L. D., The University and the Times, 530
College, Policies, 19; Survey of United Lutheran Church, 72; High-school Seniors, C. D. Pierson and C. H. Nettels, 215; The Large *vs.* the Small, J. M. Stalnaker and H. H. Remmers, 302; Year, 365; Teaching, Defects and Difficulties in, C. C. Crawford, 497; of Education, G. R. Pease, 576; American, N. E. Byers, 673
Colleges, American in Foreign Countries, 8; and Secondary Schools of the Middle States and Maryland, Assoc. of, R. Walters, 827
Columbia, University, Summer Sessions of, 267; Teachers at the Summer Session, A. M. Palmer, 332; College, The Curriculum of, 460
Commercial, Teacher Training, 507; Occupation Surveys, 817
Commins, W. D., Original Differences, 488; Sex Differences, 599
Community Organization, W. W. Whitehouse, 467
Contests, Academic, C. E. Seashore, 114
Cooperation, World-Wide among Educators, C. Morley, E. R., 186
Cooperative Courses, W. H. Timbie, 709
Cornell, Univ. of, Summer School of Agriculture, 41; Appropriations for Research, 583; Report of the Comptroller, 751
Corya, F., Bust of Professor Dewey, 684
Counts, G. S., School and Society in Chicago, J. F. Reigart, 763
Courtis, S. A., Effect of Teaching, 52, 84
Cowen, P. A., A Futuristic Painting of Higher Education, 490
Cox, P. W. L., The Serious Student in Civilization, 502
Crabtree, J. W., Work of Nat. Educ. Assoc., 20
Crane, A. G., Citizenship Training, 34
Crawford, C. C., Thesis Writing and Research, 426; Defects and Difficulties in College Teaching, 497; Research in Education, 698
Criminology, in Russia, E. A. Stein, 789
Curriculum, of the College of the City of New York, 420; of Columbia College, 460; Research, E. L. Thorndike, 569

Dana, J. C., What is Education?, 238
Davis, B. E., Group Insurance, 682
Davis, H. H., Corporal Punishment and Suspension, 632
Deaf, Higher Education of, in England, 7
Dean of Men, University, H. E. Stone, 347
Debating in Our High Schools, H. A. White, 660
Degree in Education, at Stanford Univ., 9
Dewey, Professor, Bust of, F. Corya, 684; W. H. Kilpatrick, 778
Differences, Original, W. D. Commins, 488
Diploma, An Enriched, H. S. Tuttle, 98
Diplomas, in Erewhon, A. D. Weeks, 364
Discussion, 18, 49, 78, 114, 142, 177, 205, 238, 274, 302, 333, 363, 396, 428, 456, 488, 519, 546, 590, 626, 656, 682, 728, 759, 792, 823
Douglass, H. R., Teaching Effectiveness, 192
Doyle, H. G., Censorship of Publications, 78

East, Educational Dawn in, 762; Near, Education in, 825
Eaton, A. G., Japanese Education, 395
Economy, Poor, 459
Edison, Mr., Congressional Medal, 510
EDITORS, NEWSPAPER, A Review of the Views of Laymen, E. R., 10; E. R., 88; E. R., 148
Education, What is?, J. C. Dana, 238; Report of U. S. Commissioner of, 826
Educational, Events, 7, 37, 69, 101, 134, 166, 197, 227, 262, 290, 322, 350, 386, 417, 444, 474, 505, 535, 580, 613, 647, 675, 716, 749, 788, 815; Notes and News, 12, 42, 75, 107, 139, 171, 203, 233, 268, 296, 328, 355, 391, 422, 448, 480, 511, 540, 585, 618, 652, 680, 721, 754, 785, 819; Research and Statistics, 23, 52, 84, 117, 147, 182, 215, 244, 277, 308, 337, 369, 403, 443, 461, 494, 524, 549, 597, 630, 662, 689, 735, 765, 797, 829; *Educational Review*, Story of the, F. P. Graves, 529; and School and Society, 538; and W. McAndrew, 592
Effectiveness, Teaching, H. R. Douglass, 192
Egypt, American Schools in, 306
Elementary School, Pupils, M. J. Nelson, 371; Teachers, Higher Standards for, C. E. Hagie, 824
Elliott, W. Y., The Doctorate at Oxford, 685
Ellis, R. S., Constructing and Scoring Tests, 205
Endowment of Schools and Colleges, 265
Engineering, Building, of Princeton Univ., 617; Students, "Honor," 829
England, and France, Student Exchanges, 167; Education and Industry, 276; Marriage of Women Teachers in, 351; Library School Systems, 444; Scholarships in, 506; Adult Education, 535; Examinations, 647
English, School Ideas, W. McAndrew, 87; Schools, Size of Classes, 580; School Books, 731; Headmasters, Conference of, 816
Enlightenment and Emotivation, A. O. Bowden, 435
Enrolment, of Schools and Colleges, 265; School, 353
Ethics, of Teachers, S. T. Muir, E. R., 179; Code of, 431
Evans, K. E., Vocational Education, 746
Everett, L. B., The Defection of Senator Burks, E. R., 62
Evolution, Teaching of, in Arkansas, 677
Examination, New Type, D. G. Paterson, 369; Board, College Entrance, R. Walters, 687
Examinations, The Curse of, 399
Extension Teaching, J. M. Maurer, 308
Eye Strain, E. B. Notson, 760
Eyesight of School Children, 445

Fail, Why so Many Students, 629
Fay, P. J., Isaac Watts, 217
Fees, Student, L. Morey, 185
Feingold, G. A., Scholarship Attendance and Deportment, 333
Fellowships, at St. John's College, R. Pearl, 626; American Field Service, A. M. Palmer, 774
Fenton, U., Teachers and Political Life, 472; and H. C. Lehman, True-False Questions, 115
Field Columbian Museum, 354
Finances, of Wesleyan Univ., 718; of the Chicago Schools, 720; of New York Univ., 817
Financing Rural Schools, R. D. Baldwin, 341
Fire, Promethean, P. Kaufman, 121
Fishback, E. H., Character Education, 562
Flaccus, Q. H., II, The Passing of Whiskers, 49
Floating University, The, O. Maust, E. R., 122
Foreign Service, Proposed School of, 783
France, and England, Student Exchanges, 167; Teachers of, 350
Franco-British Education Congress, 198
Franklin, E. E., Graduation and the Ph.D., 182
French, Training of Teachers of, 676

Freshmen, College, Selection of, C. O. WEBER, 516; New Type of, E. K. HILLBRAND, 823
Futuristic Painting of Higher Education, P. A. COWEN, 490

GARLIN, R. E., School Surveys, 337
GARRISON, K. C., Intelligence Test Scores, 630
George Washington School of Government, 651
German, Child Labor Census, 292; School in the Crusade against Tuberculosis, 444
Germany, An Educational Tour in, 103; Exchange of School Children, 135
Gist, A. S., Elementary School, 696
GODFREY, G. H., Personnel Work at Oregon, 623
Good, C. V., Research in Education, 699
GOOD, H. G., A Spelling-book of the Sixteenth Century, 642
Grading, An Experiment in, M. KENNEDY, 18; Professors, R. S., 311
Graduation and the Ph.D., E. E. FRANKLIN, 182
Grande Chartreuse Monastery, Home for Scholars at the, 417
GRAVES, F. P., The Library of Louvain, 68; *The Educational Review*, 529
Great Britain, Public Schools, 228; Universities and Training Colleges, 243; Apprenticeship, 264; Schools, Backwardness, 522

HAGIE, C. E., Higher Standards for Elementary School Teachers, 824
"Haint Eney Place," E. N. BAKER, 547
HALL, A. B., Students and Courses at the University of Oregon, 272
HANKINSON, F., Civil Tests for Teachers, E. R., 49
HARPER, W. A., Compulsory Chapel, 627
Harvard University, Visiting Lecturers, 422; Residential Hall, 615, 659; Honors, 678
Health, Education Films, 138; Work in New York City, 170; in New York State, 477
Hearing, Children's, Tests of, 264
Hebrew Education, M. WALDMAN, 405
Heidelberg University, American Gift to, 780
Hell-Fires, W. B. SMITH, E. R., 172
HERRIOT, M. E., "Honor" Engineering Students, 829
HICKS, C. R., Instruction in Institutions of Higher Learning, 428
High Schools of City and Country, 614
HILL, C. M., Publicity for the Small College, 147
HILLBRAND, E. K., College Freshmen, 823
Hillegas, M. B., Teaching Number Fundamentals, 565
HILLS, E. C., Foreign Students in U. S., 23
HINES, H. C., Prediction and Predicament, 255
Histories of Education, State, 753
History Texts, Ancient, C. G. SHAMBAUGH, 494; Future, A. C. WILGUS, 547
HOBBS, Z. P., To School at Thirty, E. R., 118
Honors, Work, W. F. SANDERS, 455; at Harvard University, 678
HORNE, H. H., Course in the Philosophy of Education, 131
HOUGH, D. W., Yes and No for Parent-Teacher Associations, E. R., 110
House, Small, R. S. BROOKS, 46
HUNKINS, R. V., Supervision in Teaching, 728
HUNTER, W. S., Human Behavior, 701
HUSBAND, R. W., Thorndike Intelligence Examination, 521
Hygiene, Mental, American Foundation for, 616

Iceland, Schools in, 815
India, Imperial Council on Agricultural Research in, 101
Indian Service Employees, 169
INGLES, M., The High-School Library, 159
Insurance, Group, B. E. DAVIS, 682
Intelligence, Scores, Thorndike, at Columbia, in 1928, 10; R. W. HUSBAND, 521; of Students of Foreign Languages, W. KAULFERS, 597; Tests for Voters, 686; What is it?, R. P. CARROLL, 792
International Inst. of Teachers College, 354
Ireland, Lack of Teachers in, 70
Italian, Schools and the Fascists, 197; School System, Reform of, 593
Itinerant Education, H. H. NININGER, 484

JACKMAN, R. E., "American Arts," 567
Japanese Education, A. G. EATON, 395
JONES, L., Personnel Service, 765
JONES, R. W., Journalism Courses, 458
Journalism Courses, R. W. JONES, 458
Junior College, M. M. CHAMBERS, 519

Kansas, State Teachers Assoc., Convention, 40; Univ. of, Graduate Medical Courses, 138
KAUFMAN, P., Promethean Fire, 121
KAULFERS, W., Intelligence of Students of Foreign Languages, 597; Prognostic Value of General Language, 662
KEAL, H. M., Mental Ratings, 277
KELLY, F. J., The University in Prospect, 633
KELLY, R. L., The Congregational College President's Term of Service, 18
KENNEDY, M., An Experiment in Grading, 18
KILPATRICK, W. H., Dr. Dewey's Bust, 778
KIMBALL, E. P., Student Bibliographies, 174
Kindergarten Union, 72
KOLBE, P. R., Urban Influences on Higher Education in England, 153

Language, General, Prognostic Value of, W. KAULFERS, 662
Languages, Modern, the College Teacher of, C. F. SPARKMAN, 610
Latin, Achievement in, J. S. ORLEANS and H. G. THOMPSON, 549
LA VOY, K. R., Leaders, 683
Law, Research in the, 242
LAWRENCE, I., Women Teachers in Politics, 183
Laymen, A Review of the Views of, NEWSPAPER EDITORS, E. R., 10; E. R., 88; E. R., 148
Leaders, Made, K. R. LA VOY, 683
Legal Education, The Case Method of, 751
Legislation, Educational, in New York State, 146
Lehigh Univ., Salaries and Tuition Fees at, 325
LEHMAN, H. C., True-False Test, 456
Liberal Education, H. P. RAINEY, 249
Libraries, in Czechoslovakia, 37; Package, University of Wisconsin, 293
Library, American, in Paris, 136; High-school, M. INGLES, 159; School, Graduate, Chicago, 232; Systems, School, in England and America, 444
Linguistic Confusion and Science, J. W. MAVOR, E. R., 65
Literacy Law for New Voters in New York, 419
Literature Study, H. R. WILSON, E. R., 33
Loan, Agencies, L. M. N., 142; Funds, Student, 718
Logic and Persuasion, E. H. PAGET, 438
London Univ., New, 716

Longevity of Educators, G. W. A. LUCKEY, 244
Lord's Prayer, L. R. WHEELER, 735
Louvain, The Library of, F. P. GRAVES, 68
LOVETT, R. M., Meaning and Value of the Arts, 16
LUCKEY, G. W. A., Longevity of Educators, 244
LUDEMAN, W. W., Public School Teachers, E. R., 126
Lunches, School, 306
Lutheran Church, United, College Survey of, 72

MCANDREW, W., Matters of Moment, E. R., 1, E. R., 67, E. R., 129, 551, 691; Better Books, E. R., 21, E. R., 69, E. R., 136, 558, 696; A Review of Some English School Ideas, E. R., 87; The Best of Binghamton, E. R., 91; Frank Rexford, E. R., 130; An Ancient Scandal, 396
McAndrew, W., and the *Educational Review*, 592
MACCAUGHEY, V., Progressive Education, 730
MCVEY, F. L., Administrative Relations in Colleges, 705
Maguire, E. R., The Group-study Plan, 561
Maison Americaine, La, 81
Marking, Systems, College, R. B. SPENCE, 224; Students, M. F. MEYER, 546
Marks and Students, H. H. REMMERS, 759
Mathematics, Jazzing up Our, A. L. WATTS, E. R., 120; National Council of Teachers of, 566
MAUER, J. M., Extension Teaching, 308
MAUST, O., The Floating University, E. R., 122
MAVOR, J. W., Science and Our Linguistic Confusion, E. R., 65
"Me" or "I", H. RAND, 793
Medical Schools, Admission to, 242
MESSENGER, J. F., Efficient Underlings, 335
Mexico, Univ. Summer School, 228; W. M. MILLER, 545; Educational Facilities, 717
MEYER, M. F., Marking Students, 546
Michigan, Univ. of, Barbour Scholarships, 352
Milbank Memorial Fund, 230
Military Academy, U. S., 783
MILLER, G. A., Algebraization of Mathematics, 363
MILLER, W. M., Summer Session of the National University of Mexico, 545
Miners in Great Britain, University Scholarships for, 38
Minnesota, Univ. of, New Physics Building, 610; Appropriations for, 816
MOREY, L., Student Fees, 185
MORLEY, C., Cooperation among Educators, E. R., 186
Morton, R. L., Teaching Arithmetic, 564
Motion Pictures, Educational, 581
MUIR, S. T., Ethics of Teachers, E. R., 179
Mussolini as a Schoolmaster, 102

N., L. M., Are Universities Loan Agencies?, 142
Natal Natives, Education of, 535
National Education Association, Address of President, C. S. ADAIR, 1; Work of, J. W. CRABTREE, 20; Minneapolis Meeting, W. C. RYAN, JR., 25; The President of, 304
Nationalistic Education and Beyond, T. WOODY, E. R., 99
Negro Universities and Colleges, 401
NELSON, M. J., Elementary School Pupils, 371
New, York, Univ., Faculty Promotions, 74; Summer Sessions, 267; Dept. of Education of, 478; Service to Normal Schools and Teachers Colleges, 720; Finances, 817; State, Legislation, Educational, 146; Continuation School Law, 389; Literacy Law for New Voters, 419; School Health Day, 477; Conference of Normal School and Teachers Colleges Faculties, 581; City, Health Work, 170; School Budget, 201, 267; Registration, 326, 336; School Buildings, 784; Univ. of the State of, Convocation, 355; College of the City of, Curriculum, 420; Medical Center, 479; Zealand, Primary Schools, 505
Ningpo Methodist College, 262
NININGER, H. H., Itinerant Education, 484
Nobel Prizes, 717
Normal School Faculties, State Convention, 509
Northwestern Univ., Letter to Freshmen, W. D. SCOTT, 366
NORWOOD, C., Education: The Next Steps, 281, 317
NOTSON, E. B., Eye Strain, 760
Nursing Education, National League of, 818

Ohio, State, Educational Conference, 721; Univ., Dept. of Education, 651
Oklahoma, Univ. of, Graduate Medical Course at, 138
OLDFATHER, C. H., The "Bachelor of Arts with Distinction," 111
One, -teacher School, 144; School District, Lake County, Minn., as, 676
Orchestra, High-school National, Visit to Europe, 649
Oregon, Univ. of, Students and Courses at, A. B. HALL, 272
ORLEANS, J. S., and H. G. THOMPSON, Achievement in Latin, 549
ORTON, S. T., Learning to Read, 286
OSBORN, H. F., The Championship of Youth, 89
Over-simplification, P. A. WITTY and H. C. LEHMAN, E. R., 150
Oxford, Univ., American Trust Fund for, 351; Study for a Doctorate at, W. Y. ELLIOTT, 685

PAGET, E. H., Logic and Persuasion, 438
Palestine, Education in, 134; Jewish Schools in, 227, 675
PALMER, A. M., Teachers of the Columbia University Summer Session, 332; American Field Service Fellowships, 774
Palmer, A. N., An Appreciation, J. S. TAYLOR, E. R., 15
Parent-Teacher Associations, Yes and No for, D. W. HOUGH, E. R., 110
Parental Education and the Schools, 73
Paris, "University City," 322
PATERSON, D. G., New Type Examination Questions, 369
PEARL, R., The Senior Fellowships at St. John's College, 626
PEASE, G. R., The College of Education, 576
Pension Systems in the United States, 181
Pensions, Educational, Abroad, M. B. RAY, E. R., 113
Pennsylvania State College, 325
Personnel, Seminar, Intercollegiate, 107; Work at Oregon, G. H. GODFREY, 623; Service, a Project in, L. JONES, 765
Peru, New Pedagogic Institute in, R. S., 656
PHAYRE, I., The Spanish Language, 398
Phi Beta Kappa, Tests in, 10; Senate, 819
Philippines, Education in the, 169
Philosophy, of Education, H. H. HORNE, 131; International Hall at Univ. of Southern California, 719

Physics Building, Univ. of Minnesota, 678
PIERCE, D. H., Business Files Objections, E. R., 176
PIERSON, C. D., and C. H. NETTELS, High-school Seniors, 215
Pittsburgh, Univ. of, Radio Talks, 421
Playground, City, 493
Policies, New, College, 19
Porto Rico, Univ. of, 447
POTAMKIN, H. A., Exploiting the Child, E. R., 189
Predicting Success, M. E. BROOM and G. F. FOX, 689
Prediction and Predicament, H. C. HINES, 255
President's, Congregational College, Term of Service, R. L. KELLY, 18
Presidents, Service of, M. T. BOARDMAN, 429
PRESSEY, L. C., College Success, 403
Princeton Univ., Salaries, 537; New Engineering Building, 617
Profession, Teaching, C. F. ARROWOOD, 177
Professional Relations, Women's Inst., of, 781
Progressive Education, V. MACCAUGHEY, 730
Propaganda in the Public Schools, 582
Prosperity, The Schools as an Index of, 795
Psychology of Citizenship Training, A. G. CRANE, 34
Publicity for the Small College, C. M. HILL, 147
Punishment, Corporal, and Suspension, H. H. DAVIS, 632
Punjab, Progress in the, 166
PYLE, W. H., Educational Waste, 590
PYRTLE, E. R., Efficient Teaching, 591

Quantity, Quality and Economy in Education, 732
Quotations, 19, 81, 116, 144, 179, 207, 242, 276, 304, 336, 365, 399, 430, 459, 492, 522, 548, 592, 629, 659, 686, 731, 762, 794, 825

Radio Programs, 138, 421, 476
RAINEY, H. P., Liberal Education, 249
RAND, H., "Me" or "I", 793
Rating Our Teachers, F. M. RICH, E. R., 167
Ratings, Mental, H. M. KEAL, 277
RAY, M. B., Educational Pensions Abroad, E. R., 113
Read, Learning to, S. T. ORTON, 286
Reading Exercises, Remedial, H. H. REMMERS and J. M. STALNAKER, 797
Recreation Movement, Community, 229
REED, C. A., The New Turkish Alphabet, 758
Reform Schools, 324
Registration, in New York City Schools, 326; in American Universities and Colleges, R. WALTERS, 737
REIGART, J. F., School and Society in Chicago, J. S. Counts, 763
REMMERS, H. H., Students and Marks, 759; and J. M. STALNAKER, Remedial Reading Exercises, 797
Reports, 20, 82, 146, 181, 208, 243, 306, 401, 431, 460, 493, 593, 660, 732, 796, 826
Research, Appropriations for, at Cornell, 583
Retirement System and Teaching, E. R. PYRTLE, 591
Rexford, Frank, W. MCANDREW, E. R., 130
Rhodes, Scholars, 180, 749; Fellowships, 762
RICE, W., British Educational Matters, E. R., 12
RICH, F. M., Rating Our Teachers, E. R., 167
Rosenwald, Julius, Fund, 616
Roumania, Financial Support of Education, 474
Rousseau and Patriotism, 51
Rowantree, W. F., and M. S. Taylor, An Arithmetic for Teachers, 564
Rural, Schools, R. D. BALDWIN, 341; Education, 448, 580; School Supervisors, 677; Teacher and the Inferiority Complex, I. D. WEEKS, 714; Community Center, J. W. BARGER, 727.
Russia, The Schools, H. F. CLARK, E. R., 96; Child Vagrancy, 262; Political Education, 665
RYAN, W. C. JR., Nat. Educ. Assoc., 25; Behavior Problem Children, 208

S., R., Grading the Professors, 311; Secondary School Reforms in Chile, 361; New Pedagogic Institute in Peru, 656
St. Louis School Board, Appointments, 293
Salaries, of Elementary School Teachers, 105; and Tuition Fees at Lehigh Univ., 325; at Princeton University, 537; State, 199
SANDERS, W. F., Supervision of Instruction, 163; Honor Work, 455
Saving Money in the Schools, 459
Savings Banks, School, 508
Scandal, Ancient, W. MCANDREW, 396
Scholarship, Attendance and Deportment, G. A. FEINGOLD, 333
Scholarships, Barbour, of Univ. of Mich., 352
School, Linking with the Present, M. A. SEYMOUR, E. R., 56; Going to, at Thirty, Z. P. HOBBS, E. R., 118
Schools and Farms, 548
Scientific Study and Schools of Education, 170
Scotland, Education and Industry, 69; Agricultural Education, 386
SCOTT, W. D., Letter to Freshmen, 366
Scottish Training Colleges, 613
SEASHORE, C. E., Academic Contests, 114
Seattle, School Board and the Teachers' Union, 11; High School and University, 536
Serenity in Education, J. G. WOLCOTT, E. R., 59
Sex Differences, W. D. COMMINS, 599
SEYMOUR, M. A., Linking School with the Present, E. R., 56
SHAMBAUGH, C. G., Ancient History Texts, 494
SHANKLAND, S. D., A Review for Superintendents, E. R., 5
Singapore, Proposed College in, 7
SISSON, E. O., The Baccalaureate, 57
Smith, D. E., and W. D. Reeve, High-school Mathematics, 565; Number Stories, 566
SMITH, F. W., More Wastes in Education, 81
SMITH, W. B., Keep the Hell-Fires Burning, E. R., 172
South Africa, Exchange of Students, 229
Southern California, Univ. of, School of Education, 71
Spanish Language, I. PHAYRE, 398
SPARKMAN, C. F., The Educational Expert, 610
Special Correspondence, 16, 46, 111, 174, 272, 300, 333, 361, 395, 426, 453, 484, 516, 545, 623, 656, 685, 727, 758, 789
Spelling-book of the Sixteenth Century, H. G. GOOD, 642
SPENCE, R. B., College Marking Systems, 224
STALNAKER, J. M., and H. H. REMMERS, The Large vs. the Small, 302
STEIN, E. A., Criminology in Russia, 789
STONE, H. E., The University Dean of Men, 347
STRANG, R., How to Study, 461

STRAYER, G. D., Educational Administration, 82
Student, Exchanges, 38; Publications, H. G. DOYLE, 78; Visits, 198; Serious, P. W. L. COX, 502
Students, Foreign, E. C. HILLS, 23; Exchange, from South Africa, 229; International Exchange of, 475
Study, How to, R. STRANG, 461
STURTEVANT, S. M., Deans of Women, 259
Success, and Extra-curricular Activity, R. E. THORNHILL and C. LANDIS, 117; College, L. C. PRESSEY, 403
Summer, Play Schools, 294; School of Agriculture, Cornell, 41; Session of Univ. of California, 41; Course for Workers at Univ. of Wisconsin, 106; School of Univ. of Mexico, 228; Sessions of New York Univ., 267; Columbia Univ., 267; Sess., A. M. PALMER, 332
Superintendents, A Review for, S. D. SHANKLAND, E. R., 5
Supervision of Instruction, W. F. SANDERS, 163; in Teaching, R. V. HUNKINS, 728
Survey, Land-Grant College, 137
Surveys, School, R. E. GARLIN, 337
SWARTLEY, S. S., Bookstores in College Towns, 314
Symonds, P. M., the Nature of Conduct, 702
Syracuse University Appointments, 42

TAYLOR, J. S., A. N. Palmer: An Appreciation, E. R., 15
TEACHER, HIGH-SCHOOL, Better High-school Teachers, E. R., 45; Busy, Whither?, F. M. BAKER, E. R., 39
Teachers, Amer. Federation of, 40; High-school, A HIGH-SCHOOL TEACHER, E. R., 45; Civil Tests for, F. HANKINSON, E. R., 49; Public School, W. W. LUDEMAN, E. R., 126; and Political Life, N. FENTON, 472
Teaching, The Effect of, S. A. COURTIS, 52, 84; Elementary, W. R. WILSON, 240; Code of Ethics, 431; College, Methods of, C. R. WISEMAN, 433; Art of, A. H. UPHAM, 769
Test Scores, Intelligence, K. C. GARRISON, 630
Tests, Constructing and Scoring, R. S. ELLIS, 205; Scholastic Aptitude, in Amherst College, C. H. TOLL, 524; Intelligence, for Voters, 686
Texts, History, Ancient, C. G. SHAMBAUGH, 494
Thesis Writing, C. C. CRAWFORD, 426
THORNDIKE, E. L., Curriculum Research, 569
THORNHILL, R. E., and C. LANDIS, Extra-curricular Activity and Success, 117
Tigert's, Dr., Resignation, 179
TIMBIE, W. H., Cooperative Courses in Colleges, 709
TOLL, C. H., Scholastic Aptitude Tests, 524
Travel Tours, 323
True-False, Question, N. FENTON and H. C. LEHMAN, 115; H. C. LEHMAN, 456
Turkey, Education in, L. L. W. WILSON, 601
Turkish Alphabet, New, C. A. REED, 758
TUTTLE, H. S., An Enriched Diploma, 98; Building Character, 300

Underlings, Efficient, J. F. MESSENGER, 335
University and the Times, L. D. COFFMAN, 530; in Prospect, F. J. KELLY, 633
UPHAM, A. H., The Art of Teaching, 769
Urban, Influences on Higher Education in England, P. R. KOLBE, 153
Using What We Have, C. D. CHAMPLIN, 656

Virginia Inst. of Public Affairs, 200
Vocational, Guidance, M. BLOOMFIELD, 128; French Institute of, 386; Teachers, 446; Education, K. E. EVANS, 746

WALDMAN, M., Hebrew Education, 405
Wales, Secondary Education, 102; Student Conference, 135; School-leaving Age, 647
WALTERS, R., College Entrance Examination Board, 687; Registration in American Universities and Colleges, 737; Association of Colleges and Secondary Schools of the Middle States and Maryland, 827
Waples, D., and Others, Problem Exercises for High-school Teachers, 558
WARREN, H. A., Louis Agassiz, 442
Washington (D. C.), Child Research Center, 493
Waste, Educational, W. H. PYLE, 590
Wastes in Education, More, F. W. SMITH, 81
Watson, J. B., Psychological Care of Infant and Child, 700
WATTS, A. L., Jazzing up Our Mathematics, E. R., 120
Watts, Isaac, P. J. FAY, 217
WEBER, C. O., Selection of College Freshmen, 516
WEEKS, A. D., Diplomas in Erewhon, 364
WEEKS, I. D., the Inferiority Complex and the Rural Teacher, 714
Wesleyan Univ., Finances of, 718
Western Reserve Univ., Medical Center of, 266
WHEELER, J. L., Educational Books of 1928, 801
WHEELER, L. R., Lord's Prayer, 735
Whiskers, The Passing of, Q. H. FLACCUS, II, 49
WHITE, H. A., Debating in Our High Schools, 660
WHITEHOUSE, W. W., Community Organization, 467
Who's Who in Our Classes?, A. W. BURR, 274
WILGUS, A. C., History Text-book, 547
WILLIAMS, J. T., Bachelor of Citizenship, 383
Williamstown, Inst. of Politics, 116, 295
Wilson, G. M., What Arithmetic Shall We Teach?, 566
WILSON, H. R., Literature Study, E. R., 33
WILSON, L. L. W., Education in Turkey, 601
WILSON, W. R., Elementary Teaching, 240
Winslow, L. L., Teaching of Art, 567
Wisconsin, Univ. of, Summer Courses for Workers, 106; Experimental School, 232; Package Libraries, 293; Student Guidance at, 353
WISEMAN, C. R., Methods of College Teaching, 433
WITTY, P. A., and H. C. LEHMAN, Over-simplification, E. R., 150
WOLCOTT, J. G., Serenity in Education, E. R. 59
Women, Teachers in Politics, I. LAWRENCE, E. R., 183; Deans of, S. M. STURTEVANT, 259
Women's Colleges, Endowment, 509, 584
WOODY, T., Nationalistic Education, E. R., 99; Political Education in Russia, 665

Yale Univ., Professorships, 389; Sterling Memorial Library, 478; Earning of Students, 536; Report of the Treasurer, 650
Youth, The Championship of, H. F. OSBORN, 89
YOUTZ, P. N., Adult Education, 91

SCHOOL AND SOCIETY

Volume XXVIII SATURDAY, JULY 7, 1928 Number 706

PRESIDENTIAL ADDRESS[1]

THE time has come to render an account of my stewardship, and, like the man in the Bible, I can do so with joy and not with sorrow—for every member of the association and every circumstance have combined to make my term as president a happy one. How could I be aught but happy, when I recall the gracious manner in which you gave me this office, the charm of the lovely city of Seattle, the way in which you have welcomed me into your homes and at your meetings, your wholehearted cooperation, the work of the headquarters staff, and to crown it all, the beautiful hospitality of our hostess city, Minneapolis, whose hearty welcome has just been extended to us.

Interpreting the work of the association in the states. When in Seattle you did me the honor of electing me your president, it seemed that there were two contributions that I might try to make to upbuilding our organization. The first was to help the teachers of the country to become better acquainted with their national association, to be more familiar with the scope of its work and its intimate connection with their everyday problems, and to make each one feel that it is his, or her, association, and not a mere entity far away in Washington. To this end, I have accepted every invitation that was physically possible to accept to speak to interested groups. Whenever no definite topic for address was assigned, I have spoken of the aims of the association, of our handsome and thoroughly equipped headquarters in Washington, and of what is being done there by the eight divisions. I have told of the work of the committees and of the eighteen departments. I wish that I might picture to you the way in which this message has been received, or tell of the many special courtesies that have been shown me as the representative of our great national association. This has been a wonderful year—a year full of interesting experiences.

In Canada. Three times your president has had the pleasure of representing the National Education Association in Canada. The first occasion was an address of welcome in your name, to the delegates of the convention of the World Federation of Education Associations, which held its biennial meeting in Toronto. More than a thousand of our membership availed themselves of this great opportunity to meet and know educationists from other lands. A little later, the greetings of the National Education Association were presented to the Canadian Federation of Teachers. The last occasion was to represent you at the convention of the Ontario Education Association when they presented our fellow-teacher, Mrs. Evangeline Lodge Lindbergh, with a life membership. Perhaps you would be interested in knowing the form in which this membership was presented. It was in the shape of a box made of Canadian silver: on each corner of the lid was a maple leaf surmounted by a beaver; in the center was the seal of Ontario; within was a plate of Canadian gold, on which was engraved the certificate of membership.

[1] Address of the president of the National Education Association, delivered at Minneapolis, Minnesota, July 2, 1928.

Coordinating work of committees and departments. The second task which I undertook was to coordinate, as closely as possible, the work of the various departments and committees of the association. While each department has its own field of work, nevertheless many educational interests overlap. For example: classroom teachers are often rural teachers; superintendents, principals and teachers, are all interested in character education. It is, therefore, quite possible for the same work to be undertaken by one or more departments, causing a waste of time, energy and money. This is especially true of committee work within the groups.

Early in the fall, letters were sent to the presidents of the various departments, asking that each outline the work of his, or her, particular group for this year. These reports were carefully studied. A meeting of the officers of departments and committee chairmen was called in Boston in order that these persons might know each other and become familiar with the objectives of every group. Those present were so much pleased with the idea of a closer integration of the work of the association that they decided to make these unofficial gatherings a regular feature of convention procedure. A program has been prepared for this meeting and much good to the organization will doubtless result.

Committee work. Your president and secretary have kept in close touch with the various committees. Arrangements have been made for reports to be given both to the board of directors and to the delegate body. Let me urge that you study the official pamphlets in the envelope given you when you register; thus you will be prepared to evaluate and act upon these reports.

Informational material sent out. It is impossible for me, as president, to give you any idea of the hundreds of thousands of pieces of mail that have gone out from headquarters this year. Every effort has been made to give to our officers, committee chairmen and members, all the information that they should have in regard to the work of the association. Inquiries for additional knowledge, to supplement the material sent out, have been gratifying in that they have revealed the growing interest in education throughout the country.

Complete agenda have been sent to the directors prior to their meetings, both here and in Boston.

For the first time, adequate material in regard to committee reports, and the completed program, have been sent to state and local association secretaries prior to the convention.

Lay support of education. One of the interesting features of the work has been a more complete realization of the number of groups who stand ready and willing to help the educators of the country in their work for the schools. Frequent invitations have been received to address both men's and women's clubs of every kind and description: social, civic and business —local, state, national and international. Every one of these groups has an educational committee. You have only to think of the work for crippled children done by the Shriners and Rotarians, the health work and provisions for the wiser use of leisure time fostered by the Kiwanians and Civitans, the emphasis placed on vocational educational guidance by the Altrusa and Quota Clubs, the slogan of the National Federation of Business and Professional Women's Clubs, "at least a high-school education for every business woman"; the highly significant work of the parent-teacher associations, and so on through the civic, semi-civic and social clubs. Bulletins have come from many kinds of organizations, setting forth their interest in the field of education. What an army to call to our aid in interpreting to the public the work of the schools!

Removal of illiteracy. In 1914 the National Education Association was the first group to sound the challenge to the states for the removal of illiteracy. Two years ago the Chamber of Commerce of the United States published a bulletin called "Four Years of Opportunity." It contained a discussion of the illiteracy problem in the United States and urged each state to endeavor to reduce the number of its illiterates before the 1930 census. Much of the material in this bulletin was gleaned from the reports of our own illiteracy commission. It hardly seems possible that we should have so long remained inactive in the face of the immense financial, social and spiritual losses we were suffering in this country through the illiteracy of our people. In every state there are literally thousands of native-born illiterates, both white and colored. The "Four Years of Opportunity" have dwindled to two. Please let me urge each one of you to go back to your state determined to do all within your power to remove from America the stigma of five million illiterates.

Homes for retired teachers. Last summer, just after the Seattle convention, we received an offer of a thousand acres of land and a hundred thousand dollars in money for the establishment of a national teachers' home. This offer, which has since been duplicated, brought us to the realization that many questions must be answered before we could actually establish homes for teachers. How many teachers would want to go to a home? Would one large national home be better, or several regional homes? Perhaps state homes would be best. In any case, how would the applicants be selected? Where could the money be secured? Plans have been made for collecting and tabulating all this information. Soon we shall be able to speak with authority as to desirability, location, types and costs of homes for retired teachers.

Research. This is a day of research. Every business of any size has such a department. Our own research division has grown immensely in scope and influence in the five years it has been in existence. Because of the wide-spread desire for definite information, and because of the lack of sufficient data as to what has been, and is being done, the executive committee has recommended that we set up within our research division a plan for the coordination of educational research. This will necessitate the employment of an additional research assistant and the extension of our present contacts with the Bureau of Education, the universities and other agencies. We hope, for example, to secure the interest and cooperation of specialists in different phases of educational research who will list and evaluate current material. Periodic, annotated bibliographies will be published and much duplication of effort and expense will be eliminated. Thus we will help to carry on until the passage of our bill for the establishment of the Federal Department of Education.

The education bill. Much has been accomplished in the past year in extending the knowledge of the education bill. With this knowledge has come increased support for the measure. The hearing before the Congressional Education Committee in Washington last April was most encouraging. When all educators are informed and working for the bill—then, and only then, will we have a Department of Education with a secretary in the President's cabinet. This is as it should be.

There is but one constitutional justification for expending the tax funds of the people upon the public schools. It is to insure the general welfare by increasing the common knowledge and common ability to think accurately and straight. The public schools of the United States are attended by more than twenty million Americans at the most impressionable periods of their lives. The slant of their thinking will determine the public policy of to-morrow. For this reason, the utmost care must be taken to avoid the introduction into the public schools of propaganda of a kind that will bias their future judgments.

College faculties and the National Education Association. The statement that members of college faculties are individualists interested in nothing outside of their own fields has been frequently made. It has also been said that they are not interested in the National Education Association. Our efficient secretary has in his office literally hundreds of letters that would disprove both of these statements. As a result of the resolution in regard to tenure of office and salaries of college teachers a new cooperative relationship has been established with colleges and universities. The outlook in this direction is most favorable.

Exchange of credits and certificates. Due to the shift in industry from one section to another, and other causes, there has been an apparent over-supply of trained teachers in some states and a deficit in others. This necessitates provision for an exchange of professional certificates. A special committee, under the chairmanship of Mr. E. C. Doudna, secretary of the Board of Regents of the State of Wisconsin, is in charge of this work. Later in the week you will hear a report from this committee.

Relation between higher standards of training for teachers, and salaries. The progress made in raising the standard of training for teachers is astonishing, but with a few exceptions, salaries have not increased in an equal proportion. Unless the public can be made to appreciate the direct relation between better teachers and better salaries, these well-trained young people will be forced to go into other lines of work.

Your committee on the economic status of the teachers, of which Dr. B. R. Buckingham is chairman, is studying this question in all its phases. We may confidently expect to hear, in a year or two, an authoritative statement on the subjects of supply and demand, equalization of salaries for rural teachers and kindred topics.

Cooperation with other organizations. The National Education Association has cooperated in every way possible with other educational groups. Representatives have gone to many conventions. The relations between the National Education Association and the Bureau of Education have been most friendly and helpful. You will be called upon later to authorize the continued support by your officers and headquarters staff of a movement for an increased appropriation for the Bureau.

The National Association of Teachers in Colored Schools. Six years ago, in Boston, the National Education Association committee on problems in colored schools was organized. Because of an unfortunate choice of title, this committee has been unable to accomplish much. It seemed expedient, therefore, to adopt a plan of reorganization. We now have a committee on cooperation between the National Education Association and the National Association of Teachers in Colored Schools. The membership of this committee is composed of representatives of both organizations. Their president, Dr. W. J. Hale, will bring to us here the greetings of the National Association of Teachers in Colored Schools, and we will send a representative to their convention in Charleston.

It is the opinion of your president, and the executive committee, that more can be accomplished by cooperation with this group than by a special committee of the National Education Association.

Degree requirements for mature teachers. The question has been raised, but little actually accomplished, on the subject of requirements for bachelors degrees for mature teacher-students. Perhaps next year something will eventuate from this year's work. It is indeed distressing to see a social science or history teacher spending her precious sabbatical leave studying Greek, French and mathematics. Not that the study of Greek, French or mathematics is unimportant, but the whole matter seems a question of objectives.

Publicity. The National Education Association has had an unusual amount of favorable publicity in the past year. This has been due to several causes. The employment at headquarters of an exceptionally good publicity man, who has established contacts with the various press associations; the cooperation of the official organs of state and local educational associations, as well as other educational journals; the stand that the National Education Association has taken on several matters of importance and the addresses of the officials in various places. In other words, the affairs of the National Education Association have had news value.

Objectives of the National Education Association. Seventy years ago the National Education Association was organized "to elevate the character and advance the interest of the profession of teaching and to promote the cause of education in the United States." As has been stated, this movement had two closely allied objectives. One has sought to create the tools of good teaching—courses of study incorporating subject-matter and activities suited to the needs of all children, teaching techniques based upon experience and scientific experiment. The other has endeavored to recruit the teaching profession from the intellectually elite among the young people of the nation and to secure social and economic recognition for teachers comparable to that accorded to the members of other professions that demand the equivalent in character, training and responsibility.

The attainment of these objectives calls for leadership of the highest quality, unselfish, persevering, idealistic leadership worthy of the descendants of pioneers.

Some accomplishments. What are some of the things that have been accomplished? Between the years of 1917 and 1927 our high-school enrolment has increased from 1,600,000 to 4,000,000; teacher attendance at summer school has increased from 40,000 to 250,000. There are now four times as many teachers colleges authorized to grant degrees as there were in 1917 (25 to 100). The number of consolidated schools has increased from 8,000 to 16,000. Curriculum research has been fundamental and far-reaching. Twenty-six states, as opposed to four or five, now have sound retirement laws and the teachers of thirteen states have some form of tenure law. The value of school property has increased from $2,000,000,000 to $4,800,000,000; and the average salary of teachers has increased from $600 to $1,300 a year.

Finance. The National Education Association is now a million dollar corporation. To be absolutely accurate, our June 1 report shows that on that date our income and assets totalled $1,019,397. Our membership (181,350) and our cash balance of June 1 ($88,311) are the largest we have ever had. Life memberships are increasing rapidly (1,748). With a few insignificant exceptions, our divisions at headquarters have lived within their budgets. A large part of this gain is due to the efficient work of our secretary, Mr. Crabtree, and of his able corps of assistants.

Growth in membership. The growth in membership of the National Education Association from 10,104 in 1918 to 181,350 in 1928 is amazing, but the growth of the state associations from 200,000 in 1917 to more than 600,000 in 1927 presents an astounding figure. Several state associations and many local organizations count within their membership 100 per cent. of the teachers in the given area. We have more 100 per cent. schools in the National Education Association to-day than we had members ten years ago.

Work of state secretaries and directors. Too much can not be said in commendation of the efficient work of the state secretaries and of our state directors. They are our field agents in education.

The end is not yet. While much has been accomplished, much more remains to be done. Of the 900,000 persons engaged in educational work in America, only 181,350 (about 20 per cent.) are members of the National Education Association. A tabulation in the report of the secretary indicates that while our percentage of possible membership now equals that of the American Bar Association, the American Medical Association with its 61 per cent. of possible membership is still in the lead. We are far from our goal of a united profession at work on its problems. We do not yet realize our potential strength for progressive and constructive educational legislation.

The convention program. For the past year, I have traveled to and fro and up and down this vast country of ours. I have visited historic Jamestown. I have stood at sunset on Burial Hill. I have knelt in spirit before the defenders of the stockade at Harrodsburg. I have traveled the Oregon and the Santa Fe Trails. In my heart there has grown up a deeper respect and reverence for those, our pioneer ancestors, whose courage and steadfastness have given us this wonderful heritage.

I have visited schools, big schools and little schools, one-room schools and schools whose magnificent masonry and many chambered walls would put to shame an ancient palace.

Everywhere, I have seen teachers at their work training the children of America—helping them to establish within themselves those cardinal virtues that marked our founders. So it was inevitable that the convention topic this year should be "Education for Citizenship."

The program has been carefully built. Each speaker has his contribution to make. It is my hope that all of us will go away from this meeting with a deeper conviction and a wider vision of the part that we, as teachers, may play in the building of a greater America.

The challenge of the National Education Association. Perhaps the greatest service that our national association is rendering is helping local and state associations in developing within us teachers a finer professional spirit—a larger vision of the place of education in the social, civic and economic life of our communities. It challenges us to further professional study that we may better fit ourselves for our daily tasks, to painstaking experimentation that we may improve our methods of teaching; to scientific study of child life, that we may better understand the abilities, interests, ambitions and accomplishments of each individual pupil. Our National Education Association challenges us to live life on a high plane, and to live it abundantly, in order that we may interpret it more accurately to the developing boys and girls with whom we work. Our National Education Association inspires us with new courage because of the cooperative effort of its 181,350 members. It binds the teachers of the nation together in one great professional organization, with a common understanding, common ideals and one common purpose—namely—service to the children of America.

The teachers' opportunity. The opportunity for service yet before our association is greater than you and I even dream. Yet we need not be disheartened by the size of our task, for "We believe that the education of youth is the finest of the fine arts and that our task as interpreter of life to youth is a great trust placed in us. We believe in aspirations and enthusiasms of youth. We believe in the power of example. We believe in cooperation with all humanizing agencies. We believe in patience and perseverance and faith in the final outcome of education and of life."

It has been said that a task without a vision is drudgery—a vision without a task is a dream—but a task and a vision is joy unspeakable. The teachers of America have a great task but they have also a vision of the result of that task rightly performed upon the future of America and of the world.

CORNELIA STORRS ADAIR
RICHMOND, VIRGINIA

EDUCATIONAL EVENTS

THE PROPOSED COLLEGE IN SINGAPORE

ABOUT ten years ago it was decided to commemorate the centenary of Singapore by the foundation of an institution for higher education in Malaya that should bear the name of the founder of the Straits Settlements, Thomas Stamford Raffles. A boys' school, with accommodation for 700, known as the Raffles Institution, has long been in existence, and it is reported by a correspondent of the London *Times* that the proposed college is now under construction.

The college grounds comprise over fifty acres, which were formerly the Government Economic Gardens and which were donated by the colonial government. Plans for the college include an administration block, a science block, two halls of residence for sixty students each, a sports pavilion equipped with a gymnasium and swimming bath, and ten acres of playing fields. Developments of the future, to be undertaken as funds become available, include arts and engineering buildings, and a third hall of residence.

The main architectural feature of the college is the great hall, which is situated on the first floor of the administration block, and is said to be the finest hall to be found in Malaya. In commemoration of a donation of $150,000 from a Java sugar and shipping magnate, it is to be called the Oei Tiong Ham Hall. One hall of residence is already completed.

At the outset, the subjects of instruction will include English, science, mathematics, geography, history and education. There will be five or six courses for student-teachers, and the local candidates for the teaching profession who were formerly sent to the University of Hongkong at the expense of the colonial government will go in future to the college. One of the most useful activities of the college will consist in providing an improved course of training for Malayan teachers. It is hoped that the time is not far distant when the college will form part of the University of Singapore, and the successful student will receive a diploma at the end of his (or her) three years' course. Until that time the college will be prepared to accept students who wish to read for the degrees of the University of London, and this will afford an opportunity for obtaining a degree without going outside Malaya to read for it.

HIGHER EDUCATION OF THE DEAF IN ENGLAND

A CONFERENCE on the higher education and further technical training of the deaf has been held at University College, London. The London *Times Educational Supplement* reports that Lord Charnwood, president of the National Institute for the Deaf, presided, and that delegates from the following bodies were present: *Universities:* London, Liverpool, Manchester; *Education authorities:* London, Kent, Staffordshire, Durham County, Birmingham, Bradford, Leicester, Bristol, Stoke-on-Trent and Glasgow; *Schools:* Manchester, Derby, Stoke-on-Trent, Margate, Edinburgh, Dundee, Northampton, etc.; *Special Welfare Societies:* Birmingham, Leeds, Leicester and London. A number of other bodies also interested in the deaf were represented.

Lord Charnwood, in opening the conference, said that no provisions comparable to those abounding for hearing children were available for the higher education of the deaf in England, and the conference was called by the National

Institute in the hope that steps would be taken to fill up this gap in the national system of educating that class.

Miss Mary Hare, chairman of the National College of Teachers of the Deaf, briefly indicated the suitability of deaf children for more advanced culture and achievement than were possible in the existing primary schools.

Mr. W. Carey Roe, vice-chairman of the college, then gave a short review of the present facilities for educating the deaf. He emphasized the complete absence in England of any public provision for post-primary education, of which there was ample evidence to prove that the deaf were as capable as other children. He gave instances of the success of the deaf in attaining educational distinction in America and in the private schools of England. He then proceeded to outline the nature of the proposal, ages, curricula and courses, and specially emphasized the fact that the latter should be sufficiently liberal to meet the varying conditions of those who undertake them. What was wanted was the establishment of a residential college, initially for some fifty students; and, inasmuch as this college could not expect to cater for all the types of study required, that the services of existing colleges or technical institutions should be utilized, the special staff supplementing as necessary the work of these. The proposed college could be established by contributions from local education authorities or, as was the case in the lectureship at the University of Manchester, by private beneficence. He hoped that at no distant date the deaf would enjoy equal advantages with the hearing in the pursuit of knowledge and culture.

The conference debated the subject at some length, and the following resolution was passed without dissent:

> That this conference is of opinion that the time has arrived for the extension of the national system of education for the deaf by the establishment of provisions for further education than can be given in the present schools for such children.

It was unanimously decided to request the National Institute for the Deaf to constitute a suitable committee to consider and report upon the proposals placed before the conference and the best methods by which they may be made effective, and that the report of this committee be submitted to a further conference to be held later.

AMERICAN COLLEGES IN FOREIGN COUNTRIES

NATIONALISTIC tendencies in "backward" countries have led to a transformation of the organization of American colleges in these countries, according to Dr. Stephen P. Duggan, director of the Institute of International Education, who makes the statement in his eighth annual report, published recently. More natives are being admitted to the faculties and native studies and courses are constantly increasing.

Under the heading, "American Education in Backward Countries," Dr. Duggan writes that in no place on earth is the doctrine of self-determination so enthusiastically acclaimed as in the so-called backward countries, as China, Persia, Turkey and Egypt. These peoples, through education, have become earnest advocates of education, and now hold up their own national ideals.

In China in higher education, insistence now is upon the teaching of the principles of the revolution, the elimination of subjects considered antagonistic to them, the introduction into the curriculum of more elements of Chinese culture and the use of the national tongue as the medium of instruction. Stringent regulations have been made and enforced to realize these aims. An even more rigid and uncompromising attitude has been adopted in Turkey.

Such an attitude would naturally have a profound effect upon foreign institutions of learning in these countries, and especially upon American schools and colleges, since Americans have been most successful in establishing such educational institutions. Most of these institutions were of mission origin and have had a great and direct influence upon the life of those countries, but they were essentially American schools. The curriculum was almost identical with that in the United States; the organization and administration was American; attendance at divine worship was required in most of them. In Turkey, no courses in the Turkish language, history or institutions were given, and in China only a small number.

The new nationalistic tendencies have caused a transformation. Dr. Duggan writes in part:

In China, Canton Christian College, which some time ago became Lingnan University, and Peking Christian University, which became Yenching University, now have Chinese deans and a majority of the faculty are Chinese. The actual control has been transferred to Boards of Managers on the field instead of Boards of Trustees in the United States, and the majority of these Boards of Managers are Chinese. A similar change is taking place in most of the other American educational institutions in China. Of even greater significance is the movement which has already succeeded in integrating the religious activities of the missions of the different Protestant denominations into the Chinese Christian Church to be administered by native Christians.

In Turkey the same story is to be told. Robert College, the Constantinople College for Women and the International College at Smyrna have added the Turkish language, Turkish literature, Turkish history and Turkish institutions to the prescribed curriculum. Turkish teachers have become members of the faculties. Compulsory chapel attendance has been abolished. Turkish national holidays have been honored. The results of these changes have been marked. Whereas, before 1922, American institutions in Turkey were attended almost exclusively by Greeks, Armenians, Bulgarians and other non-Moslems, the majority of the students to-day are Moslem Turks. Moreover, whereas these American institutions under the old régime were regarded by the Turks with great suspicion, they are favored to-day as against institutions of the other nations, because of the evident desire and purpose to conform to the new education regulations of the government.

Those who are familiar with the history of the Near East during the past fifty years know how much the Balkan people owe to Robert College for providing them with leaders of intelligence and character. The opportunity is now offered to these American institutions to assist the new Turkey in a similar way.

A NEW EDUCATION DEGREE AT STANFORD UNIVERSITY

THE board of trustees of Stanford University has recently approved a plan, submitted by the faculty of the school of education, for the establishment of a three-year graduate program of study leading to the professional degree of doctor of education (Ed. D.), and after much the same plan as that now followed at Harvard. The new degree is to be primarily a professional degree, analogous to J.D., M.D. and D.D.

The proposal to create such a degree was considered some three years ago, but was decided against at that time. The recent reconsideration and final adoption of the plan has been due largely to the interest of President Wilbur in the idea. Knowing of the previous discussion, last October President Wilbur, in a communication to the faculty of the school of education, pointed out the need for the new degree in part as a means for enabling Stanford to provide the rising junior colleges with a better type of subject-matter teacher, and asked that the faculty reconsider the proposal and try to formulate a workable plan for such a degree.

As a result of a careful reconsideration of the idea, a complete plan for two types of the degree has been worked out, the proposed plan has been considered and criticized by the proper university committees and in turn amended by the faculty, and the entire plan was approved at a recent meeting of the board of trustees of the university.

According to Dean Ellwood P. Cubberley, of the school of education, three main reasons for the new degree were influential in its establishment. First was the desire to create a professional degree of equal weight and difficulty with the present Ph.D. degree, but with the emphasis on professional preparation and mastery of educational materials rather than primarily on research; second was the desire to provide a master-teacher type of degree to prepare a better teacher in subject-matter fields for the rising junior colleges, and third was the desire to create a new university degree that would relieve all departments of the university from the pressure of those older candidates for the Ph.D. degree who are not primarily interested in research, but who are good teachers in colleges and normal schools and who seek the degree due to pressure from the institutions with which they are connected rather than from any deep interest in the advancement of knowledge through research.

The new degree is to be of two types, one to be known as the school administrator type and primarily designed to prepare for school administration and the teaching of education in universities, colleges and normal schools, and the other is to be known as the master-teacher type and primarily designed to prepare a new type of teacher in subject-matter fields for the junior colleges and for small colleges generally.

The time requirement for the two types is the same, viz., a minimum of three years of study beyond the A.B. degree. Each type likewise is based on the completion of the A.B. and A.M. requirements for graduation in the school of education, except that A.B. graduates from other schools or departments may be permitted to make up undergraduate deficiencies in education by individual study, as well as by taking courses.

Each type will call for the completion of the requirements for a state teacher's certificate, including major and minor teaching subjects and at least two years of successful experience as a teacher, one of which must have been subsequent to taking the A.B. degree. For the master-teacher type, the equivalent of one year of advanced study in education will be waived, and the candidate will be expected to devote this time to advanced work in a teaching minor, such as history, mathematics or chemistry, and with a view to perfecting himself in the subject-matter field as well as in educational theory and practice.

The chief differences between the new degree and the general university degree of doctor of philosophy will lie in that the emphasis for the new degree will be placed more on a broad and systematic knowledge of education as a field rather than on research; that the thesis may be an organization or application of existing knowledge, as well as a contribution, instead of being exclusively a contribution as for the Ph.D. degree; and that the reading knowledge of German and French now required for the Ph.D. degree is changed to one modern language for the master-teacher type, and may be waived entirely for the administrator type of degree. In place of the language requirement, the candidate will be expected to evidence a wide mastery of selected fields in education, and to extend his reading and study beyond the scope of the courses given, much as does the English university student in the honors courses.

Comprehensive written examinations, and the same type of three-hour oral and one-hour thesis examinations as now required for the Ph.D. degree, will be expected. The aim will be to make the new degree as difficult to secure as is the Ph.D. degree, but to substitute a different type of difficulty and one of much more value as preparation for junior college and college teaching and professional work in education. The creation of a teachers' degree by the leading universities, analogous to the Ph.D. degree in time and scope, was recently recommended by a committee of the American Historical Association as desirable from the point of view of historical study. Harvard and California have recently established the degree of doctor of education.

THORNDIKE INTELLIGENCE SCORES OF COLUMBIA COLLEGE SENIORS ELECTED TO PHI BETA KAPPA IN 1928

DEAN HERBERT E. HAWKES, in a recent interview, reported that the median of Thorndike intelligence scores of Columbia College seniors whose college record will make them eligible for consideration for Phi Beta Kappa is 85. He pointed out that the median of the thirty men who are actually elected to Phi Beta Kappa is only one or two points higher. This median score is based on the intelligence test which the seniors took four years ago at entrance to Columbia College and is only two or three points above the average of students admitted. The distribution of their scores is as follows:

SCORES ON THORNDIKE INTELLIGENCE EXAMINATION FOR HIGH SCHOOL GRADUATES

60– 64.9	3
65– 69.9	3
70– 74.9	7
75– 79.9	6
80– 84.9	15
85– 89.9	20
90– 94.9	17
95– 99.9	14
100–104.9	7
105–109.9	6
110–114.9	2
115–119.9	1
	101 Median 84.125

The range of the scores is from 60 to 120. The six men scoring below 70 are bilingual or multilingual students who had some difficulty with English when they entered college four years ago. It is shown that Phi Beta Kappa men average only slightly above the general average for students admitted to Columbia College. The further fact is brought out that "the form of the distribution for college freshmen furnishes an interesting indication of the extent to which factors other than whatever is measured by the Thorndike Intelligence Test contribute to the type of success in college work leading to the highest academic honor within the power of the college to confer."

THE SEATTLE SCHOOL BOARD AND THE TEACHERS' UNION

THE question of the expediency, if not the right, of school teachers to organize themselves into a labor union has been definitely answered in the negative by school officials and sustained by state courts in Washington. According to an editorial correspondent of the New York *Times,* the decision has ended the struggle which covered a period of more than six months between the Seattle District School Board on the one hand and the organization of teachers and interested labor officials on the other.

The teachers' movement began last fall, when the Seattle High School League appealed to the District School Board for a general increase in salaries, which, as estimated at the time, would represent an increase in the school budget of approximately a million dollars. The board, which functions as the administrative body for the public schools of Seattle and certain suburban districts which are incorporated for administrative purposes into a single school district, took the appeal under advisement pending the making up of its budget for the school year of 1928–29, which was reached last March. The board then announced an inability to grant the increases because of state laws restricting its power to levy further taxation.

A few days later it was announced on behalf of the Teachers' League that a large majority of its members had been taken into the Seattle High School Teachers' Union, No. 200, affiliated with the American Federation of Labor. The School Board immediately announced that they would have no dealings with teachers through union officials and a little later declared that in the new contracts for teachers for the next year they would insert a clause in which the applicant for a teaching position should declare that he or she was not affiliated with a teachers' labor union and would make no such affiliation during the period of the contract.

Labor leaders at once asserted that this clause was in violation of constitutional rights of the employed. Attorneys employed by the Central Labor Council of Seattle obtained an order from a Superior Court judge restraining the School Board from issuing the contracts and sought to have the order made permanent.

On this basis the case went into the courts. The contentions of labor leaders were that the school board, as a public body, did not have the same right to refuse in the selection of the personnel of its employes that a private firm or other employer of labor might exercise. The court, however, ruled that the vocation of teaching in the public schools of Seattle is of a public character, under control of the state and its governmental agency, the board of directors, and it is for the latter to prescribe the conditions under which those whom it selects may teach in the schools.

The case was immediately appealed to the State Supreme Court, which sustained the ruling of the lower court. There was talk of taking the case to the Federal Court, and in the meantime the school board sent out its contracts containing the anti-union clause, the charter of the union was surrendered and every one of the teachers decided to accept the new contract.

Assurance was given by the School Board that there would be no retributive action on the part of the board toward any teacher who had engaged in the movement for unionization.

ADULT ALIEN SCHOOLS IN NEW YORK CITY

INCREASED budgetary appropriations for evening schools, smaller classes, higher standards and better methods in the selection, training and appointment of teachers, and better physical equipment, have been urged by the Council on Adult Education for the Foreign Born. In its plea for a greater number of evening elementary schools for the adult aliens of the city, the council points out that the present equipment and curriculum of the night schools "do not adequately meet the needs" of New York City's 250,000 non-English speaking adults.

The council maintains that these schools are Americanization centers, and urges that they be made attractive to the aliens of the city.

The report as quoted in the New York *Sun* follows in part:

> Good as they are—and they are increasingly better—these schools do not enroll enough adults and do not hold them adequately when enrolled. The evening elementary schools are not sufficiently attractive; seating and equipment is not appropriate; curriculum and program is not sufficiently elastic; classes are too large; social and other than regular curriculum features are lacking; adults should not be handled as children; many principals and teachers are not professionally minded about their work.

Suggestions for improvement by the council are as follows:

> Reduction of arbitrary and questionable figure of 30 per class as basis for budget making and apportionment of teachers; also adoption of rules allowing smaller classes, depending upon conditions and needs.
>
> Higher standards and better methods in the selection, training and appointment of teachers, coupled with progressive salary schedules depending upon satisfactory experience and quality of service. Similar standards, coupled with progressive salary schedules, for principals.
>
> Better facilities, equipment and materials for instruction. Selected buildings, well located with larger seats and well lighted. Up-to-date textbooks and materials.
>
> A socialized curriculum. By this is meant, not an arbitrary course of study, but an elastic scheme of educational service based upon deliberately discovered conditions and needs of adults.
>
> The development of a few selected schools, with special facilities, selected principals and teachers, modified or elastic rules and regulations, for purposes of experiment and demonstration, is imperative. Does any one pretend to know all about adult education in public evening schools?

EDUCATIONAL NOTES AND NEWS

WILLIAM J. BOGAN, for the last nine months acting head of the Chicago public schools and formerly first assistant superintendent, has been elected superintendent of schools in Chicago to succeed Dr. William McAndrew.

DR. FREDERICK MAURICE HUNTER, since 1917 superintendent of the schools of Oakland, California, took up his work as chancellor of the University of Denver on July 1. He succeeds Dr. Heber Harper, who tendered his resignation last fall. Dr. Hunter was president of the National Education Association in 1920.

THE inauguration of Dr. James E. Coons as president of Iowa Wesleyan College was held last month. President Walter Dill Scott, of Northwestern University, delivered the inaugural address.

IRA N. CHILES, acting president of Central Wesleyan College, Warrenton, Mo., has been elected president of the college. Dr. John Helmers, professor of history, has been chosen dean.

THE REVEREND J. TAYLOR HAMILTON, president of the Moravian College and Theological Seminary, Bethlehem, Pa., has retired. He will be succeeded by the Reverend Dr. W. N. Schwarze, resident professor at the school for the past twenty-five years.

FRANK M. RUSSELL, associate professor of political science at the University of California, has been appointed dean of the undergraduate division of the university, to succeed Thomas M. Putnam, who has held the position for fourteen years. Dean Putnam will devote himself to the duties of dean of the summer session at Los Angeles.

H. E. CHANDLER, superintendent of schools of Junction City, Kans., has been appointed head of the appointment bureau of the school of education at the University of Kansas, Lawrence, Kans.

J. E. HANSEN, superintendent of schools of Westby, Wis., has been appointed to the University of Wisconsin extension division at Madison. He will serve as assistant chief of the new bureau of visual education.

DR. GEORGE B. MANGOLD, since 1912 director of the Missouri School of Social Economy in St. Louis, has been named professor of sociology at the University of Southern California.

PAUL S. MILLER has recently been elected to the faculty of the school of education of New York University. He has been the principal of high schools in Pennsylvania, New Jersey and Connecticut for the past fifteen years.

JAMES H. HANFORD, professor of English at the University of Michigan, has been appointed graduate professor of English literature at Western Reserve University.

MILLET HENSHAW, of the University of Chicago, has been appointed assistant professor of English at St. Louis University.

J. C. W. CHESSEX, head of the French department at Brandon College, Manitoba, will be acting assistant professor of French at the University of Washington, Seattle, for the next academic year. He will take the place of Professor Charles L. Helmlinge, who will study in Paris.

FRANK H. BOREN, since 1919 principal of the University High School in Oakland, California, has been appointed to the superintendency of the San Mateo, Calif., Union High School District, to succeed William L. Glascock. The appointment includes the supervision of the San Mateo Junior College District.

BURTIS E. WHITTAKER, superintendent of schools at Oyster Bay, N. Y., has been appointed to the principalship at Philadelphia, N. Y.

ADDIE V. HOYT, teacher of the third grade at the Judson School, Malden, Mass., is retiring after thirty years of service. Her sister, Frances Hoyt, since 1894 head of the French and German departments of the Everett High School, Everett, Mass., is also retiring.

MISS MARY E. GALLAGHER, for fifty-two years a teacher in the public schools of Fitchburg, Mass., and the oldest school teacher in point of service in the city, has retired. For forty-two years Miss Gallagher was principal of the Maverick Street School, and the Fitchburg school board has voted to change the name of the school to the Gallagher School as an act of appreciation of her service. The board has also voted to erect a memorial tablet for her at the school.

AT the thirty-sixth commencement of the Rhode Island State College, at Kingston, the honorary degree of doctor of letters was conferred upon Edward M. Lewis, president of the University of New Hampshire, and that of doctor of engineering upon Harold S. Boardman, president of the University of Maine.

HARVEY NATHANIEL DAVIS, president-elect of the Stevens Institute of Technology, has been awarded the honorary Sc.D. by Brown University and the honorary LL.D by Rutgers University. Arthur Fiske Warren, headmaster of the Collegiate School, New York, received the degree of doctor of humane letters from Rutgers.

AT its recent jubilee commencement exercises, Duquesne University conferred the degree of doctor of science upon Dr. Thomas Stockham Baker, president of the Carnegie Institute of Technology.

JOHN J. TIGERT, United States commissioner of education, received the honorary degree of doctor of laws from Dickinson College, Carlisle, Pa., at its commencement last month. He delivered the commencement address.

THE honorary degree of doctor of education has been conferred by Ohio University on Albert Leonard, superintendent of schools at New Rochelle, N. Y.

MRS. MARY C. BARKER, of Atlanta, Ga., was unanimously reelected president of the American Federation of Teachers at its twelfth annual convention in Chicago on June 28. Mrs. Florence Curtis Hanson, of Chicago, was named secretary-treasurer. Eleven vice-presidents, completing the executive committee, were Lucie W. Allen, of Chicago; Selma M. Borchardt, of Washington, D. C.; W. Everett, of Sacramento, Calif.; Amy Fox, of Minneapolis; Abraham Lefkowitz, of New York City; A. J. Muste, of Brookwood Labor College, Katonah, N. Y.; Florence Rood, of St. Paul; W. B. Satterthwaite, of Seattle; W. J. Scott, of Atlanta, and F. G. Stecker and C. B. Stillman, of Chicago.

Dr. J. Edgar Park, president of Wheaton College, Norton, Mass., delivered the commencement address at Radcliffe College.

Dr. Paul Shorey, professor of Greek at Chicago University, was the commencement speaker at Mt. Holyoke College last month.

Victor K. La Mer, of Columbia University, has been appointed a lecturer at the American Chemical Society Institute, which will meet in Evanston, Illinois, from July 23 to August 18, 1928. He will give several series of lectures in physical chemistry.

Dr. John L. Stenquist, director of the Bureau of Research of the Baltimore Public Schools, Baltimore, Md., and lecturer at the Johns Hopkins University, is again giving courses at the University of California during the summer session.

W. O. Allen, head of the department of philosophy and education at Lafayette College, Easton, Pa., will be on sabbatic leave during the first term of 1928–29. He will spend it in France and England. Professor Allen is giving courses in education this summer at the Pennsylvania State College.

Dr. Robert D. Leigh, president of the proposed college for women at Bennington, Vermont, has sailed for Europe to study higher educational institutions for women in European countries.

Dr. Charles R. Skinner, from 1895 to 1904 New York state superintendent of public instruction and from 1915 to 1925 legislative librarian at Albany, N. Y., died on June 30, at the age of eighty-three years. In 1897 Dr. Skinner was president of the National Education Association.

Mark Keppel, for more than twenty-five years superintendent of the Los Angeles county schools, died recently at the age of sixty-one years.

Miss Mary J. Foley, senior member of the teaching staff of the Girls' Latin School, Boston, died on June 21. She had taught at the Latin school for forty years.

Mrs. Eva L. Jones, principal of Ruperts Land Ladies' College, Winnipeg, died recently in California, where she had gone for reasons of health. Mrs. Jones was formerly school principal of Havergal College, Toronto.

Henry W. C. Davis, regius professor of modern history at the University of Oxford, died in Edinburgh, on June 28, aged fifty-four years.

The northwest session of the Institute of International Relations will be held at the University of Washington, Seattle, Washington, from July 22 to 27, 1928. The institute has for its purpose the serious study of the problems involved in international relations, in the belief that an understanding of such problems is the greatest single need of the present decade. While the interest of the institute is in general international relations, the summer conference will stress the problems of the Pacific and the Orient, relations with the British Empire, and problems in international education, international organization, international commerce and finance. It is an attempt to provide on a modest scale, for the people of the Pacific Coast, such opportunities for instruction and discussion as are provided through the Institute of Pacific Relations at Honolulu, Hawaii, and the Institute of Politics at Williamstown, Massachusetts.

The New York State Museum at Albany has again cooperated with the Buffalo Society of Natural Science in arranging for the Allegany School of Natural History, at the Allegany State park, in Cattaraugus County, N. Y. The school is opening on July 7.

The third summer institute of euthenics at Vassar College opened on June 27, to continue for a month. Dr. Annie Louise MacLeod, who was recently appointed warden at the University of Syracuse, to succeed Mrs. Florence Knapp, is the director.

The Second Annual State Conference on Child Development and Parent Education was held from June 20 to 22 at the State University of Iowa, Iowa City.

The League of the Empire, associated with the Imperial Union of Teachers, has arranged a Franco-British Congress, which will be held at University College, London, from July 17 to July 20, inclusive. There will be about fifty delegates from France and over one hundred from the Oversea Dominions. The French delegates will include the heads of both secondary and primary education in the ministry, the rector of the University of Paris, rectors of several other universities in France, deans of faculties, and professors. The Duke of Connaught will preside at the opening meeting, and Lord Eustace Percy, president of the Board of Education, and the vice-chancellor of London University will be among those who will give addresses of welcome.

President Henry Noble MacCracken, of Vassar College, announced at the college commencement that gifts during the past year amounted to $891,686.

Gifts to Williams College totaling $374,243 have been announced by President Garfield. He has also announced that Williams College has definitely decided on an increase in faculty salaries to the following maximums: Professors, $6,000; associate professors, $5,000; assistant professors, $4,500, and instructors, $3,000. The plan is to take effect not later than 1930, and to begin with those professors who have been longest in the service.

More than $500,000 has been raised in the campaign of the Newton Theological Institution, Boston, for $1,000,000, according to an announcement made by President Everett C. Herrick, of the institution.

An appropriation of $290,000 to the University of Washington for an aeronautics building has been made by the trustees of the Daniel Guggenheim Fund for the Promotion of Aeronautics. The appropriation was made at the request of the president of the university, Dr. M. Lyle Spencer, and was granted in view of the fact that a course in aeronautical engineering has already been established, and the importance of the engineering institution. The state will provide funds for equipment and staff.

The Board of Education of New York City has created the new post of secretary to the superintendent of schools at an annual salary of $7,500.

According to the Bureau of Education the establishment in the University of London, England, of a chair for teaching and research in American history is being planned by committees appointed in New York and London to raise an endowment of approximately $150,000. The funds are to be used to provide the salary of a professor, and to some extent for the maintenance of a library in connection with the department.

A library course will be given this summer at Fordham University under the direction of Miss Mary McDonnell, librarian of the Wadleigh High School. This is a ninety-hour course, and gives eight points university credit. It is accepted by the regents of the State of New York for certification of school librarians in secondary schools of certain sizes, and is approved by the American Library Association. Cataloguing will be taught by Miss Ellen Hedrick, formerly catalogue reviser in the Yale University library. Reference work will be taught by Miss Jerusha Meigs, librarian of the Seward Park High School. Children's literature and story telling will be taught by Miss Mary T. Haugh, children's librarian of the Fordham branch of the New York Public Library. Book selection and school library administration will be taught by Miss McDonnell.

Bowdoin College, Brunswick, Me., has been made an associated institution of the University of Cambridge. This carries with it the benefits of affiliation with the great English university and will permit Bowdoin men who wish to carry on graduate work at Cambridge to be exempted from a portion of the customary examinations for admittance. Bowdoin has for some time been an associated institution of the University of Oxford.

In recognition of the effectiveness and usefulness of its past achievements in promoting world friendship through school teachers, the National Council of Teachers of English at its annual meeting in Chicago increased the appropriation for its Committee on International Relations and broadened the scope of its activities. More than 500 educators from every state and 42 libraries are cooperating with the committee in promoting its program, it was announced. To carry on study of American speech, cooperating with the Linguist Society and the Modern Language Association of America, the Committee on American Speech was continued with Charles E. Fries, professor of education at the University of Michigan, as chairman. Professor Fries was elected president of the National Council, succeeding Dudley H. Miles, of Evander Childs High School, New York City.

SPECIAL CORRESPONDENCE

THE MEANING AND VALUE OF THE ARTS

THE course in the meaning and value of the arts at the University of Chicago was established as one of a series of general survey courses offered for junior college students. The course in the arts is at present limited to forty students whose record in three quarters is B or above.

It is obvious that the course in the arts has to do with a set of values quite different from those of the earlier survey courses with the worth of things in themselves apart from functional or practical considerations, a worth felt as a matter of immediate response, not of knowing or reason. The fine arts taken collectively represent man's conscious endeavor to give expression to this world of beauty. The effort in this course is to present the arts not historically or philosophically but as immediate subjects of appreciation. Accordingly, the ordinary academic standards and tests are difficult of application. The interest and responsiveness of the student as shown in private conferences, group discussions and practical exercises are the best means which the instructors have of estimating the success of the course in each individual case.

The course, as given in 1928, occupied ten weeks of five exercises each week. The first three weeks were given to a consideration of painting, by E. F. Rothschild, instructor in fine arts, the University of Chicago. In addition, there were given three lectures on the historical development of painting by Professor Oscar Hagen, of the University of Wisconsin, and two lectures on prints by Miss Ethel Hahn, of the University of Chicago. A week and a half were devoted to architecture with lectures by Mr. Rothschild, and a concluding lecture on the architecture of Chicago was given by Mr. Ernest Grunsfeld, a practising architect. A week and a half were given to sculpture, with lectures by Mr. Lorado Taft; two weeks to music under the direction of Mr. Mack Evans, with additional lectures by Mr. Glenn Dillard Gunn, Mr. Felix Borowski, and demonstration by the University Choir and the Ebba Lindstrom quartet; and a final two weeks to literature, with lectures on poetry by Mr. George Dillon, on drama by Professor Frank H. O'Hara, on fiction by Professor Tom Peete Cross, and on criticism by Professor Percy H. Boynton. In the first three subjects, the lantern provided illustration, and in the fourth division musical instruments and the voice were freely used. Readings were assigned, both required and suggested, in connection with each division of the course. The general direction of the course was in the hands of Professor R. M. Lovett, who attended practically all the lectures, consulted with students, and acted as intermediary between them and the instructors.

Formal instruction was largely by lectures. A question which has been discussed from the initiation of the course, three years ago, is whether the approach to the several arts should be made by the analytic or the historical method. Conversation with students reveals the fact that they too are of different opinions. It is pointed out that they are used to the historical approach, that the history of art connects itself readily with their other historical studies, that being more at home and secure in this method they can give themselves with more zest to esthetic enjoyment. On the other hand, students confess that the analytic method, though more difficult, gives them new sources and methods of appreciation. The plan followed this year was a combination of the two. The introduction to painting was conducted by Mr. Rothschild by the analytic method, with Professor Hagen's lectures tracing the development of certain principles from the Renaissance to the present. Architecture was presented according to the same combination. Sculpture was treated historically, after a preliminary visit to Mr. Taft's studio to allow students to acquaint themselves with the practical work of the sculptor. Music was approached analytically and practically; and literature in the same fashion. The interest of students in technique and processes was evident. It had been intended to have a practising artist give one of the lectures on painting, but the plan unfortunately was not carried out. Mr. Grunsfeld in architecture, Mr. Taft in sculpture, Mr. Evans and his colleagues in music, and Mr. Dillon in poetry, supplied this important practical element.

A difficulty, which was not unforeseen, is that of breaking habits of appreciating works of art in terms of literary association, or of approaching them as subjects to be *studied about* rather than immediately perceived and felt. To meet it, great stress was laid on the collateral activities of the student, who was encouraged to visit art exhibitions, to attend concerts and plays, and to read poetry and fiction as means of esthetic experience. Reports on these collateral activities, as well as upon formal reading, were handed weekly to the director. Students met the director each week in three groups, at hours arranged for their convenience, for discussion of these reports and of various questions arising in regard to the course. To promote the association of students in their collateral activities, and to secure their cooperation in the conduct of the course, each group was further divided into three committees, interested respectively in the plastic arts, in music and in drama. Occasionally, in addition to the regular group meetings, joint meetings of the several special committees of the three groups were held. Though it was not possible for all students to attend, each committee was usually represented. There was also a committee on architecture, and one of the plastic arts committees devoted itself to the applied arts and crafts. It was the purpose of each committee to investigate some phase of the contemporary esthetic life of the city, and report on it for the benefit of the class as a whole. Thus the three committees in plastic arts investigated the exhibitions at the art clubs, art stores, department stores and craft shops. The committees respectively followed the newspapers of the city in their art, dramatic and musical news and criticism, and reported their findings at the close of the quarter. The chief object of these arrangements, however, was to promote and stimulate social enjoyment of esthetic experience. Special occasions for this enjoyment have been provided, in many instances at the suggestion of the students. A visit of the class to the Art Institute under direction of Mr. Rothschild admirably supplemented his presentation of his subject. A visit of the arts and crafts committee to shops and exhibitions was directed by Miss Mildred Chamberlain. Attendance at a performance of the Goodman Theatre gave students a view of the working of a modern stage and lighting system. The class made an inspection of the new chapel under the guidance of the architect on the ground. The committee on architecture, after inspecting important buildings in Chicago according to a list furnished by Mr. Grunsfeld, invited him to dinner (open to the class as a whole), and engaged him in informing conversation for the evening. Those interested in music attended the Chinese opera with Mr. Evans, etc.

An important feature of the course, as may be inferred from the foregoing description, is the cooperation of the students in moulding it to their desires and needs. Within the framework of regular appointments arranged in advance, it is possible to have great flexibility. Suggestions and criticisms have been made freely. All that were practicable have been adopted at once; and others filed for future use. In this connection, the position of the director of the course is one of large possibilities. As an expert in none of the fields presented, he is able to adopt the attitude of the student and judge the presentation of his colleagues from that point of view. In consultation with him, students express themselves freely in regard to the course, almost always helpfully. He is naturally responsible for the mechanism of the course, and supplies a principle of continuity in its conduct and interpretation.

The chief criticisms made by students upon the course as at present planned have to do with what is left out. In particular, photography should be given a place, and the photoplay. There has been a demand for more consideration of the applied arts and crafts, especially furniture. To secure opportunity for these, it will be necessary to eliminate literature, except for drama, or reduce its presentation to a single week. This course is recommended by the present instructors, on the ground that the approach to literature as a fine art is made the basis of courses introductory to poetry, fiction and drama, which are widely elected.

Altogether, the course, in the opinion of students, has been successful in conducing to the discovery of new interests and to the enrichment of experience. It is justified, according to the opinion of instructors, in giving opportunity for a variety of pedagogical experiments, in particular that of making collateral and group activities on the part of students contributory to the course. It is an expensive course, chiefly on account of outside lectures and demonstrators. These advantages could be shared by a larger number of students than enrolled this year. It is desirable that the course be open by election to all students of sophomore standing; but it should be emphasized that the basic work of the course should be maintained in small sections. The present number, forty, seems the natural unit.

Robert Morss Lovett

University of Chicago

DISCUSSION

THE CONGREGATIONAL COLLEGE PRESIDENT'S TERM OF SERVICE

The colleges with Congregational affiliations are properly considered among our most stable institutions. Dr. Herbert W. Gates, of the Congregational Education Society, at our request, has recently submitted data as to the term of service of the Congregational college presidents. Their relatively long service has much to do with the stability of these institutions.

President Wilkins has been at Oberlin one year, but President King, his predecessor, held office twenty-five years.

Presidents Vestling, of Olivet, and Buswell, of Wheaton, have served two years each. Presidents Mierow, of Colorado College, Dean, of Doane, Britt, of Knox, Holt, of Rollins, and Nash, of Yankton, have been at the helm in their respective institutions for three years each. President Warren, whose resignation occurred in 1924–25, served at Yankton thirty years.

On the other hand, President Penrose has served at Whitman for thirty-four years, President Wooley at Mount Holyoke for twenty-seven, President Rammelkamp at Illinois for twenty-three, President Garfield at Williams for twenty, President Pendleton at Wellesley for seventeen, President Blaisdell at Pomona for eighteen, President Cowling at Carleton for nineteen, President Main at Grinnell for twenty-two, President McGown, American International College, eighteen.

Omitting those who have served between two and three years, of whom there are nine, the average term of the other Congregational college presidents (twenty-six) is fourteen years. This is about double the average life of an American college president. There are few groups of colleges in the same class on the basis of term of executive service.

Robert L. Kelly

Association of American Colleges,
New York City

AN EXPERIMENT IN GRADING

At faculty meetings there had been considerable discussion of grades and grading. There was the usual criticism that a B grade under one teacher might represent work which would be graded A by another teacher or C by still another.

Throughout the school there seemed to be too much emphasis on grades. A pupil was more concerned with getting a high grade than with getting something worth while out of the class or in doing good work and aiming at high scholarship.

As one professor said, "If a girl gets back a piece of written work with an A or a B on it she takes it and in the hall falls on the neck of her chum with a shriek of delight and pays no attention to any criticisms or corrections."

The following experiment was tried with a biology class. This was an elective class in entomology made up of sophomores and juniors. There were forty-one in the class.

It was announced at the beginning of the term that no grades would be given on any work done during the term, but that as far as possible such criticisms would be made as would help the student to evaluate and improve her own work. All work, oral and written, would be recorded and at the end of the term as just a grade as possible would be given to the registrar. They were asked to try to forget grades and see how interesting all could make the class.

The work of the class consisted of assigned reading, lectures, class discussions, laboratory work, collecting and classifying insects, special reports. There was a small library of entomological books which was freely used. Individuals brought in magazine and newspaper articles and interesting specimens. A collection of insects belonging to the school was used for study and comparison. One test was given during the term. No text-book was used. Each student made her own text-book by writing up class notes, reports on reading, drawings and clippings and bulletins. Most of these notebooks were very good and showed work and thought.

There was unusual interest and cooperation. The class was certainly an enjoyable one to the teacher and seemed to be so to the pupils.

At the end of the term the grades handed to the registrar included no failures and an unusually high percentage of A's and B's. I think that the result would have been the same if the only report going in to the registrar had been ratings of passed and failed or their equivalents.

MARGARET KENNEDY
STATE TEACHERS COLLEGE,
FARMVILLE, VA.

QUOTATIONS

NEW COLLEGE POLICIES

A VISITOR to one of the commencements which are an outstanding feature of June, even in a year of political conventions, might receive the impression that colleges and universities are pretty well satisfied with themselves. The campus is permeated with an atmosphere of general congratulations and success. That this is a misleading notion becomes evident before one has turned more than a few pages of a group of addresses and papers which have been brought together in a volume entitled "The Effective College," edited by Robert Lincoln Kelly and published by the Association of American Colleges.

In the opening chapter President Aydelotte, of Swarthmore, speaks of "the saving discontent which we all of us feel, students and teachers alike, with the empty hurly-burly of college life." It has been the fashion to lay the blame for this condition upon the undergraduate, who has been charged with a predilection for "college activities" rather than for the serious business of acquiring an education.

Dr. Aydelotte does not hold this view. Heads of colleges, he suggests, should feel for the harassed undergraduate "not contempt, nor quite admiration, but rather a deep sympathy—his life is so much like that of a college president." The undergraduate did not originate the quantitative theory of culture. "He takes it as he finds it, and often gets more out of it than its architects had any right to expect."

How is the college to emancipate itself from the slough of this confusion? It has begun its escape by shifting its attention from numbers to quality. The emphasis is away from "healthy growth," which too often meant as rapid an increase in the number of students as could be attained, to competition for the best students, with limitation upon the number as an inevitable condition. Students are feeling this changed situation in the fact that even first-rate candidates are not always able to get into the college of their choice.

More striking is Dr. Aydelotte's suggestion regarding the enlargement of educational facilities. Despite limitation upon numbers, the demand for a college training is bound to force some kind of expansion. At present the youth must choose between a college and a university. Whichever he selects, he loses in one way or another.

The Englishman is not compelled to make such a choice. "He becomes a member of a small college, of from two to four hundred, and gets all the advantages of life in a small group. He is at the same time, by virtue of his membership in his college, a part of a large university with all that that may mean." Two or three American institutions are planning to adopt this arrangement as their method of growth. The results will be decidedly interesting to watch.

It is also within the bounds of possibility that tuition fees will be materially increased. Preparatory schools have gone much further in this direction than have colleges, although new colleges are announcing a much higher scale of charges, the youth with meager resources being assisted by correspondingly liberal scholarships.

At present we have the incongruous spectacle of a student's expenses being reduced by as much as half when he goes from preparatory school to college.

Entrance requirements—that ancient battleground of preparatory school and college—are undoubtedly in for drastic changes sooner or later. Why should a student who has an unmistakable bent for music or some other art be actually penalized because of his gift, while one who is content with the staple curriculum is smiled upon?

The Greeks knew better. They would have been scandalized by a system under which credit for entrance to college was gladly accorded for a year's work in botany, for instance, and denied for any number of years' work in music. Such a policy is a reflection upon a college's professed devotion to culture.—*The New York Evening Post.*

REPORTS

THE WORK OF THE NATIONAL EDUCATION ASSOCIATION[1]

CONSTRUCTIVE TENDENCIES IN EDUCATION

A FEW years ago the National Education Association adopted the ideal, "A stabilized all-inclusive membership and the entire profession at work on its problems." Many thought it a beautiful sentiment but not an ideal to be realized. Each year, however, members are impressed with the gain made during the preceding year. Teachers in all types of work are members—teachers in the kindergarten, in the elementary grades, in the junior and senior high school, in the college and university. The gain in professional spirit and in the study of the problems of the profession are among the outstanding achievements of the year.

Many school systems now have a continuous plan for the study of the curriculum. In some systems of schools there is a director for curriculum study. The building of the course of a study is no longer done by the clipping process. The study is on a truly scientific basis in a few cities, and in most cities careful, intelligent thought enters into the discussions and decisions. The yearbooks issued by the Department of Superintendence lead the way. These are on a scientific basis and contain the best practices and the best thought in the profession. The large number of orders received for these yearbooks is a fair indication of the trend of thinking along these lines.

The cooperative plan of studying questions in the preparation of committee reports aids materially in getting the profession at work on its problems. The definite effort to interest principals in holding meetings of the teachers in their buildings, printing for them in pamphlet form suggested programs for the work and urging organization and study in the *Journal* and in the *Research Bulletin* have had a tremendous influence in establishing the practice of studying professional problems. Henry van Dyke says: "Knowledge may be gained from books; but the love of knowledge is transmitted only by personal contact." In like manner professional knowledge may be found in libraries, but professional ideals come only from the exchange of views and from the inspiration of personal contacts such as these meetings and educational conventions afford.

The association has advanced the interests of the profession much more rapidly by getting into the current of the best educational tendencies and by contributing what it could to these tendencies and to others growing out of them. Has not the gain been much more pronounced than would have been possible by spending its energies in trying to start new trends and theories? In 1917 there was plainly a movement for giving the classroom teacher a larger share in working out educational programs and policies. Believing it to be a tendency in the right direction, the association took it up as a part of its program. The momentum of the movement has increased rapidly from year to year. It has developed greater professional spirit among teachers. It has increased the membership of the association. It has resulted in the movements to improve the curriculum and to secure a better balanced articulation between subjects, courses and institutions, as well as to lead to other constructive tendencies.

If it is true that the unparalleled growth and success of the association is largely due to its

[1] From the annual report of the secretary, Dr. J. W. Crabtree, to the executive committee, board of directors and the representative assembly.

taking hold of and promoting the best trends of the day, it becomes important to know which are the most fundamental trends and to follow them from year to year as in the case of the one just mentioned. In order to get a list of worthwhile tendencies we wrote to a number of the leading educators of the nation asking each to mention two or three to which the association could give attention. The replies brought in a long list, the same ones being mentioned time after time in different phraseology. Those in the following paragraphs are the ones that were most frequently mentioned in these letters. There is no attempt to list them in the order of importance. The wording is as a rule that given in the letters.

There is a distinct movement toward unity on the part of those engaged in education. Even the ranks of higher education are feeling the impress of it now. This movement is an outgrowth of an awakened professional consciousness and a realization that the teaching of youth and the cause of education have a fundamental place in the success and social progress of the republic. That consciousness in pervading the ranks of those who teach the youngest children and those who do the expert work in the laboratories of great research institutions. There is already a marked increase of confidence on the part of the lay public and a willingness to take the advice of those in professional ranks as to educational policies. The teacher, the superintendent and the professor are becoming the nation's expert advisers on school problems in their relation to national prosperity and individual happiness.

There is a marked tendency to recognize education as a governmental issue separate and apart from the usual functions of government. This tendency recognizes that education has a fundamental relationship to the welfare of society and to the state. It is not simply passive and protective. It is not a mere incident to the forward movement of society. It is more than all that. It places education as the foundation of human progress. It tends to establish in the several states educational machinery, which is responsible to the people through the chief state school official and which in each state and community separates school issues from all others of state and municipal control. If the tendency in this direction develops, as it bids fair to do, it will ultimately bring about in this country a popular habit of mind which will enable citizens and voters to solve school problems in the terms of school issues, separate from the other issues of politics and government. No more wholesome tendency is evident than this one.

The fuller meaning of the state's function in the preparation of teachers for the public schools is recognized as never before. Associated with this are better salaries and longer tenure. The possibility of still better preparation is thus made possible. Are we expecting too much to look forward to the day when four years of preparation beyond the senior high school will be the minimum for teaching in the elementary schools? Tulsa, Oklahoma, and a few other cities require four years' training as a minimum.

Another movement is in the eagerness to find an equalization principle in state plans for subsidizing public education—with a square deal for all communities. Perhaps the provision in the earlier Education Bill of a $50,000,000 fund for equalizing educational opportunities had much to do with bringing this topic forward for discussion. The work of the Finance Inquiry gave the fact basis. Certain technics have recently been developed and there is now going on a revision of state subsidy plans in New York, Florida, Kansas, Nebraska, Connecticut, Wisconsin, Pennsylvania and possibly many other states. The economic ability of the weaker districts must be brought up to par in order that the children may not suffer from inferior teachers or inferior school opportunities of any kind. A square deal will bring this about and people are trying to find it.

Great gain has been made in the extension of local public educational programs to adult education and in the utilization of the public-school plant for evening work to meet the needs of all citizens. The part-time school, libraries, lyceums, clubs, chautauquas, the radio, the motion picture are some of the many out-of-school agencies contributing to the intellectual growth of the individual. There is a very decided tendency to develop the first two years of college work in the immediate environment of students. Some interesting experiments are now being made in the field of the junior college. This tendency is moving rapidly. It needs to be wisely directed or it might do harm as well as good.

There is an increasing tendency to regard all school education as a continuous whole, and thus to lessen emphasis on the former arbitrary breaks between the parts of the educational system. This is particularly noticeable in the college. Colleges are taking a very different attitude toward secondary and even elementary education than they did a few years ago. This is true whether the institutions be state or private. Regional associations, such as the North Central, Middle States and Maryland, Southern, New England, *et cetera,* are experiencing a great change in the spirit which animates and dominates them. Higher institutions must serve the ends of society. Therefore, they are coming into closer relationship with state-supporting education. The whole nation is ready to profit from the report being prepared by the committee on articulation.

Provision has been made in many colleges for freshman orientation or guidance. Provision has also been made in a number of secondary schools for helping high-school freshmen to find themselves. This service naturally extends itself to other high-school and college students. It was organized first to meet an emergency need for freshmen and then extended in places to meet an urgent need in other classes. Guidance and help becomes more and more necessary as larger and larger numbers attend the high school and college. Is not the time ripe for a study of this tendency and to have the practices and findings of those working on the problem published for general distribution?

One outstanding leader of educational progress cites these desirable trends. "A move towards the county unit in administration, abolition of elected county and state superintendents, improved systems of taxation, part-time education, vocational education for all, child welfare, preschool and junior college." Another one gives this list: "Vitalizing courses of study, improved efficiency in teaching and in administration, increased attention to character education, a deeper appreciation of our own profession and the observance of its standards and ideals and an all-inclusive association and understanding." Still another says: "Improvement in teaching personality and in extending character education, organizing and supervising extracurriculum activities, but nothing else means more than the movement for retirement allowances and for fairer tenure regulations."

The following movements have either been set in motion by the association or at least stimulated by it:

1. The enlistment of all teachers and administrators in a great program of service and the formation of an all-inclusive profession.

2. Definite progress in getting the entire profession at work on its problems.

3. A united movement for a Department of Education.

4. Promotion of the principle, the equalization of educational opportunity.

5. Movement for an adequate supply of educated and professionally trained teachers for all the schools.

6. Scientific salary studies leading to the adoption of the much better salary schedules now in operation.

7. Development of educational research and publicity on a nationwide basis and the use of the central office as a clearinghouse.

8. Definitely relating the central organization to the larger public interests of America.

9. Improved plans and policies for the Americanization of the foreign-born, and for doing away with illiteracy among the American-born.

10. Development of a closer relationship between the school and the public.

11. Development of international ideals in education and the organization of the World Federation of Education Associations.

12. A more scientific basis of testing and measuring as applied to work in the schools.

13. Thrift savings, and the general diffusion of financial knowledge and practises.

14. The junior high school, the junior college and increased vocational advantages.

15. Development of a plan of keeping pace with the advancing curriculum and for continuous attention to the integration of courses in the curriculum and of the various divisions in the school system.

The College and the Association

The statement "Colleges are not interested in the National Education Association" has been made many times during recent years. In arranging to carry out the instructions of the board of directors and of the representative assembly to use the association's influence for better salaries for college instructors and professors, the thought of a new relationship between the association and colleges was developed. The plan of working through a committee chairman for each college was worked out and submitted to college presidents. It was accepted by 635 institutions representing practically all leading colleges and universities in the United States. The plan provides for a committee chairman in each college who receives information concerning the work of the association and who passes on to the president and faculty only such questions as he considers advisable. He appoints members of his committee as necessary.

The correspondence back and forth has been heavy. Each general letter brought replies from hundreds of committee members. Many have asked for special information on other professional problems. The following statement by a committee chairman is typical of letters which have been received during the last month:

> We have taken a very different interest in the N. E. A. at this university since you began your efforts to enlist the college people in the association. We had come to think of the organization as belonging to the public schools and only those interested more directly in the preparation of teachers. We are convinced now that your organization may be of great benefit to all colleges and that possibly we can be of some help to the N. E. A. We have had discussion of the various items taken up in your letters and have planned to have interested groups go more into detail at another meeting and during next year. Of course we are interested in your efforts to have salaries placed upon a proper basis. This question is quite a serious one in colleges of this type. Also the maximum load for the instructor is an important item where the funds for the budget are inadequate. We are interested in all that you have to offer and will continue to look forward to your communications.

The publicity given to the low salaries paid to instructors and professors, and particularly to those in charge of freshman and sophomore classes, has led colleges and universities to plan to increase salaries. Many have actually taken steps for giving increases. A few have already adopted new schedules providing more adequate salaries. The charge that the staggering freshman mortality of recent years was largely due to inferior teaching in freshman year is causing colleges to give careful consideration to the whole question of teacher preparation, personality, tact and to salary. The committee chairman who knows the point of view of the profession and who appreciates the conditions and handicaps that must be overcome in the college proves to be the one to call the attention of college authorities to the question.

This is one of the most important movements of the year. It could not have been accomplished had it not been preceded by the outstanding work of the research division. The gain has already been so great that no one can longer make the statement that colleges are not participating in the study of professional problems. The ease and alacrity with which the interest and cooperation of the college have been secured is cause for congratulation when one realizes the full meaning of having such highly trained specialists at work on the problems of the profession. It is hoped that the board of directors will approve of the plan and authorize that it be continued.

EDUCATIONAL RESEARCH AND STATISTICS

FOREIGN STUDENTS IN THE UNITED STATES

THE eighth annual report of the director of the Institute of International Education (New York, December 31, 1927) gives a table showing the number of foreign students in the colleges and universities of the United States. An analysis of this table shows that the number of Latin-American students enrolled during the past five years is as follows:

	1922–23	23–24	24–25	25–26	26–27
Mexico	232	198	201	188	211
West Indies (not including Porto Rico)					
Cuba	158	139	120	80	109
Santo Domingo	8	5	......	4	7
Haiti	5	4	5	6	6
Total	171	148	125	90	122

Central America (country not specified)	6	9	4	2	......
Costa Rica	18	13	13	9	18
Guatemala	21	18	17	20	21
Honduras	19	22	20	23	12
Nicaragua	12	10	11	8	8
Panama	28	33	30	42	56
Salvador	7	6	9	8	9
Total	111	111	104	112	124
South America (country not specified)	6	12	6	1	8
Argentina	57	33	38	35	27
Bolivia	31	19	26	14	15
Brazil	56	52	43	31	43
Chile	42	33	25	23	34
Colombia	57	34	33	34	50
Ecuador	12	9	8	10	8
Paraguay	2	1	......	......	1
Peru	69	52	59	37	35
Uruguay	19	13	12	6	4
Venezuela	13	15	18	20	19
Total	364	273	268	211	244
Latin America (exclusive of Porto Rico)	878	730	698	601	701
Porto Rico	224	181	190	183	261
Grand total	1102	911	888	784	962

The enrolment of students from Latin America (exclusive of Porto Rico) has fallen to a little less than 80 per cent. of what it was five years ago. This is discouraging to those who would like to see closer cultural relations established between Latin America and the United States; but, on the other hand, it is encouraging to note that the enrolment in 1926–27 was considerably larger than in 1925–26. Porto Rico, however, sent more students to the United States in 1926–27 than in 1922–23.

It is interesting to observe, as shown by the following figures, that it is the British Empire that sends us the largest number of students, and, with the exception of 1923–24, there has been a steady growth from year to year. Curiously, it is Germany that shows the largest percentage of increase during the five-year period, although the total in 1926–27 amounted to only 183.

	1922–23	23–24	24–25	25–26	26–27
British Empire					
England	120	170	236	202	229
Australia	39	25	39	47	37
British East Africa	......	......	......	2	......
British Honduras	1	......	1	1	......
British West Indies	144	98	103	125	121
Canada	827	684	737	733	984
India	218	231	202	170	193
Ireland	38	31	50	49	46
Newfoundland	......	......	......	......	3
New Zealand	17	18	18	15	19
Scotland	29	38	44	52	54
Wales	2	5	7	7	13
Total	1435	1300	1437	1403	1699
Some Other Countries					
France	144	126	128	90	103
Germany	63	79	121	124	183
Italy	74	89	79	117	89
Russia	344	391	433	515	340
Spain	47	52	36	34	42
Total	672	737	797	880	757
China	1507	1467	1561	1317	1298
Japan	658	708	793	685	619
Total	2165	2175	2354	2002	1917

The courses taken by students from Latin America (exclusive of Porto Rico) are as follows: Agriculture, 32; architecture, 11; commerce, 37; dentistry, 18; education, 12; engineering, 255; journalism, 3; law, 16; liberal arts, 145; library science, 3; medicine, 34; pharmacy, 3; theology, 30; unclassified, 117.

The enrolment of students from Porto Rico differs from the above chiefly in that a much larger proportion of Porto Ricans study medicine in the United States, namely, 67 out of a total of 261. In general, with Latin-American students engineering is the most popular course, and liberal arts is second. But among Canadians and students from Europe and Asia the course in liberal arts is by far the most popular.

E. C. HILLS
UNIVERSITY OF CALIFORNIA

SCHOOL AND SOCIETY

Volume XXVIII | Saturday, July 14, 1928 | Number 707

THE MINNEAPOLIS MEETING OF THE NATIONAL EDUCATION ASSOCIATION

Rather more attention than usual was paid to the concerns of the profession of teaching at the annual meeting of the National Education Association, held at Minneapolis, Minnesota, from July first to sixth. It is true that "Education for citizenship" had been selected by President Cornelia Adair as the main theme of the convention, and the programs of most of the main sessions and many of the departmental meetings were definitely organized around this theme, but various factors combined to bring to the fore certain questions directly affecting teachers as members of the organized teaching body.

Plans for Reorganization

In the first place, there was the problem of reorganization of the association itself. A growth in membership from 8,000 to 181,000 in a decade could hardly come about without some complications, especially since the largest part of this increased membership had come after the organization of the delegate assembly seven years ago. On the whole it is felt that the plan has worked well, but certain developments that have come as the result of experience had never been actually recorded in written rules; there was a certain amount of duplication in representation because of overlapping membership, and some felt that the delegate assembly had grown too large. A committee headed by Dr. P. P. Claxton, superintendent of schools of Tulsa, Oklahoma, worked hard on a revision of the by-laws and made its report at Minneapolis. The delegate assembly rejected the proposal to reduce the number of delegates, evidently feeling that an assembly of potentially 1,700 or 2,000 was no more unwieldy than one of a thousand—both presumably being out of the deliberative-body class. The remainder of the report was accepted by the delegates.

Professional Reports

The professional character of the summer meeting was further emphasized by the printed reports submitted. Time was when reports, even in printed form, represented chiefly opinion, and seldom concerned themselves directly with teachers' interests. Among the reports presented for the consideration of the delegates were those on tenure and ethics of the teaching profession, both of which showed the results of direct study of the questions, assisted by the headquarters research division of the association.

"For a school official to fail to recommend one of his teachers for a position in another community because he does not want to lose her services" was adjudged to be the most unethical thing that could be done in the teaching profession, according to the report of the committee on ethics. Other unethical things that followed close at hand in getting almost unanimous vote of the four thousand teachers who were polled were: to violate official correspondence or conversation among teachers; to dismiss, or recommend for dismissal, a teacher without giving her ample notice and an opportunity to be heard; to discuss deficiencies of pupils in such a way as would embarrass them or their parents; to act as an agent for, or receive a commission, royalty, or anything of value from books or supplies in the purchase of which he or she exercises official decision; to endeavor to secure or to maintain one's position by innuendo, exploitation, complimentary press notices, or advertising; to teach one's religious, political or other private beliefs to pupils. Contrary to the expectations of some teachers, the ideas of school executives with regard to these major ethical offenses were in accord with those of the teachers, at least as reported to the committee. Sarah T. Muir, of Lincoln, Nebraska, who was chairman of the committee which made the investigation, announced that the committee intends to recommend a code when the study has been completed.

For and Against Tenure

The committee on tenure reported two groups of persons opposed to permanent or indefinite tenure for teachers—one group composed of those who for selfish reasons, frequently political, desire to retain arbitrary control of the schools and the school system; the other made up of persons who honestly believe that permanent or indefinite tenure has unfortunate results on teaching efficiency. The committee believes that the efforts of the first group can be nullified by organizations of teachers and by the force of public opinon. In consideration of the objections of the second group the committee is carefully studying the experience of states and cities that have had tenure for a long period, in particular calling attention to a report on the results of permanent tenure in New Jersey now being made by Assistant Professor Willard S. Elsbree, of Teachers College, Columbia University.

Several reports presented before the National Council on Education showed the same attention to fact-gathering in the field of education. Dr. Strayer's report on the relation between the educational and business administration of schools; Mrs. Cora Wilson Stewart's final report on the illiteracy situation, and the report on the "preparation of teachers for handling behavior-problem children," which attempted to show objectively, by an array of descriptions of courses, what is being done by teacher-training institutions in this important new field.

For a Unified Profession

Both the reports by President Adair and by Secretary J. W. Crabtree were similarly of business-like character, dealing, to be sure, with matters of education in the large, but directed rather specifically to the work of the teachers and the association. Miss Adair told of the work she had done during the year in coordinating the efforts of the various departments and committees of the association. She spoke particularly of lay support of education as she had observed it in this year of her presidency, of the immense number of groups outside the teaching profession who at present "stand ready and willing to help the educators of the country in their work for the schools." She urged immediate action in all the states to get rid of as many illiterates as possible in the less than two years that remain before the census of 1930. "We must," she said, "remove from America the stigma of five million illiterates." She paid special tribute to educational journals and to daily newspapers for their increasing interest in school news. She called attention to the fact that amazing as was the growth of the National Education Association in the past ten years, still more significant was the growth in membership of the state teachers associations, from 200,000 in 1917 to over 600,000 in 1928. "We are still far from our goal, however," she added. "We are not yet a united profession at work on our problems. We do not yet realize our potential strength for progressive and constructive educational legislation."

In his report as secretary, Mr. Crabtree stressed the recent tendency of the association to put time and money into study and research, instancing particularly the cooperative study of the curriculum that is going on under association leadership. He called attention to the vigorous movement for unity in the educational profession and described the successful efforts of the association during the past year to secure closer relations than heretofore with the teachers in colleges and universities.

THE "POWER LOBBY" AND "PROPAGANDA"

For the most part matters of this sort are of real significance to the profession, but they do not make as good newspaper "copy" as the older less specific and less reliable stuff. Indeed, it would seem to be almost axiomatic that getting down to business in this fashion means sacrificing a good deal of the explosive kind of newspaper publicity that annual meetings of the National Education Association sometimes get. There was one notable exception at Minneapolis, however, Secretary Crabtree's analysis of the situation that had developed as the result of recent evidence on the so-called "power lobby" before the Federal Trade Commission in Washington proved sufficiently startling to bring some of the "public relations" people to explain what they had been doing and to stir the board of directors of the association to the adoption, on the eve of the convention, of the following resolution:

Resolved, That the board of directors condemn the policy and efforts of agencies to put propaganda into the schools and hereby authorize the president of the association to appoint a committee of ten to prepare a report for the meeting of the association in 1929 on the following points: (1) What principles of school administration should guide school authorities and what principles of school procedure should guide teachers in handling material which might be classed as propaganda; and (2) what machinery, if any, needs to be set up on a local, state or national basis to serve as a protection to individual school officers and teachers.

THE PROGRAMS

Any attempt to summarize addresses or points of view presented at the programs, whether of the main sessions or of the thirty or forty departmental and affiliated groups, must be largely a matter of personal interest or chance, or both. No one could attend many of the sessions, however, without realizing how real a grip international affairs have on the teachers of America. Nearly every speaker on "citizenship" included "world-citizenship" as part of his program. Following a meeting of the committee on international relations on Sunday, July first, under the chairmanship of Dean William F. Russell, of Teachers College, Columbia University, Mr. Uel W. Lamkin, of Missouri, destined later in the week to be elected president of the association, presented to the board of directors of the association recommendations covering the meeting of the World Federation of Education Associations at Geneva next summer, at which some two thousand American teachers are expected to be present. The National Education Association itself expects to have a delegation of two hundred or more, though the number has been left undeterminate. It is probable that Dean Russell will be selected to head the American delegation to Geneva.

Still another indication of international interest was the dinner given Sunday evening in honor of Dr. James C. Yen, of China, at which President Adair, H. B. Wilson, of the Junior Red Cross, Henry L. Smith, of the National Council of Education, Caroline Woodruff, of the Council of Administrative Women, Mrs. S. M. N. Marrs, president of the Parent Teachers Associations, and Mrs. Cora Wilson Stewart, head of the National Illiteracy Crusade, paid tribute to the mass education movement in China, and the remarkable reception Mr. Yen had when he spoke before an evening meeting later in the week.

International courtesies again played their part at the first general session of the convention, when Dr. E. A. Hardy, head of the Canadian Teachers Federation, speaking in behalf of the 20,000 Canadian teachers, said he hoped that the Canadian teachers would take as active a part in their national development as American teachers were now taking in the United States.

Other reports dealt with teacher-participation in world affairs and with the Pan-American Child Congress at Havana. That education must be the basis for any attempt at world understanding was the assertion of Dr. A. O. Thomas, president of the World Federation of Education Associations, in presenting his report. He stated:

> No matter what cooperation is undertaken, education must be the supporting column of the edifice itself. Cooperation, not rivalry, must be the answer. A universal program of education is needed. Federated education is a cooperative enterprise for the promotion of this new point of view, but it is not an organization of propaganda. Propaganda should never find a place in education. We should give the children the truth as we have it and not seek to fasten too many of our dogmas and creeds upon them, else there will be no progress.

THE HAVANA CONGRESS

Francisco Vizcarrondo, assistant commissioner of education of Porto Rico, described the work of the Havana child-welfare congress. He said:

> Such congresses as these bring a necessary unity in purpose and action among the nations of America. The school systems of South America, though coming from a common source in Europe, show a great variation from each other and also from the system of their origin. Similarly each state in North America has its own type of school, organization and administration. Out of this seemingly chaotic situation there must come standards as to purposes, ideals, methods and procedures. If uniformity is secured both in aims and methods, then details as to subject-matter can be left to the judgment and aspiration of each country.

One report which attracted considerable attention among school administrators attending the convention has already been referred to. It was that made by Professor George D. Strayer before the National Council of Education, and dealt with the perennial subject of the independent business manager *versus* the business manager under the superintendent of schools. Dr. Strayer pointed out that investigations had shown that even in the ordinary business details there was no improvement in systems that had an independent business manager; that on the contrary there was real waste of time, money and energy, for the superintendent of schools under this arrangement had to spend a large part of his time educating the business manager to the real educational needs of the children in the schools. Business managers of the type he had in mind, he said, were chiefly concerned with such things as saving ten cents on kindergarten chairs rather than on purchasing the kind of equipment that was necessary for the proper education of the children.

Favorable results of the use of classroom motion pictures were reported by Dr. Thomas E. Finegan, following the study made in twelve American cities during the past year. That the pupils were more interested, that further reading was stimulated as a result of the films, and that greater originality seemed to result from the lessons based upon the motion pictures, were some of the conclusions reached by the teachers in whose schools the experiment was carried on. In not a single case was there an unfavorable report from a teacher, principal, supervisor or superintendent.

THE FARMER AND EDUCATION

Florence Hale, state supervisor of rural education of Maine, sought to bring to the convention something of the interest in the farm question that agitated the political leaders at Kansas City and Houston. She stated:

When the farmers of this country are relieved from the burden of excessive taxation, when they are given a proper market for their products, and when they are assured protection in the adequate profits for their labor, then they will be ready to listen to those things which we know are necessary if the rural child is to have his opportunity with that of the city boy and girl. I believe the farmer would be willing to cooperate in needed consolidation of schools if it were not for the burden of present economic conditions. Country people desire the best for their children and are just as keen in appreciating it as are any parents, but for many years the financial problem has been uppermost in their minds.

Miss Hale urged the kind of education in rural regions that would enrich the lives of farm children in music, art, appreciation of the heroic and fine points in life.

Parental education is bound to spread rapidly in the next few years, according to a prediction of Miss Adelaide Steele Baylor, of the federal board for vocational education. She said:

We have thought too much of the home as a center where people are fed, clothed and sheltered, and too little of its function as a center for solving problems of relationships, a function that is fundamental in citizenship. The family is the first social group of which the child is a member. Here he experiences the relations of himself to adults, of adults to him and of himself to others near his own age, and while he does not experience the relationship of adults to adults, he constantly observes this. The home is responsible for at least three fourths of the child's time even after he leaves school, and its influence continues throughout life.

THE EDUCATION BILL

That the association is just as determined as ever on the subject of the federal department of education bill was early indicated at an enthusiastic meeting of the legislative commission, under the leadership of Superintendent William M. Davidson, of Pittsburgh, and Miss Charl O. Williams, field secretary of the National Education Association. With one of the authors of the present education bill, Senator Curtis, running as vice-presidential candidate on the Republican national ticket and a statement in the Democratic platform at Houston more favorable to education than any before presented, the school people interested in federal legislation in behalf of education naturally feel more than ordinarily confident of eventual action, and this was clearly in the air at Minneapolis. Publications distributed at the convention included opinons for and against federal legislation, in order to meet the argument sometimes heard that the association has not been willing to present both sides of the case. Reports to the meeting indicated that forty-four states are now organized under state chairmen in support of the bill. New Jersey is one of four states, the officials stated, where it has been so far impossible to set up an organization with a state chairman to push the measure. At the meeting of the delegate assembly where the report of the legislative commission was presented, one delegate, from Rhode Island, spoke against the bill, and a single vote, apparently, prevented the approval from being unanimous.

Tuesday morning's general session, which was separate from the meeting of delegates, gave special attention to the citizenship theme set by President Adair. The psychological aspects of education for citizenship were set forth by President A. G. Crane, of the University of Wyoming; F. M. Gregg, of Nebraska Wesleyan University, described a plan of character training in use in his state; Miss Agnes Samuelson, state superintendent of schools of Iowa, analyzed the spiritual elements in citizenship-training, and Miss Sally Lucas Jean, of New York, spoke on "Laying the cornerstone of to-morrow's healthy citizen." That the schools of to-day have the greatest opportunity ever offered in the history of the world for the building of healthy human beings was her contention:

All departments in a school system, from the janitor to the superintendent, contribute to the health of the child. They must be coordinated. It is the duty of the schools, not only to see that the school environment is not harmful to the child, but to see that it actually helps the child in every possible way. Adequate play space, proper toilet and washing facilities and above all the hygienic arrangement of the program—the balancing of work and recreation—are all essential factors in a healthful environment.

SECONDARY EDUCATION

One of the largest of the department meetings was that of the department of secondary school principals, which dealt particularly with the relations of the high school to the elementary and junior high school on the one hand, and the colleges and universities on the other. Speakers on the junior high-school program told of the difficulties of articulating the units, and in some instances questioned whether the junior high school as now organized was really carrying out the objectives originally set for it. The need for bridging the gap at the upper end, between high school and college, was emphasized by Dean J. B. Johnston, of the University of Minnesota. Both colleges and students usually go about the selection of a higher educational institution for a given student in the wrong way, Dean Johnston said:

The college to which students are sent is usually selected on the basis of location or for financial, social or religious reasons, not in consideration of the student's own talents, interests and needs. Students choose to go to college for a great variety of reasons, but seldom think much about their fitness for the kind of thing they are attempting to do. Highly dependable means of predicting success in college are now available, and professional schools should also make use of tests of aptitude for their work.

Before the department of rural education, Superintendent Milton C. Potter, of Milwaukee, urged that city school systems should try to be of special help to rural teachers in matters of curriculum making, since that is where the city schools have themselves made the best progress in recent years. He thought cities ought to help the rural schools financially, but not by taking away money which the city needs for the education of its children.

PRINCIPLES AND POLICIES

At the final meeting of the delegate assembly on Friday, July 6, the resolutions committee presented the following declaration of principles and policies, which was adopted:

(1) *Education for a democracy.* Our American democracy is based firmly on the principle of the equal inalienable right of all to life, liberty and the pursuit of happiness. But there can be no equal right for all, no best achievement for any without full and equal opportunity for education. To give this opportunity to all in fullest measure, both as the means and as the end of democracy, is the great purpose of the American public school. Through the public school we have undertaken to free, develop, inform, inspire, guide and direct all the energies of all the people to the service of man and of society in all its forms. From the public school the American people expect and demand the promotion of individual welfare, public health, material wealth, social purity, political wisdom, safety and strength of state and nation, world vision and preparation for the most effective service of humanity. It is for these results that the people pay ever more willingly rapidly increasing sums of money for the support of the schools. That the money of the people may be well spent, the work of the schools well done and their purposes finally attained, we, for ourselves and fellow teachers, pledge the fullest devotion of all our energies as our patriotic duty and highest service to state and nation.

(2) *Parent-teacher associations.* No greater movement in the field of education has been fostered during the last quarter of a century than the organization of parent-teacher associations. This movement has for its purpose the welfare of children, and it has held steadfastly to this high endeavor and has become one of the most efficient agencies in the promotion of all activities which contribute to the successful training of the child in its relations to the home, school, church and state. In every commonwealth it exerts much influence in the field of the curriculum and in the

assumption of a proper attitude toward extra-curricular subjects. Without its influence there would have been less progress in securing adequate funds for buildings, equipment and maintenance of the public schools. The social intercourse of parents and teachers contributes to a better understanding and appreciation of child nature and brings about united action in every community resulting in democracy in education.

The National Education Association commends this great organization upon the work already accomplished and assures its cooperation in all efforts to promote a closer relationship between the home and the school.

(3) *Financing education.* The long-established and widely accepted principle of equalizing educational opportunity is closely allied with financing education. Provisions for education based on abilities and needs of children are generally directly proportional to school revenues. The real problem, therefore, of financing education is to devise a system of school revenue that will assure equal educational opportunity, which is the birthright of every American boy and girl. The state has the sovereign right and the inescapable duty to organize, supervise and administer education. Inequalities in educational opportunities exist in almost every state because of inequalities and inequities in taxation necessary to produce school revenue. In those states where the lack of school revenue is most noticeable, invariably, taxing possibilities have not been exhausted. There should be made a study and investigation of additional sources of school revenue, with special attention to indirect forms of taxation.

The state should accept the responsibility for seeing that a satisfactory program of education is offered to all children and it should, in a businesslike manner, set about the task of seeing that the burden of support of the program is distributed in such a manner that it will fall upon the people in all localities according to their ability to furnish school revenues.

(4) *Retirement.* Sound teacher retirement systems increase school efficiency. The fact that twenty-two states and the District of Columbia now have state-wide laws, with eleven more states with laws that apply to certain cities only, and that the other sixteen states are working diligently towards state-wide retirement legislation, shows that the public and the teaching profession recognize the value of this movement. We believe in a retirement system that is absolutely fair to the teacher and to the public. The efficiency of the teacher is increased by a retirement system, because it lengthens the period of teaching efficiency by relieving the teacher's mind of a fear of destitute old age and by making it possible for a teacher to invest in study, training and travel without endangering the provision made for his later years.

The National Education Association endorses legislation providing for a fair and just retirement of teachers and believes that a sound plan for this purpose will contribute greatly to the growth and the stability of the teaching profession.

(5) *Tenure.* The development of the teaching profession depends in a very large measure upon the permanence of teaching positions and the freedom of teachers from those disturbances and petty annoyances that cause unrest and dissatisfaction. For these reasons this association gives its support to all legislative movements for the securing of tenure of position for the teachers of our country. We commend those states and cities that have safeguarded their schools by creating laws for teacher-tenure. We believe that we can not have the teaching profession that is desirable until teachers throughout the country have reasonable assurance of tenure.

This association pledges its support to legislation for the purpose of improving conditions of tenure, and urges upon cities and states the importance of permanence in teaching positions to insure the stability and progress of the teaching profession.

(6) *The curriculum.* The National Education Association recognizes the study and investigation of school curricula as one of the important educational projects in present-day education. The increase in knowledge in all fields of human endeavor has made necessary the selection of subjects for use in the school programs of the country. The efficiency and the value of modern educational programs will depend upon a wise selection of material for use in the instruction of children. This association notes with interest and approval the many studies and reports on the curriculum that have been made in recent years. We believe that the determination of educational objectives growing out of the study of the school curriculum and the selection of subjects with proper objectives are essential in the development of present-day school programs.

The greatest objective in all educational training is the growth and development of the child in all those qualities that make for complete living. We hold to the principle that all programs of study should be subordinate to the advancement of this great purpose.

(7) *Illiteracy.* The National Education Association has stood consistently for the removal of adult illiteracy from the United States and has

fostered the movement as one in keeping with the high ideals and patriotic spirit of the teachers of America, as well as one that fulfils the meaning and true purpose of democracy.

The year 1930 will be a momentous one in educational history, marking as it does the new census and the rank which our country will occupy among others in literacy. The best possible use should be made of the intervening time both to enlighten mankind and to lift our nation to the place which it deserves to occupy.

The challenge is to all America, but to the teachers it is insistent. We call upon the teaching forces of America to enlist in a united effort to rid their communities and the nation of illiteracy by 1930.

(8) *Americanization.* The adaptation of persons of foreign ancestry and the naturalization of the foreign-born into American citizenship is a matter of such importance to the welfare of the nation that it should be handled with the greatest intelligence. We commend all movements for the true and sound Americanization of those who do not possess by inheritance the spirit of our American institutions without bringing upon those who seek American citizenship through the process of naturalization any hardship. We hold that the full rights of American citizenship should not be conferred upon those who have not come into full possession of the American spirit and American ideals. We approve those institutions and agencies that by instruction, training and inspiration are striving to bring the foreign-born into a loyal and understanding relation of our American institutions and a loyalty to our national ideals.

(9) *International relations.* The National Education Association declares its interest in all movements for the promotion of more amicable relations among the nations of the world. We believe that the nations have much more to gain through the practice of amity and peace than through misunderstanding and discord. We especially commend the work of the World Federation of Education Associations, and we pledge our support and cooperation in its various movements for the establishment of a better understanding among the peoples of the earth. We believe that world peace can only be established through a process of education in all nations and that the establishment of universal educational ideals among the nations will be the greatest force for creating international understanding and peace.

To attain these results we recommend that educational institutions provide courses of instruction in international relations and that all available materials for the cultivation of good-will among the nations be fully utilized. Such instruction should be especially emphasized in the teacher-training institutions.

(10) *Freedom of the teacher.* The National Education Association believes that there is urgent need for recognizing the influence of the teacher's status on the whole process of education in the public school. This is especially true in the nature of the contract, the status of the teacher in the school and in the community, and in relation to those in authority. We believe there should be more genuine freedom for the teacher, freedom in mind and spirit to achieve and create and to take pride in the art of teaching, so that he may have the same satisfaction in achievement and recognition that the lawyer, the doctor and the engineer have in the practice of their professions. Such freedom should be accompanied by a proper restraint and a sense of obligation and responsibility in all relations.

This association approves for all those engaged in public education that academic freedom which means, not the propagation of unsound or revolutionary theories, but rather the exercise of initiative and independence in the preparation of individuals for freedom in a democracy. The men and women engaged in the work of education in our country should illustrate in their professional activities the finest type of American citizen.

(11) *Convention attendance.* We call the attention of managers of summer schools for teachers and summer sessions of colleges and universities attended by teachers to the importance of so arranging their work as not to deprive their students of the opportunity of attending the meetings of the National Education Association.

(12) *Health and physical education.* Health is winning increasing and clearer recognition as the fundamental objective in the entire program of public education. We recognize health education and health service for children as a definite and appropriate function of the public school. This objective should be defined as health of body, health of mind and health of character. It is a primary function of the school to discover the health assets and health liabilities of the child, to conduct health inspection for the prevention and control of communicable diseases, to keep a record of the health and growth of each child as a part of an educational record, to provide a healthful school environment and to safeguard the life and health of the pupils in promoting all first aid and safety provisions against accident.

The purpose of health education is to bring to bear upon every child in the school the greatest possible number of influences favorable to the inculcation of habits, attitudes and knowledge desirable for individual and community health. Physical education should put the major emphasis upon an extensive program of wholesome activities for all pupils rather than the devotion of the facilities of instruction primarily to the more highly gifted and intensively developed few capable of winning victories and contests.

We endorse all movements in the communities and in the schools of the country for the promotion of physical education and mental health. We believe there is no greater objective in education than the ideal of a sound mind in a sound body.

(13) *Postage rates for books.* This association gives its endorsement to the proposal to amend the postal law so that more favorable rates may be granted for the circulation of books through the mails. The diffusion of knowledge and the advancement of culture are dependent largely upon the wide distribution of books. For this reason no unnecessary restrictions should be placed upon the circulation of books among the people.

(14) *Unity of educational administration.* In recent years it has been suggested that the business administration of schools can to advantage be divorced from their professional management. It has been argued that the construction of school buildings, their maintenance and operation, the purchase, storage and distribution of supplies, the making of the budget and the like, can be best handled by one trained in business affairs. In a considerable number of school systems the business manager has been made an officer coordinate with the superintendent of schools reporting directly to the board of education. This type of organization ignores the fact that every act of the business manager is worthy of approval only as it contributes directly to the furtherance of the educational program adopted by the board of education.

All affirm the necessity for adequate business procedures in the administration of a school system. The board of education in our larger communities should elect, upon the nomination of the superintendent of schools, an assistant superintendent in charge of business affairs. This man should be highly trained as a business executive and should cooperate with the superintendent of schools in the making of the budget, in the development of plans and the supervision of the construction of buildings, in the purchase, storage and distribution of supplies, in the handling of the payroll, and the like. His efficiency will be increased by virtue of the relationship which he bears to the chief executive officer of the board of education. The administration of the school system will profit from a relationship which is sound in theory and which has been successfully established in practice.

(15) *Bureau of Education.* We commend the work of the United States Bureau of Education, done too often with meager funds and inadequate equipment. We urge upon Congress the importance of making to the Bureau of Education such adequate appropriations as will enable it to do effectively and in the plane of present needs all the work of investigation, information, advice and promotion for which it was established. Because of the rapid growth of the public high school as a part of our system of education, we urge the need of a comparatively large appropriation for the special purpose of enabling the bureau, in cooperation with state and local authorities and agencies, to make a thorough and comprehensive study of public secondary education, its organization and methods, and its relation to and articulation with elementary education and with higher education.

(16) *The education bill.* Efficiency and economy demand that the several agencies of the federal government dealing with education, now distributed among the several executive departments, be consolidated in a department of education.

The welfare of the children enrolled in our schools is dependent upon our ability to make available to boards of education, to superintendents of schools and to teachers throughout the nation, the results of current practice, of experiments wherever they are conducted, and of scientific investigations.

We urge that a department of education be created under the leadership of a secretary, with a seat in the president's cabinet. We urge that adequate support be provided for this department in order that it may conduct such inquiries and disseminate such information as will make for the highest degree of efficiency in all of our schools. This service can be rendered by a federal department of education without in any way interfering with the constitutional rights of the several states to control, administer and supervise their own schools.

We urge the Congress of the United States to create a department of education in accordance with the principles embodied in the Curtis-Reed Bill which was before the last session of Congress.

W. CARSON RYAN, JR.
SWARTHMORE COLLEGE

PSYCHOLOGY OF CITIZENSHIP TRAINING[1]

THE psychology of citizenship training sounds fearfully technical. The speaker, however, is not qualified to treat the subject in a scientifically technical fashion. The speaker's point of view is that of an ordinary student of education. Viewing the problem from the standpoint of the public school administrator, I may perhaps be charged with being in the position of the boy who was apparently deeply interested in the sand-lot game of baseball. A bystander accosted him and said, "Young man, I suppose you know all about this game of baseball?" The reply was, "No, sir, I don't know a t'ing about it; I'se only de umpire." The administrator is often required to be the umpire and as such he should know the general rules of the game, though perhaps those whom he supervises are vastly better detailed technicians than himself.

During the past few decades the attention of educators has been closely centered upon the content of courses, the making of syllabi and curricula. Vocational and professional training have brought in the reign of the specialist, until in higher education and measurably in secondary education, we have seen the hyper-specialization of courses and the creation of student programs made up of highly specialized fragments in the various fields of knowledge. Educators are now beginning to cry that the graduates' schooling has failed to give an integrated whole; that there has been no coordination; that his acquaintance with the fields of human knowledge is scrappy and confused. The emphasis upon specialized subject-matter has over-emphasized the intellectual, often neglecting the social and moral needs of students. There is a refreshing reaction from this attitude now becoming evident in educational thought. Educators are recognizing that students and citizens are more than intellectual machines; that qualities of heart and soul and personality are fully as important as keen intellectual power. This trend of thought is showing itself in the establishment of student personnel departments, in the creation of new testing devices to show individual differences, in the student health programs, in an insistent demand for better citizenship training. The very presence on the program of this great association of the topic of citizenship shows the attention being given to this topic by educators.

From the school administrator's standpoint, two very basic false assumptions have often been made in the plans for training citizens. The first false assumption has been a too narrow concept of citizenship. Citizenship is more than a knowledge of machinery of the government, more than the mere performance of voting, holding office or watching government activities. We have had notable examples in the last decade of men who are highly successful in all these particulars and yet were arrant knaves in high places. Citizenship is a more complex thing. Essentially it means harmonious and efficient team work in society. Good citizens are good neighbors, good friends. The sum total of a man's social reactions determine his citizenship. His character, personality, his attitude toward public welfare, are all parts of his citizenship.

A second false assumption in which the schools have readily fallen because it is the line of least resistance is the undue emphasis placed upon preachment. It has been assumed that an intellectual knowledge of right conduct would assure performance. It is the old mistake made in our boyhood days when the lad who recited

[1] Address before the general meeting of the National Education Association, at Minneapolis, Minn., July 3, 1928.

the ten commandments most glibly was given the prize Bible and it was easily supposed that he would be the best boy. As a matter of fact, we lads knew him as the ringleader in all the deviltry. The emphasis has been put upon intellectual knowledge. Americanization courses have relied for their efficiency upon a knowledge of the mechanics of government, a smattering of American history, a knowledge of the functions of county officers, as if this information would make good citizens. We have overlooked the fact that the best training agencies in America to make our foreign-born peoples good citizens are the cooperative societies in which these men and women participate and experience the satisfactions of good team work. Codes of ethics, courses of instruction in morals, have been largely preachment giving information as to right conduct. It is true to-day as in days of old that he who knows best is not always the one who does best. Eyes they may have but they see not; ears they may have but they hear not. They may be hearers of the word only and not doers.

Citizenship depends upon the sum total of man's personality which has been described as the sum total of his habits, attitudes, ideals and prejudices, which determine his daily reactions. One's daily reactions are mostly a matter of habit and only partly a matter of formulated intellectual code. One might say that roughly one's social conduct is seventy-five per cent. habit, fifteen per cent. standards, and ten per cent. ideals. Habits, however, are not acquired by an enforced intellectual assent, by the ability to repeat at examination time preachments given by the teacher. They are not acquired by memory exercises, not by discussion of cases, but habits are acquired by satisfying experiences oft repeated. To acquire a personality which shall assure the proper social responses of a good citizen, one must test the satisfactions of good citizenship through good reactions. If the schools then are to train their students to become good citizens, the schools must afford the students opportunity to acquire habits of good citizenship, and these habits must be acquired through oft-repeated satisfying experiences.

Habits alone, however, however automatic they may become, are not reliable in times of stress. A mere automaton does not possess the necessary flexibility required by changing conditions. The actions of an automaton will break in times of sore temptation. The habits must have for their support and as an aid in their acquisition some formulated standards. It is here that the intellectual guide of citizenship training makes its appearance. The standards will probably be highly specific, simple and applicable to a limited situation. Here again, in a new complex situation, the standards may break down and we need for the fullest assurance of right reaction that the standards of conduct shall be illuminated and inspired by the light of ideals. We thus have a triumvirate of habits, standards and ideals, working together and a three-fold cord is not easily broken. We are most of us reasonably honest in small matters of money. We will return excessive change and we do it without any great mental struggle, almost automatically from a matter of habit. We would probably be honest to the extent of $5. If it were a transaction involving $100, we might give some serious thought to the question of returning the money. In this case the habits are threatened and the standard comes to their rescue and says: "A mistake in your favor should be rectified as readily as you would wish a mistake against you to be corrected." If the amount, however, should reach into the thousands there might be a very severe mental struggle. None of our existing standards would fit a situation of such magnitude. We would be tempted to find reasons and justifications for keeping the money. Here the thing which might save the situation would be a high ideal of honesty as an abstract virtue. Like some famous men, you might decide that you would rather be poor and honest than rich and a thief. Your ideal will say "It is not right" or "You must live with yourself, your self-respect; your contentment is worth more than mere money." In the triumvirate of habits, standards and ideals each is reinforced by the others. The ideal makes possible the transfer from one situation to another. It is an intellectual thing which can be taught by the schools, but the mistake in the past has been in teaching this to the neglect of the acquisition of good habits or even in the face of contradictory habits. The mistake has been in teaching the ideal without the proper foundation of experience from which the ideal might have been built inductively.

Little Mary comes to the table with dirty hands. Her mother says: "Mary, you must go to the bathroom at once and wash your hands. The little dog next door wouldn't eat his dinner with such dirty paws. It is not nice to come to the table with such dirty hands. Other people do not like to see such a dirty little girl." This experience is repeated inexorably on each day of the week, and it is surprising the amount of innate resistance which Mary possesses. After weeks and months of this training, however, she decides that it is more comfortable for her to wash her hands before she comes to the table. She reluctantly gives assent to the standard of clean hands at the table. She has acquired a habit of neatness, specific and exceedingly limited, which does not extend beyond meal time. She has acquired a standard equally limited which says: "Your hands must be clean when you appear at the table." Later she goes to school and here the teacher insists upon clean hands and Mary has repeated experiences formed perhaps a little more easily now than the first one, which forms habits of clean hands at school, and the standard which says: "Your hands must be clean when you go to school." Later she forms another specific habit by the same process which says that she must have clean hands when company appears and later again a habit of clean hands when playing with her pretty playthings. From these habits and along with them she has also acquired four standards which can be stated in intellectual terms; hands must be clean at table; hands must be clean at school; hands must be clean when company comes, and when playing with soilable playthings. Later in life when more specific habits and standards of neatness have been formed, there may come a day when Mary will catch a glimpse of an ideal of neatness in the abstract; neatness and cleanliness of person, of mind, of thought, of her home and her surroundings. From habits there came a generalized standard, not a generalized habit, but a formulated set of specific standards. From this set of standards, by process of abstraction, comes the ideal of cleanliness. This is a process of training, starting with experience and working out inductively to the highest thing—the ideal. Many of the attempts to teach morals, character, personality, citizenship, in the schools, have tended to reverse the process and force upon little children ideals first before there is comprehension or acceptance. The result has been mere memoriter acquisition of the information—unassimilated, unaccepted and functionless.

How can the schools then obey these simple laws of citizenship training and afford their students opportunity to acquire harmonious social habits, useful formulated standards and inspired guiding ideals? Unconsciously in most cases, the schools are already doing much in this line and their most successful results are secured when following this psychological order of habits first, standards and ideals later. Punctuality, regularity, accuracy, honesty in individual class work, courtesy, consideration for others, are all being taught in our public schools by the daily discipline of the schools. Our supervised playgrounds, our extra-curricular activities of students, are giving students first-hand experience of good citizenship. My little boy came home proudly from the first grade and stated that he was mayor. I said, "Mayor of what?" and he said "Mayor of Happy Town." "Where is Happy Town?" "Why, Happy Town is our school and I am Mayor. We have policemen and hostesses and other officers in our town." Later he came back with the proud announcement that he had been reelected Mayor of Happy Town. In his little childish way, he and the others were participating in the pleasures and satisfactions of good citizenship. The schools are indeed affording opportunity for their students to become good citizens, but much is being overlooked and neglected. Much more must be done. The schools must be true social communities. The teacher must be the manipulator and creator of social situations. The teacher must thoroughly understand the laws of personality training, the standards and ideals to be secured. The teacher must look upon the students as individuals and the task of teaching as one greater and nobler than that of a mere impartation of subject-matter. The harmful tendencies which the little Marys and Johns and Pauls show must be suppressed, discouraged. The positively helpful attitudes must be put in their stead by creating situations in which the young people may primarily acquire correct habits. With the formation of the habits must go the formulation of standards, and as the standards multiply and the upper levels of the school life are reached, ideals must be abstracted and made to illuminate and interpret and strengthen the standards.

The object of this address is to endeavor to bring to the consciousness of our teaching profession the true and natural process whereby young people acquire harmonious social personalities. There must be in the forefront of the teacher's consciousness the realization that good habits are primary, but that good habits can not be effectively formed or reliably maintained unless there accompanies these habits a stated standard, and that standard will in times of great stress be ineffective unless the whole is illuminated, interpreted and inspired by ideals. This triumvirate must be vividly in the teacher's mind as manipulator, creator and director of situations. The work of the school—the teaching of readin', writin' and 'rithmetic—must be made to afford the young people opportunities to acquire the pleasing habits which shall assure the student's individual happiness and success and make them a blessing to society.

A. G. CRANE

UNIVERSITY OF WYOMING

EDUCATIONAL EVENTS

LIBRARIES IN CZECHOSLOVAKIA

IN Czechoslovakia all communities are now required by law to maintain public libraries. According to the Department of the Interior, this nation is the first in the world to make the support of libraries mandatory.

Under the Czechoslovakian law every town having 10,000 inhabitants must appoint a librarian. This officer must have completed secondary school education and have had a one-year course for librarians. In smaller communities, a teacher who has acquired the librarian's technique by taking a month's training in library work may be appointed. The ministry of education sends a practical handbook on administering small libraries to the librarians in small parishes, and the inspection of all libraries is performed by instructors of the ministry. The law provides that a fifth of all books in every library must have instructive content. Greater towns are obliged to open a reading room of journals at the library, and the greatest towns also must have a local public library of musical compositions.

In the year 1920, 3,400 private libraries had 1,650,000 books; in the year 1926, 16,200 public libraries had more than 5,000,000 books. Thus there has been provided one library for each 894 inhabitants and 44 books for each 100 persons. In the American public libraries, according to the U. S. Bureau of Education, there are 60 books for every 100 persons. The libraries in Czechoslovakia are financed by the communities and the state; the communities paying ninety per cent. and the state ten per cent. of the cost.

UNIVERSITY SCHOLARSHIPS FOR MINERS IN GREAT BRITAIN

The report of the Miners' Welfare Fund of Great Britain for 1927 contains an account of the granting of university scholarships, offered for the first time early in that year. The account is quoted in part in the New York *Times*. Two kinds of scholarships were offered, the first for working miners and the second for children of miners. The principal requirement was that candidates must either be ready to enter a university degree course, or be so far advanced in this preparation that they could qualify for entrance before the beginning of the next university year. The plan was well advertised and the response was immediate and large. Altogether 1,209 applications were received from miners and 1,050 from miners' children. The degree of preparation shown by working miners was unexpected. The report states:

> More than a hundred proved to be already qualified to enter on university degree courses, nearly another hundred were taking a qualifying examination during the year with reasonable prospects of success, and more than a hundred more had acquired such a degree of education that, so far as the selection committee were able to judge, they would have had little difficulty in passing one of the qualifying tests for persons of mature age which are now held by practically all the British universities. There were thus more than three hundred working miner candidates whose applications demanded serious consideration. Among the second group, the children of miners, more than five hundred, were already qualified to enter on degree courses.
>
> Only eleven scholarships were available, and after much selection and elimination, eight of these were awarded to miners and three to children of miners. The successful candidates in the first group ranged from 22 to 40 years of age, only three being under 25. Six of them wished the scholarships in order to obtain a degree in economics; one wished to study commerce, and one, desiring to become a Methodist minister, was awarded a scholarship to enable him to complete his studies in Hebrew.
>
> Of the three successful contestants in the second group, two were lads of 17, who were given scholarships to obtain honors degrees, one in English and one in the classics. The third was a girl of 18, whose scholarship would enable her to complete the medical course which she was following.

The report emphasizes that to a great extent the miner candidates desired courses which would bear upon the mining industry, stating that in view of the widespread unemployment in coal mining at present in England it might have been anticipated that many would seek an opportunity to fit themselves for careers other than mining, but the proportion was much smaller than was expected.

Among the candidates of the second group the situation was very different, the largest group, 57 per cent., wishing to enter some branch of the teaching profession, and the remainder being scattered among a variety of occupations, or not specifying what career they wished to follow.

THE INSTITUTE OF INTERNATIONAL EDUCATION AND STUDENT EXCHANGES

The growth of the movement for the international exchange of college students has been described by Dr. Stephen P. Duggan in his eighth annual report as director of the Institute of International Education. He states that one of the most important functions of the institute has been the development and administration of a series of student exchanges between the United States and the countries of Europe.

At the present time, he reports, there are exchanges between the United States and five

European countries: Czechoslovakia, France, Germany, Hungary and Switzerland, and negotiations are pending with Austria and with Spain. The fellowship exchanges are for graduate study only.

The Franco-American exchange, administered by the institute, provided last fall for the bringing over of sixteen French students to study in American colleges and universities, and the sending of twenty-two Americans to France. The Americans have been attending the universities of Bordeaux, Grenoble, Lyons, Nancy, Paris, Cherbourg and Toulouse, and the École Normale Supérieure de Sevres.

Four years ago the institute organized the American-German student exchange to provide Americans with information regarding German universities and academic opportunities, and to furnish Germans with corresponding information concerning American educational institutions. One of the outstanding achievements of the American-German student exchange has been the establishment and administration of a series of exchange fellowships offered by American universities for German students and by German universities for American students. The exchange is represented in Germany by the Akademischer Austauschdienst in Berlin, an organization established by prominent educators in Germany, which effects the exchange of students between German universities and those of other countries.

The development of this activity, conceived as a movement toward fostering and stimulating international friendship and good-will by creating a tradition of cooperation between the United States and Germany, is illustrated by the fact that in four years the number of fellowships has grown from fourteen to fifty-nine. Thirty-three German students have been in the United States on these fellowships during the past year. Twenty-six Americans have been spending the year in Germany at the universities of Berlin, Bonn, Breslau, Frankfurt, Giessen, Göttingen, Heidelberg, Marburg, Münich and Tübingen and at the technological institutes at Berlin, Charlottenburg and Dresden.

The American Czechoslovak students exchange began in 1922–23, when five students came to the United States. The exchange has become definitely established on a reciprocal basis whereby each year five Czechoslovak scholars are awarded fellowships at American colleges and universities and American students are offered by the Czechoslovak ministry of education a corresponding number. The American fellows have been studying at the University of Prague, the opportunities being available there in Charles University, the University of Technological Sciences, the Arts Academy and the Commercial College.

Three years ago a similar exchange of students between Hungary and the United States was initiated, the Hungarian ministry of education offering several scholarships covering tuition, lodging in the Nicholas Horthy College, and lunch and dinner at one of the students' messes. Although these scholarships are available in the University of Budapest, the University Faculty of Economic Sciences, the Polytechnic High School, the Veterinary College and the Music Academy, all at Budapest, the number of Americans eligible to enjoy these fine opportunities is limited by the requirement of a sufficient knowledge of Hungarian to enable the student to understand lectures. One American has been in Hungary this year, studying at the University of Budapest; five Hungarians have been in the United States.

Last fall a Swiss-American student exchange was launched. The Swiss universities offered to American students desiring to study in that country a number of tuition scholarships, and in several instances these scholarships were supplemented by stipends covering board and lodging, or their equivalent, provided in the university communities. Six Swiss scholarship holders are in this country and two American scholars went over last fall and are studying at the Eidgenossische Technische Hochschule at Zurich and at the University of Zurich. Two others entered upon their work in Switzerland this spring.

INDUSTRIAL TRAINING FOR ALASKAN NATIVES

FACILITIES for industrial training in Alaska will be extended as rapidly as funds will permit, according to a statement by the Bureau of Education, printed in the *United States Daily*. It is the policy of the bureau to give vocational training in the territory instead of sending natives to the United States for such education, as was formerly done. The full text of the statement follows:

Until recently no systematic form of industrial education for Alaskan natives was provided within the territory. Young Alaskans were sent to the states for vocational training. This policy did not prove satisfactory for the reason that after a stay in the states many of these boys and girls found it difficult to adapt themselves to their home environment. It was also deemed unwise and uneconomic because the change of climate frequently was deleterious to their health.

To meet the foregoing situation, the policy has been adopted of establishing industrial schools within Alaska. Hence industrial schools have been organized at Eklutna, near Anchorage, on the Alaska Railroad; at Kanakanak, on Bristol Bay; and at White Mountain, on Seward Peninsula—all of which are strategic points. Eklutna, being near the Alaska Railroad, is readily accessible for pupils from the interior and from the Upper Yukon region; it can also be easily reached from the settlements on the southern coast. Kanakanak will be the center for vocational training for the Aleuts and for the Eskimos of southwestern Alaska. To White Mountain will come the Eskimos of the northwestern region as far north as Point Barrow.

Included in the curriculum of these vocational schools are such industries as house building, carpentry, boat building, furniture making, sled construction, operation and repair of gas engines, marine engineering, navigation, tanning, ivory carving and basket weaving.

Centuries of experience in the use of tools of their own contrivance has developed in the native races mechanical skill of a high order. This skill enables them to carry out in various modern industries the instruction received in these vocational schools. With very little training the natives excel in mechanical operations. They are especially gifted in ivory carving and basketry.

The three vocational schools in Alaska have proved such a success that it is proposed to extend the facilities for industrial training there as rapidly as funds will permit.

RESOLUTIONS OF THE EXECUTIVE COUNCIL OF THE AMERICAN FEDERATION OF TEACHERS

The position of the executive council of the American Federation of Teachers on two questions has been determined in resolutions presented before the twelfth annual convention. According to the New York *Times*, the resolutions dealt with what is known as the "yellow dog" case and with propaganda. The "yellow dog" case concerns W. B. Satterthwaite, of Seattle, Wash., who was summarily dismissed from the public-school system of Seattle because he admitted being a member of the American Federation of Teachers. The resolution, in effect, promised financial support to carry his case to the United States Supreme Court if necessary. The case involves, in addition, 260 teachers in the Seattle public schools who were dismissed when they refused to sign a contract denying them the right of admission to the American Federation of Teachers.

The propaganda resolution arose from the discharge of Wesley H. Maurer, professor of journalism at Ohio State University. According to W. Walter Ludwig, chairman of the conference committee of Ohio State University, Professor Maurer was discharged, without an opportunity for explanation, on charges of taking sides in a labor controversy in articles while associate editor of the Athens *Messenger*. Ludwig declares the charges were without foundation. The resolution recommended taking up the case with the Ohio State Federation of Labor and with President Bryan, of Ohio State University, and an endeavor to obtain enactment of tenure law making it necessary to give a teacher a fair trial before dismissal during contract.

THE ANNUAL CONVENTION OF THE KANSAS STATE TEACHERS ASSOCIATION

The Sixty-fifth Annual Session of the Kansas State Teachers Association will be held in Topeka, Hays, Fort Scott and Hutchinson on November 8 and 9, 1928. The complete list of speakers, as given in the *Kansas Teacher*, is as follows:

General Sessions

Judge Florence Allen, Ohio Supreme Court, Cleveland, Ohio.

Cameron Beck, New York Stock Exchange, New York City.

President Aurelia Henry Reinhardt, Mills College, California.

Tom Skeyhill, Famous Speakers, Inc., Steinway Hall, New York City.

Vilhjalmur Stefansson, Emerson Bureau, 850 Orchestra Bldg., Chicago.

Honorable J. J. Tigert, United States Bureau of Education, Washington, D. C.

DEPARTMENT MEETINGS

College and high school:

Dr. C. E. Germane, University of Missouri, Columbia.

Professor James M. Glass, Rollins College, Winter Park, Florida.

Professor Herbert B. Bruner, Columbia University, New York City.

Frederick M. Hunter, chancellor of the University of Denver.

Professor C. E. Rugh, University of California, Berkeley, California.

Professor Edward O. Sisson, Reed College, Portland, Oregon.

Grade School:

State Superintendent F. C. Blair, Springfield, Illinois.

Mrs. Helen Fischer, Shenandoah, Iowa.

Eugene Lies, Playground Association of America, 315 Fourth Avenue, New York City (only Hays and Fort Scott).

Rural School:

Professor I. D. Weeks, Northern Normal and Industrial School, Aberdeen, South Dakota.

Professor J. L. McBrien, Central State Teachers College, Edmond, Oklahoma.

Primary:

Miss Laura Zirbes, Columbia University, New York City.

Miss Jean Betzner, Columbia University, New York City.

THE UNIVERSITY OF CALIFORNIA SUMMER SESSION

REGISTRATION at the University of California Summer Session at Berkeley this year is approximately the same as in 1927, according to an estimate made by T. B. Steel, assistant recorder of the faculties. The summer session opened on July 2 for six weeks and will close on August 11.

A total of 5,049 students registered for the summer last year.

Among the visiting faculty members are Dr. E. G. Nourse, of the Institute of Economics, Washington, D. C.; Vaclav Vytlacil, artist-lecturer of Munich, Germany; Karl Buehr, of the Chicago Art Institute; Dr. Herman Adler, criminologist at the University of Illinois; Archibald Bowman, professor of philosophy at the University of Glasgow, Scotland; Tucker Brook, professor of English at Yale; Dr. Constantine Caratheodory, mathematician at the University of Munich; Dr. A. Feuillerat, of the University of Rennes, France; S. W. Gilman, professor of business administration at the University of Wisconsin; Frederick Koch, professor of dramatic literature, University of North Carolina; Charles Koechlin, composer and former lecturer in music at the Sorbonne, Paris; Harry A. Overstreet, professor of philosophy in the College of the City of New York; Dr. Albrecht Penck, professor of geography at the University of Berlin; Dr. R. S. Rait, professor of Scottish history and literature at Glasgow University and historiographer-royal for Scotland, and Dr. William R. Vance, professor of law at Yale University.

VISITING LECTURERS AT THE CORNELL SUMMER SCHOOL OF AGRICULTURE

DR. HENRY C. TAYLOR, head of the Institute of Land Economics and Public Utilities at Northwestern University, will lecture during the third week in "Public Problems of Agriculture."

Dr. George A. Works, formerly head of the department of rural education, now dean of the graduate school of library science at the University of Chicago, will lecture during the fifth week on "Public Problems in Agriculture" and "The Curriculum in Vocational Agriculture."

Professor C. B. Gentry, state supervisor of vocational agriculture and head of the department of agricultural education at the Connecticut Agricultural College, will conduct classes in agricultural education during the second and third weeks.

The Hon. Arthur W. Ashby, lecturer in agricultural economics at the University College of Wales, is scheduled to lecture in agricultural economics.

Dr. C. H. Lane, chief of the agricultural service of the Federal Board for Vocational Education, lectured on "Agricultural Education" during the first week.

Miss Virginia Bonser, who, with Miss Josephine Wright, is to conduct the class work in the demonstration school of rural education at Forest Home, is arriving from England.

Several special unit courses have been provided for teachers of agriculture, county agents and leaders of junior extension, who by the nature of their positions have difficulty in being away from their posts for a period as long as six weeks. Special courses are offered this year in agricultural economics and farm management, forestry, hotel administration, pomology, poultry, rural education, rural engineering and vegetable gardening.

NEW APPOINTMENTS AT THE UNIVERSITY OF SYRACUSE

At Syracuse University the following appointments have been made: Ernest Thelin, Florida State College, Tallahassee, to be associate professor of psychology and director of the psychological laboratory; John H. Washburne, New York City, to be associate professor of educational psychology; Cardinal Goodwin, professor of American history and dean of the graduate school of Mills College, Calif., to be professor of American history; Earl T. Appel, head of the department of geology at Illinois Wesleyan University, to be associate professor of geology; Herman K. Beyle, associate professor at the University of Minnesota, to be professor of political science; Dr. Annie L. Macleod, director of euthenics at Vassar, to be dean of the College of Home Economics; Donald B. Watt, personnel officer at Yale University, to be personnel officer.

EDUCATIONAL NOTES AND NEWS

Dr. Uel Walter Lamkin, since 1921 president of the Northwest Missouri State Teachers College at Maryville, has been chosen president of the National Education Association for the coming year. Miss Cornelia S. Adair, of Richmond, Va., the retiring president, automatically has become first vice-president, and H. L. Smith, dean of the Indiana School of Education at Bloomington, has been reelected treasurer. Atlanta, Georgia, has been selected as the 1929 convention city.

Dr. Mervin Grant Filler, since 1899 professor of Latin and since 1914 dean of Dickinson College, Carlisle, Pa., has been chosen president of Dickinson. He will take office on July 31, succeeding Dr. James H. Morgan, whose resignation was announced last month.

Dr. Claude B. Miller, a Missouri minister, has been selected as head of Hardin College, Mexico, Mo.

Dr. W. L. Uhl, professor of education and director of the school of education at the University of Wisconsin, has been appointed dean of the school of education at the University of Washington, Seattle, to take the place of Dr. Frederick E. Bolton, who has been made dean emeritus. At Wisconsin, C. J. Anderson, associate professor of education, has been appointed to succeed Dr. Uhl as director.

Edward E. Rockwell, dean of the college of engineering at Rutgers University, has been appointed professor of civil engineering at Lafayette University, to succeed Professor Frank O. Dufour, who is returning to active engineering work.

Mrs. Florence Schee Robnett, of Evanston, Ill., has been named dean of women at Northwestern University, succeeding Mrs. Winifred G. Richardson, resigned.

Zoe Bayliss, of the Whitewater Normal School, has been appointed assistant to the dean of women at the University of Wisconsin.

William Voas, of Northwestern University, has been appointed professor of psychology at Iowa State College at Ames, to succeed Professor Paul Fields.

At Cornell University, Allen Nevins, professor of American history, has resigned to return to the editorial staff of the New York *World*. Harry Isler Lane, instructor in mathematics, is leaving to become acting head of the department of mathematics at the University of South Dakota.

Edward L. Adams has been promoted from associate professor to professor of Romance languages at the University of Michigan.

Paul Hazard, professor of the comparative history of the literatures of Southern Europe and Latin America at the Collége de France, Paris, is to be exchange professor from France to Harvard University during the first half of the year 1928–29. He will give a series of twelve lectures on "L'Évolution de la Poésia Française de 1815 à nos Jours."

SIR GEOFFREY BUTLER, senior burgess in Parliament for the University of Cambridge, has been appointed president of Corpus Christi College, Cambridge, to succeed the Reverend C. A. E. Pollock.

GEORGE SMITH, since 1914 master of Dulwich College, has been appointed director of the department for the training of teachers at Oxford University. The appointment is effective October 15.

DR. CONRAD GILL, a graduate of the universities of Cambridge and Leeds, has been appointed professor of history in University College, Hull, England.

SIR WALTER BUCHANAN RIDDELL, principal of Hertford College, Oxford, has been made chairman of a commission which is to be appointed in Ceylon to work out a scheme for the establishment of a university.

M. E. BRANDON, for eight years superintendent of schools at Holgate, Ohio, and a former district supervisor of Defiance County, Ohio, will succeed William L. Manahan as county superintendent of schools in Defiance County, on August 1.

FRANK L. EVERSULL, for six years principal of the Woodward Elementary School, St. Louis, has been named principal of the Junior and Senior High School, East St. Louis.

JAMES E. WARDLE, instructor in mathematics at the Dwight School, New York City, has been appointed supervising principal of the new high school at South Huntington, L. I., and in addition will have charge of two grade-school buildings.

CHARLES M. EATON will retire at the end of the present calendar year as superintendent of schools at Weston, Mass. He has served the Weston schools for thirty-two years.

ERNEST HATCH WILKINS, president of Oberlin College, has been awarded the honorary LL.D. by the University of Chicago. President Wilkins was formerly professor of Romance languages at Chicago and from 1923 to 1926 was dean of the colleges of arts, literature and science.

M. LYLE SPENCER, president of the University of Washington, received the honorary degree of doctor of laws from Northwestern University, Evanston, Ill., at its recent commencement exercises.

AT the 107th commencement of Amherst College, on June 18, Professor Allen Rogers Benner, of the Phillips Academy, Andover, Mass., received the honorary degree of master of arts; Edwin Hallock Byington, for forty-five years an educational worker in Turkey, was the recipient of the degree of doctor of divinity, and Lewis Perry, for fourteen years principal of the Phillips Exeter Academy at Exeter, N. H., received the honorary degree of humane letters.

ARTHUR C. BOYDEN, principal of the Massachusetts State Normal School at Bridgewater, and Wallace Mason, principal of the Keene Normal School, Keene, N. H., received the honorary degree of doctor of education at the commencement exercises of the Rhode Island College of Education last month. Dr. Boyden was one of the principal speakers at the ceremonies. He gave a talk on the history of the foundation of normal schools.

DR. EDWARD C. ELLIOTT, president of Purdue University, Lafayette, Indiana, delivered the commencement address at Butler University, Indianapolis, on June 18. His address was entitled "The Fewness of the Many."

DR. JOHN H. FINLEY, of New York, was the commencement speaker at Stanford University and at Reed College, Portland, Ore. His subject at Reed was "The New Pioneers."

GROUND was broken for a new two hundred thousand dollar library building at Illinois College, Jacksonville, during commencement week. The speaker of the day was President William M. Hudson, of Blackburn College, upon whom the honorary degree of doctor of laws was conferred.

DR. DAVID EUGENE SMITH, professor of mathematics at Columbia University, has returned from Europe, where he served as a visiting Carnegie professor of international relations. As a representative of the Carnegie Endowment for International Peace, he lectured at University College, London, at the University of Toulouse and at the University of Montpellier.

DR. JAMES R. ANGELL, president of Yale University, and Dr. Livingston Farrand, president of Cornell University, sailed on July 8 for Europe.

PROFESSOR CLARK P. BISSETT, of the University of Washington Law School, and Professor Linden A. Mander, of the political science department of the University of Washington, left June 1 for Europe for the summer. Professor Bissett has been asked by Premier Benito Mussolini to deliver a series of lectures in Rome. Professor Mander expects to attend the League and to make a study of Empire government in England.

FRANCIS H. SMITH, professor emeritus of natural philosophy at the University of Virginia, died on July 5, in his ninety-ninth year.

WARREN NEVIN DRUM, formerly principal of the Central State Normal School, Lock Haven, Pa., and for the past three years dean of instruction at the State Teachers College, Indiana, Pa., died on June 11. His book, "A Preview of Teaching," will shortly be published by Ginn and Company.

MARY E. DEAN, for twenty-five years a teacher in the Northampton, Massachusetts, public schools and later principal of the Julia Ward Howe School in Revere, Mass., died on June 30, at the age of seventy years.

LOUISE KROMER, one of the oldest and best-known of the public school teachers in Philadelphia, died on June 26. For more than forty-five years she held positions of responsibility in the schools, having been principal for nine years of one of the first of the schools for Negro children connected with the school system, and for twenty-five years was in charge of the science classes at the Girls' High School until her resignation in 1909.

MRS. MARGARET MADDEN, for twenty years a district superintendent of the Chicago public schools, died on June 28.

A SCHOOL of adult education at Mills College, California, will be held from August 13 to 25. The first week will be devoted to contemporary problems concerning the family, and the second week to race and immigration problems.

HARVARD UNIVERSITY and the University of Rochester will share jointly a bequest of $640,988 from the estate of Dr. Charles A. Dewey, a Rochester physician.

WORK has been started on a dormitory for women attending the University of Vermont, to cost $50,000. The building is the gift of the late Mrs. William Geary Slade, of New York, in memory of her daughter, Mrs. Harriet Slade Crombie.

THE Chicago School Board has adopted a budget, calling for expenditure of $84,000,000 for the maintenance of the school system during the coming year.

The Board of Education for New York City has requested the board of estimate to authorize the expenditure of over $21,500,000 for the erection of public school buildings to be built this summer. This is more than half of the total sum recently set aside for new schools.

MISSISSIPPI has made its first appropriation for state library extension work, $5,000 a year for the coming biennium for the State Library Commission created in 1926. The commission plans to emphasize field work with the libraries of the state, and especially the development of county libraries.

COURSES in commercial training for girl graduates of elementary schools have been established by a public school in Manhattan, New York City, the U. S. Bureau of Education has stated. This one-year school, offering training in typewriting, shorthand and bookkeeping, and designed to make it possible for girls who can not attend high school to take positions in offices, is said to be the only one of its kind. There is no age limit.

COURSES in printing may be obtained in 369 institutions in the United States and Canada.

During 1926–27, 28,537 students were enrolled in such courses, under the instruction of 443 teachers, as shown by a recent survey of printing instruction made by the department of education of the United Typothetae of America. Of the institutions in which printing courses are offered, the largest number, 88, are academic high schools; 86 are junior high schools, 22 are technical high schools, 44 are trade or vocational schools and 31 are evening schools. Nine are colleges or normal schools, 10 are "plant" schools, 29 are elementary schools and 17 each are continuation and part-time schools. The time devoted to the subject varies from 1 to 48 hours per week, and from 5 weeks to 6 years. The age-range of students is from 11 to 16 years in elementary schools, and from 12 to 18, to 30, and even to 60 years of age in other schools and institutions. Equipment to the value of $3,316,960 is available for use of students.

HIGH-SCHOOL students are considerably better prepared to do college work in English now than they were ten years ago, according to a compilation made by Miss C. R. Wood, instructor under Professor H. B. Lathrop, of the English Department at the University of Wisconsin. At Wisconsin, first-year students who are found deficient in the ability to express themselves in good English are demoted to a subfreshman class. Miss Wood's figures reveal that since 1917 the percentage of freshman demoted has decreased from 18 to 7. In 1917–18, 191 of the 1,057 freshmen were demoted, 18 per cent.; in 1919, 264 of the 2,199, 12 per cent.; 1920, 217 of the 1,702, 12.75 per cent.; 1921, 198 of the 1,659, 12 per cent.; in 1922, 161 of the 1,479, 10.88 per cent.; in 1923, 153 of the 1,736, 8.81 per cent.; 1924, 124 of the 1,639, 7.56 per cent.; 1925, 115 of the 1,578, 7.29 per cent.; 1926, 130 of the 1,922, 6.9 per cent.; in 1927, 139 of the 2,341, 6.8 per cent.

OF the million persons engaged in teaching in this country in 1926, 17 per cent. were men, an increase of 3 per cent. over the number in 1920, the Federal Bureau of Education has stated. The bureau attributed a decrease in the number of male teachers between 1860 and 1920 to small salaries, better opportunities in other pursuits and to the entrance of a greater number of women into the profession. Forty-three per cent. of the teachers in 1880 were male, 34.5 per cent. in 1890, 30 per cent. in 1900, 21 per cent. in 1910, and 14 in 1920.

BECAUSE "too much money and energy are spent on conferences which overlap each other and have the same aims," five women's colleges, Smith, Vassar, Wellesley, Bryn Mawr and Mount Holyoke, have resigned from the Women's Intercollegiate Association for Student Government. The five colleges will support only two conferences on student government in the future, one to be held in the spring and attended only by delegates of the five, and the other a meeting of the National Students' Federation. The conference, representing about sixty women's colleges, voted to hold its next session at Western Reserve University. The five colleges which withdrew will, upon invitation of the present association, continue to keep in touch with it by sending one representative to its conferences.

COURSES in Spanish-American and Latin-American literature are being introduced in a number of colleges in the United States, the Bureau of Education reports. A chair of Spanish-American literature has recently been established in Yale University. In the majority of courses in the department, instruction is given from the Spanish-American point of view. A chair of Spanish-American literature has been established at Stanford University, California, and a chair of Latin-American literature at the University of Texas. Courses in Latin-American literature have also been introduced in connection with the study of Spanish in a number of colleges.

THE "traveling schools" which have been tried out experimentally by the Provincial Government of Ontario, Canada, in remote sections of the province, have proved so successful that the minister of education has arranged for two more, to operate between Fort William and Superior Junction. Night classes for adults will form a part of their program. There is a report that the government of British Columbia is planning to make it possible for every pupil in the province to have a high-school education by supplying correspondence courses for children who live in places too remote for them to attend school.

IN memory of the late Lord Northcliffe, his brothers, Lord Rothermere and Mr. Cecil Harmsworth, have presented the sum of £30,000 to the Centenary Fund of University College, London. The income from the fund is to be utilized to endow "The Lord Northcliffe Chair of Modern English Literature" and "The Lord Northcliffe Lectureship in Literature." The Lord Northcliffe chair of modern English literature will be a companion chair to the Quain chair of English language and literature, and its holder, with the Quain professor, will be joint head of the department of English language and literature at University College. The Lord Northcliffe lectureship in literature will be held normally for one year, and in no case for longer than three years. The lecturer is to be an eminent man of letters and his duty will be to deliver six public lectures in the academic year in which he holds office.

SPECIAL CORRESPONDENCE

THE PERFECT SMALL HOUSE

SWARTHMORE'S ADVENTURE IN HOUSING HER PROFESSORS

ONE of the problems confronting most colleges, or rather most professors—particularly those in or near great cities—is that of finding houses, suitable and comfortable, at a price within the reach of academic salaries. Intent on solving this problem, so that her professors may work under the pleasantest of conditions, Swarthmore College, in the suburbs of Philadelphia, has undertaken to build a number of faculty houses on land belonging to the college, charging, by way of rent, a certain percentage of the cost of the building, not including the value of the ground. This, of course, is not a new idea; Swarthmore already has several campus houses, as many other places have; but the type of house they are building—compact, convenient, even luxurious, yet small withal, is very interesting—not to college circles alone but to people in general, for it is an able and attractive solution of the small house problem.

There were limitations of two kinds to be faced: First, the possible amount of rent which the professors could or should pay, and second, the quality and durability of materials, which, quite rightly, was insisted upon. The question resolved itself into getting the utmost space for the money, with the greatest number of conveniences. The original intention was to build the houses to suit as nearly as possible the needs of those who were to live in them. If one presented a good and desirable plan within the above limits, the house would be built accordingly.

The first house, so built, was from the accompanying sketch—completed within three and one half months of starting. The plan has proved so economical, both of building cost and available space, so attractive, so easily adaptable to differing needs, so complete, so compact

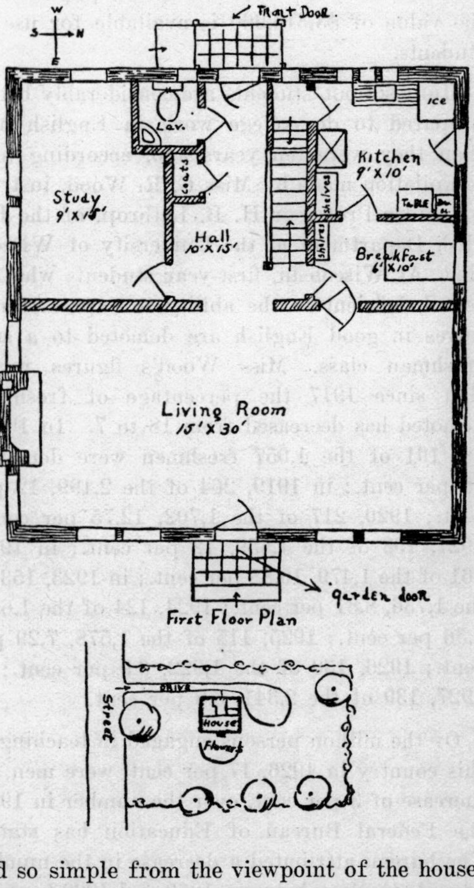

and so simple from the viewpoint of the housekeeper, that every one else wants one like it! The result is that four more with slight varia-

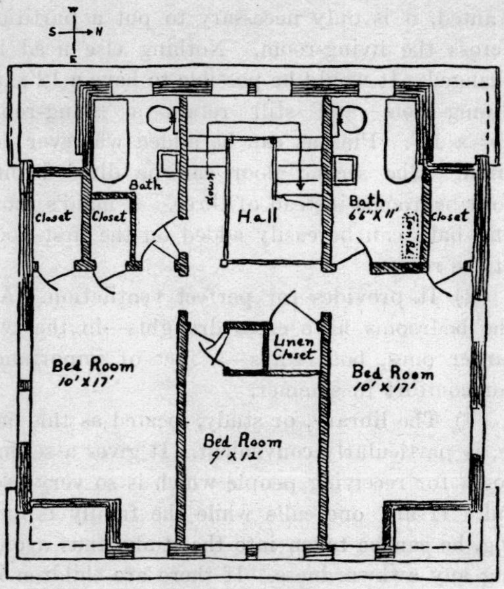

Second Floor Plan

tions have just been built. From experience in building, this seems directly contrary to the usual house psychology. Ordinarily, when looking over a new house with the thought of one's own needs, there is apt to be the feeling, "of course this is very nice, but if I were building it I would," etc., etc.

But let the house speak for itself. It is a cottage type, with broad gable-end to the street, of concrete stucco on cement block, warm yellow in color. It contains a good-sized entrance hall, study, living room, breakfast room and kitchen on the first floor; three bedrooms and two baths upstairs.

To take the plan in detail; the hall is ten feet wide, with stairs on the left as you enter. These rise from a point near the entrance into the living room and are carried on a landing over the front door. On the right are two doors, the first into a comfortable-sized lavatory, the second into an ample coat closet. Further down on the right is the door into the study. Well-lighted by three windows, the side walls lined with book shelves, there is still room enough for two desks and a full-sized couch. The latter, with the lavatory so near, makes it available as an emergency bedroom, giving that sense of stretchableness, of always being able to take in one more, which a small house so often lacks.

The living room is the surprising feature—a well-proportioned room 15′ x 30′—it annihilates immediately all one's impression of being in a cottage! This sense of spaciousness is obtained by doing away with a dining room, as such, and by using one end of the living room for that purpose. The small breakfast room—wholly separate from the kitchen—proves so attractive and convenient that most of the three meals a day are served there. It is airy and pleasant with a full-sized window looking into the garden and a door leading both to the living room and to the front hall, the latter a direct short cut to the front door. An attractive built-in cupboard holds all the china, silver and linen needed for breakfast and luncheon. When one dines in the living room, the breakfast room makes an ideal serving pantry, giving ample space for laying out salad and dessert courses, coffee tray, etc. It acts as a buffer, too, for the smells and noise of the kitchen, an important point which is rarely taken into consideration in the small house.

Off the breakfast room, the kitchen is a marvel of compactness; cupboards and broom closet built in; sink with drain board on either side, well-lighted by the three casement windows directly above; a space just right for the electric refrigerator; the whole quickly and easily ventilated. The window at the head of the cellar stairs, close by, serves both to facilitate airing the kitchen and to light the cellar steps, in many houses dangerously dark. In the basement are the laundry tubs and service toilet.

One of the first comments on the house—after the surprise of finding it so large inside—is on the amount of plumbing. This, too, has been most carefully planned for, so that the pipes go up in two direct lines, thus saving much expense. It is a house planned to minimize housework, to be run for the most part by the mistress herself. The lavatory, for example, is an essential in the small house, regardless of an architect who said they never put them in houses costing less than sixteen thousand dollars. If one's husband brings a colleague home for luncheon, he can be turned in there to wash his hands without the hostess running upstairs to make sure there are fresh towels, or that the children have left everything in order! And we all know what comfort the two bathrooms mean! These are clearly arranged off each of the two large bedrooms (one of them with a door into the hall, so that it can be used by the occupants of the third, or middle bedroom) and at opposite ends of the house, so that no sound is heard through as is so often the case when bathrooms are back to back.

The structural details of the house were all most carefully considered, on the basis of the best of materials (iron girders, slate roof, copper gutters and flashing, etc.) but eliminating the fancinesses which so often add to the cost and, alas! so often detract from the appearance. It will be simpler to list a few of these points which made such a house as this possible for the sum expended. But first of all I should mention the satisfaction of having a contractor who took as much interest in helping solve the problem of a good small house at a reasonable figure as if it had been his own.

(1) Windows and doors all stock sizes—a substantial economy which architects are apt to oppose on the ground of too much regularity.

(2) Mouldings on woodwork, base-boards, etc., are simple flat finish without the ridges and curves which serve to catch the dust and increase the cost.

(3) Stairway is built with a "closed string," instead of open, saving thereby quite a sum, yet making a pleasing effect when completed. Banister and spindles are well proportioned but unornamented.

(4) Hard-wood floors are of best oak—yet not all exactly matching in color—another saving, and certainly more attractive than a perfectly uniform tone.

(5) Interior woodwork is gum, not the least expensive, but a delightful wood when left unstained and unpainted, dressed only with an oil shellac. The color and grain are altogether charming. Kitchen, lavatory and bathrooms are white enamel.

(6) A hot-air furnace proves ample for heating purposes—a marked saving in cost as well as in the space usually given to radiators, a particularly important matter in a small house.

A similar list of some of the advantages of the plan will conduce to brevity.

(1) It will allow of many variations to suit differing needs. If a separate dining-room is wanted, it is only necessary to put a partition across the living-room. Nothing else need be changed. It would be possible to have a 12′x15′ dining-room and still retain a living-room 15′ x 18′. Piazzas can be added wherever desired. The second floor can be divided into four bedrooms instead of three. A maid's room and bath can be easily added on the first floor at the rear.

(2) It provides for perfect ventilation. All the bedrooms have cross draughts—in the two larger ones, both ways—a fact of importance for comfort in summer.

(3) The library, or study, located as this one is, is particularly convenient. It gives a second room for receiving people which is so very useful. If any one calls while the family is dining, he can be taken into the study, thus avoiding any awkwardness. If there are children in the family, it gives a room where they can study or play without being under foot.

(4) There is not a dark corner in the house. Even the upper hall has two full-sized windows. The bathroom windows are likewise full-size and do not obviously shriek "bathroom," as one approaches—which is so often the case when a small window is used.

(5) It is possible to go from the kitchen and breakfast room upstairs without being seen from the living-room.

(6) The coat closet is convenient to the front door—which is not always the case.

(7) The linen closet is beautifully light—opening not into a bathroom but into the upper hall so that linen and blankets are always available.

(8) A folding ironing board in the second bathroom is a great convenience. If one wants to press a frock there is no need to run down and up two flights of stairs.

(9) On entering the front door one gets a charming view across the hall and living-room, through the glass door opposite, to the garden beyond, greatly adding to the sense of size. The fact that the hall increases in width before you reach the door into the living-room augments this air of spaciousness.

(10) The combination of dining-room and living-room is much more simple and workable than most people imagine, particularly when, as

here, there is a breakfast-room in addition. A three- or four-fold screen, which can be drawn to conceal the table when set for dinner, and folded back when dinner is announced, answers quite as well as a permanent partition, with the added advantage that when one wants a large room it is there. One of the worst faults a house can have is to be "cut up"—we all know the phrase—it is almost impossible to create an effect no matter what the furnishings may be.

(11) Every foot of space is accounted for, well-lighted, well-aired and easy to get at.

(12) A well-planned house will always appear its true size—a skilfully planned house seems larger than it really is. The universal comment when friends enter is, "But how large!" "How do you get such a big room into such a small house," "What a pleasant hall," etc., etc. An Irish maid put her finger on it, with the deftness of her race, when she remarked, "It's a very large house for the size of it."

Cost of building varies so greatly in different localities that figures can not be relied upon. However, the fact that this house, in the neighborhood of Philadelphia, could be built for eleven thousand dollars, of the best of materials, stucco on concrete block, iron girders, slate roof with copper flashings and gutters, built-in bath tubs, etc., gives some basis for calculating. It could of course be considerably reduced by changing any of these materials, while still giving a good house. Last but not least the whole is pleasing and attractive in appearance—with the dignity which simple well-proportioned mass always gives. Set close to the ground, with the broad gable and generous chimney facing the street, it looks to belong where it is—to be already a part of its surroundings.

RUTH S. BROOKS
SWARTHMORE, PA.

DISCUSSION

ON THE PASSING OF WHISKERS IN EDUCATION

AT a recent meeting of leading school administrators I was impressed by their physical size. The great majority were not only tall but also comfortably filled out,—men of eminence, I should say, above the general crowd. The thought occurred to me that in administration physical size must be highly correlated with intelligence or else a substitute for it. The latter would be a shocking alternative.

This meeting was the first that I ever attended, being impelled to it by recent interest in professional education. A striking characteristic of the modern educator is that he is beardless. Here and there was a mustache, a tribute to vanity; or a Van Dyck, an excuse for not shaving daily; but for the most part the faces were bare. The educational leaders of my day, in marked contrast, wore long, full beards, which besides giving them an appearance of great impressiveness, had several other marked advantages. For example, when one of these patriarchs was asked a question he had only to look wise, stroke his beard, while the questioner waited, and then oracularly reply "It is my impression. . . ." What could be more effective —or convenient? He had no need of facts or even of philosophy: a beard and impressions were sufficient. He was one of those *barbae tenus sapientes*. I suspect that there is a real significance in the passing of whiskers in educators, although to-day some have lost the beard but kept the gesture.

My observation set up, as any observation should do for a scholar, an interesting train of reflection. I recalled the Roman senator who sat statue-like before the conquering Goth curious at the stately beard, but when the Vandal stroked it he instantly was slain, such was and is man's sensitiveness to his personal adornments. David's ambassadors had their beards despitefully shorn off by a bold and perspicacious heathen, and humiliated they had to tarry in Jericho until their beards were grown. Alexander the Great, on the other hand, had no such pride. Being a practical man he ordered his Macedonians to shave off the handle by which an enemy might seize them. (What septuagenarian does not recall the plot that he made when a boy thus to conquer the master if called up for a flogging?)

Adam, Zeus, Jahweh, Woden, Abraham, Moses and Agamemnon have all been imagined and pictured with beards, evidence that dignity and might were not formerly associated with smooth faces. In history it is easy to recall leaders who were bearded more than the pard:

Charlemagne, Ivan the Terrible, Leopold II, Henry III, Henry VII, Kaiser Wilhelm, and, of course, Barbarossa.[1] It is an interesting list. Those scientifically inclined are challenged to find some common cause. The medieval Franciscans were bearded, the Dominicans were not.

We are accustomed to think of some nations as bearded and others with smooth faces. But my researches[2] seem to show that, except with the people whom nature has not blessed (or cursed) with fast growing hair on their faces, beards wax and wane in fashions. The heroes of the Revolution—Washington, Adams, Jefferson, Franklin—were all smooth-shaven; those of the Civil War—Grant, Lee, Mead, Jackson, Sherman—were all bearded; those of the World War were beardless. The erudite Dr. Reisner calls my attention to the fact that a bearded laborer at Brook Farm had to be locked up in the local jail to protect him from a mob of neighbors, at that time conventionally smooth-faced, who were infuriated by his hirsute adornment. It is evident that man is sensitive and jealous of efforts to conceal or to beautify the human face.

As fashions wax and wane, may we not confidently and hopefully look forward to a return of whiskers in education? Although, as the Germans say, it is not the beard that makes the philosopher, it certainly is the beard that makes an ordinary man look like one. In education we have seen the passing fashions of correlation, projects, measurements, standardized tests, and curriculum reconstruction; each flourishes for a few years and then has its reaction. Studying these waves of fashion I go on record as prophesying that soon educators will again begin *sapientem pascere barbam*.

Quintus H. Flaccus, II.

THE SITUATION AT CLARK UNIVERSITY

Commenting upon the discussion of "The Situation at Clark University," by Professor Charles Roger Hicks, of the University of Nevada, printed in the issue of School and Society for April 21, 1928, a correspondent has sent the editor the following letter by Mr. Bradley Stone, of Boston, which recently appeared in the Boston *Transcript:*

It seems almost incredible that the trustees of Clark University, after meditating for a month on the petition of the students for redress of grievances in connection with the action of the president about their monthly magazine, should dismiss the matter in the way they do. The secretary of the trustees, in his curt letter, refers to the petition as that of "some students" of the university. The petition, as is well known, was signed by a majority of the student body. In declining to act on the petition, the trustees characterize the president's action on the controversy as a case of "discipline" and observe that "discipline lies with the president and the faculty, in whom we have entire confidence." They clearly found themselves in a very embarrassing position, shrank from stirring the muddy pools more deeply, and concluded that the least said the soonest mended.

Is this an adequate or creditable way of shelving this now notorious trouble? Does it show a decent respect for the opinion of mankind? Do older scholars and the press do their duty if they allow the fine young fellows at Clark University to be treated in this cavalier fashion without protest or more light? Do the members of the faculty, whom the trustees in their decision associate with the president in responsibility in the "disciplinary" action taken, unanimously and without exceptions accept the position assigned them? To simple souls, this seems remarkable.

Recalling the controversy as succinctly as the trustees dismiss it, the facts seem to be these: The president of the university surreptitiously secured from the printers the proofs of the students' magazine, a thing itself impossible to conceive a man like President Lowell, of Harvard, or President Butler, of Columbia, doing. He came upon proofs of an article which went against his stomach; and he dismissed the three editors who controlled the magazine. It immediately appeared that both the managing editor and the writer of the offending article had themselves decided against its publication as not in good taste; and the other two editors had never seen the article nor known of its existence. Yet the ban was not withdrawn from them. Three of their fellow students, men of high standing in their classes, incensed at the injustice, promptly resigned from the university by way of protest; and the majority

[1] Mr. Flaccus has evidently overlooked Brigham Young and the Smith brothers.

[2] Like many other educational researches as yet incomplete. My conclusions are still tentative. Q. H. F. II.

of the student body expressed their sympathy by signing a petition to the trustees asking them to review the situation and do justice to the students. If this is not a true statement of the facts, it is incumbent on the faculty of the university, whom the trustees now associate with the president in responsibility for his course, to tell the public wherein the reports so widely published in the press are wrong.

No one surely would wish to do injustice to the president and faculty of this honored university, to which Dr. G. Stanley Hall gave world-wide renown as a seat of academic freedom. But equally no red-blooded person can condone the treatment of an American student body as the students of Clark University, if the public has been rightly informed, appear to have been treated. The recent letter of the secretary of the trustees seems to plain people, on the basis of the facts given them, the worst piece of snobbery in the whole business. There have been others. One apologist for the president, a graduate student who sports "LL.B." after his name, reproached the spokesmen of the protesting students, in a letter to the Boston *Transcript,* for objecting to the president's course as "un-American." What business, asked this LL.B., have these young men to talk of Americanisms, when half of them have foreign names? This particular "100 percenter" might profitably devote a few hours in his summer holiday to compiling a list of a hundred citizens with "un-American" names, from Peter Faneuil and Albert Gallatin to Carl Schurz and Theodore Roosevelt, who have rendered the country patriotic service which we are not yet ready to despise.

It will be remembered that half a dozen years ago the president of Clark University, finding a group of students in one of the halls listening to a lecture on socialism by an accomplished scholar whom they had invited to inform them about the principles and aims of that movement, ordered the young chairman to adjourn the meeting; and when the student properly refused to do it, he himself turned off the lights, breaking up the meeting. He didn't like socialism, and would have none of it. Perhaps the president of Harvard does not like socialism; but he would only applaud any student group seeking to learn about it from a scholarly specialist in a proper way. At Clark, three or four professors resigned from their place on the faculty in indignant protest. At the present grosser performance we hear of no faculty protest, although the protesting students state that certain members of the faculty have assured them of their sympathy. Has the faculty in these half dozen years grown pusillanimous; or is the public, after all the notoriety, still uninformed as to the real facts? On the basis of the published facts, the university officials certainly have no case.

QUOTATIONS

ROUSSEAU AND PATRIOTISM

THE seven thousand teachers at the meeting of the National Education Association in Minneapolis took preparation for citizenship as their central theme this year. They would find material for its treatment in Rousseau's writings, if they were to turn from "Emile" to some of his less-known writings. Pertinent extracts from these have been presented in the current number of SCHOOL AND SOCIETY by Professor Edward H. Reisner, of Teachers College. Far from thinking solely of the individual, Rousseau was "the first important modern exponent of the use of education to create and consolidate human cultures." What warmer praise of patriotism is to be found than in an encyclopedic article on "Political Economy" written by him a few years after he came into public notice from winning the prize of the Academy of Dijon?

> It is certain that the most miraculous effects of virtue have taken rise from patriotism, this agreeable and lively sentiment which gives to the force of self-love all the beauty of virtue, gives it also an energy which without making it unnatural renders it the most heroic of all passions.

A nation is not a mere aggregation of individuals; it is an "adventure in human welfare" in which they may have an active part, but have no right to be called citizens unless they do participate. To prepare citizens through education is "the most important business of the state." Yet so to prepare them is not the work of a day, and must begin with the children:

> If they were early accustomed to regard the individual only according to his relations with the body of the state and to be sensible of their own existence only as it forms a part of the public, they may at length come to identify themselves in a degree with the great whole, to feel themselves members of their country and to love it with that exquisite sensibility which every isolated being has for itself . . . and thus transform into a sublime virtue that dangerous disposition which gives rise to all our vices.

Of this theory Rousseau made specific application when many years later he was asked by one of the parties in Poland to suggest a plan of government. He deliberately advised fostering of nationalism and the creating of "a national physiognomy"—such teaching that at fifteen the youth would know all his country's history and at sixteen all its laws, and that there should not have taken place in all his country a fine action or exist an illustrious man that was not in his mind and heart as he came into maturity and citizenship. But to enter most potently into that relationship, Rousseau would still insist that first of all each individual should have his faculties and innate capacities as highly developed as is possible.

The century and a half since Rousseau has seen patriotism work its miracle and lead men of every nation to sublime heights. But it has also given glimpse of even greater heights beyond, which are reached only through the love of country. To Rousseau the sentiment of humanity was not strong enough to embrace all mankind. It "evaporated and grew feeble" in its diffusion. In his time the "calamities of Tartary or Japan" could make no such appeal as those of a European country. To-day human sympathy knows no national bounds, and the intensity of one's patriotic devotion is to some degree indicated and measured by what he is ready to do for others. The field of adventure in human welfare is now as wide as the world.—*The New York Times.*

EDUCATIONAL RESEARCH AND STATISTICS

THE MEASUREMENT OF THE EFFECT OF TEACHING[1]

The measurement, by objective tests, of the effects produced by teaching has long been recognized as an important problem. However, no very satisfactory solution of the problem has yet been devised. The methods in common use are two. The unsophisticated user of tests is content to report, as the products of teaching, merely the achievement of children in terms of gross scores in tests. Those who have a little better understanding of the science of measurement give tests both at the beginning and at the end of the teaching period and consider that "changes in score" reflect the effects of teaching effort. The point of view of the writer, however, is that both of these measures tell only the magnitudes of the resultant effects of *many* factors, of which teaching is but one. To be entirely satisfactory, the measure of teaching employed must be a "single-variable" measure. It is the purpose of this paper to propose a new analytical technique by means of which, with proper control of the conditions of measurement, a truly satisfactory measurement of the effects of teaching may be made.

To prove that both measures of achievement and measures of growth are influenced by many factors other than teaching, it is only necessary to compare a development curve based on scores in a standard test (such as the Stanford Achievement Test) with a growth curve for a purely physiological development (such as the cutting of the lower right canine tooth in boys) or with the development of educational abilities which are not the direct products of teaching (such as the spelling of the word "front" which does not occur in the course of study in the schools tested.) (Table I, Fig. 1.)

TABLE I–A

ILLUSTRATIONS OF THE "MANY-VARIABLE"-NESS OF CONVENTIONAL MEASURES OF TEACHING

1. *Physiological Development*—Per cent. of boys of various ages possessing the lower right canine tooth.

Age	8	9	10	11	12	13	14	15
Per cent. Mature	0	12.6	32	65	83.7	92.7	97.2	100

2. *General Educational Development*—Per cent. of children in age-grade groups spelling the word "front" correctly. The word does not occur in their course of study.

Age-Grade	6–1B	7–2B	8–3B	9–4B	10–5B	11–6B
Per cent. Correct	0	5	52	88	98	100

3. *Specific Educational Development*—Age norms for Stanford Achievement Tests (Manual of Directions).

Age	9	10	11	12	13	14	15	16	17	18
Norms	25	39	53	64	71	76	80	81.5	83.5	84

[1] An address delivered before Section Q, American Association for the Advancement of Science, Nashville, December 26, 1927.

TABLE I–B

THE DATA ABOVE SMOOTHED AND MADE COMPARABLE BY EXPRESSING THEM AS PERCENTAGES OF MATURITY AT TEN EQUAL INTERVALS BETWEEN ZERO AND 100 PER CENT. A SCORE OF 86 IN THE STANFORD ACHIEVEMENT TEST IS ASSUMED TO REPRESENT MATURITY

Time Intervals	0	1	2	3	4	5	6	7	8	9	10
Physiological	0	3	14	38	60	74	86	92	95	97	100
Spelling	0	.5	5	25	52	73	88	94	98	99	100
Stanford	0	.3	2	13	33	55	71	83	90	96	100

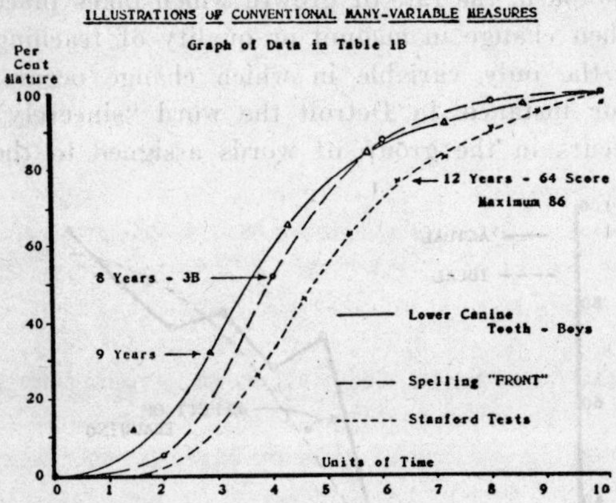

FIG. 1

Note the similarity in the form of the three curves. To say that a twelve-year-old child makes a score of 64 in the Stanford Achievement Test, or that in one year he has grown from a score of 53 to a score of 64 is to describe merely his status or his rate of development. Teaching is but one of many factors affecting such status and development.

The cutting of teeth by boys can scarcely be considered to reflect the effect of teaching. Differences in the time of eruption of teeth in different individuals are ordinarily ascribed to differences in the hereditary and environmental influences acting. Yet the curves for the development of general (untaught) educational ability, and for abilities which are ordinarily regarded as the direct products of teaching, are very similar in character. Development is a natural process to which teaching merely contributes as one among the many factors involved. The fact of the matter is that live children inevitably grow. The training given in school affects growth in educational abilities somewhat, but the actual change in score that takes place in any individual is determined, not alone by the teaching, but by the natural growth-rate of that individual as well.

Further proof of the "many-variable"-ness of conventional scores is readily secured by sorting into homogeneous age-grade groups the scores for success in any single item, as the spelling of the word "army" (untaught,) and then finding the central tendency for *each* age-grade group separately. (Table II.)

TABLE II

A FURTHER ILLUSTRATION OF THE COMPLEX CHARACTER OF CONVENTIONAL SCORES

An age-grade-ability table of scores in terms of percentages of correct spelling of the word "army" (untaught). Based on tests of 2,395 boys. The scores given in the table are the scores of the various age-grade groups. From the 1926 Survey of Spelling in the public schools of Hamtramck, Michigan.

Grades	7	8	9	10	11	12	13	
1A	0	0	0					
2B	4	2	-	0				
2A	25	33	22	24				
3B		53	39	25	25	→ A		
3A		62	57	38	32	40		
4B			86	74	51	39	67	D
4A			90	86	86	84	48	
5B			95	100	92	78	74	
5A				100	92	94	92	
6B				100	100	98	93	
6A					100	98	100	I_2
7B						100	100	
					B	I_1	C	

The table is to be read as follows: The average score of a group of boys eight years old, in the 2B grade, was 2 per cent. of correct spelling of the word "army." Arrow A indicates change in scores caused by age and intelligence, training being constant. Arrow B indicates change in score caused by intelligence and training, age being constant. Arrow C indicates change in score caused by age and training, intelligence being constant. (?) Arrow D indicates change in score caused by increased age, decreased intelligence and decreased training. No score indicates solely the effect of teaching.

Now "grade attained" is, of course, a rough measure of amount of schooling. Similarly, "age" is a rough measure of maturity. Age and grade together furnish a rough measure of intelligence. That is, other things being equal, the eight-year-old boy who attains the 3A grade, when most of the eight-year-old boys are in the 2A grade and some are still in the 1A grade, has a mental endowment of superior quality. If we examine the age-grade-ability table with these facts in mind, it is readily seen that as we compare score with score a move in any direction from any selected starting point involves changes in at least two factors.

No score in the entire table reflects, solely and uniquely, the effect of teaching. Hence it may not be out of place, in passing, to call the attention of test makers and norm setters to the advantages of expressing standards in terms of age-grade-ability grouping. If age were measured in half years, schooling in half grades, comparison from system to system could be made on a less ambiguous basis than at present. If the further refinements were made of expressing norms in terms of sex-age-grade rate of promotion-ability scores, and of making comparisons in terms of the development curves for defined groups, ambiguity and unreliability (under proper control of the testing conditions) would be almost completely removed. For instance, a comparison of the development curves for superior, normal and inferior intelligence along the line indicated by the arrows I^1, C and I^2 in Table II enables one to see that, in general, changes in intelligence produce corresponding changes in rate of development. (Fig. 2.)

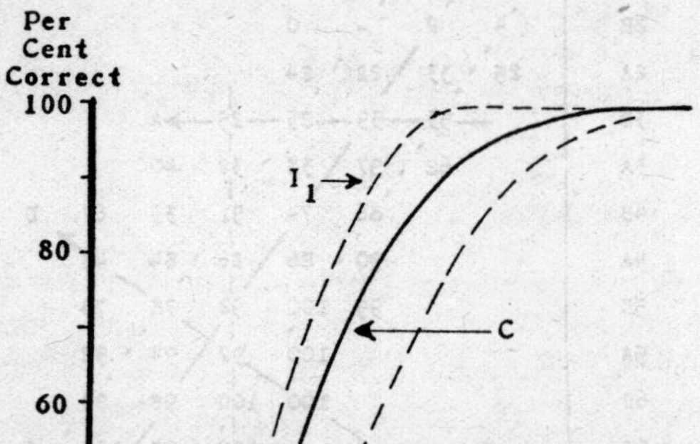

Fig. 2. Comparison of age-grade-ability development curves along lines of superior, normal and inferior intelligence, Table II. The greater the intelligence the greater the rate of development.

To secure a "single variable" measure of teaching, it is only necessary to measure the *change* in the rate of growth which takes place when change in amount or quality of teaching is the only variable in which change occurs. For instance, in Detroit the word "sincerely" occurs in the group of words assigned to the

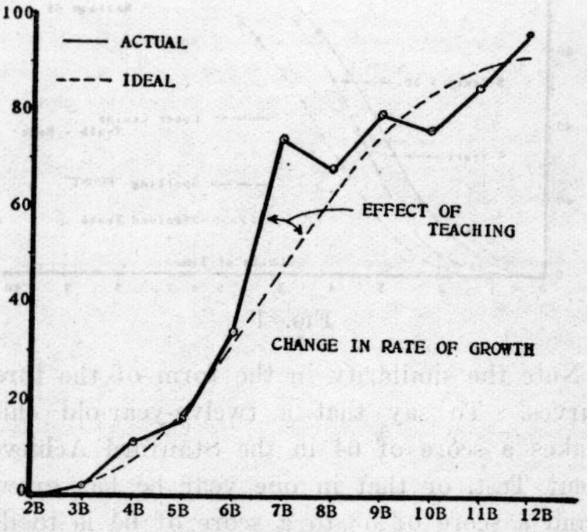

Fig. 3

TABLE III

The Development of the Ability to Spell "Sincerely"

Scores in per cent. of correct spelling of word "sincerely" made by age-grade groups of boys and girls differing one year in age and one grade in training in regular sequence, Detroit Public Schools. The word is taught in the seventh grade Groups.

Age	7	8	9	10	11	12	13	14	15	16	17
Grade	2B	3B	4B	5B	6B	7B	8B	9B	10B	11B	12B
Per cent. correct.											
	0[1]	2	11	16	34	74	68	79	76	85	96
Similar data for "customary" (untaught) for comparison											
	0[1]	5	13	18	42	60	66	80	87	90	97

[1] Estimated.

seventh grade course of study in spelling, but long before the seventh grade some of the children through incidental contact learn to spell the word, and grade by grade more and more children are able to spell it successfully. (Table III, Fig. 3.)

If now one estimates what the development curve would have been if the word had not been taught (broken line, Fig. 3) one can see that the teaching operated to increase the rate of growth and that after the teaching was over

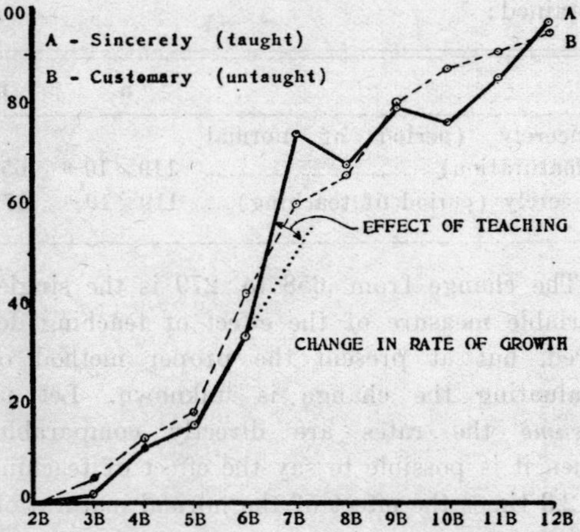

FIG. 4. Note that in the lower grades the curve for "customary" (Curve B) is slightly above the curve for "sincerely" (Curve A). If "sincerely" had not been taught in the seventh grade, it is assumed from the form of Curve B that Curve A would have continued as indicated by the dotted line. The change in the rate of growth which occurs when teaching begins is thus the true measure of the effect of teaching.

changing from elementary to high-school level.)

Information in regard to what the development curve would have been had there been no teaching was gained by comparing the scores for the word "customary," which does not occur in the course of study, with that for "sincerely," which does. (Fig. 4.)

However, the precise measurement of the effect of teaching rests upon a more solid foundation than mere estimation of probable curves of development. Last year I had the pleasure of presenting to this section the evidence which proves that the Gompertz formula, developed in 1825, expresses the general law of biologic growth. Whenever either an individual or a group made up of a normal distribution of nature elements grows toward a defined maturity, under conditions such that neither nature nor nurture changes in amount or quality during the period of growth, the development curve is accurately represented by the formula

$$y = n^{r^t}$$

in which

y = per cent. of maturity attained at the end of any given time interval,

n = quality of mechanism acted upon (nature).

r = rate of growth (effect of nurture under the given conditions).

t = intervals of time during which nurture acts.

For instance, in Table 2 consider the development curve for the spelling of the word "army" represented by the arrow C. (Table IV).

TABLE IV

THE DEVELOPMENT OF ABILITY UNDER (NEARLY) STANDARD CONDITIONS

Observed per cents. of correct spelling of word "ARMY" by groups of boys in-grade-at-age.

Time units	0	1	2	3	4	5	6	Total
Age-Grade groups	7–1B	8–2B	9–3B	10–4B	11–5B	12–6B	13–7B	......
Number of cases	.....	139	82	88	90	87	40	526
Per cent. of correct spellings	0[2]	2.1	39.0	73.8	92.2	97.7	100	.....

[2] Estimated.

the ability promptly "slumped" to the normal level. (The irregularities in the upper end of the curve are assumed to be due to the difference in selection, and in the meaning of "grade," in

The constants for "nature" and "rate of growth" derived by conventional statistical procedure from the data (using the nearest whole per cent. in each case) are

$n = .000,023,26$ or 2326×10^{-8}
$r = .3003$

The complete series of equations for computing the per cent. of development attained at the end of each of the time intervals, and the resulting values of y, actual scores, errors, etc., are as follows:

Equations	Resulting value	Actual score	Error
$y_0 = (2326 \times 10^{-8})\ .3003^0 =$	0.0	0.0	0.0
$y_1 = (2326 \times 10^{-8})\ .3003^1 =$	4.1	2.1	2.0
$y_2 = (2326 \times 10^{-8})\ .3003^2 =$	38.2	39.0	.8
$y_3 = (2326 \times 10^{-8})\ .3003^3 =$	74.9	73.8	1.1
$y_4 = (2326 \times 10^{-8})\ .3003^4 =$	91.7	92.2	.5
$y_5 = (2326 \times 10^{-8})\ .3003^5 =$	97.4	97.7	.3
$y_6 = (2326 \times 10^{-8})\ .3003^6 =$	99.2	100.0	.8
Standard error = 1.0 per cent.			

The equations are given in full that the reader may have the opportunity to develop for himself the concept that *constant teaching* acting on a group of normal boys of (nearly) *constant nature* results in a *constant rate of growth*, .3003. Many persons find it difficult to conceive of human or biologic growth in exact mathematical terms, but the evidence in my possession seems to prove beyond question that all growth under the conditions stated above is well represented by the Gompertz law. However that may be, it is sufficient for present purposes to see that the constant, r, summarizes in a single quantity the resultant effects of all the variables determining the effect of nurture on nature, that is, *the rate of growth*.

Under such conditions, if all the other variables are held constant and only teaching varied, it follows that the resulting "changes in rate of growth" will be a "single-variable" measure of the effect of the changes made in the teaching procedure.

For instance, to return to the two words "sincerely" and "customary," the constants computed for the periods unaffected by teaching are:

Constants		n	r	Standard error[3]
Words:	Sincerely	119×10^{-6}	.658	3.2
	Customary	989×10^{-6}	.658	3.2

"Sincerely" is a word of greater complexity (intrinsic difficulty) than "customary," and for convenience in computation, adjustment for this fact has been made in the "n" constant; this accounts for the large difference in the "n" values. The "r" values, being closely the same, are in conformity with the similarity in the development curves of the two words.

If now, for the word "sincerely" the value of "n" is held constant and a new "r" computed for the portion of the curve during which direct teaching took place, the following results are obtained:

	n	r
Sincerely (period of normal maturation)	119×10^{-6}	.658
Sincerely (period of teaching)	119×10^{-6}	.279

The change from .658 to .279 is the single-variable measure of the effect of teaching desired, but at present the proper method of evaluating the change is unknown. Let us *assume* the rates are directly comparable. Then it is possible to say the effect of teaching is 2.3 times the effect of the normal maturation influences.

A better form of comparison, however, is to compare the times taken to produce the same amount of growth at the two rates. Thus, for the word "sincerely" and a given group of children, one year of teaching produced a gain that it would have taken 3.1 years of normal maturation to achieve.[4]

It should be evident from the foregoing that it is possible to measure only the relative, not the absolute, value of the effect of teaching. The need immediately arises for standard development rates, derived from standardized teaching, from which to measure relative values.

S. A. COURTIS
UNIVERSITY OF MICHIGAN

(To be concluded)

[3] The data on which the constants are based are not as ''pure'' as those for the word ''army''; hence the larger standard error.

[4] In general, the time ratio of the single-variable measure of the effect of teaching is the ratio of the logarithm of its rate of growth to the logarithm of the basic rate of growth.

SCHOOL AND SOCIETY

Volume XXVIII | Saturday, July 21, 1928 | Number 708

THE MEANING OF THE BACCALAUREATE[1]

Baccalaureate—a curious, almost ironic word. No laurel wreath; quite other is the etymology of the word, and the history of the idea. It is so odd and humorous as to be worth setting out in some detail; we may read in the lexicon:

Bachelor: from Low Latin *baccalarius*, a holder of a small farm or estate called *baccalaria*. The latter probably derived from Low Latin *bacca*, corruption of Latin *vacca*.

Vacca—cow! How words do travel! Moreover, the rest of the dictionary's lore is not much more flattering: for the etymologically true *baccalarius*, and the transmogrified bachelor or baccalaureate run the following course of meanings:

1. Tenants holding a fee of an inferior kind. 2. Monks who had not yet taken the full vows. 3. Knights who, for lack of means, had not yet raised their banner in the field. 4. Students who had taken their first degree in the university. And finally, 5. unmarried men, who, because of their solitary condition, were regarded as candidates or probationers for marriage.

Still worse, these innocent not-yet-married men were often looked on askance and put under disabilities or penalties, as being in some grave manner imperfect or even guilty! What wonder that somewhere in the long line of linguistic flow, kindly scribes shaded the vowels—a most gracious ablaut or umlaut—to get away from or at least around the lowly wet-nurse of the human race, and arrive instead at the laurel wreath of victory! But it seems really to have begun with the cow.

[1] Baccalaureate address at Reed College, Portland, Oregon, June 10, 1928.

How much of this is jest and how much earnest may perhaps be guessed by what shall follow. But I hasten to assure you that you have come far and arrived somewhere when you become baccalaureate; it is a long cry from that little patch of land, with, it must be supposed, *a* cow as its complement of livestock, to where you stand this momentous week. When you receive on the last day of the week the bachelor's degree and the parchment testimonium which certifies it to the world, and move the tassel of your academic headgear ninety degrees to the right, at that moment no agricolar, still less a bovine symbol could do justice to the occasion, but truly a laurel wreath; here at least reformed spelling is justified, even though it obscures literal etymology. Nobody will call you *baccalaurius;* indeed I am almost frightened by my own temerity to have torn the kindly veil from off the now noble word and exposed its lowly origin; yet I really mean something by so doing and may be able to hint that meaning to you in due time.

You have come far and have arrived. There are in the ordinary run of lives three great universally waited-for days: birth, in which the waiting is indeed vicarious; marriage, and death; the day of graduation may well be, for those who experience it, a modest fourth to these great three. In one respect it probably surpasses them; in being consciously looked for through a longer period. A degree is after all just a grade, technically the sixteenth on the American plan; and being graduated is just another promotion; indeed that is exactly what the Germans call it. But the baccalaureate promotion is a sort of node in the long stream of school-going, a thick place running back into prior time and forward into the time to come. It is a striking of the clock, long-expected, eagerly listened to and then lapsing into relative silence, yet still echoing vibrant among other waves of experience. The decided beginning of the node for you of Reed College was the ordeal of the junior qualifying examination; it widened into the heavy labor of thesis writing, and culminated in the final stress of the senior oral.

Behind and alongside of these special phases of the pre-graduation course are the broad curriculum of the lower division, and the expanded freedom and strenuous requirements of the upper division. All these marked features of the college serve to consolidate the realism and substance of the course; the two formal examinations have another virtue, less fully recognized but vital: they enhance the ritual of the whole procedure and so greatly add to the impressiveness of the final act of graduation.

It is true that the baccalaureate is the first degree, that is, the lowest degree, given by American colleges and universities. Nevertheless, in some sense it is the most interesting and perhaps the most important degree. At least it is doubtful whether the attaining of any higher degree will produce an impression upon your mind equal to that connected with this first degree. For generations it was the only degree conferred by American institutions, at least "in course;" and honorary degrees are quite another story. The great mass of those who graduate from college never take any higher degree; for them the bachelor's degree is not only the first, but also the last and final academic arrival. Mostly then because it is the first, and comes early in life, partly also on the grounds just indicated and some to be pointed out directly, the attainment of the baccalaureate bulks very large spiritually and emotionally, with both the recipients and their friends: hence the greatness of the commencement exercises, at which these degrees are conferred. Hence also the practice which calls us together this afternoon, the "baccalaureate" address, originally called sermon, and invariably delivered by a clergyman; even after higher degrees came to bulk large in higher education, and universities, or at least their faculties, transferred much of their interest to the "masters" and "doctors," still the exercises of commencement week opened with the baccalaureate address.

It is concerning the meaning of the baccalaureate, then, that I invite you to reflect; at least the invitation is surely appropriate, and I pray to the gods of discourse that my words may not hinder your reflections from being profitable. John Dewey, in one of his most trenchant utterances, says that meaning is greater than truth, in that truth is but one of the many elements or forms of meaning. So let me try to speak truth and let your baccalaureate intelligence perceive still greater meanings.

In arriving at the baccalaureate, then, there are at least two aspects in which you have arrived definitely and finally: you are college graduate and alumnus of your alma mater; from these two points of vantage or disvantage you cannot be dislodged any more than you can from your birth to certain parents and to a certain station in life. Neither church nor state can grant either party a dissolution of this union. When on the eve of our entrance into the world war, David Starr Jordan braved the whirlwind by challenging the aims of the war, some of his Cornell classmates met and expelled him from the class: it was a sorry joke upon the self-appointed inquisitors. But even if Jordan had been a traitor instead of an admirable patriot, no disclaimer would have been open to nor any defense needed by the great institution which is his spiritual foster-mother. Your college is entitled to share in the merit of your achievements, but only at the cost of bearing the onus of your delinquencies. The peevish old men who excommunicated Jordan should have known that neither they nor the university could enjoy the reflected glory of the great scientist and administrator and yet incontinently throw the pacifist overboard.

The intense attachment between alumni and their alma mater is rather distinctive of our country. Like all intense affections it is likely to gender evil as well as good. The good is found in such things as warmth of mutual affection and common pride, and lasting reciprocal interest and aid. The college can never lose its love for you and interest in you and your career; it will be very natural for you to keep always a place in your heart for the college; it happens that Reed alumni thus far have set a rather high standard of gratitude and appreciation. You do not need me to tell you that a college so young and so charged with pioneer enterprise stands in unique need of your support.

But the basic meaning of the baccalaureate and of course of any degree transcends the institution which confers the degree. The historic formula of the rite makes no mention of the particular institution, but "admits you to the degree of bachelor, with all the rights, privileges and immunities which pertain thereto." And the document which certifies to the act is addressed to all those to whom it may concern. Both formula and document were in Latin, the universal language, to emphasize this cosmopolitan reference. The candidate is "admitted to the fellowship of scholars;" and that fellowship is as wide as the civilized world. Your diploma opens doors to you everywhere. It is a passport with almost no geographical limitation. It is pleasant to assure you that college graduation initiates you into a sort of spiritual freemasonry, and furnishes clues to fine associations and friendships in any cultured community.

It is trite to say that you have arrived with a small minority of your age-fellows, most of whom have dropped out of the academic march much earlier. There are in the United States well over two million persons of your age, or, more strictly, of the average age for college graduation; of these more than 1,850,000 are not graduating and will not graduate. The group has been much worse than "decimated," but not in the ordinary sense, for the fraction, about one in fourteen, have not been killed but only graduated. But your minority situation in the world is far more marked than this: for the relative number graduated was far smaller in the past than it is now; I know of no reliable statistics of the total number of college graduates in the population as a whole, but it is far below seven per cent.: indeed, so rapid has been the recent increase in college attendance and graduation that it is probably not more than five; you may well belong to a privileged group forming only one twentieth part of the people of the country. Even if the present rate of increase in higher education should keep up, which is far from probable, you will be well along in years before graduates number one tenth of the whole people. Outside of the United States the proportion of persons so educated falls far below the level here.

Another way to mark the point at which you have arrived is to say that it denotes, better than any other common experience, *the end of youth and immaturity*. You have surrendered all claims and all exemptions which can be based on infancy, imbecility, or illiteracy, at least in law or logic: I add the qualifying phrase to safeguard myself against having to guarantee all academic bachelors against folly or ignorance. You cannot take refuge in lack of schooling; nor, what goes much deeper, in deficiency of that mysterious but very real capacity which the intelligence-tests test, concerning which I may repeat what I have said before from this desk, that whatever it is and howsoever important, it is not, or at least not yet, intelligence. Out of a random sampling of your fellow-citizens you stand in the top quarter in IQ and the top seven per cent. in academic training. This is a rather tight place to be, and should add to one's qualms about standing before the judgment-seat; but it is where you have arrived; it is part of the meaning of the baccalaureate. It is true that in some sense you arrived here long ago, even perhaps in your fortunate choice of ancestors; but graduation, even with the lowly baccalaureate degree, certifies the fact to you and to the world, and makes it of record for all time.

In the second place—and coming on the heels of the comprehensive final senior orals this may surprise you and even possibly the faculty—in the second place you have accumulated, by long process, and with many losses in transit, a mighty stock of—of what? Of knowledge? Of information? Call it what you please; you have it. It is one of the gifts of the college course, and you ought to be duly grateful: at least for some of it. After all it is true that "no man's thinking is better than his information:" or at least no thinking, however good, can elicit truth out of false or erroneous or missing data. Let me bear a bit of testimony here on the vexed question of senior theses, as relevant to my present point: every year I learn from one or more of the theses something which I never knew before; sometimes it is something which nobody ever knew before, and yet quite true; and sometimes fruitful and vital. Of course, in stressing the very considerable character of the knowledge you have accumulated, I do not mean to deny that you have infinitely more to learn, and that many of the things which will be most vital in your careers not only are not included in your college curriculum, but are not even discovered yet.

I wish I were as sure about the increase of power as I am about the increase of knowledge; at least I am far surer at Reed than at many other places. But we face a sort of paradox here: information, facts, data, particulars, statistics, dates, formulae—these are the indispensable raw material for thought, for profitable reflection, for intelligence in the true sense of that word. In one sense one can not have too much of this material; in another sense too much of it wrecks the intellectual life. Burke says that every man who is ruined is ruined on the side of his natural propensity: the very first natural propensity of the thinker is the gathering of facts; if, for any reason, inner or from without, he becomes engrossed and absorbed in collecting, to the exclusion or diminishing of the higher process of reflection and organization, his intellectual life lingers in a barren erudition. The actuality is likely to be even worse, for facts bereft of the integrating function of organization dribble and leak out of memory and are lost in oblivion. The very word oblivion is a sort of knell in our pedagogy, tolling the fate which befalls how much of what we learn?

But time forbids dwelling on this question; it is gratifying to note that education in general and higher education in particular are attacking the problem as never before; whether their efforts will avail to outweigh the ever-increasing difficulty due to the swelling flood of the tide of knowledge in every direction, time alone can tell. For our present purpose let us take heart of hope, and believe that you have arrived in both information and power; that knowledge has come and wisdom has not lingered.

This arrival in knowledge and mental power signifies that you live in an illuminated world, or at least a better-lighted world than if you had not so arrived. There are fewer dark regions in it, and a whole visible and understandable topography, with boundaries and contours, and, best of all, roads and other means of communication.

There are some things that your school education, and probably all your education, has gravely neglected. This because you have had nothing more than a particularly high grade variety of typical modern education; in other words you have been born too early to have the education of the future.

The first and most specific of these arrears is *politics.* The noblest of Plato's works is his politics, commonly called the Republic, in which he teaches that philosophers should be kings. But the philosophers, meaning of course the thinkers in general, have chosen mostly to follow his defeatist counsel and hide behind a wall, a monastery or university wall usually, until the sandstorm of the actual world of affairs shall blow itself out. But in twenty-three centuries it has not blown itself out. The philosophers have begun to come out from behind the walls. What will you do? In other words, who is going to think for Portland, for Multnomah County, for Oregon, the United States of America—which the little girl called "Tissofee"—meaning of course "My Country:" and finally—a practical question now for the first time in history—who is going to think for the *orbis terrarum,* the ecumene or inhabited world—the family of nations, whether League of Nations or not? There is an obligation of some proportion for millions of thinkers. What about you? Lest the word *think,* used so freely here, may mislead, let me put a whole corrective consideration into a pregnant sentence of Carlyle's: "The end of Man is never a Thought but an Action."

The next point of neglect is beauty and joy, and of the phase of life that cultivates these, art. "Bachelors of arts" for centuries back have been marked by their ignorance of art and their consequent indifference to it. Beauty and joy are not in the curriculum. Play, which is almost another name for all of these, is the pet aversion, the *bete noir,* of the pedagog. This in spite of all the greatest educators from Plato down to John Dewey, who agree that the child must learn "as if playing." Bosanquet gives as the source of manifold ills in the social order that "we enjoy what we ought to use, and use what we ought to enjoy." The first clause denotes the lowness of our tastes; the second the commercialization of the arts and of recreation. I am not throwing stones at football or baseball or even boxing bouts; nor implying that we are worse than our fathers: it is not so far back to the Roman circus with its bloody shows, and still less far to the time when public executions were the most popular of spectacles.

You see both of these deficiencies are in the field of *values;* in other words, human meanings. The leaders of the intellectual life have shrunk from their functions in this field and left it to suffer from superficiality, traditionalism, even quackery and charlatanism.

More art, more beauty, more joy, and especially better joys—a better and richer realm of values—these lie on the forward road. You owe an obligation to yourself to cultivate this neglected area of your personal lives, and to your race to promote it socially.

But while much more might be said of arrival at the baccalaureate, I have no more time to give to that phase; I turn to my next, which is of course the only thing it could be—*departure.* After all the baccalaureate is, or at least was, just baccalariat, and had more to do with a cow than with a laurel wreath. It meant a man with the smallest kind of farm, a knight who had not yet raised his own banner on the field, a solitary man looking for a better-half to make an entity out of his fragmentary existence. It is not a status to be dwelt in any longer than necessary, and certainly no destination for anybody, but only a point in transit.

Since I am a college professor I should clear my skirts at once of the suspicion of special pleading: I am not talking about "higher degrees," at least of the academic variety. My own suspicion is that on the whole you are likely enough to "do graduate work," and get your master or doctor. Surely you will not suspect me of speaking disrespectfully of these; I assure you nothing of the sort is in my mind. But I am just not bringing them up now. They are after all only more degrees or steps, and are no more status or destination than the baccalaureate. So let us genuflect to them and pass on.

First, then, let me swap the cold and negative term departure for a warmer and more positive one, which will far better suggest my meaning: that term is *expectancy.*

First then, as human beings living in a highly civilized and economically prosperous community, and of ages ranging near twenty-one years, and quite regardless of your being college graduates, you have an impressive life expectancy: forty years. It is true that the actuarial tables from which this figure is taken, with all their wonderful scientific quality, have not the slightest power to predict the life-span of any single individual; in a group as small as this graduating class even the average actual term of life might vary considerably from the statistical norm. Moreover, it is possible, nay probable, that the progress of hygienic knowledge, medical skill, and the improvement in the habitual forms of life, may still further increase the average span of life measurably even within your lifetime. Still, if any one of you were sitting down to frame the most careful and rational plan of life, and needed to use a figure for length of life in the process, the figure of forty years would be the only one with any general validity. You might properly modify it in the light of your family history, your present state of health, your intended course of life, but that would be all individual and personal to you. For my purpose it is sufficient as it is.

Now it is quite common for people to talk of the shortness of life, especially those who are themselves no longer young. I must demur to all such talk; *life is very long;* you are due to have sixty years in all, forty being still before you. Certainly as compared with the periods of history or the cycles of stellar evolution forty years is a mere tick of the clock. But all such comparisons are totally inept and really ridiculous. They are like proving that a man is a very small creature because the star Betelgeuse is so vast. This kind of argument has just as much force as proving that man is gigantic because an amoeba is microscopic; that is no force or meaning at all.

Nor am I talking in mere subjective terms. That might turn out to be mere praise of tedium; I am not predicting and certainly not wishing that life should seem long to you. But forty years is an immense span of happening, of reality, of movement and change. Range back over the forty years now elapsed, to 1888: as you move backward see how things drop out of the picture—aviation entire, with all its wealth of invention, of daring, of romance, of prophetic outlook in peace and war; the world war entire, with its complete redrawing and recoloring of the map of human life, and its supermagical transformations worked upon our own country. Why, it was forty years ago yesterday that William II ascended the imperial and royal throne, with all the world wondering what this rather brash and egotistical young man would do in Germany and Europe! So the astounding parabola of his erratic trajectory through history got itself pretty well drawn to a finis within the first three quarters of this forty-year span, and has been trailing along at nadir for the last quarter. Depart for a moment from our own particular dates, and note that the whole life-period of that mighty German Empire, of which this William was so brilliant a symbol, was only forty-seven years, from its haughty inauguration in Versailles in 1871 to its catastrophic downfall in that same place in 1918. If you live out your due time, your life from boyhood or girlhood on will be longer than the whole epoch of that Empire. But this sort of theme is a fearful temptation to garrulity: I leave the rest of it to your own historical erudition and vivid memory.

Turn now to the future: if the forty years just gone have been so crammed with substance and meaning, and if so much of our *now* lay forty years ago unknown and even unsuspected in the womb of time, what may not emerge, evolve, come true, write itself into history, in the forty years looming before you and belonging to you and your generation? Can you imagine that in 1968 when you look back to this great year of 1928, this 1928 and its world will look as small, as petty, as old-fashioned and out-of-date, as 1888 and its world look to us now? It seems absurd; but the simple probability is that you will then gaze back over an even vaster stream of events and evolvements than we can even dream of now. In all this we are talking only of the average span: but men live far beyond this average; there are, I suppose, some scattered few among the army of college graduates—bachelors—this year, who will actually see with their own eyes the dawn of the next century, the twenty-first. I do not recall hearing it even mentioned before! Yet measured in the span of human lives it is so near.

Arrival and *expectancy;* these two are the pattern of life, and of course are really merged into one. Their meaning—and it is meanings we seek—is quite ineffable and transcendent. What are you looking forward into? Certainly something you do not see; if you saw it, it would be present, or past. Still you are looking mainly forward, into the future, contradictory as the mere words are. Yet the only thing you can expect with certainty is the unexpected; the expected may or may not happen; if it does not happen then the unexpected happens instead of it; if it does happen then the unexpected happens with it. Who was wise enough in 1888, when some few of us elders were "baccalaureates," to know the future? The future was once pictured as a sphinx, who knew but would not tell; to-day it is freely suspected that the sphinx not only does not tell, but does not know.

With all this talk about expectancy I do not mean to commit myself to either "optimism" or "pessimism"—whatever these shibboleths may mean. When I exercise my "will to believe," I might confess to meliorism, as George Eliot dubbed it; but it is a volition, not logic; but mark well, *not illogical;* since the Book of Genesis has been supplemented by the book of nature the best logic is after all on the side of hope, or, at least, expectancy. The great and indisputable fact is that things are going on and we with them. As Whitman says:

This day before dawn I ascended a hill and look't at the crowded heaven,
And I said to my spirit, When we become the enfolders of those orbs, and the pleasure and

knowledge of every thing in them, shall we be fill'd and satisfied then?
And my spirit said No, we but level that lift to pass and continue beyond.
You are also asking me questions and I hear you,
I answer that I can not answer, you must find out for yourself.

In the interest of a fuller conception of expectancy I must further appeal to the vigor and reach of your imagination in saying that life must be not merely long—indeed it need not be long by the calendar at all—but it must be wide, and deep, and high, and rich. It may seem foolish to tempt the scorn of the cynic and the wrath of the pessimist by such talk; but I point out that I too may have my say just as they do. It is very smart to say, as Balfour does, that life is a disreputable episode on a minor planet; but it is also a very foolish thing to say. If Mr. Balfour knows of anything more reputable than human life he has not told us of it. If he will be frank and tell us that this is really just an expression of his emotions, then we must be very sorry for him; if he really means it as a true description then he should favor us with a little rigorous logic in support. But even if he could—and he really couldn't—the logic of his own life would refute both his arguments and his proposition; how could his political career, his lifelong scholarship, the persistent earnestness of his attack on problems both practical and theoretical, be squared with any such view of life as a whole? Of course we do think with our emotions—or at least we don't think without them: and according to James-Lange that means that we think partly with our livers; and sometimes the liver is out of order. This is almost the same as to say that all the most vital questions about life are answered by the will. It is perhaps fortunate that most of the cynics change color completely when they act, especially in their families, with their friends, in their vocations and avocations. So I repeat without hesitation or apology, that any expectancy worth while must look for a life wide and deep and high and rich.

This is not to say that life is to be happy, or prosperous, or successful, or what we hope for; it is not likely to be "all beer and skittles"; or to Americanize it, all golf and cocktails. I may digress here to utter one of my gravest anxieties about schooling, and especially higher schooling, that it educates to luxury and extravagance, to the wearing of fine clothes, the enjoying of comfortable jobs and easy money, the indulgence of aristocratic tastes. It may even be that the tendency to cynicism among the intelligent is partly due to the failure of education to lead to affluence. To deny indignantly that life is a disreputable episode is not to declare that it is soft, easy, comfortable, simple, a sure thing, a game in which everybody always wins. Oscar Wilde lost terribly and had to write "De Profundis" and "Ballad of Reading Gaol"; but his life was not a disreputable episode, even though it contained one. The world war had crooked diplomacy behind it and through it, devilish cruelty in it, contemptible profiteering accompanying it, but neither was it a disreputable episode.

The life of man is well supplied with hazard, pain, suffering, loss; in these respects, as in everything else of consequence, he completely outranges the rest of the animals. In belonging to the race you fall heir inevitably to this part of the bequeathed endowment. They are integral to his type of life, probably to all life. So your expectancy, whether for four years, or forty, or many more, embraces these things; they, too, are part of "What Men Live By."

What we are here involved in is probably the profoundest question open to the mind of man: a great man was asked, if he could put one question to omniscience, what it would be; he said: I would ask if the universe is friendly? Well, we can not ask omniscience: but the case is not totally dark; in the first place, men seem to want these more somber things; at least they want and will have hazard, danger, peril, and these are just potential and imaginative wounds and pain and death. This is a very simple fact of ordinary observation and history; Nobile with the *Italia* in polar ice and the *Southern Cross* battling hurricanes across the Southern seas are just two "modern instances." Another fact is less simple and even more paradoxical, that pain and loss are so integral to life that life can not be wide or deep or high or rich without them. Well did the old Greek proverb say "Whom the gods love, to them they give great joys and great sorrows." There are few truer sayings than that a fight is good enough to win only when it is good enough to lose.

Utilitarian ethics is as great an escape from the mores and the "categorical imperative" as democracy is from divine right of kings; but the utilitarians fell victim to a profound fallacy which has confused minds ever since, in that they taught that the value of life is measured by subtracting the sum of sorrows from the sum of joys; of course by such computation it is easy to reduce most values to zero or even a net minus quantity. The truth is totally different, that the value of life is a sort of sum or rather consummation of joys and sorrows. This is far from the smug and comfortable morals and religion which have dominated the last hundred and fifty years, but it has the great superiority of being realistic and tenable. Instinct and history both confirm it; art and literature celebrate it; any sound philosophy and program of life must embrace it. "Blessedness," says Spinoza, "is not the reward of virtue; it is virtue itself." Only we must remember that Spinoza was writing and thinking in Latin and *virtus* is militant as well as moral.

Two very brief comments and then we must be done with our present topic of expectancy. First, your immediate future is of course always paramount: it is what you have and what you must seize. The third decade of life is marked in a peculiar way: it is the golden time for the demonstration of your genius; in it you must probably achieve a real beginning of whatever worthy work you are to perform. Osler said this must be done before forty; nearly all case material points to thirty as the usual deadline. Cromwells and U. S. Grants are rare and wide variants. Newton, Watt, Fulton, Bell, Darwin, Wallace—all were deep in their tasks in their twenties. There is probably a definite clock-strike somewhere near thirty. Artists often achieve their acme well within the third decade; but in most callings and activities it is enough to make a good beginning.

But away with all foolish talk of childhood and youth being "the best time of life." When a middle-aged or elderly college graduate declares that his four years in college were the best years of his life, he passes a sad verdict upon himself, his fate and his college. It is a satisfaction to know that youth in the twenties rarely if ever suspects that he is living the best part of his life; he is looking toward it. Your expectancy must include the element of progressive expansion if it is to serve your present needs; no matter how many actual lives there may be in which "youth is the best time," you can not content yourselves with any such pattern. For one reason youth is already on the wing and will soon be gone; maturity, elderhood, stretch out in a long vista. It is part of the very distinction of human life that it binds time, as Korzybski says: it is the long rich train of memory and the far-shooting beams of expectancy that mark you as man instead of mere zoön. You must expect your twenties to be better than teens, your thirties better than twenties, forties better still, and—yes, I will say it, fifties better than forties—so much I dare assert; even further I hurl my heave of faith, that sixties and even seventies may still broaden and deepen and brighten the earth and skies of life. It need hardly be said that we praise old age, not senility; we make the calendar an ally, but arteriosclerosis and neuro-degeneration are shocking foes of all we desire. Rip van Winkle's toast is just right: "May you live long and prosper"; that is, may you live as long as your expectancy reaches, not in mere actuarial period, but in breadth and depth and height and richness. In such case what we call death may come as a welcome and blessed requiescat—or it may even be unexpectedly a reveille.

"Man can be explained only in terms of what he is trying to become and not in terms of his origins," says the scholarly and saintly Clutton-Brock. The expectancy of man is his only hope; but the expectancy of man is a synthesis and summation of the rationally grounded but resolutely willed expectations of individuals like you and me; how great and positive—or alas, how small or negative, is to prove your contribution or mine to this summation—the only knowable and incarnate form of eternal life? This points directly to my next and last theme: *obligation.*

Obligation: what a disappointing finale; again what dubious and almost humiliating verbal associations, ligature and ligament; perhaps, although very questionable, religion. But certainly bonds, limitations, the logical contrary of freedom, and, be it noted, of looseness, laxity, license. True, this is a liberal college of liberal arts, giving, it is assumed, a liberal education. Moreover Reed is even among liberal colleges rather more than usually liberal—too free, some suspect. Nor can I avail myself here of the ancient Latin formula with which the degree used to be conferred; it speaks much of rights, privileges, immunities; but nothing of obligations; and that in an age when duty and obligation, law and rules and vows played a leading rôle in life and culture. Nevertheless I find myself still obliged to stress obligation.

Let us begin with an obligation that is specially marked in youth: gratitude. This does not mean that youth should have more gratitude than maturity or old age; but only that it has so much less of other and higher forms of obligation. It is the one native, original, basic obligation of any young person. But it is not instinctive; it had to be cultivated from the beginning, as is well indicated by that magna charta of our occidental morals, the ten commandments: no command to parents, but one, occupying a high place, being placed at the top of the second or human table to youth: Thou shalt honor thy Father and thy Mother. It is so hard for youth to look back. Most of the testimonies to filial and educational indebtedness are given by mature persons: consider that long chapter in which Marcus Aurelius, emperor, recounts what he owes to the many elders who surrounded him in childhood. There is sense as well as nonsense in that old paternal remark: "You will thank me for this twenty years from now." It would be more meticulously accurate to say: "You will not thank me within much less than twenty years."

It may be a slight digression, but I desire here to point out a subtle and dangerous evasion of this form of obligation. We gather that even the Hebrews themselves used it: it consists in thanking God and forgetting men. The son who was anxious to get free from the duty of supporting his aged parents "offered" his substance to God, and so made it immune from all human demands; a convenient legal fiction, and the remoteness of the substitute recipient, made the procedure very inexpensive and very popular. Not a little that goes by the name of religion and charity even to-day falls under suspicion of being an attempt to buy immunity from very real gratitude and obligations to human beings by performing much easier litanies and graces to God.

I am keenly aware of the distastefulness of all this talk about gratitude. In a certain sense it is worse than futile to talk about gratitude, or even obligation. But let me say one more word about it: To whom or what is gratitude due? How far back does it reach? Here we are, in Reed College, getting the bachelor's degree, in the City of Portland, State of Oregon, United States of America, and so on. "Heirs of all the ages, foremost in the files of time." What a cloud of potential claimants, ancestors clear back to protoplasm, pioneers, founders, patriots, prophets, inventors, and so on *ad libitum, ad infinitum* and so very soon *ad nauseam!* Every time I have attacked this part of the problem it has run off into a *reductio ad absurdum* in a vivid memory of Italian laborers digging the ditches for sewer and water around Reed College in 1912. Is it possible that here to-day in the elegant and artistic seclusion of this beautiful chapel we are in any way obligated to vouchsafe even a moment's consideration to such an irrelevant and undignified mental image? I have truly no well-worded answer to the question; if it has confused your minds a little I am satisfied to let it pass.

I suppose the most universally admitted obligation of a graduate is to *think*. Now it is true that you will be likely to do thinking enough, after a fashion, as do most of those who arrive at the baccalaureate. But be warned that being classified in the census as brain-worker is no guarantee on this head. Many a supposed brain-worker could offer only negative evidence of the activity of his mind, namely that his arms and legs are idle. The mechanization of industry does not stop with turning the craftsman into a robot; it reaches out to the brain-worker and standardizes him too, so that he is soon almost as much of an automaton as the operative who tightens the nut on bolt No. 23 on a Ford chassis. Indeed the mass of the activity in most callings tends to hinder rather than to foster the habit of genuine thinking. The powers of perception, reflection and mental initiative will dwindle and die if unexercised; when they do, life narrows to a mere thread of dimensionless time, which the shears of Atropos might as well cut now as later. The sole hope of preserving these powers is to *keep on widening them;* this demands new images, new concepts, new principles, new action. The two great foes of this expanding experience are the ones already indicated—the routine of daily tasks in one's vocation and *fear*. On the score of routine you are likely to occupy rather favored situations; but you will be exposed, perhaps more than most men, to the fear of the new. Courage and the spirit of adventure are indispensable to the widening and deepening of expectancy and of experience.

All this, and all else of consequence, sums up in one great concept, *man.* "Homo sum; et nihil humani mihi alienum est"; Let us English it in the positive instead of the negative: I am man; and everything that pertains to man is relevant and congenial to me. Humanism has been the motto and maxim of all the Renascences; most of all of the one now dawning, the brightening light which you may see and to which you may contribute. It is true that we have been threatened with a modern scholasticism in every field of knowledge, and it is well to recognize the danger. But since the Renaissance and the enlightenment we could never fall so deep into dehumanized erudition and logistics as did the historical scholasticism—or at least as it has been commonly supposed to have done. "No virtue is safe if it is not enthusiastic." Not our disgusts but our admiration are the effective forces of progress. There is only one fatal scepticism, that is unfaith in man.

"Ships are all right," said Conrad's sailor; and Conrad tells us this is the very gist of the sailor's creed. Now ships are not all right: they are often dirty; the sailors themselves call some of them "hell-ships"; they even founder or split on rocks. But not one whit the less ships are the sailor's very home and life, and are all that come between him and the depths of the sea. Moreover the romance and passion and heroism of the sea are far more closely linked to whalers and tramps than to ferry-boats or even liners. Every individual man or woman is embarked on the ship of the race, and in it must make his voyage, to happy landfall or disaster. For us "man is all right"—must be all right. Not however as judged by his origins, nor even by what he is, but, as Clutton-Brock says, by what he is trying to be.

The great Jesuit order has for its motto "Ad majorem Dei gloriam." But the sainted Chrysostom gave us, long before Loyola's time, another formula which we may include in our calculations: "The True Presence of God is—Man." Still earlier in sacred lore we read: "If a man love not his brother whom he hath seen, how shall he love God whom he hath not seen?" And earlier still, at a most sacred source, "Inasmuch as ye did it to one of the least of these my brethren"—my human brethren, that is—"Ye did it unto me." Earliest of all, echoing from a primitive and instinctive age, comes the most sweeping and profound of all these insights, far more prophetic than historical: "In the beginning—God made—Man—in His Own Image." So we may write an instructive and inspiring variant of the Jesuit motto—Ad Majorem Hominum Gloriam—to the greater glory of the visible image of God, man. This is, at least for here and now, the acme and summation of all our arrivals, all our expectancies, all our obligations, whether as "Bachelors," or just as men and women.

Edward O. Sisson

Reed College

THE LIBRARY OF THE UNIVERSITY OF LOUVAIN[1]

Your Royal Highness, Leopold, Prince of Belgium; Your Eminence, Ernesto Cardinal Van Roey, Archbishop of Malines; Very Reverend Monseigneur P. Ladeuze, rector of the University of Louvain; learned members of the faculties; distinguished guests; ladies and gentlemen:

Upon this most significant occasion I have been commissioned to bear the greetings of my fellow citizens to the people of Belgium, whom all Americans ever hold in profoundest respect. In particular, as visiting professor to the University of Louvain I have the honor to represent the Carnegie Endowment for International Peace, and as president of The University of the State of New York and state commissioner of education I am the delegate of the Board of Regents and the state department of education. It is, further, my great pleasure to serve as personal representative of the distinguished president of Columbia University, Dr. Nicholas Murray Butler, who first beheld the vision of this magnificent building and directed its materialization, and of the thousands of contributors, who have with alacrity offered to Belgium and its renowned university such objective testi-

[1] Address given in French at the dedication of the Louvain Library, July 4, 1928.

mony to their sympathy with her, and their indignation and protest against the outrages and horrors of war.

Fourteen years ago the civilized world was shocked from center to circumference by the destruction of the library of this historic University of Louvain. In the entire record of mankind there has been no clearer evidence of the extremities to which the madness of war would hurl itself. It was a demonstration of the utter futility of warfare and the destructiveness and ruin that fell upon humanity when the primitive instincts and passions of our infra-human ancestry have once slipped the leash. No act of Vandal or Goth was ever more ruthless and blindly unreasoning. The destruction served absolutely no purpose, not even that of the exigencies of warfare or of robbery and pillage. It was the avatar of wantonness. It was the natural offspring of the war demon.

For half a millennium the University of Louvain had stood as a most notable center in every advanced movement of civilization and education. It had furnished leaders in each new epoch of progress—the renascence of learning, the renovation of religion and the development of realism, and had become the permanent abode of literature, science and all life in the spirit. It had given birth to the genius of such leaders as Erasmus, Vives, Rescius, Lipsius, Clenard, Vesalius, Dodonee, Mercator and Jansen. The heart of the university and its wellspring of inspiration was in the library. For five hundred years the collections here had been accumulating, and they contained the world-famed books of all Christendom. And to this library the scholars of the world turned when they wished to examine the invaluable manuscripts of the Middle Ages, hundreds of incunabula, precious books of the hours, early publications of the reformers, historic and politico-religious pamphlets, polemic writings of the seventeenth century, various editions of the Bible, and other rare works that distinguished it among all libraries.

Such was the store of intellectual and spiritual riches that war and the most brutish of instincts laid waste. Never has there been a more striking demonstration of ruthlessness than this, and never before has there existed a grander opportunity for service to humanity and progress than that of restoring these walls and furnishing anew this treasure-house of civilization. The United States will ever rejoice that her claim to succor stricken Belgium and the world of intellect and culture was heard, and that the assembled nations granted to her the right and the privilege to erect a structure that would be emblematic of the highest aspirations and achievements of mankind. The presentation of this library building, then, is accompanied with the lively and abiding admiration, affection and good-will of the United States for Belgium, and for that noble soul and friend of humanity, Desideratus Cardinal Mercier, at whose behest and in whose honor this memorial was erected.

FRANK PIERREPONT GRAVES
THE UNIVERSITY OF THE
STATE OF NEW YORK

EDUCATIONAL EVENTS

EDUCATION AND INDUSTRY IN SCOTLAND

THE second report has been published of Lord Salvesen's committee on education and industry in Scotland. The first report, dated January, 1927, dealt with the second portion of the reference to the adequacy of the arrangements for enabling young persons to enter into and retain suitable employment. The other subject referred to the committee for consideration was the relation of the public system of education to the requirements of trade and industry. It is stated in the London *Times Educational Supplement* that the two Scottish reports are alike in their general conclusion that things are not by any means so bad as irresponsible critics would make them out to be, and that the trend of policy and effort is in the right direction. There may be room for improvement in detail, but education authorities and other administrative bodies are fully alive to the situation, and the schools are contributing their share toward the solid foundation on which all specialized instruction must be built.

If any section of the community comes in for blame, it is the parents, who fail to keep their children at school until an appropriate curriculum can be completed. This will be generally recognized as one of the main drawbacks to a satisfactory training being secured for each child before he or she enters on the actual business of life. In a certain class of family, and that a very numerous class, the child is regarded mainly as an economic agent, a means whereby the family income may be augmented at the earliest possible moment. Pupils enrolled for a secondary course, which the parents pledge themselves to have carried through, are tempted by the prospect of an immediate opening in an office or factory. The parents allow or force them to leave school, to the immediate dislocation of studies and the ultimate detriment of both parent and child. The committee recommends the strongest possible support should therefore be given to education authorities which insist on reasonable grounds that parents should fulfil the obligations under which they have brought themselves. The recommendation applies alike to courses leading to the universities and alternate courses in any and every class of school.

Other recommendations are in line with recent developments and with the aims of the department and of H. M. inspectors, as expressed in recent annual reports. The first essential of public education is a thorough grounding in the three R's, without which further progress is seriously handicapped, if not absolutely barred. Special measures should be adopted to deal with boys and girls who fail by the age of thirteen to earn promotion from the senior division of the school. While increased provision should be made for manual work in both elementary and secondary schools, the committee does not approve of the early introduction of vocational subjects as such. But the practice in some schools of devoting a fourth year of the course, after the completion of the general curriculum, to an intensive commercial or industrial course is one that ought to be more widely adopted. When young people have actually entered on their occupation, a necessary condition of the continuation of their education is the limitation of the hours of employment, a proviso on which due stress is laid. Suggestions are made for the constitution of a committee of the Advisory Council to work in cooperation with the National Council for Juvenile Employment, and for the stimulating of cooperation between education authorities and industrial organizations—all on sound lines already adopted by the more progressive authorities.

THE LACK OF TEACHERS IN IRELAND

The Reverend Wm. Anderson (headmaster of Mountjoy School, Dublin), whose suggested plan for increasing the supply of properly prepared candidates for the training college entrance examination was sympathetically received at the recent meeting of the Dublin Diocesan Synod of the Church of Ireland, has sent to the press a statement of his views on the situation and the means of overcoming its difficulties. These difficulties affect the Protestant primary schools chiefly. In recent years it has been several times stated in public that Catholic teachers have been appointed to Protestant schools, and with the repetition of this statement the number of such teachers seems to have grown. One thing at least is certain: there is a shortage of Protestant primary teachers, and it seems hardly less certain that, under present conditions, the shortage is bound to continue, if not to increase.

Mr. Anderson, in his statement, names the three sources from which the supply of teachers is supposed to come—the new preparatory colleges, the secondary schools and the primary schools. The first of these sources may in time prove reliable, but at present it does not count. The secondary schools have already sent students to the training colleges, but Mr. Anderson believes that the primary schools must always be looked to as the chief source of supply. He does not mean that the primary schools can be expected to prepare pupils for the colleges' entrance examination. A gap will remain between the primary school's highest standard and the standard for college entrance, and as Mr. Anderson believes that the greater number of young people who have the college entrance in view will continue to come from the primary schools, he urges the bridging of the gap as a matter of very great importance. In Northern Ireland, as well as in the Free State, he sees that the secondary school leaving certificate is coming to be regarded as the standard for training college entrance candidates, and he therefore regards it as pretty certain that primary-school pupils will cease to consider teaching as a possible profession unless, on leaving school, they have a fair prospect of obtaining a secondary education. They can not get this in the ordinary secondary schools, which are too expensive, and Mr. Anderson therefore suggests the opening of a special secondary school for such candidates within the training college buildings. He thinks that the school might be recognized by the department and, accordingly, obtain the usual capitation grant of a secondary school. The normal age of pupils entering this school would be seventeen, and the course of preparation for the college entrance would last two years.

Whether the department recognizes a school of this kind or not—and it is doubtful whether it could recognize a school which must be run on lines quite different from those of the preparatory colleges, if it is to accomplish what is expected of it—it is clear that the church, which is complaining of the necessity of appointing Catholic teachers to posts in its schools, must adopt some plan such as that suggested by Mr. Anderson. There will be differences respecting details. Seventeen as the age for entering the college's secondary school seems somewhat late, and one may doubt whether a two-years' course will be long enough to enable the pupils to reach the standard of the secondary school leaving certificate. Mr. Anderson does not consider the question of expense, but he suggests that the Candidate Teachers' Fund, established some years ago by the Church of Ireland, might become the nucleus of the fund that would be needed for putting his scheme into operation.

THE SCHOOL OF EDUCATION OF THE UNIVERSITY OF SOUTHERN CALIFORNIA

ON the recommendation of the faculty of the school of education and endorsement of the graduate council, the board of trustees of the University of Southern California, at a meeting held last month, took the following action:

> Upon the recommendation of the president, it was moved and unanimously carried that the school of education, which has hitherto in its work for advanced degrees been regarded as a part of the graduate school be henceforth recognized as one of the separate professional schools of the university, operating on the same basis as the school of law and the school of medicine, and that the faculty be empowered to recommend for appropriate degrees those who complete satisfactorily the courses laid down for such recognition.

Under this action, the faculty of the school of education was authorized to outline a three-year professional program leading to the degree of doctor of education. According to Dean Lester B. Rogers, of the School of Education, two factors have led to the establishment of the new degree. One was the desire to create a professional degree of equal weight and merit with the present Ph.D. degree, but with the emphasis on advanced professional preparation and mastery of educational principles and procedures rather than primarily on research. The other was to provide a master-teacher type of degree for the better preparation of teachers in subject-matter fields for junior and other colleges. The new program will meet the needs of men and women in teaching positions who wish to continue their scientific study of education, but who are not interested primarily in research.

As in the plan recently approved by the board of trustees at Stanford University for the Stanford School of Education (see issue of SCHOOL AND SOCIETY for July 7), two curricula have been organized which lead to the degree of doctor of education. One is known as the administrator type and the other will be known as the master-teacher type and will be primarily designed to prepare a new type of teacher on subject-matter fields. The chief differences between the requirements for the new degree, and the general university degree of doctor of philosophy will be in the emphasis placed on a broad and systematic knowledge of education as a field of professional service, rather than on research. The thesis may be an interpretation or the organization and application of existing experience, as well as a contribution.

The reading knowledge of French and German now required for the Ph.D. degree will be changed to one modern language for the master-teacher curriculum, and may be waived entirely for the administrator curriculum. In place of the language requirement, the candidate will be expected to have full command of the tools that will be needed in his thesis work, including statistical methods. The quality of work, preliminary, major and final examinations will be required as for the degree of doctor of philosophy.

The school of education will continue to give work leading to the doctor of philosophy degree under the general regulations of the graduate council. Hereafter, all candidates for credentials, candidates for the master of arts degree in education and candidates for the doctor of education degree will be admitted by way of the admissions committee, and will be under the entire direction of the faculty of the school of education.

THE ANNUAL CONVENTION OF THE INTERNATIONAL KINDERGARTEN UNION

The thirty-fifth annual convention of the International Kindergarten Union, held recently in Grand Rapids, Mich., brought together more than 2,000 educators, nearly 1,000 more than the number enrolled for any previous meeting of the organization.

As reported by the U. S. Bureau of Education, some who attended the convention had nursery schools as their special interest, others the kindergarten, and still others the primary grades. All were equally interested in presenting, discussing or hearing about methods of teaching children from babyhood throughout the entire school life. Continuity in educational experience was the central thought throughout the entire program.

In the regular meetings the topics under consideration included supervision of teaching from the standpoint of the classroom teacher and the supervisor, nursery school and parental education, classroom activities of young children, significance of the beginnings of education and opportunities for national and international cooperation in their relation to world fellowship through education.

The exhibit of commercial products and that of the work of children in the early elementary grades of the Grand Rapids schools gave helpful information to all who saw them. The children's exhibit featured units of activities. For example, one booth demonstrated work with farm life and showed how interrelated construction work, reading, number work, nature study and other curriculum subjects are essential to the first-grade child's process of learning.

One morning was spent in visiting Grand Rapids schools. This part of the program was so organized that each person might select the work he wished to see demonstrated, join a group interested in the same phase of teaching, and visit a designated school under the guidance of a group leader. Subjects for observation included social studies, oral language, health activities and music and rhythms. The development of each of these subjects was followed by the group from the nursery school to the kindergarten and on into the first and second grades. The morning's observation was followed by valuable discussion directed by the group leader.

THE COLLEGE SURVEY OF THE UNITED LUTHERAN CHURCH

Meeting at Teachers College, Columbia University, from June 27 to 29, the Board of Education of the United Lutheran Church in America received the final report of its college survey commission, representing two years' investigation of the work, personnel and equipment of twenty-one United Lutheran Church colleges, junior colleges and academies throughout the United States and Canada. The report, consisting of more than 2,000 typewritten sheets bound in nine volumes, was presented in person by the three members of the survey staff—Dr. R. J. Leonard, head of the school of education of Teachers College, Columbia University, and Dr. E. S. Evenden, of the department of education, as co-directors, and Dr. F. B. O'Rear, of Teachers College, assistant director.

In presenting the report Dr. Leonard called particular attention to the fact that the educational work of the United Lutheran Church in America is based upon a progressive underlying principle. He cited that section from the constitution of the board of education adopted in 1918 which states:

It shall have authority to prepare general surveys of educational standards; to investigate any phase of educational work and make recommendations to institutions and synods; to appoint pastors and other agencies for the prosecution of religious work among students; to publish literature covering the various phases of its work under the direction of the executive board (of the United Lutheran Church in America); to cooperate with synods in the establishment of new institutions where approved by the United Lutheran Church; to receive and disburse contributions for educational purposes and to hold and administer bequests and trusts for such purposes and to perform such other tasks as the United Lutheran Church may assign it.

Various chapters in the report of the commission are an intensive study of the effectiveness of administrative work, the curricula, buildings and equipment of the institutions, the student life and activities with reference to extra-curricular student activities and their relation to scholarship, endowments and methods of financing, salaries of faculty members and "teaching load," the relationship of location of each institution to its supporting Lutheran and non-Lutheran constituency, the work of the church at various non-Lutheran institutions throughout the country, and a comparative study of denominational boards of education. It is said to be the first time in the history of American education that such a study of denominational boards has been made. Throughout the nine volumes charts, maps and graphs illustrate and compare the institutions surveyed. Each institution has been visited personally by two of the directors and at least three other experts from among the graduate students at Teachers College. Throughout the period of the survey, the professional staff has had the cooperation of a survey commission consisting of Dr. Howard R. Gold, chairman, New Rochelle, N. Y.; Glen M. Cummings, Esq., Cleveland, O.; Dr. J. Henry Harms, Philadelphia, Pa.; the Reverend C. F. W. Hoppe, New York City; Dr. Marion J. Kline, Altoona, Pa.; Mrs. Wythe F. Morehead, Salem, Va.; Dr. E. P. Pfatteicher, Philadelphia, Pa., and Professor Hugo C. M. Wendel, New York University.

PARENTAL EDUCATION AND THE SCHOOLS

A JOINT conference is to be held from July 24 to 26 at Teachers College, Columbia University, under the joint auspices of the college and the Child Study Association of America, to discuss "Parental Education and the Public Schools."

On the opening day, parental education as a distinctive aspect of adult education will be discussed by the following speakers: Chairman—Mrs. Howard S. Gans, president of the Child Study Association of America; "Parental Education To-day" by Mrs. Sidonie Matsner Gruenberg, director of the Child Study Association of America; "The Parents' Place in the Education of Children" by Dr. Robert J. Leonard, director of the school of education, Teachers College, Columbia University; "The Cooperation of Parents in Child Welfare Research" by Dr. W. E. Blatz, director of the St. George's School for Child Study, University of Toronto; "The Discussion Method as an Instrument in Parental Education" by Dr. Harrison S. Elliott, director of the department of religious education and psychology, Union Theological Seminary.

The topic for Wednesday, July 25, will be: "Parental Education: An Opportunity and a Responsibility for the Educator" and the program is as follows: Chairman—Dr. William Heard Kilpatrick, professor of education, Teachers College, Columbia University; "What a System of Public Education can Offer in Continuous Parental Education" by Dr. Clyde R. Miller, director of the Bureau of Educational Service, Teachers College, Columbia University; "How Parental Education may Promote the Effectiveness of the Public Schools" by Dr. Jesse H. Newlon, director of the Lincoln School, Teachers College, Columbia University; "A Sampling of Parents' Inquiries" by Dr. Elsie O. Bregman, assistant director of the Child Study Association of America; "The Function in Parental Education," (a) "of the Parent-Teacher Association" by Mrs. A. H. Reeve, president of the International Federation of Home and School, and (b) "of Parents' Study Groups" by Mrs. Cécile Pilpel, director of study groups of the Child Study Association of America.

"Current Programs in Parental Education" will be the subject of the session on Thursday,

July 26, with the following program: Chairman—Ralph P. Bridgman, director of the Parents' Council of Philadelphia; "Volunteer Organization Programs" by Dr. Lois Hayden Meek, educational secretary of the American Association of University Women, and Miss Margaret J. Quilliard, director of field work of the Child Study Association of America; "State Program" by Mrs. May Pardee Youtz, head of the division of Child Study and Parent Education of the State University of Iowa; "Public School Programs" by Dr. Eugene S. Briggs, superintendent of Schools, Okmulgee, Oklahoma, and Miss Helen Wightman, teacher in the public schools, Kalamazoo, Michigan; "Training for Leadership Program" by Dr. Ruth Andrus, acting director of the Institute of Child Welfare Research, Teachers College, Columbia University.

The Headquarters Office of the Child Study Association at 54 West 74th Street, New York City, and the Extension Office, 509 West 121st Street, will be open to visitors during the forenoons. Individual conferences may be arranged during this time with members of the staff of the association. There will be an exhibit of materials used in parental education on display at each office. Tickets of admission may be had on application to the secretary of Teachers College or to the Child Study Association of America.

FACULTY PROMOTIONS AT NEW YORK UNIVERSITY

Among the recent promotions on the faculty of New York University are the following:

School of education:

John R. Clark, associate professor of education to professor of education.

Howard R. Driggs, associate professor of education to professor of education.

J. Andrew Drushel, associate professor of education to professor of education.

Charles M. Gill, associate professor of education to professor of education.

Vincent Jones, assistant professor of music education to associate professor of music education.

Frank S. Lloyd, instructor in physical education to professor of physical education.

Paul S. Lomax, associate professor of commercial education to professor of commercial education.

Jay B. Nash, associate professor of physical education to professor of physical education.

Albert S. Pegues, assistant professor of English to associate professor of English.

Ralph E. Pickett, associate professor of vocational education to professor of vocational education.

Charles E. Skinner, assistant professor of educational psychology to associate professor of educational psychology.

Paul V. West, assistant professor of educational psychology to associate professor of educational psychology.

Arthur D. Whitman, assistant professor of education to associate professor of education and supervisor of student teaching.

Andrew T. Wylie, instructor in education to assistant professor of educational psychology.

Washington Square College:

Leland W. Crafts, instructor in psychology to assistant professor of psychology.

Clarence G. Dittmer, associate professor of sociology to professor of sociology and chairman of the department of sociology in Washington Square College.

Joseph W. Barlow, associate professor of Spanish to professor of Spanish and chairman of the department of Spanish in Washington Square College.

Philip E. Wheelwright, assistant professor of philosophy to associate professor of philosophy and chairman of the department of philosophy and adviser to freshmen.

Rufus D. Smith, assistant dean to associate dean.

University College of Arts and Pure Science:

Douglas H. Fryer, assistant professor of psychology to associate professor of psychology and chairman of the department of psychology.

Albert S. Borgman, associate professor of English to professor of English (on leave of absence during 1928–1929).

Joseph H. Park, associate professor of history to professor of history.

EDUCATIONAL NOTES AND NEWS

DR. JOSEPH EUGENE ROWE, head of the department of mathematics and director of extension in the College of William and Mary, has been chosen president of the Clarkson Memorial Institute of Technology at Potsdam, N. Y. He succeeds Dr. John P. Brooks, who resigned last year.

DR. G. I. CHRISTIE, director of the Agricultural Experiment Station at Purdue University, Lafayette, Indiana, has been elected president of the Ontario Agricultural College, to succeed Dr. J. B. Reynolds.

THE REVEREND DR. C. R. MYERS, president of Hartwick Seminary, Oneonta, N. Y., has been made president of Hartwick College, Oneonta.

THE inauguration of Royal C. Agne as president of Huron College, Huron, S. Dak., took place during the college commencement week last month.

WILLIAM D. TRAUTMANN, associate professor of German at Adelbert College, has been appointed dean of the college.

PROFESSOR ROBERT R. AURNER, of the school of commerce of the University of Wisconsin, has been appointed acting dean of men. He will replace Dean S. H. Goodnight, who will be on leave of absence next year to be executive head of the "floating university."

FRANK W. CLELLAND, registrar and executive secretary of the Boston University School of Social Service, has been appointed assistant dean, and will serve during the next academic year as acting-dean, of the school of religious education at Boston University. He received the honorary degree of D.D. at the recent commencement exercises of Missouri Wesleyan College.

DEAN PRISCILLA FOWLE, of the Newton Theological Institution, Boston, has been appointed dean of women at Denison University, Granville, Ohio.

DR. FORMAN T. MCLEAN, of the governmental experiment station at the Rhode Island State College, has been appointed supervisor of public education at the New York botanical gardens in Bronx Park, New York. Dr. McLean was formerly professor of botany at the University of the Philippines.

MEYER NIMKOFF, who received his Ph.D. degree in sociology at the University of Southern California, has been appointed assistant professor of sociology at Bucknell University, Lewisburg, Pa. Clarence Richard Johnson, professor of sociology at Bucknell, is returning to the university after two years' leave of absence.

N. BURTON PARADISE and Benjamin C. Nangle have been promoted from the rank of instructor to that of assistant professor of English at Yale University; Robert J. Menner has been promoted to be associate professor of English.

DR. VAN METER AMES has been promoted to the rank of assistant professor of philosophy in the University of Cincinnati.

GLENN R. BARR, assistant professor in the department of Spanish at Oberlin College, Oberlin, Ohio, has been appointed assistant professor at Miami University, Oxford, Ohio.

VIRGIL S. MALLORY, head of the mathematics department of the East Orange high school, N. J., has been appointed associate professor of mathematics at the New Jersey State Teachers College, Upper Montclair, N. J.

DR. NANCY BAYLEY, of the University of Wyoming, has been appointed research associate at the University of California Institute of Child Welfare. Her work will be in connection with a survey of the development of young children which the institute is now fostering.

JEAN GONTARD, a French scholar, will lecture on contemporary French literature at the University of California, Los Angeles, next year. He has been a professor at the College of the City of New York.

H. L. ROTH, lecturer in philosophy at the University of Manchester, England, has been elected professor of philosophy at the University of Jerusalem.

EDWARD A. MILNE, Beyer professor of applied mathematics at the University of Manchester, England, has been elected the first

Rouse Ball professor of mathematics at the University of Oxford.

Andrew Cowper Lawson, professor of geology and at one time dean of the College of Mining of the University of California, will retire on July 25, after thirty-eight years of service on the faculty. He will become emeritus professor of geology and mineralogy.

Evan Thomas, professor of mathematics at the University of Vermont, has retired. He had taught at Vermont for thirty-two years.

Walter R. Hepner, superintendent of schools at Fresno, Calif., has been elected superintendent of schools at San Diego.

R. H. Licking, assistant principal of the high school at Kewaunee, Wis., has been elected superintendent of schools, to succeed W. F. Kruschke.

James C. Boudreau, director of art instruction at Pittsburgh, Pa., has been appointed director of the school of fine and applied arts at Pratt Institute, Brooklyn, N. Y., to succeed Walter Scott Perry, who retires after forty-one years of service.

Dr. George D. Olds, president emeritus of Amherst College, delivered the commencement address at Trinity College last month. He received the honorary degree of doctor of laws from the college. Professor Henry Marvin Belden, head of the department of English at the University of Missouri, received the honorary degree of doctor of letters. The honorary M.A. was conferred upon Robert Hillyer, a member of the Trinity College English department, who is to succeed Professor Charles T. Copeland at Harvard University next year, and upon R. Eston Phyfe, assistant principal of the Hartford Public High School.

Kathryn Newell Adams, president of the Constantinople Woman's College, has received the honorary L.H.D. from Wheaton College, Norton, Mass.

Nebraska Wesleyan University, Lincoln, Nebr., has conferred the honorary degree of doctor of divinity upon Earl Enyeart Harper, president of Evansville College.

Dr. David P. Barrows, professor of political science at the University of California, has been given an honorary degree of doctor of laws by the University of Bolivia. Dr. Barrows has been in Argentina in the course of a trip through South America where he is studying political and economic situations and endeavoring to assist in promotion of better understanding between Latin America and the United States.

Yu-chuen James Yen, general director of the Chinese National Association of the Mass Education Movement, was awarded the honorary M.A. at the Yale University commencement exercises.

Miss Mabel E. Adams, principal of the Horace Mann School, New York City, has received from Gallaudet College for the Deaf, Kendall Green, Washington, an honorary master's degree in recognition of her services for the deaf. Gallaudet is the only college for the deaf and is maintained by the United States government.

Mrs. Mary Tate Smith, a member of the faculty of Public School 54, Brooklyn, was recently honored by a dinner on her seventieth birthday. She has been a teacher for fifty years and will now retire under the statutory age limit.

Dr. J. V. Breitweiser, dean of the school of education and director of the graduate division of the University of North Dakota, will be exchange lecturer at the University of Manitoba in 1929. He will give four lectures in January on the following subjects: "Economy of Time and Mental Energy or Personal Efficiency"; "The Use and Abuse of Mental Tests in Education"; "The Integration Concept in Human Behavior"; "The Development of the Junior College."

Dr. John A. Lapp, head of the department of social sciences at Marquette University, Milwaukee, Wis., was the commencement speaker at Creighton University, Omaha, Nebr.

Dr. David Starr Jordan, chancellor emeritus of Stanford University, has been named chairman of the Northern California committee of the Near East College Association, which will endeavor to bring to public attention the work being done by six American colleges in the Near East, and to promote interest in their permanent endowment. Other members of the committee are: Dr. W. W. Campbell, president of the University of California; Chester Rowell, Paul Shoup, Fred W. Bradley, Wallace Alexander, Charles W. Merrill, F. L. Lipman, Dr. Ray Lyman Wilbur, Platt Kent, Bishop Edward L. Parsons, Dr. Philip King Brown, C. K. McIntosh, and Paige Monteagle.

DR. WALTER BOOTH ADAMS, for thirty-eight years a member of the faculty of the American University at Beirut, Syria, died on July 9. Dr. Adams was sixty-four years old.

LUCY CROSBY BEDLOW, supervisor of practical arts in the New Bedford, Mass., public schools, died on July 5, at the age of sixty-seven years. She had been a supervisor in the New Bedford schools for twenty-seven years.

MARY M. FORSTER, for more than fifty years a teacher in the schools of New York City, died recently at the age of eighty-four years. She retired in 1912.

A VISUAL Education Conference was held at Drake University, Des Moines, Iowa, from June 25 to 29. The following are among those who took part in the program: Dr. W. H. Dudley, University of Wisconsin; Dr. Ellsworth C. Dent, University of Kansas; Dr. C. F. Hoban, Harrisburg, Pa.; August O. Oddleifson, Rochester, N. Y.; B. W. Kelley, Rock Island, Ill.; Dr. Herbert Martin, University of Iowa, and H. L. Kooser, Iowa State College. Dean W. F. Barr, of the college of education of Drake University, who has for several years been active in the promotion of visual education, reports that this is the first of a series of annual conferences to be held under the auspices of Drake University.

AN exhibition in commemoration of the tenth anniversary of the founding of the Czechoslovak Republic has been inaugurated in the city of Brno. It will continue until September 30. According to information received by the U. S. Bureau of Education, the exhibition is so arranged as to present a complete history of the cultural, educational and industrial development of Czechoslovakia during the past decade. Particular attention is devoted to the educational progress of the nation.

WASHINGTON UNIVERSITY, St. Louis, Mo., is offering two fellowships in timber research for the school year 1928–29, which have been established by the American Creosoting Co., of Louisville, Ky. This work has been in progress during the current year, and special equipment is being installed for the further investigation of the elastic properties of timber. The fellowships pay $1,000 and tuition yearly. Time will be available for other graduate study. Engineers who have done one or more years of graduate laboratory work are desired.

THREE parties of Cuban public school teachers are coming to the United States on an instructional tour of Eastern schools. One group will go to Niagara Falls and the New England states. The second group, members of the School of Pedagogy, will go to Washington, and the third, formed by 300 teachers, will visit Key West, Palm Beach, Miami, Daytona, Tampa and Ybor City.

THE Board of Regents of the University of the State of New York have granted a provisional charter to the Santiago College for Girls in Santiago, Chile. This is the second South American institution that has been chartered by the Board of Regents, the other being Mackenzie College at São Paulo, Brazil. Santiago College for Girls was established in 1880 by Dr. Hiram Hayes La Fetra to afford educational facilities to the daughters of American and English families residing in Chile. It has had rapid expansion, since the best Chilean families have also sent their girls to this school, which has offered training from kindergarten through high school and is now about to offer higher education. The principal office of the college will be in New York City.

"STUDENTSHIPS" for teachers who desire to attend full-time courses of advanced specialized study or research in universities or other institutions have been established by the British Board of Education. The studentships are limited in number, and applicants must have had not less than five years of experience in schools recognized by the board. The purpose is to assist suitable teachers in recognized schools—which may be elementary, secondary, technical, or institutes, art schools, or training colleges—who wish to improve their teaching ability. The course of study must be approved by the board. Grants will be made for a term or for the academic year, and may be extended for a period of not more than two years, not to exceed £100 a year. Research work necessitating travel or practical study of industrial conditions in connection with instruction in technical subjects will be considered by the board in making awards.

The Permanent Court of International Justice at The Hague decided, by eight against four votes, mainly in favor of Poland in the Polish-German dispute over minority rights in Silesia. The court, while rejecting the Polish denial of the court's competency, sustained Poland's thesis that only children whose mother tongue is German were entitled to use the minority schools—that is, schools where the language of the minority population, namely, German, is used as a medium for instruction. Germany maintained that parents, whether Poles or Germans, could freely decide whether their children should attend minority German or majority Polish schools. The court, however, upheld the German plea that the declarations by the parents as to whether their mother tongue was Polish or German must not be questioned. Poles had claimed that these declarations should be given on oath and the parents be liable to cross-examination.

The Council of State in France has annulled the decision of the Minister of Public Instruction to fuse the individual schools for each of the sexes at Mauroux, a commune of less than 500 inhabitants. The decision of the French State Council was rendered on the complaint of a parent residing in the commune of Mauroux (Lot) and the parents' association of the Department of Lot. Although the Ministry acted in accordance with the request of the municipal council of Mauroux that the schools for boys and girls be combined the Council of State rendered the opinion that the mixed schools authorized by the law of October 30, 1886, should be considered an economic and not a pedagogic measure. Had the resources of the commune of Mauroux been insufficient to maintain separate schools for the sexes, the mixed school would have been authorized. As, however, the commune was already provided with two schools, the question was pedagogic and not economic, and the council decides that the commune was obliged to continue to maintain both.

DISCUSSION

CENSORSHIP OF STUDENT PUBLICATIONS

This paper finds its starting-point in a remark recently made by a student of a sister institution, a member of the staff of its college weekly, to the effect that the faculty adviser read every word in every issue before the paper was printed. Every sheet of copy, every page of proof, he said, had to bear the censor's initials; and the printers had been instructed not to go to press until the faculty adviser had given his official O. K.

In another recent instance a college president is alleged to have had a secret arrangement whereby galley proof of the college literary publication was submitted to him by the printer, without the knowledge of the staff.

Inquiry of college presidents, deans of men, heads of schools of journalism and students active in publications, reveals that this sort of thing is fortunately not very common in American colleges. Only in a few cases that have come to my attention do college authorities indicate that they approve of censorship in any form. On the other hand, almost without exception they appear to believe that student editors should be given complete authority, but authority accompanied by the complete responsibility that must accompany lawful authority in every activity of life.

Many of the answers emphasize the fact that censorship is not only contrary to American ideals of free speech and a free press, but also that censorship is bad psychology and bad educational policy. I have had an opportunity not long since to test the psychological effect of censorship in the case of a "razz" sheet published by the George Washington University chapter of Pi Delta Epsilon, the national honorary journalistic fraternity.

The editors believed—and rightly, as events proved—that the suggestion of censorship or suppression would increase their sales. Accordingly, the paper was printed with one corner perfectly blank and with a similar blank space taking up about one third of the editorial column. These blanks were then painstakingly cut out by members of the staff and it was whispered about that I had suppressed an offensive story and editorial. The paper "sold like wildfire" and its appearance was followed by visits to the printer in search of the missing portions, offers of high prices for "unexpurgated" copies—as much as ten dollars was offered—and sales almost double those of other years.

If this "suppression" had not been a hoax to increase circulation, if there had really been a suppressed story to serve as its background, the results would undoubtedly have been similar but vastly greater in degree. The curiosity of readers would have had something substantial to feed upon, and suppression would have defeated its own purposes, as I believe it usually does.

That censorship is educationally bad seems to be pretty generally agreed. Even those who are forced to practice it usually apologize for it. If college publications have a place in the educational scheme of things—as I am sure they have—we should not apply to them the autocratic and paternalistic methods of rod and rote that education in general has long since discarded.

The ideal system, my inquiries seem to indicate, is one of complete editorial control by students, with strict accountability for the exercise of that control both as members of the college community and as citizens. Only in this way, in my opinion, will student editors be enabled to develop genuine standards of editorial judgment, discrimination and taste. As long as standards are imposed by faculty or administrative fiat they are bound to be educationally and psychologically unsound and to be accepted by students grudgingly, if at all.

On the contrary, if such standards are developed from within, they will have every prospect of being sincerely applied and scrupulously maintained.

These suggestions, however, do not mean that there ought to be no contact whatever between student boards of editors and deans, faculty advisers, instructors in journalism and other officers. Far from it. Indeed, I believe that student editors will seek such advice and will appeal to maturer judgment to a far greater degree when such consultation is voluntary and spontaneous than when they feel that the adviser or censor is their natural enemy and that it is part of the game to trick him by any legitimate—or illegitimate—means.

Of course, editors will frequently not accept this advice. That must be expected. Sometimes I am afraid events will prove that they are right in not accepting it, that they are wiser than the adviser. In any case, they should be free to accept or reject it as they choose, with the understanding that they accept full responsibility for the outcome.

The advantages of a system under which frank, friendly and intimate conference between student boards and university officials is substituted for arbitrary and autocratic control so far outweigh the disadvantages due to the inevitable and sometimes serious mistakes that editors will make, that I am convinced we ought to take the chance courageously for the sake of the greater good. Unpleasant incidents are bound to happen, but they are part of the price we must be prepared to pay for what I am sure student editors will ultimately accomplish: the development—by the trial-and-error method—of sound and acceptable journalistic standards.

I have had an interesting communication from Mr. H. N. Higinbotham, formerly editorial chairman of the *Harvard Lampoon,* from which I am going to quote:

> I can say that we have had no faculty intervention during the last five years in connection with the *Lampoon.* This does not mean that there have not been instances where faculty intervention would have been quite justifiable. Three years ago we issued a parody on the *Literary Digest* which met with the disfavor of the police and we were prohibited from putting it through the mails, because of a picture which was considered by the police to express unpatriotic sentiments.
>
> Slightly over a year ago the *Lampoon* was involved in difficulties, because of its Princeton Game Number, which were somewhat embarrassing to the college. I can say from my own experience in this connection that the lessons which one learns in such affairs are far more valuable than what would be gained through student publication censorship.

One of the most difficult problems of college journalism is of course the so-called "college comic," which is sometimes the journalistic outlaw of an otherwise respectable campus. It is my opinion that current misconceptions, both inside and outside of educational circles, with regard to the conduct and morals of college students are often primarily due to the impression given by a few so-called "comics." The emphasis upon alcohol and sex in would-be "funny" magazines has done more to give decent college men and women a bad name than any other single factor. No one who is at all familiar with the fine boys and girls who constitute the great majority of our student bodies is willing to admit that the picture of them given by certain "comics" has any substantial basis in fact. Whatever foundation may exist —if any really does exist—for the distorted and gross caricature of college life given by these "comics" is undoubtedly due to attempts on the part of unthinking and immature students to be "collegiate," as misguided readers of these publications sometimes conceive of the term. It is a pity that these "comics" should ever be accepted as genuinely representative of college life, and doubly a pity that college students or officers themselves should ever so accept them.

Most of the difficulty here, I believe, is due to misplaced emphasis. Ten or fifteen years ago a college student who was arrested appeared in the papers under "Arrests" and was handled in a minor way by the regular police reporter. To-day he is "front-page stuff" and rates a "scare headline." This is probably partly due to the misrepresentation of college life and morals to which I have referred, and partly to our heightened interest as a nation in education, and particularly higher education, in all its manifestations.

College editors realize that a wrong impression of college students is abroad. This is evident from discussion at the meetings of college journalists. For instance, at a recent meeting at the University of Washington in Seattle, the Western Association of College Comics went on record as opposing the popular notion of college men and women as dissipated youths and even went out of their special field to attack college moving-pictures which emphasize the "sporty side" of college life, on the ground that such films are unjust and untrue to life. The Eastern Association of College Comics several years ago had a discussion and criticism of the prevalence of "jokes about girls walking home, petting-party jokes, and gin-flask jokes." Mr. Higinbotham, of the *Harvard Lampoon,* already quoted, was then president of this association, and declared that "there may be girls like the pictures and jokes in the humorous magazines, but they don't have dates with us." Other college editorial associations have had similar discussions.

In conclusion, let me repeat that I am in favor of giving college editors complete authority combined with accepted and acknowledged responsibility. I am sure that they will learn to exercise their authority wisely in the main and will develop more tact, good taste and discrimination under such circumstances than they ever would under a repressive system. Furthermore, they will realize that decent journalism pays. This is shown by the editorial and financial success of the New York *Times,* with its consistent policy of "All the news that's fit to print." I have seen another striking instance of it in the recent experience of the Washington *Evening Star,* which publicly announced that as a protection to its readers it would not print the harrowing details of the horrible Hickman murder case. This step, I am sure, did not cost it one penny in advertising or circulation receipts and gained it general commendation and many new friends.

College editors are likely to be among our most intelligent students. Occasionally a freak appears among them—one of those "advanced thinkers" of whom some one recently said that "they imagine that they are emancipated, when they are merely unbuttoned." In the long run, however, I believe that college editors will be just as quick to realize and accept their moral responsibility to their constituencies as editors of city dailies. In the long run, I believe that their natural idealism and desire to do worthwhile things—to my mind their dominant motive even in their worst mistakes—will help them to see that decent journalism, constructive journalism, not only pays in the financial sense and in terms of prestige, but that it also brings those more fundamental and durable returns that are without price—the satisfaction of the creative impulses of American college youth.

Henry Grattan Doyle
George Washington University

MORE WASTES IN EDUCATION

The article of Professor Jones on "Waste in Education" in the June 9 issue of School and Society is suggestive of other extravagances. The first that comes to mind, one that must impress any one that has analyzed educational conditions with any thoroughness, is the overcrowding of the content of various elementary school subjects with congesting details that tend to defeat the very purpose of such studies. I would not, as some have suggested, take a single unit from the curriculum, for I believe the elementary school is a place for wide contacts so as to permit the child's real interests to emerge. But with the vast increase in the number of study-contacts, the contents of subjects have not been judiciously and skillfully proportioned and brought within limits consistent with the educational success we ought to expect in our public schools. This is particularly true of the older studies. Instead of revising and reducing the content to meet the expanding curriculum and really put studies in a more healthy condition and a more strategic position to serve the present day, their sponsors have, in conspicuous instances, increased content even to the point of congestion. More than this, the content has frequently been chosen from the adult rather than from the child point of view. All this is bad for the studies, worse for the pupil. The elementary school pupil, judging from the requirements, is expected to be a prodigy in intellectual advancement and scientific insight to do justice to the congested and adult-formulated study-content he is expected to "pass." The deluge of quantity overwhelms quality. This is bad pedagogy and represents a particularly aggravated form of waste. The vital principle of simplicity is violated and psychological principles of education are thrown to the winds. In some cases study-content could be reduced one half to the great advantage of studies and pupils, if we consider the matter merely from the standpoint of well-assimilated knowledge, and to the great advantage of pupils from the standpoint of real growth. We must subordinate the adult attitude of mind to that of the child more rigorously than has yet been done if we are to lay claim to any genius in making school programs. Reform here would result in tangible economies.

The next thing that suggests itself is the free textbook and supply habit. Free textbooks and their accompaniments have been of inestimable value to our schools in more ways than one. The custom might well be made universal. No reasonable person would think of reverting to old conditions, but it can hardly be gainsaid that the custom has been the occasion of a great waste of public moneys. Needless expenditures have repeatedly been made which any thoroughly qualified body of educators could avoid not only without loss to pupils, but with distinct gain. Many thousands of dollars might thus be saved in a single state to the advantage of all concerned.

This is not the place to give details and further specifications. It requires only a genuine examination of the matter with heroic determination to face the facts and get at the fundamentals of the question to make a rather formidable list of obvious economies.

Such economies, and correlative ones, in housing and equipment could be made without sacrificing health, efficiency, or cheerful and attractive surroundings for the greatest of all enterprises. In fact they would enhance these conditions, and would materially help to allay the restive feeling already arising in some minds at what seems to them enormous, if not extravagant, expenditure for education. Demagogic utterances of devotion to our public schools, partly, if not wholly, for political purposes or kindred motives, have condoned and fostered these expenditures. This whole policy of economy that could be adopted without sacrificing a particle of pleasurable efficiency in education, rather increasing it, has an obvious bearing also on the matter of acquiring better paid and better equipped teachers.

Frank Webster Smith

Ridgewood, N. J.

QUOTATIONS

LA MAISON AMÉRICAINE

The first stone has been laid of the American Hostel in the University City of Paris. Lying on the outskirts of the French capital, this Cité

Universitaire groups together houses for students of all nationalities; but until recently what the French call La Maison Américaine was missing. It was, of course, impossible for the United States to be absent from the little international town which is becoming, in the twentieth century, the counterpart of the Latin Quarter of the twelfth century. In that Latin Quarter—so named because of the universal language then spoken—the youth of Europe congregated to receive instruction. Every country, every city, every tiny center is capable of giving that instruction to-day; but it is nevertheless good that there should exist a common meeting place for the students of the world. In such a common meeting place, they will learn something that can scarcely be taught as directly and as vividly elsewhere. The youth of many nations learn to understand each other and to make common cause.

When Japan, Great Britain, Scandinavia, Canada and South American republics each bring their stone to add to the pile, it is necessary that the United States, too, should bring its stone. Myron T. Herrick, the popular ambassador, referred in his discourse, on the occasion of the laying of the foundation stone, to the mechanical inventions which have brought the peoples closer together. Airplanes and railroads and swift ships, cables and radiotelegraphy have made a communication easier. Finance and commerce are international. In a hundred ways, the citizens of twoscore nations are interlocked as never before. Moreover there is a keen desire for mutual understandings, and organizations in every land are striving to establish perpetual peace. Yet amid all this machinery for the rapprochement of peoples, the Cité Universitaire of Paris, while it has a practical purpose, has also a symbolic force. In itself it will accomplish much, but by its influence it will accomplish more. The wish was expressed that other countries should, imitating the example of Paris, establish their university cities.

The very word university stands for an idea that is now generally accepted. It is derived from the Latin word *universitas*—the whole of anything, or the universe; and is therefore allied to a variety of words which signify literally the process of turning all things into one, comprehending all particulars in a single total. In its ordinary application it has been somewhat reduced but, as it is applied by the University City of Paris, something of its wider meaning is restored.

The French minister, Louis Barthou, on the same occasion rightly declared that "in the human order there is no institution, no work, no effort, from which the absence of the United States would not retard its development and diminish its hopes." Between France and the United States, he added, there might be, as between all nations, differences of opinion, but there are now surely eliminated all elements of distrust and insecurity which alone could trouble their friendship. It is with such sentiments that the United States takes its place in the Cité Universitaire. The Maison Américaine, which has benefited by the generosity of Mr. and Mrs. Homer Gage, and of many others, will not merely provide facilities for a limited number of students—it will stand as a mark set on a hill for the illumination of kindred continents. —*The Christian Science Monitor.*

REPORTS

THE BUSINESS AND PROFESSIONAL ASPECTS OF EDUCATIONAL ADMINISTRATION[1]

A MODERN school system proposes to offer to each pupil enrolled those unique opportunities for acquiring skills, for practice in precise thinking, and for growth in power of appreciation which are attainable by one of his intelligence. In the administration of a school system that seeks to achieve this desirable end, problems of personnel, of pupil records, of diagnostic and achievement test programs, of attendance and health service, of courses of study and curricula, of the planning, maintenance and operation of the school plant, and of the financing of the school system, must be integrated by the executive who relates each administrative procedure to the realization of the purposes for which the schools exist.

[1] Report of a committee of the National Council of Education submitted at Minneapolis, Minn., July, 1928.

The efficient administration of our schools depends upon the recognition of the distinction in function between the school board as a policy-determining and legislative body and the superintendent of schools as its chief executive officer. The members of a school board render their most important service when they select the ablest executive available; having rendered this service, they may continue to serve the public best by advising with him concerning the schools, by interpreting for him the will of the people whom they represent, and by requiring of him from time to time a record of the work done by the school system and proposals for its further development. The superintendent of schools, if he be competent, will present his program to the board of education and will demonstrate the wisdom of the policies which he advocates.

In recent years it has been suggested that the business administration of schools can to advantage be divorced from their professional management. It has been argued that the construction of school buildings, their maintenance and operation, the purchase, storage, and distribution of supplies, the making of the budget, and the like, can be best handled by one trained in business affairs. In a considerable number of school systems the business manager has been made an officer coordinate with the superintendent of schools, reporting directly to the board of education. This type of organization ignores the fact that every act of the business manager is worthy of approval only as it contributes directly to the furtherance of the educational program adopted by the board of education.

A budget should be adopted only after the most careful consideration of the educational program which it proposes to finance. A school building is well built only when it has been planned to serve the needs of a school offering a program of education which has been proposed by the superintendent of schools and accepted by the board of education. In our modern school systems it will seldom happen that any two buildings will accommodate exactly the same educational program. In the maintenance and operation of the building, the health and convenience of teachers and pupils are matters of primary importance. In the purchase of supplies, the needs of teachers and pupils and the demands of the educational program furnish the only sound basis for the determination of the quantity or quality of materials to be purchased.

Where the business executive has been given a place coordinate with the superintendent of schools, this action has been taken upon the assumption that better business practice would prevail and that economies would be effected. A thoroughgoing investigation covering the states of New York and New Jersey has proved that this assumption is not true, and there is no reason why it should be true. The board of education that places responsibility upon the superintendent of schools for the complete administration of the school system, and requires the assistant in charge of business affairs to report through him, may reasonably expect to secure as high efficiency in the business office as could be attained were the head of this division to be given a position coordinate with the superintendent. Other investigations have established the fact that misunderstandings and inefficiency are bound to occur where a dual system of administration has been adopted. Indeed, it not infrequently happens that under dual control the superintendent of schools, who certainly must be the leader in the educational program, supported by the board of education, spends a large part of his time in making adjustments with the business office, often on a personal basis. No good can come from this waste of the time and energy of the man responsible for the development of an efficient school system.

All affirm the necessity for adequate business procedures in the administration of a school system. The board of education in our larger communities should elect, upon the nomination of the superintendent of schools, an assistant superintendent in charge of business affairs. This man should be highly trained as a business executive and should cooperate with the superintendent of schools in the making of the budget, in the development of plans and the supervision of the construction of buildings, in the purchase, storage and distribution of supplies, in the handling of the payroll, and the like. His efficiency will be increased by virtue of the relationship which he bears to the chief executive officer of the board of education. The administration of the school system will profit from a relationship which is sound in theory and which has been successfully established in practice.

George Drayton Strayer,
Chairman

EDUCATIONAL RESEARCH AND STATISTICS

THE MEASUREMENT OF THE EFFECT OF TEACHING

II

The remainder of the paper will be devoted to a discussion of experimental attempts to solve the many problems involved in reducing the suggested method to a practical working procedure.

The field selected for experimentation was spelling. Twenty words, difficult for the fifth grade, were chosen from the Iowa Spelling Scale. For these words five study sheets were devised (Fig. 5) and six tests. (Fig.6).

UNIVERSITY OF MICHIGAN
SCHOOL OF EDUCATION

Study Lesson — Form 5

ap-pli-ca-tion

.application.............................. ....
to the study of spelling words will make them easy to spell. This word ..application.................. .. .. is a long word, but by a little ..application ... . I am sure that I shall be able to spell .application............ correctly. Its four syllables are . ap . pli ca tion...

u-ni-ver-si-ty

The second and fifth syllables of this word university...... are the hardest, so I shall write all the syllables here and notice these two a little more carefully than the others. u ni ver si - ty.. Once more, I shall write the word university ..u-nvirsity.. slowly and carefully university.

Fig. 5. A portion of one of the five study sheets designed to give "standardized" teaching of the twenty words. Each sheet takes up the same twenty words. No other teaching was permitted.

One of the tests was used as an initial test and one of the others was used after each study period. A sheet of explanation to boys and girls was also prepared. After suitable preliminary testing to determine the general spelling development of the children, their ages, etc.,

UNIVERSITY OF MICHIGAN
SCHOOL OF EDUCATION

Spelling Test — Form 5

Paul's ....(7) to enter the ....(2) has been sent. He is very ....(1) to attend in order that he may ....(11) his ....(10) in art. Paul had been ....(4) entering for some time, but it was ....(13) for him to ....(14) himself that he should take up such a ....(17) His friends, who also ....(3) the plan, told him that he would be more .. ..(16) if he attended and would be making an

Fig. 6. A portion of one of the six tests designed to be used with the study sheets. The children wrote in the proper word for each blank as the teacher read the story. Thus, "application" is written in the first blank, "university" in the second, and so on.

the study and testing sheets were carried through with many fifth grade classes.

For instance, on Monday a class was given the initial test. This was followed immediately by study sheet Number 1. No additional teaching or assistance by the teacher was permitted. The children were given one minute to fill in the blanks for each word before being told to go on to the next word. In this way, twenty minutes were spent in study. The study sheets were then collected.

On Tuesday the class was given Test 1. This was followed immediately by study sheet Number 2, and a twenty-minute period was spent in study by filling in the blanks. The same plan was followed each day, except that on Friday the test for lesson 5 was given immediately upon completion of the study.

No attempt was made to design "good" lesson sheets. The writer is sure he can construct much better ones. That they proved very effective was a surprise. The intent was merely to devise a standardized impersonal teaching (learning) procedure, and the goal was achieved. Every child was given the same opportunity to learn the twenty words.

The sheets were used with approximately fifteen hundred children, chiefly normal fifth grade classes, although some lower and some higher grades were also used.

In a few cases the procedure was varied by

having the words taught by teachers instead of by study sheets. A variety of other experiments were tried. Much data were secured which are not pertinent to the purposes of this paper. It is sufficient to say that a wealth of evidence was obtained proving that the Gompertz formula accurately represents the growth in spelling under the conditions stated.

For instance, the growth curves of three selected individuals are presented as illustrations of standard curves. (Fig. 7).

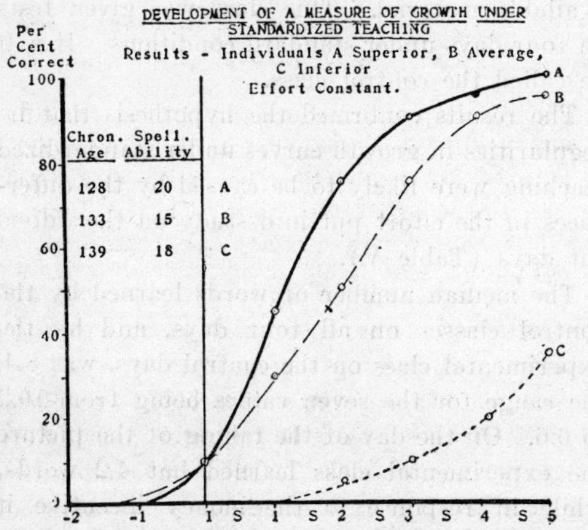

FIG. 7. Individual growth curves from the use of the study sheets under conditions of constant effort. The curves have been extended backward two days by extrapolation to show zero points. I = initial test, 1 = Test 1, 2, Test 2, etc., S = study. The curves are very perfect examples of growth under standard conditions. Children of different natures "grow" at different rates under conditions of equal training.

Values of Constants for Curves	n	r	θ
A	889×10^{-9}	.398	1.1
B	26485×10^{-9}	.467	2.4
C	5578×10^{-9}	.705	.6

The agreement between actual and computed values is remarkable considering that a variation of even a single word would have caused an error of 5 per cent. It is interesting to note in passing that individual B differs not only in ability but in type from A and C. However, not all curves, nor even many of them, were of this perfect form, although there were only one or two out of many hundred which did not exhibit the standard characteristic[5] in certain sections.

For instance, three individuals selected as resembling those of Fig. 7 had complex growth curves. (Fig. 8).

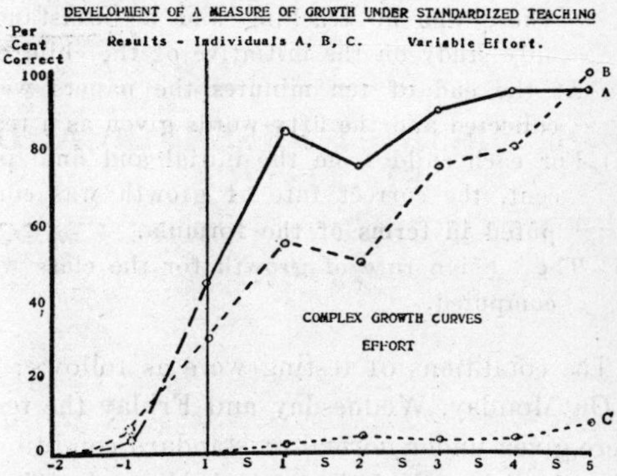

FIG. 8. Individual growth curves from the use of the study sheets under conditions of variable effort. The curves have been extended backwards two days by extrapolation to show zero points. I = initial test, 1 = Test 1, 2, Test 2, and so on. S = study. The curves vary from the standard form because the conditions did not remain constant.

Individual A especially has a curve closely resembling the curve for "sincerely," Fig. 3, in which the irregularity was described as caused by teaching. It became necessary to determine the cause of such variations.

As, in the experiments, all external conditions were controlled, the assumption was made that the variation must be due to an internal factor. After reflection upon several instances which had been observed, the hypothesis was formulated that the variation was caused by variation in effort. On certain days an individual put forth more effort than on others.

To test this hypothesis, five equal learning tests (a new type) were devised.[6] Five sets of fifty words each were so chosen from the Iowa Spelling Scale that the tests were of equal difficulty. One of these lists was used each day for five days.

The method of use of the tests was as follows:

[5] That the loglogs of the values of y form a straight line.

[6] The author is indebted to Miss Helen Miller, in charge of spelling in the Hamtramck Public Schools for the direction of the experiment, preparation of tests, tabulations, etc.

(1) The children were given the fifty words as a test and the papers collected.
(2) The children were given a printed list of the words and asked to study them for ten minutes. They were told that at the end of the study period the test would be repeated. There was no teaching and no assistance, only study on the initiative of the children.
(3) At the end of ten minutes the papers were collected and the fifty words given as a test.
(4) For each child from the initial and final per cent. the correct rate of growth was computed in terms of the formula.
(5) The median rate of growth for the class was computed.

The conditions of testing were as follows:

On Monday, Wednesday and Friday the tests were given under normal or standard conditions. These will be called the control days. On Tuesday an effort was made to *distract* the attention of the children from their study. The writer took a movie camera into the room, set up his tripod and "shot" the children from various angles. He changed films in front of the children and conversed with the teacher, in a tone loud enough to be heard by all, about his various activities. The movie, as well as the results, proved that his efforts were successful. Some children frankly abandoned all study and merely watched proceedings. All children, even the most industrious, may be seen in the movie either boldly looking up from their work from time to time or peeking up. Incidentally, it may be well to call attention to the potentialities of the motion picture as an instrument for the measurement of significant characteristics of children's actions under classroom teaching.

On Thursday, after the initial test, the teacher produced a large bag of pennies and agreed to give one to every child for every word he learned during the study period. She also offered in addition a prize of one dollar to the child who earned the largest number of pennies. The comments and behavior of the children proved that the money reward was an incentive to increased effort.

On Tuesday it was realized that a control group would add to the certainty of interpretation of the results. Accordingly, a 5B class under the same teacher was selected as the best available material. This class was given tests on four days under standard conditions. It will be called the control class.

The results confirmed the hypothesis that irregularities in growth curves under standardized teaching were likely to be caused by the differences in the effort put into study on the different days (Table V).

The median number of words learned by the control classes on all four days, and by the experimental class on the control days, was 8.4, the range for the seven values being from 10.2 to 6.6. On the day of the taking of the picture the experimental class learned but 4.2 words, while in response to the money incentive it learned 13.1 words. In general, therefore, the rate at which a child learns is affected by the effort expended, as well as by the opportunities provided.

The attempt was made to make two equal groups matched by pairs from the experimental and control classes. Twelve pairs were secured matched in age, sex and spelling ability as determined by a fifty-word performance scale. The median values of "r" differed somewhat from those given in Table V, but the results in no wise change the conclusion. (Figure 9).

TABLE V

DETERMINATION OF THE EFFECT OF CHANGES IN EFFORT

Gross scores of a 5A class (experimental) and of a 5B class (control) in five equal learning tests, one on each of five days. The attention of the experimental group was distracted on Tuesday by the taking of a motion picture and on Thursday motivated by a money reward.

	Monday Classes		Tuesday Classes		Wednesday Classes		Thursday Classes		Friday Classes	
	Exp.	Con.	Exp.	Con.	Exp.	Con.	Exp.	Con.	Exp.	Con.
Median gain in words	10.0	......	4.2	6.6	6.9	10.2	13.1	8.6	8.4	8.1
Median "r"	.56	......	.77	.61	.63	.53	.42	.58	.57	.56

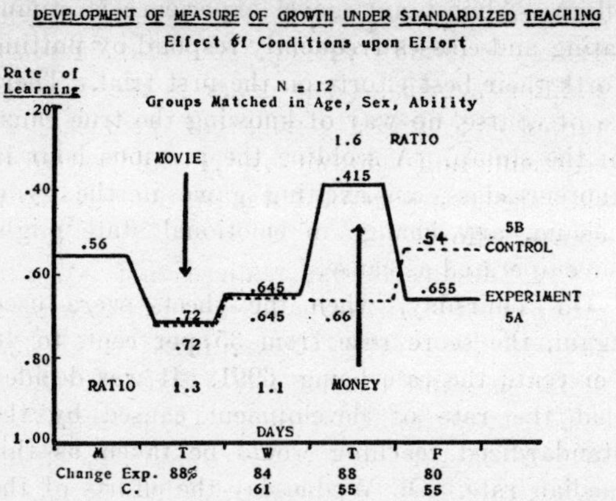

FIG. 9. Interpretation. The experimental group put forth its best effort on the first of the control days when its rate of growth was .56. Its rate on the other two control days averaged .65. The group was distracted by the movie, 88 per cent. of the children making smaller gains. The rate fell to .72. It was stimulated by the money reward, 88 per cent. of the children making larger gains. The rate rose to .41.

The control group put forth its lowest effort on the first day, had approximately the same average rate of growth as the experimental group, .65, and rose on the last day to a rate of .54. It was stimulated by the series of tests to better study effort. The number of the group who responded by making the average type of change in rate from test to test was closely 50 per cent. That is, variations in effort on different days follow the laws for chance unless there is a specific factor operating, like the movie or the money.

Rates of .415 and .72 mean that under a money incentive the class learned as much in one day as they would have learned in 2.6 days of "distraction."

They do show, however, that the experimental group put forth its best effort on the first day, while the control group began low but was stimulated by the series of learning tests to put forth greater and greater effort. Learning tests promise to prove very important instruments of investigation. They can be made to reveal internal states and qualities hitherto regarded as intangible.

A study of the changes in the experimental and control groups shows that the significant direction of change in rate of learning was quite general but not universal. For instance, of the children in the experimental group, 88 per cent. were distracted by the movie, three learning no words and one making a lower score on the final than on the initial test. On the other hand, one child learned as well and two children learned slightly better when the movie was being taken than when it was not. Similarly, the money reward called out greater effort in 88 per cent. of the children, but three children became so excited that they learned less in working for money than they did under normal classroom conditions. However, no child failed to earn at least two cents.

A feature of the work with the learning tests was the large gains made by the children. The children learned on the average almost a word a minute. Under a money incentive, the average rose to 1.3 words per minute; the words were difficult words on which the average scores of the class on the initial test were 25 per cent. and less. One child learned twenty-eight words in ten minutes when working for money, his average gains on the control days being seven. However, the record goes to two children in the control group who learned thirty-one words each in ten minutes with no more incentive than that offered by the regular testing situation. It is evident that learning under conventional school conditions takes place on a very low level of efficiency.

One other illustration will be given of the use of change in rate of growth as a measure of the effect of teachings. In cooperation with Miss Besley, director of the training department of Detroit Teachers College, the teaching ability of two student-teachers, judged by the department to be very good and very poor respectively, was measured by the new technique.

The procedure was as follows:

(1) A certain fifth grade class was chosen for the experiment.

(2) On Monday and Tuesday the class was given practice with the study sheets under standard conditions, the only change being that the test on a study lesson was given immediately after the study period. On Wednesday the poor student teacher was assigned to teach the given twenty words in fifteen minutes. She was given no instruction other than to use the time in the way that she judged would produce the best results. At the close of her teaching period the regular test for study sheet 3 was given. On Thursday study sheet 4 was used, and on Friday the good student teacher was assigned to teach the words in fifteen minutes.

The scores will be reported in terms of the per cent. of the class which spelled all twenty words correctly; that is, in this case maturity was defined as ability to spell all twenty words correctly.

The initial score of the class was 9 per cent. (Figure 10).

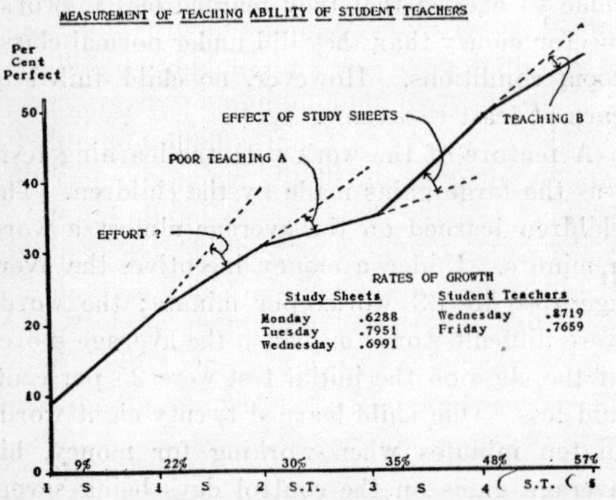

FIG. 10. Growth curve of a class where the study sheets were used Monday, Tuesday and Thursday, and student teachers on Wednesday and Friday. I = initial test, 1 = Test 1, 2 = Test 2, and so on. S indicates study sheets were used; S T that the teaching was done by student teachers. The dotted lines indicate the curve of growth had the rate the previous period been maintained. The change in the rate of growth (difference between dotted and actual lines) is the measure of the effect of the change.

The children put forth unusual effort on Monday, but ''slumped'' on Tuesday. The rate on Thursday, .6991, is taken as average or standard for the effect of the sheets. At this rate, to change the class from a score of 10 per cent. to 90 per cent. would take 8.6 days of study with the study sheets. The poor student teacher would require 22.5 days to make the same change, and the good one 11.6 days. The good student teacher was, therefore, nearly twice as able as the poor one.

The first day's study raised this to 22 per cent., corresponding to a rate of learning of .6288. The second day's study again raised the score, but only to 30 per cent. instead of to 38 per cent., which would have been reached had the initial rate of learning been maintained. The rate of learning was .7951. It would have taken two days at the second rate to accomplish as much as one day at the first rate. The drop in rate might have been caused by decrease in effort. Almost any novel experience is stimulating and classes frequently respond by putting forth their best efforts on the first trial. There is, of course, no way of knowing the true cause of the slump. A scolding the previous hour in another class, an exciting game in the gymnasium, any change in emotional state might have operated as cause.

On Thursday, when the sheets were used again, the score rose from 35 per cent. to 48 per cent., the rate being .6991. It was decided that the rate of development caused by the standardized teaching would be taken as this median rate. On Wednesday the efforts of the poor student-teacher raised the score from 30 per cent. to 35 per cent., corresponding to a rate of growth of but .8719, a rate so slow that it would require 2.6 days of similar training to achieve the same results as that produced by one day's use of the study sheets. On Friday, similarly, the good student-teacher changed the score from 48 per cent. to 57 per cent., corresponding to a rate of .7659. She would require 1.3 days to achieve the same result as one day of standarized teaching.

The good student-teacher, therefore, is to be judged to be almost twice as able as the poor student-teacher.

Much experimentation yet remains to be completed before the new technique will be available for general use, but the conclusion of the writer is that an exact scientific method has been devised by which the effect of teaching may be precisely measured. The technique will be improved by the use of matched groups, longer time intervals, repeated tests, and other similar checks, but in main outlines the procedure is complete and adequate. The greatest of the immediate needs are two:

(1) A means of measuring directly the effort being expended by a child at any instant, and (2) a direct objective measure of the "n" factors. To these must be added the need for a host of devoted workers willing to give many hours of careful research to perfect and refine the new technique as well as to render it practicable for a busy, non-mathematical superintendent or supervisor to use with safety in his daily work.

S. A. COURTIS

UNIVERSITY OF MICHIGAN

SCHOOL AND SOCIETY

Volume XXVIII | Saturday, July 28, 1928 | Number 709

THE CHAMPIONSHIP OF YOUTH[1]

In looking back over a half-century as a teacher, there is no memory which gives me more unmixed pleasure than that I have always been on the side of my students, never upon my own or upon the faculty side. In twenty-eight years of actual classwork in Princeton and Columbia I never called a roll or reported an absence; so great was the magnetism of the subject and such my unconscious enthusiasm for it, that no formal discipline was necessary. I have always been the champion of youth, and never more so than to-day when, especially during and since the world war, the valor and creative ability of American youth are being so splendidly manifested. I therefore am not in the chorus of recent attacks on American school, college and university education, in which are found my colleagues, President Butler of Columbia, President Lowell of Harvard, and Dr. Flexner of the General Education Board. I take no part in the depreciation of American youth, because in my long experience I have always found youth keenly responsive to what may be called the inspiration of the subject, eager to learn and to observe when shown how to observe, quick to distinguish between real and false values, sensitive to truth and beauty, although very deficient in the power of expression. Also, recalling the familiar sign of a far western restaurant—"Do not shoot the pianist, he is doing his best"—let us not condemn our teachers, for they are doing their best.

In the few moments which may be devoted to this address I shall endeavor to show that the blame is on our elders and college presidents, not on our youth; that it is our civilization rather than our youth which is out of joint.

First, there is the mountain of books and the forests daily turned into newspapers. Books are at once the greatest friends and the greatest enemies of modern education, for with mass education the didactic bookish system has gradually replaced the old apprentice system, with teacher and student side by side in the actual practice of an art or a profession, as our Stone Age ancestors worked with their youngsters on the flints in their caves and shelters. Direct contact with the object, in sociology, in economics, in history, as well as in literature and in science, is the most urgent need of the day. Do not first read books or listen to lectures on sociology or economics, but mingle at once with the masses of the people, make your own observations and conclusions before you see how the great minds of the past and present have dealt with these problems. In social reform, if Trotsky had spent his youth in the factories and among the working men of America instead of in the libraries amidst the vitriolic writings of social agitators his whole program for Russia would have been different; in creative literature we find Elizabeth Barrett Browning confessing, "How willingly I would as a poet exchange some of this slumbering, ponderous, helpless knowledge of books for some experience of life and man"; in science we have the two striking

[1] Address as Honorary Chancellor to the graduates of Union College, June 11, 1928.

epigrams of Louis Agassiz: "Study Nature, not books" and "If you study Nature in books, when you go out-of-doors you can not find her." I venture to say that the four thousand three hundred graduates of Columbia University on June fifth took a hundred facts from books and lectures to one fact from Nature or from man, yet one fact or truth of Nature directly observed or discovered by the student himself outweighs a thousand facts garnered from books.

The truth is, I have always been so busy observing that I have found little time to read books. I am almost ashamed to confess how little scientific reading I have done in my entire life; I preferred Nature to Herbert Spencer and even to Charles Darwin. I started as a biologist on the forceful advice of a teacher who put a hen's egg before me and commanded me to see what I could see! In the course of two and a half hours of most exciting discovery I was a confirmed biologist for life, and abandoned all thoughts of a business career. Begun in 1846, the Agassiz method of *Nature first, books afterward* created an army of zoologists and palaeontologists who dominated the biological thought of America for over half a century.

We must not only fight books but we must lead a new battle against the press, particularly against the latest output of the press, if we are to restore and refresh the environment of the youthful mind and soul, if we are to reenthrone observation and reason as the only sources of all creative endeavor and discovery. From prolonged daily observation of child life and habit and of home, school, college and university life, I believe the modern American press to be the greatest enemy of the teacher, because it destroys all the finer creative powers of the mind, establishes false standards of human endeavor, and gives a distorted perspective of current life. With certain heroic exceptions, such as the *Times* and *Herald-Tribune* of New York and *The Christian Science Monitor* of Boston, it represents the climax of the metamorphosis and metempsychosis of the modern age, the utmost revolution from the conditions which surrounded the youthful Benjamin Franklin, natural philosopher and pioneer of American science.

Literature, music, art and the stage filled 121 columns, or 28.3 per cent. of space in six issues of Franklin's *Saturday Evening Post* of 1823–5, whereas misconduct and crime filled only 20 columns, or 4.8 per cent. of space; the circulation of the paper at its best was 9,000. To-day, in the 4,731,332 newspapers circulating daily in and around New York City, literature, art, music and the stage fill 208 columns, 3.8 per cent. of space, as against 1,500 columns, or 25.6 per cent., of space devoted to fashion, athletics and sport; 191 columns, or 3.8 per cent., of space devoted to misconduct and crime; 38 columns, or only .7 per cent., devoted to religion and, at the very bottom, .4 per cent. of space devoted to education!

This newspaper analysis of the years 1764, 1823–5, 1853–4, and 1928, prepared with the aid of Charles J. Nager, of the Columbia University School of Journalism, reveals a complete revolution in the relative importance given to news matter in the past century and a half, and especially within the last ten years. In New York City to-day the "sensational" papers have a circulation four times that of the conservative papers; if this trend is trustworthy, it may be estimated that by the end of the year 1928 the sale of "sensational" papers in and about New York City will amount to more than two thirds of the total circulation.

Our newspapers are chiefly dangerous in their jazz effect upon the youthful mind. What chance has the youthful, idealistic brain in the City of New York to-day? This most delicate and sensitive of all instruments, incessantly disturbed and rocked to and fro in a whirlpool of conflicting sensations, ideas, and emotions, lacks the environment of creative repose and stimulus to artistic, literary and scientific endeavor. There is no question that there is much creative genius in America to-day, just as there has been always among a similar number of people of similar racial stocks in the past history of the world, but the intellectual environment of the age is not conducive to its best development. From well-known principles of heredity, our youth is born with all the genius and potentiality of the Golden Age of Greece, of the Quattrocento of Italy, of the Victorian Age of England.

The jazz environment destroys the youthful mind in our cities and explains the fact that the best American intellects, in both science and literature, including the Pulitzer and Nobel prizemen, are coming to-day from colleges and universities in small towns of the relatively quiet mid-west. Harvard no longer rules Boston, nor does Columbia exert any influence on New York. Neither Butler nor Lowell nor Flexner is in a position to cast stones at American youth until they devise means of protecting the youthful mind and of enforcing original thought. The nobly equipped colleges over which they preside are not filling their own graduate schools with teachers or investigators; they too are drawing recruits from the relatively small and quiet abodes of learning; the conditions of civic life are too chaotic for observation or reflection. At a recent inaugural, glittering with hoods and gowns, in one of the great Columbia schools, I asked the newly-installed dean how much original thinking was being done for a degree. "Little or none," he replied, "these people do not think; they take excellent notes and pass excellent examinations, but they do not think."

It is neither the student nor the teacher nor the underpaid college professor, but the intellectual, moral and spiritual environment of the times which is awry. Therefore, it is the irreverent and anarchical spirit of the times which must be set right, and this may be done by a truer understanding of the prehistoric and historic meaning of the word "education," namely, that its supreme purpose is the progress and ascent of man, not only in the present but in the future.

This address is not academic; it is thoroughly practical. I am preaching only what I have practiced. The young men whom it has been my privilege to teach or to whom I have been privileged to lend a helping hand, now in every part of the world—on sea and land, in laboratories and lecture rooms—have their hands on the lever of Archimedes.

On America falls the future world leadership. Pursuing the simile of Archimedes—if disciplined in incessant observation, if compelled to original thought, if guarded from a distracting intellectual environment, our young manhood is the lever which will lift the world. It is not our youth which is at fault, but our maturity.

Henry Fairfield Osborn
Columbia University

EXPERIMENTAL CLASSES IN ADULT EDUCATION[1]

In addressing so grave a body of adult educators, I feel that there can be no impropriety in quoting from Rabelais. The passage is culled from the prologue to his first book, translated by Urquhart and Motteux.

Did you ever see a dog with a marrowbone in his mouth—the beast of all other, says Plato in the second book of his Republic, the most philo-

[1] Paper read before the third annual meeting of the American Association for Adult Education at Swarthmore, Pa., May 14, 1928.

sophical? If you have seen him, you might have remarked with what devotion and circumspectness he wards and watcheth it: with what care he keeps it: how fervently he holds it: how prudently he gobbets it: with what affection he breaks it: and with what diligence he sucks it. To what end all this? What moveth him to take all these pains? What are the hopes of his labor? What doth he expect to reap thereby? Nothing but a little marrow. True it is, that this little is more savory and delicious than the great quantities of other sorts of meat, because the marrow, as Galen testifieth, is a nourishment most perfectly elaborated by nature.

In imitation of this dog, it becomes you to be wise, to smell, feel and have in estimation these fair, goodly books, stuffed with high conceptions, which, though seemingly easy in the pursuit, are in the cope and encounter somewhat difficult. And then, like him, you must, by sedulous lecture, and frequent meditation, break the bone, and suck out the marrow—that is my allegorical sense. . . .

Recent experimentation in the psychology of education has made many of its most exciting discoveries through the study of animal psychology. In starting with the study of so philosophic an animal as the dog, I feel that I am placing the psychology of adult education on a firm scientific foundation. The bone and its marrow content also have their application in this department of education. I should like to define adult education as a way of playing with books that yields the same concentrated delight that a dog finds in a bone.

Now I am rather afraid that these books included in my definition may become literally bones of contention. Some will urge that all of an adult's experience is educational and that while books are valuable enough—in libraries, for example—they are not essential in adult education. Why insist on books when so many relatively painless ways of education lie ready at hand? For example, you may lecture at adults, especially at those who look rather tired and grey; or if they are young and combative let them discuss; if you want to make education vivid, show them slides or movies; and if they won't come for love or money, invade their firesides by broadcasting education over the radio.

For a good many years Mr. Everett Dean Martin, the director of The People's Institute, has made keen use of the lecture with his Cooper Union audiences of 1,000 or more. But these are supplemented by short bibliographies of suggested reading on the programs. And in recent years they have been supplemented also by the smaller classes at the school of The People's Institute and by generous shelves of books provided through the cooperation of the New York public libraries. The lecture is simply a way of making books vocal, not a substitute.

The last decade the country has been full of later Socratics or Platonists who have made a cult of discussing and discussions. Perhaps Professor Meiklejohn sowed these seeds at Amherst College. Certainly now we are reaping the harvest. A psychologist would probably label the doctrine of education by discussion of a characteristic rationalization of a loquacious and gossip-loving race. The point may be made, however, that not all discussion is Socratic.

When I hear of an adult group which wants to discuss, I now always coldly ask, "What?" For several times a vague enthusiasm has misled me into helping to start classes that simply wanted to discuss. When this is done around a little table on the street in Paris, say between sips of *vin rouge* or *biere,* I confess the mind often encounters lofty themes. But here in America, possibly owing to the absence of the *vin* and *biere,* a mere discussion for discussion's sake, or education's sake, or as we like to say for contact's sake, is apt to be about as anemic an experience as one can well endure. Right here I should like to challenge Mr. John Watson's otherwise picturesque identification of spoken words and movements of the larynx with thinking. For if words are thoughts, then not to think is surely golden.

The difficulty with discussion, even in a well-informed group, is that after the first few sessions the repertoire of thoughts is exhausted and a dulling repetition commences. Succeeding repetitions produce dogmatic convictions and well-fortified positions, not curiosity, which you remember St. Augustine insists is a necessary ingredient for education. Live discussion groups need constantly new grist for their mill. Without reading, as well as talking, interest is sure to lag. Among the few class obituaries which mar the institute's record, nearly all, as their epitaphs record, died in the fourth or fifth week of starvation! One must have food even for thought.

When the first experimental classes were receiving skeptical consideration in the sanctum of the institute two years ago, this matter of victualling these robust learners received very serious consideration. We must not try to cram down them the heavily caloried diet of the college training table. Such stuffing would make them obese or gouty. What we wanted was the equivalent of the dog's bone, a little, good, rich marrow encased in a material that would invite much careful chewing and gobbeting. The average book that can be bolted at a bite would hardly fit the purpose.

It happened that several of us on The People's Institute lecture staff by night were teaching by day at Columbia University, and were members of the Columbia College general honors faculty. In 1919 Columbia celebrated the armistice by initiating a two-year reading course taking up in translation the principal classics of our western tradition. The course started with Homer the first year and came down as far as Shakespeare. The second year began with Galileo and finished with Freud! Why it was called honors I don't know, unless to inveigle students into electing it. The classes met one evening a week for a seminar discussion with two or three instructors. Here seemed to be promising material with plenty of marrow and solid matter, too. The institute mimeographed two lists of readings from the classics and invited the cooperation of some half dozen organizations in trying experimental classes for adults. Not only were the organizations very different, but the six groups represented striking contrasts socially, racially, economically and scholastically.

Organization was simple. The institute found six promising pairs of instructors who had taught or graduated from the Columbia honors course. It warned them that this experience was absolutely futile as far as what was ahead was concerned. The adult is a hypochondriac who must be humored. Instead of instructors disciplining students, students discipline instructors in adult education. Finally they were told that they weren't instructors at all but student leaders, and that a good class would be one in which they got little opportunity to speak and that this little must betray fundamental disagreement in views between the two. With this coaching we left everything to the two leaders.

The first night's classes ranged from eleven and a visitor to eighty-four who were mostly visitors. No adult would utter a word so the leaders staged a Homeric combat, or, if they were taking the second year, fought over Ptolemy and Galileo. As these bouts became heated, the hitherto phlegmatic adults became partisan and now and then gave a good buffet on their own account. In a week or two they were buying books and searching out intricate proofs from the classics for things they had always believed. Gradually, special pleading gave way to pleasure in dialectic dissection of ideas whether venerated or strangely new.

The test came when they encountered Erasmus and preferred his sweet reasonableness to Luther, the reformer, or found more wisdom than pornography in Rabelais. The candid willingness to follow the argument, however much it might injure cherished prejudices, showed that actual education was taking place. One group which rejoiced in its radicalism slowly began to discern that it was possible to be just as bigoted and intolerant about minority opinions as those more widely accepted. Their minds so far expanded as to be able hospitably to entertain more than one idea at a time. Their fanaticism softened into humanism.

To be honest, I should also report that while these classes have exhibited surprising vitality, many evenings have been very bad, especially in my own section. Often a lecture takes the place of discussion. Often the group arrives quite ignorant of the author to be the theme. Once, I recall, we got to arguing whether it was good to die for one's country or not. I believe Virgil was to blame. At first it was merry fun, but then quite suddenly people began to shed blood for their country. That night we lost eight members of the class. I don't think they were mortally injured in the combat, but they never returned to the class again!

But some of you are wondering why we sought the classics, why we dragged all this cold storage stuff from the university library to be served up as adult education. One would think that the college curriculum had got jolly well rid of its old-fashioned classical courses without adult educators trying to restore them. A good many moderns condemn the classics as a discipline long since obsolete.

Rather recently university professors have made a new word out of an old one that was becoming rather shabby. They may have discovered the word on the rubbish heap outside of the psychology laboratory. There it lay in the discard, an ancient thing with little or no meaning left in it. This obsolete term was the word "mind." In the days of the triumvirate, soul, mind and body, it had enjoyed great favor, but the advent of behaviorism spelled its ruin. This empty word lay ready for use. Historians and philosophers were looking for a term which would apply to the slowly accumulated concepts and habits of thought which characterize a given culture or civilization. They hit upon the term "mind" to sum up our intellectual legacy from the past. Now we hear very frequently of the western mind. Books such as "The Mind in the Making" and "The Making of the Modern Mind" trace the genesis of the habit patterns of our modern culture.

Where do our modern ways of thinking and established beliefs come from? Is their ancestry a dubious one, or do they boast of high lineage? Whence our notions of democracy, history, drama, poetry, mathematics, economics, religion? The record of these accessions to the modern mind are to be found in the books which have become the classics of our western tradition. Nearly all the more important of these books can be readily understood and enjoyed by any moderately well educated person. The language barrier of the original, not the content, has given the scholar the monopoly of them in recent times. This scholar interpretation has pointed their teaching to the past instead of to the present. Actually they contain the biography of the modern mind and offer the reader one of the best clues to modern thought.

The classics had other advantages. They totally eliminated the text-book with its lifeless style, its stereotype concepts and its predigested problems. They brought the reader into first-hand contact with the most original and able thinkers of his cultural ancestry. By avoiding the secondary and tertiary writers, the commentators and scavengers, the readings seemed likely to develop a robust taste for reading more solid books and conversely a distaste for trashy books and periodicals. Finally, they exhibited modern thought in sufficient perspective to disarm partisan thinking and permit a long-range bombardment of our more firmly entrenched beliefs.

The entire list of classics from Homer to Freud totaled seventy-six titles. In most cases they were available in dollar translations, though a good many of the better texts were more expensive. Students began to cry for books. The book shortage was aggravated by the fact that they would not stick to the assigned reading but surreptitiously explored the other volumes by the same author in the hope of confounding their leaders' arguments or exposing their superficiality. Students protested that their book bills were mounting far beyond their means.

In this crisis the institute turned to the New York public libraries. We learned that our students had been there ahead of us, showing eagerness for books long since out of print. The librarian in charge of the Muhlenberg Branch Library, Mrs. Helen W. Grannis, was good enough to assemble nearly all the books for the two courses in the classics on convenient shelves for the institute students. But in tracing our list of classics, she discovered that a few of them had never been written; that some of the translations were quite taboo because of their complete disregard for the original; that in certain cases we had not discovered the best edition. But the library collected an excellent assortment of classics in spite of these difficulties, and these books were most useful to our students.

Meanwhile, we took up the matter of a better list with the Columbia honors faculty. Their list was undergoing a revision. The new Columbia honors bibliography suggested an opportunity for compiling an authoritative readers' guide to the classics in translation. This, it seemed, would be invaluable, not only for Columbia, but also for the libraries and the institute. Negotiations were carried on with Mr. Morse A. Cartwright, Mr. Carl H. Milam and Mr. Franklin H. Hopper with the result that the bibliography was published under the title "Classics of the Western World," by the American Library Association in cooperation with the Columbia College honors faculty, The American Association for Adult Education and The Peoples Institute. Professor John Erskine and Mr. Everett Dean Martin furnished prefaces for the readings.

I have spoken with some detail about this bibliography to emphasize the importance of the public libraries and books and book lists in adult education. Our work at The Peoples Institute would be quite futile without this cooperation, for the libraries furnish the necessary bones and marrow for the educative process.

The main feature of our second year of experimental work has been a symposium on esthetics and criticism held at the Muhlenberg branch library. In a country where the pioneer ruthlessly laying waste the forests and slaying the grazing herds of the plains, or in later days exploiting our coal, oil and remaining lumber supply for his own wealth, has been our national hero, it is small wonder that we have been late in discovering art. There is little time for esthetic experience among a people which worships activity. Yet to-day the country is beginning to awaken to a new enjoyment of art. Music led the way, then architecture rose towering above the achievements of older countries, both in sheer height and in superior imagination and design. The other arts are pressing close behind.

When the institute opened its thirtieth season of classes last October, we began a careful espionage system to discover what were the hobbies and central interests of our varied student groups. The results were a little confusing. Some wanted symbolic logic, which Dr. Scott M. Buchanan proceeded to supply; some were curious about scientific method, others preferred philosophy or psychology, and a considerable number mentioned some form of art. As the classes proceeded, one scientific lecturer in particular drew many of his illustrations from the field of art. The students asked for more.

The word "art" recalled certain college fine arts courses in which an instructor with a somewhat baroque vocabulary had presented an historical catalogue of paintings or architecture from the dawn of civilization to the present. At best, genealogy, whether of kings or lesser individuals, painting or architecture, is a highly specialized subject little calculated to animate the layman. No "fine arts," we decided.

Another type of course rejoicing in the title of "art appreciation" or "introduction to art" suggested a possibility. We looked into the books of these instructors and found them redolent in such vagaries as inspiration, grandeur, balance, imagination, proportion, sensitivity. These terms were easily dated and none of them suggested the twentieth century. Again we looked farther.

Some universities offered good philosophy courses in esthetics or a laboratory course in psychology of art. These sounded more hard boiled, as the village would say, or more objective and verifiable, as the scientist would say. It began to look as if there were ways of discoursing on art without giving vent to unsuppressed emotion.

I consulted President Ernest H. Wilkins, of Oberlin College, who as dean at the University of Chicago had introduced a very interesting survey course in art last year. He stressed particularly the need of bringing the student into contact with the art around him and introducing him to the creative artists as interpreters. Perhaps Mr. Lorado Taft, one of the distinguished artists who cooperated in this course at Chicago University, will mention it in his address Wednesday evening.

What can be said about art? Is it a subject one may discuss with due regard for the laws of thought? Or must one verbalize emotion in mauve phrases? With no very firm conviction as to how these questions were to be answered we announced a symposium on esthetics and criticism during March and April. To make the function of the symposium perfectly plain, on the cover of the announcement we pictured the owl of Minerva looking quizzically at Venus, goddess of beauty. The announcement stated that the symposium was to be an experimental inquiry into the theories and methods of criticism of the various arts. It concluded by stating that this was to be a critique of criticism which would seek to clarify thinking on esthetic theory and probe into the vexed question whether the critic merited the artist's ancient privilege of madness in conversing on art or whether he should strive for rationality.

Six series of discussions made up the program. The general topics were art and esthetic experience, beauty and the beast (by a psychologist of course), cycles in literature, the mirror of the passing world (by a painter), inherited prejudices in art criticism and scientific method of esthetics. These lectures I am glad to announce are to be published in the fall by W. W. Norton & Co., Inc., as a set of five books under the general title of "Outline of Aesthetics."

Although sandwiched in at an early hour before the institute's regular school classes, attendance suggested a lively interest. The Muhlenberg Library furnished books for outside reading and various works in the Metropolitan Museum of Art offered materials of study. The arts turned out to afford very discussible subject-matter of a particularly congenial type. Most of these symposiums maintained a critical approach of high standard. A general feud enlivened the sessions over the place of subject-matter in the representative arts, a question on which the lecture staff was decidedly at odds. Critical criteria were put forward and promptly overthrown. One lecturer challenged the group to distinguish objectively between a good painting and a bad one, causing much confusion.

Again students began to ask for more books and to visit museums and exhibits. Fortunately the great Metropolitan collections were at hand to meet the latter demands. But the books again required special attention. We found the critical books on art much scattered and difficult of access. Most of the best books on art were histories or texts for student artists. Popular works on art often proved banal and unauthoritative.

So again, in the interests of adult education, we have been forced to assemble a bibliography as a readers' guide to the dimly marked paths of this shadowy subject. In its present form the list records some 500 critical books. For convenience we have classified them under nine heads, philosophy of art or esthetics, psychology of art, and criticism of architecture, drama, music, painting, poetry, prose and sculpture. Since many of the authors have rambled at liberty over more than one subject we are listing the table of contents of each book to give the reader some cue as to what he is likely to encounter. I hope very much that we may be able to publish this "Selected Bibliography of Aesthetics and Criticism" soon, for no such needed guide now exists.

Our symposium on esthetics and criticism once more demonstrates the value of library cooperation, and, in addition, points to the educational value of the museum.

And now let me sum up a few tentative conclusions. First, I should say that adult education always is an active thinking process. Professor John Dewey, in his little book on "How We Think," says that the human animal only thinks when it is uncomfortable, when it is faced by an irritating problem or situation. Applying this dictum, the conclusion would be that adult education is a form of irritation! However this may be, education is certainly not a way of filling up empty vessels with sound doctrines. It is far harder than a filling job. In the last analysis it turns out to be a way of providing the adult with the means of educating himself—teaching him to read reflectively, and placing him in the contagious environment of thinking.

Second, I do not think it necessary to dilute or popularize in order to appeal to adult students. Where this is done, it is usually out of deference to the lecturer's own limitations rather than those of his audience. Most subjects that are understood can be stated simply enough for an intelligent adult class. We have even made some fairly successful experiments with logic, mathematics and advanced science along this line, and these subjects certainly are crucial. The problem is to humanize not to popularize or cheapen knowledge.

Finally, I should like to make the point that adult education seems to have no ulterior motives. It is a way of enjoying and enriching experience. College may be preparation for life, and school for citizenship, but fortunately adult education isn't a preparation for anything. As Aristotle says in his "Ethics," the characteristic or normal function of the animal, man, is to think. This is not his duty but his function and pleasure. Adult education then is a way in which people may enjoy thinking.

Philip N. Youtz

The People's Institute,
New York City

AN ENRICHED DIPLOMA

THE past two decades have been vigorously occupied in the process of enriching the curriculum. Some, indeed, maintain that it has become so rich that, like a cake of the same quality, it is in danger of falling—or of causing indigestion. Whatever may be the conclusion on that point the time is ripe to note that there is a feature of the school system which may be enriched to the advantage of pupils, teachers and the public. It is the diploma.

This analogy between curriculum and diploma is most inept. The phrase gives no hint at the fundamental and far-reaching effect of the proposal involved. The new feature in the enriched diploma will not be added in the interests of the diploma but of the school life which it symbolizes.

At present the school diploma stands for a certain intellectual achievement. Depending upon the organization of the schools it indicates the completion of the first six or the first eight grades of the elementary school or the junior or senior high school. As the grading system has become reasonably uniform throughout the nation the meaning of graduation from a particular school unit has become correspondingly intelligible. The eighth grade diploma, for example, indicates that a child has a reasonable mastery of the simple facts of American history and of world geography and passable skills in figuring, spelling, reading and constructing sentences. He is supposed to be able to undertake the work of a standard high school.

When these attainments are analyzed into their component details, they represent a good deal for a child of fourteen to have mastered. The number of skills and amount of information imparted to children during a period of eight years is genuinely amazing, if one will contemplate it. Even more amazing is the feat when one notes the skills aside from the arts of communication in which training is given in hundreds of modern schools. Whatever disagreements there may be regarding educational policies, it can not be justly said that the schools fail to impart a surprising mass of information and to develop a remarkable array of skills. That these appropriate skills and facts have been reasonably mastered is the announcement of the eighth grade diploma. Diplomas from other grade units testify to corresponding attainments.

But are facts and skills what we chiefly want? We have come to suppose that is what the school should give, because that is what the schools have come to give. We are slaves of tradition; and we are content with traditional objectives. But are we quite satisfied?

The American school system has developed as a means of preserving our democracy. While intelligence has been stressed as a *means* of keeping our democratic institutions safe, the *aim* has been the civilization, not the intelligence. In so far as knowledge and skill fail to safeguard our national ideals, their failure must be supplemented by agencies more effective. American education is provided in the interests of its citizenship product, not of its knowledge and skill product.

Once persuade the public that the schools are not producing satisfactory results in citizenship, and support would be withdrawn from the schools. When we give the matter any thought we know that we are not providing education in order to impart information and skill as ends in themselves. Ultimately we expect our schools to safeguard our democracy.

One need not be a destructive nor an unkind critic to point out that the good must not become the enemy of the best. The citizenship of the youth in our schools and of the youth just past the doors of our schools is not so faultless as to remove all danger of criticism. With our present knowledge of the principles of character training and our high standards of teacher preparation it is possible for our schools to accomplish far greater results than we can yet show in the realm of character development and wholesome citizenship.

In this achievement the diploma may have a most significant part. The plan proposed is simple and direct. Admission to any unit of the school system is to be based upon the completion of specified subjects without reference to the diploma. The diploma is to be a personal letter of recommendation giving assurance of both scholarship and citizenship appropriate to the grade represented.

Such a plan would indeed enrich the diploma. No device for motivating good citizenship in the school has held more promise of success than this. A device, of course, it is; and only a device. And no device can ever take the place of the appealing personality and devoted efforts of the consecrated teacher. Personal influence is ever the moving force, the dynamic agency in character training. But machinery may hinder or favor the effectiveness of personal efforts.

The grading system, for example, is also a device, and a device with serious flaws; but it would be difficult to abolish it, because it reenforces the efforts of the teacher to motivate study. In spite of the fact that grades tend to take the place of achievement, to become ends in themselves, to be sought by some at the expense of justice and even of honor, still the great body of teachers would protest against abandoning this device for motivating study.

To make the diploma a testimony of citizenship and character as well as scholarship would be a device; but a device with fewer dangers than the present use of the diploma as a consummation of grades in scholarship. Without minimizing either the faults or limitations of the plan, the use of the diploma as a symbol of citizenship—attainment promises most happy results for every group affected.

As soon as the public appreciates the full significance of the change, the cause of public education will be greatly advanced. Periodical literature is asking, and many a taxpayer is wondering, just how much the schools are doing to accomplish their original purpose of training for citizenship. Any attempt on the part of the school to make a frank appraisal of its own success in this respect will strengthen the faith of the public in education.

The public will also be protected against the unreliable youth who refuse to respond to the ideals upheld by the school. When the employer can ask "Have you a diploma?" with the assurance that its possession is as reliable a guarantee of character as a personal letter from the principal, the dependable applicant will have the advantage, and the employer will be protected against the youth who can not refrain from gambling or falsehood or dishonesty. The same diploma will be a favorable recommendation to clubs or lodges when its holder moves into new localities.

Teachers will find the enriched diploma a device of double worth. On the one hand, it will justify the efforts they would gladly make, but can not afford to, in the interests of moral training. Every aspect of our present system tempts the teacher to concentrate upon the formal drill of the classroom. The curriculum is organized in terms of information and skills. The course of "study" is so crowded with requirements of this type as to exhaust the full time and strength of the teacher. Learning of facts and skills can be stimulated by means more mechanical than those required as character incentives. And the results of mechanical learning can be measured more simply and surely. When it comes to the question of promotions and salary increase, the case for moral training is still further handicapped. How far does the belief that a teacher has had an uplifting influence go to modify the criticism that her pupils have not passed in history or mathematics? Good grades, a high per cent. of pupils passing and good order in her room will expand the salary check and open the door to more desirable positions rapidly and certainly. How can a teacher afford to spend a half hour with the girl who loses her temper, at the expense of helping a dozen algebra pupils? Why should the arranging of apparatus for to-morrow's experiment in chemistry be delayed for a conference with a boy who cheated?

All the skills and facts which the teacher is employed to impart, and the grades by which their mastery is measured, are symbolized by the diploma. The call of the diploma holds the teacher to the task of coaching the pupil in the path that leads thereto.

But put citizenship into the diploma, make it stand for character attainment, and all this will be changed. The success of pupils in conduct and ideals will be as important in the reputation of a teacher as their grades in French or geometry. And the temptation to neglect the higher for the sake of the lower will be removed.

Thus the enrichment of the diploma will open the way for the teacher to give time and energy to the basic objectives of the school—a privilege which the great army of consecrated teachers of America will welcome, though it demands, by the very fact that it permits, a fuller investment of their souls in their tasks.

On the other hand, this new device will strengthen the hands of the teacher in every effort toward citizenship training. Distant motives may be limited in their force; but they are not wholly without effect. The thought of a future diploma may not be sufficient in itself to motivate conscientious study. But it often proves to be just enough incentive to tip the scale in favor of study rather than play. Similarly, the diploma alone might not hold one to ideal conduct; but it may well be just the needed addition to the not quite strong enough will of the tempted pupil. Discreetly seldom, yet just often enough, the teacher may remind the individual or the group of the value of that diploma as an "open sesame" into the business and social world, and of the handicap of going out from school unrecommended as a dependable citizen.

The "balance of power" in the will of a boy or girl need not be very great. In few cases will the knowledge of the diploma's significance prove too slight to serve as such a balance. Such a motive within reach of the teacher will serve to raise the conduct standard of any group significantly. Any teacher with imagination can readily see the vital change in the discipline of a room which would thus follow the enrichment of the diploma.

Most of all, of course, the pupils will profit by the introduction of this new motive. The majority of pupils really prefer order to chaos, cooperation to conflict, harmony to friction and accomplishment to idleness. A "balance of power" motive, such as the inclusion of citizenship in the requirements for the diploma, will lead most pupils to choose the conduct that is socially constructive rather than destructive. And having chosen they will feel better satisfied than they would have with the opposite choice. So that the motive will prove cumulatively effective, the added requirement will in no way be a big stick held over them to compel them to do what they do not wish to do. It will rather be a wholesome diet which one learns to like better and better. The briefest observation will confirm this faith in the inherent idealism of youth.

Not the least value to the pupils will be their own part in setting the standard. No resourceful teacher will overlook the opportunity of calling into conference the highest class in the school unit and asking them to work out a citizenship standard appropriate to the grade.

It would be hard to devise a project more vital for the class. Every familiar objection to ethical teaching will be removed. The project will be their own. No formal or perfunctory statements will be accepted. The justification for every item in the code will be scrutinized; they will face their own weaknesses in the very effort to set standards. The very fact that the task is cooperative adds an ethical element to the undertaking.

The analysis and recognition of ideals will clear away many false values and remove the danger of wrong-doing because of ignorance. Every temptation, in the realm involved in their study, will carry with it a reminder of the consequences involved. Having worked together they will take pride in carrying out their enterprise and will defend their standards as a matter of group pride.

But what of the really "bad" boys and girls? Will the distant, and perhaps uncertain diploma have weight enough with them to turn the scale on the side of right? To that question the negative answer may be readily conceded. But that is not the only question involved. What will be the effect upon them of the changed attitude of the large majority of normal pupils? Approval of the crowd is the most powerful motive in the school world. With the crowd increasingly satisfied with a program of order and accomplishment, approval of their daring will give place to annoyance at their interference; and school sentiment rather than the enriched diploma will, for the incorrigibles, become the "balance of power." With that backing the teacher will find this small group a much less serious problem, and will dare hope even to reform the most hopeless in time.

An established code of ideals readily becomes a part of the "traditions" of a school. Once that stage is reached the ordinary problems of discipline will be reduced to a minimum by the unconscious social pressure of the group.

For teachers, pupils and the public, then, the enriched diploma holds out reasonable promise of fundamental help by enabling the school to achieve the results which inspired its founding.

Fortunately for the stability of worth while reforms, every innovation suggests difficulties which at first seem overwhelming. Any change from the traditional basis of granting diplomas will naturally arouse questions.

Who has a right to set up a standard of character for others? The question is fair. Suppose we were to agree upon the implied negative, would there not remain this question? Is there not already some standard at least vaguely accepted by society? Is it not reasonable to try to find that standard and give it articulation on its lowest terms? No more than this is involved in the proposal. Yet the question tempts a partially affirmative answer: directly or indirectly, some spokesmen for society must set up standards, specific or vague, or civilization would be impossible. Just this process has been going on since the dawn of human consciousness. Society has been laying down restrictions upon the conduct of the individual. The state formulates the most insistent of these into laws. Public opinion enforces others, unjustly, unevenly, inconsistently, but pitilessly enough much of the time, to force a vague recognition of them upon each rising generation.

If the school can scrutinize these conventions, showing their social value where such exists and bringing the simplest of them into some semblance of consistency, it will be rendering a genuine service to its youthful citizens.

As to the practical question intended, the code should be thoroughly democratic. It has already been suggested that the most advanced class in each school unit be permitted to work out a standard. All standards so proposed should be analyzed by the cooperating principals. The superintendent should share in the discussion. His veto power should not be exercised in so important a project without the background of the groups included. Eventually a state teachers' committee should correlate the codes of several cities, seeking not formal standardization, but the adaptation of standards to grades and the improvement of each in the light of the others. The process of seeking a standard may prove the most rewarding step in the project.

One important warning is in place to those who see the possibilities of the plan and who would set about to put it in force at once: this is a public school problem. The support of the public is essential to its permanent success. The first step should be to educate the public. Two years is the briefest period in which that task can be accomplished.

In the system where the plan is contemplated the first step has been to set up a temporary citizenship standard, placing the items on the report card for home reports along with scholarship grades. Parent-teacher associations are discussing the idea of putting this citizenship standard in effect as a requirement for the diploma two years hence. If by that time the public is favorable the board will be asked to make the plan official. If more time is needed for public discussion no effort will be made to force the issue. Meanwhile the code can be revised in the light of experience.

This plan is frankly only a device. It must not be thought of as a substitute for personal influence. But as a device to supplement the efforts of the devoted teacher in building character it holds large promise.

H. S. TUTTLE

UNIVERSITY OF OREGON

EDUCATIONAL EVENTS

THE IMPERIAL COUNCIL ON AGRICULTURAL RESEARCH IN INDIA

THE Royal Commission on Agriculture in India has recommended the establishment of an Imperial Council on Agricultural Research, with a fund of $1,750,000 to "promote, guide and coordinate agricultural research throughout India," according to a report in the Manchester *Guardian*.

The report says that, with agricultural research in India still in its infancy, an efficient organization must be built up to improve the standard of living and the capacity—in terms of mental equipment and of physical health—to take advantage of the opportunities which science, wise laws and good administration may place at the disposal of the peasant, who was considered by the commission to be the most important factor in making for prosperous agriculture. The commission reports:

The demand for a better life can, in our opinion, be stimulated only by a deliberate and concerted effort to improve the general conditions of the countryside, and we have no hesitation in affirming that the responsibility for initiating the steps required to effect this improvement rests with the government. The realization of this important truth has led in recent years to a large increase in expenditure on the departments concerned with rural welfare. None the less we feel that its force is inadequately appreciated by the government of India and by local governments, and that the necessity that the rural problem should be attacked as a whole and at all points simultaneously is still insufficiently present to their minds.

It is no part of our duty to make recommendations regarding the internal organization by which governments should seek to effect coordination. We would, however, point out that in Indian conditions a very special measure of responsibility in this direction falls upon the viceroy and upon the governors of provinces. Throughout our inquiry we have been much impressed by the extent to which the viceroy can by the display of a personal interest in agricultural matters forward the cause of India's premier industry, but the immediate responsibility of provincial governors in this matter is the heavier, since it is they alone who provide a link between the reserved and the transferred departments.

MUSSOLINI AS A SCHOOLMASTER

THE days when Signor Mussolini, the Italian premier, was a school teacher have been recalled by the finding of a report in the municipal archives of Gualtieri, Italy. A recent dispatch from Rome to the London *Referee* says that the document is dated 1901–1902, when Signor Mussolini was nineteen years of age, and is entitled "Yearly report of the teacher Benito Mussolini to the Mayor of Gualtieri."

After noticing that out of thirty-five pupils there was an average attendance of thirty-three daily throughout the year, Mussolini's report states:

> But it may be a sign of the times. Education is daily more appreciated by the masses and has become a social necessity.
>
> I have always exacted and obtained discipline by very simple means—by stimulating emulation and interest in the work on hand, and by unobtrusively studying each boy's character and special inclinations.
>
> Discipline obtained by methods of coercion is no real discipline. It checks boyish individuality in the bud and gives rise to latent sentiments of revolt. Until school and home go hand in hand in the work of education, true discipline is destined to remain a pious and utterly Utopian wish. How can you expect a boy to bring a clean copy-book to school when he has probably been doing his lessons in a cow-shed?
>
> Practice has taught me to throw many ideals to the winds, and that is why I get along very well with my boys. It is a mistake to judge the teacher by the number of his pupils who get through their examinations successfully. On these occasions both teacher and pupils mainly trust to luck.

SECONDARY EDUCATION IN WALES

THE report of the board of education on the Welsh county intermediate schools, which has recently been published, shows that the demand for secondary education is steadily increasing in Wales. According to the London *Times Educational Supplement,* last year there were 24,874 pupils in these intermediate schools, an increase of 1,117 over the previous year. Thus the break which occurred during the black years of 1922–24 has now been repaired, and the number of pupils coming into the secondary schools is once more on the increase. This applies also to the other grant-earning secondary schools in Wales. The total number of pupils in secondary schools in 1927 was 35,591, or 13.1 per thousand of the population, the corresponding figures for England being 342,304, or 9.2 per thousand of the population. As in the past, so this year, Merionethshire, with its seven county intermediate schools serving a population of only 43,980 (with the sole exception of Radnorshire, the smallest county population in Wales), has 27.7 secondary pupils per thousand of its population.

This rapid growth of Welsh secondary education is probably the most remarkable feature of its educational history. For in 1895 there were only 47 county intermediate schools with some 3,367 pupils. In 1902 these had increased to 95 with 8,789 pupils and to-day they stand at 142 grant-earning secondary schools with 35,591 pupils. Satisfactory as these figures are, however, there is still much work to be done. In 1926–27, nearly one half—41.4 per cent.—of those who left the schools were under the age of 16 years. Economic conditions, which have made life in the South Wales coalfield a grim struggle for bare existence, have probably forced parents to take their children away thus early from school. In the case of the girls also, 43.2 per cent. of the leavers leave between the ages of 16 and 18 years, and of the boys 41.7 per cent. Thus there was even last year a large proportion of pupils who had stayed beyond the age of 16 years. On the other hand, 34.9 per cent. of the boys and 32.6 per cent. of the girls left between the ages of 14–16 years. This premature withdrawal prevents the proper organization of the school as a whole, for often it involves overcrowding in the lower forms and the withdrawal of teaching power from the top forms.

On the other hand, the schools do not always meet the needs of the pupils. Both in the rural and in the industrial areas many children leave school because they can not face the examinations or because the schools are not able to offer them the instruction they need. Experience has shown, the "Report on Education in England and Wales" states, that a wideawake headmaster, by providing facilities for the pursuit of other interests, has been able not only to retain such boys, but to stimulate them to appreciate the value of the extended course. Such a master has been found, for the report on the county intermediate schools gives particulars of a school in which the headmaster has developed a sixth form with classical, science, modern and commercial sides. The success of the commercial side, in the words of the report, "has been remarkable." The school has also, apparently, not lost sight of the need for corporate school work and the development of the arts and crafts. It is an important experiment, and one which deserves the publicity which it has received. The publicity, indeed, is the happiest feature of the report, for it points to the need for some central clearing house, or, if that fails, a well-organized conference, where experiments such as these might be recorded and discussed. Both Scotland and England have their educational conferences, but Wales, with its own special problems, its many-sided educational institutions, and its self-contained educational system, has as yet no central meeting-ground where the educational experience of the county may be pooled and shared.

Some information of the teaching of the classics is also given in the report. During 1926–27 17,335 pupils took Latin up to the first examination form and 224 pupils took Greek. In addition, 567 pupils took Latin and 103 took Greek beyond the stage of the first examination.

Last, but not the least important, are the notes on the provision of libraries in the schools. In the majority of the schools there is serious lack of proper library accommodation. Only eight of the 101 schools have rooms which are used solely for library work. That and the lack of adequate financial assistance appear to be the two main obstacles to the development of one of the most essential duties of the schools. Many sacrifice much to gain equipment, but money is lacking. In certain cases the local libraries have been brought in to help. One school has obtained the use of a special room at the local Carnegie library which is set aside for the use of the pupils preparing for the higher certificate.

AN EDUCATIONAL TOUR IN GERMANY

THE International Institute of Teachers College, Columbia University, and the Central Institute for Education and Instruction of Berlin have announced a tour of Germany's educational institutions for the summer of 1929. This tour has been organized by the Central Institute, which operates under the auspices of the Prussian Ministry of Education and the German Federal Ministry of the Interior.

The selection of members of the party will be in the hands of the International Institute of Teachers College, Columbia University. The tour will afford an unusual opportunity to see German schools, since it is under the official direction of the German educational authorities. It is the first time such an opportunity has been afforded American teachers as a group.

The visits to the schools will begin on June 17, 1929, either at Hamburg or Bremen, and will continue for six weeks, disbanding just before the World Federation of Educational Associations Conference in Geneva, which meets during the last week in July.

The tour will include visits to the most prominent German cities, among which will be Bremen, Hamburg, Lübeck, Kiel, Berlin, Magdeburg, Leipzig, Dresden, Chemnitz, Gera, Jena, Weimar, Nürnberg, Munich, Stuttgart, Heidelberg, Frankfort, Weisbaden, Coblenz, Mainz, Bonn, Cologne, Düsseldorf and Essen.

All types of German educational institutions will be seen, including elementary schools, secondary schools, rural schools, vocational schools, community and country boarding schools, teachers' colleges, universities and folk universities, and all types of education will be observed, such as physical education, art education, dramatics, the youth movement, school organization, methods of instruction, outdoor life, playgrounds and juvenile welfare.

The Central Institute will have complete charge of the party while in Germany, although the group will be accompanied by a member of the International Institute. The total expense for each member for the time spent in Germany (approximately six weeks) will be $350. This will include second-class railway travel, food, hotels and necessary transportation to schools and hotels within the cities.

There will be twenty-five in the party and membership will be limited to those who have some command of the German language. Those interested in the tour may secure fuller information from Dr. Thomas Alexander, Teachers College, Columbia University, New York City.

EDUCATION FOR BUSINESS

J. O. Malott, specialist in commercial education for the U. S. Bureau of Education, has issued a report on the increase in enrolment in commercial curricula in high schools and colleges. The full text of his statement as printed in the *United States Daily* follows:

There is a growing consciousness of the importance of definite preparation for business occupations. People are realizing more than ever that better preparation for these occupations usually results in greater vocational efficiency and contributes to vocational and social happiness. Business men have recently taken a greater interest in commercial education because they appreciate the relation of vocational efficiency to the efficiency of the business community. Educators have given increased attention to this phase of education in order to develop a balanced program that will meet the best interests of the individual, the business community and society.

An outstanding development in commercial education has been the increase in the number of men and women preparing to enter business occupations. Statistics were compiled during the biennium which reveal the recent trends pertaining to enrolments and the number of schools of different types offering commercial curricula.

The highest percentage of increase in enrolments in the commercial curricula from 1915 to 1924 is in the colleges and universities. During this period these enrolments increased from 9,323 to 47,552, an increase of 410 per cent. The number of schools offering these curricula increased from 58 to 129, an increase of 124 per cent. Since 1918 the number of men in these curricula increased from 14,029 to 40,734, an increase of 190 per cent., and the number of women increased from 2,982 to 6,818, an increase of 128 per cent. Eighty-three per cent. of the students enrolled in commercial curricula in 1918 and 85 per cent. of those in 1924 were men.

The greatest increase in the number of pupils enrolled in commercial curricula in the different schools from 1914 to 1924 is in the public schools. The number of these pupils increased from 161,250 in 1914 to 430,975 in 1924, which is an increase of 167 per cent. During this period the number of men in these curricula increased 109 per cent. and the number of women increased 210 per cent. The number of high schools offering commercial curricula increased from 2,191 to 3,742, an increase of 70 per cent. In 1914, 58 per cent. of the pupils enrolled in the commercial curricula in the high schools were women. By 1924 the percentage had increased to 67. Of the 685,100 pupils and students preparing for business occupations in 1924, almost two thirds were enrolled in the public high schools.

The enrolment in commercial curricula of the private high schools and academies, as well as the number of these schools offering commercial curricula, increased only 4 per cent. from 1914 to 1924. There was an increase of 54 per cent. in the number of women enrolled and a decrease of 36 per cent. in the number of men enrolled.

During the 10-year period the private business and commercial schools had a net increase of 12 per cent. in enrolments and 5 per cent. in the number of schools reporting. These schools, along with other types of schools, increased their enrolments in commercial curricula immediately before and during the world war. Due to the large number of ex-service men rehabilitated in these schools, the enrolments continued to increase until 1920. Since that date the trend of enrolments has returned to a pre-war basis.

During the school year 1919–20, a total of 336,032 pupils were enrolled in the day and evening classes of 902 schools. By 1924 the number of enrolments had decreased to 188,363, a decrease of 44 per cent.; the number of schools reporting had decreased to 739, a decrease of 38 per cent.; and there was a reduction of 40 per cent. in the number of day-school pupils and a reduction of 51 per cent. in the number of night-school pupils. In 1914, 50 per cent. of the pupils enrolled were men. By 1924 the percentage had decreased to 36.

In the schools of less than college rank, the number of women has increased more than the number of men. There are many reasons for this general trend. There is less prejudice against women in business. The evolution of much of the work in offices and stores makes possible the employment of more women. The commercial courses in the secondary schools are generally more appropriate for women than for men. Changes in the commercial curricula of the secondary schools have not been made as rapidly as changes in the requirements for office and store occupations, particularly for those occupations in which boys find initial employment.

The number of men in colleges and universities preparing for business occupations has increased more than the number of women. This is due chiefly to the fact that a greater number of men than women seek careers in business and therefore find it necessary to obtain a more thorough preparation. The colleges and universities have made remarkable progress in meeting the needs of education for business. They are offering a definite vocational education, not only for a larger number of business occupations but for the lower and intermediate as well as the upper levels of these occupations.

SALARIES OF ELEMENTARY SCHOOL TEACHERS

SALARIES paid to elementary teachers in cities of 100,000 population and over range from a minimum of $950 per year to a maximum of $3,504 per year, according to figures recently made public by the U. S. Bureau of Education. The low minimum is given for Salt Lake City, Utah, which also has the highest number of annual increases required to reach the maximum, or 17 annual increases. The highest maximum salary is given for New York City.

The figures made public by the Bureau, showing, first, the maximum salary; second, the minimum salary, and third, the number of annual increases required to reach the maximum, follow:

Alabama: Birmingham, $1,000, $2,000, 10.

California: Los Angeles, $1,400, $2,440, 13; Oakland, $1,380, $2,460, 9; San Francisco, $1,400, $2,400, 11.

Colorado: Denver, $1,200, $2,520, not specified.

Connecticut: Bridgeport, $1,000, $3,100, not specified; Hartford, $1,000, $2,000, not specified; New Haven, $1,000, $1,850, 9.

Delaware: Wilmington, $1,000, $1,800, 9.

District of Columbia: $1,400, $2,600, not specified.

Illinois: Chicago, $1,500, $2,500, 8.

Indiana: Indianapolis, $1,300, $2,800, 12.

Iowa: Des Moines, $1,200, $2,210, not specified.

Kansas: Kansas City, $1,200, $1,788, not specified.

Louisiana: New Orleans, $1,200, $2,250, 8.

Maryland: Baltimore, $1,200, $1,800, 6.

Massachusetts: Cambridge, $1,228, $1,804, 6; Fall River, $1,100, $1,700, 6; Lowell, $1,200, $1,700, 6; New Bedford, $1,000, $1,900, 10; Springfield, $1,300, $1,900, 6; Worcester, $1,200, $2,000, 8.

Michigan: Detroit, $1,200, $2,000, 5; Grand Rapids, $1,200, $2,000, not specified.

Minnesota: Minneapolis, $1,200, $2,500, not specified; St. Paul, $1,100, $1,700, 10.

Missouri: St. Louis, $1,200, $2,700, not specified.

New Jersey: Jersey City, $1,400, $2,800, 14; Paterson, $1,200, $2,800, 12.

New York: Albany, $1,100, $1,900, not specified; Buffalo, $1,200, $2,500, not specified; New York, $1,608, $3,504, 13; Rochester, $1,200, $2,400, 8; Syracuse, $1,200, $2,400, not specified; Yonkers, $1,500, $2,835, 12.

Ohio: Akron, $1,000, $2,000, 10; Cincinnati, not specified, $2,000, not specified; Cleveland, $1,200, $2,800, not specified; Toledo, $1,250, $2,240, 9.

Oregon: Portland, $1,300, $2,200, 11.

Pennsylvania: Philadelphia, $1,200, $2,400, not specified; Pittsburgh, $1,200, $2,000, 8; Scranton, $1,000, $1,800, 8.

Rhode Island: Providence, $1,000, $2,000, not specified.

Tennessee: Nashville, $1,200, $1,380, 3.

Texas: Houston, $1,000, $1,800, 8.

Utah: Salt Lake City, $950, $2,200, 17.

Virginia: Norfolk, $1,000, $1,500, 7; Richmond, $1,100, $1,800, 9.

Washington: Seattle, $1,440, $2,100, 11; Spokane, $1,200, $2,150, not specified.

Wisconsin: Milwaukee, $1,200, $2,600, 12.

THE ALLEGANY SCHOOL OF NATURAL HISTORY

In a statement issued recently, Frank P. Graves, New York state commissioner of education, calls to the attention of school teachers the opportunities for professional advancement offered by the Allegany School of Natural History.

Teachers of the branches of natural history sciences, biology, nature study, geography and physical geography will find at the school, the commissioner points out, an opportunity to study life out of doors under the supervision of unusual instructors. There is a growing appreciation of the fact that the training of students and teachers of science is not complete without a study of the living organisms in their natural environment. It is to meet this need that the Allegany School was established.

The school is conducted by the Buffalo Society of Natural Sciences, in cooperation with the commissioners of the Allegany State Park and with the educational supervision of the New York State Museum. College credit is given through affiliation with the University of Buffalo.

It is located in Allegany State Park, on the southwestern border of New York State, about forty miles east of Lake Erie. Within an area of about 65,000 acres under care of the state much of the wild life is protected so that one may occasionally observe in a wild state bear, deer, raccoon and porcupine besides observing daily many smaller mammals, such as squirrels, chipmunks, field mice and others.

The school is provided with forty cabins, including a main school building with assembly room, library, laboratories and dining room, outdoor museum and classroom and cabins for the students and staff. Each cabin for the students has two sleeping rooms and a work room.

The instruction is conducted out of doors as much as practicable and the schedule of classes is arranged to make as close a correlation as possible between indoor and outdoor work.

The school will close on August 25. The director is Dr. R. E. Coker, and the dean of women is Mrs. R. E. Coker. The geology and physiography of the region is taught by Professor A. C. Tester; the natural history of birds by A. A. Saunders; the natural history of plants by Dr. F. W. Emerson, and the nature study by W. P. Alexander.

The registration office, from which further information may be secured, is at the New York State Museum, Albany, N. Y. The cost of tuition, board and lodging is $150 for the season.

THE SUMMER COURSE FOR WORKERS AT THE UNIVERSITY OF WISCONSIN

Leaving glove-sewing, dressmaking, stitching, hand folding, and other individual employment behind them for six weeks, forty-four women and two men from six states have enrolled in the fourth annual summer course for workers in industry at the University of Wisconsin.

According to the New York *Times*, the school, which was begun as an experiment four years ago, has proved itself sound in principle and feasible in practice. The course is planned to give capable workers an insight into the world of education and its relation to industry. Such studies as economics, English, physical education and public speaking are taught by a special university staff.

Many of the students have not completed their grammar-school education. Others had a year or two in high school and several are immigrants, according to records of Professor Don D. Lescohier. Last year for the first time men were also included in the enrolment. The workers represent a variety of national backgrounds. Many are of foreign parentage, others are immigrants from Russia and Germany. The two men enrolled this year are affiliated with labor unions.

The idea already is considered a success, but the present work is regarded as a nucleus for further development in which community organizations throughout the middle west will cooperate. Such cities as Duluth and Milwaukee have already established links between civic organizations whereby funds can be raised.

The organization in Duluth is known as the Wisconsin Scholarship Association, designed to raise funds for the purpose of sending industrial girls to the University of Wisconsin summer session. Various clubs in the city support the association.

AN INTERCOLLEGIATE PERSONNEL SEMINAR

THE first intercollegiate group to assemble in the southeastern states for the consideration of educational personnel problems met at the Blue Ridge Assembly grounds at Blue Ridge, North Carolina, from June 15 to 25. The twenty-one members of the group came in answer to an invitation extended by a committee of which President H. W. Chase, of the University of North Carolina, was chairman.

The ten-day period was spent in a seminar for the discussion of college personnel and guidance problems and in actual counseling projects. In these projects each member of the group spent an average of seventy-seven hours each with four counselors who had requested such assistance. The counselors were drawn from the students of the southeastern region in attendance at the annual Young Men's Christian Association conference.

Owen E. Pence, research secretary of the committee on personnel of the national council of the Young Men's Christian Association, conducted the seminars and acted as consultant to the group concerning counseling problems. At the conclusion of the ten-day period, the faculty members in attendance voted unanimously to repeat the experiment in June, 1929.

President Chase was asked to continue as chairman of the committee and Dean Francis F. Bradshaw, of the University of North Carolina, was requested to be consultant to the group.

The general plan of a faculty seminar in conjunction with a counseling project at an association assembly was first tried in 1925 at the Geneva Conference grounds at Lake Geneva, Wisconsin.

EDUCATIONAL NOTES AND NEWS

DR. CHARLES L. O'DONNELL, since 1910 professor of English literature at the University of Notre Dame, has been chosen president of the university, to succeed the Reverend Mathew J. Walsh.

CHARLES LEWIS BEACH, since 1908 president of the Connecticut Agricultural College, Storrs, Conn., has resigned and has been made president emeritus of the college. Dr. Charles B. Gentry, dean of the division of teacher training and head of the department of education, has been named acting president.

DR. R. C. WALLACE, professor of geology and mineralogy at the University of Manitoba, has been appointed president of the University of Alberta, to succeed Dr. H. M. Tory. Dr. Wallace expects to take up his new work by September 1.

PROFESSOR HERBERT WOODROW, head of the department of psychology at the University of Oklahoma, has been appointed professor and head of the department of psychology at the University of Illinois. He succeeds Professor Madison Bentley, whose appointment as successor to the late Edward Bradford Titchener at Cornell University was announced early this year.

HENRY E. STARR, assistant professor of psychology at the University of Pennsylvania, has been appointed professor of psychology at Rutgers University.

HARRY HELSON, of the University of Kansas, has been appointed associate professor in experimental psychology and director of the laboratory of psychology at Bryn Mawr College.

DR. MANDEL SHERMAN, director of the Washington Child Research Center, has been appointed professorial lecturer on child development at George Washington University for the next academic year.

FORREST E. LONG has been appointed associate professor of secondary education at New York University.

F. H. HODDER, professor of American history at the University of Kansas, will be acting professor of American history at Cornell University during the year 1928–29.

CECIL KNIGHT JONES, staff bibliographer for the *Hispanic American Historical Review,* has been appointed assistant professor of Spanish-American literature at George Washington University, Washington, D. C.

SIR GREGORY FOSTER, provost of University College, London, has been elected vice-chancellor for 1928–29 in succession to Sir William Beveridge.

DR. L. L. JACKSON, assistant commissioner of the New Jersey state department of education, has been chosen assistant superintendent of the Newark, N. J., public schools. Dr. W. Spader, principal of the Newark Normal School, has resigned, after being connected with the public school system for forty-three years. He has been a normal school principal for thirty years.

DR. WILLIAM T. BAWDEN has resigned from his position as associate superintendent of public schools in Tulsa, Oklahoma, to become managing editor of the *Industrial Education Magazine* and vice-president of The Manual Arts Press, Peoria, Ill.

J. C. ANTHONY, of Danvers, Mass., has been elected superintendent of schools at Dedham. James Reardan has been elected superintendent of schools at East Bridgewater, Mass.

REGINALD STEVENS KIMBALL, for the last three years director of the educational department of the American Education Press, has resigned. Mr. Kimball was formerly head of the department of history and social science in the State Normal School at Worcester, Mass.

SARAH STETSON WARREN, for forty-six years a teacher in Public School 18, the Bronx, New York City, will retire on September 1.

DR. W. H. D. ROUSE, for nearly twenty-seven years head master of the Perse School, Cambridge, England, is retiring. On July 21 a complimentary dinner was given to him.

JAMES M. O'GORMAN, director of the department of education in Marquette University, Milwaukee, Wis., has been awarded the honorary Sc.D. by DePaul University, Chicago.

MARY ELLEN CHASE, professor of English at Smith College, has received an honorary degree of doctor of letters from the University of Maine.

FREDERICK KLAEBER, professor of English at the University of Minnesota, received the honorary degree of doctor of laws from the University of Wisconsin, at the commencement exercises last month.

AN endowment for purchase of books for the Widener Library at Harvard University has been created by the contributions of friends of Professor C. N. Greenough, professor of English at Harvard. The fund, to be known as the "Chester Noyes Greenough Fund," was established by more than eighty individual gifts, and is to commemorate Professor Greenough's services as dean of Harvard College from 1921 to 1927.

DR. LYNN THORNDIKE, professor of history at Columbia University, has been elected president of the History of Science Society by the council, to fill the unexpired term of Dr. Edgar Fahs Smith, who died on May 3.

DR. EDWARD PROKOSCH, professor of Germanic philology of New York University, has been appointed curator of the Ottendorfer Library of the university.

PROFESSOR C. D. ZDANOWICZ, chairman of the Romance language department at the University of Wisconsin, has been granted a leave of absence during the next academic year.

PROFESSOR HARRY FRANKLIN COVINGTON, for many years in charge of oratory and debating at Princeton University, died on July 16, at the age of fifty-eight years.

WILLIAM HAMILTON FOSTER, since 1911 vice-rector of St. Paul's School, Concord, N. H., died on July 19, at the age of sixty-seven years. He had been master of the school from 1884 to 1911.

DR. SUSAN SMITH SHERIDAN, for fifty-eight years a member of the teaching staff of the New Haven, Conn., public schools and the oldest teacher in point of service, died on July 18 at the age of seventy-five years.

MISS ADELINA A. BALLOU, for twenty-eight years a teacher in the Melrose High School, Melrose, Mass., died on July 19, at the age of eighty-four years. She had taught in other cities for some years before going to Melrose in 1887. She retired in 1915.

H. W. CARLESS DAVIS, regius professor of modern history at the University of Oxford, died of pneumonia on June 28. He was fifty-four years old.

THE Institute for Administrative Officers of Institutions of Higher Learning was held at the University of Chicago, from July 16 to 20. Trevor Arnett, president of the General Education Board, New York City; President Frank

L. McVey, of the University of Kentucky; Professor L. B. Richardson, of Dartmouth College; Professor F. W. Reeves, of the University of Kentucky; Professor E. M. Freeman, of the University of Minnesota; Charles H. Judd, director of the school of education of the University of Chicago, and Dean W. S. Gray, of the same school, were among the speakers. "Should Students Pay a Larger Part of the Cost of Education?" was Mr. Arnett's topic. Other subjects discussed were: "Responsibility of the Administration for the Moral and Religious Development of Students," "Is There a Place in American Higher Education for a Four-Year Liberal Arts College?" "Current Efforts to Improve Instruction in Higher Institutions," and "Cooperation with Organized Student Activities." A conference on religious and personnel work in colleges formed a part of the program of the institute.

THE German Institute for Foreigners at the University of Berlin has opened its summer session. There are three hundred students from thirty-five nations, the United States having a large contingent. The American professors who will teach at the institute include Karl F. Schreiber, of Yale University, M. Delmanzo, of Columbia University, and A. Busse, of Hunter College.

THE University City in Paris has been given $2,000,000 by John D. Rockefeller, Jr., for the construction and development of a central building, according to a letter just published from Raymond B. Fosdick to Senator André d'Honnorat, president of the institution. Mr. Rockefeller promises, furthermore, that during the three years following the completion of the building and while its endowment is being organized he will give three annuities of $60,000, $55,000 and $50,000. This gift will permit, almost at once, the realization of the French scheme for grouping in University City students of all nations and providing them with a common meeting place.

THE University of Chicago is to receive between $300,000 and $400,000 by the will of Adolph J. Lichstern, of Chicago.

BY the will of Captain Thomas P. Salter, of Portsmouth, N. H., who died in 1907, Dartmouth College has received $220,000. Ten thousand dollars is to be set aside for the use of two deserving students of Portsmouth, and the remainder is to be used at the discretion of the governing boards of the college. They have voted to apply the bequest to the payment of the balance of the cost of the chemistry building.

GIFTS to the University of Tennessee totaling more than $700,000 have been announced by Dr. H. A. Morgan, president of the university. The construction of a new science building to cost $200,000 has been started.

THE New York Public Library is entitled to approximately $507,000 from the $1,300,000 estate of the late John R. Slattery under a decision handed down recently by Surrogate Foley. The decision overrules the objections of nine cousins of Mr. Slattery, who asserted his will was invalid because it gave more than half of the estate to charity.

REGIONAL scholarships for students from three groups of states have been established at Yale University. The districts, in each of which one scholarship will be available for the college year of 1928–29, are the south Atlantic, south central, and far western states. The scholarships will be $750 for the freshman year and $500 for the succeeding years, to be awarded by the committee on undergraduate scholarships at Yale upon the recommendations of alumni and school authorities in the districts. The committee will select the scholarship holders on the basis of manhood, force of character and moral leadership, literary and scholastic ability, and physical soundness and vigor as demonstrated by interests in sports.

THE American Foundation for the Blind has announced the award of fifteen scholarships to blind students for the school year of 1928–1929. These awards are made annually to young persons who have shown exceptional talent and high scholastic standing. Columbia University, Syracuse University, Johns Hopkins University, Oberlin and the University of South Carolina are among the colleges which the blind students will attend.

THREE scholarships, valued at $10,000 each, have been announced at the annual meeting of the corporation of the Worcester Polytechnic

Institute. William Walter Brown, manufacturer; Charles A. Harrington and his brother, Frank C. Harrington, and Henry J. Fuller, of New York, are the donors.

WHILE plans for the distribution of the funds reserved by the Board of Education of New York City for supermaximum salary increments are still indefinite, assurances have been given by school officials that the money will not be diverted to other purposes. It will be distributed as equitably as possible among the teachers of the city.

ATHLETES at Cornell University, according to a study of the records of the class entering in 1921, which was made public recently, maintained a higher standing as students than non-athletes. A report of the study was made by David F. Hoy, registrar, to the Carnegie Foundation. It followed the college careers of the members of the class to the end. Defining "athlete" as any male undergraduate obtaining the coveted "C," or as one having been simply a member of a university or freshman team or crew even if he did not win the varsity insignia, Mr. Hoy came to the following conclusions: The athletes had a higher intelligence average; a greater proportion obtained degrees; fewer were placed on probation; they remained in college longer, carried fewer hours a semester; received a higher scholastic average; took a greater percentage of "hard" courses, receiving a higher average; took a greater percentage of "easy" courses and received a lower average, and tennis players and wrestlers stood near the top in intelligence scores and scholarship average and football players near the bottom.

COLLEGE men participating in intercollegiate athletics at Rutgers University are as good students as the non-athletes, according to the results of a survey announced at Rutgers recently. At the suggestion of the Carnegie Foundation for the advancement of teaching, an exhaustive study was undertaken several months ago at the local university, tracing the progress in college of 256 members of the class of 1926. It was found that the athletes in the class had a higher intelligence rating, that a larger percentage of athletes obtained degrees, that both groups carried approximately the same number of hours, and that the athletes had a higher total average grade for the four years. It was found also that members of the track and tennis teams stood high in scholarship, that football men were comparatively low, and that two-or-more sport men were lower than one-sport men. The conclusion drawn by George W. Fraser, who conducted the survey, is that "athletics have not harmed the academic work of the athletes."

THE Ministry of Public Instruction of Bulgaria has arranged for the school children to open accounts at the post offices. The savings department will give a little bank, without a key, to each child who wants it, and when it is full the owner may take it to the savings bank, where it will be opened; the money will be deposited in the child's name and he will receive a special bank book of his own. In inaugurating this new undertaking the Minister of Education appealed to all the teachers to encourage the pupils to begin saving.

THE Palestine government has published a draft education ordinance, the chief purpose of which is to increase its control over all types of local schools. If the ordinance is adopted, the government department of education will possess absolute rights of entry, inspection, approval and suppression of private schools of all communities. Only such schools will be allowed to continue as are inspected, approved and registered by the director of education. It will be the director's duty to scrutinize the qualifications of every teacher before registration. Further, the ordinance empowers every municipal council and certain local councils to act as the local education authority, with power to impose a local education rate.

A PROGRAM of tuition paving the way for pupils from the humblest homes to reach the highest stage of education, fewer school subjects, and concentration at an early stage on certain lines of study are among the principal features of the new and radical school reform in Sweden sanctioned by the Swedish Riksdag. The new system includes three separate stages of school education—six years (compulsory) at an elementary school, common to all classes of people; four years (optional) at a secondary school; and, finally, three years (optional) at a "gymnasium," followed by the matriculation examination admitting the student to the university. In the "gymnasium" the student is enabled to specialize at an earlier stage than hitherto, preparing himself more thoroughly for his university career and shortening the period spent at college, while the reduced number of subjects relieves the strain and overwork previously complained of, especially in the higher classes of the Swedish schools. The new plan, when fully carried into effect, will also encourage independent research work in special subjects and team work in special lines by groups of pupils.

The U. S. Bureau of Education has announced that by recent order of the Czechoslovak ministry of education, maternity leave of absence for three months may be granted to married teachers. Further leave may be allowed, but without pay, and the time of such leave will not be credited toward promotion to a higher grade nor toward service requirement for pension.

SPECIAL CORRESPONDENCE

THE "BACHELOR OF ARTS WITH DISTINCTION" AT THE UNIVERSITY OF NEBRASKA

During the acedemic year of 1925–26 the faculty of the college of arts and sciences of the University of Nebraska met informally at dinner once a month to discuss the liberal arts college, with special reference to its curriculum. Many meetings were held the following year over the report of a committee appointed to formulate the general principles upon which agreement had been reached. After much exchange of opinion—though there is little reason to mention to a circle of educators that concomitant of every faculty meeting—the outline of the new course of studies was adopted at an official meeting of the faculty at the end of the year, with but one dissenting vote, and that over a matter of wording and not against the principle of the plan. Since some features of the course appear new, a brief presentation of it may be of interest to educators.

These antecedents of the new course are of importance in any evaluation of it. It received the fullest possible discussion, from every point of view represented on a university faculty. The unanimity of approval was indeed noteworthy. Nor was it imposed from above. It arose out of a criticism, by the faculty, of the present status of the arts college in a state university of the middle west, where any restrictions upon entrance would appear undemocratic in a tax-supported institution, and would also tend to turn students in increasing numbers away from the liberal arts college into professional schools. A summary of some of the more searching of such criticisms will help clarify certain features of the new course.

Is it not possible to persuade students to study in the secondary schools subjects which belong to that stage of education and furnish the proper background for the college curriculum? This seemed possible if the college would outline a body of knowledge which it would require of every recipient of the bachelor's degree and recognize that a certain amount of this body of knowledge could be acquired in secondary schools. This would be a step towards correlating the work of the secondary schools with that of the university. Such a correlation seemed entirely feasible in the case of languages. It was agreed that the holder of the bachelor's degree should know his mother tongue and be somewhat acquainted with its literature, and have had at least two years' college work in two foreign languages. With this as a background he would take two years of advanced work in one of these languages. This background in language study could be secured in secondary schools, by four years' study of English (possibly three years for the gifted student) and by three years, study in each of two foreign languages. When a college entrance examination had shown that such work had been satisfactorily carried, the time spent in residence for the bachelor's degree might be correspondingly reduced. This course of study, it was hoped, might lead students who expect to enter the university to concentrate in their preparation upon language and literature and omit courses in science, which could be first studied with greater profit in the university.

Is it not possible to go a little farther in preventing students from "scattering" so widely in their college work? While recognizing the enormous increase in the field of human knowledge, the new course also recognizes that a student can become intimately acquainted with but a few fields of study and would emphasize this "intimate acquaintance." Hence in the required work the plan specifies at least two consecutive courses in any department and four consecutive courses in at least three departments. Thus the student in his required work would have had what might be called "preparatory majors," consisting of six courses in his mother tongue or eight in one foreign language, and of four courses in one of the basic sciences, and in history or one of the social sciences. The new course is not concerned with majors, although leaving them possible, but it would require of students a longer contact with what they do study; and the student who suddenly realizes near the end of his college work that he would like to take an advanced degree in some field with which he has just become acquainted would find to his relief that he had covered the necessary preparatory courses and had acquired some of the necessary knowledge of foreign language.

A further criticism was aimed against the departments which would allow departmental requirements to be met in any of a large number of courses. It is quite understandable that a department in a university, with the large demands made upon it by associated colleges to offer courses in various phases of its field, should be led into specialization. But it seemed that a department should have some courses especially shaped to offer the best acquaintance with the scope, significance and future development of its subject, such courses being designed not so much for the future specialist as for the general student. Hence each department is called upon by the plan to offer "designated" courses which shall meet these ends and be adapted to students who do not expect to continue their work in that department beyond that required for the bachelor's degree. The hope was expressed, that out of the congeries of courses now offered in the arts college of our university a small group might be formed which would approximate the ideal of a genuine "arts college curriculum."

The criticism, so common to all educational discussions, was voiced against granting the bachelor's degree for credit hours, or, in other words, basing it upon what is little more than a time requirement. All of the faculty, of course, agreed that students should not receive credit for a course until they had shown some mastery of the subject, more than is measured by a "pass"; and some felt that there was a fundamental difference between a numerical grade, which they would like to see abolished entirely, and a certificate of competence. And on every side protests were raised against the failure to grade courses to the level of the "gifted" student. It seemed advisable to leave the numerical grade for purposes of record in the case of students in this course who may transfer to other institutions or who may not meet the requirements. But these objections were met, in a measure, by requiring an average of 85 for all the work carried in the course. The setting of a higher standard for credit in the course, it was felt, would in practice open the classes only to the better students and raise their standards. But the principle of "competence" as a requirement for the bachelor's degree is explicitly set forth in examinations which the candidate must pass over the language study which he has carried in secondary schools, and it is implied in the average of 85 required for his work in college. This principle appeared to justify the designation of the course as one "with distinction."

One more remark, and the course can speak for itself as it was sent forth, in part, in pamphlet form to the high schools of the state.

Many on the faculty questioned whether the arts college in our state universities could meet the increasing competition of the professional schools. They felt that if it was to be saved, the salvage would come only through a frank shortening of its curriculum. The call is heard on every hand to "get down to the fundamentals" in education. Possibly the new course has helped define these "fundamentals;" its success is entirely dependent upon cooperation on the part of the secondary schools.

The college of arts and sciences of the University of Nebraska offers the degree of bachelor of arts with distinction, when the candidate shall have met the following requirements:

1. He shall present a certificate of competence in

English received from an examining committee of the department of English.

"Competence in English" is defined as ability to prepare an original manuscript in proper form, in composition grammatically correct and rhetorically appropriate, in subject-matter displaying a reasonable familiarity with the works of an assigned group of English authors.

2. He shall show to the satisfaction of the departments concerned competence to read "third year" foreign language in two languages offered in the university, one of which shall be French, German, Greek, or Latin, and the second, any foreign language offered in the university.
3. He shall meet defined universal requirements, such as freshman lecture, physical training, military drill, either under supervision or by authenticated excuse.

   Credit granted for work taken in the university leading to competence in the fields designated by 1 and 2 above, or for the meeting of the requirements set forth in 3 above shall not be counted toward the 100 hours specified in 4 below.
4. He shall complete the following work in course, with an average grade of 85.
   a. Twenty-two "designated" courses:
      Language and Literature, six (represented by the departments of Classics, English, Germanic Languages, Romance Languages), of which four shall be consecutive advanced courses in French, German, Greek, Latin, or English.
      Natural Science, six (represented by the departments of astronomy, bacteriology, botany, chemistry, geology and geography, physics, zoology), of which four shall be consecutive courses in one of the basic sciences (botany, zoology, chemistry, physics).
      History and Social Science, six, of which two shall be consecutive courses in history and four in one department of the social sciences (represented by the departments of economics, political science, sociology), or vice versa.
      Mathematics, two.
      Philosophy, two.
   b. A sufficient number of elective courses to make a total of 100 credit hours.

EXPLANATORY

"Designated" courses are defined as semester courses, selected by the respective departments and given only by instructors who are members of the faculty of the college of arts and sciences. Most of these will be three-hour courses; a few will be four- or five-hour courses. Since the courses may vary in this way, it is necessary to allow a flexibility in the requirements set forth in 4-b.

1 and 2 are concerned with tests of "competence" in the mother tongue and in two foreign languages. To meet the test of competence in English the student must have a preparation, which corresponds to that of the English courses, 1–2, or 3–4, now required of all students, and be reasonably familiar with the work of an assigned group of English authors.[1] To meet the tests of competence in foreign language his preparation should be that which corresponds to the first two years of such a language in the university. These tests, however, will expect a fairly thorough knowledge of the subject, more than is measured by a "pass." If a student has had in his preparatory school training in English and has acquainted himself with the group of authors, and if he has had at least three years in two foreign languages, he should be able to meet these tests of competence before beginning his university course. In that case he should be able to complete the work set forth in 3 and 4 in six or seven semesters. Should he have to take in the university a large part of the preparation for the competence tests, his residence in the university may be lengthened beyond the usual eight semesters. If a student is not able to meet at least two of these tests before the commencement of his third semester, it is not advisable for him to work toward this degree.

The nature of the course makes it necessary that all requirements for it shall be met in residence.

After completing the work in the twenty-two "designated" courses, the student will still have at least twenty-eight hours for elective work, which

[1] The group of authors comprises the following: Chaucer, Langland, Sir Thomas Malory, Spenser, Shakespeare, Milton, Dryden, Pope, Swift, Goldsmith, Burns, Jane Austen, Walter Scott, Wordsworth, Byron, Keats, Shelley, Browning, Tennyson, Matthew Arnold, Carlyle, Thackeray, Macaulay, Dickens, Meredith, Cooper, Poe, Emerson, Bryant, Hawthorne, Holmes, Mark Twain, Howells. The candidate will be expected (1) to know something of each author and his place in English literature, and (2) to show a fair acquaintance with the chief works of ten of these authors, of his own selection. If desired, the test over the field of authors may be taken after that in English.

will allow him to specialize in certain fields or meet the requirements for the state teacher's certificate.

C. H. Oldfather
University of Nebraska

DISCUSSION

INTERCOLLEGIATE ACADEMIC CONTESTS

Let us assume that we may apply to the development of a system of intercollegiate academic contests those principles of intercollegiate athletics which are wholesome and effective, and may avoid those features of intercollegiate athletics which are unwholesome. It should then be possible to carry into academic subjects the advantages of intercollegiate competition for the purpose of motivating the work of superior students in the regular academic subjects. In order to formulate a preliminary conception of such an organization, I desire to array a series of principles for consideration which might constitute a means of clarifying and defining our concept of such a contest.

1. The competition shall be among institutions or student teams as distinguished from isolated individuals.

2. The competition groups shall be organized somewhat on the same basis that our intercollegiate athletic units are now organized. In this part of the country, for example, we might have the Big Ten conference and similar conferences could be organized in different parts of the country and each could control a number of events.

3. The contest might be organized in one subject, for example, mathematics, and then other subjects, such as physics, chemistry, psychology and history, might be added from time to time as the general policy gradually crystalizes and interest develops.

4. The scope of events shall be limited to normal fields of achievement in the four-year course of a college of arts and sciences in such a way as not to encourage over-election of courses in the same subject, but rather to stress mastery of fundamentals, which may be tested in part in the ability "to meet new situations" on the basis of such mastery.

5. The specifications of each event shall be in harmony with the general rules of the conference and shall be made as stable as possible in order to give a well-known character to the contest and thereby encourage the early training of students for these events.

6. In scoring examinations, the total achievement for the team shall count so as to draw a large number of individuals into the sharing of victory.

7. Some cognizance should be taken of the number of students in the institution so as to put large and small institutions on a fair basis for competition. There are two ways of looking at this: one way would be to select a small team; the other way would be to draw a larger number into competition and count the total or average score. In the latter case, the size of the institution would have to be taken into account.

8. Medals, badges, prizes, or other insignia indicative of individual participation shall be awarded in addition to the general award, such as a cup, which would go to the institution.

9. There shall be joint student and faculty participation in the management of the conference.

10. The judges shall be chosen from nonparticipating groups.

11. Measures of achievement shall be built along lines of modern objective examinations, in part or whole, in order to secure impersonal scoring.

12. The contests may be held at the home institution, examiners being supplied under conference rules.

13. The conference shall be financed by institutional memberships or by some foundation or grant.

14. The annual contest shall be an occasion for gathering of teachers and students for one- or two-day programs of inspiration and motivation within the respective fields of knowledge. For example, the examinations would all be held one day, and some part of the following day would be set aside for these conferences and celebrations.

15. Place on teams, either preliminary or final, should be recognized as a part of the student's record of academic achievement.

Carl E. Seashore
State University of Iowa

THE TRUE-FALSE QUESTION AND THE STUDENT'S SENSE OF FAIRNESS

IT is an observation familiar to many persons using new-type questions that in the case of some true-false statements too much knowledge, understanding or thoughtfulness imposes a penalty. For example, the question, "Language is a good measure of intelligence" was answered negatively by one thoughtful student, because though he recognized the value of vocabulary tests, etc., he happened to think that foreigners were rather handicapped in such tests, and so had denied the universality of the statement.

Another source of unfairness to students comes from ambiguous statements. An example of such ambiguity is to be seen in the following true-false question which was used recently in an examination: "The size of the brain has something to do with intelligence." The preceding statement is true if species be compared with one another. It is false if it applies to human individuals within the limits of normality. It seems unfair to require the student to indicate his opinion of the truth or falsity of the preceding statement, and then to score his answer without giving him opportunity to define his viewpoint in the matter *if he himself recognizes the ambiguity of the statement.*

As an attempt to meet this difficulty, the following procedure was used in two examinations consisting in part of sixty-two and forty-six true-false statements respectively. The usual directions for such questions were changed to include the statement, "If you wish to qualify your answer do so on the other side of the paper." Before the examination began the instructor explained the meaning of this innovation to the class. The questions were prepared before the decision to use this procedure was made. The examination was conducted otherwise in the same manner as previous quizzes. The results will be considered under several headings:

First, how much work must the instructor do after the papers have been scored? For presumably, the qualifications made by the student would be an appeal to the instructor over the scoring key. In the longer test, 34 out of 79 qualified at least one question; in the other, 13 out of 44 did so. In the latter, six qualified one question, four two questions, one each qualified three, four and five questions. The time taken by the instructor to rescore these papers was about half an hour. In the first-mentioned test more than half merely qualified one question, the largest number of qualifications on a paper were six. The time taken in rescoring them was not estimated.

Second, what types of students make use of this device and to what extent do they use it? From the standpoint of intelligence (as measured by the Otis Self-Administering Test Advanced Examination, Form A) the students who made qualifications were superior, their median score was 54 as compared with 49 for the non-qualifiers, Q_3 59 as compared with 53, Q_1 47 as compared with 43. From the standpoint of success in the examination there is also a notable superiority of those who qualified over those who did not. The median score of the latter is 44, of the former 45; Q_3 of the qualifiers 61, of the non-qualifiers 57; Q_1 of the qualifiers 39, of the non-qualifiers 23. Of those who made a grade of D or lower in the examination, 17 did not qualify, 2 did; of those who made A, 5 qualified, 2 did not.

Whether students do or do not profit by qualifying answers is a third question to be raised. From our experience students profit little as a rule from qualifying. The main advantage to them is the feeling that they have a possible appeal, that the test is not iron-clad. That students do wish to have this privilege is made evident by the fact that during a later test on which these instructions were omitted, because of an oversight, they asked of their own initiative if they might qualify their answers. It is the opinion of the writers that this procedure is of most value in assuaging the student's feelings in taking true-false tests, in fact questionnaire returns indicated the fact that the overwhelming majority of students wish the privilege of qualifying. As one student wrote, she desired this privilege, "Because many times it is difficult to determine which way the balance of evidence coming to mind would sway the degree of truth. Also one word may so qualify the statement as to make it untrue when in general it is true, or the statement might be considered in several lights." Another wrote, "Sometimes the meaning of the question is not definite, and the student has an opportunity to show at least a part of what he understands. Also, it allows for a little self-expression and personal opinion."

Some who qualify straddle the question virtually answering both true and false to the statement. In such a case, of course, the item is counted as omitted. This type of qualification is especially true of weaker students. Of course, the amount that students would profit is dependent upon the ability of the instructor to make up the questions. In this case, the instructor had had considerable experience in the use of true-false questions. Giving students permission to qualify their answers is perhaps of most service to the instructor just beginning to use such questions as it offers a means of testing the adequacy of the questions themselves. For example, two questions in one of these tests were qualified by almost fifteen per cent. of the students; obviously the instructor should carefully consider them from the standpoint of revision before using them again; on the other hand, 18 questions were not qualified at all.

Lastly, a fact which the instructor faces in the use of the method of qualifications of true-false questions is the need to define how such qualifications are to be made. First, the length of the qualification must be limited to about two lines. It saves time and of necessity limits the amount written if qualifications are made beside or under the question on the page. The questions should be double-spaced to allow for this. If such limitations are not made, one is opening the barrier to a return to the essay answer. Second, and most important, the students should be warned against straddling the question by qualifying in such a way that both an affirmative and a negative answer are given. If they realize that they will merely get a zero for this (the question counted as omitted) they should be cured readily of this tendency. In qualifying, students should be instructed to state briefly why they think the statement as given is equivocal or indefinite, or why they accept the statement in general but wish to add something of which they have thought, which may repugn the universality of it.

Norman Fenton
Harvey C. Lehman
Ohio University

QUOTATIONS

THE SESSION AT WILLIAMSTOWN

It is in keeping with the spirit of the Institute of Politics at Williamstown that its program for the summer session, which opens on August 2, lays special stress on the problems of the Pacific and cognate subjects. Although the Far East has not been neglected previously, the comparative stability of European affairs, coupled with the critical unrest in the East, makes it appropriate that attention be given to the study of transpacific questions. Caribbean matters are to be considered in conjunction with Pacific—a new if tacit recognition of the part which the Panama Canal has played in the reorientation of American foreign policies.

It has, of course, been impossible for the Institute of Politics to continue to bring over as lecturers men of world fame like the late Lord Bryce. But it has steadily attracted specialists of knowledge and ability, who have made the sessions stimulating and informing for the many students of international affairs that gather in Williamstown each summer. Although less spectacular than the lectures open to all, the round-table conferences at which discussion is led by these experts have proved to be most helpful. There men and women acquainted with their subjects have been able to exchange ideas and discuss details, to the enlightenment of all present.

That the Institute of Politics fills a need is clear from the manner in which it has been copied in other sections of the country. Chicago and the Pacific Coast cities have established institutions for the discussion of international affairs. Apparently the American people, long indifferent to foreign affairs, are at last beginning to study them. The demand is for trustworthy information rather than for propaganda or theory. Scores of books on international affairs are turned out every year. In the maze of material it is difficult for the amateur to pick his way. Hence the special value of such courses as those given at the Institute of Politics.

It is fortunate in having as lecturers this season one of the leaders of the new movement in Turkey, Halide Edib Hanum, and two leading European economists, Mr. Graham Wallas and Dr. Hoetsch. They will lead discussions of problems other than those centering about the Pacific. It follows, therefore, that members of the institute and the visiting public will have the opportunity to hear lectures on a large variety of subjects. This is in keeping with the institute's tradition.—*The New York Times.*

EDUCATIONAL RESEARCH AND STATISTICS

EXTRA-CURRICULAR ACTIVITY AND SUCCESS

THE stress which the present day college student places upon extra-curricular activity, on athletics, college journalism, politics and other college affairs, is a most interesting phenomenon in higher education. Faculty efforts to curb this activity have not met with any marked success. Indeed popular opinion holds that the campus athletic hero, the editor of the college paper or the president of the senior class has a better chance of making a success in life than has the "greasy grind." A student with a real interest in his studies may find it advisable to conceal the real interest which he has in his scholastic work with the pose of a campus business man. Prospective employers are frequently more interested in the student's extra-curricular activities than in scholastic standing or interests.

This belief raises several questions. How much has the extra-curricular activity in college life (at Wesleyan University) increased in late years? Has this increase affected scholastic standards? To what extent is the amount, or particular variety of these activities in college, a criterion of success in later life? To what extent are college grades a criterion of success in later life? That we might obtain data which would shed light upon these questions the following compilations were made:

(1) A list was made of the Wesleyan University alumni whose names appear in the 1927 edition of "Who's Who in America."

(2) The files of "Olla Podrida," the annual undergraduate publication of Wesleyan University were consulted to gain information concerning the undergraduate extra-curricular activities of the men on our "Who's Who" list. The "Olla Podrida" gives a statement of the activities which each member of the senior class has participated in during his entire college career. Such records were available from 1870 to 1918. These activities were classified as athletic, journalistic, political, dramatic and scholastic. An arbitrary weighting was given each activity. This weighting was based on two factors, the amount of time which the activity might be expected to consume and the importance which student opinion attaches to the activity. A sample of the weightings is as follows:

Athletic.	
Varsity football	20
Varsity basketball	20
Varsity tennis	15
Class track	5, etc.
Journalistic.	
Editor of college paper	20
Member of ''Olla Podrida'' board	10, etc.
Political.	
Senior Society	2
Class president	3
College senate	3
Class prophet	1
Junior prom. committee	5
Pres. of Y. M. C. A.	5, etc.
Dramatic.	
Member of dramatic club	10
Member of glee club	10
College orchestra	5
Debating team	15
Class debate	2, etc.
Scholastic.	
Competitive prizes	3
Departmental prizes	2
Departmental societies	1, etc.

(3) For scholastic marks the college records were consulted and comparable grades were found for the members of the class from 1894 to 1918.

(4) As indices of the activity of students of years past the extra-curricular activity points of all members of the classes of 1900 and of 1910 were computed. We have used these records as comparison standards for the "Who's Who" group.

The data collected may be summarized in the following tables:

TABLE I

	Average No. of Extra-curricular Points 1885–1917						
	No. of men	Athletic	Journalistic	Political	Scholastic	Dramatic	Total
Class of 1900	51	9.7	4.4	6.4	1.3	2.8	24.6
Class of 1910	55	19.8	4.9	9.5	1.4	7.1	42.7
Who's Who Group	77	9.9	8.6	5.3	2.6	6.3	32.7
Teachers in Who's Who	68	9.0	7.3	3.7	2.9	2.8	25.8
Ministers in Who's Who	17	11.2	12.0	10.3	3.0	8.2	44.7
Journalists in Who's Who	12	2.5	20.0	5.8	1.5	4.3	34.1
Lawyers in Who's Who	8	25.1	12.1	9.1	1.4	11.5	59.2
Executives in Who's Who	33	8.1	9.9	5.4	2.5	5.5	30.4

TABLE II

	No. of men	Classes included	Average scholastic grades
Class of 1900	51	1900	2.368
Class of 1910	55	1910	2.443
Who's Who Group	77	1895–1917	2.002
Teachers in Who's Who	42	1895–1917	1.985
Ministers in Who's Who	12	1895–1913	2.163
Journalists in Who's Who	8	1895–1913	2.344
Lawyers in Who's Who	3	1895–1907	2.143
Executives in Who's Who	24	1893–1911	1.965

A study of these tables indicates the following points:

1. A comparison of the average amount of extra-curricular activity of the classes of 1900 and 1910 shows a very marked increase during this 10-year period, the average number of points for 1900 seniors being 24.6 as compared to 1910 with 42.7. The average grade for 1900 was 2.368, while in 1910 it was 2.443 on a scale where A + = 1.0, A = 1.5, A – = 1.9, B + = 2.0, B = 2.5, B – = 2.9, C + = 3.0 and C = 3.5, and C – = 3.9.

2. Those men comprising the "Who's Who" group had a higher average scholastic grade than the index classes (1900; 1910); 2.002 as compared to 2.368 and 2.443.

3. The "Who's Who" group has, as compared to the average of the two index groups:

Fewer athletic	points—9.90	compared with	14.70
More journalistic	" 8.57	" "	4.67
Fewer political	" 5.28	" "	7.91
More dramatic	" 6.26	" "	4.98
More scholastic	" 2.63	" "	1.37

When these figures were statistically treated to see if any significance may be attached to the differences, it was found that the difference in athletic points has 98 chances out of 100 of being significant, journalistic 89, political 76, dramatic 81 and scholastic 81. In order to have real significance the chances should be 100 out of 100. These differences then indicate that there is a *tendency* in favor of the campus journalist, dramatist and scholar toward the achievement of success and a *tendency* against the athlete and campus politician.

4. The total amount of extra-curricular activities engaging the college student is no criterion of the success which he may or may not gain in later life. Those men comprising the "Who's Who" group took part in slightly fewer activities (average 32.6 points) than did the average college man (average 33.3 points).

5. Dividing each of the two index classes (1900; 1910) and the "Who's Who" group into group "A," comprised of those men having the average or less than the average number of athletic points and group "B," those having more than the average number of athletic points we find that the following relationship to scholastic grades exists:

	Group A	Group B
1900	2.37	2.49
1910	2.43	2.52
Who's Who	2.00	1.99

This indicates that while athletes tend in an average group to be poorer students, it is not true in the "Who's Who" group; these latter are not affected one way or the other by participation in athletics.

6. When the "Who's Who" group (including all those from the classes between 1884 and 1918) is divided according to profession or occupation several interesting factors come to light.

(a) The 68 teachers (including college, public and private school instructors and administrative officers) closely approximate the average of the entire "Who's Who" group in extra-curricular points and in grades.

(b) The 17 ministers are somewhere near the average college group in all activities except in campus politics where they show a very strong tendency to concentrate their college interests.

(c) The 12 journalists (including editors and authors) are markedly deficient in athletic interest (or ability) and are outstanding in campus journalism. Their scholastic marks are the lowest of any "Who's Who" group, closely approximating those of the index classes, 1900 and 1910.

(d) The 8 lawyers (the group is too small for the figures to be really significant) either had marked interest or ability in athletics for their athletic point rating is by far the highest of any group considered. They are also high in most other forms of extra-curricular activity as is shown by an average total of 59.2 points compared to an average of 36.8 points for all groups in Table I.

(e) Those men in the "Who's Who" group who are holding executive positions, *e.g.*, presidents or deans of colleges, heads of business concerns, bishops of the church, were classified in one category of "Executives." This group of 33 men stand somewhere near the median for all forms of extra-curricular activity, but are the highest group which we have considered with respect to their scholastic marks while in college. The difference in marks between the executives and any other group except "Teachers," is probably statistically significant.

The everyday observation of a gradual but persistent growth in the amount of extra-curricular activities is shown quantitatively by this study. The reasons for this increase vary in their general scope and particular effectiveness so far as any individual is concerned. The most immediate cause is "social pressure." The pressure which the upper classmen bring to bear on the lower classmen is the exciting cause for the entrance of most students into one or another variety of extra-curricular activity. This pressure has to-day a marked social approval. Fraternities are usually judged on the basis of the number of varsity players, managers, members of the Glee Club, etc., included in their number. The publicity given in the daily press to college athletics and athletes is a factor leading to this social pressure in the fraternities.

A second contributing agency is the change in the major interests of the student personnel. Forty years ago the Liberal Arts College was preparatory for the professions. To-day for the most part it is becoming preparatory for business. The general educational policy of America for many years past has been away from the formal discipline of classical and mathematical training, toward a training of specific abilities. Educational authorities repeatedly point out the advantage of an educational system which is in effect a training school for specific factors, functions, trades or what not. Whether or not the faculties of liberal arts colleges agree with the wisdom of this program the students agree with it and make use of the extra-curricular activities for specific training for later life.

Another motive adding to the major importance of extra-curricular activities is that the student finds these activities more interesting than the scholastic curriculum which the college provides. A majority of the students who are planning on a professional career go to the pre-professional courses in the universities, leaving only a minority in the liberal arts college. Those students planning on going into business, or the students who have no more than the vaguest notion of what they want to do when leaving college, form the majority of the liberal arts student body. The latter group is not deeply interested in any college curriculum. A football game, the editorship of the college paper or some such activity; something "real," something "interesting," something which *seems* likely to add to their chance for that hazy goal called "success," these are the things which motivate their behavior.

It seems, then, that social pressure, educational

policy and changing student interest has given us an increased extra-curricular activity. The present-day student, his parents and his prospective employer are inclined to think it worth while. This study indicates that the past experience of Wesleyan University does not justify any great amount of faith in this present-day belief especially with the student intending to enter a profession.

There are several arguments which may be urged against the validity of our study, arguments which may negate certain findings. The first of these is the question concerning the validity of inclusion in "Who's Who" as a criterion of success or eminence. "Who's Who" is notably loaded with teachers, preachers and editors. Wesleyan University in years past had a student personnel that was directed toward these professions. This is shown by the fact that our group of 184 "Who's Who" men includes 85 teachers, 41 preachers, 14 editors, 12 lawyers and 10 business men. It seems that our study can say little or nothing concerning the desirability of extra-curricular activity for the student planning on business, but certainly the other side of the question is clear cut. We have evidence as to the desirability of extra-curricular activity for the pre-professional student.

Another fault which might be urged against this study is that, in the group of men who have achieved "Who's Who" athletic prowess may have been a question of ability more than interest. This is indicated by the lack of relationship between grades and athletic points. Because of the lack of statistical confirmation the results do not justify any clear cut statement concerning college athletics. Our evidence shows a *tendency* against the achievement of "Who's Who" by the college athlete but we repeat, it is only a tendency and a more detailed study might show the indications of this study to be entirely in error.

Perhaps the clearest fact demonstrated is that the executives have the highest college grades of any group studied, the equivalent of an average of "A –" for their four years in college. The student hoping for a career in life leading to an executive position might well consider the advisability of a stellar scholastic performance. The business man seeking executive ability should stress high scholastic standing among his requirements of a prospective employee.

That extra-curricular activity has specific training value is shown by the results from the journalist and teacher group. The training effects are indicative of value but the fact that social pressure forces many students into activities for which they have no interest or special flair causes one to be cautious in making any wholesale generalization.

That ministers were outstanding in campus politics is interesting but not as startling as it might be when one notes that we have classified such activities as President of the Y. M. C. A. and Chairman of the Honor System Committee along with class officers, speakers at commencement exercises and senior societies. It probably is to be interpreted in part as another example of the value of specific training.

We do not regard the fact that the lawyers were outstanding in athletic activity as meaning much more than a vague tendency, because of the small number of cases. With regard to the value of college athletics for specific training it seems that the team managership may be of value as business training. There is little evidence that participation in athletics as a player has either positive or negative value so far as its effect on success in life is concerned. The positive value of the physical training, team work, etc., is balanced against the fact that athletic ability has been shown in several previous studies to have practically a zero correlation with intelligence.

Generally speaking, the problem of extra-curricular activities is largely one of the intelligent guidance of the energies and interests of the student. The negative or positive value which they may possess is a question of the uses or abuses of the system.

Attention should be directed to the method which has been used in this study. Similar data are at hand in most American colleges. Properly treated the data should be useful as a mine of information for purposes of personnel research. Both the reliability and validity are far beyond that of the interest test, rating scale or similar device usually used in this work.

R. E. Thornhill
Carney Landis
Wesleyan University

SCHOOL AND SOCIETY

Volume XXVIII | Saturday, August 4, 1928 | Number 710

PROMETHEAN FIRE: A CHALLENGE TO THE AMERICAN COLLEGE

The propagation of authorship is no part of a university's responsibility.

A wholesome neutrality on the part of educational bodies would be a sound position to take with regard to the creative urge in young people.

Any success in the business of writing I have achieved is largely due to the bracing animosity of school masters.

So concludes William McFee—and for good measure he cites the experience of Kipling to bear out "the universal lesson of biography"—in a recent article,[1] already accorded a place of honor in a volume of representative American criticism. And his verdict merely voices the wide-spread prevailing sentiment among our creative writers and our critics, and in the academic world itself. Here and there, in the classrooms of the past and of the present, college teachers have quietly ignored this verdict and their students have called them blessed. But they have not become articulate in the expression of their faith. They have not protested openly against this "neutrality" toward the creative spirit which has prevailed all about them.

True enough, the American college has made "composition" or "rhetoric" the one almost universally required "subject." After ceaseless debate we have almost unanimously concluded that the aim of the course is training in the rudiments of clear and correct English. Yet few, to my knowledge, have formally challenged the common conviction that we should assume the attitude of "wholesome neutrality toward the creative urge" and that "the propagation of authorship"—the very phrase breathes disdain—"is no part of a university's responsibility."

But what if the college disclaim all responsibility of fostering the *urge* to authorship? At once the question strikes to the very heart of our educational ideal. For the creative impulse is the most precious force in human personality. It flares with peculiar and sudden light in youth. And if we quench that "flaming minister," we

> know not where is that Promethean heat
> That can thy light relume.

Ignore that creative urge or stifle it with conventional routine programs of study, and we continue merely to turn out an endless stream of machine-made products upon an over-mechanized society.

Have we forgotten the challenge and the prophetic warning of Emerson, pronounced before that rapt audience at Harvard four score and ten years ago?

> Colleges have their indispensable office—to teach elements. But they can only highly serve us, when they aim not to drill, but to create; when they gather from far every ray of various genius to their hospitable halls, and, by the concentrated fires, set the hearts of their youth on flame. Forget this, and our American colleges will recede in their public importance, whilst they grow richer every year.

No; we have not forgotten the words. We accept them as the very gospel of new world culture. And yet when faced with the practical problem of living this gospel, we begin with one accord to make excuse.

[1] "The Cheer-Leader in Literature," *Harper's Magazine,* March, 1926; reprinted in *Contemporary American Criticism,* edited by James C. Bowman, Henry Holt and Co., N. Y., 1926.

Once and for all, let us face the reasons for our practical repudiation of the ideal. Realizing that we can find the most definite field of inquiry in the one form of training which is distinctively creative in nature, let us ask what is the attitude of the American college toward instruction in writing.

Here are the arguments, one or more of which militate against the effort to achieve our ideal:

The young mind is not ready for serious training in creative writing; the college is not equipped for the task; the art of writing can not be taught.

Once and for all, as we cherish the college and its leadership in American life, let us challenge these convictions.

The art of creative writing can not be taught. Yet the art of painting and of music can. A purely self-taught painter is unknown. Wherein lies the difference? Of course the conventional answer is that schools of the fine arts do not make painters and sculptors but afford training in technique. Yet they do far more: they surround the student with models; they assist him in building up the background of individual performance in his chosen medium; they surround him with an inspiring creative atmosphere; they teach him to look at the whole spectacle of life searchingly, creatively. Only some fetish of belief can persuade us that any intrinsic distinctions thrust the art of literature beyond the pale of the very same conditions of creative environment and creative achievement.

Still, we hear the lament on all sides, college courses in writing do not produce our best authors. For a generation freshman composition has been a required subject in the American college and several millions of young Americans have passed through this mill. Never in history has instruction in a craft gone forward on such a universal scale. Yet what writer has been developed out of the vast nation-wide process? No one can answer in terms of cause and effect, not even, I submit, the authors themselves. So much of the creative processes generates in the subconscious that the source of suggestion or inspiration often remains forever unrealized and beyond the reach of detection. So the fact that the majority of the more distinguished American writers have been to college, and, in the present generation, have "taken" composition proves little one way or another. What they would have become without college training we can never know; they themselves can not determine.

All of which is but negative. Nor is much light to be derived from the fact that out of one shining course, English 5 at Harvard, have come a large number of gifted authors, most, if not all, of whom eagerly acknowledge their debt of gratitude to America's greatest teacher of creative writing, Le Baron Russell Briggs. There is only one Briggs. And if we record the rather brilliant outburst of youthful creative work at Yale during the past decade, we merely accentuate the absence of any similar results in all the other six hundred higher institutions of the country.

Does this example of the influence of one dominant personality at Harvard or of a single notable outburst at Yale merely corroborate the second contention that conditions in the American college are positively hostile to creative writing? We can hardly doubt it. Then what are these conditions? Unqualified teachers, overworked teachers, assuredly, first and foremost. Then, lack of enthusiasm for the creative aspect of the educational process in general, lack of belief in the supreme ministry of art, lack of faith in the creative possibilities of youth. That these latter defects merely reflect the same shortcomings of

American civilization will not release us from the responsibility of facing the problem of their particular expressions in the college.

I say overworked instructors first of all, because I believe this handicap comes first in importance. It is an old and wearisome subject in educational circles, I know, and I shall be suspected of special pleading in urging it here. But I have no desire to expound technical pedagogical aspects of the problem. Let a more or less typical concrete example out of my own experience suffice.

As instructor in English at one of the oldest eastern universities I once had four sections of thirty men each, one hundred and twenty students to initiate into the art of writing. Every two weeks I spent fifteen minutes in personal conference with each man on his required "themes," say four in number and totalling twelve to fifteen hundred words. . . . At ten o'clock in the morning I hasten from the classroom, where I have just spent two hours trying to teach literature, over to my office. The line is forming outside my door as I arrive. In comes Smith. "Good morning, Mr. Smith," I say as briskly as I can after two hard recitation hours, meanwhile drawing forth his unwilling efforts at composition from a huge sheaf on my desk. "Now this is a little better. But look at this awkward expression, and this, and this"—as I point rapidly down the page gory with red ink symbols, lines and numbers referring to pages in the handbook. "These sentences do not show any connection with this paragraph, and the next paragraph is not related to the preceding. And you've lost all your emphasis at the end. And you've shifted your point of view entirely here, and these sentences are all out of key with your opening. And now"—glancing at my watch I see that 10:16 has come, and I hear Brown scraping his feet outside—"rewrite these paragraphs, and hand in 'receive' spelled correctly twenty times, and also 'I should have gone' and 'its own way' without any apostrophe. Good morning. Tell Brown to come in."

Brown and I go through the similar illuminating ordeal; then Jones and sundry more for three hours until one o'clock. Five hours of steady talking, and I look out of the window, wondering whether I want any lunch or not. At 1:30 I meet a class section in composition, and go home to read daily test papers until dinner. After that I read themes for the next day's conferences for three or four hours. At eight on the following morning there I am again, ready to turn the crank. And now you will understand why they carry English instructors off to sanatoriums and asylums. You break, or you get spiritually numb—or resignedly cynical—or you get out. But we are not concerned here with the instructor's fate. I am presenting a soberly accurate picture of the process which thousands of instructors are grinding out at this very moment with some 200,000 American college freshmen. I am explaining why the American college does not produce authors.

How often I longed to sit down for an hour or so with Bill Jones and thrash out some of the shortcomings in his writing—which means, in his thinking, in his perceptions, in his immature view of the world! And what a luxury it was when Smith would linger a while after the last conference of the afternoon and just talk! But under the present system this is a seldom-snatched luxury. While you sit talking to Smith a hundred others wait and the stream of themes pours through the slot in your door. Like every other teacher I have reaped rich rewards in the appreciation of my students. It is the universal experience (I hope) of every

English teacher to have his former pupils exclaim, in after years, "I sure did receive a lot of benefit from all that hammering you gave us on sentences and paragraphs, effectiveness, you know, and all that sort of thing. I only wish we had got more of it." Yes, college composition serves a useful purpose in the automobile or the bond business. It does not make creative authors.

At this point I can see many of my colleagues shrugging their shoulders impatiently. They will exclaim, "What do you expect of freshman English? All colleges have advanced courses in writing. Students who feel any desire to go on can take those and write as much as they please." But what can they salvage out of the most ardent creative desire after being ground through this factory routine? The impulse must be powerful indeed. We must here squarely face the disagreeable truth: the majority of English departments of American colleges and universities are relatively little interested in fostering creative authorship. For a generation they have emphasized attainments in technical scholarship among the faculty and scholarly appreciation of literature among the students. Both admirable aims, to which I give ardent allegiance; both essential to the sound development of American culture particularly at this stage of our evolution. And the amount and quality of scholarly achievement in our departments elicit never-ending admiration and amazement among European professors, in view of the staggering burdens of instruction which the American scholar carries. But our enthusiasm for research has proved an enemy to other equally vital obligations resting upon our faculties of literature. It has largely ignored and subordinated the fostering of the creative spirit. And by persistent and well-nigh universal overemphasis upon the investigation and appreciation of existing literature we have deprived American youth of the priceless opportunity of making a literature of their own. What literature we have thus lost we shall never know.

I am well aware that our English departments have given lip-service to creative work. But it has been formal, half-hearted, ineffective. We have indulged the enthusiastic teacher, usually young (and without the magic Ph.D.), who has begged for a course in creative writing. But we have secretly or openly patronized him as a dilettante and promotion does not come his way—"he's not a scholar, you know."

I am also well aware of the valiant efforts of these same departments to handle the staggering problem of regimenting hordes of freshmen through required composition. Only one who has viewed the problem from the inside can conceive the difficulties of imparting even the minimum essentials of English usage and sentence structure to the droves of high school graduates who come to college, unable to spell, to punctuate, or—not to enumerate more vital aspects of writing—unable to distinguish the parts of speech. Only the initiated can realize the vast amount of energy and ingenuity expended in the experimental effort to overcome such rudimentary shortcomings in the freshman course. College presidents feel that this department would exhaust the financial resources of the whole institution in their demands for instructors. This is a vital element in the whole problem, and I shall speak of it again in a moment in no uncertain terms. But the problem is not primarily lack of money. It is our lack of vision, of sympathy with youth and of faith in them.

"But what can you expect of freshman English?" Ah, this is the question which betrays our lack of faith. And this brings me to the third and final contention of the brief against the conviction that creative authorship can be taught.

What the sceptics really mean by the question is, "What can you expect of freshmen—or college students—anyway?"

At the beginning of the second semester this year a girl came into my class from another institution. From the very outset I saw at once that she wrote with vivacity and charm—that she possessed real style; and I praised her work with enthusiasm. As the weeks wore on and I came to know her background she told me that her previous college instructor had become irritated with some deficiencies in her preparation of assignments and had been cynical about her writing. At the end of the year she won a literary prize at the university, and was kind enough to tell me afterward that she entered the contest solely because I had warmly encouraged her efforts at expression. In mentioning this recent incident I shall be absolved of personal boasting, when I say that I taught her nothing: beyond the suggestion of verbal changes and some discussion of subtler points in her writing, I did nothing. I merely encouraged her, showed that I regarded her as an individual with something important to say.

"But she is exceptional—one out of a hundred," you protest. Every individual is exceptional, I reply; and until we learn this ancient truth, we shall have missed the deepest lesson of education. "Anyhow, they don't have anything important to say. They are too immature, too irresponsible; they haven't had enough experience to write about." So runs this argument.

Not enough experience! Perhaps not; although it is not necessary to consult pages of "The Plastic Age" or "This Side of Paradise" to be persuaded that they are acquiring experience rapidly enough. Be that as it may, at what age has one accumulated sufficient experience to begin to write? And at what age does one most effectively begin to practice an art?

O we of little faith! and short memories! Have we forgotten our own "flaming youth"? (Even we academic folk "flamed" a little, I assume.) Can we forget that those years in the late teens and early twenties flare up with the creative instinct which will never afterward be so new, so wonderful, so plastic? Are we blind to those ardent, vivid, chaotic emotions which dominate those years? Are we deaf to their demand that we show them vital artistic modes of expressing these creative energies? Outlets they will find, wholesome or unwholesome, for the resistless new forces within them: athletics, dances, "parties" (à deux or en bloc), and all the other official and unofficial extracurriculum activities. Shall they find also skillful guidance and inspiration in the expression of these same forces in the enduring forms of music, drama, the fine arts, and literature?

Inevitably my query has extended to all creative activity, but having posed it, we must restrict it here to expression in language—the most common and mobile form.

And now, for the sake of clarifying our inquiry and pursuing it to a constructive conclusion, suppose you tentatively grant my assertions that authors can and should —theoretically — be developed in the American college. Then you will naturally ask, How can it be done?

Obviously not by mass production. Not by imposing a hundred students upon one instructor. Writing (and I include of course any creative expression) is a most intimate and individual human activity. A single cheer leader can sweep his frenzied thousands into the blood-curdling sound of a rushing mighty wind, but the Lord is not in the whirlwind. The divine voice speaks in the secret places of the spirit; it moves to creative expression within the solitary human breast; and help cometh from the inspired teacher when he sits alone with his student.

We wax properly rhapsodic over Mark Hopkins on the log with a single student holding down the other end. Put a hundred on the same log, if you can find room, you will have a jolly mêlée—and the end of Mark Hopkins and real education. No man has a moral right to "take on" more than thirty students if he seriously intends to teach them to write. There seems to be a kind of halo about the number thirty. (Dean Briggs for almost thirty years, I believe, limited English 5 to that number, although he was always tender-hearted toward petitions to make room for one or two more on his log, particularly so, as I gratefully remember, in the year when I made an eleventh-hour appeal for a place in the sun.) But twenty is preferable, ten better still, and best of all a Briggs on the end of the log for every ten.

Find the Briggses. Do I dream of the millennium? "Such teachers are born, not made." I do not believe it. They are created by environment sympathetic to the creative spirit. A large number of the present college teachers of composition shouldn't be instructing in the art of writing at all. They have not been trained for the undertaking and they have little or no stomach for it; they hang on in the hope that after five years or so they can drop one section and get a course in Victorian poetry, restoration drama, or modern fiction. Their graduate study, culminating in the award of the doctoral laurels, may not be the worst possible training for teaching composition; but, taken by itself, it is one of the worst. Why deprive the world of the researches of a promising young Chaucerian or Elizabethan scholar and inflict him upon groups of restless young students? He doesn't want them and they certainly don't want him. But I should qualify so cruel an indictment: many a young instructor does want, or would want, not a hundred but thirty students in writing. He could then learn to do his course justice—and his thirty would then want him. He could give his course in Chaucer besides, and realize his cherished ambition of throwing light upon some dark corner of the fourteenth century at the same time. He would then do some real teaching in the art of writing; and he would be able to enrich the domain of knowledge; and he would be able to enrich his own life—by no means a negligible element in the total life of his academic community. As he now functions, he is able to contribute little to his students, to the advancement of learning, to himself, or to his generation. Largely because he is swamped with numbers.

Numbers is one of the most vital cruxes of our educational problem, though the opportunity of education for the largest possible number is perhaps the most splendid promise of our American experiment. Just now the problem is keeping college administrations awake nights. President Lowell says that education has become too costly. It will have to be far more costly unless we sharply reduce the present inflation of numbers or substitute the radio for the old-fashioned and indispensable log.

Too costly, indeed! Too prodigal, let us say, of the energies of teaching staffs, and too meager of results, because the diffusion of knowledge and culture through so unwieldy a mass is so very diffuse. The salt that is spread too thin loses its savour. Too little leaven does not leaven the whole lump. When the head of a department asks for more leaven in the shape of more and better teachers, he is met with the monotonous reply, "We haven't the money." Meanwhile all over the land rise the gigantic forms of new stadiums, temples to the god of numbers and of noise, monuments to many a dead dream of other temples not made with hands.

Take the price of one of these and pay twenty-five new teachers a living wage for five years. Within that time they will at least begin to transform the life of your academic community. If you will find the price of another and continue their influence for another five years they will generate power enough to inspire and shape the creative impulses of youth beyond your present dream. They may even change the course of American literature.

My conclusion is, then, merely the old, old plea for more and better teachers as the simple formula for bringing forth fruits of the creative spirit in the college? Yes, if I may prescribe the specifications of these teachers, together with their "hours, wages, and conditions of labor." Upon these, however, I am sure that I need not expatiate in this place, as the ideals in all these respects are pretty generally conceded. The effective teacher of the art of writing must of course possess the knowledge, the pedagogical skill, the vision, sympathy, enthusiasm which the teacher of any subject must command. He must also possess esthetic sense and the technique of imparting craftsmanship, which are the peculiar qualification of the teacher of any art. He need not himself be a writer of distinction, but he should have the creative spirit within him. Given a group of personalities with these requisite characteristics and wonders may be wrought.

Supplementing a stationary teaching staff of this quality, however, I would add a peripatetic band of established, reputable authors—some of whom could visit the college for at least a few days every year. It would not be their public lectures upon which I should count, although these might be of great value—but the round-table and individual talks with ambitious literary neophytes, bringing them into close contact with accomplished practitioners of the art of writing. All professional schools preparing for divinity, law, medicine, or engineering, and schools of fine arts, music, and drama draw heavily upon the prominent exponents of these arts and professions in their course of training. Creative literature alone is not so represented in our scheme of higher education. So exceptional is an annual appointment of a writer as a visiting member of a faculty that the item is front page news in the daily press; and the pioneer policy of planting a poet in the midst of an academic community at Amherst, Princeton, and Michigan has inspired no end of admiration for so radical a departure. Among authors I should, moreover, include editors. Hence the arrangement which permits Mr. Canby, of the *Saturday Review,* to continue a course in literary composition at Yale (limited, be it noted, to ten students) seems to me ideal. Through such contacts ambitious youth may derive at least first-hand, inside information about the grueling game of writing, much practical and technical knowledge which few teachers are at present prepared to impart, and the inspiration which emanates from the presence of creative personalities. Even the authors themselves may conceivably find no little interest in the mysteries of initiating young candidates into the fraternity of authorship. I can see nothing against this proposal and everything for it. Is it not a potential means of reconciling the ancient antagonism between the academic and the creative?

If all these Utopian conditions might suddenly be realized I am not so deluded as to suppose that we should as suddenly—or ever—produce a crop of literary geniuses. I should not expect that work of great merit or even best sellers would pour forth from the campus dormitories upon an astonished world. Under ideal conditions, undergraduate writing must perforce be derivative and bookish, half-baked and jejune—as well as often fresh and clever. (The marks of immaturity are, incidentally, not unknown in the work of older people.) Nor do I urge training in authorship as any substitute for experience of life. But there are two ways to learn about life: one is to live it; the other is to pursue its ever elusive aspects for the purpose of fixing them in the forms of enduring significance and beauty. It is a mere commonplace that nothing so sharpens an idea, an emotion, an impression as the effort to give it shape in words. Nothing makes us so keenly aware of ourselves and of the world as the creative spirit. Once awakened by the creative impulse the "finished and finite clod untroubled by a spark" is moved with an eager transforming aspiration. If, therefore, we could stir the academic waters with this spirit we need not worry so much about graduating incipient writers. The lasting powers thus released in our youth could not be measured, and the reflex tonic effect upon our whole academic life would be past reckoning.

Just now it is the students themselves who are showing us the way. Within a decade college courses in short-story writing, in dramatic technique, and in journalism have increased prodigiously, not so much because faculties have experienced a sudden desire to teach composition in more advanced, specialized creative fields, but because the undergraduates themselves have voiced a new and wide-spread demand for such training. The groundswell of a national renaissance of the creative impulse which is inspiring a new American literature has swept over the academic barriers and lifted the spirit of responsive youth. That the rising generation eagerly seeks to understand current interpretations of their world is clear from the many new and crowded courses in contemporary literature. They are looking at sex, religion, social forms, with a fearless, clear-eyed candor—and sophistication—that often startles us. But they are not only looking critically; they are feeling creatively.

So, not always in articulate words but none the less insistently, youth is saying to us: "We ask you for more than information, more than knowledge, more than discipline of seeing and thinking clearly, more than training in methods of enlarging the boundaries of exact knowledge, more than preparation for vocational success and good citizenship. We ask you for sympathetic encouragement of our creative powers, for guidance of our strivings after creative expression, for an atmosphere which stimulates the creative spirit." This plea we dare not ignore or evade. It is youth's challenge to the American college.

PAUL KAUFMAN
AMERICAN UNIVERSITY

TWENTY YEARS OF VOCATIONAL GUIDANCE[1]

FROM the modest, individual work which Professor Frank Parsons started in a little neighborhood-house on Salem Street in the north end of Boston, twenty years ago, two professions have emerged. One is that of the trained vocational-counselor in school and college; the other, that of the trained personnel-supervisor in business and industrial organizations. There were gifted people before, of course, who gave this kind of service. But what they did was to be brought within the focus of intelligent interest and study. Systematic attention to guidance and placement problems gave form and content to the vocational-guidance movement.

[1] Address at the annual meeting of the National Vocational Guidance Association, Boston, Mass., February 24, 1928.

Perhaps the most important of all the contributions made possible by this work was the realization that human nature is the most precious, as well as most elusive, material that school and shop have to deal with, and that what happens to it is the acid test for measuring how well or ill they serve.

It won't do to claim too much for vocational-guidance work by itself. What is fortunate about it is that its birth coincided with a good deal of stir in both the fields of education and of employment. Many causes account for this stir, and they are not all of a sentimental or theoretical nature.

The fact is that along with the effort of our schools to do a better job as builders of character and of lives, there have been and are similar efforts on the part of employers and of industrial managers to lift "employed hands," so-called, into self-respecting and cooperating human beings. Among enlightened executives that is the modern conception of a working organization.

I have said that causes other than philanthropic account for the changes in employment-practice that run parallel to the vocational-guidance and other present-day educational objectives. These changes are of profound interest, as their fulfilment promises more success to the effort of our schools.

The gratifying truth is that the waster of human energies in employment is no longer looked upon as a practical man. He is less and less tolerated in any position that places him over men. He has been found to be too expensive to keep. To be practical to-day as an executive is to know how to be a builder of fellow-workers.

Reasons of a hard-headed sort, illuminated by contributions of modern physiology and psychology, have made this notion a lively one in the working establishments of the present time. Costly stoppages and dislocation of work in organizations where a different conception prevailed told the story in the balance sheet.

What has the vocational-guidance motive in employment shown? It has made clear, in the first place, that a sound employment-plan knows in advance the qualifications for work and makes adjustment between work and worker in the least wasteful way.

Productive efficiency is never adequate or hardly possible where such considerations are ignored.

In the second place, it has shown that sustained working-power is not something that happens by itself; it must be nourished by intelligent provision in the way of incentives, understanding and mutual interchanges among the working family.

You would suppose that these truisms are known everywhere as a matter of course. This is far from being so. Where these simple human management fundamentals are regarded, the success of the organization is cited as something phenomenal.

MEN AND MACHINES

Thus far, a *laissez-faire* policy with respect to human energies and abilities has been for the most part followed in the field of employment. If machines had been handled as has human nature, our country would be an economic wilderness to-day.

Nothing is left to chance when a machine is designed, bought, installed and operated. Its load capacity is known in advance, lubrication points marked, speed and fitness constantly checked up, the repair and resting periods set and a charge of obsolescence fixed from the outset.

Perhaps one of the triumphs of the vocational and educational stimulus to industry has been to encourage the idea of treating men almost as well as if they were machines. Perhaps a first step in making proper use of human energy is to become sensitive to the bookkeeping item of human depreciation.

Science has been the great ally in all recent progress, humanly speaking. Where the cry of the idealist went unheeded, the lesson of the laboratory could not be disregarded, for arithmetic told the story.

Thus, in recent years, to the general aspirations of the teacher and vocational-counselor have been added the findings of tests, measurements, analysis, from varied sources of scientific exploration and experiment—medicine, engineering, economics, legislative and managerial initiative. Vocational guidance no longer works in an atmosphere of generalizations. The fortification of hard facts from a wide range of researches is available.

We can confidently attack the problems of education and of career in the light of data. These are by no means complete data, of course; but the work is going forward with approved instruments for fact-finding and it speaks the language of reality.

These explorations in the field of school and employment relationship go down to minute but significant phenomena.

Forgotten Children

A fairly good measure of the intelligence level of any given group of people is the accuracy of the age statistics. This is the conclusion of specialists in what is known as human geography. The delicacy of this test of intelligence, they have shown, is evident from the fact that in practically all our states people who are intelligent and therefore careful report the ages and the number of their children correctly. If they are unintelligent and so usually careless, they report them wrongly.

The area of forgotten children, then, is a fairly good index of the stage of community enlightenment. The age report, decisive from many points of view, especially that of school administration, is a starting-point for sound planning right through the occupational career.

Ellsworth Huntington, of Yale, can show by the simplest of map-making methods that the general measure of community alertness and education in any given locality reveals itself in the percentage of children who are in school, the proportion graduating from high school, the length of the school year, regularity of attendance, *the pay of the teachers* and the number of boys and girls who keep up some form of study after eighteen.

Forgotten Grownups

Forgotten adults, as well, give a true measure of the social and industrial standards of any given locality, and it is possible in terms of employment to plot similar revealing maps of intelligence and efficiency levels. The number of steadily-employed, the provision for advancement, the stability of the job, as well as of the employee, the absenteeism whether self-willed or from preventable sickness and accident, the needless hirings, uncontrolled discharge, the compensation and other incentives and the number of growingly-fit—in short, the record of labor turnover and of industrial relations in any given establishment reveals managerial competence or its opposite.

There is no need to guess to-day at what is good management. A sound business grows with a growing personnel. No business can flourish on a foundation of stagnating human nature. Industrial success has brought this fact home with startling impressiveness. Those who will not face this lesson while it is still in black ink will have the pleasure of having it brought home in red ink, the banner of deficit.

In recent years, an increasing number of executives have been incorporating the guidance-motive, phrased, of course, in other terms, in their dealing with the human wills and assets which they engage.

School people will profit by a study of the methods now in use in some of the stores and factories of the country. The schools of business are giving a professional basis to management and this means a scientific basis.

Able men have come to the top by responding to the professional appeal. They understand the language of those who would deal with human nature in the light of understanding.

Never before have school and business come closer than they do to-day in the common outlook of vocational advisers in school and college and of men of affairs such as Owen D. Young, A. Lincoln Filene, Henry Dennison, Harry Kendall, Haley Fiske, Henry Bruere and others that may well be included in a roll of honor.

Men of this type will not be few as the increasing magnitude of business goes on. To avert waste of human effort and direct and coordinate this effort is an absolute economic necessity.

Both the complexities of modern business problems and the spread of guidance and training opportunities compel the appointment of executives who can deal with the new situations.

It is not an accident that attention to the life-career motive, as President Eliot called it, has been developing these twenty years past, while at the same time, employing organizations have taken on functions hitherto relegated to school and college.

It is no accident that the spread of education has gone along with the growth in the number of professionally-minded business leaders.

If you list what is done to-day in the businesses managed by men such as I have named and contrast with activities extant when Professor Parsons started his work you will believe that we have had but a foretaste of what is possible when school and employment take their cue from human nature and its capabilities.

After all, what we all try to do is to live, and it is the glory of our United States that we mean to live on as high-rising a level as we can bring about.

To interrelate effort, result and reward in work is to take the surest step upward. This is a basic thought in all vocational guidance. If this is not fulness of life, it is at least the rock-bottom foundation for it. On this foundation both school and employment can build. This foundation gives teacher and business man a common aim.

To secure such fulfilment on some such foundation has long been an avowed duty of the school; it now has come to be recognized as a precondition of business success where the leadership is competent.

One present task is to make such leadership less rare, and this, if for no other reason, because the business in question will be the better off for it.

That a development such as this must vastly enhance the guidance and training interests of the school only means that school and business are never safely far apart in their main job, which is that of giving human nature its chance.

MEYER BLOOMFIELD

NEW YORK CITY

THE BASIC CONTENT OF A COURSE IN THE PHILOSOPHY OF EDUCATION[1]

THE purpose of this paper is to suggest from the writer's standpoint what the content of a basic course in the philosophy of education should be. There is no intention to standardize

[1] Revision of portion of a paper on this subject presented at the 1928 meeting of the National Society of College Teachers of Education, in Boston.

such a course, which would probably be neither possible nor desirable.

A few preliminaries dealing with related matters will serve to introduce and give a setting to our answer.

From what sources is our answer to be derived? Partly from our knowledge of the situation regarding educational philosophy as it exists, and partly from our own philosophy of life. The texts commonly used, their points of view, their contents, the views of teachers of the subject, the common content of lectures and syllabi on the subject, the necessary relations of the subject to other adjoining subjects—these all have their worthwhile suggestions to make. But from facts as they exist we can never finally determine what should exist. The latter involves an application by means of judgment drawn from one's own philosophy of life.

What do we mean by a philosophy of education? It is something more definite than general views about education. It is something richer in content than "applied sociology," however valuable the latter may be. It is something deeper even than those general regulative points of view commonly called "principles of education." As we understand it, *the philosophy of education is an intellectual interpretation of the meaning of education in the light of a world-view.* This world-view includes the cosmic as well as the social process. Such a world-view is indeed one's philosophy of life, including his philosophy of education. It is derived through seeking reflectively an adequate ground or explanation for known phenomena. In finding its answers, it utilizes all forms of acknowledged human experience, whether scientific, aesthetic, moral, social, recreative, vocational or spiritual. One's world-view is more than the widest possible generalization based on experience; it is a reasonable and adequate explanation of such experience. A philosophic explanation tries to be ultimate When the usual principles of education become indeed first principles, then they are philosophical. What does education really and truly mean? That is the question raised by a philosophy of education. And meanings are not fully defined apart from purpose.

Why have such a course? It is a good thing to try to see the educational problem whole. This involves seeing life whole, seeing the cosmos whole, and seeing education as a part of the whole process. Such a view tends to eliminate narrow-mindedness, helps us to see all around an educational question, tends to improve our evaluations of conflicting tendencies and opinions, and sheds some guiding light on what to do next.

A philosophy of education may be taunted with being repetitious and overlapping other courses. This taunt is often justified. The novelty in a philosophy of education is not its facts but its point of view and its treatment of the known facts. Its treatment is synthesizing and its point of view is critical, evaluating and interpretative. Though intellectually unifying, philosophy would emotionally harmonize and practically direct.

It is not the function of a given course in philosophy of education to indoctrinate; rather to stimulate. Philosophy is rather thinking than knowing. No philosopher knows enough to be justified in teaching his system, or that of the text, as the final truth. The usual text has its own philosophical point of view. The usual instructor has his own philosophical bias. Yet there are philosophies many, and philosophers may genuinely and honestly disagree as to the better theory of human existence. In the face of such a situation it is better to adopt a democratic and scientific attitude. The democratic attitude lets each philosophy speak for itself as fully and as fairly as time allows. It is comparative in method. The scientific attitude traces out the causes and the consequences of each philosophy in an objective way. The student well-guided in this way may well be left to find and to formulate his own philosophy of education. He will appreciate the compliment of being permitted to think for himself. And his teacher will eschew the risk of making the student's mistake for him.

Who then should undertake to teach a course in the philosophy of education?

The teacher of the philosophy of education should, ideally speaking, be well grounded in biology, physiology, sociology, psychology and philosophy, including logic, aesthetics, ethics and metaphysics. He should be a man with a philosophy and a program but not a propagandist, or a proselytizer or an indoctrinator. He should not tell his pupils what to think in philosophical matters but train them how to think. He should be able to state sympathetically views he does not personally hold. He should use largely the method of discussion. His personal views should be kept in the background in classroom discussion, though he should not hesitate to commit himself on any question when the class wants to know where he stands. And any view of life may properly be introduced and discussed.

Concerning the outline now to be presented, let me add that it is arranged logically, not necessarily in the order of learning. Also that no text-book or syllabus known to me is so composed. Further, a course such as that outlined would preferably require sixty classroom hours. It might be given in forty-five hours but not satisfactorily in thirty.

What then should be the basic content of the course in the philosophy of education? Its first main division should be concerned with the concept of a philosophy of education (see outline at end of this paper). This can hardly be developed without using such biological and physiological concepts as evolution, organism, environment, adjustment and growth. Adequate notions of what education fundamentally is, for example, adjustment or right growth, should be contrasted with inadequate, though partially true notions, such as training the mind, or preparation for adult life, or recapitulation of the past. The concept of philosophizing as the unifying and evaluating function in human experience must necessarily be developed. One's philosophy of education will be his interpretation of the meaning of education in the light of his world-view; it will be the ultimate answer to the question, why educate? As there are philosophers many and philosophies several and varying, at this point the main typical philosophical points of view that have been used in interpreting the meaning of education should be sketched, particularly the pragmatic, the idealistic, the behavioristic, the realistic and the eclectic.

Given this orientation in the field of philosophy of education, attention may next be directed to the four main questions with which any general theory of education must be concerned. These are (1) What is the goal of education? For answer we turn mainly to ethics: (2) With what does the educative process start? For the answer we turn mainly to psychology: (3) What are the means of education? For answer we turn mainly to sociology; and (4) How shall we measure our educational progress from starting-point toward the goal? For answer both scientific method and careful judgment are necessary. These four questions give us the succeeding main divisions of our course, each with important subdivisions of its own.

Let us consider them in order.

Under "the goal of education" we may well inquire into the chief values of life, such as health, recreation, truth, beauty, character, vocation, worthy citizenship and spirituality; the corresponding main aims of education; whether democracy is the social goal, and, if so, what is meant by it; whether a self-realized personality is the individual goal, and, if so, whether it is immortal; how the individual and the social goals are related; the correct conception of vocation, and how education is the process of realizing the ends of living.

In answer to the question, "With what does the educative process start?" we must inquire into the varying views of the original nature of the educand, individual differences, education as redirecting impulses already at work, the individual's need for education and society's need for education.

Under "the means of education," we should take account of the use of social controls, education as a function of society, the meaning of experience, the use of the racial inheritance, the proper content of the curriculum, the method of education, the function of thinking, the rôle of the teacher, the contributions of educational organization and administration to the process, the significance of the nature and kinds of school support, and the actual and potential educational services of state and church as social institutions.

Under "the measurement of our educational progress," we have to come to terms with the testing movement, our manifold scales for measuring attainment, our historical comparisons between past and present school accomplishment, and our evaluations of the actual in terms of the ideal. The nature of progress is to be determined. Contemporary educational tendencies, literature and schools, experimental and other, are to be estimated in terms of our philosophy of life.

Finally, with a look back at our concept of a philosophy of education, the educational goal, the educational starting-point, the measurement of educational progress, we ask ourselves the meaning of the whole process in terms of varying world views and our own.

Our students, in the process of the course, should have been led to grapple with the great issues for themselves, should have felt our own point of view, should have come through somewhat better educated themselves for the intellectual experiences they have had, and, if we are good teachers and they are cooperative, they should have found that good thing known as a personal philosophy of education and of life—one that most convinces their own reasons, truly awakens their interests and best guides their personal and professional conduct.

SUGGESTED CONTENT OF THE BASIC COURSE (60 HRS.) IN THE PHILOSOPHY OF EDUCATION

I. *What is a philosophy of education?*
   1. The concepts of evolution, organism and environment.
   2. The concepts of education: adjustment? growth? or what?
   3. Inadequate concepts of education.
   4. The concepts of philosophy and philosophy of education.
   5. Different typical philosophies of education.
      (1) Pragmatism (2) Idealism (3) Behaviorism (4) Realism (5) Eclecticism.

II. *What is the goal of education?*
   1. What are the chief values of life?
   2. What are the main aims of education?
   3. The social goal—Democracy? Its implications?
   4. The individual goal—Personality? Immortality?
   5. The individual and society—how related?
   6. Education as vocational.
   7. Education as the realization of the ends of living.

III. *With what does the educative process start?*
   1. The original nature of the educand.
   2. Individual differences.
   3. Education as redirection.
   4. The individual's need for education.
   5. Society's need for education.

IV. *What are the means of education?*
   1. Social controls.
   2. Education as social.
   3. The meaning of experience.
   4. The racial inheritance.
   5. The curriculum.
   6. The method of educating.
   7. The function of thinking.
   8. The rôle of the teacher.
   9. Educational organization, administration and support.
   10. The state and education.
   11. The church and education.

V. *How shall we measure our educational progress?*
   1. Tests, measurements, historical comparisons, and evaluations.
   2. The nature of progress.
   3. Estimates of contemporary, educational tendencies, literature and experimental schools.

VI. *Summary and conclusions:*
   The meaning of education in the light of various world-views.

HERMAN H. HORNE
NEW YORK UNIVERSITY

EDUCATIONAL EVENTS

EDUCATION IN PALESTINE

THE genuine demand for education among Arab peasants is illustrated in the annual report on education, recently published by the Palestine Government for the school year 1926–27, by the fact that twenty-one villages completed the construction of school buildings at their own expense in 1927, while eleven more village schools were then being built.

According to a special despatch to the *Christian Science Monitor*, the main efforts of the government have been concentrated on providing elementary education for the Arabs and especially the Moslem Arabs, who form the largest and at the same time the most backward part of the population. The need was particularly pressing in the villages, and of the 317 schools maintained by the government 266 are in rural areas. The language of instruction at all the government schools is Arabic, English being taught as a foreign language from the third class of the elementary schools upward. It is interesting to note that among the pupils recently admitted to one of the government schools in Jerusalem are the sons of the Emir Abdullah of Transjordan and of ex-King Ali of the Hejaz.

One of the main difficulties of the government department of education is the serious shortage of trained and experienced native-born teachers. To meet this need the government has established two training colleges—one for men and one for women. In 1927 there were 142 students, of whom 64 were women. A few selected students are also being assisted by the government to obtain higher education at various institutions abroad, including the American University at Beirut, the Bulaq Training College at Cairo and the universities of Oxford and London.

In addition to the government schools, there are also 520 denominational schools, which, provided that they reach a prescribed standard, receive grants-in-aid from public funds. These grants have until recently been very small, but in 1927 they were increased to the more substantial sum of £12,430. The Zionist schools now number 191 and have an attendance of about two thirds of the total number of Jewish school children and one fourth of the total number of school children in the country. There are only 23 Jewish children at the government schools, and the remainder of the total of 26,557 are provided for by such bodies as the Alliance Israelite of Paris and the Anglo-Jewish Association of London. There are also a large number of Christian schools, with a total attendance of 15,782.

A notable and interesting feature of school life in Palestine is the growth of the Boy Scout movement, and it is stated that a training course for Girl Guide leaders, presumably Moslems, was recently held in Jerusalem, "under strictly harem conditions."

THE EXCHANGE OF SCHOOL CHILDREN BETWEEN GERMANY AND NORTHERN EUROPE

Finland participated last summer for the first time in the exchange of pupils between the northern European countries and Germany. The initiative was taken by the German association, Deutscher Philologenverband, according to the U. S. Bureau of Education. The association provides for free transportation in Germany. Two hundred pupils from Sweden participated in 1925; this number increased to 700 in 1926 and to 800 in 1927. Next summer, when Norway and Denmark will follow the example of Finland and Sweden, it is expected that the number will increase to 1,500. The school administration took the lead in this movement in Finland in the spring of 1927.

On account of limited time for arrangements, it was necessary to restrict the exchange of pupils to those from Helsingfors and its immediate vicinity. In 1927, a total of 31 girls and 27 boys from 14 to 17 years of age participated from Finland. The pupils were located in homes equal in social and educational standing to the homes of the visitors; the girls were placed with families with daughters of the same age, and the boys with families with sons of equal age. The visit was of a month's duration, after which the German pupils accompanied the Finnish pupils to Finland as the latter's guests.

The purpose of this exchange is to give the young people a chance for recreation and at the same time to widen their vision by acquainting them with the ways and customs of a foreign country by teaching them its language and fostering friendly relations with that country. An agreement for the exchange of pupils during next summer has already been concluded with the German committee.

In connection with this exchange of pupils it is planned to arrange for a trip for a number of students from the more advanced classes for the purpose of more intensive study. This trip will take eight or ten days. The maximum number of participants will be fifteen. The main purpose of the trip is to visit Weimar to study the intellectual atmosphere there.

STUDENT CONFERENCES IN WALES

Conferences of students of university tutorial classes have been held lately both in South and North Wales. It is reported in the London *Times Educational Supplement* that in North Wales the work under the guidance of Mr.

Silyn Roberts is showing rapid growth. Thirty-one classes were organized and of these 24 earned the full grant of the Board of Education. The total number of extra-mural classes reached 65, as compared with 23 in 1924. One-day schools have also been organized with considerable success. Principal Evans, who addressed the students, emphasized the importance of regarding the work as an essential duty of the university. The classes are now evidently well established in the counties of North Wales. At present it is stronger on the upland areas than in the valleys. But the movement as a whole is a vigorous one—the extra-mural students are twice the number of the internal students—and as the connection between these classes and the university is made strong and effective, so will the number of students continue to increase. Principal Evans mentioned the desirability of greater variety in the choice of subjects. But this, and indeed the future of the work, is dependent upon increased financial aid. Throughout the country the demand for adult education can not be stimulated overmuch lest the university prove unable to cope with it. Already there is a lack of teachers, and a grave lack of funds to help deserving students in their progress from the classes to the university colleges. Scholarships are needed, and more help might also be forthcoming from the local authorities.

Principal Evans suggests that the system of state scholarships which now helps pupils in the secondary schools should be extended to give opportunities for study to those adult students. The residential college at Harlech exists to carry on the work of the tutorial classes, but first the paths to this and the other colleges must be made easier by grants from the local authorities and by a more generous system of state aid. In the Swansea area the same tale is told. There the number of students has increased from 551 last year to 689 for the present session, and it is believed that many more classes could be held if the money were available to provide more tutors. Here, as elsewhere, the supply of tutors does not meet the demand for classes, nor is there money to pay for their services. There is little doubt that tutorial work in these extra-mural classes will have to be placed upon the same basis as that of the full-time university tutor. If this were done more of the graduates would take up the work as a career. At present much of the supply of tutors is too haphazard to make the work as effective as it should be.

THE AMERICAN LIBRARY IN PARIS

THE extension work of the American Library in Paris is growing rapidly. Close cooperation with the various universities and institutions of higher instruction throughout France has been established for some time, and quite recently, at the suggestion of Burton Stevenson, director of the library, an official circular concerning the library's service was sent to all lycées by M. Francisque Vial, in charge of French secondary instruction. Monsieur Vial calls the attention of all teachers to the value of this service, speaks of it in the warmest terms, and asks that the entire personnel of the secondary schools be informed of it. As a result the library has received numerous letters from teachers asking for books, and many applications from students requesting borrowers' cards.

The library offers, through its extension service, to send to any teacher or student for a loan of two months any books relating to any American subject which they may wish to see, and to procure any such book not already in its collections. Books on other subjects are also loaned. These loans are sent by mail post-free, by the courtesy of the ministry of public instruction, through its Service des Prêts d'Imprimés. The same service is offered to the whole of Europe, but since the postal charges for countries outside of France must be met by the borrower, it has not developed as rapidly as the service within France.

The library is about to issue a bibliography of books important to the study of American history, which will be sent to all libraries and universities of Europe, with the offer of a long-term loan of any of the books listed, and this will be followed by a bibliography of American literature, and by others covering other American subjects. Special bibliographies upon any American subject will be prepared upon request. Meanwhile, as this service develops, Mr. Stevenson hopes to secure the cooperation of the ministry of public instruction in other European countries in forwarding these books through diplomatic channels, so that there will be no charge on the borrower.

The main purpose of the American Library in Paris is to "become the recognized center of information about America for Europeans, and to promote among students, journalists and men of letters in Europe a closer acquaintance with American literature, institutions and thought."

THE PROGRESS OF THE LAND-GRANT COLLEGE SURVEY

THE survey of land-grant colleges in the United States, which is being conducted by the bureau of education, Department of the Interior, is making good progress, according to the director of the survey, Dr. Arthur J. Klein. The full text of the recent statement, taken from the *United States Daily,* is as follows:

The land-grant college survey is progressing rapidly. Cooperation in the work and interest in its success are wide-spread. Large numbers are actively participating in the survey as members of local committees and of the field staff.

Since the issuance of the initial circular of information describing the plan and scope of this undertaking, many of the questionnaires have been prepared and distributed to the colleges for final filling out. Approximately two thirds of the work in this connection has been completed, much of it in advance of the original schedule. The bureau's field staffs to handle four of the questionnaires have been organized and their members have started to make visits to the institutions.

The questionnaire on graduates and ex-students, which is designed to secure information concerning the human product of the land-grant colleges, has been completed in printed form. One hundred and fifty thousand copies have been printed and are now being forwarded to the institutions to be sent to their former students. Already thirty-four institutions have submitted estimates of the number they will require.

The questionnaire on control and finance has been prepared, reproduced and distributed to the institutions.

Carl E. Steeb, business manager of Ohio State University, and D. W. Springer, secretary of the Association of Governing Boards of State Universities and Allied Institutions, are largely responsible for its preparation. Before its final adoption, the questionnaire was reviewed by the advisory committee on the financial aspect of the study. This committee includes Robert G. Sproul, vice-president, comptroller and secretary of the regents of the University of California; Fay E. Smith, secretary of the board of trustees of the University of Wyoming; Alfred S. Brower, comptroller of North Carolina State College of Agriculture and Engineering; Robert L. Himes, business manager of Louisiana State University and Agricultural and Mechanical College, and Charles H. Gorman, comptroller of the University of Nevada.

In addition, the questionnaire was reviewed by the advisory committee representing the governing boards of the colleges composed of the following members: John Callahan, regent, University of Wisconsin; Junius E. Beal, regent, University of Michigan; William S. Myers, trustee, Rutgers University; David E. Ross, Purdue University, and Alma W. Paterson, trustee, Ohio State University.

At a recent meeting of the Association of University and College Business Officers held at the University of Minnesota, J. C. Christiansen, of the University of Michigan, and Lloyd Morey, of the University of Illinois, led the discussion of a paper read by Mr. Steeb on the land-grant college survey. As a result, the organization adopted the following resolutions:

Resolved, That this association, comprising many institutions other than land-grant colleges, commends the survey of those colleges now being made by the U. S. Bureau of Education, and that we pledge the support and assistance of our members in this undertaking.

And, since the results of the survey will be of value to all of our institutions whether land-grant or otherwise, be it further

Resolved, That the bureau be requested to make available, if possible, to all members of this association the various questionnaires that will be prepared, in order that they may, if they so desire, make similar studies of their own institution for their own benefit, in comparison with the results obtained by the survey.

Copies of the questionnaire on registrar's information have been forwarded to the institutions to be filled out. This questionnaire was prepared by Ezra L. Gillis, registrar of the University of Kentucky, who submitted it to many other registrars for criticism and revision. At a meeting of the registrars' national organization held at Cleveland in May, the questionnaire was also presented to several special groups of registrars from the land-grant institutions of Minnesota, Illinois, Nebraska, Missouri, Maine and Colorado, in order that they might make a complete analysis. A number of registrars outside the land-grant college group also examined it. Before final adoption, therefore, the questionnaire was the subject of critical study by almost three fourths of the registrars by whom it is to be filled out. The registrar's questionnaire is particularly important as it contributes to every portion and phase of the survey.

GRADUATE MEDICAL COURSES AT THE UNIVERSITIES OF KANSAS AND OKLAHOMA

A cooperative effort by two state universities became effective when the Kansas Board of Regents approved the employment of Luther Wesley Kibler, as manager of post graduate medical study, in cooperation with the University of Oklahoma. Mr. Kibler, who has been a member of the extension faculty of the University of Oklahoma for three years, will be in charge of the organization of special courses for physicians of the two states, and is already organizing a half dozen intensive courses to be given this winter at the medical schools of the two universities.

For two years or more the University of Oklahoma, and for the past year the University of Kansas, have been conducting circuit classes in graduate medical instruction, but when it was found difficult to obtain the type of instructor desired to conduct circuit classes—meeting weekly in six or seven cities for a two months' term—it was decided to attempt a program of five-day schools, approximately once a month, with a different phase of graduate medicine to be taught at each. The faculties for these intensive courses are now being assembled by Mr. Kibler.

H. G. Ingham, director of the University of Kansas extension division, said:

> So far as I know, no other American universities are attempting a cooperative program of instruction. In fact, I know of no instance in which universities in adjoining states are carrying on a program of graduate study for the medical profession.

THE RADIO EDUCATIONAL PROGRAM OF WALTER DAMROSCH

The Radio Corporation of America has arranged with Walter Damrosch to give twenty-four of his famous children's and young people's concerts over the radio on Friday morning at 11 o'clock Eastern time, through a chain of twenty or more stations, beginning on October 26th.

Mr. Damrosch, a pioneer in music appreciation, has given such concerts in New York since 1891. He will now be able to reach fifteen million young people with his musical message. His programs will be graded to conform to the development of this young audience, and verbal comments will serve to create the mood for the understanding and enjoyment of the music played by his orchestra. The various instruments of a symphony orchestra, their special characteristics and groupings will be illustrated by appropriate excerpts and solos.

The Radio Corporation states:

> It should be understood that these concerts are in no way to take the place of regular musical instruction. The average time allotted to each individual child is fifteen minutes weekly, not an unfair amount of time to be taken from a crowded curriculum and devoted to the world's greatest music. Mr. Damrosch's object is to increase the interest and appreciation of good music and thereby to stimulate the cultivation of school singing and school orchestras. No great achievement in performance is possible without a background of familiarity with the best in music literature.

In September the Radio Corporation of America will publish all the symphony programs in book form, and each program will be accompanied by ten or twelve questions and answers personally prepared by Mr. Damrosch which will embody the explanatory comments made by him during the concert. Classroom visual aid will also be suggested. If teachers desire, they may use these questions in their classes after each concert, and rate their pupils accordingly. Proper school authorities may obtain the program books free of charge by writing to the Educational Division of the Radio Corporation of America, 233 Broadway, New York City.

HEALTH EDUCATION FILMS

Plans for a complete series of health education films designed specifically for classroom use in public schools have been completed under an agreement by which the department of biology and public health of the Massachusetts Institute of Technology will cooperate with the Eastman Teaching Films, Inc., in what is said to be the most comprehensive program of its kind ever undertaken.

According to the report of the plans in the Boston *Evening Transcript,* the films will be produced under the direction of Dr. C. E. Turner, professor of biology and public health at the institute, and one of the leading authorities on child health education. He will have as his assistant Miss Georgie B. Collins, who has resigned as director of health education in the public schools of Malden, to begin work on the first of the health education films.

The series of films, Dr. Turner said, will be extensive and complete, and will present teaching material in the field of health in much the same way that the recent Eastman films have contributed to the teaching of geography, civics and other subjects. He stated:

> The motion picture has a tremendous contribution to make to public education. Its possibilities have been little realized up to the present because very few films have been made specifically for classroom use. The type of film adapted for general and adult audiences has little value as a definite tool in education.
>
> The program will include films showing the nature and functions of the body and problems in health control of the environment, all presented with the greatest scientific accuracy and so produced as to interest the child.

One of the great opportunities offered by this method of education, Professor Turner pointed out, is that films present life in motion. The child will be shown those basic facts of physiology and health procedures which are now a part of the best health education programs of the country. These will be presented within the scope of his understanding and in a manner which would be impossible without the aid of the motion picture.

Every film will be prepared for a particular grade level and will definitely recognize the extent and limitations of the health knowledge already acquired by the child. It is expected that the first productions will be for the use of upper, intermediate and junior high schools. When completed, the series will present a complete program of health education for public schools.

Special equipment for microscopic motion picture photography is now being installed at the institute. The new work will proceed hand in hand with further developments in the biocinema research laboratory, established in 1921 for motion picture research and for the production of educational films dealing with the nature of bacteria, the disposal of sewage, the diphtheria organism, the preparation of antitoxin and other subjects. The classroom films produced at the institute on biological and public health subjects were the first contributions of the kind to be made at an American educational institution.

EDUCATIONAL NOTES AND NEWS

THE Right Reverend James H. Ryan, professor of philosophy at the Catholic University of America, Washington, D. C., has been made rector of the university, to succeed Bishop Thomas J. Shahan, who resigned in March.

DR. IRA N. HOLLIS, who retired three years ago from the presidency of the Worcester Polytechnic Institute, has been made president emeritus of the institute. He was awarded the honorary degree of doctor of engineering at the commencement exercises of the institute.

G. C. L. RIEMER has been elected principal of the State Teachers College at Clarion, Pa.

THE Reverend Brother Albert, president of St. John's College, Washington, D. C., has been named president of La Salle College, Philadelphia.

WALTER J. SHEPARD, professor of political science of the Brookings Graduate School, Washington, D. C., has been appointed dean of the college of liberal arts at Ohio State University.

DR. ALEXANDER G. RUTHVEN, director of museums at the University of Michigan, has been appointed dean of administration of the university, to succeed Dean Edmund E. Day, whose resignation took place in June.

LUTHER A. WEIGLE, professor of religious education at Yale University, has been appointed dean of the Yale Divinity School, to succeed Dean Charles R. Brown, who has retired.

JAMES L. PARKS, professor of law at the University of Missouri, who recently accepted a professorship at the University of Washington, has been released to become dean of the law school of the University of Missouri. He will succeed Dean J. P. McBaine, who goes to the University of California School of Law.

PROFESSOR E. B. MCGILVARY, of the philosophy department of the University of Wisconsin, has been called to the University of California, Berkeley.

DR. RICHARD T. HAINES, trustee of the American wing of the Metropolitan Museum of Art, New York, has been appointed professor of fine arts at St. John's College, Annapolis.

HARLEY L. LUTZ, professor of economics at Leland Stanford University, has been appointed professor of public finance at Princeton University.

HAZELTON SPENCER, director of the English department at Washington State College, Pullman, has been appointed associate professor of English at Johns Hopkins University, where he will direct research in the Shakespearean drama. Dr. Murray W. Bundy, formerly assistant professor of English at the University of Illinois, will succeed Dr. Spencer at Washington State College.

DR. PAUL V. KREIDER, instructor of English at the University of Michigan, has been appointed assistant professor at the University of Cincinnati.

LESTER M. BEATTIE, formerly instructor of English at the University of Wisconsin, has been made assistant professor of English at the Carnegie Institute of Technology, Pittsburgh, Pa.

CECIL KNIGHT JONES has been appointed assistant professor of Spanish American literature at George Washington University, Washington, D. C.

DR. JAMES M. YARD, for nearly twenty years a religious educational leader in China, has been appointed to the new post of director of religious activities at Northwestern University.

PROFESSOR BENJAMIN W. BACON, of the Yale Divinity School, retired on July 1. The Yale corporation has voted that he be appointed professor emeritus in appreciation of his thirty-two years of distinguished service as a teacher, and his many contributions to theological scholarship.

JOHN T. SYMONS has been chosen superintendent of schools at Coldwater, Mich., to succeed Charles F. Hamilton.

C. C. CROSSWHITE, for the past two years principal of the Simonsen Junior High School, Jefferson City, Mo., has been elected superintendent of schools at Cameron, Mo.

H. W. HODSON, superintendent of the Clinton county schools, Ohio, has been elected superintendent of schools at Wilmington, Ohio.

WILLIAM AUGUSTINE PERRY, formerly principal of St. Athanasius' School in Brunswick, Ga., has been appointed principal of the Waverly School at Columbia, S. C.

FANNY WYLES, for fifty-seven years a teacher in the Detroit public schools, is retiring at the age of seventy-seven years.

H. F. COLLINS, head of the modern side of Manchester Grammar School, Manchester, England, has been appointed headmaster of the Chichester Secondary School for Boys.

PRESIDENT W. A. JESSUP, of the University of Iowa, and Dr. John A. Miller, vice-president of Swarthmore College, have received the honorary LL.D. from Indiana University.

WALTER THOMAS, research professor in agricultural and biological chemistry at the Pennsylvania State College, will receive the honorary Sc.D. from the University of Wales at the coming congregation of the university.

MARGARET JUSTIN, dean of the division of home economics of the Kansas State Agricultural College, has been elected president of the American Home Economics Association. Other officers elected were Effie I. Raitt, of the University of Washington, *vice-president;* Frances Zuill, of Iowa University, *secretary;* H. Gale

Turpin, of Baltimore, *treasurer;* Lita Bane, of the University of Wisconsin, *councillor,* and S. Agnes Donham, Boston, *controller.*

GERTRUDE HODGMAN, assistant professor in the Yale School of Nursing, has been giving a course in "Principles of Teaching Applied to Schools of Nursing" at the summer school held at the Bedford College for Women, University of London, from July 16 to August 4.

DR. C. F. SANDERS, of Gettysburg College, is to be on sabbatical leave for the coming year. He left on July 15 for a trip around the world.

GEORGE COLVIN, president of the University of Louisville, Louisville, Ky., and former state superintendent of public instruction, died on July 23, at the age of fifty-three years.

EMILIE MCVEA, from 1916 to 1925 president of Sweet Briar College in Virginia, and formerly dean of women at the University of Cincinnati, died on July 27, at the age of sixty-one years.

THE Reverend Joseph Bonahue, formerly president of Columbia University, Portland, Ore., died on July 27, aged thirty-nine years.

GEORGE MARTIN DUNCAN, from 1894 to 1923 a professor in the department of philosophy at Yale University, died on July 27, at the age of seventy years. Dr. Duncan had been made professor emeritus in 1923.

CHARLES WESLEY HOBBS, editor and supervisor of instruction in the division of university extension of the Massachusetts State Department of Education, died on July 28, at the age of fifty-four years.

JAMES A. O'DONNELL, principal of the Isaac Remsen Junior High School, Brooklyn, died in Germany on July 20, at the age of sixty-two years. He had been a teacher for forty years.

THE annual conference of county and district school superintendents of Pennsylvania will be held at the Pennsylvania State College from August 9 to 11. The conference, conducted by the state department of public instruction and the college, is held for the purpose of enabling superintendents to keep in touch with the latest developments in education and to meet outstanding leaders in the field of education just before they resume active work with their own schools in the fall. Among those who will appear on the program for this year's conference are Dr. Walter S. Monroe, director of educational research at the University of Illinois; William McAndrew, editor of the *Educational Review;* Joseph F. Noonan, president of the State Education Association; W. R. Straughn, of the Mansfield schools; A. D. Thomas, superintendent of schools at Hazleton; and R. C. Shaw and C. F. Hoban, of the state department of public instruction.

CONFERENCES on new educational tendencies in Russia, Germany, Italy and Czechoslovakia are being held at Columbia University this summer under the auspices of the University of the State of New York. On July 18, the first of these conferences, a study of adult education among the Russian peasants, was conducted by Dr. George S. Counts, professor of education at Columbia University. On July 25, Dr. Franz Hilker, of the staff of the Central Institute for Instruction and Education of Berlin, discussed new forms of adult education in Germany. Recent tendencies in public school education in Italy were discussed on August 1 by Edward Corsi, publicist and educational director of Harlem House, while Dr. Otokar Vocadlo, lecturer in Czechoslovakia, school of Slavonic studies, University of London, conducted the conference on adult education in Czechoslovakia.

THE Hampton Institute of Virginia will receive $2,500, and Constantinople College, Turkey, $2,500, through the will of Mrs. Fannie Garrison Villard.

THE trustees and alumni of Lehigh University have pledged a fund of $500,000 for the building of a Gothic addition to the university library.

THE University of Latvia, Riga, is to receive $1,000,000 through the will of Kristap Morberg.

FOR the accommodation of married graduate students at Harvard University, the Harvard Housing Trust is erecting a building at Holden Green, Cambridge. Provision will be made for twenty-two apartments and one small house. Rents will be from $39 to $59, and occupancy is promised by September 15.

BUILDING materials are on the way to Point Barrow, Alaska, for the rebuilding of the schoolhouse, which was burned last January. The Eskimo schoolboys are expected to aid in the building of the school.

OWNERS of farms, mines, factories and other enterprises in remote sections of Guatemala are required to maintain schools at their own expense if as many as ten children in the families of their employes are without opportunities for education, according to the U. S. Bureau of Education. Public education in Guatemala will also be promoted by the prohibition of work during school hours by children of school age. A scholarship for a complete course in government schools will be available for at least one child of any parent who has taught more than ten years in government schools. Schools receiving government aid will hereafter be secular.

THE work of the children's libraries which goes under the name of "Les Heures Joyeuses" is developing rapidly in Belgium. It started under American initiative and the first library for children was named "Brand Whitlock," in honor of the former United States Ambassador to Belgium. The third of these children's libraries has been opened in Brussels. At the opening ceremony Burgomaster Max thanked Mr. Gibson, the new United States Ambassador, for the support his country is giving to the children's libraries in Belgium.

AMERICAN citizens of Japanese parentage increased their enrolment in the Hawaiian school system by 2,326 during 1927, according to figures compiled by the Hawaiian Department of Education. The total enrolment of Japanese students in the island schools during 1927 was 34,450, which compares with a total enrolment of 32,224 for 1926. There are but 3,017 Caucasians enrolled in the territorial schools, the report indicates. Contrasted with the increase of the Japanese students, the enrolment of Spanish, Portuguese and Porto Rican students shows a decrease for last year.

EVERY community in Bulgaria is, by a recent law, obliged to set aside public land for the upkeep of a public library, the state contributing in each case 12½ acres of land for the same purpose. Further support for the library is made up of appropriations from municipal governments and contributions from the schools. Thanks to this law, libraries and reading rooms have increased in one year from 800 to 2,000. The whole enterprise is directed by the ministry of education.

DISCUSSION

ARE UNIVERSITIES LOAN AGENCIES?

THE logical if not the humanistic limit of academic begging probably has been attained in a printed appeal for funds recently sent to the graduates of an institution of learning. It begins with these words in large type: "Can you now pay for your scholarship? (Your education cost more than you paid for it)." And then after a sentence omitted here, "You did get a scholarship, you know." Certainly; but the question is, must every one who receives a gift, a prize, or a reward pay it back in cash?

Did the deans and things, chairmen and so on, of some of the big colleges and universities, men and women fired red hot with the rah, rah, rah, rah spirit of emulation, get closer to the secret and real heart and opinion of their respective graduates-as-a-whole, they would realize all too keenly the disgust of the latter at the shameless alms-campaign now reaching, it must be, toward some kind of a climax. Ambitious as they are (and have to be, to keep their rah rah positions) to outdo the other colleges and universities in wealth and publicity, they simply could not, many of them, buckle themselves down to such undignified mendicancy, in season and out, insistently year after year. Told that certain graduates have no idea, ever, of contributing, they send them sedulous cries for money just the same.

Familiar with many alumnae and alumni of many such institutions, I am certain that the latter can not realize the still politely restrained protest that is fomenting and fermenting legally in thousands of folk *neither stingy nor indigent*, but merely sordidly disgusted, and perhaps (as is mankind's nature, is it not?) stubbornly repelled so that they even write anonymous letters to prominent journals, vulgar as the habit surely is. Some of these fermenting souls even go so far as to think, privately for the most part, that the graduates of a college or university can help it in more productive ways, and without this insistent and myopic annoyance.

The ethical casuistry of the matter seems to the writer, at least, plain enough. Many students on entering college are well aware that, as this present appeal sets forth, their tuition, room-rent, and board are not going to pay for what they are about to have a chance to get; but probably not one student was ever told on admission that this difference in cost he would have to repay in money—if the students were told this, some of them would prefer a different source of their borrowings. I have read over the notice of my own prized scholarship and it contains no hint that it was made me as a loan. And as a matter of fact, in my particular case it was bestowed on me with all its glittering tuition-credit of one hundred and fifty dollars, six years after the end of the course which seems to be most referred to in this appeal, and in an entirely different department of the university. But the office-files and cross-files and cross-cut-files are so formidably and unescapably efficient nowadays! And the pound of flesh means so much: "biggest and best"! like the circus.

In some institutions undergraduates are asked, and induced in many cases, to sign agreements, small and innocent-looking, but morally as binding as the witnessed judgment of God against an acknowledged sinner, that they will pay a definite and often considerable sum each year as long as they shall succeed in living—for richer, for poorer, in health and sickness, out of a family of well-fed leisure or out of one full of half-fed children, or out of the lean flat purse of one who has not been successful in earning or in keeping money. This procedure, taking advantage of the impulsive and suggested urge to sign on the dotted line, until death do you part, thinking about its intent and reasonableness afterwards rather than before, reminds one of the olden time when, it is said, boys of ten or eight, members of various organizations of "cadets," were asked to sign a pledge that never, never would they smoke, or take a drink of any liquid that would intoxicate. In this latter case big men and women stood around, but in the former case the persuasion was far more persuasive, it being nothing less than that rah-rah, good-feller, generous-girl spirit that dominates the morale of every wide-awake college in all this land of quick enthusiasms. In both cases the average will of those who signed so thoughtlessly certainly was not "free," properly speaking, at all.

Many academic institutions are not guilty of this undignified mendicancy so like the wearing of one's academic gown in the commencement procession hind-side-fore. Other great universities do it, but so skilfully and academically that no one shouts aloud or cares. But when an alumnus (or alumna?) like myself gets these illegal duns from several institutions month in and month out, it is almost inevitable that he (or she) should be one of the worms that turn.

And I wonder if the "average" graduates do really owe so infinitely much to their respective colleges as some of the latter try to make them believe? The best I can say is that for one I do not believe it. I paid my way and if I was awarded two small scholarships, it certainly was because I seemed to have earned them by being fit for them according to academic standards. And some institutions of learning owe some of their alumni or alumnae many times as much for the advertising afforded them and the prestige of having had them as students and graduates as any system of sophisticated bookkeeping could show their education cost the institutions —though this is wholly inapropos of the present instance.

And of course the theory is wrong, and debased from its earlier high estate, that shouts aloud to every graduate for endless growth in size and wealth and power. The teacher-log-student triumvirate of education still has just a wee bit yet to say for itself in this whirr of propeller wings and wireless in which we now live. Commercialism repels the most desirable scholars and sends them into some less efficient but happier environment with their books.

And what is the younger generation of future academic folk, now in grammar and "prep" schools, going to think of this begging-system about which they hear their parents complain and joke and likely enough, not too seldom, swear? Are they going complacently to enter college expecting to pay not only tuition and perhaps board and room-rent but interest on all that sum "loaned" to them by endowments intended for them alone? I suspect that complications may arise in this connection somehow, sooner or later, not wholly academic—for plain common-sense intelligence is not dead despite the impression gained as one superficially looks about him.

One thing seems certain in our academic-weather forecast: There's more disgust seething in the minds, partly "subconscious," of American alumnae and alumni than will prove profitable or expedient in the long run for certain colleges and universities. This storm will have a two-fold manifestation: first, moral and sentimental, and, second, financial. Or perhaps it may be *true* that "so long as the cheque-ordered yellow floods of coin pour in, the moral atmosphere breathing on the cheque-books matters not at all."

Yet some would say to these deans and chairmen academic that were the tuitions increased three-fold or more, or else a clear understanding had with every new student that he is not buying a loan when he thinks he's paying his tuition at college so that it is, in part, his own, the moral atmosphere would be more agreeable and academic and it well may be a bit more honest, too.

L. M. N.

THE ART MUSEUM AND THE UNIVERSITY

THE annual report of the Fogg Art Museum of Harvard University, 1926–27, gives an indication of what the museum as an institution may accomplish when affiliated with a university. The record shows great evidence of progress, particularly in the occupation of its new building especially designed to serve its needs and making possible increased efficiency in all its varied activities. The report carries notes on special lectures and exhibitions, the growth of the departments of prints, photographs and slides and the museum library; the cooperation of the museum with various departments of instruction in the university; a record of special gifts which a foundation such as the museum would naturally attract, and the work of exploration and excavation carried on under museum auspices. The reach of the enterprise is indicated by the staff of forty called for under the conditions which the new building makes possible and by the estimated necessary budget of $96,000 with a guaranteed income of $67,000. Mr. Edward W. Forbes, the director, says in the conclusion of his report:

> The new building offers every opportunity for carrying on the work under almost ideal conditions. It proves how successfully the architect accomplished the difficult task of combining the functions of a small art museum open to the public and a fine arts laboratory for students.

The museum movement in America has in it great potential promise for enriching our civilization. It is indeed already making a great contribution of this character. The museum should become a universal institution present in every community as is the public library. If some generous philanthropist would seize the social opportunity for serving America on a grand scale by promoting museums as Carnegie promoted libraries by cooperation with local communities, the museum movement would spring ahead as did the library movement a score of years ago. The report from Harvard shows that the art museum can render a great service in a university community and helps make plain the validity and worth of the museum as a social institution.

BENJAMIN R. ANDREWS

TEACHERS COLLEGE,
COLUMBIA UNIVERSITY

QUOTATIONS

EDUCATION IN THE ONE-TEACHER SCHOOL

THE one-teacher school is not entirely bad. Neither is it all that can be desired. Let us consider some of the reasons why the latter is true.

First: The wages paid in country one-teacher schools do not attract teachers as do the wages of schools in cities and towns. As a rule, wages of teachers in the urban communities are higher than in the rural districts. This fact has a tendency to take the better class of rural teachers into the cities, and since a school can not be first class without a first-class teacher, the rural school necessarily can not, in the great majority of cases, equal those schools which have, all other things being equal, superior teachers.

Second: Usually the conditions of the home life of teachers in the country are not equal to those of the teachers in the cities or towns. The rural home is seldom modern. Rarely has the rural home modern toilets, the bath, furnace or steam heat, or the electric light, while these may all be had in the city and all but the smallest towns and villages. Thus conveniences in home surroundings tend to make city positions more sought for and far preferable.

Third: The social life of the country is, for most teachers, less attractive. This is obvious, for in the city there is every form of amusement and entertainment and advantages for increasing the cultural life of the teacher, which, if one is a real teacher, has become an important part of daily life.

Fourth: Teachers, like men and women of other professions, desire recognition as belonging to a profession. A city position is regarded as establishing a teacher as a *teacher,* and thus at once making her an integral part of a great and honorable profession. A *teacher* has had special training like a doctor, a lawyer or a minister, and thus feels a professional pride. Teachers of rural, and especially of one-teacher rural schools, are thought of as belonging to a class of novices, inexperienced, poorly qualified and, as a class, unable to qualify as worthy of a professional title. Is it any wonder, therefore, that teachers seek positions other than in one-teacher schools?

Fifth: There is lack of equipment in many rural schools: no maps, no globe, seats dilapidated, no janitor service, no adequate playground, little or no playground equipment, no water supply, no conveniences for pupils or teacher to keep clean.

We could go on enumerating a sixth and a seventh; and where would it end? It is sufficient if we have established that there are conditions which, at present, are keeping the rural schools from measuring up in quality to our city and town schools.

From these facts we conclude that those teachers of rural schools who hold the best credentials and secure from their supervising officer good recommendations, and are thus classed as the best teachers, are the most likely to be selected for the more desirable urban positions. The result is that the younger, less experienced and least qualified teachers are constantly in the rural schools. There are notable exceptions, but we must admit that our poorest teachers are in the rural one-teacher schools. It would be much more diplomatic to put it differently and say that our better teachers are in our city and town schools, but for this discussion let it stand as we first expressed it.

What appears above, reduced to its lowest terms, simply says our rural schools, as a class, are taught by inferior teachers, housed in unsuitable buildings, without proper sanitary conditions, without grounds for the proper and necessary development of the play instinct, without play equipment, without desirable school and library supplies and without a social life sufficient to assist in making the school equal to the schools of the nearby cities. We admit it all. The rural one-teacher school has not impressed educators as equal in efficiency to the well graded, better taught, thoroughly supervised, beautifully housed, finely equipped city school.

But the one-teacher rural school is not all bad. It may be judged partly, if not wholly, by its product. Are the boys and girls, the men and women who have come up through these schools, and these schools only, a class of inferior, uncultured citizens? Emphatically no! No class of urban educated citizens can be characterized as more substantial, more patriotic, more hard headed, more industrious, better politicians, better Christians, or better citizens than the product of our rural schools.

No class of children take higher rank in our high schools than the children who graduate from the rural elementary schools. No college students, as a class, excel those who come from the country. The universities and professional schools bear adequate testimony to the mental ability, industry and superior scholarship of our one time rural pupil. Nor is it in business that the city trained youth excels. The captains of industry, in large measure, are the product of the rural community, the output of the rural school. Science and invention both testify to the efficiency of the thinker from the farm. Legislative halls abound with men who have been, and in many cases still are, from the country. County, state and national offices are filled with men and women whose early training was secured in the one-room, one-teacher, rural school, often lacking every vestige of equipment except books for the study of the three "R's," and such books would not now be regarded as fit for duty.

Teachers in rural schools may not equal in experience, scholarship and professional training their colaborers in urban schools, but in the great majority of cases these same unappreciated teachers have had educational inspiration and have splendidly imparted to their pupils the desire and purpose to advance. These same poorly equipped teachers have been like the pick, shovel and wash pan of the placer miner, not very good tools. But nevertheless from the application of these poor tools to the pay dirt of rural youth has come a gold product of human intelligence world wide, influencing for better every activity of education, science, invention, government and Christian life and development.

The rural school is not all bad. It has value. Its value is as far removed from zero as the east is from the west. It has a value to human life; it brings opportunity to youth; it inspires youth to action; it encourages action into accomplishment and accomplishment into character and character into life.

The rural school is not all bad. It may not be idealistic to teach from ten to forty pupils, ranging in age from six to twenty-one, varying in grades from the first to the eighth, all housed in one room for five and one half hours, while the teacher conducts from thirty to forty recitations per day, with recitation periods of from three to ten minutes, and at the same time disciplines the whole school. But even so it gives results.

It is to be regretted that the best conditions do not surround the rural school but even at its worst there are redeeming features. In the city school, one grade only is housed in a room. Perhaps as high as eight or ten recitations are heard in a day. When the class, that is, the whole school, is not reciting, the whole room is a room for study. And frequently, during these study periods, the minds of the children are not active to an extent which makes for education. It may be a time for drowsiness or wool gathering.

But this is not so in the one-teacher school. Every minute is a recitation period for some class and a study period for all others. There is no quiet hour. If, during what for any student is the study period, his mind turns from his lesson, his attention is almost necessarily drawn to the work being presented by the reciting class. As such class is never of his grade his lapse from his appointed study task and his attention to what is going on at the recitation benches, gives him either a review of something he has already passed over, or coaches him in advanced work which he will be taking another year. Thus, almost every minute of the five and one half school hours his mind is active and he is receiving an education. Mind activity, sustained, directed and intensive, results in education. And intensive mind application is a most valuable exchange for class quizzes and fancy school equipment, and may even more than offset the difference between superior and mediocre teachers.

Surely the organization, conduct and results of rural one-teacher education is not all bad.—*Rural School Board Magazine.*

REPORTS

EDUCATIONAL LEGISLATION IN NEW YORK STATE

EDUCATIONAL legislation of general interest enacted by the New York Legislature this year has been summarized by the law division of the State Department of Education as follows:

Chapter 450 of the Laws of 1928 applies to cities having a population of more than 35,000 in which the title to the school property is vested in the city. By its terms it relieves such city boards of education from the duty of carrying fire insurance upon school property, which property may be insured by the city authorities.

Chapter 499 amends the tax law by adding to it Section 70c, and requires that school taxes and other taxes be separately indicated in the tax bills in cities in which the annual estimate and budget of the board of education are not subject to change by some other city authority and in which the bills for taxes include school taxes and taxes to be raised for general city purposes.

Chapter 591 amends Section 491b of the education law so as to include part-time or continuation schools in computing the amount of the equalization quotas to be apportioned.

Chapter 592, applying only to city school districts, adds a new subdivision to Section 877 of the education law and in substance requires city boards of education to levy school taxes in all those cities in which the budget of the board is not subject to reduction, increase or change by any other officer, board or body of the city.

Chapter 593 adds another subdivision to Section 877 of the education law relating to city school districts. In substance, it requires boards of education to place in their annual budgets detailed schedules for all purposes indicating the entire amount to be expended by the board for school purposes, including the amount to be levied for debt service on account of bonds or certificates of indebtedness issued for school purposes, whether the amount to be expended is on account of local revenues or to be derived from state aid. It also requires the total amount on account of local revenues and the total amount to be derived from state aid to be listed separately in such budget.

Chapter 594 adds a new subdivision to Section 877 of the education law. It relates only to city school districts, and in effect requires the board of education to publish its annual estimate and budget prior to action thereon in all those cities in which the estimate and budget are not required to be submitted to any other officer, board or body for revision or change. It also provides that the board shall appoint a time and place for a hearing on the estimate and budget.

Chapter 595 adds Section 877a to the education law, and requires the board of education of all cities in which the annual financial report does not already contain the information, to publish annually a full and detailed account of all moneys received by the board and all moneys expended. It must also contain a full and complete statement of any bonds issued the preceding year for school purposes and the disposition made or to be made of the proceeds of such bonds.

Chapter 646 repeals former Article 23 of the education law relating to compulsory education and substitutes a new article. By its terms it increases the number of school days during which school is required to be in session from 180 to 190, exclusive of holidays and vacation periods. Attendance upon part-time instruction of minors 14 to 17 years of age, who are employed, is required in cities having a population of 20,000 or more and also in districts where there are 200 or more such employed minors under seventeen years of age. A minor who is a graduate of a four-year high-school course of study, however, is not required to attend part-time instruction. A minor is required to attend school only if in proper physical and mental condition. Provision is made that the school authorities, the superintendent of schools, or the district superintendent may suspend a minor who is insubordinate or disorderly, who is endangering the health, safety or morals of others by his presence, or who is feeble-minded. The statute also fixes the procedure to be followed when such suspension takes place.

Applicants for employment certificates must present (a) certificate of physical fitness, (b) schooling record, (c) evidence of age, (d) literary test, (e) pledge of employment. A birth certificate, baptismal certificate and passport may be accepted as evidence of age. If these are not obtainable, documentary evidence satisfactory to the certificating officer may be accepted, except that an affidavit of age is not to be accepted.

EDUCATIONAL RESEARCH AND STATISTICS

THE PUBLICITY PROGRAM OF THE SMALL COLLEGE

A STATE of almost universal criticism of the American college prevails at present, and the front rank of the critics consists largely of successful business men, men whom it is important for the college to convince of its own value, but who are too frequently inadequately acquainted with the mechanism, objectives and accomplishments of the collegiate institution. They are firmly entrenched in the misconception that college life is characterized by a series of athletic and social programs which occupy the student's attention throughout his college career, and to which a superficial study of highly impractical theory is, at best, incidental. It is little wonder that they should have these ideas, since collegiate athletic and social activities are continually brought to their attention by the newspapers, while those of an intellectual and practical value are conspicuously absent, or relegated to a position of unimportance. This, together with a preconceived notion that the subject-matter presented to the student is entirely irrelevant, and that as soon as he has entered the business world, though his degree may be considered in the process of his selection, his first official procedure should be to forget this superfluous learning, gives rise to a deplorable situation. The lack of confidence of these men has risen to such proportions that the college should no longer sit back and view it with indifference, when we consider that in an Eastern city, the seat of a large university, not only they, but professional men as well, believe that the institution is an incubus upon municipal development, since it pays no taxes, takes up ground admirably suited for commercial purposes, and since it appears to turn out individuals whom they consider spoiled by their four years of "academic leisure." Not only has the public a right to information proving that the youths in colleges are not wasting their time, but it is necessary for the salutary existence of the colleges themselves that it be furnished with such information. It is interesting to see just what has been, and is being done in this matter, especially by the smaller institutions, to which a favorable public opinion is necessary for expansion and recognition. With this purpose in view, a questionnaire was recently sent to 136 colleges ranging in enrolment from 300 to 1,000 students, and of these, 100 replied. The following tabulations were made from these replies, and in some instances, they are compared with data from "Newspaper Publicity for the Public Schools" by Dr. R. G. Reynolds.

It appears that many colleges have no definitely organized system for cooperating with the newspapers in matters of publicity, for only 51 per cent. of them have arranged for special officers or committees to function in this capacity. Their means are quite variegated, since practically every administrative officer is represented in this list; and they seem for the most part to be casting about for convenient expedients rather than carefully working them out. As to the other 49 per cent., their attitude may be inferred from the fact that they think either that the public has little or no interest in their affairs, and that their collegiate activities, therefore, have no practical news value, or perhaps that no real benefits will accrue as a result of such publicity, and consequently they maintain a traditional state of apathy in this respect.

A comparison of these findings with those in Dr. Reynolds' study of city school system publicity in 250 cities affords some interest. Though 28 per cent. of these school systems employ officers to collect school news, but 16 per cent. of the colleges reporting employ a director of publicity. There is more agreement of figures with regard to the use of publicity committees, for 12 per cent. of the school systems and 10 per cent. of the colleges make use of them. Thirty-five per cent. of the schools use student reporters, while only 9 per cent. of the colleges do, and 26 per cent. of the former and 11 per cent. of the latter use individual teachers. In 13 per cent. of the city systems and 3 per cent. of the colleges, journalism classes collect and report the news.

TABLE I

AGENCIES RESPONSIBLE FOR COLLECTING AND REPORTING COLLEGE NEWS

Agencies	Number	Per cent.
1. Publicity committee composed of faculty members	10	10
2. Director of publicity	16	16
3. Journalism class	8	8
4. Individual faculty members	11	11
5. Joint faculty-student committee	1	1
6. President	5	5
7. Alumni secretary	6	6
8. Individual student	9	9
9. Student press board	1	1
10. Director of extension	4	4
11. Local newspaper man, paid by college	1	1
12. Secretary to the president	3	3
13. Registrar	3	3
14. Dean of women	2	2
15. Department of athletics	3	3
16. Graduate assistant	2	2
17. Not reporting	15	15
Total	100	100

In two important respects there is a marked discrepancy. The superintendents in 79 per cent. of the cities represented in Dr. Reynolds' survey collect school news, while only 59 per cent. of the college presidents are reported as doing so, and this in spite of the fact that so much of the college work of real news value has to do with administrative procedure. The superintendents evidently recognize this fact; and so does public opinion, and an account is rendered faithfully by a direct employee of the public to prove that his procedure is unimpeachable and progressive. The college president evidently doesn't consider himself as a public employee, though in many cases his college receives state aid. Because of this inclination, a large part of the public does not realize how its money is being spent by the college, for the college is not quite as near to the public as are the elementary and secondary school, and there is no pressing demand on its part for information. The same reasons, perhaps, may be offered to explain why no colleges report that news is collected by board members, whereas 37 per cent. of the city schools have news released by the clerks of the school boards. It is at any rate lamentable that such good publicity opportunities are ignored merely because there is felt no external stimulus of a public group to be satisfied.

TABLE II

Comparison Between Colleges and City School Systems as Regards Agencies for Collecting and Reporting News

Agencies	Colleges Per cent. using	City systems Per cent. using[1]
1. Having individual paid officers	16	28
2. Having publicity committees	11	12
3. Superintendent or president	5	79
4. Board members	0	37
5. Individual teachers	11	26
6. Individual students	9	35
7. Journalism classes	8	13

Fifty-four per cent. of the colleges report no special plans for the collection of the news, and of those that do, in no case do the plans show any particular originality; there is no definite organization, and haphazard methods seem to be the order of the day. The plan used by 16 per cent. of the colleges is that of having the staff

[1] "Newspaper Publicity for Public Schools," Reynolds, pp. 45–46.

TABLE III

Special Plans for Collecting School News

Special plans	Number	Per cent.
1. Staff of college paper writes special stories for the city papers	16	16
2. Printed news sheet prepared at the college and sent out to the papers of the state for simultaneous release	4	4
3. Staff maintained by the alumni	4	4
4. Student from each county of state sends news to the county papers	11	11
5. Correspondent for metropolitan papers	7	7
6. All departments are organized for news, president's office used as clearing house	3	3
7. Page from college paper appears in local papers	1	1
8. Colleges having no special plan	54	54
Total	100	100

of the college paper prepare articles of special interest to be published in the city papers. A practice of reporting college activities to the home papers of the students has arisen, and 11 per cent. of the institutions consider this type of publicity to be of sufficient importance to provide student reporters for it. This news, probably personal, and relating to the achievements of students resident in the respective communities, possibly received its impetus from a tendency on the part of the students themselves or their families to promulgate their

TABLE IV

Difficulty in Getting College News Printed

Colleges	Number	Per cent.
1. Having no difficulty	38	38
2. Having slight difficulty	11	11
3. Having much difficulty	28	28
4. Not reporting	23	23
Total	100	100

academic successes, but if it is used systematically, it indeed offers a good opportunity for productive advertising. It is seen that 4 per cent. send out printed news sheets to all the newspapers in the state, but only at irregular intervals.

On the whole, the newspapers are quite willing to publish college news, and in the cases where there is difficulty, the burden of responsibility seems not to lie entirely, if at all, upon the newspapers, but rather on the colleges themselves. Among the 28 per cent. reporting much difficulty in getting news printed are listed those who do not value the attitude of the press, those who have neglected to cultivate friendly relations with the newspapers and those who feel that money spent in newspaper publicity is wasted.

Exactly 50 of the colleges reporting paid advertising definitely do not advertise, and the remaining half do not advertise extensively.

TABLE V

REASONS ASSIGNED FOR NEWSPAPER ADVERTISING

Reasons	Number
1. Special announcements to supplement the catalogue	8
2. Courtesy to papers	7
3. To get good will of papers	10
4. Attract students	19
5. Seek financial support	1
6. Announce special college events	8
7. To find boarding places for students	2

Seventeen per cent. advertise as a mere matter of courtesy to the press, for they feel that its favorable attitude, gained by the presence of the college on its advertisers' list, is desirable though they do not believe that there are any material results to be expected. Although students are sought and local college events are made public by advertising, only 28 per cent. use the opportunity offered by the newspapers for advertising their actual work, and this takes the form, usually, of announcement of courses, calendars and faculty appointments.

With relation to the question whether certain types of college activities get undue publicity, quite at the expense of others which may, or may not, be more worthy, there seems to be an almost equal division of opinion. Forty-six per cent. feel that such an undesirable attitude of the press exists, while as many more do not find it so. It will be of interest to examine the following table and observe just what activities are believed to be attracting too much attention.

TABLE VI

TYPES OF ACTIVITIES WHICH SEEM TO GET AN UNDUE AMOUNT OF NEWSPAPER PUBLICITY

Activity	Number
1. Athletics	32
2. Extravagant student utterances	3
3. Fashions and student regulations	3
4. Personal and sensational	11
5. Social items	5
6. No report	46
Total	100

An explanation of these discrepancies is that the papers are not as well supplied with news concerning certain activities as they are with news regarding others. But perhaps the fault may lie to some extent in the want of comprehension on the part of the colleges as to just what sort of news interests the public. If we study Table VIII, we may feel confirmed in this conclusion, for we find that the colleges do not agree among themselves as to what constitutes news.

Most numerous among these complaints may be mentioned those directed against extreme athletic publicity and personal and sensational news. But in the final analysis, precisely such is news; there is no doubt that the great majority of newspaper readers are interested much more in accounts of college athletic events, and "dope" on coming contests, than they are in doctors' theses, for example. Likewise, editors, as men of business, can not be criticized for publishing "college scandal" because that also is strongly demanded by their subscribers. Such news is easy to gather, and quite popular with the public, whereas types more desirable from the standpoint of the college authorities are more difficult to collect and are little likely to be widely read, much less to be widely demanded.

A large majority of the colleges (70 per cent.) recognized the importance of the attitude of the press toward them, but as many as 26 per cent. regard it as of no importance. Of course, all publicly supported institutions reporting fall into the first group. The latter group is constituted of the endowed colleges, since by their position, they may feel independent of public opinion. But many of them, too, feel the necessity of the good will of the press. It is strange however that these institutions can consider as negligible the greatest agency for interpreting their work to a prospective and actual clientele.

TABLE VII

Reasons Assigned for Including Publicity as an Item in the Budget

Reasons	Number
1. Good business	14
2. Owe publicity of activities to the public	12
3. Makes possible better cooperation with homes	1
4. Increases enrolment	22
5. Has wholesome effect on faculty	2
6. Only way to get truthful reports in the paper is to pay for them	6
7. Forced to compete with advertising colleges	2
8. Consider such expenditure as wasted money	4
9. There is no good reason	5
10. Positively do not include such an item	7
11. No report	41

Forty-three per cent. of the colleges either include the publicity item in their budget, provide for it in some other item, or express the wish that their finances would permit such an item, while 20 per cent. include it reluctantly, or are emphatically opposed to such an inclusion. Thirty-six per cent. use publicity because it is good business (if it is assumed that the 22 per cent. that regard it as useful for increasing enrolment may be classified in this category), while only 12 per cent. feel that they owe any information concerning their activities to the public that makes their existence possible.

TABLE VIII

Most Valuable Types of College News

Types	Number
1. Student activities	31
2. Enrolment statistics	3
3. Social events	10
4. Faculty changes	4
5. Gifts	7
6. Curriculum	6
7. Straight educational stories relating to educational progress and college accomplishment	13
8. Personal items	2
9. Work of the college	4
10. Extension activities of the college	2
11. College programs (literary, musical)	1
12. College history	1
13. Personal student items for home papers	5
14. Alumni activities	11
15. Athletics	12
16. Articles praising the college	8
17. Needs of the college	2
18. Achievements of students	6
19. Achievements of faculty	6

About one third of the colleges value news concerning student activity, under that specific designation, most highly; but if there are added such other news items as school events, personal items for home papers, athletics and achievements of students which may all be legitimately classified under the general heading *student ac-*

TABLE IX

Types of Publicity Desired, but Difficult to Get Printed in the Paper

Types	Number
1. Reports of experts in the field of education	1
2. Parents' sacrifice to educate their children	2
3. Scientific articles	5
4. Scholarly and research articles	7
5. Courses of study	4
6. Theses of students	6
7. Statistical reports	5
8. None that do not now appear	44
9. No report	32

tivity, there are in all 64 per cent. ranking this type of news as being of the most importance.

It is evident according to this table that 30 per cent. of the colleges do not comprehend clearly the audience appealed to by the newspaper. Although investigation, which may be of general interest, should, if properly presented, be accorded a place in the columns of a newspaper, the public in general has no interest in statistical presentation or discussions of research technique. The difficulty in the case of such colleges is that they do not understand the editor's conception of what the public wants.

TABLE X

METHODS RECOMMENDED FOR CULTIVATING FRIENDLY RELATIONS WITH NEWSPAPERS

Methods	Number
1. Make no conscious attempt to do it	14
2. Be friendly with them	3
3. Call annually but do not wear your welcome out	1
4. Make confidants of the editors	1
5. Cooperate with them	15
6. Give them the news	16
7. Be courteous	11
8. Through civic organizations	5
9. Courteous to all, friendly with none	2
10. Personal contacts	11
11. Advertise freely	13
12. Tell them the truth	2
13. Have neglected to do it	5
14. No report	12

The chief point of interest here is that practically all reporting are convinced of the importance of being on friendly terms with editors, and each seems to believe that he has discovered the precise means by which such relations should be cultivated.

CONCLUSIONS

The reports seem to justify the following conclusions:

1. The small colleges throughout the country, as a rule, have no satisfactory organization for collecting and reporting college news.

2. About one fourth of the colleges have special officers or committees to whom are definitely assigned duties in connection with newspaper publicity.

3. Although city school systems have failed to take full advantage of newspaper publicity, they have advanced far beyond the colleges.

4. Colleges should cultivate the cooperation of the newspapers which comes from mutual understanding, frankness and honesty. It is not necessary to buy the influence of papers through bribery with money, or an insincere display of cordiality, or through business pressure.

5. The policy of colleges regarding paid advertising must be determined by individual institutions because it is dependent upon local conditions. It is pointed out that paid advertising is perfectly legitimate for colleges and can be used without impairing institutional dignity provided good taste is used and the advertisements express the personality of the college.

6. Colleges should take as much pains in providing facts regarding other activities as they do regarding athletics if they expect these activities to receive their share of newspaper publicity. Care should be taken to provide the press with calendars of events and admission tickets for all activities of general interest.

7. Unless there is someone on the college staff who understands newspaper writing, it is better to provide regular reporters with all the facts than to write the articles for publication. Stories are more frequently garbled because of inadequate information than because the newspapers wish to distort the facts.

8. Small colleges could well afford to secure the services of an expert reporter, at least until they became acquainted with sources of news within the college and until they learn what is regarded as "news" by the newspaper.

9. The public has a right to know all about the activities of the colleges who are training its youth even though they are privately endowed. The colleges should be engaged in no activities that they could not defend before the public. The better appreciation of the college and its work which would come from such acquaintance would doubtless help to increase its resources.

CLYDE M. HILL

YALE UNIVERSITY

SCHOOL AND SOCIETY

Volume XXVIII SATURDAY, AUGUST 11, 1928 Number 711

URBAN INFLUENCES ON HIGHER EDUCATION IN ENGLAND

VII. THE URBAN UNIVERSITY OF TO-DAY

IN preceding chapters an attempt has been made to describe the forces which have paved the way for the modern English urban university and moulded it to its present form. Enough has perhaps been said to give a reasonably clear picture of its formal organization and of the various services which it has assumed at the wish of the people. These things have been largely matters of fact rather than of personal observation or opinion. The writer realizes that any attempt by a mere observer from another country to interpret the spirit and success of these universities is subject to the possibility, even probability, of grave error. Such an attempt is necessarily based upon the personal interpretation of unfamiliar conditions and is subject therefore to all the well-known fallibility of the traveler's tale. Nevertheless it would be wrong to exclude from the picture all traces of the direct impressions received in visiting these institutions and in meeting the men who are directing the various phases of their activity. Much of what is to follow has come from these men themselves in personal conversations or through correspondence. It is the hope of the writer that he may prove to be a reasonably accurate reporter and interpreter of the impressions thus received.

To the visitor from the United States the outstanding fact is the spiritual kinship of the English and the American urban universities. Not only is the material form of the service effort largely identical in the two countries, but the motive which actuates it is the same. So true is this that one may picture a delegation of English urban university men as entirely at home in a meeting of the American Association of Urban Universities. So familiar to them would be the subjects discussed that only the difference of local conditions and of academic nomenclature might interpose a temporary obstacle. To both countries the same urban growth has brought similar problems and naturally the methods of solution are largely the same. Though the absence of state universities in England imposes upon the urban institutions certain duties of service to a considerable geographical area, they are nevertheless to be identified with our own urban rather than with our state universities. There is lacking in most of them anything equivalent to the multifarious activities usually designated as "extension-work" at our own state institutions. In most cases, too, a larger part of their financial support comes from national and local urban sources than from other geographical or educational units outside the cities of their location. For this reason there is not the same utter dependence upon the bounty of, for example, a county as is the case of our state institutions in their relation to the state. Hence the non-curricular activities of the English urban university are actually predominantly urban in character. The one exception is the work of the extension lecturer and the tutorial classes which, as already stated, covers considerable areas.

Generally speaking, the tutorial classes are remarkably successful and are enthusiastically encouraged by the cooperating universities. In most cases the university men who make the direct contacts with the representatives of the Workers' Educational Association report that excellent relations are maintained and that a most friendly feeling exists. Practically there are usually two leading figures, the university faculty member in charge of the work and the representative of the W. E. A.[1] These two, if they work together harmoniously, are able to satisfy the requirements of both academic procedure and of labor demand. In some institutions the university representative is quite evidently in supreme command, while at one university, at least, the major direction of affairs[2] is in the hands of the W. E. A. secretary, who has his office in the university buildings. Much of course depends on personality, and the system is flexible enough to allow natural leadership to be developed on either side.

While the relations between the universities and the labor movement are for the most part harmonious, even a casual observer must detect certain tendencies which are not without danger to the existing tutorial class system. These are traceable directly to the more radical labor element, which is by no means negligible in England. This wing of the party believes that little good can come to labor from the existing universities. A visible result of this protest is the foundation of the labor colleges, which endeavor to furnish education for work-people without the assistance of the universities. Naturally a "specialized" system of economics and political science forms the basis of this education. The aim of this element of labor is frankly materialistic, and class consciousness is emphasized. The movement is openly a belligerent one and has been a source of considerable embarrassment to the W. E. A., which must, of necessity, stand well with both the trades unions and the universities. During its earlier years considerable emphasis was put upon the fact that the W. E. A. was primarily an *educational* organization, which had no desire nor reason to participate in political or economic disputes. With the growing strength of labor in political life and with the direct challenge of radicalism in education, this position has become more difficult to maintain. Recently, yielding to labor pressure, the W. E. A. has become party to an agreement ratified by the trades union congress, which involves some coordination beween the various types of working-class education. In a statement explaining its position, the W. E. A. organization says, in part:

> The Trades Union Congress invited the four bodies concerned, *viz.*, the Workers' Educational Association, the National Council of Labour Colleges, Labour College, and Ruskin College, to come together, along with a representative of the Cooperative Union, Ltd., as a committee under its auspices, on the strict understanding that each body should fully preserve its freedom in both principles and teaching methods. This coordination was thus definitely based upon a recognition of the fundamental differences of principle and policy among these bodies. If the W. E. A. had not been convinced that its established educational principles and methods were in no way jeopardized by the agreement, it would not have entered into it.

This association with the opposed school of thought in labor education, has caused considerable annoyance and apprehension in the universities and among local education authorities and has even led to some question whether the present cooperative arrangement for the conduct of tutorial classes can be permanently maintained. However, the importance of the existing difficulty must not be too seriously estimated. It is of interest rather as an indication of certain disrupting tendencies which are inherent in the system and which are unfortunately always to be regarded as

[1] The usual practice is for the joint committee to have two secretaries—one a university member and the other the secretary of the W. E. A. district concerned.

[2] Subject, of course, to the authority of the joint committee.

sources of potential danger. It is to be sincerely hoped that they may never become a serious menace to one of the finest achievements of modern English university development.

Excellent as the tutorial class system has proved itself to be, it has not as yet realized all the hopes of the joint committee which published in 1908 the remarkable report on "Oxford and Working-Class Education." This fact is due not only to economic conditions, but also to certain unavoidable difficulties inherent in the plan. They may be summed up in the statement that tutorial class education is not, and at present can not be, regarded as equivalent to regular university training. For example, only those subjects can be studied which presuppose no secondary-school preparation. Thus the natural sciences,[3] mathematics and the languages, at least on a university basis, are largely eliminated as possibilities, and an undue emphasis is given to the social sciences and those subjects which do not depend upon previous periods of rigorous mental discipline. Also, the work is not recognized as leading to a degree, although in some cases the necessary residence period may be shortened and the student's career furthered by scholarship grants. As a matter of fact, however, the number of tutorial students eventually attaining the degree has never been large. Mansbridge describes the tutorial class student as follows:[4]

Two main types of persons join the classes, one consisting of men and women who are convinced that their work as citizens is accomplished inadequately because of their lack of knowledge, and who decide deliberately to give a great portion of three years to the acquisition of such knowledge; the other consisting of those who join the classes as the result of pure educational impulse. These types do not remain fixed throughout the years of the class. Men pass from one to the other. In any case, it frequently happens that the class becomes so large a portion of the lives of the students that they can not with equanimity contemplate ceasing attendance.

Undoubtedly the tutorial class has attained its greatest success in reaching considerable numbers of work-people and in elevating the class rather than the individual. It has therefore come nearer to realizing this educational ideal of the labor movement than it has to opening up a way for work-people, either adolescent or adult, to enter the university. For our purpose it is of interest to try to analyze the reaction of the tutorial class system on the university itself. Unlike the earlier extension classes, it can not claim credit for the founding of new universities, but it undoubtedly has brought the already-existing universities before the English people in a very favorable light and has gained approval from wide classes of population. Perhaps the most important influence has been that exercised upon the teaching staff. There can be no question of the salutary effect upon any teacher of occasional contact with adult minds in the practice of his profession. In all the universities visited, the men engaged in tutorial classwork emphasized this point and seemed to find a large measure of satisfaction in the opportunity offered them for acquaintance, and often friendship, with their maturer students. The increased number of teaching positions also has served as a valuable outlet in providing careers for ambitious young scholars, thus bringing new blood and new ideas into English university life. It is perhaps still too early to detect any marked influence in curriculum or subject-matter. However, faculty members were encountered who professed to see in this contact with the working classes a potential source of reorganization in the teaching of certain branches of the social sciences. At any rate the workingman has, in the tutorial classes, a hitherto unknown opportunity to present his political, social and economic views to the

[3] Except, perhaps, biology.

[4] University Tutorial Classes, p. 93.

university world. These classes are also responsible for the creation of a new genus of teacher at the English university, namely, the staff tutor, who devotes his entire time to the extramural classwork. Opinions differ as to the desirability of this arrangement. Proponents argue that the interest of such a man is undivided and his work therefore more effective than that of the regular university teacher whose tutorial class is a side issue. Opponents, on the other hand, complain that the staff tutor is too remotely associated with university life and that he can not therefore truly represent the university before his classes.

A short digression may be allowable here to consider the viewpoint of the English people toward the tutorial classes in so far as they manifest any attitude at all. As we have already seen, it is generally a favorable one. Strangely enough, the opposition, unimportant though it may be, comes from the most widely separated classes of society. The radical labor element, as has already been stated, looks with distrust upon the "capitalistic" tendency of university training and prefers to teach its own system of economics in the labor colleges. At the other end, a small element of the aristocracy and plutocracy still disbelieves in education for the working classes, and regards these efforts as a foolish and even dangerous experiment. Into this feeling is injected some of the traditional difference in viewpoint between the older aristocracy of the county and the newer democracy of the city. Thus we see these tutorial classes accused of aristocratic or capitalistic tendencies by the radicals, and of radicalism by the aristocrats. Fortunately the great mass of the people pays no attention to these divergent opinions and is fully in sympathy with the universities.

A vital factor of the success of the tutorial classes is to be found in the fact that the student pays but a nominal fee. This is explained by the desire to make the work available to even the poorest workman, and is justly regarded as an important step in educational democracy. It is noticeable, however, that the fees charged regular university students are considerably higher than the tutorial class fees and there seems here to exist an unjustifiable discrimination against the adolescent student. The explanation has been offered that the adult classes are *non-vocational* and are given in direct preparation for citizenship rather than in preparation for a profession or vocation, as is predominantly the case in the regular session. While this reasoning may not be universally regarded as sound, there is in our own country an exact parallel to be found in the law of the state of Ohio governing municipal universities. This law provides in effect that, in such institutions, tuition may be charged in all courses except in the college of liberal arts, *i.e.*, a student may receive a liberal education without expense, but he must pay for instruction in those branches of knowledge by which he expects to earn his living.

At only one English university, Liverpool, does there seem to be a tendency to work independently in offering tutorial classes (or their equivalent), as well as with the W. E. A.[5] It is argued with some justice that all trade unions have not cared to affiliate with the W. E. A. and that there is no reason why the university should refuse to grant a direct appeal from these organizations. Thus classes have been given direct, for example, to the dock workers' union, at their own request, without reference to the W. E. A. organization. The same independent tendency is marked also in the Scotch universities. In England, however, it is the exception to the general rule, and the W. E. A. is, almost every-

[5] Nottingham has a number of classes in connection with a special miners' welfare adult education committee, which is a joint committee with the department of adult education, and is financed out of the welfare fund.

where, the officially-recognized agency for cooperation.

The question has often been asked whether the English tutorial class-system could be successfully transferred to the United States. As a matter of fact, sporadic attempts have been made to interest certain American colleges in teaching a peculiarly "labor" type of political and economic science, but the response from both workmen and colleges has been small. The two reasons which render the success of tutorial classes doubtful in our own country are to be found in the material prosperity of the American workman and the democracy of educational opportunity. American labor is more adequately rewarded and hence more content with existing conditions than is the case in England. More important, however, is the fact that opportunity is open in every large city for the workman not only to secure adult education of any type he desires, but also to send his children to college after they have received a free secondary education. A workers' educational association, as a connecting link between labor and the universities, would be an anomaly in the United States, for no such link is necessary. The great state and city universities belong to the work-people as freely as to the rest of the population, and are by them as freely used. Useful, even indispensable, as is the W. E. A. in England, it must be regarded as the product of purely English conditions. Thus it has met with some measure of success in the British dominions and colonies, where English tradition prevails. But in the United States adult education must develop not merely as a workmen's enterprise, but in terms of the entire population.

Several efforts to provide education for work-people by some phase of the part-time method have been made at the English universities, but these have never assumed large proportions. At Birmingham the plan is outlined as follows:[6]

Industrial Certificate Department

As the result of an agreement made with certain trade unions, the University of Birmingham has established a special department for the systematic instruction of students nominated by the unions. The course occupies two full days—Monday and Tuesday—of each week during the twenty-six weeks of the university session. The scheme has been approved by a representative body of Birmingham trade unionists; and the administrative committee includes, along with academic members, one representative of each union sending six or more members.

The lectures and tutorial assistance are provided by the university without charge; and note-books and text-books are also supplied freely to the students. The unions, for their part, undertake to make compensation, where necessary, for loss of wages, and in the case of union officials, to free them from all duties on the days they attend the university. Further, the unions are expected to make the necessary arrangements with employers as to leave of absence from work.

The subjects of study are:

1. Modern European history
2. National and local government
3. Modern industry and economics
4. Social philosophy
5. English literature.

In addition to these courses of lectures tutorial assistance is given to students in the principal subjects; and special stress is laid on the preparation of essays and practice in clear expression.

An industrial certificate is awarded after the examination, which is held in June.

The plan outlined above has evidently not satisfied the expectations of those concerned, since it is just now in abeyance.

A somewhat similar opportunity is offered by the university college of Nottingham for adult working-class students. The course takes up two whole days in each week and is planned to cover two years:[7]

First Year

Economics
Economic organization
Industrial history
General history
English

Second Year

Advanced economics and economic organization
Statistics

[6] Calendar of the University of Birmingham for the Session 1925–26, p. 187.

[7] University College, Nottingham, "Prospectus of Day Classes," 1925–26, p. 79–80.

Political history
Social psychology
Logical method.

Other subjects may be added, if time allows. A certificate is granted for satisfactory completion of the work, and free studentships are granted by the college to selected students on condition that the trades union or other organization makes arrangements for absence from employment and for maintenance where necessary. The plan differs essentially in many ways from our own cooperative engineering system, but particularly in the fact that the college deals with the organizations rather than the employer directly.

The University College of Nottingham, which was the first college developed directly from extension teaching, has the distinction of possessing the only department of adult education in England.[8] Thus its head, Professor R. Peers, M. C., M. A., is the only professor of adult education at an English higher institution. The department, according to its constitution, is organized for the following activities:

(a) The provision of three-year university tutorial classes and one-year preparatory classes leading up to tutorial classes.

(b) The provision of university extension courses and other courses of lectures of a university character in non-vocational subjects.

(c) The arrangement of internal courses at the university college and other approved centers for adult working-class students, more particularly for students in extra-mural classes and similar students who might profit by continuous training, but whose circumstances do not permit them to take advantage of the ordinary facilities for full-time study.

(d) The training and provision of tutors and lecturers for extra-mural classes and courses.

(e) The investigation of problems connected with adult education, and the publication of such reports and information as may be approved by the departmental committee.

Two factors at least distinguish the work in adult education at Nottingham: (a) its organization as an independent department, rather than as a subsidiary function, drawing upon other departments; this means the creation of a staff whose whole time and energy is given to this highly-specialized work; and (b) its expressed conception of adult education in England as eventually capable of development into a science covering all classes and widely-extended fields of knowledge, in distinction to its present commonly accepted limitation to work-people. The success of this department of adult education, expressly organized with a single object in view, is witnessed by the fact that Nottingham has more tutorial classes than any other English college or university.[9]

The efforts just mentioned, supported by government grants for the education of work-people, are typical of the attitude of the state toward higher education in England. There exists a feeling of *national* responsibility, which is entirely absent in the United States. In England the urban universities lean heavily on the national exchequer for support, as well as on the councils of their own city and adjacent communities. In fact, as has been previously stated, every university and university college in England is now in receipt of income from national sources. This is not surprising in a nation which has subsidized a great industry (mining) and which maintains an unemployment relief system. In our own country it is the in-

[8] However, a number of other universities (Cambridge, London, etc.), have approximately the same thing under other names. University College at Exeter has a "Department of Extra-Mural Studies."

[9] See table on p. 743, SCHOOL AND SOCIETY, June 23, 1928.

dividual state and the city, not the nation, which have adopted higher education as a function. There are, however, certain important differences. In America no state is called upon to support, even in part, eleven great universities, as well as numerous colleges of different kinds. Nor is the plan of joint university support by state and city known in America generally.[10] The English system is particularly interesting to us in view of the efforts made in recent years to establish a department of education in our national government, and the initial desire of its proponents to link up with it a plan for national subsidies to certain forms of education. The failure to extend this latter phase of the attempt, beyond its already long-established usage in the Department of Agriculture, seems to prove that the American people do not believe in joint support of universities by several political units. Thus it is probable that state and municipal universities will continue to keep their individual characters in the United States. The English urban university, however, partakes of the nature of both, in so far as its financial support is concerned.

If we put aside consideration of purely formal differences in organization and source of income, the new English university remains the spiritual brother of the American municipal institution. Both are free from religious prejudice or test, both are the result of local pride and industrial or economic need, and both find their highest expression in service to the students of their own communities. They may be justly ranked among the best creations of modern urban civilization.

PARKE REXFORD KOLBE

THE POLYTECHNIC INSTITUTE
OF BROOKLYN, N. Y.

[10] The Georgia School of Technology receives a grant from the city of Atlanta in addition to its income from the state.

THE PLACE OF THE HIGH-SCHOOL LIBRARY IN A NATIONAL LIBRARY SERVICE

THE influence of social and economic conditions on business, industry, education and government has made nothing short of a revolution in educational procedure the world over. In no division of our educational system has this change been more revolutionary than in secondary schools and in no other division has such rapid progress been made.

To our old high schools came a fairly homogeneous mass of pupils with well-established traditions, language and vocabulary. Few came with any intelligent interest—many with a real distaste for scholarship, although scholarship was all the old type of school offered. To the school of this day comes a heterogeneous mass with many diverging interests, all of which our schools try to satisfy, for while scholarship must be emphasized, the development of the individual so that he may fill his rightful place in society is the great work of the school. We no longer think of pupils in the mass but as individuals. How can they, within the brief span of high-school years, be given right attitudes of responsibility and self-guidance toward right standards of living? Education which sends its pupils out with the ideals of free competitive struggle instead of ideals and practice of social cooperation which enables the individual to be of greatest service falls far short of its opportunity.

Librarians speak with pride of the contribution the library is making to adult education. "When boys and girls are taught to like and depend upon books, the problem of adult education will be largely solved," an educational leader has said. Obviously then if books are to be the tools of the age, we must teach the use of them. We know that all learning is a slow process, brought about only by careful direction and systematic training. The lack of this systematic training during school years accounts for the necessity of now trying to bridge the gap—beginning at the wrong end. Never can skill so acquired bring the satisfaction, the joy, the spontaneity of that begun or originated, in the readers' youthful impulses. The game belongs to them and their joy in their ability to hunt out their own material and select their books will develop a power and even a leadership much needed in this day. As we are dealing with the individual, the library must find a way to recognize the pupil's initiative, his capacity for study, his interests, and thus prepare him for self-directed personal development beyond the school. His natural urges and curiosities must be conserved and directed in such a way as to bring to him the joy of work and the power of self-direction which go to make a successful adult.

The cardinal principles of secondary education as set forth by the American National Education Association as objectives of modern education in a democracy are worthy home membership, health, mastery of the tools and technique of learning, vocational effectiveness, useful citizenship, wise use of leisure time and ethical character. In the light of these objectives, the high-school library assumes new importance in the field of education, and becomes one of the most vital factors in the achievement of this goal.

The challenge of worthy home membership carries with it the art of living together. The home of to-day, reflecting the influence of motion pictures, the automobile, the increasing rights of women and children, is very different from the home of yesterday. To see a typical American girl, well dressed and speaking excellent English, escorting her mother wearing a shawl over her head, speaking broken English, or none at all, gives a new conception of what the school is meaning in the lives of these people, as well as a new conception of the tremendous opportunity and responsibilities of the institution. These children become the interpreters of our customs, ideals and standards to their homes. Through our books on domestic science, woodworking, cooking, sewing, study of color, textiles and laundry work, the library can do much for them.

Health has never received the proper attention from youth. The library must cooperate in the effort to raise health standards. A healthy body is necessary to a healthy mind. Books—good books—are our most powerful factors for producing a healthy mind. Only a healthy mind can be an active one. Lazy thinking and habits break down mentality and morality. The school library can do much to inspire the individual to read, to investigate, to make his own life and that of his fellow men healthier. The discoveries of science furnish great inspiration for independent reading. What normal youth will not devour books on athletics, swimming, golf, tennis, track? Through these books he soon learns where he is weak, and what corrective measures he can use. This is the great object of all our education—to make it carry over into living. Too many times there is a gap between what we know and what we do.

Mastery of tools and technique of learning is of great importance. We are just beginning to realize that the library is a storehouse of the sharpest, finest tools, and to avail ourselves of their assistance. For fifty years the library has stood ready to help, but has been used only in the most indifferent way. Books used to be for the scholar, the student and the man of leisure, only. To-day, all must turn to books. The housekeeper must study home sanitation, food values, domestic economy; the public official must know how to study municipal statistics, city planning, recreation, welfare work. All are realizing slowly the value of books. We can no longer expect youth to accept the coin of our wisdom. We have learned that the only way is to place in his hand the tools, teach him how to use them and leave him to get the experience, the wisdom for himself. This method alone will make cultivated practical citizens.

Vocational effectiveness is demanded by the industrial world. Only through books will be opened the great field of human interests and information to broaden and develop habit and ability for any work. Books will help every one to choose wisely the service which he will render, and to continue development in chosen lines. The right to find what he can do best, to labor, to produce, to the end that he will not be a burden on society is the birthright of every child.

The challenge to citizenship must give to all a new vision of our responsibilities. Not every youth can take courses in civics, economics and sociology while in high school, but the library is open to all, and much can be done to influence his reading along these lines. The children of to-day are our citizens of to-morrow—they will elect our officials, plan our cities, man our industries. Somehow they must be taught what they have inherited and how to carry their share of the burden. No classroom can develop citizens of this type, but the lives of Lincoln, Gladstone, Washington, Franklin do teach the long struggle to make the safer civilization in which we now live.

The use of leisure time is closely allied with home membership. Many of our problems of social and economic life will be solved when the home has been made attractive enough for people to find pleasure within it. The school library may prove a most powerful factor here; a taste for books, a habit of finding entertainment in them, is no longer the privilege of a leisured few. In other days only these few could read and develop libraries, of which there are such magnificent examples all over Europe. To-day this privilege extends to the masses and is about the only force against commercialized leisure controlled by men whose only interest is money making. Unless we can systematically foster this privilege, teach our youth the joy of reading, give an appetite for something better, their impressions and desires can lead to nothing but deterioration in thinking and mental vigor.

To develop character, which is the culmination of all other objectives, we must give these youths the experience of putting into practice again and again the principles of conduct which are the guarantee of good character. It is those who leave school with unformed characters who become tools of the unscrupulous boss. Companionship with books has long been recognized as the corner-stone of character. Never has our moral obligation to be intelligent been greater than now; to be intelligent to guard, to preserve, to improve, to transmit institutions and ideals handed down by generations. Our greatest task is to equip our youth with such education that they will develop attitudes of fair play, and a regard for rights of others, which eventually grow from a sense of cooperation and of responsibility toward society. This can come only from working in an atmosphere of proper stimulation, and to provide this atmosphere the school library exists. Every pupil must fashion some philosophy of life; we need to help him to see and feel some of the thrills and joys of those who have lived and served for the good they could do, and not for the material reward. The story of Pasteur, happy in study and service; of Grenfell, living a life of hardship because Labrador needed his skill, and the stories of the lives of many others will help to make his life less sordid and selfish. The eminent French psychologist and philosopher, Le Bon, in his book "Revolt of the World," says, "The principal function of all education should be to create those habits which are guides of every day life. The future will belong not to those whose intellect is greatest, but to those whose character is strongest." What a challenge to the school library! The public library alone will not do; the habit forming library must be inside, not outside the school. We must begin with the youth of the day.

The modern high-school library is rapidly developing into a specialized form adapted to its own peculiar needs. One of the most important factors of its success is the appreciation by the principal and teaching staff of the functions of the library, and their whole-hearted cooperation in helping to achieve these functions. To become a vital unit of the school, the libary must establish its identity and have its functions recognized and respected; it must be free to work out its own salvation. The giving out of information, through books and other materials used to supplement class work, is a most important function, but not the whole function. Classes in history read widely in fiction, travel, biography and sociology as well as history. English classes add biography, history and sociology to literature. All use every means to enrich the class work. Thus the library becomes a vital part of the life of the school, and pupils learn to appreciate and possess the library. The high-school library needs a tremendously live collection of materials of various kinds: books, magazines, clippings, pamphlets, pictures, victrola records and maps. It is just as important to be able to furnish a model of a boat for a boy who is making one as it is to have a classical dictionary on the reference shelves.

Only about forty-seven per cent. of those who enter American secondary schools complete the course. In our own school, about fifty per cent. are foreign born. The process of making a living, the adjustment into the environment of a new country constitutes a positive struggle, and supersedes all other activities for culture. All the finest antecedents of birth, custom and social position of their own race are lost in the confused order of evaluation of the new distractions of the day. Some agency, logically the high-school library, must arouse them to an appreciation of true valuation and delight in reading for recreation. Youth has the happy faculty of projecting itself into characters which interest it. The thrill the adolescent boy or girl gets from reading is an experience that comes once in a lifetime. To have a girl in tears because Jo did not marry Laurie; to have a boy describe "The Talisman" as a "Whiz of a book. I sat up till two o'clock to finish it"; or another to call Barrie "The guy who writes keen plays"; to have "Cloister and the Hearth" described as the "Swellest book I ever read; it made me cry," serves to give us a renewed appreciation of literature branded as old-fashioned, which is too often buried under the mass of modern production.

The really efficient high-school library surely has its place in any system of national library service. In America, we find the following types: First, that linking the public library system to the school system by cooperative arrangement, whereby the public library administers the school library, housed and financed by the board of education. Second, the school library under the supervision of the school division of the public library, usually under an agreement whereby book collection, transportation, supplies and equipment are furnished largely at expense of the board of education. These partnership plans should furnish only temporary relief and can only be justified when there are no other means by which a school library can be obtained. It is difficult to find concentration to-day under favorable conditions. The coming and going of the public can not be otherwise than most distracting to school atmosphere and discipline. The school library will lose, too, by the lowering of the tone of the book collection, and the librarian, if she understands the need of the high-school work, will have no time for the general public. Third, the type par excellence, the library belonging wholly to the school. Each school is different, and each group of teachers will work to the same ends along entirely different paths. Each library must have the most advantageous location, and must adapt itself to its type of school, class of pupils and plans of teachers—ever vital coworker. For is it not the mental workshop, the laboratory, the center of the intellectual and cultural life of the school? Therefore there must be freedom, easy access to shelves and every encouragement to browse, with shelves showing quality more than quantity, and a recognition that what pupils want they want at once. Interest lost may never be regained. The library must work, primarily, always to interest, to make pupils want more and more, better and better.

And what are the results? Who can tell? "Life is a lot bigger than it looks" is the comment recently heard from a high-school junior, who had just finished reading DeMille's "Strongheart." One of our late encyclopedias says "The most potent and most economical influence exerted for good on young and old is through reading." Is not our chief task to create in our pupils such a love for books, such an appreciation of libraries and dependence upon them, that when school days are over, they will turn instinctively to other libraries at their disposal for all they have come to expect from the library in their school? The child of to-day has a right to receive while in school that experience and training which will obviate confusion and embarrassment in furthering his self-education in the years to come.

The field of the high school is a fascinating one for library service, rich in opportunity and rewards. It gives a chance to contribute to the well-being of good citizens, through the fostering of good reading habits, and cultivates a connection with public libraries and those of other institutions. "Preparation for participation in the ever increasingly complex social life of our times demands a training as wide as life itself." Surely no type of library service can be more inspiring, or can be more worthy of the best efforts of our profession.

MAY INGLES

TECHNICAL HIGH SCHOOL,
OMAHA, NEBRASKA

SUPERVISION OF INSTRUCTION IN HIGHER EDUCATION

THAT poor teaching characterizes much of the work in higher education is a generally accepted fact. This situation is especially true in the liberal arts college. In elementary and secondary education the problem of instruction has been carefully studied, and great progress has been made in attaining effective means of instruction and in perfecting objective measurements to test the results of instruction. This is not the case in higher education. In general, it may be said that instruction in higher education is not as effective as in elementary and secondary education. The statements of careful observers and investigators in this field confirm the existence of this real weakness of the college:

Scientific method in college administration and college teaching must still be mainly a prophecy.

Not much can be said about its application up to date.[1]

> I have long contended that the source of half of the ills to which the modern college is heir, lies in the prevailing methods of instruction. . . . If the content of college courses was more closely related to the demands of after life, if the objectives, in other words, were clear to those who pursued them, the intellectual tempo of the institution would be immediately quickened. But the college courses should also be reorganized so as to stimulate independent activity on the part of students.[2]

> The best teaching is found in the lowest grades of our educational system. Much teaching in the college is sterile.[3]

> Teaching in elementary and secondary schools is superior to instruction in institutions of higher learning.[4]

There appears to be good evidence that college teaching is not as successful and effective as it ought to be. The reason for this situation, and the conditions that have made it difficult to supervise college teaching and to measure the results of instruction will be discussed in the following paragraphs.

The lack of definite objectives on the part of the college is partly responsible for ineffective teaching. Furthermore, the evaluation of the results of instruction, when the purpose is cultural, is very difficult. Certain traditions have also grown up respecting college teaching that hamper any constructive plan of supervision. Since little or no professional training has been demanded for college teaching, college teachers themselves have had little interest in any scientific study of college teaching. In considering prospective teachers scholarship and the possession of degrees have been emphasized. Apparently, college administrators believe firmly in the time-worn principle *"he who knows can teach."*

Klapper[5] gives the following causes of ineffective teaching: (1) only equipment necessary for successful teaching, thorough knowledge of the subject; (2) lack of sympathetic understanding of the student's viewpoints; (3) absence of constructive supervision. "In a college such supervision would stir deep resentment. The college teacher is, in all matters of teaching, a law unto himself. He sees little of the actual teaching of his colleagues; they see little of his . . . methods of teaching are rarely, if ever, brought up for discussion. The results are inevitable. Weaknesses of teaching are perpetuated, while the devices and practices of an effective teacher remain unknown to his colleagues." (4) No standards required for college teaching, except scholarship and character, and no knowledge of educational technique required.

In a recent bulletin[6] of the Association of American Colleges, Dean Randall, of Brown University, chairman of the commission on "The Enlistment and Training of College Teachers," gives the results of a questionnaire sent to 267 institutions. In reply to this question, "What do you consider the most essential qualification for teaching in college?" two hundred and twenty-five or 84.3 per cent., mentioned scholarship; seventy-seven or 28.8 per cent. teaching ability; sixty-seven or 25.1 per cent. professional training.

In the small college there is danger that the members of the teaching staff may not make contacts with the leaders and investigators in their own field. The very organization of these institutions makes such a condition a common one. This inevitably results in ineffective teaching, since no teacher, at least on this level, can do his best without a knowledge of the development and progress in his field of study and without the intellectual stimulus that comes from contacts with those who interest themselves in the problems of teaching and research in his special field. In the denominational college a considerable number of the teaching staff are

[1] Kelly, F. J., "Scientific Method in College Administration and College Teaching," SCHOOL AND SOCIETY, Vol. 20, 1924, Sept. 27.

[2] Capen, S. P., "Dilemma of College of Arts and Sciences," *Educational Review*, Vol. 61, pp. 277–285 (1921).

[3] Klapper, Paul, "The College Teacher and His Professional Status," "Educational Administration and Supervision," Vol. II (1925), pp. 73–91.

[4] Taylor, W. S., "Supervision of College Instruction," Bulletin No. 7, University of Kentucky (1926).

[5] Klapper, Paul, "College Teaching." New York: World Book Co. Chap. 3 (1920).

[6] Vol. XIII, No. 2, April, 1927.

graduates of theological seminaries. Frequently their training is limited to this type of education. Unfortunately, this training has made many of them firm believers in the "ex-cathedra" method of imparting information. College teachers who have had some experience in the public school system or whose graduate work has had some contact with the professional schools of education usually show a fine professional spirit.

The dangers of turning inexperienced teachers loose to do as they please is pointed out by Flexner.[7]

> For instance, a newly-made doctor whose personal fortune and interest lie elsewhere is appointed to teach college boys: in the name of academic freedom he is turned loose in the classroom to follow his own bent. He teaches what and as he thinks fit. As a result much of the instruction given to undergraduates is far too highly specialized in content and method of presentation to be adapted to any but expert use . . . Can the untrained instructor be left free to take such account of these facts as he pleases, whether in the substance offered or the method pursued? . . . A college instructor in English, frankly confessed himself appalled by the difficulties he encountered, told me recently that no superior officer had ever set foot in his classroom, that he knew only in a general way what other men were doing with the problems with which he was contending—that he was, in a word, academically free to do what he could or would.

Supervision of instruction as a general program in higher education evidently does not exist. Objection is made to supervision on the grounds that it means a loss of freedom for the teacher. On the contrary, supervision of the right kind will free the teachers from worries regarding the judgment or evaluation of their work. It is a most undesirable situation when the president of an institution has no better means of receiving information regarding the efficiency of the teachers than the reports of students.

In vocational and professional training, the results of instruction are being tested by objective measurements like practice courses, practice teaching, medical and dental clinics. Various other experiments have been attempted to measure the results of college education. In 1923–24,[8] the School of Education of Oklahoma Agricultural and Mechanical College devised a method of supervising instruction by means of the opinions of students. Questionnaires were sent to all the students, requesting them to evaluate the methods used by the instructors. No definite information is given as to the success of the experiment, except a statement that it resulted in an improvement in their instruction. Former President Mezes,[9] of the College of the City of New York, suggests a method of training college teachers in which professional training, practice teaching and study or research in their special field, each takes a definite portion of the candidate's time. Dean Randall,[10] in his report in a recent bulletin of the Association of American Colleges, received the following answers to question 13 of his questionnaire: "What type of instruction do you offer to prospective teachers?"—"Some institutions reported it their practice to send a delegate from each department to supervise or instruct the young instructors who are conducting freshman courses. Some reported that they held bi-monthly meetings among the various departments where papers were read on problems relating to teaching. One institution reported that the faculty formed a class each year for the purpose of making a careful study of the teachers' problems. Another reported that they made an attempt through the dean's office to assist and interest young teachers in their work. Another reported that graduate assistants serve as apprentices to senior professors." Dean Taylor,[11] of the University of Kentucky, recommends that in large institutions a dean of instruction be appointed who will be responsible for improving instruction in the institution. R. M. Hughes, formerly president of Miami University, reported the following interesting plan tried in Miami. Some experienced member of the teaching staff was relieved of all

[7] Flexner, Abraham, "The American College," 1908, pp. 189–193.

[8] Patterson, Herbert, "An Experiment in Supervising College Teaching," School and Society, Vol. 21 (1925), pp. 146–147.

[9] Klapper, *ibid.*, Chap. II.

[10] *Ibid.*

[11] *Ibid.*, pp. 98–106.

duties on a certain day and spent this day visiting the institution and reported his findings at the end of the day to the president.

At the Institute for Administrative Officers of Institutions of Higher Education held at the University of Chicago, July 18 to 22, 1927, the deans in conference expressed themselves in favor of some practical plan of supervision and improvement of instruction.

There is abundant evidence to show that there is much ineffective teaching in college. The constant use of the lecture method in some institutions; the failure to make application in teaching to the everyday life of the student; the lack of knowledge of educational technique; all tend to substantiate the charge of ineffective teaching against the college. There is great need of improvement in instruction. Supervision of the right kind will doubtless bring about a change. A good deal of information regarding teaching can be secured from students, but it will hardly suffice as a constructive plan of supervision. In large institutions a special officer known as dean of instruction, who could devote all his time to this work, appears to be a practical plan of supervision. In smaller institutions, the head of the department of education might be relieved of a part of his duties and assigned to the dean's office to assist in this important work—in case the representative of this department has had the professional training that would fit him to do this work effectively.

Improvement of teaching will be one of the main objectives in the program of college administrators of the future. They will agree with this statement: "Ineffective college teaching will not improve until professional teaching standards are set up by respected institutions."[12]

W. F. Sanders

Park College

EDUCATIONAL EVENTS

PROGRESS IN THE PUNJAB

The quinquennial "Report on the Progress of Education in the Punjab" for the period ended March 31, 1927, has recently been printed. According to the London *Times Educational Supplement,* the report shows that the number of pupils in attendance at institutions of all grades increased in the five years by 88.7 per cent. The percentage of pupils under instruction to the total population rose from 3 to 5.72. If girls are left out of account, the percentage for boys alone works up to 9.32, a figure unsurpassed by any other Indian province. Experience in Indian elementary education shows, however, that it is quite possible for such figures to give a far too pleasing impression of the real measure of progress.

The increases recorded in the Punjab have been accompanied by measures to ensure the development of elementary education on sound lines. It is a commonplace of the problem that few of the pupils enrolled in Indian primary schools have the persistence or inclination to stay the course. In the five years the increase of enrolment in Class 1 has been on a much larger scale than in Class 4. This is inevitable since almost all new pupils must necessarily take their places in the first class. The significant feature of the returns is that the proportions of enrolment in the upper classes have been improved, especially in the last year of the quinquennium.

A potent cause of the withdrawal of children after only a year or so at school has been the inefficiency of the work in the infants' class, more particularly in the one-teacher school. This type of school is extravagant as well as inefficient, if the average cost of educating a literate is calculated. In 1922 there were as many as 2,754 single-teacher schools, but this large number was reduced before the end of the quinquennium to 1,000. It will be recalled that the Linlithgow Commission has recommended that wherever possible in British India the Punjab plan of establishing "central" schools and converting single-teacher schools into branch schools should be adopted. Another direction in which the commission commends Punjab progress to the consideration of other local governments is that of the conversion of primary schools into lower middle schools. The Punjab report states that, in spite of the forebodings of a few years ago, the lower middle school is fast increasing in popularity, and that parents usually prefer this type of school to the similar classes of an Anglo-vernacular school.

[12] Klapper, *ibid.*

The vernacular system is far stronger and more stable than it was at the beginning of the quinquennium.

Lord Linlithgow and his colleagues came to the conclusion that the effective remedy for the unsatisfactory state of primary education in India is the introduction of the compulsory system as rapidly as local conditions permit. Here again the Punjab has led the way. Sir George Anderson points out that the somewhat clumsy term "voluntary compulsion" is open to misconstruction. Compulsion is voluntary only in so far as the parents in any given area apply for the enforcement of compulsion on their own initiative, but once the application has been approved by government the attendance of the pupils concerned is compulsory. He describes the system in the Punjab as having the support of popular opinion and constituting "a powerful means of encouraging the growing enthusiasm for education which is filling the minds of the masses." In 1921 there were only two municipal areas in which compulsion was in force. By last September the system had been applied to 52 urban and 1,118 rural areas.

The difficulties of enforcing attendance in areas where education is compulsory are by no means as great as were originally anticipated. Sir George Anderson writes that it is comparatively easy to ensure the attendance of 80 per cent. of the boys who should be at school. The difficult problem is to bring prompt action against the few remaining defaulters. The effect of compulsion is very largely the filling up of the sparsely attended upper classes of a primary school or department. Therefore the appointment of the additional teachers required would not only increase the roll, but also ensure far greater stability in the teaching. Rightly understood, compulsion means economy, for it prevents wastage of effort through early leakage.

The beneficent effects of the revised system of grants assessed in accordance with the needs of each district, the institution of schools for adults and of village libraries, the provincialization of schools, and the establishment of intermediate colleges in remote parts of the province have been greatly enhanced by the new activities passing under the name of community work. These activities, the resolution states, "have imparted to our school education the reality it lacked before by bringing it into close relation with rural life and pursuits."

STUDENT EXCHANGES BETWEEN FRANCE AND ENGLAND

Seven years ago the Association France-Grande Bretagne, in order to cement the trans-Channel rapprochement, was organized for the purpose of making arrangements by which young French people, between the ages of 14 and 18 years, could be received into English homes in exchange for English girls and boys who would be taken into French families. There was no question of payment on either side. The time of sojourn was ten months.

The New York *Times* reports that M. Desclos, assistant director of the National University office at Paris, has drawn attention to the fact that the project has worked out in a very one-sided manner—for every seven French children who now want to go to England, there is only one English child desirous of going to France. For the first four years the exchange was about even; then in 1925, 211 French students applied for admission to English homes, while 203 English sought to sojourn in French homes; in 1926, the figures were respectively 267 and 164; in 1927, 266 and 155; while this year it is 350 and 50.

While M. Desclos confesses that he has not fathomed the cause for the change, Captain B. S. Townroe, the secretary of the association in London, is more outspoken. He flatly says that the English people have no appreciation of the advantages offered—they are too insular, particularly in regard to language. He admits, however, that the difference in the standard of living may have something to do with it. The English boys and girls miss the customary porridge or bacon and eggs that so often form the English breakfast. Then, again, while the tea habit is growing in France, it has not yet become a family institution. Furthermore, the French are said to be more adaptable and cross the Channel with the idea of getting the best out of whatever may be in store, while English youth crosses doubtfully and predisposed to have an unhappy time.

THE INTERNATIONAL CHILD WELFARE CONGRESS

The International Child Welfare Congress, which was held recently in Paris, attracted delegates from countries in most parts of the civilized world. Considerable attention was given during the congress to open-air schools and kindred institutions.

One interesting fact which came out in the discussion was that the open-air movement is destined to have an effect not merely in its own specialized sphere but on methods of education generally. The Times *Educational Supplement* reports that M. Ad. Ferrière, of the International Bureau of Education of Geneva, who made a general survey of the subject from the pedagogic point of view, insisted on the necessity of new methods in the open-air school. He was extremely critical of the open-air schools for delicate children, which imposed on their pupils the same curriculum as that obtaining in the regular elementary schools. "To profit intelligently by the resources of the open-air," said M. Ferrière, "constitutes a science and an art which have to be learnt," and his survey showed a remarkable tendency of open-air schools in various countries to develop on special lines, involving a departure from the commonly practised methods of schooling. The common principle which he discovers as being followed is that of the interaction of the health of the intelligence and the health of the body.

M. Lemonier, who carried out an inquiry on French open-air schools, found that their curriculum covered less superficial area than that of the elementary schools, but had greater depth. "Few books, little writing, few essays and similar tasks, but much talking on the direct observation of nature, sensory exercises, much drawing, singing, light manual work, gardening, physical training." As to the method of teaching, it is "analytic, Socratic, active with the participation of the pupils . . . centres of daily interest adapted to the seasons . . . exercise of judgment, verification by experiment, encouragement of initiative."

M. Emilio Fournie, of Montevideo, also insisted that education in the open-air school takes on "an essentially experimental or intuitive character; the child spontaneously observes the nature which surrounds him; he observes and discovers for himself."

Miss Margaret MacMillan, in an enthusiastic picture of the Rachel MacMillan Nursery and Camp Schools, said that to-day the open-air school was a kind of sanatorium, but ventured to predict that soon nearly all the schools would be open-air institutions.

According to Miss Mary E. Murphy, of the Elizabeth McCormick Memorial Fund, the trend in the United States in the last few years has been towards open-window rooms instead of open-air schools. This is due at once to the desire to meet the growing demand for fresh-air facilities, and the need felt by school boards to satisfy it as much as they can without a crushing expenditure. In Belgium the open-air schools seem to have retained for the most part the ordinary curriculum of the public elementary school. In Italy, Germany, Switzerland and Greece open-air schools are places of educational initiative and experiment, with no strict adhesion to the ordinary school programs.

A comparison of reports from various countries shows a notable similarity in time-tables in schools for children of defective health. In most of them lessons in class occupy three hours a day. There are four meals a day, with a siesta of 1½ to 2 hours after the mid-day meal. One speaker said, however, that in New York the rest was taken immediately before mid-day in order to avoid the loss of appetite resulting from fatigue. Cleanliness is everywhere one of the chief subjects in teaching and practice. Clothing varies with climate and season, with the maximum exposure to sun and air. The child's stay in the school, or period of daily attendance if he is living at home, ranges from two months (which seems to be generally considered too short a period) to five months, or even, as in certain boarding schools in France, one year.

Complete statistics showing the progress of the open-air movement are not available, and because of the great variety of institutions, ranging from holiday camps to permanent schools, and including establishments which merely have open-windowed class rooms, figures would have to be carefully analyzed to be of real use.

EDUCATION IN THE PHILIPPINES

AN idea, however inadequate, of the extent of the educational system which has been established in the Philippine Islands since their occupation by the United States, may be had from a glance at the figures given in an editorial article in *The Christian Science Monitor*. There are employed at present in the public schools of the Philippines more than 26,000 teachers, only 325 of whom are Americans. The great majority are graduates of the insular schools, and a few have received their education abroad. While approximately 1,000,000 children are in school attendance, 2,000,000 more are still without school facilities, and great as has been the educational progress during the last quarter century, the problem of reaching the balance of the unschooled children is vast.

The culmination of the educational system of the islands is the University of the Philippines in Manila, with an enrolment last year of 6,464. A branch of the university established at Cebu has an enrolment of 1,000. There are also three other universities in Manila, the oldest of which, the University of Santa Toma, was established in 1611, thus antedating Harvard.

Two major educational problems, yet to be solved—problems which are causing the authorities much concern—are the raising of funds to provide the facilities for reaching the 2,000,000 unschooled children, and the extension of practical education to enable the Filipinos to employ the arts of civilization to the best advantage. Much encouragement as to the acquiring of needed funds, however, is found in the increasing revenues available from the three sources of income upon which the system depends: *i.e.*, the national, provincial and municipal governments, respectively. While in recent years the amounts derived from all these sources have increased several fold, yet much larger sums are necessary to make education available in the remote parts of the archipelago. The government of the United States provides no money for school purposes.

The second of the major problems is the necessity of furnishing an education which will fit the native to be a successful farmer. He must not be educated out of his environment. Already there is an oversupply of natives in the "white collar jobs," while millions of acres of fertile land are lying fallow. The need to educate the native to a love for the soil and to an understanding of the possibilities which result from its tillage is not unlike that of the Negro in the southern states of the American Union.

That this practical side of education, however, has not been neglected, is seen in the fact that last year 243,678 students cultivated 12,968 acres, selling their product for upward of $750,000. The bureau of education is keenly awake to the need for manual training especially as applied to agriculture, for the economic welfare of the islands lies emphatically in that direction. The fertile soil, combined with favorable climate, makes a most promising outlook for the agriculturist. The difficulty lies in inculcating a love for and interest in this most fundamental of all industries, the tilling of the soil. Education along practical lines seems to be the only solution.

EDUCATIONAL LEAVE FOR THE INDIAN SERVICE EMPLOYES

UNDER a law recently approved by the president, the Department of the Interior has been authorized to extend to instructors and physicians in the Indian Service educational leave of not more than thirty days in one fiscal year, or sixty days in alternate years only. Heretofore such leave had been granted only to instructors in the Indian schools and could not exceed thirty days in length, even though none had been taken in the previous year. According to the Secretary of the Interior, Hubert Work, the thirty-day period was usually insufficient for instructors to attend summer school courses. He says:

> The practice of allowing educational leave to instructors of the Indian service has proved to be of great value in enhancing the character and efficiency of the service rendered by employes of this class. It has been required that the instructor attend a college or normal institution during the summer vacation months at least every other year unless excused for good and sufficient reasons. However, the summer courses conducted by the schools and colleges are of longer duration than thirty days, usually requiring attendance for at least forty-two days.
>
> In order that a student entering these courses may secure credits for actual work given, it is

necessary for him to attend during the entire course and the institutions mentioned were not entirely complacent with respect to an attendance of shorter duration than the entire period. It is the purpose of the Indian Bureau to require the performance of actual work which will be of definite value rather than mere attendance for observation only.

Every year conventions and meetings of teachers and of educational organizations, as, for instance, the National Education Association, are held. It is of importance occasionally that teachers or members of the organizations, and especially officials of the bureau associated with the administrative or supervisory activities of the school service, should attend these gatherings.

SCHOOLS OF EDUCATION AND SCIENTIFIC STUDY

THE schools and colleges of education are among the most important factors in promoting scientific study of the problems of higher education, according to the U. S. Bureau of Education. These institutions are turning out an ever-increasing stream of studies produced by faculties and by graduate students.

The bibliographical difficulties in handling masters' and doctors' theses, combined with the feeling that graduate-student work is not of much significance, prevents full utilization of studies of these types, although they are now usually produced under the direction of the trained faculties of the college of education. The bureau states that a few of the larger institutions, such as Columbia, Chicago and Ohio State University, have arranged systematic methods of making such work available to their own students, but on the whole the vast amount of information collected and treated by graduate students under competent direction serves little useful purpose except to the student himself and perhaps to the professor directing his work.

Since many of these studies are careful treatments of well-defined subsectors of higher educational fields, it is unfortunate that we should have no system of reporting them similar to that used by the law reviews. Such reporting might as a by-product also serve to raise the tone of some of the work now done for the master's and the doctor's degrees.

The tendency to rely upon careful scientific study of the internal problems of the institution is expressed most effectively in the growing development of the new profession of educational adviser to the president. Some of our larger institutions are setting up research bureaus, or in less formal ways are assigning to persons freed from departmental responsibilities the task of study and presentation of the internal problems of the institution.

One important result of research of this kind is a decided reduction of the tendency to regard an educational device, or means of accomplishing an educational end, as an end in itself. The purpose or use of procedure considered is kept more prominently in mind and the method of accomplishment is more frequently subjected to criticism and test.

There is still room for further application of the scientific spirit to use of popular devices and adaptions of organization introduced to the educational world under the auspices of agencies which command respect. It is still cause for amazement, for instance, to discover the number of institutions which give psychological tests to freshmen upon entrance and then make no or little use of the results. The illustration chosen is perhaps not entirely happy, since psychological testing has been promoted by the American Council on Education as a means of collecting data to be used for purpose of cooperative research in this field.

THE PROPOSED REORGANIZATION OF HEALTH WORK IN NEW YORK CITY

MARKED changes in the health work in the public schools of New York City have been recommended by Superintendent of Schools Emeritus Dr. William L. Ettinger in a report to Superintendent of Schools Dr. William J. O'Shea made after an investigation covering a year.

Last year Dr. O'Shea requested Dr. Ettinger to investigate health conditions in the schools—how health education could best be promoted and whether medical inspection and pupil examination should be regarded as health education. The investigation was a part of Dr. O'Shea's plan to develop health work in the schools.

As reported in the New York *Times,* Dr. Ettinger's first recommendation is that "the board of education should assume control of the medical examination of school children." At the present time all of the health work in the schools, including the examination of children by physicians and nurses, is in charge of the board of health. The recommendation by Dr. Ettinger revives a movement dating back to the time of the late Dr. Maxwell, who as superintendent of schools vigorously advocated that supervision of health work in the schools be under the administration of the board of education. Dr. Ettinger expressed the opinion that supervision of this activity by the board of education would result in greater efficiency and economy. He stated also:

A staff of physicians (part-time service) should be appointed for this work. A medical report should be required of each child entering school, said report to be on a blank provided by the board of education and approved as to form by the board of health. This report should be made as a result of an examination made by physicians designated by the parent or by a physician of the board of health.

A reorganization of the department of health education should be made along the following lines: health service, health instruction and physical activities, all these branches to be under the supervision of the present director of health education.

A reassignment of the present staff should be effected to conform to the new organization. Assistant directors of health education should be named to direct and supervise a staff of physicians and nurses in the conduct of health service activities; assistant directors of health education to direct and supervise a staff of special teachers in the conduct of health instruction; assistant directors of health education to direct and supervise a staff of special teachers of physical training in the conduct of physical activities.

A survey should be made of all clinical agencies throughout the city available for cooperation in follow-up work, and a list of these agencies and their location and other necessary information should be made available for use by all heads of schools.

Dr. Harris, former health commissioner, sent to Dr. O'Shea a reply to Dr. Ettinger's report. He said in part as follows:

From time to time alarms have been sounded by persons who are interested in public health, advising me that Dr. Ettinger had set out to justify the taking over of the health department's functions in the medical examination of school children by the department of education.

I did not credit these alarms, because, as you no doubt recall, at the beginning of my term of office, as commissioner of health, I visited you at your home, and had a conference with you at which time we agreed as to the proper division of functions of the two departments of the city government. Insofar as health work for school children is concerned, we agreed that it was proper to allocate to the health department the technical work of diagnosis of communicable diseases and the medical examination of school children and that the department of education, in consonance with its name and its purposes, should educate the children with respect to the things that they ought to know about personal and community health as a part of the regular curriculum.

It is not only my personal belief but that of the foremost public health men in the country that this is a proper division of functions, and that wherever the department of education has invaded the field of technical medical service, it has resulted in a serious setback of preventive medical work of the health department of such community. . . . I am, therefore, pained and surprised if Dr. Ettinger's recommendation be correctly reported.

EDUCATIONAL NOTES AND NEWS

Dr. John J. Tigert, since 1921 U. S. commissioner of education, has resigned to become president of the University of Florida, Gainesville, Fla. The resignation will be effective September 1. Dr. Tigert was formerly president of Kentucky Wesleyan College, and for ten years was professor of psychology and education at the University of Kentucky.

Dr. J. L. Beeson, since 1925 dean of the college of arts and sciences and for thirty years professor of chemistry at the Georgia State College for Women at Milledgeville, has been named president of the college.

Dr. C. T. Dowell, dean of the school of agriculture of the Oklahoma Agricultural and Mechanical College at Stillwater, has been appointed dean of the school of agriculture and director of the experiment station at the Louisiana State University.

At a meeting of the board of administrators of Tulane University, Judge Rufus E. Foster was made dean emeritus and professor of law emeritus, and Dr. Max Heller was made professor of Hebrew emeritus.

The current number of the University of Chicago *Record* announces the following appointments and changes at the university: Nelson B. Henry, Jr., of the Lewis Institute, to be assistant professor of education and assistant to the director of the school of education; Clarence William Brown, to be instructor in psychology; H. F. McNair, of the University of Washington, to be professor of history; Helen R. Wright, of the Robert Brookings Graduate School, to be associate professor of social economy in the school of social service administration; I. N. Edwards has been promoted to be professor of education; Grace E. Storm to be assistant professor of education, and Robert Redfield to be assistant professor of sociology. Professor Henry C. Morrison has resigned as superintendent of the laboratory schools, but will remain as professor of school administration in the school of education.

The following promotions at the University of Washington, Seattle, have been ratified by the board of regents: from associate professor to professor, Edwin R. Guthrie, in psychology; Wesley F. Orr, in English; Ralph M. Blake, in philosophy; from assistant professor to associate professor: Curtis T. Williams, in education; Maurice T. Price, in sociology; Louis De Vries, in Romanic languages; Harvey B. Densmore, in classical languages; James Arbuthnot, in physical education for men; from instructor to assistant professor: Sophus Winther, in English.

Dr. J. P. Guilford, of the University of Kansas, has been appointed associate professor of psychology and director of the psychological laboratory of the University of Nebraska.

Laurence F. Shaffer, research associate of the Lincoln School, Teachers College, Columbia University, has been appointed assistant professor in the department of education and psychology at the Carnegie Institute of Technology.

Dr. Clarence E. Ayres, from 1920 to 1923 associate professor of philosophy at Amherst College and formerly associate editor of the *New Republic,* has been appointed lecturer in philosophy and professor in the experimental college at the University of Wisconsin for the first semester of 1928–29.

Professor Carlo Formichi, of the University of Rome, will be the first occupant of the chair of Italian languages and culture at the University of California, recently founded by residents of the state of Italian descent.

Professor Clayton Carus, of the faculty of the school of commerce of the University of Southern California, is to teach at the University of Virginia next year.

Professor Anna H. Palmié has retired recently, after thirty-six years as a teacher of mathematics in the college for women at Western Reserve University, Cleveland, Ohio.

Dr. Ferdinand Zinsser has been elected to the rectorship of Cologne University for the year 1928–29.

The Reverend George Bernard Cronshaw, chaplain, bursar and fellow of Queens College, Oxford University, has been elected principal of St. Edmund Hall, Oxford.

W. E. Soothill, professor of Chinese in the University of Oxford, has been appointed a member of the governing body of the School of Oriental Studies (London Institution) until August 31, 1930, to succeed the late D. G. Hogarth.

O. S. Hubbard, since 1921 assistant superintendent of schools at Fresno, Calif., has been elected superintendent to succeed W. R. Hepner, who was recently appointed superintendent of schools at San Diego.

Dr. George Melcher, assistant superintendent of schools of Kansas City, Mo., has been appointed superintendent, to succeed I. I. Cammack, who has been made a superintendent emeritus.

In Wyoming the following school appointments have taken place: Raymond H. White, superintendent of schools of Wisner, Nebr., has been elected city superintendent of the Douglas schools to succeed R. L. Markley; Alfred Anderson, principal of the school at Savery, has been elected superintendent of the Clearmont schools; S. N. Erwin, formerly city superintendent of Powell, has been elected to head the school system in Glenrock.

H. F. Hunt has been elected assistant superintendent of schools at Tacoma, Wash.

Everett W. Ireland has been elected superintendent of schools at Somerville, Mass., at an annual salary of $5,500.

Gustave Staubenmuller has been reelected associate superintendent of schools in New York City for the fifth term. He has been in the school system for forty-eight years.

H. Richardson, principal of the Bradford Technical College, England, has been made Officier d'Académie by the French government.

The Reverend Alfred Edwin Craig, from 1911 to 1918 president of Morningside College, Sioux City, Ia., died on August 1, at the age of sixty-seven years.

Samuel Fessenden Clarke, professor emeritus of natural history at Williams College, died on August 1, at the age of seventy-seven years. He had been professor of natural history at Williams from 1881 until his retirement twelve years ago.

Dr. John Daly McCarthy, director of health education for the board of education in New York City, died on July 30, at the age of forty-one years.

Katherine Ann Steir, for twenty-three years principal of the Wadleigh High School annex, New York City, and more recently a teacher in the Jersey City and Montclair, N. J., high schools, died on July 30.

The National Council of State Superintendents and Commissioners of Education will convene in Washington on December 11 and 12 to discuss educational questions with federal authorities. Problems to be considered include educational statistics, uniform reports and cooperation between the federal bureau and the state bureaus of education.

The Mary Institute, a school for girls, associated with Washington University, St. Louis, Mo., has been given $300,000 and a $60,000 site for a new building by Mrs. Newton R. Wilson.

The Tuskegee Normal and Industrial Institute has received $20,000 from the estate of Aaron Naumburg, of New York. Harvard College received a like amount "for the purposes of the Fogg Art Museum and to be spent in the training of curators."

Smith College and Radcliffe College are each to receive $1,000, by the terms of the will of Lucy J. Russell, of Lynn, Mass. The purpose of the bequest is to aid deserving young women to attain an education.

The council of New York University has authorized the erection of a twelve-story building to occupy a plot 100 feet square on the northwest corner of Fourth and Green streets, near Washington Square. The erection of this building is the first step in a program of development for the school of education. The building will be Gothic in design and will set a standard for the university's architecture at Washington Square. Plans have been completed and filed, and the demolition of the structures now occupying the site of the new building will begin as soon as the leases of the occupants of the present building expire. It is expected that the new building will be ready in the fall of 1929.

The Benedictine Foundation recently opened in Washington the first school in the country to teach the arts and crafts to retarded children. The hope is to make them self-supporting, and, where possible, to bring some of them up to the average mental standards. It is to be known as St. Gertrude's School of Arts and Crafts. It opens with ten girls. Some applications have come from boys, and it is hoped to have a house for boys at an early date. The ages of the girls are between eight and thirteen. The new venture has no connection with the Catholic University at Brookland, but hopes are entertained that the latter may open its doors to any students which the new school develops sufficiently.

Some of the most important work done by the International Confederation of Students is in connection with foreign travel; and the student identity card, available to every *bona fide* student through his National Union of Students, is regarded as a triumph of international cooperation. Issued originally in July, 1926, its success may be gauged from the fact that during the first six months of its existence over nine hundred applications were dealt with. It is now officially recognized by fourteen governments, and carries with it certain privileges. Austria, Italy and Denmark grant free visas, while France allows a reduction of 50 per cent. in the cost of the visa and Great Britain extends the visiting period from three to six months. The air lines, too, make a special reduction, varying from 5 per cent. in Sweden to 25 per cent. in Poland. The Students' International Club at Geneva offers free membership for a week in each year to all holders of the card. A guarantee of student's status, and issued by the National Unions of Students of seventeen countries, the card serves as a letter of introduction to all student bodies and assures a friendly welcome in any foreign university.

THE fifth central school of agriculture in Mexico has been inaugurated at Champusco, State of Puebla, and will serve as a technical and practical agricultural education center for some 200 young men, the sons of farmers in the states of Puebla, Mexico, Guerrero and Texacala. The school was opened by President Calles with ceremonies attended by several thousand people including high government officials. This school is modern in every respect and its faculty includes some of the best known agricultural experts in Mexico. Building and equipment represents an investment of more than $150,000, and the school plant occupies a tract of about 750 acres. The government plans to open two more schools, one in the state of Mexico and the other in the state of Chihuahua.

COMPULSORY military service for illiterates over twenty-one years of age is provided in a bill presented to the Cuban congress. The bill also provides for a check of census figures on illiteracy in order that no unlettered individual may escape compulsory education. The term of service in the army would be the time needed by each individual to absorb the "three R's," it being understood that several hours of instruction in the elements of education will be given by non-commissioned officers, in addition to the usual drill. Another provision of the bill is the creation of cash prizes for rural school teachers who succeed in teaching groups of one hundred illiterates of more than the usual school age, but under voting age, to read and write.

THE public schools of Hawaii, during the last academic year, cost the taxpayers a little more than $5,000,000—more than half the government's budget for the period in question. The public schools cared for 66,434 children of varying ages during the same year. In the private schools 9,497 youngsters proceeded with their education. Children of Japanese ancestry dominated in numbers in the attendance at the public schools, 34,621 of them being listed by the Department of Public Instruction. They represented 52.11 per cent. of the entire school population. The University of Hawaii, supported by the territory, has more than 800 students. The Kamehameha schools, instituted through the foresight of Bernice Pauahi Bishop, the last of the line of the Kamehamehas, have recently started work on a new $3,000,000 plant. The students are those only with Hawaiian blood in their veins, no matter how small the quantity may be. The first schools in Hawaii were more or less select. But in 1841 compulsory free education was decreed by the ruling monarch to include all children from 4 to 14 years of age.

THE teaching of geography, history and civics in schools and universities of Salvador by other than native-born teachers has been prohibited by law.

AN order has been issued by the Czechoslovak minister of education abolishing, as from October 1, the admissibility of the University of Hungary degrees in Czechoslovakia. It is stated that the measure is strongly resented in Hungarian circles in Slovakia and Carpathian Ruthenia, as over 500 students from these parts annually frequent Hungarian universities. Under this order an M.D. degree, for example, from the University of Hungary, can not be recognized in Czechoslovakia.

SPECIAL CORRESPONDENCE

THE STUDENT MAKES HIS OWN BIBLIOGRAPHY

ALL college teachers hope sooner or later that they may be able to arouse such interest in some phase of their work that their students will at some time be impelled to read and study independently either for enjoyment or in pursuit of some definite object. A thirst for more intensive study is often aroused through personal contacts between teachers and students. Admiration or respect and devotion for the instructor may create deep intellectual enjoyment. All good teachers have the ability to kindle activity and interest in a certain number of their students. But is it not possible to increase the number of those so kindled?

Certain well known devices are used to get the student to read. Written book reports, critical papers, tests, oral discussions and written statements are demanded. Other instructors, less rigid, spend much effort in preparing reading lists for classes which many students clamp into their note-books and never examine except as may be obligatory for the term grade.

It is probably necessary to require a certain number of fundamental books to be read and these must be indicated somewhat dogmatically. Also evidence of some sort ought to be required of students showing that this work has been done. Aside from these demands it is an unusual teacher who can get students to read further, and this is not due entirely to laziness of the pupil or to pressure of other courses or competition with outside attractions, but perhaps more than all else to a sort of mental anesthesia which has prevented the student from ever guessing the keen pleasure of intellectual adventure.

It would seem that in addition to the required reading a cumulative bibliography compiled by the students themselves might be a definite part of the work of certain courses. If a few books were examined each month of the year from September to June by the end of the nine months a collection of worthwhile impressions would be made which would give the student some idea of what there was in the whole field to interest him. In spite of himself he would often be led in his ramblings and browsings to read entire books. Moreover, it is a good habit to acquire a taste for recording one's impressions and information found in clear and tangible form and for perfectly obvious reasons a bibliography made by oneself for oneself means infinitely more than one prepared by the instructor.

Such a cumulative bibliography has been prepared for the last two years by a class at Smith College composed of juniors and seniors in a year's course on the history and evolution of the family. Fourteen books were required through the year. Written reports and discussions were based on these selected books. Some choice in definite fields was allowed. Besides these books read and reported upon the cumulative bibliography was made on cards or stiff paper five by eight inches, each card to contain one title only. It was suggested that the books (or articles) examined should bear the full name of the author, complete title of the book, publishing company, number of pages, price if possible, date examined, for whom intended, general contents and purpose and personal comments on the general impression of the book. Special features were to be noted, as, for instance, good supplementary reading lists, excellent illustrations or ample and reliable foot notes.

The student was to keep in mind that his views only were to be expressed except as he otherwise indicated, and that the list was for himself and not for the instructor although the instructor was to look it over on completion. Therefore it was to be expected that occasionally the student's impressions obtained on examining a book twenty minutes or longer might prove on actual reading to be somewhat different. Nevertheless the student would have an idea where to go for definite material at any future time and incidentally, perhaps, his interest might be much quickened.

Although the results will show that all the suggested points were seldom covered, the practice of making the bibliography and the actual handling of numbers of books has met with considerable enthusiasm and interest. Class discussion has shown, it is thought, a far wider knowledge and critical ability along this line than would probably have resulted without this system.

After examination of these lists which ranged from about thirty to sixty cards, no limit being set, the instructor took occasion to state general defects of method, but not of impression, and ways of improvement both by written comment on the cards and by general class discussion. The lists showed considerable discernment in giving titles on the basic phases of this course on the evolution and history of the family, such as studies on the ancient and medieval family, ethnological, legal and sociological; studies on the effects of the industrial revolution on the work of the home; the woman movement and problems as to sex differences; careers for women; juvenile delinquency; divorce and the general changing conceptions of the family and its members. A certain amount of perceived correlation with other fields of college work was shown as in presenting titles from literature, particularly of the novel, autobiography, biography and drama, from history, also from studies in abnormal and child psychology and social maladjustment.

The close ties between the social sciences themselves and between the social and biological sciences and of drama and the stage were easily noted. Many students appeared to get real enjoyment in seeing the many ramifications of their subject which, in many cases, because of their scope could be no more than touched upon in class hours.

A few samples of these cards are here given, not because of the soundness of the impressions of the students or even for completeness of record, but merely to indicate the possibilities of a method by which the student finds out partly by himself the significance and importance of the field in question, of acquiring a reading list more alive and meaningful and as one way to start early the habit of keeping a card file. Personal taste and a more independent critical judgment, it is thought, might be thus somewhat developed.

Mencken, H. L.

THE DEFENCE OF WOMEN

Alfred A. Knopf, N. Y.
1918. 210 pages.

Contents: The feminine mind; the war between the sexes; marriage; woman suffrage; the new age.

Comments: Very much exaggerated and radical but the book contains a certain amount of truth. Rather amusing to read. Should be taken more or less with a grain of salt.

Examined January 15, 1928.

Filene, Catherine.

CAREERS FOR WOMEN

Houghton Mifflin Co.
Cambridge, Mass.
1920. 569 pp.

A series of articles by different experts to show the positions open to women and the necessary qualifications. An attempt to help girls and women to choose their life work. Gives description, qualifications, training, salaries, advantages, disadvantages, and books to read along this line.

Very useful and helpful for a woman entering the business world.

Examined October 10, 1927.

Howard, George Elliot.

A HISTORY OF MATRIMONIAL INSTITUTIONS

University of Chicago.
1904, 3 vols.

Large divisions are:

Analysis of the literature and theories of primitive marriage and family.

Matrimonial institutions in England.

Matrimonial institutions in the United States.

Howard pays particular attention to the *legal* aspect. Excellent final chapter on present problems of marriage and the family.

I would not care to read the three volumes in their entirety but the parts I did read were interesting. I should think this would be a very good authority in which to look up specific points.

Very complete bibliography. October, 1927.

Langdon-Davies, John.

A SHORT HISTORY OF WOMEN

Literary Guild, N.Y.
1927. 382 pages.

Examined: February, 1928.

Contents: History of the career of women and their part in society from primitive times to modern times including a look into the future.

Chapter headings:

1. Biological Background of Woman's History.
2. Women in Primitive Society.
3. Ancient Civilizations.
4. Early Christian Church.
5. Middle Ages.
6. Modern Times.
7. The Future.

Comments: Book got a violent roasting in the New York Times Book Review on Nov. 27, 1927. Reviewed by Simeon Strunsky. Said by some not to be entirely accurate. Written for the layman.

These samples, although far from being as complete as they might have been, show how students went about the brief examination of books for further information and reading and lead one to think that the requiring of some such individual effort might develop in many students a keener appreciation of what a reader has a right to expect from an author once he has avowed his aim and purpose.

The college-bred person need not be a walking encyclopedia at graduation and even if he could be made so we know how soon the information and knowledge accumulated would slip away. But he should know where authoritative information may be found and how critically to evaluate it. The A.B. degree ought to mean among other things that one has acquired the habit of knowing readily the earmarks of a good book.

E. P. KIMBALL

SMITH COLLEGE

DISCUSSION

PERMANENT MEMBERSHIP IN THE TEACHING PROFESSION

IN an address before the department of superintendence of the National Education Association in 1921 President Walter A. Jessup maintained that better teaching is the greatest need of American schools;[1] with this position, surely no one would be inclined to disagree. We must agree, too, with the statement of Charles W. Eliot, "The American schools will never equal the schools of Germany and France until well-proved teachers can secure a tenure during behavior and efficiency, like teachers in those countries."[2] No defect of American schools is more striking, and none carries more evils in its train, than the astounding rush of inexperienced persons through teaching positions. Contrasted with the permanent or indefinite tenure enjoyed by teachers in England, France and Germany is the annual election or short term contract of American teachers; and contrasted with the stability of the teaching force in the European countries mentioned, is a teacher-turnover in the United States of 16 per cent. each year,[3] and a local turnover which reaches much greater proportions than this; in Washington for example 76.9 per cent. of rural teachers were, in 1924, reported new in their places,[4] and it is said that in the same year 68 per cent. of teachers in similar communities were new to their positions in Wisconsin.[3] No important gathering of educators, no set of proceedings of leading educational associations, but notes the need of real professional status for teachers, and every extended notice of this need leads to comment upon the matter of permanent participation in the work of teaching.

The dignity, independence and standard of performance which give high ranking to an occupation can never be secured for a profession the members of which regard it as a temporary expedient. Adequate normal and college training for entering teachers is so exacting and expensive that no one can afford it without permanently committing himself to the profession,[5] and experience plays so important a rôle in forming the teacher that even the individual who has had excellent training in college and professional school reaches a high level of performance only after years spent in the practice of teaching—and that under favorable conditions.

Adequate professional standards for teachers are conditioned by factors which may be classified as follows:

(1) Salaries which will justify the large initial outlay of time and money required for proper training, which will enable teachers to maintain proper standards of living, recreation and advanced study, and which will make possible substantial savings

(2) Opportunities for professional training

(3) Buildings, equipment and living conditions favorable to good work

(4) Self-direction and independence

(5) Security of tenure

The first, second and third of these conditions are being met. As regards the first: salaries,

[1] *N. E. A. Addresses and Proceedings,* Vol. 59, pp. 779–782.

[2] *Educational Reform,* 1898.

[3] *N. E. A. Addresses and Proceedings,* Vol. 62, pp. 252, 253.

[4] *N. E. A. Addresses and Proceedings,* Vol. 62, p. 477.

[5] See Taeusch, *Professional and Business Ethics,* p. 149 ff.

while far too low in many quarters, have on the whole, been steadily advanced over a period of years and are attractive to great numbers of able persons. Opportunities for professional training in education have been made available in all parts of the country, and for most groups of teachers, through the recent growth of a body of scientific knowledge in the fields of psychology and pedagogy and through the development of normal schools and of departments and schools of education in universities. The third condition of effective teaching—supplying to teachers proper living conditions, and proper buildings and equipment for teaching—engages the efforts of school boards and executives everywhere. Achievement in all these directions holds promise of better things to come; and one feels warranted in saying that in all these respects conditions favorable to effective teaching have been established, or are being established.

Low salaries, unsatisfactory living quarters, poor equipment and buildings and inability to teach well due to inadequate training, however, while perhaps the most ponderable causes of the unrest of teachers are by no means the only conditions which contribute to it. The recurrent tensions due to annual or biennial elections to teaching positions, interference with one's work by officious persons outside the schools, chagrin over positions unjustly lost, competition for positions, difficulties attending transfer from one community to another and desire for professional advancement all contribute to unsettle teachers in their work. Loss of efficiency due to this unrest is so universally recognized as to make comment on it superfluous.

Discussions of short tenure in teaching positions and brief membership in the teaching profession narrow, for the most part, to consideration of tenure laws and of the discharge of teachers for insufficient cause.[6] These matters are vital, but they by no means exhaust the possibilities of this situation. Most proposals relating to tenure in teaching positions, moreover, are formulated to meet conditions in large cities.

The problem of permanent educational service in rural communities, villages and small cities is a very different one from that faced in large cities. The board of education of a large city, having a great number of positions to fill, can transfer teachers from one school or type of educational service to another, and thus provide promotions, place teachers in congenial work and relieve difficult local situations, without interrupting tenure. The board controlling a small system of schools, on the other hand, faced with a situation in which a good teacher has reached the limit of promotion or has lost effectiveness through conditions wholly local, has no recourse except to retain a teacher in a situation unsatisfactory to him and to the board, to discharge him or to advise him to apply elsewhere. Quite generally rural teachers regard removal to larger towns and cities as the only road to professional advancement, and they quite generally resign to avoid situations growing out of local control of schools.

The small unit of school administration is a great obstacle in the way of checking the migration of teachers out of the profession and in stabilizing the teaching force in smaller communities. In this as in many other respects the local unit of school administration has outlived his usefulness.[7] So long as teachers are employed by boards controlling districts having at most a few hundred pupils, just so long will they feel tenure and promotion insecure and their work hampered by pressure from without the school system. Since boards which appoint teachers must retain power to discharge those who, in their view, have outlived their usefulness to the schools which employ them,[8] it is hard to see how any tenure law could protect teachers from dismissal for local causes while their tenure depends upon local boards.

Any plan designed to promote permanent membership of teachers in their profession and to encourage teachers to remain for long periods in the same locality must face the problem of the small unit of school administration. If we

[6] See articles on tenure in the teaching profession in the *Addresses and Proceedings* and in the *Journal of the National Education Society,* 1921–1927.

[7] *N. E. A. Addresses and Proceedings,* Vol. 59, pp. 362–363.

[8] *The Journal of the National Education Association,* Jan., 1928.

are to have the permanence of teacher tenure which is so attractive a feature of the school situation in Australia, England, France and Germany, we must have also something of the centralization of administrative functions which characterizes the school systems of these countries.

To avoid the difficulties growing out of the lack of centralized administration of schools in the United States, let the state, or at least a division of the state having a population of not less than half a million persons, be made the unit of school administration, so far as certification, employment, transfer and promotion of teachers are concerned. Let teachers be appointed to a waiting-list for positions on the basis of training and of standing in examinations and let appointments to positions as probationer teacher be made as vacancies occur. Having taught as probationers for a given period those who demonstrate their fitness would be eligible to appointment with permanent tenure. Once placed on permanent tenure questions relating to the teacher's promotion, transfer or discharge should rest with trained and responsible school officials, as in France and Australia.[9]

Local certification has long been recognized as unsatisfactory, and the adoption of state certification laws has contributed enormously to the improvement of schools; but certification laws have not sufficed to protect the teachers against unjust dismissal, unwarranted interference with their work, nor against the competition of the inexperienced products of colleges and normal schools, who in increasing numbers knock at the doors of the profession.

The advantages of complete centralization of educational administration is well stated by Dr. P. R. Cole in the "Educational Yearbook," 1924.[10] Having pointed out the disadvantages of centralization, Professor Cole says:

> Yet the general opinion is that such limitations are more than compensated by the fact that every teacher is a civil servant, with practically certain employment, regular promotion, state pension rights, general security of tenure and exemption from those petty and mischievous attempts at interference that often proceed from the envy and malice of mediocrity and the spite of ignorance, especially in small provincial centers."

9 A teacher would, of course, have the privilege of applying for transfer, as she now has the privilege of applying for positions.

10 "Australia, Educational Yearbook," 1924, International Institute of Teachers College, Columbia University, pp. 9, 10.

C. F. ARROWOOD

THE RICE INSTITUTE,
HOUSTON, TEXAS

QUOTATIONS

DR. TIGERT'S RESIGNATION

UNITED STATES COMMISSIONER OF EDUCATION DR. JOHN J. TIGERT has resigned in order to accept the presidency of a university maintained by one of the states. This emphasizes the fact that education is still regarded primarily as a state function. Even the highest educational office in the federal government, concerned with the welfare of 27,000,000 children and a million teachers, is regarded as of less importance professionally than the executive headship of a minor university. Dr. Tigert's immediate predecessor resigned to take the provostship of another state university and then the superintendency of schools in Tulsa, Okla. Another predecessor quitted office to accept the presidency of a private university.

Whether, as has been strongly and widely urged by the National Education Association and other organizations, there should be a Federal Department of Education, with or without cabinet representation, it must be felt that even with its present title and function the United States commissionership of education should in dignity and in influence be preeminent among the educational offices in America and invite to its occupancy foremost men. Horace Mann accomplished his great work in Massachusetts, which mightily promoted the development of the public-school system throughout the United States, under a title which seemed to belittle his office, but which he magnified by his service. The United States commissioner is not clothed with much administrative power, but his opportunity to serve the schools of all the states is great, if he is supremely qualified for the office (and willing to live on its meager salary).

The function of the Bureau of Education (which is a division of the Department of the Interior) is

to collect statistics and facts showing the condition and progress of education in the several states and territories and to diffuse such information respecting the organization and management of school systems and methods of teaching as shall aid the people of the United States in the establishment and maintenance of efficient school systems and otherwise promote the cause of education through the country.

About its only definite ministerial duties are those which relate to the management of the schools for natives in Alaska and the supervision of "the government reindeer industry" in that territory, and to the oversight of the agricultural colleges and schools of mechanic arts under the Morrill act. But there is an undefined work of collection, diffusion, assistance and promotion—a field extending across all state lines but erasing none, bounded only by the ability of the commissioner and of the staff at his command. Such service as the bureau can give in making available to all the states the experience of each and in bringing to them the counsel of other lands and times should not and need not impair the state's obligation to its children. It should rather intensify the state's sense of responsibility as well as improve its educational theory and effort.

It were better, perhaps, that one should be called to the position who has not only had technical training as a teacher and a cultural background, but who has also had his experience largely within the range of the public schools. No university president or city or state superintendent is "too good" for this office. It will be difficult to find an educator in any field good enough. Dr. Tigert, educational soldier that he is, with an excellent record, has chosen to go back into action—to the educational front. The position calls for one who will be content to ponder over the grand plan of campaign and give counsel to those who carry on as teachers in this greatest of democracy's undertakings.—*The New York Times.*

A DEFENSE OF RHODES SCHOLARS

KIND words have not so frequently come the way of Rhodes scholars at Oxford that a phrase on their behalf by Louis M. Jiggitts in the London *Spectator* will not be welcome to them and their friends. Examining the records of twenty-two years, Mr. Jiggitts finds that if Rhodes scholars from the United States have not developed into geniuses of the first rank they have made a decidedly good showing.

As students, the Rhodes scholars have made better records as a whole than the records of Americans who have gone to Oxford independently. Although their attainments in scholarship are declared to have fallen somewhat behind those of British "open" scholars, they have done better than Oxford commoners. Last year they attained to more firsts and seconds combined than did the "open" scholars.

Glancing at the records of former Rhodes scholars who have completed their work at Oxford and returned to America, Mr. Jiggitts finds that in general they have managed to get along. Among them there are "a dozen educational executives, several outstanding literary figures, a judge of a state supreme court, the United States commissioner of education, at least thirty promising lawyers, six outstanding physicians, a United States district attorney, nine college deans and forty-three full professors." In addition there are "some twelve who are numbered among the successful business men of the nation, four distinguished in journalism and about half a dozen in politics." One is considered a leading authority on Elizabethan literature, another is "one of the two or three leading authorities in the United States on the diplomatic background of the world war," at least two have achieved international distinction.

Considering that Americans have numbered slightly more than half of the 1,250 Rhodes scholars who have entered Oxford and that of these a large proportion are still too young to have had sufficient opportunity to distinguish themselves in business or the professions, this showing is really excellent. About 40 per cent. of all of the beneficiaries of Cecil Rhodes's project have become teachers and about 25 per cent. have been admitted to the bar. It commonly takes many years in either profession—teaching or the law—for a man to arrive at genuine distinction, so it may be admitted that full returns are yet to be received. Nineteen

United States scholars entered the ministry; this relatively small number casts an interesting sidelight on the ambitions that spur modern youth on in pursuit of general culture, for only a short time ago the proportion would have been expected to be higher.—*The New York Sun.*

REPORTS

PENSION SYSTEMS IN THE UNITED STATES

ACCORDING to an investigation recently completed by the U. S. Department of Labor there were twenty-one state systems of retirement for teachers and seven city systems independent of the state organizations in force at the end of the school year on June 30. Most of these limit membership to teachers, but the New Jersey and Pennsylvania systems include janitors and engineers.

Teachers, states and cities contribute jointly to the pension funds in nearly all the states. Michigan and Montana contribute nothing, while on the other hand Rhode Island provides all the pension funds, the teachers contributing nothing.

In Arizona there is also a non-contributory system under which the teacher is permitted to retire after twenty-five years' service with an allowance of $600 a year. Nevada provides for an annual contribution of $12 from each teacher and retirement after thirty years' service on $600 a year.

Maine has an optional system under which teachers may retire when sixty years old on pensions after thirty years. Members contribute five per cent. of their salaries and the state gives annually an amount equal to the combined contributions of the members. Only seven teachers have elected to come under its terms. The amount of the pension depends on an allowance bought by the combined contributions.

The accompanying table shows the date of establishment and the approximate membership of the systems included.

The membership figures merely give an approximate idea of the size of the different groups. Owing to the change of the system in Maryland the number of participants was not obtainable; those in Virginia also were not

STATE SYSTEMS

	*Year established	Membership
California	1913	36,108
Connecticut	1917	9,749
Illinois	1915	38,888
Indiana	1915 (1921)	12,341
Maryland	1927	....
Massachusetts	1914	20,019
Michigan	1917	24,471
Minnesota	1915	16,866
Montana	1915	5,600
New Jersey	1903 (1919)	19,830
New York	1921	39,648
North Dakota	1913	8,226
Ohio	1920	42,972
Pennsylvania	1921	58,409
Rhode Island	1908	3,599
Vermont	1919	2,956
Virginia	1908	....
Wisconsin	1911 (1921)	18,054

CITY SYSTEMS

Chicago	1896 (1907)	11,927
Detroit	1895 (1923)	6,300
Milwaukee	1909 (1921)	2,054
Minneapolis	1909 (1924)	2,344
New Orleans	1910 (1918)	1,619
New York	1894 (1917)	25,995
New York Board of Education	1921	2,507
Washington, D. C.	1920	2,761

* Figures in parentheses indicate year of change in system.

ascertained. Teachers generally share in the management, but in five systems have no representation.

In three of these, California, Rhode Island and Virginia, the system is administered by state boards; in Washington, D. C., it is in the hands of the District of Columbia. In Chicago, Minneapolis and New Orleans representatives of the teachers form a majority of the pension board. In New York City and Detroit the teachers elect three of the seven members of the board and in Milwaukee four of the nine.

In three states the contribution is a percentage of the salary, based on sex and age at entrance, which will produce, after normal requirements as to age and length of service have been fulfilled, a sum sufficient to purchase a specified annuity. In these states the percentage ranges, according to age at entrance, are as follows:

	Men	Women
Maryland	4.28 to 6.28	4.08 to 7.75
New Jersey	3.6 to 6.11	3.91 to 7.42
Pennsylvania	3.33 to 5.30	3.69 to 6.59

The city systems show much the same kind of arrangements. Chicago and Milwaukee teachers pay graded flat sums. Chicago requires monthly payments of $1 for the first four years of teaching, of $1.50 for the second four, $2.50 for the third four and thereafter $5 a month for as long as the teacher continues in service. In Milwaukee the contribution is $4 a month for the first ten years of service, $6 a month for the next five years and $8 a month thereafter. Both cities count ten months to a school year.

EDUCATIONAL RESEARCH AND STATISTICS

AGE OF GRADUATION AND THE PH.D.

At what age is the degree of doctor of philosophy normally secured? Is this age increasing or decreasing? Does the age of its securance vary with the field of study majored in? Is the age of graduation prognostic of success? Does the department of specialization condition the probability of success? This study is an effort to answer these questions. The Johns Hopkins Press has recently published a list of dissertations with additional information concerning all of the graduates of the Johns Hopkins University granted the Ph.D. degree for the first fifty years of the university's existence, 1876–1926, inclusive.[1] The data therein provided are used as the basis of this study.

During the first fifty years of its existence, the Johns Hopkins University awarded the doctorate to thirteen hundred eighty-one men and women. For this study we shall classify the graduates according to the five decades of the period.

Table I shows the limits of each decade, the Roman numbers by which the decades shall hereinafter be referred to, and the number of people graduating during each decade.

TABLE I

Decade	Years	Number of graduates
I	1877–1886	84
II	1887–1896	310
III	1897–1906	327
IV	1907–1916	305
V	1917–1926	355
Total		1381

The following example will indicate the method that was used in determining ages: An individual born in 1870 and graduating in 1897 may be assumed to be twenty-seven years old. Inasmuch as graduation occurs in June, this may be considered the middle of the year. Therefore, the students graduating in 1897 (born in 1870) will vary in age from twenty-six years, six months to twenty-seven years, six months. Given a sufficiently large number, they will average 27. Such a method seems sufficiently accurate for the purposes of the study and the month and date of birth are not given, only the year. The range of the age of the graduates is from 20 to 79.

Table II shows the findings.

TABLE II

Decade	Age range of graduation	Average age of graduation	Number of cases	Number with no birth date
I	23–38	25.83 yrs.	75	9
II	20–53	27.19 yrs.	307	3
III	21–50	27.88 yrs.	327	0
IV	21–52	27.52 yrs.	304	1
V	21–79	28.25 yrs.	352	3
Total group	20–79	27.53 yrs.	1365	16

This table shows only 1,365 graduates; for sixteen of the graduates no birth date is given:

[1] The Johns Hopkins University Circular. New Series, 1926, No. 8. Whole No. 373. Baltimore, Maryland, August, 1926.

therefore, they were automatically eliminated from consideration. With the exception of Decade IV, this table exhibits a consistent tendency, a marked increase in ages from Decade I to Decade V. One suggested explanation for the exception found in Decade IV may be made: the withdrawal of the older men to enter various war activities; these men returning later would naturally raise the average of Decade V.

Does the age of graduation vary with the department of study? If so how can this be explained? It may be that some departments attract younger students while others attract older ones. Or some departments may place heavier requirements upon their students and hence force them to spend more than the average amount of time in securing their degrees. One more factor may be considered. Many students devote only part of their time to graduate study and therefore secure their doctorate at a more advanced age. Perhaps these students tend to choose one or just a few departments. Table III shows the average age of the graduate of each department.

TABLE III

Department	Number of graduates	Median age
Philosophy, psychology, education	59	31.50
History, political economy, political science	220	27.29
Ancient languages	163	28.34
Modern languages	177	28.33
Mathematics and astronomy	87	28.21
Physics	128	27.67
Chemistry	315	26.44
Geology, mineralogy	75	27.68
Biology	141	28.71
Totals	1365	27.53

Apparently it takes much longer to turn out a philosopher than it does a chemist. But among the other seven departments there is a range of only 1.42 years.

Is the age of graduation prognostic of success? The criterion of success here used is being listed in "Who's Who in America." While this is admittedly not a perfect measure of success, it is the best one available. The graduates are divided into four quartiles in accordance with their ages, as indicated in Table IV.

TABLE IV

	Age range	Number of cases	Number listed in "Who's Who"	Percentage in "Who's Who"
Quartile one	20–25 yrs.	349	131	37.5
Quartile two	26–27 yrs.	331	128	38.7
Quartile three	28–31 yrs.	370	125	33.8
Quartile four	32–79 yrs.	315	86	27.3
Totals		1365	470	34.4

Inasmuch as the exact ages of the graduates were not obtainable, it was necessary to divide the quartiles at the end of age groups. Therefore, the quartiles are not exact, but approximate. This table tends to prove that the younger graduates have a better chance of achieving "Who's Who" than do the older ones. These data are simplified in Table V; the first and second quartiles being combined, as are the third and fourth.

TABLE V

	Age range	Number of cases	Number listed in "Who's Who"	Percentage listed in "Who's Who"
Younger half	20–27	680	259	38.1
Older half	28–79	685	211	30.8

Here is indicated a quite definite distinction. A student who is twenty-eight or older at graduation has only four fifths as good a chance of attaining "Who's Who" as his younger rival.

To study the same data from another angle, let us see what relationship obtains between date of graduation and admission to "Who's Who." We can secure this information by using our original decade groups. This is done in Table VI.

TABLE VI

Decade	Number of graduates	Number listed in "Who's Who"[2]	Percentage listed in "Who's Who"
I	75	54	72.0
II	307	196	63.8
III	327	150	45.9
IV	304	61	20.1
V	352	9	2.6[3]
Totals	1365	470	34.4

This table tells a straightforward story. It takes time to obtain success. The longer the students have been away from the university the better is their chance of obtaining eminence. Only a negligible percentage of Ph.D. graduates achieve "Who's Who" in the first five to ten years after their graduation.

Does his department of study condition the student's probability of achieving "Who's Who"? Table VII is an effort to answer this question.

We saw in Table VI that only 2.6 per cent. of the graduates of the fifth decade had attained "Who's Who." Therefore, to include data for this fifth decade in the following table would be to penalize the rapidly growing departments.

For this reason the data in Table VII are for the graduates of the first four decades only. This table reveals a very great range in percentages. Practically three out of every five of the graduates of the history, political economy and political science departments are found to have attained "Who's Who." It is interesting that in five of the nine departments 50 per cent. of the graduates of the first four decades have attained "Who's Who."

[2] "Who's Who in America" first appeared in 1898. Prior to that date, six of the graduates had died. One of these was in Decade I and five in Decade II. Exclusion of their records would raise slightly the percentages for the first two decade groups.

[3] Of these nine, four had obtained mention in "Who's Who" before they secured their Ph.D's. Therefore, really only 1.4 per cent. of the graduates of Decade V have achieved "Who's Who" since graduation.

TABLE VII

	Number of graduates	Number listed in "Who's Who"	Percentage listed in "Who's Who"
Philosophy, psychology, education	22	11	50.0
History, political economy, political science	168	100	59.5
Ancient languages	140	59	42.1
Modern languages	137	60	43.8
Mathematics and astronomy	70	24	34.3
Physics	90	47	52.2
Chemistry	226	72	31.9
Geology and mineralogy	54	29	53.7
Biology	106	59	55.7

SUMMARY OF FINDINGS

The average Ph.D. graduate of the Johns Hopkins University secured his doctorate at the age of twenty-seven and one-half years.

The age at which the doctorate is secured is increasing, and has been doing so more or less consistently for the past half century.

The age of graduation varies with the department of specialization. However, except in the cases of philosophy and chemistry, this variation is not great.

The age of graduation is somewhat prognostic of success. Those students graduating at twenty-eight or older have only four fifths as good a chance of achieving "Who's Who" as do their younger rivals.

The longer a man has had his Ph.D., the better are his chances of being included in "Who's Who." The chances of a graduate's being listed within the first five or ten years are practically negligible.

Apparently the department in which one specializes somewhat influences a man's chances of attaining "Who's Who."

E. EARLE FRANKLIN
DETROIT TEACHERS COLLEGE

SCHOOL AND SOCIETY

Volume XXVIII SATURDAY, AUGUST 18, 1928 Number 712

STUDENT FEES IN STATE UNIVERSITIES AND COLLEGES

THIS is not a statistical presentation; abundant and accurate information of that character concerning the subject is readily available.[1] My purpose is to endeavor to get at the principles which do or should hold in regard to student fees in state universities and colleges and to determine to what extent the present practice and attitude conform to these principles.

The state university, including the land grant college, is a comparatively new experiment in education. Its development is within the memory of some living persons and its greatest growth within that of many. There is little question that it was founded primarily on the basis of providing an equal educational opportunity for all at little or no cost to the individual.

The idea was a new one both in respect to its universality and in respect to the allocation of its cost. Education prior to that time was "a privilege for the few."[2] The state had made some contribution to such schools as Harvard, Yale, William and Mary and Pennsylvania, but the burden of expense had been primarily on the individual student. As a result, those who could take advantage of the opportunity were both limited in number and confined to a restricted social group.

The newly proposed state university was clearly intended to be an integral part of the publicly supported system of education. Its main support was undoubtedly intended to come from public funds. In most states it is the expressed or implied desire of the people that state-supported higher education be as free to the student as elementary education.[3]

Yet the idea of fees or tuition was not entirely absent from the state university plan even in the beginning. The Federal Land Grant Act does not make any restriction against fees. Very few laws relating to the establishment of state-supported universities and colleges specify that no fees shall be charged. The organic act of the University of Illinois provides that one of the powers of the board of trustees shall be "to fix the rates of tuition." At the first meeting the board adopted "rates of tuition," although soon after it voted that "tuition should be free to students pursuing work exclusively in the agricultural, polytechnic, and military departments."

Probably the idea of having tuition carried over naturally from the private institution, the only kind of institution of "higher" grade previously existing and in which tuition was an established practice. However, in the majority of cases no tuition as such was introduced in the new type of institution and such fees as were created were nominal in amount. Probably the boards found then, as now, that other sources of income were not sufficient and that a charge of some kind

1 Proceedings of the Association of University and College Business Officers and Bulletins of United States Bureau of Education.

2 W. O. Thompson, president emeritus, Ohio State University. "The Educational Budget." *Illinois Alumni News*, April, 1928.

3 C. H. Thurber, executive secretary, University of Buffalo, "Fiscal Support of State Universities and Colleges." United States Bureau of Education Bulletin, 1924, No. 28.

against the student was a necessity. Probably they felt that the student would appreciate his work more if he paid something for it.

Generally speaking, then, some fees were in force from the beginning in the majority of state universities and colleges. As is well known, there has been a gradual increase in these fees, the greatest increase occurring in the past ten to fifteen years, in which the enrolment and the expense have likewise shown the largest increases. The statistics seem to indicate that a period of stability may have been reached, as such increases as have been made in the past two or three years have been for the most part only nominal.

During the period of greatest increase in fees, from 1914 to 1924, fees in state-supported institutions approached closer to the fees charged in endowed schools. The very recent past, however, has seen a marked tendency toward further material increase in the fees of the latter group, so that the present tendency seems to be toward such a relationship between the fees of the two groups as existed some fifteen years ago.

In spite of increases, fees in state universities and colleges are still comparatively small in amount. They still represent a comparatively small portion of the total incomes of most of these institutions, the average for all being about 12 per cent.;[4] not that this income might be easily dispensed with or replaced, but it continues to be a minor item. It is usually insignificant as compared with the state appropriations. It is also a moderate part of the total expense of instruction per student and a still smaller part of the total cost of a student's college education.

A study of the fees in force at various state institutions indicates that, while some variations in amount exist, a remarkable similarity and approach to uniformity have grown up. The headings under which fees are charged are generally the same; the relationship between fees of different kinds, such as resident and non-resident, is similar in the various places. The rate of fees charged in the same departments of different institutions is similar as is the relationship of fees in different departments. Thus, without concerted action, a reasonable uniformity has come about in the practices of schools of similar conditions and stages of development.

The question of fees in state-supported schools of higher learning has been a subject of considerable discussion pro and con through the years. As late as 1901 a resolution was introduced in the board of trustees of the University of Illinois calling for the complete abolition of all fees. The resolution did not pass. President James, of Illinois, said in 1918:

> I venture to mention a few points in which the University of Illinois in 1968 will be different from the University of to-day. We think now of a university with low fees for instruction, then we shall see a university with no fees; now a university in which boys and girls with little money can come and make their way, then we shall see a university in which every boy and girl who is able and willing to profit by a university education will be able to get it, no matter how poor their parents, no matter how difficult the conditions under which they have lived.[5]

J. H. Holst, writing in 1923 in the *Educational Review*, said:

> We should abolish all tuition fees in state- and federal-supported educational institutions because we ought to deal honestly with the law or with the implied spirit of the law; and we ought to commit ourselves definitely in practice as well as in theory to the principle of free education and equality of educational opportunity.

[4] United States Bureau of Education Bulletin, 1927, No. 37.

[5] B. E. Powell, University of Illinois Semi-Centennial History.

The advocacy of a half principle is never justified except as an expedient to a full recognition of the principle. If education at public expense is a sound principle of government it ought then to be put into practice whenever and wherever possible.[6]

Generally speaking, proposals to put upon the resident student at least an increased burden of the expense of his college education have met with disfavor in the state legislatures, and among the press and general public, in all states.

There are some, however, who hold a different view. Among them are those who consider that the state is expending too much on education. Taxation has become, presumably for that reason, a very heavy burden. President Emeritus Thompson, of Ohio State University, said recently:

They tell us that we are expending such enormous sums of money as to threaten the solvency of society. They tell us that this enormous program of education will eventually bankrupt the people and thus take away from them the very things that we seek to strengthen through education.[7]

Others insist that the student, being the chief beneficiary, should pay a larger part of the expense incurred on his account. They raise the question, for example, as to whether the individual who wants any type of education above the high school should not pay at least the current expense thereof.

The eastern colleges and universities and the foundations have taken up this idea with vigor. A thorough presentation of this subject was made by the distinguished leader in educational finance, Mr. Trevor Arnett, at a recent meeting of the Eastern Association of College and University Business Officers.[8] Although he dealt more directly with the endowed institutions, he raised the question as to whether the principle of placing on the student the burden of the current expense of his instruction should not be seriously considered by the state institutions.

In the minds of some the contrast between the fees of state and private institutions stands out. These persons are inclined to put the state in somewhat the same relation to the state university as the benefactor of a private school.

There are those who think that if the state pays any of the expense it should pay all. Others find, and perhaps correctly enough in many cases, that our fees are not based upon any well-defined policy, or upon any careful cost accounting system. They call for a "thorough examination of the whole situation, to the end that we may base student fees upon something more than the university's need for a little more income."[9]

It appears entirely logical and reasonable that some fees should be charged in a state-supported university or college. It is true that it is the university of the people. Its benefits extend to the entire commonwealth; yet, not every one who might be entitled to attend it can do so, and those that do, get greater benefits than those who can not. Hence, they should pay something for this privilege.

The university does not stand on the same footing as the common school. It is

[6] J. H. Holst, professor of psychology and education, Montana State College, "The Imposition of Fees in State-Supported Institutions." *Educational Review,* January, 1923.

[7] W. O. Thompson, president emeritus, Ohio State University, "The Educational Budget." *Illinois Alumni News,* April, 1928.

[8] Trevor Arnett, member of the General Education Board, "To What Extent Should College Students Pay the Cost of Their Education," Proceedings of the Association of University and College Business Officers of the Eastern States, December, 1927.

[9] J. B. Sears, associate professor of education, Leland Stanford University, "Our Theory of Free Higher Education," *Educational Review,* January, 1923.

not within the reach of every citizen's home. The courses of study are much more diversified and specialized and the consequent attention to the individual student and the resulting expense of instruction per student many times greater than in the lower schools. Consequently, the individual should bear some direct part of the expenditure thus made for him, and the fact that instruction is entirely free in the lower schools does not necessitate the application of the same plan in the higher divisions of the state school system.

The fees charged have not thus far in most cases amounted to a substantial part of the total cost borne by the student and are, therefore, not burdensome. Those who have to pay the fees do not as a rule complain of them. On the contrary, there is probably some feeling of satisfaction in making some definite contribution to the support of the enterprise from which they get a major share of the benefits.

There are certain services of a non-instructional character, more or less individual, for which the student should properly pay. Certain penalties must be charged to prevent abuse of privilege and rule. Courses in which the quantity of consumable supplies used or apparatus broken is considerably governed by the student call for fees or breakage charges. Instruction in the professional branches has generally been considered as warranting a higher charge.

Even a lower scale of fees than those charged by private schools helps to maintain a balance between them and the state-supported schools. The omission of all fees at state schools would tend to take students from other schools, particularly the small colleges within the state, and be detrimental to them as well as to education in the state.

It seems reasonable and proper that students from other states be required to make a larger contribution to the expense of their instruction than the resident student. This idea appears to be universally established among the state institutions. There are limitations, however, to the extent to which even this charge should be carried, and an excessive rate of non-resident fee may work to the detriment of the institution and the state charging it.[10]

In the application of any scale of fees it must be kept in mind that there will be some who will desire the privileges of the school and are entitled to it, but who can not pay. All agree that for these individuals provision should be made so that they will not be deprived of the opportunity. Scholarships and loans are the established and practical methods by which this condition can, to some extent, be met. The funds for these purposes are now generally inadequate even for the present range of expense.

It does not follow, however, that because there are sound reasons why fees should be charged, in state universities and colleges these fees should be increased to a maximum point and made to approach the cost of the service rendered to the student. It may be granted that the amount being expended from the public treasury for higher education is of itself a large sum; but it has always been and continues to be but a small portion of the total public expenditures for education. In Illinois the appropriations to the University of Illinois from state taxes represent only 4 per cent. of the total taxes raised in the state for all educational purposes. A similar condition would doubtless be found in every state. Thus, it is evident that whatever burden of taxes may result from educational expenses is placed by the people

10 Marion L. Burton, former president of the University of Michigan, "Bulletin on Non-resident Fees." David Kinley, president of the University of Illinois, "The President's Report for the Year 1921–22."

upon themselves for their local undertakings; and few would be found who would want to be known as wishing to hinder or retard the development of our common school system. "The masses of people throughout the country believe in education and because they believe in it they are willing to pay the expense."[11]

A similar situation is found in the relation that the state tax bears to the total taxes. The average property tax rate in urban communities in Illinois is about four dollars per one hundred dollars assessed valuation, the assessed valuation being supposedly based on full value. Of this sum the amount levied for all state purposes is thirty cents, of which about seven cents goes to the support of the university, or about 1.75 per cent. of the total. The tax schedules of two rural townships for this spring came to my attention recently; the state taxes represented 9.3 per cent. and 11.3 per cent., respectively, of the total taxes assessed. The university portion of the state tax amounts to about 2 per cent. of the total taxes assessed. Out of all taxes paid by citizens of Illinois for every purpose, approximately 17 per cent. represents the amount applicable to the university. These figures clearly indicate that the expense of higher education does not contribute noticeably to the total tax burden.

Furthermore, the expense to the state for maintaining the state schools of higher education is not as a rule even a major part of the total expense of the state government. Out of total appropriations of the current biennium by the Illinois legislature payable out of the revenues of the biennium and not including those payable out of proceeds of bond issues, the university appropriations represented 9.9 per cent.

[11] W. O. Thompson, president emeritus, Ohio State University, "The Educational Budget." *Illinois Alumni News*, April, 1928.

Every comparison will tend further to substantiate the fact that in this country expenditures from the public treasury for education, and for higher education in particular, are not a financial burden and are moderate or negligible as compared with expenditures for other public purposes; and when compared with expenditures made for objects other than government or public welfare they fade into insignificance.

A major reason for maintaining a low scale of fees at state-supported institutions is to carry out the original and fundamental purpose of these institutions, namely, to make higher education available to the largest possible number. Prior to the coming of this system higher education was available only to those who could pay. The great purpose of the state university has been to change that condition; nothing should divert it from that noble mission.

Every increase in fees in state universities and colleges tends to hinder the carrying out of this original purpose. A scheme of larger fees would place a much greater handicap on those less able to pay. An added cost of two hundred dollars and more per year would put a college education beyond the reach of no small number who can now take advantage of it.

The tendency toward an aristocracy in circles of higher education is increased by increased costs. In the past a thoroughly democratic condition has generally prevailed in our state institutions. They have not proven uninviting to young people from homes of wealth, and at the same time have been within the reach of those of less means or, in fact, without resources at all. This is the condition that is most desirable.

It is pointed out by some that there are many students who attend state institutions who could well afford to pay the full cost of their education. It must be borne in mind, however, that these are the very persons who are now probably paying the bulk of the tax money required for university support. They are not less entitled to the advantages of the plan because of their ability to pay more than they are called upon to pay. The fact that some students seem to spend increasing sums on personal and social matters and that this money could easily be applied to increased fees does not warrant a large scale of fees. These personal expenditures are entirely optional with the individual; if he does not have the means, he can curtail them and adjust them to his resources. Fees, however, must be assessed uniformly against all, and all must pay alike; if they are increased the students less able to pay suffer, while those with adequate means do not reduce other expenditures. Thus the burden falls solely on those least able to meet it.

Every suggestion for the increase of fees in colleges and universities has been accompanied by the recognition of the fact that many can not pay the increases. Because of that fact it is acknowledged that provision must be made whereby help is made available to those not able to meet the charges. As Dr. C. H. Thurber points out in his exhaustive "Fiscal Support of State Universities and Colleges":

> Anyone who views America's democratic institutions as a whole must advocate that the states make fiscal provision so that the highly capable, qualified resident student who happens to lack funds may gain a college education.[12]

Those who raise the question concerning the present scale, or advocate a scale more nearly approaching "cost" (whatever that may mean) point out that institutions adopting such a plan have a responsibility to provide a way by which every individual may secure the desired education. Thus, they acknowledge that the strong must bear the burdens of the weak; and that is the exact purpose and present plan of publicly supported higher education. How much better can its financing be accomplished than by the present method?

No discussion of this subject can fail to take account of the fact that the service of the state university or college is by no means limited to the instruction given by it to those who attend it in person. Its work is much broader and more far-reaching than that. "It is to uplift every intellectual and industrial and commercial and professional interest of the commonwealth."[13]

> The state university is more than a teaching institution. In fact, teaching represents but a fraction of its service and expense. It is a center of learning for the teaching of old truths and the discovery of new ones, a place for the discussion of present day problems, and an organization for the solution of these problems.[14]

> The great democratically controlled institutions like the land grant colleges, our state universities, our public high schools, introduce a modifying force. They become the agency through which the popular interest in education finds a more or less adequate expression. By virtue of their origin and their maintenance they can not lose sight of the public welfare as one of the great objectives in education.[15]

To quote again from Dr. Thurber's bulletin:

> It should also be emphasized that whatever part of the cost of higher education is paid by the state is not made as a gift, but as an investment.

[12] C. H. Thurber, executive secretary, University of Buffalo, "Fiscal Support of State Universities and Colleges." United States Bureau of Education Bulletin, 1924, No. 28.

[13] A. S. Draper, former president, University of Illinois, Proceedings of the Board of Trustees for March 10, 1903.

[14] David Kinley, president of the University of Illinois, Bulletin on "The University of Illinois," 1927.

[15] W. O. Thompson, president emeritus, Ohio State University, "The Educational Budget." *Illinois Alumni News,* April, 1928.

The state expects an intellectual return upon all its appropriations for education that will result in increasing the public well-being.[16]

The suggestion is sometimes offered that state-supported schools bring their fees into approximate agreement with those of privately endowed institutions. It seems to me that such a proposal shows lack of appreciation of the difference in origin, purpose and scope of activity of the two types of schools. I do not emphasize distinctions for the purpose of promoting competition; but it seems clear to me that the privately endowed school is established primarily for the welfare and service of those who attend it. From its earliest times it has in one way and another selected those whom it would serve. It has served them in a more intimate and intensive manner than is ordinarily possible and perhaps even desirable in a publicly supported school. To-day, when its doors and those of the state schools alike are crowded, it may select in its own manner those whom it will admit; the state school must take all.

For these distinctions, it seems to me, the student may well pay a major part of the cost of the service rendered him. I do not mean by this to suggest that I think the private gifts and endowments for our private colleges and universities should be lessened or less sought after; these gifts are an investment in world uplift the same as the investment that the state makes in its schools. They have borne and will continue to bear abundant fruit. The larger their extent, the lower will be the fees which have to be charged even in these schools, and consequently the larger the number of students who may have the advantage of attending them, and the larger the opportunity those institutions will have to further increase their contributions to the public welfare through research and discovery.

[16] C. H. Thurber, executive secretary, University of Buffalo, "Fiscal Support of State Universities and Colleges." United States Bureau of Education Bulletin, 1924, No. 28.

The achievements of our private institutions, their time-honored traditions, their high standards, have set models and goals for all institutions of higher learning. Their increasing scales of salaries have set marks toward which all are obliged to move, if for no other reason than in self-defense. All are engaged in the same great undertaking, and should work in close harmony. The different relationships, obligations and scope of activities of the respective groups, however, it seems to me, should be kept in mind.

Proposals for the increase of fees have rather generally brought up the difficult subject of "per capita cost." The suggestion is frequently offered that fees should be based on the "cost of instruction per student," and should cover all or a certain portion of that cost. Such a proposal immediately calls for definition and explanation of what is meant by and included in "cost" as thus used. Usually it is found that the term is not to be taken literally. If it were, all items of expense would be covered—teachers' salaries, administration, library, physical operation, supplies and equipment, depreciation and interest on investment. Ordinarily it is frankly admitted that only some of these items are intended to be covered. Thus, it becomes evident that the proposal is not what it first seems to be, but merely means a further increase in the scale of fees beyond that now in force without any real intent of covering the cost of the service rendered in the way that a commercial or professional concern would set about fixing the selling price of its goods or services.

It has been pointed out by some, and with some justification, that there has been no well-defined policy in the establishment of fees in state-supported institutions;

that changes are made without definite basis or clear purpose; that the fees charged should be based on a carefully analyzed statement of costs, and checked against a carefully determined policy. Probably some imperfections would be ironed out by the exercise of greater care in these regards. Doubtless, however, Dr. Thurber is right when he says that:

> No matter what our theory in respect to higher education may be, the question of charging larger fees at the different state institutions will be decided by the economic and practical situations existing in the state and at the state institutions.[17]

To summarize: Our state universities and land-grant colleges are an integral part of our publicly supported school system, and their major support should come from the state; fees have been charged from the beginning, and no federal law and few state laws prohibit them; they have increased somewhat, but still represent a small part of the total expense, either of the institutions or of the student; a considerable uniformity exists in the practices of the various institutions, and the period of considerable increase appears to be at an end.

There are sound reasons why some fees should be charged; but the fees should be moderate in order to maintain and further encourage democracy and equal opportunity in these institutions, and to prevent departure from one of the cherished principles upon which they are founded.

From a standpoint of the burden of expense of higher education on the public treasury and on the public itself, there is no occasion for alarm or for feeling that this should not continue and increase.

It is reasonable to expect that the fees in privately endowed institutions should be materially higher than in state institutions.

The state university and land grant college is the world's greatest experiment in education. It is the nineteenth century contribution of America to the most democratic and inclusive educational system in the world. Every proposal to increase fees endangers the ideals and principles upon which the experiment is founded, and tends to shut the door of opportunity which the state should keep open, to those who need it most.

LLOYD MOREY
UNIVERSITY OF ILLINOIS

[17] C. H. Thurber, executive secretary, University of Buffalo, "Fiscal Support of State Universities and Colleges." United States Bureau of Education Bulletin, 1924, No. 28.

RATING THE TEACHING EFFECTIVENESS OF COLLEGE INSTRUCTORS

PERHAPS in such a time or institution when or where only students capable of directing their own learning activities and only students of superior learning capacities are to be found in college classes, the importance of effective teaching technique might be regarded as not of paramount importance. Since the coming of flood waves of students into colleges and universities in the country within the past years, such a time, if it ever existed, has passed and such institutions are rare if there are any at all.

While no one can show definitely to what extent it is true, there can hardly be any question that the doubling and redoubling of college and university enrolments within a few years, during which time the population of the country has increased only a few per cent., has resulted in lowering the general level of ability among college students. If we grant the reasonable assumption that a fairly high degree of selection took place in college entrants a generation or so ago, it follows naturally that a large proportion of students of average or less than average ability is now attempting higher education than formerly. Whatever may have been the relative importance of effective teaching in the good old days, it is certain that to maintain the standards with a less able group of students, teaching activity must be more effective.

The Tendency to Under-rate the Importance of Good Teaching

Yet, it does not seem at all certain that this situation has been generally sensed or that much definite effort has been made to refine and improve college methods of instruction. In fact, certain developments have taken place which have operated to divert attention from teaching and to lessen its importance in the eyes of college instructors and administrators. Prominent among these has been the growing importance attached to the function of a college faculty in the field of research. Among American institutions of higher learning the tendency has been to imitate the German university of the later nineteenth century with its emphasis upon research. This has resulted in a very material increase in the intellectual morale and the spirit of research among college and university institutions. On the other hand, it has given rise to an unfortunate attitude towards the importance of teaching.

The belief that the greater service lies in research activity and that to do research of significance gives evidence of a higher order of genius than to do superior teaching became wide-spread. It approached a conviction that the gift or ability to do superior teaching was a common one and not worthy of demonstration. It became apparent that one's research activities were much more likely than one's teaching activities to result in a desirable reputation among one's fellows nationally. The quality of one's teaching is not likely to spread far beyond the campus bounds, while researches are published. In the effort to maintain and to improve the standing of their respective institutions, administrators have in the majority of instances been quick to reward the researcher and slow to recognize in a satisfying way the teacher.

The emphasis placed upon research has been very fortunate. It has contributed to the raising of a number of American colleges and institutions to the level of real universities. But it is not logical or desirable that it be accepted as a matter of legitimate consequence that teaching became a matter of little significance, that one need be ashamed of being an effective teacher, or even that one may offer as an excuse for bungling teaching the belief that research, not teaching, only is worthy of the true university professor. In fact, it is not difficult at all to show that many of the greatest research contributions have been made by men and women stimulated by great teachers.

Few are still able to deceive themselves with the traditional myth that the mere presence of the master of great learning in the classroom will result in hastening the intellectual advance or even quickening the intellectual pulse of his students. Many have put aside, along with Santa Claus and superstitions, the comforting myth that nature has provided for the linking together in the zygote the gifts of genius in learning and effectiveness in teaching. Even that most soothing human tendency to rationalize one's beliefs and conduct leaves some dregs of bitterness and futility in the cup of the learned professor who, because of sloven or ineffective teaching, finds himself in the seminar room or laboratory with but the occasional student, who alone has had the persistence or other uncommon quality of character to wander through the haze and maze of unskilful teaching of the time-serving sort which has been his lot to bear in the classroom of the misunderstood teacher, while his classmates deserted to the ranks of those under the leadership of better teachers—those teachers who radiated inspiration by their apparent clear-cut understanding of both subject-matter and human nature and who generated that enthusiasm for the possibilities of advanced and research work which can be possessed only by those who have mastered the elementary and intermediate facts, skills, ideals, attitudes and concepts, and feel, therefore, the appetite for conquest, which takes hold securely only in the heart of the student who sees clearly the field and knows where the uncharted areas are and their significance to the whole field, to say nothing of his ability to chart them.

The neglect of teaching by this type of research man has not only resulted in the decreased effectiveness of his own teaching but has operated to lower the standard of teaching generally in the institution in which he is employed. It has become fashionable in many institutions to teach poorly. To do so is regarded as the badge of intellectual superiority. Thus the lazy or inexpert instructor turns weakness into strength by the simple process of rationalization. In any institution in which many such instructors are found, the average or normal level of teaching ability is consequently sufficiently low to constitute a rather ordinary standard of what is expected in the way of skill in the classroom.

Whatever may be regarded as the paramount function of the college or university, funds are made available to state and endowed institutions for the purpose of teaching well all those who are accepted for enrolment. Students do not pay tuition for the promotion of research in those institutions supported largely by tuition. Common honesty and a pride in work well done demands that instructors teach well and learn to teach well and that a premium be placed on good teaching in salaries and other recognitions.

How Teaching is Rated

Perhaps in no institution is no attention paid to the teaching efficiency of instructors, though it is certain that in many the prevailing standards are too low. It is also a matter of interest to what extent and by what means those in charge of the administration of colleges and universities evaluate the teaching skill and results of the instructors composing the faculties. The author of this article could not contain his curiosity longer on this point and sent to the deans of some thirty colleges and universities, north, south, east and west, large and small, state-supported and endowed, the following request for information.

The replies from fifteen of these institutions indicated the head of the department is the sole or chief judge of the teaching effectiveness of the members of the staff. Undoubtedly the same situation exists in a number of the other institutions, the replies from which did not indicate who passed judgment on the merit of the instructors. In two others it was stated the opinions of colleagues as well as heads are considered. Without doubt in the majority of the fifteen institutions in which the head of the department does the evaluating, the opinions of colleagues play an important part.

One reply mentions that one source of data is the opinion and comments of other instructors based upon the apparent preparedness of students having taken courses with the instructors being judged. Another gave as a means faculty opinion based upon the free intellectual activities of the various members. Three replies mention the enrolment and the number of advanced students as a criterion. One of these suggests that these figures are considered in the light of a number of pertinent factors, the grades assigned by the instructor, for example. In at least four of the institutions replying, studies of marks assigned and the number of failures have been employed in furnishing pertinent data. In one reply it was stated that a study of the examination questions employed by the instructors were considered.

A number of those replying were frank enough to mention student opinion as a source of data. There can be little doubt but that it is influential in all institutions, though in but few is it formally sought and scientifically gathered and interpreted. To do the latter would seem to offend the dignity of many college professors, who apparently prefer to "bury their heads in the sand" and prefer accidental, incidental, chance, student opinion by circuitous and devious routes to be brought to bear upon their reputations as teachers. They prefer to judge rather than to be judged to such an extent that they place their professional fortunes at the mercy of chance, anecdotal, back-door information.

THE NEED OF FAIRER MEANS OF RATING

It is the firm conviction of the author that most college deans and administrators feel clearly the need of a fairer and more adequate means of evaluating the teaching of individual instructors. The following typical excerpts from replies contribute to this conviction.

> We have no plans or devices for obtaining information as to the efficiency of the members of our faculty as teachers that are perfectly satisfactory.
>
> Permit me to say that we can offer very little that is of any use in that connection. . . . If you reach any helpful conclusions in connection with this inquiry, we should be very glad indeed if you could let us have the benefit of your study.
>
> We do not therefore have a device or plan to determine the teaching efficiency of the members of our faculty.
>
> To learn at first hand the teaching efficiency of the members of the faculty is a problem that is continually before us.
>
> If you can acquire any light in your research and can give it to those of us who are working at the problem, you will be rendering a great service.
>
> I regret to say we have no definite plans or devices to obtain information as to the teaching efficiency of the members of the faculty.
>
> I can not say that they (the methods of obtaining information as to the teaching efficiency of the members of our faculty) are as good as they should be.

It is also his conviction that college professors in general are not satisfied to have so little scientific effort expended in evaluating their efforts. It is none the less obvious that the thought of being visited by superior officers or being rated by students is not attractive to college teachers. It is not unreasonable, however, to entertain a suspicion that we would eventually become accustomed to it and feel no more offended under fire than when the clerk carefully counts the change we give him in payment for a purchase or when the auditing committee inspects the books we have been keeping as treasurer of the church, school or community organization.

Various plans and devices have been proposed and used for determining the teaching efficiency. Among these, in addition to those mentioned in the summary of replies, are the following:

1. The objective measurement of the results of teaching. To formulate objective, valid, and reliable tests for a great many college courses would be practically impossible. The problem of constructing such tests which would give proper weight to various objectives of the course, of preventing coaching, of establishing comparable norms, of allowing for the differences in the quality and preparation between classes and sections make this method impractical, to say nothing of the effort and expense incidental to the employment of such a program. The use of such tests for this purpose have not proven satisfactory even in the elementary and high school, where this problem is much simpler.
2. The use of formally collected student opinions, ratings, rankings.
3. The use of formally collected opinions, ratings, and rankings of colleagues.
4. Formal visitation and rating by some rating

officer, *e.g.*, a dean, a head of department, a specialist in theory and practice of instructional procedure.

Some beginnings in the use of the last three named methods have been made, though the use of the student opinion has been limited and cautious. Whether or not such a plebiscite would bring pressure to bear upon teachers to curry favor may be debated. The abler and bright students, as indeed may be said of less intellectual but shrewd students, are not so easily deceived as we often think they are. The laughs which take place about the fraternity fireplace over some of our "clever" jokes, stories or devices give support to a suspicion that they understand us better than we know. The possibility of the development of student tendency to rate the easy instructor high and less favorably the instructor who believes in the principle of self-activity (for the pupil as well as the instructor) is not negligible, though the resourcefulness of a faculty and student committee to meet this situation seems quite adequate.

At any rate, it does seem that there is need for more adequate machinery for giving recognition to good classroom work skillfully done and that student opinion seems reasonably valid and certainly much more reliable than the catch-as-catch-can incidental methods now employed.

No one has yet shown that the opinions of students are valid judgments of teaching ability. No one has shown that they are not. In fact, a very good argument may be made for their validity, though space will not be taken here to go into the details of it. It is certain, though, that students of college grades are as able to judge whether they are being well taught and inspired as can be estimated by colleagues from their few intellectual activities and by the heads of departments from an occasional visitation or from interviews.

Not all faculty members will care to have their teaching formally rated by students. Yet there can be no doubt that it is so being rated informally constantly and that while no record is made of such judgments, general impressions as to the teaching efficiency of instructors get all over the campus, by way of gossip, passing conversation, etc.

The chief differences between the existing condition and the formal student rating are (1) the increased emphasis likely to be placed on formal recorded student opinion, and (2) the increased accuracy and reliability[1] of it as compared with the present subterranean routes of information regarding the efficiency of instructors. It is certain that no great emphasis should be placed on student ratings alone, or on the ratings of colleagues alone, or for that matter on any source or kind of data alone. The contributions of the instruction in other directions must be recognized and evaluated particularly in (1) research and investigation, and (2) service to the school and the state in various ways. The influence of the instructor upon morality and character must not be ignored, as in fact it is not. The ability to work peacefully with colleagues must be given some consideration.

Reliability of Students' and Colleagues' Ratings

It also seems reasonable that it is much more scientific and reliable to collect the opinions of a large and representative number of students, rather than to place reliance upon the few chance remarks upon occasions which may in themselves color these remarks.

From a series of very interesting experiments in this direction, conducted by Dr. E. R. Guthrie, of the department of psychology of the University of Washington,

[1] To be discussed in a later paragraph.

he was able to show that the reliability of student opinion was quite high and materially higher than the reliability of fellow members of the faculty. The student ratings were obtained from members of large classes in psychology who each rated from five to twelve instructors. By use of the Brown-Spearman prophecy formula the reliability of the average judgment of sixteen students on a given instructor was estimated from the reliability of two sets of eight ranks to be .88. A repetition of the experiment a month later enabled the reliability to be calculated directly. For the average judgments of sixteen students, it was found to be .89. With a later group the estimated reliability (by use of the prophecy formula) was .72. The use of a rating sheet or score card was found to result in even greater reliability, namely, .30 for one student as compared with .26 for one judgment without the rating card, would give an estimated reliability of .87 for the average of sixteen ratings. The reliability of judgments of sixteen members of the faculty even on the teaching effectiveness of colleagues was also .26, which would require the judgments of nineteen equally reliable colleagues to produce an average rating as reliable as the average judgment of sixteen students.

The relative ease with which the ratings of a fairly large number (fifteen or twenty students or more) may be obtained as compared with the difficulty of obtaining a like number of judgments of members of the faculty competent to rate any given instructor favors the use of student opinion, whatever may be said of the relative validity of student judgments as compared with those of colleagues.

At any rate, it seems certain that (1) the question of raising the standards in college and university teaching should not be ignored to the extent that it has been in many American institutions; (2) there is much room for the improvement of the methods of evaluating the teaching effectiveness of university teachers, in fairness to the capable instructor and in interests of the institution; (3) because of its higher reliability and the ease with which it may be gathered, formal student opinion should be investigated as a source of data.

Equally certain does it seem that efforts should be expended to improve the technique and spirit of instruction in university classes.

HARL R. DOUGLASS

PROFESSOR OF EDUCATION,
UNIVERSITY OF OREGON

EDUCATIONAL EVENTS

THE FASCISTS AND ITALIAN SCHOOLS

ITALIANS living in foreign countries have been ordered to send their children to Italian schools, instead of to those of the nations in which they reside, under pain of being summarily expelled from the Fascist party in case they already belong to it. According to the New York *Herald Tribune,* this order was issued by Piero Parini, secretary general of the Foreign Fascist Organization, presumably with Premier Mussolini's approval. The section dealing with this subject follows:

The secretariat general of the Foreign Fascist Organization unfortunately has been obliged to observe that various compatriots residing abroad continue to prefer sending their children to foreign schools instead of to local Italian schools. These cases are all the more deplorable, since it is inconceivable that a good Italian would forego having his own children grow up with instruction in the language of the mother country, thus forming a spirit according to our secular culture.

Whoever does not feel these duties regarding the education and spiritual formation of his own children and does not see that in preferring foreign schools to our excellent Italian schools abroad is guilty of authentic defection and the lack of one of the essential duties of Italians who live beyond the confines of the mother country, and is without doubt a person incapable of comprehending the spirit and ideality of Fascism. I direct, therefore, that those to whom the action in question may be imputed and who do not change their conduct following the warning by the secretaries of the various Fascios—and if they be inscribed in the party abroad—be summarily expelled for lack of national sentiment.

THE FRANCO-BRITISH EDUCATION CONGRESS

THE Franco-British Education Congress has been held recently at University College, London. A report of it in the London *Times* states that the delegates from the British Empire numbered 200, while there were about fifty French delegates, including prominent educationists from various parts of France.

In the absence of the Duke of Connaught (the honorary president of the League of the Empire), Prince Arthur of Connaught received the delegates. He was accompanied by the French ambassador (M. de Fleuriau), Lord Eustace Percy (president of the board of education for Great Britain), Lord Meath (vice-president of the league), and Sir William Beveridge (representing Sir Gregory Foster, vice-chancellor of the University of London).

Prince Arthur of Connaught, in welcoming the delegates, said he trusted that their meeting would lead to much light being thrown upon educational questions of the highest importance to both Great Britain and France. These two great countries had for generations influenced each other through their literature and their social relations, but their educational systems differed so widely that it was not easy for the one to appreciate and understand that of the other. He trusted that this occasion for comparing first-hand information as to the ideals of the two nations and the educational means by which they were severally endeavoring to reach them would be of great value to both of them. He hoped it might be possible to devise means for closer educational cooperation and for an extension of the interchange which already took place between professors and students on both sides of the Channel on lines such as were already in operation between the various countries of the British Empire.

At the opening session the subject for discussion was, "The work of the home universities in connection with the empire and with foreign countries."

Professor E. A. Gardner said there were at present about 5,000 students from overseas in British universities, and about 2,000 of these came from foreign countries. Nearly half of the total were students of the University of London. He advocated an extension of the interchange of professors and students.

"The University of Paris and its Relation to Other Universities in France and in Foreign Countries" was the subject discussed at the afternoon session, at which the principal speaker was M. Desclos. He pointed out that Great Britain was among the thirty-four nations who had decided to house their students in Paris in hostels which would form part of the Cité Universitaire. In Paris they were thinking of cooperating with the University of London in the project of erecting hostels for students on the Bloomsbury site. They could not afford to build a great French house, but they hoped to be able to contribute to the building of one of the hostels. They would then ask that there should be reserved a certain number of rooms to be occupied by properly selected French students. In that way they would have a counterpart of the great hostel which Britain was going to build at the Cité Universitaire. The two universities of London and Paris would then still better promote the extension of good feeling and mutual understanding between the two countries.

INTERNATIONAL STUDENT VISITS

SIXTY French school children have recently left Paris to spend a month in the homes of German families and an equal number of German children have gone to French homes. Officials in charge of selection of students in France report that they have had many more applications than they could satisfy.

Nine German professors and fifty-two girl students from the Hohenzollern Lyceum University, Berlin, are visiting Ireland this summer on a tour. This is not merely a sight-seeing tour, although the places of historic interest are visited. Lectures are given and opportunities taken to reconstruct and discuss the history of the country in the light of the daily observations. So far there has been no indication on the part of Irish students to reciprocate the visit.

Fourteen Japanese students from Doshisha University of Kyoto, Japan, under the direction of Raymond K. Oshimo, the first American-born Japanese teacher to go to the university, are on a forty-day friendship tour to the United States. Doshisha University is the oldest Christian university in Japan and has an enrolment of 4,700 students. Many leaders of Japanese education, journalism and politics are among its graduates, and it has been known as a potent factor in transmitting American ideas into the Orient. The boys making this tour are from twenty to twenty-four years of age and are financing the trip themselves.

A party of 170 Canadian women and 40 men students are visiting Great Britain, as members of the Overseas Educational League. This is the fifth annual tour to Great Britain organized by the league. It is stated that the object of the tour is to introduce members of the party to university life in Great Britain and France. The league itself desires to assist those engaged in education to interpret its purpose in the broader terms of human fellowship and understanding; to emphasize the significance attaching to citizenship in the British Commonwealth of Nations; to endeavor in some small measure to interpret Britain and France, the respective mother countries of the two great branches of the Canadian people, and to develop a consciousness of the international rôle of education as a means to peace among the nations.

The party was conducted by Mrs. R. F. McWilliams, past president of the Canadian Federation of University Women. Included in the party were Major F. J. Ney, executive secretary of the National Council of Education of Canada, and honorary organizer and founder of the Overseas Education League; Professor N. N. Evans, McGill University; Professor Vincent Bladen, Toronto University, and Dr. Joseph Graham, who is traveling as honorary medical officer. All the universities of the Dominion had representatives in the party.

The students hoped to visit Glasgow, St. Andrews, Oxford and Cambridge Universities, as well as places of interest in England and Scotland. Before returning to Canada the party will also visit France and Belgium.

STATE SALARY SCHEDULES

The statement is often made, according to a report by the U. S. Bureau of Education, that the salaries paid teachers chiefly determine the quality of young people attracted to the profession, the quality of professional preparation they receive, and the length of time they remain in the service. In states without well-planned salary schedules, there will be found little relationship existing between the salaries paid and the teachers' professional preparation. Teachers with a minimum of professional training are paid nearly as much as those with much training, and increases in salaries have come about mostly because of length of service. The amount of professional preparation has had apparently little influence on the attainment of a maximum salary.

To remedy this condition it is recommended that a state salary schedule be formulated that is adaptable to the varying needs of the state. Such a schedule, scientifically prepared, should make provision for increases in salaries on the bases of such factors as professional improvement, experience and teaching efficiency.

According to investigations made by the bureau, the states that have enacted minimum salary schedules are North Dakota and New York. The North Dakota law, passed in 1921, provides a minimum amount of training and a minimum salary for teachers; and that after August 31, 1923, any entering teacher shall, as a minimum requirement, hold a diploma from an approved four-year high school, or the equivalent, and meet all certificating requirements as to professional study. That for such preparation the minimum salary be $810 per year of nine months, and that no less than $50 per year shall be added for each year of service in the profession for a period not to exceed five years.

The New York State law, which became effective on August 1, 1923, provides that the salary for teachers of kindergarten and first to eighth year grades shall be $800 the first year, with an annual increment of not less than $75, the number of annual increments not less than eight; and for high-school teachers, $900 for first year, with an annual increment of not less than $75, and the number of increments not less than eight.

The question of equal pay for men and women teachers doing the same work continues to occupy the attention of many boards of education. The granting of more pay to men is defended by some boards on the ground that in order to get men teachers they must be paid more than women, for women will work for less. Such boards contend that supply and demand should regulate the salary.

If competent men are to be retained in the profession, any equal pay schedule should provide that the salaries of the women be made equal to those paid men rather than that there be any averaging of the salaries of the two.

THE EDUCATION DEBATE AT THE VIRGINIA INSTITUTE OF PUBLIC AFFAIRS

The Curtis-Reed bill, establishing a federal department of education, was discussed in a forum debate at the Institute of Public Affairs at the University of Virginia on August 9. The discussion was under the leadership of Miss Charl Orville Williams, legislative field secretary of the National Education Association, who opened the debate with an outline of the historical course which has led to the presentation to Congress of this bill which provides for a cabinet member on education but not for federal financial aid.

As reported in *The Christian Science Monitor* the debate centered about the question of whether a federal department of education would enable the government at Washington to lay a controlling hand on state educational activities.

Every speaker against the bill based his objections on alleged "infringement of states' rights"; every advocate of the project, however, denied the possibility of such infringement under the terms of the bill.

Miss Williams emphasized that no federal aid to the states is provided in the bill; that its chief aim is to give to education the same importance which is given to agriculture, industry and labor, each of which has a spokesman in the cabinet, and to enable the government to undertake adequate research in this field which would then be available to the states in drawing up their own educational programs.

Dr. Bradford Knapp, president of the Alabama Polytechnic Institute, characterized the states' rights argument as "a smoke-screen put up for the purpose of defeating the bill."

Those who have studied its terms, he said, do not believe it could result in undesirable uniformity of educational methods, but only of standards. He pointed out that, in many localities, 40 per cent. of the local taxes goes into the upkeep of schools, and is often unwisely spent because the state can not afford to engage in comprehensive research as could be undertaken at Washington.

William M. Davidson, superintendent of public schools in Pittsburgh, said that "education has become the biggest business in America. The present status as maintained by the Bureau of Education," he said, "does not meet the needs of this business, which represents a capital of $10,000,000,000 invested in educational plants and $2,000,000 spent on personnel."

Dr. Charles G. Maphis, director of the institute, speaking in favor of the Curtis-Reed bill, said that the states are doing valiant service to education, but need the assistance of the federal government. Inadequate citizens, he pointed out, are liabilities not only of the state, but of the nation.

Three reasons for supporting the bill were advanced by Dr. A. R. Hatton, professor of political science at Northwestern University, as follows:

> It would permit the federal government to perform its work in the educational field more effectively, but the government would in no way assume direction of state activities.
>
> It would meet the tremendous need for some one central agency of research to act as a national clearing house of information.
>
> It would eliminate duplication of efforts by the states and enable them to spend state funds more wisely.

It was learned that seven congressmen who have consistently fought the Curtis-Reed bill in Washington were invited to present the case for the opposition, but declined to participate. Dr. John H. Latane, of Johns Hopkins University, based his opposition on the belief that establishment of a federal department would be the entering wedge for a constantly increasing jurisdiction exercised by a secretary of education; that it would result in undesirable standardization, which has no place in the educational field, and that there is much educational research now being ably carried on in universities.

Judge Oscar Leaser, tax commissioner of Maryland, declared that he opposed the project for three reasons: That the cabinet is already big enough; that education is a matter for the states; and that the tendency toward bureaucracy should be curbed.

THE SELECTION OF TEACHERS IN BOSTON

By vote of the Boston school committee on August 6, the order presented by Edward M. Sullivan, providing that candidates to teach in Boston high and intermediate schools shall be chosen from one list to be established according to the candidates' ratings and without regard to the college from which they were graduated, was passed.

It was on June 11 that the school committee, in private conference, decided to establish two lists, one for Boston Teachers College graduates, commonly known as the "inside list," and the other for graduates of other colleges, the "outside list."

This caused much criticism. The Boston *Post* editorially asked: "Why should Boston girls who have been graduated from Bryn Mawr, Radcliffe, Smith, Vassar or Wellesley find it very much harder to secure positions as teachers in the schools of Boston than girls who hold diplomas from the Teachers College in this city?" The Boston *Transcript* editorially remarked that "it would be preposterous to suggest that the Boston girl who graduates from the Boston Teachers College is any better prepared, in general education and training, than the Boston girl who earns a diploma, with high scholastic rating, from such a distinguished college as Bryn Mawr, or from any other of the important colleges where women receive degrees."

It is said that vigorous newspaper editorial attacks led Mr. Sullivan to seek a change in policy. At the meeting on August 6, he was opposed by two members, Joseph J. Hurley and Dr. Joseph V. Lyons, while he was supported by the chairman, Francis C. Gray, and Mrs. J. F. Barron.

The session was lively through efforts of Mr. Hurley to block the order by objections. Roll call was delayed two hours.

The secretary read at the request of Mr. Sullivan a statement of his in which he charged that the Boston public schools are being dominated by a group of Teachers College graduates, that they are suffering from a consequent lack of outside stimuli, and that in recent years educational methods have not advanced as fast here as they should. He also maintained that there was strong opposition against the graduates of Catholic or non-sectarian schools.

Superintendent Jeremiah E. Burke replied to this attack, which he termed "a wholesale condemnation of the Boston public schools."

"The service of our teachers is continually improving, not deteriorating," Dr. Burke declared. "The rating lists have been in use since 1906, they have been held inviolate, and there has emphatically been no letting down in our standards. Appointment has been only by merit, and that system will continue as long as I am your superintendent."

Mr. Gray and Mrs. Barron said that they favored the single list because they wanted the best teachers regardless of where they were educated or where they lived. Mr. Sullivan's frequent and emphatic utterances were in the same vein. Mr. Hurley said, however, that he opposed it because "the entire agitation overlooks the fact that Teachers College is a college for embryonic teachers," where the science and art of teaching is inculcated, not as a part of the course, but as the course.

THE NEW YORK CITY SCHOOL BUDGET

The Board of Education of New York City has adopted a budget for the maintenance of the city school system during 1929, totalling $131,700,680, an increase of $7,153,453 over this year's appropriations. In addition, the board voted $33,000,000 for the acquisition of sites and the enlarging and construction of school buildings during the coming year.

According to the New York *Times* the largest single item in the budget is $75,953,999 for the maintenance of the day elementary and junior high schools, an increase of $1,779,710. Next in size comes the appropriation for day high schools, $22,100,989, an increase of $1,306,528. The compulsory continuation schools will cost $1,955,895, and the training schools for teachers will require $1,445,808, a decrease of $123,-321, due to an anticipated smaller attendance because of the lengthening of the course of study. The cost of all the day schools and classes for the coming year will be $102,914,-152. The evening schools will be operated for a total of $2,162,091.

While the public-school budget must be approved by the board of estimate and apportionment, that body generally accepts the estimates of the board of education with little change. The budget represents the work of two months by the finance and budget committee of the board of education, a representative of the board of estimate and representatives of every department in the school system.

The total cost to the city and state of the city's public school system is not represented in the budget of the board of education. In addition to the $131,700,680 required for the maintenance of the school system during 1929, the board of education will contribute $360,-808 to the trust funds of the board of education retirement system. Expenditures by other branches of the city government toward the maintenance of the public-school system during the coming year must be guessed at from past years. The city controller certified to the budget committee of the board that during the school year August 1, 1927, to July 31, 1928, the expenditures for debt service for the schools aggregated $19,695,869.

Annual instalments paid by the city into the trust funds of the Teachers' Retirement System and the administration expenses of the system were certified by the controller to aggregate $5,674,893. The expenditures in the same period by the department of health for nurses, doctors and clinical service for school children, as certified by the commissioner of health, aggregated $667,749. The expenditures by the department of water supply, gas and electricity for gas, electricity, power and lamps for the schools, certified by the commissioner of the department, aggregated $1,159,993. If these expenditures remain the same for the coming year, the total cost of the school system would approximate $159,259,995, or more than $150 for each of the 1,000,000 school children registered in the city schools.

In the day elementary schools the board of education has provided for 100 teachers for the reduction of oversize classes during 1929 and sixty-two positions for new buildings to be opened, in addition to the usual provision for increased register.

The appropriation for the free public lectures which the board of education has maintained for many years, but which have disappointed the school authorities recently because of the small attendance, was cut down again this year, provision being made for only 196 lectures.

To repair old school buildings the board has allowed $3,525,000 for foreseen repairs, as against $2,475,000 for this year. This increase was believed all that the building department of the board could absorb during the coming year. The budget for unforeseen repairs was increased from $863,000 to $1,075,000.

The budget committee reported that:

Both as to numbers of pupils and as to cost, your committee, of course, has to give primary attention to the needs of normal children. At the same time those who are suffering from physical or mental infirmities have not been neglected. The community owes its handicapped children an equal opportunity with normal children to acquire an education and become self-supporting and self-respecting.

The following table shows the number of classes for the handicapped.

	1928	1929
Open air classes	167	177
Tuberculosis	36	35
Crippled children	135	133
In hospitals	2	1
In homes	76	82
Cardiopathic	39	42
Blind	7	7
Sight conservation	74	79
Deaf	49	49
Speech improvement	27	28
Mentally defective	401	431
Mentally and physically defective	0	40

The forty classes for mentally and physically defective children are to be experimental. One class will be established in each school district for the instruction of "floating" boys and girls of too little ability to keep abreast in the ungraded classes.

EDUCATIONAL NOTES AND NEWS

DR. HARVEY NATHANIEL DAVIS, professor of mechanical engineering at Harvard University, takes up his new work as president of the Stevens Institute of Technology, at Hoboken, New Jersey, on September 1. Dr. Davis succeeds the late Dr. Alexander C. Humphreys, who had been president of the institute for twenty-five years.

R. W. BARDWELL, superintendent of schools at Rock Island, Ill., has been elected head of the schools at Madison, Wis., to succeed Dr. Thomas W. Gosling, who has become superintendent of schools at Akron, Ohio.

RAYMOND E. PINKHAM, principal of the West Orange, N. J., Junior High School, has been appointed superintendent of the Weehawken, N. J., schools. Raymond E. Hearn has been appointed acting principal of the West Orange school, to succeed Mr. Pinkham.

CHARLES E. TEACH, of Bakersfield, Calif., has been elected superintendent of schools at San Luis Obispo.

DELBERT BRUNTON, of the department of history and social science at the Chico State Teachers College, has been appointed principal of the high school and superintendent of the Mountain View school district in California, to succeed William A. Otto.

DR. ROKURO NAKASEKO, of Doshisha University, Japan, will be the first occupant of the chair of international relations recently established at the University of Hawaii, Honolulu, by the Carnegie Endowment for International Peace.

WALTER REYNOLDS BOOTH, head master of Wolverhampton Grammar School, England, has been appointed master of Dulwich College, in succession to George Smith, who on October 15 becomes director of the department for the training of teachers at Oxford University.

V. T. HARLOW, lecturer in history at University College, Southampton, England, has been appointed keeper of the Rhodes House Library, Oxford.

DR. GEORGE FILLMORE SWAIN, of the faculty of the Harvard Engineering School, has received the Benjamin G. Lamme medal for "accomplishment in technical teaching," awarded at the annual meeting of the Society for the Promotion of Engineering Education.

ERNA GRASSMUCK, of the faculty of the Pennsylvania State Teachers College, Indiana, Pa., has been awarded the Nathan C. Schaeffer Memorial Fund scholarship, and will spend a year in study at the University of Chicago. The scholarship is from a fund of $14,000 contributed by teachers of Pennsylvania in memory of the late Dr. Schaeffer, former Pennsylvania state superintendent of public instruction.

MISS A. LUCILLA MCCALMONT, director of handwriting at Utica, N. Y., has been elected president of the National Association of Penmanship Supervisors.

DR. WILLIAM MCANDREW, editor of the *Educational Review* and formerly superintendent of the schools of Chicago, delivered the commencement address at the Pennsylvania State College at the close of the summer session on August 9.

PROFESSOR R. V. D. MAGOFFIN, head of the classics department at New York University, left on August 12 for Sante Fe, N. Mex., to spend a month at conferences of the trustees of the School of American Research. This is one of the schools of the Archeological Institute of America, of which Professor Magoffin is president.

DR. EDWARD CARY HAYES, since 1907 professor and head of the department of sociology at the University of Illinois, died on August 7, aged sixty years.

THE REVEREND HENRY CLAY SHELDON, formerly professor of systematic theology at Boston University, died on August 4, in his eighty-fourth year. He had been a professor at the university from 1875 to the time of his retirement about five years ago.

MISS JESSIE CLAIRE MCDONALD, for fifteen years principal of the National Cathedral School for Girls, Washington, D. C., died on August 12, aged fifty-nine years. Miss McDonald was formerly a member of the faculty of the Farmington School, Farmington, Conn.

EDWIN SMITH RICHARDS, for fifty years connected with school work in New Jersey, died on August 9, at the age of seventy-two years. He had retired three years ago from the principalship of the Winfield Scott School, Number 2, of Elizabeth, N. J.

THE University of Southern California, at Los Angeles, held an Institute of Municipal Administration from August 13 to 18. It included lectures and round-table discussions on city planning, municipal finance, street traffic control, public health, municipal engineering, social welfare, legal problems of municipalities, public institution, recreation and park administration, city clerkship administration, councilmanic problems and county administration.

THE congress of the International Confederation of Students opened in Paris on August 11. The object of the confederation is in general the defense of student interests at home and abroad and the development of facilities for foreign travel. This year the congress has discussed the subject of international recognition for all college diplomas.

A SUMMER school whose object is a study of the Victorian Age was held at the University of Cambridge from July 27 to August 16. The schedule each day was allotted to lectures by authorities on the different phases of education, art, literature, political activity, science and religion during the Victorian era.

THE University of Chicago has received $120,000 from Robert Law, Jr., which makes Mr. Law's gifts to the Development Fund total $200,000. The total is to be used as endowment for a distinguished service professorship. A pledge for $50,000 has also been received, from the Leila Houghteling Fund, for establishing a fellowship and scholarship fund in the school of social service administration.

THE University of Michigan is to be benefitted by the will of Avery Hopwood, playwright. Mr. Hopwood's estate is valued at approximately $1,000,000. Three fourths of this has been left in trust to the playwright's mother. At her death one fifth of this trust goes in another trust to the University of Michigan, the income to be distributed among students who excel in dramatic and fiction writing. The will reads: "It is especially desired that students shall not be confined to academic subjects but shall be allowed the widest possible latitude. The new, the unusual and the radical shall be especially encouraged."

ON September 1, 1928, a division of school architecture will be established in the Texas State Department of Education to render free service to the smaller school districts. This has been made possible through an appropriation of the General Education Board of New York City. Superintendent Marrs, on his return early in March from Boston, where he attended the meeting of the Council of State Superintendents, called upon Dr. Wycliffe Rose, who was then president of the General Education Board in New York City, and as a result of the interview the board at a recent meeting made a sufficient appropriation to finance the division for a period of three years, at the end of which time it is believed the legislature will recognize its importance and make adequate appropriations for its support. Personnel of the division and details of administration will be announced later.

A DIVISION of school attendance has been created in the North Carolina Board of Charities and Public Welfare for the purpose of increasing the daily school attendance in the state. The county units of the division consist of the county superintendent of public welfare and the truant officers as administrators and the superintendents of schools and the rural supervisors as advisory members. The county boards will seek the cooperation of local groups, which will be urged to appoint a committee in each community whose duties will be to arouse public interest in school attendance, help the teachers get the real reasons for absences, help to make adjustments in the homes when needed to permit the child's return to school, and make the parents realize the importance of education.

ENROLMENT at Columbia University this summer was 150 higher than last year with a total of 14,007 students registered. More than half of the summer students were teachers. The largest increase in enrolment was from the central and western states, with the number from the North Atlantic states less than last year. There are 4,203 students from New York State. Nevada has the smallest number with two students. There are sixty-nine students from Hawaii, the Philippines, Porto Rico, the Canal Zone and Alaska.

THE example set by the Royal University of Perugia in establishing a course in journalism has been followed by the University of Ferrara, where Signor Nello Quilici, the editor of the *Corriere Padano,* has been intrusted with the chair of journalism, and by the University of Milan.

BRITISH Instructional Films Limited, who are installing themselves in their new studios at Welwyn, Herts, have issued a catalogue of films which they are prepared to hire out at lectures, at institutions, colleges and schools. They include travel films and war films, and may yet include a series of historical films.

THE Scottish National Library in Edinburgh has received a second donation of £100,000 from Sir Alexander Grant. Among the conditions under which this second £100,000 has been given are: That the government be prepared shortly to take in hand the first portion of the new buildings; that the donor is to be the sole private donor contributing to the work; that the building be erected on the existing site or an adjacent one, fronting, and having a public entry from George IV Bridge and communicating directly with the buildings in which the National Library (formerly the Advocates' Library) is at present housed, and that the plans ultimately adopted are approved by the donor.

THE Jugoslav minister of education, Milan Groll, has introduced into the National Assembly a bill which provides that any woman teacher who marries any one not a teacher shall lose her position. In other words, in the future, the only married women teachers will be teachers' wives.

DISCUSSION

A METHOD OF CONSTRUCTING AND SCORING TESTS GIVEN WITH TIME LIMITS TO ELIMINATE OR WEIGHT THE EFFECT OF SPEED

SEVERAL recent studies have shown that the correlation between speed and level of ability is only moderately high, and hence that tests in which speed is an important factor will in particular cases be inaccurate enough to work a real hardship on individuals who are slow but able to do very difficult problems. At the same time there are conditions in which it is desirable to give tests with time limits so adjusted that few if any students finish the test. In testing large groups, it is very distracting to have some students finish the test and leave the room while the other students are still working. If those who finish early do not leave the room they are much more likely to look around and investigate the answers made by their neighbors or otherwise interfere with the discipline in the room. At times this difficulty might be met by having those who finish early begin studying some previously given assignment, but very often this is not possible or practicable. In tests of subject-matter there is a further important reason for giving tests with limited time in that this places a premium on thorough knowledge. The student who has mastered a subject can, other things being equal, answer questions on it more rapidly than on a subject he knows less about. Reduction in the time required for recall is one of the most important results of thoroughness. If, however, a test is constructed in the usual fashion and given with a time limit so adjusted that no pupil finishes the test the ordinary result is that none is measured on the entire subject, and the slower and less proficient ones especially are measured on only a part, perhaps only half, of it—the latter part of the test not having been attempted by them at all.

The method explained here makes it possible to meet these difficulties. By appropriate methods of constructing and scoring tests it is possible to give them with time limits but to eliminate or control the weight given to speed and at the same time secure a measure of each student's knowledge of the entire subject, or, in case of intelligence tests, to secure a measure of the ability of the slow students to do difficult problems.

In using this method the questions or items of the test should be of the "new type" variety such as true-false, completion, multiple choice and so forth. In making out the questions we begin at the first of the subject to be covered and make out 100 (or other large number) items arranged to follow some systematic plan. Each of these questions is to be independent of the others. It must not depend for meaning or construction on its neighbors. Next we go through the test and rearrange the items so that, using the original numbers, they are in the order: 1, 3, 5, . . . 99, 2, 4, 6, . . . 100. In other words, we take the odd-numbered items for the first half of the test and the even-numbered items for the last half of the test, with the result that we really have one test consisting of two approximately equivalent forms covering the same material. The rearranged test may naturally be renumbered 1, 2, 3 to 100 so as to conceal its method of manufacture and not confuse the students.

The test constructed as above is given with a time limit so adjusted that nearly all of the group tested will attempt the first fifty items, but so that few if any will finish all of the test. If the group is reasonably homogeneous this time adjustment will not be difficult to make. For heterogeneous groups it may be necessary to divide the whole test into three equivalent parts instead of two, so that nearly all will finish the first part, but few, if any, will finish the third part.

The result of giving a test in this way is that all students have been measured on the entire field covered by the test, but that the faster ones have been measured twice on a considerable part of the field. This fact is taken into account in making up the test score. If, for example, in the assumed case of a test of 100 items divided into two equivalent parts of 50 items, a student attempts the first 75 items we determine the total score on items 1 to 25, inclusive, plus items 51 to 75, inclusive, and divide this sum by two in order to get the average score on the part of the subject covered by those equivalent parts of the test. To this is added the score on items 26 to 50, inclusive. This gives a maximum total score of 50 points instead of 100 points as with ordinary methods of scoring. When a test is scored in this way no premium at all is placed on speed. The only difference between the scores of the most rapid workers and those of the slowest workers is that the former are more reliable because the abilities of the most rapid workers have been measured almost twice while the abilities of the slowest workers have been measured only about once.

If now we wish to place a premium on speed we may do so by adding to the total score just secured some fractional part of the score made on the second part of the test or on the whole test. We may, for example, add 20 per cent. of the score made on items 51 to 75, inclusive, in the case assumed. If 20 of these items are correct, we would then add 4 points to the previous total. The weight to be given to speed may be determined arbitrarily or, in particular cases where suitable criteria exist, the proper weighting can be determined by the method of multiple correlation. In cases where a test is divided into three parts instead of two the same general principles of arriving at scores can be followed. Those parts of the whole test which cover the same part of the subject are averaged, although in some cases two parts must be averaged and in others three parts in order to arrive at the correct figure.

Because of the method of constructing and scoring these tests it is necessary to caution the students against skipping wildly around in taking the test. Rather they should begin at the first and go straight through and should not spend an excessive amount of time on any single item. If an item is too difficult it should be skipped but no known items should be passed over. When a premium is placed on speed it will doubtless be wise to tell the class how the tests are to be scored so that the work will be rapidly done.

In tests of subject-matter the material can in some cases be arranged so that the most important parts are in the first of the two equivalent parts of the test. This will insure that most of the class will be more accurately measured on that part of the work.

There may be cases where it is desirable to have a measure of speed of work as well as a measure of level of ability or of extent of knowledge. If such is desired it can be based on the number of items attempted or preferably on the total number correct. It would probably be advisable, for example, if we were to take speed of work into account in determining the amount of work a student is permitted to attempt in high school or college. Where the average student takes 15 hours, the slow student might well take 12 or 9, while the rapid worker might be permitted to do 18. Certainly some students work twice as rapidly as others who do a similar quality of work. While this difference is related to differences in level of intelligence, there is adequate reason to consider it as a separate factor.

ROBERT S. ELLIS

COLORADO COLLEGE

QUOTATIONS

EDUCATION FOR EDUCATED ADULTS

THE exchange of amenities between American colleges and universities and their alumni has been for many years under suspicion of being over a one-way street. Through it the alumnus is encouraged to give as liberally as possible of his funds for the university's support. He is permitted a certain amount of latitude in recommending prospective students. He is even permitted a voice in the management of the corporate body by electing a quarter of the trustees, who theoretically have a voice in the educational system by virtue of control of the budget and the physical plant.

In exchange for this he is permitted the freedom of the campus and the classroom if he chooses to pay a visit; certain social gatherings are arranged from time to time for his benefit; and always he is a welcome visitor to any and every event where spectators go through a turnstile. From time to time he is scolded in the "unconscious funnies" by editors looking for a subject and staff writers who always scold about human group weaknesses as the most comfortable method of earning a livelihood.

There is a rising feeling almost potent enough to be called a conviction, that many alumni of many colleges are intellectually competent and worthy of a closer and more equitable relationship with the college; that the college owes them a greater return for their interest; and for the developing of that interest, for its own good, should build for the exchange of amenities a two-way street over which tho alumnus could continue, after graduation, to receive certain services looking toward his intellectual preservation.

Much groundwork has been done along these lines by pioneers in the movement, with Amherst, Michigan, Smith, Vassar, Pennsylvania and a few others leading the attack. Where a real effort has been made it has been met with enough success to justify it.

Among the services offered by these various colleges may be listed: reading courses, reading lists, loan libraries and personal advisory service; short courses, institutes and intellectual home comings; vocational advice and radio hours. All these are organized primarily for the alumnus, but open to a certain extent to the general public.

The idea offers a splendid opportunity for a new relationship between the college and the alumnus. It may eventually displace the notion, often stated if not actually believed, that the alumnus, if not a psychopathic, is at least a well-intentioned but permanent idiot.

These advanced ideas on the "education of the adult educated" meet with many difficulties. The idea is new, and not yet completely demonstrated. The cooperation of the teaching staff is never easy to secure. Many of these still regard one big intellectual breakfast for each student as sufficient. The addition of a considerable item to the budget for a mere frill might not appeal to either the trustee or the alumni fund subscriber. Finally, there has been no spontaneous insistence by any powerful group of important alumni for a continuation of education beyond commencement.

A pioneer must, of course, have vision enough to proceed without mathematical demonstrations, guided by the faith in his reasoning. Gradually the problems are being met. Questionnaires give assurance of the strength of the demand. A willingness to pay for services has in some instances solved the financial problem. These two questions settled, the cooperation of the teaching staff has become less difficult. The movement is undoubtedly gaining headway.—*The Cornell Alumni News.*

The recent investigations of Professor Thorndike at Columbia, mentioned by President Glenn Frank in his address at the Triennial, show that the capacity for learning does not cease as we have been thinking, subconsciously at least, at any given period, say when one graduates from college. In fact it appears that the man or woman of forty or more is just about as good a subject for the learning process as an undergraduate. Put these ideas all together and you have a basis for a new deal all around in university education.

It suggests the reason why so much interest is developing in what is called "adult education." As far as the continuation of college education is concerned, this term doesn't seem to fit precisely, but it does express an idea, which, of course, is bigger than merely continuing the impetus toward learning which should begin with a college course. In other words, any effort to stimulate further interest in study on the part of college graduates is only part of a bigger movement, which is not only national, but international in its scope.

All over the country, university men, presidents, faculty and alumni are considering this question of adult education. The Carnegie Foundation is vitally interested in it through the American Association for Adult Education, a body supported by a Carnegie grant. The American Alumni Council, in a series of resolutions passed at the last annual conference held at Minneapolis in May, also voted to study this very important question and pledged its support and cooperation in any effort toward further study of the movement. Just recently the new president of the Alumni Council, Miss Florence Snow, alumnae secretary at Smith College, has announced that the aims and policies committee of the council will join with a committee of the American Association of Adult Education in the study of the possibilities of continuing education after graduation.

The first meeting of these two committees will be held early in October, with President Little, President Coffman, of Minnesota, President Neilson, of Smith, President Jessup, of Iowa, Director Leonard, of Teachers' College, Columbia, representing the Association for Adult Education. The committee representing the American Alumni Council are Levering Tyson, Columbia, chairman; Frederick Allis, Amherst; Miss Harriet Sawyer, Vassar; J. L. Morrill, Ohio State, and Wilfred B. Shaw, Michigan.

The field before this larger committee is as yet more or less uncharted. Their problem is to find what, and how great, is the interest in this question of continuing study on the part of the alumni bodies on the one hand, and of the universities themselves on the other.—*The Michigan Alumnus.*

REPORTS

THE PREPARATION OF TEACHERS FOR DEALING WITH BEHAVIOR PROBLEM CHILDREN[1]

Few recent changes in education are as significant as those that have to do with behavior problems. What may fairly be called the scientific attitude—that of patient observation, recording of data, interpretation, understanding—is beginning to replace older methods of handling difficult children. The situation has been clearly stated by Howard W. Nudd, of New York City, chairman of the National Committee on Visiting Teachers:

> Every teacher, every social worker, and many a parent is familiar with the problem child—the boy or girl whose school progress or whose reactions to normal requirements point toward later inefficiency, delinquency, or some other failure in personal or social adjustment.
>
> What is the trouble with such children, and what can be done for them? How can the school obtain and utilize a knowledge of the forces that are affecting their success, and give them in fullest measure the benefits of their educational experience? Puzzles or pests at home, in school, or elsewhere, their personal welfare and the welfare of

[1] Presented before the National Council of Education, Minneapolis, Minn., July 3, 1928, as part of a report of the Committee on Behavior Problems of Children.

society require painstaking effort in their behalf. They can not wisely be regarded as temporary nuisances, whose present weaknesses a kindly fate will in some way heal with the balm of time, nor can they wisely be ignored, without serious study and effort, as inevitable liabilities which society must expect along with its blessings. To-morrow they will be citizens, for weal or for woe, and their shortcomings to-day, if left uncorrected, may have dire effect upon the character of their citizenship to-morrow. They present the most baffling, the most urgent, and the most interesting problems in the field of education.

The Visiting Teacher and the Regular Teacher

During the past few years the visiting teachers, or counsellors, as they are called in some localities, have made a very important contribution to the task of dealing with behavior problem children. With their study of home background, their application of the principles of social case work, their understanding of mental hygiene, they have helped the schools and the teachers greatly in this difficult situation. It has become clear, however, that, important though the services of the visiting teachers have been and will continue to be, ultimately the problem becomes one of giving to all teachers, in their preliminary preparation if possible, something of the same basic understanding of human behavior that visiting teachers are obliged to have, to the end that they may better understand individual boys and girls in school. That a real beginning has been made in this direction is indicated by the fact that, of some two hundred universities, colleges and normal schools whose catalogue announcements were examined, at least twenty are giving special courses definitely intended to prepare teachers for handling difficult children, and another score or more are offering courses in mental hygiene with something of the same purpose.

These courses have nearly all made their appearance in the past year or two. Most of them are the direct outgrowth of the work of the National Committee of Visiting Teachers. The committee emphasizes the distinction between courses that are merely theoretical in character, given by persons who have had no actual experience in handling problem children, and courses conducted by persons who have had such experience and who put pupils up against actual cases. All courses conducted under its auspices are therefore given by experienced visiting teachers and are based on actual cases which the visiting teachers have handled. During the summer of 1927, such courses were provided in seven teacher-training institutions. For 1928, courses have been arranged with the help of the committee in the following universities and colleges: University of Alabama; University of California; George Peabody College for Teachers, Nashville, Tenn.; Michigan State Normal College, Ypsilanti, Mich.; University of Minnesota; University of Missouri; New York University; University of North Carolina; University of Washington; Western Reserve University, Cleveland, Ohio, and the University of Wyoming. Courses of the same type, given by visiting teachers, are also being offered independently at the University of Colorado. "The purpose of these courses," says a statement from the committee, "is not in any sense to train visiting teachers, but primarily to assist the class teachers to understand and teach puzzling and difficult children."[2]

Typical Courses

One of the newer courses which clearly shows the influence of the visiting teacher movement is the course called "The Problem Child in School," given at the summer session of the school of education of Western Reserve University, Cleveland, Ohio. This course is described as follows:

> A study of the school problem of the individual child based upon actual class material drawn from the experiences of visiting teachers. The relation of behavior and scholarship to developmental history, mental ability, personality makeup, environment, family relationships, recreation and other causative factors. The adjustment of their problems through adaptation or change of attitude in home or community and schools. Utilization of community resources. Adaptation of the curriculum to special needs.

[2] For teachers who wish to acquire a full technical training for visiting teacher work the committee offers fourteen fellowships at the New York School of Social Work and at the Chicago Graduate School of Social Service Administration, University of Chicago.

Another course at the Cleveland School is the "Seminar on the School's Responsibility for Adjustment of the Individual Child." It includes "intensive study of several types of problem children, such as the dull, normal, superior, emotionally unstable, neglected and socially unadjusted," and provides for "additional case material drawn from the experience of visiting teachers."

The school of education of the College of the City of New York calls its course "Problems of Child Behavior":

The aim of this course is to train teachers in the technique of dealing with the behavior problems of school children through actual study of cases reported by child-guidance bureaus, habit clinics, disciplinary schools, and similar agencies. Emphasis is placed on methods of gathering, assembling and interpreting data. Fundamental laws of behavior are formulated as a result of these case studies.

At the University of Utah courses of the newer type are illustrated by the following two:

Case Work and the Schools. (a) An application of the technique of social case work in dealing with normal and "problem" children. (b) The rôle of the child-guidance clinic in facilitating the behavior adjustment of children. (c) The visiting teacher and her work.

Mental Hygiene (Advanced). An attempt to formulate the established principles of mental health. An advanced course for teachers, hygienists, counselors, and others, looking toward the development of mental hygiene guidance and instruction in the schools.

At the New York State College for Teachers, Albany, a course intended for graduate students and seniors is labeled "Psychological Study of Problem Children." It includes "study of intellectual, emotional and other characteristics of children who differ from the average"; it attempts to "trace various causes of unsatisfactory work, truancy, lying, destruction of property and other forms of undesirable behavior"; and it "considers constructive measures for aiding children to adjust to life situations."

Besides a number of courses dealing with child psychology, child development and mental hygiene, the National Kindergarten and Elementary College, Evanston, Illinois, offers the following:

Child Guidance. A series of lectures stressing the necessity of observing carefully the reactions of normal children in normal situations in order to help individual children realize their greatest potentialities.

In the summer session the same institution offers a course in the "Scientific Method in Handling Behavior Problems," in which "a study is made of the outstanding behavior problems with young children and the application of the principles of mental hygiene and psychology to their successful solution." A survey of the current literature in case studies and observation in the demonstration school of the college are required.

"The growing conviction that the school must concern itself with the entire personality of the child, and not merely with his intellect" is the reason announced by the Central State Teachers College, Mount Pleasant, Michigan, for its course on "Mental and Sex Hygiene." Another state teachers' college that has shown its interest in the newer approach is Marshall College, Huntington, West Virginia, which offers a three-hour course in the summer session on "The Problem Child." The college of education of the University of Minnesota calls its course in the regular session "The Psychology of Behavior Problems in Children." The University of Cincinnati, in its college of education, offers, in addition to courses on personality and education, the study of personality differences, psychology of character and principles of mental hygiene, a special course on "The Problem Child in Home and School," which is described as "a review, through case discussion, of the typical social and psychological factors leading to undesirable behavior in children; types of motivation; remedial measures." The course on mental hygiene in the summer session of the same institution covers:

Meaning and scope of mental hygiene; need for it in the schools; what has been done; human nature and social adjustment; practical suggestions for use in the schoolroom; for leaders of youth movement and for adults.

Field-work Experience for Teachers in Training

In a few instances field work is offered as a major part of the work of the course.

This is the chief element in the plans that have been worked out by the White-Williams Foundation, of Philadelphia, particularly in cooperation with the Philadelphia Normal School, but also with other institutions. "The chief emphasis of our work," says a report of the director dated February, 1928, "is coming to be upon cooperation with teacher-training courses in order that the problems of children's behavior may be better understood and handled by classroom teachers." Accordingly "counselors" ("visiting teachers") are placed in the schools of practice and a course in behavior problems is given by one of the counselors to a selected group of students who in connection with this are doing field work with the school counselors in their schools. Miss Emma Rannells furnishes the following description of the work done under the senior sociology course:

A small group of students, instead of doing the regular senior work in sociology, are having all their class and field work with the White-Williams Foundation, gaining in a very practical way further knowledge of child psychology and mental hygiene principles. This group of students, for a nine-weeks' period (the other nine weeks of the term they are doing practice teaching) meets for an hour a week of class discussion and spends two afternoons a week in field work in the two schools of practice and in the other elementary schools in which we are working.

Since starting the work in February, 1927, we have had five such groups, and a sixth group is starting this spring (April, 1928). Because of the practical difficulty of offering field work to many students, our largest group so far has consisted of twelve girls. Altogether so far we have had forty-eight girls. In our new group we have thirteen. The group having this special work is selected by the sociology department of the Normal School on the basis of high averages in the two departments of psychology and sociology.

In the class period our method has been that of discussion. The aim has been to give the students the point of view that behavior, troublesome and irritating to the teacher, is *symptomatical* and that to affect the behavior we must understand and treat the causes of the symptoms. Each group of students have chosen their own list of problems to discuss in the nine class periods. The following is the list of one group:

The rude, fresh child
The bully
The shy, backward child (the one who cries often)
The lazy, indifferent child
The defiant child
The child who steals
The child who lies
The fussy child
The tale bearer
The self-assertive child
The nervous child

In class the counselor presents a case referred to her by the teacher because the child has been exhibiting the particular type of behavior under discussion. In this way the fundamental causes of the behavior and the treatment applied in one case are clearly brought out. There is free discussion of the case, of other possible causes for the same type of behavior, and of other treatment measures. We choose the case carefully. The case of the *lazy, indifferent child,* for example, was selected from among a number of such cases, for several reasons—it was the case of an only child, in which problem the class had expressed interest, the child was of a well-to-do family, and, too, it offered the opportunity of presenting the work of the child guidance clinic, as Thomas was studied there. In this case the chief causative factors of the laziness and indifference Thomas was exhibiting were found to be hyperfatigue-ability and immaturity, both of these factors in turn having causes in both the physical and the emotional realm. For instance, one factor accounting for immaturity was the tremendous care and protection the boy had always had. This had made it difficult in school for him to apply himself because the teacher could not give him the constant stimulation which he had so depended upon in the home. In considering cases the students think in terms of which factors in the situation are assets and which are liabilities, and treatment, of course, is modification of the liabilities.

When the students first come to the school for field work they meet the principal and teachers, have a trip through the school, learn about the neighborhood, and consider the problems one might well expect to arise because of neighborhood conditions, such as lack of play space, factory neighborhood, etc. Field-work experiences consist of conferences with children referred as problems of one kind or another, consultation with their teachers, visits to their homes and visits to social agencies at the time, or formerly, interested in the family. Home visits are made only to those homes well known to the counselor and for a special purpose, such as giving the date of a hospital appointment previously consented to. However, because of the familiarity of the students with the situation as a whole, she invariably brings back information which is helpful in an understanding of the case. Before sending the student to a social agency the counselor explains every phase of the problem as we know it. She confers with the agency worker, telling her of the student's background, and so the worker gives the student not only a report of the agency's contact with the family, but also an interpretation of their work in general, the aims and ideals of the agency. When the student comes back with the report from an agency she goes over all the material secured with the counselor and the part the information plays in an understanding of the present situation is thought out by counselor and student together.

A course in which field work is the major element has been carried on during the past five years by the education department of Swarthmore College in cooperation with the White-Williams Foundation. The course is called "Social Work and the School," and is described in the Swarthmore College catalogue as follows:

> This course is given in cooperation with the department of school counseling and training of the White-Williams Foundation of Philadelphia. It consists of at least one half-day each week of supervised field work with the counselors in the public schools; and a fortnightly conference with the supervisor of the department for discussion of particular problems and interpretation of the work. The aim of the course is (1) to enable those who intend to be teachers to enter teaching with an understanding of some of the social causes of school difficulties, and some knowledge of social resources, and (2) to give those students who are interested in social work as a profession an opportunity to get a brief practical contact with one kind of social case work.

What can be Done through Existing Courses

It is, of course, quite possible to help prospective teachers for handling behavior problems by modifying existing courses, without necessarily introducing entirely new ones. Indeed, there is something to be said for this method of making the needed changes in the preparation of teachers in normal schools and colleges. An introductory course in educational psychology may, of course, help little or much in preparing teachers for the work they have to do. It may merely be the old psychology of the nineteenth century, with little or no relation to teaching; it may be modern in its point of view on laws of learning and scientific measurement; and it may—and of course should—include the contributions of what is sometimes called the newer psychology in respect to emotional life and human behavior. If prospective teachers can actually get their introduction to psychology and teaching from college and normal school teachers who themselves have the modern approach and are equipped with the newer psychology and mental hygiene—a real advance will have been made toward preparing teachers adequately to handle the problems of behavior. Dean William S. Gray, of the University of Chicago, points out that while at Chicago, for example, no special emphasis is given to courses on behavior problems, actually "a very large number of our courses in the school of education give attention to behavior problems of children." He cites the following titles: "Mental and Physical Growth of Children"; "Psychology of Elementary Education"; "Psychology and Treatment of Exceptional Children"; "Psychopathic Retarded and Mentally Defective Children," and remarks: "I seriously question the advisability of organizing special sequences of courses to take care of this particular field. I believe the best results can be secured by incorporating the necessary training into the basic courses which a department gives."

That significant case material can be introduced into courses bearing rather conventional titles is the experience of a number of institutions. Supplementary notes on the published announcements at Johns Hopkins University indicate that "in the regular educational psychology courses teachers and students make case studies of individuals having adaptive difficulties"; the course in clinical methods includes the purpose of "helping those who take it to increase their ability to understand the behavior problems of children and to help in the solution of these"; and the educational clinic "has for its aim the discovery and diagnosis of behavior problems of individual children," including "follow-up and recommendations of remedial treatment."

"School Use of Social Agencies" is the title of a course given at Teachers College, Columbia University. This is:

A course especially designed to orient superintendents, principals, and teachers in the problems of personality as they arise in the field of education, which, while not primarily involved in teaching, fundamentally condition the total experience of the child. A consideration of the resources that exist at present to meet such problems: the visiting teacher; the pupil's life-history record; the home; the neighborhood; the community and its social work agencies, especially child clinics and bureaus of welfare, research bureaus, agencies for the prevention of delinquency. Guidance, its methods and values for the child and the community. Throughout, discussion will proceed so far as possible from the consideration of actual cases.

The inadequacy of any course, whether of the special sort of regular courses in which the newer point of view is incorporated, unless contact with social agencies is made possible, is emphasized by Dr. Elizabeth L. Woods, director of the psychology and educational research department of the Los Angeles schools:

Few of our teacher-training institutions give much if any work which is definitely practical on this subject. Some mention is made of conduct difficulties in certain of the courses in educational psychology. The best help is usually obtained, however, in careful work under supervision from such laboratories as a child guidance clinic or a psychological clinic dealing with behavior problems. I believe that we are on the right track here in our system. We are loaning a school counselor each year to the child guidance clinic to do intensive case work on problem and behavior cases under careful supervision. This counselor comes back at the end of the year to us and assumes her own duties, but with new enthusiasm and point of view.

Child guidance clinics, such as Dr. Woods mentions, are now in operation in seven communities, following the five-year demonstration of the Commonwealth Fund, which came to a close in 1927, and visiting teachers are at work in fifty-five communities, in twenty-one of which a demonstration had previously been made by the fund. The opportunities, therefore, for cooperation between teacher-training institutions and social agencies interested in the schools are better than ever before, both for teachers in training and for teachers already in service.

Minimum Essentials in Preparing Teachers for Behavior Problems

In his report to the National Conference of Social Work in May, 1928, Dr. Henry W. Thurston, who served as chairman of the subcommittee on training of his organization and has cooperated throughout with the subcommittee of the National Education Association, presented a number of statements he had secured in answer to the question: "What are the minimum essentials regarding the problem child and his treatment which social workers in general and school teachers ought to know." Because of their direct bearing upon the topic of this report summaries of several of these statements are included.

Dr. William Healy, of the Judge Baker Foundation, sums up the needs as follows:

1. Some knowledge of physiology and medicine is needed by social workers and school teachers.

2. They also need a very considerable acquaintance with the values and weaknesses of social backgrounds.

3. Thoughtful consideration of the following facts will serve to enrich the knowledge and aid the every-day judgments of any who wish to deal understandingly with delinquents:

The problem of *mental capacities* in terms of standardized norms as far as these have been established.

The problem of mental *balance.*

Certain *dynamic* qualities of mental life, such as states of temporary or constitutional lethargy and laziness, as contrasted with alertness and forcefulness.

The qualities of mental life which are subsumed under the head of *personality characteristics,* etc., love of adventure, revengefulness, stubbornness, rebelliousness, or loyalty, generosity, kindness, responsiveness, etc.

Certain traits and trends as related to characteristics of the individual's group.

Of immense significance frequently for the study of delinquency is the mental content—ideation or imagery.

Mental experiences, plus repressions, are worthy of much attention in many cases showing the most persistent trends toward delinquency.

The fact and force of *mental habit* should never be lost sight of.

General mental attitudes, such as grudge formations against individuals or groups or against society as a whole.

Mental impulsions.

Dr. Lawson G. Lowrey, of the Institute for Child Guidance, New York City, lists the following statement of essentials:

Every social worker, and teacher, should have a knowledge of psychology, reading Burnham's "The Normal Mind" as a foundation.

Social workers and teachers should know a great deal about modern dynamic psychiatry, reading such books as White's "Outline of Psychiatry," Alfred Adler's "Individual Psychology," Freud's "General Introduction to Psycho-Analysis," and Bleuler's "Textbook of Psychiatry."

They should know a great deal about how children get to be problem children, reading such books as Healy's "Individual Delinquent," and "Mental Conflict and Misconduct," as well as the Commonwealth Fund publications—"The Problem Child in School," "Three Problem Children," and "Teachers' Attitudes."

All this reading should be tied together by courses of lectures on the dynamics of behavior and by actual case experience. The worker should carry at least one case through a clinic and attempt to work it out in detail, particularly with treatment.

One of the most important things such work must accomplish is to give the worker and teacher some insight into her own personality trends and the meaning of those trends in stimulating responses from those with whom she comes in contact, particularly children.

A brief summary of the needs is the following from Dr. Marian Kenworthy, of the New York School of Social Work:

Teacher and social worker should feel unsatisfied until they gain enough insight into the total experiences of the child to evaluate what these experiences have done in the development of the child's personality.

Social worker and teacher should feel challenged with the necessity of discovering what need lies behind the child's behavior, and what his behavior actually means to the child in his attempt to work out his adjustment to life.

Teacher and social worker need to know causes in the child's environment, as well as in his personality. They need contact with family background and knowledge of interaction between parents and children, sisters and brothers, their attitudes, interests, and prejudices relative to the child.

Teacher and social worker need to know the child's habits; the methods of handling him, and his educational experiences, beginning with the methods used in habit training and including his school experiences, both academic and in social adjustment.

Teacher and social worker should feel the necessity of planning treatment based upon knowledge of physical and psychological treatment of the child and directed toward the causes of behavior, whether physical, academic, social or environmental.

Conclusion

The past decade has been the period of scientific measurement of capacity and achievement as applied mainly to the traditional school subjects. With something of the same scientific spirit teachers are now giving attention to the problems of children as human beings. It seems likely that teacher-training institutions are about to expand and modify their existing programs to include the recent contributions of psychologists, social case workers and mental hygienists in the field of human behavior. It is important to emphasize, however, that to be truly effective this work must not only be based on sound theory but on actual living case material. For this reason workers in this field are insisting that the courses be given as far as possible by persons actually experienced in the work and not by those who are merely academically prepared. Some of the results that may be looked for from this new development have been summed up by Miss Edith Everett, former president of the National Association of Visiting Teachers:

For the teacher already in service, the scientific attitude toward undesirable behavior, as a fact for which the cause may be sought and found in earlier experiences, and the remedy for which may be provided through a change of conditions, making possible a more genuinely satisfying success, puts a new dynamic quality into her classroom relationships. For the student in training for teaching, it often removes effectively a bug-bear which has been hanging over her—her fear of meeting disciplinary problems. For when all behavior becomes, not a subject for praise and blame, opinion and judgment, but for thoughtful study and analysis, it leaves no room for fear, unless it be fear that we have not yet skill and understanding enough to give it the wisest treatment.

W. CARSON RYAN, JR.
SWARTHMORE COLLEGE

EDUCATIONAL RESEARCH AND STATISTICS

A STUDY OF HIGH-SCHOOL SENIORS TO DETERMINE WHO SHALL BE RECOMMENDED TO COLLEGE

FOR a period of three years the principal and counselor of one of the Los Angeles high schools have been interested and concerned in the problem of recommending high-school pupils to college. Nearly all colleges of this state hold a high-school principal responsible for determining the ability of a graduate to do college work. The pupil, the school and the college—to all three the principal must be fair. The principal of this school, being a progressive, forward-looking educator, determined to discover, if possible, a scientific method of recommending pupils to college. A study of the individual differences of any senior high-school class shows that all are not prepared for college work. It falls upon the principal, with the help of his counselor or whoever carries on the personnel work of his school, to decide whom to recommend to college. Of course, it is understood by all pupils in advance that certain marks and subjects are required for automatic recommendation to college. The fulfillment of these requirements, however, is arbitrary and does not necessarily indicate or predict college success.

In order to effect a more scientific method of arriving at a decision of individual recommendations, a procedure was set up for a more thorough study of the personnel of each senior class. The information concerning each pupil was secured by the counselor through private interviews, written questionnaires, the Terman Group Test, the Miller Test of Mental Ability and the Otis Self-Administering Test, the Stanford Achievement Test in Arithmetic, character rating charts, school marks and ratings on the scholastic ability by teachers.

These surveys were made for a number of reasons, of which but one will be discussed here: viz., to help discover the fitness of the members of the class for college recommendation.

For two years this plan was followed. There were, at the end of this time, returned to the high school, college freshman scholarship reports in sufficient numbers to make a statistical study possible.

The number of grade points earned in the freshman year was then figured for each of the fifty returned freshman reports from college.

The high-school scholarship rating was obtained by listing all of the marks earned and credits given in all academic courses taken in high school. A mark of "A" was given three points, "B" two points, "C" one point, "D" no points, "E" (failure) minus one point. The total number was divided by the total number of credits.

In the personnel files of the school, there were character ratings for each of the pupils under consideration. The traits which had been selected were: (1) regularity and persistency, (2) control of attention, (3) respect for authority, (4) application and industry, (5) coöperation in group activities, (6) ability to learn, (7) speed in work, (8) sense of accuracy, (9) trustworthiness and responsibility and (10) initiative and aggressiveness. Ten or more teachers had been asked (while these graduates were still in high school) to rate them in these traits, *1* if very superior, *2* if superior, *3* if average, *4* if inferior, and *5* if very inferior. The total of the very superior ratings was added to one-half the total of the superior ratings, added to one-third the total of the average ratings, added to one-fourth of the inferior ratings, added to one-fifth of the very inferior ratings. This number was then divided by the total number of ratings and multiplied by one hundred, and might be called the character rating index.

The intelligence rating used was the Intelligence Quotient on the Terman Test of Mental Ability. Thus there are four ratings for each of the fifty pupils for whom college scholarship reports were returned.

The problem is to use the foregoing data on 50 cases in order, first, to determine for the principal who is recommending high-school graduates for college the relationship between achievement in college during the freshman year and the best combination of achievement in the academic subjects in high school, in character rating and in intelligence rating, and secondly to ascertain the regression equation in these four variables in order to know the best weight to assign to the known ratings that may best predict success in the freshman year of college.

For this purpose it is necessary to use multiple correlation technique. For clearness and convenience we denote college scholarship in the freshman year by the letter "G," high-school scholarship in academic subjects by the letter "H," intelligence rating by the letter "I" and character rating by the letter "C."

The zero order coefficients are:

$r_{IG} = .429 \pm .07$

$r_{IH} = .420 \pm .08$ $r_{HC} = .690 \pm .05$

$r_{HG} = .523 \pm .07$ $r_{IC} = .326 \pm .08$

$r_{GC} = .410 \pm .08$

Thus the relationship between intelligence quotient and college scholarship for the freshman year and that between the intelligence quotient and high-school scholarship in the academic subjects are practically the same; the highest degree of relationship is between high-school scholarship and character rating, and the lowest is between intelligence quotients and character rating.

Partials of the first order necessary to the solution of the problem at hand are:

$r_{IC.H} = .055 \pm .09$ $r_{GC.H} = .080 \pm .09$

$r_{IG.H} = .272 \pm .09$ $r_{HC.I} = .644 \pm .06$

$r_{IH.C} = .285 \pm .09$ $r_{GC.I} = .316 \pm .09$

$r_{GH.I} = .418 \pm .08$

Partials of the second order are:

$r_{GI.HC} = .270 \pm .09$

$r_{GH.IC} = .457 \pm .08$

$r_{GC.IH} = .079 \pm .09$

And finally, the coefficient desired is

$r_{G.IHC} = .650 \pm .06$

The coefficient between college scholarship in the first year and intelligence has been raised from .429 to .650 by adding in the effect of character rating and high-school scholarship in academic subjects, while that between college scholarship and high-school scholarship has been raised from .523 to .650, and that between college scholarship and character rating from .326 to .650 by adding in the other two variables in each case.

The regression equation desired is found to be:

$$(\overline{G} - 17.14) = .23\ (I - 107.8) + .96\ (H - 20.06) + .47\ (C - 65.06)$$

$$\overline{G} = .23\ I + .96\ H + 0.47\ C - 29.97$$

Summary.

I. The problem is to ascertain how best a principal may know whom to recommend for college entrance. In attempting to solve the problem three facts ascertainable by a principal are used to predict success in the first year of college; high-school scholarship in the academic subjects, intelligence rating as determined by the Terman Group Test and the combined character rating in ten traits by several teachers.

II. The coefficient of correlation between college scholarship and high-school scholarship was found to be .523; that between college scholarship and intelligence .429, and that between college scholarship and character rating, .326; while the multiple coefficient between college scholarship and a combination of the other three variables was .650.

III. The regression equation to predict college scholarship for the first year knowing the other three variables was found to be

$$\overline{G} = .23\ I + .96\ H + .047\ C - 29.97$$

The standard error of estimate based on such a coefficient is quite high; and yet evidence such as this is certainly much better than intuition or guess.

IV. The study is merely preliminary to what might and should be done in this direction. A better selection of character traits, perhaps, and different evaluation of the character ratings would probably prove beneficial to a higher prognostic index; other significant data might well be obtained through the better standardized tests. The problem is a compelling one and will doubtless become more so as more and more young people clamor for higher education.

CELIA D. PIERSON
CHARLES H. NETTELS
LOS ANGELES CITY SCHOOLS

SCHOOL AND SOCIETY

Volume XXVIII | SATURDAY, AUGUST 25, 1928 | Number 713

ISAAC WATTS—AN UNSUNG SINGER OF EDUCATION

THE passing of the centuries reveals an interesting tendency to revaluate the achievements of individuals in the light of new points of view. This is well exemplified in the case of Isaac Watts, whose claim to immortality has been heretofore based upon his contributions as a divine and poet. With a diminution of interest in the religious themes he treated and with a dismissal of his poetry as "doggerel," he seems about to be forgotten. But there is one phase of his activity that has been largely overlooked; that is, his educational writings. Their popularity among early American schoolmen should win some recognition for their author in this country to-day.

Young Isaac entered at birth into a stimulating and stirring environment. During the last decades of the seventeenth century the struggle between the dissenters and the Anglican Church was still at a high pitch. Charles II was ruthlessly suppressing all traces of the Puritan Commonwealth and Watts' parents were among those who felt the weight of the royal hand. Some of the infant's earliest contacts with life were made at the breast of his mother, while she sat on prison steps; within, his father languished, suffering "for conscience's sake."[1] With such a background it would have been surprising if the life and thought of young Watts had not become permeated with religion. The impress of Calvin was still potent among English dissenters.

Education likewise played a prominent part in his early life. No less profound and significant changes were being felt in that realm than in religion. The formalized humanism of the schools was being subjected to critical attacks by educational thinkers. Educators were being forced to reexamine their axioms and their aims in the light of the new realism. As advances in science were undermining the naive acceptance of authority, so were the writings of Bacon and Locke undermining the Ciceronian curricula. Even writers friendly to humanism, such as Erasmus and Milton, had warned against the barrenness of formalism. And nowhere in England was there a greater interest in the problems of education than among the Calvinistic dissenters.

Watts' first experience as a teacher began in 1694; in that year he became a tutor to the son of Sir John Hartopp at Stoke Newington, a position he retained for five years. For his pupil he drew up the rudiments of logic; these notes he later enlarged into the volume, "Logick." The work was based principally on that of Leclerc and was published in 1725. It so well met the needs of the time that it was accepted in the English universities.

He began his clerical career as an assistant to Dr. Chauncey in Mark Lane, London, and two years later he was made pastor. Overstudy in his youth had undermined his health, however, and in 1712 a fever forced him to relinquish his pastorate. The last thirty-six years of his

[1] Robert Anderson, "Poets of Great Britain," Vol. IX, London, 1794, p. 287.

life Watts spent as a guest at the home of Sir Thomas Abney. The latter had been lord mayor of London and was one of the wealthiest and most influential of the dissenters. These years were particularly happy ones for Watts. He still retained his connection with his original church, but ill-health kept his pastoral duties light.

For the daughters of Sir Thomas he wrote "The Art of Reading and Writing English" (1721). Through motives of gratitude to his patron he seriously took up the writing of educational works. His catechisms, one for children of three or four years, and one for those of seven or eight, were composed for the use of his benefactor's daughters. Both of them were preparatory to the shorter catechism and represented an attempt to reach the child's understanding. They were accompanied by "A Preservative from the Sins and Follies of Childhood and Youth," also in catechetical form. Watts loved children and liked to write for them.

In 1728 he wrote "An Essay Towards the Encouragement of Charity Schools," a plea to the dissenters to establish schools for the poor. "The Improvement of the Mind" (1741) was probably his most widely used book. In "A Discourse on the Education of Children and Youth" (2nd Ed., 1769) Watts expounded his ideas on educational methods. "The Knowledge of the Heavens and the Earth Made Easy" (1726) indicated the breadth of his interests, from theology to science.

The pedagogical ideas of Watts are at times paradoxical. In general he was a product of his age, but here and there are flashes which bespeak the Romantic rather than the Rationalist. And some of his pronouncements are as sound to-day as they were in the eighteenth century.

In natural philosophy he bowed to Newton, in logic to Locke. He especially agreed with the latter upon the supreme importance of the reason to mankind. Nor did he overlook the educational implications of rationalism; of all the faculties of mankind the one most important and most worthy of training was the understanding. Frequently he was tempted to indulge in rhapsody over this, "the glory of human nature."[2] Children should be taught by reason; they should be given reasons for doing things. Only in this way did he believe the right type of conduct could be evolved. After his model child had arrived at the age of fifteen, "he was suffered to admit nothing into his full assent, till his mind saw the rational evidence of the proposition itself."[3] The boy's tutor was very careful never to indoctrinate him "with a magisterial air," a care that is practiced by few parents in this age of propaganda. Even in matters of theology the boy was urged to test all dogmas in the light of reason, and to accept only those which passed the test.

But Watts would not put his trust in exercise of the understanding alone. He was wise enough to realize the importance of the child's native curiosity in the development of reason. He pointed out the novelty of all life to a child; and that novelty is attractive. Enrichment of the understanding, he believed, should be attained by a wide acquaintance with the facts of nature. The rôle of the parent or teacher would then largely be a matter of answering questions and of stimulating further questions from the spontaneous interest of the child. He wrote:

> You who instruct them should allure their young curiosity to ask many questions, encourage them in it, and gratify their inquiries, by giving them the best and most satisfactory answers you can frame, and accommodate all your language to their capacity.[4]

[2] Isaac Watts, "A Discourse on the Education of Children and Youth," London, 1798, p. 336.

[3] *Ibid.*, 364.

[4] *Ibid.*, 303.

Since in general Watts agreed with Locke, it is not surprising that he should accept the latter's ideas on faculty psychology. He quite explicitly divided the mind into "faculties," or "natural powers." These included understanding, memory, judgment, reasoning, conscience.[5] That he did not consider this division a mere matter of verbal technique is indicated by the fact that he quite clearly prescribed definite types of training for each faculty. Exercise he stressed as the most important factor in the development of each power.

One difficulty in determining any writer's opinion on the question of formal discipline or transfer of training is the ambiguity attached to those terms by modern writers on the subject. Frequently educational theorists engage in spirited discussions of transfer—discussions colored deeply with emotion—and yet no serious attempt is made to delimit the subject of their debates. Opponents of formal discipline almost invariably accuse its defenders of accepting far more than they actually do. Effigies of straw are often set up by the militant-minded of both sides and then gleefully demolished. Don Quixotes are no less ridiculous in the field of intellect than in that of chivalry.

Unfortunately, Watts was less clear in his educational deductions than in his basic assumptions. When he made the statement that "the general principles [of mathematics and the sciences] have . . . valuable and excellent uses . . . for the exercise and improvement of the faculties of the mind,"[6] it is not quite clear to what he referred. Nor did he clarify the situation by hastening to include the fact that they "are often made of admirable service in human life." Somewhat less vague was his insistence that the sciences and poetry enlarge the capacity of the mind. In the case of the sciences he emphasized the value of a knowledge of the wonders of the universe in order that future reading might be better comprehended. Poetry he advocated because of the sublime ideas contained in it; the mind thus became familiarized with the beauties of the imagination. It seems more probable that instead of transfer Watts had in mind in this instance some crude concept of apperception. The aim of these studies implied in his discussion is remarkably similar to that later expressed by the Herbartians.

The real concept which Watts held regarding the matter of general transfer was probably best implied in his statement that

> Clear and distinct apprehension of the things which we commit to memory is necessary in order to make them stick and dwell there. . . . Many a lad forgets what has been taught him, merely because he never well understood it: he never clearly and distinctly took in the meanings of those sounds and syllables which he was required to get by heart.[7]

And conversely,

> It must be acknowledged that where a happy memory is found in any person, there is one good foundation laid for a wise and just judgment of things, wheresoever the natural genius has anything of sagacity and brightness to make a right use of it.[8]

Here, quite probably, is the heart of the matter. The development and use of one faculty may aid in the development of another, inasmuch as it formulates techniques valuable to the second; to that extent it may be called "transfer." The distinction is merely a verbal one. It most assuredly does not suppose any general and mystical improvement of the whole mind with the improvement of one faculty.

Watts' recommended course of study was rather remarkable for its extensiveness and its versatility. In these respects, though

[5] *Ibid.*

[6] Watts, "The Improvement of the Mind," London, 1798, p. 209.

[7] *Ibid.*, 170.

[8] *Ibid.*, 162.

not in its content, it approached the famous curriculum of Milton. At the basis of any education he placed the common arts—reading, writing, spelling and accounts. Even in a social way their utility was readily discernible. The study of spelling, for example, he advised in order to avoid blunders in writing letters.[9]

Following this basic training he would have children given a good knowledge of life, of themselves, of others, and of the world in general. This instruction, he insisted, should be of a useful nature, information that would aid them in their social intercourse and in their life work.

Young persons should apply themselves to know those things which most nearly concern them, and which have the most immediate relation to their own business and duty, to their own interest and welfare: and it is a valuable part of wisdom to neglect other things, and not to waste our time and spirits in them, when they stand in any competition with our proper and most important work.[10]

The principal part of Watts' course of study included what he termed the "ornaments and accomplishments." Because of their social value and the impossibility of an elegant education without them, children should be taught logic, arithmetic, algebra, geometry, geography, astronomy, natural philosophy, history, poesy, singing, drawing, painting, fencing, riding and dancing.[11] French might be added because of its aid in understanding English, but he did not consider it particularly valuable. Likewise those with plenty of leisure might include Latin and Greek. The climax of all this, however, was training in deportment. He insisted that:

Among all the accomplishments of youth there is none preferable to a decent and agreeable behavior among men, a modest freedom of speech, a soft and elegant manner of address, a graceful and lovely deportment, a cheerful gravity and good humor, with a mind appearing ever serene under the ruffling accidents of human life.[12]

The study of the sciences he believed should be begun at an early age, preferably at nine or ten. They would be very easily learned at that time, because the natural imagination of the child would assist in the understanding of them. Their content would be interesting and the pupil would not need any urging to master them. That Watts was familiar with the Latin texts of Comenius was indicated by his advice to mingle science with Latin to make the latter more "tolerable" to the youth learning it. It was particularly important, he believed, to teach the sciences early, because of their great usefulness.

And surely it is best as far as possible to train up children in the knowledge of those things which they should never forget rather than to let them waste years of life in trifles or in hard words which are not worth remembering.[13]

Watts did not share with his age the popular fallacy that a child was merely a miniature adult, in mind as well as in body. He followed his master, Locke, and preceded Rousseau, in his insistence on the recognition of mental growth. "The teachers of children," he wrote, "should have some prudence to distinguish their ages."[14] That he did not carry the idea to its extreme logical conclusions is scarcely to be wondered at; Watts had neither the genius of Locke nor the rebellious spirit of Rousseau.

If one reads of the attitude toward children in early New England, he would envisage the Puritan Watts as a stern disciplinarian. But the severities of Puritan-

9 Watts, "A Discourse on the Education of Children and Youth," p. 319.

10 *Ibid.*, 325 f.

11 *Ibid.*, 328 ff.

12 *Ibid.*, 335.

13 Watts, "The Improvement of the Mind," p. 206.

14 Watts, "A Discourse on the Education of Children and Youth," p. 305.

ism had somewhat spent their force by the beginning of the eighteenth century. And in many ways this mild divine reflected the joyous attitude of the first century rather than the harsh austerities of Geneva.

One disciplinary suggestion that he made was particularly noteworthy, because of the sound psychology involved in it; modern parents and teachers might frequently make judicious use of it. Speaking of his fictitious child, he said:

> He was enticed sometimes to the love of letters, by making his lesson a reward of some domestic duty; and a permission to pursue some parts of learning was the appointed recompense of his diligence and improvement in others.[15]

How many children have had their love of learning or of labor forever destroyed, because study had been prescribed for them as a punishment and not permitted them as a reward; of such a delicate mechanism is the child's mind constituted.

Whipping, Watts considered particularly ill-advised. This was a revolutionary doctrine in the eighteenth century, when every school had its whipping-post and when every parent took the dictum of the Hebrew epigrammatist to heart. They had yet to learn that epigrams should be read, not obeyed. Watts, wiser than Solomon in this, realized that a smile is more potent than a threat. His model child was

> Never driven to practice anything by a frown or a hasty word, where it was possible for kinder affections to work the same effect by indulgence and delay.[16]

That Watts' influence was wide-spread in the educational circles of England is, of course, to be expected. That his "Logick" was considered valuable enough to be accepted by the universities speaks well for its merit. But his greatest influence was among the dissenters and especially in their academies. His fame as a divine and as a theological writer would almost insure the acceptance of his text-books. Then, too, his popularization of Locke was welcome; the latter was very favorably received by the nonconformists.

It is not so well known that Watts' influence was also very extensive in the American colonies. Nor was the influence limited to the Congregationalists; as in England he was popular in all sects. Thomas Hollis, the famous Baptist benefactor of Harvard College, numbered Watts among his intimate friends. When in 1727 Hollis founded the first Harvard professorship of mathematics and natural philosophy, he wished it established upon sound principles. To secure these he called upon his educated acquaintances for plans and suggestions. Among the five complete plans submitted was one from Watts. These were forwarded by Hollis to the College Corporation for their selection and approval.[17]

Casting about for a candidate for the chair he had endowed, Hollis' interest was attracted to Isaac Greenwood. Not trusting his own judgment in scientific matters, he again consulted his friends. And Watts was one of the four who examined Greenwood in regard to his fitness for the position. As a result, the latter received the position.[18] He was shortly afterward discharged, but not because of academic unfitness.

Through Hollis, Watts acquired considerable interest in the Massachusetts college and made several donations to it. The Harvard records show a gift from him as early as 1724.[19] Again in 1737 he gave several books to the college library.

[15] *Ibid.*, 356 f.

[16] *Ibid.*, 361.

[17] Josiah Quincy, "History of Harvard University," Vol. I, Cambridge, 1840, p. 399.

[18] *Ibid.*, Vol. II, p. 15.

[19] Samuel B. Eliot, "History of Harvard College," Boston, 1848, p. 169.

Copies of his own works he sent across as soon as they were published.[20]

Yale was likewise a recipient of the good-hearted Watts' benefactions. He sent a gift of all his works and later a pair of globes to that institution. The college also used his text-books; in 1779 his "Logick" was being used in the sophomore class.

Other than the Puritan colleges made use of Watts' text-books; their clearness and simplicity evidently appealed to instructors. Originality is not demanded of a text-book writer. In 1756 Provost William Smith published a proposed curriculum for Pennsylvania College. Here one would expect to find no trace of Puritan influence. Yet the course of study for freshmen listed Watts' "Logick," "Improvement of the Mind," "Ontology," and "Essays."

In the neighboring colony to the north the College of New Jersey introduced into its curriculum in 1750 Watts' "Ontology," "Astronomy," and "Logick."[21] Evidence of the wide dessemination of his writings can also be found in the early records of Brown University. Among the gifts which that college received in 1771 were two of Watts' books. Its total library consisted of about 250 volumes and among these were his "Philosophical Essays" and "On the Passions."[22]

Probably the most surprising and convincing bit of evidence as to how thoroughly the works of this English divine had permeated the colonial society is found in connection with Dartmouth College. When that institution was established in the wilderness of New Hampshire, clear beyond the outskirts of civilization, the books of Watts had preceded it. A member of the first class at Dartmouth in 1770 was Samuel Gray, who had prepared for college in the "Indian Charity School" at Lebanon. And at this institution he had studied and mastered Watts' "Logick."[23] Two years later the Reverend Simeon Williams, of Windham, New Hampshire, was preparing students to be juniors at Dartmouth. He likewise grounded them in the "Logick."[24] From New Hampshire to Pennsylvania was truly a broad field. It is doubtful if there were many authors who enjoyed a greater dissemination among these pioneering peoples.

Watts was no less well known in the early American academies than in the universities. This was to be expected in view of the close relationship between the New England institutions and their prototypes in the mother country. His influence was especially noticeable in those pioneer schools of New England, the Phillips academies. Judge Samuel Phillips was intensely interested in the work of the outstanding English dissenters. Especially beloved were Matthew Henry and the two friends, Isaac Watts and Philip Doddridge. It is reported that the judge memorized most of Watts' poetry.

Many of the educational ideas of Samuel Phillips reveal a similarity to those of Locke; it is probable that he obtained them largely through Watts' popularizations. His original platform for the policy of Andover was distinctly realistic. The judge, in fact, opposed the study of Latin entirely; but Eliphalet Pearson, the first preceptor, converted him to the idea of its inclusion. The text-books of Watts were, of course, used in the schools. The students were even required to learn by heart some of his hymns for children and parts of his catechism.

Since the Phillips academies were to a great extent the models for many later

[20] *Ibid.*, 171.

[21] U. S. Bureau of Education, "Circular of Information," No. 1, 1899, p. 57.

[22] Reuben A. Guild, "History of Brown University," Providence, 1867, p. 82.

[23] Baxter P. Smith, "History of Dartmouth College," Boston, 1878, p. 59.

[24] *Ibid.*, 60.

ones, it was to be expected that their espousal of Watts' text-books would be imitated by the more recent schools. The works seem to have been especially popular in the female seminaries that began to spring up in the first quarter of the nineteenth century. Quite possibly Watts' progressive attitude toward the education of girls favorably inclined the sex to him. When Catherine Fiske began to teach young women at Keene, New Hampshire, Watts' "Improvement of the Mind" was used in her school. One of the outstanding institutions of this type was Joseph Emerson's Female Seminary at Wethersfield, Connecticut. And his prospectus, published in 1826, listed "The Improvement of the Mind" as a text in the senior class.[25] Emerson, in fact, edited the work and published it with a series of questions based on each chapter. So extensively was this American edition used that at least one revision was published.

From the academies and seminaries Watts' works passed over into some of the early high schools. "The Improvement of the Mind" was being used in the Providence High School in 1828. Some of his educational ideas attained a strong hold upon teachers of that period. Instructors in this Rhode Island school at the time agreed upon "the necessity of mental discipline"; adding, "that algebra and geometry have this tendency, none will pretend to deny."[26] In the very book they were using Watts had insisted strongly upon the disciplinary value of mathematics.

The influence of Watts in America extended even beyond the confines of the schools. So versatile had been his productions that both young and old found interest and profit in them. Not only did American children study from his "Compleat Spelling-Book," but at an even earlier age they learned his "Young Child's Catechism." An author could scarcely desire a more wide-spread diffusion of his writings than would be effected by their inclusion in the ubiquitous "New England Primer." At least one edition of that work, that of 1777, contained four contributions from Watts' pen.[27]

The almost universal knowledge of his writings among adults is evidenced by the frequent mention of, or quotation from them, found in early nineteenth-century writers. James G. Carter in his "Letters . . . on the Free Schools of New England" quoted from "The Improvement of the Mind" in support of the value of arithmetic. He agreed with Watts on the disciplinary value of that subject.[28]

Even a generation later Watts was still well known. In 1856 a contributor to Barnard's *American Journal of Education* in an article on reading presented ten different quotations from the English divine's work on the mind.[29] His educational influence was probably as wide-spread as his theological; and, concerning the latter, one writer remarked, "Watts' influence as a theologian with the ministers in New England . . . was hardly less than it was in England."[30]

In 1865, when Henry Barnard published his list of text-books used in America, nine

25 *American Journal of Education,* I (1826), p. 507.

26 G. A. Dewitt and J. Kingsbury, "Providence High School," *American Journal of Education,* III (1828), p. 428.

27 "The New England Primer," Boston, 1777. Facsimile in Barnard's *American Journal of Education,* V (1880), pp. 381, 385.

28 James G. Carter, "Improvement in Arithmetical Instruction," *American Journal of Education,* II (1827), p. 32.

29 T. H. Vail, "Hints on Reading," Barnard's *American Journal of Education,* II (1856), p. 216 ff.

30 Charles Hammond, "New England Academies and Classical Schools," Barnard's *American Journal of Education,* XVI (1866), p. 414.

of Watts' works were included.[31] Several significant facts can be gleaned from this list. All but two of the nine books had been published in America and several had gone through two or more editions. Possibly even more significant is the fact that the "Logick" and "The Improvement of the Mind" had been published in this country after the Revolution. Strong indeed must have been his hold upon American hearts to retain his popularity through the post-war nationalism. "American texts for American schools" was the cry of the period, a cry that seems to rise with cyclic persistence from first-generation autochthons. Most British writers were banned. But Isaac Watts, ever genial and ever versatile, remained. His position was secure—even against the storms of hysteria.

PAUL J. FAY

OHIO STATE UNIVERSITY

THE IMPROVEMENT OF COLLEGE MARKING SYSTEMS

DURING the last twenty years there has been considerable agitation by various educators for improvement of marking systems. Undoubtedly the problem was discussed prior to this period, but up until about 1905[1] practically nothing was written. The increase in numbers of students has had much to do with the increased agitation. As long as the president and the faculty could know all the students there was less need for a reliable marking system, but when students began to come by hundreds where before they had come by tens, the problem became one of prime importance.

While there has been in the last few years much agitation, some hard feelings and several hundred pages of periodical literature in connection with the problem, very little has been accomplished. The whole problem is surrounded by an emotional feeling which is very likely indicative of the unsound basis on which the matter rests. Are there any clues which might help to clear up this situation? I would like to make a few suggestions which may have some bearing in this connection.

It is assumed in this discussion that it is desirable to get one figure which best represents the composite work of the student. This is open to question, but can not be discussed here. It would seem to be the assumption that practically every institution in this country takes for granted.

I am not going to discuss the improvement of the process of differentiating between pupils in any single course. That problem has been discussed elsewhere; I shall limit myself to the problem of getting a composite indicator from all the student's courses. The marking within one course is fundamental, but it is not necessary to wait until it is perfect before attacking the problem of combining single marks.

When one examines the literature on marking systems at present available, one finds that almost all the material can be classified under the following headings: (a) "Presentation of Evidence to Show Variability between Instructors"; (b) "An Exhortation for Improvement"; (c) "A Suggested Plan for Bringing about the Improvement." Some papers include all three phases, some limit themselves to a or b. The objective evidence is limited in most cases to a presentation of present conditions. We can be certain wide variations in marking exist. It would seem that these wide variations which do now exist ought to make some differences, but do they, and if so, how much?

The suggested plans are for the most part based upon the use of the normal curve. Do the suggested plans improve the situation and if so, how much? What is the distribution of ability? Are the variations in ability from group to group of enough significance to warrant treatment? Do groups vary from year to year? Instructors insist they do. The answer to all these questions is that we do not know. But isn't it desirable that we set about to find out?

[31] Henry Barnard, "American Text-Books," Barnard's *American Journal of Education*, XV (1856), p. 568.

[1] *Cf.* "Examinations, Grades and Credits," J. McKeen Cattell, *The Popular Science Monthly*, February, 1905.

THE NATURE OF THE DISTRIBUTION OF ABILITY

The data with regard to the distribution of ability are mainly of the logical or inspection type. The logical deduces the shape of the curve by adding certain assumptions to the known fact that large random groups tend to give a normal curve. The difficulties are apparent, especially when various persons get opposite results.

The inspectionists go one step further objectively. They get distributions plotted and then by looking at them decide whether or not the normal curve is applicable. This too can not be accepted as a scientific procedure—it is too easy to alter quite markedly the appearance by such a simple thing as a change in the method of grouping scores. The process that should be applied is to test out the goodness of it and get a reportable result.

There is practically nothing available in this form. Thorndike and Bregman[2] have shown that the distribution of the ninth grade is normal, although some logicalites have assumed that even at that point it should be slightly skewed. Additional data on the form of distribution are given in Thorndike's "Measurement of Intelligence." It is possible to move the central tendency up or down and still keep the curve normal. In working with mental ability tests collected in a graduate institution, the author[3] found P equal to 695, which indicates the distribution is well described by the normal curve.

It is not enough, however, to show the distribution of native ability to be normal; we need to know about the distribution of specific abilities like Latin, English, mathematics, chemistry, etc. The answer to this problem will come only when there are available objective tests for all those subjects. One can not use present results because in a group in which ability is distributed according to the normal curve, if the test is too easy or too hard, the true picture is not forthcoming. Pressey[4] has called attention to the fact that even though the distribution of measures of native ability be normal, the distribution for any subject will not be normal unless certain factors like teaching emphasis and incentives are the same for all students.

One other factor that always enters into the practical situation is the administrative feasibility of any particular device. If I found that I could increase the correlation of a marking system with my criterion from .50 to .55 with an increase of about two hundred hours' labor per year, I might or might not use the system. If I were engaged in statistical research, I probably would; if I were in the position of the usual college officer, I almost certainly would not.

In our present state of darkness the normal curve is probably the best one to use. It is probably safer than to allow each instructor to determine subjectively his own distribution. We must admit, however, that we have no scientific justification for it; it should be tested out as fast as possible.

AMOUNT OF IMPROVEMENT

The next lack of evidence is in regard to the amount and nature of the improvement resulting from the installation of a supposedly better plan. One difficulty here is the fact that many of the plans never get off paper. But even when they have, people have been too prone to assume that decreased variability among instructors was desirable and a step in the right direction.

One thing that always can be done is to try out plans simultaneously and compare the differences or correlate the results. In the study mentioned the author found a correlation of .93 between an unweighted average of grades and system designed to correct for the variations between instructors. The r between the unweighted scores and a very elaborate score designed to correct not only variability but also differences in level was .91. It seemed that while there were wide variations between the way that instructors marked, when the results were balanced there was a sort of collective justice. This does not mean that such would always be the case; it would not. There were certain factors which made this situation distinc-

[2] *J. Ed. Res.*, 1924, 10: 271–8.

[3] "The Improvement of College Marking Systems," Bureau of Publications, Teachers College, 1927.

[4] Pressey, S. L., "Fundamental Misconceptions Involved in Current Marking Systems," SCHOOL AND SOCIETY, 1925, 21: 738.

tive. The point here is that one can not tell *a priori;* one must measure the difference.

It is not enough, however, to know that there is a difference; it is also necessary to be sure that it is in the right direction. Here is an exceedingly important field waiting for investigation. What are the criteria against which these composite scores are to be weighted; what, in other words, are marking systems for and how can one tell when the aims are achieved?

I will simply call attention to the need for study in regard to such problems as the weighting of marks from the senior year as compared with marks from the freshman year, or the weighting of marks from the engineering school as compared with the marks from the agricultural school. Are these differences measurable and significant? Techniques have been suggested for this purpose, but the usefulness of any technique must be actually tested for each institution.

The Handling of Marking Systems

The results from attempts to improve marking systems by assigning arbitrary percentages have not produced very satisfactory results and does not seem to be the desirable method at the present time. Under present plans an instructor is asked to do two things—rank the students in his class, which is a legitimate request, and secondly, to assign weights to the ranks, a task which he is not in position to do. This latter function requires seeing the particular group in comparison with all the other groups in the college. This is not the task for an instructor; it belongs to an administrator. The instructor should have a part in determining the policy to be followed, but the carrying out of the policy should be left to one person. He would use the devices suggested above to help him determine how to weight the ranks.

If there were available for every subject a series of standardized achievement tests, it would be possible for an instructor to weight his grades, objectively and easily, but it will be some time before that point is reached, although progress is certainly being made. It will be objected that such a plan will mechanize education and impersonalize it. It will impersonalize it only at a point where it is desirable to do just such a thing. From previous experiments one has some grounds for believing that just to the extent marking is impersonalized will the validity of the measures increase.

The criticism of mechanization is a fair one. It is possible to become so engrossed in watching the wheels run that one forgets what they are running for, but this need not be the case. If educators know just what they want marks for, there will be little danger at this point.

Marking systems in the final analysis have only one justification—to help the students. This help may be given in a number of ways. The student may be given an indication of his relative ability, the instructor may be helped properly to adjust his work to his students, the administration may be guided in its decisions about degrees, but in every case these things should be done for the students' benefit—immediate or ultimate. At present the chief use of marking systems is to determine who gets or does not get degrees and honors—mainly the matter of degrees. One reason that keeps marks from being more widely used is probably the difficulty in handling them in the present form. If colleges were to adopt a readily available system of marking, it would be possible to find out whether marks had any other possibilities. We especially need to emphasize their prognostic value.

This availability is another advantage for the suggestion for having the instructors rank the students and a single administrative officer turn these ranks into usable units. The ranks could be scaled in terms of a standard deviation unit in such a way that at any time it would be possible to get a single figure representing the student's position in comparison with the rest of the student body. One difficulty in connection with the use of letter grades is the problem of combining the various grades.

A final point in connection with marking systems is the present over-weighted gap between pass and fail. The differences in achievement between those just above and those just below the passing mark is not great, but the difference in effect is considerable. If there were some scientifically determined point such that people falling below that were known to be unable to succeed in the things that follow, there might be some justification for such a sharp demarcation; but under existing conditions where the dividing line depends very largely upon the professor's own subjective opinion, the importance of this division would seem to be grossly over-weighted.

If the instructors are simply asked to rank their students, they are freed from the onus of making this distinction between those who can and those who can not. One of the biggest difficulties in connection with arbitrarily assigned percentages of grades has been around the percentages of failures. Instructors realize the weight attached to this mark and they hesitate to assume the burden of the responsibility. If the instructors simply ranked the students, it would be possible to do away with the specific mark of failure for each separate course and judge the student on the basis of his total work for the semester or for his college career.

The points I have tried to emphasize in connection with the improvement of marking systems have been: (1) The necessity for controlled study of the assumptions and the results; (2) the distinction between ranking and assigning weight; (3) the necessity for making marks really usable by putting them into the form in which they can be used; (4) the reduction of the gap between pass and fail.

The inculcation of all these things into a marking system is not easy and will not come perfectly in one step. When such a system or any part of it is attempted, it should be understood as tentative and careful records should be kept so that it will be possible to know after a period of several years the successes and failures of the plan.

Ralph B. Spence
Teachers College,
Columbia University

EDUCATIONAL EVENTS

JEWISH SCHOOLS IN PALESTINE

A special correspondent to the New York *Times* writes that one of the first branches of development emphasized by the Zionist executive in Palestine was that of education. The government now recognizes the Palestine Zionist executive as the official educational agency for the Jews. About 65 per cent. of the Jewish children in the country are enrolled in the Zionist schools. The total enrolment amounts to about 18,000, distributed among kindergartens, elementary, secondary, vocational and teachers training schools. The remaining minority of Jewish children, about 8,000, are divided in the schools of the Alliance Israelite Universelle and the old-fashioned "Chedorim" and "Yeshivoth" (Jewish religious schools).

In the Zionist system of education there is a division, allowing for three different points of view. The majority of the children attend what are called the general schools; in the Mizrahi, or orthodox schools, there is an enrolment of about 30 per cent. and there is also a small minority in the schools of the Labor Federation.

In the general schools the system of education is similar to that which exists in Europe and America. In addition to the Bible and Hebrew literature, the children are taught the usual subjects. Particular emphasis is put on home geography. Frequent expeditions and observation lessons serve to bind the pupils to the land.

The Mizrahi schools are more definitely religious in character and orthodox in point of view. The course of study is a synthesis between the traditional course of Jewish study of the "Chedar" and "Yeshivah," wholly religious in character and based on the Bible and the Talmud, and the modern secular subjects.

The schools of the Federation of Labor are making perhaps the most evident attempt to readapt the Jew to the soil and to manual labor.

Of importance not only to the Jewish world, but to the cultural world at large, is the development and growth of the Hebrew University in Jerusalem. Up to the present the various faculties of the university have been engaged only in research and postgraduate work. As a result of the recent meeting of the board of governors in London the university has now been authorized to introduce systematic degree instruction for undergraduates, and two faculties—one in arts and the second in science—have been sanctioned.

Thus far the theory has been that so long as no diplomas or degrees are conferred, the university has no right to charge tuition fees. It has been dependent wholly upon endowments and yearly contributions, the largest part of which have come from the United States. Now there are committees of friends of the university in England, Germany, Poland, Rumania and Lithuania. A number of scholarships have been established and there is also a loan fund.

The student's organization is divided into a number of study groups trying to organize outside the university opportunity for study in the subjects that the university is not as yet able to provide.

With emphasis laid on the fact that the university is to be strictly non-sectarian in character, it is believed that this institution will fulfil the long-felt need of the hundreds of young men and women of the country for a center of learning ranking with the foremost universities of the western world.

THE PUBLIC SCHOOLS OF GREAT BRITAIN AND INDUSTRIAL TRAINING

According to a despatch from the London bureau of *The Christian Science Monitor*, the committee set up by the Minister for Education and the Minister of Labor to inquire into education in relation to trade reports that what trade and industry want from the elementary schools is general intelligence and adaptability, not specialized vocational training. The intellectual and moral characteristics which are required are those which would be produced by a sound general education, including an adequate amount of handicraft, and supplemented by physical training and organized games. They point out to the critics that it will be impossible to get the best results until the classes are reduced in size and until playing fields are more commonly provided.

The committee deprecates the introduction of more than a small proportion of special subjects into the school curriculum. On the commercial side, for instance, it declares, it would be deplorable if such mechanical subjects as shorthand and typewriting overshadowed the general education, which must remain the chief object of the school.

All the witnesses emphasized strongly the value of relating school instruction to the environment of the pupil. The treatment of such subjects as English, arithmetic, history and geography is steadily becoming more realistic in this sense. The extension of handicraft teaching, too, is warmly recommended.

The committee comments upon the suddenness of the plunge into employment for the ordinary child. To move at one step at the tender age of fourteen from the atmosphere of the school, with its comparatively easy hours and light discipline, to that of the factory, to move without an interval from the childish to adult surroundings, is to undergo a very disturbing experience. The committee approves of those firms who set up an "initiation school" for children to attend during the first few days of their employment in order to become generally familiar with the industry. Where such a course can not be adopted, the committee recommends visits to factories by school children under the supervision of a teacher and in close relation to the ordinary work of the school.

The committee thinks it likely that industry, including agriculture, would benefit by recruiting from the secondary schools. It recommends that the age entry into apprenticeship should be adjusted in order to allow of secondary-school children becoming apprentices after the termination of their school course at the age of sixteen.

The committee points out that there is an absence of effective contact between those responsible for the boys and girls as school pupils and those responsible for the same boys and girls as young workers. The first is due to ignorance on the part of employers of the school system; the second is a tendency, now disappearing, for teachers to forget their close relations with industry.

The committee recommends that the Board of Education establish a small special body representative of the views of employers, workers, local education authorities and teachers to undertake national negotiations between the various interests concerned—teachers, local authorities, federations of employers and trade unions.

THE SUMMER SCHOOL OF THE NATIONAL UNIVERSITY OF MEXICO

The eighth summer school of the National University of Mexico was one of the best attended sessions since the school was inaugurated in 1921. Students from three countries have taken courses this year—Mexico, the United States and Canada.

There were nearly 300 students from the United States, while Canada was represented by three students. About 90 per cent. of the American delegation were women, most of them school teachers. The largest contingent in the American delegation, which represents 39 states, came from California and Texas. These states furnished 81 students.

Sixty per cent. of the American students will receive credits in colleges and universities of the United States for their work at the summer school. During the eight years the school has been in existence, more than 2,000 teachers and students from American educational institutions have attended the classes.

The object of the school is to make available to professors of Spanish in other countries, particularly the United States, the most efficacious means of learning this language and practicing it. The tuition fee for the course is $30.

The courses in English at the school have been especially popular with all the students. Great interest has been shown in the lectures on general sociology in English by Dr. Edward Ross, of the University of Wisconsin, as have been the lectures on Aztec literature by Professor John H. Cernyn, of the faculty of the National University of Mexico and the course on Mexican folklore by Professor Fernando Ramirez de Aguilar.

EXCHANGE STUDENTS FROM SOUTH AFRICA

TWELVE South African educational and cultural leaders will visit the United States during the next year under the auspices of the Carnegie Corporation of New York. President F. P. Keppel has announced that they will study American public-school systems, technical and commercial schools, parks and museums, libraries, community welfare, hospitals, city management, rural poor relief and other features of American activity.

South African educators advertised publicly for applicants and chose the following: S. C. Butler, principal, Tsolo School of Agriculture, to study Negro agricultural education; R. J. W. Charlton, assistant superintendent, Johannesburg General Hospital, to study hospital organization; E. C. Chubb, curator of Durban Public Museums and Art Gallery, to study educational use of museums; W. H. Hemar, principal, Cape Technical College, Cape Town, to study technical education; L. Hotz, secretary, Union Advisory Council of Labor, Pretoria, to study labor and industrial problems; E. P. M. Long, assistant in the public service labor department, Pretoria, to study wage regulation; A. D. Luckhoff, secretary, Algemene Armesorg Committee, Dutch Reformed Church, to study rural poor relief work; J. M. Meiring, head master, Gray College School, to study the organization of secondary education; O. J. P. Oxley, professor of fine arts, Natal University, to study art education; O. H. Howe, teacher in the Girls' High School, St. James, to study vocational guidance for girls; S. H. Scaife, inspector, Cape Education Department, to study agricultural education; M. S. Walsh, member of Cape Town City Council, to study aspects of city management.

The visits of the South Africans are part of an exchange plan being put into effect by the Carnegie Corporation whereby American educators are to spend a period in Africa making studies for the corporation.

THE COMMUNITY RECREATION MOVEMENT

THE Bureau of Labor has made public a summary of community recreation activities in the United States in 1927, according to which the movement made substantial progress during 1927. Reports have been received from 815 cities throughout the country which maintain community recreation plans under trained leadership. The number of cities reporting recreation programs for the community had increased from 505 in 1922 to 815 in 1927, and the number of trained workers from approximately 11,000 to nearly 20,000. In addition to these paid workers, 203 cities reported that 7,025 trained volunteers assisted in carrying out the recreation programs. The number of cities employing workers throughout the year had increased from 215 in 1922 to 321 in 1927. Training classes for paid workers were maintained by 146 cities and for volunteer workers by 82 cities.

Separate play areas in charge of recreation leaders numbered 10,770, an increase of 647 over those reported in 1926. The faculties provided include 6,301 outdoor playgrounds, 2,156 indoor recreation centers and 349 community houses, part of these facilities being provided for colored residents. The out-of-door playgrounds had an average daily attendance of more than 1,400,000 persons, including both participants in the sports or games and spectators. The indoor recreation centers had an average daily attendance of nearly 300,000 and the community houses an average attendance of 46,000.

Other recreation facilities reported include 403 bathing beaches in 214 cities, 840 swimming pools in 364 cities, 227 streets closed for play in 31 cities, 263 golf courses in 180 cities, 231 summer camps in 82 cities, and 694 play areas which do not come under the foregoing classifications in 52 cities. In addition a large proportion of the cities report tennis courts, baseball fields and athletic fields.

The majority of the recreation programs are under the direction of municipal recreation commissions, departments or boards, and in a number of cities municipal and private departments are combined in the management of playgrounds and community centers. About 280 cities report that private organizations maintain part or all of the recreation facilities.

Of 658 cities reporting on the sources of support for community recreation, 394 were carried on by means of municipal funds, 97 by private funds and the remainder by a combination of municipal and private funds and appropriations from the county or state. The total expenditure for public recreation in 1927 as reported by these cities amounted to $32,191,763.

THE MILBANK MEMORIAL FUND

John H. Kingsbury, secretary of the Milbank Memorial Fund, has made public a report on the results of intensive work carried out in three health demonstration areas in the attempt to reduce to a minimum the sickness and death rate from preventable diseases. The three areas chosen were two square miles in the Bellevue-Yorkville section of New York City, in Syracuse and in rural Cattaraugus County. The work, for which an appropriation of $2,000,000 was made, was begun in New York in 1925 and in the up-state areas in 1923.

In the last five years deaths from non-pulmonary tuberculosis in Cattaraugus County have averaged one third of what they were during the preceding nine years. Three successive low death rates constitute an unparalleled record in that region, which formerly failed to show a downward trend even when tuberculosis mortality in the United States registration area and in New York State was on the decline.

The average death rate from this disease in Cattaraugus County was formerly 71.7 per 100,000 population. In 1923, the year the experiment began, it was 68.1. By 1925 it had dropped to 45.3. In 1925 it was 43.7, and in 1927 had dropped still further to 42.1.

During 1924, 1925 and 1926 the infant mortality rates were lower than in any of the previous eight years, the decline marking a definite departure from an upward trend which had been evident from 1916 to 1923. A study of the causes of death revealed that the three-year decline was due chiefly to the reduction in the number of deaths from preventable diseases.

More than one half of all the children under ten years in the rural schools of the county have been immunized against diphtheria. The Cattaraugus County Board of Health has established a maternity, infancy and child health service under direction of a trained specialist, who is cooperating with similar state and federal health services in attempting to utilize the methods employed by health departments of world-wide reputation to reduce maternal and infant mortality and to safeguard the health of the child not yet old enough to attend school.

The 1927 death rate from tuberculosis in Syracuse was the lowest the city has ever had. The rate of fifty-nine deaths to 100,000 population during the year represents a reduction of 60 per cent. from the rate of 146 in 1908. Syracuse has the lowest tuberculosis death rate on record among the large cities of the United States.

As a result of an intensive campaign there to protect children from measles, the mortality from this illness was 69 per cent. lower among children under three years of age during the 1926–27 epidemic than it was in the preceding outbreak. It is pointed out in the Milbank Fund report that fully 70 per cent. of all deaths from measles occur within the first three years of life.

More than 20,000 Syracuse children, chiefly of school age, have been immunized from diphtheria within the last three years. Judging from the periodicity of the disease in the past, the report points out, another wave of diphtheria is about due.

The infant mortality rate in Syracuse has exhibited a continuous decline during the entire period of 1916–27. The maternal mortality rate, on the other hand, has shown an upward course for the last two years.

Last year was the first full twelve months of activity on the part of the health center at 325 East Thirty-eighth Street, which is now under development by the Bellevue-Yorkville health demonstration. It is estimated that 109,000 contacts were made during the year. The work in this region was started too recently to show results as positive as those found up-state.

A study made in this area showed that the third-grade school children have a higher average of physical defects than those of the city as a whole and that the medical and nursing staffs now available are inadequate for school medical inspection.

The death rate in this district was 16.74 in 1,000 in 1924, 18.62 in 1925 and 19.13 in 1926. Organic disease was the principal cause of death, followed by pneumonia, cancer and accidents.

The appropriations made by the Milbank Memorial Fund during 1927 bring the total of its contributions since incorporation to $5,388,-007.32. Aside from the sum of $325,000 set aside for the New York health demonstrations, the fund made appropriations in 1927 amounting to $193,450, chiefly to agencies working in the field of public health.

THE CHICAGO SUPERINTENDENCY

The correspondent of the *School Board Journal* writes as follows:

William J. Bogan is Chicago's new superintendent of schools. After the Chicago schools had completed one entire school year without an official head of the educational department, the school board on June 27 unanimously elected the man who was unofficial acting superintendent throughout that period. Mr. Bogan has been in the Chicago system for 35 years. Prior to his promotion to the position of assistant superintendent in 1924, he was principal of Lane Technical High School. The new superintendent is 58 years old and has four children. It is likely that the new leader will be very well received by the teachers and principals.

At the time of his election, Mr. H. Wallace Caldwell, the new president of the board of education, lauded Superintendent Bogan as follows: "In paying you this most perfect tribute, the board of education has given its vote of confidence and its complete trust in placing in your hands the educational welfare of Chicago school children. No political interference will be placed in your path. You are the chief."

Mr. Bogan responded, saying, "The honor conferred upon me today is as great as any one who believes in children could receive. The responsibility is great. It would be too great did I not know that I will share it with you."

Although 25 candidates were considered, the choice is said to have resulted from a recommendation of the Mayor's Advisory Committee and the personal regard of a majority of the board members for the man who successfully piloted by careful leadership the great Chicago public-school system without real authority.

It is interesting to note that the Public School Emergency Committee, which turned loose several scorching statements against the school board during the past year, has, through two of its most noted representatives, Rev. Charles W. Gilkey and Rabbi Louis Mann, expressed satisfaction at the selection of Mr. Bogan. They stated, "We congratulate Superintendent Bogan on the great opportunity that is his to give Chicago a school administration that will restore to the city and its public schools their rightful place in the esteem and confidence of the nation."

Confronted with so many piled-up problems awaiting settlement, the new superintendent decided to forego any vacation this summer. He has intimated that the junior-high-school program, which has been "under his wing" since its start four years ago, will be pushed. He held out the hope that as soon as the school board's finances can be strengthened, there will be an increase in salaries for the teaching force. Between now and September there are many important teaching and executive positions to be filled, chief among them the presidency of the Chicago Normal College.

THE GRADUATE LIBRARY SCHOOL OF THE UNIVERSITY OF CHICAGO

The new graduate library school of the University of Chicago, which is an outgrowth of a movement on the part of the library profession for an institution devoted exclusively to research and graduate study, will open with the autumn quarter of the university on October 1, according to Dean George Alan Works.

J. C. M. Hanson, recently acting director of the University of Chicago libraries and now in charge of the recataloguing of the Vatican Library in Rome, will be professor of bibliography, classification and cataloguing in the new school; Harriet E. Howe will be associate professor of library science, and Douglas Waples, professor of educational method. Dr. Pierce Butler, of the Newberry Library, Chicago, will be a lecturer for the autumn quarter, and the special lecturers already engaged include J. Christian Bay, librarian of the John Crerar Library; Theodore W. Koch, librarian of Northwestern University; Carl H. Milam, secretary of the American Library Association; Carl B. Roden, librarian of the Chicago Public Library, and George B. Utley, librarian of the Newberry Library.

The kinds of positions for which the new library school will give preparation include those of administrators of public, college and university libraries, teachers for library schools and of library science in teachers' colleges, and librarians of special collections such as law, history, medicine, science, Americana and manuscripts. Chicago has many important library interests that will be invaluable to the school. The American Library Association has its headquarters in Chicago, which makes cooperation in certain types of studies readily possible, and the library science student will find unusual facilities for his work in the great libraries for which Chicago is famous—the Crerar, Newberry, Public, University of Chicago and Northwestern, and other notable collections like those of the Chicago Historical Society, the Chicago Law Institute and the Municipal Library.

THE EXPERIMENTAL SCHOOL OF THE UNIVERSITY OF WISCONSIN

Additions to the teaching staff of the experimental college of the University of Wisconsin, under direction of Dr. Alexander Meiklejohn, will include nine men when the fall session opens. Coming of a second year class necessitates an increase of instructors or "advisers" to a total of about 20.

At the close in June of the regular session, 111 freshmen finished the first year of the new college. Total enrollment during the entire year was 119. Of the original group of students, 108 reserved rooms for the second year, according to Carl Bogholt, who is serving as secretary during the summer. Three of these have withdrawn, leaving 105 who are expected to be included in the second year class.

Rooms in the dormitories will accommodate 256 men. With 105 expected to return as sophomores, and 20 advisers, room for 131 freshmen is available. The exact figure may vary before the session opens.

Inquiries regarding admission to the college are now being received, says Mr. Bogholt, and a considerable number of freshmen have already definitely enrolled in the college. Prospective students are indicating their desire to enroll in applications for admission sent to the registrar of the university.

New members of the staff include Professor Carl Russell Fish, professor of American history at the university; Clarence E. Ayres, lecturer in philosophy, former student at Brown University, University of Chicago and Harvard University, and associate editor of *The New Republic;* Robert J. Havighurst, assistant professor of physics, graduate of Ohio Wesleyan and Ohio State University, formerly fellow with the Rockefeller Council of Research at Harvard, and recently assistant professor of chemistry at Miami University; Francis Steegmuller, instructor in English, formerly at Columbia University, author of "O Rare Ben Jonson," which he wrote under a pen name, and other books; Ralph M. Crowley, assistant in psychology, who received a master of arts degree at the University of Wisconsin; Paul M. Herzog, assistant in history, from Harvard University; Douglas Orr, Swarthmore College. Another addition to the staff is expected to be announced shortly.

Advisers already on the staff include Dr. Meiklejohn, former president of Amherst College; Walter R. Agard, professor of Greek civilization; John M. Gaus, professor of political science; Percy M. Dawson, associated professor of physiology; Samuel G. A. Rogers, associate professor of French; Laurance J. Saunders, associated professor of history; Paul A. Rausenbush, assistant professor of economics; Malcolm P. Sharp, assistant professor of law; Carl M. Bogholt, instructor in philosophy; John Powell, Jr., assistant in philosophy.

These advisers give most of their time to the experimental college, but each gives some instruction in regular classes of the university.

The freshman course of study will again be concerned this year with Athenian civilization. The subject for study in the sophomore year will be the life, thought and organization of modern America.

EDUCATIONAL NOTES AND NEWS

Professor Andrew Fleming West, dean and founder of the Graduate College of Princeton University, whose resignation was presented to the trustees in the spring, will pass over his administrative work to his successor, Professor Augustus Trowbridge, at the beginning of the college year.

Dr. Frank P. Graves, New York State commissioner of education, has returned to the United States from Belgium, where he attended the dedication of the library of Louvain University.

Dr. James Earl Russell, dean emeritus of Teachers College, Columbia University, who returned on August 12 from a world tour, was on the same day the guest of honor at the annual men's steak dinner of Teachers College. Dr. Russell gave a brief account of the trip, which he took in the interest of the Carnegie Foundation. One thousand students of education attending the summer session of Teachers College were at the dinner.

Before leaving California to take up his work as chancellor of the University of Denver, Dr. F. M. Hunter, since 1917 superintendent of schools at Oakland, was the guest of honor at a testimonial dinner given by five hundred colleagues and friends.

Professor W. A. Bratton, for thirty-one years head of the department of mathematics in Whitman College, has been granted the degree of doctor of science by Williams College, his alma mater. Professor Bratton studied in Columbia University during the academic year just closed.

Robert E. Bacon, assistant dean of Harvard College, has resigned to become dean of St. John's College, Annapolis, Maryland. Besides the deanship, he will be vice-president of the college and assistant professor of English.

Dr. Charles Hugh Neilson has been appointed associate dean at the St. Louis University School of Medicine, to fill the vacancy left by the death on July 11 of Dr. Don R. Joseph.

Frank W. Clelland has been appointed assistant dean and will act as dean of the school of religious education of Boston University during the coming year. He was formerly secretary and registrar of the university's school of social service.

Professor William D. Trautmann, associate professor of German, has been appointed dean of Adelbert College, Western Reserve University.

Dr. Hervin U. Roop, for the past five years head of the department of philosophy and education and director of the summer school of Wheaton College, has resigned to accept the position of dean of Lincoln Memorial University at Harrogate, Tennessee, and head of the department of philosophy and psychology. Dr. Roop was for a number of years president of Lebanon Valley College, Pennsylvania. Lincoln Memorial University is a non-sectarian, coeducational institution of a thousand students, an endowment of two million, and thirty buildings. The B. A. Duke Hall of Citizenship has just been dedicated.

The Reverend H. S. Ficke, of the Presbytery of Boston, has accepted the position of professor of English and head of the department at the University of Dubuque, Iowa, an institution set aside by the General Assembly of the Presbyterian Church for the training of leaders in Americanization.

Dr. H. R. Laslett, professor of psychology in Whitman College, goes to the Oregon State College, Corvallis, in a similar capacity this autumn.

In the department of zoology of the University of Pittsburgh, the following changes in rank are in effect for the coming year: Robert T. Hance, from acting head to head of the department; P. W. Whiting, from assistant to associate professor; E. Alfred Wolf, from instructor to assistant professor; A. W. Kozelka, from instructor to assistant professor at the Erie Center of the University of Pittsburgh; E. P. Jones, from graduate assistant to instructor at the Uniontown Center of the university. New appointments to graduate assistantships include: Dorothy Binns, Carey H. Bostian, Donald Charles, George Dambach, Paul R. David, Eward McCrady, Jr., George E. Snyder and Ruth Thompson.

Additions have been made to the faculty of the department of French of the University of California at Los Angeles as follows: Professor Paul Bonnet, who for the past three years has been a lecturer in the University of Sydney, Australia. He was president of the Alliance Française in Sydney and took an active part in the cultural and civic life of the community. Dr. Maxwell Smith, of the University of Chattanooga, Tennessee, will occupy the post of lecturer in French. Jean Jontard, formerly a professor in the City College of New York, will also join the faculty in the fall; as also Miss Julia Broquet, who has been teaching French at Mills College, who has been appointed associate.

Esson M. Gale, for twenty years a resident of China and lately an administrative officer in the Chinese government, has returned to America to accept a position as lecturer in Oriental languages at the University of California.

Frederick Maurice Powicke, professor of medieval history in the University of Manchester, has been appointed regius professor of modern history in the University of Oxford in the room of the late Mr. H. W. C. Davis.

Ernest Camp, Jr., formerly state news editor of the southern divisional offices of the Associated Press, Atlanta, has been appointed an instructor in journalism in the Henry W. Grady school of journalism, University of Georgia.

J. E. Hansen, formerly superintendent of schools at Westby, Wis., has been appointed assistant chief of the bureau of visual education in the extension division of the University of Wisconsin.

Dr. M. G. Neale, of the school of education of the University of Missouri, who in June accepted the position of assistant commissioner of education of New York State, has reconsidered his decision and will remain at the University of Missouri. The assistant commissioner will be head of the finance division, a position created at the last session of the New York Legislature.

The school board of Indianapolis has appointed successors to three assistant superintendents, whose positions were abolished last October. The new assistants are Mr. F. T. Glidden, formerly assistant state superintendent; Mr. B. B. Williams, statistician of the state education department, and Mr. C. C. Underwood, formerly of the Crawfordsville schools.

We learn from *The School Board Journal* that William Dick, secretary of the board of education at Philadelphia, Pa., has retired with the completion of fifty years of service. Mr. Dick became connected with the school system of Philadelphia in June, 1875, with his appointment as clerk. In 1891 he was made paymaster, and in 1906 he became secretary of the board. Mr. Dick is a member of the National Association of School Business Officials and had served as president and secretary of the association.

Dr. C. W. Merriman has resigned as a member of the school board at Beloit, Wis., after a service of more than fifty years.

V. T. Harlow, late of Brasenose College, Oxford, and recently lecturer in history at University College, Southampton, has been appointed keeper of Rhodes House Library.

Dr. E. R. A. Seligman, McVicker professor of economics at Columbia University, has undertaken to make for John J. Raskob, national Democratic chairman, a complete study of the farm relief problem.

Two British students are to make world tours as the result of awards made by Arthur Jenkins and Mrs. Barbara Wootton, representing the British Labor Party, and E. R. Palmer and Miss Bradley, of the cooperative movement. These awards are the first under a scheme endowed by Sir Arthur Dyke Acland for providing deserving scholars with means to travel. They go to Paul Winterton, of Warlingham, Surrey, who proposes to study the conditions of the peasants in southern Russia, with special reference to agricultural and industrial cooperation; and to May Louisa Dhonau, of New Cross, London, who will investigate German and Austrian local government with special reference to recent developments in rating and municipal enterprises.

Samuel J. Beck and Carl H. Rogers, fellows in psychology of the National Committee for Mental Hygiene, under grant of the Commonwealth Fund, and in training at the Institute for Child Guidance in New York City during the past year, completed their fellowships on June 1. Mr. Beck has been appointed psychologist to the Jewish Board of Guardians, committee on field activities, in New York City. Mr. Rogers has taken a position as psychologist in the department of child study of the Society for Prevention of Cruelty to Children, in Rochester, N. Y.

Dr. Ira S. Wile, of New York, has been invited to give a series of five lectures on "The Problem Child" from July 2 to July 6, 1929, under the auspices of the Tavistock Square Clinic for Functional Diseases in London.

Sir James Irving, of St. Andrew's University, Scotland, gave an address recently before the English-speaking Union at Chicago, on the desirability of establishing fellowships for American students in universities other than Oxford and Cambridge. He believes that "such students will return to America with a fairer view of Britain and a better understanding of the British people than is possible by the restricted method of sending men to Oxford only."

Nathan Lamport, president of the Yeshiva College of America, a Jewish institution now being built in New York City, died on August 14 at the age of seventy-four years.

I. F. Hall, for twenty-five years superintendent of schools at North Adams and more than sixty years engaged in educational work in Massachusetts, died on May 27 at the age of eighty-one years.

Edwin Smith Richards, a retired school principal, who served the public schools of New Jersey for fifty years, died on August 11 at the age of seventy-two years.

Jessie Claire McDonald, for fifteen years principal of the National Cathedral School for Girls, died on August 12 at the age of fifty-nine years.

Viscount Haldane, of Cloan, British Secretary of War from 1905 to 1912 and twice Lord Chancellor—once as a liberal and once as a laborite—died at his home in Perthshire, Scotland, on August 18. Lord Haldane, like Lord Balfour, was the author of works on philosophy, science and education. His books include in addition to a biography of Adam Smith, "Education and Empire," "The Pathway to Reality," "The Reign of Relativity," "The Philosophy of Humanism" and "Human Experience." During the war Lord Haldane was accused of sympathy with Germany and was obliged to retire from political activity. Again like Lord Balfour, Lord Haldane was a member of a distinguished family. His mother, a woman of great intellect, died three years ago, a few weeks after she had celebrated her 100th birthday. His sister, Elizabeth Sanderson Haldane, LL.D., is known for her civic and literary work. His brother, John Scott Haldane, has been director of the mining research laboratory of Birmingham University. Another brother, Sir William Stowell Haldane, is a leader in the law. His nephew, J. B. S. Haldane, is a well-known biological chemist and author.

Sir George Otto Trevelyan, like Lord Haldane a distinguished statesman, author and historian, died on August 16, aged ninety years, at his home in Northumberland, England. He was the last survivor but one, namely, Lord Rosebery, of all those who sat in the cabinet with Gladstone.

Providing for the erection and equipment of a new Hall of Philosophy, the University of

Southern California has received a gift of $265,000 in memory of the late Colonel Seeley W. Mudd, former mining engineer and leading citizen of Los Angeles. The new Seeley Mudd memorial building will house the philosophy offices, classrooms, the enlarged library of philosophy, and periodical reading rooms, as well as special rooms for the use of research fellows and graduate students. $240,000 will be expended in the erection of the building and $25,000 will be used for its furnishings and equipment.

A GYMNASIUM for the elementary and high schools of the University of Chicago has been made possible through the gift, amounting to $400,000, of Mr. B. E. Sunny, chairman of the board of the Illinois Bell Telephone Company.

THE national endowment fund of the American Historical Association now amounts to $300,000, according to a report by Professor Harry J. Carman, of Columbia University, executive secretary of the fund committee. The goal for the fund is $1,000,000. Despite its losses from floods, Vermont has subscribed $6,305, or more than twice its quota, Professor Carman said. Indiana also has exceeded its quota with subscriptions totaling $8,530. Other subscriptions are as follows: Connecticut, $6,419; the District of Columbia, $3,426.28; Illinois, $5,602.82; Maine, $1,035; Maryland, $3,336.36; Massachusetts, $8,977; Michigan, $3,195; Minnesota, $2,821; New Jersey, $1,365; New York, $45,170; Ohio, $2,756.42; Pennsylvania, $27,919.25; Rhode Island, $2,125.

DR. CHARLES H. ELLIOTT, commissioner of education of New Jersey, has ruled that Benton F. Allen has not qualified for protection under the tenure act. Accordingly, his appeal from a notice terminating his services at the end of June was dismissed. Dr. Elliott ruled that the services of a teacher must be continued beyond three calendar years to gain tenure protection. He pointed out that Allen, except in the first instance, had been employed for the school year and that the initial contract had been dated back to July 1, 1925, whereas it was actually executed on August 3.

THE executive board of Brookwood Labor College at Katonah, N. Y., has sent a message to William Green, president of the American Federation of Labor, asking that it be allowed to reply to charges that the college teaches communistic doctrines. The charges were made by speakers at the quarterly meeting of the federation's executive council, just held at Atlantic City. Referring to the council's announcement that branches of the federation and its affiliations would be asked to discontinue all forms of support to the college, including supplying of scholarships, the board requested Mr. Green not to notify the international unions until it had had an opportunity to present its case.

THE Northern Library Congress, which recently took place in Stockholm in the Commercial High School, included delegates from Norway, Finland and Denmark, numbering 250, besides a large number of representatives from Sweden.

ENGLISH has been made the principal foreign language to be taught in Estonian public schools, according to the latest instructions from the Ministry of Education. English will thus take the place of German, which was intensively taught heretofore.

A BUREAU to supervise the physical and mental development of children during their school life was created recently by a decree of the Minister of Public Instruction of Chile. A division of education will provide courses in school hygiene for teachers and for the general public and training courses for nurses and home visitors. A division of school hygiene will be in charge of medical inspection of school children and will also make studies of their physical and mental development. Free dental and medical treatment will be provided for children whose parents are unable to pay. Laboratories, clinics and other facilities for carrying on the work of the institute will be maintained by the public authorities.

IT is proposed to establish a federation of Balkan universities under the title of the University Union of Southeastern Europe, comprising the Universities of Bucharest, Prague, Belgrade, Zagreb, Sofia, Athens and Constantinople. "The union," the idea of which is credited to the Bucharest faculty, will center in Belgrade, and proposes to provide a clearing house for scientific and medical discoveries, especially those which will ameliorate public health, prosperity, social and economic conditions. An interchange of professors and students among union members is a chief feature, and a monthly publication in French is also proposed. The annual meetings will be held in the various Balkan capitals. Turkey will send the president of Stamboul University and three professors to the preliminary conference at Bucharest.

AFTER gradually dropping more and more in arrears, so that it finally owed its whole teaching staff twenty-six months' salary, the Peking National University has made a "new beginning" by formally repudiating these old debts, and starting all over again, with promises of regular full salary payments in the future. This repudiation, which with most of the teachers averages well above $4,000 each, has created serious individual problems. Many of the teachers had been virtually existing on long-time credit, and others had borrowed money from friends and from banks. Now these teachers must personally shoulder these debts or go through bankruptcy proceedings. The salary repudiation has been received with great bitterness by all of the staff, and many able professors have refused to continue teaching and have sought other situations.

THE U. S. Children's Bureau reports that, under a decree recently promulgated, school attendance in Chile is made compulsory for all children during the years between the ages of seven and fifteen. Under the previous law school attendance was required for four years only. The decree directs that the schools be equipped as far as possible with playgrounds, gymnasiums, baths and libraries, as well as with school gardens, workshops and other facilities for manual training. Provision is also made for institutional schools of the cottage type for dependent and handicapped children and for traveling schools which will go from place to place in rural districts having no permanent schools. The employment of children of school age in factories, workshops and other establishments when school is in session is prohibited, and the administrative authorities of the provinces are ordered to inspect establishments employing young persons and report violations of the law. Penalties are provided for failure of parents to send their children to school and for the employment of children in violation of the provisions of the decree.

ELEMENTARY schools in Cardiganshire, Wales, will hereafter be taught only the Welsh language, according to the U. S. Bureau of Education. The last English-speaking teacher serving in an elementary school in the county has resigned, and hereafter no teacher will be appointed who can not teach in Welsh. This is the outcome of a popular movement in Wales, fostered by the Federation of Welsh Education committees and other organizations, for the teaching of Welsh in the schools of Wales by Welsh teachers. Welsh has become the language of instruction in most infant schools of Carnarvonshire, and its use in senior departments of elementary schools is increasing. In Glamorganshire, a rule was passed in 1923 that in five years only teachers qualified to teach Welsh should be employed in the elementary schools of the county. Vacation courses and special classes, in the meantime, were organized throughout the county, and it is now proposed to enforce the requirement, beginning on January 1, 1929. Notwithstanding the cooperation of Welsh training colleges, local school authorities have difficulty in obtaining competent teachers able to teach Welsh and to give instruction in that language.

THE claim of the secondary teachers of the Irish Free State to pensions was urged at the General Synod of the Church of Ireland by the headmaster of Mountjoy School, Dublin, who proposed a resolution in which the synod expressed regret at the government's delay in legislating, and asked for the introduction of a pension bill before the end of the present year. Mr. Anderson gave the minister for education credit for having at heart the interests of the teachers, but he emphasized the inconsistency of stopping short of providing them with pensions. Secondary teachers in the Free State, he said, were civil servants in everything but name, and they were the only body of the kind in the British Isles who were without pensions.

The pension question had been shelved during the last three years, but the government had recently given orders for the preparation of a bill. Mr. Anderson wishes the government to realize that the need for a bill is urgent.

DISCUSSION

WHAT IS EDUCATION?

ASK that question and always the answer will be: "It is what one gets from school"; or, expanding that statement, "It is that which a person gains in schools, colleges, universities, lectures and the like, through reading, studying, listening, taking notes and being examined, all in close submission to teachers and text-books." That is to say, the word education is almost universally limited in its meaning to the effect of a "course," a teacher, a text-book and an examination. We are so fixed in the habit of thinking of education in the style above suggested that, even when we say a man is "self-educated," we have in mind the thought that he has pursued a "course" of reading and study laid down by an expert.

The fact is that a very small part of the whole mass of knowledge, experience, skill and wisdom that an adult possesses has come to him through "education," as it is almost universally defined.

A grown man's knowledge, skill and wisdom depend more upon the gifts that were his at the moment of his birth than upon any influences that affected him thereafter. "As a man is born, so is he," is still true, in spite of the strange dreams and claims of behaviorists to the contrary.

And, after the influence of one's own inborn qualities, next in importance comes, not the influence of "education" as defined above, but the influence of environment. By environment is here meant, of course, all that affects a person from the moment of birth. "Education" is part of this environment, but a small part only. The inbred and now most persistent habit of thinking that formal education, by school, teacher, course of study and text-book, is all of the education training that the average individual enjoys in his earlier years, has turned the discussion of "Adult Education," which is now so fashionable and persistent, away from all rational studies that might lead to conclusions of value. Nearly all of that discussion is concerned with ways and means for supplying to young people a little addendum to that special, occasional and usually distasteful training, driving, boosting and guiding which formed the education of the school.

So strong is the hold on us of the commonly accepted theory that "education," as above defined, can be and should be the most potent influence in making men intelligent, thoughtful, interested and wise, that we are continually charging our schools and colleges with gross stupidity of management because so few "educated" persons display any evidences of having received the wisdom and other good qualities which the current superstition says they should have acquired in school.

For example: a writer in a recent *Atlantic Monthly* says, "the intellectual mediocrity of our people today, *mostly due to this defective system of higher education . . .!*"

It is more than probable that not one person in a hundred of those who may read those words would think for a moment of objecting to them. If an occasional reader does object it will be because he thinks our system is not quite as defective as the writer assumes, and does not leave its students in a state of intellectual mediocrity, and not because he sees that to lay the mental inferiority of most of us to defects in our higher education, is to assume that birth, and all environmental doings outside of "higher education" are of no importance as factors in creating wise men! Yet what could be more stupid than to ascribe the mediocrity of the people of this country to a defective system of higher education. No mediocre people ever lifted themselves out of mediocrity by setting up good schools. Good schools are fundamentally results and not causes!

Few will deny that parentage, home surroundings, play, companions, influence of adults and a thousand other items that go into the life of any boy or girl in the first 18 years, are of tremendous influence in fashioning the creature who, at 18, enters a "system of higher education." Few in fact will deny that the 18-year old was largely fashioned at the moment of birth. Most of us will, after a moment's thought, come to the opinion that we are, in these days, a little education-mad; are intoxicated with the notion that a few hours in school are making the next generation just precisely what the schools intend them to be. Even those who are education-mad, or pedagogically intoxicated, should look for a moment at certain facts of life.

In the time between the moment of birth and his eighteenth year, a boy of average health has had, at the rate of 16 per day, over 105,000 waking hours. During those hours he has had countless thousands of experiences, has made countless thousands of observations, has asked thousands of questions and been answered, and has obeyed and disobeyed, has touched life in endless ways and has learned, learned, learned. He has had endless lessons in manual training, in games and plays. He has been subject to that instruction in manners and morals which goes perforce with companionship.

But it is idle to try even to suggest the items of learning that have been driven into him in his thousands of waking hours.

Of all this learning, a little has come by way of that "education" which we now so venerate. For consider, the average child is subject to the educational machine, during all these 105,000 hours of waking life, for a scant 8,000 hours only—one hour in thirteen. And, for many reasons, the training and the discipline of those hours have been far less effective than they are generally assumed to be. The boy often finds school distasteful. He learns his lesson because he must, whereas he meets with great zest and pleasure much of the training of his environment, from the time he explores his own periphery in the cradle, until he develops the use of hand and eye on the ball field. During many school hours he is subject to the will of a teacher who is by nature, study and experience poorly equipped for her work. This discipline of life, out of school, goes steadily on for twelve times as many hours as does that of school. The school hours are not in one continuous series. They are interrupted by every Saturday and Sunday, by many holidays and by prolonged vacations. The due progress of training and of the acquisition of helpful habits by school is broken on every Friday, to be resumed with difficulty on every Monday; and is still more broken at every term's end and laboriously patched again at the opening of each term.

While this is not a plea for a more rational time arrangement of our schools and colleges, it may be proper here to note that the Saturday holiday and the long and frequent vacations, which were adopted by our schools several generations ago largely for economic reasons that had nothing to do with education, are needless and absurd obstacles to the effective working of our schools. But that is in parenthesis.

The delusion that education is a rather remote and esoteric yet most desirable thing, to be gained only through the ministrations of teacher or lecturer and "course" and book, is in no part of the skill-and-wisdom-gaining field more harmful than it has proved to be in the department of adult education. Nearly every discussion of this movement, and well-nigh every organized effort to promote it, begins with the assumption that adults who wish to learn must all be taught; must form classes; must adopt courses; must acquire text-books, and must be examined and must aim for degrees, or diplomas or certificates. And, unfortunately, this obsession that learning-something must always mean being-taught-something, has so possessed us all, that the adult-who-wants-to-learn almost instinctively feels that, to fulfil his desire, he must begin by becoming one who wishes-to-be-taught.

As long as this notion persists—and of course all formal-education people will help it to persist and to grow stronger—adults wishing to learn will look about for some approved method of being educated! But, thanks to Mr. Gutenberg and others, our new world is crowded with print, in words, pictures, diagrams and charts; this print lies ready to the hand of all inquiring minds; inquiring minds increase in number as modern industry each day more fully and plainly declares that better wages await the better-informed; and every day we see grow larger a vast army of students who—masterless, classless, without study-courses and not asking for diplomas—begin with the daily paper, graduate to the trade organ, promote themselves to the technical journal, then advance to the standard treatise, and in due course become educated adults.

But if, one may ask, in spite of a wide-spread delusion as to the part that formal education plays in the process of learning, countless thousands are learning without the pale of formal education, why complain?

Well, perhaps I am moved in good part to give forth this protest by the effort my library colleagues are making to take the teacher's part in "education." In effect, we are urged to set up in our libraries Departments of Adult Education! I am convinced this effort is unwise because of the teaching form of education the country already has a fair sufficiency and a sure continuous growth; institutions whose business it is to gather print and make it ready for use have already in hand all the work they can do, and do well; and to enter the field of the school and the teacher as other than a handmaid thereto is a needless and unwise diversion of energy. J. C. Dana

November, 1927

CAN SUPERIOR MEN BE SECURED FOR ELEMENTARY TEACHING?

A considerable number of colleges and universities have recently announced that in the future unusual emphasis will be given to the instruction of the first two years. One of the chief proposals of these programs is the selection and retention of superior men for the instruction of freshmen and sophomores. It can hardly be doubted that no program for the improvement of undergraduate teaching is likely to go very far unless the men in contact with these students are of high quality. In fact, the success or failure of these ambitious programs will probably rest upon the quality of the men who will carry them out. If undergraduate instruction remains the province of second-rate men no change in the mechanics of courses or the addition of "Freshmen Weeks" or courses in "How to Study" is likely to have more than a superficial effect. If, however, colleges find it possible to turn their beginning students over to strictly first-class men the remaining problems of first- and second-year teaching will shrink very greatly since the majority of these classroom problems arise from the fact that, in the larger universities at least, the larger part of this teaching is done either by students whose major interest is in an advanced degree or by disillusioned older men who have failed to get something better.

It is difficult to persuade really excellent men to devote any considerable part of their time to undergraduate teaching. It is almost impossible to find a really good man who will devote the larger part of his time to classroom work with freshmen and sophomores. It will pay administrators who are interested in such men for this service to consider the reasons why men of ability find it unattractive. It is not likely that any considerable number of superior men will be drawn into undergraduate work until these reasons are fully recognized and adequately met.

There are many reasons why the superior man finds undergraduate instruction unattractive. The chief of these are the absence of prestige in elementary teaching, the fact that the work of the elementary classroom does not contribute to the advancement of professional research, the long hours in the classroom, the inordinate time that the conscientious teacher gives to personal conferences with students and the fact that however much administrators may pay lip-service to teaching, academic rewards are likely to go to the fertile publisher rather than to the less spectacular pedagogue.

The absence of prestige in elementary teaching is a fact so obvious as to require no elaborate demonstration. There are few men devoting themselves largely to undergraduate instruction who are not apologetic about their assignment, particularly if they are members of a department in which many courses are offered for upperclassmen and graduates. The low esteem in which elementary teaching is held is due, in part at least, to the fact that the majority of men do it for want of something better. For a man in a large department to devote himself year after year to teaching freshmen is ordinarily an admission that he is incapable of getting something better. Just as free, unskilled labor is degraded by slavery, so all elementary teaching is degraded by the fact that elementary teaching is, in large departments at least, a pretty good indication either of immaturity or of professional failure. A position from which the successful man escapes to something better is never held in high esteem and elementary teaching is no exception. It is interesting to secure the lofty explanations of men who through choice or necessity add an occasional elementary section to their other more pretentious duties. "I like to keep up some contact with undergraduates." "I fill in with an elementary section." "I believe that it is my duty to give freshmen some contact with a graduate-school man." Prestige plays an inordinate part in the academic world since it is one of the few inexpensive luxuries of the teacher. Unfortunately elementary teaching pays no dividends in this pitiable commodity.

A number of other unattractive conditions of elementary teaching are so bound up together that it is unprofitable to consider them separately. These are the absence of topical relation between elementary teaching and professional research, the inability of elementary students to cooperate with research and the consequent reduction in research and resulting publication. These conditions constitute a serious drawback to the elementary teacher. Material for elementary instruction is organized under the influence of educational aims and this organization contributes little or nothing to research organization. Elementary teaching requires one pattern of organization, research quite another. The question might even be raised whether the man who throws himself heart and soul into teaching is not thereby reducing his research effectiveness.

Certainly the shift in pattern is not an easy one to make. The organization of material for graduates is, however, a research organization. From this organization comes naturally the sort of "productive scholarship" that gets one's name on the author's line. Furthermore, the upperclassman or graduate is a potent research assistant. He is invaluable in a variety of ways. His cooperative value is so great that a considerable amount of publication by recognized scientists is "with so and so" or at least carries the student's name in a grateful footnote. This is particularly true of research requiring great drudgery. The elementary teacher has none of these facilitations. The result is that, being entirely on his own, investigation on a large scale is difficult and his scanty bibliography wins him little honor.

Of itself this condition need not be serious. The man who has a sincere interest in scholarly investigations will find his satisfaction in the amount of time that he can devote to that activity. The fact that the mass of work to which he can append his name is less than it would be under more favorable conditions need bring him no concern. But there is one cause for concern here. Recognition among one's colleagues, the notice of administrators, the consequent proffers of other positions with the opportunity for betterment either through acceptance or barter, rest in no small part upon the amount of publication rather than the time devoted to research. The perfect flower that blooms unseen will never be transplanted to a richer garden. Herein lies a profound disadvantage for the elementary teacher. He may find in his investigations complete satisfaction for his own nature even if he is forced to do much hack work that would ordinarily be turned over to an advanced student, but he will not ordinarily be able to do the prolific publishing that is the surest road to fortune.

It is held, in theory, that such is not the case. It has been frequently stated in the past two years that successful elementary teaching will be rewarded and that the research difficulties of the undergraduate teacher will be taken into consideration. Time alone will show whether or not this is true. In the meantime the fact remains that the weightiest argument for advancement (in some institutions almost the only one) lies in offers from other institutions. The fact also remains that before good teaching can be rewarded it will be necessary for colleges to discover what good teaching is and who is doing it. At present, since few colleges have any reliable information as to the sort of teaching being done the tendency is to rationalize this ignorance by weighting heavily the "objective" evidences of activity. That is to say, publication. A certain amount of shrewdness characterizes the superior man. Just at present he seems to be doubtful as to the future of the college teacher who depends for his advancement upon such possibilities.

Certain other unattractive concomitants of undergraduate teaching must be summarized without discussion. Teaching schedules for elementary instructors are ordinarily longer than for advanced classes. In many institutions they are nearly as long as for high-school teachers. The time spent in preparation for a really good elementary lecture, demonstration or class discussion, may be very great. Yet there is no spectacular or tangible result of this expenditure of time. If one is even moderately clever no time need be spent in preparation without either class or administration being the wiser. To make virtue forever its own reward is to expect too much of human nature. The endless conferences with students demanded of the elementary teacher raise the same problem of unrewarded energy. Finally, one serious objection of superior men to elementary teaching must be noted. In our larger departments with a huge staff, the content of the elementary course is rapidly being rigidly organized through syllabi, outlines, group conferences, assigned readings and the like. There are many departments in which the topics to be discussed are set forth in detail and the time allotment for each is specified. Any member of the staff who deviates from this program is subject to discipline. One mark of the superior man is likely to be an unwillingness to be regimented. Even as a young instructor he is likely to find the retailing of the cut-and-dried course of some one else irksome. As an older man he is likely to demand the fullest freedom to conduct his courses in his own way. If he does not insist upon this freedom he is either indifferent about his teaching or is not really a superior man after all.

The administrative procedures necessary to remove the objectionable features that keep the better sort of men out of elementary teaching seem fairly obvious. The problem is, first, to see clearly why it is hard to build up a permanent staff of first rate men for undergraduate courses, second, to decide whether, in view of the absence of the more passive virtues such men are really wanted after all, and lastly, if they really are wanted, to provide conditions that will attract them.

Wm. R. Wilson

Ohio State University,
Columbus, Ohio

QUOTATIONS

RESEARCH IN THE LAW

Establishment by the Johns Hopkins University of an institute for the study of the law is in keeping with modern thought in regard to the legal profession. This will not be a school to train men to practice law. It will devote itself to research. Under supervision of men of high scholarship it will study scientifically the economic and social effects of law; the clarification and simplification of law; the training of jurists and codifiers, and the guidance of writers of text-books and thinkers upon the human effects of law.

The standing of the Johns Hopkins and the character of the men selected for the faculty are guaranties that the proposed work will be carried on with high skill. Men of prestige in the legal profession and noted educators have indorsed the plan. The cost of operation has been underwritten for three years and there is assurance of financial backing for five years. When these have passed, it is hoped a permanent endowment can be obtained. No students will be enrolled for the first academic year, although properly qualified persons who desire to assist in research may apply for the privilege of so doing.

The public in the United States is dissatisfied with the administration of criminal law and is by no means satisfied with that of civil law. The nation is struggling under an antiquated system of criminal jurisprudence ill adapted to the needs of modern urban civilization. The cry of the hour is for law reform such as that which England has long since put into effect.

As yet there is no agreement either as to what changes are needed or how they can be put into effect. Lawyers and judges have written notably on the subject and considerable research has already been done. But a vast amount of this kind of work remains. Johns Hopkins can help importantly.—*The New York Evening Sun.*

MULTIPLE APPLICATIONS FOR ADMISSION TO MEDICAL SCHOOLS

Reports that great numbers of students are being turned away from medical schools, while true in a sense, greatly exaggerate the situation.

An investigation, two years ago, showed that 8,500 individual students made in all 20,093 applications, or an average of about 2½ applications per student. In a second report showing the applications for the last session, 11,282 individual applicants made 23,590 applications at about the same average as the year before. In the fall of 1926, 6,420 applications were accepted but of these there were only 5,020 actual enrolments, indicating that 1,400 students had been accepted in two or more schools. Thus, at the beginning of the session in the fall of 1926, vacancies still existed to the extent of one fourth of the entire enrolment. Fortunately, some of the schools had waiting lists whereby many of these vacancies were filled. Authentic reports show that, in the fall of 1926, 6,009 students were admitted to the first-year class. Of the 6,397 applications rejected in the fall of 1926, 2,622 individuals were rejected because of unsatisfactory qualifications. Of these, according to later investigations, 1,340 reapplied in the fall of 1927 and 750 were accepted, many of whom had secured additional preliminary qualifications. It is interesting to note that of the 750 whose credentials were reinvestigated on the second trial in 1927 and were accepted, only thirty-two had applied in 1926 to as many as from five to eleven different schools, while forty-three others who had applied in 1926 to five or more colleges and whose qualifications were reexamined in 1927 were again refused. In brief, the sifting processes during these two years resulted in the admission of the better element and the rejection of students less well qualified. The statistics published indicate that as the numbers of properly qualified students seeking admission to medical schools increase, the medical schools are also gradually adding to their teaching staffs, equipment or clinical facilities whereby larger numbers of students are being enrolled.

REPORTS

THE UNIVERSITIES AND TRAINING COLLEGES OF GREAT BRITAIN

THE report has recently appeared of the British Committee on Universities and Training Colleges. This committee was appointed by the conference which the president of the Board of Education called in February, 1926, which consisted of representatives of universities and university colleges, training colleges, local education authorities and other bodies interested in the training of teachers. The conference resulted in the appointment of the committee "to consider in what way cooperation between the universities and training colleges can be best effected." The committee consisted of eighteen members, the Universities of Oxford, Cambridge, London and Wales have each a member; the combined English universities have two members; the local education authorities four; the governing bodies of voluntary training colleges two, and the training college associations and teachers six members. The chairman is Mr. R. J. G. Mayor, formerly the principal assistant secretary in the universities and training of teachers branch of the Board of Education, and his colleagues are all experts.

The following are the recommendations made by the committee:

(1) That the schemes for the establishment of joint examining boards for the various areas which have been provisionally approved by the board continue in operation for a period not exceeding five years from September, 1928, in any case.

(2) That copies of all such schemes be communicated by the Board to the bodies represented on the conference for their consideration.

(3) That any representations made by these bodies with regard to the schemes provisionally approved be considered before final approval is given to the schemes which are to come into effect at the end of the period of provisional approval.

(4) That the board appoint a Central Advisory Committee for the Certification of Teachers, which shall be representative of the various bodies and interests chiefly concerned in the training and recognition of teachers, and that it be the duty of this committee to maintain a general survey over the examinations instituted under Circular 1372 and to advise the board upon questions arising thereon.

(5) That, with a view to ensuring the maintenance of a proper continuity of standard during the

early years of the working of the new examination system, the board and the new examining bodies cooperate in making such arrangements as will enable representatives of the Board to give active assistance to the new examining bodies, as well as to the Central Advisory Committee, of which the establishment is recommended under (4) above.

(6) That it is desirable that the training colleges and the new examining bodies, in putting forward proposals for schemes of study and syllabuses, should for the present make no abrupt departure from the general scope and standard of the existing arrangements.

(7) (*a*) That the board's inspectors continue, in concert with the training college authorities, to test the proficiency of students in the practice of teaching and in physical training, and that the marks assigned by them to the students for these subjects be communicated to the new examining bodies for inclusion in the general results of the examinations.

(*b*) That the board's inspectors should similarly continue for the present to test the proficiency of students in advanced handwork for men students, and also, where desired by the new examining bodies, in practical work in domestic subjects.

(8) That the new examining bodies should endeavor, as soon as may be conveniently practicable in each case, to make provision in their own examinations for the other subjects which are at present tested practically by the board's inspectors—namely, science, music, drawing, needlework, and handwork (other than advanced handwork for men students).

(9) That the new examining bodies should for the present continue the Board's practice of granting two chances of reexamination to students who fail at their first examination, and that they should afford facilities in 1930 and 1931 for the reexamination of students who fail at the last examinations conducted by the board, on the understanding that the cost of the reexamination of the latter students shall not fall either on the examining bodies or on the students themselves.

(10) That the board be requested to raise the overriding maximum for their proposed grant from 30s. to £2 for each student examined.

EDUCATIONAL RESEARCH AND STATISTICS

LONGEVITY OF EMINENT EDUCATORS

IN a study of the longevity of eminent individuals covering different occupations and periods of history, the writer had occasion to use the biographical information found in Monroe's "Cyclopedia of Education." The data thus obtained seemed to have sufficient intrinsic worth to be of special interest to educators and scientific students. This is considered especially true of two tables which are submitted here with the necessary explanation and comment.

Monroe's "Cyclopedia of Education," published in 1911, is so familiar to educators of the United States that any comment on that score seems unnecessary. Its readiness of access to all students of education makes it rather easy to one so inclined, if interest and time are sufficient, to verify the truth of the data and thought here set forth.

For the purposes of the study it is necessary to have at hand the dates of birth and death of every individual considered. Failure to obtain such knowledge frequently leaves out of account many eminent persons. In the "Cyclopedia of Education" there are brief biographical sketches of one thousand one hundred and seventy-two educators available for the present study, forty-one women and one thousand one hundred and thirty-one men. The biographies of no individuals living at the time of publications were inserted, thus adding to the reliability of the data in reference to the true average life-span of the class or group of persons concerned.

In the writer's more extended study of longevity, the effect of education and occupation on lengthening life have been under consideration; but here, only such facts as seem clearly involved in the two tables, selected from others, of that branch of the larger study pertaining to a certain designated group of educators will be considered. The data have been classified with reference to nationality or country of activity, period of activity, age at death, average life span, and the rank according to the highest average length of life by countries and periods.

The countries included and specially named are the United States with 518 persons; England with 229; France with 84; Germany with 167; Italy with 50; Greece with 38; Scotland with 30; Switzerland with 23; "all others" (including Spain with 9, average age at death 62; Ireland with 6, average age at death 69.5) with

TABLE I

LIFE-SPAN OF EMINENT EDUCATORS OF DIFFERENT COUNTRIES AND PERIODS OF ACTIVITY

Nation	B. C.			1 to 1000 A. D.			1000 to 1600			1600 to 1800			
	Number	Sum of ages	Average	Number	Sum of ages	Average	Number	Sum of ages	Average	Number	Sum of ages	Average	Rank by nations
Greece ...	17	1241	73.00	17	1179	69.35	3	231	77.00	......	......	......	1
Italy	5	320	64.00	14	955	68.21	26	1733	66.65	4	273	68.25	6
Scotland	......	......	......	......	......	......	6	408	68.00	18	1299	72.16	2
Switzerland ...	......	......	......	......	......	......	7	423	60.43	15	1002	66.80	9
Other nations	2	144	72.00	6	365	60.83	8	500	62.50	13	903	69.46	7
France	......	......	......	3	213	71.00	25	1591	63.64	46	3278	68.23	5
Germany	......	......	......	5	334	66.80	39	2470	63.33	87	5953	68.42	8
England	......	......	......	8	544	68.00	67	4352	64.95	98	6594	67.28	4
United States	......	......	......	......	......	......	1	80		202	14126	69.93	3
Totals ...	24	1705	71.04	53	3590	67.73	182	11788	64.77	483	33428	69.21	
Period rank			1			4			5			2	

Nation	After 1800			Women			Men			Totals			
	Number	Sum of ages	Average	Number	Sum of ages	Average	Number	Sum of ages	Average	Number	Sum of ages	Average	Rank by nations
Greece ...	1	69	......	......	......	......	38	2720	71.58	38	2720	71.58	1
Italy	1	76	......	1	51	......	49	3306	67.26	50	3357	67.14	6
Scotland	6	418	69.66	......	......	......	30	2125	70.83	30	2125	70.83	2
Switzerland ...	1	66	......	......	......	......	23	1491	64.83	23	1491	64.83	9
Other nations	4	276	69.00				33	2188	66.30	33	2188	66.30	7
France	10	650	65.00	6	394	65.66	78	5338	68.43	84	5732	68.23	5
Germany	36	2313	64.25	3	214	71.33	164	10856	66.20	167	11070	66.28	8
England	56	4145	74.00	13	918	70.61	216	14717	68.13	229	15635	68.27	4
United States	315	21616	68.62	18	1237	68.72	500	34585	69.17	518	35822	68.76	3
Totals ...	430	29629	68.90	41	2814	68.63	1131	77326	68.37	1172	80140	68.38	
Period rank			3										

33. The difficulty of correctly classifying educators in regard to nationality is quite marked. This is especially true in the colonial and earlier periods of the United States, the days of the Church Fathers and the period of the Renaissance. Educators are and have nearly always been cosmopolitan. As regards England and the United States, it was generally necessary to classify the educator as belonging to that country wherein he gave his principal service. It is natural that the United States should be favored with the inclusion of the largest number of names in a publication of its own country. The lists from other countries, being more selective, tend to add slightly to the average length of life of those thus included.

The five periods of activity, as here designated, are but arbitrary divisions of time which may or may not be best. They seem, however, quite suited to the material involved and interestingly indicate forward movements of society and progress of civilization. The first period, covering the time before the Christian era, contains but 24 names, too few for safe generalization, but sufficient in a selective class, as under consideration, to show trend. The second period, that from 1 to 1000 A. D. inclusive, contains 53 names, still too few to show more than pronounced trend. The third period, that representing the time between 1000 to 1600 A. D., contains 182 names, a number which considered in connection with the selective material gives rather reliable data. The fourth period, that between 1600 to 1800 A. D., contains 483 names, a number quite sufficient, taking into consideration the general nature of the material, to give reliable conclusions. The fifth period, that covering the time since 1800, or more specifically between 1800 and 1910, contains 430 names, 53 less than the fourth period, but again sufficient for reliable deductions.

As already mentioned the material has been organized under the special heading of eight different nations: Greece, Italy, Scotland, Switzerland, France, Germany, England, and the United States; a ninth rubric, "other nations," is given to include all names of other countries, in which Spain is represented with nine names and an average length of life of 62 years, Ireland with six names and an average length of life of 69.5 years, and all others, eighteen names, with an average length of life of 67.39 years. This furnishes the material and steps for nine grades or ranks according to the highest average length of life by nations and five special ranks as to the periods of time.

In the latter, the period preceding the Christian era ranks first with a general average of 71.04 years; that between 1600 to 1800, second, with a general average of 69.21 years; the period since 1800 ranks third with a general average of 68.9 years; the period between 1 and 1000 A. D. ranks fourth with a general average of 67.73 years, and that between 1000 and 1600 ranking fifth, or last, with a general average of 64.77 years. Noting now the ranks by nations, it is seen that Greece ranks first with an average length of life of 71.58 years; Scot-

TABLE II

The Age at Death of 1172 Educators Recorded in Monroe's "Cyclopedia of Education," Classified as to Nationality or Country of Activity

Age at death	United States	England	France	Germany	Italy	Greece	Scotland	Switzerland	Other nations	Totals
20										
21										
22										
23										
24										
25										
26										
27				1						1
28										
29		3								3
Totals		3		1						4
30										
31		1		1						2
32		1								1
33		1				1				2
34			1							1
35				1						1
36	3	1	1							5
37	3								1	4
38	1	2								3
39	1									1
Totals	8	6	2	2		1			1	20
40	2								1	3
41	1			1						2
42	3									3
43	4	1		1						6
44	3	3								6
45	3	1		1	1			1	1	8
46	3	2	2	1						8
47	8	6	1	3				1		19
48	5	1	1	2				1	1	11
49	4	2		1	1			1		9
Totals	36	16	4	10	2			4	3	75
50	10	2	2	1	2	1			1	19
51	7	2	3	2	3					17
52	6	5		2	2		1			16
53	5	3	1	2	1	2			1	15
54	7	4	1	4				1		17
55	10	3		3		1		2		19
56	2	3	2	4	1					12
57	5	5	2	3					1	16
58	3	2	1	5	2		1			14
59	10	1	4	6	2					23
Totals	65	30	16	32	13	4	2	3	3	168

Age at death	United States	England	France	Germany	Italy	Greece	Scotland	Switzerland	Other nations	Totals
60	9	7	2	2	1	2	3	1	2	29
61	7	4	2	4	1			1	1	20
62	7	2	1	4	2	1			2	19
63	13	7	3	8	1		1	1	3	37
64	14	7	2	4	1	2			1	31
65	16	9	2	5		2	2	2		38
66	9	4	4	6	2			1		26
67	18	3		3	1	1	6	1		33
68	21	4	2	6			1		1	35
69	14	6	1	4	1	2		1	2	31
Totals	128	53	19	46	10	10	13	8	12	299
70	14	7	5	12	4	2	3			47
71	20	5	1	4	1	2	1		1	35
72	13	10	4	9			1	1	2	40
73	25	12	1	6	2		1	2		49
74	17	8	2	11	1	1		1	1	42
75	17	3	1	3	4	6	1		1	36
76	20	9	3	4	4		1	1		42
77	15	2	2	2	1				2	24
78	24	5	1	4	1		1		1	37
79	12	5	1	2	1	1			1	23
Totals	177	66	21	57	19	12	9	5	9	375
80	13	6	4	3	2	4			1	33
81	13	10	1	4		1				29
82	14	3	3	3					1	24
83	5	3	3	4	1		1	1		18
84	9	2	6	1					2	20
85	13	9	2		1	1		1		27
86	9	2	1	1	1		3	1		18
87	3	3	1	1			1			9
88	4	6	1							11
89	6	5		1		1	1		1	15
Totals	89	49	22	18	5	7	6	3	5	204
90	2	2				2				6
91	6	2		1						9
92	3									3
93	1					1				2
94	2									2
95		2								2
96										
97	1									1
98						1				1
99										
100					1					1
Totals	15	6	0	1	1	4				27

Grand totals: United States, 518; England, 229; France, 84; Germany, 167; Italy, 50; Greece, 38; Scotland, 30; Switzerland, 23; other countries, 33; 1172—41 women, 1131 men.

land second with an average of 70.83 years; the United States third with an average of 68.76 years; England fourth with an average of 68.27 years; France fifth with an average of 68.23 years; Italy sixth with an average of 67.14 years; "other nations" seventh with an average of 66.3 years; Germany eighth with an average of 66.28 years; Switzerland ninth with an average of 64.83 years, six years below the highest and less than four years below the average.

The ranks according to historical periods or the era in which the educator lived may bring surprises to many readers. They, at least, do not offer encouragement to the thought that the span of life is being lengthened through education, science and medical and surgical knowledge and skill. Advances in these directions seem apparent, but their influence, if any, on lengthening the span of life is less marked than many have been led to believe. Such improvement as has been made has been felt chiefly in saving and prolonging to adult age the lives of children and youth; thus changing life's expectancy tables without materially affecting the normal specific longevity. The advance in intelligence and medical and surgical science may be scarcely more than sufficient to keep the balance and overcome the hazardous life and depressing effects caused by the more strenuous, nerve-racking activity demanded of modern social organizations.

The ranks according to nations, also, are quite interesting. It will be seen that the variation in averages among the nations is slight. England, France and the United States differ less than one half year, or less than one per cent. This closeness of averages is quite apparent on examination of the columns marked "averages," especially the column of final "averages." Biologically considered, the tangential forces and artificial boundary lines set up between nations are not of themselves sufficient to prevent intermarriage, race intermixture, the crossing and recrossing of peoples, so that even in blood, inheritance, common and approaching ideals, the entire human family is fast becoming but a single race, an intellectually united people.

The few women that found biographical mention in the "Cyclopedia of Education" have been tabulated and added to the tables for such information as the numbers warrant. The number here is too small to be of more than suggestive value, but when added to those gathered from other sources and given as part of the larger study, they become of special interest and value. Table I contains other facts of interest, but they seem sufficiently clear as represented in the table and do not call for further mention.

In Table II effort is made to show by years and nations the particular ages at death of the 1,172 educators under consideration, collated and summarized in periods of ten years each and as a whole. There are but four deaths occurring in the twenties and one at a hundred; 20 in the thirties; 75 in the forties; 168 in the fifties; 299 in the sixties; 375 in the seventies; 204 in the eighties, and 27 in the nineties. The largest number of deaths occurring within any ten-year period was 375 in the seventies; then follow in order the sixties, eighties, fifties, forties, nineties, thirties and twenties. The ten highest death years, given in order, are as follows: (1) seventy-three with 49 cases; (2) seventy with 47 cases; (3) seventy-four and seventy-six with 42 cases each; (4) seventy-two with 40 cases; (5) sixty-five with 38 cases; (6) sixty-three and seventy-eight with 37 cases each; (7) seventy-five with 36 cases; (8) sixty-eight and seventy-one with 35 cases each; (9) sixty-seven and eighty with 33 cases each, and (10) sixty-four and sixty-nine with 31 cases each. Thus of the fifteen years mentioned as having the highest death averages, eight belong to the seventies, six to the sixties and one to the eighties. The first five years showing the greatest number of deaths all fall within the seventies. Other observations might be made, but the tables are sufficiently clear to any one particularly interested.

A few general observations may not be wholly amiss:

1. Heredity, though an important factor in determining the span of life, is not the only factor and in many instances not the dominant factor. The three more important factors in affecting the span of life are heredity, environment and intelligent control. There are, however, many other factors, mostly within control, the proper balance and mutual interaction of which tend to affect favorably the span of life.

2. There does not seem to be any fixed limit to the span of life beyond which one can not go. If nature establishes such a norm, it is not now being reached by any appreciable number of the human family. There is a feeling among scholars, reaching almost to a conviction, that by taking thought, barring certain limitations, observing and utilizing ordinary intelligence in conduct and modes of living, it is quite possible for the average individual, under or within the fifties, to extend his span of life and usefulness at least ten and more probably twenty years.

3. In the field of vital statistics it is shown that more males than females are born, but women live on the average from two to six years longer than men, thus balancing the account. It is quite probable that the longer life of women is due, for the most part, to the nature of their occupation and saner living; and it may be that as women take on the occupations, struggles and more hazardous life of men their span of life will be materially shortened, possibly even below that of men engaged in similar activity. Such a thesis is supported by the data here given and corroborated by much additional evidence gathered from the biographies of eminent women.

4. In the processes of growth and development the individual's tenacity of life varies considerably from year to year. On a much larger scale this fluctuation in the tenacity of life is also seen in the growth of groups of individuals and nations, racial periods of weakened vitality when nearly the whole people are affected. This ebb and flow of human vitality, as seen in the large, seems to operate in cycles, sometimes within great cycles of fifty or a hundred years. In the individual development, man passes through a period of weakened vitality in the early fifties which, if successfully passed, gives promise of many more years of usefulness. Medical aid, if intelligently applied in protecting one over these danger periods of weakened vitality, would surely be felt in time in lengthening the span of human life. Courage and a fascinating, fertile problem give tenacity to life, while worry and discouragements sap vitality.

G. W. A. Luckey

Washington, D. C.

SCHOOL AND SOCIETY

Volume XXVIII | SATURDAY, SEPTEMBER 1, 1928 | Number 714

THE CRISIS IN LIBERAL EDUCATION

THE liberal arts college in America is a sick institution. There has never been a time when there was as much genuine concern for the future of this educational institution as there is at present. Educational leaders and interested laymen from one end of the country to the other are raising their voices in lamentation over the condition of traditional educational ideals. The leading journals of the country carry articles in almost every issue dealing with some aspect of the problem. It requires only casual observation of the trends in American education to discover that fundamental changes are taking place in the realms of higher education. This is inevitable. A corresponding transformation began in elementary and secondary education in the last decade of the last century which has culminated in an entirely new educational system. These last forty years have witnessed a complete reorganization of America's common school system. This period is particularly characterized by the rise of the junior high school and the junior college, plus a thorough reorganization of the entire curriculum based upon the application of a scientific study of the educational process and the needs of society. Until the last decade of the nineteenth century our educational system was constructed from above downwards, that is, we assumed a certain type of higher institution and built the entire system below it to fit its pattern. The outstanding objective of secondary education was to prepare for college and university, and colleges and universities dictated the kind of education it should be. The curricula of the secondary schools were determined by college entrance requirements, and high-school text-books were written almost entirely by college professors. As long as the secondary schools submitted to this autocratic state of affairs there were no particular college problems. But once secondary education began to assert its independence and to chart its own course in the light of its own chosen objectives, troubles for the traditional type of higher education began. The point is that the common schools broke with tradition and began to adjust themselves to modern life. This adjustment was hastened and put upon a sound educational and sociological basis by the application of a scientific study of the problems facing the common schools. The traditional college is sick unto death to-day because it has made little or no attempt to study its problems scientifically in an effort to adapt itself to twentieth century life. Everything else in society might change, but not the liberal arts college. Its position and objectives in the scheme of things must not be challenged. Liberal education has become traditional scholasticism. This is one of the great ironies of history, says Everett Dean Martin:[1]

> The classical tradition in education is one of the ironies of history. That pedants should have succeeded in making this tradition into a mere convention is almost incredible. In the poetry, drama and philosophy which we have inherited from ancient Athens there is a spirit of youth, of

[1] "The Meaning of a Liberal Education," page 197, W. W. Norton & Co.

freedom, of inquiry, of adventure. In the estimation of Egypt or of India, the culture of Greece was *parvenu*. The striking thing about the Greek spirit is its humanism, its lack of priestly tradition, its independence of religious authority. The men of the fifth century before Christianity were creators, not imitators. They were following many lines of inquiry for the first time, unhampered by the prestige of orthodoxy. A noisy populace could condemn the philosopher but could not secure his deference to its beliefs. No idea, no institution was so venerable or sacred as to escape critical examination. The practice of examining all things was the method of education; its aim was the life of reason. There was no official instruction, no established truth, no traditionally recognized knowledge. Student and teacher together pursued wisdom not as scribes and custodians of ancient and hallowed doctrine, but rather in the spirit of those who enter upon a voyage of new discovery. Such is the spirit of the classical tradition and no education is liberal which loses that spirit.

In diagnosing the malady of the liberal arts education, therefore, I should say first of all that it has ceased to be *liberal*. It has lost the true meaning of the word. The greatest problem that we are confronting with respect to liberal education is that of restoring it to its original meaning and purposes.

There has been the general feeling that the traditional type of liberal education was not in any real sense functioning in solving the problems of contemporary life. Our liberal college curricula through the last two or three centuries have been largely determined for us by the ancient classical traditions and the psychological theory of discipline. This condition also characterized the curriculum of our public schools until recent times. With the beginning of the twentieth century and the application of scientific methods to the solution of educational problems, American educators began to realize as they had never realized before that the school was out of harmony with life and was not contributing in any vital way to the solution of contemporary problems. With this belief firmly established in their minds, they began the process of eliminating dead material from the curriculum and the positive process of adapting the school to life conditions. This effort to adapt the school to life, and to cause the school to function in solving the problems of life, is a fundamental assumption upon which modern educators are attempting to define the objectives of education and to build the curricula and to select activities for the accomplishment of these objectives. The great objective, therefore, of modern education may be said to be the effort to train youth to deal masterfully with existing conditions, or, in other words, to acquaint youth with contemporary life and its most outstanding human values.

The statement of this objective is the true objective to be sought in a liberal education. This has been true throughout the entire history of education. Where education thrived and flourished, we find its great objective being the effort to adapt itself to existing conditions. A short review of some of the outstanding periods in the history of education will make this more clear. Perhaps the greatest example of this thesis is to be found in Greek education at the time of the golden period at Athens. It is a noteworthy fact that there has never been a civilization that has so influenced the intellectual life of the world as did the Athenian civilization during this wonderful era. The secret, I believe, of the intellectual enthusiasm is to be found in the Greek's passion to solve all the problems of life which were confronting him. The outstanding characteristic of Greek education during this great period was that it was trying to adapt itself to its environment, and further than this, making a determined effort to control and direct its environment to the most worthy ends. There were three important facts in the environment of the Greek youth to which the educator had to assist the student to adapt himself. There was, first, the psychological fact. The Greek mind was just beginning to free itself from its own classical mythology and to begin to conceive of Greek gods and their mythology as mere poetry. In freeing themselves from this mythology they began to study seriously the experiences of life and to discover for themselves their meaning. In order to do this, they began to employ reason and the development of logical ways of thinking and the best scientific method that they knew. The second great fact of the Greek environment was the political life of the times. Every Greek youth of the upper class was expected to take some active part in the political life and institutions of his day. In order to do this intelligently, he must be a student of politics and government. Consequently, there developed among Greek leaders an outstanding interest in politics and government. There fell to them the great responsibility of working out in their state the best and most permanent type of political institutions. The third great fact which influenced Greek education was sociological, and had to do with the development of the best society possible. These three facts, therefore, psychological, political and social, were the basis for all Greek education. The significant point in this connection is that these facts were outstanding in their life and in that sense constituted the true basis for a liberal education. The fact that the environment greatly influenced Greek education is readily seen when we study the curriculum found in their schools. The simplicity of the curriculum was one of its marked features. One writer, speaking of this condition, remarks that,

> In a manner seldom witnessed in the world's education history, the Greeks used their religion, literature, government, and the natural activities of young men to impart an education of wonderful effectiveness. They taught no arithmetic or grammar, no science, no drawing, no higher mathematics, and no foreign tongue. Music, the literature and religion of their own people, careful physical training, and instruction in the duties and the practices of citizenship, constituted the entire curriculum.

The very opposite of this situation characterized the education of the middle ages. Many writers and thinkers have tried in numerous ways to explain that great period of intellectual darkness known as the dark ages. Of all the factors which produced it, it is my belief that a departure from this Greek concept of a liberal education was without doubt one of the chief factors. In support of this contention, let us consider a few facts. In the first place, the medieval attitude of mind was one entirely opposed to this conception of a liberal education. In studying the declining of education during this long period, certain facts relative to the medieval attitude of mind should be remembered. The first one of these is the complete suppression of individuality. The individual in the middle ages was not free to express himself. He was a member of some group and was dominated by that group. The outstanding example of this is the medieval church which held almost complete sway over the entire individual, his spiritual life, his political life, and his intellectual concepts. Life for him was institutionalized and there was little chance for individual expression. A second characteristic of this medieval attitude of mind was obedience to authority. This was an age of faith. There was no such thing as intellectual curiosity or the application of scientific methods to the solution of their daily problems. All things were controlled by God and there was nothing for man to do but obey. This attitude of mind is illustrated by the type of architecture of the age. The Greeks and Romans were interested in the present, and their architecture took the form of large, massive columns, more or less low. In the medieval ages this type of architecture changed to tall, vertical columns, looking upward and pointing to the other world. The cathedral spires are an outstanding example also of this attitude of mind. A third characteristic of this medieval attitude of mind was the lack of scientific inquiry or lack of imagination. Reason was subject to faith and man must conform to the authority of the age and that principal authority was the Roman church. A fourth characteristic of this attitude of mind may be termed "other-worldliness," the general concept being that this world was but an anteroom to heaven. All things pertaining to this life were not to be considered. To enjoy pleasure and beauty was sinful. The ideal man of the middle ages was the monk who spent his life in self-denial and complete isolation from society. He lived a life of meditation; not upon the problems of contemporary life, but upon the other world. It is said of Thomas À Becket that he wore camel's hair underneath his fine clothes as a constant reminder that his thoughts should be on the other world. The story is also told of bishops riding over the beautiful Alpine mountains on their donkeys, that they would always ride with their heads bent down beside the necks of their donkeys, so as not to notice the beauty of the scenery. Education under these conditions became scholasticism. It was not liberal in any sense. It was a knowledge set apart from ordinary human interests and affairs. It did not include proficiency in any of the arts of contemporary life, but rather in book-learning and in disputation. Its aim was to mold the mind of man to a fixed type, rather than to develop in him the free spirit.

The next great period in our educational history was that great humanistic period known as the Renaissance. This movement was fundamentally a revival of interest in human affairs. As we know, it was largely produced by a rediscovery of the Latin and Roman classics, and since these classics dealt with human affairs and the problems of contemporary life it was perfectly natural that there should be this great revival of humanistic interest. It meant, first of all, a revival of individualism, a rediscovery of the individual. Men freed themselves from corporal control and became highly conscious of selfhood. In the second place, reason and scientific inquiry supplanted obedience to authority. Men were little inclined to be subject to or led by authority. They began seriously to question the theological dogmatism of the medieval church, and besides being possessed of this new scientific spirit they began the development of scientific method. This method as we all know has formed the basis for our modern scientific era. Furthermore, this humanistic period brought a new interest in this life. They began to turn their minds from the things of the other world, and to find enjoyment in all that this world had to offer. This is the crux of the whole matter so far as liberal education is concerned. It meant that education growing out of this new concept of life was again to become liberal in the truest sense of the term. It represented a fundamental difference between the ideals of the middle ages and this new period. There accompanied this Renaissance the development of a new social structure commonly known to us to-day as the middle class. This class was largely made up of men of affairs, of industry, of commerce. This created a new purpose in education, a new objective. The old objective had been to train priests and officials in the Roman church; the new objective was to train men for commerce and for society in general. There entered a practical purpose in education. People must be trained in government, in art and in commerce. Thus we find growing out of this period what might be called a two-fold purpose of education, namely, liberal education and practical education. These new objectives in education demanded a new curriculum; the seven liberal arts of the middle ages were no longer sufficient.

They were not fundamentally related to life. Where were they to find the subject-matter for this new curriculum? They found it in a return to the Greek and Roman classics, and out of this great body of classical literature they found their intense enthusiasm for things related to human life. The study of this classical literature was nothing short of a passion. It was believed that this great storehouse held all the secrets for the solution of the world's problems. The situation for liberal education was most hopeful. There was also a practical side to the study of Latin. Books were all written in Latin. It was the language of the scholars. It was the language of the legal profession in the court room. All bookkeeping was done in Latin and any person must know Latin in order to become a man of affairs.

Two things happened to spoil the great opportunities for liberal education. The first one of these was the mistake which was made of believing that they could reproduce the Athenian civilization and the conditions of the golden period. In other words, it failed because they tried to transplant a civilization of two thousand years into modern conditions and the attempt of course was futile. The other thing which proved disastrous to the classical studies was the development of the vernacular of all the western European countries. When this was done, the practical use of Latin disappeared, and in order that Latin might be saved for the curriculum, its friends began to claim for it great values growing out of the Latin style and also emphasizing the psychological theory of mental discipline. The teaching of Latin, therefore, became highly formalized and consequently devitalized. As a result of this process, it may be said that what chiefly survived the Renaissance was the traditional education in which the ancient classics are taught as tedious drill in language with the aim of improving a student's literary style and also of disciplining his soul by compelling him to master something thoroughly disagreeable to himself. In this process education became anything but liberal. In this formal study of the classical literature it is impossible to get behind the language to literary appreciation or back of the literature into the ways and values of ancient life. In other words, we have simply acquired a very imperfect use of the instrument without using that instrument for acquiring any of the great values which it might unfold for us. Education, therefore, became a most artificial process, entirely separate from reality and from human affairs. That was the condition in which American educators found themselves fifty years ago.

The next period in American education I should term the scientific period. The modern scientific movement, as in the early Renaissance period, offers high hope that education will again become liberal. The objective of modern science in any field in which you care to take it seems to be a discovery of all the laws of nature and human institutions for the purpose of directing human life toward its own highest end. In other words, modern science is committed to an analysis of all things that are related to contemporary life with a view to improving that life. A few examples will make this point clear. Modern physicists are busying themselves discovering every possible law of the material universe and then using these discoveries for the benefit of mankind. The laws of electricity have been mastered and directed to human needs. The gas and steam engine have been perfected and directed toward human benefits. The same thing is true of modern chemistry and modern biology and physiology. We are applying discoveries in all these fields to the relief of human suffering and the direction of human life toward happier goals. The same thing is true in psychology. We are trying to discover the laws that control and motivate human conduct in order that we may direct our conduct toward the great human values. Modern education, therefore, is intensely humanistic. It is concerned chiefly with human values. It is seeking the discovery of truth in every field of human activity. Back of this search is the fundamental belief that the discovery of truth will bring freedom. We believe that once we have discovered all the laws of the physical universe we shall thereby become masters of that universe. We shall thus be liberated from the bonds which have held us all these centuries. We believe that when we discover all the laws of bodily health we shall thereby be able to free ourselves from disease and the consequences of it. We believe that when we discover all the laws of social institutions and the things that motivate and control human behavior we shall thereby be able to perfect for ourselves a society and civilization which shall be free from all the social evils that have marred the civilization of the past. In other words, we believe that we are seeking for a truth, which, in the words of Christ, will make us free. This, then, restores liberal education to its original meaning—that of producing freedom.

What then constitutes a liberal education in our twentieth century? If the thesis which I have been trying to develop is true, it follows that a liberal education fundamentally is a study of contemporary life and all the problems growing out of that life. It has to do with every problem related to human life and human destiny. I believe that here is the possibility for the liberal college again to come into its rightful place among the educational institutions of our day. The problem, therefore, of the liberal college is to adjust itself and adapt itself to human affairs. It can no longer separate itself from the normal activities of human life and expect the patronage of a twentieth century civilization. On the other hand, it must vitally relate itself to life and to the solution of all human problems.

The starting-point, therefore, in a liberal education seems to be the study of individual and social problems. In other words, it becomes a study of the environment and conditions which surround us. I return to a statement which I made earlier, that it must teach youth to deal masterfully with its environment.

Beyond all doubt, the greatest problem upon the horizon of our modern environment is the problem of human relations. During all the centuries of civilized man the one great outstanding problem which humanity has failed to solve is the problem of how we shall live together and promote the best ends of the race. So far the failure to solve this problem has been miserable. The recent world war is a colossal example of the failure of men to live together in harmony and to promote the great human values. We are engaged at the present time in a cut-throat economic competition which holds for the future nothing but strife and contention. I believe, therefore, that the core of a liberal education in our day must be the study of human relationships. This seems to me to be the point of departure in building a curriculum for the modern liberal college. It must, as it has always done, center its attention upon human and social values. Our great fields of study, therefore, are necessarily sociology, politics, government, psychology, and most of all religion, because in religion we are to find the highest objectives of human destinies and it is commonly believed that the principles of Christianity afford the only basis for a human society which shall be able to attain the highest objectives of the human race.

The one great objective, therefore, of a study of contemporary life and human and social problems is to direct our civilization toward its chosen ends. In other words, the great objective of a liberal education is to enable man to become a master of his environment and to develop in him the ability to control his environment and direct it toward his own purposes and to choose worthy purposes. There is a large group in our society at the present time who are making a fundamental challenge to this objective. They are telling us that man is a product of his environment and that the ends of life are predetermined. They are telling us that the will of man is a myth and that there is no such thing as purposive consciousness and no ability of man to direct his behavior toward his own chosen ends. They carry this philosophy of life to this extreme, that man is not a free moral agent and consequently is not responsible for his acts. Therefore, when man commits a crime against society, he is not to be punished for the reason that society has produced his criminality. This conception of life is the direct antithesis of all that is implied in liberal education. It resolves itself into the conflict of whether man is a product of his environment and can not escape certain predetermined ends or whether man is to be the master of his environment and capable of directing it for his own ends and purposes. In the latter case, moral responsibility is restored; man is responsible for his environment and for changing that environment for the good of mankind, and he is also responsible for the ends toward which the human race should be striving constantly. Thus is liberal education restored to its place of highest importance among the institutions of civilization.

HOMER P. RAINEY

FRANKLIN COLLEGE

PREDICTION AND PREDICAMENT

IN a way it is strange how psychological science has upset so many things formerly accepted as being worth while. With its new assumptions and new truths, it seems to have done to educational training somewhat the same thing that Mrs. O'Leary's cow did to Chicago. After kindling a fire of enthusiasm for new techniques in teaching, it has proceeded to destroy the teacher's effectiveness in utilizing them. Through the analysis of a child's intelligence and vocational fitness, it has tried to show how it is possible not only to predict what his future conduct is likely to be but to safely point out the line of endeavor that will result in the greatest gain. Then, at almost the same time, it has proclaimed, first, that a child revolts against too close mental and physical confinement and, for that reason, should not be repressed and his future determined; and second, if he be among those who are classed as geniuses as a result of their intelligence ratings, he must be set aside to be watered, tended and watched. These opposing truths, whether or not they have emanated from the same sources, have left teachers stranded high and dry above the turbulent waters of modern education, so that, when confronted with a complexity of conditions from which they see no immediate rescue, they have essayed in their own names or under the indirect guidance of psychological experimentalists a few rather feeble attempts at vocational counseling and the analysis of intelligence, and the formulation of a few rules for success in modern life.

It is easy to see how this confusion might make potential failures of many children. Evidence that this is actually happening was brought to my attention a few days ago when a prominent surgeon described to me the predicament into which his son had been thrown. The boy, now eighteen, had been an average student in school and, although never in serious trouble, had always resented advice and direction from his parents. From the time not long ago when he completed his high-school course, they have been much concerned over the selection of a vocation or profession, the immediate problem being the choice of a training school. The school psychologists, who tested the boy, reported that he had exhibited strong tendencies toward mechanical pursuits and, because of that, should follow his father's profession, but that he was suffering from an *inferiority complex,* a condition which, they stated, must be remedied before he possibly could succeed in professional work. Free from economic pressure, the boy not only has remained adverse to advice but has developed a pronounced hesitancy in deciding for himself. Then, to add to these complexities, having learned of the findings of the psychologists, he suddenly has become more apathetic about his whole future and has surprised his parents by obtaining passage on a tramp steamer bound for foreign ports.

Since the boy has been gone from home the father has had time to think the matter over. He admits that the boy has pronounced aptitudes for mechanical manipulation; he even is willing to assume that these may have been inherited. In this he might be wrong, of course —it is natural for *any* boy to work with his hands, and whether or not he exhibits tendencies in that direction as he grows older depends upon the need and opportunity for engaging in mechanical work and upon interests consciously or unconsciously cultivated or developed. In any event, all concerned agree that *this* boy would do well in handling the lighter and finer tools.

But what is a father to do when his boy will not take his advice? For one reason and another he has not looked with favor upon the possibility of the younger man following his profession; and the latter could not be caused to come to a decision. Could this have been due to his so-called inferiority complex? As a surgeon he had not had much time to devote to the new theories proposed by psychologists. The latter had stated that in professional work a feeling and attitude of positive assurance is essential and that at all times the professional man must be in complete control of any situation that may arise. Certainly they had been right in that.

I have known the surgeon and his family for ten years and if the boy is suffering from an inferiority complex I am all wrong in just what that ailment is. Prior to his departure from the parental roof I dined in their home and, when the boy came in, dressed in a perfectly fitted tuxedo and smoking one of his father's expensive cigarettes, he had the air if not the age of a man of the world. When his studies were uppermost in his mind he might have had a *feeling* of inferiority, but even this I doubt. One may have such feeling without having a complex—the complex does not enter until he develops concomitantly strong tendencies toward selfishness and egotism. Then, too, the complex nearly always originates in some physical deficiency, such as imperfect eyes, a weak stomach and kindred ailments or in a suppression that results from poor environment. This boy had had no such weaknesses. While still a member of the Boy Scouts he had won all the merit badges that organization had to offer. And his home environment had been almost ideal. Outside of certain sport activities in which he was able to excel, he had displayed no signs of egotism and was markedly unselfish.

If I were asked for a simple but comprehensive definition of psychology, I would say that it is *common sense put in scientific terms.* If it *is* common sense, then it should be used in common-sense fashion. In doing so, one would find it next to impossible either to be dogmatic or to become strongly partisan.

Just why the school psychologists have not learned to use the facts and principles of common sense in common-sense fashion is hard to fathom. Perhaps it is due to the mystery with which psychological science so recently has surrounded itself. But, if we are thoroughly psychological, we must admit that there is a place for all the sciences and for all the persons engaged in scientific research, provided their relative worth to our general scheme of growth and evolution can be plainly seen.

Naturally, then, one must go slowly in passing judgment upon the school psychologists and upon the educationists who are striving valiantly to be scientific. They serve just as important ends as other professional workers or as those engaged in commercial, agricultural or industrial enterprises. But science, with all its simplicity, with all its tendencies to get down to brass tacks, seems thus far to have helped some of them little, and it is well to consider for a moment how this might be.

Psychology is a comparatively young science; in fact, it is so young that it has not been freely and generally admitted into the company of the older sciences. Then, its subject-matter is the human mind, and this is so variable, so wavering, so vacillating and so irregular in its reactions that it can not be observed (and generalized upon scientifically) with so much confidence as when dealing with inanimate objects or with elements that may be at least temporarily controlled.

Again, it is so difficult a subject that few are able to master it thoroughly, and even these find themselves fairly well lined up with some narrow phase of the subject or with some one school of thought or interpretation. The very nature of the subject, too, carries one far afield in his thinking, even at times to the dangerous point of throwing a haze over his entire mental outlook.

It is natural that a science having to do with the human mind, with consciousness and learning, should be called upon to help in the training of the young, to explain how the child mind works and to meet the new demands of teaching large numbers. This leads naturally also to the professional preparation of many psychologists, no two of whom, because of the nature of their subject and the nature of their training, would be in complete agreement.

The overcrowded schools of the past ten years have been responsible for the teacher's neglect of the individual pupil and the former has found it necessary, in cases seeming to need special attention, to turn them to the psychologist for observation and study; and a parallel condition exists outside the schools where life is moving at such a rapid rate and our increasingly complex modes of living have put such a strain upon the individual's power of adaptation that public interest has been forced into a rather superficial study of psychology as it may interpret the many idiosyncrasies we seem to have so suddenly developed.

Overcrowded conditions, lack of individual attention to pupils, and the schemes of rapid promotion devised by the psychologists of learning have tended to fill the higher schools with students who are noticeably immature both in body and mind, and this has lowered the level of teaching in these schools to a point on a plane with that of the grammar schools of twenty years ago.

It will readily be seen, then, how difficult it has been to tie up scientific procedure with a study of the human mind in action and how easy it has been to confuse the school child in his thinking. Bewildered by the elaborate program of studies before him, unable in school to turn to anybody sincerely in sympathy with his situation and unable at home to find anybody thoroughly conversant with modern school problems, lost in the masses of pupils who crowd the classrooms, the child may come to hold himself aloof from his classmates and, in extreme cases, brood over his condition to the point of self-destruction, or may join those who lightly ridicule the ones who have succumbed to introversion. In either event he is on the road to intellectual suicide.

But to get back to the surgeon's son. Had he come to the age of eighteen twenty years ago, he *might* have been advised to enter the mechanical pursuits, but there would have been nobody to gratuitously classify him as a victim of an inferiority complex; nor would there have been anybody to invite particular attention to his exceptional brightness had he shown flashes of brilliancy in his studies. There even would have been nobody to offer standardized guidance looking toward vocational success. Under such limiting conditions what would have happened to him? If he were an average boy he would have kept within the law and, if he had seen fit to sow a few wild oats, most persons would have expected him to get over it and seriously to go to work at something. This would have been applied common sense. Had he run away from home, as a general result of immaturity in thinking, it would have been because there life was too simple, too monotonous, too lacking in thrills. At least, he would have understood most of the things that were going on around him.

But the simplicity of living of twenty years ago is passed and with it some good phases of training that the newer psychologists have caused us to discard. As a result, it is likely, although they may not be conscious of it, many children are driven from school to-day because they are "fed up" with trying to find out what it is all about—the business of making a vocational choice, in instances as early as the sixth grade; the inability to take courses friends are taking or to have any knowledge of the subject-matter covered by them; the narrow path that leads either to one type of higher training or into the trades if one is dumb in the classics; the testing, the classifying, the shunting, the labeling, the enforced counsel; the speeding up of learning, of religion, of all life—it would be little wonder if they have sought release from these conditions by means they have deemed expedient. Older students everywhere *are* seeking such relief through the agencies they can find or create. Their gay abandon at athletic contests is but testimony that this is something they can comprehend. And, as for rules for success in life, such as were written twenty years ago, who is able to formulate them now? Does anybody maintain that he knows where we are going? A Harvard professor has removed permanently to Carolina that there, where there is peace and quiet, he may be able to concentrate; and it was he who in his writings and lectures helped us over so many of the rough spots a few years ago.

The speeding up of education and throwing open the doors of the schools to everybody made the school psychologist and the vocational counsellor persons of professional importance. As schools are now organized and supported, such specialists are as certain to be needed as a lighthouse on a rocky coast. When useful for no other purpose, it is they to whom the buck always may be passed. But they, as a class, have need for more caution in their recommendations. When their judgment is weak, as in the case of the surgeon's son, somebody should tell them that a straight line is the shortest distance between two points and that, if they will follow it to the basic cause of any child's difficulty, without such evident meanderings, they will find themselves suddenly free from the constant stalkings of the ghosts of their too hasty conclusions.

In the case cited (and it is but one of many) a serious condition has been produced which the psychologists themselves would not be able and will never have the opportunity to remedy. The worst phase of it is, there was nothing unusual in the boy's condition from the start. Most boys, while passing through the age of adolescence, are inclined to discredit and disdain the advice of their parents, and many, because they are so familiar with the hardships that attach themselves to the occupations of their fathers, do not care to follow in their footsteps. At the age of adolescence, too, their greatest and almost consuming desire is to wander away from their accustomed surroundings, and it is a characteristic trait to be wavering in decision. Add to these conditions the complexity of modern educational training and we are not to be astonished at anything that may happen. The only difference between the modern eighteen-year-old boy and a boy of the same age in preceding generations is that the former experienced simpler contacts and had a much smaller number of occupations from which to choose. If the latter is faring badly from a moral standpoint, this may be attributed to his inability, because of the speed with which we move, to detect likenesses and differences, to separate the good from the bad and the beautiful from the ugly. Such states of affairs *may* develop complexes, but they need not, and to hand out labels promiscuously is not only reprehensible but highly dangerous.

The surgeon's son has passed from under the surveillance of the school psychologists, possibly from the schools for all time, and seems to have left nothing in his wake but disquiet and distress. At best, a year of his time, when he needs it most for more profitable ventures, is likely to be wasted; and this as a result of the school specialists' attempts to prevent waste. But the situation is not without hope for the parents. If the boy continues to be much like other boys, he will get over his desire to roam the world, will return home and, after repeated trials, find a satisfactory job ashore. His early home training may be depended upon to guarantee that. But he will never experience a feeling of satisfaction when he looks back upon the efforts of the specialists to guide and direct him into a niche previously selected—such efforts were based too much upon snap judgments and surmise.

If the public, through its boards of education, should see fit to employ more teachers, see that they are trained more thoroughly in commonsense methods and practices, and pay them enough to enable them to give all their energies to the help and guidance of individual children, the school psychologist and the vocational counsellor would not be needed. Then, if, when erecting new school buildings, these should be located as far as possible from the highly congested districts of our cities, the children would be afforded the quiet that permits of contemplation and reflection, and not, as now, confined to educational Towers of Babel. Under these conditions they might also be allowed a longer time for training for life outside the school. The quick promotion schemes are, in a sense, but temporary expedients; they have done little but to fill open jobs and higher institutions with educationally delinquent juveniles. And it might be a part of wisdom to see to it that each child gets more general, classical education, rather than to be shunted into special school divisions for vocational training before he is intellectually dry behind the ears.

Finally, whether the boy goes to the job from the vocational school or from the classical school, his real education has just begun; and, no matter what has gone before, he will find, with Solomon, that the race is not to the swift, and that time and chance are the real psychological determiners. If he has the usual experience, it will be necessary for him to be tried out on each job until he finds the right one; and how soon that will be depends upon how readily he is able to adapt himself, what habits of work he has formed, and the amount of faith he has been able to create in and command from his parents, teachers and employers.

HARLAN C. HINES
COLLEGE OF EDUCATION,
UNIVERSITY OF CINCINNATI

WHAT IS A PROFESSIONAL COURSE FOR DEANS OF WOMEN?

AN eminent authority in education has said:

> The growth of professional schools is perhaps the most striking characteristic of recent university history. Their growth is adduced by increased wealth in our land, which means ability to pay for expert service, and the inability of most people to cope with the increasing complexity of modern life. This willingness of the public to employ graduates of professional schools and to pay them for expert service is the correlative factor in the development of professional education.

It is, therefore, not out of place to ask, *"What does 'profession' mean as applied to the field of the dean of women?"*

In the first place, the question presupposes the assumption that the work of the dean is a profession in its own right. It is not a side line of activity appended to the profession of teaching or of nursing or of vocational guidance or of being a vice-principal or a principal or a matron, but has those three characteristics which mark the profession as different from the vocation. It requires a sound liberal education as a basis for professional training; it has a body of professionalized subject-matter worthy to be the material of a curriculum; it is rapidly developing a code of ethics by which the members of the profession govern their relations one with another. It is only fair to say, however, that the work of dean has so recently emerged from the position of being an incidental activity of almost any school factotum, and the body of professional material is so small compared with that of law or medicine or theology that some do not admit its claims to professional status. The assumption of the paper is, nevertheless, that, young as it is, the work of deans has become a profession with a professionalized subject-matter. The results of Jones' study of "The Status and Function of Women Deans in Colleges and Universities" tend strongly to substantiate this assumption.

What then is a professional course?

A professional course is one designed to provide a worker with what he needs in the practice of his profession. It is not a salmagundi of courses selected from the liberal arts college, because they furnish general information necessary to the dean. Psychology, sociology, history, literature, science and religion are part of the cultural background conceded to be necessary equipment of every professional worker, without which success in professional work is doubtful. Such educational background should, however, not be confused with professional training which has its own categories and its own curricula worked out in terms of function. It is not possible, for instance, to train a surgeon by giving him an academic course in history, though it be the history of medicine, or the account of the development of the science of anatomy. He must learn how to hold a scalpel, make an incision and suture a wound.

The content of a professional course must be built on the basis of a functional analysis of the work involved. Such analyses of the work of the dean have been made in recent studies of the function of deans in colleges and teacher-training institutions.[1] They indicate the following duties performed by deans, which in turn suggest some of the categories in use.

(1) *Work with individuals on personal problems.* This is the most universally performed duty of deans of both colleges and teacher-training institutions and takes the most time. Eighty-four per cent. of deans in colleges and universities spent time in the performance of this duty. Few deans would doubt that improved skill in this important function might be learned.

(2) *The organization and management of social activities,* including supervision of student participation in government, sororities and other student organizations. Seventy-nine per cent. of deans work intimately with student government and 75 per cent. supervise extra-curricular activities. There are certainly techniques involved here that, were they known ahead of time, might save the waste of the trial-and-error method of procedure.

(3) *The supervision of housing,* with all that it means of planning, equipment, organization and social values of dormitories, to say nothing of other forms of housing. Sixty per cent. of the deans approve plans for dormitories.

(4) *The organization and direction of part-time employment of students,* which involves standards of academic work, health and social development. Forty-three per cent. of the deans perform this duty.

(5) *Research.* One might mention other duties which are performed by many deans. Fifty-six per cent. handle discipline cases; many have administrative functions and influence the development of curricula and educational policies in general; most give numerous public addresses; many have to do with the selection and orientation of freshmen. These are the functions which become the basis on which a professional course for deans should be constructed.

A consideration of the functions of deans of women as a basis for a professional course suggests the second question, *"What particular skills does one need to perform these functions?"* A satisfactory answer entails further analysis. Discipline, for instance, involves skill in case study and in the art of bringing about recovery from wrong-doing. The student interview, if successful, assumes skill in getting "contact" with the interviewee. Successful administration demands skill in the planning of work and in the use of devices for accomplishing work.

A third question demanding attention is, *What information is needed in order to do the work?* Such information immediately divides itself into knowledge directly pertaining to and knowledge merely relating to the work in question. For example, the standards of adequate housing, the comparative number of women graduates now as compared with that of twenty years ago, the application of psychology to the work with the adolescent, a conception of the place of habit, impulse and intelligence in conduct are kinds of information needed to perform the dean's tasks, while the history of education or Greek literature might be called related knowledge. In such work as that of the dean to which the humanities contribute so much, there is, of course, no such sharp division between direct and related knowledge as exists in the case of the trades, but there is without doubt specific knowledge which should be a part of the professional course and which as a part of a professional course should be treated from quite a different standpoint from that of the academic subject. The academic subject is taught logically, developed as a whole. Professional subject-matter is treated with reference to its usefulness in a practical situation. It has been said that in liberal education the question is, "What will the subject do to the student?" The question in professional education is, "What will the student do with the subject." This difference between the academic and professional attitude toward subject-matter

[1] Jones, Jane L., "The Status and Function of Women Deans in Colleges and Universities," Bureau of Publications, Teachers College, New York, 1928; Sturtevant, Sarah M., and Strang, Ruth M., "The Status and Function of Women Deans in Teacher Training Institutions," Bureau of Publications, Teachers College, New York, 1928.

is further illustrated by a question once asked by a superintendent of schools, "Can you tell me why people who have had a major interest in psychology so often can not teach successfully?" That phenomenon is easily explained on the basis of the difference between the academic interest in the subject as such and the professional attitude which *uses* the subject material in a specific situation.

The professional course therefore must develop its own curriculum in terms of its own problems. The test of what is to go into a course of study is whether it is needed in practice, whether it fits one to take the successive steps in this work with confidence, skill and intelligence. There is no such thing consequently as logical development of subject-matter, or of progressing from the simple to the complex. What is needed to meet a given situation may involve a dozen different fields of subject-matter which are useful as applied to the problem in hand.

This implies that *the method of the professional course is different from that of the academic course.* Its uses the concrete problem which should be skilfully selected by the leader because it is common to the profession under consideration and points to principles of procedure. One might list any number of problems which might become the stuff of a professional course for deans of women, the solution of which would take the student into many fields of subject-matter for her information. The method is that of problem solving.

If one were to say that each can learn as the case requires, the answer would be "yes," but the purpose of a professional course is to short-cut the way to an end by working under a leader who knows the field as a whole and the various methods of approach. The amount of professional subject-matter and the expert knowledge of the leader depends somewhat on the age of the profession. The dean's field is new as compared with law, medicine and theology, but even so there is material that could not be exhausted in three years of graduate work.

This suggests another problem connected with a professional course. The economic return that may reasonably be expected will determine the amount of time that one will feel he can spend on preparation. In the last analysis professional education is an investment upon which one must rely for definite economic return as well as for satisfaction in work. Jones' study showed that the median salary for deans in 263 colleges and universities reporting is $2,766.66. The median salary for deans in institutions for teacher training is slightly higher, $3,054. In most cases these facts mean that training will be confined to one year of graduate work. *What selection of material then shall be made?* It is difficult to find a way to give students what they need for successful practice and advancement in their profession in a limited time. In making such selection, the teacher must ask, "What have they had before they came by way of education and experience? What can they get for themselves elsewhere? What in technique can better be supplied by other courses in the college?" It is clear, for example, that a critical study of the Bible can better be made under a specialist in the Bible, that speechmaking and writing and research, all techniques much needed by the dean, can be satisfactorily obtained in other well-organized departments of the college. And finally he must ask, "What can most advantageously be given in this course in a limited time?"

The full development of a professional course for deans of women entails not only theoretical knowledge but also a practice period or interneship. This is hard to arrange in a field where one has to deal with people who have to be learned, but there is no reason why such practice could not be provided in time. Opportunity to serve as assistant to a dean or as head of a hall is in effect an apprenticeship which is being more and more asked for by young women themselves.

In conclusion, then, a professional course is one which seeks to provide the knowledge, skills and techniques which are necessary to the practice of the profession in question. Its purpose is to shorten the way to an end by offering the opportunity for study under competent leadership, for survey of such materials as are available and for knowledge of the whole field as well as of specific problems. Its value as a course for a particular person, will depend in part on what the person is and knows to begin with, and what use he can make of his training.

In my opinion, the continuance of the professional status of the work of the dean depends upon the rapid development of the specific information and skills and techniques which comprise professional subject-matter. There is more and more demand for those who have learned to use expertly the tools of service in the field of personnel, in the field of housing, in administration.

As James E. Russell says, "The leadership of the olden time may have been dependent upon the accident of birth, but the leadership that is ahead is a matter of professional training."

SARAH M. STURTEVANT
TEACHERS COLLEGE,
COLUMBIA UNIVERSITY

EDUCATIONAL EVENTS

THE NINGPO METHODIST COLLEGE

THE special correspondent of the New York *Times,* at Peking, writes under the date of July 24 that following the closing of the Hangchow Christian College because of the attitude of the Nanking government toward missionary educational institutions comes a revelation of injuries to the Ningpo Methodist College, the properties of which have been held for fifteen months by a Chinese educational institution and are still illegally occupied despite many protests to the Nationalist régime.

The Ningpo Methodist College, which has been in operation for twenty-six years, met, it is stated, every requirement of the Nationalist Ministry of Education. Even before the Nationalists took Ningpo the board of trustees boasted a majority of Chinese members, and a Chinese president had been elected.

Attendance at religious exercises was made optional for all students, this being one of the Nationalist requirements, and the college was thrown open to all Kuomintang speakers and lecturers who wanted to expound Dr. Sun Yatsen's doctrines to the students.

According to the correspondent, the Kuomintang propagandists demanded the right to call out the student body at will for participation in mass meetings and parades. Then they demanded that the students have representation on the board of directors, later that they control the board. The final act was an order that students must obey their Student Union in all matters before obeying the orders of the college. This made discipline and order impossible to maintain.

After the "Nanking incident" of March of last year the forces of disruption became so strong that the Chinese trustees voted to close the college until conditions returned to normal. The students received back their tuition fees and were sent home.

On May 1 last a Chinese-owned private school, run for profit, boldly invaded and took over the Ningpo Methodist College grounds and buildings. The invaders remain there to this day, in spite of the fact that Chinese and foreign trustees of the original institution have repeatedly petitioned the Nanking government for the ousting of the interlopers. The provincial government's aid has also been sought, but in vain, and the local Ningpo authorities will do nothing.

Meanwhile the buildings have suffered deterioration. Plaster has fallen from the ceilings. Unbroken window panes are the exception. The costly equipment of the science laboratory is ruined. The grounds and tennis courts are knee high with weeds. The walls are all scrawled over with writing and plastered with Nationalist posters, inside and outside.

CHILD VAGRANCY IN RUSSIA

IN connection with the campaign in Russia to provide homes and educational opportunities for homeless and stray children in the Soviet Union the following circular letter has been sent out by the Central Committee of the Communist Party of the Soviet Union to district committees and local organizations.

Child vagrancy in the country continues to be a great evil. Although its dimensions have been considerably diminished, nevertheless the thousands of socially neglected children and youths in the streets of the cities constitute a sharp contrast to the increasing economic prosperity of the country and the growth of its cultural level. Nevertheless the party and the state have at their disposal sufficient means, if backed with the proper attention and energy, to liquidate the essential features of child vagrancy, if not to dispose of it entirely within the next year or two.

It is believed by the central committee that the liquidation of child vagrancy, and of street vagrancy to begin with, represents a task of tremendous social and political importance, and in compliance with the decisions adopted by the political bureau of the central committee on this question, it is suggested that local party organizations devote particular attention to the following:

1. To endeavor to achieve in the course of the coming year the total liquidation of street vagrancy in places where it is particularly prevalent, and in order to avoid the repetition of vagrancy by children picked up in the streets, to organize systematic observation of the street.

2. To give a decided trend to the whole activity of the children's homes, in which children over twelve years of age are educated, towards the teaching of crafts so that the homeless children may be prepared for independent industrial life in the quickest possible period of time, for which purpose particular attention should be devoted to the organization of workshops in connection with children's homes.

3. To take steps towards improving the quality of the personnel in charge of the children's homes and of the organs of the district educational boards, superintending the campaign against vagrancy. To select a body of industrial instructors for the homes from among the foremost skilled workers of the factories.

4. To secure the progress of the exceptionally important work on preventing the growth of vagrancy in the country by means of more determined legal protection of children, the organization of industrial workshops for unemployed children, the organization of material aid to children in destitute families, and the wider attraction of the youths into the handicraft and artisan workshops and into peasant agriculture.

5. To secure the material basis of the children's homes and the rational economic utilization of the funds granted for their upkeep, so that they might become institutions which really educate and train homeless children, and not merely give them shelter.

6. To attract into the campaign against child vagrancy and child neglect all public organizations, particularly the Young Communist organizations, the trade unions and the delegate meetings of working women and peasant women.

7. To intensify the activity of the press in the matter of arousing public interest in the combatting of child vagrancy.

The party organizations should strengthen the leadership of this campaign against child vagrancy, and systematically examine the activities of Soviet and public organizations by reports by such bodies delivered before meetings of the committees.

THE TEACHING OF MODERN LANGUAGES IN CANADA

THE Canadian Committee on Modern Languages, with the aid of the Carnegie Corporation, has issued an exhaustive report on the problem of modern language teaching in Canada, which is summarized in the *Times Educational Supplement*. The general committee, the secretary of which is Professor Shaw, of the University of Toronto, includes university professors and school teachers of modern languages, inspectors of schools and others, and regional committees have also been at work.

The language (other than English) chiefly taught in Canada is French. Spanish is taught in about ten schools in Ontario, but is not offered elsewhere except in a few private schools, commercial schools and in some of the universities. German fell off rapidly during the war, recovered about one third by 1921, declined again, and now seems to be gradually recovering some of the ground lost. The 2,000 or so pupils who learn Italian are mostly the children of Italians in the large cities. Among the recommendations which the committee have made are the following:

Research and experimental work should be encouraged, especially in teachers' training colleges. Where new colleges or departments are established they should be closely connected with universities which can control their policy and make appointments. Such colleges or departments should be adequately provided with books and apparatus. The committee does not find that any training college in Canada is now engaged in experimental work in modern languages.

It is suggested that a modern language journal should be established to keep teachers abreast of progress, but it is admitted that the lack of a national organization of modern language teachers in Canada makes the founding of such a publication difficult. The establishment of a laboratory for experimental work in phonetics is advised, and the appointment of modern language supervisors in cities and counties, or groups of counties, whose duty it will be to determine the nature of the work advisable under local conditions, to provide syllabuses, and to direct and appoint or nominate teachers, and supervise their work.

Modern language libraries, it is suggested, should be created in secondary schools, to contain, besides reference books, at least one current periodical for each language, and a selection of interesting books which will encourage pupils to read for themselves. Model collections of books should be kept on display in training colleges. Few such libraries now exist, and the schools need better equipment in the way of maps and phonetic charts. Statistics are given indicating that the libraries of many Canadian universities are inadequate, so far as modern languages are concerned. It is suggested that more modern language text-books should be published in Canada as a stimulus to teachers.

In the matter of curriculum it is recommended that there should be a transfer of emphasis from grammar to reading. Written examinations, it is stated, have become a fetish in the Canadian educational system, and in modern languages encourage excessively the grammar-translation method. In the second volume of the report some space is given to describing tests of a modern kind, which are published and distributed by the Canadian Committee on Modern Languages.

APPRENTICESHIP IN GREAT BRITAIN

THE place of apprenticeship in British industry is reviewed in a recent issue of the *Educational Supplement* of the London *Times*. The discussion is based on a series of handbooks now being issued by the Ministry of Labor, dealing with the report of an inquiry into apprenticeship and training for the skilled occupations in Great Britain and Northern Ireland during 1925–1926. The handbooks constitute the first adequate survey since before the war and present material to make clear the situation resulting from post-war industrial depression.

Questionnaires were sent out and of the 7,493 employers furnishing returns 59 per cent. did not employ either apprentices or improvers. The proportion of London employers having apprentices was 15.7 per cent., as against 63.5 per cent. in Scotland and nearly 60 per cent. in the northern counties.

Apprenticeship is not considered "dead," but it has changed in form. The model scheme used by employers with adequate facilities permits a boy who has had two years in a technical school to begin workshop apprenticeship in the third year at third-year wages. Boys with less than two years in technical school remove the deficiency by the necessary school attendance during their apprenticeship.

In many of the trades, few or no provisions are made for apprenticeship training. The smaller firms, notably among printers, do far more than their share in developing boys and girls into skilled workers. In only a few branches of the textile industry are there apprenticeship provisions and these are in limited fields. In many instances, long hours of labor prevent school attendance even when the opportunity exists. The secretary of a union writes: "Many boys and girls are left to pick up the trade as well as they can. The best is not obtained from our young people and never will be under our slipshod method."

It is believed that more should be done for the young workers, not only for their benefit but for greater business efficiency, since it is evident that the much larger number of older men engaged in industry now than before the war are misplaced in positions demanding quickness and physical strength.

TESTS OF CHILDREN'S HEARING

DR. HARVEY FLETCHER, of the Bell Telephone Laboratories, writing in *The Bell Laboratories Record,* calls attention to the large number of American school children who are partially deaf, and outlines a method by which the defect may be measured.

The detection of partial deafness in children is of importance in relation to their school work, since those with defective hearing may appear to learn slowly. When partial deafness is determined, teaching methods may be altered to advantage and medical attention given when it is necessary.

Plans for developing a simple testing method requiring little or no apparatus were taken up by Dr. Wendell Phillips, of the American Federation of Leagues for the Hard of Hearing, president of the American Medical Association, Dr. William J. O'Shea, superintendent of schools of New York City, and Dr. Fletcher.

The method finally chosen as most satisfactory involves the use of a phonograph audiometer—an ordinary phonograph with an electromagnetic reproducer, and a group of telephone receivers. Dr. Fletcher thus describes the method and results:

After the telephone receivers have been distributed and properly adjusted, the children are told that they are about to hear numbers called, first by a woman and then by a man, who seem to be moving farther and farther away, so that the sounds will grow weaker and weaker. They are asked to write as many of these numbers as they can hear. . . . Then they hear numbers spoken, the loudness of each sound being less than that of the preceding one. The test is given twice by a woman's voice and then twice by a man's voice. The receivers are then changed to the other ear and the test repeated. In the upper grades, a record of three-digit numbers is used, while for the earlier grades the record is one of two-digit numbers. Master sheets for correcting the papers are so arranged that for easy comparison they may be placed alongside the numbers written on the blank form by the child. The hearing-loss for any test is found in the outside columns opposite the last number heard correctly.

With the apparatus and method outlined above, it was found that there could be tested per hour seventy-five to a hundred and fifty children, depending upon the degree of efficiency in organizing them into groups of forty, and getting them to and from the classroom provided for the tests. Of over 4,000 school children thus tested it was found that 595, or 14.4 per cent., were hard of hearing, 3.2 per cent. had defects in both ears, and 11.2 per cent. had defects in one ear only.

Of the 595 deaf children, a medical examiner chose fifty-seven from the same school, and in every case but one found some definite ear trouble, such as running ears, catarrhal deafness, nerve deafness, adhesions and congestion of the ear-drums, and results of mastoid operations. In one case a bead was found lodged against the ear-drum.

The school records showed that these fifty-seven students had repeated sixty-six classes, while the same number of normal students selected at random from the same grade had repeated only eighteen classes. Dr. Fletcher observes that probably more money will be saved by preventing the children from repeating classes than would be used in finding and treating deficient children.

THE ENDOWMENT AND ENROLMENT OF SCHOOLS AND COLLEGES IN THE UNITED STATES

A STATEMENT has been issued by the U. S. Bureau of Education giving a valuation of school property throughout the country and the enrolment in all types of schools.

The bureau reports that in 1926 the colleges and universities received in benefactions a total of $118,144,082, of which amount $72,374,608 was for additions to endowments and the balance for current expenses and buildings. During the same year teacher-training institutions received a total of $8,728,950 in benefactions, of which amount $6,682,023 was for additions to endowments.

The total amount of endowments reported by schools in 1926 is as follows: Colleges and universities, $987,012,929; teachers colleges and normal schools, $19,425,113; private high schools and academies, $67,151,000; all of which makes a total of $1,061,589,042. The amount received annually by private high schools has not been reported since 1918.

The state departments of education report a total value of public elementary and secondary school property for 1926 of $4,676,603,539. Private high schools report $511,544,000. Teacher-training institutions, including endowments, have a total valuation of $202,630,512, and colleges and universities of $2,334,307,421. If the private elementary schools have property valued at as much as $400,000,000, this would make a total value for these institutions of $8,125,085,472 for grounds, buildings, contents and productive funds.

It is not possible to state with any degree of certainty the number of elementary schools. No data exist for private elementary schools. In 1926 the states reported 256,104 public-school buildings. A total of 215,439 of these are designated as elementary school buildings and 9,538 as high-school buildings.

This leaves more than 31,000 undistributed as to use. Of the total, 256,104 buildings, the number used in consolidated schools is 16,291 and the number of one-room buildings is 161,531.

There are approximately 21,700 public high schools, 2,500 private high schools, 386 preparatory departments of colleges and 125 secondary departments in teacher-training institutions. The teacher-training institutions number 402, of which number 101 are teachers colleges, 102 state normal schools, 27 city normal schools, 108 county normal schools and 64 private normal schools. The colleges and universities number 975, of which number 153 are junior colleges.

There are 5,920 students enrolled in private schools for the Indians, 188,363 students enrolled (1925) in private commercial and business schools, 187,828 enrolled (1925) in trade and industrial schools and 77,768 enrolled (1927) in nurse-training schools. Data on expenditures are not available for these four types of schools.

There are enrolled also 29,647 elementary students in practice and model schools in teachers colleges; 11,174 students in extension courses and 28,433 in practice and model schools in state normal schools; 334 in extension courses and 4,524 in practice and model schools in private normal schools, and 209,454 in summer schools, 268,481 in extension courses and 3,772 in winter short courses in colleges and universities.

Enrolments in elementary schools, high schools, normal schools and in colleges and universities in the outlying parts of the United States amount to 1,496,928. This makes a grand total of enrolments in all types of schools mentioned in this report of 31,037,736.

THE MEDICAL CENTER OF WESTERN RESERVE UNIVERSITY

THE great medical center that is now in process of organization and construction at Western Reserve University was the main theme of a luncheon address given recently by President Robert E. Vinson to the members of the American Association of Collegiate Registrars at their annual meeting in Cleveland. According to a report in the New York *Times*, he said that when the present plans are brought to fruition the university will have a combination of instructional and research facilities in medical and health education that will be equaled by few other institutions.

Since the inception of the plan more than $30,000,000 have been raised and spent on the development of the center. Besides several gifts, a campaign was carried on in Cleveland last year to raise $6,000,000 to complete the hospital and school of nursing buildings. A total of $8,250,000, or $2,250,000 beyond the amount set, was contributed and all of it came from the City of Cleveland with the exception of $1,000,000 from a citizen of New York.

In 1927, at the inauguration of its president, the university dedicated a new medical building as a part of a comprehensive plan for improving its already strong school of medicine. Dr. Vinson spoke as follows:

> The building was given by a member of the Board of Trustees. It is an interesting story, perhaps the first of its kind, that Western Reserve University had practically *carte blanche* in building its School of Medicine, and every head of department was told simply to sit down and write out his bill of requirements for his department, with the assurance that the things he thought he needed could and would be provided.
>
> It is even a more interesting story that when the building was completed the university turned back to this generous donor—probably it was the first time in all educational history that such a thing has been done—about $1,000,000 of the money he had set aside to complete the building.

In describing the center, James F. Abel, associate specialist of the United States Bureau of Education, said:

> This is only one building of a group that will bring together on the university campus a series of closely related agencies, all now being coordinated in one outstanding enterprise, to work toward the general purpose of offering the finest kind of medical and health education. The major elements combining to form the medical center are the university with its graduate school and its laboratory facilities for teaching the fundamental sciences, the school of medicine, the school of dentistry, the school of nursing and the school of pharmacy.
>
> For hospital service and training, the maternity hospital and the children's and babies' hospital, each with 150 beds, were erected near to and shortly after the medical building at a cost of approximately $3,500,000. Accommodation is being provided this year to bring to the university Lakeside General Hospital, with about 160 beds for general medicine and surgery, and 140 for specialties under each of these general departments. More-

over, the university has control of the convalescent hospital in a suburb of Cleveland, the City Hospital, and the Charity Hospital, so that for the development of medical education alone 2,250 beds will be available and under the immediate control of the faculty of the School of Medicine.

A nurses' training school was formerly maintained by each of the hospitals connected with the university. These are now united in one school of nursing in which all the scientific training of the young women is taken over and given by the university, and the hospitals furnish the facilities for practical experience.

The new medical library, with a capacity of 200,000 volumes, was brought to the medical center through agreement between the university and the Cleveland Medical Library Association. When the association was beginning its campaign in 1924 for funds for a building the university invited it to join the medical group, offered to give the land upon which to locate the building, and the wife of a university trustee donated $400,000 on the condition that the library be placed on the campus.

An institute of pathology, the gift of the General Education Board, will be placed in the midst of the medical center. It will provide room for the laboratory facilities necessary to the teaching of pathology and the investigative work of that department. It will also be the research laboratory for the hospital group and the men connected with it. This arrangement will free considerable space in the medical building for the department of surgery.

THE SUMMER SESSIONS OF COLUMBIA AND NEW YORK UNIVERSITIES

A TOTAL of 14,007 students took courses at Columbia University this summer—an increase of 150 over last year's registration, when 13,857 were enrolled. New York University enrolled 4,716 students, an increase of 263 over last year and an increase of 2,830 over the registration in 1922, when 1,986 students were enrolled.

At Columbia University the number of women students was more than twice that of the men, the figures being 9,735 women as compared to 4,272 men. More than half the women students are engaged in teaching, while 7,435 are matriculated students working for degrees.

Practically every country in the world and every part of the United States were represented in the enrolment. The largest increase in registration over last year came from the central and western states. A decrease was marked in the north Atlantic states. As was to be expected, New York state sent the largest number of students, 4,203. Pennsylvania came next with 1,189.

The territories were also well represented. Hawaii, the Philippines, Porto Rico, the Canal Zone and Alaska sent 69 students. Canada headed the foreign delegation of 322 with a total of 127 students. Included in the group of 322 were 48 Chinese, 26 Cubans and 20 Japanese.

Many supervisors and administrators took advantage of the courses offered. There were 151 superintendents, 472 principals, 15 deans of women in high schools and 16 deans of college women.

Forty-one states and six foreign countries sent students to the New York University summer session. Of these students, 3,146 came from New York state, and 550 came from points outside New York City. In spite of the fact that the Washington Square Center of the university has limited dormitory facilities, an increasing number of students from other parts of the country are attending the school each year.

A total of 402 courses were given in forty-eight different subject groups in the 1928 session. This was an increase of more than one hundred courses over last year.

THE BUDGET OF THE NEW YORK CITY SCHOOLS

THE city spent $125,258,403.22 on its school system in 1927, according to the annual financial and statistical report of the Board of Education. The report was compiled by the auditor's office of the board under the general supervision of Frederick D. Chambers, the head auditor.

According to press notices, the expenditures left a balance of $28,428,529 on December 31, 1927, including $14,000,000 set aside for salary increases effective January 1. The greater portion of the balance consisted of funds appropriated for capital outlay, which had not been expended during the year.

The expenditures were $92,090,038 for cost of instruction; $4,174,737 for maintenance; $5,799,766 for operation; $2,425,478 for administration; $18,059,254 for capital outlay, and $2,709,127 for auxiliary agencies.

The report shows that teachers' salaries form the bulk of the board's expenditures, amounting last year to 82.675 per cent. of the total outlay. That was one per cent. more than the corresponding percentages for the three preceding years and nearly two per cent. more than the percentage for 1923. While the relative share of the teacher is rising, the percentage expenditure for equipment is going down, the reduction being, on the average, one tenth of one per cent. a year.

Graphs printed in the report show that the total enrolment of 946,068 last year was only 77,000 less than the combined registration of Chicago, Philadelphia, Los Angeles, Detroit and Cleveland and about equal to the combined school populations of Boston, Baltimore, St. Louis, Pittsburgh, Minneapolis, Buffalo, Newark, Milwaukee, Washington, San Francisco, Kansas City, Seattle and Cincinnati.

Enrolment figures by boroughs and comparisons with past years show the drift of school population from Manhattan to the other boroughs. During 1927 alone Manhattan lost 5.52 per cent. of its high-school population and during 1926 more than 8 per cent. Brooklyn and Queens have been gaining, as has the Bronx, which increased its day high-school enrolment in 1927 by 21.87 per cent. The corresponding percentage for Richmond is 19.08.

The number of pupil-hours of instruction given during the year was almost 1,000,000,000. The total cost of the physical plants, including about 900 buildings and their sites, is $354,282,337. The figure has more than doubled in the last decade.

The value of vocational work undertaken in the schools is discussed in the report, which says:

> In the Parental School, several practical industries are operated as part of the education of the pupils. The subjects embrace laundry work, baking, farm work, tailoring, shoe shop practice, ice plant, etc. The products of these industries are distributed mainly among the different truant schools and have a certain practical value.

The value of the output of these industries during 1927 was estimated by the principal of the school to be as follows: Laundry work, $41,486; bakery, $21,382; farm, $16,265; tailor shop, $9,025; plumbing shop, $3,080; printing shop, $9,022; carpenter shop, $6,589; shoe shop, $2,425; repairs, $5,000; ice plant, $4,650; auto mechanics, $1,450; barber, $2,500; piggery, $1,802; hennery, $702, and tinsmith, $641, making a total of $126,024.

The products of the pupils in the regular vocational and trade schools, exclusive of the Manhattan Trade School for Girls, was valued at $13,808. The Manhattan Trade School for Girls sold the work of its pupils for $13,941.

Odd items of income to the board for the year were $131,938 from the sale of lunches, compared with $80,000 five years ago and $20,004 from tuition from non-resident students, compared with $5,439 in 1926.

EDUCATIONAL NOTES AND NEWS

Trevor Arnett, business manager of the University of Chicago, will succeed Dr. Wickliffe Rose as president of the General Education Board. Mr. Arnett was secretary of the board from 1920 to 1924. Dr. Rose has been president of the board since 1923, and will still unofficially represent the board in various directions.

Allen C. Blaisdell, assistant director of the Students' International House in New York City, has been appointed director of the similar institution established in Berkeley, California, and endowed by Mr. John D. Rockefeller, Jr., with the sum of two million dollars. The building is expected to be ready in the autumn of 1930.

Professor C. H. Haring, head of the department of Latin-American history and economics at Harvard University, sailed for the United States from Lima, Peru, on August 24. Professor Haring has completed a tour of South America to study the establishment of a fund by the Guggenheim Foundation to give scholarships at American universities to selected South American students. It is also expected that the fund will provide money for South American professors and writers to visit the United States.

Dr. Arthur T. Hadley, president emeritus of Yale University, has expressed a willingness to accept the Democratic nomination for United States Senator from Connecticut.

DR. O. R. LATHAM will take up his work as president of the Iowa State Teachers College at Cedar Falls at the beginning of the college year. He succeeds Dr. Homer H. Seerley, who recently retired at the age of eighty years.

B. O. SKINNER, superintendent of schools at Marietta, Ohio, for fourteen years, has been appointed president of Wilmington College in Wilmington, Ohio.

PROFESSOR JAMES H. HANCE, head of the department of geology at the Agricultural and Mechanical College at College Station, Texas, has been appointed dean of the Oregon State Agricultural College, to succeed Dr. Charles E. Newton, who recently resigned.

DEAN J. H. SKINNER, of the school of agriculture of Purdue University, Indiana, has been appointed director of the Purdue University Agricultural Experiment Station and of the agricultural extension department of the university, to succeed Dr. G. I. Christie, who has resigned, after twenty-three years of service, to become president of Ontario Agricultural College at Guelph.

DR. SHIRLEY W. WYNNE, deputy health commissioner of New York City, has been appointed commissioner, to succeed Dr. Louis I. Harris, who recently resigned to accept the position of consultant to the National Dairy Products Corporation.

DR. GEORGE C. RUHLAND has been appointed commissioner of health of the city of Syracuse, at a salary of $10,000, succeeding Dr. Herman G. Weiskotten, dean of the college of medicine of Syracuse University, who resigned on August 1. Dr. Ruhland, who since 1924 has been deputy commissioner, is to give his whole time to the work.

DR. WILLIAM T. BAWDEN, for the past five years associate superintendent of schools at Tulsa, Oklahoma, has accepted the position of managing editor of the *Industrial Education Magazine,* published by the Manual Arts Press in Peoria.

DR. J. B. EDMONSON, professor of secondary education at the University of Michigan, has been appointed to the editorial board of the *Michigan Educational Journal.*

DR. DANIEL A. PRESCOTT, formerly of the Harvard Graduate School of Education, has joined the faculty of the school of education of Rutgers University.

DR. G. H. YEUELL, associate professor of education in the University of Cincinnati, has accepted a professorship of education at the University of Alabama, the appointment to take effect on September 1.

DR. HARRY BEAL TORREY has been appointed professor of hygiene and physical education and director of the health service at Stanford University. Paul T. Cherington, director of research, J. Walter Thompson Company, and formerly professor of marketing in the Harvard Graduate School of Business Administration, has been appointed professor of marketing in the Stanford Graduate School of Business.

DR. HARRY R. MCPHEE, of the Iowa State College at Ames, will join the department of physical education at Princeton University at the opening of the academic year.

DR. HAROLD ELLIS JONES, director of research in the institute of child welfare of the University of California, has been appointed associate professor of psychology in that institution.

DR. JOHANNES LINDWORSKY, professor of psychology at the University at Cologne, has been called to Prague.

PROFESSOR JOHN MACMURRAY has been appointed, as from August 1, to the Grote chair of philosophy of mind and logic tenable at University College, London. Mr. Macmurray was in 1919–20 lecturer in philosophy in the University of Manchester, and from 1920 to 1922 professor of philosophy at University College, Johannesburg. Since 1922 he has been fellow, classical tutor and Jowett lecturer in philosophy at Balliol College, Oxford.

PROFESSOR JOSEF SUSTA, of Czechoslovakia, minister of public instruction since 1920, has been appointed by the council of the League of Nations a member of the International Committee on Intellectual Cooperation, in the place of the late Professor H. A. Lorentz, the Dutch physicist, who died last February. Dr. Susta was appointed in 1900 assistant professor at the University of Prague, and in 1905 became professor of general history. In the beginning of his academic career he devoted himself to the study of the economic history of Bohemia, but later relinquished this study for that of religious history.

Dr. F. Aguilar, founder of the dental school in the College of Medicine of Madrid, has been given the title of Viscount de Casa Aguilar by the government. This is said to be the first time that a physician has been so honored.

The retirement is announced at the age of seventy years of Thomas B. Bronson, head of the department of German at the Lawrenceville School, New Jersey. Dr. Bronson has been a member of the faculty for thirty-six years.

The Journal of Education reports that "Frederic Allison Tupper, who retires from the Brighton High School of Boston because he has reached the 'retiring age,' is welcomed by a prominent Investment Securities Company, J. W. Brown & Company, of Boston." Mr. Tupper has been principal of the school for twenty-seven years and on his retirement the head masters of Boston gave him a dinner at the Boston City Club. At the annual dinner given by the mayor to the higher cadet officers and instructors he was officially eulogized. Teachers of the school, past and present, gave a dinner "seasoned with gold coin." The alumni gave a reception at which there were more presents. The Girls Council of the school presented him with more gold. The class of 1928 presented a beautiful painting and still more gold. Among other gifts was a volume with the names of all graduates for twenty-seven years duly engraved.

Dr. L. W. Smith, superintendent of the township schools of Joliet, Illinois, has been appointed superintendent of schools at Berkeley, California, to succeed Dr. H. B. Wilson, who resigned to accept the national directorship of the Junior Red Cross, with headquarters at Washington, D. C.

Raymond E. Pinkham, principal of the West Orange, N. J., junior high school, has been elected superintendent of schools in Weehawken, N. J. Raymond E. Hearn has been made acting principal of the junior high school, succeeding Mr. Pinkham.

James E. Blue, for two years principal of the high school at Ironwood, Michigan, has been elected principal of the high school at Rockford, Illinois.

L. A. Packard has been elected superintendent of schools at Port Huron, Mich., to succeed H. A. Davis, who resigned to enter business. Mr. Packard was principal of the high school for the last five years.

Robert G. Sproul, vice-president and comptroller of the University of California, has been named by the board of education of Berkeley, Calif., as a member of that body.

It is stated in the *School Board Journal* that William H. Maddock, who has for many years represented the educational department of the G. and C. Merriam Company, publishers of the Webster Dictionary, has retired. Mr. Maddock succeeded the late Major A. J. Cheney in 1902. He now goes to Rochester, N. Y., to become the sales manager of the educational department of the Eastman Kodak Company. He is a native of Iowa and has been in the educational field since 1894.

William J. Bogan, the newly-elected superintendent of the Chicago schools, has invited fifty representative citizens to form an advisory committee for the public schools. *The Journal of Education* reports that the following citizens have accepted his invitation: Dr. C. S. Bacon, Mrs. W. S. Brewster, H. P. Chandler, Mrs. A. MacLeish, A. L. Foster, Dr. A. Kegel, Mrs. S. T. Lawton, Rabbi L. L. Mann, F. A. Moore, V. A. Olander, A. S. Peabody, Mrs. C. E. Shearman, S. C. Simms, Leah Taylor, C. W. Barnes, E. L. Burchard, Mrs. H. W. Cheney, G. W. Dixon, Mrs. E. W. Jackson, Mrs. B. F. Langworthy, Mrs. E. L. Loewenthal, W. J. Mee, Agnes Nestor, W. J. Parker, Msgr. C. J. Quille, Mrs. G. C. Sikes, F. Streyckmans, J. H. Witter. The first meeting of this advisory board will be early in September.

The American Bar Association celebrated its fiftieth anniversary at the recent annual meeting in Seattle in a symposium which expressed the community of interest of the professions.

Medicine was represented by Dr. William Allen Pusey, Chicago, a former president of the American Medical Association, who reviewed its progress in the last fifty years; Associate Justice Harlan F. Stone, Washington, D. C., spoke on fifty years' work of the Supreme Court of the United States; Reverend Ozora S. Davis, president of the Chicago Theological Seminary, on the progress of theology; Dr. John H. Finley, editor, New York *Times,* on the progress of education, and Mr. F. B. Jewett, vice-president, American Telephone and Telegraph Company, on progress in engineering. Silas H. Strawn's presidential address was on the progress of law.

DR. OTTO HONETCH, a member of the Reichstag and professor of history in the University of Berlin, arrived in New York on August 13 on his way to Williamstown to take part in the sessions of the Institute of Politics.

PROFESSOR FRED D. FAGG, of the University of Southern California, has been appointed exchange professor to the University of Königsberg, Germany, where he is to be associated with the Institute of Air Law headed by Dr. Otto H. Schreiber. Dr. Rudolf Hirshberg, of the Air Institute, is to be at the University of Southern California during the year Dr. Fagg is in Europe.

LECTURERS in psychology at the New School for Social Research in New York City during the autumn season will include Dr. Fritz Wittels, consulting psychologist of the Psychotechnical Institute of Austria; Dr. Joseph Jastrow, professor of psychology, University of Wisconsin; Dr. Frankwood E. Williams, lecturer in psychiatry at the Yale Medical School; Dr. Ira S. Wile, former member of the Board of Education, and Dr. David M. Levy, of the Institute for Child Guidance.

DR. EDWIN O. JORDAN, professor of bacteriology and chairman, department of hygiene and bacteriology, University of Chicago, has been appointed Cutter lecturer on preventive medicine at Harvard University for the year 1928–29.

MRS. GEORGE F. ZOOK is giving a series of child welfare lectures under the auspices of Akron and Summit County Federation of Women's Clubs. Mrs. Zook served as president of the Child Study Association in Washington, D. C., for two years before going to Akron, where her husband, Dr. Zook, has become president of the university.

DR. SAMUEL WALLACE WELCH, past president of the State and Provincial Health Officers of America, and health officer for Alabama for more than ten years, died suddenly on August 22. Dr. Welch was in 1922 chairman of the Public Health Medical Association and was chairman of the National Malaria Commission.

WILLIAM TRICKETT, dean of the law school at Dickinson College, at Carlisle, Pennsylvania, since 1890, died on August 1 at the age of eighty-eight years.

AS a memorial to the late James J. Storrow, Mrs. Storrow has given $1,000,000 toward a playground in the Charles River basin in Boston to provide boating, bathing, skating and yachting in crowded areas.

BY his recent gift of $120,000, Robert Law, Jr., has raised his donations to the development fund of the University of Chicago to $200,000. The entire sum will be used as endowment for a distinguished service professorship. The Leila Houghteling Fund has also pledged the sum of $50,000, to be used for establishing a fellowship and scholarship fund in the school of social service administration.

CHARLES H. ELLIOTT, commissioner of education of New Jersey, has reported to the state board of education that 1,146 of 1,519 applicants for admission to the normal schools passed the examination in May. He recommended that the test be made more difficult so that fewer students will be admitted. There is a surplus of teachers in northern New Jersey. Mr. Elliott suggested that the examination include American history and a uniform intelligence test.

THE *Journal* of the American Medical Association reports that, as a preparation for entering school, the child health conferences that have been held this summer throughout Maryland, under the auspices of the state department of health, have encouraged parents to have their preschool children examined as to their weight, posture, teeth, throat, vision and hearing. Few in a total of 2,100 children examined made a perfect score; 1,825 of them were in need of some special care; the teeth of 1,188 needed attention; 859 had enlarged or infected tonsils; 305 had adenoids, and 161 were mouth breathers; unfavorable heart conditions were found in sixty-four, and thirty-seven had defective vision. Only about thirteen in every hundred children were in the 100 per cent. healthy class.

It is reported in the daily press that the American history text-books, attacked during the trial of Superintendent William McAndrew, of Chicago, for their alleged pro-British taint, have been discarded from the public-school system by a unanimous vote of the Board of Education.

It is announced that the cruise around the world of the "University Afloat," under the presidency of Dr. J. C. Jones, of the University of Missouri, has been postponed until 1929, owing to failure to obtain a registration of three hundred students.

An International Congress of Design and Applied Art, which was attended by delegates from 26 nations, including Great Britain, the United States and Japan, closed at Prague on August 11 after six days of work. The delegates were received by President Masaryk, who gave a garden party in their honor.

Plans are being made by the Ministry of Public Education of Mexico for an international exhibition of drawings to be held in Mexico City, opening on September 1.

SPECIAL CORRESPONDENCE

STUDENTS AND COURSES AT THE UNIVERSITY OF OREGON

During the last academic year two significant programs have been adopted at the University of Oregon, both of which will be of far-reaching interest to the student body and especially to the entering class in 1928. The first of these is an improved organization and procedure for handling problems of personnel and vocational guidance. The second of the programs effects a distinct change in the lower division of the university that goes by the name of the College of Literature, Science and the Arts.

I

In recent years psychology has thrown considerable light on the problem of securing better adjustments of the individual to the useful pursuits of life. Modern business, following the lead of the psychologist, has done much, through proper placement, to enhance the effectiveness and increase contentment among the numerous body of workers. For those whose active participation in business or professional work is postponed until the end of a university course the problems of adjustment must receive attention at the hands of university authorities. Indeed, the whole task of education is, in a sense, preparation for intelligent choice and pursuit of vocations in which the individual realizes his highest usefulness to society.

Students enrolled in the university are in a sense passing through the critical period of their lives. Conflicting interests and impulses often interfere with concentration of effort and steadiness of purpose so necessary to the process of learning. Energy expended in the futile or aimless attempt to making adjustments too often detracts from the process of mental growth.

To assist in the process of finding proper adjustments at the earliest possible stage, to supply as far as possible an intelligent and scientific basis for selection of life's work and the choice of an educational program best suited to that end, to discover and stimulate students of unusual capacity, while devising sympathetic methods for dealing with backward students who may be gifted in some particular direction are some of the duties of the newly created personnel council. The composition of this council has been carefully determined and it is the purpose of the administration to bring to bear on these vital and fundamental problems the best scientific training and approved technique. Around the activity of this important organization will center some of the larger questions of educational policy.

An interesting departure has been made by the scholarship committee in conjunction with the offices of dean of men and dean of women in passing judgment upon the students of superior promise. Students whose unusual gifts are clearly indicated by mental test scores and enviable records in the secondary schools are carefully followed to see how near their university records come to fulfilling the promise. Any conspicuous slump in scholastic achievement is made a subject of expert inquiry with a view to removing causes and elevating the standard of work. Only by applying the rule "from each according to capacity" can the university conserve its most precious material, cultivate a pride in thoroughness and forestall habits of idleness on the part of superior students who could easily achieve a passing standard. Under the new honors system lower division students are carefully sifted for scholars of promise and these students enrolled in upper division courses that constitute a continuing challenge to their powers.

II

One year ago the faculty, in line with the newer developments in education, created a committee to study and report on the question of organizing the first two years of university work on a junior college basis. While rejecting the phrase "junior college" and substituting the designation "lower division work" the legislation nevertheless embodies the junior college principle in effect. The first two years of the college curriculum are recognized as a unit related in a way to the high-school work that has gone before and intended to facilitate the transition from secondary school work to specialized university training which begins with the junior year. The first two years of the college of literature, science and the arts as reorganized are intended to lay broadly the foundation for a liberal education and prepare the student for specialized study or entrance into the professional schools later on.

During the freshman year while the student is finding himself, the course will consist, in addition to the required work in English, foreign languages and physical education and hygiene, largely of survey courses intended to lay a foundation much broader than the courses hitherto offered by departments. The aim in these courses will be to emphasize relationships that are broader than the boundary lines of single disciplines. These relationships made clear at the outset will serve as a wholesome corrective for a certain narrowness or intellectual blindness resulting from specialization begun before the student has had a chance to broaden out.

To facilitate the work of giving these survey courses, the departments were classified into four affiliated groups: (1) Languages and literature, (2) social science, (3) physical sciences and (4) biological sciences. Each of these groups is provided with survey courses broadly introductory to the work of the several disciplines included in the group. During the first two years, a student who has not chosen a major in one of the professional schools will not have a department major at all. He will merely designate one of the groups as a field of principal interest. Moreover, he will be compelled to distribute his freshman and sophomore work in such a way as to insure contact in a broad way with three of the four groups into which the college is divided.

At the beginning of the junior year the student will choose a major at a time when his wider acquaintance with the field of university work should facilitate an intelligent choice. During the first two years students will be assigned in small groups to professors who will act in the double capacity of adviser and instructor in the survey courses indicated above. Perhaps one of the most significant features of the plan is that it will bring the freshmen at once into contact with some of the outstanding members of the faculty at a time when the influence of such instructors will count the most in the training of intellect and the moulding of character.

At the same time the course of the first two years was reorganized the line was more sharply drawn between upper and lower division. At the end of his first two years the student will be given a junior certificate or, if he prefers, a certificate of graduation from the lower division. Provided the student has maintained a high average in his work, he will be given a junior certificate with honors privileges and be entitled to enroll in honors courses. The work from this point to the receipt of his bachelor's degree will be more intensive and more highly specialized. Nearly two thirds of the courses must be of advanced nature and designated as upper division work.

At a recent meeting of the faculty, steps were taken to make more rigid the scholarship requirements to remain in the university. In the lower division students on probation for poor scholarship showing are required to carry and successfully pass at least twelve hours or be dropped from the university. In the upper division the status of probation is abolished and the student failing to make ten hours (as against seven formerly required) will be dropped from the university and denied the privilege of petitioning for reinstatement until a period of nine months has elapsed.

Both because a certificate of graduation can be obtained at the end of two years and the student in the upper two years must face a rigorous program of intensive study, many students of average ability or below will find the end of the second year a convenient stopping place in their university careers. The prospect of obtaining at least the foundation of a liberal education in two years and securing a certificate of graduation in a shorter time will doubtless attract many who might regard a four-year course too costly or too formidable. In the long run, the new departures are not likely to make any material change in the number who receive instruction at the university. A rising standard of university achievement has always been a challenge to students of superior ability who come in increasing numbers, and the periods following the stiffening of scholarship requirements have been, at the University of Oregon, marked by material increases in enrolment.

ARNOLD BENNETT HALL

DISCUSSION

WHO'S WHO IN OUR CLASSES?

WE all know that there is a large book containing thousands of names of those who have marked themselves by some unusual achievement, by doing more for their fellows than the average man or woman. They are but thousands among the many millions of the world.

Every community, society, group having a common purpose has its "Who's Who," those who do and can do more than others. A teacher and a class are a group with a common purpose in which some do, and can do, more than others of the group, and can serve their group. One fourth, sometimes one third, can do three times the work of the poorest fourth, twice that of most of the average in ability, and with no more time and effort than they. Though this has been proven true again and again, school classes are generally conducted on the theory of equal tasks for all, with some doing better than others. But the doing better by no means takes up the slack of the ablest fourth, often contributes to it; for one who can do more is likely to do less work poorly; he needs more, to do his work well.

A duty and a privilege that most of us teachers neglect is finding out who is or can be a "Who's Who" in our classes, and so marking them in our class books.

HOW CAN WE FIND OUT WHO THEY ARE?

Not always by their class record. Some of the highest in record may be doing all they can, all they ought to do. The slack are often among those doing average work, or even poor work. This is our field for personal interest and inquiry. Some day an unusual reply, or piece of work, may lead us to suspect that there is unusual ability there, and we follow up with a personal inquiry into habits of study.

We shall learn much by now and then having an oral or written quiz on how the lesson of the day was prepared. If oral, a personal experience session, a comparison of individual ways will be revealing.

If a student comes up with his difficulties we can go into the question of how he studies. A better way may be without warning to omit the recitation for the day; assign the next day's lesson, and say to the class, "You may study this lesson while I talk with some of you about how you study." After you have waited to see who are slow in getting to work, you call Henry to you and say quietly: "What did you do first, Henry, in preparing to-day's lesson? What next? What next? When? Where? What help? How did you know you had the lesson?" Commend his better ways, make a suggestion or two, and send him back to his studying. Call Mary, and so a dozen or more others. Near the close, pass around to a number to see how much they have done. Then give two or three suggestions, and say to the class, "To-morrow we shall take up to-day's lesson and the one you have been studying." When you have gone around the class with your mental diagnosis, you will know better what each one can do.

Timing study will reveal ability. Assign ten or fifteen minutes study to a new piece of work. Then get at the results by their writing what they have done, or by a set of questions covering the work. To test permanence of impression, put the study at the first of the period and getting the results at the close, or the next day. This will be a far better test of ability in a study than any of the usual "intelligence tests."

The effort of the teacher is to learn in every way possible "Who's Who" in the class, the aptitudes of each, and so mark them in the class book.

WHAT SHALL WE DO WITH THEM?

Do exactly what was done with many a man or woman whose name is in "Who's Who." They were drafted for service because they were known to have more ability than their fellows. Mark the names of the half dozen or so in your class book who can do more than the task for the average of the class, as you discover them, and assign them not more work of the same kind, but those services that shall be of value to the class, duties in which they will take satisfaction and pride, because they are given place before their mates. Following are some of the duties which may be assigned:

1. One or two may be asked to follow a periodical, or another text-book, for added light upon the lessons.

2. One or two may prepare and hand in questions, topics, for the teacher's use, or select points worth discussing.

3. Two may be told that for a week all calls for explanations will be referred to them first, or they may select points and explain them.

4. To some may be given for a time the correction or criticism of all oral work. Sometimes a part of papers handed in will be given them to correct.

5. For every two or three working at the blackboard, one of these may follow the work and be ready to help or correct at signal by the teacher.

6. From these best a running mate in study may be assigned for a week or more to a slow or failing pupil to help, and to report what is the trouble with him.

7. In older classes, now and then, one may be asked to hand in, or give a lesson assignment; and he may next day teach his assignment.

8. One or two may have the duty of getting ready the material needed for the class, specimens, etc.

9. The care of temperature and ventilation of the room may be another's duty.

10. The usual lost time of roll calling by the teacher may be saved to the class by having it the duty of one to hand in at the close of class the names of those absent and of those late.

Any teacher can find other ways of service, can use some or all of those suggested. No student should do one thing continuously. He needs the experience of a wider range of service.

But will not some object? They may; the equality point of view is old and fixed. It must be changed. A student has no more right to be an idler on his job, to keep pace with the slower than has an employee in shop or field to do no more work than the slowest. School and life are to be alike.

A class is not a corporal's guard with the teacher the corporal, too often the present conception, but it is a company with parts serving other parts and a captain at its head to direct.

WHAT WILL THIS FINDING "WHO'S WHO" IN OUR CLASSES DO?

1. It will reveal and develop abilities. That is what school is for.

2. It gives all new points of view, wider relations of lesson and of teacher. It is not all, "teacher asks, pupil recites."

3. The average pupil will be waked up, spurred to his best. He says, "If John can do that, I can."[1]

[1] The help of the teacher lacks that stimulus. A teacher wrote to her professor in education, ''My beginning algebra class is in the dumps, though I explain and explain.'' The professor wrote back, ''That class is making you carry them. Say privately to two of the best, 'I shall call on you for three days to do the explaining in class.' Then pass on the service to two others.'' Six weeks

4. It saves the present waste of time in having those recite who always know. It gives more time to those who need the time.

5. It gives the slow a larger service; instead of the service of one, the teacher, the service of many, and of those who having just found their way, can understand their difficulties.

6. It opens the way for giving a higher record for higher service. It recognizes both kind and quality of performance, a great gain.

7. It brings personal interest, and personal relations into the classroom. It changes the atmosphere of task giving, and task accounting, to that of personal service.

8. It makes the classroom game a practice game for the life game to come. The school is a social unit with experiences and duties like those to come. It is practical civics.

9. No revolution in methods is necessary. It adds to what the teacher is already doing. It can start with one of the ten suggestions and go on to others.

10. It opens a way for the teacher to study the classroom game, the greatest need in education to-day. The game is not more than half played in most classrooms.

This is one solution of the problem of "individual differences" in a class.

A. W. BURR

BELOIT COLLEGE

after, the report came, "My algebra class is my best, all want to explain." It was the same class and the same teacher; but that was the difference between teacher-explaining and pupil-explaining.

QUOTATIONS

CONTACTS OF EDUCATION AND INDUSTRY IN ENGLAND

THE committee appointed by the president of the Board of Education and the Minister of Labor "to inquire into and advise upon the public system of education in relation to the requirements of trade and industry, with particular reference to the adequacy of the arrangements for enabling young persons to enter into and retain suitable employment," has now presented its second report, which deals with the first part of the terms of reference. Already details of its recommendations have appeared in the press, and already certain criticisms of those recommendations, particularly with regard to their cautious framing, have been made.

It is not our purpose to attempt a defense against such criticisms. There can, indeed, be little doubt as to the cautious framing of the report. Its attitude towards the raising of the school leaving age, for example ("for the reasons given in the body of our report, we do not submit any recommendations . . ."), is doubtless disappointing when the weight of other opinion is considered. Its attitude, too, towards the development of full-time instruction in technical schools (which "must be considered with due regard to the factors of supply and demand") may not be very heartening. That the result of the growth of the internal system of examination is regarded as satisfactory; that "criticisms relating to basic subjects [taught in elementary schools] are too sweeping and are frequently made on insufficient ground"; that authoritative industrial opinion does not favor vocational training in primary schools; that the educational principles formulated by the Hadow Committee are accepted; that industry would benefit by a larger intake of pupils from secondary schools, and that to accomplish this the difficulty occasioned by the age of entry into apprenticeship, namely, sixteen years, "should be examined by the industries concerned"; that the grouped course system in evening schools is justifiable but should be more elastic, and that the system of advisory committees in connection with technical schools "should as far as possible be made universal": all these points will be noted perhaps with a little impatience by those to whom the problems are familiar, and in their search for recommendations which shall show means of swift solution of these problems they may be apt to overlook not only the profounder significances of this report, but also the fact that another committee, which has presented its report recently, has been dealing with the same terms of reference applied to Scotland.

The two reports have been cast along similar lines, but the Scottish report seems bolder in its decisions. If the English committee hesitates concerning the school-leaving age, the Scottish committee does not: in its first report it supported the raising of that age; in preparing this report the evidence "has confirmed us in the opinions therein expressed." Unlike the

English report, too, it says clearly "attention should be given to the need for further development of whole-time technical education."

Probably the most disappointing feature of the English report is the fact that definite views were difficult to obtain from industrial sources. Yet both committees emphasize the need for employers to interest themselves in educational provision. The Scottish report puts it well:

It is not merely that they have an interest in seeing that the money they provide is intelligently spent. They depend for their success on the mental caliber of their workers. The employer takes every care to obtain good raw material and machinery that is economical and efficient; he should be equally careful to obtain workers who will be able to use their brains as well as their hands in the fashioning of the material and the tending of the machinery.

We would commend that passage to the National Confederation of Employers' Organizations, which appears to have found itself unable to give authoritative answers to any questions except those of the raising of the school-leaving age and the establishment of compulsory day continuation schools—both of which it opposed.

In spite of the fact, however, that the confederation was unable to submit its views to the test of examination by oral evidence, we would underline its view that "the absence of collective views on the part of employers is due largely to lack of knowledge of the system," and its hope "that some way may be found of increasing that knowledge and securing contact and practical cooperation." We quote these two statements because we agree with the committee that they "remove the suspicion that the employers of this country had already formulated a body of definite views and requirements which were being ignored by those responsible for education." We agree also with the committee's view that, since educational nomenclature is a source of difficulty, the Board of Education should issue a short handbook descriptive of the educational system. Anything which will help employers to repair their lack of knowledge of the system and so enable them to contribute their views must be done speedily—particularly since the committee has rightly insisted that "industries must define their needs, and no other body can do it for them." Not entirely unconnected with this is the indifference of employers to technical education, and the fact that its importance is missed also by many educationists.

Valuable as all this may be to clear the ground for the *rapprochement* between education and industry, it does not present what we have called the profounder significances of the reports. There are pointers in both to the wider and deeper aspects of the problems under review.

The employer is recommended to look on primary, secondary, continuation and technical education not as four distinct types, but as mutually related elements in a coherent system. He is advised to do this immediately, because "unless there is a totally unforeseen reversal of educational ideals this conception of education above the age of eleven is likely to be put into practice within a generation." No employer ought to miss the point of that quotation, particularly the last phrase.

There is good reason, too, for the warning sounded concerning the urgency of a solution to these problems: "any special measures which can be taken to secure the contact which every one desires should be taken with all possible speed before the educational position becomes so solidified that any modifications, however desirable, will be extremely difficult if not impossible to make."

With such significant prophecy and warning before us, it becomes ever more urgent that we should not regard education and industry as two self-contained and separate matters which have in some way to be joined together. The reports do not fail, therefore, to indicate matters not always clearly visualized.—*Nature*.

EDUCATIONAL RESEARCH AND STATISTICS

MENTAL RATINGS, SCHOLARSHIP AND HEALTH

FOR several years, mental ratings, as determined by group tests, have been available for all pupils entering the high schools of Detroit. These ratings have been used as a basis for study of scholarship in the Cass Technical High School. It has been found that there is a wide variation between them and the school accomplishment as shown by teachers' ratings of classroom work. A study of these variations, however, has proved the value of the ratings as one of the factors which determine the probable success of pupils.

When this study was begun in September, 1924, it was assumed that the pupils of low rating, as determined by group tests, would not continue in school after the compulsory education age. It was found that many of them persisted throughout the four years. Many of them graduated with good records from difficult technical courses requiring four years of mathematics and several semesters of advanced science. In June, 1927, out of a graduating class of nearly one hundred and fifty students, thirteen finished with "honor" or "highest honors." Of these honor graduates, seven had entered the high school with group test ratings of either "D" or "E."

Originally, it was planned to follow a group of boys through the four years of high-school life, studying them individually and advising them as to their educational and vocational futures. A diagnosis and a prognosis were to be made in each case and the school and placement history was to be recorded to discover the truth or falsity of the findings. The group was taken from three newly organized classes of 9B English containing only pupils who had not failed the course. The classes had been formed without regard to mental ratings or any other indications of mental capacity.

This group numbered one hundred and thirty-five pupils at the start, but changes in classes and transfers at the beginning of the first semester reduced the number of fairly complete records to one hundred and seven. The records of the group tests (Detroit Alpha) were furnished by the Detroit Public School Psychological Clinic, and the scholarship and physical records of the grade schools were available for the study of the group.

In order to arrive at a composite score, it was determined to give to the group a battery of tests chosen to fit the probable needs of technical students. It was hoped that this composite score would indicate the probable success of individual students and also test the value of the Detroit Alpha ratings. This was done under the supervision of the psychology department of the University of Michigan, and the following tests were given to the group:

Link arithmetic I
Link arithmetic II
Army Alpha 6, test 2
Army Alpha 9, test 2
Constructive visual imagination I
Constructive visual imagination II
Cancellation
Army Alpha
Detroit Alpha II

The results of the tests were correlated with each other and with the original Detroit Alpha ratings, and, at the end of the semester, with the scholarship records of the group. A personal history blank was filled out for each case by individual interviews. These contained data concerning parentage, home conditions, vocational and educational likes and dislikes, educational plans and any employment records.

With the above information at their disposal, the experimenters felt competent to predict the probable success or failure of the individuals. The composite scores, on the whole, confirmed the Detroit Alpha ratings, and changed the order given by the original data but very little. The distribution of the Detroit Alpha ratings follows:

A	19	High rating group 33
B	14	
C+	18	Medium rating group 35
C	17	
C–	18	Low rating group 39
D	11	
E	10	
Total	107	

The pupils of the high rating group were expected to finish their chosen curricula without many dropping out of school, those of the medium group were expected to maintain an average number throughout the four years and those of the low group were expected to disappear before the history should be complete. The record of the four years with respect to those leaving school is shown in Table I.

It is apparent that the high rating group fulfilled the prediction, but the medium and low groups reversed the expected results. The whole

TABLE I

Mental ratings	Original group	Number who left: 1st year	2nd year	3rd year	4th year	Total who left	Number remaining	Per cent. remaining
A	19	2	5	4	0	11	8	48
B	14	4	2	0	0	6	8	
C+	18	4	7	5	1*	16	3	17
C	17	4	8	2	0	14	3	
C–	18	8	3	3	1*	14	5	
D	11	2	3	1	0	6	5	33
E	10	6	1	0	0	7	3	
Totals	107	30	29	15	2	74		
Remaining		77	48	33	35			35

* Returned to school.

group showed 35 per cent. remaining at the end of the four years. The low group kept the same average as the whole, and of the medium group only 17 per cent. remained. With the exception of the high group, the mental ratings seemed to have little in common with the pupils remaining in school. An investigation as to the reasons for leaving school was begun in order to discover a possible explanation.

First, where did they go? Our records show that they transferred to other schools, to part time continuation school, to trade school, or were marked "over age" when they left. The

TABLE II

Mental ratings	Lefts: To other schools	To part time or trade schools	Over age; work	Moved; no trace	Totals
A	3	3	3	2	11
B	2	4	0	0	6
C+	4	7	3	2	16
C	6	2	3	3	14
C–	2	6	6	0	14
D	0	4	1	1	6
E	1	2	3	1	7
Totals	18	28	19	9	74

last three indicate that the pupils were leaving school to become wage earners. Table II shows the distribution.

The fact that 47 of 74 left to go to work would seem to point to economic necessity as a reason for leaving. A study of their average scholarship records for the whole time that they remained in school shows that failure in school is another factor. See Table III.

TABLE III

Mental rating	Scholarship: High	Medium	Not passing	Total
High	4	3*	10*	17
Medium	3	13	14*	30
Low	2	7	18	27
Totals	9	23	42	74

* Scholarship below mental rating.

It is seen that 42 of the 74 "lefts" were not passing in their school work. The low rating group was the most consistent in its scholarship, 18 of the 27 doing work of low grade, but the excessive failures in the high and medium groups demand an explanation. The numbers marked (*) show that 27 pupils were doing work of a grade below that consistent with their ratings. It seems safe to assume that failure in class work is a reason for a large part of the student mortality. There remains for investigation the reasons for the failure of pupils of high mentality and the success in school of pupils of low mental ratings.

At the end of the first year of this study, it was thought advisable to segregate the pupils of low mental rating, to give them programs consistent with their abilities and study them as a group. This has been done for three years and about one thousand pupils have been in this group up to the present time. Each semester, a physical examination has been given by the Detroit Board of Health and 94 per cent. of the group have been found to have physical defects. Many of the group have been returned to regular classes after corrective work has been done and have been able to carry regular work successfully. These results led directly to two conclusions: that health is the greatest single factor governing success in school, and that mental ratings which do not take physical condition into consideration are not a true index of the learning ability of high-school pupils. The study of the backward group has shown that the ratings were a fair index at the time the tests were given, but that school training and corrective work caused radical changes in learning ability.

A study of failing pupils of normal mental rating has proved that almost 100 per cent. of them are suffering from physical defects.

The group of honor graduates mentioned in this report, who entered high school with low mental ratings, were found to have had corrective work done in every case. The school success of these pupils was equalled by their mental ratings as determined in their senior semester by another Detroit Alpha group test. In this test, they all received high ratings.

This investigation of the physical condition of pupils was not started in time to allow a complete report of the four-year group to be made, as many had left when the physical examinations were begun, but the 35 of the group remaining have been examined. Table IV shows their physical condition compared with the scholarship and mental ratings. Those marked (X) are physically defective and those marked (O) are in good physical condition.

TABLE IV

Students Remaining at End of Four Years

Mental ratings	Average scholarship A	B	C+	C	C−	D	E
A	OOOO	XX	X	X			
B	O	OO	O	OXX			X
C+				O	XX		
C			O	OO			
C−		OO	O	OO			
D			OOO			OX	
E		O		O	O		

Of the pupils of low rating who remain in school, every case has a record of corrected physical defects and most of them are doing work of a grade which shows that the original ratings no longer are of value for predictive purposes. The large number of high-rating pupils remaining is explained by the fact that their physical defects were not a sufficient handicap to make them fail. The medium-rating group found the handicap too great and almost disappeared in the four years. These two groups were not given the physical attention that was given to the low-rating group during the first two years. The latter was watched as the group needing physical attention, and corrective work was done almost from the beginning. How many of the others could have been saved, educationally, by having had the same attention, is a question that can not be answered now. The study and correction of physical defects is being carried on in a more scientific manner now and the results are becoming apparent. It has been found that more than one-fourth of all pupils enrolled at the Cass Technical High School have physical defects and these are being followed up and corrected in increasing numbers.

TABLE V

Summary of Table IV

Average scholarship	Physical condition Good	Defective
Equal to or above mental rating	22	1
Below mental rating	3	9

The results of this study are summarized as follows:

In many cases, mental ratings, as determined by group tests, are not permanent.

Therefore, mental ratings alone, as determined by group tests, are not a reliable basis for predicting high school success or failure or for predicting the duration of school life.

The greatest reason for the variation in mental ratings is to be found in physical condition.

Physical condition is one of the greatest factors affecting school success and the duration of school life.

Correction of physical defects constitutes one of the most important problems in education.

Harry M. Keal

Cass Technical High School of Detroit

EDUCATIONAL BOOKS PUBLISHED IN 1928—Continued

Tests and measurements (education). HENRY LESTER SMITH and WENDELL W. WRIGHT. 555 pp. $3.00.

Zur Psychologie der Vorstellungstypen mit bes. Berücks. d. motor. u. musikal. Anlage. RICHARD BAERWALD. Reprint 1928. 444 pp. Paper bound. $5.04.

Reaching other minds. DAVIDA MCCASLIN. 296 pp. $1.75.

Building character; proceedings of the Mid-West Conference on Parent Education, February, 1928. Chicago Association for Child Study and Parent Education. 351 pp. Paper bound. $1.00.

Elementary psychology. ARTHUR IRVING GATES. Revised edition. 629 pp. $2.60.

Hans Andersen the man. ELITH REUMERT. Translated by JESSIE BRÖCHNER. 208 pp. Illustrated. $3.50.

Goethe, the history of a man. EMIL LUDWIG. 657 pp. Illustrated. $5.00.

Modern German reader; Deutschland in Wort und Bild. FREDERICK BETZ and GOTTLIEB A. BETZ. 293 pp. Illustrated. $1.40.

Gesundheitspflege des Kindes im Elternhause. CARL HOCHSINGER. Sixth edition. 288 pp. 20 illustrations. $2.40.

History of mankind. HUTTON WEBSTER. 712 pp. Illustrated. $2.12.

Greek history for young readers. New edition. ALICE ZIMMERN. 397 pp. Illustrated. $1.90.

The growth of a nation, the United States of America. EUGENE CAMPBELL BARKER, and others. 734 pp. Illustrated. $1.80.

The foundations of the Constitution. DAVID HUTCHISON. 414 pp. $3.50.

The year's work in English studies. Volume VII, 1926. Edited by F. S. BOAS and C. H. HERFORD. (English Association.) 322 pp. $2.50.

Prose models, for use with classes in English composition. Edited by EDWIN LONG BECK and WILLIAM LUCIUS GRAVES. 671 pp. $2.00.

Heine; edited by S. LIPTZIN. HEINRICH HEINE. 338 pp. Illustrated. (Johnson's German series.) $1.60.

Deutsche Stunden; Lehrbuch nach der direkten Methode. LYDIA MARIE SCHMIDT and ELSE GLOKKE. 397 pp. Illustrated. $1.60.

The American renaissance. ROBERT LUTHER DUFFUS. 321 pp. $4.00.

More things to draw. EDWIN GEORGE LUTZ. 96 pp. Illustrated. $2.00.

Play areas; their design and equipment. Playground and Recreation Association of America. 222 pp. Illustrated. $2.00.

The lantern, and other plays for children. ABBIE FARWELL BROWN. 152 pp. $1.75.

SCHOOL AND SOCIETY

Volume XXVIII — Saturday, September 8, 1928 — Number 715

EDUCATION: THE NEXT STEPS[1]

The chief advance made in the first quarter of the twentieth century has been that the nation as a whole has been converted to belief in the value of education. When the century began there were still very many who had received little or no schooling in their youth, but had won their way, not without a considerable measure of self-satisfaction, to substantial positions. That perhaps legitimate pride was based on a certain misunderstanding of the values of life, and it involved the fallacy vividly exhibited by a certain local millionaire of my acquaintance who was asked to support the movement for the establishment of the local university. "University," he said: "what do you want with a university? I left school when I was thirteen, and look at me." Now it was just because we *were* looking at him that we desired the means of higher education to be at the command of the community, though at that particular interview it was hard to say so. To-day, nearly a generation later, that particular type—a type usually of sturdy independence, strong character and material outlook—has largely been gathered to its fathers; there have been twenty-five years of constantly extending further education; the war has taken place. Opposition to education as such, at any rate to education after the age of fourteen, is now confined to the National Confederation of Employers' Organizations, and to the farmers, both of which circles are mostly interested in the continuance of the supply of young labor under the conditions to which they have been hitherto accustomed. But they represent now a definite minority of the nation, which as a whole is unwilling to think of a large mass of its members as merely raw material to be utilized in its course from the school to the scrap-heap; it believes that each boy and girl has a right to be trained as an individual. There flourishes to-day a living and growing belief in the value of human personality; it dominates all that is best in our education, and I believe it will soon be unquestioned in any quarter. It must so dominate the general mind if our democracy is to justify itself, if, indeed, it is to survive.

Any one who studies the growth of our education during the last century can not fail to be impressed by the fact that it has been developed to meet needs which made themselves felt in practice, and not to satisfy preconceived theories, or a logical perfection. Its history is that of a soldiers' battle: it has been the creation of actual combatants, and not of a general staff. As a result it has all the vitality which comes from springing direct from the national life, so that the life of the schools is interwoven with that of the people; but as a system it is not logical, and it is not complete. There have been remarkable and successful achievements in some directions, but gaps have been left unfilled in others. It has been well said that the landscape of English education is one of peaks and valleys rather than that of a uniform tableland. It is our business now to think nationally as well as locally, and to apply our minds to the filling up of those valleys, some of them deep, which still exist, and it is the purpose of this paper to indicate what, in the opinion of one who has spent more than twenty-five years in service in one field of our education, are the next steps which we should take if we are to move towards the creation of a system which is really national, and will provide for all the varying and complicated needs of a great nation of the twentieth century.

Right across the path of advance lies a lion, at the moment only apparently asleep, which has already devoured imprudent wayfarers, and may devour more: I need not say that I refer to the existing system of dual control in elementary education. It is as well to know what is the

[1] Address of the president of Section L—Educational Science, British Association for the Advancement of Science, Glasgow, 1928.

size of this problem. According to the last published figures, those for 1926–27, out of 22,629 public elementary schools in England and Wales, 10,478 were council schools and 12,151 were voluntary schools; of these 12,151 again 10,457 were Church of England, 135 Wesleyan, 1,196 Roman Catholic, 12 Jewish, and 351 of other types. Taking it another way, by the numbers of children in attendance, there were 4,924,102 in the council schools and 2,711,244 in the voluntary. It is therefore a very large problem, the solution of which can not be left to time, as is our national way when we are in the presence of a difficulty; for, while it is true that the number of council schools tends steadily to increase, and the number of voluntary schools to dwindle, yet the process is so slow that it would take very much more than a century before the voluntary schools became negligible. The position is this: that the act of 1902 left the buildings of the voluntary schools in the possession of the denominations, and the religious teaching of the schools under the authority of the school managers, who retain also the right to appoint the teacher. Those who to-day have to organize the whole of education in any district find themselves hampered at every turn by the fact that they do not control all the schools. If, on the authority of the Education Act of 1921, they want to take the older children from a number of schools and group them for better teaching into one, they may find that the non-provided schools will not part with the very children for whom the system is designed. They may desire to reorganize, reequip or rebuild a school, and find that the managers may very probably not possess the means, and in some cases not the will, to bear the expenditure involved. They may be aware, as in some cases they are aware, that the buildings to which the children have to go are ill-equipped, badly planned, far below the standards of the present day, but there is very little which they can in practice do to remedy this state of affairs. Even if they are willing to build a totally new school they have to face the fact that, without the good-will of the managers of the non-provided school, they may fail to obtain the attendance of a proportion of the children large enough to jusify the expenditure. Thus there is at present neither simplicity, economy, nor efficiency. On the denominations themselves the system plainly imposes burdens which are in general beyond their means. A settlement of the question is demanded in spite of the fact that any attempt at a solution brings the solver up against what some would call religious conviction and others sectarian prejudice. Nevertheless there is more general good-will in the air and a greater spirit of reason, and we ought to go forward. I submit that advance can go forward on lines which have been proposed, and found pretty general support, that the voluntary schools should be transferred to the local authorities, who in return should allow at certain times and on certain days facilities of entry. Religious instruction would be given at definite periods, during which, if it were desired, certain children could be withdrawn for denominational instruction to be provided by the denominations. So far as Church of England and Nonconformist schools are concerned, I do not believe the withdrawal would in practice prove necessary or desirable, for I think that a very strong majority of the nation desires that the basis of all our education should be religious and Christian. These religious bodies are near enough together to arrive at a concordat as to the syllabus of religious instruction which should be followed, and the principles of the denomination could well and fitly be taught in the Sunday schools. I would submit that the educational enthusiasm and beneficence of the denominations could from their own point of view be most usefully directed to the provision of a certain number of schools for post-primary education and of training colleges for teachers. At any rate the scheme which I have thus briefly outlined is not one which disturbs the position and functions of teachers on the one hand, or one which need create friction between the churches and the local authorities on the other. But it does give the local authority effective control over buildings and organization, and that is a necessary condition if further advance is to be made.

That further advance is outlined in the Report on the Education of the Adolescent, which has come to be known as the Hadow Report; since its publication it has commanded an unusual amount of support and interest. I give my unqualified adherence to the proposals which it makes, though I do not agree with the nomenclature which it suggests. Primary education should in future be a stage which ends at about the age of 11+, and this for the best of reasons, because at about that age childhood closes and the first beginnings of adolescence set in. A second stage of education should therefore start at this point, going on for the majority to 15+, for many to 16+, for some to 18 or 19, this stage being regarded as a single whole, designed to meet the needs of the adolescent, and therefore containing within itself a considerable variety of type. This is not simply a question of adding one year to the course as it exists at present: it means rethinking the whole of our education on a psychological basis, and designing the primary course for the years of childhood, the post-primary courses for the ensuing years. It means as an ideal that all children would go forward after eleven on parallel lines, following the course best suited to each. The Hadow Report therefore states in its second conclusion that, "while taking the country as a whole, many more children should pass to 'secondary' schools in the current sense of the term than pass at present, it is necessary that the post-primary grade of education should include other types of post-primary schools, with curricula varying according to both the age up to which the majority of pupils will remain at school and the different interests and utilities of the pupils to which the bias and objective of each school will normally be related." They envisage, therefore, besides the secondary schools of literary and scientific type, selective central schools with a four-year course, and a practical trend in the last two, non-selective central schools, which may exist either by themselves in some areas, or in other areas side by side with the selective schools, and a variety of other arrangements, which I think they only insert in their report because they realize that there must be a temporary period of makeshifts. Quite rightly, as I think, they do not believe that this system, if established, would hamper or cripple our already existing secondary schools, for the desire for education, once it is established, grows of itself. Quite rightly they realize that the education of adolescence is something wider than that which is given through books alone, and the new schools, while they begin with their eleven-year old pupils in much the same way as the secondary schools, will always seek to develop the hand and the eye, and in their last two years will develop a practical bias.

There is an immense gap which the promoters of this report seek to fill, and only those who have studied facts and figures know how large it is, so large, indeed, that it prevents us from making any claim at present that we have a system of education which deserves to be called national. In any one year the total school population is very slightly above 700,000. At the age of 14+ there are at least 300,000 children who are outside the system altogether, and receiving no continued instruction; at the age of 15+ this figure has risen to 520,000. This means that the effort and the money which have been devoted to the training of those children up to the age of 14 are in very considerable measure wasted; and though I have not time to argue it now, or to advance the evidence, here in this gap may be found the reasons for much of the unemployment, and still more of the unemployability, which exist within our society to-day. It is of the most vital importance that those years of adolescence should be safeguarded by all that is of inspiration and of good report. Which of us would willingly allow a child of his own to pass to the work of the world at this age without further help? Not one of us. It is not a question of the interest of employers, or of the interest of parents; it is a question of the interest of the child, and of the nation, whose main wealth is the men and women which it produces. And since, if it were a matter of the interest of our own children, we could only answer that question in one way, it seems to me a plain matter of social duty to strive to bring it about that the same safeguards and help should exist for all, and that we shall not continue to neglect a full half of the children who are born into our country.

But before I pass from the region of primary education there are a few further points which I should like to make, though I must make them briefly. We take our children into school at the age of five, a year earlier than any other country, and after a good deal of past blundering we have developed in many of our infant schools institutions which seem to me to be of peculiar merit. In them the children are active, not passive, happy, and not dull: the atmosphere is that which is proper to early childhood, an atmosphere of freedom, spontaneity, and joy. I should like to see the policy steadily followed of developing and increasing the number of these admirable places. I have no doubt, too, that the policy will be steadily followed of reducing the size of classes in the primary school. I need not labor this, for to this audience it will be obvious that a teacher confronted by sixty, seventy or more pupils can not follow the same methods, or seek the same ends, as the teacher who deals with thirty-five. The teacher of the large class can seek only discipline and a certain amount of mechanical accuracy; as the numbers fall he can begin to treat his pupils as individuals. He can develop those methods, for instance, which I believe are admirably suited to the stage of the primary school, which are associated with the name of Miss Charlotte Mason, and the Parents' National Educational Union. Promising experiments have been made on these lines in Gloucestershire, Kent and elsewhere, and during our sessions we shall hear more of them. Other experiments also can be tried so long as the teacher is not overborne by numbers. But of primary education as a whole —and I am speaking of the stage that ends at 11 +, not at 14—I would say that it is no longer the region of the three R's; it is the region of another trinity, the hand, the eye, and the voice. It is the business of the primary school to teach the child to see and observe, to make and to do, and to speak and to sing. And then the child will be much more fit to enter into the great inheritance of the world, with more capacity for true happiness, and more capacity for true intelligence.

In passing from this digression once again to the consideration of post-primary and secondary education, it is in place not to omit the mention of one other administrative reform, and that is the rearrangement of local authorities so that in any given area there should be one authority for the whole work of education. At present there are 318 authorities for elementary education and 145 for higher education; the mere mention of the fact shows that in many districts it is impossible to organize the education as a whole. Clearly the areas should be wide, for to-day communities spread over great distances, and their members sleep in one place and work in another; not only in education it is beginning to be found that units which are too small do not make for cheapness or efficiency.

To turn to the problems of secondary education proper—by which I mean education of boys and girls up to the age of 18—it is advisable first to survey the present position and to see how that position has arisen. The public schools and the great day schools of the nineteenth century were inspired both in regard to curriculum and method by Oxford and Cambridge, and they were largely classical; a reaction against this undue narrowness led to the experiment of the organized science schools of the last ten years of that century. These in their turn certainly carried the reaction too far, and produced juvenile chemists and physicists without culture or general education. In 1907 the Board of Education issued its first regulations for secondary schools, and sought something broader than either of these two rival institutions; they established a four-year course in which English, geography and history, at least one language other than English, mathematics, science, and drawing should be studied, together with manual work, physical exercises, and, for girls, housewifery. As that course has been worked in practice in the last twenty-five years, it has been in the main academic in spirit, and the important subjects have come to be the native tongue, the foreign language or languages, and mathematics and science; the schools have continued to look to the universities, and to the development of those advanced courses which lead up to university studies. All this effort has been directed and stabilized, and some would say stereotyped, by the setting up of the system of school certificates, for which in England and Wales eight university authorities examine. All the secondary schools, therefore, have in the main the same outlook, which is primarily that each pupil should at the end of the first stage of the course be able to matriculate at a university; the school certificates have been brought into relation with the matriculation examinations, and the system is now organized in all its details.

Meantime the number of schools, and the number of pupils at each school, have greatly increased. In 1904 in England the number of secondary schools for boys, for girls, and for boys and girls together was 575; there are now 1,184 recognized for grant by the Board of Education and 305 recognized as efficient, but not eligible for grant. In 1904 the number of pupils was 97,698; in October, 1927, it was 349,430, and if you add the 57,655 in the schools not eligible for grant you get a total of 400,000 boys and girls who are in England pursuing a course of secondary education. Now the reason why I have troubled you with these figures is to point out that, while the content of secondary education has not changed, and remains academic in spirit and outlook, the number of schools has more than doubled, and the number of pupils has increased by more than four times. To put it clearly in another way, in the first year in which the school certificates examination was held, there were 14,232 candidates; for the last one for which figures are available there were 54,593, again very nearly an increase of four times.

The result of pouring all this mass of new material into a single mould has produced a slowly increasing volume of protest, but those who protest are much more sure in describing the symptoms of the distresses of the secondary schools than they are in pointing to their cause or in finding the cure. It is said that there is a good deal of overstrain among the pupils of the secondary schools, particularly among the girls, and that for the average the effort of reaching a satisfactory level in English and English subjects, in a foreign language or languages, and in mathematics and sciences is too much. That this is so is shown by the fact that when the examination was established it was supposed that nearly all would be successful at the end of their course in obtaining a school certificate, but as a matter of experience less than two out of three have been able to do so. It is alleged that the examination hampers the freedom of the teacher, who during the whole four years' course can never turn aside to browse in the pleasant paths of literature or to pursue interests common to himself and his class, but must concentrate the attention of his class and himself wholly upon what will pay in the examination room. Great schoolmasters of the past are quoted who could never have pursued their favorite methods with success under present conditions. It is asserted that for many boys, and for still more girls, the present curriculum is unsuitable, that they are not all, or indeed comparatively many, of them going to the universities, and that they ought not to be sacrificed to the interests of the few who do contemplate that course. The question is raised whether as a matter of fact this intellectual training of the girl ought to be the same as that of the boy, and whether the tyranny of imposing the preparatory curriculum of the university upon the girls is not even more unreasonable than it is asserted to be in the case of the boys. On this point the committee which reported on the differentiation of the curricula as between the sexes spoke with an uncertain voice, probably because they knew that there were many feminine associations ready to tear and devour any committee or any individual who said anything which might be taken to imply that women were not the full equals of men, and girls of boys.

The practical outcome of all this is the suggestion that boys and girls should be awarded a school certificate even if they omit a foreign language entirely, or mathematics and science entirely, so long as they make up for it by proficiency in subjects such as music, art, handicraft, housecraft and other subjects of more motley character and more dubious claim. On this proposal the English teaching profession is divided, the Headmasters' Conference and the Assistant Masters' Association being against it, the Headmasters' Association doubtfully in favor, and the Headmistresses' Association and the Assistant Mistresses almost as one woman in favor also. From this state of affairs one can judge where the shoe pinches most, but there is no doubt that it does pinch, and any one who remembers the figures I have just quoted will quitely readily understand why. There are more boys and girls taking the full secondary course to-day than are either fit for it or fitted by it. The malcontents are quite right in the criticisms which they level against the system and its present results, but they are in my opinion wrong as to the nature of the cure and the method by which they would bring it about.

Cyril Norwood
Headmaster of
Harrow School

(*To be continued*)

AN IMPEDIMENT TO LEARNING TO READ—A NEUROLOGICAL EXPLANATION OF THE READING DISABILITY

Since reading forms so early an acquisition in academic education and since facility in this subject is usually acquired even by children who quite obviously are below the average in brightness, we are prone to assume that any child who is not grossly defective in intelligence can learn to read. Like all generalities this assumption has its exceptions. That certain physical defects such as very faulty vision or hearing may serve as a hindrance to easy acquisition of reading is self-evident but it requires more explanation when the statement is made that children with normal or even superior intelligence and with normal vision and audition and even with normal use of ordinary pictorial material may yet have great difficulty in learning to read, or may even prove to be unable to learn from ordinary teaching methods. This statement is, however, demonstrably true and suggests a problem on which the neurologist may throw some light.

That children with a specific reading disability but with normal intelligence do exist has been known in medical literature for approximately thirty years and in that period studies have been made of many cases by physicians, psychologists, and teachers. In general, however, there has been a strong tendency to differentiate between those who learn to read with great difficulty and those who never learn to read at all, and to cases of this latter group (those whom no amount of ordinary teaching will train to read) was given in 1895 the name of congenital word-blindness. This term was applied first by an English ophthalmologist and its use was suggested by the similarity between this difficulty and that of persons who had lost the capacity to read because of disease of the brain and who were known as cases of acquired word-blindness. In such cases destruction of a small part of the brain by a tumor, an injury or a hemorrhage gives rise to a practically complete loss of the power to read, and this loss exists as an isolated defect, that is, the individual does not lose the power to understand spoken words or to speak or to do arithmetic or other mental tasks. Later a second English ophthalmologist, Hinshelwood, studied more extensively a number of children who could not learn to read, and because the symptoms which they presented were so closely parallel to those of acquired word-blindness he suggested that probably a defective development of part of their brain—the so-called area for word memories—lay back of their failure. This was pure inference from comparison with the acquired cases and not only has no proof of such a development-defect been brought forward in these cases but there is strong evidence to suggest that there is no such fixed predestination of brain-areas to serve a given purpose as this assumption would entail. Hinshelwood further attempted to divide poor readers into two groups—those of congenital word-blindness who did not learn to read at all under regular school training and whom he considered to be pathological or disease cases, and those who were merely slow in learning this particular subject whom he rated as physiological and hence not as disease cases. Hinshelwood's separation into these two groups has dominated consideration of the reading disability to a very considerable degree although there have been many investigators who have felt that this division into two classes was artificial and that children of normal mind who had difficulty in reading all belonged to the same group and that the cases of "congenital word-blindness" were merely those of greater severity.

In my own work in this field I was from the first rather strongly impressed with the idea that specifically retarded readers formed a homogeneous group who differed only in the degree of their handicap and not in type. I was further convinced that the nature of their errors in attempting to read indicated the reason for their disability, offered a means of recognizing their handicap early, and, further, might serve as an indicator for methods for training them to read. These views have now been put to the test of an extended study of a comparatively large number of cases and I think that the above assumptions are strongly supported by these further observations.

The explanation of the cause of the handicap rests on well-known facts of brain anatomy and brain pathology. Unlike many of the organs of the body, the brain is made of two symmetrical halves or hemispheres separated from each other by a deep cleft or fissure and connected only by a massive bridge of fibers. It is thus more nearly comparable to the two arms than to the heart or liver and this simile may be carried further since the two hemispheres are exactly like each other but are an antitropic right and left like the two hands. While we recognize that structurally these two halves are quite distinct, we yet know that they do not work as separate units. Nor are their relations to each other exactly the same in the various functions in which the brain participates. For example, the way the two halves function in control of voluntary motion is not like the way in which they function in the reception of visual impressions and in neither of these are their relations to each other the same as in reading and writing. This will be more clear from a consideration of these various functions separately.

With regard to control of voluntary motion, each hemisphere acts on the opposite side of the body exclusively. While there is exceedingly close coordination between movements of right and left hands, for example, yet each is independently governed by nerve-cells situated in a narrow strip of gray matter, the so-called motor area, of the opposite hemisphere. This independence of the two sides is demonstrated when disease or injury destroys the motor area of one hemisphere. This results in a loss of voluntary movement of the opposite half of the body but does not interfere with voluntary movement on the same side. Thus in the common one-sided paralysis which so often follows a stroke of apoplexy, destruction of the motor area or of the fibers leading from it, in the left hemisphere, paralyzes the right arm but does not affect the left. This relative independence of operation of the two hemispheres also characterizes the brain's registration of the sensation of touch. A touch on either thumb is registered in the opposite hemisphere only. This is quite in accord with the physiological needs of the situation, for in order to respond accurately the brain must be informed not only that a thumb has been touched, but also whether it was the right or left thumb.

With regard to sight and hearing the situation is quite different. Here, obviously, to enable proper response it is important that a single object or a single sound shall give rise to only a single impression and not to a separate sensation of the messages from each eye or each ear as in the case of the touch-messages from the thumbs. The nerve-fibers which run from the center for acute vision in the retina of each eye divide so that each eye is connected with both hemispheres and thus whether an image falls on either retina or on both, its message is immediately relayed to both hemispheres of the brain. A comparable situation exists in hearing. The single conscious impression that results from this double activity is probably not brought about by inactivity or elision of the effect produced in one half but by the fusion of the effect in both. This is supported by physiological studies and also by observations where disease or injury has caused destruction in that part of one hemisphere which receives messages from the eyes or ears. As we have seen above, when one motor area is destroyed a paralysis in one half of the body (hemiplegia) results but when one visual area or one auditory area in the brain is destroyed there is no loss of central vision or of hearing. Thus we must assume that either half of the brain alone is competent for sight and hearing.

We must, however, restrict the foregoing statements to the registration of the simpler material brought in by sight and hearing such as objects and noises. When we reach the much more complicated processes which underlie understanding of written and spoken words we find still another type of relationship between the two hemispheres. The four activities which constitute the "language faculty"—understanding the spoken word, understanding the printed word (reading), speech and writing—seem to be controlled exclusively from one hemisphere since destruction of certain areas of one hemisphere causes loss of one or more of these functions while destruction of exactly similar degree and in exactly the same part of the other hemisphere gives no demonstrable result. This striking difference in functional importance of the two hemispheres in the more complex functions underlying language constitutes the problem of cerebral dominance and while much of the older view of the exact pigeonholing of these functions into restricted areas, predestined for that particular purpose, is under challenge to-day, yet the general view of control of these functions from one hemisphere is practically universally accepted.

As we have seen above, however, there is no such striking structural difference between the two hemispheres as we see between their functional duties. The two halves are about equal in size and in complexity and since the studies of Dr. Kappers of Amsterdam and his followers have demonstrated that completed growth of nerve-cells is very largely influenced by the stimuli which they receive, we must assume that the inactive (or non-dominant) hemisphere has been stimulated as freely as the active (or dominant) side and we may further assume that such stimulation has left a record behind it in the nerve-cells of both hemispheres. In other words, we feel that both halves have been equally irradiated by nerve-currents and that both bear impress thereof, but since the destruction of one side brings no aftermath we believe that one of these sets of records is elided or inactive in the language-faculty and that normally a physiological habit is established of using only one set in reading, writing and speech. The two halves of the brain, however, while alike in size and design, are reversed in pattern, that is, the left hemisphere bears the same relation to the right hemisphere that the left hand does to the right hand. It seems logical, therefore, to conclude that the records (or engrams, as they are called) of one hemisphere would be mirrored copies or antitropes of those in its mate. If then there should be failure in establishment of the normal physiological habit of using exclusively those of one hemisphere there might easily result a confusion in orientation which would exhibit itself as a tendency toward an alternate sinistrad and dextrad direction in reading and in a lack of prompt recognition of the differences between pairs of words which can be spelled backwards or forwards, such as *was* and *saw, not* and *ton, on* and *no*, etc.

These alternations and confusions are exactly what characterize the efforts of retarded readers and moreover the frequency of their occurrence bears a very clear relation to the severity of the condition. Extended studies have shown that while many other types of errors occur, such as faulty vowel-sounds, faulty consonant-sounds, etc., confusion in direction bears a most significant relationship not only to reading-retardation in children of normal intelligence (specific reading-disability) but also to the amount of their handicap. In their earlier years these children have greater trouble than the average in telling *b* from *d* and *p* from *q*. Later they learn to tell these letters apart quite readily when seen alone, but are very apt to get them mixed when encountered as parts of words, or this may evince itself in written spelling as when a boy writes *bady* for *baby* and *septemder* for *september* and can not see the error on re-reading it. Still later these simpler confusions between letter-forms are entirely corrected, but errors due to wrong sequence or direction of reading are common. Here the most frequent are confusions of short pallidromic words like *was* and *saw*, as mentioned above, but we also very often find a few letters turned around in the middle of a word. Of this type my recent case-records show *pardon* read as *pradon, maple* as *malpe, story* as *sorty* and *target* as *targret*. Obviously such a failure of the printed word to call up its sounds in proper sequence forms an obstacle to arousing that auditory memory of the word to which its meaning is attached, and reading is sadly blocked. Still later in the milder cases and especially in those children who have had a great deal of intensive help from special teachers or at home, I have found a fair facility in reading accustomed words, so that reading-tests comparable to the child's placement in school would show a passable result, but an almost complete blocking when new words were encountered. Thus one girl of thirteen read *architectural* without hesitation but was completely stampeded by *archaeological* although she knew the word by ear and read *logical* instantly when the first half of the word was covered up and then read the whole word with ease. This child has advanced in grade by dint of extra work, but her schooling has failed so far to give her the reading-tools that make fluency possible and that would permit her to increase her reading-vocabulary outside of school drill even to a degree equivalent to the word-meanings which she has stored by auditory implantation. Other facts in her performance and in that of similar cases lead me to believe that these children have suffered from a distinct reading-disability which has been partially corrected but not sufficiently so to make reading a useful accomplishment to them. The influence of slow and insecure reading on all other academic studies need scarcely be elaborated. One child tells me for example, "I can do my arithmetic if I understand the problem and I can understand it if the teacher reads it to me, but it's lots harder if I have to read it myself." These cases show a very much better auditory than visual memory and have often in the past been listed in the psychological literature as cases with predominant auditory-imagery or even as cases with defective visual-imagery. Such characterizations are, however, merely descriptive of the observed symptoms and all too often bear the implication of an inherent constitution which may block hope of remedy or at best suggests the use of the more facile path for training rather than a corrective frontal attack on the weaker one.

The conception of this whole group of retarded readers here presented, resting as it does on a physiological basis, offers a much more constructive approach to training than do its predecessors, that of brain disease, brain defect, or even that of an inherent psychological type. The errors which such children make in a test-situation not only will serve to determine whether this factor is the stumbling block in their reading, but will indicate the relative severity of the disability and give excellent clues to special methods of retraining. The test of such an hypothesis lies largely in its application and a fair number of retraining experiments have now been carried out to the point where I think we can say with fair security that this disability can be very largely overcome when it is recognized at an early period and proper training measures are immediately instituted and consistently carried out. Such retraining, for example, resulted in a full year's advance in reading after eight weeks of special work in a group of children who had fallen behind on an average of over two years in reading while in the regular schools. The giving of an adequate skill in reading to the older cases is still in an experimental stage. I am undertaking the direction of a retraining program in two such cases, but too recently to estimate the results which may accrue.

One factor which lends its aid to the process of training is the earnest cooperation and willingness of most of these children as soon as they realize that they are no longer under suspicion of being "dumb-bells" or of not working. This is easy to understand. The reading-disability does not correlate with intelligence,—our cases are found to cover practically the entire range of intelligence as usually measured. When a child of average or even superior mind finds himself able to keep up with his class in arithmetic and to compete successfully in social relations with his playmates, but sees most of his fellow pupils, including some who are obviously more stupid than himself, making progress in reading while he is failing, and where, since the obstacle which has blocked him in this particular task is not understood, he is exposed to criticism, punishment and pressure from parent and teacher and the characteristically brutal frankness of other children, the effect on his emotional life is apt to be far-reaching. From these emotional stresses we have seen the development of several reaction patterns. Some children become apathetic and indifferent to school. Others build a marked feeling of inferiority, while a few develop an antagonism toward their teachers and not infrequently become disciplinary problems. The emotional load seems to be particularly troublesome when a younger brother or sister is making more rapid progress. Thus one nine-year-old boy who was entering the third grade in school but who was almost two years retarded in reading, showed very little evidence of strain until his six-year-old brother entered school and began to make headway in reading and then the strain began to be apparent. When such a child, who has been accused of inattention, laziness or stupidity, to explain his slowness, is told that there is a real reason for his delay and that he can probably learn to read as well as the others the response is such as to be very illuminative of the deep-seated feeling which his troubles have engendered. His attitude frequently changes at once and his hearty cooperation in the work is almost immediately forthcoming. Not infrequently the relief of the parents is also quite revealing.

There are many other implications of interest in this approach to educational difficulties by way of our knowledge of brain-physiology and brain-pathology. My choice of the term "impediment" in the title of this review was for the double purpose of implying something of less severity than a true defect and at the same time of relating this condition to certain speech disturbances. We now have reason to believe that many cases of stuttering rest on a different but comparable physiological confusion and in certain of these cases also our results in retraining are very promising. In spelling also many interesting data are accumulating. Where a child has a striking reading-disability, spelling also suffers and improvement in spelling results incidentally with reading-training, but in some children a failure of harmonious interplay between visual and auditory material as evinced in faulty spelling seems to exist more or less independently of difficulty in reading. Thus one small boy read aloud two pages of a story book for me with only three rather insignificant errors, yet made twenty-eight bad errors in spelling orally words selected from the material which he had just read. (Among these were such bizarre mistakes as *qulkey* for *quickly*, *enmuouse* for *enormous* and *trounth* for *through*). Retraining in this type of handicap would also seem to offer great promise although our work in that direction has not as yet been carried far enough to be conclusive.

NEW YORK CITY SAMUEL T. ORTON

EDUCATIONAL EVENTS

THE INTERNATIONAL CONGRESS ON CHILD WELFARE

THE International Congress on Child Welfare was held in Paris, July 8–12, and was attended by a large number of French and foreign representatives. The *Journal* of the American Medical Association reports that the congress was organized by la Ligue des Sociétés de la Croix-Rouge, l'Association internationale pour la protection de l'Enfance, l'Union internationale pour la protection de l'enfance du premier âge, l'Union internationale de secours aux enfants, and le Comité national de l'Enfance. M. Paul Strauss, former minister, was president of the congress, and Dr. Lesage, member of the Academy of Medicine, served as general secretary. It was held the same week and in the same section of the city as three other French congresses discussing similar problems: Congrès d'assistance publique et privée, with M. Rondel as chairman; Congrès des habitations à bon marché, with M. Henri Sellier as chairman, and Congrès du "Service social," with M. Sand as chairman. The contributions of the four congresses were combined in one common exhibit. The Congress of Child Welfare had selected five chief topics for discussion, which were treated in papers of some length and awakened real interest. The papers were published in both French and English, and corresponded to the work of the special sections. The maternity section discussed *maisons maternelles,* or maternity homes and retreats for pregnant women and nursing mothers, with Dr. Trillat, agrégé professor of the Faculté de médecine de Lyon, as the principal speaker, and with papers on special subjects by Miss Halford, of England, and Madame Dr. Marthe Ehrlich, of Poland. The section on early childhood dealt with a comparative study of the best means of promoting breast feeding, with the principal paper presented by Professor Lereboullet, of Paris, and special papers presented by Dr. Matija Ambrosiee, Serbia; Professor Brandt, Sweden; Professor Cacade, Italy; Professor de Groer, Poland; Dr. Growski, Poland; Dr. Helen MacMurchy, Canada, and Dr. S. Ver, Greece. The section on the second period of childhood occupied itself with the organization of open-air establishments for children. The chief speakers were Dr. Dufestel, of France, for the medical point of view; A. Ferrière, of Switzerland, for the pedagogic side, and Dr. Dequidt for the presentation on the vacation colonies. Among the speakers on special topics were: M. Demazeures, Belgium; Dr. Kita, Japan; Professor Lampadarios, Greece; M. Lemonier, France; Miss Margaret MacMillan, England; Dr. Eduardo Masip, Spain; Miss Mary Murphy, United States, and Professor Mario Ragazzi, Italy. Madame Mascart gave a hygienic study on the pupil. Another section presented a paper on social service, the topic being "The Guiding Conceptions of Social Service in Infant Welfare." The principal speaker on this topic was Miss Grace Abbott, of Washington, with the presentation of special topics by Dr. Gonsalès Alvarez, Spain; Mlle. Haye, Netherlands; M. Von Kock, Norway; Madame Mulle, Belgium; Professor Morquio, South America; Reverend S. C. Pringle, England; Miss Hester Viney, England. The final section took up the subject of unfortunate and neglected children, and discussed the practical functioning of juvenile courts. The chief paper was presented by M. Donnedieu de Vabres, which was followed by discussions by Professor Ugo Conti, Italy; M. G. Jongh, the Netherlands; M. A. Komorowky, Poland; Madame Dr. Mende, Germany; M. Edouard Neymark, Poland; M. Wets, Belgium, and M. de Casabianca, France. All resolutions proposed by the chief speakers were adopted as being of practical value.

THE ARGENTINE NORTH AMERICAN INSTITUTE

The Pan American Union has given out a statement concerning the plans of the newly established Argentine North American Cultural Institute, which is given publicity by the *U. S. Daily*.

The institute was founded on May 9, when certain prominent residents of Buenos Aires interested in the cultural progress of the United States gathered together to take formal action on plans that had already been discussed. A constitution previously prepared by a provisional committee was approved and an executive committee and officers were chosen for the club.

Although yet young, the institute has proved itself very successful. It consists of more than a hundred members, among whom are distinguished educators, lawyers, engineers and authors. The treasury contains over 10,000 pesos, collected both from dues and voluntary contributions to the work which the club is promoting. On May 19 the first of a series of lectures under the auspices of the club was given by Dr. David P. Barrows, former president of the University of California, who is now visiting Latin-American universities on behalf of the Carnegie Endowment for International Peace. Dr. Barrows spoke at length on university education in the United States.

Besides sponsoring such lectures, the institute endorses the interchange of students and teachers of both nations, as well as the exchange of collections for libraries, museums and art galleries. It is also planned to establish scholarships for Argentine and United States students who wish to continue their studies in the other country. In this way it is hoped that interest will be developed in the study of the Spanish language in the United States and in the study of English in Argentina.

Similar associations have already been established in Argentina for the purpose of acquainting the nation with the intellectual life of various foreign countries. Among these the French group has been particularly active for some time. The new institute, however, is the first one formed in Latin-America for the purpose of cultural interchange with the United States.

The institute's representative now in the United States, Dr. del Campo, is a distinguished judge, professor and writer. He is well known in Argentina for being a public-spirited man, and among the many organizations with which he is connected is the Rotary Club of Buenos Aires, of which he is the past president, and he is also governor for the International Rotary for Brazil, Uruguay, Argentina and Paraguay. Although he is interested in all phases of culture, his specialty lies in the field of art. As director of the Museum of Fine Arts of Buenos Aires, he has a commission from his government to visit expositions, museums and art centers of the United States and to make contracts with as many artists and collectors as possible. He is arranging for the exchange of exhibitions between institutions in this country and Argentina. While here he hopes to obtain a clear understanding of the spirit of United States art and of the work of the institutions developing art. Upon returning to his own country, Dr. del Campo expects to be called upon to interpret to the Argentines the artistic and cultural side of the United States.

A CANADIAN TRAVELING SCHOOL

The New York *Sun* reports that in order to provide educational facilities for children living in the scantily populated districts around Lake Superior in Ontario, the Canadian government during the last few months has made the experiment of turning a railway passenger coach into a traveling school. The plan met from the outset the hearty cooperation of the authorities of the Canadian Railway, who agreed to look after transportation and provide a special passenger coach. This coach is divided into two parts, one with desks for the children and the other with sleeping and living quarters for the teacher.

School starts at 9 o'clock. The day is begun with prayer and then a record of the national anthem is played on the school phonograph. The pupils at all the little towns and way stations visited vary from six to seventeen years. A library of five hundred books is provided. The car visits seven communities a month, the stops varying from two to four days, according to the number of pupils in the community. The teacher gives out extra lessons for home work to be done between the calls of the railway schoolhouse.

The majority of the scholars attending the school are French Canadians, and during the first few months all orders and explanations had in large part to be given in the French language. In addition, explanations had to be made in Italian, Rumanian and other languages.

Around the teacher and the car the social life of the little communities centers. Concerts and other forms of entertainment in the evening are held in the car. Sometimes the evening is also devoted to night classes for parents of the young pupils, many of whom have learned to write English for the first time. Mr. Walter McNally has been placed in charge of this work, which has proved so successful that it is planned to extend the service to other parts of the Dominion.

THE GERMAN CHILD LABOR CENSUS

A decrease of nearly 25 per cent. in twenty years in the number of children under 14 employed on the land is shown by a recent census in Germany, an analysis of which has just been published by the International Labor Office, according to a summary in *The Christian Science Monitor*. The decrease is in contrast to an increase of roughly 1,400,000 in the numbers of persons of all ages engaged in agriculture in the country. The exact figures of the 1925 census were 390,412 children—202,098 boys and 188,313 girls—and 14,338,433 persons of all ages. The corresponding figures in 1907 were 512,328 (280,069 boys and 232,259 girls) and 12,893,148.

Examination of the figures shows that whereas there has been such a large aggregate decrease in agricultural child labor, there has been an actual increase of over 90 per cent. in the number of children in the permanent employment of their families. On the other hand, the number permanently in the employ of strangers is 66 per cent. lower. The largest decrease took place both in family and outside employment, on the medium-sized estates—the peasant holdings of 50 to 250 acres. Far more children are now being permanently employed than formerly but on the other hand there is not a single farm which does not report a decrease in temporary child labor.

An investigation carried out in Baden by the Association for Infant and Child Welfare showed that children employed by their own parents are as a rule set to work at an earlier age than those employed by strangers. Of 78 boys and 22 girls reported under the latter category, one was eight years and five were nine years old. The average, however, showed four children of six years, three of seven, three of eight and 19 of nine years. The work done is described as fairly exacting, requiring constant watchfulness to prevent cattle straying from unfenced pastures. The children themselves stated that the young cattle and the sheep and goats gave them the most trouble. The investigator noted that the brighter children avoided this class of employment and found something else to do. As a result, it is said, of this investigation new regulations were issued by the Baden Children's Bureau last January concerning the employment of children for cattle tending.

RULES GOVERNING APPOINTMENTS OF THE ST. LOUIS SCHOOL BOARD

THE school board of St. Louis, Mo., has adopted new rules governing the appointments and duties of the assistant superintendents-emeritus, the supervisors-emeritus, the principals-emeritus and the tutor-assistant. The rules are as follows:

1. It shall be the duty of assistant superintendents-emeritus, supervisors-emeritus and principals-emeritus, under the direction of the superintendent, to act as substitutes respectively for regular assistant superintendents, supervisors and principals and to perform such other duties as the superintendent of instruction may require.

2. It shall be the duty of tutor-assistants, under the direction of the superintendent, to act as substitutes for regular teachers, to give individual or small groups instruction, to assist the principal in making reports and the like, and to perform such other duties as the superintendent of instruction may require.

3. Assistant superintendents-emeritus, supervisors-emeritus, principals-emeritus and tutor-assistants shall be appointed by the board upon recommendation of the superintendent. No person shall be appointed to any of said positions who shall not have attained the age of 65 years.

4. Persons holding the said positions shall be subject to suspension or removal as provided by law.

5. The tenure of assistant superintendents-emeritus shall be as provided by law for assistant superintendents. The tenure of supervisors-emeritus, principals-emeritus and tutor-assistants shall be as provided by law for teachers.

6. Whenever any assistant superintendent, supervisor, principal or teacher shall attain the age of 70 years, he shall be transferred upon his own application, if an assistant superintendent to the rank of assistant superintendent-emeritus, if a principal to the rank of principal-emeritus, if a teacher to the rank of tutor-assistant, and if he shall not so apply he shall be subjected to an annual examination, physical and otherwise, to be conducted under the direction of the superintendent of instruction, to determine his fitness to continue his duties in the position he then occupies. The results of such examination shall be reported to the board.

PACKAGE LIBRARIES FROM THE UNIVERSITY OF WISCONSIN

A MESSENGER service of library material reaching communities in every county of Wisconsin delivered 7,791 packages to 2,112 addresses in 786 communities during the last 12 months.

Demands for loan package libraries, as they are called, were increased by about 1,300 during the year, according to the report of Almere L. Scott, who is in charge of this activity of the University of Wisconsin extension division.

Ten trained searchers, with access to the university library and files, and to reference lists of thousands of magazines, newspapers and documents, are constantly at work sorting and indexing information and preparing packages to answer requests coming in from every corner of the state.

Seventy-four per cent. of communities to which packages were sent have no public library, and the value of the service to persons and organizations in these places is emphasized. Users include men's, women's and children's clubs, parent-teacher associations, church organizations, more than 350 of the states' 429 high schools, 353 other schools, colleges and academies, other groups and many individual inquirers.

Hundreds of packages were used in preparing topics and debates, the report shows. Hundreds more were used for educational and cultural purposes. Thirty packages went to persons preparing public addresses, 27 to writers of articles for publication, 151 to persons requesting business information.

The package library service is free to all citizens of Wisconsin and gives inquirers, regardless of location, the assistance of library specialists in locating needed information.

A package library is made up of standard books and documents on a given subject, together with authoritative articles clipped from periodicals or copied from books or other sources. The average weight is about three pounds. Reference lists to guide the reader in further study of the subject are often included. The aim is not quantity but quality and definiteness of the information furnished, it is stated.

No loan package is ever considered complete and closed. After its return, the next inquiry may cause its contents to be increased, rearranged or taken apart for making up a new package.

Special fields in which large numbers of loan package libraries were requested, selected and lent this year were agriculture, industries, sociology, music, education, forestry, fur farming, women's work, women's clubs, interior decoration, food and diet, biography, history, literature, architecture, prohibition, recreation, drama, taxation and tariff. Subjects relating directly to Wisconsin and its interests were also numerous. In 93 special fields at least 25 packages each were lent.

SUMMER PLAY SCHOOLS

Friday of last week brought to a close the twelfth season of the Summer Play Schools under the direction of the Child Study Association of America. According to a report sent us by Miss Lucy Retting, the director, these play schools are different from the playgrounds and offer many opportunities in health and recreation and specialized programs not offered in the yearly program of the city child. Over 2,000 children have been benefited in this way.

In addition to the preliminary medical examination given the children before registration, nearly every child has had completed dental and other remedial work recommended at that time. One of the "high spots" of this season has been the services of a special health supervisor who has given her sole attention to assisting the schools to realize the best their situation offers toward mental and emotional, as well as social and physical, health.

The Play School Committee again conducted the Children's Canteen, from which over six hundred luncheons went out daily to those schools which had no kitchen facilities. The dietitian in charge also gave consultant service to many of the centers preparing their own food.

Farming and gardening were again emphasized, and two schools sent groups of children to country camps with their play school teachers for periods of two to four weeks. While the usual manual, art, music, dramatics, dancing, games and nature study subjects have had their share of the children's happy attention, homemaking in a fine and wide sense has been emphasized in several of the centers. In one instance the children made jams and jellies, and prepared and enjoyed small luncheon parties in the home of their local director. In another, four neighborhood homes were thrown open to groups of boys and girls who, with their teachers, decided upon the need of extra shelves, curtains and other manual and art products, made them in their school workshops, and had the joy of seeing them in use before play school closed. Two organizations rented near-by empty apartments, and used the cleaning and furnishing of them as school projects. In one of these the children grappled with real problems of worn-out plaster and rotten flooring, coming off victorious in every instance. After the rooms were in good sanitary condition furniture was made, or purchased in second-hand shops and renovated—books donated for the carefully contrived book cases, vases, lampshades and curtains made in the craft classes, and to crown their efforts, a charming if tiny rock garden was built just outside the kitchen door.

The parents of the play schools children were called together two or more times during the summer to discuss problems of child training with an experienced leader of child study work employed by the Summer Play Schools Committee. A meeting of delegates from these groups was so successful that requests were made by the delegates for at least two more in the fall, one of them to be held in the evening in order that fathers might also attend.

It is said that teaching methods were progressive, partly due to the program of teacher-training work of the Summer Play Schools Committee, which hopes to put more time, effort and money into this part of its spring program each season. This will serve not only to raise the teaching standards of existing summer play schools, but may provide a field from which new schools in or outside New York City may draw personnel understanding of child study aims and methods.

Both New York and Cleveland gave assistance to the Summer Play Schools as before, and there is every reason to believe that this assistance will be increased next year. The sympathy and co-operation of the Board of Education of New York City not only serves as a stimulus for like interest in other cities, but gives hope to the Summer Play Schools Committee that the time is not far distant when it will assume entire responsibility for giving to every child who does not get away for country care during the summer vacation the privileges of a summer play school.

THE WILLIAMSTOWN INSTITUTE OF POLITICS

THE staff correspondent of the New York *Herald Tribune,* Mr. Walter Miller, reports that plans are being considered to establish the Williamstown Institute of Politics upon a permanent endowment.

Dr. Harry A. Garfield, president of Williams College, stated in an interview that if this was done the purpose of the institute would remain unchanged, but he intimated that when such an endowment was created it might be appropriate to consider changes in method and procedure based upon the institute's past experience.

Dr. Garfield also announced that continued financial support had been provided for the present and that the institute would hold its next session here in August, 1929, upon substantially the same lines as heretofore.

Each session of the Institute of Politics costs $50,000. For the last five years the cost has been borne by Bernard M. Baruch, the General Education Board and the Carnegie Foundation under a five-year program, which expires with the present session.

Dr. Garfield is reported to have said:

The institute was organized as a fact-finding agency and a place of exchange of ideas to aid in arousing public opinion to an understanding of the points of view of other nationals. The conference idea of threshing out international problems has been proved of value. This method has been recognized in the organization of many other institutes in widely separated sections of the country and abroad.

The suggestion has been made that institutes of this kind might profitably coordinate their efforts; that in bringing speakers of international reputation from abroad arrangements might be made to hear them at centers other than Williamstown. This suggestion would be welcomed by the Institute of Politics should it prove feasible.

Here at Williamstown we are serving a progressively growing constituency each year. This is shown by an increasing demand for the reports of the proceeding. It is significant that this demand comes not only from educators, lecturers, business organizations and students of international affairs but from many other groups in all parts of the country. Due in part at least to the agency of these institutions our citizenship is outgrowing its old insularity and isolation.

Altogether some sixty different institutions or similar organizations have sprung up throughout the country in imitation of the pioneer effort here at Williamstown.

Dr. Garfield implied that some suggestions for modification in present methods have been advanced, and if the institute should be given a permanent endowment they would have to be considered. It has been suggested that the small round-table conferences should be kept closed and the general conferences, at which all members of the institute take part, alone be thrown open to the public.

Another question which has arisen is the relative value of the general discussions, which tend rather to bring out the trends of opinion among the membership than to add any facts of general interest, and the more formal addresses by recognized authorities which may bring out definite contributions to the questions being discussed but which lack the flexibility of the open debate.

THE UNIVERSITY OF CALIFORNIA AT LOS ANGELES

BY the decision of the regents of the University of California, the Teachers' College, as well as the College of Letters and Science, is to be moved to the new Westwood site of the University of California at Los Angeles. The move is to be made during the summer vacation of 1929.

The University of California at Los Angeles had its beginning in the State Teachers' College at Los Angeles, which was founded in 1881 as the Branch State Normal School of California, a branch of the Normal School at San Jose. Five years later its catalogue was entitled State Normal School at Los Angeles. In 1919 the legislature transferred the property of the institution to the regents of the University of California, Southern Branch. Only freshman and sophomore courses were given at first, but in 1923 a third year was added and in 1924 the fourth year was provided; and two colleges, Letters and Science, and the Teachers' College, each with a four-year course and leading to a baccalaureate degree, were operated.

In 1924 the institution had grown so large that President Campbell recommended that the regents seek a larger site. He also recommended that when this site was secured only the College of Letters and Science be moved to it, and this latter recommendation was unanimously adopted by the regents. The new site at Westwood, of approximately 385 acres, was donated to the university by the municipalities of the County of Los Angeles and the county itself. In 1926 a bond issue was voted by the people providing $3,000,000 for buildings on the new site. These buildings are in the course of construction.

At the February meeting of the regents this year, in Los Angeles, a citizens' committee appeared, asking that the Teachers' College be moved to the new site. President Campbell and Regent William John Cooper, state superintendent of public instruction, were instructed to report on the proposition. These reports were presented at the June meeting, but action was deferred until August, owing to the fact that several regents were not in attendance.

The University of California at Los Angeles, given that name a year and a half ago, has about 6,000 students, about half in each college.

EDUCATIONAL NOTES AND NEWS

Dr. Edmund D. Soper, vice-president of Duke University, has been elected president of Ohio Wesleyan University, succeeding Dr. John W. Hoffman, who recently retired because of ill health.

The Reverend Coleman Nevils, S.J., has been appointed president of Georgetown University, to succeed the Reverend Charles W. Lyons, who has served in that capacity for the last four years.

Dr. Montgomery Porter Sellers, professor of rhetoric and the English language, has been appointed dean of Dickinson College. He succeeds Dr. Marvin Grant Filler, who is now president.

Dr. William Dick Cutter, for the past five years dean of the New York Post-Graduate Medical School, has been appointed acting dean of the new school of medicine at the University of Southern California.

W. G. Taggart, assistant director, has been appointed acting director of the agricultural experiment stations and acting dean of the college of agriculture of Louisiana University. He succeeds Dr. R. W. Dodson, who resigned in June. Dr. W. R. Perkins, director of the extension service, and Dr. E. L. Jordan, professor of animal industry, resigned at the same time as Dr. Dodson.

Miss Florence M. Nicholson, dean of women at Coe College, Cedar Rapids, Iowa, has been appointed associate dean of women and member of the personnel staff of Syracuse University.

Morrill Bishop Buckner, who was formerly associate pastor of the First Methodist Church, Portland, Oregon, has resigned his position to become dean of men at Gooding College at Wesleyan, Idaho. His wife will serve as matron of the men's dormitory.

Dr. Clemens Pirquet, specialist in the diseases of children, was on August 29 nominated for the presidency of Austria, to succeed President Michael Hainisch, whose term expires at the end of November. Dr. Richard Wettstein, professor of systematic botany in the University of Vienna, was the only other candidate.

Dr. Bayard Dodge, president of the American College at Beirut, has returned to Syria, after spending a year in the United States. Dr. Dodge will arrive in Beirut in time for the opening of the academic year at the university. It is the largest of the six American colleges in that section of the world, for which a $15,000,000 endowment fund is being raised, according to a plan outlined by the late Cleveland H. Dodge.

DR. J. G. NEEDHAM, head of the department of entomology at Cornell University, has returned after spending a year in China, under the auspices of the China Foundation to Promote Culture and Education. Dr. Needham was the third guest of the foundation, the first guest being Professor John Dewey and the second Professor Paul Monroe.

DR. WALTER S. ATHEARN, dean of the school of religious education of Boston University and chairman of the division of character, moral and religious education of the World Federation of Educational Associations, will go to Europe next month, visiting the missionary schools in Egypt and the Near East.

DR. J. M. D. OLMSTED, professor of physiology and chairman of the department at the University of California, has returned to Berkeley, after having spent the summer in Belgium and England. He spent six weeks at the Physiological Institute of Liége, Belgium, where he delivered two lectures on the history of insulin.

DR. and MRS. HORACE EATON were guests of honor at a dinner given recently by the English department celebrating the completion of Dr. Eaton's twenty-fifth year of service to Syracuse University. The dinner was planned as a recognition of the outstanding contributions made by both Dr. and Mrs. Eaton to the city community as well as to the university.

DR. T. WINGATE TODD, professor of anatomy in Western Reserve University, has been appointed a member of the board of managers of the Brush Foundation, recently established in the interests of race betterment by a gift of $500,000 from Charles F. Brush as a memorial to his son.

DR. F. T. MCLEAN, plant physiologist at the Rhode Island Agricultural Experiment Station at Kingston, has resigned to become director of public education of the New York Botanical Garden.

AT the University of Chicago, Drs. Warder C. Allee and Carl R. Moore, zoology; Edwin A. Burtt, philosophy; W. J. G. Land, botany; Harvey B. Lemon, physics, and Frank E. Ross, astronomy, have been promoted to full professorships.

IN the department of zoology of the University of Pittsburgh, the following changes in rank are in effect for the coming year: Robert T. Hance, from acting head to head of the department; P. W. Whiting, from assistant to associate professor; E. Alfred Wolf, from instructor to assistant professor; A. W. Kozelka, from instructor to assistant professor at the Erie Center; E. P. Jones, from graduate assistant to instructor at the Uniontown Center.

DR. ROBERT FEIS, head of the department of economics at the University of Cincinnati, has resigned in order to devote his time exclusively to writing and research.

DR. DAISY ALFORD HETHERINGTON, assistant professor of educational psychology at New York University and director of the University of California Play School during the recent summer session, will remain in California during the winter. She will offer lectures on various aspects of education, under the auspices of the University Extension Division.

PROFESSOR MARTIN H. FISCHER, head of the department of physiology at the University of Cincinnati College of Medicine, spoke recently at the annual meeting of Phi Beta Kappa on "Scholarship and Main Street."

DR. M. L. LOWERY has withdrawn his resignation as superintendent of schools in Middlesex County, New Jersey. He was tendered the post of head of the English department of Girard College, Philadelphia, but has decided to remain in Middlesex County.

LEWIS C. TIDBALL, Wyoming commissioner of education, attended the summer session of the University of Washington, taking advanced work for a doctor's degree.

THE John Newbery medal, given annually for the most distinguished children's book of the past year, has been awarded to Dhan Gopal Mukerji for "Gay-Neck." The presentation was made by Annabel Porter, chairman of the children librarians section of the American Library Association, at the fiftieth annual conference of the association held recently in West Baden, Indiana. John Newbery, in whose honor the medal is named, was an eighteenth century publisher and bookseller and one of the first publishers to devote attention to children's books. The medal is the gift of Frederic G. Melcher, of New York City.

George Martin Duncan, who for twenty years, until his retirement in 1923, held the chair of logic and metaphysics in Yale University and who had previously for fifteen years been a member of the staff, died on July 26 at the age of sixty-five years.

The first unit in the two and a half million building program at the University of Tennessee is now in process of erection. The building is for physics and geology and with its furnishings will cost about $200,000. Plans for a chemistry building are under way and other buildings projected include a program calling for about $500,000 annually for the next five years.

The college of letters and science of the University of Wisconsin enrolled during the academic year 1927–28 7,306 students, including graduate students. There were 4,229 men and 3,077 women, not including those registered in summer sessions. Contributing to the total were fellows, 43; scholars, 36; graduates, 773; seniors, 1,345; juniors, 1,349; sophomores, 1,630; freshmen, 2,114; adult specials, 16. Included are students in the course in applied arts, 202; course in chemistry, 127; chemistry commerce course, 59; B.A. general course, 4,111; Ph.B. general course, 541; course in humanities, 53; course in industrial education, 28; course for normal-school graduates, 60; course in pharmacy, 63; three-year course, 54; course in physical education, 271; pre-medic course, 422; experimental college, 119; course in commerce, 201; school of journalism, 128; school of nursing, 37; three-year nursing course, 68.

It is reported in the daily press that a grandmother, three of her daughters and three granddaughters were enrolled at the summer session of the Kansas State Teachers' College. The grandmother, Mrs. E. E. Shipley, who is principal of the Lincoln School at Miami, Okla., received her degree this summer. The three daughters who are attending school are all teachers. Mrs. R. B. Walker teaches in Treece, Kans.; Mrs. Wayne Loafman teaches near her mother's building in Miami, and Miss Elizabeth Shipley is a primary teacher in Picher, Okla. Catherine Walker, Regina Walker and Sue Wayne Loafman are the granddaughters. Catherine and Regina attend the college high school and Sue Wayne is in the grade training school.

The Michigan College of Mining and Technology is offering for the academic year of 1928–1929 twelve graduate fellowships carrying stipends of $1,200 each. Holders of these fellowships will be engaged in the study of various problems in connection with the general research program at the college for which the State of Michigan has provided the sum of $50,000 for the coming year. This program deals with the iron and copper resources of northern Michigan and with their utilization. Appropriate parts of this research program are conducted in cooperation with mining companies, the United States Bureau of Mines, the United States Coast and Geodetic Survey and the Carnegie Institution Department of Terrestrial Magnetism.

The Experiment Station Record calls attention to the work of the Coyocutena Agricultural College of Honduras, which was established in 1926 near La Libertad in the Department of Comayagua, Honduras. A tract of about 6,000 acres 2,000 feet above sea level, owned by Pompilio Ortega, founder of the school, has been made available for the institution. Two main buildings have been erected by the students themselves, one an administration building of adobe brick housing the office, library and living quarters of the staff, and the second a students' dormitory of logs. A science building and a manual training building are projected. At the present time 16 students are enrolled, ranging in age from 12 to 20 years, and the curriculum has been restricted to Spanish, English, arithmetic, geography and history of Honduras, free-hand drawing and elementary agriculture. An abandoned coffee plantation near by has been acquired, and about 20,000 young coffee trees have been planted by the students. A beginning has been made in purebred livestock, a rain gage has been installed, and data on rainfall have been collected.

THE abstracts of dissertations approved for the Ph.D., M.Sc., and M.Litt. degrees in Cambridge University for the year 1926–27 show the use that is made of these degrees to encourage research among the graduates of Cambridge and other universities. Only 14 out of 55 degrees were awarded in the literary faculties and only 2 of these went to Cambridge graduates. Of the 41 science degrees, 15 were awarded to students trained wholly at Cambridge. The following are the figures for the different departments: Physics 10, mathematics 6, biochemistry 5, physiology 4, botany 4, history 4, while fine arts, music, law, moral science, geography, architecture and anthropology are all unrepresented in the list. The difference is reflected also in the colleges: Trinity with 10, Emmanuel and Caius with 9 each, and St. John's with 7, head the list, while Magdalene, Pembroke, Peterhouse, Queens', St. Catherine's, Selwyn and Trinity Hall are absent. Of the graduates educated elsewhere who came to Cambridge only for post-graduate work, 13 came from other universities in England, 5 each from Canada and Scotland, 4 from India, 3 each from the United States and Wales, 2 each from Australia and Ireland and 1 from New Zealand.

COMMERCIAL and agricultural enterprises operating in Mexico have established 1,704 schools for their employees and their children, according to an announcement of the Department of Public Education. The statement says that these schools were established in compliance with specifications of the Constitution of Mexico. A total of 70,901 persons are receiving instruction in these schools, and they employ 2,010 teachers.

FOR the year 1928–29, Glasgow rate-payers will be called upon to meet a charge of £1,477,-278 for education, this being an increase of £71,483 as compared with the previous year. The estimates, which were approved at a recent meeting of the education authorities of Glasgow, forecasted a total expenditure of £2,797,047, total income being shown as £1,319,769, leaving the deficiency to be met out of the rates.

A REUTER despatch to the London *Times* stated that Signor Mussolini, the prime minister, and Signor Belluzzo, the minister of education for Italy, have issued a number of orders with regard to all branches of education. Italian elementary schools will be given new textbooks calculated to rear children in a healthful spirit of Fascism. Universities and high schools are to be investigated with regard to the needs of their respective districts. New laboratories are to be established for the universities. Archeological discoveries will also come under fresh regulations. In general the aim of the government is to "complete" the Fascistization of all the schools, and not only their curricula but also the teaching staffs. Signor Mussolini has arranged that the Villa Falconieri Frascati shall be made the headquarters of the International Institute of Educational Cinematography.

THE Hungarian minister of public instruction, Count Kuno Kleberlsberg, according to a German press report, has recently issued a decree by which "film teaching" is declared obligatory for more than 200 schools. The films are to be shown in the schools themselves, and the exhibitors are bound to put their cinemas at the disposal of such schools as have no adequate show rooms. Conferences will be held in the provinces by the Hungarian-Dutch Cultural and Economic Company. In Budapest, obligatory film shows have been organized for public and secondary schools, for the past fifteen years. These will be intensified in the coming season. The Pedagogical Film Factory in Budapest is responsible for these conferences. The German reporter deplores that similar measures have not been taken in Germany. While Hungary has officially recognized that the film is the most important educational factor of to-day, in Germany only occasional conference speeches are made in this connection, and a small number of pioneer school people with insufficient subventions are endeavoring to introduce film tuition in their establishments. In Hungary, the film is introduced in schools as an obligatory and regular tuition means, while in Germany the school film movement is nothing but a feature film competition for cinemas.

WORK is to be started immediately on the new Metropolitan Library of Peiping, China, financed by Boxer indemnity money remitted by the United States. It is the aim of the directors of the library not to duplicate the special collections of other institutions established at Peiping. It subscribes for 360 American and British periodicals, most of which are not otherwise obtainable in Peiping, and it also receives and binds many Russian, Japanese, and other technical journals. Its collection of Bibles in many languages, books on Occidental and Oriental music, and rare old Chinese manuscripts is noteworthy. T. L. Yuan, the head librarian and acting director, is a former student of Harvard and Oxford Universities.

THE Moscow Theater for Children is now celebrating the completion of ten years' activity in organizing theatrical performances for the children of school and pre-school age. It is said that the theater has now gathered sufficient experience towards working out a regular repertoire of plays that will be of interest to the children. Their attitude and attention at the different performances is carefully observed and studied, and in this manner material is gathered for the purpose of working out a program of theatrical performances that will be appreciated by the children. The experience of the Moscow Theater for Children has been useful to similar theaters organized in Kharkov, Kiev, Tiflis, Krasnodar, Omsk and elsewhere.

Two new pavilions destined for the use of students of Argentina have been erected at the Cité Universitaire in Paris. There will be accommodation for 200 students. The French, Belgian and Canadian dormitories are already occupied; that of Japan will be opened next year, and the pavilion of the United States in two years. In 1931, England, Spain, the Netherlands and Sweden will also have their buildings completed. Plans are also being made for the erection of dormitories for Armenian and for Indo-Chinese students.

A SPECIAL correspondent of *The Christian Science Monitor* states that a Bombay philanthropist, Sir Cowasji Jehangir, has donated a sum of 1,500,000 rupees for the founding of a public school for Parsi boys, the first of its kind in India. The donor has appointed a committee for carrying out the scheme. This body has been intrusted with the task of settling all details, unfettered by any conditions from the donor, including the decision as to the location of the school. If the amount offered does not cover the whole cost of founding the proposed school, the committee will appeal for funds from the Parsi public.

A BY-PRODUCT of the resentment felt by the inhabitants of the Austrian Tyrol at the iron rule of the Fascist government over their Teutonic brothers in the Alto Adige is likely to be the selection of English as the obligatory foreign language in the higher schools of that province. A Vienna dispatch to the *Frankfurter Zeitung* tells of a public meeting in Innsbruck, attended by nearly everyone of importance in educational and governmental circles, at which a resolution was passed by a big majority asking the provincial school authorities to make English the second language instead of Italian. It was contended that English was more useful in view of the increasing numbers of British and Americans visiting the Tyrol and that the tourists from Italy were but few.

SPECIAL CORRESPONDENCE

WHAT MATERIALS BUILD CHARACTER

AMONG the applications of educational measurements not the least significant is that of testing methods of religious education. A considerable mass of literature has already sprung up and a significant number of careful studies have already been made in the field of religion.

One problem which has come to public attention in recent years is that of the material to be used in the week-day schools of religion. This movement sprang up so rapidly and has won such popular favor that its place in the general program of religious education is now assured. Because of its very newness and freedom from slavery to past tradition the week-day school of religion offers a unique challenge to the modern educator.

Apparently the public feels the need of some religious training beyond that which is given through denominational agencies, and of moral training beyond that which results from the public school program. Indeed the public probably does not distinguish between these two objectives. Character is the thing desired. If the churches secure it, well and good; if the schools can cultivate it, that too is good. If either fails, the problem is increased; if both fail the situation is critical. Society wishes the rising generation to be educated for ethical conduct. A considerable part of society is not convinced that this object can be obtained without the motivation of religion, and so the week-day school of religion is meeting approval and rapidly growing.

The practical question has already become apparent to both religious and educational leaders, "What shall be taught in these week-day schools of religion, and how shall it be taught? Shall the movement become a means of intensifying sectarian differences and cultivating a consciousness of the division of religion, or shall the churches unite in a common program furnishing the children of the schools with such common essentials of morality and religion as all can accept as indispensable, leaving sectarian emphasis for the Sunday schools?"

The curriculum introduced in the week-day schools generally has been made up chiefly of biblical material. This very fact has constituted a problem, partially overcome only because there is so strong a sentiment against sectarianism. The cause for disagreement still exists so long as the basic material is taken from the Bible; for sectarian differences arise primarily from variant interpretations of the Bible. But what alternatives are there? Do we not face a hopeless dilemma?

Dare we consider the alternative of omitting the biblical material from a school of religion? The answer depends upon the motive. If the motive is that of modernist propaganda, such a policy will fail; for the week-day school of religion can not succeed if it becomes an agency for propaganda of any kind. If, on the other hand, the motive is to find religious material upon which all religious agencies can agree, it is entirely possible that this effort may succeed.

Three other types of material suggest themselves because they are already being used in some degree by nearly every agency of religious education. Worship is a feature of all religion. Religious schools are training children in worship, and providing for higher art on the part of our leaders of worship. Worship is coming to be looked upon not as a source of instruction but as an agency for cultivating attitudes and ideals. In the interests of consistency didactic elements are more and more being excluded from the worship service. Hymns are being selected for their musical qualities rather than for their mere vivacity. Responsive readings and other forms of antiphonal services are being introduced for their beauty and reverential effect, not for teaching content. Here is a possibility of religious training involving no basic disagreement in theory of church organization, in doctrine, or in interpretation of the Bible.

A second feature that has increased in favor among all religious agencies in recent years is the practical project in Christian service. The slogan "learn by doing" has been accepted as applying to religious life. Children who are organized into groups and stimulated to serve, to give, to cooperate in some altruistic effort become more religious in that very process. Here is a second possibility of religious education involving no sectarian disagreement.

A third type of material is that of direct ethical instruction. In recent years the suggestion has often been repeated that character is caught not taught. Many modern teachers protest against any form of direct ethical instruction; yet the last decade has seen the creation of a large number of codes of morals with a resultant increase rather than decrease in the vital outcomes for which they stand. And one or two careful researches seem to show that practical conduct is improved by direct ethical instruction. So that here is a third possibility of material on which there can be no denominational quarrel.

Now if these three types of material could be utilized by the united agencies of religion in the week-day schools, leaving the biblical material for the Sunday schools, a most significant increase in efficiency in the total program of education could be brought about.

The present purpose is not to discuss the partisan viewpoints or to refute the arguments against such a program, but only to answer, and that but partially, the one question, "Would such a program, from which biblical teaching was omitted, produce the desired effects upon character in a degree at all comparable to the effects produced by biblical teaching?" Manifestly, the gains in such a cooperative program, free from sources of disagreement or friction, would be very great. If the losses were not correspondingly great, the plan would commend itself to all thoughtful educators.

The attempt to measure with some care, even though on a small scale, the relative effectiveness upon character of these three types of teaching as compared with biblical teaching was recently made by the author.[1] In six groups of sixth-grade children, totaling one hundred fifty, the four types of material which have been mentioned were presented in different carefully-controlled combinations. Three forms of tests were used to determine the effect upon character. One test sought to measure religious ideas, a second social attitudes, and a third indicated actual performance in the form of honesty or cheating in scoring papers in a contest.

The results of the study were most convincing in showing that of the four elements studied, direct ethical training had far the greatest effect upon immediate honesty. In the group in which all four elements were included, seven out of nineteen pupils cheated in the opening test. Of these seven, five did not cheat at the end of four months' training. In the group which was trained by the use of the code of ethics, Christian service and Bible teaching, twelve out of twenty-two cheated in the preliminary test, eight of whom refrained from cheating at the end of the term. In the group in which ethical training, worship and Bible teaching were included, ten of the twenty-four cheated at the beginning, four of whom did not cheat at the end. But in the first group from which ethical training was omitted only one reformed, while eight who had not cheated at the start cheated at the end. In the other group from which ethical training was omitted, there were no cases of reform, but a slight increase in cheating.

The conclusions which seem inevitable, insofar as this small group is typical, quite reverse the commonly accepted idea that ethics must be taught indirectly rather than directly.

[1] Reference is made to a study of selected types of material for a curriculum of religious education in connection with the week-day school of religion of Eugene, Oregon.

Just what value religious knowledge and ideas have in actual conduct is problematical, as is also the value of social attitudes, which may indicate not what the subject would do, but what he thinks the examiner thinks he ought to do. The improvement in regard to ideas and attitudes in the study of this small group did not correlate at all closely. While there were some consistent gains in attitude, they were too small to be dependable without wider confirmation. Religious ideas tended toward mature judgments more rapidly on the part of those who did not study the Bible than on the part of those who did; but there was no consistent gain under any one of the other elements.

No evidence that can be gathered from the study here reported shows any advantage in character growth among those who were trained in Bible study as compared with those who were trained in worship, Christian service and direct ethical instruction.

While of course the chief conclusion to be drawn from this study is that a more extensive study is necessary before recommendations can be given with confidence, at least there is a strong suggestion that the way may be open to harmonious and effective cooperation by all religious agencies in the week-day and vacation schools of religion without the use of biblical material, which is the source of greatest friction and disagreement, and at the same time without loss of effectiveness in the cultivation of Christian character.

Harold S. Tuttle

University of Oregon

DISCUSSION

THE LARGE COLLEGE VS. THE SMALL

The question of the relative value of the large university or college as contrasted with the small in producing leadership has long been the matter of heated argument, while the factual evidence on the subject is even less than that on the heredity-environment question. The advantages of the small college are continually emphasized. Indeed, one is impressed with the fact that the small college expends a good deal of energy in the effort to become something else. Mr. Newton D. Baker in his address at the ceremony of inauguration of Ernest J. Jaqua as president of Scripps College said:

> . . . the best we could do was expand our educational facilities until they became Montgomery Wards, or Sears Roebucks—mammoth educational institutions, standardized in part, with microphones in the classrooms in order to reach outlying students.
>
> What was lost? The intimacy of personal contact between instructor and student. What have we gotten? We have gotten, in a great many instances, instead of education a mass of unassimilated and unorganized information. This is not a substitute for education.
>
> Here . . . you are limiting the number of students. You are going to bring them into direct and immediate personal contact with the personalities of their teachers. You are going to educate and cultivate them so that they will have minds, ornamented it is true with knowledge, but with ordered knowledge, and so that they will have spirits restrained and disciplined by contact with experienced people.[1]

The implication made here, and strongly emphasized in the advertising matter of most of the smaller colleges, is that in the large universities something of great value is lost: the "warm, nourishing life of cultured, inspired, competent personalities" is lacking.

If an educational institution, large or small, aids in developing its students into leaders in their work, then the degree of success of the institution may be measured by the number of its recognized outstanding graduates. "Leadership" can be usefully thought of only as leadership in something—not leadership in general. In the field of science, for example, the men who have made the contributions to their respective fields are widely recognized. In "American Men of Science," a biographical dictionary edited by J. McKeen Cattell, practically all the living American scientists are listed. Approximately 1,400 of these names have a star affixed, indicating that they have been selected by their fellow-scientists as the most outstanding men in their particular field. These men, without question, represent a very competently selected group of "successful" men—leaders—in the fields of science.

If the men who graduate from the small schools received some added inspiration from the personal contact which is supposedly there afforded, then a larger proportion of them should be fired with a greater desire for knowledge than is the case with the graduates of the larger institutions. In the case of scientists this is an approachable problem, as the starred men in "American Men of Science" serve as an excellent and unparalleled criterion of leadership.[2] Let us consider the size of the colleges from which these men graduated.

The median year in which these scientists received their first degree, in most cases their bachelor's degree, was found to be 1893–94. In the "Report of the Commissioner of Education" for this year (Vol. II, pp. 2017ff) the size of all colleges in the United States for the year is given. For the purposes of this study each college was assigned the size it had during this year.[3]

If there is any relation between success in the field of science and the size of the college from which one graduated, it should be brought out best by a consideration of the extremes, the very large colleges and universities, and the very small ones. A distribution of the sizes of all colleges and universities as listed in the commissioner's report for the year 1893–94 was made. The colleges were then divided into four groups of equal number on the basis of size: the quartile points were computed. A large university was defined as one which fell in the upper one fourth of size of all colleges for this median year, while a small college was defined as one which fell in the lower or first one fourth. The medium-sized college was the one which fell between these two groups, *i.e.,* in the middle half.

The scientists who graduated from foreign institutions or who received no degrees were not considered. This leaves a group of 1,240 scientists who received their first degree in this country. Of these 35 were graduates of the small schools, 208 of the medium-sized schools, and 997 of the large schools. The 35 graduates of

[1] SCHOOL AND SOCIETY, XXVI, No. 673 (November 19, 1927) p. 644.

[2] We are indebted to Edmund O. Seagrave for transferring onto cards the names of the starred men, and for the grouping of these cards according to the schools from which the men graduated.

[3] In the few cases where the colleges were not listed for this year, the size given for the nearest year was used.

the small schools represent $0.39 \pm .04$ per cent. of all graduates from these colleges during this year.[4] The 208 graduates of the medium-sized schools represent 0.44 ($\pm .02$) per cent. of all the graduates of these schools, while the 997 graduates of the large schools represent 1.16 ($\pm .02$) per cent. of the graduates of the large institutions.

The difference between the percentage graduating from the larger institutions, and that graduating from the smaller ones is (1.16–0.39) 0.77 per cent., while the probable error of this difference is 0.04 per cent. This difference is over 19 times its probable error, which indicates a statistically significant difference.

The conclusion is that the large universities and colleges (as here defined) have a greater tendency to graduate men who later become leaders in science (*i.e.*, have their names starred in "American Men of Science") than do the small colleges.

This same method of attack was also carried out using appearance in "Who's Who in America" (edited by Albert N. Marquis) as the criterion of leadership. While the individuals appearing in "Who's Who" are probably not nearly as competently chosen as the starred scientists in "American Men of Science," appearance in "Who's Who" very likely more nearly represents what the lay person means by "leadership." Inasmuch as there are 26,915 names in "Who's Who," only a sampling was used.[5] This was obtained by taking the first name on every other page, provided such person had a university degree. Otherwise the next name was used. When the graduates of foreign universities were eliminated a sampling of 1,021 names was left. Of these 720 or 0.84 ($\pm .03$) per cent. of all graduates of large colleges for the median year, graduated from the large college group; 260 ($0.55 \pm .03$ per cent.) graduated from the medium-sized college group; and 41 ($0.46 \pm .07$ per cent.) graduated from the small college group. The difference of the percentages graduating from the large and the small colleges is nearly five times the probable error of the difference. While this is not as pronounced a difference as was found in the study of the scientists, it indicates a real difference. It is interesting to note that of the group who graduated from the small colleges 19.5 per cent. are classified as clergymen, contrasted with the 7.4 per cent. of the large college group who are thus classified. Perhaps the small colleges, while not stimulating men to scientific leadership, do stimulate them to moral and spiritual leadership of the sort typified by the clergy.

This study seems to indicate that the large colleges and universities have an advantage over the small ones in that a larger proportion of their graduates are leaders, when leadership is measured by appearance as a starred scientist in "American Men of Science," or by appearance in "Who's Who in America."

John M. Stalnaker
H. H. Remmers

Purdue University

[4] A frequency distribution of the size of the colleges for the year 1893–94 was made. A class interval of 100 was used: 0–99, 100–199, etc. To compute the number of graduates the frequency of each interval was multiplied by the mid-point of the interval. In the case of the first interval, 0–99, a mid-point of 50 was used, although this number is actually too small as practically every school had at least 50. Had a mid-point of 75 or 80 or some more justifiable number been used, the number of graduates from the lower quartile schools would have been increased, making the percentage of starred scientists who graduated from these schools even less than the 0.39 which is here used.

[5] We are indebted to Miss G. Washburn for transferring onto cards the names from "Who's Who."

QUOTATIONS

THE PRESIDENT OF THE NATIONAL EDUCATION ASSOCIATION

"Be ye doers of the word and not hearers only." That is the spirit which has brought Mr. Lamkin up the ladder from a pioneer Missouri home to the presidency of the National Education Association. He has done well whatever his hand found to do. Persons who visit the fine institution over which he presides speak often of the discriminating sense of values that has been built up among the students and of the abiding loyalty and integrity of both students and faculty. Tens of thousands of Missouri children are better taught because of the work Mr. Lamkin is doing in their midst. His life is firmer in its values for having come out of the soil of democracy. Members of the association may well be proud that their new president is descended from a line of forefathers who have taught school in America since the days of Washington and Franklin.

The all-inclusive character of the association is suggested by its choice of presidents. Many points of view and diverse gifts have come to this influential office. Calling the roll of recent officers in reverse order, one has a classroom teacher, a state superintendent, an elementary school principal and a city superintendent; one has representatives of Virginia, Illinois, Massachusetts and Colorado, and one understands why America has achieved a degree of unity found over no other similar area on the face of the globe. It has been inspired in the schools.

Uel W. Lamkin was born in Missouri. His father, E. P. Lamkin, was for many years associated with the Clinton, Missouri, Academy. Mr. Lamkin's schooling was obtained in this academy and in the University of Missouri. His professional experience began with the principalship of the Washington School at Clinton. Since then he has been high-school teacher and principal, state high-school inspector, county superintendent of schools, state superintendent of schools, chief of civilian rehabilitation service and director of the Federal Board for Vocational Education. Since 1921 he has been president of the Northwest Missouri State Teachers College at Maryville.

All his life Mr. Lamkin has been a builder. His gift for constructive work as revealed at Maryville is a prophecy of what his leadership in the National Education Association will mean. Under his guiding hand the Maryville State Teachers College has developed in both spirit and plant. On the campus have been erected two new buildings, one for physical education and one a girls' residence that is considered a model of its kind. Here is a school where dormitory life sets a standard of what the best home life should be. This college has won a class A ranking by the American Association of Teachers Colleges and has been recognized a member by the North Central Association of Colleges and Secondary Schools for its work in liberal arts leading to the A.B. degree. Here is a faculty which believes that every teacher must be a good scholar as well as a master of teaching technique.

President Lamkin has been a worker in professional organizations for many years. While superintendent of schools in Henry County, Missouri, he was elected president of the State Teachers Association. For the past three years he has been a member of the executive committee of the Missouri Association. He also served as a member of the building committee which directed the erection of a $50,000 headquarters' building for the State Association, in Columbia.

Mr. Lamkin has been active for many years in the National Education Association and has contributed much to its growth and the development of its policy. For two years he served as chairman of the committee on resolutions and in 1926–27 he was a member of the association's executive committee. He helped in the development of the headquarters retirement system, which is considered a model for teacher retirement systems throughout the country.

Mr. Lamkin is the fourth representative of Missouri to be elected to the presidency of the association. The others were William T. Harris, 1875; F. Louis Soldan, 1885, and J. M. Greenwood, 1898.

It is a tribute to Mr. Lamkin and a promise of growth for the association that he was elected without opposition. That a large number of delegates came to the polls to cast their ballot when there was no contest and no special campaign was a compliment both to the delegates and to the new president.

At the close of the final session of the Representative Assembly, the new president was escorted to the platform by Past-President Francis G. Blair. President Adair thanked the delegates for their cooperation throughout the year and bespoke the same loyalty for the new president, whom she then introduced. Said President Lamkin: "I have no hope of carrying out the work of this association as efficiently as has been done by the daughter of Virginia, who through her courtesy and ease of manner and good judgment and her kindly feeling has brought about this spirit of good-will in this association. I come to the office with some appreciation of the difficulties that confront me and with the hope and belief that I shall have the hearty cooperation of every member of this association in seeing that it continues to lead in bringing about such conditions in America as will provide better teaching for children in this country that they may have life more abundantly and better serve this great Republic in which we live and which we all love."

In a conference with newspaper men following his election, President Lamkin emphasized the welfare of the pupil in the classroom and suggested that the keynote of his work for the year would be the slogan of the association, "A fair start in life for every child."—*From advance proof of the Journal of the National Education Association.*

AMERICAN SCHOOLS IN EGYPT

AMERICAN schools in Egypt receive high praise from Pierre Crabitès in the *Nineteenth Century.* The article is intended to support a project of the British High Commissioner to Egypt for a fund to maintain English schools in the Valley of the Nile. Italian, Greek and especially French and American schools are having an influence there which, as it seems to Mr. Crabitès, places the English cause at a disadvantage. It is not that these are anti-British, or anti-Egyptian, but that their "kindness, their sense of fair play, their moral ascendency so impress themselves upon their student body that these children instinctively come to love the land of those who personify to them all that is noblest in life."

The influence of the American schools is described as all-pervading. They dot the land from one end to the other with an average daily enrolment of some 20,000 pupils. Their curriculum begins with the primary department and ends with the college. The student body is Egyptian, including "Muslims, Jews, Copts, Syrians, Armenians and Greeks." There are foreigners from neighboring Levantine lands. "They," says Mr. Crabitès of the pupils, "are not Americans. But they all learn to love the United States. Children are remarkably astute. They recognize virtue. They detect sham. They know that no sordid, no ulterior, no hidden motive has inspired those who are looking after their education. It has thus come to pass that, while their unformed vocal cords are being attuned to a nasal twang, their receptive minds become impressed with an abiding confidence in the idealism of America."

French schools in Egypt, the writer says, have served since the times of Louis XIV to spread French culture in that land. They have served to make of it a "cultural dominion of France." The teachings of the Jesuits and Christian Brothers, of nuns of the Sacred Heart and Mère de Dieu, have given to literate Egypt "a mental horizon which is largely French." But while Catholic French schools have been busy trying to implant French culture on Egyptian soil, as Mr. Crabitès sees it, the American Protestant schools have sought the sole objective of making useful Egyptians of their students. Both are reported as having been singularly successful in their undertakings.

American schools are supported by the United Presbyterian Church of the United States. Because of them and their cultural activities and the French schools, which seek the peaceful penetration of Egypt by French culture, Mr. Crabitès thinks England has been sadly negligent of its own educational responsibilities toward Egypt. France, he says, has created in the Levant, and particularly in Egypt, "an intellectual, a spiritual, a cultural dominion" that tends to strain to the breaking point Kipling's Anglo-Indian conviction that east and west shall never meet.—*The New York Sun.*

REPORTS

SCHOOL LUNCHES[1]

PUBLIC-SCHOOL lunch rooms in dark, poorly ventilated, musty basements are rapidly being replaced by well-lighted, ventilated and cheerful ones, equipped with the most modern appliances and supervised by trained dietitians, who not only prepare food suitable for growing boys and girls, and serve it in an environment conducive to the development of high ideals and

[1] Report of the U. S. Bureau of Education.

standards of conduct, but make the essential food products so appealing to the eye and appetizing to the taste that food selection by children becomes a pleasurable exercise.

Too often the lunch is hurriedly swallowed and is devoid of nutriment needed for muscle and bone building, formation of good blood, teeth and all the other factors which help to produce health. This is one of the important reasons why the person in charge of school feeding should be a trained dietitian, so that the right kind of foods will be supplied.

If the breakfast is insufficient, there is every reason why the school lunch should make up the deficiencies. Investigations concerning the breakfasts of school children show that from one fourth to one half of the children go to school without breakfast, and many of them go after having had only a cup of coffee. This situation may be due to poverty, slovenly habits of living (not rising in time to eat properly), or ignorance on the part of the parents of the needs of growing children.

It is the duty of the school, in so far as its educational resources will permit, to counteract these deficiencies. For this purpose the school lunch room is gradually being recognized as one of the greatest health agencies in the entire school system.

In 1926 the New York lunch inquiry committee studied school lunch rooms in 120 cities of 50,000 population and more. This committee found that 43 of the 120 lunch rooms were under the direct supervision of departments of home economics, 29 under cafeteria managers, 21 under lunch-room directors, 7 under parent-teacher associations, 3 under the principal of the school and the others under miscellaneous management.

According to this study, several cities have their lunch rooms organized according to the following combinations: Joint directorship of the cafeteria director and penny-lunch association; the home-economics department and parent-teacher association; supply commission and penny-lunch association; cafeteria manager and home-economics department, and one of several other combinations.

The home-economics committee of the 1926–1927 commission of curricula, appointed by the department of superintendence of the National Education Association, made a survey of the lunch rooms in the 130 public schools enrolled in the cooperative plan of curriculum revision of that association.

This committee found that 65 schools have lunch rooms managed or the menus directed by home-economics teachers; 78 schools have the assistance of home-economics girls especially trained for this project; 78 or more schools have the home-economics girls prepare all or some of the food served in the lunch rooms; 32 schools give the home-economics girls an opportunity to assist with the marketing for the lunch rooms; 65 or more schools teach guidance in food selection by means of posters, publicity in the school papers and class instruction; 43 schools provide extra nourishment for the malnourished, destitute and anemic children, and the expense entailed for these purposes is met either by the school board, philanthropic organizations or the parent-teacher associations; 93 or more schools train students in proper conduct while serving in the lunch room, and 78 of the schools give training in proper conduct to the students served; 32 schools cooperate with the department of agriculture of the school in securing vegetables and flowers, with the art department in making posters and in giving suggestions for beautifying the room, and with the commercial department in securing assistance with accounts.

This study indicates that in a large proportion of the cities in the cooperative plan of curriculum revision the departments of home economics either manage or cooperate with the lunch rooms; that in a number of cases the lunch room is of mutual benefit to the departments concerned with it, either as offering opportunities for subsidiary instruction in home economics, health, conduct and accounts, or for utilizing the salable products of home economics and agriculture. This study found no exploitation of home-economics students for the benefit of lunch rooms.

The report of the Massachusetts committee of home economics in elementary and secondary schools shows questionnaires were sent to 197 superintendents. Of these, 167 reported on the school lunch; 85 reported that home-economics teachers are responsible for the school lunch; 65 made a negative reply on this question, and 18 did not report on it. The recommendations of this committee concerning home economics and the school lunch room are given below as to:

(a) *Organization.*—Unless the schools are large enough to employ the service of a full-time lunch-room manager, the lunch room should be under the management of the home-economics teachers, for this arrangement gives better coordination and cooperation between the foods department and the lunch room; gives control of food standards; gives students an opportunity to apply knowledge learned in the classroom; and affords a better salary arrangement for the lunch-room director, as she is not obliged to make her salary, but is paid from school funds like any other teacher.

If the above arrangement is in effect, the lunch-room manager should not be expected to carry a full teaching load. If she is not a foods teacher, she should have received training in home economics with reference to the health point of view, and she should be in entire charge of the lunch room, with the principal of the school acting in an advisory capacity. The lunch-room manager should have the same status as the teachers.

The school lunch-room manager, even if she has received home-economics training, is recommended to have an advisory committee composed of the principal of the school, a mother, a member each of the home-economics department and of the student advisory organization.

Home-economics departments should not be expected to prepare all the food served in the lunch room. This custom produces a hardship on the students and lowers the quality of the food served, but the surplus food from the home-economics departments may find a profitable outlet in the lunch room. However, it should be kept in mind that the purpose of the lunch room is not to make money to defray the expenses of other school activities, but to produce wholesome food for growing boys and girls at a reasonable price.

(b) *Qualifications of manager.*—The lunch-room manager should be a person of excellent health, executive ability and imagination. She should have a knowledge of the costs, values and preparation of food, and of the psychology of selling foods to growing boys and girls. She should be experienced in the buying and managing of food supplies, and in keeping daily records, and she should have the ability to produce artistic surroundings.

(c) *Location of lunch room.*—The lunch room should not be in the basement, because of the insanitation and unattractiveness of dark, inadequately ventilated rooms, but, if possible, on the same floor with the foods division of the home-economics department.

(d) *Equipment and serving facilities.*—These should be of such a type as to provide arrangements for the students to wash their hands and to insure rapid service. The length of time for serving should not be less than 20 minutes; 30 minutes is preferable.

(e) *Kinds of foods.*—Only foods healthful for growing boys and girls should be served. Candies of any kinds, pastries, rich desserts, doughnuts, frankfurters, pickles, tea and coffee should have no place in the school lunch room, even though they may be good sellers and profitable. In certain localities where children insist on having candy and frankfurters and will buy them outside, it is preferable to provide them in the lunch room, and of good quality.

EDUCATIONAL RESEARCH AND STATISTICS

METHODS USED TO COMPENSATE INSTRUCTORS FOR EXTENSION TEACHING

It is interesting to note that various wage-payment plans, some more or less complicated, others quite simple, are used by colleges and universities in the United States to compensate instructors for extension teaching. Whereas the amount of compensation for regular instruction, carried on for the most part during the day, is based chiefly upon three factors, academic training, experience and rank, compensation for extension teaching in the majority of colleges and universities in this country has no similar basis.

The material reported in this paper is based upon the summary of a questionnaire that was sent to eighty-five colleges and universities. Included in the list are all of the members of the National University Extension Association and forty-four additional colleges and universities that have extension departments of sufficient size to make the answers worthy of notice. Seventy-seven answers were received.

The specific questions with which this study is concerned are as follows: Describe the method used to compensate instructors for evening work; is the plan in use acceptable? If not, what suggestions have you to offer for its modification?

A study of the answers to the first question shows a large number of plans, which appear to fall into six groups. Group one includes those schools that pay a salary to the instructor, including evening work as part of the regular load of the instructor. In this group will be found a few schools that find it necessary to take care of their overload in extension by employing part-time instructors who are paid according to rank and the number of teaching hours.

Group two includes those schools that compensate their instructors for evening-class work on the basis of a percentage of tuition received from evening classes. The percentage of fees given to the instructor ranged from fifty to ninety-five. Some schools guarantee a minimum amount per teaching hour under their plan, while others make no guarantee. This group also includes those schools that give their instructors all of the receipts up to a certain maximum and above that retain a percentage for overhead expenses.

Group three includes those schools wherein instructors are compensated for evening-class work on the basis of the number of hours of work and according to the rank of the instructor. In some cases the amount paid per hour is calculated on a basis of a certain percentage of the yearly salary. In the majority of cases, however, the amount has no definite relation to the yearly salary received, but appears to be determined on a basis of the receipts from evening-class work.

In group four are included those schools that reported paying their instructors for evening-class work a certain sum per semester hour irrespective of the rank of the instructor. The amount per hour paid the instructor in this group appears to be determined according to a plan similar to the plan described in group three.

Schools that report paying their instructors on a basis which appears to be best described as a sliding-scale-according-to-rank plan are included in group five. Under this plan the amount paid each instructor is determined by his particular rank and the number of students in his class.

Group six includes those schools that compensate their instructors for evening-class work according to a plan which can be described as a sliding-scale-without-regard-to-rank plan. The amount paid each instructor under this plan is determined according to a plan similar to the one described in group five.

The outcome of the questionnaire is shown in Table 1.

TABLE 1

Wage-payment method	Number of schools using plan	Number of schools reporting plan acceptable	Number of schools reporting plan not acceptable	Number of schools reporting plan "not very" acceptable
I. Part of regular load	18	16	2	
II. Percentage plan	21	16	3	2
III. Per hour according to rank	9	5	2	2
IV. Per hour without regard to rank	21	17	1	3
V. Sliding scale according to rank	4	2	2	
VI. Sliding scale without regard to rank	4	2	2	
Total	77	58	12	7

Let us consider the results of the question: "If not (acceptable), what suggestions have you to offer for its modification?" The two schools that were dissatisfied with the plan under group one had no suggestions to offer and no new plan to propose. The modifications or changes in method suggested by those who were dissatisfied with the plan designated in group two included the following: A plan whereby instructors would be paid as much for small classes as for large classes; a plan whereby the instructor would be guaranteed his compensation for evening-class work.

Those schools that pay their instructors on a basis of a certain amount per semester hour according to the rank of the instructor and that are dissatisfied with their method of payment gave the following suggestions for change: Should have special instructors for evening-class work; large classes should pay more than small classes; salaries are inadequate to attract the best teachers.

The modifications or changes suggested by those who were dissatisfied with the plan designated as group four included the following: The work should be made a part of the regular load; special instructors should be employed for evening-class work; salaries are inadequate to attract the best teachers.

The schools dissatisfied with the method of payment described in group five and group six appeared to agree upon the plan which would best meet their objections; namely, the plan whereby evening-class work is made a part of the regular teaching load.

THE SIGNIFICANCE OF THE FINDINGS

A cursory glance at Table 1 will be sufficient to impress upon the reader the fact that there is no one outstanding plan of payment for evening-class work of collegiate rank. And what appears to be even more significant is the fact that the schools using the same plan of payment defy classification. There are large schools and small schools using the same plan; there are old extension departments and new extension departments using the same plan; and there are schools located in the same city using different plans.

It appears that a large percentage of colleges and universities with well-established extension departments did not plan the method of paying instructors for evening-class work according to the method used for regular instructors, nor according to any accepted best plan for paying extension instructors. Rather it appears that the majority of plans now in use are the result of an effort, organized or unorganized, to enlist the direct aid of the instructor in developing the size of his class.

If those schools using the plan called "part of the regular load" and the plan designated as "per hour according to rank" are combined, it is found that there are twenty-seven schools or approximately 35 per cent. of the schools that use a wage-payment plan similar in many respects to the method used to pay regular instructors for day work.

Consider next the plan called "per hour without regard to rank." It is found that twenty-one schools, or approximately 27 per cent., use a method of payment which differs somewhat from the method used to pay instructors for day work in that no rank is recognized.

Turning our attention next to the plan called "percentage" and the two sliding-scale plans, it is found that twenty-nine schools, or approximately 38 per cent., employ methods of payment based directly upon the number of students in each extension class.

A significant fact to note in respect to the answers received to the second question, "Is the plan in use acceptable?" is that little variation is found between plans when the ratio of acceptability of the plan in use to the number of schools using a particular plan is considered. A glance at the table will make that fact clear.

Although there appears to be no general agreement as to the best plan, it is worth while to note the results of the question, "If not acceptable, what suggestions have you to offer for its modifications?" Here we find a somewhat general agreement among the answers. All schools dissatisfied with the method of payment in use appear to agree upon a method which would include one or several of the following factors: To pay instructors as much for small classes as for large classes; to guarantee the salary of the instructor for evening work; to employ special instructors for evening-class work; to make the work a part of the regular load.

JAMES M. MAURER

UNIVERSITY OF TULSA

SCHOOL AND SOCIETY

Volume XXVIII   Saturday, September 15, 1928   Number 716

GRADING THE PROFESSORS

A new fashion has been set in educational circles, hailed by many as a "great step in advance." The professor is being graded by the students.[1] We smile. Turn about is fair play. Now the professors will come to realize how it feels to get "marked." What is sauce for the goose should be sauce for the gander—or the goslings—so there you are. A Daniel has come to judgment.

The professors are being graded with a difference however. The grades are not being filed where they can be scrutinized by interested parties. No indeed! The results must be kept a dark mystery. They are for the eyes of college administrators and student councils alone. No one else has access to them. Each professor is sometimes presented with his own marks, but in the "improved" style of professor-grading this is dispensed with as unnecessary. And where the mark is actually given him, with the gracious permission of the student council, is the professor allowed to examine each ballot and question each grader as to why the particular mark was accorded? No, again. It is only students who have such prerogatives. Only they by inalienable right are allowed to go to their graders and ask impertinent and possibly embarrassing questions as to why a particular mark was given.

Professors must not be permitted to face their accusers. In the first place it is usually impossible, since no names are as a rule signed to the student-ballots (just to make the poll more "impartial"). And in the second place to allow the professor to ask questions would not be entirely fair, do you think? Would not some professors tend to carry a grudge, determine to get even and retaliate when it came their "turn" to grade? Which, of course, is a very serious matter, for a student's whole "career" is involved in the grades he gets, whereas only the professor's job is involved in the student-grading, and what is one job more or less in the lifetime of a professor.

Furthermore, it is hardly in the nature of a student to carry a grudge, or to aim to get even with a professor. No student, especially in this "enlightened" generation, would think of doing such a thing. He is—well, for one thing, he is still too young and the responsibilities of the world weigh very heavily upon him. He would not think of grading the professor down because his "line" had proved unacceptable, or because he had been taken to task for chronic indolence or tardiness or because the professor had been sarcastic and had made him feel foolish for whispering in the back of the room. If the professor were allowed to see the results of the student-gradings and if names had to be attached to the ballots, it might even look as though the faculty were suspicious of the students or questioned their good intentions, their very honor in fact!

But what measuring-rod could students possibly find to apply to their professors? Why, of course, those matters with which students are most familiar, both by experience and training. And those are obviously a knowledge of the professor's subject, a knowledge of pedagogy and teaching ability and a knowledge of the professor's reliability. Time was when these matters were decided in advance of appointing a professor to a position, by inquiry among his colleagues and among those with whom he had previously worked. But under the new dispensation such crude and old-fashioned methods are done away with. Regarding the professor's field of special study, what should his colleagues know about it? Why, they can not see the forest for the trees. They are of an older generation which has not the insight of the present one. And, most important of all, is it not logical to presume that those who have had no contact whatsoever with a subject are freest of bias and prejudice re-

[1] *Cf.* J. P. Gavit's, *College*, Harcourt, Brace & Co., 1925, pp. 196 ff.

garding it and are thus best able to judge "instinctively" as to who has real knowledge concerning it? Hence, the students grade their professors regarding "knowledge of subject."

Similar arguments can be submitted to demonstrate that students are in an excellent position to determine a professor's ability to teach. Having observed a number of high-school and grammar-school teachers in action, college students come to their tasks with infallible criteria. For example, a certain procedure enabled one to "get by" at high school; if the same procedure enables one to "get by" at college in a given course, the professor is quite apparently a good teacher—and, incidentally, a good fellow. Another criterion is whether or not a course is made "interesting." Here the student finds a simple test. "If the professor can not make the course interesting, he is not a good teacher," we hear stated on every hand. What difference does it make whether the subject is Latin composition or sex-relations, trigonometry or how to play the stock market, Greek grammar or folk-dancing? "Show me an interested class and I will show you a good teacher," says Benny Arnold, president of the freshman class of X College, because he was right guard on his high-school team; and he, of course, ought to know. There are other important reasons for depending upon students to size up the professor's ability to teach, but those given will suffice.

And what could be more fitting than to ask students to pass judgment on a professor's "reliability?" From earliest childhood, in his important worldly activities, the growing boy or girl, especially in the "new" generation, has acquired a full knowledge of the meaning of reliability—particularly through an extended practice of its antithesis. Still this is neither here nor there. What the student means, in the main, by a professor's reliability is peculiar to the student himself. Naturally he wishes his professor to be "reliable." How else could he determine in advance what question the professor will ask him in class to-morrow or what the examination questions will be? Any unpredictability in this respect is highly undesirable, from the student point of view. Hence "reliability" in a professor is a good quality; and, of course, the student knows best how to size this up.

And so the students are grading the professors. A very fitting procedure, as has been indicated. But there is an even more fitting side to it; and that is that some college authorities take it seriously and set considerable store by it. For here is an excellent device, ready at hand, for "getting a line" on the value of a professor to the institution. All the administration has to do is to listen carefully to the unbiased estimates of students who get low marks in their courses, for students who do well in college rarely express an opinion unsolicited; and the ones who get low marks are, after all, in the best position to "size up" a professor, since others are too absorbed in the subject-matter under discussion, and thus in getting better grades, to make a scientific study of the professor's knowledge of subject, ability to teach and reliability. Also, by letting it be openly known that student opinion carries considerable weight with the administration, quite a plethora of expert knowledge regarding the professors is forthcoming. And as a result how the professors in such colleges must be toeing the mark, not to say trembling in their shoes!

Should the system of student-grading become firmly established, the potent effect upon teaching methods, in adapting them to modern "needs," should be apparent to all. Other interesting developments are already in evidence here and there.

One of the most significant is that the new order of things furnishes an excellent environment for the training of faculty-politicians. The barroom of saloons, though in a very crude way, of course, used to provide such a place; that is, there the embryo wardheeler could experiment and gather lieutenants and followers about him, making promises of how he would change the *status quo* if elected. Obviously, these promises were made to secure adherents and not to be kept; in fact, most of them were sheer impossibilities on their very face. Under the genial influence of liquor—when men become like little children again or like unsophisticated students—many things are believable which otherwise might be questioned. But the open saloon is gone now and it has been a real problem to find an adequate substitute as a training-ground for politicians.

Under the new order of student control in colleges, a body of students is just such a substitute. What an ideal environment for the development of political strategy and experience it now becomes!

The ideal faculty-politician will be a young bachelor, not too far removed in age from the students themselves, good looking, a hail-fellow-well-met, interested in youth movements, fraternities and extracurricular activities of every variety. The subject he teaches and the length of his teaching experience are entirely irrelevant in the new régime. He will be present at all fraternity- and sorority-dances, but never as a chaperon, will drop in casually but regularly at fraternity houses and dormitories to fraternize, will speak often at chapel and at all possible student-functions but always on a light subject or one complimentary to the new dispensation and the power (not the potentialities) of youth. Above all, he will be a big brother to the students; not too old a brother, you understand, but in reality "one of them," sympathetic to their problems, especially sympathetic to those who receive low grades in their courses or who have been disciplined by the dean or otherwise; and of course he himself will never give a student a low mark nor mete out disciplinary action under any circumstances.

Such an ideal faculty-politician will soon find himself popular. He will have many sweethearts among the girls and many ardent supporters among the boys. He need not go further; his admirers will do the rest, for student opinion of this character spreads rapidly. At the eating-houses and in the get-togethers in students' rooms—where in any college the faculty-members are constantly discussed and where, in colleges under the new régime of student-grading, there is even more occasion for frank discussion, the word is passed around that so-and-so is the "right sort." His good fellowship and fine personality are made clear to all, by emphatic statement and repetition, and he is at the proper time voted the most popular teacher on the campus; and, of course, in the student-grading he stands ace-high. Not that all students will give him a good grade; some of the high-brows lack discernment in this respect; but the vast majority are not high-brows (thank goodness!) and so the régime of student-grading, supplemented by a receptive administration and the presence of a faculty-politician, moves forward on the road to destiny.

The faculty-politician need go no further than just indicated, for if the administration is discerning he will forthwith be promoted to a full professorship and receive an increase in salary. He is evidently a valuable man, despite the fact that he has only an M.A. degree and regardless of the protests of the dean that no other member of the faculty has been made a full professor in recent years until he has received his doctorate. Some deans are entirely out of step with these new developments anyhow. They are too old, undoubtedly.

But the faculty-politician, if he is a real dyed-in-the-wool politician, will go further. Why should he fail to take full advantage of this exceedingly fertile field for political experimentation? He may aspire to political honors in the broader arena of democratic government later on, and his experience at college will stand him in good stead. In any event, he can go further even at college.

He need not stop at a professorship. In fact, this should be but a beginning under the new dispensation. He has his ardent supporters among the students. Some of them have confided personal matters in him which puts them more completely under his control. He can suggest to those who are most in his confidence that the college should, for example, have a new dean, that the present incumbent is too harsh in his methods, is out of step with modern youth and that the students should have more freedom. He need not say that *he* is the logical man for the place; it would be unwise to go that far, for he must be in a position always to "get out from under" should too strong an opposition to his plans develop; but his admirers will understand. Student opinion will take form. Soon it will be the talk of the campus that the present dean is old and fossilized and that so-and-so would be the right man for the place. Quickly that sentiment will reach the administration. The outcome, where conditions are favorable to the new order, should be easy to predict. And this is but one illustration of the opportunities for training in political strategy made possible by the development of college control through student opinion, as expressed in the grading of professors and otherwise. Other possibilities will readily occur to the reader.

Another development of the new régime worth noting is its effect upon the younger members of a faculty. Tutors and instructors are, of course, slightly older than the students —two to five years perhaps—and thus have lost some of the purity of thought and completeness of knowledge which students still possess. But at the same time they are not so far removed from such pristine all-sufficiency as are the full professors, and they are, therefore, in an excellent position to keep their superiors from ossifying too fast. There are, it is true, many tutors and instructors who are unable as yet to shake off tradition and who still show deference and respect to the professors; but, where student-grading is becoming an established institution, this old-fashioned esteem is being rapidly done away with. In such institutions, where a professor holds a conference with a group of young instructors for the purpose of clarifying an issue about to be presented to the students, do the younger men wait until their senior has outlined the issue and then ask him questions in order to clear up their own thinking? Certainly not, except for those who are not yet enlightened enough, for that would be an admission that the professor knows more about the subject than they do. He may have done his graduate work at the same big university from which they have just graduated. But he took his work twenty to forty years ago, whereas they took theirs last year; he has not only forgotten a whole lot which is still fresh—exceedingly fresh!—in their minds, but he has doubtless also had poorer teachers two to four decades back than they had last year; or if some of the same teachers are still at the big university!—but why pursue the thought further? Obviously, with the coming of the "new" generation, young instructors know more than the professors—this deference and respect is all the "bunk" anyhow—so why should they not exercise their superior knowledge and tell the professors how the issue should be clarified and taught? Why not, indeed!

Well, these are some of the developments of the control of colleges by student opinion, the grading of professors being its most recent expression. A new day for higher education is dawning!

It would, of course, be irrelevant—not to say irreverent—to suggest that, since members of boards of trustees are often even older than the professors and therefore still farther removed from the knowledge, sagacity, discernment, etc., of students, that the latter might some day be persuaded to take over the college-administrative function as well as the grading function. But one thing at a time. Student-grading of professors is still in its infancy. There is really no saying how far-reaching the effects of the present revolution in educational methods are to be. Time alone will tell.

R. S.

BOOKSTORES IN COLLEGE TOWNS

Whether a college is better off located in a small community or in a city is one of those questions forever debatable and never decided—at least, to everybody's satisfaction. There are, however, certain defects in the life of the small community that must be recognized by any fair-minded person; and it should be apparent that it is the duty of the institution most vitally concerned, namely, the college, to see to it, if it can, that the weaknesses are corrected.

It should first of all recognize what is meant by the term "small communities." By "small communities" I mean to imply not simply a limitation of population, though that is frequently an adequate criterion. That community is small, as I mean to use the term, that is without certain advantages that encourage and foster a cultivated life. Most communities, though not all, with small populations are lacking in these advantages; unfortunately, on the other hand, many communities with fairly large populations—with forty or fifty thousand inhabitants—are not uncommonly little better off than towns with a few thousand souls; and all too frequently the situation is no better in cities with populations of one hundred thousand. These "small communities" suffer, of course, from several disadvantages of a sort that will occur to any reader upon a moment's reflection; but I propose to consider only one of them.

An educated and cultivated person, and such a person a college graduate is supposed to be, may reasonably be expected to have an acquaintance with books. It is obvious that our knowledge of the past is gathered, for the most part, from books; and books, too, account for much of the deepening of our understanding of human nature, the refining of our emotions and the softening of our sensibilities; in short, they are invaluable instruments for making us intelligent, reflective and sensitive men and women. But more than that, an educated and cultivated person should be an owner of books, for how else can he continuously be under their pervading and mellowing influence? Indeed, is it too much to ask that he be, as nearly as it is possible, a lover of books? For only as he is a lover of books will he surrender himself repeatedly to their mysterious power. If a student has been reared in a home where good books are bought and read it is possible that he will come to college with an interest already kindled; if so, he will in this respect give the college no particular concern. But more than ever before the American student body is recruited from homes with commonplace and materialistic interests; and a student from such a home is unlikely to be alive to the appeal of books. Any one who knows undergraduates knows that the facts support this contention. Go into the average college student's room and what do you see? A talking machine, a radio set, ill-assorted pictures and photographs, "college" pillows—and a pitiably small row of dull, drab text-books. Try to find, if you can, any enthusiasm for building up a small library of choice books—standard novels, poetry, history, biography! Sudents, you say, have no money to spend for books; but they will spend from fifteen to fifty dollars and even more for a party. No, they have the money; they lack the directed incentive.

If, then, on the one hand, books have so vital a part in the education and the cultivation of students' personalities; and if, on the other hand, many students seem to be without any genuine and deep interest in this influence, is it not clear that the college has a heavy responsibility in this direction?

"To be sure it has," answer the college instructors, "and have we not been exerting ourselves in this matter? Have we not been sending students to the libraries and assigning readings and reports?" But the general apathy among students is a sufficient commentary upon the effectiveness of the system.

"The difficulty," continue the instructors in self-defence, "is that we have not made sure that students have done the reading. Let's devise a system to do that, and all will be well!"

No, the difficulty lies far deeper. To be sure, students "skim" books—if indeed they read them at all. But even if they do read the books, they read listlessly unless they have brought to the reading an interest already existent. Moreover, library copies are often worn and not infrequently shabby; and such books rouse in their readers no eager curiosity. Again, libraries find it impracticable to do the one thing that might stir an interest in books, that is, to admit the run of students to the stacks, where they can handle the volumes, get in touch with them and feel their fascination. The problems of administration involved seem too great to permit this freedom. Thus because of human frailty books have to be doled out from the "reserve desk." A book has become simply a conveyor of information, an article of merchandise. And finally readers, even mature readers, often find a college or public library so uninspiring because of uncomfortable chairs or drab surroundings or unhygienic temperature that they have no pleasure in using it as a workshop. No, in the nature of the case the college library can never provide the ease and the informality of the student's study or the home. It would seem clear, then, from all these considerations that it is doubtful whether the college library can develop an abiding interest in books where that interest does not already exist.

If, then, the library does not develop that interest, what can? The bookstore can. Not the bookstore that sells victrola records and sporting goods and also books, but the bookstore that exists to sell books primarily. Such a store has not only the latest novels and cheap reprints of popular stories; it has also the best of general contemporary literature and a generous selection of standard books. The collection need not be a large one, though naturally the larger the better; but it should be representative of many tastes. Into such a store the visitor should be free to come without feeling the necessity of buying; he should feel free to roam about, take books from shelves or tables, look over the pages—and if he finds nothing interesting, go out without buying and without being trailed by a clerk. Such freedom is essential, for many students are shy and will not venture into the store if they know they are being shadowed by a misguided employee or that they are expected to make a purchase. Any one who often comes into such a bookstore will at last find a book and then another and another that he will want to buy and read and own.

The importance of the right kind of bookstore in an education is a commonplace with many thoughtful persons. Writing about one of the best of such stores in a great university town, Basil Blackwell's at Oxford, England, a writer in the *Morning Post* of London said:

> Many men will aver that the greatest educative influence of Oxford resides neither in Bodleian, nor schools, nor tutors, nor lectures, nor college societies, but in the excellent management and most liberal facilities of one of the best bookshops in the world—Mr. Blackwell's.

And a writer in the *Evening Standard* of London wrote to similar effect as follows:

> Undergraduates at Oxford were accustomed to spend their afternoons in three ways: either they indulged in some kind of athletics, or else they took a walk, or else they went to Mr. Blackwell's shop in the Broad. When they went there, they read any book that occurred to them. All the shelves were open. . . . Generations of undergraduates have done their reading there without cost.

Persons who have been in Mr. Blackwell's shop will acknowledge at once that these writers have not exaggerated the fascination that the shop has for the Oxford man. They will remember that students linger over the tables, that they leaf through the books, that they even read as much as they want—and that they then buy or not, as it suits them. No officious or ill-advised clerk ever offers "Can I help you?" You speak to him first if you want help. And there are half a dozen other bookstores in Oxford that are just as hospitable and generous.

But that is Oxford; it is, as a matter of fact, typical of many English and Continental towns and cities. Indeed, one of the first observations of an open-eyed American traveler in Europe is the number of really good bookstores. One finds bookstores—well stocked and intelligently managed—on many streets of the great cities. And even the small communities have shops of a quality that surprise and shame the American observer. Our best city in such matters, New York, is in no way to be compared with London or Paris in the number of excellent stores or in their distribution through various parts of the city. And as for the smaller communities, the situation is almost ludicrous. How many American cities of five thousand population have even one respectable bookstore? How many of twenty-five thousand have one? How many even of seventy-five or one hundred thousand? Every reader knows the answer: almost none. He knows the answer because he has only to consider the small towns—and the large ones too—that he is acquainted with. I could name a score of eastern cities with populations of one hundred thousand for the bookstores of which a cultivated resident has to make apology. And I see no reason to believe that western or southern cities, whether college towns or not, are any better off in this respect. Whether the fault is with a non-book-buying public or with visionless storekeepers is beside the point; the situation as pictured is deplorably obvious.

And so the responsibility comes back to the college. If the town—large or small— can not or will not support a bookstore, then the college should. I do not, of course, mean a store that sells merely text-books; they may be included, and probably would be. No, I mean a store that stocks all classes of literature, that makes itself enticing to students, that provides such an atmosphere that students will look forward to returning again and again. Such a store would have more the appearance of a private library than of a bookstore. On the floor would be some rugs, not necessarily expensive, but harmonious in color; on the walls would be a few pictures. If there could be an open fire-place, of what inestimable advantage it would be! The shelves would be, if possible, those of an open bookcase. Books would be invitingly arranged. On small tables would be placed a tempting display of new books; and the cheery glow of a reading lamp and a cosy chair set nearby would invite a reader to inspect at his leisure a book that he had found of interest. Such a store would require also a tactful, sympathetic manager—a college graduate, of course, and a man or woman who also knows how to get along with students and who knows and loves books.

The question naturally arises, "The bookstore is all very well for such persons as will visit it, but just how are you going to get into the store those very persons who most need it but are unlikely to come?" Well, even in these days when students have discovered how to make one text-book do the duty of three, they have to go to some bookstore occasionally—for books, for stationery, and the like. And just there the manager has a great opportunity through making his store as attractive as possible—a point that has already been made. Even the dullest person will ultimately be influenced by effective arrangement. Furthermore, an instructor can, if he will, do a great deal to encourage students to frequent a bookstore. It requires no ingenuity—only a little thought and patience—for an instructor to tuck into a lecture a reference to a new book he saw on sale, to bring a desirable book to class and to read from it, to refer to a bargain in Stevenson he saw there this morning or to give the direct suggestion that it is worth while looking into the bookstore occasionally. Finally, judicious and repeated advertising of the bookstore in the college papers can not fail to attract students, just as advertising in the general press does not fail to win the general public. It seems almost certain that a combination of influences is bound to tell ultimately.

Finally, the administrative officials of many colleges will raise an important practical question, "Will such a venture pay?" The answer would depend somewhat upon the student body and upon the type of encouragement given the venture. For a year or two it possibly might not pay; it might even lose money. But ultimately it would be almost sure to pay for itself and would probably show some profit. But, after all, such a question, if it is to be taken as hinting at objection, shows a failure to appreciate the significance of the proposal. It is the contention that a bookstore of the kind suggested would help to do that very thing for which the college exists. So do professors; but they do not pay for themselves; they are paid in part out of endowment. Very well; let endowment be used, if necessary, to pay for another type of educational activity—a college bookstore.

STANLEY S. SWARTLEY

ALLEGHENY COLLEGE

EDUCATION: THE NEXT STEPS
II

THE standard of secondary education in England is high, and is something of which we have a right to be proud. Its methods and objects are the fruit of long experience and of the efforts of several generations. The boy or girl who has taken a school certificate before the age of sixteen, followed an advanced course, or specialization in a sixth form, to the age of 18+, has reached a level attained in few educational systems other than our own. I question indeed whether any country is producing boys and girls of as high a level of intellectual excellence and training as those hundreds who go up every year to compete for scholarships and places at Oxford and Cambridge. I believe this to be true of the boys, and it is certainly true of the girls. This system is now built on the general education of the school certificate and the specialized education of the higher certificate, and I hold that it should stand unimpaired, and not be tampered with; for it is far easier to relax a standard than ever to recover it. To say that every boy and girl who goes to a secondary school for four years should be awarded the same certificate, whatever subjects they may have studied and offered, is to say that things which are not equal to one another are equal to the same thing; it is to say that the boy who has been successful in English, history, geography, Latin, French, mathematics and science is *prima facie* the same article as the boy who has been successful in English, general elementary science, drawing, handicraft and shorthand, or the girl who has offered English, botany, music, drawing and needlework. I am not representing either course as better than the other; one may be right for A and the other for B. I hold no brief to argue that the high-brow is better than the low-brow, or the blue stocking than the flesh-colored stocking. All that I maintain is that they are palpably not the same, that it is illogical therefore to call them the same, and that nothing but confusion will result from calling them the same. It may be democratic and in accordance with the spirit of the age to hold that we are all the same as one another, and ought therefore to be labelled with the same labels; but no man who has taught a class for one term can really hold that nature gives any warrant to such nonsense. Surely the logical course is to award two kinds of certificate, one which shall fulfil the academic conditions and maintain unlowered the existing system which causes no difficulty to the boy or girl of average academic ability, and the other which shall be a proof that the boy or girl has taken at school that course of education which in the particular case was the most fitted.

I would therefore have in any secondary school these two types definitely recognized to be different, not superior or inferior, the one to the other, but different. It would be recognized at the school-certificate stage by the one type sitting for the school certificate awarded as it now is, and the other for a general certificate which shall show that they have made good use of a good and sensible type of education. If they stay at school the one type will continue to go on to the higher certificate, again organized as it now is, and the other to a second certificate, which shall again test the subjects of a quite unspecialized education, designed to meet the individual need in each case. There will then be a good deal of variety inside secondary education, and when the central schools become more numerous and more organized, and the modern schools come into existence in increasing quantity, there will be a good deal of variety outside the old secondary schools as well. And when you consider the variety which must exist among that more than half-million boys and girls with whom we shall have to deal, I think you will agree with me that the more variety there is the better.

Even so my discussion of the problem of the right curriculum for the higher forms of the secondary school is not complete. In saying that the standard should remain unimpaired, and not be tampered with, I have in mind the work of the best boys and girls. But many more than the best go on to the universities, and it is right that they should do so; I am not convinced that any of these should attempt specialized study before they enter the classes of the university. On the one hand the colleges of Oxford and Cambridge, through their open scholarship examinations, enforce on the schools the attempt to reach a very high standard along narrow lines; some universities, by allowing their intermediate examinations to be taken through the higher certificate, confuse the courses proper to themselves and to the schools; some universities admit their students too early; the higher-certificate courses themselves often involve specialization built on a very slender foundation of general knowledge. On the other hand many professors and university teachers are loud in their condemnation of the state in which their pupils come to them, with minds ill-balanced and ill-furnished. I submit that this region of the last two years of school is insufficiently explored, and the nature of the work that should be done by the average student not thought out. I submit further that it is a matter which might well engage the attention of all the universities of the country in conference. They have perhaps no common mind, but I do not know that they have attempted to arrive at one: they have never clearly stated what they want; they have never faced the fact that through their scholarships they make extreme specialization necessary, and through their professors complain of the result. I regard the matter as urgent, for as chairman of the Secondary Schools Examination Council I know that the curriculum and the examinations proper to this later period of school life stand in great need of definition, and that in proceeding to the work, which can not long be deferred, we have no clear guidance from the universities as to what they really want.

However, it is not only in the secondary schools that some thinking needs to be done about the requirements of the immediate future; there is also some advance that needs to be made after due thought in that very complicated field which is known as technical and further education. There has just lately been issued the second part of the report of the Committee on Education and Industry in England and Wales, to which I would commend this audience if they would like to go deeply into the matter. In this department of education the next steps which require to be taken are all of them steps to secure better contact with other branches of the educational system, and with industry and employment. Technical education is a field which has been developed all by itself, and in isolation from almost everything else. Each part has grown to meet a need, and usually a local need. It is cut off from the elementary education which precedes it, for elementary and technical education have been controlled by different departments of the Board of Education, and it is cut off from the university education, which in the case of the best students ought to follow. There is frequently a gap of one, two, or even more years between the end of the elementary course and the beginning of technical instruction, and that instruction is frequently sterilized by the fact that students have to come to it tired, late in the evening, and in the center of cities. Finally, there is need of much fuller contact, of more mutual knowledge and sympathy, not only between technical education and industry, but also between all forms of industry and commerce and all forms of education. There ought to be a full inquiry into this difficult and complicated problem; educationists ought to know and consider more thoroughly what is wanted, and employers ought to take much more trouble to find out what is being done. May I quote in this connection a paragraph from the recent report of the Committee on Education and Industry with which I thoroughly agree? "We do not consider," they say, "that educational policy should be determined by industrial requirements, however legitimate in themselves. What we do feel most strongly is that in the interests of the boys and girls, quite as much as in the interests of industry, educational policy, and still more important its application in detail, ought not to be settled without full knowledge of occupational conditions, prospects and needs. It can not be said that educational administrators are in as close touch with trade and industry as they would wish to be at this important stage in educational history. We are therefore forced to two conclusions. In the first place, any measures which can be taken to secure the contact which every one desires should be taken with all possible speed, before the educational position becomes so solidified that any modifications, however desirable, will be extremely difficult, if not impossible, to make. In the second place, local authorities and all others concerned should obtain, so far as is possible, the views of representatives of trade and industry, employers and workers alike, before committing themselves to any reorganization which might have direct or indirect effects on industrial conditions. The connection between school arrangements and circumstances of employment are not always apparent at first sight, and too great care can not be expended in investigating the industrial implication of educational changes."

There is a large question of very general interest which I can state, though I do not know that I can supply an answer. What is the proper part which formal and external examination should play in our educational courses? Examinations at the present time play a very large part. In a great many places there is competition and examination for scholarships and for free places at the secondary schools; some four years later there follows the school certificate, theoretically for all. One or two years later follows the higher-certificate examination, and then there are for some all the university and professional examinations in prospect. Entrance to the public schools is obtained by an examination known as the common entrance examination, which is said in some cases to be competitive, but in all cases involves the reaching by the candidate of a certain definite standard. Competitive examination admits to the Army, Navy and the Civil Service. The system is so thorough and so universal that the victim, if that is the right word, may never be out of the shadow of an examination from eleven years old to twenty-three, or even later. It is argued, first, that this gives almost inevitably a totally wrong view of knowledge, and makes a boy or a girl from school days on feel that his or her object is not to study a subject, but to acquire the capacity to answer on paper examination questions about it, and that therefore, once examinations are over, he or she learns no more. It is argued, secondly, that the teacher's freedom is destroyed, since he has to teach his subject not in the best way, but in the way which will pay best in the examination, and that the more inspiring, original, and fresh he is in presentment, the less he is likely to succeed on a mechanical system. It is alleged, thirdly, that the system is really unsuccessful, that it picks out for honor those who have the examination faculty and can write fast and to the point, but that, judging by what happens in after-life, it does not really pick the best men and women, and those who will go furthest in their study.

There is a certain amount of truth, but a good deal of unreasonableness and lack of practical common sense, in all this attack which is so frequently made to-day. My own profession, the schoolmasters, are not inconsistent, though the schoolmistresses dispute the palm with them, for they insist on a certificate to mark the successful completion of all their courses, and do not rest until all the subjects which they teach have been brought, for instance, within the ambit of the school certificate. The subjects which of all others ought to be the most free, and are in my opinion in their own interests least examinable—music and art—are, I suppose, the means for awarding more certificates by examination than any other, and the blame for this I lay largely at the door of my professional brothers and sisters. It is not, I think, seriously true that teachers are cramped by the examinations; on the whole, examinations follow the school curricula, and do not control them; the teachers, moreover, are well represented on the examining authorities, and can make their voices heard. It is not possible to say whether a boy or girl knows a subject save by asking questions; there must be the same for all, answered under the same conditions in the same time, and that makes a written examination necessary. No one suggests that examinations are more than they are, a very human and sometimes fallible means of finding out whether a candidate knows what he ought to know, and no one in his senses claims that they pick out the person who will be ultimately the most successful. What is true is that in early years they tend to dull the edge of the desire for true knowledge, and that throughout school life there are plenty who are quite incapable of showing on paper what they have in their head; they are not fools, though they may be written down as such, but they are bad examinees. Moreover, in any system of examination which is more or less universal—as is the case with the school certificate—we have to think of the dull and of the slow developers, who suffer badly when they are crammed and forced to an unnatural level.

I believe, therefore, though the time is not yet, that the right course will be to abolish all external examination for the average boy and girl, though leaving it as the avenue to the universities and the professions. In the case of the average boy and girl the properly inspected and efficient school will issue its own certificate that A or B has attended for four or six years as the case may be, and has reached a satisfactory level of performance. The power to make such an award implies a high standard of professional honor, and perhaps a higher level of efficiency than yet exists, but it would enable the schools to teach a pupil what he could learn, to teach him in the right way, and not drive him in the wrong way to a wrong standard. The mere size and complication of the examination system will tend to break it down. Doubtless 55,000 candidates have sat for the school certificate this summer, each doing six, seven, or eight papers; the number of qualified examiners free to undertake the work is very limited. In another twenty years there may be 100,000 candidates, for the Hadow Report asks for a special leaving examination for all the pupils at those modern schools which it hopes to see established. Certainly the question will become acute, whether so great an effort will be repaid by any advantage which can accrue from the issue of tens of thousands of certificates each year, certificates which state that the holders have in effect reached a very moderate standard of knowledge, such as you might expect from an average person of their years. Would not the issue of a similar statement by a responsible school have a precisely equal value?

To see the examination system at its worst it should be studied in the common entrance examination to the public schools. This examines four to five thousand candidates yearly, and is designed to ascertain whether those thirteen-year-olds know enough English, scripture, history, geography, Latin, French, arithmetic, algebra and geometry to be admitted to the bottom form of a public school. Much of the boy's future depends upon the result of this examination, for the doors to the schools which he desires will remain locked if he does not qualify. The object, therefore, of what is a most expensive form of education and of what should be the best, carried out as it is with small classes and in good buildings, is to enable little boys to answer questions on paper with great rapidity, and to switch their small minds with accuracy from Genesis to Ivanhoe, from Henry VIII to the causes of rainfall, from quotations to problems, from Latin to French, and so on, for two momentous days. The bright boy finds it easy, the average boy in many cases, the dull boy in all cases, finds it terribly hard. The result on the teaching is remarkable, for there is a handbook issued, which commands a large sale and a free use in many schools, which has reduced the whole thing to cram by analysis of all the best papers. I have in my possession a leaflet which bears the inscription "To the preparatory schools is dedicated this sample of the Common Entrance Handbook in the sincere belief that the latter will prove a boon to all who possess it." David and Jonathan, publishers, 60 pages, price 5s. I turn the page and find all the sovereigns of England ranged in order according to the frequency of their occurrence in the last thirty-three papers, from Victoria, ninety-seven, to Edward V, who has failed to score; the same with English literature, from "Westward Ho!" with fourteen occurrences to "Rip Van Winkle" with one, "Idylls of the King," twenty-one, to "John Gilpin," one; it is very thorough, for it treats languages and geography in the same way. Truly the preface may well say that the handbook was written not with a view to publication: it was written to supply a need. That need was the necessity of cramming, and not educating—a process degrading to the teacher, hurtful to the taught, and a cause for hanging the head to all who are responsible for the system which has produced this travesty of our art. It is no surprise to learn that there are schools where the boys read no authors, but only do examination papers; read no history, but memorize answers about names, and treat literature and geography in the same way. I conceive that there is no method of reform save the abolition of so indefensible a system, and I believe that it is, or ought to be, an educational axiom that there should never be any examination of a child under fifteen save by his own teachers. If any one doubts this I would ask him to estimate the improvement of elementary education in this country which has taken place since payment by results was done away with and the inspector's examination was abolished.

I must draw to a close. Whatever reforms of administration, whatever changes of curriculum, whatever increase of expenditure are approved, the last word lies with the teachers, and all depends on the spirit which animates them and the ideals which move them. This country is committed to the experiment of unrestricted democracy, ideally the highest form of government if the quality of the citizens is good, in practice capable of being the worst, where the citizens are uneducated and incapable of discerning the true values of life. Everything seems to me to depend upon whether the teachers in the next generation rise to the full measure of their responsibility and opportunity, whether they carry through every part and parcel of our educational system the highest and truest English tradition, that education is more than instruction, that character counts for more than brains and lives more than learning, that the true basis of life is religious, and the only real values spiritual. I would say that the main end and aim is to train boys and girls for service to the community, and to make clear that their lives can be lived in this spirit, whether they are tradesmen or merchants, engineers or manufacturers, clergymen or doctors, or followers of any career whatever, and that the only life deserving of contempt is the life that contributes nothing, or contributes evil, to the common stock. We have a fine traditional method to follow, which has been handed down to us from the best of our predecessors; we can build our school lives on fellowship and the sense of honor, on the team-spirit and not on individualism. We can point our pupils forward to the quest of seeking to establish among the citizens of this country a more equitable division of the things that matter, not by the self-destructive method of class-war, but by the mutual help of classes. We can save them from the fallacy that money is the thing that matters most, for we can show them that the values of eternal life are among us now, and now can be sought.

There is no nobler calling than that of the teacher, and the hope of the future lies in this, that none can escape the teacher's influence. The highest education is the gift of personality to personality, where in freedom one leads, and others are fired to follow; and this can not occur unless schools are free and individual, and the teachers within them no less free to develop and give the best of which they are capable. Education can and must be organized in Whitehall and the county town, but it can not there be given; it can only pass from living men and women to living boys and girls, where each is known to each. This personal relation based on freedom is the most precious tradition that has come to us from the greatest of the past, and any advance of organization and extended scope would be too dearly bought if it brought into question, or rendered impossible, the spontaneity and independence without which no school can be great.

Cyril Norwood

Headmaster of
Harrow School

EDUCATIONAL EVENTS

THE PARIS "UNIVERSITY CITY"

Mr. John D. Rockefeller, Jr., has made a gift of $2,000,000 to the "University City." According to the Paris correspondent of the *Journal* of the American Medical Association his secretary, Mr. Raymond B. Fosdick, has acquainted Senator Honnorat, the president of that institution, with the terms of the gift in a letter in which it is specified that the money shall be used for the construction of a central building and for the administration of services that will assure a common bond between the various nations represented there. During the first three years following the completion of this building, Mr. Rockefeller will place further sums at the disposal of the institution to facilitate the organization of its functions: $60,000 for the first year, $55,000 for the second year, and $50,000 for the third year. He previously furnished the funds for the restoration of the palace of Louis XIV in Versailles. These examples of American generosity have had a great effect in France, where the prolonged discussions over the regulation of the expenses of the war have awakened some bitterness. Last winter, at Mr. Rockefeller's invitation, M. Honnorat inspected university buildings in the United States similar to the one that is to be built here. He is planning to use the Rockefeller gift to organize besides the central administrative services a common foyer, with restaurant, libraries, recreation rooms, rooms for physical culture, promenades, athletic grounds, information bureau, lecture halls and a theater and concert hall. The various dormitories that continue to be erected within the large area known as the University City will furnish complete accommodations for 10,000 students. The creation of a central building in which the students of various nations, segregated in their own special dormitories, can meet together will constitute an important factor in developing a feeling of understanding among the representatives of the younger generation destined to constitute the intellectual élite of the future.

According to the New York *Herald Tribune* approximately $100,000 is still needed to build, equip and open the American building. Each of the nations of the world has been invited by the University of Paris to accept a gift of land and put up a dormitory for its own nationals. About forty nations have accepted and more than a dozen dormitories will be in use this season.

Dr. Homer Gage, of Worcester, Mass., chairman of the American committee, has made an appeal to Americans to complete the fund for this country's dormitory. Three additional educational institutions have provided a room each —the College of the City of New York, Brown University and Duke University. Among universities and colleges which have contributed one or more rooms are Harvard, Yale, Dartmouth, Smith College, Vassar, Cornell, Rutgers, Williams, the University of Pennsylvania, the University of California, the University of Wisconsin, Rice Institute, Mount Holyoke and Purdue University.

Plans are under way for the raising of funds at Princeton, the University of Chicago, Columbia, Radcliffe, Bryn Mawr and the Pennsylvania College for Women.

Most of the fund to date has come in the form of room subscriptions, although smaller donations are welcome. For $2,500 a university, community or individual has the privilege of placing a suitably inscribed tablet in a student's room, indicating the source of the gift and carrying a preference in the assignment of that room. Among those represented by one or more rooms are Mr. and Mrs. Edsel Ford, Mr. and Mrs. Charles P. Taft, the late Miss Belle Skinner, Dr. William S. Thayer, Edwin S. Webster, Mr. and Mrs. George C. Lee and Dr. A. Lawrence Lowell, president of Harvard University. In addition to individuals, a number of cities will be represented by rooms. Among them are Evanston, St. Paul, Minneapolis, Cincinnati, Baltimore and Washington.

THE FINANCIAL DIFFICULTIES OF THE CHINESE SCHOOLS

THE Peking correspondent of the New York *Times* reports that Chinese educational leaders in Peking are now violently at outs with the Nanking Ministry of Education because certain specified funds long earmarked for the use of schools and colleges are being held up, or else are being diverted to unknown uses. Specific charges are that the Nanking authorities have taken and retained the special one tenth of the Hatamen Octroi tax, a levy which for years has gone to pay the salaries of teachers in the Peking primary schools, and that moreover they have sequestered the $150,000 a month of the returned Russian Boxer Indemnity funds—payments which under China's agreement with M. Karakhan, when he was Russian ambassador, were always to be used only for the support of the nine government universities in Peking.

Schools and universities in the old capital are due to reopen on October 1, but at present there is no money on hand for fuel and janitor pay, much less for paying the teachers and professors. Another dispute will rage around paying the salaries of teachers for the last two months, since the Nationalists took over Peking. The teachers have received no pay, though the Hatamen Octroi has been steadily collected, and though the Russian Boxer funds have been regularly remitted from the customs.

Members of the faculty of the Peking National University are reported to be in serious straits due to the fact that the university, which owes its whole teaching staff twenty-six months' salary, has decided to repudiate these debts and to start all over again, with promises of regular full salary payments in the future.

Serious individual problems have arisen because of this repudiation, which means a loss of more than $4,000 to most of the teachers, many of whom have been existing on long-time credit or have been borrowing from banks and from their friends.

These teachers must now shoulder these debts themselves or must go through bankruptcy proceedings. The entire staff has received the salary repudiation with great bitterness. Many of the best professors have refused to continue teaching and have sought other positions.

TRAVEL TOURS OF THE NATIONAL UNION OF STUDENTS

THE system of travel tours combining recreation with instruction, which are organized by the National Union of Students for the benefit of university and university college students in all the countries of Europe and in America, has this summer, according to the London *Times*, shown a very marked extension. The number of university students who have visited Great Britain from abroad has exceeded all records, the increase being threefold, and particularly in students of both sexes from Germany and America.

The tours from England have also been increased in number, France, Germany, Switzerland and Austria being the most popular objectives. The system rests on the idea of the student of different countries entertaining each other. Walking expeditions in Austria "with rucksack and ice axe" have been very popular this summer with English students. American students visiting England have mainly devoted themselves to pleasure trips, the round including London, Oxford and Cambridge, and Stratford-on-Avon; Carnarvon, Snowdon and the Menai Straits in Wales; Dublin and Belfast in Ireland, and Glasgow, Inverness, Aberdeen and Edinburgh in Scotland, before further travel on the continent.

"Faculty tours" in which the program has included visits to large business works in all parts of England have been the most popular with German students. Similar tours have at the same time been carried out by English parties, there being a "pharmacy" tour to Paris, a mining tour for Birmingham students to Bethune, Lens and Lille, a geography tour to Holland, Germany and Belgium, a librarians' tour to Rome, and a textile tour from Leeds to Antwerp. Students of law from the university at Würzburg now in London are including in their tour a visit to the printing department of *The Times* on August 27, and a party of Berlin motorcyclists have carried out a tour of England which has included visits to several dirt-track racing events.

Students visiting England so far this summer have numbered about 450, and over 500 have gone from England to the continent and to America. There is an elaborate system of providing hospitality in large cities through influential special committees who are able in many cases to accommodate tourists in private homes.

REFORM SCHOOLS

Statistics for 1926–27 of schools for delinquents have been made by the U. S. Bureau of Education. These institutions are of a reformatory nature, and receive inmates committed to their care by juvenile and other courts. Reports were received from 158 institutions out of 173 believed to exist.

The number of instructors reported for the year is 1,488, of which number 582 are men. These persons are engaged primarily in the instruction of inmates. The assistants numbered 4,677 in 1927, of whom 2,529 were men. These assistants do no teaching, but care for the inmates.

The total number of inmates reported for 1926–27 is 84,317, of which number 65,174 are boys and 19,143 are girls. Of the total number of inmates, 72,803 are white and 11,514 are colored. Since 1922 the number of inmates has increased 28.6 per cent., which is an increase of 30.2 per cent. for boys and 23.5 per cent. for girls.

White inmates have increased 31.4 per cent. in the last five years, and colored inmates have increased 25.7 per cent. Instruction was given to 61,740 inmates, or 74 per cent. of the total number in institutions reporting this item. Some trade or occupation was taught to 48,646, or 75 per cent. of all inmates in institutions reporting this item.

The percentages of those inmates which are native-born of native parents, and of those which are native-born of foreign or mixed parents, are about the same as the percentages for corresponding groups in the 5- to 20-year class of the general population. Foreign-born inmates comprise about 6 per cent. of the total number of inmates in institutions reporting foreign-born, while the foreign-born children comprise about 7 per cent. of the whole number of children in the United States.

Ninety-one schools reported both the number of inmates committed (24,110) and the number that could neither read nor write (2,271). This is 9.4 per cent. of those committed in these institutions. In 1920 among children 10 to 20 years of age in the United States, 2.7 per cent. were illiterate. One hundred and thirty-nine institutions report both the number of inmates discharged (27,530) and the number discharged that could read and write (27,385). This would indicate that 145, or 0.5 per cent. of those discharged from these institutions, were illiterate. This is considerably below the average for the United States, although there are probably differences in the definition of illiteracy in each group.

THE PENNSYLVANIA STATE COLLEGE

THE voters of Pennsylvania will on November 6 be asked to approve a bond issue of $8,000,000 for the erection of buildings at Pennsylvania State College. A bulletin issued by the college states that:

For years the need for expansion to meet demands made by the people has been felt keenly at the State College. Thousands of student applicants have been refused admission in the past ten years, and the valuable research and extension services of the college that reach every county and community in the state have been handicapped, all because building space is so limited.

The State College plea for buildings through the bond-issue method is to be based largely on the fact that this method will provide an immediate and assured means for the construction of buildings, resulting in economies that otherwise might not be available. A definite building program has been completed by trustees and is now ready to be put under way. A steady and definite income over a period of years is an important factor in efficiency, trustees declare.

Hearty endorsement of the State College bond-issue has come from more than a score of state-wide organizations, including the State Grange, the State Education Association and many farmer and industrial groups. Students and alumni are prepared to distribute information in every county, their goal being not less than a million favorable votes for the constitutional amendment.

Any movement that assures increased service not only to the agricultural groups but to commerce and industry as well is bound to win approval, it is pointed out by those who have become familiar with the State College situation and its needs.

Fifteen years ago most of the work of the State College was confined to the campus. An occasional printed bulletin told of agricultural research work. Then came the establishment of the agricultural extension service, which slowly but surely convinced farmers that in the county agents they had real friends and progressive representatives of the college right at their own front doors. There followed visits by specialists from the college, demonstrations were started on farms, boys and girls became interested in calves, pigs and truck crops, until to-day thousands of rural communities are proud of new records, new achievements and better farming conditions where frequent mention is made of State College and its service.

SALARIES AND TUITION FEES AT LEHIGH UNIVERSITY

DURING the collegiate year of 1928–29, the tuition fees of students of Lehigh University will have reached a point where they just equal the salaries of the professors and instructors, according to a statement issued by the university. The statement points out that the administrative expenses and the cost of operation and maintenance of the physical plant, as well as the many other items of expense incurred in the operation of the university, are paid principally from income from endowment and from a few additional sources. The salary item is said to amount to approximately half the total expenditures of the university, the other half being expended principally on administration and operation.

While the administrative costs and those of operation and maintenance of the physical plant are the two largest items which are paid from sources other than tuition, there are a number of other items for which considerable amounts are appropriated, such as the student health service, the library, the institute of research and general welfare and entertainment.

The funds of the board of control of athletics at Lehigh are entirely separate from the other funds of the university.

The expenditure for the operation and maintenance of the physical plant has no bearing on the cost of new construction now in progress on the campus, the cost of which approaches two million dollars. The two principal building projects under way are the James Ward Packard electrical and mechanical engineering laboratory, the gift of the late founder of the motor car company bearing his name, and the large addition to the Lucy Packer Linderman Memorial Library. The former will cost more than a million dollars and the latter, which will be paid for by alumni and trustees, will exceed half that amount. An entire new heating plant is now being installed and will be ready for operation by October 1.

During the last five years Lehigh University has received more than $2,600,000 from its alumni in the form of gifts. This sum does not include an additional million which was given by persons other than alumni in a drive for increased endowment. The total gifts during the past year amounted to $350,000. During this five-year period nearly 60 per cent. of the alumni have participated with contributions. The largest single gift was made by the late James Ward Packard, of Warren, Ohio. It amounted to more than $1,200,000. In addition, Mr. Packard made substantial bequests in his will.

THE BOSTON PUBLIC SCHOOLS

The public schools of Boston opened officially on September 13. It was estimated that approximately 131,500 children would be in attendance.

While the exact figures are not known and will not be known until the actual figures are available some time in October, this estimate is based on the enrolment for last year, to which has been added 1,500, the anticipated increase for this year.

The increase is expected to be largely in the high and Latin schools. In these schools an enrolment of 24,400 is anticipated; in the Teachers College, 800; elementary and intermediate schools, 95,500; kindergartens, 9,000, and special schools, 1,800.

The number of teachers will be 4,450, an increase of 100 over last year, and three new schools will begin work, increasing the total number of school buildings to 300.

Robert B. Masterson, former member of the board of examiners of the school committee, will be in charge of the boys' unit of Memorial High School in Roxbury, opening for the first time. Herbert T. Rich, former head of the German department at the Public Latin School, will take the place of Frederic A. Tupper at Brighton High. The latter has reached the age limit after serving as headmaster of that school for many years.

Charles H. Early, former submaster in charge of the Damon School in Readville, will be the new principal of the Wendell Phillips School in the West End, taking the place of Cyrus B. Collins, whose retirement because of having reached the age limit was announced last June.

The new schools that will open are the three-room boys' unit of the Memorial High School in Roxbury; Patrick F. Lyndon School in West Roxbury, named in memory of Reverend Patrick F. Lyndon, who died in 1878 and who was a member of the school committee in 1875; Henry Abrahams School, Jamaica Plain, named after Henry Abrahams, prominent for his communal welfare and labor work in this city and who was a member of the school committee from 1917 to 1919. He died in 1923.

The Lyndon School is a thirteen-room building, which will house grades one to six and kindergartens. Henry Abrahams School will open as a five-room unit, for use by grades one, two, four and kindergarten. This building is intended eventually to be an eleven-room unit.

The new Hyde Park High School will not open until October or November.

REGISTRATION IN THE NEW YORK CITY SCHOOLS

There was a registration of more than 1,050,000 children for the school year opening on September 10 in 900 elementary and secondary schools throughout the five New York city boroughs. Tabulation of registration figures show an estimated increase or about 25,000 pupils over the 1,034,822 registered last year.

Eleven new school buildings with a total capacity of 16,650 have been opened to handle the increase. Approximately 400 teachers have been appointed in addition to the 34,000 required last year.

In response to a plea from Mr. O'Shea, 40,000 parents, members of the 152 Parents' Associations affiliated with the United Parents' Association of Greater New York, cooperated in obtaining early registration.

"A pupil who enters school late—even one day late—is likely to miss some essential instruction in a new subject," Dr. O'Shea wrote the association. "Although such omissions are frequently caught by instructors, the loss of the first few hours' class work may cause the pupil to fail and be forced to repeat a whole term."

In the evening schools, the attendance for the coming year was estimated at 70,000 by Morris E. Siegel, director of evening and continuation schools. The estimate included 30,000 for the evening high schools, 25,000 for elementary and 15,000 for grade schools.

New schools to be opened this month with the number of sittings follow:

Schools	Sittings
P. S. 152, Manhattan	1,398
P. S. 14 (addition), Bronx	1,032
P. S. 90, Bronx	2,329
Theodore Roosevelt H. S., Bronx	4,620
P. S. 104 (addition), Brooklyn	1,250
P. S. 225, Brooklyn	1,348
P. S. 14 (addition), Queens	884
P. S. 29, Queens	1,078
P. S. 45 (addition), Queens	1,029
P. S. 113, Queens	703
P. S. 30 (addition), Richmond	985

The annual decrease in the number of children enrolling in the Manhattan schools will continue this year, it was said. Eighty teachers have been transferred to Queens and the Bronx.

APPOINTMENTS IN THE CHICAGO SCHOOLS

UPON recommendation of Superintendent William J. Bogan, the Chicago school board has made a large number of transfers and new appointments in the school system. The following are recorded in the *School Board Journal:*

Chicago Normal College: (Salary, $8,500 per year.)

Butler Laughlin, principal of Parker Senior High School, was chosen to succeed Dr. William B. Owen (deceased) as president.

Assistant Superintendents: (Salary, $10,000 per year.)

Benjamin F. Buck, principal of Senn Senior High School, was named for the vacancy caused by Mr. Bogan's elevation to the superintendency. Mr. Buck will be in charge of junior and senior high schools, continuation schools, etc.

Isabella Dolton, principal of the Farragut Junior High School supplanted Mr. Morgan G. Hogge as assistant superintendent in charge of evening schools, Americanization classes, community centers, summer-vacation schools, etc.

Charles J. Lunak, principal of Hirsch Junior High School, supplanted Mr. Charles D. Lowry, and assumes responsibility for the annual school budget, buildings and repairs, research, etc.

James E. McDade, principal of the Wentworth Elementary School, supplanted Elizabeth Murphy, and will be in charge of truancy, defective children, special subjects, etc.

Rosa A. Pesta, principal of the West Pullman School, succeeds Clarence E. DeButts, in charge of the assignment of teachers and principals, the listing of text-books and supplies, rules, etc.

District Superintendents: (Salary, $6,500 per year.)

Jane A. Neil, principal of the Spaulding School for Crippled Children, was placed in charge of the city's schools for cripples.

Lillian Tobin, principal of the Mozart Elementary School.

James E. Bache, principal of the continuation schools.

Special Assistant to the Superintendent: (Salary, $5,720.)

Fred J. Lane, principal of the Jenner Elementary School.

Heads of Bureaus: (Salary, $6,000 per year.)

J. Lewis Browne, organist, choirmaster and musical composer, named director of music.

Florence Swain, named director of household arts.

Eston V. Tubbs, principal of the Chase Elementary School, named director of curriculum.

Don C. Rogers, principal of the Smyth Elementary School, named director of the bureau of building survey.

Senior-High-School Principalships: (Salary ranges from $4,300 to $5,700.)

Thomas E. Johnson, principal of the Haugen Elementary School, to Medill High School.

Junior-High-School Principalships: (Salary ranges from $4,600 to $5,400.)

William T. McCoy, from principalship of the Earle Elementary School to that of the Curtis Junior High School.

Bertha Armbruster, from principal of the Hilton Elementary to the Farragut Junior High.

Edward Wildeman, from principal of the Shields Elementary to the Kelly Junior High.

Daniel J. Beeby, from principal of the Oglesby Elementary to the Hirsch Junior High.

Elementary Principalships: (Salary ranges from $3,000 to $4,800.)

Laurence G. Collins to the Hamline School; Mina S. Rogers to the Motley; Harold H. Postel to the Drake; Ada M. Andrews to the Plamondon; Josephine K. Liska to the Haven; Howard Bradley Smith to the Greene; Earl L. Koehler to the Walsh, and Mary I. Reynolds to the Onahan. Nellie F. Ryan was elected principal of a continuation school.

EDUCATIONAL NOTES AND NEWS

Rear Admiral Samuel S. Robinson has assumed the superintendency of the United States Naval Academy at Annapolis, succeeding Rear Admiral Louis Nulton.

It is reported that Dr. George R. Throop will continue for another year as acting chancellor of Washington University at St. Louis.

Professor W. W. Packer, of the Missouri Teachers College at Warrensburg, has been appointed principal of the State Teachers College at Alva, Oklahoma, to succeed Dr. J. P. Battenberg.

Ralph C. Jenkins, superintendent of schools at Putnam, Connecticut, has become principal of the Normal Training School at Johnson, Vermont.

W. Spader Willis, principal of the Newark, New Jersey, Normal School, has retired after serving for forty-three years.

Professor Henry Brayton Gardner, head of the department of economics at Brown University, and Professor James Q. Dealey, head of the department of political and social science, have retired from active service.

Dr. Charles Wharton, assistant director of physical education at the University of Pennsylvania, has been unanimously nominated by the Democratic state convention as the Democratic candidate for governor.

The honorary degree of doctor of philosophy has been conferred on Professor F. W. Taussig, of Harvard University, by the University of Bonn in recognition of his eminent work in the field of economics.

The University of St. Simon has conferred the honorary doctorate of laws on The Honorable David E. Kaufman, minister to Bolivia. This is the first time that this degree has been conferred on an American.

Dr. George D. Olds, president emeritus of Amherst College, and Mrs. Olds have returned to Amherst after a trip to Europe, which included a visit to Russia for the study of its educational and scientific institutions.

Dr. Hamilton Holt, president of Rollins College, Winter Park, Florida, was the guest of honor on September 6 at a dinner given by alumni and students of the college at the Fraternities Club, New York City.

President Coolidge, upon invitation of the League of Nations' Secretariat, has appointed Professor T. S. Adams, of Yale University, as expert to attend an international meeting on double taxation and tax evasion opening at Geneva on October 22.

The engineering staff of the survey of Land-Grant Colleges has been increased by the appointment of A. A. Potter, dean of the engineering school of Purdue University, Lafayette, Indiana, and Arthur N. Johnson, dean of the engineering school of the University of Maryland, College Park, Maryland.

Albert F. Vandergrift, head of the department of mathematics of Belmont High School, Los Angeles, has been appointed a member of the Committee on International Relations in the National Education Association.

An advisory committee of experts has been asked to cooperate with the new Chicago city school administration, under a plan initiated jointly by Superintendent William S. Bogan and President H. Wallace Caldwell. This committee consists of Walter Dill Scott, president of Northwestern University; Frederick Woodward, acting president of the University of Chicago; David H. Kinley, president of the University of Illinois; Henry M. Raymond, dean of Armour Institute of Technology; Thomas S. Levan, president of DePaul University; George N. Carmen, president of the Lewis Institute, and Dr. Robert Kelly, president of Loyola University.

Dr. George E. Carrothers, of Rollins College, Florida, has joined the faculty of the school of education of the University of Michigan. Before going to Florida Dr. Carrothers worked at the Ohio State University.

Dr. T. V. Smith and Dr. E. A. Burtt have been promoted to full professorships at the University of Chicago.

DR. LEONARD CARMICHAEL has been promoted to be professor of psychology and director of the laboratory at Brown University.

DR. ROLAND CHARLES TRAVIS has been appointed research associate in psychology with the rank of assistant professor at Yale University.

AT Hamline University, St. Paul, Minnesota, Dr. Paul E. Johnson, of Boston University, has been appointed head of the department of philosophy, and Dr. Alfred R. Root, of the University of Iowa, acting head of the department of psychology in the absence of Professor C. F. Echterbecker, who has been granted sabbatical leave for research and study in Berlin.

DEAN R. P. BROOKS, of the school of commerce of the University of Georgia, has been appointed director of the bureau of business research at that university.

MISS MARIE MELZER has been appointed dean of women at the school of commerce, accounts and finance of the University of Denver. Miss Melzer was graduated from the university in 1921. Since then she has been traveling around the world. She spent two years in the South Pacific Ocean as secretary to the vice-president of the Pacific Commercial Company and taught in Hawaii for a time.

MISS JESSICA FOSTER, formerly acting dean of women at the Ohio State University, has been appointed to the position of adviser of women at Long Island University, Brooklyn, New York.

THE nursery play school established as an experiment last winter at Drexel Institute, Philadelphia, will be made a permanent feature of the curriculum and Miss Myra de Haven Woodruff, a member of the staff of the nursery school at Vassar College, has been added to the Drexel faculty and will be director of the play school.

EDWARD F. MCCULLOUGH, now principal of the Woodrow Wilson Junior High School, Pasadena, California, is now principal in charge of special teachers in that city in the department of Child Welfare and Guidance.

JOSEPH G. COWELL, sculptor and painter, has been elected associate director in the Designers' Art School of Boston. He has been connected with the school since its foundation.

DR. J. E. W. WALLIN, director of the bureau of special education of Miami University, has been loaned until January to the Ohio State Department of Education to make an investigation of the problems of special education and the examination of handicapped children which the state must solve. Since its establishment under Dr. Wallin in 1921, the bureau has made over 5,000 clinical examinations of mentally handicapped children in all sections of the state, and has had a registration of 975 students from about fifteen states and Canada.

PROFESSOR RALPH MASON BLAKE has leave of absence from the University of Washington during the next academic year, when he will be visiting lecturer at Harvard University.

DR. LAMBERT L. JACKSON, formerly assistant commissioner of education for New Jersey, has accepted the position of first assistant superintendent in charge of instruction in the Newark school system.

L. E. CHENOWETH, Kern County, California, superintendent of schools, has accepted appointment as Bakersfield city superintendent at a salary of $6,000 a year for a four-year term. James Parker has accepted reappointment as assistant superintendent for a four-year term at $4,000.

IRA C. LANDIS, assistant superintendent of the schools of Riverside, California, has been promoted to the superintendency.

CARL B. MOORE has resigned as superintendent of schools at Fairbury, Illinois, and will go to Urbana, which will be his headquarters as traveling salesman for a school-supply company.

DR. PAUL R. RIDER, associate professor of mathematics in Washington University, has been given a year's leave of absence, to enable him to accept a Sterling Research Fellowship at Yale University.

PROFESSOR ROGER H. WELLS, who has been in Germany for the past year studying German city governments on a Guggenheim Fellowship, is returning in October to resume his work at Bryn Mawr College.

A NUMBER of visiting scientific men will work in the research department of biochemistry of the University of California during the coming academic year. These include Dr. Werner Schmidt, one of the seven men sent from Germany to America each year by the International Education Board; Professor W. M. Hoskins, associate professor of chemistry at the University of Nevada; C. V. Smythe, who for the past two years has been connected with the Institute for Animal Nutrition at Pennsylvania State College, and O. E. Emerson, from Hawaii, who has been awarded a university fellowship in biochemistry to work under Dr. L. R. Cerecedo.

MRS. EVANGELINE LINDBERGH has sailed for Turkey, where she has accepted an appointment to act as visiting professor of chemistry at the Constantinople Woman's College. She was accompanied by Miss Alice Morrow, sister of Dwight W. Morrow, United States Ambassador to Mexico. Miss Morrow has accepted an appointment to act as hostess at the same institution.

WALTER BERGEN CRANE, principal of the Metropolitan High School in Los Angeles, president of the California Teachers Association, died on August 3, at the age of forty-eight years.

THE general session of the eleventh annual Conference of the State Normal Schools was held at Bridgewater, Massachusetts, on September 7. Officers were elected as follows: Miss M. Harriette Bishop, Worcester, *president;* Dr. Stewart Foster, Framingham, *vice-president;* Miss Anna Crowell, Hyannis, *treasurer;* Miss Grace Pickett, Westfield, *secretary.*

THE congress has provided increased salaries throughout the Bureau of Education, except that of the commissioner. According to the *School Board Journal,* the increases vary from $60 per year to $400. Two specialists now receive $5,800 per year, and two $5,600 per year. There are nine specialists in so-called Grade 5, receiving $4,600 to $4,800 per year; seven in Grade 3, receiving $3,200 or $3,300; seven in Grade 2, at $2,600 to $2,900, and one at $2,100. The chief clerk, who is also acting commissioner whenever the commissioner is away from Washington, receives $4,800, and the chief editor, $3,500. In addition, there are in the Washington office a total of 58 men and women in clerical work of all sorts, including stenographers, typists, statistical clerks, mail clerks, library assistants, etc. Salaries for these 58 vary from $1,380 to $2,800 per year; 20 of them in Grade 3, at $1,620 to $1,860 per year; 29 in Grades 4, 5 and 6; the other 12 in lower grades. The total amount of money necessary to cover these increases is $18,460. The average increase in salary is, therefore, close to $200 per year for each employee of the bureau.

REPRESENTATIVES of Maine colleges and of the Associated Industries of Maine, at a recent meeting at Lewiston, discussed plans to install schools in four educational centers in the state for the instruction of selected foremen and second hands in the economics of industry and management. According to preliminary plans schools will be established near the University of Maine, Bowdoin College, Bates College and Colby College, with professors from these institutions in charge. Groups will be limited to fifteen or twenty-five students each.

PROTESTS against the action of the executive council of the American Federation of Labor for its recent decision to advise affiliated unions to withdraw support from Brookwood Labor College at Katonah, N. Y., have led President William Green to notify the Brookwood Board of Directors that final action will be delayed until the members of the council have had ample opportunity to acquaint themselves with the protests filed. Whereas the council has held that the college teaches doctrines opposed to those of the American Federation of Labor, A. J. Muste, of the college faculty, says that as an educational institution the college does not teach any particular doctrine. The college authorities take the stand that theirs is a fight for freedom in education.

The Christian Science Monitor prints the following: "Following a visit by the chief of Harvard's college yard police, and after several complaints from neighbors, the Harvard Liberal Club has been ordered closed indefinitely by Matthew Luce, director of morals of Harvard University. The Harvard Liberal Club, which has been mentioned at various times in connection with radical movements both within and without the college, was the summer residence of five graduate students, all of whom have now moved elsewhere. The direct reason for the 'padlock' was given as the presence of a young woman unchaperoned in the library of the club, contrary to college regulations. This disciplinary measure is regarded by some members of the club as a move to impede further radical movements on their part. Others, however, point out that there are no club activities during the summer months, and that after the beginning of the school term the club will still exist, even though its clubhouse is closed."

Upward of 275,000 public school children in Philadelphia have resumed their school work, many of them in new and improved quarters and several thousand fewer of them under the compulsion of attending part-time classes. This year the night schools began simultaneously with the day classes, and afford opportunities for adults to the number of more than 30,000. With the new schools now ready and with the four buildings which are expected to be finished by December, the public schools are in better shape, so far as accommodations are concerned, than for some years. They have not yet caught up with the increase in school population, but they are making good progress.

The New Jersey Department of Education estimates that the army of boys and girls returning to studies this month numbers more than 500,000 and that an additional 125,000 are entering school for the first time. These pupils are housed in 2,300 buildings and 26,000 teachers are required for their instruction. Some students will attend one-room buildings, which are fast disappearing before centralized township schools, but the greater number will be found in schools that are modern in every respect. As a result of the centralization and the desire of boys and girls living in the rural districts to gain high-school education, more than 50,000 children are transported in buses to and from school daily.

The establishment of several new Catholic parish schools is announced by the Reverend Dr. John J. Bonner, superintendent, in connection with the opening of the Catholic schools in Philadelphia and throughout the diocese for the registration of pupils in elementary grades and first year students in high schools. It is estimated that about 87,000 children will be enrolled in the Catholic schools of the city. The five diocesan high schools are the Northeast Boys, West Philadelphia Boys, Boys Catholic, John W. Hallahan Catholic and the West Philadelphia Catholic Girls High Schools. The two parish high schools are St. John the Baptist High and St. John the Baptist High School for girls.

The trustees of the La Verne Noyes Scholarship Foundation, 2500 Roosevelt Road, Chicago, have announced an additional list of twenty-seven schools where world war veterans and their children may obtain free tuition, making in all sixty schools from which applicants for scholarships may choose. Depending on the needs of the applicant, all, or part, tuition is paid by the foundation for general courses, medical, engineering, teaching and other special branches. In all, 1,200 scholarships are offered. Mr. Noyes established in 1918 a scholarship foundation of $2,000,000 at the University of Chicago. The trustees now are Lewis C. Walker, Frederick L. Dole and Joseph J. Fraser.

The first unit of the two and a half million building program at the University of Tennessee is now in process of erection. The building is for physics and geology, and with its furnishings, will cost about $200,000. Plans for a chemistry building are under way, and other buildings projected include a program calling for about $500,000 annually for the next five years.

In addition to other bequests the late Dr. Joseph Schneider, Milwaukee, left $271,000 to the University of Würzburg, Germany.

By the will of the late Lord Haldane, £6,000 is divided among the Universities of Edinburgh and Bristol, Birbeck College and the British Institute of Adult Education, and £1,000 is left to the University of Göttingen, which he attended as a student.

An Associated Press dispatch reports that a course in the "history of journalism" was opened recently at the Perugia University by order of Premier Mussolini. The university offered Premier Mussolini the honor of being the first holder of the chair, but he declined in favor of Deputy Paolo Orano, who is a militant newspaper man, 35 years of age. The first lecture is entitled "Toward a Historical Doctrine of Journalism." The announcement of the new department was accompanied by an official statement in which it was described as an indication of the highest consideration in which the régime holds journalism and of the profoundly revolutionary transformation undergone by Italian newspaperdom under Fascism.

SPECIAL CORRESPONDENCE

THE TEACHERS OF THE COLUMBIA UNIVERSITY SUMMER SESSION

One explanation of the popularity of the summer sessions held at Columbia University, which each year attract more than thirteen thousand students and teachers from all states of the Union and from foreign lands, is to be found in the caliber of the instructional staff. A study of the men of science who are giving instruction in the various courses which are offered is indeed illuminating. Of the 582 persons teaching in the 1928 Columbia summer session the names of eighty are to be found in the fourth edition of the Biographical Directory of American Men of Science.

This edition of the directory, which was published in December 1927, contains the records of about 13,000 men of science—both men and women are included under this heading. It is believed by the editors of the directory that the entries are tolerably complete for those in North America who have carried on research work in the natural and exact sciences. Some are admitted "who are supposed to have advanced science by teaching, by administrative work or by the preparation of textbooks and compilations." There are also some whose work has been chiefly in engineering, medicine or other applied sciences, and a few whose work is in education, economics and other subjects not commonly included under the natural and exact sciences. "The names are included because they are supposed to represent work that has contributed to the advancement of pure science—the term being used in the narrower sense—or because they are found in the membership lists of certain national societies."

Just about one out of every seven persons, ranging in rank from associate or instructor to full professor, teaching in the summer session, is recognized as a contributor to the advancement of science. A similar study of "Who's Who in America" or of other reference works in the non-scientific fields would undoubtedly swell the total of outstanding figures on the staff and give further indication of the attractiveness of the opportunities available at Columbia University during the summer.

In the directory a star is prefixed to the subject of research in the case of about one thousand notes, indicating that the subject of the biographical sketch is one of a thousand students of the natural and exact sciences in the United States whose work is supposed to be the most important. A star appears in the biography of twenty of the eighty persons listed in the directory, and sixteen of the twenty are members of the regular instructional staff of the university.

In analyzing the distribution of the eighty outstanding men of science it is found that the largest group is in the field of chemistry, fourteen of whom are teaching chemistry and one chemical engineering. Pure psychology follows with nine, while eight others are in the field of educational psychology. Physics musters nine and mathematics six. In the natural sciences there are five in zoology, four in geology and geography, two each in biology, botany and physiology, one in anthropology, and two are classified under the general heading of the natural sciences. Medicine contributes six, education four, electrical engineering two, and astronomy and nutrition one each.

It is interesting to note that one of the chemists, a college teacher in his field, is giving work in college administration under the title of "Educational Problems of the College," that one of the educational psychologists is to be found in the law department, giving a course on the "Psychology of Legal Institutions," and that one of the botanists, by profession the director of a museum, is teaching the "Principles of Museum Administration and Public Instruction."

A Ph.D. degree is held by sixty-two of the eighty, an M.D. by five, and a British D.Sc. by one. Of the balance six have the M.A. degree, two E.E., one Ch.E., and two B.S. Only one of the group does not possess a college degree and he had attended a university for several years.

Sixty-six are of professorial rank; thirty-seven of them are full professors, seventeen associate professors and twelve assistant professors. There are also among the college teachers eight instructors, one lecturer and one associate. Two of the others are museum directors and the third is a computer and associate mathematician with the U. S. Coast and Geodetic Survey.

It is natural to expect that a large proportion of the summer session teachers would be drawn from the regular instructional staff of Columbia University, but it bespeaks well of that staff that sixty-two of its members teaching in the summer session are among this select list of eighty. Dartmouth contributes three and North Carolina two, while one comes from each of the following institutions: Agnes Scott, California Institute of Technology, the College of the City of New York, Denison, Harvard, Massachusetts Institute of Technology, Minnesota, Syracuse and Wyoming in the United States and Toronto in Canada. Of the eighteen from other institutions eight had previously taught at Columbia and two of the others had pursued graduate work at that institution.

The ages of the group range from twenty-five to sixty-three, the average age being just slightly above forty-five with the Q1 at 38+ and the Q3 at 52+. Within age groups four were below thirty, five between thirty and thirty-five, thirteen between thirty-five and forty, fifteen between forty and forty-five, thirteen between forty-five and fifty, fourteen between fifty and fifty-five, eleven between fifty-five and sixty, and three above sixty.

It has already been stated that sixty-two possessed the Ph.D. degree. Of these forty received that degree from Columbia, five from Chicago, four from Harvard, three from Cornell, two each from Johns Hopkins and Minnesota, and one each from Illinois, Pennsylvania, Syracuse and Yale in the United States and from Leipzig and Munich abroad. Two of the five M.D. degrees were from Columbia, the others being from Chicago, Iowa and Syracuse. The D.Sc. degree was awarded by the University of London. The two E.E. degrees came from Columbia and Syracuse, the Ch.E. from Columbia, and the B.S. from Massachusetts Institute of Technology. Four of the six M.A. degrees were from Columbia and the other two were from Dartmouth.

In the light of James McKeen Cattell's studies of the distribution of American men of science according to place of birth it is interesting to note the distribution of this group on that basis. New York leads with fourteen and is followed by Ohio with seven, by Indiana with six, by Massachusetts and New Jersey with five each, by Illinois with four, by Maryland, Nebraska and Pennsylvania with three each, by Michigan, Missouri, Kansas, New Hampshire, Virginia and Wisconsin with two each, and by Arkansas, Connecticut, Delaware, North Carolina, Texas, Utah, Vermont and Wyoming with one each. Nine of the group are foreign born: Three in England and one each in Scotland, Canada, Germany, Austria, Poland and the Baltic Provinces. Birth statistics are lacking in the sketch of one of the group. By sectional distribution: Thirty-one were born in the North Atlantic states; nine of them in New England states; seven in the South Atlantic states; twenty-eight in the North Central states; two in the South Central states, and two in the Western states.

Archie M. Palmer

DISCUSSION

SCHOLARSHIP, ATTENDANCE AND DEPORTMENT

The relation between scholarship and school attendance, on the one hand, and scholarship and conduct, on the other, is one that interests school principals to no small extent. Time and again, pupils are urged to be regular in attendance and watchful of their conduct, because both of these in one way or another affect scholarship. There is no question that attendance does, though whether the relation is uniform is something that can be answered by figures only. Similarly, the reasonable assumption exists that the pupil who is not interested in his school work is usually the one who is most mischievous in the classroom, and most prone to disregard school rules. As far as the writer is aware, however, no figures on this subject have thus far been published.

With respect to school attendance, it is obvious that even when a pupil is absent one day, he actually misses two recitations: the recitation of the day when he is absent, and the recitation of the day when he returns, since on that day also he is usually unprepared to recite.

In order to ascertain to what extent the two assumptions mentioned above are true, the writer made a careful analysis of the scholarship, attendance and deportment records of the two classes which were graduated from his school[1] in June, 1927, and January, 1928. Complete attendance and deportment records are kept at this school for every pupil; the former in the customary way; the latter, however, is rather unique. Instead of sending pupils to the office when they misbehave, the teachers demerit them, either by giving one, two or three demerits for the offense, depending upon the severity of its nature. Among the "offenses" for which pupils are demerited may be mentioned such as creating disturbance in the classroom, dishonesty, insolence, coming late to class without a written excuse, failing to bring textbooks to classroom, failing to keep appointments after school, eating or creating disturbance in corridors, cutting class, etc. The offending pupil is instructed by his teacher to report the necessary demerits, and these are noted on his permanent record card in the office.

The matter of determining the relationship between the three factors was very simple. All that one had to do was to set up the scholarship scale in multiple units of 5, as is shown in the first column of Table I. Then, note the final scholarship average of each pupil in each of his eight semesters and record in the proper

[1] Bulkeley High School.

TABLE I

Scholarship grades	Average No. times absent per semester	Average No. demerits per semester	No. cases
95–100	....	....	......
90– 94	1.5	.1	15
85– 89	1.8	.7	62
80– 84	1.5	.8	116
75– 79	1.9	1.5	159
70– 74	1.8	3.0	227
65– 69	2.2	3.5	272
60– 64	2.6	4.8	265
55– 59	4.3	8.5	141
50– 54	4.1	7.9	113
45– 49	4.9	10.2	47
40– 44	5.1	7.1	15
35– 39	4.4	10.9	9
30– 34	21.7	2.7	3
Av.	2.6	4.1	1444 (Total)

level his absences and demerits for each semester. Dividing the total number of absences or demerits by the number of cases in each scholarship level gave the respective averages, as is shown in columns 2 and 3.

Thus, there were fifteen cases of final scholarship averages which ranked between ninety and ninety-four. The average number of absences per semester for the pupils in that group was 1.5. The average number of demerits for each pupil per semester in that group was 0.1. There were sixty-two cases of final scholarship averages which ranged between eighty-five and eighty-nine. The average number of absences per semester for the pupils in that group was 1.8; the average number of demerits was 0.7. And so on clear down the scale until we come to the pupils whose final scholarship average, for instance, was between 45 and 49. There were forty-seven of such cases; the average number of absences per semester in that group was 4.9; the average number of demerits, 10.2.

A careful study of the table will show conclusively that there is a most direct relationship between attendance and scholarship, as well as between conduct and scholarship. This study bears out similar findings with respect to the first two factors reported in the February issue of *The School Review*. The present study was based on the complete school records of 183 graduates, and represents a total of 1,444 cases. Generally speaking, the vagaries of the teachers giving demerits—that is to say, passing judgment on conduct—were not extreme; for practically all these pupils had passed fully three of their four years under the same group of teachers—teachers who had been long in the service and who did not give demerits except for good cause.

Let no one make the mistake of drawing the conclusion from the above figures that scholarship depends on attendance only. For it is more than likely that the conditions, physical and otherwise, which interfere with perfect attendance, also hinder high scholastic attainment. Nevertheless, the relationship is too uniform not to force upon one the conclusion that frequent absence from school, whatever the cause may be, is in part responsible for poor achievement. Similarly, the poor scholar is also the poor school citizen; or it may be *vice versa*.

GUSTAVE A. FEINGOLD

BULKELEY HIGH SCHOOL,
HARTFORD, CONN.

EDUCATING EFFICIENT UNDERLINGS

THE writer passed to members of the faculty of the University of Idaho a paper asking each professor to enumerate the outstanding characteristics of his three best students. The characteristics given were then arranged in order, according to the number of times each was mentioned. While the amount of data collected was very small, it is probably typical, and hence suggestive. The results indicated that, in the minds of these professors, attention and industry stood at the head of the list; next in order came promptness and neatness; third in rank came interest, accuracy and good expression; fourth in rank came thoroughness, system, enthusiasm and confidence.

These are all desirable characteristics, and any student possessing them is practically sure to receive a good grade. Any one would know that without asking faculty opinion. These statements, however, are interesting when compared with the characteristics rarely mentioned. Each of the following was mentioned only once: appreciation, conscientiousness, discrimination, earnestness, courtesy, thoughtfulness, resourcefulness, stability, loyalty, originality, leadership and ability to get along with others. The following were mentioned twice: ambition, openmindedness, balance, independence, imagination.

The placement bureau of the university asked the superintendents of the state what characteristics they most desired in those whom they expected to employ as teachers. Tact, sympathy, loyalty, cooperation, judgment, honesty, cheerfulness and scholarship were named by almost every superintendent. Reports from business men, on file but not tabulated, tally almost completely with these.

A comparison of the qualities chiefly desired by instructors with those chiefly desired by employers forces us to ask the question, "Are we trying to develop men and women of the highest type, or are we trying merely to develop receptacles of erudition capable of retaining and returning intact whatever is given to them?"

The qualities mentioned as most important by the professors will make efficient workers under direction, but without some additional strong qualities will not make leaders of thought nor of action, will not make creators, nor men and women of pronounced success. Perhaps receptacles of erudition are all the college can produce. Perhaps the qualities which make leaders are not fostered in regular college work, but are merely native endowments which survive college requirements. Perhaps our job is to educate efficient underlings and trust to nature to produce a few superior human beings.

Erudition is easy to pass on and easy to measure. It is a necessary part of education. The fault is not so much in what we do as in what we leave undone. The greatest of the unsolved problems in education is how to teach men. We know better how to teach subjects than we know how to teach men and women. Books on methods of teaching usually refer to methods of teaching subjects. A few great educational theorists have stressed the other side, but it is hard to get many to use their theories. It is so much easier to deal with the abstract and the formal than it is with the concrete and the human. The small amount of data just presented shows the need of a change of emphasis. I am optimistic enough to believe it will come, though it will no doubt come slowly.

UNIVERSITY OF IDAHO J. F. MESSENGER

QUOTATIONS

THE NEW YORK CITY SCHOOLS

IF registration for the public schools, now under way, shows the same annual increase of approximately 20,000 which it has maintained during the last five years there will be something like 1,045,000 pupils on the rolls of elementary, high and special schools at the beginning of the new school year. The average attendance for 1928–29 will be about 100,000 less if the precedent of last year is maintained. For the support of this school army of close to a million the Board of Education has adopted a budget of nearly $129,000,000, exclusive of $33,000,000 appropriated for new construction. Critics of the board's bookkeeping insist that in reckoning the total cost of the school system there should be included $27,000,000 disbursed through other city departments in the form of interest on construction bonds, teachers' pensions and light and water service. The city's total outlay on the education of its children would thus be approaching the $200,000,000 mark.

The part-time problem has not yet been solved. Last September the number of part-time pupils was 66,381. For the new year the board announces the opening of eleven schools with 16,658 seats, which will probably fall short by a few thousands of taking care of the increased enrolment. The situation is somewhat better than the figures would suggest, to the extent that, relatively, part time is more prevalent in the high schools. The hardship of an irregular school day falls more heavily on the older children. In the elementary schools a year ago one pupil in forty-five was on part time. In the high schools it was one pupil in seven. It is also in the high schools that attendance has grown most rapidly. The annual increase in enrolment for the entire school system would be less than 2 per cent., but the high-school pupils last year showed an increase of 7 per cent. over the preceding year. The indication is that a greater number of elementary school pupils enter high school. Twice a year, in January and June, the schools send out 60,000 graduates.

The present registration is expected to show the same trend in geographical redistribution that has been under way for a decade. Last year Manhattan had a loss of more than 12,000 pupils, whereas Brooklyn and the Bronx gained 10,000 apiece and Queens added no less than 13,000. Of the eleven new school buildings only one is in Manhattan, in the far-north Dyckman section. A number of districts have lost population to the extent of permitting the abandonment of schools. Though local Manhattan pride may suffer, the city as a whole should be grateful for the boon of modern accommodations in the newer and less congested districts. The city's million children of to-day, receiving instruction from an army of 33,000 teachers, and financed by almost a $200,000,000 budget, enjoy the great advantage of incomparably better physical surroundings than a generation ago.—*The New York Times.*

LAST year, in the public schools of this city, one dollar in every seventy-five dollars spent went into "health education." This includes the sums spent on baths, community and recreation centers, athletic activities and playgrounds.

On one day in the year, known as "Health Day," every pupil is examined for external signs of disease and for easily found defects. It is estimated that as a result of this one examination one pupil in each ten is relieved of physical defects which might otherwise develop into permanent and in many instances serious handicaps.

The assertion is made, and it may be true, that the schools of New York are as solicitous of the health and do as much to promote the physical well being of pupils as the schools of any other city in the world.

We are not meditating criticism of the good work now done in our schools in this important direction.

We are wondering what the return would be if, instead of spending one dollar in each seventy-five dollars on health, the school system could double or treble its outlay on health.

Beginning Monday more than a million young people will come into our schools for approximately five hours each day during five days of each week.

There is no other place that we know of in the world where so fine an opportunity exists to do fundamental health work on a similarly large scale.

Our courts, prisons, hospitals and other corrective institutions are costing each year an increased sum, staggering in its total, to cope with various phases of mental, moral and physical disease while this great fountain source of possible betterment is receiving by no means the amount of attention we might profitably give it.

When shall we realize the importance of making every school a complete health center?—*The New York American.*

EDUCATIONAL RESEARCH AND STATISTICS

FACTORS CONDITIONING THE SUCCESS OF SCHOOL SURVEYS[1]

THE purpose of this article is to set forth both the factors which have contributed to the success of school surveys and those which have presented obstacles to success. Emphasis will be placed upon such factors as are seemingly under the control of proper and adequate school publicity. The data, which were collected by means of several inquiry forms, represent the survey publicity experiences of twenty-one states and forty-eight cities.[2]

In Table I are shown the factors which have been found to contribute to the success of school surveys, together with the number of states and cities reporting each. Table II gives similar information about the obstacles that have been encountered in efforts to secure school improvement based on surveys. There were reported a total of twenty-five factors of success and a total of thirty-six obstacles. There is no doubt much overlapping among the items in each table, but it was impossible to eliminate this condition and at the same time accurately describe the experiences of the states and cities.

The reader will notice that many of the obstacles are the direct opposites of corresponding factors of success. For example, "hard times" is the opposite of "general prosperity." Other obstacles which have direct opposites are the following: A lack of organized publicity, a lack of adequate publicity, extreme recommendations, the attitude of school boards, a delay in the publication of the survey report, the school needs not being very evident, the failure to place copies of the survey report into the hands of the leaders, poor support by the newspapers, propa-

TABLE I

SHOWING THE FACTORS THAT HAVE CONTRIBUTED TO THE SUCCESS OF SCHOOL SURVEYS

Factors	Number of states reporting	Number of cities reporting
Support of leading citizens	14	23
Support of the newspapers	18	25
Support of board members	0	27
Work of school children	3	6
Evident school needs	11	17
Leadership of teachers	15	12
Reasonable recommendations	16	25
Outside survey staff	12	18
No delay in the survey	8	14
Presenting actual facts	17	24
Copies of survey report in hands of leaders	17	23
Sane view of the surveyors	12	19
Adequate publicity	7	17
Support of the women	12	15
Complete organization of publicity	4	8
Support of lodges and clubs	3	8
Cooperation of city superintendents	1	0
Support of religious organizations	2	4
General prosperity	4	2
Publicity for a long time before the survey	2	0
Presenting a complete school code	10	0
Cooperation of the state dept. of education	18	0

[1] This study was made under the advice and criticism of Dean B. F. Pittenger, of the School of Education of the University of Texas.

[2] For a list of the states, see *Educational Administration and Supervision*, February, 1927, p. 109; for the cities, see SCHOOL AND SOCIETY, August 27, 1927, p. 278.

Cooperation of county and township superintendents	15	0
Maintaining a legislative lobby	9	0
Active interest of governor and members of the survey commission	2	0
Totals	232	287

TABLE II

SHOWING THE FACTORS THAT HAVE HINDERED THE SUCCESS OF SCHOOL SURVEYS

Factors	Number of states reporting	Number of cities reporting
Hard times	6	4
Complete success is a matter of time	14	9
Reaction against taxes	15	9
Lack of funds for publicity purposes	5	11
Large Negro population	2	3
Lack of organized publicity	7	3
Lack of adequate publicity	4	6
Increased cost of education	11	7
Lack of public interest	9	8
Politics	12	8
Extreme recommendations	1	2
Jealousy of the power of school officers	7	2
Desire to do too much at one time	6	1
Survey lacking in a practical purpose	0	1
Attitude of school boards	6	6
Constitutional limitations	9	2
Distrust and indifference of the people	6	3
Delay in the publication of the survey report	3	3
Conservatism of the people	13	6
Backwardness of the people	8	2
School needs not very evident	2	1
Failure to place copies of the survey report into the hands of leaders	0	1
Poor support by the newspapers	0	1
Propaganda	0	1
Poor support by the leading citizens	1	1
Lack of harmony between surveyors and teachers	0	1
Recommendations not clear	1	0
Surveyors from home state	1	0
Failure to prepare enough local leaders	10	0
Failure to enlist help of children	2	0
Conservative legislature	7	0
Lack of cooperation in general	5	0
Opposition of county and township superintendents	3	0
Isolated communities	6	0
Fear of school consolidation	8	0
Sectional and institutional interests	3	0
Totals	193	102

ganda, poor support by the leading citizens, selecting the surveyors from the home state or locality, failure to enlist the help of school children and the opposition of county and district superintendents.

In general, the factors of success reported most often by the states are also the ones reported most frequently by the cities. This correspondence is also found in the reports on obstacles to success. It is true, however, that the states reported more factors of success and also more obstacles than the cities. This is probably due to the fact that the state, because of its larger area and more diverse interests, has more varied conditions and problems to meet than the city has.

If frequency of mention is any indication of the relative importance of the various factors of success, then it must be concluded that, for the states, the most important factor was the support of the newspapers. For the cities, on the other hand, the most frequently mentioned factor was the support of board members; this factor, however, is closely followed by that of the support of the press. On the same basis, other important factors of success for both states and cities are the following: Securing the support of the leading citizens, making the school needs evident, securing the leadership of the teachers, making reasonable the recommendations for the improvement of school conditions, employing an outside survey staff, preventing delay in the survey, presenting actual facts of school conditions, placing copies of the survey report into the hands of the leaders, employing a survey staff which has a "sane" view of school conditions and problems, giving adequate publicity to the findings of school surveys, obtaining the support of the women and securing cooperation in general. Those in charge of school surveys should make sure that these factors are operative in the efforts made to secure school improvement.

On the basis of frequency of mention, the greatest obstacle encountered by the states was that of reactions against taxes. The obstacle reported most often by the cities was a lack of funds for publicity purposes. Evaluated on the same basis, other significant obstacles for both states and cities are the following: The fact that it takes time to reap the full benefits of school surveys, a lack of organized publicity, a lack of adequate publicity, the increased cost of education, a lack of public interest, politics, jealousy of the power of school officers, a desire to do too much at one time, the attitude of school boards, constitutional limitations, the distrust and indifference of the people, the conservatism and backwardness of the people, a failure to prepare enough local leaders, a conservative legislature, a lack of cooperation in general, the geographical isolation of some communities and the fear of school consolidation. Survey commissions should be particularly alert to take the necessary steps to minimize and counteract the obstacles here enumerated.

This question might be raised: Are the obstacles encountered by school surveys more potent than the factors favoring success? As stated above, the tables show that there were reported a total of thirty-six different obstacles, and only twenty-five factors of success. On the basis of these totals, then, it could be held that the obstacles were the most powerful factors influencing the success of school surveys. The totals at the foot of each table, however, tell a different story, for the sum of the frequencies of the factors of success is, in the case of the states as well as in the case of the cities, much greater than the sum of the frequencies of the obstacles to success. This would suggest that the influence of the factors of success outweighed that of the obstacles to success. For the cities in particular, the total for the factors contributing to success is much larger—in fact, several times as large—as the total for the factors hindering success. This seems to indicate that city surveys are meeting with less opposition than state surveys, a condition which can be explained partly by the fact that the cities have always taken the lead in educational progress.

The discussion up to this point has suggested that many of the factors of success and many of the obstacles to success are related to school publicity. This article aims to emphasize such factors as are under the control of publicity; for this reason all other factors may now be excluded from the discussion.

The factors which are under the control of or pertain to school publicity may be conveniently grouped and discussed under the following heads: (1) The need for organization in survey publicity, (2) the need for adequate publicity, (3) the importance of securing the leadership and active help of certain groups, and (4) the need for observing certain general methods in school survey publicity.

(1) It goes without saying that the survey publicity efforts should be properly and thoroughly organized. This is necessary in order that such efforts may be consistently directed toward the same general end. The work must be thoroughly planned in order that the publicity program may accomplish the best results. To this end, some group or committee must be made responsible for the organization and control of survey publicity.

(2) That survey publicity must be adequate is suggested by a number of the factors listed in the accompanying tables. This means not only telling the story of the schools completely, but it also means reaching all the people. Probably one of the main reasons why certain communities were reported as isolated and opposed to the general program of school improvement was because such communities were not thoroughly informed on school matters. Why is there a lack of public interest in school affairs? Why are the people conservative and backward when it comes to solving our school problems? Why are they often jealous of the

power of school officers? Why is it that the people can not understand the needs of their schools? Why is it that politics is so often a stumbling block in the way of school progress? Such difficulties are due mainly to the fact that school officials so often are not careful to inform the people thoroughly about their schools, so that they might keep pace in their thinking with modern educational progress. Education will always have numerous opponents as long as its story is not made known far and wide.

(3) The tables have suggested that the success of survey publicity is largely dependent upon the support and leadership of certain organizations or groups of people. In this connection were mentioned the leading citizens, women's clubs, lodges and civic clubs, religious organizations, local leaders, teachers, board members, school children and newspapers. The people need leadership in educational matters as much as in other public affairs. They can not be expected to give their support to proposals for school improvement until the active support of their leaders has been enlisted in behalf of the schools. But experience has shown that such leadership must be intelligent. To this end, the leaders must be thoroughly informed first. This probably means that, for one thing, copies of the published reports of surveys be placed into the hands of the leaders.

The states and the cities have found that the support of the newspapers in particular is most important in securing the improvements outlined by school surveys. The charge has often been made that the press is not friendly to the schools and does not accord them proper support. Experience does not confirm this charge. None of the twenty-one states and only one of the forty-eight cities referred to above reported that the press gave poor support in getting the survey findings before the public. If school officials will show the press a little courtesy and consideration, they can rest assured to get its support in matters of school improvement.

(4) The final group of factors conditioning the success of school surveys consists of various general methods of procedure in publicity. It has been found of value to inform the people thoroughly before the survey is ever undertaken. The survey must be the result of the public's own thinking on the matter. It has been found unwise by some to attempt too many changes at one time; complete success, in other words, is a matter of time. However, in the case of state surveys, some states reported that the success of their surveys was partly due to the fact that they presented a complete school code for adoption to the legislature, instead of presenting "piecemeal" legislation. No doubt the success of such a method depends very largely upon the readiness of the people to accept the proposals contained in the school code. Another factor to be mentioned in this connection is the legislative lobby. Whatever one may believe as to the wisdom of maintaining a legislative lobby for the purpose of securing school legislation, experience has shown that lobbying is often effective in stimulating a conservative legislature to favorable action in behalf of the schools. Still another factor of importance is that of not delaying the publication of the survey report. Experience has shown that a delay in this matter may cause much of the cumulative effect of earlier publicity efforts to be lost. Finally, no program of school publicity can succeed unless those engaged in carrying it forward work in thorough harmony and cooperation. There is a need for cooperation in general; but the reports of the states and cities show that, in particular, there is a need for cooperation on the part of the state department of education, county and township superintendents, survey commissions and survey staffs.

The purpose of this article has been to point out the factors conditioning the success of school surveys and to suggest that many of these, perhaps most of them, are under the control of school publicity. The aim has not been to show specifically how the various factors may be controlled. The aim has been to outline problems, not solve them. The discussion has indicated, however, that, because so many obstacles are encountered in carrying out the improvement sought by school surveys and because many of these obstacles seem to be under the control of school publicity present-day school survey publicity is not as effective as it might be.

R. E. Garlin

Texas Technological College,
Lubbock, Texas

SCHOOL AND SOCIETY

Volume XXVIII SATURDAY, SEPTEMBER 22, 1928 Number 717

ADEQUATE FINANCING OF RURAL SCHOOLS: IT IS SOLELY THE FARMERS' PROBLEMS?[1]

THE question as stated is surely rhetorical, since the answer to it must necessarily be, from the view-point of any American who believes in his country's essentially democratic program and in a system of universal education, an emphatic "No!" However, the problem which is up for discussion is not so entirely simple that it can be emphatically answered in the negative. The elements entering into it are sufficiently complex to give us reason to pause and to cause us to analyze the question a bit more thoroughly.

The word adequate itself suggests primarily to the quantitative American mind the idea of sufficiency or enoughness. However, a more careful consideration of the term shows that it involves the idea not only of sufficiency but also of that even and carefully balanced adjustment which avoids partiality and attains equity. As related to the problem of financing rural education, it must be interpreted primarily in the latter sense, although certainly there should be no ignoring of the importance of sufficiency or the quantitative aspect of the term.

School financing can hardly be called a new problem. It has been with us since the beginnings of public education in the western hemisphere with the Massachusetts laws of 1642 and 1647, up to the present time, when the principle of universal public education, publicly supported, seems to be rather firmly established. The conception of universal education, like the ideal of democracy itself, has been a persistent, restless and compelling growth. Time was when its staunchest advocates thought only in terms of rudiments, the three R's, for a three or four months' session during the winter. Then came graded work, an expanding curriculum, the high school, the state universities and agricultural and mechanical colleges, extension and adult education—to name a few of the elements that have come to be comprehended in the concept "universal education." As the conception has grown there has come also the insistent demand for more money to supply the material foundation upon which extensions might be securely and firmly established.

One aspect of this broadened conception of universal education constitutes our problem. Universal education should guarantee educational opportunities of such extent as present economic status and general appreciation of the need for education may dictate, to children living on farms, in mining, fishing, and lumber-camp villages and in small hamlets and towns, equal to those provided in urban territory, in so far as this may be possible. This is and must be the ideal. The path to its realization is rough, beset with many truly formidable problems. Financing is one of these. That it is the only one would be a hasty conclusion. That its solution or closer approximations thereto will clear the path for a more sure-footed approach to the other problems involved is a conclusion which the modern economic organization of society does not permit us to dodge.

[1] Address delivered before the Rural Schools Section of the American Country Life Association, Urbana, Illinois, June 21, 1928.

School financing, in the last analysis, is a pressing problem in the United States because: (1) In broad outline our ideals of education are *national*; (2) the final control of education is a *state* function; (3) the support of education is preponderantly a *local* obligation. If the three factors—ideals, control and support—were unified on either the national or the state level, the problem would be less complex, because the problem of the apportionment of the burdens and the benefits of education would be much simplified. If unification were on the national level, there would be no apportionment problem. If it were on the state level, the apportionment problem would be that of distributing the benefits and burdens of education among the states. But, as it is now, as described at the beginning of the paragraph, the local community must pay, largely out of its own resources, for that which is constantly stimulated by broadening national ideals as to what constitutes adequate educational advantages and which the state may require it to provide. Were wealth rather evenly distributed, the problem might still be fairly simple. But the fact is that there is no such even distribution of wealth among communities. Consequently, many communities labor under very serious economic handicaps when they strive to provide what ideals suggest or the state requires with regard to schools. It is the reduction or the removal of these handicaps which constitutes the big problem of school financing.

Having thus outlined in a general way the problem of school financing, may I suggest certain respects in which adequate rural school financing presents special difficulties, as follows:

(1) Provision of adequate schooling of elementary grade in areas of sparse population, where school population and attendance are small.

(2) Provision of adequate schooling of secondary grade in areas of sparse population, where area served by the high school must be extensive and where such a school will probably be located in a village or town, involving transportation of pupils, in addition to the higher cost of secondary schooling. The problem is accentuated in that the village or town often bears the burden alone, or tries to make ends meet by charging tuition to children from outlying districts. A recent study of high-school opportunities in Colorado points out that it is in the areas where the smaller high schools are located that inability to pay this tuition cost works a deprivation of high-school privileges to young people.

(3) Concentration of population tends to reduce unit costs of standard educational opportunities, while sparseness of population tends to increase them. A study by Dr. Staffelbach, of the San Jose State Teachers College, indicated that the average costs per child per day for schooling in states having fewer than seventeen children per square mile gradually increased from forty-one cents in states having a school population of more than seventeen per square mile to sixty-eight cents in states having fewer than one child per square mile. Evidence of this same sort exists in profusion to show the same sort of variation in costs per child between districts in the same state and in the same county.

(4) Concentration of population is generally attended by concentration of real valuation, while sparseness of population is often attended by scant real valuation. If we consider wealth as we should, in terms of personal property, stocks, bonds, securities, etc., then the concentration of wealth accompanying concentration of population becomes still more evident, and the relative amount of wealth available per functioning unit, *i.e.*, the teacher, in

sparsely populated areas generally becomes still less.

(5) Some sparseness of population is almost, if not entirely, irremediable by consolidating territory for school purposes, at least as far as elementary education is concerned. Transportation of little folks in certain parts of the country at certain seasons of the year is quite inadvisable.

(6) Some sparseness of population is almost, if not entirely, remediable by consolidating territory, at least for secondary, and largely for elementary education. Consolidation gives, artificially, the same result practically as is obtained in urban centers where concentration of population tends to reduce unit costs of standard educational offering. Thus the financing of rural education is seen to cut squarely across into the problem of properly functioning administrative units for rural schools.

From what has been said up to now no doubt it has become evident that the adequate financing of rural schools is a rather knotty and complicated problem. Now that some of its complexities have been analyzed, shall we return a moment to the statement of our question, before attempting to answer somewhat in detail the rhetorical question? May I sum up my understanding of the phrase "adequate financing" as related to the enterprise of public education? I take it to imply:

(1) Sufficiency of funds to maintain a high-standard educational program.
(2) Equity of the tax burden necessary to provide this sufficiency.
(3) Equity of educational benefits enjoyed.

The first element requires little or no explanation. It is probably enough to say that to-day's high-standard program will be superseded by one of considerably larger dimensions and loftier aspirations to-morrow. Such is the nature of life, and it is quite unthinkable that education should cease to grow.

Equity of tax burden to support education implies not only a uniform tax rate on real and personal property, and that the bulk of taxes be levied on a state-wide basis, but also (and perhaps this is of at least as great importance) that taxes be levied on those items which are guarantees of ability to pay and in amounts proportional to ability to pay. In one sense at least these are the farmer's problems. At least they concern him vitally. I shall not intrude upon the subject of the next speaker[2] farther than to suggest that the farmer pays a far higher proportion of the nation's taxes than his aggregate wealth justifies, largely because the basic taxing methods now in use generally are still those prevalent in the days when one's homestead and herds represented all he had in the world. In other words, the farmer pays on visible property, which constitutes his chief wealth, full tax, while his city cousin owns stocks, bonds and other securities, and mayhap even, through a mortgage, a large part of the very farm upon which the farmer pays taxes up to its full assessment. This is the farmer's concern, if not his problem, and he has both a right and a duty to make his inequitable status in this matter fully and convincingly known. But it is not his problem alone. It is a problem for the nicest study of the economist and the expert on taxation. Nor can the urban dweller afford to ignore it, even though present tax methods may temporarily work an economic advantage to him, for, if economic necessity should continue to cause the abandonment of farming to the alarming extent that it has in the past few years, the time will not be far off when, both from the standpoint of increased proportion of tax upon him and from the standpoint of higher prices for a lessened food supply, the city dweller will find himself in the position of the man who

[2] Professor B. H. Hibbard, University of Wisconsin, "A Tax Program for Rural Schools."

killed the goose that laid the golden egg. This is a problem of the statesman, too, for no nation in all history has permanently survived which has failed to solve the problem of the land, and which has failed to maintain an independent, upstanding population on the farm. So much for the tax problem, very sketchy and quite incomplete.

Equity of educational benefits implies not necessarily the same kind of teachers, buildings, equipment, supervision, etc., as city schools provide, but teachers as well trained for rural work as city graded and high-school teachers are trained for their work; buildings as well appointed for rural educational, recreational and community purposes as city buildings are appointed for like purposes in the city environment; a curriculum as rich and as well conceived in terms of the educative resources of rural and village life as is the curriculum of urban schools in terms of urban life; and supervision as well adapted for and as fairly apportioned to the rather trying conditions met by the rural supervisor, as city supervision is adapted to relatively less trying conditions in the city. I would not like to be misunderstood to mean that rural life is altogether different from urban life, certainly not that it is less satisfying or genuinely attractive, but rather that there are elements of difference of sufficient moment to justify our careful attempts to conserve their educational advantages, at the same time that we weave them into the fine, strong fabric of national life. This perhaps deserves further discussion, but time demands that it rest with this statement.

Now, of course, this equity of educational benefits is a matter of profound concern to the farmer. His hope for the future rests upon it more perhaps than even the most enthusiastic of us who stand sponsors for better rural education realize. I shall only suggest that Denmark gives some little hint as to the possibilities of well-planned and administered rural education.

Assuming a sufficiency of funds to maintain a high-standard educational program, and a tax scheme which distributes the burden of school support equitably, the achievement of an equity of educational benefits depends upon two factors: (1) An equitable scheme of state school fund apportionment; (2) an intelligent scheme of rural school administration. But is this solely the farmer's problem? It is surely due for more thorough-going and intelligent consideration than he has given it in the past. Prejudice and tradition must give way to willingness to make adjustment in a progressive way to a changing rural and world order. But the villager and urban dweller are concerned as well, and their counsel and cooperation must be sought. Indeed, these two factors upon which an equity of educational benefits depends, calling as they do for an enlistment of the cooperation of so many groups, a fine adjustment of so many seeming conflicts of interests and rights and an adventure upon the uncharted open spaces of new financial arrangements, new group alignments and community reorganizations, as well as new purely educational reorganizations, provide a nice problem for the best educational leadership and statesmanship that America can produce. This equity rural boys and girls have seldom enjoyed, but to it, according to all our undergirding American political and social standards, they have always been entitled. To achieve it will require patient study, well-chosen and forceful publicity, consummate courage, unfailing friendliness, incisive insight, dogged determination and constant courtesy on the part of rural school leaders. They must avoid the error so easily made of regarding this as their sole problem. They must enlist both the interest and the active cooperation of farmer, villager, city dweller, and last, but by no means least, their professional associates, in this growing undertaking. Time does not permit my going into an extensive discussion of what constitutes an equitable scheme of state school fund apportionment. Numerous studies have been made of this matter which furnish an almost unlimited variety of suggestions. I shall, therefore, be content to append hereto a tentative scheme for state school fund apportionment which follows rather closely a plan suggested in my volume, "Financing Rural Education," issued by the Rural Service Press.

Turning now to the problem of an intelligent scheme of rural school administration, I shall have time to suggest only a few type problems which it will have to attack. This is by no means an exhaustive list, but it suggests the variety of issues which a rural school administrator must study and meet.

(1) What constitutes a proper balance between the legislative or policy-making power representing the people of a community and the executive and policy-advising power representing trained educational authority?

(2) What is a proper and workable distribution of function between centralized state control and local control?

(3) What, under varying local conditions, is a proper unit for effective rural school administration?

(4) How rapidly can teacher certification requirements be raised? Shall these requirements precede, accompany, or follow, salary adjustments?

(5) Shall consolidation and the frequently consequent transportation requirement contemplate all grades, or only secondary education? What local conditions will help to determine?

(6) How can rural supervision be made most effective throughout the year?

Once again the question arises whether these matters are the concern of others than the farmer. I submit that they are of distinct concern to villagers and urban dwellers as well as to farmers. First, let me state it from the theoretical standpoint. In the words of Woodrow Wilson, "No authority less inclusive than the state may be entrusted with the control of education." The state is in America all of the people. Thus we see quite simply expressed and briefly stated the democratic political and social theory of education.

Secondly, from the practical standpoint, we may point out that to date failure to achieve the objectives set forth as constituting adequate financing of rural schools has resulted in:

(1) A rather distinct drag on village and city secondary school progress, and on the progress in the state teachers colleges and universities, caused by the relatively ineffective preparation had by so many pupils in rural schools. When these students with somewhat defective foundation come to the high schools, if the teachers give them even a part of the attention necessary to enable them to make reasonable progress, the rest of the class is slowed up. In many cases the ineffectiveness of rural school preparation constitutes a handicap which is almost impossible for the boy or girl to overcome. The drag is social and personal as well.

(2) Comparatively less adequate rural school teachers. These are the cause of the drag mentioned above. As a rule we get very little more than we pay for. The salaries paid in rural schools, partly because of an inequitable apportionment of state school funds, are notoriously low. The way in which these teachers affect city schools, and therefore the urban population generally, is that usually, after a few months of teaching in rural schools, they go into city school positions for which they have been inadequately prepared, as a general thing, both by training and by experience.

(3) A dearth of rural leadership in religion, in social life, and in political fields. This is a very serious matter because it deprives rural people of effective representation in these important concerns. It is also a serious matter for village and city people because it renders too difficult the cooperative activity which should characterize the relationships between rural and urban folks. That is to say, when rural leadership or representation fails to be effective it means that authoritative communication and cooperation between city and country are lacking.

(4) Inability of rural people to attack and solve their problem. It is scarcely open to argument that a more adequate system of rural education would have resulted in these times of rural

economic stress in a more thorough-going and efficient handling of his problem and working out of his salvation by the farmer himself.

(5) Closely related to (4) is the relative economic and political ignorance on the part of much of our farming population resulting in willingness to follow those who, either for personal gain or with sincere but misinformed motives, have offered panaceas which have not and can not work. Worse yet, farmers have been continually hoodwinked by both major political parties into supporting a high protective tariff founded on the "catchy" slogan that "cheap labor produces cheap goods." Analysis of this slogan, definition of its terms fairly and frankly and subjecting honest terms to the test of honest facts will readily demonstrate its basic fallacy.

To sum up this matter from the practical standpoint: I should be the last to claim that rural people are lacking in intelligence. But rural people must have, in addition to a high degree of native intelligence, information upon the trends of modern life and training in thinking with this information at their disposal. An adequate system of rural schools is indispensable to such a program; and an adequate system of rural schools is unthinkable without adequate rural school financing. No argument is needed to point out the real, practical importance of these matters to urban dwellers as well as to those who make their homes on the farms of the land, for whether we will or no, rural and urban America are members of one body. Each group has differing and varying functions, but the task of developing a complete and satisfying American life, both in the cities and on the farm, is one of cooperation. A nation divided against itself can not stand. On the other hand, rural people and city people, looking into each other's faces with level eyes, backed by the confidence of equity of opportunity in education, and in economic, political, religious and social life, can build a nation to furnish the world both with material wealth and with spiritual leadership.

We are not pessimistic about the outcome, for there are many hopeful signs that merchants and bankers, captains of industry and leaders of labor, as well as educational and social welfare workers, are more and more coming to recognize that these problems, including adequate financing of rural schools, challenge the intelligence of America as a comprehensive national problem.

PLAN OF STATE SCHOOL FUND APPORTIONMENT FOR THE STATE OF YAKIMA[3]

I

(a) Any district unable to operate its schools in the following items:

(1) Minimum salary per teacher allowed of $1,200. (Not more than one teacher shall be allowed for each thirty or fraction thereof in ADA in the elementary school and one for each twenty or fraction thereof in ADA in high schools in the district during the preceding year.)

(2) Tuition to another district approved by state superintendent.

(3) Transportation either within or without district, if routes and costs are approved by state superintendent.

(4) Janitor service in accord with standards set up by the state superintendent.

(5) Supplies and reference books.

(6) Administration and supervision (one supervisor to each thirty teachers or fraction thereof not less than eight employed in the district).

(7) Fuel and equipment.

with a levy of five mills on true valuation, shall be entitled to an apportionment from the state current fund sufficient to cover the difference between the amount needed and the proceeds of such levy.

(b) In addition to the above apportionment, for each additional .5 mill beyond five mills levied by the district toward increasing the amount expended per teacher allowed by corresponding additional amounts of $100 beyond $1,500, there shall be apportioned from the state current fund an amount sufficient to cover the difference between the additional amounts of $100, $200, $300, etc., and the proceeds of the levies of .5 mill, 1 mill, 1.5 mills, etc., respectively: provided (1) Not less

[3] "Financing Rural Education" (Rural Service Press, Stevens Point, Wis.), pp. 208–210.

than 70 per cent. of the additional amounts shall be used to increase the teacher's salary; and (2) state apportionment on this basis shall cease when the teacher's salary reaches $2,000.

II

Apportionment shall be made to each county from the state current fund to reimburse the county for three fourths of the salaries of supervisors. Provided that (1) No county shall employ less than one supervisor for each thirty teachers or major fraction thereof in the county in districts outside districts where there are eight or more teachers; and (2) the salaries of supervisors shall be based on a schedule which makes allowance for successful experience and advanced training, beginning with a minimum salary of $2,400 and advancing to at least $4,200.

III

The State of Yakima shall issue bonds in three series, of a value of $8,000,000 in each series, dated July 1 of the years 1926, 1928 and 1930, respectively. These bonds shall bear 4 per cent. interest, compounded semi-annually. They shall be sold at not less than par, and the proceeds used for a state rural and consolidated building loan fund. Any district in the state which submits plans for the building of a rural or consolidated building, if these plans and specifications meet with the approval of the state superintendent and the state school architect, may borrow from the state rural and consolidated building loan fund an amount sufficient to erect and equip its buildings. The amount thus borrowed becomes an obligation upon such district. It shall be repaid annually to the rural and consolidated building loan fund, in amounts equal to one twentieth of the total, plus interest on the unpaid balance at 4 per cent., interest compounded semi-annually. If a special building levy of 3.5 mills is not sufficient to cover these payments, and the levy under I is five mills, there shall be apportioned from the state current fund an amount sufficient to meet the difference between the payment due and the proceeds of the special 3.5 mill levy.

IV

Any district maintaining a one-, two- or three-room school which meets the requirements for state standard schools as to teacher qualifications, length of term, character of building, equipment, sanitation and grounds, shall be entitled to a standard school bonus of $100 in addition to all other apportionments. No school shall receive this special bonus for more than five years.

ROBERT DODGE BALDWIN
CENTRAL STATE TEACHERS COLLEGE,
STEVENS POINT, WIS.

THE UNIVERSITY DEAN OF MEN

"WHAT are the duties of a dean of men?" I am sometimes asked. The answer can not be given in a sentence. In general, it may be said that his work is both educational and social, that it is both administrative and personal. He is the contact officer between the administration and the men of the university. He exercises a friendly supervision over the moral, social and intellectual life of undergraduates. He confers with them on questions affecting their personal or group interests. He seeks to enlist cooperation of all who can further these ends.

Among the state universities that have added deans of men to their staffs since the university of Illinois led the way nearly thirty years ago are Kentucky, Tennessee, Indiana, Iowa, Colorado, Montana, Nevada, Kansas, Oregon, Washington, California, Arkansas, New Mexico, Arizona, Pennsylvania, New Hampshire, North Dakota, South Dakota, Wisconsin, Utah, Wyoming and West Virginia. Scores of colleges, technical schools and endowed universities have done likewise, as, for example, Allegheny College, University of Pittsburgh, Georgia Institute of Technology, Stanford University, De Pauw University, Ohio Wesleyan University, Purdue University, Carleton College, Leland Stanford, Jr., University, Oberlin College, College of Wooster, Morningside College, the College of the Pacific and Occidental College.

Other institutions of higher learning have added officers known as deans of students and advisers of men. They include the state universities of North Carolina, Michigan, Texas, Nebraska and Minnesota, and Toledo University, Iowa State Teachers College, the Missouri School of Mines and South Dakota State College of Agriculture and Mechanic Arts. These officers are members of the national association of deans and advisers of men, which held its first meeting in 1918. Their duties are not to be distinguished from those of deans of men.

Northwestern University has a dean of men in addition to a personnel department. The University of Illinois and the University of Pittsburgh have assistant deans of men to aid the deans of men in their work, especially with organizations. The University of North Carolina has established a bureau of vocational information as a part of the office of dean of students with a director in charge. Yale, Princeton and Brown have deans of freshmen. Princeton has also a director of personnel and an assistant director. Carnegie Institute of Technology has a bureau of personnel research, whose director has done work attempted by a few deans of men. The University of North Dakota has both a dean of freshmen and a dean of men. The University of South Carolina has a director of student activities.

Some idea of the varying activities of deans of men may be obtained from the following statements taken from official bulletins:

University of Colorado: The dean of men is particularly interested in the physical and moral welfare of the men of the university. He is a member of the faculty committee on student organizations and social life, and is also an advisory member of the committee on discipline. He is ready at all times to consult with students about their living conditions, social affairs and scholarship. Any student who needs help of any kind should feel free to call upon him.

University of Washington: The dean of men is concerned with the welfare of the men students of the university. He confers with them on all questions affecting their personal or group interests. Among other duties he prepares reports on students failing in scholastic work, arranges schedules, helps to obtain students part-time employment and examines housing conditions. A list of approved boarding places is kept in his office.

University of Pittsburgh: The work of the student during the first and second year is under the supervision of the dean of men. He receives frequent reports of the academic standing of each student and is constantly engaged in conferences with students, instructors and parents for the purpose of improving the standard of this work. He devotes considerable time to advising students who have not yet decided upon their careers, finding what their interests are and making it possible for them to obtain information concerning the vocations in which they are interested.

At the University of Tennessee the dean of men is chairman of the committee on social affairs. He is a member of the council of administration. He assists in the operation of attendance regulations. Absences are sent to him by instructors.

At Pennsylvania State College the dean of men has some oversight over student morale, student conduct, community conditions, housing, orientation of freshmen and the conduct and financing of student activities.

The dean of men of the University of Arkansas is adviser for all men students and looks after the general college life of these students.

At the University of Kansas the dean of men is chairman of the division of vocations, chairman of the committee on convocations and lectures and assistant to the president.

The dean of men of Ohio Wesleyan University is a member of the committee on discipline, the committee on fraternities and sororities, the committee on social activities and the committee on student loans and scholarship. He is chairman of the committee on eligibility and special adviser to foreign students.

At the University of North Carolina the dean of students is a member of the faculty committee on fraternities, the committee on student mortality and the committee on cooperation with alumni. He is chairman of the committee on student employment, chairman of the committee on student life and activities and chairman of the chapel committee.

The administrative officer at Harvard who does the work of the dean of men is known as the regent. I quote from the Harvard bulletin:

The regent is a university officer who exercises a general supervision over the conduct and welfare of students. It is his duty to direct the proctors who reside in the university buildings or in buildings to which the superintendence of the university extends. He is expected to inform himself of the condition and management of all buildings in which five or more students are lodged or in which student societies meet. He is also expected to inform himself fully about all students' societies and clubs, and to enforce the responsibility of the officers and members thereof for their proceedings.

Into the office of the dean of men of a state university like West Virginia University, where two thirds of the twenty-nine hundred students are men and where there are no dormitories for men, comes a stream of students on missions so varied that they provide a veritable panorama—a changing, shifting scene—comedy, tragedy, joy, sorrow, hope, fear—the assortment seemingly made by some inexorable law of chance.

I have stood with fraternity men before the grave of a dead brother. I have accompanied the body of a student, accidentally killed, as it was being carried to its last home in a little cemetery nestled among the beautiful hills of West Virginia. I have stood at the bedside of a student about to die in our infirmary and sought to comfort his father and mother. I have broken the news to instructors and students of the serious illness and death of parents. I remember staying up nearly all night with one young instructor to whom, in the absence of the president, I had conveyed the news of the death of his father in an automobile accident. Quite as vivid is my memory of a night-ride by train with a father whose boy had run away from college and taken a room at a hotel in a nearby city. I recall seeking to quiet the nerves of a fine young fellow who one afternoon had accidentally killed a fellow-student and friend while, with loaded guns, they were climbing under a fence. I shall never forget the sessions with a student who lost his mind and was reported to me after he had threatened the life of a local teacher. I remember more than one call from the local police department to come down to see students who had been arrested.

The office of the dean of men is a haven to which students, faculty members, parents, landladies and others go when they have a real or fancied grievance or a request they hesitate to take to instructors or to other administrative officers. His office is a general clearing-house for students who seek information about rules and regulations. He is the university trouble man. He is not a policeman. His business is helping young men and in this he gets his chief satisfaction.

Perhaps a more definite idea of the varied activities of the dean of men will be gained from the following paragraphs concerning my own activities and experience from day to day:

A large number of men call to fill out personnel-record blanks which are filed in our office. These are used constantly to supply to instructors and to others information about students other than that on record in the office of the registrar. These blanks are used as a basis for individual interviews for purposes of educational, personal and occupational guidance and readjustment.

Students are called into conference concerning excessive absences from classes, irregular withdrawal from courses and irregular habits reported by landladies, neighbors, merchants and others. Some of these students are supplied with information concerning university rules and regulations. Others are given kindly advice. A few are warned that their dismissal will be recommended if reports of irregular habits continue to come in.

Many students come to ask for leaflets on law, medicine, pharmacy, engineering careers, agricultural occupations, careers in business, etc. Leaflets prepared by our office, together with those supplied by the National Research Council and by other universities, supply the information. They are also directed to the vocations-shelf in the library, which was established three years ago on the recommendation of the dean of men. Among the books in this collection are: "The Training and Rewards of a Physician," by Richard C. Cabot; "The Law as a Vocation," by Frederick J. Allen; "The Engineer," by John Hays Hammond; "The Training of a Forester," by Gifford Pinchot; "Training for the Newspaper Trade," by Don C. Seitz; "The Teacher," by George Herbert Palmer; "The Young Man and His Vocation," by F. H. Harris, and "Choosing Your Life-Work," by William Rosengarten.

The regular weekly required guidance-meeting for the men of the freshman class is held. One of the professors in the college of medicine talks on social hygiene. After the talk several of the men remain for personal conferences and advice. Other talks and conferences on the use of the library, the choice of a life-career, how to study, keeping mentally fit, keeping physically fit, etc., are arranged.

The chairman of the social committee of the inter-fraternity council, which is composed of representatives of seventeen national Greek-letter social fraternities on our campus, calls to talk over ways in which the fraternity open-house dances can be improved. The dean of men at West Virginia University is a member of the university social committee and assists in the preparation of the social calendar, confers with representatives of men's organizations desiring to hold dances and attends many dances each semester as patron or chaperon.

The prep-master of one of our twenty-four fraternities for men calls for information as to the attendance of its eleven freshman "preps" and for my estimate of their progress, habits, etc. The administration of attendance-regulations is in the hands of the dean of men at West Virginia. Through it much light is thrown on the habits, health, punctuality and reliability of both men and women attending the university.

The executive secretary of one of the national Greek-letter social fraternities announces that he will visit the university on a date set to confer with the dean of men and others concerning the application of a local group for a charter in his fraternity. The members of the national fraternity in Morgantown and nearby towns are called together for a luncheon and a conference is held. After the luncheon the local fraternity is visited and inspected.

The student president of the university Y .M. C. A. calls to talk over his program for the year. The student in charge of the university directory which is issued by the Y. M. C. A. also calls to talk over progress being made with the directory. A member of the faculty advisory board comes to confer on Y. M. C. A. finances. The dean of men is chairman of the faculty advisory board, consisting of six faculty members.

A letter arrives from a nearby city asking for personal information concerning the character, habits and qualities of a graduate of last year's class, who is an applicant for a position. The letter is written and a conversation with the mother of the young man assures her of the interest of the university in his welfare.

A landlady informs me that a freshman boy has left town under circumstances that should be investigated. A telegram is sent to his parents. A telephone message from his father later in the day thanks me and states that an effort to find him will be made at once. Since the boy has been away from his room but one night, I feel confident that these parents will have little difficulty in tracing their son.

A hundred paragraphs like the above could be written, all different. The work of the dean of men in a great university is never done, is never the same and is always with human beings. That's why it's so fascinating.

HARRY E. STONE

WEST VIRGINIA UNIVERSITY,
MORGANTOWN, WEST VIRGINIA

EDUCATIONAL EVENTS

RECOMMENDATIONS OF THE NATIONAL SYNDICATE OF TEACHERS OF FRANCE

THE Paris correspondent of *The Christian Science Monitor* writes "that a large and important body known as the National Syndicate of Teachers of France and the Colonies, in meeting assembled, has voted unanimously for the creation of a separate Ministry of Education. With equal unanimity they pressed also for the abolishment of all confessional schools. This is the same group which recently advocated the cleaning from all school history books of any taint of animosity toward Germany.

"Education is at present treated as a branch of the Ministry of Public Instruction and Fine Arts—the main branch, of course. The teachers feel that educational matters are of such great importance to progress in this country that they should be handled by a ministry devoting full time to these questions. The present Minister of Public Instruction and Fine Arts, Edouard Herriot, former premier and for many years the able Mayor of Lyons, sees eye-to-eye with the teachers generally. The resolutions passed at their congress are not, therefore, meant as criticisms of him, but rather as assisting him in his liberal policies by giving as striking a manifestation as possible of the current views of the vast majority of teachers.

"Sentiment was strong in favor of doing away entirely with all private schools, so that there should be only one school system in the state, and only one set of laws. Wiser heads knew this goal could not be arrived at to-day, and the congress was persuaded to vote simply that private schools be no longer allowed any of the special privileges of the past, such as a different requirement for teachers and the right of religious instruction by representatives of a church. Religion and education, the teachers felt, should be kept apart.

"Prolongation of the period of teaching for all children was requested by this body of teachers, as well as a continuation in some form of public instruction of children who had been graduated. "Nationalization of education" was demanded, by which is meant presumably that education should be regarded nationally and organized in this way, every one being treated in the same way and all schools open freely to all classes of pupils. Finally, the congress expressed the need for the creation of regional, department and local educational councils to discuss and advise on educational affairs."

THE MARRIAGE OF WOMEN TEACHERS IN ENGLAND

ACCORDING to the London *Times,* a new phase of the difficulty in school administration which often arises when women teachers marry is presented by a case at Leigh, a Lancashire non-county borough, where the local education committee has failed to pay the month's salary due to a woman teacher employed at the Pennington Church Mission Infants' School on the ground that she had recently married. The refusal to pay the salary due to Miss Varley, as she was until her marriage two months ago, is the act of the Leigh Education Committee, which pays the salaries of the teachers in the elementary schools in its area, whether the school is provided or non-provided.

The committee justifies its refusal to recognize Miss Varley since her marriage because it is alleged that she, in common with other unmarried women teachers in the borough, signed an agreement to resign on marriage. That stipulation was made by the Leigh Education Committee over a year ago. Women teachers in the Leigh schools who were already married were not affected by the new regulation, which was designed to prevent the continuance in their vocation of single women teachers if they married. Two teachers who have married during the last twelve months have duly resigned, and it is contended by the Leigh Education Committee that Miss Varley should also have done so. Her case is complicated by the fact that, unlike the others, she is a teacher in a non-provided school, and therefore does not owe her appointment to the Leigh Education Committee but to the managers of the school, and this body is apparently supporting her in seeking to ignore the Leigh Education Committee's new regulation.

The Education Commitee acknowledges that it has no power to give notice to any teacher in a non-provided school, but assert their right to refuse to recognize any teacher, such refusal taking the form of striking her off the pay roll.

The correspondent of the Pennington Church Mission School is the Reverend L. S. Murdoch, who has declined to give the teacher notice of the termination of her engagement at the school. Mr. Murdoch has stated that he was not necessarily fighting the case of married women teachers in general, but he was desirous of upholding the rights of non-provided school managers to appoint or dismiss teachers except on educational grounds. Marriage had not been held to be in itself an educational ground for dismissal. Miss Varley had neither resigned nor been dismissed, nor had she, in his opinion, broken any agreement.

A special meeting of the commtitee of the National Union of Teachers will consider the Leigh case. It is understood that the union upholds the attitude of the managers and the teacher, and may decide to make a test case of it if litigation should become necessary to uphold the teacher in her position.

THE AMERICAN TRUST FUND FOR OXFORD UNIVERSITY

THE American Trust Fund for Oxford University was formally established on September 12, by a gathering of Rhodes scholars at the Bank of the Manhattan Company, New York City, trustee of the fund. According to the account in The New York *Times* the trust deed establishing the fund was signed by Franklin F. Russell, secretary of the Association of American Rhodes Scholars, and delivered to J. Stewart Baker, president of the Bank of the Manhattan Company, who accepted and signed it on behalf of the trustee. John W. Davis, former Ambassador to Great Britain, and J. D. Scott,

British Consul at New York, were also present. Both signed the deed as witnesses.

The purpose of the fund is wide, including scholarships, exchange professorships, fellowships, contributions to building funds or such other uses as may be determined by an American committee in consultation with Oxford authorities. No fixed sum has been set for the fund, nor will any concerted drive be made for contributions, but it is hoped that considerable sums will be obtained from Rhodes scholars and others.

Mr. Russell said:

In creating this fund we Rhodes scholars had in mind two objects: first, to make some return to Oxford for the benefits we all feel we derived from our residence there, and secondly, to establish a medium through which gifts of any size, large or small, could be received from Rhodes scholars or others interested in Oxford and in international education and cooperation.

We deem it peculiarly appropriate that a trust fund for the oldest university in the English-speaking world should be entrusted to the oldest banking institution in the United States.

On behalf of the bank Mr. Baker expressed pleasure in accepting the trusteeship:

The Bank of the Manhattan Company is delighted to have a part in a movement which has for its purpose the interchange of educational facilities between this country and Great Britain, believing that through education better understanding will result.

Rhodes scholars present included Henry A. Moe, secretary of the John Simon Guggenheim Foundation, and Carroll Wilson, general counsel of Guggenheim Brothers. Together with Mr. Russell, they have taken a prominent part in the organization of the movement.

It was recalled at the meeting that the creation of the trust coincides with the seventy-fifth anniversary of the birth of Cecil Rhodes and with the twenty-fifth anniversary of the establishment of the Rhodes scholarships. During the last twenty-five years more than 600 students have gone to Oxford as Rhodes scholars from the United States, more than 500 from the British Dominion and about sixty from Germany.

THE BARBOUR SCHOLARSHIPS AT THE UNIVERSITY OF MICHIGAN

More than seventy women from oriental countries, according to a statement made to the U. S. Bureau of Education, have already availed themselves of the Barbour scholarships, which provide $800 per annum and university fees for attendance at the University of Michigan. The authorities seek to interest graduates of Russian and Turkish universities to join those from Chinese, Japanese, Indian and Korean universities, as well as the representatives of oriental races from the outlying parts of the United States.

Clarence C. Little, president of the university, states that the benefits already received from the occidental training applied by oriental women to service in their own communities is great, is in fact a "priceless experience of contact of American students with young people from a diversity of foreign countries."

The Honorable Levi L. Barbour, formerly regent of the University of Michigan, while traveling in the Orient some years ago, recognized the need there of scientifically and broadly trained women, particularly of women trained in medicine. He was so firmly convinced that such training was a success by the remarkable careers of three women, two from China and one from Japan, early graduates of the University of Michigan, that on returning to Michigan he made provision for the scholarships now offered.

Mr. Barbour died in 1925, but the income from the fund he set aside will provide for a larger number of students in the near future. The scholarships, yielding $800 per annum, and the university fees are expected to defray the living expenses during the college year. Travel, personal expenses and vacations must be provided for from personal resources, and funds sufficient for the student's return trip should be kept on deposit with the university. An estimate of the expenses at the University of Michigan for the college year of 36 weeks is $745.

In making the award of a scholarship (which is done annually by a committee upon a basis of merit), consideration is given to the character of the candidate, her physical condition, her scholastic attainment, her fitness for classroom purposes, marked ability in some special field and desire to return to her native land for service after suitable preparation shall have been made. On account of the rapid progress in the education of women in the Orient, preference is given to applicants who are graduates of oriental colleges. No definite number has been allotted to any one country, and race restrictions or religious requirements are not imposed.

STUDENT GUIDANCE AT THE UNIVERSITY OF WISCONSIN

ACCORDING to a correspondent of the New York *Sun*, a new and far-reaching program of student guidance, which in time is expected to affect elementary and high schools not only in Wisconsin but throughout the country, is being put into effect with the freshman class entering this fall at the University of Wisconsin. Classes will not open until September 26, but during the entire preceding week the freshmen will have the benefit of the new program of college counseling and vocational guidance.

The first step toward this end has already been taken through the distribution of handbooks containing ninety pages of information about student life, scholarships and vocational opportunities. These handbooks have been distributed to all prospective freshmen, to 135 faculty counselors and to 225 upper class or graduate students, who will assist in the work. These latter have received preliminary instructions in how to proceed.

New admission blanks which the university will use this year for the first time will be placed in the hands of faculty counselors before the freshman period. These blanks, the result of numerous conferences by a statewide committee of cooperation, representing officials of colleges and secondary schools, call for data on interests, aptitudes and past records of the new students.

The blanks are regarded as a step toward a plan for vocational guidance which will eventually start in the elementary schools and continue through the school life of students.

More natural and easy adjustments of freshmen to college life is the purpose of the freshman period. President Glenn Frank will meet faculty counselors and student advisers on the day preceding opening of the period. Individual conferences with faculty members will be arranged for the freshmen, and no counselor will have more than twenty pupils to guide. Choice of subjects, advice and interpretations of college life and procedures, use of the library and other matters will be discussed. The problem of how to study and the matter of vocational guidance will be presented during the special period, but the project will be continued throughout the year.

Educational tests not related to admission will be supplemented by convocations and by contacts between freshmen and advisers chosen from upperclassmen.

Because of the new policy freshmen who enter the university this fall are expected to start with a decided advantage over those who came as new students in former years.

SCHOOL ENROLMENT

WHEN the schools open this month about 30,000,000 students will answer the summons, according to the U. S. Education Bureau.

By far the largest proportion of this huge student body are elementary school pupils, whose numbers the bureau estimates at a total of more than 23,000,000.

High and preparatory schools are next with an enrolment of about 4,500,000, and colleges and universities will absorb another 1,000,000. Normal schools, commercial schools and special institutions account for the remaining 1,500,000.

Measured by the number of persons engaged in the educational field, education is the country's biggest business. In addition to the 30,000,000 students there are about 1,000,000 teachers. No other single industry employs or engages the full time of so many persons.

Expenditures for education, which have been constantly on the upgrade since the war, will aggregate $3,000,000,000 this year, in the opinion of Dr. Frank M. Phillips, chief statistician of the bureau. Reports to the bureau gave the total expenditures for 1925–1926 as $2,744,979,698, and Dr. Phillips believes a conservative estimate of the increase will bring it to three billions for this fiscal year.

A declining birth rate in this country materially has lowered the rate of increase in attendance at elementary schools in recent years. A graph of the attendance rate increase shows a tendency to flatten out since 1924, though the birth rate decline has been in progress since 1915. This lowered birth rate is expected to be felt in the high schools and colleges in a few years.

Illustrating the lessened attendance in elementary schools, the first-grade enrolment in 1918 was 4,281,013, in 1922 it was 4,084,145, and in 1926 it declined to 3,923,492. A part of this reduction may be charged to better schemes of promotion by which nearly all pupils are moved on a grade. Available statistics indicate that the 1930 census may show little if any increase in the number of children ready to enter school over the number shown in the 1920 census.

THE EDUCATIONAL WORK OF THE FIELD COLUMBIAN MUSEUM

How virtually every child in the schools of Chicago is constantly reached throughout the school year by supplementary educational activities of the Field Museum of Natural History is described in a booklet, "Field Museum and the Child," published by the museum and summarized in the *Public Ledger*, Philadelphia.

Three hundred and eighty-six schools in the city, with a combined enrolment of 600,000 children, are being supplied with two traveling museum exhibition cases, changed every two weeks during the school year, by the N. W. Harris public school extension department of the museum. A total of more than 1,000 such cases, containing botanical, geological, zoological and economic specimens, are circulated by the museum. All the subjects represented pertain to the plants, mineralogy, fossils, animals and industries of the Chicago region.

The work of the James Nelson and Anna Louise Raymond public school and children's lecture division of the museum provides free moving pictures, lantern slides, illustrated lectures, guide lecture tours and other educational entertainment, both in the schools themselves and at the museum. Through the activities of this division 265,649 children were reached directly during 1927.

This pamphlet is to be distributed to school officials, principals and others. It contains thirty-four pages of text describing in detail all of these activities on behalf of children and is illustrated with eight photogravures and five half-tones. A complete list of the subjects represented in the traveling exhibit cases, and a complete outline of the plan correlating the museum exhibits and lectures with the curriculum prescribed for the public schools by the Board of Education, are included in the pamphlet.

The Harris extension department has been built up on an endowment of $250,000 established in 1911 by the late Norman Wait Harris, to which contributions amounting to $125,000 have since been added by members of Mr. Harris' family. The Raymond division is founded on a $500,000 endowment provided by Mrs. Anna Louise Raymond as a memorial to her husband, James Nelson Raymond.

LECTURES AT THE INTERNATIONAL INSTITUTE OF TEACHERS COLLEGE

STUDENTS from foreign countries who have been coming to America to study educational institutions will have an opportunity of following a fundamental course which has been organized by the International Institute of Teachers College, Columbia University. It will consist of a series of lectures by a group of distinguished educators drawn from American universities. Following is a list of the speakers and subjects of the different lectures:

October 2.—Paul Monroe, "Historical Foundations of American Education."

October 8.—George D. Strayer, "Administration of Public Education in the United States."

October 16.—Alvin S. Johnson, "The Material Basis of Education in the United States."

October 23.—William H. Kilpatrick, "The American Elementary School."

October 29.—Charles H. Judd, "The American Secondary School."

November 6.—Ernest H. Wilkins, "The American College of Liberal Arts."

November 13.—James E. Russell, "Vocational and Professional Education in the United States."

November 20.—Walter A. Jessup, "The American State University."

November 27.—William F. Russell, "The American Teachers College."

December 4.—Harold Rugg, "The American Experimental School."

December 11.—Edward L. Thorndike, "The Science of Education in the United States."

December 18.—William C. Bagley, "The Profession of Teaching in the United States."

January 8.—Mary E. Woolley, "The Education of Women in the United States."

January 15.—Robert R. Moton, "The Education of the Negro in the United States."

January 22.—Albert R. Mann, "Education and Rural Life in the United States."

January 29.—John Dewey, "Education and Industrialism in the United States."

February 5.—Boyd H. Bode, "Contemporary Educational Theory in the United States."

February 12.—Nicholas Murray Butler, "Education and World Citizenship."

THE CONVOCATION OF THE UNIVERSITY OF THE STATE OF NEW YORK

IN response to the request of school officials throughout the state, the committee in charge of the sixty-fourth Convocation of the University of the State of New York has selected the subject of "Research in Education" as the general theme of the sessions. To present this subject, which is receiving increased attention, the committee has secured as speakers outstanding leaders in educational research and also in the fields of business and industrial research. The convocation will he held on October 18 and 19 in chancellor's hall of the State Education Building in Albany. In view of the interest in the topics to be presented and the preeminence of the speakers, it is expected that the sessions will be more largely attended than ever before.

Three general sessions will be conducted, on Thursday evening, October 18, and on Friday morning and afternoon, October 19.

The subject on Thursday evening will be the "Value of Research." The speakers will be Dr. B. R. Buckingham, lecturer in the graduate school of education at Harvard University, and Dr. Frederick P. Keppel, president of the Carnegie Corporation.

The session on Friday morning will be devoted to the consideration of the topic, "Research in Industry and Business." Addresses will be given by Owen D. Young, chairman of the board of the General Electric Company, and by Edward A. Filene, president of William Filene's Sons, Boston.

"Curriculum Research" will be the theme of the session on Friday evening. At this meeting addresses will be given by Dr. W. W. Charters, professor of education at the Ohio State University, and by Dr. Edward Lee Thorndike, professor of educational psychology at Teachers College, Columbia University.

A number of interesting features have been planned for the convocation. These include a reception on Thursday afternoon, the dedication of the Joseph Henry Monument in Capitol Park, musical selections by school orchestras and a motion picture based on some phase of industrial research.

The convocation committee consists of the following: Walter Guest Kellogg, board of regents, *chairman;* Ernest C. Hartwell, president of the State Teachers Association, *vice-chairman;* Frank P. Graves, commissioner of education; James Sullivan, George M. Wiley, J. Cayce Morrison and Lewis A. Wilson, all of the department of education; Burtis E. Whittaker, president of the Associated Academic Principals; Henry D. Fearon, president of the Associated School Boards and Trustees; Wilbur H. Lynch, president of the Council of Superintendents; Mrs. Dorothy B. Connolly, president of the State Association of District Superintendents; Harry W. Langworthy, superintendent of schools, Gloversville, and Randolph T. Congdon, principal of the Normal School, Potsdam.

EDUCATIONAL NOTES AND NEWS

THE newly elected president of the British Association for the Advancement of Science is Sir Thomas Holland, rector of the London College of Science and Technology. He will preside at the meeting to be held next year in South Africa.

DR. CLARK S. NORTHRUP, professor of English at Cornell University, has been elected president of Phi Beta Kappa at the sixteenth national council of the honorary scholastic fraternity in session in Ohio Wesleyan University. President Ellen F. Pendleton, of Wellesley College, was elected vice-president. Dr. Oscar M. Voorhees, New York, secretary, and David Layton, New York, treasurer, were reelected. The following were elected senators to serve six years: President James R. Angell, Yale University; John W. Davis, New York City; Dr. John H. Finley, associate editor of the New York *Times;* Dr. Raymond B. Fosdick, New York City; Dr. Frank P. Graves, New York State Commissioner of Education; Dwight W. Morrow, U. S. Ambassador to Mexico; Dr. Clark S. Northrup, Dr. Ellen F. Pendleton, Dr. Albert Shaw, editor of the *Review of Reviews,* and Owen D. Young, New York.

Dr. Lynn Thorndike, professor of history at Columbia University, has been elected president of the History of Science Society, to fill the unexpired term of the late Dr. Edgar F. Smith.

Dr. Jacob Gould Schurman, U. S. Ambassador to Germany, formerly president of Cornell University, is visiting the United States.

Stephen C. Simms, who since 1913 has been curator of public-school extension of the Field Columbian Museum, Chicago, has been elected director of the museum, to succeed the late David Charles Davies, who died on July 14.

G. Bromley Oxnam will be inaugurated as president of De Pauw University on October 12. The inauguration will be a part of a two-day celebration at the university. Among other events will be the dedication of Lucy Rowland Hall, the new dormitory for women. Bishop Edwin Holt Hughes, a former president of De Pauw University, will give the inaugural address. Ed Jackson, governor of Indiana; William Lowe Bryan, president of Indiana University, and Bishop Edgar Blake, of the Indianapolis Area, will make short addresses.

Dr. William Allen Wilbur, for twenty-four years dean of Columbian College, George Washington University, has been appointed provost of the university. Dr. Charles Edward Hill, professor of political science, has been appointed acting dean in place of Dr. Wilbur.

Dr. Frank Washington Ballou, superintendent of schools at Washington, D. C., has been appointed professorial lecturer in education at George Washington University.

Dr. H. W. Distad, of Emory University, has been appointed head of the department of education and director of teacher training in the University of New Mexico. He has had a number of years experience in connection with research and teaching in Northwestern University and in the city schools of Minneapolis.

Reverend John M. Ratcliff has been appointed assistant professor of religious education in the school of religion and in the department of education in the school of liberal arts of Tufts College.

Dr. Edwin G. Fleming will leave Columbia University this autumn to become associate professor of psychology at William and Mary College.

At the University of Virginia, Frank A. Geldard, formerly of Clark University, has been appointed associate professor of psychology. Miss Louisa Oates will occupy the newly established Sadie Heath Cabiness chair of nursing education. Miss Adelaide A. Mayor, of Teachers College, Columbia University, has been appointed assistant professor in the same subject.

Harry F. Fore, associate professor of English at Purdue University, has become head of the English department and chairman of the committee on graduate study at Creighton University.

Mrs. Alma Tyler Perkins, for the past two years dean of women at Carroll College, Waukesha, Wisconsin, has been appointed dean of women at Rockford College and assumed her new office on September 15. Dean Perkins is a graduate of Wellesley and Simmons Colleges.

Peter A. Mortensen, formerly superintendent of the Chicago schools, has returned to the school system as principal of an elementary school.

The National Council of Education has announced the election of Superintendent Frank G. Pickell, of Montclair, New Jersey, to membership in the council.

Miss Jane C. Allen, for the last two years general director of the National Organization for Public Health Nursing, recently presented her resignation and it has been accepted with regret by the directors.

L. DICKERSON, executive assistant of the board on library and adult education of the American Library Association, has accepted the librarianship of the Indianapolis Public Library and will assume his new work sometime after October 1.

THE Mississippi Library Commission has appointed Elizabeth N. Robinson to the new position of secretary. Miss Robinson is a graduate of the Carnegie Library School, Pittsburgh, has been children's librarian and branch librarian in the Seattle Public Library, librarian of the Medford, Oregon, Public Library, and head of the school division of the St. Paul Public Library.

DR. HARL R. DOUGLASS, of the University of Oregon, is spending a year's leave of absence as visiting lecturer in secondary education at the University of Pennsylvania.

PROFESSOR C. I. LEWIS, of Harvard University, will conduct a seminar in logic during the spring term at Columbia University.

DR. H. H. PORTER, professor of economics at the University of Washington at Seattle, has been appointed exchange professor at Dartmouth College.

DR. GEORGE HOLLISTER, Hinghua, China, has been appointed professor of missions at Ohio Wesleyan University during the year's leave of absence of Professor Albert E. Suthers.

MISS IDA M. TARBELL will be the first occupant of the newly created William L. Honnold lectureship at Knox College, Galesburg, Illinois, the establishment of which was announced last spring. Her term of residence will be for six weeks during the first semester. The subjects of Miss Tarbell's lectures will be "The Growth of Big Business in America."

DR. JOHN ELOF BOODIN will join the department of philosophy of the University of California at Los Angeles during the coming year. It is expected that Dr. Ferdinand Casper Schiller, of Oxford University, will lecture during the second semester.

ERNEST W. LINDSTROM, professor of genetics at the Iowa State College at Ames, has returned after a year in Europe. He was assistant director of the International Board in Biology and Agriculture. Professor Lindstrom traveled in most of the countries of Europe where there is important research, except in Russia, in order that the board, through fellowships and assistance to laboratories, might best assist the progress of science.

DR. F. W. HART, of the department of education of the University of California, has returned to Berkeley after conducting summer-session courses at Utah Agricultural College in education administration. In the early part of the summer, Dr. Hart conducted round table discussions of New Mexico city and county school superintendents at their annual conference at Albuquerque, held under the auspices of the University of New Mexico.

DR. O. D. FOSTER, university secretary of the Council of Church Boards of Education, has returned to his work after five months spent in the recuperation of his health, most of the time in Europe. Dr. Foster visited Italy, Switzerland, Austria, Bohemia, Germany, Holland, Belgium, France, England, Ireland and Scotland.

DR. E. A. BIRGE, president emeritus of the University of Wisconsin, has returned from northeastern Wisconsin where his party of ten men studied the contents of 229 lakes. Dr. Birge spent his seventy-seventh birthday unpacking boxes containing hundreds of samples of lake water and low forms of lake life, collected during the summer in the comprehensive study of lake productivity which he began about thirty years ago.

DR. ROBERT L. KELLY, executive secretary of the Council of Church Boards of Education and permanent executive officer of the Association of American Colleges, gave lectures on college administration at the summer sessions of Columbia University, New York University and the University of Minnesota.

SEVEN courses for the Lowell Institute lectures have been announced. Vilhjalmur Stefansson will give eight lectures on the Arctic regions during January. He will be preceded by M. Paul Havard, professor of the College of France, who will give the opening course on "La sensibilité française au dix-huitieme siècle" in French; Professor Robert DeCourcy Ward, professor of climatology at Harvard University, who will discuss "Man and his Climate," in eight lectures, and Dr. Paul J. Sachs, professor of fine arts at Harvard University, whose subject is not ready for announcement. The three remaining lectures will be by Dr. Chester N. Greenough, professor of English at Harvard, on "The Influence of English on American Literature in the Eighteenth Century"; R. G. Hawtrey, on "Economics and Sovereignty," and Ernest Barker, professor of political science in the University of Cambridge, on "English Political Ideas during the American Revolution."

WILLIAM MILLIGAN SLOANE, from 1896 to 1916 when he became professor emeritus, Seth Low professor of history at Columbia University, died on September 10, aged seventy-seven years.

DR. ANDREW HENRY PATTERSON, professor of physics of the University of North Carolina for twenty years and for the last seventeen dean of the school of applied sciences, has died at the age of fifty-eight years. Dr. Paterson had leave of absence from the university and was resting at Little Boar's Head, New Hampshire, in the hope of recovering his health.

HENRY LANE ENO, research associate in psychology at Princeton University and a member of the American Psychological Association, died on September 10. Mr. Eno gave to Princeton University the building for the department of psychology.

ROBERT FORSYTH, who prior to his retirement twenty-four years ago was superintendent of schools and principal of the high school in Lebanon, New Hampshire, for sixteen years, died on September 13 at the age of eighty-seven years.

THE National Recreation Congress will be held in Atlantic City, New Jersey, from October 1 to 6. In addition to the group discussions nationally known leaders are being invited to speak at general evening sessions. There will be opportunity to participate in music programs, mass games and recreation evenings; unusual recreation activities will be shown in the exhibit room, and on Friday and Saturday the national finals of the Model Aircraft Tournament will be held.

From June 15 to June 30, 1929, an international library conference will be held in Rome. The conference, which has received the approval of the Prime Minister of Italy, will be convened by the International Library and Bibliographical Committee, a committee formed by representatives of fifteen nations at the fiftieth annual meeting of the British Library Association in 1927. Invitations will be extended to different countries to send official delegates as guests of the Italian government. As the meeting of the American Library Association will be held in the southeastern part of the United States in the spring, it is probable that a special party will sail for the international conference within a few days after the close of the meeting.

WASHINGTON UNIVERSITY, ST. LOUIS, is the recipient of the residue of the estate of the late George Warren Brown, shoe manufacturer, which amounts to $630,000.

BETWEEN $500,000 and $1,000,000 is left by the late Robert H. Ingersoll, manufacturer of dollar watches to create the "Robert and Roberta Ingersoll Foundation" in New York City within the next two years, to aid "worthy boys" in obtaining a "college, university or professional education."

LONG ISLAND UNIVERSITY has moved to its new building in Brooklyn. The Brooklyn College of Pharmacy which was established in 1887 by the Kings County Pharmaceutical Society as a lecture center has become a part of the university. It became a full-fledged technical school in 1891. It has graduated about 3,000 students and its classes number about 250 each year.

EACH year the Iota chapter of Phi Sigma Sigma fraternity, at the University of Pittsburgh, Pittsburgh, Pennsylvania, presents a scholarship of one hundred dollars to a Jewish girl, not a member of a fraternity, who is entered as a junior or senior student in the university. The recipient of the scholarship is selected on the basis of scholastic attainment, leadership and personality. A committee composed of the dean of women, two members of the faculty and two members of the fraternity select the girl best deserving of the award. The scholarship is awarded annually at the June commencement, and is known as the Iota of Phi Sigma Sigma Scholarship Award.

THE city council of Oakland, California, has voted an increase of approximately 25 per cent. to the Board of Library Directors for the use of the Oakland Free Library, Oakland Public Museum and Oakland Art Gallery. This will increase the available funds about $50,000 over last year's revenues. The city of Piedmont, California, entirely within the geographical area of the city of Oakland, which has been paying to the city of Oakland $1,500 a year for service from the Oakland Library, is increasing its payment this year to $4,770. The commissioner of revenue and finance of the city of Oakland in his letter transmitting the proposed city budget to the council said, among other things: "The library performs a great and useful work in the community. Furthermore, it is in the hands of a trained and competent personnel and I am convinced that any money given to this fund will be wisely and advantageously spent."

TWENTY-FIVE seniors in the school of education at the Pennsylvania State College are now in Johnstown for a nine-weeks' period of practice teaching, in which they will take complete charge of certain high-school classes, under the supervision of the resident teacher and a college staff faculty member. This is the second year that the Johnstown schools have been used for this purpose. Professor Frank A. Butler, formerly on the faculty of the University of Wisconsin, is in charge of the resident supervision. A second group will go to Johnstown for nine weeks beginning with November 12.

THE University of Wisconsin School of Education, including various teacher training courses, enrolled 1,418 students during the last academic year, excluding the summer session. Because most of the students in the school register as juniors, after two years of regular university work, the upper classes show the heavier enrolment. Seniors numbered 589, juniors 421, sophomores 142, freshmen 169. There were also two adult specials, 90 graduate students, three fellows and two scholars.

STATISTICAL analysis of the registration records for new undergraduate students at the University of California this semester show that women outnumber the men by twenty-eight and that although the total registration of new undergraduates is 116 greater than last year, there is a decrease in the number entering the medical school, the college of mechanics, the college of chemistry and the school of jurisprudence. Divided into classes, the new undergraduates, all undergraduate students who have never attended the university before, appear as follows: 73 seniors, 536 juniors, 216 sophomores, 1,580 freshmen and 83 special students, making a total of 2,488. Of this total, 1,231 are men and 1,257 women. The number of students entering the university with advanced standing, that is, sophomore rating or higher, has steadily increased during the last fourteen years from 21 per cent. in 1914, to 34.3 per cent. in 1928. The women have consistently outnumbered the men for the past three years. Among the new undergraduates about 8.2 per cent. are registered from outside the state.

THE School Board of Pottsville, Pennsylvania, and the Parent-Teacher Association will jointly conduct an investigation into conditions in the schools, following the resignation of F. W. Moser, principal of the high school. The board has refused to accept his resignation. Mr. Moser made the following statement: "My resignation as principal of the Pottsville High School has been under consideration by me for a long time and did not come suddenly. I have no statement to make as to the reason which caused my resignation, but if pressed by the school board will be only too willing to disclose my reasons. I believe that my resignation will be for the good of the high school and those concerned."

SUPERINTENDENT ROBINSON G. JONES, announces that steps toward shortening Cleveland's school course from twelve years to ten will be started this year. The action is in line with the policy extensively discussed at the last convention of the National Education Association and in other educational organizations. Cleveland is one of the first cities in the country to try the experiment. It will probably require several years to make the change.

THE school grades of unemployed pupils in the high school at Joliet, Illinois, are only one per cent. higher than the school grades of the employed pupils, according to a study reported to the United States Bureau of Education in connection with its survey of part-time education. Those pupils who were employed devoted approximately two hours per day to employment outside of school hours, that is, before school, after school and on Saturday. The study was made of the school grades of 250 employed and 1,650 unemployed pupils in the Joliet Township High School, Joliet, Illinois, for the school year 1927–28. The reasons the pupils gave for work were as follows: 58 per cent. of the pupils wanted spending money; 27 per cent. gave as their reasons, "necessary to stay in school," "to help parents," and "to buy clothes and books"; 6 per cent. wanted to occupy their spare time, and 9 per cent. referred to car fare, savings accounts, money for college, vacation funds or experience. Eighty-two per cent. of the employed pupils stated that the work did not interfere with their accomplishments in school. The average weekly earnings per pupil employed was $4.82 for the boys and $2.87 for the girls.

THE *Journal* of the American Medical Association states that one new case of infantile paralysis was recently reported from Baltimore County, but no new cases from Baltimore City. The outbreak appears to be on a downward trend. Eighty-nine cases in all have been reported in Baltimore since the first of the year. Six of these cases resulted fatally, the last death having been reported, August 30. The total in the state numbered 117 during August. The public schools of Baltimore did not reopen until September 17. This decision was actuated by the Parent-Teacher Association expressing opposition to opening on September 5 Serious administrative difficulties in the delayed return of a large number of pupils would have been encountered had the schools opened on schedule, and after a two and a half hour debate, the Baltimore City School Board decided on postponement. The board, however, is convinced that there is no necessity for this postponement, and, if there were no other consideration than the public health involved, it feels that it would have been its duty to open the schools as planned. Parents on the advice of their family physicians refused to allow the children to resume their classes on the fifth.

THE tercentenary of the laying of the foundation stone of George Heriot's Hospital, a famous old Edinburgh school, has recently been celebrated. The school is one of the oldest institutions of Edinburgh, having been founded by George Heriot, court jeweler to King James VI of Scotland.

A REUTER despatch reports that six French professors have been engaged by the Turkish government to teach in the Constantinople and Smyrna schools and that one hundred young Turks are going to France for study.

THE municipality of Berlin is planning to increase the number of infant welfare centers and to equip them with irradiation apparatus against rickets. All children who are rachitic or show evidence of becoming so will receive treatment free of charge. Children will also be given orthopedic treatment when needed. As the orthopedic department of the university clinic is overburdened at present, new orthopedic centers are to be established in the municipal hospitals.

DEMONSTRATION trains and traveling motion pictures are two innovations in India by means of which officials of that country hope to spread information to the illiterate millions regarding cooperation and other subjects. It has been found that in this way large areas can be covered and that everywhere large and interested crowds are attracted by the pictures and exhibits. The first demonstration train was introduced last year. It consisted of seven cars, including one each for agriculture, public health, industries and cooperation. The agricultural car was an effort to show the producer how the quality and quantity of his output could be improved by scientific methods. It contained samples of cereals and other products, implements, fodder and feeds for cattle, fertilizers, insecticides, etc. The cooperative car contained exhibits designed to show the benefits of cooperative enterprises in Bengal, and officials were present to explain the exhibits and give out information.

THE Peking correspondent of the London *Times* cables that "students of Tsinghua College —an institution which owes its existence to America in devoting to its upkeep the undisbursed portion of the Boxer indemnity—are making hay of the organization, built up after years of educational effort. They claim that the college is full of accumulated evils, and, as comers from afar in pursuit of learning, they are distressed by the sorry spectacle. Their association, determined to get rid of the domineering elements—the masters who prescribe the lessons—has telegraphed to Shanghai for a new president, who will be agreeable to manage the college according to the ideas of the students. Meanwhile, the students are carrying on a campaign against the masters, who insist on a fixed curriculum, regular hours, periodical examinations and all the other hindrances to youthful enjoyment, and have compelled five of them to resign by swarming into their homes in the dead of night. Their particular complaint against the professor of chemistry is that he did not know enough about Sun Yatsen's 'three people's principles.' It is understood that practically all the staff intends to resign if the new president arrives."

ACCORDING to a recent report of the national society in Germany organized to provide vacations for children, there are in that country 1,300 vacation colonies with accommodations for 100,000 children. Every year through them about 370,000 school children, one tenth of the school population of Germany, get holidays in the country, the total number since the organization of the agency being about 4,000,000. The work is done through private welfare societies in cooperation with municipalities, public school insurance agencies and other organizations. About 70,000 of these children are provided for in farm families. Special rest homes are provided for those in need of medical supervision. A new development in Germany is the "forest school" system, by means of which entire classes with their teachers are transferred to the country for several months. The railroads which in Germany belong to the government, furnish free transportation for the vacation trips. A follow-up system has been established to check the results of the plan. A complete change of climate and surroundings is found to have produced good effects in 90 per cent. of the cases, and vacations spent near home produce good effects in 40 per cent. A special committee was recently organized in Austria for the purpose of arranging vacations for Austrian children in Germany and German children in Austria.

SPECIAL CORRESPONDENCE

RECENT SECONDARY SCHOOL REFORMS IN CHILE

DEVELOPMENT of all sides of the child's intellectual and physical well-being and freedom to express his own personality are the outstanding features of the new general regulations for secondary schools issued by the Chilean government during the month of July. These regulations, which reflect some of the modern trends of education which have been entering Chile from Europe and the United States, also show a sincere desire to adapt the schools of Chile to the special needs of the nation.

According to the new regulations special attention is paid to health in the schools and classes are to be held out of doors wherever the health of the pupils and the nature of the subject studied permit. In so far as possible all studying is to be done in the school, and no teacher can require a student under fifteen years of age to do work at home. Furthermore, all new pupils are required to take a physical as well as a mental examination.

Special attention is given in the new regulations to developing the personality of the student. The child's personality should not be curbed by too rigid discipline, and no corporal punishment should be administered in the schools. Individual thinking should be developed, and for this purpose text-books are considered as an aid but not as an essential part of education. Teachers can not require the students to buy them. Furthermore, the lecture system is to be abandoned, except in the few cases where the subject itself requires presentation of the work in this manner.

In the regulations stress is laid on forming a spirit of cooperation among the students, cooperation with the students and teachers and also cooperation with the community outside. For this purpose the establishment of Boy Scout units is favored, and approval is given to plans for implanting habits of temperance and of school savings. The school is considered the nucleus of a school community bearing the same name as that of the school. This community is formed of students, teachers, parents and guardians, and is governed by a board chosen annually. Like most parent teacher associations, the organization deals with matters of health, spiritual culture, moral development and productive efficiency of the child. At first the community considers some of the internal problems of the school, which are brought to its attention by the principal of the school. But it is expected that in time the scope of its work will be enlarged: improving conditions around the school building and grounds, helping needy students, carrying on a sort of community extension work outside of the school itself.

These general regulations come as a sequel to several decrees, which, beginning with that of January 20 of this year, have revolutionized the secondary schools of Chile. Of the 117 secondary schools previously open, several have been closed, giving way to schools of the new order, while many have added or substituted new courses. The schools formerly were a heterogeneous group, but under the new laws they are classified and arranged into an orderly system.

The new program of the schools is arranged so as to open a field of productive activity to Chilean youth, and consequently the schools now meet in a better way the economic needs of the country. The introduction of technical courses in most of the *liceos* or high schools is the outstanding feature of the new program. There are twenty-one purely technical highs, which have a five-year course, during the last three years of which majors are offered in commerce, industries, agriculture, mining and feminine trades. Although the other lyceums are not primarily technical, each has a technical major in which the student can specialize during the last three years of the six-year course. The fifty so-called *liceos semi-integrales* have two sections or majors: one technical and one of either arts or sciences. The seven so-called *liceos integrales* have all three majors: technical, arts and sciences.

The two purely cultural high schools are the National Institute and the Diego Barros Arana Boarding School, where the students specialize during the last three years in one of the following sciences—mathematics, physics, chemistry, biology; or in one of the following humanities—literature, philosophy, history.

Specialized secondary education is also given in the following types of schools: Commercial institutes, schools of commerce, industrial schools, vocational schools for girls and schools for abnormals.

Entrance requirements for the secondary schools include a diploma from the six-year primary school course or the passing of an examination on those subjects. At present pupils of eleven years of age are admitted, but it is expected that after the new system has been in operation a few years the minimum age will be placed at from thirteen to fifteen. Upon completion of the high school course the pupil will receive a *Licencia Secundaria* (secondary school certificate) if he graduates from the scientific or arts course, or a *Certificado de Competencia* (certificate of competency) if he graduates from a technical high or a technical course. The former diploma will admit the possessor to the university institutes connected with the University of Chile at Santiago, which are professional preparatory schools.

The new curricula for the secondary schools were put into practice when the Chilean schools opened this year in March. The department of education claims that the reforms have already proved themselves successful. The enrolment this year was larger than last year, so large that several parallel classes had to be formed to take care of the students. The enrolment in many of the schools shows a marked preference for scientific and technical majors, and, according to the school authorities, this justifies the new changes. The following enrolment figures are given to illustrate this preference: In No. 3 Girls' Lyceum eighty-one enrolled in the scientific course, seventy-nine in the technical course and thirty-three in the arts; in the fourth-year course of the Amunátegui Lyceum fifty-one scientific majors enrolled, twelve in the arts and eleven in the technical course. The government is spending five million pesos in equipping schools for the new technical courses, and it is hoped that the present school system will adequately meet the needs of the secondary school education of the nation.

R. S.

DIVISION OF EDUCATION,
PAN AMERICAN UNION

DISCUSSION

THE ALGEBRAIZATION OF MATHEMATICS

THE term arithmetization of mathematics seems to have been introduced by the late Felix Klein, who directed attention to a marked tendency in the development of mathematics since the time of A. L. Cauchy towards an emphasis on arithmetic concepts. Recently it has been pointed out that the tendency towards arithmetization can clearly be traced back to the time of Euclid and that it furnishes one of the most useful unifying principles in the study of the history of elementary mathematics.[1] In the present article we aim to direct attention to a closely related tendency which may be denoted by the term *algebraization of mathematics,* and which can be as clearly distinguished from the tendency towards arithmetization as the subject of algebra can be distinguished from that of arithmetic. The existence of the former tendency has been frequently recognized indirectly, and its marked development in modern elementary mathematics was forcibly expressed by Sir Oliver Lodge in his "Easy Mathematics," 1906, page 127, where it is stated that "An equation is the most serious and important thing in mathematics."

One of the clearest instances of algebraization is exhibited by the works of I. Newton and G. W. Leibniz relating to the founding of the broad subject now commonly known as Calculus. It is now easy to see traces of this subject in some of the works of Archimedes, and especially in many of the writings of the first half of the seventeenth century. Near the end of volume two of the well-known "Vorlesungen über Geschichte der Mathematik" by M. Cantor it is stated that the infinitesimal calculus may be said to have been discovered during the half century 1615–1668, and that Fermat was especially successful in developing differential calculus while Pascal took a leading part in the development of the integral calculus. While traces of the algebraization of this subject may be found in the works of these French mathematicians it remained for Newton and Leibniz to inaugurate a real algebra of this calculus, and hence the credit of the discovery of the broad subject of Calculus is now commonly given to these men. It would be more nearly correct to say that they algebraized some of the earlier developments relating to Calculus and thus stimulated an active interest in a very fertile field of research at that time.

The algebraization of trigonometry may be said to have been inaugurated by Vieta even before the concepts of the trigonometric functions had been arithmetized. Traces of much earlier steps towards algebraization in trigonometry are numerous, especially in the works of Arabian mathematicians. In fact, it has been recently discovered that a work by Archimedes on the heptagon contains various steps in this direction.[2] These earlier steps seem, however, to relate to special problems rather than to the development of a general method for the study of the subject of goniometry. In the study of this subject the algebraic equation plays a very fundamental rôle. In particular, Vieta observed the relation between a cubic equation having three real roots and the goniometry formula by means of which the cosine of $3A$ can be expressed in terms of the cosine of A, and thus he threw much light on the so-called irreducible case in the general solution of the cubic equation. In this and in various other developments the algebraization of trigonometry led to important advances in the subject of algebra itself just as the arithmetization of various ele-

[1] *Cf.* H. Wieleitner, *Jahresbericht der Deutschen Mathematiker-Vereinigung,* Vol. 36 (1927), p. 74; G. A. Miller, *Science,* Vol. 62 (1925), p. 328.

[2] *Science,* Volume 67 (1928), page 555.

mentary concepts has led to new advances in the subject of the theory of numbers.

The second book of Euclid's "Elements" is commonly regarded as a kind of geometrical algebra, and hence it results that the contact between algebra and geometry was implicitly recognized already in ancient times. This contact was especially emphasized by R. Descartes, and his work aroused a wide interest in the general problem of the algebraization of geometry. Efforts along this line gave rise to the vast subject of analytic geometry, which has close contact with the various graphical methods of calculation and of conveying with striking clearness by means of graphs various scientific facts. Just as the arithmetization of elementary mathematics was greatly aided by the choice of related units of linear, surface and solid measures, so the algebraization of more advanced mathematics has been aided by an increasing emphasis on the laws of combination of the elements under consideration irrespective of the wide range of meanings which may be attached to these elements. Hence algebraization tends to economize thought and it is this feature thereof that has been largely responsible for the growth of this tendency and will probably insure its permanency. At any rate, the history of mathematics appears more connected if it is noted that arithmetization and algebraization have been fundamental tendencies in many of the developments of mathematics of the widest scope.

G. A. MILLER
UNIVERSITY OF ILLINOIS

DIPLOMAS IN EREWHON[1]

HE had been out from Erewhon, had Professor Egsin, and was now returning to the land, beyond the Range, when as luck would have it, I chanced to have from his lips an account, brief indeed but to me most telling, of the way they do in Erewhon, about diplomas. The professor's account of the Erewhonian diploma procedure was upsetting to me; for it seems that in his land the graduates of high schools were always expected to secure two diplomas. As soon as I got his drift I resolved to hide the fact that our own high-school (and college) graduates receive but one diploma; they are not required to capture two.

Had it not been for the incompatibility of practice on diplomas, here, and there, the professor and I might have spent our forty minutes in the gentle bliss of noting that our minds moved along on parallel tracks, for we were both sold on education. But on diplomas, diplomas and attendant circumstance, we were far apart, or, as one is to two.

As one might surmise, the difference in number of diplomas connoted a difference in educational theory. And in the talk something would occur every little while to leave me perplexed or staring. "Conditioned in lightning" was one of the jolts. Now just what might "conditioned in lightning" be, I asked myself. I inferred that a pupil who showed too much fear of this electrical phenomenon might draw less than a passing mark in emotional development, whether or not he succeeded in passing all the tests for academic subject-matter graduation and getting *that* diploma.

Egsin must have divined my confusion; he veered more and more to particulars. It seems he had had the duty thrust upon him of running down and bringing to book parents whose reprehensible tantrums and stodgy fixations proved a handicap to the children of their gangrenous households, for a child from an emotionally non-integrated home had about as much chance to get his Mot-Cult (Emotional Culture) diploma in June as a grizzly bear would have of being mistaken for a hummingbird. Hence, the pursuit of the parents by the educators. No more rough stuff in the homes.

This tutor, or combination tutor and domestic Nemesis, went on to say that the Erewhonians had begun with the academic standard, but that an epidemic of murders had rocked the teaching profession. It was palpable, ran on Egsin, that a man might hold a subject-matter diploma in one hand and an automatic in the other. Something had been overlooked. The Mot-Cult diploma was the culmination of a reform that went to the very roots of things; education now, in Erewhon, was not what it was; it was improved.

Now in my day it was the commonest occurrence to damn the teacher if you did not like

[1] Butler, Samuel, "Erewhon, or Over the Range."

the subject. It was only when Egsin was unrolling his exposition that it dawned on me how unjust this proclivity was to the teacher. Here I was, a man of forty, perceiving, and for the first time, that there must have been a flaw in my emotional structure for having fallen so readily into the vice of getting mad at the wrong object or so often at anything; I recalled with shame how I had fallen over chairs, and blamed the chairs; and in the benign presence of Egsin I felt like a student of statute law who discovers that the legislature has repealed his information. How many omissions and perversions may not have fallen to my lot, a graduate of merely the subject-matter side, as it were?

As I am a pacifist, at least to the extent of believing that war is uneconomical and messy, I felt out the professor on war.

"I'll venture to say," answered Egsin, "that in every war you have ever had there have been among the brawlers the most highly educated men of the time; anyhow that was true in ancient days in Erewhon; men with our highest degrees showed few generic differences in emotion from the ordinary run; it was as if the scholars were on a height for learning but on a primitive level for feeling. The Mot-Cult diploma is a tangible evidence of an appreciation of a consistent cultural elevation. While we always give subject-matter diplomas at commencements, the Mot-Cults get the hand."

The time was upon us when Egsin would take off. But my eagerness was greater than ever. "Pardon me," said I, "but tell me this; I must be frank. Never have I met a person, never have I dreamed of meeting a human being who seemed to have such adroit facility for laughing at the right time." (I had sprung two or three little jokes.)

"It's in the curriculum," replied Egsin, eying the aluminum bird that would bear him beyond the Statues and into Erewhon. "The Mot-Cult diploma is not granted simply for avoiding rages, fears and envies; it goes to him in whom are built up appreciations and kinds of sensibility. The world is made by praise."

The propeller whirred, the multiple motors roared and a tornado of rushing air drowned my words, Egsin waved farewell, and did even that in a manner giving a subtle charm to leave-taking, dismal by convention, and possibly soon afterwards may have been presiding at commencements, passing out diplomas with both hands—the subject-matter diploma with one, and the emotional culture sheepskin with the other.

ARLAND D. WEEKS

STATE COLLEGE,
FARGO, NORTH DAKOTA

QUOTATIONS

THE COLLEGE YEAR

UNTROUBLED by anxious questions what is wrong with the American college, or even by definite findings that pretty nearly everything is wrong, something like 300,000 young men and women have made all necessary preparations for becoming freshmen within the next fortnight. In this respect they behave very like their adult relatives who continue to get married despite the breakdown of marriage, to earn their livings in the offices of shops despite the crisis of the white-collar class, to raise cotton, wheat and hogs despite the prostration of agriculture and to vote the party ticket despite the disintegration of the parties. As an index to national prosperity the extraordinary growth of higher popular education may be considered at least as significant as the increase of automobiles.

In 1890 high-school attendance accounted for 5½ per cent. of all children of high-school age; in 1926 the percentage was 35. In 1890 the number of college students was 1½ per cent. of the total population of college age; in 1926 it was 9 per cent. The new academic year will probably find 1,000,000 students in the colleges, universities and professional schools. This enormous gain has been effected in the face of mounting costs of college education far beyond the rise in the general level of prices. Last June President Emeritus Thwing stated in the New York *Times* that the average annual cost of tuition for men and women twenty years ago was $136; to-day it is $336. Even when allowance is made for the relatively greater amount of self-support among college students, it is obvious that a high condition of family well-being stands behind a four-fold increase in the number of students purchasing college education at double the cost.

The rush to the colleges has not been an unmixed blessing; certainly not from the point of view of harassed college administrations and faculties compelled to face a problem both numerically and qualitatively complex. The opinion has been expressed in competent quarters that 50 per cent. of the students now in college do not belong there. Thirty years ago there were many men in college who did not belong, and the ratio has undoubtedly risen. But until we have agreed upon a definite formula of what colleges are for, and what is success in college and what is failure, and until the psychologists and the personnel experts have perfected a really satisfactory measuring rod for fit and unfit, we are justified in refusing to be discouraged. In every great social forward surge there are involved waste and error. The wise man waits for stabilization and ultimate results, and in the meanwhile buckles down to the day's task.

That actually is what the college administrators and teachers are doing. Experimentation is the order of the day; in dealing with the mere pressure of numbers; in providing opportunity for the exceptional student; in new pedagogical method; in adapting curriculum to new social conditions. The things that are wrong with the American college arise largely out of things that are well with the American people—an increasing material well-being exploited for a broader intellectual development.—*The New York Times.*

LETTER TO THE FRESHMEN OF NORTHWESTERN UNIVERSITY

You have applied for entrance to the freshman class of the College of this University. We have considered your credentials carefully, have judged that you are capable of performing all our required tasks, and have accordingly accepted your application.

If we had the opportunity to sit down together for a few moments it is probable that you would ask me pertinent questions about the University and about the college life here at Northwestern. You would want to know the attitude the University takes toward the freshmen and the probabilities you might have of a successful college career.

The ideal of this college is to select only those applicants who by aptitude and training are capable of meeting the demands of the college. But this college has assumed the further responsibility of so cooperating with the individual student that he may actually accomplish the end which he has been adjudged able to attain. We have accepted you as a freshman and we will attempt to give you every possible form of assistance in order that you may succeed as a student at Northwestern University. In our attempt to assist you I desire to make certain suggestions which I trust you will welcome.

For you, as a freshman student, this year is possibly the most critical in your life. It marks a turning point, it is the measure of your progress, and is the beginning of a new epoch. You have ceased to be a child and have entered into adult life. You will be less shielded and protected than in the past, and you will be affected by a richer and more complex environment. Your safety will not be provided by parental care but must be sought in your own strengthened will power and in your enlightened self-determination.

Unfortunately, many students in our American colleges have lacked the requisite strength of will and enlightened self-determination, and their college careers have ended in failure. According to the report of the U. S. Department of Education, out of every 1,000 students who enter college, 678 fall by the wayside and only 322 secure a degree of any kind. The record at Northwestern is much better than the average for the nation, so that of each thousand that enters more than 322 succeed in securing a degree, but in every entering class, even at Northwestern, there are many who fail in completing the course and securing a degree. In each freshman class many fail to complete the work of the year and to appear as fully accredited sophomores the following year. Many of these failures are unnecessary and are due to the fact that the entering student fails to comprehend the nature of his environment, and accordingly the environment is his undoing, although it might be his source of strength.

In the hope of increasing your chances of success I want to call your attention to certain phases of the environment at Northwestern that experience has shown to be important in the careers of our students.

The first phase of your environment to which I call your attention is one that will press in on our students very hard this year and may threaten you. This phase is the one that may be spoken of as the economic or the financial. The cost of living is not as high in Evanston as it is in some college communities, but it is very high. Disaster can be avoided only by economy and wisdom in all financial matters. You will be tempted as never before to spend more than you can afford. There will be no guardian to restrain you, and you are in great danger of spending your money needlessly and thus sacrificing your opportunity to remain in college.

Certainly as many as one half of all our entering students will find it necessary or desirable to earn a part or all of the money required to meet expenses. We have just appointed one man who will devote his entire time to securing part-time employment for the students in Evanston. Remunerative work will be found for many of our students—possibly for all who desire such opportunities. For many of our students the time devoted to earning money may be so wisely distributed that it will not seriously interfere with other duties. The nature of the work may also be such that it forms a helpful supplement to the training in the classroom.

Many students who possess insufficient ready cash realize that their earning power will be much greater after graduation, and so have the wisdom to borrow a part of the necessary funds. The University has an inadequate number of scholarships but it will this year grant $175,000 in scholarships, loans, and fellowships to students. You should feel free to apply for any financial assistance available.

We welcome the young men and women of limited means who earn part or all the money required to meet the university expenses, but we warn you to avoid the work that in its nature or its amount injures your health or interferes with your other duties. We urge upon you the most scrupulous care in all your financial matters and the practice of rigid economy in all the non-essentials. Where additional funds are required we urge the borrowing of money, if possible, rather than to engage many hours daily in earning money during the academic year. If you happen to be one who has abundant financial resources, we urge upon you the importance of conforming to the democratic habits of thrift that characterizes every ideal college community.

The second phase of our environment to which I desire to call your attention is a complex one including bodily health, physical training and athletics. These three should constitute a mutually connected whole.

Although you are required to present data from your family physician, you will be given a physical examination immediately after arrival in Evanston by our physicians. You will be under more or less constant supervision by our medical staff. If conditions demand, the Department of Physical Education will give you corrective exercise in keeping with the findings of our physicians. Before you take part in competitive athletics you will be examined as to your capacity for such strains.

Spencer Hall is conveniently located and properly equipped to take care of your physical ailments. You are asked to call there in order that expert service may be given to your physical needs. We desire that you should call at this health center for such apparently minor ailments as slight wounds, colds and general indisposition. Here our doctors and nurses will be at your service and if conditions warrant you will be given hospitalization.

All students are required to take a course in physical training. The character of the work for each student is determined by the department after careful consideration of individual needs, and it may include athletic sports, swimming, or indoor gymnastics. If you so desire you may elect that your physical training should be taken in either the Army R. O. T. C. or the Navy R. O. T. C.

Athletics are a regular branch of our Department of Physical Education. Athletics are made interesting and all are encouraged to participate. We believe in competitive games, whether intercollegiate or intramural. We believe that the best physical training is had in competitive games. While in college it is quite as unwise to give too much attention to athletics as to give too little. You should not allow athletics to absorb a large part of your time, your thought, or your energy. Excessive interest in athletics is suicidal to many a college student. Because of this excessive interest the work of the classroom is often neglected with the resultant ineligibility for participation in games, and finally the exclusion from college for failure to attain our standard of scholarship. Beware lest athletics become an end and not merely a means to the greater end for which you have entered this college.

The third phase of your environment to which I refer is the social. This includes most of the field spoken of locally as "Student Activities." We have come to appreciate the importance of the social environment more and more during recent decades. The historians of the future may well refer to the past century as the period of extreme individualism, and to the present century as the period of the awakening of the social. This, your first year in the University, will be your greatest opportunity for the development of your social nature. We want you to begin to think and to act in terms of the many rather than in the narrow and childish terms of individual selfishness. We advise you to cooperate with your fellow students in all helpful ways. Join at once your class organizations, the local church organization of your faith, the Y. M. C. A., a civic, a dramatic, a literary, a musical, a social, or such other organizations as are provided to meet the needs of all the members of your class. My advice to every student is to join at least two different organizations. Many of our students find it desirable to join also some smaller group where the social contact is especially intimate.

Although the social environment may be very helpful, it is too often overemphasized and perverted into a detriment. During the first days of your attendance at college the social environment will in many ways assume an undue importance. Do not allow it to blind you to the other and the more important phases of your environment. The social is important and helpful when properly subordinated. Beware lest the social should be regarded by you as the aim of your college career instead of merely as a means to a higher end. The Dean of Men will be ready to give you advice concerning your social relationships. He will appreciate an opportunity to discuss with you any question that you may raise concerning "activities" on this campus.

The fourth phase of your environment to which attention should be called is the religious. A religious interpretation of life is inherent in the traditions of Northwestern. We believe in the Fatherhood of God and the Brotherhood of man. Your Alma Mater is proud of those children alone who in a small way or a large way help in the work of civilization, who contribute something to promote human weal, who strive to advance the Kingdom of God on earth. She seeks as her children those who find such an environment congenial, and who enter the University better to equip themselves for such a service. We urge you to take advantage of this phase of your environment by cooperating with it. You may have been cooperating with the religious institutions in your home community, and by leaving your home and coming to Northwestern you may sever that relationship. In your application blank for admission you indicated the church of which you are a member or which you are accustomed to attend. This information will be forwarded to the local church of the denomination you mentioned. We will urge the members of that church to get in touch with you, and we are sure you will welcome any invitation they may extend to you. We most heartily recommend that you hasten to establish the most helpful cooperation possible with those religious organizations in this new environment that in your judgment are most effective in promoting the Kingdom of God on earth. The Director of Religious Activities will be prepared to advise you on any problems that may arise in connection with your religious life here in college.

The last but the most important phase of your environment to be mentioned is the educational. Northwestern is not an economic or a money-making institution; it is not an athletic association; it is not a social club, and it is not a church. It was not founded and is not conducted as any of these or as a substitute for them. Northwestern University is exclusively an educational institution. We welcome as students only those that come because they desire to learn. The subjects of instruction, the classrooms and the laboratories—these are the center and the objects of supreme importance in your university career. If it were not for these, the University would not have been founded or you would not have entered Northwestern, or you certainly would not remain here.

Regular attendance at classes and completion of daily assignments are habits that may be acquired, and which ordinarily assure success in an educational career. The professors in charge of your classes will welcome an opportunity to help you over any difficulties arising in the classroom. The entire staff of the Personnel Department devotes all its energy to helping students to solve their college difficulties. You will be required to call once at the personnel office, and to state facts concerning your progress. It is most desirable that you should feel free to call there for help in solving any difficulty that arises and affects your progress in college.

If you have the strength to keep the educational aim from being eclipsed by the other phases of your environment, your student days will fulfil all your expectations. You will be true to the cause that brought you to Northwestern. You will continue to report present at the roll-call of those who have the will power and the enlightened self-determination to profit by a university training.

WALTER DILL SCOTT

OFFICE OF THE PRESIDENT

EDUCATIONAL RESEARCH AND STATISTICS

USE OF NEW-TYPE EXAMINATION QUESTIONS IN PSYCHOLOGY AT THE UNIVERSITY OF MINNESOTA

IN 1925 the writer described the attempt of the department of psychology to build up a large file of new-type questions so that "a reservoir of from 1,500 to 2,000 objective questions could be developed from which examinations in endless variety could be quickly assembled and used as occasion demanded."[1] A methodology for determining the diagnostic significance of each question (the extent to which a given question differentiates between good students and poor students in a given course) was also described. The present brief article is in the nature of an accounting regarding the extent to which the department, over a period of some five years, has been able to carry out the plan as outlined. It is believed that the publication of this material at the present time may be of interest to many instructors contemplating a similar venture.

Altogether, our file of questions for introductory general psychology (a three credit, two quarter course for sophomores) now contains 2,261 new-type questions. Of these, 662 or 29 per cent. have been statistically analyzed to determine their diagnostic value.[2] Ultimately we hope to complete the analysis of all questions, placing in one file those which have proved most valid and effective and the remainder in another file. With this aim accomplished, we should be able to make up examinations including both valid and non-valid questions, but scoring only the valid questions in determining a student's mark. This would decrease the time and cost of scoring and would also increase the validity of our examinations. Enough work has been done to indicate that our present examinations contain much dead wood which not only adds to costs but also detracts from their value.

Each question used in an examination is typed on a card three by five inches, together with a notation regarding the right answer. The cards are then classified as to topic and form of question. In making up new examinations the committee of instructors pulls from the file a representative group of cards cover-

[1] Donald G. Paterson, "The Preparation and Use of New Type Examinations." Pub. by World Book Co., Yonkers, N. Y. 1925. pp. 60–64.

[2] These statistical evaluations are made possible by a special grant authorized by President L. D. Coffman. Two major students in psychology (Josephine Conger and Cornelia Taylor) have been in charge of this project and the tabulations contained in this article were made by them as part of their report of progress.

ing the topics to be included in the examination, arranging them according to the form of the question. These are then placed in the hands of the department stenographer, who proceeds to cut the stencils for mimeographing.

TABULATION OF AVAILABLE QUESTIONS IN GENERAL PSYCHOLOGY ON FILE, AUGUST 1, 1928

Topic	Form of question: Single choice	Matching	True-false	Analogies	Completion and single word answers	Total
Introduction to psychology	33	......	0	18	46	97
Nervous system	85	......	5	65	95	250
Reaction tendencies	11	......	8	6	14	39
Native and acquired traits	39	......	4	19	26	88
Emotion	29	......	4	32	32	97
Learning	67	......	8	38	73	186
Memory	23	......	14	3	12	52
Association	4	......	0	0	3	7
Attention	16	......	7	9	24	56
Sensation	0	......	0	1	0	1
Fall quarter topics	......	214	......	......	......	214
Total	307	214	50	191	325	1087
Sensation	7	......	23	0	0	30
Perception	5	......	2	0	0	7
Imagery	22	......	4	5	20	51
Association	22	......	5	20	28	75
Testimony	7	......	3	6	10	26
Suggestion	16	......	3	5	15	39
Efficiency	13	......	3	0	3	19
Will and personality	30	......	8	17	49	104
Intelligence and individual differences	97	......	80	56	85	318
Abnormal psychology	70	......	73	54	117	314
Winter quarters topics	......	191	......	......	......	191
Total	289	191	204	163	327	1174
Grand total	596	405	254	354	652	2261

By shuffling the cards a new stencil can be cut yielding a duplicate copy. Two or more duplicate copies are then mimeographed and when used are passed out alternately so that copying from one's neighbor is well nigh impossible.

The following table shows the distribution of the questions according to form and topic.

The topics in the table are arranged in the order of their presentation during the fall and winter quarters. The questions are all based on the lectures and on the study assignments in R. S. Woodworth, "Psychology;" A. I. Gates, "Elementary Psychology;" R. Pintner, "Intelligence Testing," and B. Hart "The Psychology of Insanity." The small number of questions dealing with sensation and perception is due to the elimination of these two topics from the elementary course shortly following the introduction of new type examinations. These two topics are now covered in a specialized course elected by students planning to major in psychology.

Scrutiny of the table reveals a fair picture of the relative emphasis placed upon various topics in our present elementary course. The following consolidation will perhaps indicate this emphasis more definitely:

	Number of questions
Introductory topics	97
Nervous system	250
Reaction tendencies, native traits and emotion	234
Learning and memory	238
Imagery and Association, Testimony and suggestion	191
Will and personality	104
Intelligence and individual differences	318
Abnormal psychology	314

It is apparent that the department makes liberal use of all forms of questions with the exception of the true-false type. The 254 true-false questions were used only during 1922 and 1923. Analysis of these questions showed such a small proportion to be effective in differentiating the several levels of ability that it was decided to abandon them. The 405 matching questions have not been distributed by topic because they are usually presented in blocks of twenty or twenty-five paired items covering a wide number of topics. In view of the difficulty experienced in the devising of satisfactory analogy questions it is gratifying that 354 such questions have now been accumulated. Increasing emphasis is being placed upon matching and analogies questions since available analyses point to these forms as unusually effective.

The task of preparing an adequate file of new-type questions for the introductory course may be said to be fairly complete. With this achievement behind them, members of the department are now making the examinations for the advanced courses equally objective.

DONALD G. PATERSON
UNIVERSITY OF MINNESOTA

THE ABILITIES AND ACHIEVEMENTS OF ELEMENTARY SCHOOL PUPILS BEFORE AND AFTER A VACATION

MUCH evidence is now to be had concerning the differences in test scores of elementary school pupils before and after the summer vacation. Most of the experimenters have not concerned themselves, however, with the changes which occur in the period immediately following the vacation period. This article is written for the purpose of reporting a portion of such a study[1] and in the hope of stimulating further investigation of this character.

The summer vacation in the schools in which the writer did his testing was sixteen weeks in length. Tests were given on the three days preceding the closing day in the spring, and alternate forms of the same tests were given on the three days following the opening day of school in the fall. Finally, the same tests as those administered in the fall were again given on the three days prior to the closing day for the Christmas holidays. This made the school period fifteen weeks in length as compared with the sixteen weeks of vacation.

The tests used for intelligence were, in grades 7B and 5A, the Otis Self-Administering Tests of Mental Ability, Intermediate Examination, and in grade 3A, the National Intelligence Tests, Scale A. In reading, the Stanford Achievement Tests were used throughout; in spelling, the Morrison-McCall Spelling Scales; and in arithmetic, the Courtis Standard Research Tests, Series B. The results for approximately fifty cases in each grade are given in the accompanying table, the mental or education levels having been determined by comparing the scores with the norms for various ages as reported in the test manuals and elsewhere.

[1] The complete study is reported as Research Bulletin Number 10, Bureau of Educational Research, Madison, Wisconsin. It is entitled "Differences in the Achievements of Elementary School Pupils Before and After the Summer Vacation." 1928.

CHANGES IN MEAN ACHIEVEMENT IN TERMS OF MONTHS OF MENTAL AND EDUCATIONAL AGES

	Over vacation period. (16 weeks)	Over school period. (15 weeks)	Net change in both periods combined. (31 weeks)
Intelligence			
Grade 7B	+11 mos.	+ 6 mos.	+17 mos.
Grade 5A	+ 8 mos.	+ 7 mos.	+15 mos.
Grade 3A	+ 4 mos.	+14 mos.	+18 mos.
Reading			
Grade 7B	+ 5 mos.	+ 6 mos.	+11 mos.
Grade 5A	− 2 mos.	+ 6 mos.	+ 4 mos.
Grade 3A	− 4 mos.	+ 8 mos.	+ 4 mos.
Spelling			
Grade 7B	0 mos.	+ 2 mos.	+ 2 mos.
Grade 5A	− 7 mos.	+ 9 mos.	+ 2 mos.
Grade 3A	− 7 mos.	+10 mos.	+ 3 mos.
Arithmetic attempts			
Grade 7B	0 mos.	+18 mos.*	+18 mos.*
Grade 5A	−12 mos.	+20 mos.	+ 8 mos.
Arithmetic rights			
Grade 7B	0 mos.	+18 mos.*	+18 mos.*
Grade 5A	−12 mos.	+13 mos.	+ 1 mo.

* Extrapolated values.

Read the above table as follows: Grade 7B gained in intelligence during the summer vacation an amount which represents the normal gain for about eleven months. During the school period the same grade gained an amount equal to the normal gain for six months. The total gain during the vacation and the following school period (a total of less than eight months) was equivalent to the normal gain for seventeen months.

It will be noted that grades 7B and 5A, using the Otis test in intelligence, gained more during the vacation period than during the school period. In both periods, however, they gained considerably more than the normal amount of gain for that length of time. In grade 3A the situation is different. Here a normal gain was made during the vacation period whereas an enormous gain was made during the following period of schooling. Taking the two periods together, the gain in intelligence in all grades is considerably above the normal gain for that length of time. This would tend to verify the conclusions of Miss Patterson[2] that "summer vacation seemed to have a beneficial effect on the intelligence of all children," and of Dr. Morrison[3] that "the summer's vacation sent the children back to school capable of making a very much better record on intelligence tests."

The fact that grade 3A shows such large gains during the school period as compared with the vacation period may mean that the National Intelligence Tests are affected by schooling to a greater extent than is true of the Otis Tests.

The fact that in every case except one the gains in educational achievement during the school period are greater than those which one might normally expect from any other school period of equal length is worthy of note. This is not true in the case of spelling in grade 7B, but this may be due to the fact that the pupil achievement is too near the limit of achievement which is possible on this test. The reasons for this increased achievement are no doubt many but may be attributed in part to the fact that the pupils are relearning much material which would naturally take less time than the original learning. It is also quite likely that the elimination of fatigue and a different attitude on the part of the pupils toward their tasks play a large part. Only in the case of intelligence scores in all grades and arithmetic scores in grade 7B is the net gain for both the vacation and the school periods as great as or greater than the normal gain for the same length of time.

The reader may well be cautioned not to make the assumption that the gains during the summer would have been comparable to those made in the fall had schooling been continuous. Numerous factors such as climatic conditions, the elimination of fatigue and difference in pupil attitude must be taken into account. More evidence is required concerning the effect of the all-year school as compared with the summer vacation custom before any conclusions concerning their relative merits can be drawn.

Comparing the changes in achievement over the summer vacation with the changes over a similar period of schooling, we may summarize as follows:

(1) The gains of the school period are greater than those of the vacation period in the case of all school subjects and in the case of intelligence in grade 3A.

(2) Grades 5A and 7B made greater gains in intelligence during the summer than during the school period.

(3) The gains in intelligence for all grades was much greater during the two periods studied (vacation plus following school period) than one would expect in any period of similar length. The seventh grade also gained more in reading and arithmetic than the normal gains for the same length of time. In all other school subjects the gains were smaller during the two periods than one might normally expect for a similar period of schooling.

(4) The gains of the school period were greater than one would normally expect for the same length of time in all tests except spelling in grade 7B. The construction of the test may have caused this exception to occur.

(5) During the vacation all grades lost or remained unchanged in school achievements with the exception of reading ability in grade 7B. During the school period all grades gained in all tests.

M. J. Nelson

Iowa State Teachers College,
Cedar Falls, Iowa

[2] Patterson, Mildred V. W., "The Effect of the Summer Vacation on Children's Mental Ability and on Their Retention of Arithmetic and Reading," *Education*, 46, 222–228, December, 1925.

[3] Morrison, J. Cayce, "What Effect has the Summer Vacation upon Children's Learning and Ability to Learn?" Educational Research Bulletin, Ohio State University, Vol. III, pp. 245–249, October, 1924.

SCHOOL AND SOCIETY

Volume XXVIII | Saturday, September 29, 1928 | Number 718

THE BACKWOODS SCHOOL IN AMERICAN FICTION

Backwoods communities are of two sorts. There are some which deserve the name only while they are new: of this sort are Woodville, seat of the state college in "The New Purchase,"[1] and Montacute, of Mrs. Kirkland's tale of the early Michigan settlements, "A New Home—Who'll Follow?"[2] There are other backwoods localities which have been settled for years, but which cling—one is sure it is from choice—to the ideas, speech and manners of a day when they lay just behind the frontier. Flat Creek, of "The Hoosier Schoolmaster,"[3] Pigwacket Center, where the young hero of "Elsie Venner"[4] served his apprenticeship as pedagogue, and the Horn of the Moon, where Locke Amsden[5] taught his first school, are types of such long-settled communities which have escaped the march of progress. All of them, however, those on the way to become cities and those which cling to the old life, possess identical characteristics which mark them as belonging to the backwoods.

I speak of the backwoods in the present tense, but the truth is they no longer exist, for they were banished by the mail-order store, the telephone, the automobile, rural free delivery and the radio. Little by little the differences which set them off as backwoods vanished. These differences were quite intangible, or rather, they differed by possessing rather intangible qualities in a degree not found elsewhere. The dweller in the backwoods was a bit more independent, more aggressive in his democracy, more inclined to admire feats of physical strength and courage and more interested in his neighbors than persons in other communities, and that was all. Democracy and independence were his most boasted traits. He carried his dislike of aristocrats and their manners to great extremes, and he resented bitterly every attempt to restrain him or to limit what he conceived to be his rights. Mrs. Kirkland is speaking for the backwoods when she says, "we all do as we like." "The New Purchase" contains many references to the bumptious democracy and independence of early Hoosiers, and to their contempt for all they deemed "big bug" and "stuck up." This distrust of all aristocrats and of all that pertained to aristocrats betrayed the backwoodsman at times into crudity, although he was on occasion capable of tact and of great consideration for the feelings of others; and it certainly contributed to his neglect of some of life's

[1] Baynard Rush Hall, "The New Purchase; or, Seven and a Half Years in the Far West." First published in 1843 this book, by the first principal of the seminary which grew into Indiana College and later into the University of Indiana, is one of the most valuable sources for the early history of Indiana. The Indiana Centennial edition, edited by Professor James Albert Woodburn and containing an exceedingly interesting essay and body of notes from his pen, was published in 1916 by the Princeton University Press.

[2] Caroline M. Kirkland, "A New Home—Who'll Follow? or, Glimpses of Western Life." First published in 1839, it enjoyed considerable popularity in this country and in England.

[3] Edward Eggleston, "The Hoosier Schoolmaster." This book gives by far the most interesting and accurate picture anywhere to be found of the backwoods school of eighty years ago. All quotations from "The Hoosier Schoolmaster" are by kind permission of the publishers, the Orange Judd Publishing Company, New York.

[4] Oliver Wendell Holmes, "Elsie Venner," 1861.

[5] Daniel Pierce Thompson, "Locke Amsden; or, the Schoolmaster." Published in 1847, this is one of the few American novels written with intent to reform education.

refinements which might have been his in spite of the difficulties imposed upon him by poverty and isolation. The backwoods admired strength and hardihood. To say that a person was a "right smart man" meant in the language of Flat Creek[6] that he was fit for a fight or a frolic or for the rough, heavy work with which life on lonely farms is filled. The unhappy individual who was physically weak was "sorry" and "no account," no matter what fine qualities of mind and spirit he might possess. In the backwoods people knew each other, and took toward each other very definite attitudes. One might be counted as an enemy or as a friend, but he was counted.

Schools were of great importance in the backwoods. Not that backwoods youths went to school a great deal, or learned a great deal while there, or made in after life any considerable use of what they gained by association with pedagogues. No, in such localities a boy learned from his father or from other farmers and hunters the things that really determined his earnings and local standing. The arts and knowledge that were of most worth to him had to do with handling a gun or axe, with ability to stand up for his rights with his fists if need arose, and with the crude farming by which, principally, the backwoods lived. The importance of a school in a backwoods community was due to its social values. The coming to a remote rural settlement of a teacher, especially if he were young and unmarried, was of itself an event of first importance; and once the struggle for mastery of the school was joined between the master and the older boys, or once the master began to show especial interest in some young woman, the community was supplied with a subject for speculation and comment that was a real boon. There were school games, too; hat ball, cat, bull pen, shinny, prisoner's base, pop-the-whip and coasting.[7] Three or four times a year, at least, all gathered at the schoolhouse for singing school or spelling school, and at the close of each session there was an exhibition. The school brought social play and glimpses of a world beyond limited horizons to people who had too little of either.

[6] Edward Eggleston, *op. cit.*

American writers of fiction have not neglected the backwoods school. The most interesting and accurate picture, indeed, that we have of the institution is that which they furnish us.

The typical backwoods school was housed in a log building of one room; its curriculum was elementary, being confined to reading, spelling, arithmetic, writing and a very little history and geography. There was usually a summer session taught by a woman and attended by the younger children, and a winter session for the older boys and girls over which a master presided. In newly settled communities more pretentious institutions might be opened, as the college at Woodville, in "The New Purchase," but such institutions, while in the backwoods, were not of them.

Augustus Baldwin Longstreet furnishes in his "Georgia Scenes"[8] a short but very interesting and quite accurate description of a hut typical of those in which schools were held.

> It was a simple log pen, about twenty feet square, with a door-way cut out of the logs, to

[7] Edward Eggleston's story of village school life, "The Hoosier Schoolboy," contains accurate accounts of some of the games played by boys eighty years ago. He is wrong in thinking that bull pen was played only in the old west; it was a favorite game in North Carolina until about 1900.

[8] Augustus Baldwin Longstreet, "Georgia Scenes, Characters, Incidents, etc., in the First Half Century of the Republic." This book was brought out first in 1835. The last edition was published, with the delightful illustrations of the second edition, in 1906. The description of the log schoolhouse quoted here is used by kind permission of Harper and Brothers, publishers of the last edition.

which was fitted a rude door made of clapboards and swung on wooden hinges. The roof was covered with clapboards also, and retained in their places by heavy logs placed on them. The chimney was built of logs, diminishing in size from the ground to the top, and overspread inside and out with red clay mortar. The classic hut occupied a lovely spot, overshadowed by majestic hickories, towering poplars, and strong-armed oaks. . . .

A large three-inch plank (if it deserves that name, for it was wrought from half a tree's trunk entirely with the axe) attached to the logs by means of wooden pins, served the whole school for a writing desk. At a convenient distance below it, and on a line with it stretched a smooth log, resting upon the logs of the house, which answered for the writer's seat.

Where stone was plentiful rock chimneys took the place of those of clay and sticks. Fireplaces were wide and high, so wide and high that a boy could step fairly into them, and rain and snow fell quite freely into the fire and upon the wide hearth on stormy days. Aside from the writing desk and bench of which Longstreet speaks, buildings of this sort were furnished with a pail and dipper, the latter usually a gourd, backless benches made of rough slabs or planks set on pegs which formed their legs, some crude tables of home manufacture and rows of wooden pegs driven into the walls, upon which the pupil's hats, caps and wraps were hung.

"Forest Life"[9] describes a western school of the forties.

The school-house still serves all denominations as a place of worship, and its walls, venerable with the gathered blackness of two years, have as yet no taste of paint. The various lawsuits, to which its location, construction, erection, and furnishing, gave rise being still undecided, the building remains an object of the first interest. The library which ought to decorate its western wall is still unpurchased, nor have I heard anything lately said of an appropriation for the purpose. Nor is there yet a tree planted whose shade may soften to the rising generation the fervors of the noon-spell.

The school of "Georgia Scenes" is fortunate in its location. All through the last century it was the fashion to regard land fit for no other purpose as good enough for a school site; and so generally were district schools located in abandoned fields that they came to be known, in the south and west at least, as old-field schools. The schoolhouse of "The Hoosier Schoolmaster" was placed over a pond. Strickland, in his "Pioneers of the West; or, Life in the Woods,"[10] describes a schoolhouse which stood on the narrow corner where two ways met, with no tree to shade it, "no fence except the one to cut it off from the green fields, with its high windows sprinkled with shingle-panes, and its high slab-benches, and rickety writing-tables." Land, it is ironically explained, "is too scarce in a new country, or, . . . it will one day be too valuable to waste much on a schoolhouse site."

Backwoods schools were ungraded; the simplest organization of classes was difficult. Only recently have texts been generally prescribed for use in schools. Mrs. Kirkland tells us:

The purchase of books, where there is nothing to control the whim of the teacher, and where every three months teacher is sure to have a new fancy, becomes quite an inconvenience among people of very limited means; and the effect of this is an utter impossibility of classifying the scholars and enabling the instructor to make the most of his time. Some parents insist on having the school books which served former teachers used as long as they last, and as we all do as we like, this makes fine confusion, and helps along the master's temper by thwarting his plans at every move.

"The Hoosier Schoolmaster" contains references to the doing of "sums" in school and to a learned young lady who had ciphered all the way to fractions, and was, as a natural consequence of such unnatural behavior, "stuck up." A schoolmaster is quoted in "The New Purchase," who declared, "I can teach sifering, reading,

[9] Caroline M. Kirkland, "Forest Life," 1842.

[10] William Peter Strickland, "Pioneers of the West; or, Life in the Woods," 1856.

writing, joggerfree, surveying, grammar, definitions, parsin—.'' But the great subject of study in these schools was spelling, and the favorite text, stronger even than ''McGuffey'' in the affections of the backwoods, was the ''Blue Back Speller,'' Webster's immortal ''Elementary.'' Edward Eggleston knew the backwoods and wrote of them as has no other novelist; his ''The Hoosier Schoolmaster'' furnishes the most accurate as well as the most interesting picture of the life of which he wrote. Of the place of spelling in the work of these schools Eggleston says:[11]

> There is one branch diligently taught in a backwoods school. The public mind seems impressed with the difficulties of English orthography, and there is a solemn conviction that the chief end of man is to learn to spell. '' 'Know Webster's Elementary' came down from Heaven,'' would be the backwoods version of the Greek saying but that, unfortunately for the Greeks, their fame has not reached so far. It often happens that the pupil does not know the meaning of a single word in the lesson. This is of no consequence. What do you want to know the meaning of a word for? Words were made to be spelled, and men were probably created that they might spell them. Hence the necessity of sending a pupil through the spelling-book five times before you allow him to begin to read, or indeed to do anything else. Hence the necessity for those long spelling-classes at the close of each forenoon and afternoon session of the school, to stand at the head of which is the cherished ambition of every scholar. Hence, too, the necessity for devoting the whole of the afternoon session of each Friday to a ''spelling-match.''

Schools were locally administered. County commissioners or district committeemen examined and certified teachers in the west and south, while in some New England states the settled minister of each town discharged this duty until well into the nineteenth century. Writers of fiction sustain the character given these examinations by Mrs. Kirkland in the following passage, ''Our law provides examinations, but forgets to provide for the competency of examiners; so that few better farces offer than the course of question and answer on such occasions.''

Teachers seeking certification in Wisconsin about the middle of the last century were, so Strickland tells us, rarely subjected to rigid examinations.[12] He describes two examinations. On one occasion the examiner had evidently ''grown rusty on the 'rudiments.' '' ''The examination consisted of a few common-place questions on geography and arithmetic, and an attempt at orthography, which after proceeding as far as the number of letters in the alphabet and their divisions, was rounded off with a laugh and the remark that he had really forgotten the first part of the spelling book.'' ''Locke Amsden; or, The Schoolmaster'' contains accounts of two examinations to which the hero of the tale was subjected, both of which were conducted by district committeemen. Captain Bunker, of the Horn of the Moon, refused to pay any attention to certificates of proficiency furnished the applicant by the schools he had attended, and examined him after a method of his own. Amsden's examination at Mill Town Emporium served only to reveal the vanity, ignorance and incompetence of the school committee. Jack Means[13] dispensed with an examination altogether, a procedure not at all unusual where certificates were issued by local authorities.

Mention has been made of the custom of conducting two schools in the same district, a summer school for the smaller children, taught by a woman, and a winter school, attended by the older pupils, which was taught by a man. ''The Algerine Captive,''[14] ''A New Home—Who'll Fol-

[11] Edward Eggleston, ''The Hoosier Schoolmaster.''

[12] W. P. Strickland, *op. cit.*

[13] E. Eggleston, ''The Hoosier Schoolmaster.''

[14] Royall Tyler, ''The Algerine Captive; or, The Life and Adventures of Dr. Updike Underhill, Six Years a Prisoner among the Algerines,'' 1797.

low?''[15] ''Forest Life,''[16] ''The Hoosier Schoolmaster''[17] and ''Pioneers of the West''[18] contain references to this practice. The Civil War drew men away from the schoolroom and women were drafted to fill places in winter schools. Academies and women's colleges were, after the first quarter of the last century, offering to women opportunity to prepare for teaching. The rapid expansion of the school system created a demand for teachers too great to be supplied by the men available. ''The Reign of Law''[19] furnishes the only discussion to be found in American fiction of the general opening to women of teaching positions in the schools.

McConnell's ''Western Characters'' contains an essay, ''The Schoolmistress,'' which reflects the popular idea of a summer school teacher of eighty years ago. She was, if this account can be trusted, usually a product of New England, and burned with zeal to carry the light of that blessed region to the dark west; her name was either Grace, Charity or Prudence; she had never known youth, was prim, angular and loose-jointed; she was a fast walker and an equally rapid talker; her piety was sincere and a bit rigid; and, finally, she ultimately left the schoolroom to preside over a home of her own, the real goal, some are unkind enough to hint, of her going west at all.

The Wisconsin schoolma'am as described by Strickland is a less competent but much more attractive figure; and one has the feeling that the author has drawn from life, a feeling lacking after reading McConnell.

> The universal schoolmistress that we used to see in our childish days, was young, somewhere between fifteen and eighteen, romping and wild, though good-hearted enough; by some chance unmarried, but by no chance without a beau to take her to parties, hops, and huskings. She had enjoyed all the advantages of a district school since she was twelve years old; and now—well, she made no secret and I see no reason why I should—the gist of the matter was she was to be married in the fall; and while her ''feller'' was ''breaking up'' a few acres, and chinking his cabin for the winter, she must teach a three-months' school as the only means at her command for getting a little money to buy her a smart wedding gown, and a table, or a high-post bedstead, or a looking glass, or something of the kind, as a sort of apology for the setting-out her poor squatter father, with his half a dozen children, could not give her.[20]

Pay was small. That Strickland's heroine received a dollar and twelve and a half cents a week was proof of her excellence, for such high pay was exceptional. Cleory Jenkins, of ''A New Home,'' was willing to supplement her salary by doing chores for a neighbor.

The lot of the rural schoolmaster in America has been a hard one, and while excellent men have served these schools few of the more able have remained long in them. Often these positions have been filled, in spite of the fistic prowess desired in a master, by the lame and physically weak. Thomas Jefferson expected that the elementary schools in Virginia should be taught by men unfit for hard work. American fiction furnishes pictures of schoolmasters who are admirable. John Gray, of ''The Choir Invisible,''[21] is strong and well trained; Ralph Hartsook[22] and Locke Amsden[23] are capable and men of fine character.

The typical backwoods schoolmaster of American fiction is, however, very different. The tradition of Ichabod Crane rules the

15 C. M. Kirkland, *op. cit.*

16 C. M. Kirkland, *op. cit.*

17 E. Eggleston, *op. cit.*

18 W. P. Strickland, *op. cit.*

19 James Lane Allen, ''The Reign of Law,'' Macmillan, 1900.

20 W. P. Strickland, *op. cit.*

21 James Lane Allen, ''The Choir Invisible,'' Macmillan, 1897.

22 E. Eggleston, ''The Hoosier Schoolmaster.''

23 D. P. Thompson, ''Locke Amsden; or, the Schoolmaster.''

American story. Updike Underhill,[24] the first schoolmaster to appear in an American novel, is a pedantic prig; Mr. Michael St. John, whose difficulties with his pupils furnish the theme for a rollicking chapter in Longstreet's "Georgia Scenes," is a ludicrous and rather contemptible figure. Cyrus Whicher, the ill-bred and ill-nourished schoolmaster of "A New Home," and William Horner, of "Western Clearings,"[25] were Michigan teachers of a day when, so Mrs. Kirkland tells us, "a plane, a chisel, and two dollars a day make a carpenter," and even less qualified a person to keep a school.

"The Schoolmaster's Progress," a sketch in "Western Clearings," is rich in details, and, in spite of the author's reliance upon exaggeration for the effects she hopes to produce, a valuable picture of schools and schoolmasters in the west eighty years ago. A quotation will indicate its nature.

> Master William Horner came to our village to keep school when he was about eighteen years old: tall, lank, straight-sided, and straight-haired, with a mouth of the most puckered and solemn kind. His figure and movements were those of a puppet cut out of a shingle and jerked by a string, and his address corresponded with his appearance. Never did that prim mouth give way before a laugh. . . .
>
> Truly he had a grave time that first winter. The rod of power was new to him, and he felt it his "duty" to use it more frequently than might have been thought necessary by those upon whose sense the privilege had palled. Tears and sulky faces were the rewards of his conscientiousness; and the boys—and girls, too—were glad when working time came around again, and the master went home to help his father on the farm.

In spite of a large boy who defied him the whole of his first year and of his ignorance—his scholarship was so meager that he could never decide whether Hannibal was a Roman or an enemy of Rome—Master Horner was a successful teacher, being reelected annually, until, quite of his own accord, he retired to the farm on which he had filed upon reaching his twenty-first birthday. His success was due in part to his circumspection, in part to his earnestness in the discharge of his duties and in part to his good judgment in never wearing his coat while teaching, a habit which left him unencumbered in settling the more serious problems of discipline and which impressed upon his employers the fact that he, like they, earned his bread by physical exertion.

Mrs. Kirkland explains the low order of ability attracted to the backwoods school. She asks:

> What man in his senses who is capable of earning a decent livelihood—"who has arms to pare and burn a moss"—will undertake a most vexatious and thankless task, for wages inferior to those of a common laborer? Who but the lame or the lazy can afford to work every day and all day, and "board round" besides, all for eight or nine dollars a month?
>
> And what inducement [she continues] can there be for study or any effort at improvement on the part of such young persons as may wish to become teachers, when they know that it will probably be their fate to be "examined" by persons totally incompetent, and that these posts are usually let out, like railway contracts, to the lowest bidder?

The tradition of the backwoods schoolmaster begins in American fiction with Updike Underhill, of "The Algerine Captive," while Tom Brainless, of Trumbull's "The Progress of Dulness," is the first figure of the kind in our poetry. "The Algerine Captive," published in 1797, is the fictitious biography of Dr. Updike Underhill, who was born in New England, worked on his father's farm, received his schooling in the district school and in the home of his minister, taught a backwoods school, read medicine and was captured by the pirates

[24] R. Tyler, *op. cit.*

[25] Caroline M. Kirkland, "Western Clearings," published in 1845, describes life in Michigan in the early days of its settlement. One chapter is entitled "The Schoolmaster's Progress."

of Algiers, among whom he remained for seven years a prisoner. The book affords Tyler opportunity to discuss education, duelling, the practice of medicine, Virginia parsons and various other topics. His views on the subject of Latin are of considerable interest. He is in substantial agreement with Trumbull, Freneau and Francis Hopkinson on the subject.

Updike Underhill read the classics with his minister and was in consequence of no further use on the farm. Upon recommendation of his minister he was employed to teach a school; there his life was so hard that his mother believed that a dream of hers of his falling among savages "was now out." Updike's poor pay, his conceit and general inefficiency, his struggles with his pupils and his deserting teaching after a very short trial are in what came to be the accepted tradition of the rural schoolmaster.

In fiction and in life rural schoolmasters of ability and ambition have a way of leaving the schoolroom for more lucrative and congenial lines of work. John Gray, schoolmaster of "The Choir Invisible,"[26] turned to the law, Ralph Hartsook[27] and Locke Amsden[28] took charge of village schools, William Horner took up government land. In his picture of men and manners of a century ago, "The Kentuckian in New York,"[29] Caruthers tells very briefly of a young man who made the district school a stepping-stone to a physician's practice. "When he came to these parts he drove what we call a Yankee cart, half wagon, half carriage, full of all sorts of odds and ends; when he had sold them out, he sold his horse and cart too, and then turned to keepin' a little old-field school." The Yankee "got considerable ahead," sold out the school, read medicine for four months, received his degree and set up in practice.

An important prerequisite of the backwoods teacher was the privilege of boarding without cost at the home of his pupils, his stay at each home being proportioned to the number of children it sent to his school. Many masters took advantage of this custom to make firm friends of the families of their districts; as did Ralph Hartsook[30] on that first Sunday at the home of his principal trustee, and as did the merry young master of "Snowbound," whose violin, stories, athletic skill, genial manners and willingness to make himself useful won him a warm welcome everywhere. "Boarding round" was frequently a trial to teachers; no doubt it was to hostesses as well, but backwoods people are too hospitable to breathe so much as a hint that a guest could cause trouble. We hear from the teachers often. Ralph Hartsook[31] was forced to board with Pete Jones and to sleep with young Pete, who had an annoying habit of taking his half of the bed in the middle. Mary Catlin[32] found beds not all they should be. Poor Cyrus Whicher[33] "'boarded round' till there was very little left for him." When he came to the home of Mrs. Clavers he had been reduced by slim fare to "a mere cuticle—a 'skellinton' as Mr. Weller would say—shaped like a starved greyhound in the collapsed stage, his very eyes faded to the color of skim-milk, which had doubtless been his richest potation since he attained the empty honors of a district school."

When one recalls the pay received by rural teachers the desertion of the work by all who could establish themselves in other

[26] J. L. Allen, *op. cit.*

[27] E. Eggleston, "The Hoosier Schoolmaster."

[28] D. P. Thompson, *op. cit.*

[29] William Alexander Caruthers, "The Kentuckian in New York," 1834.

[30] E. Eggleston, "The Hoosier Schoolmaster."

[31] *Loc. cit.*

[32] W. P. Strickland, *op. cit.*

[33] C. M. Kirkland, "A New Home—Who'll Follow?"

lines can not be wondered at. A dialogue in "The Columbian Orator"[34] mentions ten dollars a month as the wage of a master who had just been let go, and the majority of the committee which had discharged him regarded this remuneration as too high. The same committee employed a worthless applicant at five dollars a month. Mrs. Kirkland mentions eight dollars a month as the wage of a male teacher in Michigan during the forties. William Horner[35] in his third year received sixteen dollars a month, one dollar more than a New England school of the same period paid Locke Amsden[36] for his first school.

It will be recalled that Ichabod Crane sought to establish himself in comfort by marrying the daughter of a substantial farmer. McConnell[37] declares that many western masters followed this road to affluence. Sometimes, if fiction is as reliable here as in other matters, the heiress sought the schoolmaster. Mirandy Means set her cap for Ralph Hartsook,[38] and her mother undertook to advance her daughter's fortunes by reciting to the teacher the story of the happy lot of Squire Hawkins, who had come to Indiana a poor teacher and had married rich Flat Creek acres.

> Twenty year ago, when he come to these 'ere diggin's, that air Squire Hawkins was a poar Yankee school-master, . . . He didn't stay poar long. Not he. He jest married a right rich girl! . . . His wife hadn't no book-larnin'. She'd been through the spellin' book wunst, and had got as far as 'asperity' on it a second time. But she couldn't read a word when she was married, and never could. . . . Squire Hawkins jest put eddication agin the gal's farm and traded even, an' ef ary one of 'em got swindled, I never heerd no complaints.

Little in the way of scholarship was expected of these men. "The New Purchase" contains amusing accounts of the ignorance and pretensions of applicants for positions at the state college at its opening. One gentleman, seeing mention of chairs in the publications of the committee having charge of the selection of a faculty, offered to "*find his own chair,*" provided he was elected to a position. Another proposed to make a name as a literary man by publishing a spelling book, the distinctive feature of which was to be a column of "exemplyfying illustrations" parallel to each column of words to be spelled. Opposite to the word cream was to be placed the "exemplyfying illustration," "*Unctious part of milk.*" Another applicant who understood no language save his own offered to prepare for the chair of foreign languages at the rate of one language every three weeks.

Discipline in backwoods schools was severe. There isn't a novel in which they figure but the birch and the struggle between master and pupils holds a prominent place. In the oldest copy of "Ben Bolt" that I have seen a couplet runs:

> And don't you remember the school, Ben Bolt;
> And the master, so cruel and stern?

Daniel Pierce Thompson and Edward Eggleston were advocates of milder and more enlightened methods of discipline in schools. Eggleston records Mr. Pete Jones's formula for the complete education: "Lay it on good is what I says to a master. Lay it on good. Don't do no harm. Lickin' and l'arnin' goes together. No lickin', no l'arnin', says I. Lickin' and l'arnin', lickin' and l'arnin', is the good ole way."[39] But it is evident that he does

[34] Caleb Bingham, "The Columbian Orator." In the preparation of this paper an imprint of 1817 was used.

[35] C. M. Kirkland, "Western Clearings."

[36] D. P. Thompson, *op. cit.*

[37] J. L. McConnell, "Western Characters; or, Types of Border Life in the Western States." Particularly interesting for two sketches, "The Schoolmaster" and "The Schoolmistress," and for Darley's inimitable drawings of these characters.

[38] E. Eggleston, "The Hoosier Schoolmaster."

[39] *Loc. cit.*

not approve of it. Rough tactics had been resorted to by Locke Amsden's predecessors in the Horn of the Moon district,[40] but Locke managed his school without cruelty and without fights; and Thompson halts his story to advocate more intelligent methods of ruling schools. Both "The Hoosier Schoolmaster" and "Locke Amsden," however, reflect the rough ways found in backwoods schools. Amsden, when applying for a school, was told bluntly, "The question first to be decided is, whether you will be equal to managing our rough boys in the mountains." Jack Means[41] told Ralph Hartsook, "it takes a right smart *man* to be school-master in Flat Crick in the winter. They'd pitch you out of doors, sonny, neck and heels, afore Christmas." In the face of this warning and of the further declaration, "ef you git licked, don't come on us. Flat Crick don't pay no 'nsurance." Ralph persisted, and accepted Mr. Means's permission to "roll up and wade in." The young master did find that it took a "right smart man" to overcome the surly suspicions of the ignorant and to cope with the plots of the malicious. He defeated by a trick a scheme to duck him, and met an attempt to bar him out of his school after the manner of a young master of whom Greeley tells in his reminiscences, by smoking out the rebels.

There was real need that teachers in rural districts be men of considerable physical strength. Of all the hardships to which a backwoods schoolmaster was exposed, none was more severe and none made greater appeal to the imagination of the novelist than the ever recurring conflicts with the older boys of the school. Rural America loved rough sports, admired the man who could take care of himself and had no patience with the man who lacked strength or courage to stand up for his rights. A new master was sure to have these important traits tested before he had been long in a school, and it is not surprising that the tradition in American fiction runs that one of the important qualifications for teaching a district school was the ability to fight. The warnings issued Ralph Hartsook and Locke Amsden have been mentioned. It is easy to show that the tradition has grounds. In the winter of 1837 some hundreds of schools in Massachusetts were broken up by the warfare between masters and pupils.[42] Fithian records a barring out that took place in Virginia just before the Revolution. Horace Greeley describes the custom of barring out, as does Ramsey in his "Annals of Tennessee." A "barring out" or "turn out" was managed as follows: The older boys would agree among themselves to keep the master out of the school building, and so prevent the holding of regular sessions of the school. This might be done to force the master to grant a holiday, as in "Georgia Scenes"; it might be done to force the master to stand treat, as in Ramsey's "Annals of Tennessee"; or, as in "The Hoosier Schoolmaster," the object might be to humiliate the master and disrupt the school. At the time set for the "turn out" the older boys would take possession of the schoolhouse in the absence of the master, send the girls and younger boys out of doors, bar the doors and windows, and prepare to resist by force the entrance of the master. When the master appeared he usually made some attempt to enter, then, if the terms offered by the rebels were not too hard, capitulated. Masters too insistent upon their rights were likely to be ducked in the nearest creek. Parents and school trustees were usually neutral in

[40] D. P. Thompson, *op. cit.*

[41] E. Eggleston, "The Hoosier Schoolmaster."

[42] See Professor Norton's introductory essay in "The First State Normal School in America," p. xliii. About four hundred of the twenty-eight hundred winter schools in rural Massachusetts were broken up by the warfare between "big boys" and teachers in 1837.

these contests, the notion being that it was the master's business to manage his school. In "Georgia Scenes" the elders umpire the affair; but I find no record of this happening in real life.

Novels which deal with the backwoods school do ample justice to the spelling school. Mrs. Kirkland gives a full account of one held in William Horner's district, prefacing her story with a general account of the institution.

> The spelling-school is one of the ordinary winter amusements of the country. It occurs once in a fortnight, or so, and has power to draw out all the young people for miles round, arrayed in their best clothes and their holiday behaviour. When all is ready, the umpires are elected, and after these have taken the distinguished place usually occupied by the teacher, the young people of the school choose the two best scholars to head the opposing classes. These leaders choose their followers from the mass, each calling a name in turn, until all the spellers are ranked on one side or the other, lining the sides of the room, and all standing. The schoolmaster, standing too, takes his spelling-book, and gives a placid, yet awe-inspiring look along the ranks, remarking that he intends to be very impartial, and that he shall give out nothing *that is not in the spelling-book.* For the first half hour or so he chooses the common and easy words, that the spirit of the evening may not be damped by the too early thinning of the classes. When a word is missed, the blunderer has to sit down, and be a spectator for the rest of the evening. At certain intervals some of the best speakers mount the platform, and "speak a piece," which is generally as declamatory as possible.
>
> The excitement of the scene is equal to that afforded by any city spectacle whatever; and towards the close of the evening, when difficult and unusual words are chosen to confound the small number who still keep the floor, it becomes scarcely less than painful. When perhaps only one or two remain to be puzzled, the master, weary at last of his task, though a favorite one, tries by tricks to put down those whom he cannot overcome in fair fight.

By far the best account of a backwoods spelling school is found in "The Hoosier Schoolmaster." The story of the eventful evening which witnessed the victory of Ralph Hartsook over the champion speller of Hoopole County is too long to be quoted and so rich in humor and in color that no summary can do justice to it, but Eggleston's statement of what the spelling school meant to the backwoods can be lifted from its context without loss of interest.[43]

> There had to be a spelling school. . . . It is the only public literary exercise known to Hoopole County. It takes the place of lyceum lecture and debating club. Sis Means, or as she now wished to be called, Mirandy Means, expressed herself most positively in favor of it. She said that she 'lowed the folks in that district couldn't in no wise do without it. But it was rather to its social than to its intellectual benefits that she referred.

Nothing short of the full account can do justice to Jeems Phillips, conqueror of three masters, who was "spelled down" by the schoolmaster, to the Squire, to Jack Means and "ole Miss Means," or to the loves and hates and enthusiasms that run through the story.

The spelling school flowered in the backwoods and passed with the passing of the backwoods; pretended revivals of the institution have no root in the soil. The school exhibition, however, reached its greatest development in the village school, and American novels contain many references to it, by far the most delightful of which is that found in "Tom Sawyer." "The Schoolmaster's Progress" provides the only description of an exhibition in a backwoods school.

The exhibition took place usually on the last day of school, though in some schools they occurred three or four times a year. On these occasions pupils displayed their proficiency in reading, writing, spelling, arithmetic, history and geography. Prizes were distributed, and there were dialogues, declamations and songs; the performance lasting until well into the night. The whole countryside attended; and how people without theaters, professional singers or athletes did thrill to the efforts of

[43] E. Eggleston, "The Hoosier Schoolmaster."

their own entertainers! Compilers of school books had an eye to these occasions. Bingham's two books, "The American Preceptor" and "The Columbian Orator," McGuffey's readers and less famous books as well were filled with selections from plays and orations, and with homespun declamations and dialogues as well. "The Columbian Orator" contains Everett's old favorite, "Lines Spoken at a School-Exhibition, by a Little Boy Seven Years Old." The opening lines still linger in many a memory.

> You'd scarce expect one of my age,
> To speak in public on the stage;
> And if I chance to fall below
> Demosthenes and Cicero,
> Don't view me with a critic's eye,
> But pass my imperfections by.

Toward the close of the school year the pages of text-books and collections of declamations and dialogues were ransacked, parts were allotted to every pupil; and preparation, quite as delightful as the final presentation, occupied every mind and most of the time of the school. Not until teachers from colleges and normal schools introduced the more sophisticated graduation exercises, and motion pictures came to furnish amusement that could be had without effort, was the exhibition finally banished from the district school.

CHARLES F. ARROWOOD
THE UNIVERSITY OF TEXAS

THE NEW COLLEGE DEGREE—BACHELOR OF CITIZENSHIP

THE liberal arts colleges to-day are confronted with an impossible situation. They are overrun with students from all walks of life. "Don't miss a college education," is advice freely given. College is supposed to give a unique life experience not to be missed if possibly obtainable. It is seen as the avenue to material, social and spiritual opportunity. Although tuition fees have doubled, applicants to colleges have far more than doubled. So long as the country remains prosperous, young people will continue to swarm to college doors. Sons and daughters, not only of professional men, but of farmers, plumbers and storekeepers, aspire to scholarship and to degrees in arts and sciences.

While rejecting a few, the colleges accept the great majority of the aspirants to learning. They are started on a four years' journey presumably to terminate in the degree of bachelor of arts or of sciences. Of course a large number never reach the happy ending. They have not been able to keep up, or they have not found college what they expected it to be. Some have been "weeded out" (an abominable term), because not found to be "college material." Some return to their homes with indifference; others with bitter disappointment. All these young people have good capacity, but not the kind the college requires and stimulates. Others stay on the four years and acquire with difficulty the necessary quantity of credits, to be voted by a reluctant faculty the coveted degree.

Scholarship is what the institution has to offer, but of course the youth of this group never become scholars in any worth-while sense. While designated bachelors of arts or of sciences their studies have never sunk deep enough to become vital in their lives. The degree is like an emblem worn on the sleeve, or like a feather in the hat. Only a portion of those who go to college, possibly 30 per cent. of the entering group, are capable of using the college opportunity, and gaining by merit the learned degree.

What about the 70 per cent. not destined to become scholars? Let us listen a minute to the faculty discussing them. Shall we lower standards in order to retain them? Can we let them by with their inferior accomplishment? Shall we make concessions for evident lack of ability in particular subjects, mathematics, foreign language, laboratory science or written English. Faculty members become gray-haired attempting to teach persons of limited wits what they can not appreciate, and compromise themselves and their college by graduating those who should not graduate, incidentally giving to the student a wrong sense of values and a wrong estimate of himself. But I should insist, these young people are not nit-wits, even though the college with its traditional curriculum of arts and sciences has little to offer them. It is because the college curriculum is the Procrustean bed requiring conformity that they are found misfits. But who shall say that the conventional college subjects are the only things that can benefit the mind of youth?

Many of these young people have no clear motive in coming to college. They believe that the college experience is in some way desirable. An interest in scholarship they certainly have not. They do prize the company of the picked group of students and faculty members who become their associates during four pleasant years. They enjoy books of a kind. Of course they will enjoy college activities, such as dramatics, music and athletics. Plenty of these young people do aspire to a high type of life and citizenship, whether or not they ever can be scholars or care to be.

But the college says to them: "This is an institution of learning. Acquire mastery of the curriculum and remain. If you can not become learned, get out." But that the exodus be not too great the college is willing to compromise. It stamps persons with the insignia of a learned degree whose learning is superficial, even some who fail to catch even in slightest degree the spirit of science and of art. Teachers justify the compromise by saying, "The college experience did him good; remember what he was when he came, college life has developed him." This is often very true. But letting him remain is one thing, crowning him with the laurel of the bachelor of arts is something else. By so doing the college has cheapened its product and confused its purpose.

The thesis of this paper is that the time-honored degrees in arts and sciences should be limited to those who can earn them. Only they truly walk in the holy places. Such degrees are not for the 70 per cent. But these, if they are earnest and are prepared to use opportunities, we will not put out. There can be a new degree, new holy places for those willing to walk therein. These young people of the 70 per cent. wish to go to college. Society is anxious for a high type of citizenship. Why not retain them and provide new types of college activities? Why not create the degree of bachelor of citizenship?

What should be the requirements for the proposed degree and what are the advantages of the plan? It would require a student to remain in college four years as he now does, or possibly three years. It would require him to be a consistent, cooperable member of the college fraternity, by which is meant not a secret segregated clique, but the entire membership of students and faculty. It would require him to live up to a high standard of morals both in and outside of college, since character is the aim to be achieved. He would be stimulated to adjust himself to his fellows, to learn to appreciate them, get along with them and lead them according to his abilities. To-day many students whose limited ability makes their work drudgery, or who overestimate the value of grades, fail to get any social experience worth while in college. The new degree will aim at social power properly directed.

The student will be encouraged to enter extra-curricular activities such as discussion clubs, music clubs, dramatic work and athletics. He will enter them regardless of his scholastic standing. There are students who do well in such activities who have not much ability for scholastic attainment. Surely, then, these are the ones for extra-curricular activities. But, no! It is one of the ironies of present college practice that these are the ones kept out. They are ineligible because "down" in scholarship, and thus prevented from doing the only things they can perhaps do well. The activities undoubtedly bring out the student in many ways. They give him new appreciations and insights, afford expression and develop the social nature. But this is not to assume that college life is to become a round of pleasure. On the contrary, the pleasure aim is to be strictly subordinated, the same as is necessarily so in normal living.

Activities of college character, however, are not sufficient. They must be supplemented by work in the community. In fact, to confer a degree in citizenship on one without knowledge and skill in the problems and practices of good citizenship would be absurd. Certainly there are many grave social defects requiring the attention of a devoted citizenship. These can be studied and suggestions made to correct them. The studies should be made not merely by means of books, but by investigations, observation and contacts. One of the sad commentaries on the present college is that many of the students to whom we give the highest grades are utterly ignorant of current affairs. Another is that the public knows the college only through its football games and other recreational activities. The citizenship student will especially study current events. And the public may come to know him because of his participation in community affairs.

Adequate attention to the vocational interest must be prominent in the plan. A young man or woman who leaves college without definite vocational plan or with little economic capability is not only a useless citizen but may become a menace to society. At present a great many students work for a living while attending college. This practice can be encouraged for citizenship students. In fact, whatever the work may be, the student's attitude, diligence and sincerity in pursuit of it indicate the quality of his citizenship.

Of course the reader will ask what becomes of the curriculum for the candidate in citizenship. The answer is that the curriculum is optional and that examinations are not required. The student should be supplied bountifully with books and magazines and encouraged to use them. In fact, he should be required to make investigations and reports, to present theses and maintain logical arguments in discussion. To this end books will be necessary. Books will be used not for set lessons but to answer problems. The student will be advised to follow certain courses but without formal examinations.

Culture studies for the citizenship student will not be neglected. He may take the regular courses with the A.B. students. He should be particularly provided with interesting lecture courses covering the classics, such as Homer, Dante, Chaucer, Shakespeare, Molière, the Book of Job; also lectures on great periods or events of history, or achievements in science, and he should enter into discussions concerning them. He should be stimulated to an acquaintance with the great works of art and music. A student unappreciative of culture will not care to remain in college atmosphere, and one who is lazy can not acquire the degree in citizenship.

The faculty whose responsibility it is to train a body of students in citizenship will quickly formulate aims and develop methods. Of course a new technique of teaching will be required. The teacher himself should be a model citizen participating in community affairs. He should have high moral aims and gifts of leadership. The public may welcome young people trained in efficient citizenship more than the academic type whose minds are often educated away from real affairs.

The college student is sometimes represented as frivolous, and occasionally even as immoral. The citizenship student can be neither one and be retained in college. It is therefore upon moral qualities rather than intellectual ones that his retention depends. No longer can the college ignore the personal life outside of college halls. Whether on the campus or beyond the moral life is one. Possibly even activities of the kind mentioned by James in his "Moral Equivalent of War" could be pursued under college supervision. Certainly James' ideal, that the youth through labor become familiar with the hard foundations of our civilization, is a good one.

An advantage of the plan is that it eliminates the present hypocrisy of granting learned degrees to persons not earning them. What will the arts degree amount to in a few years if the present tendency of reckless conferring is continued? Compared with other countries, Germany, France, England, Japan and China, scholarship is not highly honored in America. This may be due in part to the cheapening of the A.B. degree. The plan suggested makes it a real and high honor to attain the scholastic degree for the 30 per cent. who can attain it.

The plan also affords the person of less brilliant mind the opportunity to taste of college life and to be moulded by it. It would train him in a somewhat direct way for community service; also to use the opportunities the community affords. It would reduce complexities in the athletic situation. Every college professor knows that a man who goes in hard for sports can not achieve in scholarship, and most of the athletes are without ambition to do so. There are occasional exceptions. We can say to the athlete: "Very well. You may continue to concentrate your attention and use up your energy on football, track and basketball, and if your attitudes are right, you may find citizenship value therein and receive credit on the citizenship degree. But most likely you can not remain a candidate for the arts degree."

And most important of all the candidate for the arts degree will find that scholarship is honored as it has not been recently. He will find himself in a group apart, as he is in reality. His loyalty to the college will not be challenged if he prefers absence from the athletic cheering squad. As he is qualitatively different he is not relegated to an inferior place in competition with sporting popularity. Furthermore, the degree in arts will be restored to its traditional place of honor, and a wondering public will be less confused in what a college is for.

JOSEPH T. WILLIAMS

WHITTIER COLLEGE,
WHITTIER, CALIFORNIA

EDUCATIONAL EVENTS

A FRENCH INSTITUTE OF VOCATIONAL GUIDANCE

THE establishment at the Sorbonne of the Institut National d'Orientation Professionnelle provides France with a national center for research and training in vocational guidance. The announcement of courses and staff states that the institute is a center of instruction regarding all subjects related to psychology in its application to vocational selection and guidance. The institute also encourages researches necessary to the development of scientific methods and to the control of their applications in employment, placement and counseling.

Courses of instruction are given by a distinguished faculty in physiology, pathology, psychology, child study, economics, industrial management and organization of guidance; and facilities are provided for observation and practice in vocational counseling bureaus.

MM. Fontegne, Laugier and Pieron are joint directors of the institute. M. J. Fontegne is general inspector of technical instruction and assistant director of instruction of the Seine; M. H. Laugier is chief of staff of the Sorbonne and director of the laboratory of physiology applied to mental hygiene, and M. H. Pieron is professor in the College of France and in the psychological institute of the University of Paris and director of the psychological laboratory at the Sorbonne.

The officers of the administrative council are as follows: *President*, M. Labbe; *Vice-presidents*, MM. Barrie, Gaillard, Luc and Sellier; *General Secretary*, M. Fontegne; *Treasurer*, M. Oualid.

Further information concerning this development in vocational guidance may be secured from Mlle. M. Lichbenberger, secrétaire-archiviste, Institut National d'Orientation Professionnelle, Musée Pédagogique, 41 Rue Gay-Lussac, Paris.

AGRICULTURAL EDUCATION IN SCOTLAND

A REPORT, in which the whole system of Scottish agricultural education was reviewed, was issued in September, 1924, by the Departmental Committee on Agricultural Education and Research in Scotland. The London *Times* states that it was later decided by the Scottish Board of Agriculture to institute an inquiry for the purpose of ascertaining how far agricultural education is reaching those actually engaged in farming or farm work, and is immediately effective in the improvement of farming practice. It was deemed desirable that the inquirer should not have been intimately associated with the existing educational system in Scotland, and accordingly Mr. J. R. Campbell, late assistant secretary of the Department of Agriculture and Technical Instruction for Ireland, was invited to undertake the inquiry. Mr. Campbell's report has now been issued by the Scottish Board of Agriculture.

The following are among the conclusions and recommendations made by Mr. Campbell in a long report:

> Agricultural education has effected very great improvements in farm practice, and especially in those branches to which most attention has been given, *viz.*, dairying, manuring, seeding, and poultry-keeping. The value of these improvements

amply justifies the expenditure that has been incurred.

Agricultural education is not reaching a sufficiently large proportion of those engaged in farming. This, Mr. Campbell says, is due to the fact that, so far as the less progressive farmers are concerned, too much time has been spent in trying to instruct in scientific subjects men whose habits and minds were already formed and fixed before the attempt to educate them in technical agriculture commenced. "It is more than doubtful if any useful purpose is served by instruction of a scientific nature except when it operates upon young minds already prepared by a sound general elementary education, without which scientific instruction, bulletins, and field experiments will be barren of educational results. On the other hand, the educated progressive farmer who reads and thinks will not attend courses dealing with subjects that are, to him, well worn. He is interested in the results of research, and can be reached best by means of lectures and demonstrations by specialists.

In order to reach the mass of farmers it is essential that the local winter courses should be developed intensively, and, it is clear, must have for their objective not only education, but organization directed to self-education of young farmers and farm-workers of, say, from 20 to 30 years of age. For these the type of instruction given by county organizers is likely to yield fruit, but even here the isolated short winter course, if the work ceases with the last lecture, can not be expected to have an adequate permanent effect.

Mr. Campbell suggests that before the end of a course the organizer should encourage the students attending it to constitute themselves a circle, club or society for the purpose of extending their studies after the close of the course. The organizers should deal specifically with the aims and objects of such an organization, should sketch its possible constitution, and outline the work it should undertake. Its primary work should be the continuation of their studies, and this might, with advantage, take the form of discussions initiated by one of their number on articles in agricultural journals, etc., or any matter of common interest to farmers.

PUBLIC AND PRIVATE SCHOOLS IN THE UNITED STATES

A steady increase in the percentage of school pupils attending public schools in preference to private schools is shown in a recent study made by the United States Bureau of Education, and reported in the *U. S. Daily*.

The study shows a rapid decline in the birth rate in the United States since 1915.

The American public school is experiencing a stupendous growth and prosperity. The percentage of pupils in public schools in the United States as compared to private schools is steadily increasing through the years. The latest figures on the subject show that of elementary pupils about 92 per cent. are now in public schools while 89 per cent. were in such institutions a generation ago. Sixty per cent. of the pupils in secondary schools attended institutions supported by the public in 1890, while 91 per cent. of such pupils attended public school in 1926. Seventy-seven per cent. of normal pupils went to public schools in 1890, but that number had grown to 93 per cent. by 1923. Where 13 per cent. of college students attended institutions supported by the public in 1890, 36 per cent. now attend institutions so supported.

The amount of money spent per pupil in the public elementary schools is rapidly increasing. In 1920, for instance, about $40 per pupil was being spent. The amount had increased to $59 by 1924 and in 1926 it was $63.

In the 36 years that followed 1890 the attendance at colleges and universities increased 529 per cent. During the same period the attendance at normal schools increased 676 per cent. These increases were strikingly great but were below those of high schools (not including junior high schools), which had more than 10 pupils in 1926 where they had one in 1890. The increase here was 1,055 per cent.

The most striking fact in the study, however, is the steadily and rapidly decreasing birth rate in the United States, which affects the number of pupils entering the schools each year and which may become an outstanding racial phenomenon in the near future. That number may become stationary, despite an increasing population.

The reduction in the birth rate is a fact that should not be overlooked. This rate has dropped from 25.1 per 1,000 population in 1915 in the registration area to 20.6 in 1926. This area included 31 per cent. of the whole population in 1915, and 76 per cent. in 1925. Infant mortality rates have dropped off materially during this 10-year period. The rate was approximately 102 per 1,000 live births in 1915, and 71.7 in 1925.

Applying the birth rate and the infant mortality rate for each year, this means that 22.5 children per thousand of the population reached the age of one year in 1916, and less than 20 per thousand in 1926. Applying the same rates to the estimated population for each year indicates that 2,239,000 children reached their first birthday in 1916, and 2,292,000 reached it in 1926. This is an increase of a little over 50,-000,000 in 10 years.

Any material decrease in the birth rate must in time have its influence upon the number of children who are old enough to enter school for the first time each year. Restricted immigration further reduces the number of, say, six-year-old children. It is quite evident that the number of six-year-old children is not increasing very rapidly from year to year. The 1930 census may show little, if any, increase in the number of children ready to enter school over the number shown in the 1920 census. If these same conditions exist for a number of years, school enrolments will reach a stationary period, especially in the lower grades.

The enrolment in all classes of schools combined amounted in 1926 to 31,000,000 pupils.

EXCLUSION OF CHINESE FROM MISSISSIPPI SCHOOLS

EFFORTS of a Chinese boy to enter the white schools of Mississippi has resulted in a ruling by the Supreme Court of that state reversing a decision of the Circuit Court and denying a mandamus plea by one Joe Tin Lun to compel the state superintendent of education and the teachers of the Dublin Consolidated School to permit him to enroll in that school.

According to the report in the New York *Times,* Joe Tin Lun contended, in substance, that if he were excluded from the school he would be denied the "privilege of the most favored nation" as provided for in the Burlingame treaty; that he was entitled to be admitted as a pupil in a white school because the United States government, with proceeds of school lands granted to the state, supports and maintains such school, in part, and that depriving him of the right to go to school violates a property right guaranteed by the Fourteenth Amendment to the Federal Constitution.

The first two contentions of appellee were summarily disposed of by Associate Justice McGowen, who delivered the opinion of the court, dismissing the petition by holding that the bare assertion in the record that a Chinese boy was not granted "privilege of the most favored nation," under Burlingame treaty, constitutes neither proof nor argument, and that funds derived from sixteenth section lands are in no manner controlled by the United States government, but constitute the state's own contribution to its own schools.

As to the third contention, the justice commented on the recent case of Rice *vs.* Gong Lum, in which it was pointed out that in the Constitution of Mississippi providing for separate schools for white and colored races, the term "white races" is limited to the Caucasian race, that the term "colored race" includes all other races, and that the "dominant purpose" of this provision "was to preserve the purity and integrity of the white race, and prevent amalgamation, and to preserve, as far as possible, the social system of race segregation."

He further said that "under the constitution," both state and federal, "the negro is an American citizen. . . . Then how can an alien Chinaman complain when he is assigned to a school provided, under our law, for the colored races? We thus permit him to share with our own American citizens our benefits and privileges, and enjoy all of the benefits and privileges accorded to one of our own citizens.

"We belong to that class of people who believe that there are no two things created exactly alike. Things are similar to each other. So it is with schools. They have a similarity, but it is certain that no two schools in Mississippi, or any other state, are exactly alike. The testimony of the county superintendent of education in this case shows that equal facilities are furnished to the two races, white and colored, and, in our opinion, that is all that is required under the Fourteenth Amendment."

THE CONTINUATION SCHOOL LAW OF NEW YORK STATE

THE Bureau of Labor Statistics has made public the following statement dealing with the decision of the Court of Appeals of New York holding the continuation school law of the state to be constitutional.

The New York law requiring certain employed minors between the ages of 14 and 18 to attend continuation schools has been held constitutional by the Court of Appeals of New York. Abraham Braunstein was convicted in New York for a violation of Section 601 of the Education Law in that his son failed to attend a continuation school in New York City.

The boy was over 16 years of age, had successfully graduated from a public school and had attended the high school for six months, but because of his father's financial losses he was obliged to leave school and go to work. He had attended a continuation school for a time. In addition, he attended a night school and a night preparatory school, as he was anxious to obtain the necessary educational qualifications to begin the study of law.

His employer informed him that his absence at the continuation school during office hours was so serious a handicap that he would be obliged to discharge him. Thereupon the boy, to save his position, ceased to attend the continuation school. The case was taken to the Court of Appeals on constitutional objections to the statute. The chief complaint against the statute was that as night schools had been created and are recognized and regulated by the department of education, the boy should be excused from the continuation day school if he attends the night school.

The Court of Appeals, in upholding the constitutionality of the law, gave the following opinion:

> There is a reason for the distinction. That children, at work all day, should also be compelled to study at nights is an evil in itself. Probably, under present conditions, it is an evil that may not be wholly corrected. So far as possible it should be minimized. Day-school attendance should be encouraged. Many employers may cooperate in carrying out the policy of the department. Others might not. They might insist that their employees attend night schools to avoid the interruption, thus making such attendance in effect compulsory.
>
> Once we had a law requiring children working in the daytime to attend evening school. The experiment was abandoned. It was found that their health was injured out of all proportion to the value of the education they received. The requirements as to girls also involved moral hazard. That should not be done indirectly which was found unwise when done directly. In truth, the evening schools are intended primarily for those who have reached maturity. And even four hours a week in a continuation school is not a mere waste of time. They do not confine themselves to vocational training. Optional courses may be taken leading to general education. For these reasons we think the distinction made by the legislature between day and night schools is justified.
>
> All minors in districts where continuation schools exist are treated alike. And treated as a labor law rather than as one affecting education solely, it is not discriminatory. It separates those who have completed a four-year secondary course from those who have not. It seeks to induce all to do so. If they will not or can not, it makes their right to work subject to the necessity of acquiring some further daytime instruction. The legislature might forbid all minors under 18 to engage in regular work during the hours of the school day. It might require them to spend those hours in study. It may do less.

NEW PROFESSORSHIPS AT YALE UNIVERSITY

YALE UNIVERSITY opened its 228th year on Thursday with several professors added to its faculties. Among these is Dr. F. d'Herelle, of Paris, France, who becomes professor of bacteriology in the Yale School of Medicine. In addition to having discovered bacteriophage, Dr. d'Herelle, who is one of the world's leading bacteriologists, has made important contributions in many fields of pure and applied bacteriology.

Dr. Wallace Notestein, who has held the Goldwin Smith chair of English History at Cornell University, has been appointed Sterling professor of English history at Yale. This appointment was made possible by the trustees of the estate of John W. Sterling, who in June, 1927, established four additional Sterling professorships, one each in the fields of law, English history, biology and vertebrate paleontology.

Dr. Walter Theodore Brown has been appointed professor of religion, with assignment to Yale College, as part of the university's program for the development of the religious life of its students. Professor Brown is a graduate of the University of Toronto and received the degree of doctor of philosophy from Harvard University in 1911. He has been for fifteen years a member of the faculty of Victoria College, University of Toronto. Three of the new professors will join the faculty of the Yale Divinity School, two as visiting professors. Halford E. Luccock, D.D., of New York, becomes professor of homilectics. Professor Luccock has been a member of the Hartford Theological Seminary and of Drew Theological Seminary. Dr. Terret Reaveley Glover, fellow of St. John's College, University of Cambridge, has been appointed visiting professor of New Testament in the Divinity School, and Wilfred Evans Powell, B.D., of Phillips University, has been appointed visiting professor of religious education.

Three of the new professors who have joined the Yale faculty will teach in the School of Law. They are Frederick Charles Hicks, of New York City, who becomes law librarian and professor of legal bibliography; Walton Hale Hamilton, professor of law, and Arthur L. Goodhart, visiting professor of law.

Professor Hicks has been law librarian and professor of legal bibliography at Columbia University. Professor Hamilton goes to Yale from the Robert Brookings Graduate School of Economics and Government of Washington, D. C., where he was professor of economics and government. Professor Goodhart, who succeeded Sir Frederick Pollock as editor of the *Law Review Quarterly,* England's leading legal publication, is a native of New York City and graduated from Yale in 1912. Later he went to England, where he became barrister at law of the Inner Temple and a fellow and lecturer at Corpus Christi College of the University of Cambridge.

Dr. Herbert Spencer Harned, who has been a member of the faculty of the University of Pennsylvania since 1913, has been appointed professor of physical chemistry. Elliott Dunlap Smith, a graduate of Harvard and of the Harvard Law School, has been appointed professor of industrial engineering in the Sheffield Scientific School. While in the employ of the Dennison Manufacturing Company he taught at Harvard, giving a course on "Social Psychology in its Industrial Aspects."

ART IN THE SCHOOLS

Interest in art among the school children of New York City is increasing, according to the annual report of the School Art League. Miss Florence N. Levy, secretary of the league, which maintains headquarters at the Barbizon, 140 East 63rd Street, New York City, said that 21,027 public, senior and junior high school pupils attended 48 lectures given by the School Art League at museums and exhibitions during the 1926–1927 school year. The league now has 14,811 junior members.

The organization maintained five Saturday morning drawing, modeling and craft classes, which held 145 sessions during the school year and gave in all 4,666 lessons in these subjects. Under the guidance of Mrs. Laurent Oppenheim, chairman of the scholarship committee, industrial arts scholarships were awarded in January and June, 1928, to 42 boys and girls graduating from high school who were entitled to a year's tuition at a professional art school. The Haney Fine Craftsmanship Medals were awarded to 820 pupils in elementary work shops, while 45 Art-and-Trades Club Medals for designs were awarded in the high schools of this city. The Alexander Medal for work in the second high-school year was awarded to 68 students, and 62 Saint Gaudens Medals were given for work in third year high-school classes.

An exhibition of work from the art departments of the city high schools was organized by the league and circulated throughout the United States by the American Federation of Arts. The work of gifted children was shown at the Art Center. The league also announces the following additions to the board of trustees: Miss M. Rose Collins, chairman of the art department of George Washington High School; DeWitt Lockman, member of the National Academy of Design and former chairman of the committee on education of that body; Miss Kate E. Turner, principal of the Bay Ridge High School, and Mrs. William H. Allen.

In addition to the above the following are members of the board: Mrs. John W. Alexander; Hermon A. MacNeal, sculptor; Mrs. Laurent Oppenheim; Mrs. S. T. R. Cheney, chairman of the Art Department, Washington Irving High School; Florence N. Levy, director of the design department, Arts Council of the City of New York; Huger Elliott, director of the department of education, Metropolitan Museum of Art; Forest Grant, director of art in high schools; Florence A. Newcomb, chairman of the art department of Haaren High School, and Otto H. Kahn.

THE CHILD STUDY ASSOCIATION OF AMERICA

THIS fall marks the fortieth anniversary of the Child Study Association of America which, for the greater part of that time, was known as the Federation for Child Study. Out of a small group of women who met to discuss their individual problems has grown a national organization whose work has extended to the far corners of the earth. As a fitting celebration a one day conference has been planned to be held on November 20 at the Hotel Pennsylvania, with a morning and afternoon session, followed by a dinner. Mrs. Howard S. Gans has been president for over thirty years and Mrs. Sidonie M. Gruenberg is the director of the organization.

Parental education and child study will be presented from two distinctive points of view at the conference. General principles and outstanding tendencies in the rapid development now going on will be discussed by leading authorities. In addition to this analysis of fundamental ideas, the actual working programs of state, university and volunteer organizations engaged in child study and parental education will be presented by their own staff members. Together these two portions of the program will give an authoritative survey both of the ideals and objectives and of the practical work of various types of organizations throughout the country.

At both the conference and the dinner, prominent leaders will bring to special aspects of child study and parental education the vital contribution of their own experience. Owing to the absence abroad of many of those closely associated with parental education, no complete announcement of these speakers can be made at the time the annual program goes to press. The full announcement will, however, be mailed in the early autumn to association members and others who are interested. Among the speakers of whom announcement can be made at this time are: Mr. and Mrs. Felix Adler, Dr. John Lovejoy Elliott, Dr. Bernard Glueck, Mrs. Sidonie Matsner Gruenberg, Porter R. Lee, Dr. E. C. Lindeman, Mrs. Henry Moskowitz, Dean William Russell, Dr. Edward L. Thorndike, Ralph P. Bridgman, Mrs. Cora Trawick Court, Miss Gertrude Laws, Mrs. S. M. N. Marrs, Robert E. Simon and Miss Edna Noble White.

EDUCATIONAL NOTES AND NEWS

ON the occasion of the recent meeting of the British Association for the Advancement of Science, honorary degrees were conferred by the University of Glasgow as follows: The Reverend Professor Shailer Mathews, dean of the Divinity School of the University of Chicago, received the doctorate of divinity. The doctorate of laws was conferred on Sir William Bragg, president of the association; Sir Thomas Henry Holland, president elect; Dr. Adrien Loir, director of the Natural History Museum at Havre, representing the French Association for the Advancement of Science; Dr. Frank Lincoln Stevens, professor of plant pathology in the University of Illinois, representing the American Association for the Advancement of Science; Dr. Franz Eduard Suess, professor of geology at Vienna; Professor E. Westermarck, professor of sociology in the University of London, and Professor P. Zeeman, the physicist, of the University of Amsterdam.

THE title of emeritus professor has been conferred by Cornell University on the following members of the faculty who retire this year: H. C. Elmer, professor of Latin; Frederick Whiting, professor of clinical surgery; H. H. Wing, professor of animal husbandry, and E. H. Woodruff, professor of law.

THE HONORABLE M. L. DUGGAN has been reelected state superintendent of Georgia.

DR. N. D. SHOWALTER, president of the State Teachers College at Cheney, Washington, is

Republican candidate for state superintendent of Washington, to succeed Dr. Josephine Corliss Preston, who has been state superintendent for sixteen years.

Dr. William A. Messler, principal of the Jersey City Teachers Training School, has been appointed by the New Jersey State Board of Education to be principal of the new state normal school to be opened next September in Jersey City.

Dr. Howard Dare White, assistant superintendent of schools of Jersey City, has resigned to become assistant state commissioner of education. Dr. White will succeed Lambert L. Jackson, of Princeton, who will become assistant superintendent of schools at Newark.

Dr. W. J. Osburn, formerly director of the division of tests and measurements in the Wisconsin State Department of Education, is now associated with Ohio State University as professor in school administration. He will give half of his time to work in the State Department of Public Instruction. Dr. H. H. Davis has been appointed assistant professor. He will also give half his time to the state department.

Dr. A. T. Stanforth, who for the past year has been a teacher in the Jamaica Training School for Teachers, New York City, has been appointed director of supervised teaching at Indiana University.

The board of superintendents of New York City has nominated Dr. Albert A. Aldinger for the health education directorship; Frederick L. Holtz for the principalship of the Maxwell Training School for Teachers, and Mrs. Letitia Raubicheck to the post of director of speech improvement. The post of director of health education became vacant a month ago when Dr. John D. McCarthy died suddenly. Dr. Aldinger, who has been nominated to succeed him, held the position until his retirement from the system in November, 1925. The speech directorship became vacant a few months ago when the Board of Examiners announced that Miss Agnes Birmingham had failed to pass the necessary test for the director's license. Mrs. Raubicheck is at present chairman of the elocution department of the Julia Richman High School. Miss Emma Johnson resigned as principal of the Maxwell Training School on September 7. Mr. Holtz was designated acting principal on her retirement. He has been head of the model school of the institution since 1913.

At Teachers College, Columbia University, Dr. Harold L. Clark has been appointed professor of education; Dr. John R. Clark, associate professor, and Dr. Clarence Linton, assistant professor.

Willard L. Chase, of Teachers College, has been appointed assistant professor of education at Boston University. J. Stevens Kadesch, principal of the Medford High School and president of the National Association of Secondary School Principals, has been appointed instructor in education at the college of practical arts and letters.

The Reverend Robert Russell Wicks, since 1925 chaplain of Mount Holyoke College, is to take up at the beginning of the academic year his work at Princeton University as dean of the chapel, a position recently established. He will be in charge of the undergraduate religious activities and will conduct the regular Sunday services in the new chapel built at a cost of $2,000,000.

Hermann Diederichs, for many years professor of experimental engineering and director of the Sibley School of Mechanical Engineering of Cornell University, will join the faculty of Princeton University as the first incumbent of the John E. Sweet memorial professorship in engineering at the opening of the academic year.

Dr. Charles Edward Hill, professor of political science, has been made acting dean of Columbian College, George Washington University.

Edwin F. Bradford, formerly registrar and director of admissions at Syracuse University, will open the new office of director of admissions at Cornell University. Registrar David Fletcher Hoy, who has combined the duties of registration and admissions at Cornell for almost thirty-five years, will continue as registrar, while Professor Bradford will handle admissions.

THE recently established Knox Taylor professorship of geography at Princeton University, which was founded with an anonymous gift of $150,000, will be filled by Professor Paul MacClintock, who was formerly associate professor of geology at the University of Chicago.

APPOINTMENTS at George Washington University include: George F. Bowerman, public librarian of the District of Columbia, who has been appointed professorial lecturer in library science; William Armstrong Hunter, formerly of the University of Florida, associate professor of law, and Richard Norman Owens, formerly of Emory University, professor of accounting.

JOHN WINFIELD VOORHIS has been appointed professor of Bible and religious education at Park College. The following instructors have been appointed: Virginia Lee Cole, journalism; Charles D. Flory, education; Charles F. Metz, chemistry and physics; John R. Jackson, biology, and Samuel T. Lenters, art.

THE University of Arkansas, at Fayetteville, announces that an appropriation has been made for an extensive enlargement of the equipment and space of the psychological laboratory. Facilities for both teaching and research have been made available, and the department has moved into a suite of eleven rooms on the second floor of the old engineering building. Three new men have been added to the staff of the department of philosophy and psychology, under the headship of Professor W. B. Mahan. The new appointees are: Dr. John A. McGeoch (Chicago), professor of psychology and director of the psychological laboratory; Dr. R. H. Waters (Chicago), associate professor of psychology, and Dr. Cecil DeBoer (Michigan), instructor in philosophy and psychology. The library of the university has also acquired sets of all the important English, German and French psychological and philosophical journals.

THE *American Economic Review* states that Dr. Frank A. Fetter, of Princeton, and Dr. Horace Secrist, of the Bureau of Business Research at Northwestern University, have received appointments in the new graduate department of economics which is being formed at Claremont Colleges in California. The first step will be the organization of research in economics, specializing in problems of business. A limited number of advanced students will be accepted. Dr. Kenneth Duncan, Dr. George S. Burgess and Mr. Norman T. Ness, of the Pomona College faculty, will be associated with Drs. Fetter and Secrist for the coming year. The seminar system will be used exclusively in this new department. The college is offering five scholarships for the coming year to students of high scholastic attainment for graduate work in economics.

PROFESSOR GODFREY HAROLD HARDY, Savillian professor of geometry at Oxford, is taking up his work at Princeton University. He is exchanging with Professor Oswald Veblen, of the department of mathematics. Professor Hermann Weyl, of Switzerland, will occupy the Thomas D. Jones research professorship of mathematical physics.

MISS CHARL O. WILLIAMS, of Washington, has been appointed chairman of education of the National Federation of Business and Professional Women's Clubs for 1928–29. Miss Williams was formerly a county superintendent of schools in Tennessee. She served as president of the National Education Association in 1921–22 and is now its field secretary. The Federation of Business and Professional Women's Clubs handles scholarships providing secondary school education or specialized training for business women.

DR. S. J. HOLMES, professor of zoology in the University of California, was elected president of the university chapter of the Phi Beta Kappa scholarship honor society at the annual meeting of the organization held recently. Other officers are: *first vice-president,* Dr. J. H. Hildebrand, professor of chemistry; *second vice-president,* Dr. P. B. Fay, chairman of the French department; *third vice-president,* Dr. P. O. Ray, chairman of the political science department.

THE officers of all Radcliffe undergraduate organizations recently entertained President Ada L. Comstock, Dean Bernice V. Brown and

Miss Priscilla Gough, college marshal and director of publicity, for the purpose of holding an informal discussion of undergraduate activities and problems, and also for creating more intimate relations between the students and heads of the college.

Cleveland P. Grant has been appointed acting curator of the N. W. Harris Public School Extension of the Field Museum of Natural History, in Chicago. Mr. Grant has formerly held the post of staff lecturer.

Dr. James Rowland Angell, president of Yale University, has returned to New Haven, after a summer spent in Ireland and England.

The War Department announces that Governor-General Stimson, of the Philippine Islands, has requested the board of regents of the University of Wisconsin to extend the leave of absence of Dr. Eugene Allen Gilmore, vice-governor of the Philippines, for one year. Dr. Gilmore is professor of law and has had leave of absence from the university since 1922.

Dr. Waldemar Kaempffert, director of the Rosenwald Industrial Museum, in Chicago, will sail for Europe in October. Mr. Kaempffert will spend about three months in visiting the industrial museums of Munich, Vienna and London.

Dr. Merton K. Cameron, of the University of Oregon, has accepted an appointment for one year as head of the department of economics at the University of Hawaii. He expects to return to Oregon at the expiration of his leave of one year.

Professor Alzada Comstock, of Mt. Holyoke College, has been granted a semester's leave for the first half of 1928–29 for a study of land reform laws, which she will begin in Estonia.

Miss Georgiana Gollock, formerly joint editor with S. J. H. Oldham, of *The International Review of Missions,* is now *en route* to Canada and the United States, where, at the invitation of the Phelps Stokes Fund of New York, she will make a special study of Negro education.

Students of education who will visit the United States this autumn include: M. Auguste Désclos, associate director of the Office National des Universités et Écoles Françaises, who was a member of the commission that visited the United States last year on behalf of the Cité Universitaire; Dr. Georg Kartzke, assistant director of the Deutsches Institut für Ausländer of the University of Berlin and professor for eight years at Yale University and for one year each at California and Toronto; Dr. Paul L. Dengler, director of the Austro-American Institute of Education in Vienna; Dr. Dora Wagner, who came to the United States last spring as a member of a group of German educators invited by the International Institute of Teachers College, Columbia University, and Miss Minna G. Gowan, graduate of Girton College, Cambridge, chairman of the Higher Education Committee of Edinburgh. Lectures at universities and colleges by any one of this group can be arranged through the Institute of International Education of New York, of which Dr. Stephen P. Duggan is the director.

Dr. H. Foster Bain, secretary of the American Institute of Mining and Metallurgical Engineers, was the speaker at the convocation exercises on September 27 of the Case School of Applied Science at Cleveland.

The death is announced at the age of sixty-one years of Dr. Herbert Burnham Davis, principal of the Henry Clay Frick Training School for Teachers at Pittsburgh.

Dr. Benjamin Warner Snow, professor of physics at the University of Wisconsin, died on September 21 at the age of sixty-eight years.

The annual meeting of the American Psychological Association will be held in New York City in affiliation with the American Association for the Advancement of Science on December 27, 28 and 29. The sessions will be held in Schermerhorn Hall, Columbia University. The Pennsylvania Hotel has been designated as headquarters. Professor Edwin G. Boring, of Harvard University, is president of the association.

The forty-first annual meeting of the American Economic Association will be held in Chicago, from December 26–29, with headquarters at the Stevens Hotel. There will be one session on unemployment; one on banking policy as a remedial agency in business cycles; one on government control of public utilities, with special reference to electric light and power, and motor transportation; one on installment selling, and one on the Russian situation. Joint sessions will be held with the American Statistical Association and the American Association for Labor Legislation, and a round table conference with the Association of Collegiate Schools of Business. Professor James W. Bell, of Northwestern University, is the chairman of the committee on local arrangements.

THE program for the 1929 convention of the National Congress of Parents and Teachers, to be held in Washington in the spring, 1929, was one of the subjects for consideration at the meeting of its executive committee on September 24, at Fort Sumter Hotel, Charleston, South Carolina. The committee also gave attention to the reports and plans of officers, bureau managers and committee chairmen; field service; the matter of cooperation with national agencies; the summer round-up of the children, and other matters relating to the activities of the association.

THE forty-fourth annual meeting of the Associated Academic Principals of the State of New York will be held on December 27, 28 and 29, at Syracuse.

STUDENTS of agriculture from schools in all parts of the nation will meet in Kansas City, Missouri, from November 17 to 23 for the third annual national congress of vocational agricultural students, which is to be held in connection with the American Royal Livestock Show.

FENN HALL, a new building erected for the Cleveland Young Men's Christian Association School of Technology, was dedicated on September 13. The building, designed for adult students, cost equipped $201,000. It contains nineteen classrooms, nine laboratories and a library. It is said to be the first building to be erected by a Young Men's Christian Association for educational purposes only. $100,000 for the building was given by Mr. Sereno P. Fenn, formerly president of the Young Men's Christian Association, and $101,000 was secured from former students, teachers and board members of the school.

A PROVISIONAL charter for the Santiago College for Girls, at Santiago, Chile, has been granted by the board of regents of the University of the State of New York. The institution was established in 1880 as a school for the education of girls from American and English families, but it now includes among its students many Chilean girls. Courses from kindergarten through high school have been offered, and the curriculum will hereafter include higher studies. This is the second institution in South America which has been chartered by the Board of Regents, the first being Mackenzie College of São Paulo, Brazil.

SPECIAL CORRESPONDENCE

DEVELOPMENTS IN JAPANESE EDUCATION

JAPAN very wisely and democratically started her system at the bottom and provided six years of primary education for every child in the empire. However, although there are many secondary schools and both government and private schools are increasing rapidly, yet there have never been and will not be for many years enough secondary schools to take care of all those who wish to have secondary education. This is the underlying reason for the difficult entrance examinations for all schools above the primary, for secondary and higher schools must choose somehow or other whom they will admit out of the large number of eager applicants. To give an idea of educational facilities: in our city of 150,000 people in the west central part of Japan, which is less modernized than many other parts, there are 12 kindergartens with 60 to 100 children each; 17 primary schools with 240 to 600 pupils each; seven girls' high schools with 400 to 700 pupils each; five boys' middle schools with about 700 pupils each; one normal school each for women and men primary teachers; one high school for men (junior college grade) with 600 students; one technical college with 600 students, and one medical university with 150 students. These all are well equipped and have high standing. It may seem that to provide all these separate schools causes waste in buildings and equipment, but in fact each school is so nearly filled to capacity every year that it would be difficult to effect much economy by combining.

As was stated in a recent number of School and Society entrance examinations were to be abolished for girls' high schools and boys' middle schools. However, the burden of choice could not be eliminated by a mere gesture, and this year pupils were selected according to their primary school records and in reference to their general health. Instead of making life easier for the children and teachers, the result was that the children were harassed continually, for one day's absence or failure might have dire effect; and the teacher's responsibility for grading and recommending the pupils was onerous. This year the no-examination method will be tested. Meanwhile educators are seriously thinking about the problem, and are watching the results in the secondary schools.

Another innovation is the abolishing of the term examinations in secondary schools. The general custom has been to have no tests during the term, but to set apart two periods of three days or more for mid-term and final examinations in each of the twelve or more subjects that each pupil studies. The pupils usually have studied very little until a few days before these periods and then for a week or ten days have burned midnight electricity and crammed frantically. This method presupposed the lecture system in almost all subjects. This year it was agreed by the authorities that unexpected tests given often during the term and no finals would be better for the pupils both mentally and physically. A few schools began to try out this plan from January and with the beginning of the school year in April practically every school in Japan adopted it. After having used the plan only one or two terms very few pupils or teachers say they like it. The pupils say the "surprise" tests force them to study for every day's lessons, and the teachers say they are busier also. However, the authorities agree that in theory the new plan is much better than the old.

One of the most admirable points in primary and secondary education here is the attention given to health. The climate in the west central district is very damp, and tuberculosis is especially prevalent. But the schools are taking particular pains to spread information about hygiene. Each school has a physician employed to examine the pupils at intervals; the Department of Education provides illustrated lectures, moving pictures and posters on health; and the pupils are urged to take plenty of outdoor exercise. Tennis courts, outdoor basketball space and equipment besides indoor ping-pong tables and all the usual gymnasium equipment are required and much used. Each school holds an annual field day when the classes compete, and sometimes interschool contests are held. The girls excel in esthetic dancing and calisthenics, though many do well also in tennis, basketball, running and skiing.

The rule is for each primary and secondary school to dismiss classes one day each month on a fine day and the whole school take lunches and go for a walk into the country. The pupils may walk from two to seven miles and return. Our school usually chooses for its destination some historical spot, or some place of special scenery. There is no lack of such places, so that the pupils get much pleasure and information as well as healthful exercise. Most schools plan and supervise mountain climbing trips for the summer vacation also. Such monthly outings and vacation trips are financed by the student association wholly or in part. The provincial authorities schedule and supervise ten days of swimming for the pupils and teachers of each school during the summer vacation. The teachers must supervise the pupils of their respective schools to some extent, but all responsibility for safety is borne by the provincial education authorities. In such ways as this the paternalistic features of the school system are shown, but democratic tendencies also can be clearly seen.

Alma G. Eaton

Hokuriku Girls' High School,
Kanazawa, Japan

DISCUSSION

THE PASSING OF AN ANCIENT SCANDAL

Schools opened this year with a remarkable conversion of newspaper editors to the better life. Five years ago Milton Potter's resolutions that our public-school teachers are attractive men and women followed a protest by William H. Allen against the ungallant cartoons and flings of newspapers insulting to the intelligence of teachers, children and citizens generally. Each year the *Educational Review* has urged superintendents to see editors early and to take a bevy of teachers along. The idea is working. The News Enterprise Association reports upwards of nine hundred newspapers as complimenting their readers on the resumption of school service. I have seen no more graceful or understanding recognition of the schools than this editorial in the Boston *Transcript,* which appeared under the caption: "Hate it? They love it."

If ever a tradition needed debunking, it is the notion that children "hate to go back to school." Year after year, as the city schools open, newspapers continue to describe the event in the old-fashioned manner, wholly ignoring the facts as they now exist. Bright-minded reporters—who usually think it unpardonable to write even one sentence in a mid-Victorian manner—fill long articles about the school-openings with stale "atmosphere" from the nineteenth century, allowing never one breath to blow in from the twentieth. They picture thousands of children dragged home from the highways and byways of summer leisure, forcibly washed and starched by fond but grim mothers, and then marched off to school as though to jail, against their wills, against their pleasures, against everything in them which is normal and characteristic of the nature of childhood.

If this ever was a correct picture—and we doubt if it ever was, so far as concerns the first few days of the school session, which have always been so flavored with excitement and with the interest of changed occupation as to make them quite attractive to all healthy children—the general impression conveyed by contemporary descriptions of the school opening is incorrect "old hat," completely out of touch with the times. Nearly all of the younger children to-day seem to enjoy going to school. Ask them whether they "like school," and you will have an affirmative answer from nine children of ten. Even the one dissenter sometimes refuses to confess his enjoyment merely because he has come to think—probably from hearing the remarks of his elders—that it is the proper thing to say that he does not like school. Apart from such cases, and from "problem" children who may be finding their path to the school door beset by real difficulties of adjustment, there is a quite universal relish among American children to-day for the work of the first few years in school.

Assuredly the credit for this new zest among school-pupils flows to those leaders in the field of education who have thought out the ways and means of making children like their early studies. It is not merely true that large new emphasis has come to be placed in recent years upon the educative value of play, and upon the extent to which children can so be led to work almost without consciousness that they are working. The deeper secret of the success of modern pedagogy in the elementary grades is that great teachers have now come to know, in a clear and true way, the elements of the child-mind which they are striving to educate. They know, through intense study and by thousands of measurements, what the capacities of the six, seven and eight-year-old minds really are, and in what ways the competence which they already possess can be made more competent. In a word, they do not begin a child's education by asking of it the impossible—they seek always the possible, a graded ascent of the ladder, not a sudden leap upward.

Fifty years ago children entering a rural school in New England were confronted on the first day of admission with twenty-six Roman hieroglyphs drawn on the blackboard by the teacher. They were immediately set to learning these strange symbols by rote. No one asked or cared whether there was a child in the room whose mind was yet prepared to grasp any sequence running to more than ten or eleven—let alone twenty-six in an unbroken series. No one considered whether the child had yet been trained to know a left curve from a right curve. Thousands of children enter school without ever having grasped this distinction, but time was when they were expected to identify a long series of letters full of lines and curves before they knew one from the other. To-day as all parents know, there is no such sudden introduction of a six-year-old child to a set of letters which civilization itself took many centuries to evolve. The approach is made in an altogether different manner, and most children love it. Of course they are glad when the school term ends in June, just as their predecessors were. But teachers have learned how to postpone until very late the evil day of fatigue, and how to substitute, during most of the year, delight in the stead of despair.

May I suggest to you who read this that it is your pleasant duty to take it to your local editor and to persuade him to absorb it? It would also be a public service to write the editor of the *Transcript* what you think of him.

Wm. McAndrew

THE SPANISH LANGUAGE AS AN AMERICAN ASSET—ITS VALUE IN POLITICS, CULTURE AND TRADE

In a flaming discourse, lashing out at Pershing and his staff down there in Arica, Don Agustin Edwards, the Chilean delegate, once declared: "They are men who know nothing of our language!"

I'm afraid they don't. So they must needs depend upon interpreters and translators for all intercourse with the people and knowledge of the facts—spoken, written and read. This is a serious disability in an international dispute, in which the peace of twenty nations is more or less involved, as well as the whole moral authority of the United States under the Monroe Doctrine.

At every Pan-American Congress—political, scientific, literary, medical or commercial—it is tacitly expected that "the other people will speak 'English.'" Which, of course, they do, and often perfectly. That same delegate in Arica, when he was minister in London, showed me the sheets of a book he was writing on Chile in English for simultaneous publication in Great Britain and the United States. I could only look at the typescript in wonder!

Similarly, Dr. Alberto Salamón, one of the Peruvian delegates in that plebiscite, has also written a book in English on the economics and resources in Inca-land under President Leguia—the ablest statesman in Latin-America to-day.

In fact, from Havana down to Buenos Aires, and from Bogotá to Valparaiso, you will meet hundreds of thousands of people who speak at least a little English, and read and write it as well. But for the most part, Americans down here are pretty weak at Spanish, even after long residence. I met an important official in Panama who boasted he had been there twenty years and—"his own language was good enough for him!"

Here enters the question of good manners. That man, and many more like him, are making their living in Spanish-speaking countries, and it is surely a matter of courtesy to acquire this magnificent vehicle of expression. How many times have I seen American men and ladies at banquets, receptions, dances, lectures and so on, looking very forlorn amid all the voluble gaiety around them! Many of the native guests spoke English, of course; but it can not be expected from a whole nation, which a few foreigners visit as delegates or business men.

One is utterly lost—crippled at every turn, without Spanish in these fascinating lands of clever men, beautiful women and vast undeveloped spaces, which offer marvelous chances to capital and enterprise.

I can speak English with President Leguia, of Peru, and with President Ospina, of Colombia. But I must use Spanish with Machado, of Cuba, with Chiari, of Panama, and Vasquéz, of Santo Domingo. And I must speak French with President Louis Borno, of Haiti—whom I take this opportunity of thanking for his many courtesies in the vast "White House" on the Champs de Mars.

"Geographical propinquity"—to use Lloyd George's pedantic phrase in the Irish negotiations—ordain and impose the Spanish language upon all Americans. These Hispanic peoples have elaborate and beautiful manners. I present a letter of introduction in Madrid, and at once receive a "Besa-la-Mano" or "Kiss-thy-hand" from the statesman in question. The appointment is made at "this, your house"; and your "assured servant" takes this, the first opportunity, to present the expressions of an esteem which seems to reach the skies!

Something more than mere commercial correspondence is called for among a people of such elaborate ritual. A pious "God guard you!" concludes even the official letter which informs you that you have been heavily fined, and given twenty-four hours to pay!

It is very necessary also that we keep in touch with the journalism, art and letters of Latin-America, apart from the classic poesy and prose of Spain. Here is a young literature of new and powerful thought; here are poets and essayists, novelists and political writers of great originality. How is the United States to keep in sympathetic touch with her sister-continent unless she is *en rapport* with the spiritual side?

In round figures we have now $15,000,000,000 invested in these wonderful lands. They look up to us; our influence pervades all their cities and small towns, from Santiago de Cuba to La Paz by means of the cinema-reel. They turn to us also for loans. It is an American—William Pulliam—who controls the finances of Santo Domingo. Another American—Dr. Cumberland—holds the purse-strings of Haiti. A third American—Charles Sutton—turns Andean rivers into the dry pampas of Peru. I could fill a column with names and great positions. American machinery runs the sugar-mills in all these republics. A single smelter of the great Cerro de Pasco copper concern at Oroya, Peru (12,000 feet above the Pacific), cost nearly $15,000,000! And every Latin-American shop is filled from floor to ceiling with American goods.

I have said enough to show the Spanish language as an all-round asset. A good stenographer with two languages can command $200 a month here in Lima in the big banks and business houses. So Spanish is also a worth-while investment for any clerk of either sex, at home or abroad.

It is not a difficult language; it is much less complicated than French, and far more sonorous in the orator's mouth than the softer, more "feminine" Italian. Our schools ought to make Spanish a compulsory study; and certainly no commercial traveler—to say nothing of our diplomats—ought to pass south of the Rio Grande without a fair grounding in the glorious tongue of Cervantes.

The Spanish *ambiente,* or environment, may be trusted to do the rest—especially if the newcomer has a real love for this magnificent vehicle of thought and sentiment, whose very essence and spirit are poles apart from the Anglo-Saxon psyche.

IGNATIUS PHAYRE

QUOTATIONS

THE CURSE OF EXAMINATIONS

EVERYBODY acknowledges that examinations are "a curse." The child who has to present himself for an examination is encouraged to crowd his memory with disconnected facts instead of to understand the spirit and meaning of history; he is encouraged to memorize instead of to reason. And yet examinations—or, at all events, a great many examinations—belong to the category of inevitable things. They go on existing, not because the world and his wife have much good to say of them, but because they fulfil some function for which no adequate alternative has been discovered.

And, after all, we suppose it will be admitted that in some circumstances no alternative is needed. It is impossible to conceive how universities could confer a degree except as the result of examination; and it is not easy to conceive how the professions of the law, medicine and so on could award their diplomas of competence except as the result of examination.

We must distinguish. And Dr. Norwood, the admired head-master of Harrow, distinguished in a very inspiring if sometimes very rash manner in an address which he delivered to the British Association. He spoke in particular of the school certificates and the common entrance examination to the public schools. In the first year of the school certificate examinations there were 14,232 candidates, but in the last year for which the figures are available there were 54,593 candidates. Candidates for the school certificate can pick and choose between subjects, but the tendency has been for the examination to become, in the main, academic. The universities naturally insist upon certain subjects being taken, as the winning of the school certificate is generally accepted as entitling the pupil to enter the university, and as relieving him of the first minor university examination. Dr. Norwood argues that there should be two distinct kinds of school certificate—that for the universities and that for the ordinary boy or girl of a secondary school. There would be no question of calling one class superior to another; it would be merely a case of acknowledging that there was a difference. One certificate would satisfy the universities, and the other would merely be a proof that the boy or girl had taken at school that course of education which had been considered most suitable. This seems entirely reasonable.

Dr. Norwood was on dangerous ground when he went on to discuss the common entrance examination to the public schools. Up to about the end of last century, and perhaps for a few years longer, there was no such competition to get into the public schools as there is now. A boy was frequently accepted by a public school on the accounts given of his work at his private school. The examination for which he had to sit when he arrived at the public school was merely to decide in what division or form he should be placed. To-day entrance to the principal public schools is practically an affair of competition. Dr. Norwood does not forget, however, to point out that, as so much of the boy's future depends upon his success in the entrance examination, it is natural that at his private school he should be trained to answer as many questions as possible on a large variety of subjects as rapidly as possible. The boys are made "to switch their small minds with accuracy from Genesis to *Ivanhoe,* from Henry VIII to the cause of rainfall. The bright boy finds it easy; the average boy in many cases, and the dull boy in all cases, finds it terribly hard."

One of the results of this method which Dr. Norwood pillories is a handbook of mere cram. This book contains an analysis of all the past papers in the Common Entrance Examination. All the sovereigns of England are ranged in order according to the frequency of their occurrence— Queen Victoria ninety-seven times down to Edward V, who "failed to score." So, again, in English literature—*Westward Ho!* occurs fourteen times, *Idylls of the King* twenty-one times, but Rip Van Winkle and John Gilpin only once each. Dr. Norwood's comment is that it can not be wondered at that at some private schools boys "read no authors but only do examination papers, read no history but memorize names." He says that there is only one cure for such an intolerable system, and that is to abolish it. He lays it down as an educational axiom that there should never be any examination of a child under fifteen, except by his own teachers.

Dr. Norwood has the advantage of being a head-master of a public school. The masters of private schools have another story to tell, and some of them have told it in letters to the *Times.* They say that the system which immediately preceded the common entrance examination—the system which required the boy to present himself at a public school for an entrance examination—was inconvenient and expensive. The present method was introduced as a help for both parents and school-masters. It is said that the cramming of which Dr. Norwood complains applies to only two out of twelve or thirteen papers set in the entrance examination, namely, history and literature. You can not very well cram a boy, as one correspondent says, for an examination in arithmetic, algebra or geometry, or in translating Latin, Greek, French or German, or in geography as it is generally taught nowadays. Besides the cram book has been the laughing-stock of most private schools.

Let us venture our own comment. If examination papers can be so compactly analyzed as in the cramming book to which Dr. Norwood refers, is there not something wrong with the method of setting these papers? Either this must be true or the book must be a travesty of the real significance of the examination. Certainly examination papers can be devised which give a very small opening for the products of cramming. Winchester does not accept the common entrance. Nothing, therefore, seems to prevent Dr. Norwood from abolishing it at Harrow. Again, is there not room for more *viva voce* examinations? We should not care to dogmatize on this point, as it is well known that some nervous children shrink from answering questions by word of mouth even more than they shrink from the sight of empty foolscap paper, and in any kind of examination by personal interview would be very unlikely to do themselves justice. On the other hand, an examiner worthy of the name could quickly discover whether the boy or girl was "serving up" cram or answering out of a properly trained intelligence.

Last of all, there is the point of view of the parent. We believe that when all has been said and done, there is much support (as well as dislike) among parents for examinations. They say that examinations give the rewards of merit without favor.—*The Spectator.*

REPORTS

ENROLMENT IN NEGRO UNIVERSITIES AND COLLEGES

The number of institutions for the higher education of the Negro race in the United States more than doubled and enrolments have increased over six-fold during the past ten years, according to a report by the Bureau of Education after a comprehensive survey of Negro universities and colleges.

In 1917 there were 31 Negro institutions offering college work, the report shows, while in 1927, of the 79 institutions included in the survey, 77 were engaged in college work. The college enrolments in the 31 institutions ten years ago amounted to 2,132 Negro students as compared with 13,680 attending the institutions surveyed in 1927, an increase of 550 per cent. The annual income of the Negro universities and colleges in the United States has also gained at a rapid rate. For 1917 it amounted to $2,283,000, while for 1926–27 the annual income was $8,560,000, an increase of 275 per cent. The financial support being accorded Negro higher education in the country is nearly four times what it was in 1917.

Total capital investment in the real properties of the universities and colleges surveyed has likewise greatly increased. The value of the physical plants of these institutions ten years ago was fixed at $15,720,000. Their present value is $38,680,000, representing a gain of 146 per cent., due principally to the construction of modern school buildings and other improvements. The most important advance made by the institutions has been the large increase in their productive endowments, indicating the existence of a growing conviction that Negro higher education must be placed on a permanent basis through the provision of a stable annual income. In 1917, the productive endowments of the universities and colleges making up this survey amounted to $7,225,000, with an annual yield of $361,250. Since then, additions have brought this total up to $20,713,000, the annual yield being $1,071,300. The gain over the period of ten years in both endowment and annual yield, therefore, has been approximately 185 per cent.

The survey of Negro universities and colleges was conducted at the request of state departments of education of 19 states, 79 Negro institutions, the Association of Colleges for Negro Youth, the Phelps-Stokes Fund and the educational boards and foundations of seven church bodies, all of whom cooperated in arranging the study and in furnishing information. Every one of the 79 institutions was visited by representatives of the bureau. In addition to a general review of Negro higher education, the report contains individual chapters dealing in unabridged form with the academic programs, physical plants, graduation requirements, admission requirements, enrolments, training of the faculty, salaries, teaching loads, educational and scientific equipment and other functions of each of the institutions. The universities and colleges surveyed include: 5 in Alabama, 3 in Arkansas, 1 in Delaware, 1 in the District of Columbia, 3 in Florida, 9 in Georgia, 2 in Kentucky, 5 in Louisiana, 2 in Maryland, 5 in Mississippi, 1 in Missouri, 12 in North Carolina, 1 in Oklahoma, 1 in Ohio, 2 in Pennsylvania, 5 in South Carolina, 8 in Tennessee, 8 in Texas, 4 in Virginia and 1 in West Virginia.

While presenting the exceptional progress accomplished in Negro higher education during the past ten years, the report also calls attention to the fact that the immediate need of the race is more education, better education and higher education. The latest available figures show that there are approximately 48,000 Negro teachers in the United States, including those teaching in elementary schools, high schools and colleges. Of this number 1,050 are teachers in institutions of higher learning and 46,950 in elementary and high schools. Upon the latter rests the responsibility of educating 5,000,000 Negro youths under the age of 19 years, a task far beyond the capacities of such a small number. The lack of teachers is serious.

A considerable proportion of the teachers are reported as being deficient in proper training. Many have not received more than elementary school preparation, while the training of a large number of others has been limited to one or two years' work in or graduation from high school. A shortage prevails not only in the number of teachers, but also in their quality. The solution of the problem is largely centered in higher education. If more teachers adequately trained and prepared for the overwhelming undertaking of educating 5,000,000 Negro boys and girls are to be provided, the task must be done in the institutions of higher learning.

The economic salvation of the Negro is dependent to a great degree upon his training in the fields of agriculture, mechanic arts and crafts. While 1,000,000 Negroes own or operate farms, there are 1,178,000 of the race engaged in ordinary farm labor. The lack of training in mechanic arts and crafts is indicated by the fact that only 56,000 are skilled craftsmen as compared with 1,371,000 pursuing unskilled occupations or employed as day laborers. All states have established land-grant colleges offering courses in agriculture, mechanic arts and home economics. In these colleges members of the race may prepare themselves not only to become teachers in these fields, but also to enter into these vocations with all the advantages of superior specialized knowledge. If continued progress is to be made to higher economic levels, the Negro youth of the country must take advantage of these opportunities.

National social and economic life demands the training of many more Negro professional and technical leaders. This is also a question of higher education. To safeguard the health of the colored people and of their neighbors, to instruct them in hygiene, sanitation and in the measures necessary to ward off disease, care for those that fall ill, are as essential as intellectual and economic development. There are 3,500 Negro physicians and surgeons in the United States, or approximately one colored physician to every 3,343 Negroes. The white race has a physician to every 553 persons. A serious lack of Negro dentists prevails. There is only one to every 10,540 Negro inhabitants. In technical lines an even more pronounced shortage of trained men is revealed. There are in the United States only 50 Negro architects, 184 engineers, 145 designers, draftsmen and inventors and 207 chemists. Professional and technical education can be obtained in institutions of higher learning only.

Although the number of Negro clergymen serving as pastors of churches or preachers of the gospel is approximately 19,600, the training of a large number is extremely limited. Many have not had the benefit of a secondary education and others have never graduated from college, much less obtained the advantage of proper training in schools of theology. The average number of graduates from Negro theological seminaries is less than 10 a year, when the actual demand for qualified Negro ministers is over 100 annually. The responsibility of providing leadership to direct the ethical, the religious and the spiritual life of the large Negro population is one that rests upon higher education.

A considerable portion of the report is devoted to the methods of the control and administration of the institutions. Four general types of government were found among the 79 institutions participating in the survey. These included 22 publicly supported institutions under state government and control, made up of land-grant colleges, normal and teacher-training colleges; 9 universities and colleges owned, governed and controlled by independent boards of trustees and privately supported; 31 universities and colleges under ownership and control of northern white church boards and privately supported, and 17 privately supported colleges owned and governed by Negro church organizations and conferences.

Of these different types of government, the report shows that the institutions controlled by independent boards of trustees have the largest average income per institution, the amount being $261,082, while the colleges under control of state authority are second on the list with an average annual income per institution of $145,526. The colleges under the control of Negro church organizations have the third largest average income per institution with $66,977 and the institutions having the smallest average income per institution are those controlled and administered from central headquarters of northern white church boards, their average annual income being $61,075.

The survey was made under the immediate direction of Dr. Arthur J. Klein, chief of the division of higher education of the Bureau of Education, by a committee consisting of Dr. William B. Bizzell, president of the University of Oklahoma; Dr. C. C. McCracken, Ohio State University; Dean George B. Woods, American University, and from the staff of the Bureau of Education, John H. McNeely, assistant to the director, Dr. Walton C. John and M. M. Proffitt.

EDUCATIONAL RESEARCH AND STATISTICS

THE PERMANENT EFFECTS OF TRAINING IN METHODS OF STUDY ON COLLEGE SUCCESS

DURING the last five years the author has been offering a class in study methods. This class has been open primarily to probation students. The work has consisted of one lecture, one interview and one two-hour laboratory period each week. The material covered included such topics as note-taking, time-budgeting, efficient reading methods, need of adequate previous preparation, etc. During the laboratory hours opportunity was given for trial under supervision of efficient study methods. Time enough has now elapsed for any effects of this treatment to be observed. During the first year the course was given, the writer was too busy developing methods of procedure to keep adequate records, so the students of this year have been omitted from the study; students who took the course when it was last given (Winter, 1928) have also been omitted since not enough time has passed for permanent results to show. The cases included in this study are, therefore, from the years 1924–25, 1925–26 and 1926–27. During this time fifty-four students were enrolled in the class. Four of these students were at the end of their senior year at the time they took the work; these four have been eliminated since their interest was in obtaining methods for training high-school pupils rather than in raising their own college standing. The report deals, then, with the effects of training in methods of study upon fifty probation students whose training period was from one and a half to three and a half years ago.

In order to get some basis of comparison by which the results obtained might be evaluated the writer selected a "control" group of students. The fifty students of the control group were paired with the other fifty as being equal in intelligence—that is, as having scores within 2 per cent. on the intelligence tests—and as having been on probation at the same time as the other students. These "control" students did not, however, receive any training in study methods.

The results to be presented may be summarized in four tables. (1) The distribution of intelligence for the two groups will first be presented to show the type of student with whom the writer was dealing and the care with which students have been paired. (2) A second table will indicate what has become of the one hundred students involved. (3) The third table will show the relation between the success of the training and the degree of intelligence possessed by the students. (4) A final table will indicate the level of academic work done before and after training, for the trained group.

Table I shows that for each group three stu-

TABLE I

SHOWING THE DISTRIBUTION OF INTELLIGENCE TEST SCORES FOR THE TRAINED AND UNTRAINED GROUPS

Percentile rankings			Trained group	Untrained group
Highest	quarter	76–100	3	3
Second	"	51– 75	6	6
Third	"	26– 50	17	17
Lowest	"	1– 25	24	24

dents made intelligence scores in the highest quarter, and six in the second quarter; below the median, in the third quarter, there were seventeen students, and in the lowest quarter twenty-four students. It will be seen from this table that the two groups were very similar in ability and that both groups are of rather low caliber.

Table II shows the number and per cent. in each group who were "saved" from academic disaster as compared with those who were "lost" because of unsatisfactory work. In the trained group 58 per cent. were saved and 42 per cent. lost. Similar figures for the control group are 18 per cent. saved and 82 per cent. lost. The trained group shows 20 per cent. of its members as graduates, but no one in the control group has succeeded in graduating.

The third table shows the relation of the success of the training to intelligence. For the

TABLE II

SHOWING WHAT HAS BECOME OF THE STUDENTS IN THE TRAINED AND THE UNTRAINED GROUP

	Trained group	Untrained group
	Per cent.	Per cent.
Number graduated	10–20	0– 0
Number still in school and passing	7–14	4– 8
Number leaving school with passing records	12–24	5–10
Total number "Saved"	*29–58*	*9–18*
Number still in school, but not passing	4– 8	7–14
Number leaving with unsatisfactory records	2– 4	9–18
Number eliminated by rules	15–30	25–30
Total number "Lost"	*21–42*	*41–82*

trained group, the nine above the median in intelligence were all saved." Only two[1] students of the seventeen in the third quarter were eliminated. All other eliminations are of students in the lowest quarter. That is, the training has saved from failure those students who were capable enough to profit by it, since only two of the twenty-six above the 25th percentile were "lost." Of the students above the median

TABLE III

SHOWING THE RELATIONSHIP BETWEEN ACADEMIC SUCCESS AND INTELLIGENCE

	Trained group	Control group
Above median:		
Saved	9	4
Lost	0	5
In third quarter:		
Saved	15	2
Lost	2	15
In lowest quarter:		
Saved	5	3
Lost	19	21

[1] One of these students was eliminated on a technical matter and will be readmitted whenever he wishes to return.

in the control group, five were eliminated and all but two students in the third quarter were eliminated.

It seemed desirable to observe if the training period resulted in any raising of academic grades. For the trained group,[2] therefore, a table is presented showing their average standing in terms of A, B, C, D and E, the marks used at the university. In this group fourteen students dropped out of school at the end of their training quarter, so that no further study of them could be made. For the other thirty-six students, the average of *all* work done before taking the course is contrasted with the average of *all* subsequent work.

TABLE IV

SHOWING THE ACADEMIC STANDING OF THE TRAINED STUDENTS BEFORE AND AFTER THE TRAINING

	Before training	After training
C—average or better	4	15
D—average	21	13
E—average	11	8
Number passing[3]	*5*	*24*

As a result of this investigation the writer has come to two main conclusions: (1) it is not worth while to try to train students below the twenty-fifth percentile in intelligence; an occasional student is saved, but not enough to pay for the time and effort expended. (2) Students who have enough initial ability *do* learn to study. Those above the twenty-fifth percentile are almost certain to be "saved." The course for probation students appears to have justified itself by the resulting academic careers of the students electing it.

LUELLA COLE PRESSEY

THE OHIO STATE UNIVERSITY

[2] The students in the control group could not be similarly handled as the number of quarters they remained in the university varied so greatly from those students of the trained group with whom they were paired in intelligence.

[3] The passing average is a little below a C. The outstanding fact about this table is that twenty-four of these students have done passing work since taking the course.

SCHOOL AND SOCIETY

Volume XXVIII | Saturday, October 6, 1928 | Number 719

HEBREW EDUCATION

It is with nations as with individuals. Some possess particular aptitudes which others do not; some excel in one field of endeavor, others in another, so that put together they form, as it were, a complete entity.

Thus, the special domain of activity of the Greeks, in which they achieved their greatest fame, was that of the arts, philosophy and the sciences. The Romans, too strenuous and active a people for the finer arts, sought an outlet in conquests, empire-building and the establishment of special legal laws for their governments, some of which are still forming the basis of our modern codes.

The Hebrews, on the other hand, to whom art was taboo, and who entertained no dreams of world empires, chose, so to speak, the province of spiritual activity which dominated their every move and mode of life.

In modern times we draw a close distinction between secular and religious instruction. In ancient Israel such a differentiation was made utterly impossible, for everything was viewed "subspecie religionis."

Inasmuch as the starting point of the Hebrew nation was, as amongst others, the family, elementary education as such, at the very beginning, commenced with the family and was carried on within it through centuries up to the time of Simeon ben Shetah (126–72 B. C.).

Since the Hebrew nation is supposed to have had its inception in the patriarch Abraham, he must, therefore, be regarded as the initiator of its education. And, indeed, an injunction went forth to him to teach his children so that "they may keep the way of Jehovah to do Justice and Righteousness."[1]

It is justice and righteousness that run through all the stages of Jewish existence from the patriarchal through the Mosaic, the prophetic, the exilic, up to the close of the talmudic period (500 A. D.).

It is interesting to note that Plato in his "Republic" regards justice, "dykaiosyne," as one of the fundamental principles of his ideal state. The command issued from Abraham was made more emphatic yet by the founder of the Hebrew nation, Moses, who inculcated upon his people incessant, unflagging teaching. "Thou shalt teach them diligently unto thy children and shalt talk of them when thou liest down and when thou risest up."[2] The teacher of the Jewish child was, therefore, primarily the

[1] Gen., xviii, 19. The passion for justice and righteousness manifests itself especially in the minute legal discussions of the Talmud. To me they seemed trivial. I once happened to mention to my friend John Lovejoy Elliot, founder of the Hudson Guild, and associate leader of the Ethical Culture Society, a specific case of an ox goring a pregnant cow by whose side a dead calf was found. The discussion centers around the question as to whether the calf was birthed dead before it was gored, or as a result of it, *i.e.*, whether the owner of the ox was to be held responsible for both, calf and cow, or for the cow only. ("Baba Kama," 46b.) My friend, who is engaged in social work, saw in the detailed, hair-splitting analysis of the case a manifestation of a passion for justice. Ernest Renan, in his "Histoire du Peuple d'Israel" (p. 421), likewise regards the Jew as inbred with a passion for justice: "La trace d'Israel sera eternelle. Israel a le premier deviné une forme au cri du peuple, à la plainte du pauvre, à la reclamation de ceux qui ont soif de la justice," etc.

[2] Deut., vi, 7.

father, the pater familias, and to some extent also the mother, for in Proverbs the mother, too, is mentioned as instructress. "Do not neglect the instruction of thy mother."[3] It was, then, the duty of the father to teach his child in all the branches of knowledge known at that time and requisite for the Jew to be able to observe the laws as they developed in the course of time. Here we note at once the striking difference between the Jewish and other civilized nations, as, for instance, the Greek and the Roman. Whereas it was incumbent upon the Jewish father to teach his child himself, the Greek and the Roman entrusted their children to others—to slaves, as the very word pedagogics ("paidogogos," leader of children) indicates. It seems that the modern mother, against the like of whom Rousseau in his day fulminated, is following in the wake of the Greeks by turning over her children to the tender mercies of the nurse, the tutor or the campmaster.

The subjects taught were indubitably what in our modern age might be called the three R's. The art of reading very likely preceded that of writing, as it is today, though there was only one kind of alphabet which, as Benzinger[4] has proven, the Jews acquired from the Canaanites. In the era of the judges writing was a commonplace matter. Every one seemed to have been able to write. For when Gideon was about to chastise the authorities of Succoth for their refusal of hospitality, he picked up at random a lad from the street, who wrote down for him the names of the princes and their elders to the number of seventy-seven.[5]

That all Jewish boys were mastering the art of writing at a time when other nations were steeped in ignorance and superstition and when writing was solely confined to the priestly caste, as among the Egyptians, later the Teutons (the Druids[6]) and others, is no small matter, considering that in 1920 there were 6 per cent. male and 5.9 per cent. female illiterates in the United States, in 1921 27 per cent. in Italy and in 1924 8.89 per cent. (among the recruits) in France. In other countries, like Mexico, Brazil and others, illiteracy is appalling.

It is even assumed that women knew how to wield the quill, for it is stated that Jezebel sent out letters in the name of the king.

In view of the fact that the Jews carried on a brisk commerce with other peoples, as with the Phoenicians, Egyptians and later with the Greeks,[7] they must have been familiar with the rudiments of arithmetic at least. Moreover, their numerical as well as their weight and measure system, which are quite well developed, tend to point in this direction.

Trades as a matter of necessity were cultivated among the Jews from the very earliest times of their existence. They evidently had learned many in the land of bondage, for when they built the tabernacle in the wilderness, it is reported that all kinds of artisans were employed: carpenters, woodworkers, goldsmiths, silversmiths, dyers, etc.

Inasmuch as the Jews as a nation were surrounded by many hostile neighbors, with whom they carried on incessant wars, they had to develop a certain prowess in the game of warfare, such as handling the sling, the sword and the spear. It is related in Judges that "there were among the inhabitants of Gibeah seven hundred

[3] Prov., i, 8.

[4] I. Benzinger, "Hebräische Archäologie," p. 174.

[5] Judges, viii, 14.

[6] Of the Druids Caesar says in his sixth book (p. 144): "Graecis litteris utantur. Id mihi duabus de causis instituisse videntur quod neque in volgus disciplinam efferi velint neque eos qui discunt litteris confisos minus memoriae studere quod fere plerisque accidit ut praesido litterarum diligentiam in perdiscendo ac memoriam remittant."

[7] I Kings, v, 15 ff.; Benzinger, *ibid.*, p. 154.

chosen men lame in the right hand, every one of whom could sling a stone at a hair, and would not miss.''[8] How David manipulated the sling in his fight with Goliath is too well known.

That the Jew also indulged in a certain kind of sports, such as ball-playing and racing, is patent from a number of passages. Thus, we read in Isaiah, ''and I shall toss them like a ball,'' and in the Psalms and Ecclesiastes, ''like the strong man who runs his course'' and ''the race is not to the swift.''[9]

As some of the Psalms and Ecclesiastes were written, as it is assumed, during the Greek period, *i.e.*, during the time when Greeks attempted to impose upon the Jews their cult and culture, it is more than probable that they acquired that kind of athletics from the Greeks, notwithstanding the bitter opposition offered by the Jewish parents and the hierarchy.

That the finer arts, like music, singing and dancing, were not neglected and developed to a relatively marked degree, is self-evident, for the Jewish father had to pilgrim with the male members of his family three times a year to Jerusalem and attend the temple services which, to all accounts, were very elaborate, involving song and music in which the congregation participated.

Music played a very prominent part in the life of the Jews at large, not merely because of its use in religious services, but because of its soothing effect on the emotions in general. When Saul fell into a state of melancholy David was called in to dispel his morbid sentiments by playing for him the harp.[10] The shepherds, too, in order to guile away their loneliness played on the shawn. The variety of musical instruments which the Jews made use of is too well known.

[8] Judges, xx, 16.

[9] Isa., xxix, 3; Psalms, xix, 6; Eccles., ix, 11.

[10] I Sam., xvii, 23.

Dancing also was cultivated, both for religious as well as for entertainment purposes, especially by the fair sex. The rhythm is inherent in human nature, and, very likely, was the first expression of the soul before it could give utterance to its emotions in words.

It is related that when the Israelites had warred upon the Benjamites and sworn not to intermarry with them voluntarily because they had refused to surrender the guilty, the latter, who had felt the dearth of women, were ordered by the former, who did not wish to see them becoming extinguished, ''to go and lie in wait in the vineyards and look out and behold, if the daughters of Shiloh go out to dance in dances, to come forth out of the vineyards and snatch every man his wife.''[11]

A similar instance is reported of the Romans under Romulus, carrying off Sabinian maidens as their wives, when the indigenous Sabinians had refused to intermarry with them because of their inferior descent.

Even men indulged in the terpsichorean art, but only for religious reasons. It is said of David that, upon the return of the ark, ''he danced with all his might before the Lord.''[12]

The method of teaching, as far as can be ascertained from scattered incidents and occurrences in the Bible, was imitative, that is to say, by example. That such a procedure was in vogue and apparently popular is implied in many biblical episodes. When Yotham desired to administer a scathing rebuke to the people of Shechem for having made Abimelech king and for having exterminated his own family, he took recourse to a fable, telling how the trees went forth to choose a king and what they experienced, driving home its

[11] Judges, xxi, 21.

[12] II Sam., vi, 14.

application.[13] (I believe it is the oldest fable extant.) He felt instinctively that that was a better way to gain his point than by delivering a long harangue. This method has been frequently employed in the middle ages and even in our modern times when the people were not allowed to express their opinions openly.

When Isaiah wished to point out to the people of Judea the futility of an alliance with Egypt against Assyria he walked barefoot and in tatters for three years in the grass.[14] Jeremiah likewise endeavored to demonstrate by concrete example the uselessness of resistance to Assyria by walking through the streets of Jerusalem with a yoke on his neck, thereby indicating the disastrous consequences which were to follow. They knew well enough that the mind of the common people was much more receptive to concrete demonstrations than to mere fiery speeches. I believe that even to-day, in our advanced era of psychology and pedagogics, such processes could be utilized to great advantage.

If our pacifists, for instance, who are anxious to abolish war, would take those that have been frightfully maimed and crippled and tour the world with them, exhibiting them to the people, they would accomplish more tangible results than by fulminating anathemas and marathenas in lectures and writings.

To the credit of the Jews it must be said that they never hesitated to learn from the example of others, even though those were pagans, especially when an ethical truism was involved. In this they showed themselves genuine liberalists and not narrow nationalists. To illustrate to what extent the fourth commandment, "thou shalt honor thy father and thy mother," was to be carried, they cite the example of a heathen, who owned a precious jewel which the Jews desired to secure for the breastplate of the high priest, and whom no offer would tempt to awaken his father, who happened to be asleep on the chest in which the costly stone was locked.[15] It would be well for our modern youths, in whom there is such a woeful lack of respect and reverence for parents to be noted, to take that lesson to heart.

The father remained the teacher until the time when he could no longer fulfil the functions as such, that is to say, until he himself became too illiterate to instruct. During the Greek period when the Jews stubbornly resisted the Greek cultural and religious influences, and especially during the second century, when the Jews came into close contact with the Syrians, an appalling ignorance had gradually made inroads among them. It is a strange phenomenon that the Jew, who held on with such unusual tenacity to his traditions and religion, should have given up his native tongue and adopted that of the heathen—the Syrian. Aramaic became the vernacular of the "chosen" people, in which many of its prayers and learned works, like the Mishna and Talmud, were written. It also was the language of Jesus in which he delivered his message to the world. It had come to such a pass that interpreters had to be employed in the synagogues.

Simeon ben Shetah, president of the Synhedrion (between 126–67 B. C.), brother-in-law of king Janeus, realizing the shocking conditions and the consequences that were bound to follow, decreed that schools be established in large cities and teachers be appointed. The age of the children was fixed at from sixteen to seventeen. Those that had parents were then sent to those schools, but they were too old

13 Judges, ix, 8 ff. Sebastian Brand's "Narrenschiff," "Till Eulenspiegel"; Lessing's "Nathan der Weise." Maximilian Harden, in 1898, utilized Laboulai's "Prince Caniche" to level an attack on ex-Emperor William and his sycophants.

14 Isa., xx, 2; Jer., xxvii, 3.

15 "Abodah Zarah," 23b.

and too fixed in their habits to adapt themselves to school discipline. The orphans, however (there seems to have been quite a large contingent of them, evidently owing to the civil war that prevailed during the reign of king Janeus), did not go to school at all, for they had no one to send them. The teachers, unfortunately, did not possess the proper qualifications, they were too impatient, too irascible. The result was that the pupils would not stay in school, but would take to their heels. The Rabbis, therefore, enjoined that a man disposed to anger should not be a teacher.[16] Though this attempt of establishing public schools resulted in failure, nonetheless it marked the beginning of an organized school system.

This deplorable state of affairs endured till about the second half of the first century of our common era, when Joshua ben Gamala arose and decreed that schools be established in every city and that children enter school between the ages of six and seven. The Talmud says of him: "Verily let it be remembered too that for good, Rabbi Joshua ben Gamala is his name, for had he not been, the law would have been forgotten in Israel. At first every one that had a father received from him instruction in the law, but he that had no father learned not the law."[17]

He also laid down a law whereby a teacher should not teach more than twenty-five children; if there were more, he was to have an assistant. If the number reached fifty, two teachers were to be assigned.[18]

Such a regulation, it seems to me, would not be out of place even to-day. What a boon it would be to our overworked teachers, who not infrequently have to grapple in overcrowded classes with as many as sixty children, not too well behaved to boot.

[16] "Ethics of the Fathers," II, 6.

[17] "Baba Bathra," 21a.

[18] *Ibid.*

When we consider that compulsory education in modern times is comparatively recent, then this act of Joshua ben Gamala of almost two thousand years ago must be regarded as unusual.[19]

Ben Gamala well realized that the Jews as an entity would not endure, unless the education of the children were safeguarded. He looked upon the child as the corner-stone of the Jewish nation. "The world only exists by the breath of the school children," was the dictum of others.[20] Luther, too, realized that fact, for he asseverated: "Soll alles in den rechten Schwank kommen, so muss mit der Jugend angefangen werden."[21] That the Jesuits took the lead from him is too well known.

Whereas, formerly, at the time of Simeon ben Shetah, no curriculum is alluded to, we find now a course of study outlined in the "Ethics of the Fathers" which tends to indicate that a certain definite plan was followed. Accordingly, between the ages of five and ten, that is to say, for a period of five years, the Bible is to be taught, for another five the Mishna, which was later incorporated in the Talmud, and not until the age of fifteen was the study of the latter to begin.[22]

This course was, very likely, not strictly adhered to, at least not in the subsequent centuries, as evidenced by the "Cheder" (still extant on the East Side of New York City) which indubitably is the sequel of the original elementary school with slight modifications. The Mishna is, however, no

[19] Compulsory education was introduced in Prussia in 1717; in France in 1882; in England in 1870 and 1873; in Massachusetts not until the approach of the middle of the nineteenth century. Paul Monroe, "Cyclopedia of Education."

[20] "Sabbath," 119b.

[21] "Sendschreiben an die Ratsherren." "If everything is to proceed smoothly [that is to say, if the reformation is to succeed] we must begin with the children."

[22] "Ethics of the Fathers," 5, 21.

longer studied; the Talmud has entirely replaced it and is ordinarily begun at the age prescribed for the former. Of course, the ability of the pupil is in most instances the decisive factor.

It seems, however, that occasionally a foreign language was also taught, namely Greek. A rabbi, son of a prominent official, the Nasi (president) relates that out of a thousand children five hundred studied Greek, but finally gave it up, apparently because of its difficulty, and he was the only one left to continue its study.[23]

The Jews were very fond of the Greek language. Aristotle makes mention of the fact that he met a cultured Jew who spoke Greek.[24] The latter was not only the official language during the Greek occupation, but continued to be so under that of the Romans. Josephus, though he lived in Rome, wrote his works in Greek. Latin was held in contempt by the Jews; it was considered as only fit for soldiers, whereas Greek was held peculiarly suitable for song.[25] Latin was looked upon as being neither fit for writing nor speaking, *i.e.*, something uncouth.[26] Charles the Fifth and Voltaire entertained similar views in regard to the German language, to wit, that it was only a tongue for horses. There is very little Latin to be found in the Talmud, whereas it abounds with Greek words and expressions. The rabbis had a profound regard, bordering almost upon affection, for the Athenian savants. This seems to speak rather well for their broad-mindedness. There are even debates referred to between rabbis and Greeks.[27]

Trades, naturally, could not be taught in the schools, and there was no need for that, for this was still held to be the province of the father. The business of the school was the training of the young in spiritual matters. The son merely adopted the trade of his father, and if the latter practiced no trade, he turned him over to some artisan. This custom largely prevails in the East, Lithuania, Poland, and used to be so in Russia prior to the revolution. The rabbis maintained that the father who did not teach his son a trade was as guilty as though he had taught him to become a highway robber. They well realized that lack of trade frequently leads to idleness, and finally to crime. Hence we have rabbis who bore the surname of the trade they practiced, such as shoemaker, tailor, smith, baker, wine taster, builder, etc. St. Paul, by the way, was by trade a tentmaker. In fine, every one had to engage in some occupation. The celebrated philosopher Benedict Spinoza also owed his trade of lens-grinder, by which he eked out an independent existence, to this practice. I believe it would go far to checkmate the tendencies of crime in our modern society and to make for a more contented people if our schools were to teach our children, boys and girls, some sort of a useful craft, in view of the fact that the parents are unable or unwilling to do so. Instead of foisting upon the children all sorts of impractical subjects for which they evince no aptitude whatever, it would accrue to their blessing and to that of the commonwealth at large if they were equipped with a skilled trade. There prevailed a fine custom among the Hohenzollerns, according to which each member of the family had to acquire a manual trade. It is known that ex-Emperor William is a bookbinder by profession. He could very well earn his own living were he not maintained in luxury by his ex-subjects, upon whom he has brought so much misery and misfortune.

23 "Baba Kama," 117b.

24 "Schuerer Geschichte des juedischen Volkes im Zeitalter Jesu Christi," 3d ed., p. 9.

25 "Megilah," 71b.

26 "Abodah Zarah," 10a.

27 "Bek," 8b.

The father in ancient Israel was also obligated to teach his son swimming,[28] not for the sake of sport, nor for the sake of physical development, merely for the sake of being able to save his own life, and presumably that of others. Life was held sacred in those days from a religious point of view, and, therefore, was to be spared and preserved.

The method applied in teaching was in some respects a unique one. It was some sort of a singsong manner of instruction; everything was imparted in a singing voice, and this procedure was enjoined by the rabbis[29] and has been preserved to this day in the East. The rabbis apparently felt intuitively, or had learned by experience, that things learned by singing committed themselves more vigorously and firmly to memory than otherwise. Moreover, it served as an excellent medium to secure a proper pronunciation, and to combat stuttering.

It is noteworthy that in some of our schools and colleges singing is being utilized in the teaching of foreign languages. The College of the City of New York has been notably successful in pursuing this method, introduced by Professor John Whyte.

Inasmuch as Aramaic had become the vernacular of the Jew, just as Yiddish at the end of the middle ages and in some parts of Europe to-day, Hebrew, which was now viewed as a sacred tongue, just as Sanskrit by the Hindus and Latin by the Roman Catholic church, had necessarily to be translated into the idiom of the child. It was presumably done in the same way as it is still practiced in the "Cheder," which apparently has kept alive the traditions of the ancient school. The teacher read and translated a passage word for word which the pupil repeated until he obtained proficiency therein, when the word-translation was omitted and the passage read and translated in its entirety. By translating word for word, not only the vocables would fix themselves strongly upon the mind of the pupil, but also the grammatical forms and construction, so that there was no need for the instruction of formal grammar. The language was then learned from the language itself and not from grammar, a truism which Comenius later emphasized: "Die Sprache muss aus der Sprache gelernt werden" (language must be learned from language itself). And, indeed, a similar method was adopted, if my memory serves me right, at the Sophien Gymnasium in Berlin in the teaching of Latin. However, mere translation of the text was not thought sufficient. In addition a passage had to be memorized by the pupil each day. It was so common that when the king met a child outside the gates of Jerusalem he asked him to recite the passage he had learned by heart that day.[30] Great stress was laid upon repetition of the subject learned. The dictum of the Jewish pedagogues was: "He who repeats a hundred times is not to be compared with the one who repeats a hundred and one times."[31] The Jesuits, I believe, had a similar saying: "Repetitio mater studiorum est." They also deprecated a smattering gained of many things; they preferred rather a few things learned thoroughly. Accordingly they insisted, "Do not attempt to master many things but few."[32] Ratichius likewise stated: "Non multa sed multum."

Furthermore, they recommended to scholars, who complained of headaches, to engage in study in order to overcome that illness.[33] Headaches, as nowadays, were very likely used as a pretext to avoid study.

28 "Kidushin," 30b.

29 "Megilah," 32b.

30 "Gitn," 56b.

31 "Roshhashanah," 4b.

32 "Erubin," 54a.

33 "Chagiga," 9b.

Juvenal, who as a Roman was by no means fond of the Jews, unwittingly pays their education a compliment in his Satyra, "Romanas autem soliti contemnere leges, Iudaicum *ediscunt* et servant et metuunt ius, tradidit arcano quodcumque volumine Moyses."[34] And Professor Swift, of the University of Minnesota, one of our foremost educators, expresses himself as follows in regard to the merits of the ancient Jewish education:

> The Greeks in vain sought to induce the Jews to accept physical culture, the golden classics of Greece, and Greek science. Nevertheless, the boy who had completed the studies of the elementary school was master of one of the greatest literatures any race has ever produced. He probably knew by heart most of the Pentateuch as well as selections from many other of the scriptures, ready to explain origin and meaning of the sacred rites, customs, public and private which played a part in the events of each day. He was steeped in the religious consciousness of his people and was united with them in thought, knowledge, and sympathies.[35]

Besides the elementary schools the Jews also maintained higher institutions of learning. As a matter of fact the only favor Rabbi Johanan ben Sakkai, who at the peril of his life had managed to escape from the besieged city of Jerusalem, sought to obtain from Titus Flavius Vespasianus, was permission to establish an academy at Jamnia.[36] His desire was to rear upon the ashes of the physical temple a spiritual structure which was to become the mainstay and prop of the Jews for all ages to come.

In the academies all sorts of subjects were discussed and debated, religion, exegesis, liturgy, history, sociology, jurisprudence, philosophy, medicine, astronomy and every possible subject under the sun. They seem to have known quite a bit about medicine, for the minute laws pertaining to diseases of animals unfit for food are based upon a knowledge of anatomy and medicine. The calendar, which is rather ingenious, shows quite a familiarity with astronomy. One of the rabbis vaunted that the heavenly paths were as familiar to him as the streets of his native place.[37] This was apparently an exaggeration.

The form of instruction in the higher institutions was not the lecture, but discussion, stimulated by question and answer, and the analysis of problems by student and teacher. The students were very frequently urged to express their views, though they differed from those of the teacher.

I believe that such a method is very valuable and could be used advantageously in our colleges. Experience teaches me that discussion is by far more stimulating and inspiring than incessant lecturing. It tends to develop in the students a desire for independence of thought, self-expression and self-activity.

The academies were usually arranged like a stadium, apparently taken over from the Greeks. They contained seven rows in front of which was some kind of a dais, consisting of a stone or seven pillows on which sat the president of the academy, who was at the same time the teacher. The number seven was chosen because it was regarded as holy. The scholars occupied their seats in accordance with their ability and achievements. When they failed to keep up a certain standard they were demoted. The purpose of such an arrangement was obvious; it was to stimulate the students to greater efforts. It is related of an eminent scholar, who had fled from Persia because he had come into conflict with the authorities for having struck down a lawbreaker and had imposed silence upon himself for his rashness, that he had been gradually demoted from the first to the last seat because of lack of ability. He had been highly recommended to the

34 "Satyra," 14, 100.

35 "Education in Ancient Israel," p. 99.

36 "Gitn," 56b.

37 "Berachoth," 58b.

teacher for his scholarship and keen intellect and found wanting. When he had reached the last place, he could no longer bear the humiliation and mortification and began to put questions to the teacher, who was unable to give satisfactory answers and explanations, wherefore he quickly moved up, not only to the first place, but replaced the teacher.[38] We can imagine what would happen in our colleges and universities if such a process were followed. Perhaps many a professor would forfeit his job. On the other hand, it might work both ways; it might goad on the teachers and students to greater exertions.

The plan of having the scholars occupy seats commensurate with their achievements has been and still is, I believe, in vogue in the German gymnasia. A former friend of mine in a Berlin gymnasium, who held the fifth place, had the misfortune to have had the same error in a quiz as his neighbor. He asserted that the latter had copied from him. However, both were demoted. The effect it had on both is indescribable. The shame and disgrace they felt drove them almost to despair and suicide. It is singular that the ancient Jews, almost nineteen hundred years ago, should have adopted such a modern scheme. They, too, seem to have had an eye for pedagogical stratagems.

The position of the teacher in ancient Jewry was of the highest social standing. He was looked up to with reverence and respect, almost with awe. Whenever there was a question between father and teacher the latter took precedence, for he was regarded as giving the child or youth spiritual life, *i.e.*, something eternal, whereas the father as giving him merely physical life, something ephemeral, something passing.

The great importance of the teacher is pointedly illustrated by the following story: Several learned men were once sent from Jerusalem to establish schools and promote instruction wherever needed. They came to a town in which they found no trace of tuition whatever. Indignantly they summoned the citizens and asked them to bring before them the guardians of the town. But only magistrates and politicians (persons entrusted with the civil functions of the town) made their appearance. "These are not the protectors of the town, they are the destroyers," they exclaimed. (The esteem in which the politicians were held at that time has not undergone any material change, it seems.) "Who then?" inquired the citizens with astonishment. "The teachers," was the laconic reply.[39]

In Germany the teacher, at least up to the time of the world conflagration, held a similar position. He was held in high esteem and regard. He mingled with the best and among the select and it was deemed an honor to be in his society. His authority was never questioned. "Der Lehrer hat es gesagt," was the final word. Bismarck paid the teaching profession the highest compliment by declaring, "It was the teachers that won the war of 1870."

In this country, where success is measured in dollars and cents, the teaching profession occupies by no means an enviable position. It is looked upon as some sort of a necessary evil. The teacher is regarded by parents and students as a kind of minion, belonging to an inferior class. And this deplorable situation will continue, it seems to me, unless the economic status of the teacher will greatly be ameliorated; not until then will he be considered the equal of the merchant, doctor and lawyer. In the middle of the eighteenth century Rector Abrecht, principal of the gymnasium at Frankfort-on-the-Main, one of the most brilliant pedagogues, teacher of Goethe, upon whom he exercised the greatest influence (he is the only teacher to whom Goethe pays a high

[38] "Baba Kama," 117a.

[39] "Midrash Rabba Eicha," Chapter 1.

tribute), once remarked in an annual report in order to score the authorities on this point, "It is reported by the Jews that the tribe Simeon furnished most of the teachers and beggars; teachers and beggars are placed together apparently because the teachers at that time already were remunerated so beggarly."[40]

From the academies evolved the Mishna and Talmud, which offered mental and spiritual food to the Jew during the darkest of dark ages when he was barred from every honorable calling. To those who dwell in the east, and to some that have settled here, it still forms the only intellectual source from which they draw consolation and inspiration. It is this fact, I believe, to which their survival of nineteen hundred years of unspeakable suffering can be ascribed. According to Nietzsche, "sind die seelischen und geistigen Hilfsquellen bei den Juden ausserordentlich." He attributes it to the fact that they have passed through a schooling of "achtzehn Jahrhunderten" (eighteen hundred years) as no other people has. However, he entirely overlooks the circumstance that they were only able to emerge from that "schooling" because they had schools from which to draw strength, inspiration and aspiration; that without them they would and could never have survived. And if his vision should, perchance, come true that in consequence of their rich experiences they must produce "grosse geistige Menschen und Werke" (great spiritual men and works), which he terms "Edelsteine und goldene Gefaesse" (jewels and golden vessels) and transform their "ewige Rache in eine ewige Segnung Europas" (their eternal revenge in eternal blessing),[41] it will not be due to any other factor, I maintain, than to their schools of the past.

MARK WALDMAN
COLLEGE OF THE CITY OF NEW YORK

40 "Menzel Wolfgang und Cornelia Goethes Lehrer," p. 236.

41 "Morgenröthe Gedanken über die moralischen Vorurteile, vom Volke Israel," p. 200.

STANDARDS OF ACCREDITING

PROFESSOR REEVES' studies of standards for accrediting colleges are a valuable contribution to the subject. He has pointed out convincingly that "present standards are not resulting in a satisfactory state of excellence in every accredited college." He has suggested that the present standards be supplemented by the requirements of a reasonable minimum average faculty salary and a minimum average expenditure per student for strictly educational purposes, and that the present standard for faculty training be more strictly enforced. He has reached the conclusion also that the present method of calculating the teaching load is unfair in the case of some laboratory subjects. He is careful to say that the standards so far adopted are quantitative and do not measure quality of work or the outcome of instruction. He has made use of an independent criterion to check and supplement the formal standards, this to be based on a personal inspection of the institution with the object of evaluating the quality of instruction, the faculty personnel and the equipment of library and laboratories. And finally he suggests that comprehensive examinations and other such devices may offer a solution to the problem of actually arriving at more scientific standards.

The result of Professor Reeves' work has been wide-spread interest in the whole subject within the accrediting agencies themselves and in the Association of American Colleges and the various state college associations. Just recently a committee of the Higher Education Section of the Minnesota Education Association made a report, setting forth certain evils of standardization—the tendency to coercion, the limiting of the freedom of an institution to work out its own educational policies and the bringing about of a nation-wide uniformity which may be not an unmixed good. The charge is made that standardizing agencies have often changed their standards without first securing full data and have thus placed many of their members under a disadvantage. They have limited experimentation along lines not yet officially approved by themselves and have thus hampered rather than encouraged progress. They have made it difficult for new institutions to develop during the trying and critical first years. It is suggested that more use be made of standards of attainment of students and of methods and curricula considered best for the promotion of these results and that practical tests of attainment should be developed by the agencies for use in rating institutions and transferred students. Approval is given to the suggestion of a better criterion than that of endowment, and the opinion is voiced that this criterion may well be substituted for such standards as teachers' salaries, size of classes and teaching load. Approval is expressed of experimentation in methods and curricula.

The standardizing agencies have undoubtedly rendered great service in the development of our system of higher education. They have made it easier for new institutions to get essential endowment and equipment. Older colleges have benefited, too, even against their first desires. Just last year an old and respected college was dropped by one association because of insufficient endowment, with the result that the president went to work and raised the amount that was needed. The associations have affected the level of teacher training, even though the standard is not rigidly enforced, for my observation is that the colleges pay considerable attention to it in their employment of teachers. The standardizing bodies have served the professional school in its choice of a reasonably well-prepared entering class. They have saved the colleges an enormous amount of time and expense in classifying students transferring from other institutions. But perhaps the greatest good, though intangible and unmeasurable, has come from the formal statements of minimal essentials for an effective college, which these bodies of educational leaders have held up. It has represented an ideal, or the limit below which it was not safe for a college to remain. In no other way could the educational world have spoken so forcefully to the public.

That there have been many mistakes in judgment and unintended unfairness because of the superficiality or lack of discrimination in the standards or because of the lack of penetrating inspection, we may assume. Sometimes mistakes are made because of poor cooperation between the secondary commission and the commission on higher education. As an example, a junior college is said to have been refused admission to a standardizing association because its high-school department was not accredited. And the high school was rejected because it did not have enough full-time teachers. The institution was using combination high-school and college teachers—allowable so far as the college was concerned, but fatal for the high school.

Again, the salary scale is recognized as an unsafe index of faculty efficiency. There are undoubtedly wide differences in costs of living in towns and cities, and there are differences in family budgets. Even a standard of average faculty salary would not take care of this difficulty, but would need to be supplemented by an index of the margin left for the "higher life" after necessary living expenses. We have a vast range in our institutions to serve by way of illustration. Consider, first, a small junior college in the mountains far from any town, maintained by a church; next, a college in a small town, with its own store supplying the faculty families at cost; and last, a college with not much better salaries, in a city with no special prices to teachers and with all the social and other financial demands made on the city teacher.

Average training of teachers still leaves much to be desired by way of adequate information. We had an illustration of this just recently. Two junior colleges were visited on the same day. At the first a teacher was found who met all the standards of training, but who was old and infirm and uninspiring. At the other the visitor found one who had not yet completed work for the master's degree but who was full of enthusiasm, progressive and in every way doing a fine piece of work.

The development of the junior college and its trend toward inclusion in the secondary field rather than as a part of the old four-year college brings up new problems for the accrediting agency. Whether this spells the doom of the four-year college remains to be seen. The swing toward the secondary field seems quite strong. At present, however, the standards for junior colleges are largely set by college men and the attempt has been made to keep the work of the junior college on the level of the institution of higher education. Can this be maintained? We see the junior college in many instances developing as a part of the high-school system, yet we insist that the students shall be taught in separate classes. On the other hand, if we allow the junior college to be integrated with the senior high school, can we justify acceptance of the work as in every way equivalent to the work of the first two years of an effective college? These are questions that are vital for both the junior college and the four-year college. My prediction is that there will be no universal solution for some time, but that there will be a parting of the ways for standard colleges. The well-endowed independent colleges will be slower to accept the work of the junior college of the secondary field than will the state and city institutions.

The present situation, then, calls clearly for a reconsideration of the old quantitative standards, a supplementing of them along lines suggested by Professor Reeves. Experiences with the administration of these standards show too that they must be applied with discrimination, remembering that while the figures may be correct they do not necessarily tell the whole story. The whole story must include the qualitative factors, as has been pointed out, and these must come to light through skilful inspection and the application of attainment tests.

I believe that the next important step that the accrediting associations should take is the employment of skilled inspectors on full time to study both the institutions already in the associations and the applicants for admission. These inspectors would not have the power to damn an institution irretrievably but merely to report their findings to the already established accrediting commissions. Their work would be closely analogous to that of the high-school inspectors. It would still be a good thing to have an independent report by a visitor from another institution, as is the practice at present.

I believe also that an organized and subsidized effort should be inaugurated at once to attack the problem of attainment tests. The large standardizing agencies can without doubt obtain the needed funds to finance such a piece of research, so essential to the establishment of searching and convincing qualitative standards for the effective college.

The final solution of our problems must wait upon the discovery and application of satisfactory qualitative standards. But meanwhile we can supplement our present blank by a rating sheet that will give much pertinent information, serve as a guide for the inspector in his study, and stand out as the present-day ideal for an effective college much more powerfully than does the present questionnaire on buildings, degrees, entrance requirements and teaching load. While it would contain much of this old material, the emphasis would be changed from the "externals of excellence to excellence," as Professor Reeves puts it, from materials to the life of the institution, from machinery to spirit.

I suggest two ways to proceed. First, there are the excellent studies that have been made under the auspices of the Association of American Colleges, on the subject of "The Effective College." These papers have discussed for the effective college such topics as unit size, the business administration, the cost of education, college and university administration, personnel technique, the curriculum, honors courses, the comprehensive examination, faculty-student cooperation, athletics, records, financing the fine arts, teaching. These suggest the framework of a rating sheet that would guide in answering the all-important question, "Is the college under study an effective college?"

But I would prefer to arrange this meaty material on a different skeleton. The effective college is accomplishing certain great aims for a number of classes of people. So, I would ask first, "What is the college doing for its students?" Second, "What is it doing for its faculty?" Third, "What is it doing for its constituency?" Fourth, "What evidences are there of results?" Fifth, "What signs of progress? Do changes denote losses or gains?" Sixth, "What problems of instruction or administration are being studied?" Under these heads I would arrange the topics that at the present time meet with the approval of the association as being sound educational policy. Thus:

I. *What is the college doing for its students?*

(1) Material equipment provided—buildings, laboratories, library, athletics, endowment.
(2) Money spent on the student—unit cost per student for strictly educational purposes.
(3) Protection of the student through proper entrance requirements.
(4) Curricula provided.
(5) Training of the faculty provided.
(6) Personalities of faculty—standing in college and town.
(7) Is the principle of individual differences recognized and applied?
(8) Personnel work, faculty advisers.
(9) Sectioning of classes.
(10) Honors courses and comprehensive examinations.
(11) Teaching methods. Is the student stimulated to educate himself?
(12) Is the library *used*?
(13) Are there departmental clubs and seminars that work?
(14) Is there a stimulating faculty-student spirit of cooperation?
(15) Are extra-curricular activities reasonable and helpful?
(16) Provisions for lectures, entertainments.
(17) What attention is paid to the fine arts?
(18) What of the moral and religious atmosphere?

II. *What is the college doing for its teachers?*

(1) Salaries and margin above living.
(2) Sabbatical leaves.
(3) Retirement allowances.
(4) Academic freedom and tenure.
(5) Teaching loads.
(6) Encouragement of research.
(7) Rewards for teaching achievements.
(8) Is attention given to distribution of grades?
(9) Is experimentation and study of college problems encouraged?
(10) Is the organization democratic in theory and practice?
(11) What is the attitude of the Board of Trustees?

III. *What is the college doing for its constituency?*

(1) How does it touch the town?
(2) What does it contribute to the reading public?
(3) What is it doing for adult education?

IV. *What results of the efforts can be noted?*

(1) *As to the students*
 (a) Records in graduate and professional schools and in other colleges.
 (b) Attainment tests.
 (c) Student publications—their quality and attitude.
 (d) Records in intercollegiate contests.
 (e) Social life.
 (f) Are students fairly contented and interested in their education?
(2) *As to the faculty*
 (a) Faculty turnover.
 (b) Faculty publications.
 (c) Other faculty activities.
 (d) Membership and participation in educational organizations.
 (e) Is the faculty loyal, happy, enthusiastic?

V. *What signs of progress? Losses and gains.*

VI. *What problems of instruction or administration are being studied?*

PAUL P. BOYD
UNIVERSITY OF KENTUCKY

EDUCATIONAL EVENTS

A HOME FOR SCHOLARS AT THE GRANDE CHARTREUSE MONASTERY

ACCORDING to the New York *Times*, La Grande Chartreuse, that monastery of the Alps which was founded by Saint Bruno in 1084 A. D., is to become again the home of scholars and students, but they will not be monks.

Since 1903, when the religious orders had to leave their domains, the great monastery has been uninhabited and visited only by tourists. That liqueur, chartreuse, which the monks distilled from Alpine flowers, is no longer made within the century-old walls.

But now there is a plan on foot to make good use of the peaceful place. That part of the buildings which may be called laic, will by next year have been re-furnished and converted into a great hostel. Only university professors, scholars and scientists who wish to work quietly and in congenial company will be admitted. There will be 100 rooms and the occupants will represent almost every nation. La Grande Chartreuse will be a kind of intellectual center of the world during holiday time.

Through the Institute for Intellectual Cooperation and the Inter-University Union, a hundred professors have already had their names put down for the privilege of spending their next holidays in this monastic calm. Enough money has been obtained for the furnishing, and it is believed that by next Spring it will be ready for occupation.

The *Times* says that the Grande Chartreuse, situated in the French Alps, 3,205 feet above sea-level, was founded by Saint Bruno in 1084 and became the birthplace of the Carthusian order of monks. The friar of the monastery was the Superior of the whole order.

On the passing of the Association law in 1901, nine other houses of the order in France accepted dissolution, but the mother house applied for State recognition. This was refused and the monks, expelled in April, 1903, moved to the Certosa of Farneta, near Lucca, in Italy.

The monastery, which was burned down several times, was rebuilt in 1676. The cloister is 240 yards long and 25 yards wide. The chief points of interest are the chapter house, which holds a statute of Saint Bruno; the Chapelle St. Louis; the Prior's parlor; the library; the refectories and the monks' cells.

The cells of the Carthusian monks are really small two-storied houses, with two rooms on each floor. On the ground floor are woodsheds, and upstairs is the kitchen and a room serving as bedroom, refectory, oratory and study. The monks, who numbered about forty, never left their cells except for daily and nightly service, and once a week to walk. They took their meals in their cells and were forbidden to talk without the Prior's permission. There also lived at the monastery about 100 lay brethren. The monks wore white habits and the lay brethren were garbed in brown.

BRITISH COMMITTEE ON SCHOOL SCIENCE

Sir Richard Gregory presented to the section of education of the British Association for the Advancement of Science at the recent Glasgow meeting the report of the committee (of which he was chairman) on science in the schools certificate examinations.

According to an abstract in the London *Times,* it stated, he said, that in instituting the First School Examination the intention was that it should represent the contents of a general education up to 16 years of age, with no specialization either on the literary or on the scientific side. In the science group of subjects, however, little serious attempt had been made to devise a course of instruction suitable for all pupils, and the syllabuses of single subjects, any one of which might be included in the curriculum for the purposes of the examination, could not really represent what science for all should be in a general education. Further, large numbers of pupils in most schools never took it and therefore it did not fulfil its purpose. The committee therefore thought that the science certificate examination should be so amended as to fit the changed conditions, or, if that was impossible, that it should cease to be the normal objective of the average boy or girl.

The committee expressed themselves favorable to the establishment of a national certificate similar to that now awarded under the joint supervision of the Board of Education and the Institute of Civil Engineers. Under the system the students of each section would be examined by their own teachers in association with assessors. Questions concerning the jurisdiction or the appointment of boards of assessors presented obvious difficulties. A school which did not desire to examine its own pupils should be permitted to take the examination of another school. It was reasonable that the universities should accept this certificate as evidence of general education, but they might require a special test for admission to a chosen faculty, unless the higher certificate had been obtained. The committee wished that the second approved examination should remain an external examination so far as the schools were concerned, and were of opinion that no fundamental change was needed in the system, with one exception. There should be a broadening of the examination and the correlation of the training preliminary to it and to specialized study in the various professional groups.

The aims of the teaching of science should be—first, to train the powers of accurate observation of natural facts and phenomena and of clear description of what was observed; secondly, to impart a knowledge of the method of experimental inquiry which distinguishes modern science from the philosophy of earlier times, and by which advance is secured; thirdly, to provide a broad basis of fact as to man's environment and his relation to it; fourthly, to give an acquaintance with scientific words and with the ideas now common in progressive life and thought.

THE LITERACY LAW FOR NEW VOTERS IN NEW YORK

DR. FRANK P. GRAVES has sent the following letter to city, village and district superintendents:

The provisions of the literacy law for new voters, in practice since 1922, have naturally become the common knowledge of the school superintendents of the state. Neither this law nor the regents' rules relative thereto have been materially altered since 1923. The regents and through them the local school authorities have been charged with the full and sole responsibility for the issuance of certificates of literacy. The new voters are required to present the necessary evidence of literacy to the election authorities.

I wish especially to call your attention to the matter of properly bringing the provisions of the literacy law to the attention of new voters in your community. As this is a presidential year, new voters will be particularly interested in voting. I urge you to give frequent publicity to the times and places designated by you for the issuance of certificates of literacy. This year we are sending for the first time large posters which should be placed on the outside of school buildings in which certificates of literacy are to be issued.

In addition to cooperating with the election officials to the fullest, the following specific suggestions for carrying out your publicity campaign are made:

(1) Notify every principal and teacher under your jurisdiction of the law.

(2) Through the teaching staff notify all students and request them in turn to inform their parents, relatives and friends.

(3) After you have designated certain times and places for conducting the examination for new voters, enlist the aid of all clergymen in your community to make possible announcement of the places designated by you for issuing certificates of literacy.

(4) Inform the local newspapers both native and foreign.

(5) By means of posters in conspicuous places call attention of new voters to times and places for issuance of certificates.

(6) Cooperate with local civic clubs and agencies and local motion picture houses in informing the public of the times and places designated for the examination.

The material—bulletins containing the rules and regulations governing the issuance of certificates of literacy, tests, scoring keys, certificates of literacy, posters, blanks for reporting—necessary for the administration of the law, has been forwarded to you from the Adult Education Bureau. The secretary of state has included the regents' rules and other valuable suggestions in the election law bulletin. You are urged to cooperate with the election authorities in every possible manner.

Let us all cooperate so that there can be no justifiable criticism of the manner in which we have carried out our part of the literacy law, the aim of which coordinates with the general aim of all education.

GROWTH OF CHILD WELFARE IN CHICAGO

ANTICIPATING the annual meeting of the American Public Health Association, October 15–19, the *American Journal of Public Health* has published an article on "Child Welfare in Chicago." According to the abstract in the *Journal* of the American Medical Association, child welfare work is said to have started here in 1896 with the medical inspection of school children for contagious diseases. This was expanded in 1908 to include physical examinations for defects, and nurses were added to follow up the cases. Almost all health activities in the public and parochial schools are carried on by the city department of health. The exceptions are the special nutrition work carried on by the Elizabeth McCormick Memorial Fund and tuberculosis prevention work conducted by the municipal tuberculosis sanatorium. One hundred and twenty-two physicians visit the schools daily to inspect pupils for contagious diseases, each one of whom is permanently assigned to a district and is held responsible in that area.

Fifty-two physicians conduct physical examinations of children in the primary and kindergarten grades and routine reinspections of the higher grades. From ten to twenty physicians are assigned to the administration of toxin-antitoxin, vaccinating against smallpox and making Schick tests. They spend their time in the schools five days a week and on Saturdays at the infant welfare stations and other health centers. Defects discovered may be corrected by private family physicians, dispensaries and other special agencies. Dental care is provided through twelve dental clinics maintained in the schools by the department of health, the dental clinic at the Cook County Hospital, at the dispensaries of the municipal tuberculosis sanatorium and at the clinics of the dental colleges in the city. Hygiene courses are given to grammar school pupils of the parochial schools by the health department and the Red Cross. Infant welfare, as it is to-day, had its beginning in 1909 in a cooperative effort of the department of health, visiting nurse association, United Charities and the milk commission to lower the infant mortality rate. Later, the baby welfare stations were reorganized into a single private agency called the Chicago Infant Welfare Society, which to-day conducts twenty-three stations. The department of health, which entered this field in 1913 in cooperation with the infant welfare society, has twenty-two stations in the outlying districts. Each organization by agreement works in its own district. These two agencies have expanded infant welfare work still further to include prenatal and preschool care. The infant welfare society has ten prenatal and seventeen preschool conferences, and the department of health six prenatal and fourteen preschool conferences. The infant welfare society has added a psychiatric social worker to its staff. Now the nursery school has come into vogue, of which there are three notable examples: the University of Chicago Cooperative Nursery School, the Nursery School of the Franklin Public School and the Mary Crane Nursery at Hull House. Much duplication of effort has been eliminated by clearing all of the cases through the social service exchange and by mutual understanding and cooperation promoted through the Chicago Council of Social Agencies. The medical schools and some hospitals also are interested in child welfare. Chicago is fortunate in having in all parts of the city small parks and playgrounds which play no small part in the welfare of its children.

THE CURRICULUM AT THE COLLEGE OF THE CITY OF NEW YORK

THE new curriculum of the College of the City of New York was inaugurated at the beginning of the present academic year. The only change affecting the older students is the introduction of an alternative third year of hygiene instead of the hitherto compulsory two-year course in military training.

There have been introduced courses in science survey, appreciation of art and music and additional subjects in English for all students. Science students will be required to take a course in "Logic and the Scientific Method." Social science men must choose one additional course in philosophy.

The curriculum is divided into four groups, as follows:

1. A group of studies, prescribed for candidates for all degrees, including courses calculated to impart broad, general knowledge essential and basic to a liberal education. The subjects of this group amount to sixty credits.

2. A group of studies forming a background for the particular degree sought. Students contemplating a degree in science should have a broad and thorough preparation in all the basic sciences, considerable training in mathematics and special training in scientific technique and procedure. This second group of subjects amounts to from nineteen to twenty-four credits.

3. A specialization or concentration group of twenty-four credits calculated to make the student competent in some particular field of endeavor.

4. Free electives to stimulate interest in diverse fields of intellectual endeavor, sufficient in number to enable the student to complete the 128 credits required for graduation.

The College of Liberal Arts and Science offers courses of study leading to the degrees of bachelor of arts, bachelor of sciences and bachelor of science in social science. The fundamental aims of these various courses of study are, however, the same throughout: first, to develop the students of the college as broadly cultivated and intelligent citizens of the world in which they live and, second, to train them so that each may be able to perform some particular function in the community in a worthy manner.

RADIO TALKS OF THE UNIVERSITY OF PITTSBURGH

One of the interesting announcements concerning the fall programs of the University of Pittsburgh Studio of Westinghouse Station KDKA is of a series of talks on science that has been adapted from a college freshman course. This "radio course" is on biology and will be given on Wednesday evenings throughout the first semester by Dr. Robert T. Hance, head of the department of zoology. The general subject of the series is "The Machines we are," while the subjects of the talks beginning on October 3 are as follows: "We Chart our Course," "How do we Inherit?", "What do we Inherit?", "The Continuation of the Race," "How we Grow," "Energy and the Living Machine," "Food and its Utilization," "Circulation," "Respiration and Excretion," "The Nervous System," "Movement," "Regulating the Body," "The Body's Struggle for Life," "Our Relation with other Forms of Life," "The Balance of Nature," "In the Laboratories of Today," "What is it all about?"

"The goal of biology," according to Dr. Hance in commenting on this series, "is a knowledge of living mechanics, the result of which is greater physical comfort. This in turn leads to that rare human attribute known as common sense, which in itself is spiritual happiness. In general the subject-matter of this series of radio talks on biology parallels that which we present to our freshman classes in zoology. Needless to say, in a series as brief the radio requirements demand only the most important facts or ideas can be presented. This is perhaps not as serious as it may sound since the value of radio talks would seem to lie as much in stimulating an interest in certain subjects that will lead to further thought and study as in sending over the air a relatively complete body of information."

For the benefit of those who may wish to regard this series as a study course and, accordingly, to know in advance the subject-matter which will be treated in each talk an outline, together with suggested readings, has been issued. This is known as Radio Publication No. 42 and it is available at ten cents a copy.

The first university broadcast of the college year was given on October 3 on "Learning to Live," by Dr. John G. Bowman, chancellor of the university. Thereafter fifteen-minute programs will be broadcast from the University Studio at seven o'clock on Tuesday, Wednesday, Thursday, Friday and Saturday evenings. Daytime programs, the detailed announcement of which will be made later, will be broadcast after November 1.

THE DRAMA IN ADULT EDUCATION

Fifty-four colleges and universities in the United States report activity in teaching people to play—to interpret through pageants, folk plays and dramas the spirit and history of the state.

According to a bulletin of the Bureau of Education, the university and the college keep alive the traditions that reach far back into the history of the race by teaching community drama. The drama is nearly universal in its appeal, and participation in such dramas helps to bring about solidarity and breaks down religious and political prejudices among people who, under no other circumstances, could be induced to work together.

The acting of plays is in itself of value as a form of education, but it is of greater value when the student develops the ability to look at life through a great mind, which he does if the play is a good one.

The University of North Carolina is rendering a worthy service through its drama bureau. It is reaching all parts of the state through its pageants, its dramatization of phases of local history and its folk plays. That such extension work is appreciated is evidenced by the phenomenal growth of the drama movement in the state.

The University of Colorado gives very practical help in the selection of plays, and has arranged in the university library an extensive collection of dramas that may be borrowed for a limited period of time. A special bulletin is prepared describing this service.

The University of Indiana is another of this group of fifty-four universities that is rendering helpful service. It has a collection of more than 1,000 plays that are suitable for schools, churches and clubs.

Since a study of the art of the theater has found a place in the curriculum of American universities, there has been a great advance in the standard of the professional theater, and the "Little Theater" movement has won considerable success. Smith College and Cornell University have experimental theaters of their own which have added considerable impetus to the movement; and the Pasadena Community Playhouse Association also has a fine theater, conducted by a non-professional group and catering to a wide public taste. A whole range of drama from open-air productions of Greek plays, in replicas of Greek theaters, to modern farcical comedy or revue types of production is given by the various "Little Theater" groups.

VISITING LECTURERS AT HARVARD UNIVERSITY

THE list of visiting lecturers who are going to Harvard from other universities is considerably augumented this year by the addition of the first group of Chinese scholars under the Harvard-Yenching Institute of Chinese Studies. Founded last winter as the result of an endowment of $2,000,000 from the estate of the late Charles Martin Hall, of Niagara Falls, this institute will seek to carry out the most complete study and interpretation of Chinese culture ever undertaken.

Considerable progress has already been made in securing distinguished sinologists to teach at Harvard, as well as in correlating courses at Harvard and at the University of Yenching so that work done at either may count toward certain advanced degrees. Three professors from Yenching University—Baron Alexander von Staël-Holstein, Professor Lucius Porter and Professor William Hung—together with Professor Paul Pelliot, of the Collège de France, make up this year's contingent of visiting lecturers on Chinese culture. Professor Pelliot, one of the world's leading scholars of the language, art and archeology of Central Asia, will lecture on "The History of Chinese Art." Professor Hung is a specialist in Chinese history, Professor Porter in Chinese philosophy and Baron von Staël-Holstein in Chinese language and literature.

England, Germany and France are all represented among the other visiting lecturers who will be at Harvard this year. Professor Paul Hazard, of the Collège de France, will fill the position of exchange professor from France, held last year by Professor Andrè Koszul, of the University of Strasbourg. Professor Hazard's special field is in the comparative history of the literatures of southern Europe and Latin-America.

From England Harvard has drawn to its lecture platforms this year Charles Jasper Sisson, Lord Northcliffe professor of modern English literature at the University of London, and Ralph G. Hawtrey, assistant secretary of the treasury, who will lecture in economics. In addition to Baron von Staël-Holstein Teutonic scholarship will be represented by Professor Gustav Pauli, director of the Kunsthalle, Hamburg, who will lecture on fine arts and who will be affiliated with the Germanic Museum during his residence here.

Several American colleges and universities are also sending lecturers. Verner Winslow Crane, of Brown University, will lecture in history; Ralph Mason Blake, of the University of Washington, in philosophy and psychology; John Masson Smith, of Grinnell College, in Romance languages, and Miles Standish Sherrill, of the Massachusetts Institute of Technology, in physical chemistry.

EDUCATIONAL NOTES AND NEWS

DR. CHARLES ALEXANDER RICHMOND has resigned as president of Union College, a post that he has held for nearly twenty years. He is retiring at his own request, giving as the reason his age of seventy-six years. He will become president emeritus.

DR. EDMUND D. SOPER, dean of the Duke University School of Religion since 1926, formerly professor in Northwestern University, has been elected president of Ohio Wesleyan University.

DR. EARL A. ROADMAN will be installed as president of Dakota Wesleyan University on October 27. President John L. Seaton, of Albion College, will deliver the charge to the president. Dr. Roadman's inaugural address is entitled "The Community from which our Students come and to which our Graduates go." Speakers at the morning educational conference to be held in connection with a two-day celebration will include Dr. W. J. Early, president of the North Central Education Association, and the Honorable Alvin Waggoner, chairman of the State Board of Regents.

DR. FREDERICK J. KELLY has been installed as president of the University of Idaho. In his inaugural address Dr. Kelly outlined his program for the university. Dr. Lotus D. Coffman, president of the University of Minnesota, gave the principal address, taking as his subject "The Place of the State University in the State's Higher Educational System."

FOR the third time in succession Dr. Frank J. Goodnow, retiring president of the Johns Hopkins University, has qualified before Mayor Broening, of Baltimore, as a member of the school board. Dr. Goodnow was in Europe at the time of his last appointment. He told the mayor that, after retiring from the presidency, his plans for the future would enable him to devote more time to the schools.

DR. CAROLINE A. YALE, president emeritus of the Clarke School for the Deaf at Northampton, Massachusetts, and a pioneer in the teaching of the deaf, celebrated her eightieth birthday on September 29. Messages of congratulation received from all parts of the world, chiefly from former students who are now teachers, were presented to Dr. Yale in a leather-bound volume.

THE government of Japan has received the names of five students of education who are recommended for elevation to the peerage: They are Joji Sakurai, president of the Imperial Academy; Shosuke Sato, president of the Hokkaido Imperial University, formerly a student at the Johns Hopkins University and American exchange professor in 1914; Sanae Takata, president of Waseda University; Sankichi Sato, emeritus professor of Tokyo Imperial University, and Eikichi Kamada, ex-president of Keio University and ex-minister of education.

THE doctorate of laws was conferred on Canon Emile Chartier, vice-rector of the University of Montreal, at the recent convocation exercises of Queen's University, at Kingston, Ontario.

ELIOT WADSWORTH, Harvard, '98, honorary A.M., member of the Massachusetts Legislature and formerly assistant secretary of the United States Treasury, has been elected president of the Board of Overseers of Harvard University, to succeed the late Howard Elliott.

IT is reported that a change in the plans of the "Floating University" providing for transfer of steamers during the world cruise instead of chartering one vessel, has led Scott H. Goodnight, dean of men at the University of Wisconsin, to cancel his agreement to become educational director. Dean Goodnight will consequently be at the state university this year. Professor E. A. Ross, of the department of sociology, is expected to retain his connection with the cruise.

J. MILNOR DOREY, formerly head of the English department in the Scarborough, New York, Country Day School, has been appointed executive secretary of the Progressive Education Association, to succeed Mr. Morton Snyder, now director of the Rye, New York, Country Day School.

DR. W. L. UHL, professor of education at the University of Wisconsin since 1920 and acting head of the department of education since 1926, has become dean of the college of education of the University of Washington at Seattle. For a number of years before going to Wisconsin Dr. Uhl was professor of education at Northwestern University. During 1925 he was acting associate professor of education at Yale University.

DR. EDWARD H. ROCKWELL, of Tufts College, has been appointed head of the department of civil engineering at Lafayette College, to succeed Albert Hatton Gilmer, who has become dean of engineering at Rutgers University.

DR. PAUL A. KENNEDY has resigned the chairmanship of the department of education, Georgiancourt College, to take the position of director of the department of methods in the school of education of Fordham University. Associated with Dr. Kennedy in this work will be a faculty including John W. Davis, Dr. William A. Rabenort, Leo I. Kearney and Stephen A. Bayne.

Appointments at the Teachers College, Columbia University, include Dr. Harold F. Clark, professor of education; Charles E. Rush, professor of education and librarian; Dr. John R. Clark, associate professor of education, and Dr. Floyd B. O'Rear, Mary M. Reed, Mary E. Townsend, Willard S. Elsbree and Mrs. Elizabeth V. D. McDowell, assistant professors of education; Norval L. Church has been appointed assistant professor of music education and Dr. Clarence Linton, assistant professor of education and secretary.

Miss Hazel M. Clark, Warsaw, New York, has been appointed dean of women at Bates College, at Lewiston, Maine, taking the place of Dean Ruth V. Pope, who resigned last spring to do graduate work at Columbia. Miss Clark is a graduate of the University of Rochester and Teachers College, Columbia University, and comes from Maryland State Normal School, where she was a professor of education and social director.

Walter G. M. Buckish has in addition to governmental work been giving lectures in educational psychology in the University of the Philippines since July.

At the George Washington University, Ernest Cushing Richardson, consultant in bibliography and research of the Library of Congress and emeritus director of the Princeton University Library, has been appointed professorial lecturer in library science and consulting director of the division of library science, and Dr. Mandell Sherman, director of the Washington Child Research Center, professorial lecturer on child development.

Lafayette College will have as visiting lecturers this year Dr. John C. Merriam, director of the Carnegie Institution of Washington, and Professor Roman Dyboski, of the University of Cracow, Poland.

Dr. Stephen P. Duggan, director of the Institute of International Education, has spent six months visiting some ten countries of Western and Central Europe with the object of strengthening the educational ties between them by means of an increase in the number of exchange fellowships for students and of visiting professorships for scholars. He also discussed with foreign educational authorities plans for international conferences in particular fields of scholarship and for international support of scholarly journals that can not be expected to maintain themselves. While abroad he lectured by invitation at the universities of Berlin, Vienna and Budapest, at the Geneva School of International Relations and at the Royal Institute of International Affairs of London. He also delivered the address in English at the unveiling of the monument to Woodrow Wilson at Prague. In addition to discussing educational problems with university authorities and government officials, he had the opportunity to discuss general international questions with various statesmen, including President Masaryk, Regent Horthy, Mussolini and Lord Robert Cecil. While in Budapest, the Hungarian government conferred upon him the Order of Merit and a little later the French government made him a Chevalier of the Legion of Honor. These decorations were bestowed in recognition of his services in strengthening the cultural ties between those countries and the United States.

Visiting professors this year at Columbia University will include Louis Cazamian, professor of English language and literature at the Sorbonne, Paris, as professor of English; J. J. L. Dyvendak, of the University of Leiden, as professor of Chinese, and Pauson J. Trent, of Stanford University, as professor of history.

Contessa Maria A. Loschi, of Rome, has been appointed visiting lecturer at the University of Southern California this coming winter. She has long been identified with the social and economic problems of her own country and has served as its representative to the third and fourth congresses of the International Federation of University Women and on other important missions.

Dr. D. Simon, author of the Binet-Simon intelligence tests, at present in charge of Colonie d'Enfants Arriérés at Perray Vaucluse, France, is visiting the United States to talk with scholars and to observe the application which has been made of the intelligence tests. Dr. Simon comes from Canada, where he made similar observations in educational and social institutions. While in the United States he is making his headquarters with the Institute of International Education, New York City.

DR. FLETCHER HARPER SWIFT, professor of education in the University of California, has a year's leave of absence, during which he plans to make a study in Europe of methods of financing elementary education.

PROFESSOR W. J. H. COTTON, of Duke University, has been granted a sabbatical leave of absence for the academic year 1928–29. He will spend most of the year in travel and research in Italy, Germany, France and England, giving especial attention to the study of labor problems.

PROFESSOR JACOB H. HOLLANDER, of the Johns Hopkins University, will give a graduate course at Princeton University in the history of economic thought during the first term of 1928–1929.

PROFESSOR C. A. GREGORY, of the college of education of the University of Cincinnati, has been granted leave of absence for the first semester of the present school year.

DR. MARY COVER JONES, who was for two years research associate in the Institute of Child Welfare Research of Columbia University and who for another two years served as fellow in child development for the National Research Council, has been appointed in the nursery school of the University of California Institute of Child Welfare to take general charge of data collecting concerned with eating habits, motor activities, language development and social adjustment.

THE Board of Education of New York City recently has elected Dr. Albert K. Aldinger as director of health education, Frederick L. Holtz as principal of the Maxwell Training School for Teachers and Mrs. Letitia M. Raubicheck as director of speech improvement in the city schools, following nomination by the board of superintendents.

FRED MOSER, who has taught at Cumberland, Wisconsin, for the past three years, has resigned, to accept a position as research assistant to John R. Commons at the University of Wisconsin.

J. F. WADDELL, superintendent of schools of South Milwaukee, was appointed, on September 1, supervisor of high schools in the Wisconsin State Department of Education.

WALTER P. SWETT has been appointed assistant superintendent of schools at Somerville, Massachusetts.

SUPERINTENDENT C. C. BISHOP, of Oshkosh, Wisconsin, is chairman of a committee recently appointed by State Superintendent Callahan to study systems of grading and marking in the state. Mr. Bishop will be assisted by J. T. Giles, O. Granger, Paul Carlson and F. O. Holt. The teachers of Oshkosh have made an intensive study of marks in their own city.

THE New York Society for the Experimental Study of Education will celebrate the completion of a decade of service with an anniversary dinner to be held at the Hotel Commodore on October 20. Dr. Michael H. Lucey, principal of the Julia Richman High School and president-elect of the society, will deliver his inaugural address at the dinner. All interested in the scientific study of education are invited to attend. Reservations should be made with Secretary J. C. Bell, Townsend Harris Hall, Amsterdam Avenue and 138th Street.

MISS MARY B. C. BYRNE, teacher in the model school of the New York Training School for Teachers, appeared, according to press reports, to have won in her controversy with the New York City school authorities when the Board of Education passed on to the Board of Superintendents for action a recommendation from the medical board of the Teachers Retirement System to the effect that Miss Byrne is not incapacitated for work, but should be transferred to another school.

THE three American teachers charged with disseminating religious propaganda in Turkey have again been sentenced to three days' imprisonment and a fine of $13 when the case against them was retried. The teachers, Miss Jennie Jilson, director of the American School at Broussa; Miss Edith Sanderson, of Berkeley, California, and Miss Lucille Day, were sentenced by Judge Nizameddine, whose former identical verdict had been set aside by the Court of Appeals. Miss Jilson will not serve her sentence, pending a decision of the upper court, to which the defense has again appealed. Miss Sanderson has returned to the United States and Miss Day is teaching in Turkey.

ANNOUNCEMENT of the gift of a president's house to Evansville College, Indiana, was made on September 13, a date which marked the beginning of the second year of Dr. Earl E. Harper's administration. The house, complete with its furnishings, will be the gift of Mr. and Mrs. John L. Igleheart. The cost will be over $25,000.

THE trustees of Wiley College at Marshall, Texas, at a recent meeting formally accepted the offer of the General Education Board to donate $300,000 for endowment on the condition that a like amount be raised from other sources. A campaign for the raising of the college's share of $300,000 was planned and launched at the same time.

THE new Hilles Laboratory of Applied Science of Haverford College will be completed in time for the opening of the second semester.

OF the 142,111 resident students enrolled in land-grant institutions of the United States during the school year 1925–26, more than a third, 34 per cent., were registered for courses in arts and science, 20.5 per cent. in engineering courses, 9 per cent. in commerce and business, 8 per cent. in agriculture and 7.2 per cent. in professional education, as shown by a report on land-grant colleges by Walter J. Greenleaf, associate specialist in land-grant statistics of the United States Bureau of Education, published by the bureau of Bulletin No. 37, 1927.

SPECIAL CORRESPONDENCE

THESIS WRITING AND TRAINING IN RESEARCH AT THE UNIVERSITY OF SOUTHERN CALIFORNIA

DURING the twelve months ending June, 1928, the school of education of the University of Southern California granted a total of 168 master's degrees. The rising standards of state requirements for the high-school teachers' credential promise to keep up a very large and permanent supply of graduate students. The guidance of this number of master's theses presents a task of no small proportions. The problem is difficult for the members of the faculty as well as for the graduate students, since there tends to be overloading of the faculty with thesis work and a reduction of the amount of individual attention and help received by the student.

One way to overcome this burden would be to abandon the thesis requirement for the master's degree. This has not been done because other departments of the university do not feel the pressure so keenly and because it is felt that the writing of the thesis is a good form of training for later work for the doctorate and for practical research in the public-school system.

Heretofore the training of graduate students in thesis writing has been of two sorts: (1) Each student was required to take four semester hours of seminar courses in education. These seminars were primarily devoted to the subject-matter of education and secondarily devoted to the giving of training in scientific procedure. (2) At the opening of the year a few general meetings were held at which all candidates for master's degrees were given suggestions about thesis writing in the form of lectures by members of the faculty. Usually three or four such meetings were held each year.

The increasing size of the graduate student body has made necessary more systematic methods of training. Certain guiding principles and viewpoints have determined the direction of the efforts toward such training. (1) There was a desire to economize time. (2) There was a desire to raise the quality of the theses that were written so that the results would be more suitable for publication and more useful in solving the educational problems of the day. (3) There was a desire to give more actual training in research technique, in addition to the more immediate objective of thesis writing, in order that after theses were finished the research activities of the graduates would be continued in practical school situations. (4) There was a desire to keep up a wide variety and diversity of effort in graduate research through the promotion of many different types of research procedures. There was a fear that if all thesis writing were centralized under the training or influence of a single member of the faculty he would consciously or unconsciously limit the scope of the research endeavors of the students. This made it necessary that training in thesis writing be given by several different members of the department instead of by a single member. By this means diversity and variety could be secured within the department and at the same time the maximum advantages of concentration and specialization could be enjoyed by each faculty member.

The plan that has been worked out by Dean Lester B. Rogers and the faculty of the school of education involves the inauguration of a number of sections of thesis seminars devoted strictly to training in research procedures. Three such sections were taught during the summer school, 1928, and eight are scheduled for the fall semester, each under a different man. The policy is to limit the enrolment to twenty students in each seminar, although this could not be done during the summer school because of the smaller number of sections. The thesis seminar is treated as a two-credit course in the student's work load, although he does not receive credit on the books until the completion of the thesis in final form, at which time he receives four semester-hour credits. The seminar counts for two credits in the instructor's work load, just the same as any other class, and there is an additional allowance on the instructor's work load in proportion to the number of theses he directs.

The student selects his thesis seminar according to his personal likes and the fields of specialty of the various members of the department. Enrolment in a thesis seminar is required of all students who have not previously been admitted to candidacy, and it is a policy to postpone individual discussion and planning of a thesis with a student until he has enrolled in a thesis seminar. Admission to candidacy is the only mark or credit or grade which a student receives for satisfactory work in the seminar. Unless he makes sufficient progress to receive the recommendation to candidacy, it is expected that he will re-enroll in the thesis seminar the next semester should he care to try again. In general, it is thought best for such a person to take a thesis seminar under a different man the second time in order that the training given will not be a mere repetition, and that the influence and guidance of a new faculty member may produce results where the first one failed.

The procedures and practices within the seminar itself are somewhat in the experimental stage as yet and will naturally vary from man to man. The following points describe the procedures in the section taught by the present writer during the summer school and may be considered reasonably typical of the situation in other sections. There has been a necessity for a compromise between *thesis writing* and *training in research.* If nothing is done except simply to get theses written, general principles of scientific method may be overlooked. On the other hand, if a straight course in research technique is given, the applications to a particular thesis may be overlooked. A regular text-book is used for the course.[1] A few well-chosen theses are put on special reserve to be used as models or examples. Regular lectures are given from time to time as they are needed just as in any regular course. Since, however, each student is trying to make definite progress in the actual writing of his own thesis, it is not thought wise to follow the text-book in regular or systematic order. A very large portion of the time is spent in answering questions raised by the students. This plan interferes somewhat with the logical organization of the course but it contributes largely to the interest and value of the course because practically everything that is said or done comes as a response to a felt need on the part of the students.

In connection with the choosing of research problems, the writer has found it well to encourage some little delay in making a choice in order that a more thorough acquaintance with the available types of research procedures may be gained. There seems to be somewhat of a tendency to "order the meal without looking at the menu."

The members of the group are able to give a great deal of mutual help. They criticize each

[1] C. C. Crawford, ''The Technique of Research in Education.'' Published by the University of Southern California, Los Angeles, 1928.

other's plans and procedures, act as subjects for each other's experiments occasionally, and exchange information about sources of data on their various problems.

Most important of all, however, is the benefit which each student gains from hearing the other students' questions answered. Under the old plan of purely individual guidance there was a great deal of uniformity and repetition in the questions asked in private conferences, each student coming in and asking for information on the same points as had been covered in the previous conferences with other students. In the thesis seminar, however, questions of this sort can be answered once for all members of the class. In cases where a particular student's question is not of immediate concern to the other students, the time is not wasted, because all the members of the group are interested in research and are eager to learn everything they can about research, whether it applies to their immediate theses or not.

There was difficulty at first in breaking the ice so that students would present their difficulties in class. They seemed to be timid and afraid they would make themselves ridiculous, but this quickly disappeared when it became apparent that no one had a monopoly on personal difficulties and problems.

Recommendation to candidacy at the end of the semester hinges upon the satisfactory completion of three chapters of the thesis. The first chapter is a statement of the problem, the second a summary of related investigations, and the third a detailed description of the procedure that is to be carried out. The procedure chapter presents the greatest difficulty because of the natural tendency of graduate students to want to do the investigation and plan the procedure later. Being required to write out a minute outline of all phases of the procedure is found to be a very wholesome influence in favor of more adequate planning.

It is too early yet to judge the final results in every respect, but a few statements may be made with very definite assurance. (1) The students seem to be quite happy and well pleased with the arrangement. (2) An enormous amount of time is saved, both for the teacher and the student. (3) Out of a total of 73 students enrolled in the three seminars during the six-week summer school there were 55 students, or 75 per cent., who completed their first units of the thesis and were admitted to candidacy. (4) The tuition charge, coupled with the fact that no immediate credit is placed on the books at the end of the course, has a selective influence, and prevents the seminar from being filled with people who are not interested in theses. (5) The necessity of completing three chapters and being admitted to candidacy or else taking the course again serves as a rather effective incentive to vigorous effort upon the thesis, and thus eliminates much of the dilly-dallying so common in connection with thesis writing. (6) The completion of three chapters of the thesis during the semester leaves the students with a feeling of having invested enough time and effort in the thesis that they can not afford to fail to finish it up. (7) The thesis seminar requirement seems to have had the effect of increasing rather than decreasing the number of graduate students. In other words it seems to be considered by the students not as an additional requirement so much as an extra bit of service and help.

C. C. Crawford

Professor of Education,
University of Southern California

DISCUSSION

INSTRUCTION IN INSTITUTIONS OF HIGHER LEARNING

Men who think they know how to teach are continually telling the world about the shortcomings in teaching method of instructors in American institutions of higher learning.

The head of the department of education in a certain great university teaches the history of education. In this course he is fond of saying that the teaching of history must be revolutionized. How does *he* teach his history? He sits behind his desk with a book before him and lectures from the book. He wrote the book and uses it instead of notes. Every student in the class owns a copy of the book and supposedly can read it. But the professor tries to inject into the subject-matter some of the enthusiasm which he was unable to put into the written word. It is an admirable process, for he succeeds in enthusing his listeners. But how is the gentleman going to revolutionize the teaching of history when in practice he uses a very time-honored method of imparting knowledge and inspiration?

Another professor of education in the same university teaches in a different manner. He asks questions about the material assigned to the class at a previous session, and works up a little one-sided discussion. Certainly there is nothing new about this method.

An eminent professor in another famous university teaches educational psychology by the question and answer method coupled with the lecture and laboratory. Nothing unique about this.

The head of the department of education in still another university teaches prospective instructors methods of teaching history. He tells his students how to teach incidents in history which have absolutely no bearing on anything but military or naval history; and he is not instructing at West Point or Annapolis.

The purpose here is not to criticize exponents of the science of education for doing the best they can, but to object to the assumption on their part of an attitude of infallibility in regard to the teaching of other subjects by their colleagues. The methods actually practiced by such professional educators are not different from the methods of other instructors; and instructors in education are no better teachers than instructors in other fields, notwithstanding the misleading results of certain questionnaires. Yet they would dictate to the whole profession.

Who, after consideration, would have such men sent around to the various classrooms of young university instructors to teach them method?

The average young man who goes out to teach in a college or university has had the best training possible for a beginner; after leaving high school he has sat for four or five or seven years under many professors, whose methods he has observed, experienced and evaluated. He knows what methods students like and profit by, and now it is up to the young instructor to try to put the best methods into operation for himself. He will of necessity experiment, and his experiments will progress better if he is not pestered by any "Meddlesome Matties" sent around to observe his work. He will soon find that certain methods, successfully used by others, are unsuited to him. He will reject this method and that, retaining such methods as fit in with his temperament and personality. Perchance, he may hit upon some new method which operates well, and in any event he will develop a system somewhat individualistic. His students will recognize him as a personality. He will not be a product of a routine based in part on the weaknesses of other men's schemes.

And, whatever the strength of his methods, the teacher's personality, his interest in his work —his enthusiasms, play a most important part; and these elements can not be imparted to him by any one. Personality and enthusiasm wither under supervision, however skilful it may be.

As to the truth of the assertion that the most productive teaching is to be found outside of the colleges and universities, the writer must register a doubt; for, in his experience as a student, "sterility" of teaching is by far more characteristic of the grades and high school than of the institutions of higher learning—institutions as yet not dominated by "scientific" educators.

Is it not possible that the educational world is letting the professional, so-called scientific, educators run away with it?

CHARLES ROGER HICKS
UNIVERSITY OF NEVADA

SERVICE OF PRESIDENTS OF COLLEGES OF THE UNITED PRESBYTERIAN CHURCH

A COLLEGE president's position has been listed as a hazardous occupation. A short time ago attention was called in SCHOOL AND SOCIETY to the unusual term of service—an average of fourteen years—which characterized the presidents of colleges of congregational affiliation.

It is interesting to compare with that unusual group the service that has been and is being rendered by the presidents of the five colleges under the auspices of the United Presbyterian Church.

President J. A. Thompson, of Tarkio, has served for forty-one years; President T. H. McMichael, of Monmouth, for twenty-five years;

President R. T. Campbell, of Sterling, twenty-four years; President J. Knox Montgomery, of Muskingum, for twenty-three years, and President W. C. Wallace, of Westminster (New Wilmington, Pa.), for twelve years. The average length of service of the United Presbyterian college president is twenty-five years.

The annual report of the board of education of the United Presbyterian Church presents evidence of the efficient service rendered by showing the following institutional gain since 1920.

GROWTH (IN PERCENTAGES) FOR SEVEN YEARS

	Westminster Per cent.	Muskingum Per cent.	Monmouth Per cent.	Tarkio Per cent.	Sterling Per cent.
Plant	124	519	156	169	148
Productive endowment	44	93	195	91	169
Students	106	94	50	13	114
Average	91	235	134	91	138

M. T. BOARDMAN

OFFICE OF COUNCIL OF CHURCH BOARDS OF EDUCATION,
NEW YORK, N. Y.
SEPTEMBER 1, 1928.

QUOTATIONS

EDUCATION IN CHINA

Now that the archives of the old Ministry of Education are being prepared for removal to Nanking, there is under way a careful scrutiny of the many abortive plans adopted by China (on paper) for the modernization of her educational system.

The amount of labor involved is colossal, for the records go back to 1858, when China, defeated in war and forced to sign the Treaty of Tientsin, decided to prepare herself for contact with foreign powers. This decision resulted in the founding of the Language Institute, under the Emperor Tung Chih.

From that time on, according to the rise or ebb of the tide of reform, there have been almost countless plans, edicts and manifestoes dealing with the educational problem, but still China remains about 90 per cent. illiterate.

The great need to-day, and one which the new Nationalist Government admits is almost unsurmountable, is the tremendous shortage of teachers.

Estimating that there are 40,000,000 children of elementary school age in the country needing the services of 1,000,000 elementary teachers, the Ministry of Education is faced with the fact that, including foreigners, there are only 233,279 teachers in China—and this census includes middle school and university teachers as well as teachers of the "old style" classical education.

In quiet times the normal schools enroll about 46,000 students annually, but many of these schools are closed because of lack of funds or occupation by troops. At best there could be graduated only 10,000 qualified teachers a year—and where is the money to come from to found additional normal schools, and where are additional teachers for the normal schools to be found and how are they to be paid?

In times of peace the Protestant mission schools in China, including all grades, handle about 300,000 pupils annually, and the Catholic schools handle 400,000, but this combined total of 700,000 reaches only 8 out of every 100 of the 65,000,000 children and youths who imperatively need education.

With characteristic official Chinese disregard for the difference between planning and achievement, the educational leaders are now pointing with pride to the development of education under the so-called "Plan of 1920."

This particular plan, admirable in itself, provided for compulsory education controlled and fostered by the central government, and was to have been applied as follows:

1921—Provincial capitals and open ports; 1922—District seats and cities; 1923—Towns above 500 families in size; 1924—Towns above 300 families in size; 1925–26—Towns above 200 families in size; 1927—Villages above 100 families in size; 1928—All villages below 100 families.

Only in Shansi Province has even a serious effort been made to carry out this plan. In Shansi, until that province for the first time became involved in the civil war last August, 72 per cent. of the children under 16 years of age were actually in the schools. In no other province has the total ever exceeded 23 per cent., and in many provinces that have been continually used as battle-grounds practically all education has come to a halt, except that meritorious work carried on by the Mass Education Movement.

This mass education, or "1,000 character movement," which hopes to eliminate 200,000,000 illiterates within a generation, is doing and has done startlingly successful work and has undoubtedly profoundly influenced the lives of several millions of young and adult Chinese.

The mass education movement has the double advantage of offering a system of beginners' education which is both cheap and easy. Four "readers," which together cost only 10 cents in Chinese money (or less than 5 cents in American coin), contain a reading vocabulary of 1,200 Chinese characters, and the average dull-witted adult illiterate can master these 1,200 characters in four months' time if he or she will study for one hour a day. This equipment will enable him to read the average newspapers, ordinary letter correspondence and a great range of books upon cultural and technical subjects which have been especially compiled for mass education students.

Of course this four-months' study of one hour a day does not change the illiterate into an educated person, and the average adult graduate reads little but the newspapers. Nevertheless, even this fragmentary beginning of an education is a vast advance over absolute illiteracy and ignorance enlightened only by gossip and rumor.—*Peking Correspondent of the New York Times.*

REPORTS

A CODE OF ETHICS FOR THE TEACHING PROFESSION[1]

I. *Educational and Professional Attitude:* The strongest obligation of every member of the profession is due to those who are in his professional care. The teacher should aid in every honorable way in stabilizing and maintaining the honor, dignity and usefulness of the teaching profession.

II. *New Educational Ideas:* Every member of the profession should improve his education by reading educational literature, attending school and educational meetings and becoming an active member of local, state and national organizations of teachers.

III. *Compensation:* Members of the teaching profession should receive compensation commensurate with maximum efficiency. This should be an amount that would enable the teacher to live on a scale befitting his place in society, to improve himself professionally and to provide for himself and his famliy in old age. Regardless of compensation, a teacher should render his best services.

IV. *Contractual Relations:* It is a breach of pedagogical ethics for a teacher to violate an oral or written contract to render service. Service should be terminated by the mutual agreement between teacher, superintendent and board of education.

V. *Appointments and Promotions:*

(A) All promotions should be obtained exclusively on merit.

(B) Upon accepting an appointment a teacher is in honor bound to notify all others to whom letters of application have been sent.

(C) It is unethical:

(1) To patronize teachers' agencies that:

[1] Report of a Committee on Education, S 148, University of California, summer session, 1928. The committee composing the report was as follows: H. J. Wilcox, *chairman,* Berkeley, Calif.; E. P. Hodapp, Emerson, Neb.; Miss Edvenia Jeppson, Ogden, Utah; James A. Neilson, Upper Lake, Calif.; J. M. Nill, Dunsmuir, Calif.; R. E. Noddin, Campbell, Calif.; G. F. Purdy, Calumet, Iowa; George Rieben, McCloud, Calif.; Miss F. M. Reichle, Butte High School, Butte, Montana; M. L. Stevenson, Weber College, Ogden, Utah; Miss Hazel E. Stockton, Fairfax School, Cleveland Heights, Ohio; Miss H. M. Van Gilder, Berkeley, Calif.

(a) Encourage teachers to break contracts.
(b) Work for the promotion of unqualified teachers.
(c) Make recommendations for positions not known to be vacant.

(2) For one district to seek teachers from another district without first consulting the proper authorities.

(3) For a teacher to secure an offer elsewhere for the sole purpose of obtaining an increased salary in his present position.

(4) For a teacher to apply for another position not known to be vacant.

VI. *Relation Between Teachers, Supervisory Officers and Superintendent:*

(A) The superintendent should be administrator and adviser to all in his school system, with the right to give advice and suggestions in matters pertaining to the schools.

(B) There should exist a sympathetic bond between teachers and supervisory officers by means of which suggestions and constructive criticisms may be exchanged for the betterment of the schools.

(C) A superintendent, principal or one in authority should be willing to give accurate information to official inquiries from prospective employers pertaining to the qualifications of a teacher.

(D) Cooperation, loyalty and reliability should characterize all relations between supervisory officers and teachers.

(E) No teacher should take school matters to higher officials without the knowledge of his immediate superiors.

VII. *Relations of Teachers to Parents:* Teachers should welcome the visits of parents, maintaining a cooperative relation with them, and meet criticism with open-mindedness and courtesy. They should not discuss limitations of pupils in such a way as to cause unnecessary embarrassment; nevertheless, they should exercise the utmost candor in their discussions or communications with parents on important matters. All personal information concerning the pupils should be held in confidence by the teachers.

VIII. *Interrelation of Associates:*

(A) Committees: It is the moral obligation of every member of the profession loyally to support all policies formulated by school committees which are the legal organs of expression of the teaching corps, with the exception of policies which would clearly endanger the best interests of the pupils.

(B) Criticisms:

(1) Members of the profession should recognize and welcome the inspiration and helpfulness of constructive criticism.

(2) Verified adverse criticisms should be told only to the one criticized or his superior. The motive of this action should be helpfulness to the individual and to the profession.

(3) Adverse criticisms and insinuations passed upon a fellow teacher, predecessor, or a teacher of previous grades is condemned and regarded as non-professional.

IX. *Publishers and Supply Houses:*

(A) The profession condemns the practice of some representatives of publishing houses in going to the wrong official for orders of books or supplies without the knowledge or consent of teacher or supervisory officer, and such action should be made known to the profession.

(B) Any member of the profession who is also a representative of a publishing house should make the fact known and accept no commission in his own district.

EDUCATIONAL RESEARCH AND STATISTICS

METHODS OF COLLEGE TEACHING

DOUBTLESS the college student has ever reacted towards the educational régime to which he has been subjected. Recently considerable attention seems to have been paid to his reactions, to the extent of registering and classifying his reactions and even of soliciting further his reactions to the end of improving this régime. Various aspects of college education have been essayed in such a manner. In some cases the college students have been asked to gauge personalities. They have been asked to rate their instructors, to note their weak points or to designate those qualities indicative in their minds of a good college teacher. In other cases the students have been asked to gauge curriculum content. They have been asked to state preferences or values of college studies or courses or of different units of subject-matter with those courses. In still other cases they have been asked to evaluate in their own minds the values of certain methods and devices to which they have been subjected. Surely some values must reside in the reactions to all of these, by the real object of college teaching, the college student.

Intelligent people who have, for twelve years in the elementary and secondary schools, been subject often to the directions of many teachers and then for two or three years of college have had from fifteen to twenty-five different college instructors, are not without a considerable experiential background in the matter even if they have been "consumers" of education rather than "producers."

Breed says:

> In any campaign for the improvement of college instruction, the students of the college have something important to contribute and should be permitted to contribute it.[1]

Armentrout says:

> If we are to adapt the work of the college more closely to the needs and interests of the students it is necessary that we determine in an objective way some of the interests of the students that can be utilized in the process.[2]

The object of this article is to report a study of college students' reactions to certain methods and devices of college instruction. The returns are from one hundred and fifty college students all registered in courses in education—partly at the University of Minnesota and partly in South Dakota State College. These were predominantly juniors with more seniors than sophomores.

Each student was handed a checking list of methods and devices of thirty-one items with this written explanation:

> You are asked to check these according to their value as methods and devices of teaching as you see them as a good college student. You are not answering from your experience of this class but from your experience in college classes as a whole. Your reactions are not a part of the final grade in the course. (Most of the papers were turned in without names.) If an instructor has poorly handled an otherwise satisfactory method do not let that prejudice you against the method as such.

Each item was to be checked as "very good," "good or fair," "poor," or "very poor." In order to build up a table of rankings of these items, numerical values of 4, 3, 2, 1 respectively were given to each of these checkings. Table I shows the rankings thus obtained.

TABLE I

COLLEGE STUDENTS' PREFERENCES FOR CERTAIN METHODS AND DEVICES OF COLLEGE TEACHING

(Total of 31 ranks)

Rank	Item
	TYPE OF CONTENT
26th	Most time should be spent on facts and general principles with little time on illustrations and applications.
3rd	Considerable time should be spent in showing the functions and uses to be made of the materials given.
10th	Considerable time should be spent on concrete cases and illustrations.

[1] SCHOOL AND SOCIETY, XXIV, July 17, 1926.

[2] SCHOOL AND SOCIETY, XXIV, December 11, 1926.

INSTRUCTORS' ACTIVITY IN CLASS

13th Instructor should be the main source of facts, principles, illustration, etc.—largely lecture.

27th Instructor should be mostly a setter-of-tasks for students to master from texts and references. Class time spent on students' recitation on these.

6th Instructor should be largely explainer and evaluator of the material assigned and read by pupils.

STUDENTS' ACTIVITY IN CLASS

16th Class period should be mostly used in having students explain and evaluate the materials assigned. Instructor to act mostly as judge and guide in this student activity.

4th Students should do considerable questioning in class.

12th Students should furnish own illustrations and applications.

USE OF TEXTS AND REFERENCES

23rd Class work should stick pretty closely to a text.

8th Instructor should assign additional reference readings.

USE OF SPECIAL REPORTS

18th Written special report should be required.

14th Special reports should be given orally before the class.

USE OF CLASS TIME

22nd All the points should be taken up in class.

9th Only the main points should be taken up in class.

15th Only those points which students and instructors regard as most difficult should be taken up in class.

28th Little or no class time should be spent for drill and review.

19th Instructor should conduct practice tests in class—no scores recorded.

17th Instructor should furnish practice test material for students to use out of class—no scores recorded.

CONCERNING TESTS AND TESTING

11th Short weekly quizzes.

31st Unannounced quizzes.

2nd Quizzes over each large unit of work as completed.

21st Theme or essay type quizzes.

7th Objective tests—true-false, etc.

29th Pre-tests on entering course or taking up a new unit.

20th Use of oral tests.

24th Written tests over reference work.

25th Few or no tests.

30th Posting names and test grades on bulletin board.

1st Analysis of test questions and answers following tests.

5th Placing range of test grades on board so each individual can locate his own rank.

Evidently the students expect the instructor to furnish concrete cases and illustrations and show the applications of what is taught. Lecturing ranks higher than recitations on texts and references read, but neither ranks as high as where the instructor explains and evaluates. Students seem to feel that they should do considerable questioning in class. Utilization of references is somewhat more preferable than close application to the text. Consideration of main points in class appeals somewhat more than detailed consideration of many points.

Oral presentation of special reports by students gets a slightly higher ranking than written special reports. Abhorrence of testing as a whole is not evident from the data. In fact, of all the phases mentioned those concerned with testing secured the first, second, fifth and seventh rankings. The procedure of analyzing test questions and answers with the class following the tests secured first rank. Quizzes over each large unit of work as completed are preferred. Short weekly quizzes are not so bad. Whereas a recent statement concerning testing as a teaching skill says that no announced quizzes should be given, these students reacting in this study give unannounced quizzes the lowest rank of thirty-one items. It is somewhat of a surprise that use of objective tests gets rank of seventh from the students, while theme and essay type of questions are given a rank of twenty-first. Students like to know their own rank on a test (fifth rank), but dislike to have it publicly posted (thirtieth rank).

C. R. WISEMAN
SOUTH DAKOTA STATE COLLEGE

SCHOOL AND SOCIETY

Volume XXVIII   Saturday, October 13, 1928   Number 720

ENLIGHTENMENT AND EMOTIVATION

It is fair to say that the best possible curriculum is almost valueless in the hands of poorly trained and poorly oriented teachers. At best, a curriculum is only a tool of the teacher and pupil in the process of education. Like an ax or a saw it may even be dangerous when misused. It takes understanding workmen to use proper tools properly. A razor in the hands of a babe is dangerous.

The certification of a teacher may be a bad thing if the certificate represents qualities and training which the owner does not possess. The significance of a certificate to teach bears the same relation to teaching that a surgeon's commission to practice of his art bears to the science of surgery. A teacher is supposed to be able to present material to be learned in a psychological manner and diagnose the individual pupil's difficulties in the learning process.

The sciences of education have developed an abundance of methods of how to teach this or that subject in the curriculum. Psychology, which is one of the fundamental subjects of the sciences of education, has helped us to understand something about the workings of the mind of the student. The sciences of physiology and anatomy have helped the surgeon to know the structure and the normal functioning of the human body. But the science of psychology has only touched the fringe of the human mind and conduct. There is much that we do not know at present about the process of learning and the resulting activity. The purpose of all education culminates in a desire to modify conduct. We do not care so much about the quantity of facts the mind may be induced to acquire as we are concerned about the resulting activity. To produce desired conduct, behavior, is the object of all learning, all teaching. Here is the place where psychology should help us very greatly.

We know much about the *enlightenment* and little about the *emotivation* of the individual. It would be difficult to isolate in any given situation the enlightenment urge from the desire to emotivate individuals or groups into performing definite action. And, *vice versa,* it is almost impossible to eliminate the desire to emotivate, to indoctrinate when there is a positive effort to enlighten. Perhaps it should be so. One would find it almost impossible to ferret out the elements in any life situation which could be classed as an absolutely cold, calculating, unprejudiced attitude in presenting facts.

All missionary efforts, all theological arguments, on the part of those who are engaged in giving facts, or data assumed to be facts, are primarily concerned in emotivation. The primary purpose is to make converts to a certain point of view, toward causing individuals to act in a certain prescribed way. The Bryan "anti-evolution" propaganda is an example. The same bit of activity is true in all political parties. All advertising campaigns partake of the nature of this sort of activity. Indeed, individuals in social life in concrete situations generally act in this manner. It is the most common way of getting things done.

Perhaps the best example of enlightenment activities is that found in modern survey methods and purposes. The Cleveland school survey made several years ago, or any of the modern scientifically conducted social surveys are examples of this type. The bureau of municipal research established in many cities for the purpose of finding out the facts has been an aid to many cities in their clean-up campaigns. These are primarily for the purpose of enlightenment. Their ultimate object is to better conditions and in this they are for the purpose of emotivation.

If the survey is properly planned with the chief purpose of finding out the facts in a situation, we have an illustration of what one means by cold-blooded scientific fact investigation. But such a survey is not undertaken merely with the end in view of finding the facts. This desire to find the facts as they are furnishes a motive and a drive behind it which will look forward to selling the facts to the public concerned in order to bring about a certain reform, a change in the situation. It is hoped that in getting the facts and pitilessly publishing them we get action. Ultimately, the purpose is to get *action.* In such case there need not be an overweening desire to convert people except only in so far as showing up the situation will get activity on the part of those responsible. Else there would be no point in finding the facts. In this sense all sciences are normative. There is a lot of prattle in scientific circles about science for science' sake, but such an attitude is as elusive and ephemeral as the will-o'-the-wisp.

Most if not all scientific investigations partake of the enlightenment motive. Unusual and wide publicity in certain noted cases in court trials is for enlightenment purposes. But, in a sense, there is the desire on one or both sides to the controversy to place the public in the place of a judge or jury for the purpose of convincing it. This is an indirect way to get a certain decision through pressure from the courts.

The matter of presenting facts in textbooks and courses in school and college is for enlightenment, but there is also the desire to modify conduct. We may say that learning produces activity of one kind or another. But there are so many ways of interpreting the facts which the mind acquires, due to different mental backgrounds of experience, that much of the desired conduct is doubtful in kind and amount.

The mere acquisition of facts may produce or be the basis of exactly the opposite kind of conduct we desire. Examples of this condition are found in our recent increase of sex knowledge, which many say should be widely disseminated. Knowledge of sex matters can hurt no one as mere knowledge, if it could only stop at the accumulation of these facts. There can be no doubt, however, that much of the knowledge of these facts has resulted in harm. Neither those who have favored nor those who have opposed this type of knowledge have proved their positions.

Loose sex relations probably are the result, not of increased knowledge, but of the lack of proper motivation when the knowledge is acquired. Investigations have all pointed to the fact that loose sex practices are perhaps one of the most undermining factors of the modern family.

Another example of the statement that knowledge will not of itself condition the right conduct is found in the wide spread of chemical knowledge. Certainly chemical knowledge in itself produces no bad results, but much suffering and destruction have come from our increased knowledge of many chemical reactions. It is the emotivated purpose of those using such facts and formulae that is sometimes dangerous. The name of Nobel is known everywhere in connection with dynamite. He expected great things of dynamite. It was in his estimation a godsend to the farmer, the miner, etc. When military experts got hold of it they immediately turned its use into an instrument of destruction and desolation. The recent World War is a vivid example. The making of alcoholic drinks is another instance. These are enough examples to show that our methods of enlightenment are relatively good. Where we have failed is in giving the proper or desired emotivation. We hardly know where we are when we speak of methods of controlling conduct.

All of us who attempt to teach and in our other capacities as citizens enlighten some of those about us almost every day. We frequently see the results of our attempts at emotivation. But the best and most effective methods of emotivation are in the dark. All great teachers have been not only enlighteners but also effective and successful emotivators. Christ and Socrates are good examples of those teachers who not only could teach or present "data" but also control conduct. The old "socialized recitation method," so much in evidence in educational literature some years ago, during and since the war is wrong because it emphasizes the handing over of solutions to concrete problems which are supposed to exist. The real problem disappears. Then, we do the tricky thing by going around and hunting up problems to solve and in doing so perpetuate solutions to problems which do not exist rather than solve them. This is no way to emotivate conduct.

Probably one great mistake that modern pedagogy has made in its definition of education has been its neglect of the emotivation factor, which should certainly be a part of the definition of education. Mere learning that does not lead on to further learning, which in turn produces outcomes in the form of desired behavior, is not education in the full sense of any dependable definition of education. Enlightenment alone is not education. Education is that acquired quality of the human mind that is the product of conscious emotivated effort on the part of the one educated. All education is obtained by a learning process, but not all learning is education in our sense of the definition here given. We pick up much of our information, and much of this does not function in producing desired results. To educate one involves conscious direction. An illustration of what is here meant by education is found in the method of getting water to do certain things or to go where we choose to have it go, *i.e.,* through the pipes in a water system, and to do what we want done. This definition is in some respects diametrically opposed to the "soft pedagogy" so prevalent in our day and taught by those who would not have any indoctrination or biasing of the young student's mind.

The primitive child is not only educated but is almost completely motivated in the tribe. Primitive children cause little or no trouble in discipline. This kind of training among primitive people is necessary to the tribal survival. Civilization may yet see the necessity of following in this respect the example of its primitive ancestors.

Learning *may not* produce any desired emotivated effort on the part of the learner. Education will effect a change in behavior results. We educate ourselves both for work, vocations and for leisure purposes, or at least we should do so. The two purposes of education as here stated can not be completely separated. The one purpose merges into the other. Neither can be neglected. Education for doing necessary work furnishes its own emotivation, but education for leisure purposes is not quite so fortunate. The leisure phase is becoming increasingly more important. It is well to speak of this phase for a short time.

As civilization becomes more complex, vocational education for the individual becomes more simple and unified. This is due to multiplied and minute divisions of labor. While this simplification in requirements is taking place on the vocational side of our education the opposite is almost as true on the leisure or cultural side. That this condition is developing enormously is self-evident. It takes culture to beget culture, just as it takes grains of wheat to produce more grains of wheat. We are developing mountains of culture and as individuals we are acquiring less and less.

Our culture complexes are becoming more complicated. Minute divisions of labor give us as groups and as individuals more time to use our leisure, and our education which now prevails has not prepared us for this increasing leisure.

Dorothy Canfield Fisher has well said in one place:[1]

> We have more leisure time than any generation has ever had. We are unprepared for it—the priceless, perilous treasure of leisure time. Millions of human lives and human minds have new blank emptinesses which only a few in the race have encountered before. This is now one of the forces which drives people to reach out after more education. But it also drives them to reach out after more excitement, more sports, more noise of more sorts, more entertainment, more material possessions, more noise of any sort to fill the place in their lives formerly occupied by long hours of toil. The rising tide of suicide would seem to indicate that they are as yet not wholly successful.

America is the most lawless and at the same time the richest nation in the world to-day. Wealth helps to buy leisure. Unemotivated leisure may have some connection with our unhappy state in the midst of our plenty. Our restlessness is sometimes bewildering. Meissner pointedly says:

> This is well-called the Restless Age. Modern transportation facilities, steamships, railroads, automobiles, aircrafts have made the world our parking place. Theaters, movies, public amusement places lure the people away from their homes. The postal service, the newspaper, the telephone and telegraph, the player piano, the phonograph and radio have brought the world into the farmers' front parlor. The nation is all dressed up and no place to go. We have learned to earn but not to live. Loafing leisure is charged with explosive emotions more dangerous than dynamite.

[1] "Why Stop Learning?"

Information is easier to acquire now than at any time in the past. Our libraries, free schools, etc., are bristling with knowledge and beckoning to all to partake. We seem to be committed to the idea that knowledge is all there is to the process of education. We have adopted the Faustian theory of knowledge. We have sold our soul to the devil for knowledge.

Any kind of knowledge may be used for good or evil. What is needed along with any new knowledge obtained, and a thing more valuable than the knowledge, is the proper emotivation of those who acquire the knowledge. No science nor any great body of knowledge is either vicious or blessed. Science can not destroy nor build civilization, as has been held by some recent writers. The emotivated purpose of those using certain knowledge is the main factor.

A concluding statement may be made in this way. We all desire to enlighten some one or many and to emotivate them. We know how to enlighten by methods that are sure of results. We are uncertain about our methods of emotivation. Compared with our methods of instruction as to fact we have not yet learned the first letter of the alphabet in dependable methods of emotivation.

A. O. BOWDEN
NEW MEXICO STATE TEACHERS COLLEGE

LOGIC AND PERSUASION

EVER since the time of Socrates and Plato there has been dispute concerning the place of rhetoric in our educational systems. As the centuries passed, rhetoric, or, to use the modern and less ambiguous term, persuasion has been the victim of many bitter attacks. These attacks have varied somewhat in wording, but the underlying argument has been the same. One of the most forceful statements of this traditional view has been made recently by Professor Paul Shorey, speaking at a convocation at the University of the State of New York.

> . . . one of the most amazing illusions of modern optimism is the commonplace that science and critical scholarship have changed all this, and that our minds are no longer so easily swayed by rhetoric as were the minds of the ancients. That may be partially true of a few critical and scientific minds. But man in a mass is still as ever even more a rhetorical animal than he is a political, a logical, or a laughing animal. What deceives us is that tastes in rhetoric change, and certain forms of long-winded, sonorous, old-fashioned bombast no longer appeal to the sophisticated among us. In this sense rhetoric may be defined as the other fellow's fine writing. But *if we take rhetoric in its truer and broader sense as a misuse of any kind of fallacy, irrelevance, ornament, emotion, suggestion, wit, epigram, to gain some undue advantage over sober reason and fact, then there never has been a time in the history of mankind when the power of rhetoric was so great.* . . . The neglect of such study of rhetoric in our education is very surprising in view of the enormous and increasing part played by public speaking, directly, or in report and broadcast, and in the formation of that public opinion which is the master of us all. You will perhaps doubt this neglect. . . . What I really mean is not that we don't study rhetoric in a fashion, but that we don't study it in the right way. . . . The dominant aim in all university teaching of these subjects (propaganda and advertisement, and their chief instrument, rhetoric, in all its manifold disguises) should be the establishment of a resisting immunity. It is no legitimate function of public education to teach men how to overreach and overpersuade their fellows. It is the proper task to enlighten and harden the minds of those who make up the staple of audiences against such attempts. I have no time to prove that exploitation is in fact the spirit of our teaching of such subjects as rhetoric, public speaking, psychology, advertising, education and even history. It is a patent fact. . . .[1]

[1] SCHOOL AND SOCIETY, December 24, 1927.

Professor Shorey has given us in modern phraseology the old, old criticism of persuasion. His view will never fail to gain support in academic circles. In fact, we find that even a teacher of public speaking maintains essentially the same belief. Professor E. V. Simrell, of Dartmouth College, summarizes his distrust of persuasive methods very clearly:

> . . . The chivalrous determination that a Beautiful Theory should not be left to be murdered by a Gang of Brutal Facts frequently produces a mêlée in which theories and facts are hopelessly confused. Le Bon tells us, "The power of words is quite independent of their real significance. Words whose sense is the most ill-defined are sometimes those that possess the most influence. . . . They evoke grandiose and vague images in men's minds, but this very vagueness that wraps them in obscurity augments their mysterious power." The rhetorician constantly tends to estimate the truth of his statements by their rhetorical effectiveness. The habit of rhetorical thinking largely incapacitates him for disinterested, impartial thought. And the grandiose and vague images with which he expresses his convictions in order to influence other men's minds exert the same power upon his own mind. "As you go up in the balloon," writes Mr. Lippmann, "you throw more and more concrete objects overboard, and when you have reached the top with some phrase like the Rights of Humanity or the World Made Safe for Democracy, you see far and wide, but you see very little. . . ."[2]

Here, obviously, is an issue not to be ignored. To meet it squarely we must determine with scientific objectivity the place of persuasive methods in our twentieth century civilization. Two questions inevitably demand answers. In light of all the accredited findings of modern psychology, must we conclude that persuasion is unnecessary to social progress? And if it is necessary, should persuasive methods be taught in our schools? In seeking answers to these questions we find that for once—and perhaps the only time—psychologists

[2] *The Quarterly Journal of Speech*, June, 1928, p. 370.

are not divided in their theories concerning the fundamental basis of human behavior. Present-day psychologists are split into many schools and factions, but upon one thing they are unanimous—that most people are guided almost entirely by their desires, their emotions and their habits—by what the teacher of persuasion calls the "impelling motives." Mere logic, "sober reason and fact," will never move them very far. Life is a battle, an adventure, a possibility, and it is doubtful whether even the college professor is entirely motivated by sober reason. True, few will deny that facts, evidence, and logic are valuable aids to persuasion. They give strength and permanency to an appeal. We should certainly train our students to present the fundamental issues of any question clearly and logically whenever they speak or write. We should constantly insist that they demonstrate a reasonable skill in discovering and presenting the available evidence. We might also train them, as Professor Shorey and Professor Simrell suggest, to analyze critically all appeals, written or spoken, which are false and misleading because based on illogical assumptions or reviving dangerous prejudices. Present-day advertising offers an inexhaustible supply of specimens, including the use of every fallacy known to logic and several not yet classified. This defensive training against anti-social appeals would undoubtedly be beneficial, but we should not and we dare not stop with that. If in their speaking and writing our students are to limit themselves strictly to logic and argumentation, they will succeed only in making the better cause appear the worse. If we are willing thus to incapacitate them, we must remain content to see society governed and directed by other than educated men.

Let me cite a characteristic illustration. At a university in which I once taught, there is a partly finished student memorial union. The building is magnificent on the outside; within are bare walls and loose wood plank floors. The union has stood this way for the last four years. The logic and evidence, the sober reason of the situation, is clear to every student and faculty member. The building should be finished. As it now stands, it is a disgrace to the school and an insult to the war dead which it commemorates. One of the deans recently prepared a chart showing that if each student would contribute a fourth of the money which he spends yearly for ice-cream and candy, the memorial would soon be a thing of beauty. But as one of the faculty shrewdly observed, "The students want to eat the ice-cream, and they don't really want to complete the union. They would be glad to see the building finished, of course, but they don't want to do it themselves." And this building will remain unfinished until some master of persuasive methods conducts a campaign appealing to more than the sober reason advocated by Professor Shorey or the "disinterested, impartial thought" of Professor Simrell. When it does come, this successful campaign will present the facts and the evidence, but in conjunction with appeals to the impelling motives which influence human behavior.

I often think that this half-finished memorial union is strangely significant. It is more than a building; it is a symbol of that which the educationalists of this country are so earnestly endeavoring to accomplish. During the last fifty years knowledge has increased amazingly in every branch of learning. The social sciences, to take a single illustration, are rapidly developing a complex system in which man is placed with almost scientific precision in proper relationship to government and society. It is the high aim of the social sciences to deliver us from this age of confusion, in which society blindly staggers onward, hoping to "muddle through." Our crime waves must be met scientifically; the over-complicated machinery of law must be simplified; the remarkable expansion of large business corporations must be harmonized with the true ends of government and society; international trade must be regulated in conformity with the basic principles of economics; we must establish some form of international cooperation which will preserve world peace and save civilization itself from destruction—these and hundreds of other problems demand solution. The social sciences are working out answers. And although these answers may not be satisfactory in every respect, we may be confident that they will be fairly adequate. But what we do not know, a doubt which clouds our entire future, is whether we can persuade society to accept these answers. In public affairs, for example, most of the voters, and nearly all the politicians who pretend to serve them, know and care as little about the recent advances of history, sociology, political science and economics as they do about the language of northern Manchuria. Nor will their attention be gained by a presentation depending exclusively upon sober reason and impartial thought. Even in our colleges and universities, where the atmosphere should provoke calm deliberation, we have succeeded in gaining the permanent interest of only a very few. Why should our students be interested in the calm presentation of truth when they are constantly allured by the enticing realities of foot-ball games, auto rides, motion-picture shows, ice-cream parlors, prize fights, "spicy" magazines, dances and the countless other trivialities of our American scene? By that, I do not mean that the American public, and especially American youth, are fundamentally light-minded or empty-headed. But to be interested they must be approached by methods basic to applied psychology, persuasion and public speaking. Unless our youth are thus motivated, unless our educated men are trained to interest and motivate the uneducated or the indifferent, our most valuable learning will continue to exist in a state of futility comparable to that unfinished memorial union. Our plans for social progress will remain "on paper"; they will not be executed.

The twentieth century, we are told, is an age of specialists. But we know only too well that in many of its most important functions society is directed not by experts, but by men who possess either the ability to win the support of other people, or the financial means to employ publicity men, advertising managers, newspaper editors, and effective public speakers who will be persuasive for them. The specialist has dignity and knowledge on his side, but to gain the ascendancy he must present that knowledge, by speech and in print, in a manner pleasing to the public mind. Unless he is able to do this, the expert must continue to occupy a third or fourth rate position in our social order. When he can enrich his employers, as does a chemist, he will be given some recognition, but when he has only social service for his aim, as in sociology, the ineloquent specialist will be heeded only within his classroom, and not really heeded even there by a majority of his students. His position is a difficult one, for the specialist can never hope to present his knowledge to a popular audience in a comprehensive and understandable manner. Those few who can understand him will themselves be specialists or semi-specialists. Most people must be reached more persuasively; they should be inspired with a respect which must, of necessity, be partly an emotional reaction. This respect will give the specialist a reasonable freedom of action, just as we now allow doctors to operate upon us when we have only a faint conception of the medical practices involved. From early childhood the rôle of the doctor has been presented to us in a persuasive fashion. We have come to think of him as a man learned in a science which we can only vaguely comprehend; as a man in whom we must have complete faith in times of crisis. To a lesser degree, society looks upon the teacher—as a teacher—in the same manner. Until the other, now neglected, specialists succeed in so dramatizing the worth and dignity of their professions, they will continue weak and impotent. Our sociologists and political scientists will continue to write learned books on government; the ward politicians will continue to run the government in the old, unscientific way. We shall talk of world peace and prepare for the next war.

Thus does a realistic survey of conditions show us that if we are to gain the maximum of social progress, the teachers of public speaking and persuasion must come inevitably to hold a more prominent position in our educational systems than they do at present. The day is not far away when every progressive school system will include this invaluable training. If this country is to advance under the leadership of educated men, our students must be trained in the methods of leadership, which consist, in no small measure, in writing and speaking effectively. Nor should we forget that persuasion is of even greater importance as a complement to professional training. That is the reason the schools of engineering at Purdue University require all their engineering students to register for a fundamental course in public speaking and persuasion. And when we consider that departments of speech are growing rapidly in hundreds of colleges and universities, and that more and more secondary schools are including public speaking as a required course, taught by instructors carefully trained in the methodology of that subject—when we consider these wide-spread changes, we realize that educators generally are becoming aware of the importance of persuasion. Surely this is a hopeful sign that the social order of the future will be directed by men who know both what should be done and how to induce others to aid in doing it.

Edwin H. Paget
Syracuse University

THE SCHOOL EDUCATION OF LOUIS AGASSIZ

For several years I have maintained in addresses before public schools that America is making a great mistake in leaving the struggle for existence out of school education: in making education so free and so easy that few parents or pupils are obliged to make any personal sacrifice to secure it. Consequently, both parents and pupils fail to benefit by the struggle for existence which inevitably develops and strengthens both moral and educational greatness. The school life of Louis Agassiz, therefore, is a lesson for the pupils of our schools today, in many of which even the books are supplied at municipal or state expense and no effort or self-sacrifice at home is demanded. It is interesting that daily workmanship and garden toil are now being introduced in the private schools of Germany as an important part of a boy's education. I was myself brought up by my father in this way: to work with tools in the garden.—Henry Fairfield Osborn.

Jean Louis Rodolphe Agassiz was born in the Bernese Alps in his father's parish of Motier, on the northeast shore of the Lake of Morat, not far from the eastern extremity of the Lake of Neufchâtel, on May 28, 1807. His father, Louis Rodolphe Agassiz, was a Huguenot clergyman of old French stock but three centuries of Swiss ancestry. His mother, Rose Mayor Agassiz, was Swiss, the daughter of a physician of Cudrefin on the shore of Lake Neufchâtel, and came of a long line of physicians and lawyers who had lived for generations in the Pays de Vaud. Fifty years later, on May 28, 1857, Longfellow sang of this valley in explanation of his friend, Agassiz:

And Nature, the old nurse, took
  The child upon her knee,
Saying: "Here is a story-book
  Thy father has written for thee."

"Come wander with me," she said,
  Into regions yet untrod,
And read what is still unread
  In the manuscripts of God.

And he wandered away and away
  With Nature, the dear old nurse,
Who sang to him night and day,
  The rhymes of the universe.

And whenever the way seemed long,
  Or his heart began to fail,
She would sing a more wonderful song,
  Or tell a more marvellous tale.

So she keeps him still a child,
  And will not let him go,
Though at times his heart beats wild,
  For the beautiful Pays de Vaud.

Though at times he hears in his dreams,
  The Ranz des Vaches of old
And the rush of mountain streams,
  From glaciers clear and cold. . . .

Agassiz' father was a devout, kindly, studious man whose household was dignified though never wealthy. From his serene faith his son derived a firm belief in the omnipotence of the Creator of the universe which remained unshaken all his life and made him remarkable among the scientists of his day for his reverent reiteration of the ancient *Gratias agimus Tibi propter magnam gloriam Tuam.* From his mother, the child received affection, encouragement and understanding.

His love of the woods and fields, of the lakeshore and the whole fascinating life of the lake and of the mountains which cradled it, were early divined and helped to grow. One of his first playthings of his own selection was a small stone basin, built for a spring in the parsonage garden; here he kept pet fish which he and his brother, Auguste, had snared with their bare hands in the limpid pools at the lake's edge. More wary fish and those preferring to lurk in deeper waters, the boys caught with rod and line and Louis began his first ichthyological collections. But his tastes were not restricted to fish, for birds, mice, guinea pigs, rabbits and hares shared his affections; while he learned their habits and characteristics at first hand.

His more formal schooling was supervised during the first ten years of his life by both his father and mother. Wherever the Reverend Louis Rodolphe Agassiz served as pastor his gift for teaching soon impressed itself upon the local schools; so Louis and his younger brother, Auguste, were well trained in the rudiments of school learning. Louis also acquired considerable practical information from his close attention to the procedure of the various journeymen carpenters, coopers, masons, tailors and shoemakers who stopped at the country parsonage to do what jobs offered. The child, silently eyeing the workman, later copied his movements and learned to fashion a pair of shoes for his sister's doll, to make a water-tight barrel, and to cut cloth for a coat. In his pleasant, happy home the excitable boy learned another priceless lesson: poise and charming manners. In the life of an ambitious scientist, there are moments, when, to quote one distinguished American of the present day,[1] "shameless mendicancy" is an essential ability and when it is imperative that the appeal for funds be made by a man, not only learned, but able to inspire confidence and to speak easily with kings, executives and financiers. Inborn assurance and sincerity, trained in graciousness, are invaluable to such a man and the fortunate Agassiz received them from his parents.

When he was ten years old Louis was sent to a school for boys at Bienne where nine hours of study were required each day and where he perforce became a linguist. Yet he grew tall and straight and strong, developing a magnificent physique as well as an enormously active intelligence. After four years at the Bienne gymnasium, Louis was supposed to enter the business house of one of his uncles at Neufchâtel. He would then be fourteen years old, but when the time came he had shown such a liking for learning and begged so hard to be allowed to continue his studies, that his parents, encouraged by his masters, determined to give him the further schooling which they could ill

[1] Professor William Berryman Scott, of Princeton University.

afford. Fortunately both of them lived to see their son famous, in Europe and in America.

In another article in the *Scientific Monthly* the academic and university education of Agassiz is fully described.

Helen Ann Warren

American Museum of
Natural History

EDUCATIONAL EVENTS

THE GERMAN SCHOOL IN THE CRUSADE AGAINST TUBERCULOSIS

The great importance of the school in the crusade against tuberculosis is emphasized by Professor von Brunn in an article in the *Deutsche medizinische Wochenschrift,* which is abstracted in the *Journal* of the American Medical Association. The school is the only place in which a large group of the entire population can be given preventive and prophylactic treatment. The pupils of all the institutions of learning must be examined by the school physicians and their cases referred, if necessary, to the proper bodies for treatment. The first requisite, of course, is for the school to fulfil all hygienic demands through sensible architectural plans and interior arrangements, cleanliness of classrooms, the support of all beneficial athletic exercises, the creation of open-air schools, and the establishment of moderately priced lunches. The special training in the problems of youth is given in association with instruction in widely different subjects, and, in the last year of school, a wider survey is given by means of a course in nature study and the study of mankind. The most important task devolves on the teacher, who must not only furnish a living example to his pupils but also see that all who become sick are referred to the school physician. Four hundred out of 10,500 children examined by the author were found to have tuberculosis. Disorders of the hilum glands are frequent and should not be taken as an indication for coddling of the child. The few serious cases must be separated out from among the large number of harmless cases. Tuberculosis in a teacher is a grave menace. He exerts a harmful influence on his class. There are numerous instances in which many children have become infected by such a teacher. The timely recognition and the removal of a tuberculous teacher is exceedingly difficult, however; it is the duty of the school physician to be on the watch for such cases. If there are several cases of tuberculosis in a given class or in a small school, a thorough general examination must be instituted to discover the causes. In general, it is the duty of the school physician to look for sources of infection. He should not overlook the fact that the original focus of infection may be in an elderly person; for not infrequently the grandparents transmit the disease to their grandchildren, with whom they are wont to play.

SCHOOL LIBRARY SYSTEMS IN ENGLAND AND AMERICA

The London *Times* reports that interesting comparisons between the school-library systems of England and the United States were made at the concluding session of the Library Association Conference at Blackpool.

Mr. E. G. Savage, an inspector of the board of education, said that in a recent tour of the United States he was impressed by the deliberate way in which the Americans were teaching their young people how to use books. In America the doctrine was held that after leaving school the average citizen would have mainly to rely on books for his further education. Certain teachers were set apart, even in many poor schools, to instruct the pupils in the use of books. Their function was often characteristically expressed as "selling a library." No resource of modern advertising was neglected. The result was that Americans in daily life did support their local libraries and used them well. In New York State every school had a trained librarian on its staff. In the state of Indiana every school was required to spend 7s. per annum per scholar on books until it had a collection in the proportion of ten books per pupil. Some of the schools had collections of 10,000 books.

He had also been much struck by the cooperation that existed in America between the secondary schools and the public libraries. For example, in Cleveland there were four trained librarians all belonging to the town library. The effect of that on the youth of Cleveland was very marked indeed, and the school library was extremely popular. The people of Cleveland voted money for library purposes where they would not vote it for other things. If we in this country had that sort of cooperation we should do much better with the limited resources at our command.

English conditions, especially financial considerations, made it difficult to go as far as America had gone, but there was definitely room for greater organization of our library services within schools. Most of the public schools had a collection of books fittingly housed and worthy to be called a library, but the state of affairs in grant-aided secondary schools was generally much less satisfactory. Our next move must be in the direction of training teachers to train children how to use books; in other words, there should be a summer course for teachers who were interested in librarianship.

Miss M. Cant, librarian of the Ladies' College, Cheltenham, said that the school library, if it were to be effective, must be an integral and vital part of the school. That could not be achieved unless the librarian in charge were allowed to devote at least a half of his or her time to the management of the library. She pleaded with educational authorities to pay more attention to the value of the school librarian, "not too closely fettered by time-tables." She advocated the appointment of an advisory visiting librarian by the board of education, and the holding of summer courses for school librarians.

Mr. C. A. Scott, librarian at Aldenham School, said that the school library should not be confined to books for study, but should be as comprehensive in range as possible.

The unsatisfactory position in regard to county library headquarters was dealt with in a paper by Mr. Harry Twort, county librarian, West Sussex, who said that financial restrictions might continue to prevent many county authorities from providing proper county library buildings.

A resolution was adopted that the Carnegie United Kingdom Trustees should be asked to extend their sympathetic and practical interest to a consideration of the provision of county library buildings as the next stage in the development of the county library movement.

At the business meeting of the association, the question of the prices which libraries are called on to pay for books—the same prices as are paid by individual members of the public—was considered. Some of the bigger libraries, it was stated, spent as much as £10,000 a year on books.

The council was recommended to take up the matter with the Publishers' Association and the Booksellers' Association and to urge the necessity for some reduction of prices to libraries for their books.

It was decided to recommend the council to include the same set of subjects in the program for the next conference, to be held at Brighton in September, 1929.

THE EYESIGHT OF SCHOOL CHILDREN

The U. S. Public Health Service, with the cooperation of the Departments of Health and Education of the District of Columbia, has recently completed a thorough examination of the vision of 1,860 white school children in Washington between the ages of 6 and 16 years. These children were not a selected group and the conditions disclosed may be regarded as representative of those existing generally not only in Washington but in schools throughout the country.

This study, the significance and value of which can not be overestimated, was most thoroughly and scientifically carried out, and according to the Eyesight Conservation Council, this investigation is the most thorough and complete study of the visual condition of a large group of school children ever conducted under such favorable conditions. The work was begun under Senior Surgeon Taliaferro Clark, of the U. S. Public Health Service, and was completed under the direction of Surgeon Grover A. Kempf, the examinations of the children being made in the school buildings of Washington by Assistant Surgeon Bernard L. Jarman and comprised both the simple visual test made with the test letters of varying sizes and also a thorough refraction of the eyes of each child with the accommodation of the eyes suspended which disclosed the total amount of existing defects.

The results of these thorough eye examinations of the 1,860 school children revealed the following condition: only 3.4 per cent. of the children were found with eyes free from refractive defects; the visual defect most frequently prevailing was far-sightedness (hyperopia), of which there was 63 per cent. Near-sightedness (myopia) affected 5.5 per cent. and astigmatism 28 per cent. This extremely large proportion with eye defects included all with slight errors not needing correction but the conclusions reached by the experts in the Public Health Service were that glasses were needed by 34 per cent. of the entire group and that glasses were recommended for reading and studying for an additional 10 per cent.

An outstanding feature emphasized by this investigation is the fact that the simple visual acuity test reveals but a small percentage of the actual number of refractive errors in children. The reason for this is that the accommodation of the eye—that remarkable adaptability which enables the eye to focus instantly on objects at a distance or near by—is so strong in the young that it overcomes errors of refraction of the far-sighted (hyperopic) type. While the simple eye tests made with various sizes of letters "as conducted in the schools, are of much benefit, only the children who have marked visual defects are discovered; a great number are found to have normal vision and are so informed when in reality they are suffering with latent defects. Strains of varying amounts are present which may become worse as the child advances in its school course. The individual goes out into the commercial world much handicapped due to the effects of visual defects."

In this investigation the preliminary simple visual acuity test indicated that 34 per cent. of the children had defective vision and 66 per cent. had normal vision, whereas with the accommodation suspended and thorough examinations made an extraordinary change was shown.

The group which had standard vision or better before accommodation was suspended showed an enormous drop when the accommodation was neutralized, and nearly one fourth of those in this group dropped from standard vision to but 30 per cent. vision or worse. A most astounding change was found as to the proportion showing very defective vision. Before the accommodation was neutralized 7 per cent. of the children were in the group having but 40 per cent. of standard vision or less, but after accommodation was suspended this group increased from 7 per cent. to 43 per cent. Many of the children with standard vision or approximately 75 per cent. of standard had but 20 per cent. of standard vision when the accommodation was suspended and the hidden defects disclosed, indicating at what a burden of eye-strain and expense of nerve energy they were using their eyes.

COURSES FOR VOCATIONAL TEACHERS

A FREE evening vocational teacher-training course, open to men and women who have had trade or technical experience and who desire to teach in the public schools, is to be offered this year in New York City by the New York State Education Department. Persons eligible to take this course should write to the division of vocational and extension education, State Education Department, Albany, for forms upon which to make application for admission.

No written entrance examination is required, but admission is limited to candidates who attain a satisfactory rating in respect to general education, trade or technical experience and general fitness for teaching. The classes will be held at the High School of Commerce, 155 West Sixty-fifth Street, New York City, four evenings a week.

Many teachers of trade, technical and industrial subjects, both men and women, are required every year for service in the public schools of New York City and other cities in New York State. Such teachers must take special teacher-training work before they can secure a license to teach.

Applicants for admission to the evening vocational teacher-training course must have completed at least one full year of high-school work. Men must have had five years of journeyman experience in a trade, industrial or technical occupation. Women must have had five years' experience, of which not more than one year was spent in apprenticeship. Men should be not less than 23 or more than 35 years of age. Women should be not less than 21 or more than 35 years of age. Only citizens of the United States and residents of the State of New York may take the course.

Qualified men from the following trades are eligible: Commercial design, carpentry, bricklaying, plumbing, plastering, terra cotta work, tile setting, lithography, printing compositors, printing pressmen, jewelry making, upholstering, paper-box making, machine shop work, baking, clothing manufacturing-cutting, hand sewing and power machine operation, sheet metal work, pattern making, cabinet making, electrical work, automobile repairing, weaving, cooking, steamfitting, painting and decorating, bookbinding, paper hanging, power plant operation, candy making, fur cutting, foundry work, storage battery work and photo engraving.

Qualified women from the following vocations may be admitted to the course: Commercial design, costume design, trade dressmaking, embroidery machine operating, garment machine operating, paper-box making, millinery, novelty work, manicuring, hairdressing, tailoring and artificial flower making.

THE UNIVERSITY OF PORTO RICO

The University of Porto Rico, though its buildings were scarred and damaged by the recent hurricane which laid a major part of the island in ruins, is reported in the Boston *Evening Transcript* to have opened its doors on October 1. Before the hurricane, the enrolment of the university was 1,200, but the number who have now returned is much smaller than this. Thousands of Porto Rican families have been ruined financially, and this has tended to reduce the number of families who can afford to send their sons to college. The college authorities fear that some of the students will not be able to resume their academic studies.

Except for recitations and lectures, the university has been continuing its work since the seven o'clock classes on Thursday morning, September 13, when the oncoming cyclone first began to make itself heard and felt. The first cable received in the United States reporting the cyclone, the first request for help to the stricken thousands of Porto Rico, came from the chancellor of the university. Through its college of home economics, the university has served the refugees, preparing food and clothing for the sick and the starving. Cadets from the university R. O. T. C. have been on active guard duty over the island. Volunteers from faculty and student body have worked in many ways to relieve the situation and facilitate the reopening of the university for full-time instruction.

Three members of the faculty, José C. Rosario, Lewis Richardson and Rafael Cordero, made their way on foot on September 21 over the clogged trail from Carolina to Juncos, to determine quantitatively the damage done in that section. The *Transcript* states that they investigated the condition of 247 houses, and found that of these 143, or 57 per cent., were destroyed; 66 or 27 per cent. were unroofed, and only 38, or 16 per cent., were uninjured. Though this was not the section of the island that was worst hit, this proportion, if it held good for the entire island, would mean that of the 200,000 dwellings in the country districts, 114,000 were destroyed, 54,000 unroofed and only 32,000 uninjured. Multiplying by five these dwellings, we would have 570,000 homeless people, 270,000 with unroofed homes and only 160,000 with homes uninjured.

THE MUSEUM OF ANTHROPOLOGY OF THE UNIVERSITY OF CALIFORNIA AND THE SCHOOL CHILDREN OF SAN FRANCISCO

In conformance with the ideal of the University of California, that it shall be of as much service to the people of the state as is compatible with its function as an institution of higher education, the University Museum of Anthropology is starting a comprehensive lecture program which includes all children in the fifth, sixth, seventh and eighth grades of every school in San Francisco.

Under a plan revived by Curator E. W. Gifford definite invitations have been extended to over 5,000 school children in about 140 classes in approximately forty schools of San Francisco to attend lectures on "Ancient Peru," "Ancient Egypt," "Indians of the Southwest" or "Indians of California." The lectures are to be given by Mrs. Jean Frazeur, member of the museum staff, illustrated by material from the museum collections.

Requests for additional lectures have been received from about seventy classes containing approximately 2,400 pupils. Curator Gifford states that, in spite of increased seating accommodations in the museum lecture room, it will probably be impossible to care for these classes until next term.

The first lecture of the series was given on September 26, and lectures will continue daily until November 28. The museum collections in Peruvian culture material are considered to be the best outside of the National Museum of Peru in Lima. The Egyptian collections are also of outstanding value, and it is because of the possession of such good illustrative material that Curator Gifford and Dr. A. L. Kroeber, chairman of the department of anthropology, are interested in extending their aid to school children.

The program of lectures is carried out with the cooperation of the city school department, under Superintendent Joseph Marr Gwinn. Superintendent Gwinn sent letters to each teacher in the grades selected and those desiring to have their classes attend lectures were assigned lecture dates in groups of three or four classes totaling about 150 students. The teachers conduct their pupils to the museum in a group, and the lectures are considered as part of the classwork.

So far, Dr. Gifford says, more interest has been shown in the lectures on Ancient Egypt and Peru than on the other two, and the Indians of the southwest have attracted the least attention of all.

RURAL EDUCATION

ACCORDING to a statement issued by the U. S. Department of Agriculture, expansion of the system for rural education maintained through the agency of the cooperative extension services of the federal and state governments is reflected in some degree by the record of appropriations by Congress in support of the work. The original Smith-Lever Act, effective July 1, 1914, provided a total of $480,000, at the rate of $10,000 for each state. Gradually these appropriations have been increased to $4,602,935 for the coming year, which, with supplemental appropriations and an appropriation under the new Capper-Ketcham Act, makes available more than $7,000,000 for federal aid to the extension work.

Explaining these figures recently, C. W. Warburton, director of extension work, Department of Agriculture, said that each state and Hawaii now receives $30,000 annually without requirement that the state match this sum with additional appropriations. The remainder of the fund is divided among the states in proportion to the rural population, and with the added proviso that the state must provide an equal amount of money for extension work in order to qualify for the appropriation. Actually the states, on the average, do much more than match federal funds. For the current year state appropriations were nearly double federal appropriations.

Comparing expenditures for extension work with other activities, Director Warburton noted that the government spent approximately ten times as much in aid of roads. Extension activities cost at the rate of about $1 for each three persons on farms or about seven cents per capita for the whole population. This amounts to one twentieth of the value of farm equipment purchased in 1927, and to about one fifth of one per cent. of the value of last year's crops.

EDUCATIONAL NOTES AND NEWS

THE REVEREND CLARENCE A. BARBOUR, D.D., president of the Rochester-Colgate Divinity School, has been elected president of Brown University, from which he graduated in 1888. Dr. Barbour succeeds Dr. W. H. P. Faunce, who will retire after a service of thirty years in June, 1929, when he attains his seventieth year. He will then become president emeritus.

DR. CHARLES KEYSER EDMUNDS, formerly president of Canton Christian College and later provost of the Johns Hopkins University, was installed as president of Pomona College on the morning of October 13. Addresses were made by Dr. David Prescott Barrows, formerly president of the University of California; Dr. George White Marston, president of the Board of Trustees, and President Edmunds.

Dr. Elbert Russell, of the school of religion of Duke University, has been requested by President W. P. Few to serve as acting dean of the school for the ensuing year, to fill the vacancy caused by the election of Dr. Edmund D. Soper to the presidency of Ohio Wesleyan University.

A celebration in honor of Dr. Alpheus Baker Hervey, former president of St. Lawrence University and now in his ninetieth year, is being held this week at Canton, N. Y. Dr. Hervey entered the theological school of St. Lawrence University on October 12, 1858, and was elected the second president of the university in 1888, holding the office for six years. He has occupied pastorates at Bath, Maine, and elsewhere, and has published books on sea mosses and other fields of natural history.

In honor of A. B. Davis, who recently retired as principal of the Mount Vernon, New York, High School, the board of education has named him principal emeritus of the school and has recommended that when a second high school is erected in the city the present Mount Vernon High School be named the A. B. Davis High School. Mr. Davis has retired after thirty-five years of service to the school.

Dr. George A. McFarland, president of the Minot, North Dakota, State Teachers College, has completed his fiftieth year as an educator. He began his career as a teacher in a country school in Ohio and became president of the college in 1922.

Dr. Henry Churchill King, president emeritus of Oberlin College, is much improved in health and has returned to his home in Oberlin. He and Mrs. King spent the past year with their son in Brookline, Massachusetts.

Stephen M. Wagner, formerly president of the Board of Education of St. Louis, is a candidate for the Republican nomination for mayor of the city.

F. O. Russell, assistant superintendent of schools of Logan County, Ohio, has become associate professor of education in the University of Kansas.

Dr. Joseph A. Baer, of Columbus, Ohio, has been appointed research associate in the educational measurements bureau of the New York State Department of Education, to succeed Dr. J. S. Orleans, who recently resigned.

Dr. Howard G. Burdge has submitted his resignation as principal of the Fredonia, New York, State Normal School.

Eugene B. Butler, formerly director of elementary and high-school inspection in the Indiana state department of education, has been appointed director of statistics, reference and research, to succeed B. B. Williams, who has gone to the Indianapolis public schools.

S. M. Stouffer, superintendent at Hanover, Pa., has accepted the superintendency at Pottstown.

B. O. Skinner, formerly superintendent of schools at Marietta, Ohio, has been elected president of Wilmington College, at Wilmington, Ohio.

Resolutions declaring the services of Miss Lucille Nicol, district superintendent, as satisfactory during her probationary term of three years and recommending that her appointment be made permanent have been adopted by the New York City Board of Superintendents.

Dr. Charles H. Elliott, commissioner of education for New Jersey and secretary to the legislative commission engaged in surveying New Jersey's educational system, has announced the addition of five members to the staff. Dr. Lewis A. Wilson, assistant commissioner of education of New York, has been retained to make studies of the vocational schools, the continuation schools, provisions for retarded children and all forms of special education in New Jersey. He will develop a suggested program for the state. Dr. Edgar A. Doll, of Vineland, N. J., specialist on retarded children at the Institute for Feeble Minded at Vineland, will be associated with Dr. Wilson. He will carry on the studies dealing with special classes and other groups not now properly defined. Larger units for rural education, rural supervision and the curriculum for rural schools will be subjects which Dr. J. E. Butterworth, head of the department of rural supervision of Cornell University, will study for the commission. He will lay out a program for the next ten years. Dr. Francis A. Haas, president of the Bloomsburg Teachers College, Bloomsburg, Pennsylvania, will study problems of attendance, census, state organization and school finance. The commission has been granted an additional $25,000 appropriation by the legislature.

WILLIAM MCANDREW, formerly superintendent of the Chicago schools, has been appointed chairman of the resolutions committee of the Department of Superintendence of the National Education Association.

NEW deans appointed at Marquette University include the Reverend William Grace, S.J., dean of the Marquette College of Liberal Arts; the Reverend John Berens, S.J., dean of men; Dr. Bernard F. McGrath, dean of the school of medicine, and Professor J. L. O'Sullivan, dean of the college of journalism.

PROFESSOR J. S. P. TATLOCK will join the English department of the University of California next January. He is a graduate of Harvard University, was professor for ten years at the University of Michigan and ten years at Stanford University. During the past three years he has been professor of English at Harvard.

GEORGE K. GARDNER, at present a member of the firm of Goodwin, Proctor, Field and Hoar, of Boston, has been appointed professor of law in the Harvard Law School.

HERMANN DIEDERICHS, professor of experimental engineering and director of the Sibley School of Mechanical Engineering of Cornell University, has been appointed the first incumbent of the John Sweet memorial professorship of engineering in Cornell University, not in Princeton University, as incorrectly stated in a previous issue of SCHOOL AND SOCIETY.

FRANK R. HAMBLIN, who has been for three years assistant professor of Greek and Latin at the University of Vermont, has become a member of the faculty of Bucknell University, to be acting head of the department of Greek, taking the place of his father, who for many years has been head of the Greek department there.

THE Charles Eliot Norton chair of poetry at Harvard University, previously held by Professors Gilbert Murray and Eric R. D. Maclagan, will be filled during the academic year 1929–30 by Professor Heathcote William Garrod, professor of poetry at the University of Oxford.

DR. JOHN V. VAN SICKLE, assistant professor in the department of economics of the University of Michigan, has joined the staff of the Social Science Research Council as fellowship secretary in charge of the council's research fellowships in the social sciences.

L. L. DICKERSON, executive assistant of the board on library and adult education of the American Library Association, has accepted the librarianship of the Indianapolis Public Library.

DR. GEORGE F. BOWERMAN, librarian of the Public Library, Washington, D. C., has been appointed professorial lecturer in library science at George Washington University.

ALFRED C. POTTER has been chosen to succeed William C. Lane, who is retiring as librarian of Harvard University. Mr. Potter has been connected with the university since his graduation in 1889, first as an assistant in the library and from 1904 to the present time as assistant librarian.

WILLARD AUSTEN, librarian of Cornell University, has been named a member of the committee on resources of American libraries and the committee on the union list of periodicals of the American Library Association.

W. S. VINES, professor of English language and literature at the Keio University, Tokyo, has been appointed lecturer in English language and literature in the University College of Hull, England.

RICHARD T. LAPIERE, after a year in the London School of Economics, has returned to Stanford University to give courses in sociology.

WALTER HUG, the Swiss government scholar at Harvard University, who received his degree at the University of Zurich, has been awarded the Pugsley scholarship in the Harvard Law

School for a graduate of a law school of a foreign country, and Stephen Czako, the Hungarian government scholar, who received his degree of doctor of law in Budapest, has received the Pugsley scholarship in international law.

UNDER the auspices of the National Council of Teachers of English, Professor S. A. Leonard, of the University of Wisconsin, recently made a six-weeks' tour of research centers to ascertain what research studies helpful to teachers of English are in progress.

MRS. EDITH B. JOYNES, of Norfolk, Virginia, president of the department of classroom teachers of the National Education Association, is starting on an extensive field trip. Her itinerary will take her into Alabama, Arizona, Arkansas, the District of Columbia, Georgia, New Mexico, North Carolina, Oklahoma, South Carolina, Tennessee and Texas. The purpose of Mrs. Joynes's trip is to hold conferences with classroom teachers to acquaint them with the aims and purposes of the department and of the association.

PROFESSOR CHARLES A. ELLWOOD, who has resumed his work in the University of Missouri as chairman of the department of sociology after a sabbatical year's leave of absence, has been asked to deliver the Cole Lectures before the School of Religion of Vanderbilt University, Nashville, Tennessee, next March. The Cole lectureship aims to bring together the results of scholarship in the field of religion and the social sciences. Professor Ellwood will take as the subject of his lectures "The Destiny of Man in the Light of Modern Science."

AUGUSTE V. DESCLOS, associate director of French universities and schools, gave a public lecture on October 10 on "The International Spirit in French Education," under the auspices of the Harvard Graduate School of Education.

INAUGURAL ceremonies for the new chair of Italian culture, recently established at the University of California, with an endowment of approximately $250,000, were held on October 5. Among the speakers were Comm. Carlo Fermichi, professor of English literature and Sanskrit at the University of Rome, who has gone to California with the approval of Mussolini, as the first holder of the professorship. Other speakers were Commandatore Armande Pedrini, representing the donors; Commandatore Luigi Sillitti, royal Italian consul-general, speaking on behalf of the Italian government, and President W. W. Campbell, speaking on behalf of the university.

THE University of North Carolina announces the inauguration of a southern conference on education, to be held at the university on November 15, 16 and 17, to which are being invited state officials and leaders in educational and other public affairs. Invitations have been sent to a selected body of people throughout the southern states. This will be the first of a series of such conferences to be held annually. The conference will open with a banquet at the Carolina Inn, at which the principal addresses will be made by Dr. Douglas Freeman, editor of the *News Leader*, of Richmond, Va., and Harry W. Chase, president of the university. Sessions on the second day will be devoted to a discussion of questions of the relations of public schools and colleges. The main speakers on this day will be Dr. Lotus D. Coffman, president of the University of Minnesota, and Frank D. Boynton, superintendent at Ithaca, N. Y., president of the Department of Superintendence of the National Education Association. Sessions on the final day will be devoted to the question of financing the public-school system. A round-table discussion will be led by Dr. George D. Strayer, of Teachers College, Columbia University. A feature of the congress will be reports on educational progress in their own states by superintendents of public instruction in the southern states.

To encourage agriculture, nature study and conservation, the School Nature League is planning to bring together for public display, from October 18 to 21, in Education Hall at the American Museum a series of exhibits showing the garden and nature work of the New York City children. Schools and organizations working with boys and girls from all boroughs of New York City, as well as any New York City resident of eighteen years of age or under, are invited to take part. The fair has the combined and coordinated support and facilities of the

American Institute, the School Nature League and the American Museum. Exhibits will be judged on the basis of their educational value and prizes amounting to $2,758 will be awarded.

AN Associated Press dispatch reports that a complete investigation of the Greek letter fraternity system at the University of Texas, with a view to possible abolishment, has been ordered by the board of regents following the death of Nolte McElroy during his initiation into the Delta Kappa Epsilon fraternity. The faculty committee, which the board asked President H. Y. Benedict to appoint at once, was instructed to also investigate thoroughly the circumstances leading up to the death of Mr. McElroy, after he had collapsed while crawling over a pair of electrically-charged bed springs. The regents indicated that the McElroy case in itself did not necessarily furnish the basis for criticism of fraternities, but that it had served to bring out an undercurrent of sentiment against them in the board.

AFTER a futile attempt to negotiate a merger of Cornell College and Upper Iowa University, the two educational institutions under its patronage, the Upper Iowa Conference of the Methodist Episcopal Church has withdrawn its support of Upper Iowa University and endorsed a campaign for $1,100,000 for Cornell College. In March, an educational council, held at Waterloo, Iowa, appointed a committee of nine to work out a plan of merger of the two colleges, many being of the opinion that Methodist education could be better represented in this territory by one strong institution than by two small ones, and that it would not be possible to conduct a successful campaign in the Upper Iowa Conference for the support of the two colleges. The plan, as submitted to the board of trustees of each institution, recommended that the continuing institution should be located at Mount Vernon, Iowa, and its name should be Cornell-Upper Iowa College. The board of trustees of Cornell College unanimously endorsed the plan, while the trustees of Upper Iowa University rejected it by a vote of 17 to 7.

A DECISION favorable to the State of Vermont and Middlebury College in their case against the Central Power Corporation involving the Batel Park property has been handed down by the Vermont Supreme Court. The park property is alleged to have been given to the college and the state jointly by the late Joseph Batel. The power company has been seeking to secure condemnation of this property in order to use the land in connection with power development of the river between Ripon and East Middlebury.

YALE UNIVERSITY has received a gift of $350,000 from Mr. and Mrs. Philip B. Stewart, of Santa Barbara, Cal., Alfred Cowles, of Chicago, and Mr. and Mrs. William H. Cowles, of Spokane, Washington, to establish the Alfred Cowles Foundation for the Study of Government. Alfred Cowles, in whose memory the foundation is established, was the father of Mrs. Stewart, William H. Cowles, '87, and Alfred Cowles, '86. He was one of the owners of the Chicago *Tribune,* of which he was also business manager for many years. He died in 1889.

A BEQUEST which will amount to between $500,000 and $800,000 for the establishment of a "foundation or corporation to assist working girls" was contained in the will of the late Charles K. Eagle, silk manufacturer, which has just been filed for probate. The foundation, according to the bequest, is to aid in the development of the girls' "lives and characters in furnishing for them more comfortable living surroundings and accommodations, and generally to assist those who disclose any aptitude or ability to prosecute their studies and work along their chosen lines." The will suggests that a part of the money be used for the erection of suitably located apartments or hotels for girls who will pay moderate fees for the accommodations. The funds which will go to the foundation are composed of half of the residuary estate and a total of $220,000, made as trust bequests, the principal of which will ultimately revert to the foundation.

THREE "regional scholarships" have been established by Yale University. They are intended primarily for students from southern, southwestern and far western states, but will be withheld from those sections if properly qualified and acceptable candidates do not appear.

Rhodes scholarship standards will govern in the selection of candidates—character, capacity for leadership, intellectual ability and physical vigor. Weight will be given by the committee on award to recommendations from alumni and school authorities. The scholarships are available in Yale College and in Sheffield Scientific School, and entitle each holder to $750 in the freshman year and $500 in each of the remaining three years. Continuance of scholarship aid will depend upon the student's record at the university.

The property value of Pennsylvania's schools is $450,000,000, according to a survey made by the Department of Public Instruction at Harrisburg. There has been expended $234.25 in property value alone for each pupil enrolled for the present school year. The largest expenditure per pupil was made in Delaware County, where the investment is $385.29. Erie County ranks second with $381.18. Philadelphia's school property is valued at $81,000,000, and the pupil per capita value of property is $282.74, the city ranking twelfth in this respect. The value of school property in other eastern counties follows: Berks County, $13,634,634; Bucks, $2,414,072; Carbon, $3,297,120; Chester, $4,717,854; Cumberland, $1,780,016; Dauphin, $9,272,764; Lackawanna, $13,298,963; Lancaster, $7,217,870; Lebanon, $3,713,136; Lehigh, $8,426,257; Luzerne, $28,374,144; Lycoming, $3,820,004; Monroe, $872,980; Montgomery, $16,086,980; Northampton, $11,437,188; Northumberland, $5,124,593; Pike, $360,860; Schuylkill, $9,116,367; Susquehanna, $1,154,910; York, $6,397,753.

The tercentenary of the laying of the foundation stone of George Heriot's Hospital, a famous old Edinburgh school, has recently been celebrated. The school is one of the oldest institutions of Edinburgh, having been founded by George Heriot, court jeweler to King James VI of Scotland.

The London *Times* reports that what was described as an attempt on the part of the education committee to defeat by regulation a resolution of the Manchester City Council that women teachers on marriage should not be required to resign was recently defeated by the carrying of an amendment moved by the vice-chairman of the education committee. It was only after long debate that the resolution was carried at the last meeting of the council, that women on marriage should be allowed to remain in the service. The committee then put forward a resolution for approval that a teacher should withdraw from school five months before confinement and not return for twelve months after confinement, the salary paid to be in accordance with the committee's regulations governing absence for personal sickness. Councillor Wright Robinson, vice-chairman of the education committee, moved the amendment to this resolution that a period of three months before and three months afterwards should be substituted for the period of five months before and twelve months after confinement. He said the education committee were trying to defeat by regulation the object of the resolution which had been passed by the council, that married women teachers should be allowed to remain in the service of the committee. If the council passed this resolution they would be imposing a most vexatious condition which would do a great deal to discourage married women in the service from having children. It was, in fact, going to encourage birth control, which many members of the council had so far regarded with horror. The amendment was carried by 47 to 26.

SPECIAL CORRESPONDENCE

THE TWO CALIFORNIAS GET TOGETHER

From San Diego an hour's drive takes one into Tia Juana. To most people Tia Juana means dog races, the lure of the game, the opulence of the new Agua Caliente Hotel. But to President Hardy, of the southernmost State Teachers College of American California, and to Dr. Willis E. Johnson, director of its summer session, Tia Juana meant also "Exhibit A" of the striking educational program which Mexican California has been developing these last few years. It looked as if the two now sundered portions of the old Spanish entity might well meet together in some sort of project of rediscovery.

This summer, therefore, in cooperation with the Dirección General de Educacion Publica of the northern district of Mexican California, State College enrolled among its summer students thirty *profesores* from across the border. The Mexican-American Committee, organized to look after their reception, comfort and entertainment in this now alien land that used to be their fathers' took them quickly and painlessly through all the preliminaries that kept the other nine hundred students in line during long and weary hours, and ahead of any other group they were settled down to their summer's work.

The Dirección-General had expressed a wish that their major activity should consist in the study and observation of the best the college had to offer in modern education, and Señora Contreras had expended a good deal of time and thought in meeting its wishes. La Señora Maria Contreras was a "mexicana" who had had the good fortune to divide her childhood and youth so equally between the United States and Mexico that she had both languages at the tip of her tongue. Moreover, she had taught on both sides of the border and was an honor graduate of State College. Undoubtedly, therefore, her compatriots got a great deal from their classroom activities under her leadership. But their interest for the other students of the summer session, and for the townspeople in touch with the college, lay not so much in what they got as in what they had to give.

They left an ineradicable impression in San Diego. Not only on the campus, but at all the many affairs given in their honor, their charm of personality, their grace of manner and their varied accomplishments excited the most admiring comments. With the writer's own class, the class in "Mexican Backgrounds," they felt, naturally, allied in a very special manner. They sang and played and recited for us and, through Señora Contreras and their official interpreter, gave us several *conferencias* on the newest aspects of art, music and poetry in Mexico. Some of them were comparatively recent arrivals in Lower California and could give some delightful quarter hours on their earlier experiences in more remote and primitive parts of "la republica." A number of them already spoke English more or less fluently, and met regularly to exchange conversation with members of the "Backgrounds" class who had made some start in Spanish. As usually happens, they exchanged more ideas, information and impressions than it seemed possible that frail linguistic bridge could bear, and it came as no surprise to hear that the most valuable part of the course on Mexico had come through that delightful, difficult, direct intercourse with "los mexicanos."

"Mexican Backgrounds" was the other half of the project in rediscovery. The public schools of California enroll a high proportion of Mexican children who, it is widely felt, are not fitting into the system as well as might be desired. Perhaps, thought the administration of State College, the schools are not offering quite the conditions into which they can fit. A little more knowledge, it might be, of the land from which they come, some understanding of the long past that has produced them, a glimpse, here and there, of the home and village as it has developed beyond the Rio Grande, a few folk tales and songs—these things might open the way to modifications of attitude and technique that would make for effective adjustments. In the faith that such insight would help, some ninety men and women enrolled in the new class. They came from all over the Southwest, principals, teachers and social workers, many of them with experience which proved a real contribution to the *materia* of such a course.

It was a pity that so few of them could read Spanish. For a vivid, authentic picture of life south of the border there is nothing in print to equal that published in Mexico itself and designed primarily for home consumption. Recent monographs of the Ministry of Education and the Federal Department of Health, current copies of *El Universal* and *Excelsior,* stray numbers of this or that *Revista,* a novel of Altamirano or Federico Gamboa, the *manifesto* of some group of workers or peasants, a slender sheaf of poems, the simple primer on agriculture that the "indio" is spelling out in that incredible night school in the world-lost Sierra—these are the things that students of "Mexican Backgrounds" should read.

But even in English there is a good deal of material emanating from Mexico and representative Mexicans. Most invaluable of all, perhaps, is the "Population of the Valley of Teotihucan," an abridged translation of Manuel Gamio's celebrated study of civilization, past and present, round the region of the "City of the Gods." There is also a translation of Alberto Pani's widely-known "Hygiene en Mexico." *Folkways,* a bi-monthly review in Spanish and English, comes from Mexico City rich in ballads, art, peasant industries, customs, ancient survivals in religion and lore. The files of the *Living Age* furnish stories, articles, editorials, speeches translated from Mexican periodicals, or delivered by the nation's accredited spokesmen abroad. And a goodly collection of articles bearing the signatures of Mexican statesmen, artists and educators can be gleaned from other leading American magazines. Indeed, such sources provided more material than, with all their enthusiasm, the students could handle in the brief six weeks of the summer session, and they packed up their bibliographies with probably quite fallacious hopes of continuing their reading this winter.

Old Town in San Diego conserves many picturesque relics of its Mexican days. Ramona's Marriage Place still bears something of the impress of the "Great House" on one of those immense land holdings round which the revolution raged. Across the road stands the "Casa de Machado," still, after its century and a quarter of hospitality, offering its Spanish food and its historic memories. There the class held its farewell dinner, with Señor Antonio Villalobos, federal judge at Tia Juana, as the speaker of the evening.

The State College of San Diego believes that it is singularly favorably located for the fostering of these cultural relations between western Mexico and our own Southwest. And this summer's experience has demonstrated that such a project makes a very strong appeal on both sides of the line. There is no question as to whether it shall be continued and developed further. The only question is along just what line, of the many possible ones, next summer's work shall move.

Helen Bowyer

Detroit, Michigan

HONORS WORK IN A SMALL MIDDLE-WESTERN COLLEGE

At the present time some plan of honors work has been adopted by a considerable number of American colleges and universities. It may be said that this type of work has passed at least the early experimental stage. The introduction of honors courses has been confined largely to the eastern section of this country and in a majority of cases to the larger institutions. In a special sense, the greatest need of work of this type is found at the small college. One desirable result of honors work is a stimulus to the intellectual life of the institution. In the university and larger institutions the presence of graduate and professional schools and scholars engaged in investigation will react, at least unconsciously, on the undergraduate body in emphasizing the importance of the intellectual life.

In the small college a small number of electives is usually offered in the upper division. In the latter part of his course the serious student, who desires to concentrate, finds it impossible. In order to secure the necessary hours or credits, he must elect courses in which he has no particular interest. The small college is exposed also to the danger of isolation. Due to circumstances, the members of the teaching staff may not make the contacts, that are so desirable and necessary, with other institutions and with teachers and investigators in their field. The introduction of honors work will normally raise the level of interest in the intellectual work of the college and through the use of outside examiners will help to establish helpful and stimulating contacts with other institutions. There is every reason to believe that a small college of the first rank will increase the effectiveness of its educational program through the introduction of honors work.

In the spring of 1927, Park College adopted a plan of honors work for gifted students. Its adoption was due to a growing conviction on the part of the administrative officers and teachers of the college that the college, through its routine channels, did not offer sufficient encouragement and assistance to students in the upper division of the college. Park College is a liberal arts college with an approximate enrolment of five hundred. The college makes use of a selective admission plan, admitting, usually, students from only the upper quarter of their high-school classes, as well as the use of other methods that will insure the best quality on the part of the applicants for admission. The service of this institution is not confined to a local constituency, since more than 50 per cent. of its students come from outside the state in which the institution is located. The plan of admission enables the college to select a talented, ambitious group of students to whom it is under obligation to make the greatest possible intellectual contribution.

For the first year (1927–28) honors work was limited to members of the senior class. Ten per cent. of the membership of this class was approved by the faculty committee for this type of work. The following departments were represented: Biology, chemistry, education, English, French, physics, Spanish, sociology. The students approved were released from the routine requirements of the college, tests, class attendance and examinations, and were assigned to the departments concerned for an individual program. In order to secure unity of procedure and a discussion of common problems a meeting of all students and teachers supervising honors work was held once every month. At this meeting two or three papers were presented by honors students, followed by a general discussion. At each one of these meetings held during the year, some visitor was present, usually from one of the neighboring universities, who participated in the discussion or delivered an informal address on some topic of interest to the group. These meetings were held at the homes of the members of the faculty. They brought teachers and students together in a way that was both delightful and stimulating.

At the end of the year a comprehensive examination was given these students. The oral examinations were conducted by outside examiners, with one exception, from the two universities, Kansas and Missouri. This type of examination aroused a good deal of interest. Members of the teaching staff and students approved for honors work the following year were invited to be present, others by special invitation. One of the outside examiners made the following comment on the interest shown by the student body. "I was also favorably impressed by the interest shown by the students who attended the examination. The attitude shown by the students, I believe, is an excellent sign of the success of the plan you have adopted."

What has been the result of this special type of work adopted by the college as a part of its program? It has definitely stimulated the interest in the intellectual work of the college on the part of the student body as well as the faculty. Through the use of outside examiners it has helped to establish helpful relations with these two universities and will make the work of the college better known to them. The serious student with intellectual tastes will look forward to this type of work as a great opportunity, and as a very important part of the work of the college.

W. F. Sanders
Park College,
Parkville, Missouri

DISCUSSION

DOES IT PAY TO CHANGE INITIAL DECISIONS IN A TRUE-FALSE TEST?

As a means of answering the above question, the following procedure was employed in a true-false examination consisting of fifty-five statements. The usual directions for such quizzes were changed to include the following statement, "Indicate your answer by placing a plus or a minus sign to the right of the number that stands in front of each statement. If, after marking a given statement, you wish to reverse your decision, do not erase. Indicate your change of opinion merely by placing a second mark to the left of the number that stands in front of the statement." It is evident that, as here employed, the term "initial decision" posits the initial mark attached to a true-false statement. It is of course probable that some students may change their minds one or more times prior to making any mark at all. However, it did not seem feasible to attempt to investigate that particular phenomenon.

The purpose of the experiment was explained briefly to the members of the class and assurance was given that only final decisions would be considered in scoring the examination papers. The students were instructed to mark each statement, and the papers were scored by crediting the number of correct responses.

Study of the resultant data revealed the following facts: Of the 50 students who took the examination, 39 changed at least one initial mark. Of the latter, 10 reversed one answer, 12 two answers, 9 three answers, 3 four answers, and one each changed seven, nine, and ten answers. Of the 39 students who made one or more changes, 20 improved their scores, 14 lowered their scores, and 5 failed to effect any change in their scores. It is thus seen that approximately one half of the students who changed initial marks failed to profit thereby.

The next step was that of isolating the students who profited. An attempt was then made to discover whether such students might possess any characteristics which might account for their success.

It was found in general that the students who made few changes profited most frequently and that those who made the largest number of alterations tended more commonly to lower their scores. For example, of the ten students who reversed one answer each, eight improved their relative class standings. But the student who changed ten of his answers changed seven correct answers to incorrect ones.

It was noted that the superior students tended to improve their scores and that the inferior students tended to lower their scores when they changed initial marks. Thus, of the 20 students who increased their scores, 15 were above the median of the class. Of the 14 students who lowered their scores only 5 were above the class median. This fact may be stated in terms of class marks as follows: Of the 18 students who changed one or more initial marks, and who received a grade of B or above, 13 improved their grades by reversing decisions. On the other hand, no student who received a grade of D or less was able to improve his score.

It might be supposed that the students who were successful in altering their initial decisions were thereby enabled to rise above the median of the class and, conversely, that those who changed their minds unsuccessfully fell into the lower half of the class by reason of their unsuccess. In other words, it might be assumed that in the present discussion the term "superior student" is applied *ipso facto* to those students who were competent at reversing initial judgments, and that the term "inferior student" is applied similarly to students who were incompetent at reversing decisions.

In order to investigate this possibility, the quiz results were retabulated on the basis of the students' first decisions. The students' actual grades were then compared with the grades that would have been received had no decisions been reversed. Comparison of the two sets of grades revealed that most of the students fell either above or below the median in *both* distributions. In only two or three instances did a student fall above the median in one distribution and below in the other. It is thus clear that the superior students manifested their superior ability when they first marked the true-false statements, and that the inferior students displayed their incompetency when they expressed their initial decisions.

It is of course true that generalizations based upon a single experiment are of questionable validity. In this connection it is of interest to know that the findings herein presented are substantiated by the unpublished findings of Professor Jas. P. Porter, of Ohio University. Professor Porter studied the true-false responses of 120 college students, employing a technique not unlike that of the present writer. Porter's findings are in accord with those presented in the preceding paragraphs. At the time of initiating the present experiment, the writer did not know that Professor Porter had made a study of this problem. It is doubtless significant that two independent investigations should have yielded quite similar results.

It is interesting to speculate in reference to these findings. It seems plausible that students who know what they are about when they first answer a series of true-false statements also know what they are doing when they attempt to improve upon their initial decisions. Such students find it necessary therefore to make relatively few changes and such changes as are made are usually made intelligently. Conversely, the students who reveal a lack of ability in their initial decisions also display their incompetence when they attempt to revise these decisions. The incompetent students are therefore likely to make changes for the worse as frequently as they make changes for the better.

The question of whether or not it pays to change initial decisions in taking a true-false test thus appears to require the same answer that the more general question requires, namely, Does it ever pay to change one's mind? The answer may be simply stated: The competent thinker also shows his good judgment when he occasionally changes his mind.

Harvey C. Lehman
Ohio University

JOURNALISM COURSES

When the first school of journalism was established at the University of Missouri by Walter Williams, its present dean, in 1908, it was greeted with good-natured amusement by the newspapers. To-day some of the newspapers that ran humorous editorials about teaching journalism in a university are edited by graduates of that same school.

I was on a newspaper at the time and knew the teaching staff of the first school. Walter Williams, its founder, a former president of the National Editorial Association, is still dean there. His first staff included Silas Bent (author of "Ballyhoo") and Charles G. Ross, now the Washington correspondent of the *Post-Dispatch,* Joseph Pulitzer's St. Louis newspaper, and author of the first text on news writing.

In the pioneering stage there was uncertainty as to what the curriculum should include. Courses in the news, the editorial, reporting and in principles of journalism were among the earliest offered. General courses were given. Some schools and departments paid virtually no attention to the problems of production or management. Others were frankly training reporters and little else.

"What can you teach them?" A managing editor who asked the question was firmly convinced that all the essentials were to be learned nowhere but in the newspaper office.

To-day the tendency, the country over, is toward specialized courses that deal with some limited field so that, taking into account the required subjects, the student may fit himself for a particular phase of the work.

One of the first schools to offer specialized courses was the one at the University of Washington.

Such courses as advertising typography, publicity, trade journalism, law of the press and specialized reporting may be cited as examples of specific courses which cover a more limited field. Elements of publishing is a specialized course covering part of the mechanics of production.

The criticism, so general a few years ago, that schools of journalism were training graduates who could write but who couldn't do anything else, has been pretty well answered. News writing, copy reading, feature writing, editorial writing and short story writing cover the technique of the writing side with plenty of practice in various kinds of copy production. The business and administrative side of journalism is also given attention in the modern curriculum. At this university the courses cover business office where costs and accounting as applied to the publishing field are dealt with, newspaper administration where the student is given a broad view of the managerial problems as a whole but with more emphasis on the editorial side, trade journals wherein the mechanics of small publication work and writing for the specialized press are given attention, comparative journalism which covers the various phases of makeup, policy and presentation in the newspaper field and the courses in advertising where the theory of display advertising and copy production from the standpoint of service to the advertiser and the selling of space is emphasized.

On the broader professional and ethical side of the field of journalism there are several courses. Journalism as a profession is a course required of all beginners in the department in which the various subdivisions are pointed out and a survey given with the idea of aiding a student in selecting his objectives in the school. Community newspaper is another general course which touches on topics that later become the basis of specialized courses. In the history of American journalism, editorial writing, news writing and newspaper administration courses the student gets a view of the standards of practice, the problems of policy and the ethics of his profession. The course in law of the press is a required subject which deals with the liabilities of the newspaper and its publisher in connection with libel, advertising, contractual relationships with advertisers and subscribers and the limitation upon the right to criticise and comment which the law lays down. A course in current events deals with the news with a view to its possibilities for editorial comment upon its social, economic and political significance.

ROBERT W. JONES

UNIVERSITY OF WASHINGTON

QUOTATIONS

SAVING MONEY IN THE SCHOOLS

THE fathers and mothers of school children now have their chance to say how they think Boston's schools could save money. The special survey committee, which is investigating this question, has addressed an appeal to all citizens, requesting their cooperation. In particular, the committee asks parents to submit "specific suggestions for reducing the costs of public education without impairing the effectiveness of instruction."

If this appeal should draw forth a widespread response, nothing could be more welcome. On all sides one hears it remarked nowadays that "too much money is being spent for schools." Quite general agreement, concerning the need of retrenchment, seems to exist among those who have observed the mounting volume of municipal expenditures since the war and who know what a heavy burden has been created by the increasing weight of taxes levied to meet these expenditures. Now, if an equally general agreement, concerning the means by which economies can be accomplished in the school system, should come to be expressed by the parents for whose children the money is spent, the problem would at once be far advanced toward solution.

Frankly, we shall be much surprised, however, if any such accord of opinion develops. There is one generalized reply which may very well be expected from parents, namely, the advice, "Cut down the frills." But when it comes to a precise statement on the matter, it seems to be very difficult to discover just what constitutes a "frill" upon the fabric of modern education—what is the main garment. An element in the curriculum which one parent considers needless, another may declare is among the most valuable and helpful advantages which the public schools now offer. In principle, we believe, mothers and fathers will be extremely reluctant to declare that less money should be spent through the schools for the welfare of their offspring.—*The Boston Evening Transcript.*

POOR ECONOMY

IT has been pointed out repeatedly in the last few years that while enrolment in the lower school grades is falling—or, at best, standing still—the high schools are continuing to add large numbers to their registers. This is true not only of the day high schools but of the evening sessions as well. A count made by the Evening High and Trade School Teachers Association shows that the evening division of the secondary schools this fall has registered 5,260 more students than it did a year ago, while the names of 2,170 have been placed on a waiting list.

This, then, would be a poor time in which to enforce economies in the evening schools. Budget Director Kohler plans a cut of $70,000 from the $1,305,000 requested by the Board of Education for the evening high-school program in next year's appropriations. The reduction would still leave an increase of approximately $70,000 over the 1928 allowance, but the evening school teachers assert that this would be insufficient. The proposed cut, according to a memorandum sent to Mr. Kohler by the evening school staff, would lead to the discharge of 3,000 young men and women from the rolls, while 6,800 others would be forced to curtail their schedules of class assignments.

It would be poor economy to eliminate the $70,000. Young men and women ambitious enough to attend school after a day's work are usually of the kind most likely to benefit from instruction. In the continuation schools New York spends too much in an effort to force education down the throats of unwilling adolescents to deny with consistency a place in the evening schools to anybody really willing to study.—*The New York Sun.*

REPORTS

THE CURRICULUM OF COLUMBIA COLLEGE

THE curriculum of Columbia College has been reshaped to exclude the old theory that the college course should be wholly adapted to the scholarly type of student mind, according to the annual report of Dean Herbert E. Hawkes, made public by President Nicholas Murray Butler.

After a year of study, the College Committee on Instruction proposed eleven amendments to the curriculum, which have been adopted by the faculty. The amendments recognize that the student body consists of separate groups with special needs, and not of a single group with kindred capacity and purpose.

In effect, they discard as fallacious the doctrine that in practice the college course should regard all college students as potential scholars, and that the degree should be conferred upon the basis of a comprehensive examination which in fact goes no farther than to test the student's ability to carry on a scholar's work. Under the new régime at Columbia all are not scholars in the making. Dean Hawkes writes:

The new curriculum recognizes the fact that there are three types of students each one of which is worthy and on each one of which the degree of the college will gladly be conferred upon the completion of the requirements for the degree.

In the first place there is the student who is looking forward to a professional school and who is pointing his entire college work toward a broad and comprehensive preparation for a life of professional usefulness.

Closely related to this type is the student who by temperament and ambition is a scholar, and for whom the most effective college course is the one which gives him the opportunity to go far toward the bottom of some field of scholarly interest.

There is also the man whose best intellectual development is not obtained through research work or even through "search" work of the mind encouraged by seminars and intensive attention to the cultivation of a narrow field.

In the opinion of the committee on instruction any assumption that the students to whom we wish to give our degree are all embryo scholars who should be tested by a comprehensive examination, on a narrow field of scholarship, is unwarranted. A plan for Columbia College based on this assumption would surely result in a gradual softening of the final examination, rendering it of slight educational significance to the alleged specialist and lowering the standard of accomplishment for the genuine scholars.

The administrative advice which has been adopted automatically to take care of these various types of students consists in the requirements for the degree of sixty so-called maturity credits.

The solution of the problem of the first two collegiate years hinges upon the organization of a program permitting the student to make a wide survey of various fields of intellectual interests, in order that he may determine the directions which he should finally take.

To this end it is necessary that these years should offer material in various fields which will simultaneously provide a sound and broad basis for future scholarly work in any field which the student may select, and a sufficient survey and orientation in these various fields for the individual who does not intend to pursue them further.

The analysis of this two-fold aim so far as it had to do with the historical and social sciences has led to a surprising and remarkable result.

In the first place the departments of economics, government, history, philosophy, psychology and sociology in Columbia College have reached such a degree of mutual understanding that they are able to envisage their problem not in terms of the vested interests of the several departments, but in terms of education of young men.

In fact, members of the staff of the college in these departments are pooling their interests to such an extent that one scarcely realizes that they are representing this or that department. One merely observes that they are representing the interests of a broad and useful education.

After prolonged conference it turned out that this section of our staff felt that by an extension of the required course in contemporary civilization through the freshman and the sophomore years they could simultaneously serve both the interests of the prospective scholar who would specialize in some one of these departments, and also the general student whose intellectual interests lie in other fields.

No other course in any of these departments will be offered to freshmen or sophomores. All courses offered by these departments in the two upper years will be built upon Contemporary Civilization "A" and "B," and in these advanced courses a student will have the opportunity to carry his specialized work to any extent that his talents and desires permit.

A similar situation faced the scientific departments, and they are meeting it in a slightly different manner, probably more appropriate to the subject-matter involved. This entails the organization of a number of courses in science aimed at the man who does not propose to go into medicine or engineering, or to become a zoologist or a physicist, but who wishes to know what these subjects are about and what place they occupy in the thought of the world of to-day.

Parallel with these general courses which will be open to freshmen and to sophomores, the more intensive and thorough scientific courses in each of these departments will be offered as at present.

In the third grand division of departments, comprising the languages—both ancient and modern—fine arts and music, little change was made in the requirements for the degree.

The discussions held at the staff meetings indicated that the level of accomplishment attained by students who have passed successfully three or four years of a modern language is not too high for the needs of those who would use that language in their other academic work. It is also apparent that this amount of language study is necessary in order to afford a student an introduction to the literature and life of foreign civilizations.

Columbia College will probably be a much better college than it has been. This, however, does not tell the whole story. We want the college not merely to be one which commands the respect of its students and staff, but we want it to inspire their affection.

One does not love quality: an individual or an institution that is merely good does not necessarily possess the warmth and the spiritual qualities that cause one to love it. This can only be accomplished through the medium of personality and the material evidence of a sympathetic and friendly attitude.

The great problem before Columbia College in the years immediately before us is to supplement its excellence, by the efforts of all who have responsibility for the physical comfort of student and teacher in dormitories, offices, classroom, fraternity house and athletic field.

These are the media through which loyalty and affection can be stimulated more than through the formal work of the recitation room or the lecture hall. It is not merely a matter of money, although money is necessary in order to provide and maintain the right atmosphere in the institution.

It comes back to an appreciation on the part of administrators, teachers and alumni that the college residence is a period of training for young men who have not only minds but also bodies and spirits alive to every kind of fine influence.

EDUCATIONAL RESEARCH AND STATISTICS

ANOTHER ATTEMPT TO TEACH HOW TO STUDY

NEGATIVE as it sounds, avoiding wrong responses is an essential part of learning. Herein lies the value of the attempt reported in this article, to improve the study habits of a group of college freshmen failing in one or more subjects. Suggestions as to "what not to do" and what to try in a similar situation are the main positive results of the experiment. "Experiment" is, perhaps, a misleading word because it implies a precision and careful control of experimental factors which were not attained in this situation. The problem was one of the difficult and practical kind that educators must necessarily deal with in one way or another, as scientifically as they can under the circumstances.

The situation was a common one—a number of freshmen near the end of the year were failing in one or more of their subjects. The administration decided to require these students to drop the subjects in which failure seemed certain, and to substitute a "how to study" course lasting two periods each week for six weeks. The purpose of this course was to help the students to complete their remaining subjects with a higher level of achievement. Certain difficulties in this procedure immediately became evident. Some of the students resented having to drop one of their subjects. They felt deprived of a motive for putting forth increased effort. Other students objected to the "how to study" class because it came at a time that interfered with their other plans. Since no official credit was given for the "how to study" class, many of the students whose college work was largely motivated by marks felt the lack of this extrinsic drive.

From the standpoint of the instructor, the course had a two-fold purpose: (1) to determine what should be the content of a "how to study" course in such a situation, and (2) on the basis of the difficulties encountered to make recommendations for methods of reducing freshman mortality the following year.

Two difficulties loom large in determining the content of a "how to study" course. One is the skepticism on the part of some educators concerning the possibility of teaching any one how to study; and the other is lack of knowledge as to what constitutes effective study habits for a given individual. Dewey says that "pupils must be encouraged to utilize their own peculiarities of response to subject matter." Does this not mean that every student has a method all his own, that there is no "one best way" of studying, and that teaching how to study consists in helping each individual discover his own best way of studying? Although too much guidance in study may be dangerous, nevertheless the student may be aided in discovering the methods best for him, or, in other words, in reconstructing his study experiences by reviewing the techniques used by good students. Those methods shown by controlled experiments to be effective and those sanctioned by present-day psychology of learning, may also be suggestive to him.

Investigations of the study methods used by successful students have been well summarized by Woodring and Flemming.[1] Although there are few decided differences between the methods of successful and unsuccessful students, certain methods appear to be used more frequently by the good students. The presentation of these methods to students in a course in "how to study" might eliminate some trial and error. Certain controlled experiments have indicated the superiority of one method over another under the specific conditions of the experiment. Germane,[2] for example, found the methods of summarizing and of reading to answer definite questions superior to merely reading and rereading the material.

Butterweck[3] found specific practice exercises more helpful to dull than to bright pupils, while a discussion of study methods proved more helpful to bright than to dull pupils.

[1] Woodring, Maxie N., Flemming and Cecile White, "A Survey of Investigations on Study," *Teachers College Record*, pp. 527–549, March, 1928.

[2] C. E. Germane, "Value of Controlled Mental Summary as a Method of Studying." SCHOOL AND SOCIETY, pp. 591–593, December 11, 1920.

[3] Joseph Butterweck, "The Problem of Teaching High School Pupils how to Study."

Semi-controlled experiments have demonstrated the value for college students of courses in "how to study." Crawford[4] reports half as many students on probation, twice as many improving in their grades, and only one fifth as many continually failing among members of the class in methods of study as among the other students in the university. Book[5] also reports successful results from a similar class at the University of Indiana. The administration felt that there was sufficient evidence to justify the existence of a class in methods of study, and accordingly made plans on the basis of this evidence.

Preliminary Test. The first step was to give a preliminary test in order to discover the students' knowledge of commonly approved study habits. The following test was given to twenty-nine students who were reported as failing in one or more subjects. Opposite the responses in each exercise is the number of students marking it as (a) the answer they think best, (b) the method they usually use.

TEST OF KNOWLEDGE OF STUDY HABITS

Directions: (a) Put a check before the one answer you think is best. (b) Put a cross before the method you usually use.

	Number answering (a)	(b)
1. In reading assigned material in history, the best method is		
..........to read the entire assignment once	0	11
..........to attempt to absorb bodily the whole subject	0	4
..........to try to remember every detail in the lesson	1	2
..........to read it rapidly as a whole and then go over it to pick out important details	28	12
2. In general, the best time to read new assigned material is		
..........the same time each day for each subject	22	5

[4] C. C. Crawford, "Some Results of Teaching College Students how to Study." SCHOOL AND SOCIETY, pp. 471–472, April 10, 1926.

[5] W. F. Book, "Results Obtained in a Special 'How to Study' Course Given to College Students." SCHOOL AND SOCIETY, pp. 529–534, October 22, 1927.

........any time you feel like it	1	12
........sometimes in the morning and sometimes in the evening........	4	9
........just before the recitation period for that subject	2	3

3. In general, the best place to study is

........at home where the family are sitting	0	5
........in a room with friends	0	0
........in a quiet room free from noise and other distractions	29	22
........on a train	0	2

4. The best way to prepare for an examination is

........to reread all the material covered	9	15
........to begin to study hard the night before examination	0	5
........to study lecture and reading notes thoroughly	18	6
........to reread some of the references	1	2

5. In studying a lesson in psychology, a good plan is

........to memorize the facts one by one	0	3
........to keep each lesson separate in mind from the others	2	3
........to copy the notes taken in class each day	3	5
........to connect the important points with something in your experience	19	13

6. A good method of studying the material of an assignment, is

........to raise questions that may possibly be asked on the assignment	7	2
........to reread the assignment until every detail is mastered	11	7
........to read every word of the assignment very slowly the first time	0	6
........to make a digest of the assignment	10	13

7. In learning the important facts in a chemistry lesson, the best plan is

........at one sitting, to study the facts until you can repeat them from memory	7	14
........to study them a half hour each day and review at increasingly long intervals	20	4
........to study them ten minutes every day	0	4
........to learn as much as possible in an hour and "call it finished"	0	5

8. In reading an assignment in your own book, a good plan is

........to copy in your note-book the important points	6	7
........to make a detailed outline of each chapter	10	7
........to underscore the important points and to make notes in the margin	13	4
........to read each paragraph carefully once	0	11

9. To promote a permanent memory of a subject in a form useful for life

........keep a well-organized note-book	15	12
........review the entire subject just before examinations	3	9
........take part frequently in class discussions and discussions with friends on the subject	9	5
........reread the facts until each can be repeated from memory	2	3

10. The best way to learn a lesson is to

........memorize each paragraph just as it is in the text	0	1
........learn the material in the form in which you will most likely use it	19	16
........get a vague idea of the subject as a whole	1	8
........write a detailed outline of the lesson	9	4

Defects in this test may be readily detected. The situation in each exercise should be more specifically limited. The "best method" if there is one, is often a combination of several techniques; it depends more upon skilful use than upon mere general procedures, and varies with individual students and circumstances. It is interesting, however, to note the frank discrepancy between the methods students think are best and the ones they use.

2. *Personal Data.* The second step was to supplement the information secured from the test of study habits by additional facts obtained from a questionnaire filled out by students, by daily schedules of their activities, by a job-analysis of their present methods of study, by scores on intelligence and placement tests, by college marks and by an examination of their note-books.

The questionnaire yielded information concerning family relationships, home conditions, finances, recreational interests, reasons for coming to college, the subjects carried by the student and his own diagnosis of his failure. The facts about the student's family were useful in giving an idea of his educational and professional background. In one case both parents of the student were born in Poland. The father had eight years of schooling; the mother, four. The father is a newsdealer, the oldest sister is a bookkeeper, and the younger brother is still in high school. In another case, both parents were born in Russia, and had a negligible amount of education. Three older brothers, however, are college graduates and one a high-school graduate. They are all accountants. Very different in family background is the student whose parents belong to an old American family, and whose father is a judge.

The questions asked concerning certain home conditions throw further light on the economic, social and educational background of the students. In one case, the language usually spoken at home is Yiddish; the number of books in the home is estimated to be twenty, and these are written in Hebrew. The family has a victrola, but no radio, piano or auto. In contrast with this student is another whose family speak English, and who estimates that she has over 500 books in her library. She also has a piano, radio, victrola and auto.

The financial condition of the student is also indicated to some extent by a question on part-time employment.

The recreational interests reported, such as attending the movies, theater, parties and dances, membership in clubs, and reading other than that required by college courses—give some idea of the activities which are competing with or reenforcing the college work.

The reason the student offers for coming to college gives some indication of his general attitude toward college. The student who comes because of an intense desire and in spite of opposition from his family requires a different approach from the student who comes because his father insists upon it.

The students' own diagnoses of their failures are usually interesting rather than profound. The majority attribute their failure to spending insufficient time on their work; some, to dislike of the instructor; others, to lack of interest in the subject, and a few, to poor study methods. Many of the reasons do not indicate the underlying personality or environmental difficulties which are probably the real causes of lack of success.

From the daily schedules quantitative information concerning the total time spent in study, the distribution of time among the different subjects, regularity of the study periods and health habits might be obtained, but was not secured from this group.

The attempt to obtain an analysis of the students' study methods by asking them to notice the processes through which they went in studying different assigned material was unsuccessful. The failure to obtain a picture of the study processes may have been due to a poor presentation of the method of doing this, or to the difficulty inherent in such an introspective technique.

The students' scores on the American Council of Education psychological test and on the Columbia Research Bureau placement tests were a directly useful feature of the diagnostic process.

An examination of the students' note-books proved enlightening. It indicated that much of the lecture time was being wasted, and that little effort was being made to see facts in their logical relationships.

3. *Program for each class period.* Since the students' note-books and comments indicated that drill was needed in focusing attention and thinking logically during class periods, fifteen minutes of each hour of the "How to Study" class was spent in presenting some phase of study techniques, and in having students immediately outline this short lecture from memory. This procedure was an attempt to

"kill two birds in one shot" by giving practice in one study technique and at the same time presenting principles of study which Book, Kitson, Good, Butterweck and others have found profitable to intelligent students. As no notes were taken during the lecture, the outline was a test of concentration and memory as well as of logical thought. The score on the outline was the number of statements reproduced divided by the total number of statements in the complete outline. A correctly stated fact out of its logical position was given one half credit. Each student's score was put on a graph, which aroused considerable interest. The topics treated were:

1. Outlining
2. The daily schedule
3. Mechanical aids to study
4. Reading for different purposes
5. Speed in reading
6. Suggestions for studying special subjects
7. Reviewing for an examination
8. Psychological principles of learning
9. Motives for study

The rest of the period was devoted to practice in the phase of study previously discussed. For example, after the lecture on speed in reading, the students scored themselves on time and comprehension in reading part of one of the subjects assigned for the next day. While the students were thus engaged, the instructor attempted to hold conferences with individuals. It soon became evident, however, that this time could be spent more profitably in supervising the practice work than in holding individual conferences.

One period of the course was devoted to answering questions raised by the students. The last two periods were spent in giving the following tests:

1. Test of knowledge of study habits. This was a skeleton outline of some of the important points covered in the course, to be filled in by the students.
2. Test of ability to listen to a lecture. The same procedure was used as in the daily practice, *i.e.,* outlining the lecture from memory as soon as it was finished.
3. Test of ability in reading to answer questions on the material read. A specially prepared single paragraph was used, and also the Iowa Comprehension Test, Series D1.
4. Test of ability to get a general idea of a paragraph. A specially prepared single paragraph was used.
5. Test of ability to get the main points in their logical relationship. A specially prepared single paragraph was used and also the McClusky and Dolch, Study Outline Test, Series A, Form 1, Test 3.

Summary of Difficulties Encountered:

1. Antagonism and indifference on the part of some of the students resulted in their failure to do the assigned practice work each week, *i.e.,* to check their schedule of work daily, to make improvements in their study environment, to read for the purpose of increasing speed and comprehension, to begin reviewing two weeks early for the final examination, etc. It was from this outside practice that the greatest improvement in skill in study might be expected.
2. Poor habits of college study had already become established during the college year. The "psychological moment" to secure interest and cooperation in reorganizing the daily schedule and study habits would seem to be the first days of the freshman year, when a certain amount of adjustment to college life is being made.
3. Lack of time for individual conferences was a decided handicap.
4. Lack of close cooperation between the instructor of the study class and the teachers of the various subjects is sure to spell failure for any study program. Each teacher should give guidance and practice in specific methods of studying his own subject and should criticize his teaching method from the students' point of view. Teachers do not always demand the most desirable kind of knowledge. When the purpose of reviewing to see facts in their relationships was being discussed, one student said, "What good would it do to review in that way for a false-true test on unimportant isolated details?" Students may get in the habit of reading isolated unimportant details because these are the kind of facts that are asked for in class and in examinations. The kind of class discussions, assignments and examinations has a potent influence on the kind of studying the student does. The student studies to learn the kind of material the teacher holds him responsible for. If passing depends upon a well-organ-

ized logical grasp of the subject, the student will look for relationship among facts. If passing depends upon knowing a flock of isolated, insignificant details the student will try to learn them. If passing depends on original questions and contributions the student will make an effort to note new ideas and suggestions that occur to him. If passing depends on a reorganization of his previous experience, the student will study with this purpose in mind.

Recommendations. Out of the difficulties encountered in this experimental class, the following recommendations for the next year were made:

1. To have a regularly scheduled period each week for obtaining information about and skill in study techniques. This course should begin as soon as college opens and should be part of the program of every freshman.

2. To give academic credit for the course in methods of study.

The final mark might be a composite one based upon:

a. knowledge of study technique and principles

b. skill in study techniques

c. improvement in other subjects

d. satisfactory completion of daily assignments in the "How to study" course.

3. To carry out more thoroughly, under supervision, in smaller groups of selected students all studying the same subject, various practice exercises using the subject that is to be prepared for the next day as practice material.

4. To secure cooperation between the instructors of the course in methods of study and the teachers of other subjects and encourage these teachers to give guidance and practice in specific methods of studying their special subjects and to criticize their teaching methods from the students' point of view. There is need to reduce the gap between the ideal methods of gaining knowledge and the methods that are necessary in order to pass an examination which is petty and illogical. There is need for practice exercises in each subject. For example, informal practice material similar to the one page mimeograph tests used in this study class can be prepared. The material can be read directly from the text, the questions, skeleton outline, or choice of four general ideas mimeographed or written on the board. By these means students deficient in certain reading abilities can be detected and given more intensive practice, interest will be aroused in improving skill in reading for different purposes, and at the same time the subject-matter of the daily lesson will be mastered. The kind of practice material that Butterweck[6] found useful with the duller high-school pupils could doubtless be used successfully with college freshmen having special difficulties. This practice must be directed by the teacher of each subject.

5. To have more thorough and effective conferences with individual students concerning their study difficulties. The dean's office or specially appointed tutors might be responsible for these conferences which should include giving diagnostic tests of study difficulties, presenting to the student the facts concerning his study difficulty, getting his suggestions as to what he should do about it, helping him to make definite plans, and checking him systematically to see that these plans are being carried out.

From the experience with this class, it appears that a successful program of teaching "how to study" demands for each specific technique in each subject "motivation," information, application. Motives, or drives, in the form of a visible attainable goal, an emotion, a habit, or a physiological need are incomplete reactions for which "facilitating stimuli" must be furnished in order to bring them to a successful completion. Information about study techniques is a "facilitating stimulus" that may prevent much trial and error in completing these reactions. Application implies practice in the newly completed reaction, which in turn makes it habitual, *i.e.*, more likely to occur next time opportunity presents itself. Since each student is moved by different drives and has his own "peculiarities of response" and unique environmental conditions, teaching how to study should be largely work with individuals. As Symonds[7] has pointed out, another of the most important general factors in successful study is the assignment made by each instructor.

RUTH STRANG

TEACHERS COLLEGE,
COLUMBIA UNIVERSITY

[6] Joseph Butterweck, "The Problem of Teaching High School Pupils how to Study."

[7] Percival M. Symonds, "Study Habits of High School Pupils," *Teachers College Record*, pp. 713–724, April, 1926.

SCHOOL AND SOCIETY

Volume XXVIII SATURDAY, OCTOBER 20, 1928 Number 721

THE PRINCIPLES OF COMMUNITY ORGANIZATION

THE principles of community organization here presented have been deduced from a body of data concerning a specific community of ten thousand population, based upon a house-to-house survey, and case and topical studies. Thus it combines the photographic approach, which aims to gain a general view of the community, with the analytical, which would explore the underlying principles of the social structure. These principles are given with only such reference to their setting as clarity demands, under the following divisions: ecological factors; intercommunity relations; community solidarity; community disorganization; community inertia; community leadership; primary relationships. The way is thus open for an appraisal of the problem of promoting community organization in the specific city studied, a phase of the entire project with which the present article does not deal. The general validity of the principles submitted could best be tested by comparison with similar studies of other communities—should such a body of research be built up.

The purpose of this study is to present principles of community organization which have been gleaned from a research project in Albion, Michigan, a city of 10,000. This community combines the interests of a college town with a meeting of industrial, commercial and cultural needs of the citizens and people of contiguous territory. The population is sufficiently composite in racial elements, including negroes, to afford a type of many industrial communities. The present trend towards urbanization and regional development is found in marked fashion. A study of industrial and commercial affiliations plainly reveals tentacles of interest reaching out from Detroit, one hundred miles to the eastward, and from Chicago, two hundred miles to the west.

In presenting these principles we are attempting to analyze social facts that underlie the life of this community. In so far as the findings are in accord with previously worked out principles of community organization, we submit them as further evidence of their truth.

I. ECOLOGICAL FACTORS

An insight is gained into the meaning of the terms community and neighborhood. Albion is properly termed a community in that it is a human aggregation residing in a defined area, sensing some common ties, cooperating in some major interests, and possessing some governmental mechanism that expresses the group ideas and attitudes. The comparatively small population precludes any occasion for using the term neighborhood to designate any but a small primary group within the larger community. As they are built up around various functions within the city, the neighborhoods in Albion are eccentric circles all bounded by the common circumference of community interests.

The more constant the common interests around which the first beginnings of a settlement cluster, the more assured it is of continuity in its existence. Lumbering towns one hundred miles to the north arose and faded out in a generation. Albion's attractions were of a more permanent nature; the soil, climate, a plentiful water supply, and a prairie-like contour which did not require extensive clearing, appealed to the coming farmer. Waterways and roads gave outlet to older settlements. Census records show a steady natural growth without any of the social complications which are apt to offset the advantages of a boom.

Moreover, the attractions offered by the raw materials at hand predetermine in a large measure the type of settlers. People who came to wrest their living from the land were those of the courage, vision, patience and faith that pioneering requires. Such idealism placed the building of a church college among the primary needs, actually achieving this only two years after the founding of a grist-mill.

With the injection of new major interests and the growth of transportation came increasing freedom from the purely physical aspects of the environment. Early foundations were laid for this community as a trading center. Its later development lay largely quite as independent of this as dependent upon it. The college became a greater determinant than timber; the overflow of the auto industry from Detroit more a factor than the water-power. Industry, benefiting from the advantages of original features, now advances because of other factors, such as relationship to other centers. This is in harmony with the general law of geographic environment; man gradually creates a "technical environment" in which nature plays a constantly receding part.

II. Intercommunity Relations

Under the modern type of organization, growth and activity are largely dependent upon intercommunity relationships. Massed production requires an outlet far beyond the immediate territory. The accident of location is an important determinant in the growth of a community. Albion's factories have not been established on account of the immediate presence of natural resources, but because of market facilities. Its location upon the direct line between Detroit and Chicago has given it the advantages of their arteries of communication.

Survey of Albion's major industries—as to outlet of manufactured products, affiliated concerns, fluctuations of the market and similar phases—reveals a marked dependence upon Detroit and suggests the grip that a metropolitan area has in its regional development upon relatively distant areas. Though industrially a smaller city may be very much of a satellite of the regional center, its expanding, trading and cultural activities assume more and more a consciousness of community individuality.

The city, due to the impulse of urbanization from without, allied to its growth from within, shows a contemporary evolution from the "rurban" to the urban type—a process which is by no means completed. Schools are being built that are more in harmony with city plans. Retail stores are changing from the two-storied, red-painted type to those possessing equipment and management of a modern kind.

Albion is a trading center for an area that extends in oval shape a distance of seventeen miles north, nineteen miles south, nine and a half miles east, and twelve miles west. The rapidly increasing socialization of rural life is reflected in the needs which seek satisfaction here. It is the center for shipping, health agencies, education, religion, culture and recreation for much of the surrounding country region.

The seemingly fortuitous course of community development presents an interesting subject for speculation. We may contrast the development of four neighboring settlements in Calhoun county, all practically contemporaneous in their beginning, all lying on the same main line between Chicago and Detroit, all possessing similar water-power, climate and soil. One has almost lost its identity, and the others have populations of 46,000, 10,000 and 4,200 respectively. Community growth may be likened in homely analogy to a snowball. When through some individual or group initiative—such as founding a college or establishing an industry—a point of attraction has been established, growth is experienced in widely divergent interests. Better facilities for communication, greater advertising, more business and cultural contacts, all radiate from this center, when once the ball has been set rolling.

III. Community Solidarity

A certain community consciousness is apparent in Albion. People living within its bounds are impressed with its "folkways" and its customs, and in varying degrees are aware of its distinctive pattern. Contributing to this personality is the fact that many institutions and organizations minister to the entire population, and the residents can only express themselves in certain phases of life through these community-wide agencies. As these common interests are extended through any chosen agency, the sense of solidarity grows.

The end of all community life is the greatest possible enrichment of the individuals composing it. Under a democratic ideal, that well-being should be extended in maximum degree to every individual, the less privileged as well as the more favored. The library, the hospital, the school system, recreational and park facilities, are joint enterprises for securing for each individual what he alone could not secure. Factors of this type contribute largely to the "psychic income" of the people of the community, and are a vital part of the social culture.

Community organization harnesses potential powers to the work to be done, by furnishing the machinery of action. The twofold benefit is thus achieved: firstly, furnishing opportunities of self-expression or of exercising previously dormant abilities; and secondly, securing some concrete benefit for the community. The Chamber of Commerce, though specifically an industrial and commercial organization, out of a local membership of 570 enlisted 536 in the performance of some definite community service.

Associations of different sorts which perform some specialized function in the community can be fused to promote the general welfare or to secure a common goal. In Albion many of the smaller group loyalties, such as the clubs within the federation, and the neighborhood branches of the Parent-Teachers Association, can be enlisted to stimulate interest in a more community-wide enterprise. The better organized the community, the more clearly should each group sense its own function and cooperate to make its contribution to the general unity.

"Mutualism" is a positive factor in solidifying community forces. One's contribution will be largely commensurate with what he receives. The nucleus of social activity is invariably individual interest. The process of community building is a reciprocal one. One rejoices in a city's progress because from that accrues advantages to the citizen whose interests are identified with the place. Allegiance or town spirit is given in exchange for what the city is able to give. For each individual, the socio-centric activities are but an extension of an ego-centric consciousness.

It is interesting to note along what lines voluntary effort for the community is most easily directed. Leisure time activities are a common center of interest, as shown in the Recreational Association, Civic Music Association, etc. Safeguarding of health through community enterprise is a fruitful field for cooperation. Endeavors that appeal to civic pride or to a spirit of rivalry with neighboring towns, as in the building of the community hospital and hotel, have a powerful leverage on public interest.

IV. Community Disorganization

The social pattern depends for its maintenance and vitality upon the loyalty and centralization of the individual interests. The lack of efficient community control, the failure to achieve cohesive action on the part of individuals or groups, is a condition that may be termed social disorganization.[1] It is not to be presumed, however, that entirely cohesive action of all individuals constitutes the goal toward which programs in community organization evolve. Since the attitude of individuals is dominated by ego-centric forces, a certain degree of social disorganization prevails. There is always a conflict between the individual and society. He seeks to express himself while society seeks to coerce him within certain molds.[2]

Among causes of social waste may be competing organizations, too many of which promote disorganization. If too keen a spirit of rivalry exists—as possibly between churches—the spirit of unity essential to the best promotion of the common goal is endangered.

Too many organizations may also promote disorganization by dissipating social resources. The aim of each should be either to satisfy some immediate need of the members, or to afford a channel of accomplishing some ultimate objective through joint effort. It follows that an overlapping of societies which serve similar goals weakens community solidarity.

The presence of inadequate or outgrown social machinery makes more difficult the adoption of methods better adapted to present needs. Institutionalism is prone to perpetuate itself at the expense of progress. Officials who profit by maintaining their present status of organization may be expected to resist being set aside even for more adequate systems.

Community disorganization is revealed in the conflict of community with individual interest.

[1] C. A. Ellwood, "Psychology of Human Society," New York, 1925, pp. 177–79.

[2] E. A. Ross, "Social Control," New York, 1924, pp. 1–4.

The absence of definite city planning and zoning resulted in much haphazard development. The concentration of city improvements in desirable locations has been prompted by a consideration of group, rather than of civic needs. Those people and neighborhoods with social prestige have enclosed many improvements in their own residential spheres.

Community disorganization may be incipient organization, if guided by skilful and influential leadership.[3] When a lack becomes too glaring, the way is paved for an advance. Local attempts which have been made to organize a central charities association, so far unavailing, have at least suggested the way out.

Attention may be called to the growing demand for standards of social measurements, that the community may, to some degree, realize whether the spiritual results of certain tangible investments warrant their continuance. Are the results achieved by the combined efforts and budgets of over one hundred organizations commensurate with the social and financial cost? The greater the degree of organization within a community, the more cognizant will it become of the meaning of its own "social processes."[4]

V. Community Inertia

By community inertia we mean the inability or unwillingness to move from some accustomed condition or mode of action. The importance of this approach lies in the recognized need of striking a balance between integration on the one hand and variation on the other. On one hand, such stabilizing forces as custom and conservatism exist, which, if carried to an extreme, lead to social stagnancy. The community becomes sluggish and adjustments to new conditions are hampered. On the other hand, there is a possibility of too much change, without the ballast of the integrative factors.

Community inertia may render permanent desirable features as well as impede progress. In this fact lies room for the honest difference of opinion between the conservative and liberal. A local dinner club for Albion's business and professional men has been maintained for years, to the exclusion of such national institutions as Rotary and Kiwanis. Though the newcomer's first reaction to the preempting of the field by a purely local, loosely organized club may be one of criticism, further observation reveals the value of its peculiar features. Its democracy, inclusiveness, its unifying rather than divisive influence, its adaptability to local needs, commend it to the community, hence its striking continuance.

The psychological basis of inertia is frequently the reluctance to forego accustomed modes of action or thought. When the rapidly increasing demand for parking space outgrew the earlier provisions, more adequate arrangements were resented as meddlesome because of the failure of many readily to adjust themselves to changed conditions.

Persistent propaganda is necessary to formulate sufficient public sentiment to initiate action. During a recent period of ten years, twenty-one fatal accidents have occurred at certain of the numerous railroad crossings. The peak of zeal for safeguarding these crossings comes when the public has been shocked into attention by some particularly moving tragedy; but the interest which flares up soon tends to fade. If the initial cost of inaugurating a needed change is kept too prominently in mind, it militates against having a large enough vision to undertake the project.

Corollary to the need for sustained effort is that of organized machinery. Many of the recent achievements of the Chamber of Commerce dealt with long-felt lacks, long unsatisfied, until the necessary agencies for securing action were called into being.

VI. Community Leadership

In the institutions existent in Albion many "lengthened shadows" of past leaders are discernible. An outstanding personality sets the pattern for social action. They are the recognized leaders who through inheritance or through previous successes in their chosen lines of work possess the prestige which marks them as worthy of being followed.

Although Albion maintains its function as a primary service community, and also partakes

[3] J. F. Steiner, "Community Organization," New York, 1925, pp. 30–1.

[4] M. C. Elmer, "Interpreting Social Processes," *Journal of Applied Sociology*, 11, 247–51.

of the character of an industrial town, it is the presence of the college which most definitely affects its personality. Through numerous avenues of leadership the cultural level is raised by this institution.

The value of outside leadership is in proportion to the degree in which it adapts its program to local needs, and avails itself of the prestige of the acknowledged local leaders, while it maintains its ability to act with greater perspective. The recreational program, introduced by the national organization, has been a pronounced success because it combined the benefits of a wide experience with a careful meeting of expressed local needs. Development followed a careful sequence of stages which gradually encompassed ever-widening groups of supporters.

The use of specialists as community leaders in their own fields has been practiced considerably. Americanization work has been in charge of a committee composed of a social science teacher, a professor from the college, a clergyman and two citizens who have passed through the process of naturalization. This principle may be extended to relate to sympathetic attitude as well as to technical knowledge.

Cross-fertilization of cultures is a societal as well as a biological necessity for continued vigorous development. The steady growth of the city and college ensures a continuous filtration of new leadership of widely diverse training and experience, which keeps the current of community life flowing.

The personality element is an indispensable element in community progress. A movement which lacks the impetus of a personal driving force soon lags. Outstanding results in fire prevention, school savings systems and school absence prevention, show marked correlation with potent leadership.

Organization is not an end in itself, but is to be prized as an efficient social tool for cultivating personality. Since every individual either weakens or strengthens a community, the well-developed community affords opportunities to as many individuals as possible to unfold and enhance their own personalities in a way that shall enrich the group. The work of the recreational forces in Albion makes this ideal a reality for several hundred individuals.

VII. Primary Relationships

Adhering somewhat closely to the interpretations given the term "primary relations" by Professor Cooley, we attach the phrase to those social contacts that are "characterized by face-to-face association and cooperation." These would cover such associations as the family, the neighborhood, the closely woven interest groups and even the community in which exists a large measure of sympathetic understanding.[5] The diminishing of primary contacts which has been deplored as one of the consequences of the urbanization of modern industry is not felt in a community like Albion to nearly so marked a degree as in many larger places.

Face-to-face contacts which were woven into the fabric of primitive life may be consciously stimulated. In Albion, parks owned in common are the scene of community recreations which fuse group interests. A program for city beautification fostered civic pride and so molded individual action into a group consciousness.

Permanence of residence, which encourages neighborhood contacts, is promoted by home ownership. Real estate values here are not inflated, and 78 per cent. of the homes are owned by the occupants.

Difference in race is a marked barrier to primary relationships. The problem of assimilation of the northern European and English-speaking peoples is negligible. Barriers as they exist between native white and southern Europeans may disappear, particularly for the children born of alien parents, through a gradual process of assimilation. A more difficult problem faces the colored group, since the color line remains, even when obstacles of culture can be overcome.

The tendency exists simply to accept these outgroups as different, rather than to attempt to include them in the advantages afforded most of the citizens. Such agencies as exist for their help are prompted by a missionary spirit rather than by any consciousness of community oneness. Cases have occurred when citizens have given personal and helpful service to alien families, and bridged with noteworthy success the separating social distance.

[5] C. H. Cooley, "Social Organization," New York, 23–31, 1918; Elwood, "The Psychology of Human Society," New York, 1925, pp. 118–19.

Face-to-face contacts characterize practically all the charitable work of sixty organizations observed. The reporting of the case of need as well as administering the relief is chiefly through personal channels. This results, indeed, in much duplication of effort, and forfeits the value of modern methods of relief. Many interested helpers prefer to forego the advantages of centralization of relief, that they may retain the personal satisfaction engendered.

Obviously, one cross-section of community life such as Albion affords does not suffice for an exhaustive treatment of the principles of community organization. The general usefulness of such a project as this would be greatly enhanced by the building up of a body of similar studies, thus affording a basis for comparative observation. As to the specific community studied, the writer has extended his project to the discernment of four major lacks: need for greater coordination of effort; need of city planning; need of extending community consciousness; need of self-expression for less articulate groups. With this body of principles in the background, a critique of available agencies, such as the community council, community center, etc., for meeting these lacks was undertaken.

W. Whitcomb Whitehouse
Albion College

TEACHERS AND THE POLITICAL LIFE OF THE NATION

Among the many problems which American education now faces, none is more vital to the spiritual health of the nation than the cultivation of wholesale attitudes towards government. Important aspects of the matter are obedience to law and the spirit in which such adherence is given, understanding and respect for authority, intelligent insight into important political problems, appreciation of ideals of governmental supervision and ownership of important utilities, and so on. Furthermore, at the present time about one person in ten is said to be an employee of the government. Unless the signs of the times are deceptive, there seems to be a great likelihood that the government agencies employing men and women will increase rather than decrease in number. Thus, the problem of the school in educating the faithful government employee and cultivating in others proper attitudes towards public service is consequently going to be even greater in the future than it is to-day.

In order to cultivate, in the children in her classroom, loyalty to government and respect for it, combined with intelligent and critical interest, the teacher herself will have to have a vivid and inspired understanding of the meaning of government. She will also have to be filled perhaps with something of the crusader spirit. At a time when political corruption is being unearthed daily among government officials and when the term "honest graft" seems to be an accepted commonplace of our language, the challenge facing the teaching profession in regard to the cultivation in the coming generation of effective ideals towards the conduct of government can not be exaggerated.

A valuable approach to the problem of giving the teacher an understanding of political life is to make vivid the human character of government. Too many persons view the body politic as an impersonal thing called "the government"—losing sight of its highly personal composition and their direct relationship to it. For instance, a recent study of socially handicapped ex-service men revealed very strikingly that many of these individuals seemed to view the federal bureaus as great, all-seeing, impersonal machines, rather than as human agencies. Many of them did not make known their needs through the regular channels for such applications because they thought "Uncle Sam" would find out about their needs of his own initiative, and would see that they were cared for! Furthermore, the statement, "The present administration is corrupt," does not really mean to most citizens "*Our* present administration is corrupt." Their attitude of detachment is too strong, in such cases, for them to identify themselves with such ignominy. Though, on the contrary, it is always "*We* won the war" or "*We* have the greatest national resources in the world." All too often the weaknesses of the government are identified with the villainy of others. We do not personally claim them as we do our country's triumphs.

One way to bring before teachers the human

character of government is to allow them to see the important government officials, and to hear from them a description of their tasks. This gives the future teacher an opportunity to see these persons and to judge for herself of their capabilities for holding office as well as to obtain information regarding the duties of their offices. It is a great object-lesson in democratic government. The prospective teachers can realize something of the type of person who now chooses political life and also get a general idea of the duties which are part of the routine of government. If in addition they learn the means of selection of these officials, their salaries, and educational qualifications, and have an opportunity to observe some of the actual functioning of these officials—such as the courts in session or the legislature at work—then the activities of the government are taught to them with something like the same vividness and understanding that is obtained from demonstration exercises in a course in the physical or biological sciences.

The means by which this purpose may be accomplished are shown in the outline of a course now being given at a large teachers' college. This course was organized by the writer with the advice of the president of the institution. The proximity of this college to the capital of the state was of great advantage when inviting state officers to describe their work to the student-body. As these officials were busy during the day, the lectures were all held after dinner in the evening and were followed by receptions at which the students were given an opportunity to meet the speakers and to ask them questions. As it was planned to give the course in alternate years, members of the graduating class were required to attend these lectures; attendance for others was optional.

The governor of the state opened the course with a description of the work of his office. Following him came the state auditor, who gave concrete details of how the state finances are run. The state superintendent of public instruction spoke on the work of his department, utilizing the opportunity also to distribute copies of the state course of study and school laws, and to discuss briefly, in connection with the subject of state educational statistics, the more important blanks and forms which these future teachers were to encounter in their work in the schools of the state. The important state officers of health, child hygiene and child welfare, were also represented by officials who described the workings of their departments, and gave out copies of the literature which their agents distribute throughout the state. These latter departments are especially significant to teachers, and their active cooperation was desired by these officials in order to make their efforts more successful. The game warden described his duties, and brought along mounted specimens of the principal game animals of the state.

This course might be made more comprehensive by including descriptions of other state departments, lectures explaining the judicial features of the government, the work of a United States senator or congressman, and the duties of a senator or representative in the state legislature. Likewise, for the smaller units of government, officers of city, town, or county might be invited to discuss their work.

Of course, the personnel of speakers would be determined largely by circumstances. Institutions located at or near the state capital would have more opportunity to obtain the services of high state officials than those at more distant places. The latter might have to wait upon opportune visits or be satisfied with minor officials or even secretarial assistants. But every institution, by searching its locality, will probably be able to find some persons with the insight and experience necessary to describe the working of government as a personal, human venture, rather than as the impersonal, machine-like affair which it assumes so often in common thought.

Wherever it is convenient, future teachers should also be taken to the state capital to view the workings of government at first-hand. If at all possible, it should be arranged that these students attend the legislature frequently while it is in session. If the problems which face their state are brought to their notice in classes in history, civics, economics and politics, or in forum discussions, such visits to the legislature will be highly instructive in making vivid to them the procedures of our law-making bodies, and revealing the attitudes and the interest displayed towards these problems by the chosen representatives of the people.

Two objections might be raised to this course, first that the officials who are chosen to take part in the course may lack the fluency or ability in public speaking needed to make the course really worth while. Experience has demonstrated that those individuals who really understand their work, who are truly sensitive to the opportunities and responsibilities of their office, and feel some patriotic zeal in their work, have no difficulty in describing it to groups of future teachers. Often a man who lacks oratory will in response to questions make clear to his audience his comprehension of the duties of his office. Even though the speaker were to bore or disgust the audience, he would really be giving the future teachers a valuable lesson in government. A second objection might be that busy state officials would not have time or would not want to take part in the course. This can not be answered except by actual trial. In the course herein described no such difficulty arose.

To offer the opportunity to a group of young students, especially prospective teachers, to get this direct view of the nature and functioning of government is a very valuable object-lesson. Students still in the radiance of adolescent sentiments can often be inspired to devote their lives to public service. Those in training to become teachers usually have such ideals already aroused. A course like the one outlined above may be extremely useful in encouraging these individuals to enter the field of politics. We need not go far into the history of the American people to discover that teachers who later left the classroom and entered the government service in some other capacity have been among the most progressive and inspired public servants. Any method of encouraging more persons of this type to enter politics or the public service deserves serious consideration.

Even if the future teacher is not filled with ideals of public service in the practical way of wanting to hold public office, he will pass on to his children his own sentiments in regard to the importance of honesty, loyalty and devotion in such work. In fact, a generation of teachers inspired with high ideals of public service, and conveying them to their pupils each day in the classroom by work and deed, will do more to elevate the efficiency and moral tone of government service than many miles of civil service laws could do alone. For in the last analysis, the test of an employee is his spirit of service, not the laws, regulations and inspections which surround him.

A teacher interested in government should believe above all in human progress through education, and be truly inspired by the remarkable achievements of the human mind in developing the civilization we now enjoy. Above all, the basis of stability of thinking in regard to the prospect of political life is a scientific optimism —an optimism which recognizes the slow evolution of human institutions in the great perspective of history. One with such insight would realize moreover that it is to be expected that a democratic government would be affected by evil as well as by righteous influences, because human nature has potentialities which may lead in either direction. The oft-stated problem facing our educational system consists in developing socially desirable attitudes and behavior from the raw materials of human nature. In the last analysis the survival of democratic principles will depend upon the solution of the many problems bound up in this one.

NORMAN FENTON

CALIFORNIA BUREAU OF JUVENILE RESEARCH,
WHITTIER, CALIFORNIA

EDUCATIONAL EVENTS

FINANCIAL SUPPORT OF EDUCATION IN ROUMANIA

ACCORDING to a report from the Bureau of Education national financial support of education in Roumania is chiefly in the form of paying all teachers' and administrators' salaries, though considerable sums are appropriated for buildings, material and scholarships. The 1928 budget of the ministry amounts to 4,732,289,000 lei, as compared with 2,643,114,000 in 1926 and 4,001,000,000 in 1927. Of the increase of 731,000,000 lei in 1928 over the 1927 appropriation, 588,000,000 had already been spent in 1927 for the 1928 salary account. The additional 143,000,000 represents approximately 120,000,000 for salaries of increased personnel especially in the primary and trade schools, and 23,000,000 for material for the different institutions, particularly increased laboratory facilities in the University of Bucharest, and scholarships of various kinds. The prevailing rate of exchange since August, 1927, has been $.00625 to 1 lei.

The public school system of some 14,954 institutions includes 14,084 elementary schools enrolling 1,599,331 pupils and employing 35,199 teachers (1926–27 data); 95 normal schools with 24,877 pupils and 1,655 teachers; 127 commercial schools with 19,582 pupils and 995 teachers; 281 trade schools with 135,945 pupils and 2,763 teachers; 363 secondary schools with 114,280 pupils and 4,007 teachers (1924–25); and the four universities attended by 23,534 students and employing 4,815 faculty members (1925–26). In addition to the 1,917,549 pupils and 49,434 teachers in the public institutions, there was in 1923–24 an enrolment of 222,123 pupils taught by 7,732 teachers in 2,213 private schools of kindergarten, elementary and secondary rank, but many of these have since been discontinued or have become public schools.

The elementary school course covers a period of seven years. The child enters school at about the age of seven and for four years studies: religion and conduct; the Roumanian language; arithmetic and elementary geometry; history, civil law and the geography of Roumania; natural science and physics; hygiene; freehand drawing, singing, and physical education; and manual training, agricultural training (offered in the villages), and domestic science for girls.

THE BRITISH PRIME MINISTER ON PROGRESS IN EDUCATION

Mr. Baldwin, in an address on the issues of the coming election, given at Great Yarmouth on September 27, spoke as follows on the contributions of the conservative government to education:

There is another subject on which I want to speak for four or five minutes. It is one that plays very little part at ordinary political meetings. It is one on which I spoke a good deal myself before the last election, and that is education; and I want to pay tribute to-night to what Lord Eustace Percy has done, without advertisement, without any shouting—what he has done in the way of the fulfilment of the pledges we gave at the election. We made three or four main points. We promised to go in for the modernization of the elementary school premises; we promised to go in for a reduction of classes; we promised to improve advanced education for children between 11 and 15; we promised to increase the opportunities of young persons to get higher education if they proved themselves fitted for it—and, mind you, on all these subjects depend in no small degree the efficiency and the happiness of our country.

On all these points we have made great progress. There have been over 200 new schools built. Plans have been approved for more than 800 black-listed schools, and more than half of these plans have been carried out and executed. Large classes have been reduced by one third, and more than 8,000 of them cut down. There are 3,700 more certificated teachers, which bears out the fact that I have just related to you. All the local authorities in the country have now put forward schemes for advanced instruction for children from 11 to 15—schemes for the three years from 1927 to 1930—and they are now in the course of execution. There are 63,000 more secondary school pupils sanctioned than a year ago; 25,000 more children in the secondary schools, an increase of 16 per cent. in the free places.

That is very remarkable progress, and I do not mind confessing to you there is nothing lies nearer my heart and the hearts of my colleagues than to go on to help with the education and the health of our people, to try to convert them from a C 3 nation to an A 1 nation. Medical services in the schools have been improved, and half a million more children are being inspected every year. Schemes for crippled children for orthopedic treatment have been passed and are in action, and in conclusion—and I rejoice in this—for the first time all qualified teachers are secure under terms settled nationally and adopted by all the local authorities, and the government stand, as they have stood, for national settlement in these matters.

THE INTERNATIONAL EXCHANGE OF STUDENTS

The arrival in this country of nineteen selected students from France who will spend the academic year 1928–29 at American colleges and universities is announced by Archie M. Palmer, assistant director of the Institute of International Education. These students come to this country under the Franco-American Exchange on scholarships provided by the colleges and administered by the Institute of International Education with the cooperation of the Office National des Universités et Écoles Françaises in Paris. All the awards cover board, lodging and tuition and are tenable for the entire college year.

As an agency for bringing different countries together in points of intellectual contact, the institute has been developing and administering a series of international student exchanges between the United States and the countries of Europe, including this one with France, believing that the understanding and appreciation of one's neighbors can best be realized through an appreciation of their culture, their social life and their psychology. The Franco-American Exchange has been in operation since 1919. This year twenty-six graduates of American colleges and universities will have a corresponding opportunity to study in France during the ensuing year under the Franco-American Exchange.

On the arrival of the French students in New York the Institute of International Education entertained them at a formal luncheon at the Cornell Club. Mr. Palmer presided and welcomed them on behalf of the institute. The other speakers were M. Mongendre, the French Consul-General; Dr. Robert L. Kelly, executive secretary of the Association of American Colleges; Miss Olive Ling, assistant secretary of the International Student Committee of the Young Women's Christian Association, who will go to France this year on one of the Franco-American scholarships, and Mlle. Marguerite Mespoulet, professor of French at Wellesley College.

Nine selected Hungarian students have also arrived in the United States and will spend the ensuing academic year studying on fellowships in American colleges and universities. This group represents the fourth contingent of graduates of Hungarian universities to come to the United States under the aegis of the American Hungarian Exchange.

At the present time such exchanges are maintained between this country and seven European countries: Austria, Czechoslovakia, France, Germany, Italy and Switzerland, in addition to Hungary.

RADIO EDUCATIONAL CONCERTS

A GROUP of the country's leading educators have been selected by Walter Damrosch, the symphony conductor, to act in an advisory and cooperative capacity for the series of music educational concerts which the Radio Corporation of America is sponsoring this autumn. These concerts, which begin on October 26, are the first of their kind to be broadcast nationally and on an organized scale to the schools of the country. They will be presented on Friday mornings, during the school sessions, and graded so that students of intermediate, high-school and college age will be addressed at different periods.

The first advisory body to be called into consultation by Mr. Damrosch was the committee on music appreciation of the Music Supervisors' National Conference, consisting of specialists in music appreciation, and representing the larger cities from coast to coast. Its official duty is to formulate a standard course of study in music appreciation to coordinate with the theoretical and applied music now taught in the public schools of the country. In their new connection, the members of this committee are seeking to make the nationally broadcast concerts an integral part of the accepted public-school course in music.

The committee includes: Lenore Coffin, of Indianapolis; Edwin N. C. Barnes, of Washington, D. C.; Frances Kessler, supervisor of Bloomington, Ill.; Max Krone, of the University of Illinois; Louis Mohler, of Teachers College, Columbia University; Inez Field Damon, of the State Teachers College, Lowell, Mass.; Margaret Lowry, of Kansas City, Mo.; Helen Roberts, of Cincinnati Conservatory of Music; Sudie L. Williams, of Dallas, Texas; Frances Dickney Newenham, of Washington State University, and Grace P. Woodman, of Jacksonville, Fla.

Other nationally known music directors included in the advisory group and sponsoring the radio concerts are: Edgar Gordon, of the University of Wisconsin, and George Oscar Bowen, of Tulsa, Okla., both former presidents of the Music Supervisors' National Conference; John A. O'Shea, director of music in Boston; Joseph Maddy, whose recent organization of the National High-school Orchestra has brought him international attention; Paul Weaver, of the University of North Carolina; Sara Conlon, of

St. Louis, Mo.; Glenn Woods, of Oakland, Calif.; Helen McBride, of Louisville, Ky., and John Beattie, of Northwestern University.

Among the names of city superintendents sponsoring this first nation-wide effort in radio education may be found: David E. Weglein, of Baltimore, Md.; Paul C. Stetson, of Dayton, Ohio; J. W. Studebaker, of Des Moines, Iowa, and Willis A. Sutton, of Atlanta, Ga.

These music education concerts will be broadcast each Friday morning in half-hour periods beginning at 11 A. M. and 11:30 A. M., and will be known as the "RCA Educational Hour." The project is the consummation of a long cherished idea which Mr. Damrosch conceived in the early days of radio broadcasting when he realized the potentialities in the new medium for disseminating musical culture on a vast scale to an almost unlimited audience representing all strata of American life. He confided his hopes to David Sarnoff, vice-president and general manager of the Radio Corporation of America, who was quick to sense its possibilities, and in February two experimental broadcasts were given over the air. The response was immediate and encouraging. It was estimated that Mr. Damrosch received well over 10,000 letters from pupils, teachers and music directors all over the country, commending the programs and urging their continuance. Soon after, the Radio Corporation of America decided to sponsor the series of educational concerts under Mr. Damrosch's direction. They will be broadcast over the WJZ network of the National Broadcasting Company and its associated stations.

SCHOOL HEALTH DAY IN NEW YORK STATE

THE annual School Health Day will be observed on November 1 this year, according to an announcement made by Dr. William J. O'Shea, superintendent of schools, and printed in the New York *Times*. About 1,000,000 children in the elementary schools will be examined, health defects recorded and a follow-up system will be inaugurated to keep track of improvement or further neglect. Recitations will be suspended on that day until all pupils have been examined and observed for easily discovered physical defects.

"Principals are earnestly requested," Dr. O'Shea said in a circular issued to school administrators, "to make every effort to establish close cooperation with parents, medical inspectors and nurses in the interest of the health of the pupils, and to make certain that children with remedial physical defects receive the benefit of treatment. It is important to detect physical defects. It is still more important to correct them. In this lies the success of Health Day."

The first examination will be for eye defects. A fraction will be entered on record cards indicating individual pupils' acuity of vision, normal or abnormal. Under "easily discoverable defects," defective nasal breathing and malnutrition will be recorded. The pupils will then be weighed and their heights measured. "Children should be encouraged to compare their weights and heights with standard measurements."

The names of children showing various defects will be listed and filed in the principal's office. The following procedure of follow-up has been adopted: Each principal is requested to furnish the school medical inspector the names of all pupils found to have defects of vision or hearing. To avoid duplication, those pupils who have been examined by the medical inspector, since the opening of the school, should not be included. The results of the doctor's examinations will determine the pupils whose names will later be referred to the Inspector of Sight Conservation Classes and to the School for the Deaf.

The principal is further requested to furnish the school nurse with the names of children suspected of defective nasal breathing and defective nutrition. The nurse will refer positive cases to the medical inspector. Children with evident defects of teeth should be referred for dental treatment directly to the home.

Pending action and follow-up by the school doctor and nurse, teachers should begin their follow-up work, to the end that children with defects of vision and hearing should be seated toward the front of the room; that those with dental defects should be referred directly to the home, and that under-nourished children should receive classroom instruction in dietetics, rest, sleep, fresh air, direct sunlight, freedom from physical defects, etc.

THE DEPARTMENT OF EDUCATION OF NEW YORK UNIVERSITY

THE annual report of Dr. John W. Withers, dean of the School of Education of New York University, has been made public by Elmer Ellsworth Brown, chancellor.

Proposed expansion in the department of educational psychology includes a course in the psychology of character. Another innovation which is to become a part of this department is a psycho-educational clinic which will be established for the use of the more than 1,000 special teachers in the metropolitan district and adjoining states who deal with backward, defective or superior children. Courses will be offered in clinical psychology and in psycho-pathology for the training of these special teachers. Dr. Withers reported that the course in mental hygiene which is related to this group and is given only for graduate students has more than doubled in enrolment during the past year.

During the current year extensive revisions have been made in the curriculum of the department of secondary education. For the first time students preparing to teach in secondary schools—other than those enrolled in the Washington Square College School of Education cooperative curriculum—have been required to complete courses in secondary education. Such a change has made it possible to reach large numbers of experienced teachers with the secondary education courses and to adapt the offering to their needs and interests.

A new department including the teaching of English, the teaching of social science and history, the teaching of natural sciences and the teaching of mathematics has been introduced.

The name of the department of physical education has been changed to the department of physical education and health. The arrangement of the program for this year will offer opportunities for specialization in the following subjects: physical education, health supervision, physical therapy and recreation. In addition, other types of suggested courses have been initiated for administrators and elementary teachers.

In cooperation with the State of New York, the department has worked out in connection with the Hospital for Ruptured and Crippled a course in physical therapy which is recognized in connection with the requirements of the New York State license in physical therapy as well as for the B.S. in education. The work is being carried out through the cooperation of Dr. K. G. Hansson, head of the physical therapy clinic of the hospital, and Professor Signe E. Hagelthorn, representing the school of education.

Members of the department are cooperating with nation-wide work relating to physical education. Contacts have been made with the National Physical Education Convention, southern branch of the American Public Education Association, the Association of Women Directors of Physical Education in Colleges and Universities, the Massachusetts State Conference of Physical Directors, the Camp Fire Girls of America, and the American Posture League, as well as a number of other groups interested in play and recreation.

A plan which provides for the placement of properly qualified students in licensed positions as pupil teachers in the public high schools has been favorably received by the board of examiners and by the principals of some twenty high schools. There are three important advantages in this arrangement. First, the students get in touch with the very conditions under which most of them are going to begin working; second, the university is kept in close contact with the public schools and, finally, there is the possibility that the contact will lead to the appointment of the students as teachers-in-training and substitute teachers.

The department of personnel which was instituted at New York University in 1924 now offers a complete series of courses for the training of personnel workers on all levels of education.

THE LAYING OF THE CORNER-STONE OF STERLING MEMORIAL LIBRARY AT YALE UNIVERSITY

THE corner-stone of the Sterling Memorial Library at Yale University, which is being constructed at a cost of over $7,000,000, and which will be one of the outstanding buildings of the university, was laid on October 12. The guests included relatives and friends of the late John W. Sterling, '64, of New York City, whose bequest to Yale makes possible the building of the library. The stone was laid by Edwin M. Herr, chairman of the building committee of the Yale Corporation, assisted by James Gamble Rogers, of New York, architect of the library. The memorial address was delivered by George H. Church, of New York City, the senior trustee of the estate of Mr. Sterling. President James Rowland Angell responded in behalf of the university. The invocation and benediction were given by the Reverend Elmore M. McKee, pastor of the university church.

In the memorial address, Mr. Church said:

> I think I may repeat here for inclusion in the records to be deposited in the corner-stone, some facts which I mentioned in my address at the dedication of the Sterling Chemistry Laboratory. Mr. Sterling was a graduate from Yale in 1864, a Townsend prize winner. He took a post-graduate course, principally under Professor, afterwards President, Porter. He received his LL.B. degree from Columbia Law School in 1867, and was valedictorian of his class. In 1893 Yale conferred upon him the honorary degree of LL.D.

Mr. Church then said that Mr. Sterling had accumulated his fortune "chiefly for the benefit of Yale and to a considerable extent also for the benefit of the Miriam Osborn Memorial Home for needy gentlewomen, but his main objective and the inspiring incentive of a lifetime was his Alma Mater. He dealt with this fortune like a trustee, not using any of it for his personal benefit, but indicating quite clearly the purposes and great benefactions to which it should be applied after his decease." Mr. Church described the manner in which the portion of Mr. Sterling's estate designated for the benefit of Yale University had been administered by the trustees. He spoke of the endowment of eighteen Sterling professorships; the Sterling scholarship fund; the university fellowships; the construction and equipment of buildings, and the endowment for the permanent maintenance of buildings, a total of $12,725,974. This includes but part of the cost of the Sterling Memorial Library.

In his response for the university, President Angell said:

> This is a day to which, in imagination, we have long and eagerly looked forward. The compelling necessity for a building adequate in size and appointments for the proper housing of Yale's great library has been acutely felt for more than a decade. To realize that this crying need is now about to be met, and in a manner which will at the same time fittingly commemorate to future generations the name of Yale's devoted and distinguished son, John W. Sterling, of the class of '64, is a source of deep and abiding gratification.
>
> Yale is very grateful to the trustees of the estate of Mr. Sterling for their decision to erect this memorial and for their generous and sympathetic understanding of the problems it has presented. As stone rises upon stone in the noble and beautiful edifice which the architect has planned, we shall see our dream day by day approaching its complete realization, until presently we may expect to assemble once again for the dedication of the finished structure—an occasion which will see Yale in possession, as we believe, of the most superb and most skillfully designed of all university library buildings. Upon that day our thoughts are already fixed.

DEDICATION OF THE NEW YORK MEDICAL CENTER

THE Medical Center, 168th Street and Broadway, New York City, where eleven associated schools and hospitals have been brought together for medical research, instruction and treatment of the sick, was dedicated on Friday afternoon, October 12. An academic procession and the conferring of honorary degrees upon a group of citizens in recognition of their leadership in the movement which brought the Medical Center to its materialization marked the formal dedication.

During the past several months there has been a succession of moves to the new buildings by associated institutions, the most recent having been the School of Dental and Oral Surgery of Columbia University. The cost of the buildings so far erected is in the neighborhood of $25,000,000 and of those planned an additional $15,000,000.

Dr. Samuel W. Lambert, dean emeritus of the College of Physicians and Surgeons and president of the New York Academy of Medicine, delivered the address of dedication. Dr. Lambert, as former dean, has been connected with the Medical Center movement for eighteen years.

Dr. Nicholas Murray Butler, president of Columbia University, conferred honorary degrees upon leaders of the Medical Center movement. General Parsons conveyed to Dr. Butler authority from the trustees of Columbia University to confer upon Mr. Edward S. Harkness and Dean Sage the degree of doctor of laws; on Mr. James G. Rogers, the doctorate of science in architecture, and on Mr. Otto Eidlitz, the doctorate of science in construction.

After the exercises the public were allowed to inspect the laboratories of the new College of Physicians and Surgeons in actual operation, the new School of Dental and Oral Surgery and the Vanderbilt Clinic. Anna C. Maxwell Hall, the residence of the Presbyterian Hospital School of Nursing, was also open for inspection.

Harkness Pavilion, the Presbyterian Hospital, the Sloane Hospital for Women and the Squier Urological Clinic, being fully occupied by patients, were not open to the public. Exteriors of the Babies' Hospital, the Neurological Institute and the State Psychiatric Institute were open to inspection. These institutions will be in operation in a few months.

EDUCATIONAL NOTES AND NEWS

On the occasion of the recent celebration of Founders Day at Lehigh University the degree of doctor of humane letters was conferred on Dr. Christian Gauss, dean at Princeton University, and the degree of doctor of laws on Dr. William Mather Lewis, president of Lafayette College.

Dr. Nicholas Murray Butler, president of Columbia University, has been elected president of the American Academy of Arts and Letters in succession to the late William Milligan Sloane.

A dinner in honor of Dr. C. E. Seashore, professor of psychology and dean of the graduate college of the University of Iowa, was given in Iowa City on October 10, with an attendance of more than a hundred friends and former students. A presentation was made of a life-size portrait in oils by Mrs. Mildred M. Pellger.

Professor John Henry Schaffner, of the Ohio State University, has been appointed research professor of botany. There are two other research professors on the staff of the university, Dr. Herbert Osborn, professor of zoology and entomology, who was elected in 1916, and Professor Wilbur Henry Siebert, of the department of history, who was elected in 1926.

The Reverend Dr. John Richard Magrath, who has been provost of Queen's College, Oxford, since 1878, recently celebrated the fiftieth anniversary of his appointment. He will be ninety years old next January.

Professor Albert D. Mead, who has been serving temporarily as vice-president of Brown University, has been elected permanently to the position.

James L. Parks, professor of law at the University of Missouri, who recently accepted a professorship at the University of Washington, has been released to become dean of the law school of the University of Missouri. He will succeed Dean J. P. McBaine, who is going to the school of law of the University of California.

At the University of Florida, B. A. Tolbert, for the past year dean of freshmen, has been selected by President John J. Tigert to fill the newly created office of dean of men. Glenn Ballard Simmons, instructor in the teachers college, has been appointed assistant dean of that college.

At the Ohio State University, W. James Osburn, of the Wisconsin State Department of Education, has been added to the department of school administration as professor. Harvey H. Davis, director of the division of records and statistics of the St. Louis, Missouri, schools, joins the department as assistant professor. Dr. Osburn has been director of research for the Wisconsin State Department of Education for eight years. Professor Davis has recently received his Ph.D. degree from the University of Iowa. Two associate professors and one assistant professor were named in the department of the principles of education. The former are Howard F. Seely and Laura Zirbes. Dr. Zirbes is a doctor of philosophy of Columbia University. She formerly taught in the Cleveland schools. Amy P. Bronsky, of the Wisconsin State Teachers College at Superior, Wisconsin, has been named assistant professor.

PROFESSOR ROBERT A. DAVIS, Ed.D. (Harvard), for three years professor of secondary education at Baylor University, Waco, Texas, has been appointed assistant professor of education in the college of education, University of Colorado.

PROFESSOR H. C. COFFMAN, head of the department of philosophy and psychology in the Michigan State College, and Professor J. V. Thompson, of Boston University, have been appointed professors of religious education in Northwestern University.

H. A. KLINGBEIL, of Chicago, has been appointed professor of education at Carthage College, Illinois.

EDWIN S. LIDE, for eleven years high-school principal and city superintendent, has joined the general extension service of the University of Arkansas. He will conduct courses in curriculum building. For the purpose of teaching the new courses the towns of the state have been arranged in two circuits and Mr. Lide will meet teachers of each circuit every other week.

JEROME LLOYD LEMASTER, formerly of the University of Illinois, has joined the political science staff at Oregon State College with the rank of assistant professor. Messrs. Merritt M. Chambers and Wilbur P. Riddlesbarger have been promoted to rank as assistant professors in the same department.

DR. LOUISE BAIRD WALLACE, professor of zoology at Mount Holyoke College, has accepted the professorship of biology at Spelman College, Atlanta, Georgia. For a number of years Miss Wallace was professor of biology and dean of Constantinople College, Turkey. Her term of service in Constantinople included the years of the war, first as dean, then as vice-president and later as acting president.

PROFESSOR CHARLES S. TIPPETTS, of the University of Iowa, has charge of Professor H. H. Preston's courses in sociology at the University of Washington for the year 1928–29.

AFTER six months' sabbatical leave, Professor James F. Hosic, in charge of extramural courses at Teachers College, Columbia University, is again in residence. Leaving New York early in March in company with his wife, he made a 12,000 mile motor trip to California by way of Florida and Texas, and home by way of the national parks. He also visited the Hawaiian Islands and spent twelve weeks there, devoted in part to studying the educational situation and assisting in the development of a new program of progressive education in the islands.

PRESIDENT GUY E. SNAVELY, of Birmingham-Southern College, spent the summer traveling in Egypt, Palestine, Syria, Turkey, Greece and Central Europe.

DR. ERNEST MINER PATTERSON, professor of economics at the University of Pennsylvania, has received leave of absence for the second term of the current academic year to enable him to serve as visiting professor at the Postgraduate Institute of International Studies at Geneva. A year's leave of absence has also been granted to Asa Don Dickinson, university librarian, who will be engaged in special bibliographical work, while Dr. Charles M. Wharton, assistant professor of physical education, who is the Democratic candidate for the governorship of Delaware, has received leave of absence until November 6.

DR. FREDERICK E. CLERK will, during the coming year, study the organization and function of secondary schools in Germany, England, Belgium, Czechoslovakia and France, having been granted leave of absence for the purpose by the Board of Education in Winnetka, Illinois, where he is superintendent of the New Trier Township High School.

DR. EDWIN W. KEMMERER, of Princeton University, has been invited to go to China as adviser to the government to assist in carrying out a complete reorganization of finances and foreign loans and to inaugurate currency reform.

DR. JOY ELMER MORGAN, editor of the *Journal* of the National Education Association, made the convocation address at the opening exercises of the American University, Washington, D. C.

DR. FOWLER D. BROOKS, associate professor of education at the Johns Hopkins University, lectured before the Eastern Division of the Illinois State Teachers Association at Charleston,

Illinois, on October 12 on "Individualizing Instruction in Reading" and "The Place of Literature in Developing Personality during Childhood and Adolescence."

Professor Thomas Woody, of the University of Pennsylvania, who has returned from three months' investigation of education in Russia, will lecture during the coming summer at the University of California at Los Angeles, giving courses in the "History of American Education" and "Comparative Education in Europe at the Present Time."

Dr. F. E. Burton, professor of mechanical engineering at Purdue University, was killed in an automobile accident on October 11.

Dr. Louis A. Wood, assistant professor of economics at the University of Oregon, will be absent for a year while pursuing research work at Yale University. He has been granted a Sterling fellowship and will investigate labor conditions in the service of large railway corporations.

The National Council of State Superintendents and Commissioners of Education will hold a meeting in Washington, D. C., on December 11 and 12. They will confer with federal authorities on the following topics: educational statistics, uniform reports, and how the United States Bureau of Education can best serve as a clearing house for state departments of education.

The thirty-second annual meeting of the Association of Colleges and Secondary Schools of the Southern States will be held at the Texas Hotel, Fort Worth, Texas, from December 4 to 7. Dr. H. M. Ivy, superintendent of schools, Meridian, Mississippi, is president, and Guy E. Snavely, president of Birmingham-Southern College, is secretary-treasurer.

The New York Society for the Experimental Study of Education celebrates its tenth anniversary with a dinner at the Hotel Commodore on October 20. Superintendent of Schools William J. O'Shea is the honorary chairman. Dr. Joseph S. Taylor, former district superintendent of schools and retiring president of the society, is toastmaster. Dr. Michael H. Lucey, principal of the Julia Richman High School, newly elected president of the organization, delivers his inaugural address. Dr. J. Cayce Morrison, assistant state commissioner for elementary education, plans to discuss "The Significance of the Scientific Movement in Education"; Dr. William F. Russell, dean of Teachers College, speaks on educational progress in the past decade; F. J. Lissman, banker, on ways and means of supporting educational investigation, and District Superintendent William E. Grady, first president of the society, on educational needs in New York City.

The new biological laboratory of Wesleyan University, built at a cost of about $350,000, was dedicated on October 12 as a memorial to William Arnold Shanklin, late president of the university. Mrs. Shanklin unveiled the memorial tablet in the main hall of the building. There were two addresses, one by Professor Charles M. Child, Wesleyan, '90, of the University of Chicago, on the individual as a biological problem, and another by Professor Edwin G. Conklin, of Princeton University, on biology and human life.

Gifts to Columbia University amounting to $500,000 and payments on accounts of legacies and bequests aggregating $1,850,211 have been announced. The gifts include $250,000 given by Mrs. Nathan J. Miller, of New York City, to endow a chair for the study of Jewish culture.

The University of Kentucky has entered upon a building program which provides for the erection of eight additional buildings. The buildings planned are a large recitation hall to be called McVey Hall, a memorial auditorium, two dormitories for men, an addition to the women's residence hall, a dairy products building, an educational building and a library. Two of the buildings are under construction and will be ready for occupancy in December of this year. Bids will be called for on five other buildings in November. The plans for the library are now under way. The board of trustees authorized two years ago an extensive university plan looking to the future a quarter of a century and providing for the location of buildings that will take care of a university enrolment of eight thousand.

Illinois College at Jacksonville, Illinois, began construction of a new library building early in October. The building, which will house on its first floor a few of the administrative offices, is to cost $200,000.

Dr. Augustus O. Thomas, state commissioner of education of Maine and president of the World Federation of Education Associations, has received a letter from Dr. Thomas E. Benner, chancellor of the University of Porto Rico, expressing the gratitude of the university for assistance rendered to Porto Rico by the United States following the hurricane.

Deutsches Haus, headquarters for the advanced study of the German language and literature, is to be reopened at Columbia University. The house was first established at Columbia in 1910, but was closed up during the world war. The building at 423 West 117th Street has been assigned for its use and Dr. Frederick W. Heuser, associate professor of German languages and literatures, has been appointed director.

The first volume of the "Tercentennial History of Harvard College and University," edited by Samuel E. Morison, '08, professor of history, and entitled "The Development of the University," is going to the press in March of the coming year, and will be ready for publication next fall.

In November "Illinois College: A Centennial History," by C. H. Rammelkamp, president of the college since 1905, will be published by the Yale University Press. The publication of this volume is part of the plan adopted by the college for the observance of its centenary in 1929.

At the triennial meeting of the National Council of the Phi Beta Kappa Society held September 11 and 12 in Delaware, Ohio, a charter was granted to Mills College, California, on the application of a group of Phi Beta Kappa members of that institution. This new chapter will be called the "Zeta of California." It is the fifth to be established in the state. Dr. Oscar M. Voorhees, secretary of the United Chapters, has notified Dr. Vernette Gibbons, secretary of the Mills College members. that the formal exercises of presenting the charter and installing the chapter there will take place early in the spring semester of 1929. At that time representatives of the United Chapters and of local chapters will be present. There are eighteen charter members on the Mills staff.

Lincoln Memorial University, Harrogate, Tennessee, opened its thirty-second scholastic year with an entering freshman class of one hundred and sixty-six. To realize the most possible from the Freshman Week Period, the freshmen were divided into four sections. A faculty adviser was appointed for each section for the year; each section was given psychological tests and lectures on such topics as "Getting Adjusted," "The Budgeting of Time and Money," "How to Take Care of Health," by the resident nurse, "How to Use the Library Intelligently." The formal opening of the autumn quarter of the new year was held on October 3, with an address by the dean, Dr. Hervin U. Roop.

Atlanta University opens the present school year on a strictly college basis, the high school curriculum having been discontinued.

Under a plan intended to develop the personality of student life at New York University, a committee of eight students and eight members of the faculty will rule all campus activities for a year.

It is reported that only 750 new freshmen have been admitted to the University of Chicago, owing to the new regulation requiring applicants to have an average of eighty-five in all previous academic work.

The board of education of Minneapolis has passed a rule which requires that all remaining fraternities must immediately disband. Failure to disband means suspension or dismissal from school. The rule ends a four-year controversy over high-school fraternities.

The Louisiana legislature at its last session passed a law which makes it mandatory to equalize the salaries of men and women engaged in teaching in the public schools of the state. Under the law, parish school boards are given four years in which to make the change, so that by October 1, 1932, there will no longer exist any discrimination because of sex in the compensation of teachers in Louisiana. The law contains a provision which states "it is not the purpose of the law to require or direct the reduction of any salary or salary schedule at present in force."

ACCORDING to a recent official communication to the United States Department of State, a committee has been appointed to work out a proposal for establishing children's agricultural clubs in Finland modeled after those in the United States. The chairman of the committee is Dr. J. Jannes, former Finnish minister to Berlin. The work will be directed from a central office in Helsingfors, with the assistance of local committees. Finland already has a few agricultural clubs, six of which are experimental clubs supported by a foundation in the United States.

AN Innsbruck dispatch reported in the London *Times* reproduces the text of a notification published in the diocesan newspaper of Brixen, according to which German children may be taught the Scriptures in German in the Italian German-speaking provinces. The religious instruction of German children in public primary schools will continue to be imparted in Italian, but German priests will be allowed to repeat the instruction in German in the presbyteries or on Sunday after mass in church. This concession on the part of the Italian civil authorities is the outcome of a recent petition to the Pope signed by the clergy of more than 200 German-speaking parishes.

THE first congress of the International Federation of Students, which is under the patronage of M. Gaston Doumergue, president of France, M. Poincaré, president of the council or cabinet, and MM. Briand, Herriot, Painlevé, Tardieu and Leygues, ministers of foreign affairs, public instruction, war, public works and the navy, respectively, will be held in Paris from October 11 to 24. During recent months, according to the *Journal* of the American Medical Association, the members of the Union nationale des étudiants de France, 55 Quai des Tournelles, Paris, have exerted every effort in order that their fellow students from foreign countries may take with them, on their return home, pleasant memories of their stay in France. M. Antébi, president of the Union nationale, hopes that this first congress will mark the beginning of a rapid development of the federation organized in 1919 by the French "union." Sixteen additional countries, which brings the total number of adherents to forty-eight, have expressed a willingness to send delegates to the Paris congress. It is thought that the federation will soon include all the students in the world. It is the only international organization that represents the interests of students in general.

ACCORDING to a report recently published, the number of enrolled students in German universities for the first time exceeds 100,000 and is 20 per cent. higher than before the war.

SPECIAL CORRESPONDENCE

AN EXPERIMENT IN ITINERANT EDUCATION

IT has been my task and privilege during the school year of 1927–28 to conduct a unique, and, in the opinion of those best situated to observe it, a very successful experiment in education.

In November, 1926, the board of trustees of McPherson College, Kansas, granted the writer a traveling professorship, at the same time authorizing him to select a student group of not to exceed fourteen and to organize them for a year of camping and trekking, while pursuing courses in natural science as follows: field geology, field zoology and field botany. Credit was to be allowed not to exceed eighteen semester hours, which were to be apportioned among the above-named courses according to the judgment of the instructor at the close of the year's work. The instructor was given a free hand in organizing and arranging all the details relating to mode of travel, plans of work, itinerary, etc.

It was decided that camping should be the mode of living, since this would enable us more easily to reach out-of-the-way places where often our best work could be done. This manner of living also brought the cost of the undertaking within the reach of the average student.

Thirteen students were enrolled from those applying—nine single men, two young ladies and a man and wife. These were grouped into three companies, each company equipping itself with car, tent and the other essentials of camp life—the selection being limited and supervised in accordance with the previous experiences of my own family, when in 1924 we undertook and carried out a field excursion of a similar nature without students.

The young married couple and the two young ladies made one company, four young men a second company, the remaining five men a company and my own family of five a fourth company. Our cars and equipment were similar. All traveled in Pontiac coaches, each equipped with a capacious trunk on the rear and a combined cupboard and clothes closet on the left running board.

On August 19, 1927, the company of students gathered at Palmer Lake, Colorado, where the writer was closing the Rocky Mountain Summer School, an extension of McPherson College; and on August 22 our caravan of four cars began its nine months' trek, starting for Yellowstone National Park. Two weeks in Yellowstone were spent in the study of the geology of the park, its wild animals, the rare trumpeter swan and numerous plants.

From Yellowstone we traveled southward through the scenic Jackson Hole Country (which we trust will some day be added to the Yellowstone Park) and to the bird-inhabited marshes about Great Salt Lake, where, as guests of the Duckville Gun Club, we found abundant opportunity for the study of shore and marsh birds of many species. Visits to the University of Utah, the various museums and other notable features of the Mormon capital were all crowded into our brief stay at Salt Lake, after which we journeyed to Provo, where we visited Brigham Young University. From this point we proceeded to the study of certain geological features, among which were the ancient shore-lines of Lake Bonneville and the Tympanoogos National Monument.

We now proceeded to Cedar City, whence we turned up Cedar Canyon to the top of the range, pausing at Cedar Breaks and Bryce Canyon, two of the most perfect examples of erosional geology to be found anywhere on the continent.

From Bryce Canyon we passed southward through Kanab to the Kaibab Forest and through it to the Grand Canyon. The Kaibab Forest furnished us abundant opportunity for study of animal life, particularly the rare and unique white-tailed squirrel—probably the most remarkable zoogeographical phenomenon in North America.

Pipe Springs National Monument was the next stop and thence we went to Zion National Park, where again we were in the midst of not only one of the beauty spots of the southwest, but were surrounded on every hand by geological phenomena of the first magnitude.

Proceeding southwestward, we visited Dixie College at St. George, Utah; Eldorado Canyon, and the Piute Indians, as well as certain prehistoric ruins near Las Vegas, Nevada, and thence passed westward through the Mohave desert to southern California.

The forests of Sequoia National Park and Yosemite Valley, various museums, a half dozen colleges and universities, Mount Wilson Observatory, the beach at low tide, Catalina Submarine Gardens, the sea-lion rookeries, Los Angeles High School, Los Angeles City Library, Scripps Institution of Biological Research, a little fossil digging and a few theaters consumed six weeks of time in California, and we turned eastward from San Diego on November 15.

The Imperial Valley with its Salton Sea and tropical fruits industry, the sand desert of eastern California, the unique irrigation project at Yuma and an occasional fossil hunt broke the monotony of our trip to Arizona's capital.

From Phoenix we passed north through Prescott and over the Mingues Mountains to Jerome, whence, after visiting the great United Verde copper mine and smelter, we journeyed to Cornville Post Office, where we went into camp for a two-weeks' siege of fossil hunting and the excavation of certain large fossil footprints for the University of Arizona Museum. While here we also visited the famous Verde salt mine, which is noted for the abundant remains left by the aboriginal salt diggers, and the famous cliff dwelling known as Montezuma's Castle. Thence across the range to the Salt River Valley, stopping at the great Roosevelt Dam and at the Tonto Cliff Dwellings on our way to Globe and Miami—other great centers of the copper industry. After studying the various processes used in mining and smelting here, we topped the ridge to the westward and came to Superior, where is located the young but thriving Boyce Thompson Institute for Research on Desert Plants. We were received most cordially by Dr. Crider and his staff and were made to feel at home in the lovely camp site which had been provided for us. The nearly three thousand species of desert vegetation here under control proved a valuable asset to us in our endeavor to become somewhat acquainted with desert flora. The scenery here is grand and the institute gardens abound in bird life, rendering our stay very pleasant. The subsequent reminiscences of the events of those days convince us that some things stuck to us besides the thorns of the "jumping cactus."

We next visited the University of Arizona at Tucson, and were impressed by the exceptionally strong school of mining and engineering and the school of archeology, as well as the other departments of this thriving western university. We also visited several other points of scientific interest thereabouts. Our next stop was at Bisbee, then Douglas, from where some of the party entered Mexico *via* Naco, and proceeded as far as Cananea.

It was now approaching the holiday season and we headed for El Paso, where we were to spend Christmas. Christmas was pleasantly spent in the noted Camp Grande, where a Yule party long to be remembered was enjoyed by all.

From El Paso we went to the wonder of wonders, Carlsbad Cavern. This great cavern, which was first made known to the American public in 1924, is one of the choicest scenic gems of America. It is one of the largest and unquestionably the most gorgeously ornamented cavern ever discovered. One of the subterranean passages is occupied by swarms of bats which, together with the consequent accumulation of guano, forms an interesting biological and geological study. We visited not only the bat-inhabited portion of this great underworld, but took the seven-mile scenic tramp through this most beautiful of the world's caverns.

At Valentine, Texas, we turned aside to spend a few days on a frontier Texas cattle ranch some fifty miles from civilization. This visit gave us all a taste of the much misunderstood ranch life of the "wild west" as well as a taste of venison. The geologic aspects of this section are also uniquely interesting. And now with short stops at Alpine for the West Texas Teachers College and at the border cities of Laredo and Nuevo Laredo, we proceeded to Brownsville, which boasts of being the most southerly city in the United States. In our field excursions from this point we were privileged to study the most tropical bird population to be found within our national boundaries. It was also in south Texas that we paid a visit to the last known individuals of that handsome but almost extinct race—the whooping crane. Here also we hunted and captured the armadillo and sought out the haunts of the only truly wild pig species on the continent, namely, the peccary.

We now rounded the gulf, pausing frequently to enlarge our notes on forest trees, and brought up on the Florida Keys, where tropical vegetation and tropical animal life on sea and on land became our environment. A good low tide facilitated our work on animal life here during our two-day stay. We returned to the mainland, crossed the Everglades on the new Tamiami Trail to the Big Cypress Swamp, into which we moved our camp for a week's sojourn. Here on the shore of the beautiful little "Deep Lake" we pitched our camp and became familiar with the ways of the water turkey (*Anhinga anhinga*), the black vulture (*Catharista urubu*), the fork-tailed kite (*Elanoides forficatus*), the barred owl (*Strix varia alleni*), the wood-ibis (*Mycteria americana*), as well as many smaller birds and the alligator (*Alligator mississippiensis*), cotton-mouth moccasin (*Agkistrodon piscivorus*) and the southern fox squirrel (*Sciurus niger*). Much time was spent here in a vain search for the ill-fated ivory-billed woodpecker.

We now resumed our course to the Gulf Coast, again crossed the peninsula *via* Sebring, and thence northward along the eastern coast of Florida, visiting certain game refuges on our way. We looked about the historic St. Augustine and from Jacksonville made our way inland to Waycross, Georgia, and prepared to enter the Okefenokee Swamp, where we were to continue our search for the ivory-bill, and meanwhile to get a view of the vegetation and animal life of the greatest swamp in the United States.

By two strenuous days of driving through lowland trails we made our way to Jones' Island, where we camped on the border of Billie's Lake. By boat and on foot we penetrated into the heart of the swamp a distance of eight miles, and spent a night and a day amidst the impressive silence of the swamp jungle, which silence was occasionally broken by the bellowing of huge "gators" or the "rat-tat-tat" of the great pileated woodpecker. Though our search failed to discover the ill-fated ivory-bill, it could by no means be described as fruitless. It is generally agreed by the members of the party that this swamp experience was one of the most instructive weeks of the entire school year.

We now repaired to Waycross, whence, after a few days for laundry, baths, letter writing, car repairs and other items of rehabilitation, we proceeded to Atlanta, Georgia, arriving on March 15.

At this point our program of work was materially modified. Our field work ceased, and henceforth our entire efforts were to be directed to the study of institutions. Colleges, universities, museums, libraries, research establishments, historic points and industrial plants were now to be the subjects of our studies. Since the students were to receive but eighteen semester hours for a long year's work, great freedom was permitted in the choice of institutions so long as they were of a worthy nature, even though in no direct way related to subjects in which credit was being allowed. During the eight weeks following we visited the most important educational centers of the east, apportioning the greater part of our time to the cities of Washington, New York, Boston, Richmond and Philadelphia, with briefer stays at a score of other historic spots. Two weeks were spent in the city of Washington, where all the most important bureaus and departments received attention, and much time was spent in the Smithsonian Institution. Students were assigned work occupying about half their time and the remainder was spent according to the taste of each. Following is the program of one student during our two-weeks' stay:

March 31: A. M., in the Capitol. P. M., Congressional Library and National Museum. Evening, Lincoln Memorial.

April 1 (Sunday): A. M., in Potomac Park with the cherry blossoms. P. M., National Museum. Evening, Congressional Library.

April 2: A. M., Congressional Library, National Museum. P. M., National Museum, Congressional Library. Evening, a show.

April 3: Entire day at National Museum.

April 4: A. M., National Museum. P. M., Congressional Library.

April 5: A. M., completed assignment in museum. P. M., studied mineral collection.

April 6: Day at the zoo. Evening, Congressional Library.

April 7: A. M., Old Smithsonian Building. P. M., Bureau of Standards.

April 8: A. M., Pan-American Building and White House. P. M., Museum.

April 9: A. M., National Academy of Sciences. P. M., Museum. Evening, Congressional Library.

April 10: A. M., Mt. Vernon and Arlington Cemetery. P. M., Museum.

April 11: A. M., P. M., and evening, attending meeting of American Mammalogists.

April 12: More meetings of American Mammalogists. P. M., left for Gettysburg.

Notes were kept by each student in a notebook especially designed for the trip. A special blank form was filled out for each bird studied, another for each plant and a third form for animals other than birds. No formal classes were held, but frequent campfire discussions were a part of the program of work.

The keeping of diaries was encouraged, and most of the students did this throughout the entire nine months. Collections of specimens in geology and other lines were made by most of the students and shipped to their homes from various points. In the case of one student the collection reached several thousand specimens.

A small library, consisting of taxonomic works on botany and zoology and a few general works on geology and birds, was carried by each car.

The health of the group was far superior to that enjoyed by the same people when in residence. No serious illness of any kind was encountered, and colds were much less common than is customary under ordinary living conditions.

The expense to each student, including equipment, food, clothing, travel, entertainment, tuition and books was on the average about six hundred dollars. However, it should be remarked that the tuition charged was about one hundred dollars less than would ordinarily be charged, the instructor on this occasion depending upon other sources for a part of his income.

In closing this very brief account, the writer feels constrained to make a few suggestions relative to the possibilities and the desirability of this type of educational enterprise. Providing a suitable group can be selected, I have no hesitancy in stating that very much more useful information can be gathered during a year of supervised travel than is furnished by a year in residence in college. Various students of our group gave as their estimate that they had learned "several times as much" and "many times as much" as they had ever learned in a year in college.

It is, of course, very important that the group be selected with a full appreciation of the nature of the undertaking. A group who were not congenial or who could not cheerfully meet difficulties and hardships would certainly make success in such a program impossible. Following are some qualifications which proved of outstanding worth in making our year on wheels successful: Good health, good character, interest in the subjects studied, optimism, willingness to endure hardships, a spirit of cooperation, a spirit of toleration, courtesy, willingness to work, a sense of humor.

Having selected a suitable group, the means of travel and the mode of living must be determined upon. While there are various methods to be considered, it is the writer's opinion that camping promises the largest returns to the members of the party. It is also less expensive. As I look back upon the year's experiences, I am made to feel that some of the greatest contributions to the lives of the students came through camping.

The coeducational aspect of our group has been the subject of much inquiry on the part of educators. I wish to say that while this did not constitute a serious problem with us, I can see how the selection of a different group might do so. It is a matter which must depend largely upon the leader and his selection of students. On the whole, I should say it were safer to restrict the membership to one sex or the other.

Courses in natural history are by their very nature well adapted for such a trek. The idea of combining field studies with museum observations and library researches is well-nigh ideal. However, I see no reason why history and sociology could not be handled with equal facility. Historic spots furnish the most impressive surroundings in which to present effectively various related historical events. And surely the numerous visits to various sociological units and types forms a better subject for study than do books written upon these subjects.

On my own suggestion our college decided (before the course was begun) to allow only eighteen hours of credit for the thirty-six weeks of work. I am fully convinced, however, that a full year's credit is earned and is more fully justified than is the case when the same students are in residence.

The leader of such a group must be a person thoroughly schooled in the art of laboring under handicaps. He should be entirely at home in camp life and above all should be one who is not enslaved to the text-book or lecture method of teaching. Adaptability must be one of his strong fortes. His training must of necessity be broader than is generally required of a teacher in college in order to provide a sufficiently wide range of study for the students. Yet he must be well enough informed to feel at home with the research method in each field undertaken. For his efforts he will feel repaid by the equivalent of two or three years spent in a university.

H. H. NININGER

MCPHERSON COLLEGE

DISCUSSION

DOES EDUCATION INCREASE ORIGINAL DIFFERENCES?

"USQUOQUE, Domine?" How long, O Lord, are educational psychologists, psychologists and educators to continue naïvely to accept the now famous dictum that "practice increases individual differences"? It came into existence as an experimental conclusion sired by the two outstanding names in educational psychology about two decades ago. The startling nature of the results of the experiments, that the learning curves of different individuals did not show any tendency to approach each other after a period of practice, as seems to have been very largely assumed at that time, but that they continued to diverge as time went on, may have seemed at first glance to have warranted an unqualified conclusion. At the present time, in the light more of a different manner of interpreting the data rather than of conflicting data, a conclusion, if it is at all possible to draw one, must be very guarded and even then seems to favor a view opposite to the traditional one.

It all seems to depend upon what kind of measures we use for evaluating the data accumulated. Kincaid (in the *Psychological Review* for January, 1925), in working over the data of twenty-four experimenters who have contributed to the study of this question, suggests that there are four possibilities for evaluating the results: (1) Comparison of absolute differences at the beginning and end of practice; (2) comparison of relative differences at the beginning and end of practice; (3) relation of initial ability and gross gain; (4) relation between initial ability and relative gain. As a result of applying these measures to the data that she worked over, the author says:

> In the case of absolute measures, the indications are that differences increase with practice about as often as they decrease; in sixty-two cases an increase is shown, in fifty-eight a decrease. If relative measures are used, individuals who are initially low in achievement generally gain more with reference to their initial ability than do individuals who are superior at the start; in sixty-one cases a decrease in differences is shown as against eleven cases where an increase is indicated. . . . The weight of the summarized evidence would seem to fall in favor of the decrease in differences between individuals as being the more common result of the addition of equal amounts of practice.

The question, to say the least, is as yet surely *sub judice*. And yet the new edition of Starch still says, "All experimental results point in the direction that practice does not equalize abilities; in fact, equal practice tends to increase differences in achievement and skill rather than to decrease them." A very late text-book[1] also makes the statement: "Practice then increases individual differences" (page 212). Text-books in education that now accept this dictum as gospel truth are probably legion.

The problem, it seems, is not only far from being solved, but it is admittedly a difficult one to attack. Statistical hazards, the confusion of units of production for units of mental effort, types of functions investigated, change in function due to practice,[2] all complicate the treatment of the data. But while we are awaiting the final disposition of many of these difficulties, we may approach the whole question from another angle. The results of intelligence and achievement testing should have something to say concerning this problem of individual differences.

CORRELATION OF I.Q. AND A.Q.

In correlating the I.Q.'s of 227 fifth-grade pupils with their A.Q.'s, the author obtained a negative correlation coefficient of –.50. This shows that there is a rather considerable tendency for the high I.Q.'s to have low A.Q.'s and for the low I.Q.'s to have high A.Q.'s. This is about the same size correlation coefficient as was obtained by Franzen and reported in "Intelligence Tests and School Reorganization." He concluded that "the more stupid a child is the more he tends to get out of education in proportion to his native ability." If every pupil derived benefit from his education in proportion to his native capacity, as would have to be the case, if the original difference existing between the children were to be preserved or increased, then the bright children should not have A.Q.'s lower than 100 any oftener than the dull children, nor should the dull children have A.Q.'s higher than 100 any oftener than the bright ones. But the negative correlation coefficients show that this is not the case. The bright children are not deriving benefit from their education in proportion to their original ability, and the dull children are getting from their schooling more than we might expect of them in view of what the bright children get.

There are undoubtedly reasons for this situation, many of them defects in school procedure that might be remedied: unequal stimulation of the dull and bright, repetition of grades by

[1] Ellis, "The Psychology of Individual Differences."

[2] *Cf.* W. D. Commins, "Effect of Education on Original Differences," *Cath. Educ. Research Bulletin,* 1927.

duller pupils, retardation of the brighter pupils, etc. But the facts seem to be, nevertheless, that within the school as it is now functioning, dull children are getting more out of their schooling in proportion to their original ability than are the bright children. Hence the original differences must tend to be eliminated. The school is acting as a leveling influence, but, of course, it is not at all clear that it should or must always act in that fashion.

Comparative Dispersion of E.Q.'s and I.Q.'s, E.A.'s and M.A.'s

We may also investigate the effect that education has upon the accentuation or elimination of individual differences by comparing the variability of children in measures of intelligence and in school abilities. If school children are found to differ more among themselves in intellectual ability than they are found to do in school achievement, then we may have the right to suppose that education has tended to eliminate the differences that originally existed among them rather than to accentuate them. In the present instance we can use the standard deviation as a measure of variability or differences existing in a group of children.

In the author's study of over two hundred fifth-grade pupils, the sigma of mental ages was found to be 16.44 and the sigma of educational ages 9.84; the standard deviations of the I.Q.'s and of the A.Q.'s were found to be, respectively, 16.8 and 13.4. These facts seem to show that fifth-grade pupils are more alike when they are measured by the Stanford achievement test than when they are measured by the National intelligence test. They are more alike in educational product than they are in fundamental capacity.

In the *Journal of Educational Psychology* for March, 1925, Willson, by working over a large supply of test data from various sources, found similar results. "The sigmas of educational age in grade groups tend to be lower than the corresponding sigmas of mental." Even when taking age groups instead of grade groups, he still finds that the same tendency is shown, although not to as great a degree. School children evidently vary more in capacity among themselves than they do in achievement. It seems that we must take this as indicative of a decrease in individual differences, due to schooling.

It may not be at all necessary, as was pointed out before, or even desirable, that education should continue to reduce original differences, but it seems to be almost impossible in view of the foregoing to suppose that education is not doing that at the present time. The educational psychologist of a few years back was prepared to say that the school can not help but increase individual differences, while we of the present day may feel justified in saying that the school as now functioning is doing the very opposite, and the real question now is whether it can really do anything else. Even with this possibility in mind, the older experiments are not so helpful, because they dealt largely with unitary, simple, or linear functions, such as addition, multiplication, etc., and what the scientific educator wants to know is the effect of education upon the whole child and upon his complicated social relationships.

W. D. Commins

St. Louis University

A FUTURISTIC PAINTING OF HIGHER EDUCATION

In summarizing six weeks' (summer session) discussions on higher education one is reminded of the way Philo Vance solved the mystery of "The Greene Murder Case." Mr. Vance said:[1]

> The difference between a good painting and a photograph is this: the one is arranged, composed, organized; the other is merely the haphazard impression of a scene, or a segment of realism, just as it exists in nature.

To solve the mystery, Mr. Vance began with the segments of realism and put them into an organized composition in much the same way that an artist might create a painting from photographic details. He said that once the design of the painting were known the mystery would be solved.

We have been considering segments of realism, which, if they could be arranged, organized, or composed into a painting, might give us a different perspective, a view of the whole.

An attempt at such an organization follows:

[1] S. S. Van Dine, "The Greene Murder Case," *Scribner's*, p. 447, April, 1928.

1. The purpose of those who established Harvard College in 1836. (New England's First Fruits.)

2. A practically uniform education in colleges until 1890.

3. The spirit of American democracy characterized by "In God We Trust."

4. The increase in enrolments, especially in recent years.

5. A comparison between the proportion of population attending college in this country and in leading foreign countries.

6. The limitation of enrolment by privately controlled institutions.

7. The increase in relative numbers attending state universities as compared with private colleges.

8. The relatively open door of state universities.

9. The tremendous endowments acquired within recent decades, especially by a small number of institutions.

10. The vast sums of money spent on education.

11. A changing society demands a dynamic and flexible educational system.

12. Colleges keep pace with society in imitating some of the adult social institutions. (Colleges with their fraternities and adults with their Ku Klux Klans.)

13. The influence of "Yankee Thrift" and the scientific method upon higher education.

14. The establishment of the junior high school with the primary emphasis upon adapting the school to meet the needs of the pupil.

15. A junior college movement somewhat parallel to the junior high-school movement.

16. The rapid development of the junior colleges.

17. College personnel work as an effort to help the student.

18. Increased emphasis upon the needs of the individual as shown by the development of health work.

19. Other movements for the same purpose; (18)
   1. Adult education; 2. Specialized vocational schools; 3. Continuation schools.

20. A variation of special freshman courses called orientation courses.

21. The demand of business and industry for scholars.

22. The lack of accurate information regarding vocational, semiprofessional and professional needs.

23. The tendency toward general education in the first years and specialization in the latter years of college.

24. The trend toward greater specialization and the appearance of new professions and semi-professions.

25. The extension upward of pre-professional training.

26. The wider offering of courses and the tendency to quickly organize the knowledge in a new field. (Radio and aviation.)

27. The demand for a more practical culture and for creation in addition to the appreciation of beauty.

28. The survival of true religion in the colleges.

29. The chief limiting factor of small colleges is finance.

30. The need for greater efficiency in higher education.

31. The fact that a considerable number of students transfer from small colleges to large universities after one or two years.

32. The practice of state universities in offering cultural, professional and vocational courses.

33. The increased cost of living, making college years continually more of an economic sacrifice.

34. The limit of the possibility for the upward extension of the educative period set by the natural desire for a home life and the accompanying economic situation.

The Painting

From an inspection of the foregoing details one may deduce that a painting of higher education for the near future will have the following characteristics:

1. An emphasis upon the cultural values of knowledge with continued stress upon the practical use of culture.

2. Higher education open to all who can profit by the experience. The individual to be judged by the possibility of his making a return to society.

3. A swing of the pendulum in the direction of greater support for the smaller college together with a change in the part played by the smaller college in the scheme of things.

4. The superficial character may change because of the imitation of adult social institutions but the fundamental fiber will remain practically the same.

5. There will be increased efforts to make the individual the most socially efficient unit possible.

6. The increases which will take place in enrolment will demand greater efficiency of teaching and administration.

7. The small college may be forced to accept state support.

8. The small college may become an institution primarily for the instruction of general courses in the first two years of college.

9. There may be worked out a scheme of greater cooperation between the small college offering general training and the university offering in addition vocational, pre-professional and professional training.

10. Because of the limit placed upon the upward extension it will be necessary for higher education to provide more and more specialized training within this natural limit.

11. The higher educational institutions will have to become more and more flexible and responsive to a rapidly changing civilization.

PHILIP A. COWEN
DARTMOUTH COLLEGE

QUOTATIONS

THE OFFER TO CAMBRIDGE

IN his valedictory address the retiring vice-chancellor of the University of Cambridge had an announcement to make which must put all Cambridge men on their mettle. The International Education Board of the Rockefeller Foundation has approached the university with an offer of £700,000, on the condition that the university finds a further sum of £229,000. With this money, which is all but a million, the university would be enabled to complete at a single stroke its scheme for a new library and certain important developments which have been urged for some time past as necessary in its equipment for the pursuit of physical and biological studies. The offer, it must be clearly understood, is strictly conditional; the university must either take it on the condition attached to it or leave it; for in this case, as in others where the trust has dispensed its bounty, the trust will help only those who will help themselves. There can be no quarreling with these terms, for the offer is one of the highest compliments which can be paid to any seat of learning, while its magnitude implies a deep sense of the merits of Cambridge as a university. The terms, however, are such as must impel the university and its friends to look around them with the utmost zeal for the raising of so large a sum as £229,000. The offer has not yet actually come before the university for acceptance; but it is so attractive in itself, and would, if met, be of such enormous benefit, that it is hardly to be supposed that a supreme effort will not be made to ensure the fulfilment of the condition. Needless to say it is an offer which can be declined only with the greatest reluctance and under the pressure of overwhelming obstacles.

Perhaps the best reason for hoping that the stipulated sum may be raised lies in the earnestness and sincerity of the university in pursuing its policy of self-improvement and in the skill with which its finances are habitually husbanded. For the last seven years the university has faced with an exemplary tenacity the problem which its library presents. It has bought the ground for the new building, the plans and estimates have long been prepared and the principle has been approved that, though at present ways and means can be devised for the completion of only half the project, a beginning to that extent shall be undertaken. "This momentous decision," as the retiring vice-chancellor called it, was reached early in the present year. It was momentous because there seemed to be no clear indication when the other half of the scheme, which would cost in all £500,000, was likely to be completed. Now comes this noble offer of assistance from America, which would definitely assign to the library a contribution of not less than £250,000, and would also give the university a "new and magnificent opportunity," as the retiring vice-chancellor puts it, of advancing the studies of physiology and biology. No mention was made of a time limit to the offer; but it may be assumed that it will not be permitted to lie open indefinitely. In other words, Cambridge, which can not find the £229,000 without help, must count on the speedy support of her graduates and of others who believe that in promoting her interests they are also promoting those of the country, if not of mankind at large. The Rockefeller Trust, it is not inappropriate to recall, was established "to promote the welfare of mankind," and its benefactions are not accorded without due scrutiny of the deserts of the beneficiaries. A gift of equal munificence might conceivably come to a seat of learning from some other donor, but from no other source would the fact of its conveyance carry with it so high a testimonial towards the object of the benefaction. The truth is, however, that Cambridge is one of the most distinguished schools of science in existence; its fame is world wide, and the services which its scientific men have rendered to humanity place it in a class apart among similar institutions in Great Britain. If on other grounds Cambridge has proved herself worthy of a share of the funds which the Rockefeller Trust has at its disposal, she is unquestionably worthy on the main ground. For this reason, therefore, it is almost unnecessary to express the hope that before long means may be found to convert this splendid overture, conditional at present, into an accepted benefaction.—*The London Times.*

A CITY PLAYGROUND

MR. THOMAS ADAMS in the introduction to the report of the Regional Plan Committee on Public Recreation makes the statement that New York City has probably lost hundreds of thousands of comparatively wealthy residents because of the inadequacy of open spaces. He urges that the problem of more open space is more than a problem of recreation facilities for children. True as that is, it is concern for the children that has prompted the setting aside of $1,000,000 for play sites. It shows a determination on the part of the Mayor to do something really effective in their behalf that he has not allowed the appropriation of last year, $500,000, to be a mere gesture but has caught it up into the new budget and added another half million to it.

Sites were canvassed by the Chief Engineer of the Board of Estimate last year and recommendations made, but for one reason or another—non-concurrence on the part of borough authorities in certain conditions being one of them—they were not carried into effect. Doubtless a new survey will now be made, and with the larger sum at command there should be no further delay. Every year of postponement sees additional children deprived of what every child should have—a place to play. More thousands will be driven into the country who might be comfortable here if only there were such places for their children. One should not have to argue that adequate playgrounds for children are an essential and not a community luxury. The child's play is the "young form of work," in preparation for the business of life, and must be treated seriously—the "basis of all natural education." Moreover, it is the best antidote to crime in that period of life. If places for play are not provided in great cities, there is, beside all this, the tragic toll of death in the streets, for the child will try to play somewhere.

The Mayor and the Board of Estimate should have the support of the entire city in this step. Incidentally, the Committee on Parks and Recreation of the Mayor's committee should have thanks. The million dollars should be converted into air and sunlight and play for thousands of children as soon as it can be done. New York is far down the list of cities in its relative park and playground space—one acre for 553 inhabitants as compared with Philadelphia's 234. It is believed that more open spaces in the city would help in some measure to solve the transit problem and aid in attacking local crime problems; but it can be demonstrated beyond all question that it will minister to the safety and happiness of children. Certainly the community that invites them into its midst owes them at least this.—*The New York Times.*

REPORTS

THE WASHINGTON CHILD RESEARCH CENTER

DR. MARION DAVIS, of the U. S. Bureau of Education, has issued the following statement in regard to the work of the Washington Child Research Center. Miss Davis represents the bureau on the executive committee.

Three of the eight organizations cooperating with the Washington Child Research Center, one of the most recent projects of child development sponsored by the Laura Rockefeller Memorial, are government bureaus. Although the federal government has no part in financing the project, the Bureau of Home Economics, the Bureau of Education and the United States Public Health Service are represented on the executive committee and consulting staff. The other organizations represented on the executive committee are the American Association of University Women, the National Research Council, the American Home Economics Association, George Washington University and the University of Maryland.

A distinct need for an experimental and demonstration laboratory has been felt by the workers of these different organizations. Working together there seems to be every opportunity for representatives from these bureaus and associations interested in child development and parental education to make a definite contribution to knowledge already obtained in this field of work.

Focusing their interests in this project of the Washington Child Research Center, a nursery school enrolling twenty-five normal children, approximating a three-year age level, has been organized as a laboratory. Observation of and research in the development and growth of these young children in a most natural environment forms one part of the program of work. Four teachers, specially trained, supervise the day's program in the nursery school. The director of the center, Dr. Mandel Sherman, supervises research work and is responsible for all other activities. These include classes and conferences for the children's parents, lecture work and laboratory demonstrations for graduate university students and a consultation clinic in which children and parents needing special treatment are received and for whom remedial programs are recommended.

A nursery school is quite different from the well-known day nursery, the latter often being merely a location to place youngsters in order to relieve their parents of responsibility. The twenty-four-hour day of the children is considered in the nursery school. This involves all the home activities, and part of each day's nursery school program is given over to conferences with the parents about the children's emotional, mental, social and physical life at home.

Equipment and apparatus at the center have been planned with the greatest care to develop the children socially as well as physically and mentally. Old-fashioned building blocks in small size and in small quantities have given place to large blocks of such weight that it takes at least two children to handle them. In this way muscle tone is developed and working together is promoted. Ladders, slides, walking boards, a large sandbox, swings and a concrete walk for wheel toys make possible many kinds of play which teach independence and cooperation, and assure a coordination of muscles that leads to bodily freedom.

During the winter, as well as in the summer, over four hours' play each day is carried on outdoors. Daily physical examinations of each child forestall any contagion in the group and protect each individual.

Special problems in clothing and in nutrition for children have been worked out since the center opened last February. Other studies in the physical development of the children and in the evident effect of attendance at nursery school upon methods of handling children in the home are under way.

EDUCATIONAL RESEARCH AND STATISTICS

A STUDY OF THE VOCABULARY OF ANCIENT HISTORY TEXTS

THE word count in this study has been made for the purpose of measuring the vocabulary difficulty in high-school text-books in ancient history. Also it indicates to some degree the extent to which the content of the text is suited to the needs and capacities of the ninth grade student.

The five texts examined by the writer are presented in Table I. These texts were chosen on the basis of the extent of their use in secondary schools, as shown in information gathered from the various publishing companies. Two of the older type texts and three quite recent texts were chosen for the purpose of comparing the older with the newer texts as well as the individual texts with each other. In the general or world history texts only the part pertaining to ancient history was covered.

TABLE I

TEXTS EXAMINED IN THIS STUDY

Webster	World History
Elson	Modern Times and the Living Past
Robinson, Breasted and Smith	Our World To-day and Yesterday
Breasted	Ancient Times
Myers	General History

In order to avoid any unjust criticism of the texts examined, they are referred to by letter only. The same letter is used throughout the study to designate a certain text. However, there is no relationship between the order of the arrangement of the texts in the following tables and the order in which they are arranged in Table I.

Since all ninth grade students are supposed to be familiar with the Ayres 1,000-word list,[1] these words were not tabulated in this study. However, all words which were not found in the Ayres list were tabulated with their frequency for each text.

[1] Leonard P. Ayres, "A Measuring Scale for Ability in Spelling," Russell Sage Foundation, 1915.

In tabulating the words, separate entries were not made of plurals in s; plurals where y is replaced by ies; superlatives formed by adding er, est, or r and st; verb forms in s, d, ed, and ing; and past participles formed by adding n or en.

The entire list of words was arranged in alphabetical order and tabulated to show the frequency for each word in each test, as well as the total frequency for that word in all five texts. Furthermore, all the words checked were classified as to whether or not they appeared in the Thorndike 10,000-word list.[2]

"The Teachers Word Book," by Thorndike, is an alphabetical list of the ten thousand words which were found to occur most frequently in a count of some five million running words from forty-one different sources. The words were arranged in alphabetical order and "a measure of the range and frequency of each word's occurrence is given by the credit number following it."[3]

Since this list contains ten thousand of the most commonly used words, the writer believes it is the best measure of the strangeness or unusualness of a given word. Those words which are not found in Thorndike's list may safely be considered as unfamiliar to the average ninth grade student and should be considered as an indication of vocabulary difficulty.

TABLE II

PERCENTAGE OF TOTAL FREQUENCY OF ALL WORDS IN EACH TEXT

Text	Ayres list	Thorndike list excluding Ayres list	Thorndike list	Percentage of total number of different words in each text not found in Thorndike list
A	86.8	9.7	3.5	33.1
B	86.6	8.6	4.8	37.0
C	85.9	9.8	4.3	39.2
D	90.1	6.3	3.6	27.6
E	87.2	10.4	2.4	17.2

[2] Edward Lee Thorndike, "The Teachers Word Book," New York, Teachers College, Columbia University, 1921. 134 pp.

[3] *Ibid.*, page iii.

Table II shows what percentage of the total word frequencies of all the words appearing in each text are found within the Ayres list (see column 2), and in the Thorndike list excluding the Ayres list (column 3), while column 4 shows the percentage of the total word frequencies in the text which are found in neither the Ayres nor the Thorndike list.

The total frequencies of all words appearing in each text were computed by multiplying the number of pages by the average number of words found by counting the words on a number of sample pages. The total frequencies of all words appearing in the Ayres list were found by subtracting the total number of word frequencies tabulated from the total number of word frequencies in the text.

The second column in Table II shows that from 85.9 to 90.1 per cent. of the total word frequencies of all the words in the individual texts are found in the Ayres one-thousand-word list. It should be borne in mind that these percentages represent frequency of appearance. It it evident that the words in the Ayres list appear a large number of times and hence make up a large part of the running vocabulary.

The fourth column of the above table shows that from 2.4 to 4.8 per cent. of the total word frequencies in the various texts consist of words that are not found in Thorndike's "Word Book." This means that in reading one hundred words in running word order, the student will find, on an average, from 2.4 to 4.8 words that are unfamiliar to him. On each full page of printed matter, he will find from eight to sixteen such words.

However, the last column presents a more accurate picture.[4] It shows that from 17.2 to 39.2 per cent. of all the different words appearing in the various texts are not found in Thorndike's word list. (The number of different

[4] In computing the number of different words appearing in each text, it was assumed that all the words in the Ayres 1,000-word list appeared in the text. Consequently, 1,000 was added to the number of different words tabulated in each text. As a verification of the accuracy of this assumption, the upper 25 per cent. of the Ayres list were checked to see if they appeared in each text. All words of the upper 25 per cent. save one were found, and it appeared under a different form.

words should not be confused with the total word frequencies.)

A variation of approximately 100 per cent. in the vocabulary difficulty of the various texts is evident from the above data. Text E should be more easily read by the ninth grade student than texts B or C.

Table III gives a further analysis of the uncommon words.

TABLE III

WORDS NOT IN THORNDIKE, CLASSIFIED ACCORDING TO FREQUENCY OF APPEARANCE

Text	Total number different words	Percentage of words with frequency of: 1	2	3–5	Above 5
A	1734	46.5	16.3	16.4	20.8
B	1441	52.6	16.3	17.7	13.4
C	898	62.4	14.8	12.9	9.9
D	827	51.4	17.0	18.9	12.7
E	396	59.3	17.4	13.6	9.7
Total	5296				

In defense of the large number of uncommon words, it may be urged that these give opportunity for vocabulary enrichment. This argument might have more weight were it not for the fact, as is shown in column 3 of the above table, that from 46.5 to 62.4 per cent. of the uncommon words do not appear in any one of the texts more than once, while from 14.8 to 17.4 per cent. of the uncommon words appear but twice. It may be legitimately questioned whether the student's vocabulary will be materially enriched by him being exposed to a strange word once or even twice during a course in ancient history. In the absence of further investigation, we may question whether the value gained is commensurate with the effort on the part of the student.

Incidentally this study throws some light on the extent to which the content is suited to the needs of the ninth grade student. The vocabulary difficulty becomes all the more significant when we realize that many of the uncommon words refer to material in history with which the average student will have no further contact. This fact may be illustrated by a sampling of the words tabulated in this word count. On one single page of tabulated words appear the following:

Aegina, Aegospotami, Aemilianus, Aeneid, Aetius, Agamemnon, agglutinating, Agora, agrarian, Agrigentum, Agrippina.

For fear the writer might be accused of taking too much care in choosing the sample, let him turn to the following page in the word list, where are found:

Ahriman, Ahura, Ahuramazda, Akamantis, Akhenaten, Akkad, Aliari, alluvial, Alma-Tadema.

Samples of this kind may be duplicated many times in the ancient history vocabulary lists. If the spirit of the material represented by these words is not entirely dead, it is at least so thoroughly concealed beneath the débris of unfamiliar terminology and strange characters that the beginning ninth grade student will be able to discover but little of the supposed value.

In a word count of texts in the field of natural science, S. R. Powers[5] found that the average number of uncommon words appearing in general science texts was 1,324; the average in chemistry texts, 1,660, and in biology, 2,040. In comparison with Powers' findings it is interesting to note that in the one ancient history text which is being used in many schools throughout the ninth grade are found 1,734 uncommon words.

In conclusion, one can say that the vocabulary in ancient history offers considerable difficulty to the ninth grade student. There is a variation of 100 per cent. in the number of uncommon words that appear per page in the various texts. More than half of the uncommon words do not appear in any one text more than once. Hence the student can not be expected to become familiar with them. The content of some of the texts, as suggested by these unusual words, has little connection with the life or interests of the average ninth grade student. The field of ancient history presents as many unusual words as are found in the field of the sciences intended for the ninth grade student. It is evident that further investigation should be carried on to determine what material is essential in the field of ancient history.

C. G. SHAMBAUGH

STANFORD UNIVERSITY

[5] S. R. Powers, "The Vocabularies of High School Science Text-Books," in *Teachers College Record* 25: 368–382.

SCHOOL AND SOCIETY

Volume XXVIII SATURDAY, OCTOBER 27, 1928 Number 722

DEFECTS AND DIFFICULTIES IN COLLEGE TEACHING

As a part of the preparation for a course in methods of college teaching, which the writer was scheduled to give during the fall semester 1928–29 at the University of Southern California, a class of fifty-four college students, mostly seniors and graduates, was asked to contribute as many specific weaknesses, shortcomings, defects, faults and difficulties as they had observed or experienced in connection with college teaching. No list was given the class to be checked lest the responses might be influenced by the suggestions offered.

The replies were submitted in large part upon small cards with one point on a card. Some were submitted in the form of lists and copied later upon cards. In all there were about three thousand suggestions given.

These reports were classified by the writer according to their types. Obviously such data do not permit of strictly statistical treatment and, consequently, the present article represents qualitatively but not quantitatively the criticisms of college teaching as offered by the students.

It should be kept in mind that not all college teachers are accused of having all the defects mentioned in this article, since the list is a composite rather than a typical one. The following eighteen points represent the major lines along which criticisms were offered.

(1) DEFECTS OF PERSONALITY AND TEMPERAMENT

College teachers are criticized for a number of personality defects, such as careless personal appearance, posture and dress. Some complaint is given about unpleasant voice. The lack of physical development and too much brain development is also mentioned. Professors are said to be so engrossed in their subject-matter that they are absent-minded. They are reported sometimes to be pessimistic, sarcastic, stilted, formal, inhuman, unsocial and lacking in sense of humor. They lack tact, try to bluff students and are self-conscious. Frequently they keep in the background socially and fail to assume the position of leadership which is rightly theirs because of their training. They are also said to be susceptible to flattery, egotistical and sometimes snobbish. They enjoy telling their childhood experiences or telling about their latest European trips. They are impatient, nervous, get rattled easily and in general display a wider range of variability in matters of personal behavior than is found in the average group of men.

(2) DEFECTS REGARDING ACADEMIC FREEDOM, PROPAGANDA AND DOGMATISM

Criticism is made for all degrees of shortcomings, from undue cowardice to extreme radicalism as regards exercise of the right of free speech. Some are said to be afraid of the administration, others to fear political influences, and many to be unduly hampered by social conventions and the fear of publicity. They are commonly accused of being bound by tradition and lacking the initiative or nerve to break away from the conservatism which hampers colleges and universities. Some are even too sensitive to face the opposition of their own students. Others, lacking complete freedom of speech themselves, are said to deny it to their own students and to interfere with free discussion, weighing of evidence and drawing conclusions in their classes. A great deal of complaint is offered to the effect that college teachers are too dogmatic and sure of their own opinions so that they become outspoken and assume that their word is law. Some complaint is also made of radicalism in the social and political views as well as atheism in religious thinking.

(3) Careless and Unsatisfactory Planning of Courses

The accusation is made that college teachers have no objectives or hazy objectives for their courses. Assignments are indefinite and lacking in purpose. Teachers come to class without definite preparations, fail to connect up the lesson with previous lessons, do not stick to the point, allow too many petty details to enter, dwell upon minor points of interest to themselves and allow major problems to go unsolved, give improper balance or emphasis to topics, and even deliberately waste time because of lack of any real message to impart. Their teaching is said to lack thoroughness, to be scattered, to leave no feeling of definite accomplishment, and to fail to summarize or draw conclusions even after discussions that might have some value. A common expression is that the instructor leaves the class up in the air at the end of the lesson or the course.

(4) Lack of Study and Keeping up with the Age

College teachers are criticized for a lack of broad and basic knowledge of their subjects and the lack of rich experience in the fields taught. They are criticized further for failure to make daily preparation and to arrange for effective presentation the knowledge which they actually possess. They are said to repeat the same course so many times they get sick and tired of it. They get out of date because of lack of contact with new material that is being published, and teach theories and doctrines which were disproved years ago. A common expression is that college teachers are fossilized.

(5) Defects relating to Research, Writing, and Publication

College teachers are criticized both for too little and too much productive work. Some fail to devote time to research and creative work and thus have nothing of their own with which to supplement the books and writings of others. They fail to distinguish themselves as scholars or to experiment with new methods of teaching. They lack interest in real professional growth, even at the same time when they are striving for advanced degrees upon which salary and promotion may depend. Some are criticized for becoming so engrossed in research that teaching is neglected. Some have the art of writing more highly developed than that of speaking or teaching, and resent the interruption of work on their hobbies necessitated by class meetings. They are accused, furthermore, of log rolling in the sale of text-books which they have written and of being materialistic or commercial in connection with their publication. One student reports that college teachers have been known to acquire an undue fear of being considered materialistic and to distribute materials free which should be published and sold in a business-like way.

(6) Failure to Teach on the Student's Level

It is reported that college teachers assume more knowledge on the part of the students than they actually possess and fail to start the course upon a sufficiently simple foundation. The professor's long acquaintance with the subject leads him to forget the beginner's struggles and to clothe his instruction in the terminology of the specialist rather than in the language which students can understand. They assume that the students are all going to be specialists like themselves and they bring out too many of the fine points, technicalities, special cases and exceptions which simply confuse the beginner. They try to impart too much and proceed by steps that are too long for the student to follow. They assume that when a student has been told something he has learned it and further repetition is unnecessary. They try graduate methods on freshmen, and in rare cases make the opposite mistake of trying high-school methods on graduate students.

(7) Failure to be Practical

Such expressions as "all theory," "too academic" and "satisfied with learning for its own sake" are mentioned frequently. College professors are said to lack contact with practical men of affairs and to have too many vicarious experiences and too few real ones. They prefer to read a thing rather than to experience it and thus get too much knowledge secondhand. They are said to be unacquainted with what is going on outside of the college, to be uninformed about current events, to lack interest in politics, economics and industry, and to be so engrossed in their individual specialties as to know little even about other college subjects. They are said to lack a supply of suitable concrete illustrations to give meaning to their well-phrased statements and theories.

(8) Failure to Develop the Research Spirit in Students

There is said to be too much cramming of knowledge into students, too much teaching of facts rather than principles, too much memory and too little thought, failure to stimulate intellectual curiosity, awaken enthusiasm and arouse mental hunger. The teaching fails to create a respect for learning or to inspire a social obligation for solving the world's problems. Teachers are said to do too much of the work and leave too little for the students to do. They fail to teach students how to attack new material and do not give any definite training in the technique of research. They assume that students of the research type will become research workers automatically.

(9) Lack of Personal Interest in Students

College teachers are accused of being petty tyrants rather than master artists, of making the classroom too formal and of being too proud to teach the mediocre student. They excuse their shortcomings by saying their students lack brains, and by their attitude of contempt they alienate student confidence. They lack sympathy, are not approachable and are unwilling to give help to individuals in difficulty. They treat students as machines and do not try to get acquainted with them. They live in a world apart from students and oftentimes do not even care to know the students by name.

(10) Failure to Make Courses Interesting

Teachers in college are said to lack interest in their courses sometimes and to be unable to impart their own interest and enthusiasm at other times. A lack of any conscious effort to make the course interesting and relying upon nagging instead of real motivation are reported. Others try to "jazz up" the courses by telling stories and jokes and trying to be spectacular rather than deep or profound. There is said to be too much playing to the gallery and retelling of stale jokes which the students heard at the Orpheum last year rather than presenting substantial material that has solid merit and inherent interest.

(11) Unsatisfactory Practices regarding Measurement

College teachers are criticized for too much measurement, too little measurement and the wrong kind of measurement. Some people place so much stress on marks and examinations as to paralyze student effort, others take up time with examinations that should be devoted to instruction. Failure to measure results often enough and failure to vary the type of measurement are reported. Petty questions, vague questions and catch questions as well as unreasonably hard examinations come in for criticism. Some instructors are said to test on material completely outside of the course, others are accused of being susceptible to flattery by students who want high grades, and still others are said to base the grade on quantity rather than quality. Undue severity in grading standards is criticized, as is also the unintelligent application of the normal curve in distributing marks. Failure to designate the nature of a student's shortcomings or even to hand back papers at all comes in for criticism. Some teachers are said to encourage dishonesty by the kind of tests used and by their attitude during examinations. The practice of having papers marked by student assistants is also criticized.

(12) Defects regarding the Use of the Lecture Method

College teaching is criticized for too much use of the lecture method as well as ineffective delivery of lectures. Lectures are said to be rambling, pointless, incoherent and to fail to make the main points stand out from the mass of words. The reading of lectures from a manuscript in a droning voice is keenly criticized. Some students also mention the point that there is too little use of the lecture method on the part of teachers who really have something to give and upon certain types of subject-matter which can be handled better by lecture than by discussion.

(13) Defects in the Use of Discussion Methods

The discussion method is said to be used by college teachers too little and the art of conversation is poorly developed by them. They are reported to be unable to weld their classes into unified working groups or to create a group consciousness in the class. They do not possess skill in the chairmanship of discussions, and they assume such a prominent part in discussions as to scare the students out. They not uncommonly let some students talk too much, and they lack ability to keep the discussion on the subject. They fail to make definite previous preparation for discussion periods and they rely too much upon starting an argument as a means of killing time when unprepared. They are said to resort to student reports as substitutes for well-planned discussions or worthwhile lectures. Some teachers are criticized for keeping in the background too much during discussions and thus depriving the students of their mature and valuable viewpoints.

(14) Lack of Variety in Teaching Procedures

College teachers are said to stick to one method too tenaciously, conducting the class day after day and year after year in exactly the same manner. They are said to lack originality regarding the invention of new ways of teaching and to be afraid to adopt new methods when they are advocated by educational leaders.

(15) Failure to Adapt the Course to the Individual Student

Ignorance of the character and needs of their students and failure to study the students to find what they are interested in are also faults of college teachers. All students are treated as if they were exactly alike or as if they were all in the class of the very bright. Too little opportunity is granted for students to follow up their own special interests. The student who does not expect to take further courses in the subject is taught in exactly the same way as those who intend to major in it. There is said to be too little distinction between students who do not do their work because of laziness and those who have good reasons. Also that teachers are unreasonable in enforcing rigid and inflexible regulations regarding late work, causing hardship and injustice in the case of unfortunate and conscientious students.

(16) Improper Adjustments of Work Load

Some teachers are said to overestimate the physical endurance of students and to have no idea of the time required to prepare assignments. They demand so much work that students are tempted to dishonest methods of getting it done, and they drive so hard that students hate the course for sheer overwork. They try to monopolize the student's whole time just as if no other instructors were making assignments. Some teachers are said to pad their courses with large quantities of routine work instead of raising the quality, thus making the courses mere endurance tests. The failure to distribute the work load evenly through the course, resulting in piling up of extra work in the last few weeks, is also criticized. Some teachers are said to require so little work and to make their courses so easy that they are filled with lazy students who want easy grades but who really have little respect for the course or the teacher. College teachers are said to be overworked themselves and to be unable to give adequate attention to their teaching.

(17) Inefficient Routine Management

The number of criticisms of college teachers' management of the routine problems of the classroom was not as great as might have been supposed. Among the criticisms of this type that were offered were failure to meet the class promptly, holding class after the bell rings, being absent too often making speeches or attending meetings, wasting valuable time on announcements and purely routine matters, neglect of temperature, light and ventilation of the room, the use of laborious and time-wasting plans for checking attendance, keeping such poor records that students get passing grades even though they dropped out of the course in the second week, sitting down to teach the class, and failure to talk loud enough to be heard all over the room.

(18) Lack of Faculty Cooperation

College teachers are said to fail to get acquainted with each other or to develop institutional loyalty and school spirit as much as they should. Individual teachers do not know what the other departments in the school are doing nor how to cooperate with them. They are frequently unfamiliar with the content of courses given by members of their own department and thus allow too much overlapping of courses and too many unfilled gaps between courses. There is said to be a lack of discussion of problems between colleagues and a failure to work out a common viewpoint. The result is that two professors may make directly opposite statements and the students do not know which to believe. It is reported that two professors sometimes argue back and forth, relying upon students' reports of what the other said in his classes, and that occasionally personal and departmental quarrels will be aired unnecessarily in the classroom.

The above eighteen defects of college teachers have been made the basis for the writer's course in methods of college teaching. A syllabus has been prepared in which each of these eighteen topics is used as the basis for one week's work. Questions for discussion have been carefully planned and several selected references have been found for each topic. The course is conducted on a round-table or seminar plan and is primarily intended to permit the exchange of experience and ideas secured through reading by the members of the group. It is too early at the present writing to report anything in the way of results in the course, but it is hoped that the above outline of teaching difficulties may be of interest and value to others who are interested in the improvement of college teaching.

C. C. CRAWFORD
UNIVERSITY OF SOUTHERN CALIFORNIA

THE PLACE OF THE SERIOUS STUDENT IN CIVILIZATION[1]

HUMAN values are in a state of flux. Academic selective learning is being challenged. Mechanical revolution is resulting in a new, ill-defined culture. Something of the graciousness of the leisure class seems crowded out. Approvals for contemplation and academic interests and creative speculation seem to be limited to universities and other learned societies.

The world is in a hurry. The amount of work to be done in the world bulks so large and it impresses us so belligerently that we lose our perspectives. Few of us stop to question whether all the bustle is necessary. Almost without protest, we surrender our twentieth century world to the engineer and the specialist. We urge ourselves and our colleagues to hurry, rush, speed up, investigate, organize, publish, boast, and exploit, lest precious moments be lost. "Don't stop to argue," we say, "it takes time needed for work."

What is it all about? Are we rushing for the sake of excitement and personal glory? None of us knows. Few of us have any opinion about it. Not many of us ever give it a thought! We are just caught up in the *maelstrom* of speed and rush. If we speeded up only our work it might not be fatal. But we speed up our leisure inexcusably. Speed has become an anesthetic or a narcotic. We drive and dance and read and play cards and golf just to get the things over with. The arts of conversation and letter writing and contemplation and speculation are too seldom practiced even by college graduates and university instructors.

A machine civilization possesses us. With the added resources in wealth and in effective processes of manufacture, agriculture, and transportation, humanity might rise to new cultural heights.

In the past, the leisure classes alone have developed and encouraged such elusive traits as good taste, pleasing manners, speculative philosophy, and scientific inquiry. To be sure, many people who had little leisure also developed these traits under the encouragement of their more fortunate fellows. But such supreme exertion has called for abundant intellectual and physical resources and for a vigorous *élan vital*. And these qualities are relatively rare.

It has seemed possible that mechanical progress and democratic freedom might set free the creative impulse in the great majority of men and women. In the realms of applied science and invention, of salesmanship and exploitation, and of the mad pursuit of pleasure, there has been a veritable avalanche of creative accomplishment.

Our hopes for a release of creative energy in the fields of education, of gov-

[1] Honors Day address at the University of Arkansas.

ernment, and of literature and art and music have been less bountifully fulfilled. It is true that many more people attend our schools and colleges than ever before; many more people participate in government than formerly; more books and magazines and newspapers are read; more people dress elaborately and, to a degree, pleasingly. The phonograph and radio bring music to us with a minimum of effort on our part. Museums and photogravures and magazines make contemporary and classic art and science and literature a heritage which is easy to seize.

It remains true, however, that "you can lead a horse to water but you can not make him drink." Tabloid newspapers and true story magazines, trashy novels and airplane adventures, jazz and "glad rags" seem to the pessimist to absorb too large a share of our attentions and energies to the neglect of more permanent and significant and fundamental things. Too small a proportion of the enfranchised citizens are ready to study social and political questions; many do not even vote.

Great numbers of college and high-school students seem to the critics to be quite oblivious of the opportunities to participate in the intellectual and spiritual adventures of mankind. Vicarious football and not-so-vicarious "fussing," dancing and joy-riding, jazz and parties seem to be the emotional and intellectual diet of youth.

Freedom has been sought for mankind for four centuries or more. Its apostles have sought it, to the end that the spiritual and intellectual life of the common man might be abundant. It has been too seldom realized that freedom implies the right to waste and neglect and ruin as well as the opportunity to grow and to create and to seek the higher life.

But freedom is young. All that has been hoped may yet be attained. If that culmination is to be achieved, however, our generations will have to learn how their opportunities may be used for the greatest individual and social good.

Intolerance, self-interest, self-indulgence and indifference are attitudes and behaviors that are as old as the race. The first uses of freedom have often been the release of these undisciplined, primitive traits. Instead of bewailing conditions and berating mankind for its folly, our leaders in education and government and the arts must seek instruments for the encouragement and development of more significant and fruitful behavior.

Tolerance, unselfishness, self-discipline and altruism may be learned but they will not develop spontaneously. Freedom may open the door of opportunity, but intelligence and energy and resourcefulness on the part of our leaders are vitally necessary, if the desired characteristics are to result. The instruments and methods to be pursued are not difficult to find. But only the pioneer will discover them, and only the resourceful and the unselfish will utilize them.

Due to social inheritances, to successful teaching, to more or less chance contacts with other men and women, or to native endowment, some young men and young women in our colleges and high schools do exemplify the desired traits. A study of their practices of study and recreation and arguments would surely help us to promote like traits among all of our students. We need the active cooperation of the students whom we are met to honor to-day. They must help us plan for all students some such behavior patterns as their success indicates that they have learned.

Looking back a quarter century at my own high-school and college education, I remember with great vividness the night-long, earnest arguments that dealt with significant aspects of life. Questions of school and college politics and policies, questions of personal and social ethics, questions of religion and sex and economics and government were vigorously discussed. Frequently there was more of prejudice and heat than there was of enlightenment. But enlivenment must come to us all before enlightenment can take place. While extreme feeling and passion doubtless do interfere with intellectual contemplation, *one must care*—must feel a personal identification with a problem before he will bend his energies to contemplate it at all.

It was of relatively little importance whether we did or did not reach right conclusions regarding these questions. Indeed, it may be doubted whether any man has *right* answers for them. At the time, we probably stopped the argument without changing our convictions. Perhaps we were even more thoroughly "set" in our own opinions than before we began. But we were gaining tolerance, we were seeing that other people were honest and sincere, even though they disagreed with our own folk-opinions. And we were wholesomely disturbed that the arguments of our opponents were not always easy to answer. And we discovered that "authority" could be challenged without fear of the lightning.

The most effective and forward-looking experiment in the education of young adults is the Danish Folk High-School. Young men and young women of eighteen years or older come together to live in an environment of freedom and stimulation for a five-month period. They sing; they listen to lectures; they exercise and play; they respect their own judgments and find that their teachers respect them, too.

These young people are seeking answers to questions which have been asked by vigorous and eager minds throughout the ages. Says Hart:

> They want to know what meanings life has, if any—and if any one can tell them; they want light as to their own proper vocations in the world—if they are to have vocations; they want to know the meanings of the relentless sex-hungers that gnaw at their bodies and minds; they want to get some sense of their own relationships, or lack of relationships, to the age in which they live—and, maybe, to the ages; and for a short while at least, many of them are curious—and some are afraid—in the presence of the mystery of death. . . . As a matter of fact, these questions are mostly ignored in the years of ordinary schooling, and never answered; so that most adults carry about with them all their lives a wistfulness that has its roots in the unanswered questions of their youth. We feel that the most important task in all education is this of bringing to our young people such answers as the race has been able to find, such help as our most experienced men and women can offer. We have no fear that our young people will fail to learn. If they get wise answers to these crucial questions of their youth, they will spend their lives learning.

Dean Creager, when he was playing with me in New York, once outlined a most interesting plan for organizing the American liberal arts college on a similar basis. Something similar is actually working out at Wisconsin in the "experimental college" of which Professor Meiklejohn has charge. The tutorial plan in use at Harvard, especially the reading and study periods of several weeks preceding examinations when classes are dismissed, may permit students to educate themselves without undue interference from the professors.

If students care about attaining an objective or finding an answer to a question, they will learn. Opportunity, guidance and reward are all that are needed by such young people as we are honoring today. They form in groups comprised of earnest souls—they seek solutions for real problems. Has not the college problems enough to challenge them? If so, only encouragement and direction are needed.

At Dartmouth, five years ago or so, President Hopkins invited several serious upperclassmen to survey their own college and to report their findings and to propose improvements. Since then Harvard, Wesleyan and several other institutions have been studied by their student councils or by other groups—with the approval of the faculties. Many other institutions are under constant survey by their student bodies, too. But the faculties of some of them resent the inquiry; some expel all students who dare to think or question the adequacy and inspiration of their college requirements.

In such institutions, college loyalty is expressed by cheering the football team and subscribing for journals and meeting the expenses of the institution. But a higher loyalty to college and church and country is to question sympathetically the purpose, scope and methods of the institutions and to formulate plans for their improvement. An inquiring, skeptical, tolerant student body is the hope and the justification of a college. It is mere nonsense to assert that the college prepares students in philosophy and science, if they are not encouraged to inquire, examine, challenge and advance hypotheses regarding their classes and the institutions to which they belong.

It is because so many schools and colleges do veto initiative and skepticism that Shaw, Robinson, Sisson, William Allen White, Glenn Frank and others have doubted that education can ever aid in the advancement of civilization.

Colleges as traditional institutions do not inevitably contribute to progress. Schiller asserts that:

> No one familiar with the actual working of academic institutions is likely to fall into the error of pinning his faith to them. . . . All institutions are social mechanisms, and all mechanisms need a modicum of intelligent supervision in the absence of which they become dangerous engines of destruction.

If our colleges can see clearly what education for a twentieth-century world must be; if they can develop means for extending to all serious students the very opportunities that our most advanced colleges are furnishing for their serious students—then will the colleges safeguard and advance the democratic Christian world to which we belong.

There are over 700,000 students enrolled in our four years of college education. Tomorrow there will be a million and over. In one college generation, one per cent. of our entire population might be entering our general society with the confidence and purpose and tolerance and devotion that would grow out of such a college environment as we have sketched just now. What a leavening the lump would receive! What a future for mankind might thus be assured!

This is somewhat like the vision of Plato:

> No state, or constitution, or individual either, can ever become perfect, until these few philosophers . . . find themselves accidentally compelled . . . to accept the charge of a state, which in turn finds itself compelled to be obedient to them.

You earnest students may find yourselves compelled to take charge of your college, your churches, your cities, your clubs, your country—yes, perhaps, your worlds. These institutions may in the near future find themselves obliged to obey you. May you find yourselves ready, and know yourselves to be able to save our democracy, our Christianity, our civilization!

PHILIP W. L. COX
NEW YORK UNIVERSITY

EDUCATIONAL EVENTS

NEW ZEALAND PRIMARY SCHOOLS

THE report of the Syllabus Revision Committee set up by the New Zealand Minister of Education (the Hon. R. A. Wright), has been published by the New Zealand Government Printer, Wellington. According to an abstract in the London *Times Educational Supplement* the committee found that the present primary school syllabus was not fully suitable to present-day needs, and recommended that primary education should terminate at about the age of 12, when pupils should be transferred to post-primary schools. In the large cities it will be necessary to establish additional secondary schools to take pupils till the age of 15; in smaller towns where a high school exists pupils should go to that school. The schools should be of a single type in which there should be varied courses of instruction; and in rural areas there should be a consolidated school on the lines of district high schools. In isolated districts "tops" should be added, where possible, to existing primary schools.

Among other recommendations and resolutions passed by the committee are the following: More attention should be given to the education and the more rapid promotion of gifted pupils. The present unsatisfactory teaching of music, art and handwork, being due to the neglect of these subjects in the secondary schools, whence future teachers are drawn, intending candidates for probationships should be encouraged to pursue these subjects. Handwork should be given a more definite status Formal number-work should be abolished in the preparatory department, and a reduced amount of arithmetic should be required in the upper primary school. Increased attention should be given to the mother-tongue. Home-work in the form of set tasks should not be required from children up to 12 years of age, and only to a very limited extent up to 15. Children should be encouraged to take an active part at home in social amenities under the combined direction of parents and teachers.

With regard to post-primary education, it is recommended that attendance should be compulsory on all, irrespective of attainments, up to the age of 15. Each post-primary school should provide four courses of instruction—(*a*) an academic course; (*b*) a commercial or general course; (*c*) a handicrafts course; and (*d*) a course for those interested in domestic science and agriculture.

Administrative reforms suggested are that the Education Department should coordinate more closely all forms of education up to the university; that the control of all schools, primary and post-primary, in each district should be by one board, elected on a broad basis; that it is not in the best interests of education to have entirely different sets of inspectors for both primary and post-primary schools, and that opportunities be afforded officers of the Education Department for visiting centers of advanced educational thought. A minority report is appended, which embodies recommendations based on "investigations carried out in seeking a solution of the problem of an enrichment of the curriculum of the primary school to secure better articulation with the work of secondary and technical schools," by three members of the committee.

THE SELECTION OF CHILDREN FOR SCHOLARSHIPS IN ENGLAND

THE London correspondent of *The Christian Science Monitor* writes that educational circles in Great Britain have been greatly stirred of late by the unprecedented action taken by the Barnsley (Yorkshire) local education authority. In this town, as in most other places in England and Wales, an examination of children in the primary schools at the age of about 11-plus takes place for the purpose of selecting students of unusual ability, who are to be granted scholarships to the secondary schools. The authority has publicly expressed its disapproval of coaching children for these examinations, has reprimanded one of its head masters for coaching his pupils, and has determined to grant no scholarships to scholars in whose case it has been proved that coaching has taken place.

The reasons for this action are said to be twofold. One concerns the teachers and the other the pupils. It is not an unnatural consequence of the school examination system that individual teachers should aim at securing as many successes as possible for their own particular schools. They feel that many members of the authority and the public are noting the relative numbers of children from the various schools who achieve examination successes and they know that in applying for promotion either in their own town or elsewhere a long tale of scholarships is often a helpful and sometimes a decisive factor. Hence their concentration on the work for the examination, sometimes, it is alleged, at the expense of other work and of other pupils.

On the pupils the effect of coaching is to vitiate the impartiality of the examination. Instead of the most able pupils, instead even of the best educated pupils, being selected as the result of the examination, it is the most thoroughly prepared and the most intensively coached pupils who win through. In consequence, complaints are frequently heard from the secondary school teachers that the material they receive is not the best that could be found in the primary schools, and that many of these coached school winners, being artificially forced products, do not make good in their new environment.

The remedy that is being gradually indorsed and accepted by the authorities all over the country is that of a modified examination designed to discount special coaching. The examination is supplemented by intelligence tests; the candidates are subjected to an oral interview; their records and their back work in school are consulted, and every possible means is adopted of supporting or correcting the examination result. This out-maneuvering of coaching, it is contended, is a better method than merely to condemn coaching.

TENDENCIES IN COMMERCIAL TEACHER TRAINING

In the past two years there has been a general awakening regarding the importance of commercial teacher training. The leaders have urged that the key to the improvement of commercial education on a long-term basis is a better program for the training and certification of commercial teachers. The state departments of education and the larger universities have taken a greater interest in the preparation of commercial teachers. A number of investigations have been made to show the present status of commercial teacher training.

According to a bulletin issued by the Bureau of Education, recent developments in commercial education in the secondary schools have emphasized the urgent needs for improvements in teacher training to keep pace with and make possible further progress in the development of local programs. These needs have been particularly evident in the difficulty of obtaining teachers for the introduction of new courses, such as junior business training, clerical training, machine operating and retail selling.

A stimulating factor for the improvement of the commercial teacher-training program is the increased interest manifested by the larger colleges and universities. Some encouraging developments have been made at New York University, Harvard University, Columbia University, the University of Chicago, the University of Iowa, the University of Michigan and at many of the leading normal schools. Although the universities generally have been slow to provide for this need, many of them are interested in establishing four-year curricula, upon the completion of which recognized degrees may be obtained. Some universities recently entering this field have instituted programs of research. Concentration of commercial teacher training in the larger universities of the various states is a possibility.

A study of the comparative status of commercial and other teachers in selected counties in New Jersey showed that, "Two things at least seem inevitable in the educational preparation of commercial teachers: First, such teachers must be as well equipped as English, mathematics and science teachers, which means at least four-year college graduation; and second, the preparation of commercial teachers will tend more and more to take place in an educational center which has an acceptable college of arts and science, college of commerce and college of education, or equivalent facilities."

The emphasis on the vocational aspects of commercial education has developed a tendency toward requiring actual business experience of prospective commercial teachers. There is no doubt that such a requirement would be a large factor in the immediate improvement of preparation for business. No other single development could be more beneficial toward obtaining appropriate content, motivation in methods, appreciation of office standards and ultimate efficiency of the worker.

CHILD-HEALTH CONFERENCES

Nearly 6,000 more child-health conferences were conducted by physicians during the fiscal year 1927 than were held in the preceding year, according to figures made public by the Children's Bureau of the United States Department of Labor in its annual report of the administration of the maternity and infancy act.

Child-health conferences conducted by physicians at which children were examined and their mothers were given advice were a feature of the work in 36 of the 45 states cooperating under the act and in the Territory of Hawaii. There were 21,347 such conferences during the year, at which 136,813 infants and preschool children were examined. The number of such conferences in the fiscal year 1926 was 15,524.

Prenatal conferences conducted by physicians were included in the work of 22 states, the bureau reports. There were 3,231 such conferences, attended by 17,762 expectant mothers. Eleven states reported a total of 1,808 combined child-health and prenatal conferences conducted by physicians, at which 1,263 mothers and 27,382 infants and preschool children were examined. Over 34,000 children were inspected by nurses in 25 states in which health conferences were held with no physician present. There were 6,273 such conferences, usually held in connection with baby-weighing stations or in counties to which maternity and infancy nurses were assigned.

In all 200,223 infants and preschool children were examined by physicians, or advice as to their care was given by physicians or nurses in 43 states and the Territory of Hawaii, and in 34 states 27,377 women were given prenatal advice by physicians or nurses.

Conference work, the bureau points out, has been one of the main methods of teaching infant and child care and also prenatal care in the states cooperating under the maternity and infancy act. Through these conferences many parents have received for the first time important information on the care and hygiene of their children.

Some of the conferences are held regularly at permanent health centers. Others are itinerant conferences through which the community learns that the health conference is not a clinic for sick children, but an opportunity for mothers to learn how to keep their babies and themselves well by using intelligently available medical service and by improving the home care of themselves and their children.

Some of the states use trucks, known as healthmobiles or health cars, which carry motion pictures, exhibits, charts and posters in addition to the equipment for conference work, through the medium of which information on maternal, infant and child care may be carried to localities that are isolated and inaccessible for the more usual forms of health work.

No treatment or remedial work is done at any of these conferences. Parents whose children are found to have defects are advised to take them to the family physician.

SCHOOL SAVINGS BANKS

Savings banks are now installed in almost 14,000 schools in the United States, according to W. E. Albig, Deputy Manager of the American Bankers' Association in charge of the savings bank division.

As of June 30, there are reported 13,835 schools in which opportunity for school savings banking is offered. These schools are attended by 4,609,825 pupils, of whom 3,980,237 are participants in school savings banking, 1,687,602 each week. During the year these pupils deposited $26,005,138, received interest in the amount of $947,610 on these deposits, and at the end of the school year had net savings for the year of $9,476,391.

The year has witnessed a depression in the coal industry in several states where school savings banking is widely practiced. Unsatisfactory industrial conditions are always reflected in reports on school savings. It is to be hoped that bankers and boards of education which are financing school savings will insist that efforts to conserve school savings deposits shall be made at least equal to those in securing them in the first instance.

In the annual "honor roll" compiled in connection with the report, comprising places in which 75 per cent. or more of grammar school enrolment is participating in school savings banking, there are shown to be thirty-eight cities in which a full 100 per cent. of the attendance is taking part in the plan. These 100 per cent. cities are as follows: With grammar school enrolment over 10,000, Spokane, Wash., Hazelton, Pa.; enrolment 5,000 to 10,000, Hibbing, Minn.; 2,000 to 5,000, Pekin, Ill., Chicopee Falls, Mass.,

Iron Mountain, Mich., Auburn, N. Y., Duquesne, Pa., Luzerne, Pa., Plymouth, Pa.; under 2,000, Byron, Cal., Winsted, Conn., Belvidere, Earlville, Lake Forest and South Pekin, Ill., Warsaw, Ind, Moville, Iowa, Caspian and Stambaugh, Mich., Bloomingdale and Tenafly, N. J., Bainbridge, Catskill, Hartsdale, Hicksville, Port Jervis and Scarsdale, N. Y., Downingtown, Edgeworth, Manheim, Mayfield, Schuylkill Haven and Waymart, Pa., Mount Vernon, Wash., Wheeling, W. Va., Baraboo, Wis., Cudahy, Wis.

THE ENDOWMENT OF WOMEN'S COLLEGES

The annual report of Dr. Virginia C. Gildersleeve, dean of Barnard College, Columbia University, has been made public. Dr. Gildersleeve urges the desirability of obtaining a joint endowment of many millions for Barnard, Bryn Mawr, Mount Holyoke, Radcliffe, Smith, Vassar and Wellesley Colleges, stating that Barnard alone is in need of $1,000,000 to meet the problem of salaries, which is acute.

The seven colleges have a scheme for administering among themselves gifts that they may jointly receive. Their alliance is an "effort to make their services and needs better known to the world."

Dr. Gildersleeve writes:

The mere fact that we can cooperate instead of engaging in "cut-throat" competition, has already surprised and favorably impressed the community, and has attracted considerable attention to the whole problem of higher education of women.

The most pressing difficulty that the seven colleges face is how to pay adequate salaries to their professors, so that women students may be taught by scholars of as high quality as those that instruct their brothers. Additional endowment for increasing salaries is what we are appealing for definitely and vigorously.

Possibly no striking results will follow immediately, but we hope, in the long run, for some large donations and especially for bequests in wills. The crisis which has been threatening all seven colleges was suddenly thrust upon Barnard in an acute form this spring, when Columbia University adopted a new salary scale, making material increases in the salaries of all grades for full-time teachers.

If Barnard were to continue to maintain its scholarly standing on an equality with the rest of the university, and if the morale of our teaching staff were to be preserved, it was obviously essential for us to follow Columbia's example at once. The trustees met in May, courageously adopted the new schedule, and put it largely into effect for the next year.

This great step forward, placing our salaries on a scale which, so far as the writer knows, is higher than any ever before paid at a woman's college, will apparently cause a serious deficit.

One million dollars for endowment to increase salaries would solve this difficulty for us for the moment. From whom can we expect such a gift? What sort of donors will follow the example of our class of 1903 with its nest egg of $6,000 for this good purpose?

The problem of financing a college for women will probably always be more difficult than that of financing a college for men, because our graduates can contribute but little to our support. Women do not control, and perhaps never will control, much of the money of the world.

STATE CONVENTION OF NORMAL SCHOOL FACULTIES

The conference of New York State Normal School and Teachers College Faculties was held in Syracuse on October 11 and 12. The primary purpose of the third annual meeting was to carry on the work begun two years ago in revising the present curricula for the preparation of elementary teachers. Much progress has been made in the last two years and the work has developed to the point where tentative detailed outlines of separate courses should be in mimeograph form prior to the opening of school in September, 1929. These outlines will be used experimentally and it is hoped that some measures will be devised to find out the effectiveness of the materials and methods proposed.

Committees dealing with special subjects used the forenoon sessions in carrying on their respective committee discussions. The afternoon sessions were general in character. One speaker pleaded for the preparation of elementary teachers in terms of the work which will be required of them after graduation. Another urged that the teacher-training institutions should continuously experiment with the elementary program and that the graduates should be trained to teach in terms of what ought to be done in education rather than in terms of the present programs in public elementary education. Still another urged that training should be general and of cultural and disciplinary values. These three viewpoints deal with fundamental philosophies in teacher training and should stimulate throughout the state a great deal of discussion.

A special feature of the third annual meeting was the organization and management of the work in each of the ten schools on October 11 by the students. We have not heard of any state in which the work has been carried on in all of the teacher-training institutions by the students in the absence of the faculties. This arrangement resulted in worthwhile educational values for the students. It afforded them an excellent opportunity to assume heavy responsibilities, to exercise their powers of initiative and to meet unusual problems resourcefully.

Nearly 400 of the faculty members were present. This represents 88 per cent. of the total faculty membership. Three of the normal schools had 100 per cent. attendance. This splendid record of attendance from all the institutions is a clear expression of the professional interest of our normal schools and teachers colleges, especially in view of the fact that each member attending pays his own expenses.

THE CHILDREN'S FAIR AT THE AMERICAN MUSEUM OF NATURAL HISTORY

THE first annual Children's Fair was opened on October 18 at the American Museum of Natural History. The exhibits were arranged by the School Nature League and were drawn from the work of the public-school children in this and outside institutions. One of the sponsors of the fair was the American Institute.

The opening exercises were held in the hall of the museum. Felix M. Warburg presided. The speakers were Judge Oscar W. Ehrhorn, Commissioner Berne A. Pyrke, Dr. Gustave Straubenmuller and Dr. John L. Tildsley.

Thousands of school children visited the exhibits during the three days. More than 600 exhibits were entered. Of these eleven were group displays by schools, parks, camps and other kindred organizations. The individual exhibits were divided into six major classes: city gardens, nature study note-books and records, conservation, insects, home-made animal cages, biological principles, plaster cast and miscellaneous. The biological principles group, which was one of the most interesting of the exhibition, showed the evolution, adaptation and the protective coloring of animals. The importance of snakes, field mice and birds to the crops was shown graphically.

The bulk of entries were under Class B, the nature note-books and records. Of interest was the special display by the Newtown High School, the city's only agricultural high school. It included chickens, a swarm of bees and a model of the best types of farms, farm implements and farm buildings.

Individual exhibitors ranged in age from six to eighteen years. All the exhibits were the work of the children, both in design and execution. Among the organizations represented were the Boy Scouts, the Girl Scouts, the Campfire Girls, the West Side Y. M. C. A., the Northrop Memorial Camp, the Brooklyn Botanic Gardens, the Palisades Interstate Park Commission, the Brooklyn Children's Museum, the School Garden Association, the New York City Department of Parks, the Boy Scout Foundation of New York, the New York Plant, Flower and Fruit Guild, the Betsy Head Play Gardens and the McCarren Park School Farm.

Prizes were awarded for the best exhibits by organizations.

Besides the displays, the American Institute provided a daily program of educational entertainment for the young guests of the exposition. Among the lecturers was Paul B. Mann, head of the Department of Biology of Evander Childs High School, who spoke on the conservation of wild animals, the lecture being accompanied by moving pictures; Dr. E. Laurence Palmer, of Cornell University, gave a similar lecture. Ray Waldo Miner, curator of marine life at the museum, spoke on seashore life and Dr. George H. Sherwood, director of the museum, on the subject of trees, illustrated by moving pictures.

THE CONFERRING OF THE CONGRESSIONAL MEDAL ON MR. EDISON

MR. THOMAS A. EDISON, whose inventions have altered not only the material equipment of our schools, but also the education and occupations of all their students, received on October 20 the medal conferred on him by act of the Congress, in recognition of his services to mankind in "illuminating the path of progress through the development and application of inventions that have revolutionized civilization in the last century."

The quotation is from the congressional resolution authorizing the medal, and was repeated in the address of Andrew W. Mellon, secretary of the treasury, who made the presentation speech in the Menlo Park laboratory.

President Coolidge, speaking over the radio from Washington, sent his congratulations and the good wishes of a grateful people through a national network of forty-eight stations and by short-wave signals to foreign stations, thus giving world-wide expression to the American government's tribute. Ending his fifteen-minute address, in which he lauded the notable accomplishments of the inventor, Mr. Coolidge said: "Noble, kindly servant of the United States and benefactor of mankind, may you long be spared to continue your work and to inspire those who will carry forward your torch."

After the medal had been bestowed, Ronald Ian Campbell, of the British Embassy at Washington, acting for Sir Esmé Howard, returned the first phonograph to Mr. Edison and conveyed the greetings of his fellow countrymen on the occasion of the presentation of the congressional medal. The last address was made by Dr. John Grier Hibben, president of Princeton University.

EDUCATIONAL NOTES AND NEWS

Dr. Payson Smith, commissioner of education for the State of Massachusetts, has declined the offer of the U. S. Commissionership of Education, in succession to Dr. J. J. Tigert.

Dr. Ezra T. Franklin, president of Union College, Barbourville, Kentucky, has accepted the presidency of Southwestern College, Winfield, Kansas, to succeed Dr. Albert E. Kirk, who resigned to become head of the division of educational institutions of the Board of Education of the Methodist Episcopal Church. Dr. Franklin will take over his new work on November 10.

A tea in honor of Dr. Charles F. Thwing, president emeritus of Western Reserve University, and Mrs. Thwing, was given by the Iota chapter of Phi Beta Kappa at Radcliffe College on October 22. Dr. Thwing has been president of the United Chapters of Phi Beta Kappa. Among other guests were President Ada L. Comstock, Dean Bernice V. Brown, Dr. Fannie Fern Andrews and members of Phi Beta Kappa doing graduate work.

A dinner was given in honor of Y. C. James Yen at the Hotel Plaza, New York City, on October 23, by the American Committee of the Chinese Mass Education Association. Mr. Yen has been lecturing in this country since his arrival last spring, when he came to receive an honorary degree from Yale University.

Herbert Hoover was reelected president of the American Child Health Association at its recent joint convention with the American Public Health Association at Chicago.

Dr. Aurelia Henry Reinhardt, president of Mills College, has been appointed chairman of the department of education of the General Federation of Women's Clubs.

The Massachusetts State Normal School Teachers Association has elected Miss M. Harriet Bishop president for the ensuing year. Miss Bishop, who comes from Worcester, succeeds Dr. Edwin A. Kirkpatrick, of Fitchburg.

Dr. John A. Ceconi, director of hygiene in the Boston public schools, has been elected president of the National Association of School Physicians, a subsidiary organization of the American Public Health Association.

L. M. Hurdka succeeds Dr. J. A. Williams as head of the department of education of the State Agricultural College, Brookings, South Dakota. He has been doing graduate work in the school of education of the University of Wisconsin, and was previously a teacher in the State Teachers College, Bowling Green, Kentucky.

Arthur D. Whitman has been promoted from assistant professor of education to associate professor of education and supervisor of student teaching at New York University.

New appointments at the University of Chicago include Thomas Griffith Taylor, now head of the department of geography in the University of Sydney, Australia, as professor in the department of geography; William N. Randall as associate professor of library science in the Graduate Library School, and Dr. William Robinson, assistant professor in the department of pathology, under the Otho S. A. Sprague Memorial Institute.

At the University of Nebraska, Dr. D. A. Worcester has been advanced from associate professor to professor of educational psychology and measurements.

Glenn U. Cleeton, associate professor of education and psychology at the Carnegie Institute of Technology at Pittsburgh, has been promoted to become head of the department of industrial education. Laurance F. Shaffer, research associate, Lincoln School, New York, has been appointed assistant professor in the department of education and psychology.

Dr. C. F. Malmberg, associate professor of philosophy at Gettysburg College for the past two years, has accepted the professorship of psychology at the Illinois State Teachers College at Bloomington.

Herschel W. Arant has resigned as dean of the University of Kansas Law School to become dean of the Law School of the Ohio State University at Columbus.

Robert Elden Mathews, of the Ohio State University, is the visiting professor of law at Columbia University this year.

Elmer J. Emig has been appointed professor and head of the department of journalism at the University of Florida.

Professor Harvey L. Lutz, formerly of Stanford University, has been appointed professor of public finance at Princeton University.

Dr. Roy M. Lockenour, until recently assistant professor of political science at Oregon State College, has accepted appointment as professor of law at Willamette University, Salem, Oregon.

C. R. Atkinson has resigned from the faculty of the University of Washington to accept a position as head of the department of business administration at Hillsdale College, Michigan.

Langley C. Keyes has been appointed an assistant dean of Harvard College. He takes the place of Robert E. Bacon, who has resigned to accept an appointment as assistant professor of English at St. John's College, Annapolis, Maryland.

G. Stanley Meikle, who has been connected with the General Electric and other companies, has been appointed director of research relations with industry at Purdue University. He will represent the university as a whole and act as liaison officer between the university and industry with the object of making the university more useful to industry and industry more useful to the university. The first industrial fellowship in the School of Science has been established by the Indiana Refining Company in the department of chemistry.

Robert P. Crawford, professor of agricultural journalism and for several years a writer on finance for leading magazines, has been made assistant to the chancellor of the University of Nebraska.

Additions to the faculty of Birmingham-Southern College for the year 1928–29 include: K. E. Barnhart, Ph.D. (Chicago), professor of sociology; Leon F. Sensabaugh, Jr., Ph.D. (Johns Hopkins), assistant professor of American history; C. H. Karraker, Ph.D. (Pennsylvania), associate professor of English history; Antony Constans, Ph.D. (Harvard), professor of Romance languages; J. B. Berry, University of Edinburgh, professor of Bible and religious education; E. V. Jones, from the University of Chicago, professor of chemistry.

On receiving word of the election at San Antonio of Dean Paul V. McNutt, of the Indiana University Law School, as national commander of the American Legion for 1928–29, Secretary J. W. Crabtree sent the following telegram of congratulation. "Your election as national commander of the American Legion is the source of great satisfaction to members of the teaching profession in the United States. The American Legion in cooperation with the National Education Association has rendered service of great value to education by initiating American Education Week and by promoting its observance each year. The association pledges you continued cooperation and predicts that your administration will be the most outstanding in the history of the American Legion."

HUBERT S. UPJOHN, for a number of years deputy superintendent of the Los Angeles county schools, was appointed acting superintendent by the board of supervisors shortly after the death of Superintendent Mark Keppel.

IRA W. KIBBY has been appointed chief of the bureau of business education of the State of California.

O. S. HUBBARD, formerly assistant superintendent of Fresno city schools, has been made superintendent, succeeding Walter R. Hepner, who has gone to the superintendency of San Diego City. Mr. W. B. Munson has become assistant superintendent.

E. W. IRELAND has been elected superintendent of schools at Somerville, Mass., at an annual salary of $5,500.

WE learn from *The Journal of Education* that Olga A. Jones, of Columbus, Ohio, is to be editor and publisher of *The Ohio Teacher*, which was owned and edited for many years by the late Dr. Henry G. Williams. Miss Nellie B. Scott, who has been the office manager of the *Monthly*, will be associated with Miss Jones in the work.

LEAVE of absence from the Philippine schools among the Bureau of Education officials includes Governor Carl M. Moore, of Sulu, who was at the same time division superintendent of schools; Mr. John H. Manning Butler, superintendent of schools for the Division of Cagayan and Isabela, and Mr. Sylvester C. Kelleher, former superintendent, Central Luzon Agricultural School, Muñoz, Neuva Ecija.

FREDERICK H. MEYER, director of the California School of Arts and Crafts, attended the Sixth International Art Congress held in Prague, Czecho-Slovakia. Mr. Meyer has been traveling in the eastern United States and in Europe, visiting the leading art schools and galleries.

PROFESSOR PAUL L. DENGLER, of Vienna, director of the Austro-American Institute of Education, gave a lecture on "The Spirit of the New Education in Austria" at Harvard University on October 17.

ROLLO G. REYNOLDS, principal of the Horace Mann School, New York, spoke at the opening of the seventy-fifth annual convention of the New Hampshire Teachers Association on October 19. The 1,500 teachers attending were welcomed by Hobart Pillsbury, secretary of state, on behalf of the state of New Hampshire.

MERTON C. LEONARD, retired vice-principal of the Dickinson High School, Jersey City, N. J., died on October 21, at the age of sixty-nine years. He was connected with the schools of Jersey City for twenty-one years.

AT the recent convocation of the University of the State of New York a monument to Joseph Henry was dedicated in the park before the Albany Academy, where, as a teacher, Henry made his experiments leading to the discovery of the electromagnet and eventually to the telegraph and telephone. Dr. John H. Finley, of the New York *Times*, former state commissioner of education, made the dedication speech, calling attention to the event as the culmination of an effort of twenty-five years to do honor to the great man whose statue will now stand within a few feet of the same building in which he made his notable scientific experiments.

IN commemoration of fifty years of kindergartens in Boston, 300 teachers and guests recently met at dinner in the Copley-Plaza Hotel, under the auspices of the Boston Kindergarten Association. Among the speakers were Joseph Lee, known as "The Father of American Playgrounds"; William C. Crawford, president of the Boston City Club; J. Mace Andress, of Boston University; Wallace C. Boyden, principal of the Boston Teachers' College; Miss Charlotte

Rafter and Miss Gertrude E. Bigelow. Mrs. Hetty B. Schriftgiesser, president of the Boston Kindergarten Association, presided, and Miss Caroline D. Aborn, director of kindergartens in the Boston schools, acted as toastmistress.

THE cornerstone of Curtis Hall, the engineering building of the Drexel Institute, Philadelphia, was laid on October 8 by Mr. Cyrus H. K. Curtis, who gave $600,000 to the institute for the construction of the building.

FORMAL opening of the new Graduate Library School at the University of Chicago took place with the assembling of the first class for a course in "The Origin of the Printed Book." Created by the Carnegie Foundation by a one million dollar gift to the university, the school is unique in being the only purely graduate library school in the nation. Only students who have already graduated from college with the bachelor's degree, and who have had experience in library work, are admitted for this advanced training toward the master's degree or the doctorate. The chief method of the school will be individualized research in the problems of library science and theory. Professor George Alan Works, formerly of Cornell University, is dean. New importance attributed to the library in the modern university is also indicated by changes at the University of Chicago this year. Budget appropriations for the libraries of the university amount to $380,000, as against $175,000 ten years ago. Dr. Llewellyn Raney, recently head of the Johns Hopkins University Library, is reorganizing the book distributing system, as director of libraries. The guiding principle of the new administration is that the chief function of the library is to assist and stimulate research, which involves concentration of materials at the worker's elbow. Extreme decentralization in departmental libraries and extreme concentration will be avoided. Underground stacks will eventually be abolished, except for storage.

THE endowment fund of two million dollars to be used for the increase of salaries of the faculty of Princeton University now amounts to $1,700,000, lacking only $300,000 for completion.

MR. AND MRS. GEORGE BLUMENTHAL, of New York City, have made a gift of $1,000,000 to the Metropolitan Museum of Art. The interest will be allowed to accumulate until after the death of both donors, whereupon both principal and interest must be used to buy works of art. Mr. Blumenthal is chairman of the finance committee of the museum and has made large contributions to it.

THE sum of $1,000 a year for four years has been presented to Oberlin College by James H. Causey, of Denver, Colo., for the purpose of bringing to Oberlin speakers for "lectures and conferences on important phases of international and social relations."

THE Institute of International Education announces that it has received an anonymous gift of $3,500 to be used as a prize for the teacher in a Japanese institution who writes the best essay on "The Ideals and Institutions of the American People." The prize essay will be chosen by a committee consisting of Dr. John Bassett Moore, Professor Paul Monroe, Professor James T. Shotwell, Professor William Kilpatrick and Dr. Stephen P. Duggan, director of the institute.

AT a recent meeting of the California State Board of Education the acceptance of a new site for the San Diego State Teachers College, was reported donated by the Bell-Lloyd Investment Company, consisting of 125 acres of land, together with a cash donation from the company and from Mr. Bell personally, amounting to $50,000, and the passage of a bond issue by the electors of San Diego authorizing the city schools to purchase the college for $325,000. The board directed the secretary to express its appreciation to the Bell-Lloyd Investment Company and to Mr. Bell personally; and appointed a committee of five to cooperate in developing the plans for the San Diego State Teachers College.

The Education Bulletin reports that forty-acre tracts of land near schools in three communities in Forest County, Wis., have been donated to the schools by local citizens. They become the property of the schools to which they are deeded, and will serve as laboratories for nature study. Under the supervision of extension foresters of the state university, trees will be planted by pupils of the schools at the rate of a few acres a year. Instruction will be given in thinning operations, the reduction of fire hazards, and other principles of forest management; and steps will be taken for the propagation of game and bird life. Similar projects are planned for other counties in Wisconsin.

THE Social Science Research Council invites applications before December for research fellowships in anthropology, history, sociology, economics, political science, statistics, psychology and allied fields such as law and human geography. The fellowships are open to men and women, citizens of the United States or Canada, who possess the Ph.D. degree and are not over thirty-five years of age. The stipends vary according to the amount of travel necessary and the requirements of the fellow. The choice of place to work is left to the fellow, subject to the approval of the fellowship committee. In general, appointments are for one year, during which no other remunerative work may be carried on. Mature scholars seeking aid for well-planned research projects should apply to the committee on grants-in-aid of the Social Science Research Council. For further information and application blanks, address John V. Van Sickle, fellowship secretary, Social Science Research Council, 50 East Forty-Second Street, New York City.

THE School of Education of the University of Texas has received an allowance from the Laura Spelman Rockefeller Memorial Fund for Research in the Social Sciences for a study of the education of Mexican children in Texas. The plan approved for the immediate future includes three major items: (1) A summary of previous studies relating to the problem under investigation; (2) a survey of present conditions with reference to legal provisions, school census, enrolment, attendance, health conditions, administrative plans, curricular adjustments and the like; (3) miscellaneous studies to be carried forward by interested persons—supervisors, teachers, candidates for degrees and others—with the cooperation of the director. The project is under the direction of a committee of which Dean B. F. Pittenger is chairman. Professor H. T. Manuel, of the department of educational psychology, is in immediate charge of the research and has been granted a partial release from teaching.

ST. STEPHEN'S COLLEGE, integrated last June with Columbia University, began its sixty-ninth year on September 24 and its first as a part of Columbia. The session was opened with a service in the chapel, at which Dr. Bernard Iddings Bell, warden of the college, delivered an address on "The Larger Agnosticism." Dr. Nicholas Murray Butler, president of Columbia University, greeted the students with a message.

THE French Ministry of Public Instruction has announced through the Institute of International Education the appointment of seven graduates of American colleges to positions in French lycées and écoles normales, for the academic year 1928–29. Five will occupy postes d'assistant d'Anglais in lycées and two postes de répétiteur d'Anglais in écoles normales. The assistants d'Anglais and the lycées in which they will teach are as follows: Franklin K. Guthrie, graduate of Ohio State University, in the Lycée at Roanne; H. H. Thomas, graduate of Trinity College, at the Lycée at Bourges; Robert C. Taliaferro, graduate of the University of Virginia, in the Lycée at Rochefort; Edward Philip Moreland, graduate of Stanford University and of the University of California, in the Lycée at Versailles; Edward D. Warren, graduate of Miami University, who also studied in France at the University of Aix-en-Provence and at the Sorbonne, in the Lycée Poitiers at Orleans. The répétiteurs d'Anglais and the écoles normales in which they will teach are as follows: David T. Row, graduate of the University of Wisconsin, in the École Normale at Gueret; Delbert L. Gibson, graduate of the University of Wisconsin, in the École Normale at Limoges.

The Christian Science Monitor reports that interest was lent to the final meeting of the fifty-second session of the Council of the League of Nations by intervention of Raoul Dandurand, the Canadian delegate, in a dispute which broke out between Herr Schubert, Germany, and Mr.

Sokal, Poland, concerning the closing of some of the German minority schools in upper Silesia. Mr. Dandurand pointed out that in Canada separate schools were granted for 10 children if demanded, whereas in Polish Upper Silesia 30 to 40 German children were required for a minority school. The council, after adopting the suggestion of its president, Mr. Procope, that two jurists should be appointed to assist Mr. Adachi in determining the legal aspects of the dispute, adjourned further discussion of the subject until December. In the meantime the president of the mixed court, appointed to settle such conflicts, will do his best to bring the parties together.

We learn from *Nature* that the International Federation of Intellectual Unions announced a fifth congress was held in Prague on October 1, 2 and 3. Lectures and discussions centered round the theme "The Elements of Modern Civilization." The speakers included A. Fontaine, of the Bureau International de Travail, Geneva; the architect le Corbusier, the psychoanalyst Jung and the sociologist de Man. The first congress was at Paris under the presidency of Borel; since then the federation has met in Milan, Vienna, Heidelberg and Frankfurt. As now organized, the federation is based on unions in Germany, Austria, Belgium, Spain, Esthonia, France, Hungary, Italy, Poland, Roumania and Czecho-Slovakia. It is officially registered with the International Institute of Intellectual Cooperation in Paris. The objects of the federation include the fostering of personal relationships among the "intelligenza" of Europe by opening correspondence with distinguished foreigners, by personal introductions and by hospitality to strangers, especially those on professional errands.

SPECIAL CORRESPONDENCE

METHODS AND REWARDS OF THE CORRECT SELECTION OF COLLEGE FRESHMEN

Introductory

One charge against present-day education is that we are acquiring so much pedagogy that we are forgetting how to teach. However that may be, thanks to the advent of psychometrics, American colleges are learning to *select* students—the first essential step towards educating them. The illusion that professors can "educate" students needs to be replaced by the truth that professors only furnish an opportunity for the student to become educated. If this is true, then naturally, the first task is to eliminate the candidates in whose cases self-education is impossible. Thus, the old system of admitting students to college on the basis of high-school certificates is supplemented in progressive colleges by entrance examinations and psychological tests.

That entrance examinations, whether they be tests of mental capacity or content examinations, *are* highly selective of the best material is manifest from the fact that they result in the elimination of many applicants for admission whose high-school preparation and grades seem satisfactory, and from the further fact that after freshmen have been selected by the use of such tests the appalling number of college failures has been reduced to a minimum. The financial losses due to poor selection in the past are serious enough. Lewis Terman[1] cites the instance of one college with about 2,500 students, which spends one sixth of its annual income on students who are on probation for poor scholarship. Actual tests indicated that the grade of intelligence of about 80 per cent. of these failing students was so low as to make their failure a practical certainty. More sweeping is the evidence given by the U. S. Commissioner of Education, to the effect that 66 per cent. of the applicants who entered college by certificate failed to complete the college course. On the contrary, the figures for Yale, which uses entrance examinations, show a corresponding loss of only 12 per cent. in the year 1927. Even during the period of the war, Yale's loss of students between the freshman and senior years (inclusively) was only 16 per cent.[2] The rate of loss at Wells College is much less than this.

[1] Terman, Lewis, Introduction to Ben Wood's "Measurement in Higher Education," 1923, p. 5.

[2] Corwin, R. N., "Admission to Yale," *The Yale Alumni Weekly*, p. 832.

The Selection of Freshmen at Wells College

We regard the quality of our own student body at Wells as convincing evidence of what a careful program of admissions can do. We wish to offer a brief account of the fact of superior selection at Wells; and, following this, the proof that this superior quality of our students is due to our plan of entrance examinations. It must be noted that an entrance examination is in fact a double instrument. To be sure, it selects students with superior preparation; but incidentally these examinations specify what the high-school preparation must be. But here lies the root of an ever-increasing difficulty: Colleges multiply, and in order to secure students must lower their entrance requirements. In short, whereas formerly higher education determined what secondary education should be, these rôles are now in process of reversal. Accordingly, the following data about Wells College are presented as a plea for our right to select, a right which the practices of larger colleges are compelling us to abandon.

There is, of course, an ethical issue involved, which the need for brevity forces us to shirk. There is, for instance, the thesis that the democracy of education is the root of the democracy of the state, hence, American education should be the education of the masses. But even "masses" vary from inferior to superior material. Plato in a mood of irony declared that a democracy is the best form of the state because it can do the least harm. Naturally, its incapacity for "doing good" would also follow from the same cause of its incapacity to do harm, *i.e.,* its incapacity to do anything beyond the mediocre. But Plato describes sovietism, where the confessed ideal is to allow no one to go beyond what the average person can do. A true democracy, on the contrary, requires more rather than less individual superiority, which is the strength of monarchies. Ideally, a democracy should be maintained "at the cost of the eternal watchfulness of every citizen": actually, since men are but human, democracy is maintained by the eternal and *capable* watchfulness of the few.

As direct evidence of the superiority of our group of students we will cite the attainments of our applicants in certain entrance tests. First, the reports of the National Council of Education "Cooperative Intelligence Test," published yearly in the *Educational Record,* show a consistent superiority of our students. This test, of which a new edition is published each year by a committee under the able chairmanship of L. L. Thurstone, is now given in over 160 colleges every year. Our applicants for admission in 1925 earned an average score of 537 points, while the general average score for all colleges was 500 points.[3] These averages are derived from about 16,000 cases. The Wells applicants earned an average percentile rank of 59.6, as compared with the percentile rank of 50, which is always the general average. Our applicants in 1926 were superior to the general average (of over 5,000 cases) of all schools by 25 percentile points.[4] Our last group of applicants (September, 1927) was superior to the general average (over 16,500 cases) by 43 percentile points. In fact, the Wells group led the list of colleges so far published on all tests but one, the "arithmetic test," in which Wells was exceeded by the applicants to the University of Chicago. In fact, this constant and marked superiority of our applicants suggested to us the possibility of error in the scoring of tests. However, the rescoring of sample cases reveals no errors. In all three years, tests were administered with two time-keepers, to avoid any fatal error of allowing too much time. To be sure, the superiority of the Wells group is the most marked in the case of the "artificial language test"; but there is consistent superiority to the general average on all tests.

In order to verify these findings of the National Council of Education test, we wish to cite our results with the College Entrance Board Scholastic Aptitude Tests. The number of applicants to which this test is given has grown from 1,344 cases in 1926 to 7,350 in June, 1927.[5]

The average score earned by the applicants to all colleges taking this test in 1926 and 1927 was

[3] Thurstone, L. L. *Educational Record,* April, 1926, pp. 120–126.

[4] Thurstone, L. L. *Educational Record,* April, 1927, pp. 157–161.

[5] We are indebted to Carl C. Brigham, chairman of the College Entrance Examination Board, for these data.

500 points. But the average score for the applicants to Wells College was 533 points in 1926 and 553 points in 1927. This result confirms the National Council of Education tests without a single discrepancy.

However, we face the question, are these tests, both the National Council of Education and the Scholastic Aptitude Tests, diagnostic of excellent college material? To be satisfied on this point, one needs to review the tests of reliability and diagnostic power to which these tests have been repeatedly subjected. The *r* (correlation) obtained between the National Council of Education tests and freshman grades is sometimes as low as +.24, but quite often as high as +.60.[6] These *r*'s may be low enough, but the question is, have we any other index which is a better basis for predicting what prospective students will do with college courses? Bucknell College, the University of Missouri, Transylvania College, the University of Virginia, Wells College and others find that this test is more diagnostic of what students will do in college courses than their entire four years of high school or other preparatory study. The corresponding study of the Scholastic Aptitude Tests[7] shows that, in general, high-school averages are a somewhat better index of the quality of college work than are the scores on this test; but in mitigation of this result, it must be said that the *r*'s between the College Entrance Board tests and college grades were made after selection: The *r*'s would have been much higher if all applicants had been admitted to college.

Lewis Terman[8] declares that the Thorndike intelligence tests have given *r*'s of +.70 with college success as compared with an *r* of only +.45 between four years of high-school marks and college success. "Time and again it has been shown that the scores on a single intelligence examination enable us to predict college success as accurately as we can predict it from four years of high-school marks."

The best policy, however, is not to admit students on the basis of tests alone, but to employ both criteria: we lament the tendency to abandon either the one or the other. It is a well-known fact that the reliability of any set of tests varies with its extensiveness,[9] and the need of measuring the reliability of tests is gaining universal recognition.

The Causes of Superior Average in Wells Freshmen

If Wells students are markedly above average on tests whose reliability is widely acknowledged, we may proceed on the assumption that these superior scores indicate a real superiority. To what shall it be attributed?

There is the factor of age. The average age of our 1927 freshmen was 18 years and one month. This is about the average age for women college students. Women matriculants in the Middle States average 18.19 years, which is less than the 18.4 of Southern States. Our freshmen are probably slightly younger than most college freshmen. It is an interesting fact, however, that younger applicants earn somewhat higher scores on the College Entrance Examinations. This tendency is more marked with women than it is with men.[10]

Geographically, our students do not show any unusual type of selection. Our entire student body for the year 1927–28 was distributed as follows: 46 per cent. came from New York State, and 11 per cent. from each of the two states, New Jersey and Ohio. The remaining groups, all smaller, came from 18 other states.

We are inclined to attribute the selected character of our group to our use of entrance tests; especially the severely selective character of the "Comprehensive Examinations," which we give, together with the Scholastic Aptitude Tests and the National Council of Education Intelligence Test, in our "new plan" of admission, instituted some ten years ago. The comprehensive examinations consist of four fundamental examinations as follows:

Four units of Latin,
Three units of Mathematics,
Three units of English, and
Two units of a modern language or Greek.

6 *Educational Record*, April, 1927, pp. 9–27.

7 "Second Annual Report of the Commission on Scholastic Aptitude Tests," 1927, p. 27.

8 Terman, Lewis, *op. cit.*, p. 4.

9 See Freeman's "Mental Tests," 1926, p. 256ff.

10 "Report of Scholastic Aptitude Tests," 1927, p. 20.

About the same time that this plan was instituted, Yale University adopted an almost identical entrance plan; but Wells alone seems never to have modified this plan. The four women's colleges, Vassar, Wellesley, Smith and Mt. Holyoke, united to form a new entrance plan, in which examinations were given in English or history, mathematics or science, foreign language, and a test in some optional subject. The essential defect of this plan consists in the fact that students could matriculate without examinations in English, Latin, or mathematics. All four of these colleges reduced their requirements of Latin, Vassar eliminating this requirement entirely. Bryn Mawr and Wells alone require the four units (years) of Latin. Yale, at present, requires four units of Latin of students who seek the B.A. degree, but two other degrees (B.Sc. and Ph.B.) can be secured without Latin at all. A new plan of admissions, "Plan B," examines the candidates, in one session, on "English, and three other subjects covering the work of the senior year only."[11] Dartmouth College does not give entrance examinations of any kind.[12]

Yet a committee appointed by the American Association of University Professors recently made a thorough survey of the whole subject of college entrance.[13] The result of this enquiry was the recommendation of the very battery of comprehensive tests which Wells College (apparently unknown to this committee) *has been requiring of some applicants for admission.* That the advice of this committee was sound is indicated by the following facts. We find that the students who entered Wells College in 1926 by means of the four comprehensive examinations earned an average percentile of 62 in the intelligence test, while those taking the ordinary examinations of the College Entrance Board and the tests of the regents of the State of New York earned an average intelligence percentile of only 55. But, in terms of average raw score, these figures are reversed: the comprehensive tests yielding an average of only 62 points, compared with an average score of 82 earned by those who took the ordinary examinations! This of course means that a high score on the comprehensive examinations is difficult to earn; a fact which is in complete harmony with the higher r between the scores on the comprehensive examination and the scores of the intelligence test.

Terman states that, generally speaking, students who major in Latin, philosophy, law or mathematics rank higher in intelligence than students who elect applied subjects, such as agriculture, dentistry, art, music, etc.[14]

But, the feeble defenses of the colleges against the whimsies of high-school curricula grow ever feebler. About a generation ago, says Corwin,[15] the high schools threw off what they regarded as the "college yoke." In their allegiance to the "public," they have equipped themselves with a bewildering array of "subjects" in which the old classics are lost in a vegetative proliferation of courses in "home nursing," "current events," "advanced foods," "elementary clothing," "window display," etc. The competition amongst colleges is leading to an abandonment of old entrance requirements. As a consequence, we are in a welter of "old" and "new" plans of admission, which excited President Dwight, of Yale, to offer to admit any applicant who could prove that he understood the Yale plan of admissions! It is evident that Wells College can not, when left alone, withstand the tendency to convert the struggle for "the survival of the fittest" into a struggle for "survival at all costs!"

C. Oliver Weber

Wells College

[11] *Bulletin,* "Terms of Admission," 1928–29.

[12] *Bulletin,* "The Selective Process for Admission," 1926–27, p. 16.

[13] *Bulletin of The American Association of University Professors,* Volume XII, Whole of Number 6, October, 1926.

[14] Terman, Lewis, *op. cit.,* p. 7.

[15] Corwin, R. N., *op. cit.,* p. 831.

DISCUSSION

THE JUNIOR COLLEGE AND THE "SCHOLARLY AMATEUR"

"The junior college, if generally established, will tend to extirpate the 'scholarly amateur' in American life." This statement expresses substantially the opinion voiced by the venerable Professor George Herbert Palmer in recent numbers of the *Atlantic Monthly*. With deference to the great age and magnificent services of Professor Palmer, there are those who see reasons for predicting a far different outcome of the rapid growth of the junior college movement. The assumption that the general establishment of the junior college will sound the knell of the standard American four-year liberal arts college, an institution to which we owe so much that we rightfully treasure it and regard it with peculiar affection and pride, seems not to be justified.

That the junior college movement does not mean the extinction of the standard four-year liberal arts college, but instead actually is the harbinger of a more fortunate situation than that revered institution has thus far known, becomes apparent upon examination of the facts. Four reasons in support of this conclusion are here outlined:

First, the long-established, well-endowed, liberally supported four-year colleges have so unshakable a hold upon the affections of their thousands of alumni and former students, a history so honorable and such great prestige in the eyes of the public in general that they could confidently expect to continue to prosper for generations, even though the junior college movement was assumed to be unalterably inimical to their interests.

Second, there is an increasing tendency for the professions of law, medicine, the ministry and education and business in their higher ranges to regard at least four years of liberal arts study as desirable or even prerequisite for entrance upon purely professional study.

Third, the level of general prosperity in America is so high that there will probably continue to be a substantial number of people who can afford four years of liberal arts study and who will secure it at four-year colleges of their preference, irrespective of whether or not it is regarded as necessary preparation for a profession.

Fourth, the four-year liberal arts colleges, with the exception only of the well-established colleges for women in the eastern states, now labor under a situation which makes it difficult for them to maintain desired standards of work, on account of the preponderance of underclassmen in their total enrolment. From this situation the junior college movement will certainly operate to relieve them to some extent. The typical four-year college now has from 60 to 75 per cent. of its students in the two lower classes, a fact which compels it to expend the bulk of its available resources in giving training which is admittedly secondary rather than advanced in character. Many of the horde of freshmen and sophomores are eliminated as failures, many are drawn off to the professional and semi-professional schools and many leave the institution for financial and other reasons, leaving a mere fraction of their number to continue in the four-year course. Under such circumstances it would be idle to presume that the senior college work can be done as well as it would be done if a larger proportion of the resources of the institution could be devoted to it. Now, if the junior college will care for the many students who do not have the ability, be it mental, financial or what not, to complete the four-year course, and the many others who may have the ability but for various reasons do not want more than two years of study in the liberal arts, the situation of the four-year college will be definitely better. This is the result that is contemplated by commentators who speak of the "selective function" of the junior college.

If, under such circumstances, it should transpire that from 60 to 75 per cent. of the students of the four-year college would be in the upper two classes, what college professor or administrator would not be happy at the change? It seems that the junior college may well affect the destiny of the standard four-year college in a very favorable way by making it possible for it to continue its historic work, laying more and more emphasis upon the advanced portions of it, to the benefit of its standing as an institution of higher education and to the enhancement of the quality of its service to society.

It should be admitted that the junior college movement probably will mean a change in the status of our too-numerous small, scantily-endowed, ill-equipped sub-standard colleges. These institutions need not necessarily go out of existence, but with the spread of junior colleges they may expect either to "give up the ghost" or to demote themselves to the junior college status and become accredited as such. In view of the increasing hopelessness of the financial situation of many of these schools, the latter will probably be an unmixed blessing to education in general.

Regarding our "scholarly amateur," when it is borne in mind that the junior college curriculum will include two-year liberal arts courses, either preparatory or terminal, according to the needs and plans of the student, and that as a part of the public-school system, with units in every considerable center of population, it will carry this training to uncounted thousands who would otherwise never have received it, it will appear that the "scholarly amateur" will be multiplied manyfold in American life, rather than extirpated as has been feared.

Thus far we have discussed the "scholarly amateur" as the product of the liberal arts college only. Perhaps the graduates of our four-year liberal and professional curricula such as those in agriculture, engineering, education and commerce are also "scholarly amateurs," although Professor Palmer could hardly have been referring to them when he coined the term. What will the junior college mean to the four-year colleges of agriculture, engineering, education and commerce as we now know them? Approximately the same as to the four-year liberal arts college; *i.e.*, it will relieve them of the burden of many students who can not complete four years of training or do not want it, leaving them opportunity to concentrate upon the advanced phases of their work, and perhaps to extend it upward a year or more in length, making it truly professional in character.

For those who are to engage in the "middle-level" occupations, which include operative and foremanship positions in agriculture, engineering and commerce, and at present elementary school teaching, four full years of training are either wasteful or impracticable in most cases. For these, the junior college will offer two-year terminal semi-professional courses. But this does not mean that the need for truly professional agricultural experts, engineers, educators and commercial executives will be lessened. Obviously the demand for such products of the professional schools will continue to increase, and these same professional people will be far better "scholarly amateurs" than they are to-day, because the standards of the professional schools will have been appreciably raised.

One more query apropos of the "scholarly amateur": Can the junior college really give two years of training that is the equivalent of the same amount of training in a standard four-year college? The answer for California comes from Stanford University, where the results of an investigation published in the *Faculty Bulletin* in June, 1928, indicate that the graduates of California junior colleges who come to Stanford appear somewhat superior, both in intelligence and in quality of academic work, to the so-called "native Stanford" students who have had their first two years of college work at the university.

There can scarcely be any doubt that the junior college, when it comes into its own, will produce at the end of its two-year course a very creditable "scholarly amateur," who will compare very favorably with his prototype of an earlier generation. Our "scholarly amateur" of the past, as found in the states west of the Alleghenies, was all too often the product of a struggling, meagerly staffed, poorly equipped, denomination-ridden, sub-standard "college," which was in fact a mere second-class secondary school. And even to-day he is almost universally the product of a college that is forced to spend from two thirds to three fourths of its resources in giving secondary education to a motley horde of underclassmen, half of whom will never complete its four-year course, and many of whom it must brand as academic failures. By assuming a large part of the burden of this selective function, the junior college will usher in a brighter day for the standard four-year college, and multiply and improve the "scholarly amateur."

M. M. CHAMBERS

OREGON STATE COLLEGE

THE RELIABILITY OF THE THORNDIKE INTELLIGENCE EXAMINATION

RECENT mental tests have given very high reliabilities, many being over +.90. The Stanford revision of the Binet scale has a quoted reliability of +.93; the Stanford achievement test of +.98 for a single grade; the Otis self-administering of +.92. Such high figures are brought about by each item being carefully selected and tested and by longer tests than formerly felt necessary.

Reliabilities of the Thorndike test were given by K. M. Cowdery in a recent article.[1] The figures quoted are low in contrast to many other tests and were rather disappointing to some who use this test. This was especially so, considering the great amount of work and expense put out in drawing up the examination and since it lasts three hours. By contrast the Binet scale occupies approximately one hour. Cowdery's reliability coefficients varied from +.89 for a retest by the same form within a year to +.65 for those taking a new form after a three-year interval. The correlation between first and second testings for the whole 207 cases lumped together was +.75. If we assume a reliability (say by odd-even, or split-halves methods) of +.85 at each testing, this figure corrected for attenuation would be raised to +.88.

According to these figures, the absolute difference in scores of two individuals would have to be far greater to be sure of safe discrimination in terms of ability than with the Binet scale. However, due to two factors which may readily account for a lower reliability on the part of the Thorndike, the test does not seem so inferior to the present writer.

First, the test is standardized on a very homogeneous group. Practically every one taking it is a high-school senior and an applicant for university entrance. So they are not only of the same age, but also of an equally high level of ability, and not a random sampling of that age. The test, then, if to discriminate and separate out individual differences at all, literally has to make a mountain out of a mole-hill. When the second form is taken a very slight change in score will alter the individual's standing to a considerable extent, thus lowering the correlation. In contrast to this the Binet scale was standardized on school children of all ages and of all mental abilities. Reliabilities are artificially raised by the age factor, or, taken conversely, are lowered by unusual homogeneity within the group. The reliability of +.75 for the Thorndike test obtained for a single age would probably be raised to over +.90 if computed for a large age range with normal scatter of abilities within ages. Thus, the simple coefficients of reliability are not the only features to be considered.

[1] School and Society, 27: March 24, 1928.

The second point is that the test is far more educational in nature than many other intelligence examinations. That is, it is more of a test of content learned in school than of native endowment. It must be admitted, of course, that the line between the two is difficult to draw; distinctions are more matters of proportion than of qualitative differences. The test, then, may be regarded as somewhat in the nature of a final examination for the whole high-school course. The fact that the reliabilities decrease constantly with time gives further evidence that educational content forms a considerable proportion of the test. In an examination of more psychological or intelligence nature we should expect the same results year after year, since the constancy of the I.Q. seems fairly well established. Thus, with changing knowledge and interest, scores will alter materially, and lower correlations between original and subsequent testings will result in the same manner as pointed out in the preceding paragraph. The constantly lowering coefficients seem to indicate that gains and losses in knowledge in the meantime do not counterbalance each other.

So, all things considered, the reliability of the test seems reasonably high, under present conditions. There are two factors, mentioned above, apart from the construction of the test itself, which keep reliabilities from being as high as in some other tests, which at first inspection seem to be considerably more reliable measuring instruments than the Thorndike. However, we desire a test which will have a higher reliability, since we have constant need to measure such homogeneous groups under similar conditions.

Richard W. Husband
Stanford University, Calif.

QUOTATIONS

BACKWARDNESS IN THE SCHOOLS OF GREAT BRITAIN

At a conference of teachers from the Oxford district, Dr. R. H. Crowley, senior medical officer of the Board of Education, is reported to have made the alarming statement that some half a million children, or 12 per cent. of the children of compulsory school age, are mentally retarded children. To what extent is this statement true and in so far as it is true to what extent is it due to bad school organization and teaching? A correspondent, commenting on Dr. Crowley's statement, adduces an instance in which a rural schoolmistress labeled a child of real, and perhaps unusual, intelligence as a mental deficient simply because he was of an intellectual type unusual in the district. How many children are misplaced because of the ignorance of the teachers of the elements of psychology; to what extent is mental retardation due to bad teaching and faulty psychology? This raises the question of the capacity of teachers. Dr. Crowley states that mental retardation in children is more common in rural than in urban districts. Possibly the backwardness of the rural teachers and not the backwardness of the rural children is the cause of the apparent difference in the reported percentage of mentally retarded children. A certificated teacher in a town is likely to make fewer errors in this matter than a supplementary or uncertificated teacher in a rural school. One thing, at any rate, is certain, that if children who are not suffering from defective brain power are treated as the fools of the village class they will very soon suffer from mental retardation. It is important in the interests not only of the children but of the whole community that the teaching power in the village schools be raised to the same standard as the teaching in the urban schools. At present there is a gulf fixed between the average of the town and the average of the rural teachers. That gap must be bridged or filled if national education is to become a reality.

Many country children are slower of speech, at any rate in the presence of teachers who do not speak their dialect, than town children, but in actual brain power there is reason to suppose that they, if given equal educational opportunities, are equal at least to their fellows in the towns. The superficial sharpness of the youngster in the town who from the age of eight is being crammed for scholarship purposes is not a reasonable standard from which to work. The slow and backward child of ten has very often the making of a first-class scholar or mathematician. The children with large brain capacity are often backward for that very reason. They have inhibitions from which children with small brains and active personalities do not suffer. The latter often easily and rapidly reach their maximum and appear at a very early age to be very gifted. These are the children who win scholarships and become the burden of the secondary schools. It is, in fact, very difficult to say what mental retardation really means. The term may be applied quite correctly to a child with great potentialities and equally correctly to a child, otherwise normal, who suffers from physical disabilities, such as bad sight or hearing or other troubles, or from malnutrition and bad housing. The alleged half-million of mentally retarded children includes children of every intellectual class, and at any rate some children whose mental retardation is due to wrong diagnosis in school. Mental deficiency is another matter. The reports of Sir George Newman seem to show that there are about 80,000 children in England and Wales who are apparently mentally deficient in contrast to children who are dull or backward. To what extent proper training and education in special schools can supply in each case the missing intellectual element that constitutes actual mental deficiency depends upon the school and the actual case. That much can be done to make many of these children self-supporting members of society is certain, but a greater educational problem is concerned with the 300,000 or more children who are labeled dull or backward, or both.

Sir George Newman holds that it is from this group that society inherits most of its neuropathics, delinquents, unemployables and criminals. He has pleaded for the reduction of the size of the group by education and in this way to turn off the tap of the supply of incapable and non-contributory citizens. The school medical officer can do much by indicating that portion of the group that owes dullness and backwardness to unsuspected deafness or other physical ailment. Certainly a very large number of dull children owe their dullness to these physical causes. But Dr. Crowley declares that 250,000 of the mentally retarded children are cases where the cause is "inborn and due to lack of all-round intellectual capacity or to a specific intellectual defect or other special mental disability." This conclusion seems most difficult to establish. What is meant by "lack of all-round intellectual capacity" in the case of a child of nine who has not had the advantage of highly trained teaching and has been allowed to drift because he or she does not exhibit the sharpness that crammers love? A child of great potential intellectual power in these circumstances (which are not at all unusual circumstances) would be declared to be suffering from "lack of all-round intellectual capacity." Moreover, some children with great powers have nevertheless no powers for certain subjects. That great classical scholar Shillito could do no mathematics at all. He suffered from what Dr. Crowley calls "a specific intellectual defect or other special mental disability." In fact, every specialist suffers to some extent from some intellectual defect or disability. Classification of so-called dull or backward children is what is needed, and absolutely first-class teaching coupled with insight on the part of the teachers. The problem (apart from actual physical defects) is not medical but pedagogic.—*The London Times Educational Supplement.*

EDUCATIONAL RESEARCH AND STATISTICS

SCHOLASTIC APTITUDE TESTS IN AMHERST COLLEGE

Five successive entering classes in Amherst College, ranging from 157 to 232 men, were given two or more relatively short "scholastic aptitude" or "intelligence" tests, without practice periods and requiring not over one and three quarter hours working time for each set. This was done for experimental purposes, and no administrative use was made of the scores.

The Otis Self-administering Test, Higher Examination, was given to all five classes; but the others were changed from year to year. Those used were: Army Alpha; Terman Group; three from the American Council on Education's Psychological Examination (1924 Edition), *i.e.*, the Arithmetical Reasoning, Artificial Language, and Opposites; Smith College Information (1926 Edition); C. H. T. (a sentence-completion and vocabulary test); and two editions of the Amherst Test, a revised form of the C. H. T. A combination score was also given each man, using the sum of the decile positions he had in the tests of that year. For one class this combination score included scores on three tests

TABLE 1

Correlations of Test Scores with College Grades and Ratios Based on Proportions of Inferior and Superior Students in Extreme Quarters, in Successive Classes

Freshman grades

	r	LQ Inf. / HQ Inf.	HQ Sup. / LQ Sup.
Otis	.38 ± .05	1.8	> 10.0
Alpha	.33 ± .05	1.7	> 14.0
Comb.	.38 ± .05	1.8	> 14.0
Otis	.34 ± .05	3.2	2.7
Terman	.28 ± .05	2.4	2.6
C. H. T.	.23 ± .05	1.7	2.6
Comb.	.31 ± .05	3.4	3.4
Otis	.25 ± .05	2.6	2.9
Amherst	.24 ± .05	1.4	3.0
ACE A. R.	.25 ± .05	1.8	2.3
ACE A. L.	.27 ± .05	2.1	5.0
ACE Op.	.28 ± .05	2.4	3.3
Comb.	.35 ± .04	2.3	3.8
Otis	.37 ± .04	3.6	3.5
Amherst	.27 ± .04	3.3	3.5
Comb. (incl. 3 ACE tests)	.42 ± .04	3.9	3.8
Otis	.19 ± .04	2.0	2.3
S. C. Inf.	.27 ± .04	1.6	3.1
Comb.	.22 ± .04	1.8	2.7
Entire Course			
Otis	.24 ± .07	3.6	4.8
Alpha	.32 ± .06	2.0	5.4
Comb.	.31 ± .07	3.4	5.6
Otis	.24 ± .06	2.5	2.2
Terman	.24 ± .06	2.8	2.6
C. H. T.	.32 ± .06	2.0	3.3
Comb.	.28 ± .06	3.2	3.3
Otis	.34 ± .06		
Amherst	.21 ± .06		
ACE A. R.	.16 ± .06		
ACE A. L.	.19 ± .06		
ACE Op.	.34 ± .06		
Comb.	.36 ± .05		

which were not separately studied, the Analogies I and II and the Number Series Completion, of the A.C.E. (1925 Edition). No one of the tests in the whole set was found to be strikingly superior to the others, as the data in the following tables show.

At the end of the freshman year the correlations between test scores and college grades of the men who had completed the year's work were computed; and at the end of the senior year, for the three classes now graduated, similar correlations were obtained. These coefficients, all disappointingly low, are given in Table 1.

A considerable part of our study of the tests was based on a simple three-fold classification of the scores into low quarter, middle half and high quarter. The scholastic record of the men in these groups was tabulated at the end of the freshman year, for all five classes, and again at the end of the senior year for the first two of the classes which have graduated.

A small group of six or eight men whose performance in the tests was the poorest in their class was separately listed for each test, and the scholastic record of these men, the lowest 3 per cent. to 5 per cent. of the class, has been especially interesting. Table 2 summarizes the data for these low groups, the letter A indicating a college grade of 90 or better; B, 80 to 89; etc. Sixty, or D, is the passing grade in each course, but a final average of 70 or better is required for graduation.

In order to get a simple expression for the degree to which high scholarship was concentrated towards the upper end of the test scores, the following plan was adopted. The percentage of the high quarter men who received a grade of A or B was found, and also the percentage of the low quarter who received either of these grades. The relation between these percentages was then expressed as a ratio. Men who received an A or B may be called "superior students." The more superior students there were in a high quarter, and the fewer in the low quarter, the larger the ratio became.

In a similar way an expression was formed for the degree of concentration of inferior scholarship towards the lower end of the test scores; but here the definition of "inferior students" had to be somewhat more complex. The inferior scholarship group, as we use the term,

TABLE 2

COLLEGE GRADES OF THE MEN WHO FORMED THE LOWEST 3 PER CENT. TO 5 PER CENT. IN EACH TEST, IN SUCCESSIVE CLASSES. THOSE WHO DROPPED OUT BEFORE THE END OF THE PERIOD ARE DIVIDED TO SHOW WHETHER THEIR LAST AVERAGES WERE LESS THAN C OR C AND UP

	No.	A	B	C	D	E&F	Out: <C	Out: C&up
Freshman year								
Otis	7			2	3	2		
Alpha	7			3	2	2		
Comb.	9			3	3	1	2	
Otis	6			2	4			
Terman	6		1	1	1	1	2	
C. H. T.	7		1	3	1	1	1	
Comb.	5			2	2		1	
Otis	6		1	2	2	1		
Amherst	7		1		4	2		
ACE A. R.	7			4	3			
ACE A. L.	8		1	2	3	1		1
ACE Op.	7	1	1	4		1		
Comb.	8		1	1	4	1	1	
Otis	7		1	2	3		1	
Amherst	7			3	4			
Comb. (incl. 3 ACE tests)	6			2	3	1		
Otis	7		1	3	2		1	
S. C. Inf.	7			3	1		1	2
Comb.	7			4	2		1	
Entire Course								
Otis	7			1			6	
Alpha	7			4			3	
Comb.	9			4			5	
Otis	6			3			3	
Terman	6		1	1			4	
C. H. T.	7		1	3			3	
Comb.	5			2			3	
Otis	6		2	1			2	1
Amherst	7		2	1			3	1
ACE A. R.	7			3			2	2
ACE A. L.	8			1			3	4
ACE Op.	7	1	3				1	2
Comb.	8		2	3			2	1

includes all who finished the year, or the course, with an average of D or less, all who were dropped by the college for poor work, and also all who dropped out voluntarily with a last average of D or less. The percentage of the low quarter who fell in this classification was found, and also the percentage of the high quarter; and the two percentages were expressed as a ratio. These two sets of ratios are given in Table 1, in the columns headed

$$\frac{\text{Low Quarter Inferiors}}{\text{High Quarter Inferiors}}, \quad \left(\frac{\text{L. Q. Inf.}}{\text{H. Q. Inf.}}\right),$$

and

$$\frac{\text{High Quarter Superiors}}{\text{Low Quarter Superiors}}, \quad \left(\frac{\text{H. Q. Sup.}}{\text{L. Q. Sup.}}\right).$$

An average of the two ratios for each test might be taken as a rough indication of the degree of success with which the extreme quarters of the test had picked out the men who showed the corresponding kind of scholarship.

If the high quarter contains no inferior scholars, or the low quarter no superior ones, this ratio method becomes somewhat defective, as the zero denominator gives an infinite ratio. Fortunately for the method, but unfortunately for our educational aims, we can safely expect that in every class some of the able men will do inadequate work and make poor scholastic records; so one of the possible difficulties does not actually occur. The other difficulty, that the low quarter should contain no superior students, occurred in only one class; and in that instance we have written the ratio as "larger than," >, the one which would have existed if a single man in the low quarter had made a superior grade.

Our results show that these ratios would be a weak basis on which to judge the practical utility of a test, unless over several years. But they show that even with correlations in the .20s and .30s the low quarter of a test generally contained more than twice as many inferior students as the high quarter, and the high quarter more than twice as many superior students as the low quarter.

In fairness to the tests it must, of course, always be remembered that the correlation of a perfect "intelligence" test with college grades would be badly lowered by the fact already noted, that some really competent men are indifferent towards their academic work. It would be lowered also by differences in strictness of marking by different instructors; and by a tendency in some instructors to assign grades largely in proportion to the mere industry exhibited by the students; and by a tendency in others to assign grades more or less in accordance with their likes and dislikes. But where these last two faults, at least, are probably not strong factors in the situation a test which purports to measure scholastic aptitude should give a rather high rank to nearly all the men who actually achieve scholastic success, providing always that it was given under good conditions as to interest, health, eyesight, etc. We should not blame a test if we find that some able men neglect their work and get low grades; but we must consider it as defective if men of fairly well-established scholastic ability are rated low by the test.

In this respect our results have been disappointing. The conditions under which the tests were given were not perfect, but there was no reason to believe that any considerable number of able men made low scores on account of sickness, indifference or other invalidating factors. Most of the tests were given on the first or second day of the college year, when there would be a prevalent excitement but when good effort might be expected. One study was made of the scores of the men who reported that they felt themselves physically below par to an extent which would probably affect their scores, and who named the difficulty; but in this class, whose tests came somewhat later in the month and at a time when some of the men were short of sleep, there was evidence that the scores were in fact not adversely affected: the average of the group who reported some feeling of disability was slightly above that of the entire class.

If we may suppose, then, that neither defects in the assignment of college grades nor defects in the conditions under which the tests were given, were large enough to produce any serious disturbance of the results, it is a serious count against these tests that, with two very dubious exceptions, their low quarters contained about a third as many students who actually received superior grades for freshman year as did their high quarters. In one of the two classes which have graduated and whose final grades were tabulated by this method the proportion was about the same; and in the other, where the results were much more favorable to the tests, there were still about a fifth as many superior students in the low quarters as in the high. The better showing of the Alpha, in that year, can not be attributed to any considerable superiority of the test; for the Otis also made nearly as good a record with that class, but fell down badly with the next, giving an average for both classes of 1 superior student in the low quarter to 3.5 in the high quarter. The A. C. E. Artificial Language test gave a better segregation of superior students for freshman year than any other except the Alpha and the Otis of the first class. But this interesting test can hardly be given an exceptional rating on this account. The scatter diagram of its scores and final college grades shows that in fact this test was even less successful for the entire course than the others of the set had been for the freshman year; and its final correlation was almost the lowest of the set. The requirement that practically all the students who actually win superior grades should rate well in a reliable test of scholastic aptitude was thus not well met by any test with which we dealt.

To a considerable extent this defect of the tests also appeared in the record of the six or eight men who formed the lowest 3 per cent. or 5 per cent. in each test. In all we had nineteen of these very low groups, counting each combination and each use of the Otis and Amherst tests. In every one of them at least two men finished the freshman year with a safe C average. For the entire college course we had thirteen very low groups, in the three classes which have graduated. In eleven of these groups there were at least two men who had a C average or better at the end of the four years, and graduated with their class. There was only one man who graduated in the A. C. E. Artificial Language low group, and also in one of the Otis low groups. But in the three Otis low groups combined more than one third of the men graduated all right. And in the Artificial Language low group it happened that four men dropped out of college for other reasons than scholarship, with respectable last averages; so the evidence of better discrimination is weak. Among the men already admitted to college, then, no one of these tests proved able to pick out a low 4 per cent. or 5 per cent. for whom scholastic failure could safely be predicted.

Tests which equally purport to measure general intelligence and which have about the same degree of success in predicting scholastic results, as measured by the correlations, gave very different rankings to a set of men. In picking out the forty-five men who should form the high quarter of one class the Otis and the Alpha agreed on twenty-eight. With the next class the Otis and the Terman agreed on only seven out of forty.

In spite of the unfavorable facts in our experience with these tests, it is still true that the difference between the scholastic records of the men in the low quarters and those in the high quarters is large enough to be of some practical value. Even in the least successful years, and with the least successful tests in those years, when the correlation with college grades ran down to .19, the average of the "ratio of inferiors" and of the "ratio of superiors" was more than 2/1. That is, on the average the extreme quarter might be expected to contain more than twice as large a proportion of students of the corresponding scholastic rating as would be contained in the contrasted quarter. This was true for the entire course as well as for the freshman year, so far as our data went.

The Otis test may be taken as a favorable sample of the tests used, and we may sum up some of the facts about it. The correlations with freshman grades ranged from $.38 \pm .05$ to $.19 \pm .04$, with the several classes; and with the final grades of the three classes which have graduated, from $.34 \pm .06$ to $.24 \pm .07$. In the prediction value of its extreme quarters it worked comparatively well with the final scholastic results in one class, and comparatively poorly with those in the next. The average of the results in these two classes shows that the men in the low quarters received about 1/3 as many superior final grades as did those in the high quarters and that more than three times as many of the low quarters men dropped out of the class with grades below seventy. The low quarters of these classes contained 15 per cent. of the total number of superior students and contained 39 per cent. of the inferior students. Table 3 shows the five-year average of the percentages of the college grades in the three divisions of the test, for the freshman year only.

TABLE 3

FIVE-YEAR AVERAGES OF THE PERCENTAGES OF DIFFERENT GRADES RECEIVED FOR FRESHMAN YEAR BY THE LOW QUARTER, MIDDLE HALF, AND HIGH QUARTER IN THE OTIS S-A TEST. THOSE WHO LEFT BEFORE END OF YEAR DIVIDED ACCORDING TO LAST AVERAGE

	A	B	C	D	E&F	Out: <C	Out: C&up
L.	1.0	12.7	33.0	32.0	9.0	9.6	2.8
M.	1.3	21.1	37.9	27.5	4.2	6.4	1.6
H.	6.7	35.5	34.6	16.9	2.2	1.9	2.2

The percentile curves of the Otis scores showed strikingly that the maximum score in this test is too low to allow of proper differentiation within the upper 15 per cent. of these college classes, their scores being crowded together in the last five points of the scale. Even then the last point was not useful, as no one made the perfect score of 75. To indicate the general level of performance of the freshmen in this test, to readers who are familiar with it, the medians for the five successive classes were: 61.25, 60.63, 58.22, 59.00, 61.17 and 59.90. The scholastic averages of these freshman classes varied more than their test medians, but had little correspondence with them, the superiority of one class in the test being no reliable indication that its college work would also be superior.

Some critics think that such tests are discredited when one can show that advice or administrative decisions based on the test scores would be wrong in a considerable percentage of the cases. It is not sufficiently recognized that decisions based in the conventional way on high school grades, entrance examination marks, and personal impressions, are also certainly mistaken in a considerable percentage of the cases. It happens that we know the degree of fallibility of the tests and that we generally ignore the evidence of the great fallibility of the accepted methods. Under such conditions one should welcome the aid of tests, even if no more successful than the ones we used. But in dealing with an individual one should generally try to get the score translated into a statement of degree of probability of a particular result. There is nothing undesirable in having a student learn how many chances there are against the scholastic success of those in his section of the test scores and how many chances in favor. Perhaps the chief value of studies of such tests in colleges is to furnish more information of this supplementary sort to those who advise high-school students about undertaking a higher education.

CONCLUSIONS

(1) Results with a series of tests, including the Alpha, Otis S-A, Terman, three from one set of the American Council on Education, the Smith Information, and the Amherst test, did not indicate that any one of them was especially reliable for predicting scholastic standing. The correlations with college grades were all low, both for freshman year and for the entire course.

(2) None of these tests picked out a lowest 4 per cent. or 5 per cent. for whom one could safely predict scholastic failure, either for freshman year or the entire course. Among men already admitted to college by the current methods the tests did not discover any groups who were incapable of obtaining passing grades.

(3) Considered as tests of scholastic aptitude these tests were faulty in rating relatively low a considerable proportion of the men whose scholastic accomplishment proved to be actually superior.

(4) There was a considerable variability of predictive value of one test repeated with different classes. For freshman grades the correlation of the Otis varied from $.38 \pm .05$ to $.19 \pm .04$; and predictions based on the upper and lower quarters of the test were almost twice as successful for the entire course of one class as for that of another.

(5) The degree of success of the extreme quarters in predicting freshman grades did not reliably indicate the degree of success in predicting final grades.

(6) In spite of the unfavorable facts in our experience, it is still true that the difference between the scholastic performance of men in the low quarter and of men in the high quarter was enough to give nearly all these tests some practical utility.

CHARLES H. TOLL

AMHERST COLLEGE

SCHOOL AND SOCIETY

WITH WHICH IS COMBINED THE

EDUCATIONAL REVIEW

Volume XXVIII | Saturday, November 3, 1928 | Number 723

THE STORY OF THE EDUCATIONAL REVIEW

By Dr. FRANK PIERREPONT GRAVES

NEW YORK STATE COMMISSIONER OF EDUCATION AND PRESIDENT OF THE UNIVERSITY OF THE STATE OF NEW YORK

The *Educational Review* was the brain child of Nicholas Murray Butler. It was started by him nearly two score years ago and for nearly a generation he directed its career. During the other nine years of its existence the editorial responsibility has been carried for almost equal periods by the writer and by William McAndrew. McAndrew gave it a somewhat wider appeal and succeeded in imparting to it some of his native spice, but it remained essentially the same sort of a journal.

The first number appeared in January, 1891, with Nicholas Murray Butler as editor, assisted by E. H. Cook, William H. Maxwell and Addison B. Poland. The founder was then still in the twenties but already a distinguished professor at Columbia, and, although numerous responsibilities induced him to transfer the care of his creation to others almost a decade ago, he is now most vigorous and at the zenith of his career.

In this opening number the five articles were from the pens of Daniel C. Gilman, William T. Harris, Josiah Royce, Andrew S. Draper and Charles DeGarmo. At that time an article from any one of these thinkers would have been sufficient to make the reputation of an issue of the ordinary magazine. And throughout the years that followed the material in the *Educational Review* was kept on this plane just as far as it was humanly possible. Regardless of popularity and cost, it was intended to be a missionary organ. It was written distinctly for earnest and scientific students of education in a period when scientific study of the subject was a suspected industry, and it was the bitter opponent of personal and partisan politics in education, when political influences were rampant. It has raised the intellectual tone of the teaching profession, and has helped to give it new courage and a unity of thought and purpose.

Joy Morgan, editor of the *National Education Association Journal,* has called the *Educational Review* "the *Atlantic Monthly* of the educational group." Does it not seem an unhappy circumstance that such a magazine should lose its identity? Its place as a technical journal has now been taken by a dozen specialized publications, which have arisen in the past twenty years, and the journalistic sources of educational news are far more numerous and effective than they used to be, but there ought still to be room for one general magazine of such distinctly literary and idealistic character. Since, however, it has been decreed that the name and form must vanish, it is most fortunate that the spirit and substance are to be preserved in a journal that has so clearly won its way to educational leadership as School and Society.

THE UNIVERSITY AND THE TIMES[1]

By Dr. LOTUS DELTA COFFMAN
PRESIDENT OF THE UNIVERSITY OF MINNESOTA

The theme of these exercises is the relation of a State university to the State.

Upon such an occasion as this and with this theme in mind, the natural thing would be for one to discuss questions of finance and the responsibilities of the university as a teaching, research, and service institution. I have, however, decided to do something quite different. It is my purpose to discuss some of the significant tendencies and movements in American life that have a bearing upon universities.

America is not a country of traditions. We are near the frontier in time and much of the blood of the pioneer still flows in our veins. We have acquired few national habits or attitudes of mind. We still believe that the road to progress is the road into the untraveled and the unknown, while the road to safety is the road of custom. Both men and nations who traverse the beaten paths of safety discover nothing new. The paths of safety reveal their goals from the very outset; they never lead beyond the plateaus into the undiscovered regions. When men assume that what they think is profoundly and irrevocably right and that what they do should set the standards of conduct and of action for all others, then we may be sure that life has lost its charm for them. The blood of the adventurer, of the discoverer and of the inventor no longer warms them into action. The spirit of youth has ceased to beckon them on and the zest of the scientist does not disturb them. They sleep tranquilly on while the chariot of progress moves swiftly by.

America is a country in which change is the order of the day. The steam engine, the automobile, and the aeroplane, together with electricity and its offspring, the telephone and the radio, have practically annihilated both time and space. Transformations equally revolutionary and quite as far-reaching are occurring in almost every field of human thought. The stories of modern science read like romance. One hundred years ago the following sciences did not exist or were known only superficially: chemistry, biology, psychology, electricity, sociology, bacteriology, zoology, physical astronomy. Now disease has been almost if not quite conquered, distance annihilated, and the forces of nature made docile under the hand of man.

And yet we are not satisfied. There is the constant urge for new achievements, and particularly as they may contribute to our material comforts. We demand better cars, improved means of transportation of all kinds; greater facility of communication; time and labor saving machinery for industry, agriculture, the home; mechanical devices of every imaginable use. The demand for improvements in these respects brings powerful, absorbing, and consuming pressures to bear upon physical scientists everywhere. The whole social order at present, in this country at least, feels the impelling impacts of industry. Indeed industry has reached its long arms, under the name of efficiency, into every institution. It has multiplied the products of life and improved their quality to such an extent as to modify profoundly our philosophy of living. We want "bigger and better" things because they add to our comfort and increase our dividends. Experiment for industry is the order of the day. Millions are spent in subsidizing it. We boastfully

[1] Address given on the occasion of the installation of Dr. Frederick James Kelly as president of the University of Idaho.

exploit it and then immediately impose additional tributes upon it.

It cannot be claimed, of course, that Americans are wholly neglectful of the spiritual rewards and values of life or that they bow in constant worship before the gods of industry. Industry has contributed in numerous and subtle ways and to an enormous extent to the humanizing of life. We are living in an atmosphere of growing altruism, partly because industry is teaching us the lessons of cooperation. Many of the old values of life are being restated in social rather than in individual terms. Economic stability and industrial efficiency provide leisure and opportunity for the consideration of the more intangible values of life.

Industry moulds things according to a pattern. It seeks a standardized product. It prospers on mass production. Standard products have helped both the manufacturer and the consumer. They help the manufacturer because they enable him to produce more; they help the consumer because they cost less than other products and because they are easily remembered.

The movement for standardized products has extended far beyond industry. Although highly beneficial to infant industry it can not be said that it is equally propitious in the fields of the more strictly social institutions. When it reaches over into the educational field and insists that all children shall be fitted to a common mould, taught the same material and in the same way, it is probably destroying the goose, or at least one of the geese, that lays the golden eggs of human progress. When the demands for economy, the introduction of similar systems of accounting, and the comparison of one university with another on the basis of square feet or square unit of something or other, become the basis for university administration, then we may be reasonably sure that these things are standing in their own light. Whenever educational institutions become so industrialized that they think in terms of common units and common products, that day they will become the victims rather than the leaders of the social order they are supposed to serve.

While American industry is producing standardized articles in uncountable quantities, there is, nevertheless, a saving factor in the situation, a factor which is purely psychological in character. Although we like to secure things as cheaply as possible, we like to be different. To have incontrovertible evidence of the presence of this desire, one needs only to call attention to the hours of fatiguing shopping women will undergo in order that their spring hats may be unlike those of their neighbors. What is true of spring hats is equally true of everything else. Even Henry Ford has discovered that men will not be satisfied with the Model T; they demanded a new car, and he is responding to the demand. This eternal conflict between efficiency on the one hand and initiative on the other, between sameness and dissimilarity, will continue to be waged. The battle will never be won. If it were, it would mean stagnation, on the one hand, or chaos, on the other.

It must be clear that the greatest asset of standardization is also its greatest menace, for uniformity tends to destroy freedom and the right to experiment. Uniformity is more easily obtained in material than in spiritual things, but we will not submit to it indefinitely in any realm. While we reach out with one hand for the cheap standardized products, we reach out with the other for the new and the uncopied. Constant experiment and uniformity, two antithetical things, must remain in close association. We shall live forever, we hope, in a world that is eternally trying to improve itself. We shall continue to foster and encourage experiment in everything which pertains to our physical comfort and needs. Whether we shall be equally open to experiment in the social and political fields is still subject to some doubt. When national affairs are considered we are disposed to view with suspicion and alarm many of the governmental practices of foreign countries and to view our own with certain pride and satisfaction in comparison. And yet it must be clear that if all art or all social theories or all governments were alike there would be no further progress.

Variation in the social and political fields is as essential to human progress as biological variation is essential to the improvement of the human race. Nations have always differed from one another enormously in customs, economic life, religious practices, national ideals, and forms of government. The world probably never saw a greater number of interesting social and political programs than exist to-day. Witness, for example, the League of Nations, the International Court of Justice, the dole for the unemployed in England, the marriage and divorce laws of Norway and Sweden, the socialistic theories of Austria, the dictatorships of Spain and of Italy, and the communistic government of Russia.

Of all these the one that seems to be attracting the most attention is Russia. Whether this is due to the fact that it seems so remote and its doctrines are so radically different from ours, I do not know. It [illegible] my privilege to visit this country [illegible] with a group of American educators and to see at first hand many of the novel features of this gigantic experiment. It is an attempt to impose a philosophy wholly foreign to American thought, and untenable according to our opinion, upon 140,000,000 people. It is no wonder that we have a deep interest in what is transpiring there.

For ten years now we have been expecting and predicting chaos in this stricken land. Meantime the government apparently has grown more secure. The economic theories of the Russians are abhorrent to us. In fact, we can never reconcile ourselves to the confiscation of private property, nor to the assumption that all types of labor are of equal value and should be rewarded alike. This doctrine, we maintain, destroys competition and initiative, both of which are necessary for progress. And yet with these doctrines still prominent throughout Russia, American trade with her is increasing and she is paying her bills. We maintain, and with vigor, that art, science, industry, all progress, both spiritual and material, depend upon a clear recognition of individual differences and upon freeing those who possess such qualities to pursue genius where she listeth. We know that the great things of life flow from talent and genius rather than from the masses, and yet there never was such apparent interest in and knowledge of art in all of its forms among the populace as exists in Russia to-day. We do not countenance murder in any form of kings or queens or czars, nor the execution of the ruling classes. We stand unreservedly against revolution by bloodshed in all of its forms everywhere. And yet we can not fail to rejoice somewhat in the fact that the common man, who for five centuries has been the abject slave of these rulers, has freed himself from this enslavement and is now enjoying a new and exalted status. Every American would, I presume, maintain that any country that teaches a social philosophy, the essence of which is world revolution and the ultimate destruction of capitalism, is inimical to our government and to the peace of the world. And yet one gets some satisfaction from the fact that education is becoming the great passion of this people, both old and young.

There are many strange theories and doctrines in this far distant country. They are strange to us partly because we are not familiar with the background and other circumstances which explain them and partly because they are so remote from our accustomed modes of thinking. For example, we can scarcely imagine all the lawyers of our country being suddenly disbarred and a committee of citizens, none of whom was informed in the technique of the law, being chosen to hear and try cases as they arise. And yet that is exactly what has happened in Russia, and millions of the common people are laboring under the pleasant delusion that justice is now being expedited.

Suppose state medicine were suddenly introduced in America and the doctors were employed by the state at stipulated salaries to care for the health of the people, what a wave of protest would be heard from the representatives of this profession, and yet that very thing seems to be coming to pass in Russia.

Even in the field of university education we find equally strange things happening. The universities are controlled by committees, consisting of professors, workmen and students. This arrangement might prove acceptable to many American students, for this committee chooses the professors, prepares the schedule of classes, determines the content of the courses, and votes on whether a student shall or shall not be promoted. I hope this will not convert the students of the University of Idaho to the Russian system, for I have not told all of the story.

And so I might go on reciting inconsistencies and incongruities, for, after all, Russia is a land of strange contradictions. She destroys or exiles many of her artists but saves her arts; she sustains a communistic government which confiscates private property, but pays a wage to everybody; her government is autocratic, but the right of assembly is recognized; the government suppresses the religion of the established church, but seeks by subtle methods to canonize Lenin. Men speak with bated breath about some things, while youth in the workingmen's theaters ridicules many communistic doctrines. A government perhaps as autocratic as any the world has ever seen is undermining itself and digging its own grave by providing the most democratic system of education the world has ever beheld.

My purpose in calling attention to these matters upon this occasion is simply to emphasize the fact that the greatest political experiment of a thousand years is probably unfolding itself before our very eyes. The man who thinks it is all bad does not know his facts and the man who thinks it is all good has forgotten some of the important lessons of experience. There is in process here a gigantic struggle for the emancipation of the human spirit, to free it from ignorance and superstition, to acquire political liberties hitherto denied, and to possess more of the blessings of civilization. The struggle is merciless, ruthless, terrible at times. Its instruments are the instruments of espionage, exile, destruction of property and of life itself. These are the implements of power and of force, of coercion and of authority. Here is a great experiment on a magnificent scale in the laboratory of human experience, pursuing its uncharted way, employing agencies we condemn; it is small wonder that we are skeptical of it. But if intelligent progress is to be made in the fields of the social and political sciences the same tolerant, sympathetic, questioning attitude must be brought to bear upon these matters as is brought to bear upon problems in the field of the physical sciences. When standards, usage, habits and customs mould thought and guide action in any field, it will become intolerant of other forms of action and unprogressive within its own territory. Acceptance of the opinions of others is not necessary for one to be tolerant of them. If the aim of life is to produce a better civilization, then every possibility and every problem should be considered in the light of experience and of the factors affecting it. And this is what education is for. It tries to make one open-minded, not the advocate of some half-understood problem; it teaches tolerance; it exalts experiment.

Whether the Russians have understood this I can not say. Their philosophy is like a great dragon. Every time you cut off one of its heads, two spring forth in its place. The only way to destroy the animal is to strike at the body, and the instrument with which to strike is education. From democratic education must inevitably issue popular government. The more widely distributed the schools, the freer the government will be. It is no mere accident of time and place that Russian despotism destroyed the schools for the people and maintained a secret surveillance over a militant police. The chief means of control in a despotism has always been some form of coercion, whereas the chief means of control in a democracy has always been some form of popular education.

One of the inherent faiths and fundamental principles of Americans from the pioneer fathers on has rested upon education. They believed it to be necessary to give strength and stability to their institutions. The brave men and women who settled on the eastern coast and their equally brave descendants who trekked across the plains and western mountains declared time and again that the common schools were the hope of the country. Wherever they settled they soon built a school and not long thereafter they founded a university in which the arts and sciences were to be taught.

The struggle which these institutions of learning have had at times to train free men for the intelligent exercise of their responsibilities in a free republic has been heroic, and sometimes, I regret to say, not without its tragedies. The efforts on the part of certain classes or groups and occasional powerful individuals to control and dictate the policies of these institutions for special rather than public purposes, to make of the students advocates rather than free thinking, free acting individuals—some of these efforts would do credit to Russia in her palmiest Czaristic or Soviet days.

America has staked her future on free and independent public education. This is the greatest social heritage, the most priceless possession our fathers had to transmit. Now what is this thing we call education? We speak of it as freeing the mind, liberating the spirit, making one more cosmopolitan and catholic in his sympathies. Education cherishes and preserves that which experience has tested but it refuses to remain static. It is constantly undermining old faiths and establishing new points of view. By its very nature it is dependent upon liberty to search for the truth and its very essence is found in the right to teach the truth. Human happiness is resident in achievement, but achievement is impossible in a satisfied world. The problem which the modern world has is that of maintaining her schools and universities in the spirit in which her founders conceived them. A university, we like to think, is a laboratory of thought, a republic of scholars, a place where social theories are checked and tested, where everything that is of human interest and pertains to human welfare receives dispassionate consideration, where natural and social sciences proceed hand in hand and side by side in their study of all those problems and theories which are basic to human progress, to higher achievement, to better living. The test is whether we in this era of physical change, with its demand for more material comforts, its attempts to standardize the processes of life, and its intolerance of unfamiliar social practices, will allow these institutions to pursue truth where truth leads and to teach it when it is found. If Idaho will do that and that alone, no matter what her shortcomings may be in other respects, she will be a truly distinguished university.

EDUCATIONAL EVENTS

ADULT EDUCATION IN ENGLAND

"THE Tutor in Adult Education" is the title of a report, published by the Carnegie United Kingdom Trustees, of a joint committee appointed by the British Institute of Adult Education and the Tutors' Association to inquire into the problems of the supply and training of tutors. A summary in the London *Times* states that the inquiry has extended over nearly two years, and the committee, after setting forth their conclusions and recommendations, state their belief that "adult education has a contribution to make to national life that is of steadily growing importance—a contribution far greater than is, even yet, generally realized. But if this is true it is essential that an adequate supply of properly qualified tutors should be assured; for on that more than any other single factor the immediate future of adult education seems to depend." The report says:

In the committee's opinion, while the part-time tutor will remain indispensable, it is imperative, in order to insure the progressive development of the Adult Education Movement in both town and country, to secure a steady increase in the number of full-time appointments, including staff tutors, resident tutors and organizing tutors. It is essential to maintain the voluntary element in adult education by continuing to use the services of men and women who are not engaged in it professionally, by providing them with any training necessary for this work, and by enlisting the voluntary services of part-time tutors engaged in the higher types of class work for pioneer work to a much larger extent than at present. The solution of many problems of adult education in the countryside lies in the appointment of resident tutors to serve particular rural areas.

All full-time tutors engaged in extra-mural work under a university should be paid a regular salary, the committee considers. After a period of probation they should be given full status as teachers on the staff of the university, including pension rights and reasonable security of employment over a period of years. It is important that extra-mural tutors working under a university should be brought into close contact with the university, and also be made to feel their membership of a corporate group of teachers engaged in adult education.

For experienced staff tutors £400 to £450 per annum is recommended as a reasonable minimum salary. For less experienced tutors a minimum probationary rate of £320, calculated on a basis of four classes at £80, is recommended, the probationary period not to exceed two years. These rates should also apply to tutors in residential colleges and similar institutions. In the case of tutors employed by local education authorities the problem is regarded by the committee as too complex for them to make detailed recommendations, but they recommend generally that the rate of pay should be high enough to attract and train really capable and well-qualified tutors.

The committee think that much teaching ability is at present unused through lack of opportunity for its development, and that if this ability is not to be wasted a more adequate provision, both in number and amount, of scholarships and bursaries to admit adult students to internal university degree courses is urgently required. In the direction of finance the committee finds that the existing Adult Education Regulations of the Board of Education have certain serious effects on the supply of tutors because of the limits which, in effect, they impose on the appointment of salaried tutors. In order to remedy this it is suggested that the Board of Education should pay by way of grant three quarters of any reasonable salary (up to a fixed maximum) paid by a responsible body to a full-time tutor while still paying grant on a class basis for classes taken by part-time tutors. The development of adult education would also be materially promoted by increased financial assistance from local education authorities. The principle already in effect conceded in the case of the universities of Oxford and Cambridge, of making special grants from state funds with a view to the development of extra-mural work, should be extended to the newer universities and university colleges.

EDUCATION OF NATAL NATIVES

THE correspondent of *The Christian Science Monitor* in Durban writes that Dr. C. T. Loram, acting superintendent of education for Natal, holds that it is necessary in South Africa for the natives to develop along the same lines as the European section of the people because, he added, quoting Booker Washington, the American Negro leader, "If you are to keep one section of a people down, you must stay down with them."

The native education policies in the various provinces varied, Dr. Loram pointed out. In the Cape the native was regarded as a potential white man and native children were taught in exactly the same way as white children. In Natal, however, he was regarded as a separate person and the tendency was rather to make the very best native possible than try to bring him right up to the level of the white man.

The question of industrial development among the natives was far from satisfactory. They were taught in their schools the rudiments of agriculture or of carpentry, or of boot-making, yet as a result of the action which had invariably been taken by the various trade unions affected, they were given no scope whatever after leaving school.

"I hope people in South Africa will realize," said Dr. Loram, "that it is in their own interest that a place should be found in the industrial world for their black fellow citizens."

It was of interest that of over 1,000,000 native children, ready for education, only one fifth of that number were attending school. Native education at present costs the state about £2 10s. per child per year. To educate all the native children possible at this low figure would cost the state something like £2,500,000. In taxation the natives of the country paid something like £1,200,000.

The cost of Indian education on the other hand was £5 per year per child and that of white children £17. It was commonly argued, he said, that as he belonged to the country the native was entitled to receive a grant as big as if not bigger than that enjoyed by the Indian community.

The love of the native for education was so great, Dr. Loram said, that he was sure they would be willing to pay even more in taxes, if they could be assured of a bigger educational grant.

THE SEATTLE COMMITTEE ON THE CORRELATION OF HIGH SCHOOL AND UNIVERSITY WORK

In the report of a joint committee from high-school and university faculties in five departments, appointed by Dr. M. Lyle Spencer, president of the University of Washington, Seattle, and T. R. Cole, city superintendent of schools, Seattle, to consider ways and means for effecting a better correlation between high-school and university work, are set forth the following weaknesses of university freshmen in English:

1. Freshmen entering the university, generally, lack the ability to react to their reading.
2. Freshmen lack the ability, generally, to obtain information on a given topic and to organize the information logically. Consequently, their written expression lacks clearness, force and precision.
3. Freshmen, generally, are both ignorant and careless as to correct composition form; that is—grammar, punctuation, paragraphing and spelling.
4. Too often freshmen lack pride in meeting accepted standards of expression, both in speaking and in writing.
5. Many freshmen are able to write original, short compositions that have commendable qualities, but such compositions do not fulfil university requirements as concerns organization, outlining and expression.

To correct these faults the committee suggests that:

1. More attention in high school should be given to informational writing.
2. Senior composition should take on more of the university attitude, which consists of gathering information, digesting it, and organizing a logical and intelligent presentation of the material.
3. Teachers in high school should refuse to accept compositions written by pupils who persist in making the same mistakes day after day.
4. There should be continued drill upon the minimum essentials.
5. High-school teachers should stress the use of the library in gathering material. Let pupils learn how to use library helps.
6. In high school there should be more written compositions and more carefully planned oral composition, especially in connection with the study of literature.

The report also considers in the same manner the subjects of mathematics, history, social science, natural science and foreign languages.

THE EARNINGS OF YALE STUDENTS

According to the annual report of Albert B. Crawford, director of the Bureau of Appointments and of the Department of Personnel Study at Yale, a total of $594,187.28 was earned last year by the Yale University students who wholly or partially support themselves. These students represent one third of the university enrolment. Financial aid extended during the year by the university to them through scholarships, long-term tuition loans and short-term emergency loans amounted to $404,983.27, bringing the grand total of all scholarship aid and reported earnings to a new peak of $1,000,-564. Over two thirds of this amount, or $766,-503.36, represents assistance through the university agency, either in financial aid by scholarships and loans, or in employment secured for students directly by the Bureau of Appointments.

Of the $594,187.28 earned by the students, $387,066.88 was earned while the university was in session; the balance, $207,120.40, was earned during the summer time. A total of 1,352 individuals received employment through the bureau during the academic year and the summer. This is seventy-three per cent. of the total registration for employment.

Term earnings from work secured for students by the Bureau of Appointments exceeded all previous records, reaching a total of nearly a quarter of a million dollars. This represents 6,227 positions filled during the college year by 1,265 different individuals. The increase resulted chiefly from more effective organization by the bureau, of Christmas vacation employment, through which over 400 students earned some $20,000, for the most part as post-office and railway-mail "extras" during the holiday rush. With assistance of the postal authorities, who sent representatives to New Haven for that purpose, the bureau was able to arrange for qualifying and bonding these student workers at its office in advance of the vacation period. Many more men were thus placed for the Christmas period than formerly, when a special advance trip to New York was necessary in order to obtain such work.

Earnings from work during the college year reported to the bureau as secured independently also showed an increase, amounting to over $138,000. Though much of this employment is obtained through the university, all such earnings from positions not directly referred to students by the bureau are classified separately as "independently" secured. Adding these figures to those for work secured directly through the bureau gives a total of $387,000 reported earned last year during term-time alone. Summer vacation earnings through both sources raise this sum to nearly $600,000 for the entire college year.

The student agencies, which serve various student needs, enjoyed a banner year. Approximately $35,000 was earned by 273 students through the various agencies. The Student Laundry Agency, with twenty-nine men, earned $3,812. This group of students collects and delivers laundry with its own automobile truck. The Student Suit Pressing Agency, with forty-two men employed, and operating its own plant, earned $12,326. By waiting on table in the university and other dining-halls, 528 students earned board which would have represented an outlay of $121,584. Thirty-three students organized eating tables and earned $9,850. By selling neckties, nine students earned $848. Others sold raincoats, shoes, furniture, and ten earned $1,201 by selling newspaper subscriptions to their fellow students. The baseball and football programs, as usual, offered desirable opportunities for earnings.

The varied occupations the students pursue in their efforts to earn all or a part of their expenses is shown in the following media of employment: advertising agent, artist's model, blood-transfusion donor, pallbearer, bookkeeper, caretaker, chauffeur, Christmas worker, entertainer, janitor, gardener, guide, proofreader, messenger, reader to blind, draftsman, stereopticon operator, teacher, tutor, translator, companion, salesman, musician and supernumerary.

During the year three students earned over $3,000 during their spare time, and one earned over $2,000; three earned over $1,500; fourteen earned between $1,500 and $1,000; sixty-two earned between $1,000 and $500, and 544 earned between $500 and $100.

SALARIES AT PRINCETON UNIVERSITY

A GIFT of $60,000 has been made to Princeton University by Mr. and Mrs. Ellis B. Earle, of Newark, N. J. This gift marks the close of the campaign for the two million endowment fund and enables the university to claim the conditional gift of $1,000,000 made by the General Education Board about three years ago.

The new scale of salaries made possible through this endowment gives a range of $6,000 to $9,000 for professors and will affect over 100 members of the faculty. The range for associate professors will be from $4,500 to $5,750, affecting over forty teachers. More than sixty assistant professors will have salaries ranging between $3,000 and $4,250 under the new scale, while nearly ninety instructors will have salaries amounting to from $1,800 to $2,750. The old salary scale averaged from $2,000 to $500 less than the new scale.

In his recent annual report President Hibben described the strengthening of the teaching power of Princeton through the addition of new courses, the calling of new professors and a more adequate provision for the salaries of those members of the faculty "who have given abundant proof of the value of their long-continued service to the university as scholars and teachers" as "the most characteristic and gratifying feature of the progress" of Princeton during the past year.

Attacking those critics of Princeton's recent building program who maintain that "we are 'putting all our resources in stone and mortar and neglecting the man power of Princeton,'" Dr. Hibben says in his report, "Such criticism results from an ignorance or lack of appreciation of the reinforcement of the intellectual resources of the university. Most of the buildings on our campus just completed or now approaching completion have been made possible by special gifts and do not require any expenditure from our general funds. Some of them are sources of revenue."

Among the new men who have been added to the Princeton faculty are Colonel Augustus Trowbridge as dean of the Graduate School; Dr. Robert Russell Wicks as dean of the chapel; Professor Herman Weyl, of Zurich, Switzerland, to the new Thomas D. Jones Professorship of Mathematical Physics; Professor Godfrey H. Hardy, of Oxford University, in exchange for the first half year for Professor Oswald Veblen; Professor Harley Leist Lutz, of Stanford University, to the chair of public finance, and Professor Paul MacClintock, of the University of Chicago, to the Knox Taylor chair of geography.

THE EDUCATIONAL REVIEW AND SCHOOL AND SOCIETY

The *Educational Review* was established in January, 1891, by Dr. Nicholas Murray Butler, now president of Columbia University, and was published by Henry Holt and Company. The editorial introduction reads:

The Educational Review has been undertaken in the belief that the time has arrived when a periodical of its scope and character is demanded and will be sustained. There are enough earnest and enthusiastic students of education in America to provide it with a constituency. Inasmuch as all leading articles, discussions, and notices of new books that appear in the Review are to be signed by their authors, it seems proper to announce that the publication of such signed contributions does not necessarily involve editorial endorsement of opinions that may find expression therein. The Review has no policy that is not consistent with the scientific study and discussion of education.

The *Review* was edited for twenty-nine years by Dr. Butler. On relinquishing the control at the end of 1919 to the George H. Doran Company, he wrote:

This issue of the Educational Review, bearing date December, 1919, is numbered 290 and completes the 58th volume. With the appearance of this issue the Review will pass from the editorial direction and responsibility which have guided it for twenty-nine years, and will hereafter be published under the auspices of the George H. Doran Company of New York.

It has not been easy for the editor to surrender an occupation and interest that have extended over nearly thirty years; but the continuing and steadily increasing pressure of other obligations has made it necessary to cast about for some that might be lightened or discontinued. The editor is assured that the Review will be conducted on a high plane and in full accord with the traditions that have been established over a generation. He wishes for the new management of the Review the fullest possible measure of success, and is glad to continue to cooperate, as adviser, in its oversight.

The Educational Review was originally planned in 1887, as one of a series of youthful projects for establishing in America the scientific study of education upon a sound philosophical basis; for raising the intellectual standard of the teaching profession, as well as for giving to its members a unity of thought and purpose; and for separating the administration of the nation's schools from the influence of personal and partisan politics. Perhaps no one who was not generally cognizant of conditions as they then existed can appreciate the change that the passing years have brought in all these respects.

The EDUCATIONAL REVIEW was announced in the autumn of 1890 for publication by the house of Messrs. Henry Holt & Company in the month of January following. It commanded from the first the support of serious and scholarly students of education in every land. In its pages are to be found the most sober and constructive contributions to educational thought that have been made anywhere during a like period. But few important names in any country are missing from its list of contributors and collaborators. The five leading articles which appeared in the first issue were written by Daniel C. Gilman, William T. Harris, Josiah Royce, Andrew S. Draper and Charles De Garmo. It would not be easy to find a stronger or more representative list of names among all those who in 1891 were active in the forward movement of American education. To the American and foreign scholars who have assisted so generously and so unceasingly to make the REVIEW representative of the best educational thought and practise of our time, the editor owes a debt of heartfelt thanks. Of the three friends who were associated with him in the conduct of the REVIEW when it was first established, only one still survives. He is none other than William H. Maxwell, Superintendent Emeritus of Schools in the city of New York, easily the most commanding figure of his time in the administration of American public education.

Dr. Frank Pierrepont Graves, then dean of the School of Education of the University of Pennsylvania and later New York State commissioner of education, succeeded Dr. Butler, and continued to edit the *Review* until June, 1924, the ownership having been transferred in 1921 to Doubleday, Page and Company. William McAndrew became editor in 1924 at about the time that he was elected superintendent of the Chicago schools. In an editorial note he wrote:

Everybody, even Frank Graves, is sorry he is giving up the editorship of the REVIEW. It is a matter of mathematics. The span of a man's working days, if you take Lecky's or Hale's or Taft's estimate at thirty-eight hours a week for forty-four weeks a year, is always, for men in educational service, stretched far beyond the standard advocated by the hygeists. For one in an administrative post to edit a professional magazine means a donation of hours never so few as estimated. The acceptance of the call is made with expectancy of sacrifice of other duties. It is a contribution one makes to the general welfare. Doctor Graves, like previous editors of the REVIEW, was willing to give his share. The sacrifice, of course, means the accumulation of undone duties growing steadily more insistent. As expected, the time comes when the steersman calls the next man of the watch to come to the wheel.

The retiring editor ought to enjoy the retrospect of the course he has steered. He has carried prize cargoes—superior goods. Joy Morgan, himself an editor of critical discrimination, writes me: "Doctor Graves has achieved his high standards in the REVIEW. It is the *Atlantic Monthly* of the educational group." This is a short equivalent of much of the shower of comments made when the retiring editor announced that his term was completed. All these verbal tributes are intended to make their recipient happy. Knowing Frank Graves I can say that they do. But I am aware that if the busy sayers of them had neglected to proffer them he would enjoy the quiet satisfaction of having accomplished quite what he set out to do when he undertook the obligation. He has the added felicity of seeing the subscription list double during the past year.

There will be no abatement of effort to maintain the REVIEW upon the high plane reached by Doctor Graves. The clientage devoted to his editorship will be devotedly served. Our readers are chiefly school men. We mean to find out what they want and to furnish it. We shall present the large issues of the educational trend and chronicle the progress of school reform. The hope and confidence of the younger writers will predominate; the steadying caution of the older ones will have its place; their lamentations, none. We shall encourage controversy which observes the courtesies of gentlemen with convictions. We shall chill no propaganda save as mutual interchange between readers may temper it.

Speaking of sacrifice, this is a good time to say out loud what is often whispered, that educational magazines (like educational workers) are not money-makers. The founder of the EDUCATIONAL REVIEW, like Henry Barnard before him with the classic journal, gave himself freely to support it and secured a publisher willing to make monthly donations to keep the project afloat. The present publishers undertook the REVIEW as their contribution to public service and in entering upon the promotion of the sixty-eighth volume they have expressed their "conviction that whatever is best in American life is mostly the result of good teaching; whatever is disappointing will be bettered by it and at length corrected.''

Beginning with the present issue the *Educational Review* and SCHOOL AND SOCIETY are combined. Previously *The School Journal*, established in 1874, and *The Teachers Magazine*, established in 1878, were merged in SCHOOL AND SOCIETY. It is hoped that the interests of education will be best served by the weekly publication of a journal having the united support of all students of education.

EDUCATIONAL NOTES AND NEWS

PRESIDENT UEL W. LAMKIN, of the National Education Association, announces the dates of June 28–July 4 for the organization's sixty-seventh annual convention at Atlanta, Georgia. The meeting will open with a general session on Friday evening, June 28, and will close with a general session on Thursday morning, July 4.

UPON the invitation of President Edward C. Elliott, Superintendent Frank D. Boynton, president of the Department of Superintendence of the National Education Association, spent October 15, 16 and 17 in studying the educational operation of Purdue University. While at the university, Dr. Boynton addressed the entire staff on "The Responsibilities and Opportunities of American Colleges."

DR. HARVEY NATHANIEL DAVIS will be installed as the third president of Stevens Institute of Technology at Hoboken, N. J., on November 23. The trustees of the institute will be hosts to the delegates at the Hotel Astor on the evening of November 22 at a dinner at which Dr. Henry Suzzallo, formerly president of the University of Washington, will preside. President W. H. P. Faunce, of Brown University, will speak. A scientific session will be held at the institute on the morning of November 23, at which papers will be presented by Professor John Johnston, director of research of the United States Steel Corporation, and Dr. Robert A. Millikan, of the California Institute of Technology. Dr. David Schenck Jacobus, a trustee of the college and past-president of the American Society of Mechanical Engineers, will preside. The inauguration ceremonies will be held in the gymnasium of the institute in the afternoon, when President A. Lawrence Lowell, of Harvard University, will deliver an address.

AT the installation of the Reverend W. Coleman Nevils as president of Georgetown University on October 27, James A. Farrell, of New York City, president of the United States Steel Corporation, introduced Dr. Nevils on behalf of the board of regents and presented him with the symbols of university authority. Ninety-three American and foreign universities, including the University of Louvain, were represented at the inauguration. The degree of doctor of divinity was conferred on President Nevils.

STANLEY BALDWIN, British prime minister, was elected lord rector of Glasgow University, in succession to Sir Austen Chamberlain, British foreign secretary, at the triennial election on October 27. The vote was as follows: Baldwin, 1,044; Cunningham Graham, Scottish Nationalist, 978; Sir Herbert Samuel, Liberal, 396, and Rosslyn Mitchell, Labor, 226.

DR. H. G. WALLACE, head of the geological department of the University of Manitoba, has been appointed president of the University of Alberta.

THE installation of Dr. Edmund D. Soper as president of the Ohio Wesleyan University will take place on February 14 and 15. The first day will be devoted to an educational conference. The formal inauguration will take place on the morning of February 15.

DR. HERMAN LEE DONOVAN was installed as president of the Eastern Kentucky State Teachers College, Richmond, Kentucky, on October 25th.

PROFESSOR E. L. THORNDIKE, of Teachers College, Columbia University, will give twelve lectures on the Messenger Foundation of Cornell University. The subject of his lectures will be "The General Field of Psychology." The Messenger lectures were established at Cornell University in 1923 as a memorial to the late Hiram J. Messenger, who died at Hartford in 1913.

DR. JAMES R. ANGELL, president of Yale University, and Rabbi Stephen S. Wise, of New York, delivered the main addresses at the annual meeting of the Northeastern Ohio Teachers Association in Cleveland.

HARRISON LYSETH, Augusta, succeeds the late Josiah W. Taylor as deputy state commissioner of education in Maine.

HENRY H. HILL has been appointed acting Arkansas state supervisor of secondary education during the absence for purposes of study of Mr. M. R. Owens.

MISS OLIVE M. JONES, past president of the National Education Association, who expects to retire as principal of the New York Probationary School, P. S. 120, Manhattan, on February 1, to assume the educational directorship of Calvary Episcopal Church, was elected president of the New York Academy of Public Education at the annual meeting held in the College of the City of New York on October 25.

MISS LAURA M. JOHNSTON, of the faculty of the Oshkosh State Teachers College, was elected president of the Northeastern Wisconsin Teachers Association for the coming year, at the meeting held in Oshkosh on October 6. Other officers named are as follows: *Vice-president,* Superintendent B. J. Rock, of Ripon; *secretary,* George O. Savage, of Oshkosh; *director,* to succeed Superintendent C. C. Bishop, Oshkosh, Miss Mabel Mayer, Manitowoc.

THE following officers of the Chicago Psychological Club have been elected for the current year: *President,* Dr. L. L. Thurstone; *vice-president,* Miss Phyllis P. Barteleme; *secretary,* Dr. Grace E. Munson; *treasurer,* Mr. J. B. Stroud.

JOHN A. H. KEITH, superintendent of public instruction of Pennsylvania, has appointed a committee of six to outline a program of statewide parental education. They are Mrs. E. E. Kiernan, Philadelphia; Arthur S. Hurrell, State College; Ralph R. Bridgman, Philadelphia; Mrs. Anna G. Green, Harold Holbrook and A. W. Castle, of the State Department at Harrisburg.

M. ELIZABETH MATTHEWS, New Castle, is the new assistant editor of *The Pennsylvania School Journal.* She was selected by a sub-committee of the executive council of the Pennsylvania State Education Association from a list of forty-eight competitors for the position.

MRS. MAUD H. MENDENHALL, formerly assistant dean at the University of Wisconsin, has become dean of women at Carroll College, Wisconsin.

DR. ALEXANDER G. RUTHVEN, professor of zoology and director of the university museum of the University of Michigan, has taken up his work as dean of administration of the university.

THE REVEREND PAUL BURT, since 1924 pastor of the First Methodist Episcopal Church at Lockport, N. Y., has been appointed to the pastorate of Trinity Methodist Episcopal Church at Urbana and to the directorship of the Wesley Foundation at the University of Illinois.

DR. E. E. LINDSAY has joined the staff of the school of education of the University of Pittsburgh. For the past four years he has been at the State College of Washington at Pullman.

DR. RICHARD H. PAYNTER, of the Philadelphia General Hospital, has been appointed to the professorship of social and abnormal psychology in Long Island University. He will also act as consultant psychologist to the student body.

ESTHER MCGINNIS, who received her Ph.D. from the University of Minnesota in June, will be associate professor in charge of the extension division of the Institute of Child Welfare at the university. She was a graduate student and fellow of the National Research Council from 1926 to 1928.

DR. JOHN H. EISENHAUER, principal of Reading High School, has joined the faculty of Bucknell University as associate professor of education and director of the summer school and extension department.

DR. K. C. GARRISON, formerly associate professor of educational psychology at Peabody College, Nashville, Tennessee, is now associate professor of psychology at North Carolina State College, Raleigh, N. C. His work is primarily in the school of education, which was established at State College in 1927 to meet a growing demand on the part of the state and the students of the college for opportunity to prepare for various types of vocational and high-school teaching positions in the secondary schools of the state.

Erna Grassmuck, formerly director of geography of the Pennsylvania State Department of Public Instruction, last year head of the department of geography of the State Teachers College, Indiana, will study this year at the University of Chicago on the Nathan C. Schaeffer scholarship. This scholarship, $600, represents the annual income on the Schaeffer Memorial Fund contributed by the teachers of the state a few years ago. While the fund is held by the authorities of Franklin and Marshall College, Lancaster, the award is made by the State Council of Education.

Dr. Albert Eduard Michotte, of the University of Louvain, has been appointed acting professor of psychology at Stanford University for the summer quarter of 1929. Since 1908 Dr. Michotte has been director of the psychological laboratory at the University of Louvain. He is the author of several books and editor of "Études de psychologie."

S. McC. Butt, associate professor of philosophy in the Pennsylvania State College, has leave of absence for the coming academic year and will be acting associate professor of philosophy in Brown University.

Dr. E. B. McGilvary, professor of philosophy at the University of Wisconsin, is visiting professor at the University of California during the fall semester, lecturing on the Mills Foundation.

Edward B. Ham, who was instructor in mathematics at Harvard University during the academic year 1924–25 and instructor in French in 1927–28, has resigned a three-year appointment as instructor in Romance languages to become research associate in the Romance department at Princeton University. He is working with a group of professors who are editing the "Roman d'Alexandre."

Dr. Samuel F. Kerfoot, president emeritus of Hamline University, St. Paul, Minnesota, has taken up his work as a special lecturer for the college. He will speak in a number of towns and cities of southeastern Minnesota on both secular and religious subjects. Several of his lectures will be organized from material gathered during his tour of Europe last winter.

Dr. B. Rush Rhees, president of the University of Rochester, was the principal speaker at the annual founders' day exercises at Swarthmore College.

Professor Zachariah Chafee, of the Harvard Law School, addressed on October 3 the Radcliffe Club of Boston on "Votes for Men," discussing some of the difficulties that still beset the voter in the use of the franchise.

John P. Frey, secretary-treasurer of the Metal Trades Department, American Federation of Labor, delivered on October 31 at Harvard University the Wertheim lecture on "The Development of Industrial Relations through Mutual Consent."

Dean Raymond Walters, of Swarthmore College, gave an address on October 22 before the faculty of Washington College, Maryland, on "The Spirit of Honors Work."

President Wallace Walton Atwood, of Clark University, delivered the address at the formal opening of Randolph-Macon Woman's College on September 24.

We learn from the *Journal of Education* that the alumni of the Mayville State Teachers College, North Dakota, have placed a tablet on the college walls in memory of Joseph Carhart, who was president of the college from 1897 to 1907.

Professor Hugh C. Frame, professor of transportation in the college of business administration of the University of Washington, was drowned off Point Monroe in Puget Sound on October 7.

The conference of the five colleges for women—Smith, Wellesley, Vassar, Mt. Holyoke and Bryn Mawr—was held at Philadelphia on November 1 and 2. The conference began with a dinner on Thursday evening, November 1, and ended with a luncheon on Friday. On Friday evening a dinner was given by the Philadelphia alumnae of the seven colleges in the Bellevue-Stratford Hotel in honor of the presidents of Mt. Holyoke, Vassar, Smith, Wellesley, Bryn Mawr, Radcliffe and Barnard. President Parks, of Bryn Mawr, was toastmistress and President William A. Neilson, of Smith, and Thomas W. Lamont made addresses. On Saturday the Wellesley alumnae gave a luncheon in honor of Miss Pendleton at the College Club; in the afternoon, Mrs. George D. Feidt, of Germantown, gave a tea for Miss Pendleton and Mrs. Henry Bonnell, of Philadelphia.

Professor Edward L. Thorndike, of Teachers College, Columbia University, spoke on October 24 at the first meeting and luncheon of the Department of Vocational Guidance and Placement of the National Council of Jewish Women. Mrs. Francis D. Pollak, head of the new department, who presided at the luncheon, announced that its purpose was to study conditions and to affiliate itself with organizations interested in vocational work. Other speakers were Dr. Meyer Bloomfield; Mrs. Alexander Kohut, director of the National Council of Jewish Women; Miss Lillian D. Wald, of the Henry Street Settlement; Dr. Mary Hayes, of the Vocational Service for Juniors, and Miss Mary Greaves, of Abraham and Straus, and Delos Walker, of R. H. Macy and Company.

The University of Chicago chapel, the gift of Mr. John D. Rockefeller, erected at a cost of nearly two million dollars, was dedicated on October 28, "that religion, pure and undefiled, may dominate all our lives, even as this structure rises above the halls of learning and bestows on them its beauty and its strength." That "the spirit of religion may grow and flourish among the students," an endowment fund of $1,000,000 has been established by the Laura Spelman Rockefeller Memorial Foundation. This announcement was made in an address by Mr. John D. Rockefeller, Jr. Dr. Charles Whitney Gilkey, newly appointed dean of the chapel, conducted the dedicatory services, together with Frederic C. Woodward, acting president of the university.

The new vocational school at Beloit, Wisconsin, was dedicated on October 2, with appropriate ceremonies. The dedication address was delivered by Robert L. Cooley, director of the Milwaukee Vocational School and president of the Wisconsin Teachers Association. An address was also delivered by George P. Hambrecht, state director of vocational education. A. G. McCreary is director of the school. Superintendent F. E. Converse is president of the board of industrial education. The building is dedicated "to the boys and girls and men and women of Beloit, who seek to add to their happiness, success and prosperity through increased knowledge."

A total of 131,210 pupils, an increase of 1,190 over last year, are enrolled in the public schools of Boston, according to the report made on October 15 by Superintendent Jeremiah E. Burke at the meeting of the school committee. In the continuation school the enrolment is 2,987, or 650 less than that of last September 30. The total attendance is 134,197. The greatest increase in the Latin day high schools showed 1,484 pupils more this year. Marked decreases in numbers were noted in the elementary schools of Charlestown, South Boston, North End, West End, city proper and the South End. In the West End schools the decrease is 371, and in the city proper, 293. Roxbury schools show a decrease of 237 as compared with last year. Alexander M. Sullivan, business manager, submitted the total expenditures for the first nine drafts of 1928 for all school purposes at $14,341,550.12.

Plans for the addition of a new division of New York University to be known as the Extension School of Adult Education, which will be established on December 2, have been announced by Elmer Ellsworth Brown, chancellor of the university. This extension school will be under the supervision of Dean Rufus D. Smith, the present director of the regular extension division. According to Dean Smith, it is the purpose of the university through the medium of this new division to offer to mature people, who possess a background of information and intellectual alertness, a group of courses which will present the cultural background of modern civilization. According to the announcement, the courses will begin in December and end in March, with fifteen weekly meetings of approximately an hour and a half each. Fees will not be charged upon a point basis since no regular credit will be given, but the charge imposed will be one that will bring the work within the means of the average person. The courses will be given at both the University Heights and Washington Square centers of the university. The Extension Division will award a certificate in cultural studies to those students satisfactorily completing the courses.

TWENTY-ONE juniors at Barnard College have been chosen for the special honors course to be given during the coming year, according to an announcement made by Dean Virginia C. Gildersleeve. The students selected are the first to be appointed under the new curriculum, which includes a minimum of required courses to be completed during the first two years. The purpose of the special honors course is "to provide for the ablest students an opportunity to do the best work of which they are capable, and to that end to relieve them of a good deal of the ordinary routine of college."

THE International Education Board of the Rockefeller Foundation has offered the sum of approximately $3,500,000 to the University of Cambridge for new developments in the physical and biological departments of the university. The offer of £700,000 included a contribution of £250,000 for the proposed new University Library. The cost of carrying out the plans prepared provisionally by Sir Giles Gilbert Scott was estimated at £500,000 for building and maintenance. The condition attached to the International Education Board's offer was that the university should raise the balance of the sum required for the completion of the whole scheme. As the resources of the university were already pledged to the provision of the new library, it would be necessary to raise from other sources the balance of £229,000 required for the fulfilment of the condition.

THE Centenary Fund of University College, London, has been presented with the sum of £30,000 by Lord Rothermere and Mr. Cecil Harmsworth, in memory of their brother, the late Lord Northcliffe. The income from the fund will endow, (1) "The Lord Northcliffe Chair of Modern English Literature," to be a companion chair to the Quain chair of English language and literature and, (2) "The Lord Northcliffe Lectureship in Literature," under which an eminent man of letters will deliver six public lectures each year, the lectureship to be held not longer than three years by one person.

THE Count Francis Vigyazo is reported to have left to the Hungarian Academy of Science his fortune, valued at lowest estimates at over $10,000,000. By this bequest the Budapest Academy of Science becomes one of the richest institutions of its kind in the world. Founded in the last century by the generosity of Count Szechenyi, the great Hungarian statesman, it suffered great losses through deflation of the currency in the post-war years. The conditions laid down in the will are that 40 per cent. of the fund should be used to further Hungarian national life, 30 per cent. in research work into the history of the Vigyazo family, and the rest in keeping with Christian and national ideals.

THOMAS WALL has presented to the British School Journey Association a large modern mansion, Fairay Court House, standing in two acres of beautiful grounds and situated in Shanklin, in the Isle of Wight. The gift includes besides the house and grounds, the sum of £3,000. The house is to be used by the School Journey Association as a holiday hostel for London school children. The association now has 400 London schools as members, and its aims are to encourage and help the undertaking of school journeys, the purpose of which is the extension of school studies by visits to places of natural, architectural or historic interest under semi-holiday conditions.

IN a statement issued with his annual report Captain Harold Goad, director of the British Institute of Florence, says that during the last session there were over 500 Italian young men and women studying English in the institute, of whom nearly half were taking a five years' course of language, literature and history with a view to teaching these subjects in the secondary schools of Italy. The British institute collaborates with the Italian University of Florence by means of a school of English philology, attended by all university students studying English for their degree. Many public lectures in English are given during the winter months, and concerts of British music and exhibitions of British art are arranged. In the reading-room are all the prominent English and Italian periodicals, and there is a library of about 12,000 English books. An annual summer school was inaugurated last year.

FOLLOWING an eight-year campaign, the City Higher Commercial School of Osaka, Japan, has been raised to the status of a university, being the first such institution in that city, the largest in the empire. The municipal assembly, the Osaka Chamber of Commerce and the alumni of the institution have been endeavoring for the past eight years to persuade the central government to take this step. In order to attain the rank of a university in Japan, it is necessary to make a deposit of $500,000 with the government.

SPECIAL CORRESPONDENCE

THE SUMMER SESSION OF THE NATIONAL UNIVERSITY OF MEXICO

THE eighth annual summer session of the National University of Mexico, which began on July 2, ended its course of instruction on July 16 after a very successful summer. As one might expect, the majority of the students attending were teachers of Spanish, but other fields, such as history, sociology, government, English and music were represented.

Thirty-three states of the United States were represented by students, Texas leading with forty-eight and California second with forty. The total enrolment of regular students was two hundred one—one hundred seventy-three women and twenty-eight men. San Salvador was the only other foreign country represented in the student body, the government of that country having sent two teachers to attend the summer session and to study Mexican schools and methods. It is said that the lack of students from other Latin-American countries is due to the poor transportation facilities between the republics south of Mexico. That country had forty-five students enrolled in the summer session.

In addition to the above enrolment, seventy-five more names were added to the school enrolment by the members of the seminar group brought to Mexico City by Dr. Hubert Herring, of Boston, director of the seminar for the study of relations with Mexico. This group ended its intensive study late in July, when most of the group returned to the United States. However, several stayed on to attend the summer session in its entirety.

Forty-six courses, divided into elementary, intermediate and advanced, were offered this summer. These courses covered the various aspects of the Spanish language and literature, phonetics, the teaching of Spanish, Spanish-American literature, life, problems, history and government, Mexican folk-lore, Mexican songs and dances, and Spanish and Mexican art and archeology. The work was given by forty-four teachers—thirty-three men and eleven women, largely recruited from the staffs of the National University, the National Preparatory School and similar institutions of Mexico City. Most of the teachers taught but one course in the summer school.

In addition to the regular university courses, but on a par with them, were special courses. Dr. Edward A. Ross, of the University of Wisconsin, gave a course on general sociology, and Professor J. H. Cornyn offered a course in Aztec literature. Dr. Fernando de los Rios came from Spain to give a series of lectures on the subject of "The Exteriorization of Justice in History," and Dr. S. Lipschitiz, of the University of Berlin, lectured on "Modern Trends in World Economics and their Relation to International Politics."

Lectures on Maya civilization were given by Dr. S. Morley, of Carnegie Institute; Dr. Carelton Beals spoke several times on Central American problems, and Dr. Juan Mackay, of the University of San Marcos, gave a series of lectures. These lectures, as well as many others, were open to the students of the summer session.

Excursions to points of interest near Mexico City were taken each week under university management, as well as visits to institutions and places of interest within the city. A typical Mexican fiesta was held each Thursday in the beautiful patio of the historic old building where the courses were offered. Mexican songs and music and Mexican folk dances in costume were features of these social gatherings.

The faculty of the summer session, the Mexican government and the Mexican people in general combined to make the summer in Mexico pleasant and profitable. It is certainly to be regretted that so few American teachers and students take advantage of the exceptional opportunity to study in a foreign land under such pleasant conditions as those offered by the summer session of the National University of Mexico.

WM. MARION MILLER

MIAMI UNIVERSITY

DISCUSSION

CAN THE "ONUS" OF MARKING ONE'S STUDENTS BE LIFTED?

HAVING been much occupied, for more than twenty years, both in theory and in practice, with "the improvement of college marking systems," I was struck with the novelty of an idea put forward under the title just quoted in the number of SCHOOL AND SOCIETY dated August 25, 1928. If we agree with the author of that article, the chief improvement needed (p. 227) consists in "freeing instructors from the onus of making the distinction between those who can and those who can not." It seems to the present writer that the author of the article quoted does nothing less than put the cart before the horse. He reverses the relative position of two things.

The "onus" of deciding, of course, by the aid of all means at his disposal, whether the pupil has or has not that minimum attainment which society expects of a person "having taken a certain course," is the very one from which society will never free the teacher. It is of relatively little social importance, for example, whether the licensed surgeon under whose hands one falls on the operating table has a little less surgical skill and anatomical knowledge than another licensed surgeon. But under no circumstances do I want a surgeon who looks for my appendix between the heart and the stomach. If his teacher did not have both the judgment and the courage necessary to decide whether his pupil "passed" or "not passed," he was not fit to be a teacher.

On the other hand, the *giving of distinguishing marks to those who pass is not essential* in educational practice. It is needed only when honors, prizes, scholarships or special privileges are to be distributed among those students who in general, that is, in all their courses or in a certain group of their courses, have a certain high *average* of scholarship. In order to establish greater justice in this respect (and scarcely at all for the purpose of preventing the abuse of failure marks or of freeing the teacher from that "onus" so dreaded by the author here criticized) we first introduced what has often been called the Missouri grading system.[1] The novel idea that "if the instructors simply ranked their students, it would be possible to do away with the specific mark of failure for each separate course," would have seemed to us nonsense if proposed.

Experience[2] has proved, however, that even (a certain, limited amount of) arbitrarily assigning *percentages* of grades, while positively and largely helpful, does not bring about as much uniformity as is desirable for *justice in the distribution of honors, prizes, scholarships and privileges.*[3] Therefore, the present writer published an elaborately designed ranking method[4] (for which credit is partly to be given also to Professor A. L. Hyde, and to which various improvements have been added later but have not been published). That "just to the extent marking is impersonalized will the validity of the measure increase" we shall readily grant to the author criticized. Also that "seeing the particular group in comparison with all the other groups in the college is not the task for an instructor; it belongs to an administrator." But all these and similar arguments become confused and worthless when we fail to see that drawing the line between "passed and not passed" is a function totally different from that of distinguishingly marking those students who have passed. The latter function should indeed be based on *ranking,* and the *teacher's* secondary duty should virtually *end there.*

[1] Compare "The Grading of Students," *Science,* 28: 243. 1908.

[2] "Experiences with the Grading System of the University of Missouri," *Science,* 33: 661. 1911.

[3] "The Limit of Uniformity in the Grading of College Students," *Science,* 40: 530. 1914.

[4] "The Administration of College Grades," SCHOOL AND SOCIETY, 2: 577–589. 1915. "The teacher reports only the rank numbers of his class, *and of course also the failures.*"

But no ranking method will ever perform the miracle of freeing the teacher from the primary "onus" of having to decide whether the student "has passed or not passed."

MAX F. MEYER
UNIVERSITY OF MISSOURI

THE FUTURE HISTORY TEXT-BOOK

WHILE agitation is in progress concerning the reorganization of the public-school system and the establishment of junior and senior high schools and colleges, perhaps it is not out of place to add a word of comment regarding the history text-book.

There have been and still are a number of criticisms of both our secondary and college history texts of which most teachers and students are aware. They are often too expensive, too brief or too detailed in the treatment of certain events, too biased or too partisan, too dry and unentertaining or too mechanical; withal, too unsuited for certain classes.

But there is one type of text which, though it may have some of the above faults, should prove of greater utility than the ones now on the market. The following characteristics might well apply to the text-book of the future. In the first place, except for the teacher's desk copy, the book should be bound in paper. This reduces its longevity, it is true, but it means that students must own their texts and can, therefore, "mark them up" in notebook fashion as much as they like, thus obtaining the greatest value from their contents. In the second place, a section should be added to the volume devoted to readings on pertinent subjects. In the third place, a division should be included in the form of an atlas containing both formal and informal maps, mainly of the black and white lined, dotted or shaded varieties using both sides of the page. The space allotted to each of these divisions would be determined by the historical field covered, but a tentative proportion might be given, as illustration, between text, readings and maps of 100 to 50 to 10.

Immediately it appears that the cost of such a work to the students must be increased over the present figure even when the book is bound in paper. Nevertheless, the advantages seem to offset the initial cost. The utility of each book would be greater, smaller schools with limited library facilities would be benefited, there would be more likelihood of a student using the readings and consulting the maps than if he had to search for them elsewhere, and finally the student would be in possession of a valuable piece of property, which after the course is completed, could be kept with future profit.

A. CURTIS WILGUS
UNIVERSITY OF SOUTH CAROLINA

"HAINT ENEY PLACE"

OPEN your ears for a few moments to the tirade of a college senior on the educational world in general. And my grievances are not entirely unfounded. Listen to my story. I set out to secure a position for next fall when I learned that I was to be graduated from my alma mater with at least the average rating. One day I took my pen in hand and wrote in my very best manner an application to a nearby school board. A few days passed and I received an answer. My application was returned and on the back of it was penciled the following, shall I say words, by the president of the school board, exactly as I have copied them here, "Haint Eney Place"—capitals, spelling, all the same and, underneath, his name.

We take our courses in college, we study four years with the aim in view of entering the teaching profession and then we come up against school boards like these. They know little or nothing of what a college education consists, they have no standard or criterion by which to judge the college graduate. When they demand an interview their interest in us is merely pecuniary; they want to know how much we demand for a salary, and if our bid is low enough we get the place.

Is it right? Should we attempt to tell them of our work in college, the words would be as Greek to them. They would need an interpreter on one side and a dictionary on the other.

If we are to have better educational systems, better schools and more thoroughly qualified teachers let's have school boards that at least know how to express themselves in English, not atrocities.

ELSIE N. BAKER
HOUGHTON COLLEGE,
HOUGHTON, N. Y.

QUOTATIONS

SCHOOLS AND FARMS

EDUCATION is not one of the footballs of national politics. Local political controversy rages often enough about the schools and sometimes school or university issues come to the front in state campaigns; but the national platforms are usually silent on educational problems of any and every sort. The major parties have never thought it worth while to adopt educational planks. Not even the continued effort of the National Education Association (the largest organization of teachers in the world) to secure the establishment of a department of education in the federal government has stirred the national leaders to make an issue of the proposal. Perhaps the reason is that politicians in both parties are opposed to national action in education. Perhaps they, and most citizens with them, have failed to realize the extent to which education is and must be a national concern; or else the practical dangers and difficulties of extending national support to schools or exerting federal influence in the development of schools have deterred the leaders from the attempt to work out safe and effective means to such an end.

In this situation, with the education bill, in one of its "emasculated" forms, still in the Congressional pigeonholes, it is interesting to note the emphasis on education in some of Mr. Hoover's speeches and the pride with which Mr. Smith is pointing to his record in support of education in New York. To Harvard men it may be still more interesting to note a connection that has been set forth by Professor T. N. Carver between one of the sharpest of the present issues of national politics, namely, farm-relief, and national action with respect to schools. Professor Carver is an authority on agricultural economics, an avowed opponent of the McNary-Haugen Bill, and a constructive thinker on farm-relief and other economic measures.

In *The World's Work* for September, Professor Carver writes on the general situation, contending that various factors beyond immediate control are tending to reduce the farming population in this country. Those who are interested should read the entire article. We quote here from the main paragraphs on rural schools. Schools, hospitals, and roads, says Professor Carver, are the three great needs of the rural community, and the greatest of these is schools. "The largest single factor in American life, either urban or rural, is the school. The greatest single advantage of life in the city over life in the country is the superiority of the city schools over those of the country. The greatest single thing that could be done toward making country life as attractive as city life would be to place within reach of every country child as good a school as is provided for the city child. . . . The nation at large has an interest in these country schools almost as vital as the rural communities themselves. . . . If the rural schools are not improved . . . the cities will suffer quite as much as the country. . . . It is a situation that calls for both state and federal action. This can be made perfectly clear as soon as we clarify our ideas as to the general purpose of education. So long as we hold to the mistaken notion that education is a kind of consumer's satisfaction, or that schools exist for the same purpose as moving-picture theaters, victrolas, and radio sets, there would seem to be no good reason why one person or one community should be taxed to provide entertainment or amusement for another. When we arrive at the true conception of a school as a means of training future workers, [we hope Professor Carver would agree that the word "workers" should be interpreted broadly to include the socially productive citizen of every type and kind] it will be easy to see why the communities that are to receive the benefit of that training should pay for it. . . . [Therefore] all cities should be called upon to pay a part of the cost of all country schools. This could easily be achieved by liberal federal support. . . . A comprehensive and nation-wide program of school building and support, standardized, administered, and partially supported from Washington, would not only be the greatest thing that could be done for the farmers; it would also be the greatest single thing that could be done for the nation as a whole . . ."

This is a strong statement, but Professor Carver is not given to statements that can not be amply defended. We venture to believe that opposition to the extension of schooling, even through federal support, is based very largely on popular misconception of the productive worth of schooling, a misconception that is fed by some of the wasted effort in the schools themselves.—*Harvard Alumni Bulletin.*

RESEARCH AND STATISTICS

THE TEXT-BOOK AND ACHIEVEMENT IN LATIN

IN January, 1926, a survey of achievement in Latin was conducted in the public high schools of New York State, under the auspices of the New York State Department of Education. The survey covered the work of the first half year as outlined in the Latin syllabus of the State Department.[1]

To make the survey a valid one, an objective test was constructed, composed of eleven parts: two parts on vocabulary, one on syllabification, one on derivation, two on verb forms, two on noun and adjective forms, one on syntax and two on translation. The test covered exhaustively all phases of the work required by the syllabus and there was nothing included in the test that was not included in the syllabus.[2]

Forty-seven schools in New York State participated in the survey. In all over 2,500 pupils, just completing the work of the first half year, took the test.

Although the syllabus outlines the work in Latin by half years, the schools were usually inclined to follow in sequence the lessons as given in the text-book that the particular school happened to be using. As a result, although schools covered the first year's work as required by the syllabus during the first year, they did not adhere strictly to the syllabus recommendations by half years. Therefore, a number of the schools felt that the test might be somewhat unfair to them since the work they covered during the first half year did not include all the subject matter that was in the test. In order to determine the extent to which this condition held, an analysis of the test was made in the light of several of the text-books used, and the test scores compared for schools using the different books.

Three books, which will hereafter be designated as X, Y and Z were used in about 90 per cent. of the schools participating in the survey that reported the name of the book used in the school. Book X was used as frequently as Books Y and Z together. Books Y and Z were used with about equal frequency. The entire test contained 196 items. Of these, Book X, the one used most frequently, covered only 157 items. Book Y covered 162 items and Book Z, 189 items, which means that the pupil using Book X could apparently obtain a score no higher than 157 points, a pupil using Book Y a score no higher than 162 points, and a pupil using Book Z a score no higher than 189 points. The statements just given concerning the number of points covered by each book are made in the light of the number of lessons which various teachers, using these books, stated that they covered during the first half year. One would expect that in schools using Book Z, the students would obtain a much higher median score on the test than would students in schools using Book X or Book Y.

Table 1 presents an analysis of the situation, showing the number of schools using each of the three books, the maximum number of points obtainable on the test for schools using each of the three books and the median score for each book. This last item means median score obtained by pupils in schools using the particular book. One striking fact stands out immediately. The median score for Book X (76.5 points) is at least ten points higher than the

[1] This survey is reported in detail in "A Survey of Achievement in First Half Year Latin in New York State" by J. S. Orleans and H. G. Thompson, Bulletin No. 892, 1927, University of the State of New York, Albany, N. Y.

[2] A revision of this test and also a test for the second half of first year Latin are now published as the New York Latin Achievement Tests, 1 and 2, World Book Company, Yonkers-on-Hudson, N. Y.

her Book Y (66.5 points) oints). In other words in sing Book X, which allowed a score of only 157 points, the median ment of the pupils is ten points higher the test than in schools using Book Y or Z, which allowed maximum scores of 162 points and 189 points respectively.

TABLE 1

RELATION OF ACHIEVEMENT ON AN OBJECTIVE LATIN TEST TO TEXT-BOOK USED

Text-book	Number of Schools Using	Number of Test Points covered by the Book	Median Score for Schools Using
X	18	157	76.5
Y	9	162	66.5
Z	9	189	66.0

Table 2 shows the distribution of median scores for the schools using the different books. The table is read as follows. Of the schools using Book X, one had a median score between 100 and 110, four had median scores between 90 and 100, two had median scores between 80 and 90, and so on. Of the schools using Book Y, one had a median score between 110 and 120, no school had a median score between 80 and 110, three schools had median scores between 70 and 80, and so on.

TABLE 2

DISTRIBUTION OF MEDIAN SCORES OF SCHOOLS USING THE DIFFERENT TEXT-BOOKS

Text-book	Median Scores for Schools using								
	110	100	90	80	70	60	50	40	30
X		1	4	2	6	2	3		
Y	1				3	2		2	2
Z			1		2	5		1	

It is apparent from this table that more than one third of the schools using Book X had median scores of 80 or over, whereas only one school using Book Y and only one school using Book Z had median scores higher than 80. In other words, the median scores for the individual schools tend to be higher in schools using the book which, for the half year's work, covered less of the test content than the other two books. But there is evidently a great deal of overlapping among the school median scores.

It would hardly be reasonable to draw the conclusion from this presentation that the less of the test material covered by a book, the better would be the score obtained by pupils using that book. Perhaps further data are needed in order to interpret the above tables adequately. The questions which naturally arise are: In what types of schools were these different books used? Or perhaps better still, What were the respective merits of the teachers using the different books? Is the method of presentation and the selection of material found in Book X considerably superior to that found in the other two books, with the result that the work is done more thoroughly by pupils using Book X, although not so much ground is covered? A tabulation of data on this point is not available, but according to the knowledge of the writers, Book X is used more generally in the larger schools, which on the whole have the better teachers and higher standards of achievement. This would tend to indicate the probability of a more careful selection of a text-book which could be effectively taught.

A valid conclusion might then be that it is not the text-book primarily but the teacher and her use of the text-book which play the most important part in determining the achievement of the students. A good teacher with a mediocre or perhaps even a poor text-book will probably obtain better results with a class than a poor teacher using a good text-book. Undoubtedly, however, the teacher using a text-book with an unusually effective method of presentation has a decided advantage over the equally good teacher using a book in which the material is not so effectively presented.

This study is perhaps too meager to make the conclusions definite. The teacher, the text-book, the type and standing of the school and differences in individual pupils and classes are all factors to be considered, yet so closely bound together as to make separation difficult for purposes of accurate comparison. It would be very interesting to see the results of a similar study along the same lines but carried out on a much wider scale and in much greater detail.

JACOB S. ORLEANS,
HAROLD G. THOMPSON

EDUCATIONAL REVIEW

Edited by WILLIAM McANDREW

MATTERS OF MOMENT

Newspaper Cheer for the First School Day.—You will recall the campaign urged by Wm. H. Allen, Institute for Public Service, protesting against the continuation of the stale newspaper joke alleging that the opening of school is, to boys and girls and teachers, like a return to prison. Dr. Allen scored the cartoonist for persisting in representing the public servants in our schools as sour-faced, unlovely specimens of decrepit humanity. Whenever one of these belated slanders appears as an editorial or a picture Allen writes the editor and asks him what school he visited on the opening day or where any teacher remotely approaching the caricature can be found?

You remember Milton Milwaukee Potter, at the Cincinnati convention of the National Association of School Superintendents, introduced a resolution, "Our women," thanking the press for its discovery that children do not hate their schools nor their teachers.

You recall that the EDUCATIONAL REVIEW sent to editors in every state an encouragement to tell the truth and furnished them with photographs depicting the manly beauty of our school men and the nobleness of our school women. Do you bear in mind that we asked you to set your own local newspaper right?

Well!!!

The thing is working. Have you seen Jo. King's drawing of the opening day of school? Who is Jo. King? He is a cheerful cartoonist of Nea. What's Nea? In this case it is not the National Education Association, although it is national and, in a wide sense, educational. The Nea is the News Enterprise Association, with headquarters in Cleveland. Young Fred Ferguson is its president and general manager. Its business for the past thirty-six years has been to furnish newspapers with every kind of news other than that known as "spot" or telegraphed intelligence that can not wait for the mails. Nea senses what is going to be seasonable in politics, science, industry, sport, education, and so forth. Its reporters, writers, and artists all over the world prepare articles and pictures. Its production plants in Cleveland, New York and San Francisco prepare the matter sent in from its bureaus there and in Boston, Chicago, Philadelphia, Atlanta, New Orleans, Detroit, Kansas City, Denver, Fort Worth, Seattle, Montreal, London and Paris. It furnishes this matter to its newspaper customers in every state of the Union, in our Colonial possessions, and in nine foreign countries. I saw, in the Lorain, Ohio, *Daily Journal* the Nea's cartoon by Jo. King. I took occasion to compliment for you, President Ferguson, on his recognition of the proprieties in connection with the schools' big day.

He beamed.

Myself: "How many newspapers carried this picture?"

Fred Ferguson: "About nine hundred."

"How did you happen to have the good sense to furnish this instead of one of those horrible representations of a poor child dragging himself into the presence of a female ogre?"

"Why, I'm an American. I'm a newspaper man. It's the business of newspapers to work public-mindedly. Schools are our best public service. Newspapers and schools should both be working for the same things: progress, advancement, a living less forlorn. It isn't fair to our teachers to represent them as unattractive to children. American boys and girls have no better friends than the public-school teachers. It is absurd to suggest that children dislike school. Even if it were true it would be poor public policy to advertise it. That would make it harder to cure. But it isn't true. American teachers have made the schoolhouse the favorite resort of children; their friends are there, their interesting work, their jolly play."

Therefore, I approve Fred Ferguson. He's a sensible chap, he agrees with me. He's a patriot. He represented American papers in foreign capitals. He was at St. Mihiel; he learned from abroad as well as at home why he has reason to be proud of his country. He approves, as one big reason, her public schools. Therefore I propose him and the Nea cartoonist, Jo. King, for membership in the free and accepted order of patriotic newspaper men, along with John Finley, of the New York *Times;* Victor Yarros, of the Chicago *Daily News;* S. J. Duncan-Clarke, of the Chicago *Post,* and John Herrick, of the Chicago *Tribune,* all of whom have shown by their pens that it is naughty to knock the schools.

I had no sooner said that than Superintendent Boone, of the Lorain schools, proposed the Lorain *Journal* and the Lorain *Times Herald* for membership because they hailed the opening of schools with editorial hurrahs. If your papers did the same send us the glad tidings.

Why is an Institute?—The Fall season of teachers' assemblies is ended in most localities. America is ready for a good searching book on the present place and functions of a teachers' institute. Beginning when apostles Mann and Barnard were crying down the fallacy that teachers are born, not made, the institute project was a school of methods. It aimed to bring the untrained instructors into line with the preparation acquired by the new workers whom the normal schools were sending into the ranks. The old days were those of the teachers' inferiority complexes. It wasn't genteel for women to work for a living. The new country offered such tempting opportunities of fortune for men that permanent acceptance of teaching as a career was repugnant to the ordinary male. Only twenty-five years ago Bardeen's "Teaching as a Business for Men" characterized the schoolmaster as a weak, good-natured mammy, tolerated and looked down upon by the merchant and the professional. The low regard for teachers, their meager pay, the absence of supervision, gave the cue to many an institute speaker and led to the abundance of "inspirational" addresses in which teaching was crowned with a cheap halo. For years we were fed with a sentimental pap the effect of which was to incline us to believe that we were devoted missionaries and devotion was enough. "No matter what you do, if your *heart* is only true, and his heart *was* true to Poll." Up to the recent period when Lotus Coffman made his study of public-school supervision, he found large areas saturated with the old theory that any one who takes up teaching has taken so noble a work that she must be petted, coaxed, praised and coddled.

Taxpayers are Asking Why.—But now that chambers of commerce, granges, associations of mayors, Prichetts, Lowells, Learneds, *et al.,* are boldly declaring we are not getting our money's worth from what is being expended on education, the searchlight of inquiry is being turned on every phase of public-school management. Within the ranks of our own workers we have developed the researchers who seem ready to attack us from the rear. "The inspirational address has passed out of the picture," says investigator Buckingham. "What we now must rely on is those who can tell us what, when, and how much." When these measurers come to try their yard-stick on the ancient and honorable institute we shall have a picturesque report. The notion that teachers when paid for attending must be rewarded by amusement finds support in the presence of "entertainers," sleight-of-hand performers, Irish comedians, jazz singers, and youthful prodigies, all of which I have seen at institutes in the past few years. If these features were originally put in as refreshment between the more solid numbers of the program they have followed the course of college athletics and have become the most striking feature of the general plan. Costing, as they do, a generous amount of taxpayers' money, institutes need reforming. Some level-headed committee needs to investigate the purposes, the methods, and, most of all, the results of institutes.

A Pennsylvania Example.—For seventy-three years Chester County has gathered its teachers annually for instruction. A study of the programs which County Superintendent Clyde Saylor has directed will show you how the institute idea has developed there through the observed experience of various years. Teamwork is evident. There is an institute committee of thirteen men and women of the county. There are subcommittees charged with special duties. Thirty instructors are assigned to places on the week's series of lessons. These include the state superintendent of schools and six of his staff. This tends to keep the schools of the county in touch with the progressive policies of the entire state. On this program were seven instructors from various Pennsylvania teachers' college, a professor from the University of Pennsylvania, a physician from the state hospital, a teacher from the state academy of fine arts and five members of the staffs of Pennsylvania school systems. As antidote to inbreeding, there were two Johns Hopkins professors, a popular lecturer on science, an editor of an educational journal, and a school supervisor from Great Britain. You who realize the need of completeness and variety will see the merit of the composition of this institute faculty.

How is the program made? The institute committee throughout the year notes what is needed in the way of stiffening the work of the schools. We want help with problem children. Dr. Horace Pike is studying this. Let's have him. Reading is moving rapidly ahead. Jessie Dotterer ought to bring us up to date. Get her. So comes Olive Hart from the live girls' high school in Philadelphia, invited to talk on English teaching; Professor Heathcote, on the new American history; Scientist Arthur Lewis, with demonstration teaching; Erna Grassmuck, with a class of school children she never saw until now, giving them geography lessons. There is theory; there is practice; there are accounts of new experiments in city, town and country. There are conferences in which the county teachers tell their plans and doings. There are many "how-to-teach" talks covering the essentials of the Chester County curriculum. There are "round-table" discussions; there are business meetings; there are reports, and, *mirabile dictu,* there is a whole day devoted to meetings of district boards of education while the various teachers' classes are progressing. To these board members the committee gave a course in which selected authorities spoke on school finances, progress in methods of teaching, ideals, forward looks, and the need of requiring efficient teaching service for what the people pay. The sections—primary teachers, high-school teachers, rural teachers, board members—nominated and elected officers and discussed plans for the year. To bring the ideas down to a focus, Superintendent Saylor called his annual message "How to begin." The instructors who were brought from outside gave a broad view of teaching problems by discussing the revolt of youth, the lure of the city, dreams of the biologist, the human teacher, looking forward, and so forth. I cite this as an example of planning an institute with intelligence, foresight and hindsight. Every teacher is paid $4 a day for attendance and loses this $4 and an additional fine of $4 for each day's absence.

If, then, you miss the five days' session you are out $40. To make it worth this to you is no mean task; Superintendent Saylor, I was told by an assistant, plans for this event throughout the whole year.

Lazy Institute Projectors.—But I was told that even in Pennsylvania there are superintendents who merely select some speakers, said to be good, and make a beautifully symmetrical program so:

Monday, 9 A. M.: music.
9.30 A. M.: address: Dr. Windy.
10.30 A. M.: recess.
11.00 A. M.: address: Dr. Chatter.
1 P. M.: music.
1.30 P. M.: address: Dr. Chatter.
2.30 P. M.: recess.
3.00 P. M.: address: Dr. Windy.
Tuesday: ditto.
Wednesday: ditto.
Thursday: ditto.
Friday: ditto.

The Superintendent and the Institute.—I remember that when Ira Bush was superintendent of the Erie, Pennsylvania, schools, I saw him conduct our institute. He abandoned the week-long plan and spread his five-day state allotment of institute bonuses through ten half-day sessions, one a month on Saturday mornings. Each teacher received two dollars for the morning and was fined two dollars for absence. No one has occasion to work up any indignation over this scheme. Millionaire directors of financial corporations use the same device to keep up attendance at their meetings. Ira insisted that a week's consecutive instituting is like taking the whole year's physical exercise in seven days. The effect does not last through the term. If the church member, said Ira, needs a weekly tonic for his soul, one a month is none too many for us. It seems to me that the bewilderment caused by a week of unrelated speeches is real. The hardened institute frequenter takes a seat not too near the front, settles into the easiest position possible, and comes out of every session as untouched by the ideas liberated by the speakers as Farragut was unharmed in Mobile Bay. The gay and lovely young things in the back seats get some amusement by exchanging pleasantries. No longer do we see the good old habit of taking notes of the proceedings.

Attention at Institutes.—I went to one affair in western Pennsylvania at which the county superintendent castigated us all at the beginning. "I want you to understand," he said, "that the state is paying good money to hire these expensive speakers to address you. I don't want that money wasted by your gossiping during the speeches. If I see any teacher communicating to her neighbor I will stop the speaker and reprimand the offender." Well, we had perfect order, but it was the order of the jail and whipping post. Butterfield was a speaker, as I recall. His gentle and pervasive humor, which mellows an ordinary audience to a point of acceptance of that gentleman's wise and profitable suggestions, had no chance. We were all scared to stiffness and didn't dare to smile. I remember an institute in McKeesport, Pennsylvania, where the gentle Ritchie began by saying, "I think you will be interested in a letter I received after your last meeting. It is from the speaker of the day. He said, 'You must let me thank you for the hospitable and courteous reception accorded by the teachers. They made it very easy and pleasant for me.' " We had perfect order. It was the attention of well-bred gentlewomen and men. You can't rely entirely on the unaided honor and good manners of us teachers in meetings of this kind. It is not many generations ago that inmates of jails and almshouses were deported to America to teach. I never saw worse manners than by some New York teachers in a meeting called by President Willcox to discuss pensions. Before that, some had hissed Superintendent Maxwell. Some Chicago teachers booed Superintendent Chadsey. Some Columbus teachers were castigated by the newspapers for bad manners. I have heard the chairman of teachers' meetings in Boston stop the speaker until whisperers could be quieted. The conductor is responsible for an efficient institute as orderly as a good teacher's classroom. If good attention doesn't come naturally as it does in Savannah, Detroit, Grand Rapids, or Minneapolis, it is his business to get it. I have seen a dozen institutes in Iowa, ten in Kansas, three in Nebraska, two in California, one in Texas, two in Virginia. They were perfect examples of attention and courtesy. Nor can attendance be uncounted. New Bedford's board of education shut down on teachers' conventions on the allegation that too many who were supposed to attend spent the time in the motion-picture houses. Wisconsin, for a time, had to devise an elaborate coupon system to be sure that the taxpayers' money was spent for attendance on institute meetings and not for roaming through department stores. But the recent institutes I have seen in Milwaukee, Racine, Madison, Appleton, Green Bay, and Oshkosh were real business. One stupidity persists in many localities except in the South; the indignity offered the speaker by giving him rows of empty seats directly in front of him. For a conductor to begin an educational meeting with the doleful exhortation: "Will those in the rear please come forward," is to admit that he doesn't know his duty. He is responsible for a courteous treatment of a speaker, whether it be one of his own official family or imported talent. Reasonable foresight will see that the front seats are filled. Henry Ward Beecher, a speaker considered of great ability, said he couldn't speak if his people had to be reached across a row of empty benches. How much more needful is it that the less able talkers who appear at institutes be freed from the ungrateful task of preaching across a no-man's land to reach an audience. In the preliminary announcements of the Connecticut State Teachers Association in Bridgeport last May was this reminder: "Our speakers are our guests. It is a courtesy for you to see that no bare spaces are in the front rows. If you make it a rule not to sit behind an empty seat you will do your share of upholding the hospitality of the association." Superintendent Gamble, of Sharon, Pennsylvania; Superintendent Boone, of Lorain, Ohio, deliver to their invited speakers a compact group of people directly in front of the platform. Principal Felter, of the Girls' High School, Brooklyn, gets this through training his ushers. But some mule-headed members of an audience know better and won't be ushered. For such the beautifully decorative rope is effective. Not in the punitive manner you think I mean, but stretching from the back, down each side of the aisle, and shutting off all but row one. As soon as this is filled row two is opened. This is the method used by competent train masters. They open fresh cars when the first offerings are filled.

Superintendent Hollis, Greenville, South Carolina, has a feature well worth while. When securing his speakers he stipulates that on each day of their service they will meet him in conference half an hour before the day's session begins. This enables him to know for sure that there will be no break in his program. If a speaker fails to appear at this preliminary assembly Hollis assigns one of those present to find the missing member. If not found, his place is filled by another speaker. Hollis has another efficiency scheme of much value. He engages experts from some department of education to spend a day in each of his schools helping the teachers. The visitor notes improvements needed, and confers with the teachers and with the superintendent. From matters discussed, features are put on the institute program so as to have direct local application. New Jersey and Michigan have "teachers' helpers" working in the schools. At institutes they borrow classes of local children and use them in demonstrations of methods needed in the particular region covered. Everywhere the demonstration or clinic is coming into vogue—actual children taught, questions of and by the teachers present. This is a method so long used in teaching physicians, in educating salesmen, and in various producing corporations that neglect of it by us would be peculiar.

The Audience and the Speaker.—The back-seat habit is discreditable to the service. It is in line with the old shabbiness of being ashamed to be known as a teacher. It is a cheap confession of lack of interest in the concerns of our profession. You never saw the conductor of a medical clinic ask the surgeons to "please come to the front seats." The spectators crowd into them. You never heard the manager of a prize fight beg: "Will those in the rear please come forward." You have seen a sales manager demonstrate to his staff the points of an automobile. You never saw his people holding off. An educational address is for improving the service. It shouldn't be subject to removable obstacles. Empty seats and listless listeners are curable by any director worth his salt. But if the institute speakers would insert in their agreement to talk: "I come on your promise that you will dispose your audience so that they sit with no empty seats in front of them," the institute director will possibly awaken to his duty. Most of them never thought how stupid, unethical, rude, inhospitable, and unprofessional the bare-bench indignity is.

While speaking of the speaker's duty, one might rap the foolish and unprofitable corrective tone too many speakers still employ in addressing teachers over whom the lecturer has no supervision. It puts them into a defensive state of mind, misses your purpose, and wastes time. The autobiographical speaker is out of date, now. He belongs only in hick towns where the audience likes to feel that the great man is telling secrets about himself. If you can get through your forty-five minutes without pronouncing your own name or telling us that you have been in Europe, if you use your time to tell us how to do the teaching we ought to do, you deserve, though you may not get, hearty applause.

The Old Institute Should Pass.—Even the best institutes I have seen violate a sound principle of teaching. The passivity of the taught is a fatal fault. Beyond that of attendance and attention there is no responsibility on the teacher. This fact kills the institute as an efficient instrument of achieving what it is set up and paid for. Classes for instruction of adults are common enough. They were long in the institute stage. Anybody could get night-school assignments to teach. Now, the efficient school manager plans his adult classes in accordance with the known facts of the learning process. Until the teachers' institute is remade with a similar aim it will continue a waste of good money, drifting along in old channels which every educated superintendent knows are clogged with traditional snags—wasteful and unscientific. A superintendent is at fault who fails to plan his institute on the observed and considered needs of his school system. It is a waste to let invited speakers choose their own general topics. It is much as though you would invite a celebrated specialist in serum to come and would let him administer adrenalin to everybody. Nobody should be so able to make an institute program as the superintendent of the schools. He should know whether arithmetic, reading, civics, or immorality needs the most immediate attention. Having fixed his topics he should select his experts for demonstrations. John Stone or Ernest Horne is worth a dozen "inspirational" speakers. Henry Morrison doesn't shout, nor purr; he hasn't a gesture in his vocabulary, but he inspires by clear demonstrable exposition of how things are done. Martin O'Shea is another. The new type of experimenter who has guided a method to success in the classroom is the Moses needed in the institute wilderness. Isn't he? He is. The fatal failure to fix or stabilize the products of institute teaching so as to prevent their speedy and complete evaporation is enough to damn it in the eyes of any economist who wants to see public money effectively spent. We wouldn't, nowadays, pay teachers merely to tell their pupils. They have to arouse thought. They have to test. Until an institute is planned with clear intent to get improved results in the schools of the districts, until the institute lessons are cerebrated in every teacher's head, the affair is only a partial step toward what is paid for. It is like laying expensive seed on the ground and failing to harrow it in.

What we must come to is this: fewer things, more thoroughly done. We shall have our program based on what the superintendent wants. He will plan the institute lessons. Different teachers will go to the sessions designated by the principals and superintendents. At the close of the lesson they will retire in groups of thirty or less to classrooms in charge of a principal or chairman charged with seeing that the essential features of the lesson are gone over by the teachers present. The psychologists have shown us so conclusively that discussion, self-activity, is so essential for clearing the mind, broadening the view, and making ideas our own, that no manager of an institute can afford the waste due to the omission of this feature so necessary to the learning process. The quiz will conclude with a requirement for each participant to write a five or ten minute outline of what he considers the main points made by the speaker. These papers will go to the principals and the superintendent.

The Teachers Won't Like It.—This will be a heartily unpopular feature. Who ever knew of any group, doctors, lawyers, or other workers, hailing with delight, unless especially rewarded, any discard of an old routine for a new procedure requiring more work? But unless this or an equally effective means of making the institute productive is employed, the researchers who examine the institute will report in favor of abolishing the project altogether, as a waste of time and money.

Conductors Should Move First.—It is much more highly creditable to us to do this ourselves than to be forced to it by pressure from without. Conductors have a real responsibility of making the institute money produce the greatest results. But beyond the financial question is the fact that improving the institute strengthens classroom teaching all along the line. It is a valuable means of reducing pupil failures and raising the value of the human product delivered to the community by the schools. Chiefly responsible for institutes is the state superintendent. The funds are allotted by his office. The institutes offer a concrete, organized project by which he can affect the whole teaching service of his state. A committee for study and recommendations appertaining to institutes is a present need of state departments of education. All of which is respectfully submitted.

A REVIEW OF BETTER BOOKS

HOI BIBLIOLOGOI

THESE are the archives of a fraternity of public-school people devoted to telling one another what of books in our craft we have found worth reading. We have no constitution. We are completely subject to the benevolent autocracy of Professor John Rose, founder, preserver and potentate of the guild. We are sifters, reviewing many works but discussing only those which each amateur considers superior.

The meeting unto which these present notes appertain was on a rainy evening. Yet every member came. The folding racks which the cunning of Steven, the shop-teacher, had made, held glistening raincoats and gave a not unpleasant odor of moist air, with some melancholy in it as our subconsciences felt the vague and misty memories of a summer gone.

Getting closer and closer.—When our manager nodded to Carolina she distributed pencils and printed sheets to each of us. We found that we were each in charge of a class of thirty pupils in suburban high school and just beginning our first day. Unknown to us, the distribution of the class is: six have well-educated parents, fathers in the professions; eighteen are children of skilled tradesmen, business men, etc. These eighteen have ability to do the school work but don't know how to study; they get no encouragement at home. The remaining six come from disrupted households. They are indifferent to usual school rewards and penalties; they are in school because of the law. They show many evil effects of parental neglect. We know nothing of this. We wish to use their first period to secure facts to help us know how to conduct the class. Which of the following procedures is best, which poorest?

(1) To ask one brief question of each pupil during the period.

(2) To give a standardized achievement test in the field to be covered in the course.

(3) To give a special test prepared by the teacher to find out what each pupil already knows about the course.

(4) To give a standardized intelligence test.

(5) To have each pupil write answers to questions about home life, special interests, his father's occupation and other significant facts.

We wrote our answers. Carolina asked: "How many consider number one the best procedure?" Nobody did. The score was:

Sixteen Bibliologoi, 88 per cent. of those present, considered the best procedure is to have the pupils write on home conditions, etc.

Two members, 12 per cent., voted for a standardized intelligence test.

All, 100 per cent., considered asking each student a brief question the poorest procedure.

"Now," said Carolina, "has any one a better procedure than any of those listed?"

The General proposed a thirty-minute essay on "Myself" by each pupil, to include "My father, my mother, our home, our family, my favorite occupation, books I have read, books I like best, why I come to school and what I expect to be." He secured, such a favorite is he, assent from almost everybody.

"Now," said the quiz-lady, "this is what it's all about. Douglas Waples, William Reavis, Irvin Poley, Harold Anderson, Howard Wilson, E. R. Breslich and Charles Stone have printed one of the most searching books[1] for high-school teachers I ever saw. It might properly be

[1] "Problem Exercises for High-school Teachers," University of Chicago Press. 99 pp. $1.00.

called 'How do you do, teacher?' They canvassed a large number of secondary-school instructors and collected a list of usual, everyday difficulties in class management: discipline, interest, thinking, preparing tests for pupils, etc. The problems cover English, reading, composition, poetic taste, slang, history and social subjects, algebra, geometry, supervised study, review, assigning lessons, science, projects, laboratory work, and so on. The authors selected situations which stimulated the most controversy. They grouped them, ten to each selected line of teaching, and they chose for each situation the five commonest answers. In the form I just tried on you they offer the 60 tests for teachers. What are they for? To furnish definite experience in training classes of high-school teachers, to provoke and direct thinking toward solution of classroom difficulties, to give a teacher in service a self-appraising guide, to give a principal a standard for his school, to help superintendents compose examinations for high-school teachers' certificates. A remarkable thing about this book is that it gives one the comforting information that his problems are not peculiar but that his brothers and sisters in high schools everywhere are meeting and solving what made him feel so perplexed and lonesome. I have made my humble attempts here to review in my amateurish way the books that have fallen to my lot. I certainly know more about good books than I did. From my angle, here is a notable piece of work, carefully planned, sedulously guarded against mere armchair theory. I think we should crown it as the French Academy of Immortals do when they find a work of very superior merit. It reaches the high mark of intelligent construction in that its problems are real, the residuum after sifting out the unusual. It has the unique distinction of preventing your indiscriminate swallowing of what it says. You have to think and judge and decide. It throws you into concrete situations instead of letting you grope among abstractions. It has the remarkable quality of exercising your common sense; the teacher of a week's experience can be as well suited by it as the old stager of many years. For the live principal who follows Mr. Gist's requirement of a course of fortnightly conferences on common educational topics with the teachers of his school it furnishes a standard program. It is the closest to everyday needs of all the books I have seen this year. I can't speak for you all, but I crown this book. After each of you has studied it the Bibliologoi, the American Academy of Immortals, Readers of the Best Books, will crown it, too."

The General, who said he was inspired in programing the fall schedule of his huge school, reported:

"I drew a varied output of the presses of the publishers who are laboring to keep us schoolmasters on the move. Again I have to compliment the Bureau of Research of Ohio State University. It publishes a volume[2] of good hard work by Harold Chapman, assistant director, Bureau of Educational Research, Baltimore Public Schools. He gives a history and the present state of that movement which, in my opinion, has done more to put our business on a respectable footing than any other single reform in education. Up to 1911 about the only regular report any school system made had to do with the attendance and absence of teachers and pupils and the total yearly cost of running the school system. The superintendent of the schools of Rochester, New York, Herbert Weet, wanted to know what was the matter with his backward schools and how to bring them definitely up to efficient service. He reminded his school board that other than educational corporations subject their output to continuous scrutiny. Their sales depend on good quality. They know where their successes and losses are and the cost of them. He got set up a permanent Bureau of School Efficiency to evaluate the methods of teaching and to report to the principals of the several schools their standing as related to the city as a whole. Promotions, age-grade conditions, absenteeism, the question of good or poor teaching and supervision were reduced from guessing to a basis of statistical facts. Each school soon had a little bureau of its own by which the principal found out where the strong and weak points of teaching are. Dr. Chapman runs over the interesting details

[2] Harold B. Chapman, "Organized Research in Education," Ohio State University Press. 221 pp. $1.50.

of the earlier storming of the fortress of educational complacency, a reform begun by that smiling and persistent magazine editor, James M. Rice, who, in the *Forum,* twenty-five years ago, had wondered why every other service was tested by its results while ours was bolstered by oratory and sentimentality. 'Teaching power, if it be power,' Rice had said in 1902, 'must produce effect. The effect is in the pupils. It ought to be pronounced enough to be measurable. Why do you rate teaching by observing the teacher? Why don't you appraise her by the results of her work? No superintendent,' he said, 'has any accurate facts about the success of his schools. The head man talks in general terms, well sweetened with buncombe about faithful, conscientious teachers. It prevents the growth of solid respect for educational service.' The *Forum* articles led to an attack on Rice by prominent school men, who castigated the editor as wishing to mechanize the schools by means of factory practice. 'The service of the schools is greater and finer than can be tested. The personality of the teacher is her greatest contribution. You can not measure it.' Paul Hanus, who had been put into the recently established chair of education in Harvard, took a view of the matter opposite to that of the conventional schoolmaster. He supported Rice, arguing that if the public-school superintendent accepts the responsibility of spending the public's money he must take the duty of knowing that it is effectively spent. Teaching must have objectives. They must be definite enough to be measured. Otherwise the most wasteful of schools can be defended by emotional slogans incapable of demonstration. Leonard Ayres, Edward Thorndike and other well-known educators refused to be hypnotized by the high-flown sentiment of the standpatters. Burdette Buckingham maintained if the teaching is good, as so many claim, it must be possible for some to be bad. Parents and taxpayers have a right to know in what respect it is good and how good it is. He and others organized a national society for educational research. Dr. Chapman tells us that the evaluation of products by means of standards experimentally determined is as much a necessity of a school system as it is of any corporation in industry or commerce. Education must utilize the methods developed by industry to improve efficiency and eliminate waste. Melville Dewey contends that the obvious economy and certainty developed in our machines must be extended to teaching. President Eliot expressed the view that the fear of destroying human character by machine efficiency is not borne out by fact. Well, the invention and use of standards won their way. New York teachers seem to have offered no opposition, but in Boston the attempt to raise the level of accomplishment met with strong protest from teachers. They saw in standardized tests something that would affect their ratings and their chances for promotion. In Kansas City the new superintendent told the board of education that the general demand for better work in the local schools should be answered by definite facts determinable by actual testing. They gave him a bureau. Chicago's board in 1916 appointed a committee to consider the advisability. It took them a year to make up their minds. Samuel Allison took up the organization of such a bureau in 1917 and prosecuted the work with such intelligence and definiteness that principals who thought it the forerunner of real supervision pretty nearly killed it, a job that Mayor Thompson's school board effected without any help, the obsequies occurring in August, 1928. Politics always fears facts. Dr. Chapman's chapter on friction is a unique and spicy contribution unusual in educational works and without any bitterness or complaint reflecting little credit upon our profession. If we could get school boards to read a book like this it would strongly tend to lift our imperfectly respected service out of the condition of a coddled infant into the place of a being able to stand erect. I am tired of seeing a tremendously expensive school system subject to the personality or popularity or politics of a superintendent, now that the science of school supervision has reached the point of determining definitely how good the service is. Salt Lake shows that its schools are superior; Duluth demonstrates that it has surpassed Detroit in some things and has not yet reached it in others. Sixty-eight city school systems maintain trained bureaus constantly checking up on the product. I agree with President Campbell, of the University of California, that a superintendent can not be held responsible for the work of the schools without adequate, independent appraisers to know, not to guess, what the work of the schools is.

A brilliant solution of the lockstep puzzle.—Report of Philip Manzer:

"I once took a summer course under Andrew W. Edson, Massachusetts educator, who was called to New York as assistant superintendent of city schools. He impressed upon us the serious defects of public-school procedure as to its failure to fit individuals. He elaborated the advantages of grouping pupils according to ability. He frequently referred to the work of a New York City principal, Edward Maguire. I have a book[4] by this last-named gentleman. It is uniquely crisp, bright and readable. This man, besides mastering the extensive techniques of teaching from baby class into the high school—in fact, Professor Miller, of the University of Wisconsin, sees the need of Maguire's methods in college classes—has a philosophy of teaching which sparkles through the book in epigrams and seeming paradoxes like these: 'Those responsible for teaching to-day are not so much interested that instructors and students know as that they know how, not so much interested in content as in ability, not so much concerned with gathering as with searching.' 'The modern teacher is concerned not so much in the pupil's learning as in his learning how to learn.' 'If children knew how to study teachers would not be needed.' 'The pupil-at-work is more valuable than the pupil-waiting-to-be-called on.' 'A great gain in school procedure is the suppression of the interfering teacher.' 'The greater the teacher's skill, the less he will apparently have to do and say.' 'An ounce of self-drill is worth a pound of instruction.' 'These are tragic days of pedagogical pessimism.' 'The child is his own best teacher.' You might say this book is a working out of the old slogan, 'divide and conquer.' No forty children were ever found who can do so well when being taught as a unit as when they are grouped according to ability. Work them in blocks of ten. Divide every period devoted to a school subject into shorter periods. The teacher takes one group of ten who are standing up and talking with her; the other three groups are at work on definite tasks according to charted plans given them previously. With her first group my lady takes up an assignment. It consists of checking the work these children have done since the previous assignment, discussing new matter and making clear the plan-charts for the work they are to do. It takes ten minutes. They then take the chart to their quarter of the room, hang it up and go to work on the assignment for thirty minutes. Madam next calls to her the second group which has meantime been working on their own assigned tasks. She does the same with them, sends them with their chart to their quarter. She takes the third and then the fourth. Each group, as you observe, works thirty minutes and confers with the teacher ten minutes. A five-minute period of general discussion completes the time. A three-group or a two-group class works on the same principle. The scheme must be worked out so as to provide for the common needs of the pupils in each group, to get all pupils working, not waiting to be called. It increases self-activity. It is utterly preventive of the recitation as we know it. It gives the teacher almost no chance to talk. Mr. Maguire says this is the main value of it. Having seen so much mental atrophy in children produced by teachers' tongues, I am inclined to agree with him. Study takes the place of listening and waiting. Individual work becomes habituated in every subject, because of the specific chart direction and because of the imminent personal report on study as made by every child every forty-five minutes. I have been sufficiently inoculated with our local anti-factoryizing rabies to react against this relentless mechanization of the school day. Maguire must have met this objection many times, for he argues it out here to a finality. 'The whole-class recitation,' he says, 'never has produced enough individual activity to satisfy the appetites of the children. Its prevailing accompaniment is boredom and stultification. Ten minutes' teacher-direction of the right kind is more than enough to furnish motive for thirty minutes' work by a child. Even condensed to ten minutes the assignment runs more of a risk of being too heavy than too light. Four ten-minute ministrations to

[4] Edward Randall Maguire, "The Group-study Plan," Charles Scribner's Sons. 203 pp. $1.80.

homogeneous groups is not so hard upon a teacher as forty minutes' control of a whole class where always some are restless at waiting for the slow and others bewildered by the success of the rapid.' Maguire's 'mechanization,' if one wishes to be hostile and call it such, is a hard-and-fast provision that every child shall be given time to do the work he can do, shall be held accountable for it at regular intervals and shall be standing on his own feet rather than be leaning on a teacher. President Eliot said the protest against mechanization of work seems to have little real justification. Even the literary men and the painters keep to a rigorous program of regular working hours. Over and again the author of this book departs from our Chicago theory that school should be run to suit the teacher. He makes no apology for proposing a program for pupil benefit rather than for teacher favor. This plan, he says, requires the teacher automatically and economically to be engaged in the proper teacher activity and not interfering with the most valuable occupation of the pupil. 'The commonest and most fatal fault that afflicts teaching is assigning too much.' In a class of forty the gifted few may blind the teacher to her error. The audience attitude of the children lures her into the talking, lecturing, scolding habit. Quiet is imposed. This isn't teaching. It's time-wasting. As long as a pupil can continue studying he does not need a teacher. In the Maguire method the teacher learns to leave the boy alone when there is no need of her.

"You do not give me time sufficient to elaborate how this book sets up the procedure for working out the proposal that the pupil, rather than the teacher, should use and train his mind. Mr. Maguire is not a free agent. He has a school of which the course of study and the hours of session are prescribed by the Olympian deities who are the school board. He takes the course, he takes the time table. By his division of every class into groups, by his program of alternate attention of teacher to each group, he secures for at least two thirds of class time a working scheme for every child unhindered by a teacher. All the rest of the project is refinement and fortification of a program so that the study by the group is kept productive, the civic function of the public school is performed, the health and happiness of the members are promoted and the school training received is thorough and efficient. Without a stumble, Maguire goes swiftly to his goal. He shows himself philosopher, seer, planner, organizer, manager and producer. When the books of the year come to be appraised I believe this one will be found worth the blue ribbon."

Dr. Batwell was next:

"Here comes Principal Elvin Fishback, of the Senior High School of Anderson, Indiana, with a short, serviceable volume[5] on the big theme of getting children to grow into the kind of men they ought to be. This, he says, is the highest achievement of the school; character training. Mere devices won't do it. Character doesn't come as a by-product of algebra. Honesty isn't spontaneous. Too much emphasis on the intellectual drove out of the upper grades half-educated children into our none too refined society. We are not doing that now. We regard every child as a potential citizen. We daren't neglect him. Moral culture is more needed than intellectual. Principal Fishback evaluates the ethical values of the different studies and activities of the junior high school and addresses himself to the need of a moral character in the teacher which must be higher than the average. How are we going to train an honest man if we permit dishonest, immoral instructors, lying about their absences, loose in their talk and habits, to be the associates of growing youth? Mr. Fishback can't subscribe to the old dictum that moral teaching is best when indirect. Pooh, pooh, says he. You're afraid of the subject. Stop arguing and improve our method. Don't fumble around the edge of morality. Let the children know that the school stands for honor, purity, service. Don't hesitate to preach as well as practice. I'm for Mr. Fishback and his specific, direct lessons in character, of which his book has many."

Respect for the respectable.—Said Polly, who was next:

5 Elvin H. Fishback, "Character Education," D. C. Heath & Co. 189 pp. $1.24.

"The experience I have had, in this revered club, with the productions of Almack and Lang lead me to assert that their hallmark on a book is a guarantee of straight, crisp, palatable nutriment, pleasant to the taste, and strengthening to the system. With that expectation I selected from the offerings of the publishers the latest contribution[6] of these two Pacific-coast producers. John Almack is a professor of education, Leland Stanford, temporarily loaned to the University of Pennsylvania. Albert Lang was superintendent of schools, Canal Zone, U. S. A., and is now head of the education department, State Teachers College, Fresno, California. These men are practical and definite in covering the multitude of things the new teacher wants to know. For example, they tell her to look out for the bargainizing school board that asks her what salary she wants. Here's the proper formula: Calculate board and lodging in the place for twelve months; multiply by two. Don't let any board get you for less. This is rock bottom. For desirable salary add fifty dollars for every year of experience and enough to pay five per cent. on the cost of your schooling since you left the high school."

"I'm for that, with my fifty years of teaching," said the General, "Twelve hundred and fifty dollars bonus!"

"But this work is for the beginning teacher," said Polly.

"These researchers," continued the General, "give us so much new matter that I'm a beginning teacher all the time."

"The book begins with getting ready to teach," continued Polly. "It has one of the plainest, soundest presentations of the reasons for taking up this life work I have ever read. Teaching can not continue to be taken as a stepping-stone. It's getting as stiff in requirements as medicine. Preparation is being made longer and longer. Teaching is now being chosen as a vocation by a large number of ambitious and capable men and women. The authors discuss its importance, opportunities, social standing, liberty, pay and realization of personal aptitudes. It's a great chapter! Listen to this: 'Every one naturally desires social approval. It is common to seek a calling that gives prestige. Distinction is probably more highly prized than anything else. Studies made of hundreds of young men and women showed this to be their highest desire.' Teaching didn't command social recognition a while ago. Success was measured by money, by the skill of the doctor and his income, by the cases won by the lawyer plus his fees. There was a feeling that recognition of ability, faithfulness and achievement was not given to teaching. What caused this? The lame ducks in the business. There are in our ranks as large a proportion of successes, as much social recognition, as in any profession. Failure to weed out the failures, the cheap, the lazy, the unprofessional, has held the rest of us back. But the social status of the teacher is on the up grade. So pressing is the popular demand for education, so great is its influence, that we are rapidly coming to our own. We are making codes of conduct for ourselves and shall soon reach the point of expelling from our association unprofessional members, as now the lawyers, ministers and doctors do. A large proportion of the world's best minds are devoting themselves to education. Its aims are more closely defined, its results more accurately measured, its failures more quickly determined. We have it in our power by organization and character to mold the whole public attitude to an approval of us and the recognition that ours is the highest of civic employments. The path to this is not through noisy protest of teachers' organizations opposing the introduction of new methods such as junior high schools, departmental teaching, platoon schools or achievement tests, but by letting the public see, as is the case in hundreds of cities, that the teachers' clubs are professional organizations hailing progressive measures with acclaim. This is the spirit of this book: study, preparation, planning, skill, team-work, improvement. These are the timely topics with which the book abounds: planning for the opening of school, the first day, organizing the routine, the problems of discipline, attendance, play and relations with the community. Then follows a survey with hints upon the new and approved principles and methods of developing the human material committed to our care by a hopeful nation. Spelling is here, the social studies, all the fundamentals, and the varied things a modern school attempts. Is this a good book for teachers' meetings? It is. To apply

6 Almack and Lang, "The Beginning Teacher," Houghton Mifflin Co. 478 pp. $2.40.

a remark just made by the General, every teacher in these days of advancement must be a beginning teacher. She can get a bookmark and refresh her mind by fifteen minutes every morning of consecutive matter here and soon become as happy, reading it, as a healthy boy is at his breakfast."

Allurement in the algorism.—"If you'll not let it go any farther than this circumspect circle," said the Viking Maid, "I'll confess to you that I have an aversion to arithmetic. My father is a carpenter and uses it. My mother is quick and accurate with figures. I never noticed any dislike when I was a little schoolgirl in Bergen, Norway, but in my American schooling somewhere along the line I got a *complexus arithmeticus*. Geometry gave me no trouble. In algebra and the required mathematics of college I cut no figure at all."

"How did you pass the principal's examination?" asked the Signpost, shielding himself with raised arm.

"The school I had was annexed to the city and all of us were validated," she replied sweetly. "Since the oncoming march of progress has given 'diagnostics' as a new fashion to the schools I have discovered not a few children in the upper grades who have a distaste similar to mine. The number of teachers who do not like the subject is considerable. Like me, they have developed a technique of concealing their aversion and their ignorance. We are unfortunates, born too early, before corrective pedagogy was invented. The departmentalized school is a godsend to us. The Lord has given my school a marvelous arithmetic teacher. She does all the top-grade work in mathematics, and, more wonderful still, she is discovering the children who hate arithmetic, why they hate it, and is mental-hygienizing their complexes away. When Papa Rose gave me these books on arithmetic I confessed. He said if a grown-up king could be taught by an Irishman to like asparagus a Bibliologa could teach herself to enjoy mathematics. I have had my eyes opened. I can read these pages with interest, every now and then with enjoyment.

"I tried the largest book first,[7] and found out from Mr. Rowantree what is wrong with me and arithmetic. 'You can't like arithmetic unless you understand the subject. You can't like a person with whom you are not acquainted. The main requisite for appreciating arithmetic is to know it. Whatever new is taught, take time to see that every child grasps the meaning. Let drills be made enjoyable and not continued to the point of boredom.' 'The ultimate goal of arithmetic is to enable the student to solve problems.' 'Success in this does not depend on any mechanical habit. The only solvent is thinking.' Much of the difficulty of making thinking have interest is due to the remoteness of the arithmetic work from the life of our time. Get problems out of the newspapers, out of everyday life. Problems that the children make are worth much more than those found in the book. Drill is inevitable. The psychologists haven't discovered a substitute. But repetition with enjoyment, drill with satisfaction, is the most efficacious. A fine way to give it interest is the self-kept graph of each pupil showing his gain in power. This gives you an idea of the reasonableness of the book. It is full of the findings of experience. I think the authors have observing minds. In speaking of the two ways of teaching they speak of the arbitrary method, the way I was taught, in which you are told how to perform a process. They speak of the rational method, in which the reason is made clear. Now, they add a new and striking reason for the rational way. It is not only a cultivation of the reason but it takes more time in the early stages and thereby reduces the number of failures, because the slower children have a better chance to master the mechanics. Rowantree and Taylor have given us a compendium of such arithmetical matters as are required in common school; twenty-two clear chapters, simple, reasonable, with no appearance of showing the authors' wide knowledge which, nevertheless, is extensive but is used solely for the purpose of helping the ordinary teacher.

"I next devoted myself to a pair of books[8] by Professor Morton, of the school of education, Ohio University. I am told that they were used

[7] Wm. F. Rowantree and Mary S. Taylor, "An Arithmetic for Teachers." The Macmillan Co. 621 pp. $2.50.

[8] Robert Lee Morton, "Teaching Arithmetic in the Primary Grades," Silver, Burdett & Co. 242 pp. $1.80; "Teaching Arithmetic in the Intermediate Grades," Silver, Burdett & Co. 354 pp. $2.16.

in mimeographed form in more than thirty schools and were checked, revised and checked again before printing. That's the way to make a practical book. Here the bugaboo of long division, the important practice of column addition, the mooted question of the best method of subtraction, are considered in the light of abundant experiment throughout the country. Professor Morton has summarized for us the results of the multitude of studies without swelling his chapters with details of the investigations. All the contents of the arithmetic courses are treated together with measurements, testing, the importance of problem solving and the use of examinations.

"Covering the same field as the last book listed is the volume[9] of two professors of Teachers College, New York. The problem before us, they say, is the matter of developing better teachers. It does seem to me that a patient, sympathetic, kindly disposition is the happy possession of each of these two men. They have a glow of enthusiasm and earnestness backed by solid learning and practical experience. We must have, they say, an adequate testing program to ascertain by proper diagnoses whether the purposes of arithmetic teaching are being fully realized. Without tests we can't know where we are on our journey. Tests reveal what can not be known by any other means. Remedial work can be determined only so. Isn't it a humiliating thing for Chicago that our Thompson Board of Education, when our Bureau of Tests was pushing ahead our arithmetic successes, disbanded the entire organization and put us back into the dark ages of guessing? We had reached a point where 100 per cent. accuracy in figuring had become the only accepted official standard. The new board threw it out. My authors repeat, 'It should never be forgotten, and it will be repeatedly emphasized here that the main purpose in teaching arithmetic is to train the pupil to compute accurately.' In the Morton books which I just mentioned I read in chapter after chapter 'proving results must be trained as a habit. The place to fix it is in the primary grades. It is incumbent on the teacher to see to it that her pupils systematically, regularly and invariably check all their work.' Over and again the Rowantree and Taylor book records: 'Accuracy is essential. It is necessary wherever computation outside of school is done. The child, if properly trained, will consider an unproved result as work half done.' I am not familiar with all the books upon arithmetic but all that I have seen put stress on this. These are familiar words to us in Chicago. The deposed superintendent spoke them on his arrival. We all assented, as usual. And then, oh my! We began to get statistics as to what teachers' classes were not proving their results and the stewing began."

"Wasn't this one of the misdemeanors on which your board of education dismissed the superintendent?" inquired the Signpost, who teaches in a suburban town.

"Oh, yes," said the Viking Maid. "Principals said he pushed 'em and the board pushed him out. We had no fuss about it in our school. When anybody failed to prove his arithmetic we told him that wasn't the way we did things. We let him stick to his problem until he proved it right. All the bosh about this making the work distasteful was directly contrary to the truth. When a child learned that he could get everything right, arithmetic became a favorite pursuit. Let me go on with my reviewing. Here comes another Teachers College man, Professor Milo Hillegas, who brought out the great series of modern methods: The Classroom Teacher. He condenses into ninety-eight pages[10] some of the most pertinent hints that every teacher needs: pupils must understand the purposes; wavering attention; the element of first importance, accuracy; the speed fallacy; counting fingers; excessive drill; waste of time, etc. If a principal puts ten minutes into reviewing this little book before he goes the rounds, he'll make his work much more worth while.

"Most of the books I read refer to Guy Wilson. He's the man who, as superintendent of schools in Connersville, Indiana, began to wonder when he went into his arithmetic classes what in the world all the fuss was about. He buttonholed every man and woman he met and

[9] David Eugene Smith, William David Reeve, "The Teaching of Junior High-school Mathematics," Ginn & Co. 411 pp. $1.60.

[10] Milo B. Hillegas, "Teaching Number Fundamentals," J. B. Lippincott Co. 98 pp. 75 cents.

sounded them upon the use they made of figures. He began, long ago, selecting things in the course of study that were unknown elsewhere than in it. He constructed a new arithmetic course for his own schools. Warwick and York printed it. He spoke at conventions. He printed pamphlets. The Federal Bureau of Education asked him to make a bulletin for general distribution. Boston University drafted him as professor of education. He tested the whole of New England in arithmetic. City schools did worse than rural ones. A year later he tested again. The improvement was astonishingly great. No matter how much Chicago is opposing tests, the inevitable fact is impressing the country at large that the people who pay for the schools are entitled to have results measured all the time. The work[11] of Dr. Wilson which the Factotum gave me to examine is a trim little volume in the Riverside Educational Monographs edited by Henry Suzzallo, whom corrupt politics ousted from the presidency of the University of Washington. Why is it, asks Henry, that this study has seemed so unresponsive? It has long been a well-organized body of thought. It is marvelously logical in progression. The scientist in education has been trying to find the answer. One of them is Wilson. I'll say at the start that the last thing in his book, a list of forty-two titles of modern treatises on this study, is not the least valuable thing in it. 'Fewer things, better done' might be the thesis of this work. Arithmetic must be based on its utility in the common affairs of life. A great deal in the texts is so rarely used that to teach it is a waste. The time could better be spent teaching children to be good citizens. Education has lagged behind industry in eliminating waste. Informational arithmetic, a term invented by the author, means the mathematics necessary to understand the quantitative situations met in general reading. This is not the most important element. But there ought to be more of it in school. He has some stimulating examples of it. You will be surprised to learn of some important neglect of arithmetic after one leaves school. Only two thirds of shoppers count their change; only 29 per cent. of customers check the additions on their bills; few women keep any account of their bank balances —they leave it to the cashier; Americans have a stupid notion that it is undignified to see whether a restaurant check is right or not. We need more Scottish immigrants in this country. My long-standing distaste for this study makes me particularly interested in Dr. Wilson's remark that the typical school-room dislike for this subject is due to lack of understanding by the children. Cut out the useless stuff that bewilders them, take time to let the necessary parts be understood, and it will be enjoyed. Enjoyed, it will be mastered. What's your hurry? Speed is the curse of arithmetic. Speaking of enjoyment, I have here a really charming arithmetical reader[12] for elementary schools. It is a set of short stories told before the fire to a lively group of children by a lively friend: how man learned to count, to write numbers, to add, subtract, multiply and divide, the astonishing, and, to me, mysterious facts about combinations of certain numbers, and the most famous of mathematical puzzles that have delighted man for centuries. I am reminded of Mr. Stefansson's query: Why leave out of your story-telling of fairies and classic myths the equally wonderful things that are facts: the magic of Edison, the wonders of science, the fascination of numbers?

"My last and pleasant duty is to remind you that there are now three year-books of a national council of mathematics teachers. The last one[13] has much to interest even a teacher who does not specialize in the study here covered. David Eugene Smith has an enthusiastic discussion of citizenship as aided by mathematics; Charles Hubbard Judd speaks on the fallacy of 'tool subjects'; Professor Slaught treats of interpretation of life; Professor Breslich, of training thought; Miss Dower, of problem solving, and Miss Kee, of a mathematical atmosphere."

The Schoolman has to know art, now.—Your recorder does not recall that our host and men-

[11] Guy Mitchell Wilson, ''What Arithmetic Shall We Teach?'' Houghton Mifflin Co. 149 pp. $1.20.

[12] David Eugene Smith, ''Number Stories of Long Ago,'' Ginn & Co. 150 pp. 60 cents.

[13] Third Year Book. National Council of Teachers of Mathematics. Bureau of Publication. Teachers College, N. Y. 276 pp. $2.50.

tor, Papa Rose, has ever reviewed a book for us. But his and our Lady Alice, she of the palette and brush, has done so. To-night her report was upon the school and art. "It is now," she said, "about two years since the Boswells—Peyton, Helen and Marcia, of that family—began sending out from Hopewell, New Jersey, their superior little compendium of art-news of the world.[14] What's in it? Paris, Munich, a great deal of Chicago, Cincinnati and New York—news, mostly—and this gives it a liveliness and interest appealing to the amateur, the professional and the teacher. It has an editor for France, one for Germany, another for Latin countries. It notes what the painters are doing. What pictures are changing hands. What the galleries are showing and the art-schools projecting. Every issue has a review of the field of art education. You certainly will want every issue on your school library reading table, for art is surely becoming as much a duty of the school as reading, writing and arithmetic. Time was when a school principal or superintendent could say without a blush, 'I don't know the difference between a Rembrandt and a Benjamin West.' No more. A manager of a motor factory might as unblushingly confess to ignorance of what a clutch is for or is. Here is a sample brick from the last issue: 'There is a theory that if a work of art is truly great it will appeal as strongly to the casual layman as to the connoisseur. To this the Detroit *News* replies, 'according to this theory although you have spent your leisure enjoying the cover pages of *Snappy Stories* you will go into ecstacies if you happen to stumble on the Hermes of Praxiteles. If you don't, worse luck for the Hermes.' 'Why, then, does the Metropolitan Museum spend the income of more than a million dollars a year telling listeners the principles and history of art? Why does the Philadelphia Museum ask for two millions to start an educational program? The simple fact is, an enriched mind is capable of finer feeling and deeper emotion than is an impoverished one. The more we know, the more deeply we can feel.' The Boswells will certainly enrich the art portion of your mind. Their abundant reproductions of pictures, their short and catchy exposition of art meanings, the variety of their presentations, can put the ordinary person on the path from which no traveler with a fair start is ever willing to depart.

"Leon Winslow wrote a first-class book on art education three years ago. He has expanded and enriched it and issued a second edition.[15] It treats of purposes, subject-matter and method. 'We have an increasing need for art,' says this Baltimore public-school director, 'For the great output of machines taking the place of hand production tends to a neglect of design, but factory goods need not be without real grace and artistry. The American school should ever seek to perfect and propagate a superior type of art. It should teach the public to appreciate and demand it. It should train designers and craftsmen to achieve the best results.' Mr. Winslow develops the objectives: appreciation, industrial intelligence, taste and skill. With complete programs he builds up an elementary school course, continuing it through the junior and senior high schools. He begins his various projects by a statement of the general, and then, of the specific aims. Actual lessons enliven the book. It is a stimulating volume and a practical guide for principals and teachers.

"We ought all to vote a civic wreath to Rilla Jackman for the service she has rendered our country by her book, 'American Arts.'[16] I have not come across any work that tells so much that an American would want to know about our progress in the path of beauty, or that tells the story so directly, so completely and with so many touches of human interest. The author is head of the public-school department, college of fine arts, Syracuse University; she has covered an immense field: crafts, glass, silverware, furniture, textiles, ceramics, painting, sculpture and architecture. She has flavored her history and facts with so much interesting anecdote and personal circumstance appertaining to her artistic people that the book, informative as it is, has the charm of a first-rate story. The five

[14] *The Art Digest.* Monthly, June to September; semi-monthly, other months, twenty issues a year. Ordinary, $2 a year; de luxe, $5 a year, Hopewell, New Jersey.

[15] Leon Loyal Winslow, "Organization and Teaching of Art," Warwick and York, Baltimore. 243 pp. $2.80.

[16] Rilla Evelyn Jackman, "American Arts," Rand, McNally & Co. 561 pp. $2.50.

hundred illustrations of American art, reproductions of painting, sculpture, etc., are beautifully rendered. There is an arrangement of matter according to style, or work, or 'school,' always a risky thing to undertake for fear of stressing one aspect of an artist's work who has done creditably in different fields. There can be no doubt that classification helps a reader, avoids the bewilderment of disconnection and aids the memory by an orderly storage of ideas in the cupboards of the mind. Its dangers this writer has avoided by mentioning each particular artist as many times as is necessary in as many classifications as cover him. Our own Lorado Taft is given the palm for doing more than any other sculptor to develop the public's art appreciation. His lectures to our soldiers in France, his services to the Art Institute and to the University of Chicago, his monuments and fountains, receive extended recognition. Our Carol Brooks, now Mrs. McNeil, is here; and Bessie Potter, now Mrs. Vonnoh; our Louis Sullivan, Daniel Burnham and John Root, pioneer of the skyscrapers; our other Chicagoans will be found in the pages. But, alas, we lose 'em. Why? Daniel French, in this book, gives a hint. 'I moved to New York because there are more models, a better atmosphere and it gives one some prestige.' Isn't it maddening! New York does not in a week do as much for art as Chicago in a day. And yet the mysterious, exasperating, unsubstantial atmosphere of prestige permits her lazily to sniff at all the rest of us. I could shout for joy that Chicago publishers issue this book. It is a superb achievement. New York has never done a comparable volume."

Poetry, man-size.—Said the Stevedore:

"Now we have an epic of the war between the states,[17] verse that clutches you, man-stuff, fire, penetration, the inside of humanity, its outside glamour, stinking slave-ships, southern mansions, thoroughbred men, women and horses, New England homespun, Virginia courthouses, pineywoods, squirrel hunters, country-store clerks and the death grips of the sixties. What is it? A powerful, clairvoyant bard projecting himself into the days of John Brown, Lincoln, Jeff Davis, McClellan, Grant and Lee, reproducing what they saw, and said, and did. It is painting, drama, history, romance, the *amor patriae*, that marches, retreats, palavers, awakens, fails, succeeds. It is the war as generals see it, as clean-shaven Websterian congressmen do, as does the heavy-footed New Hampshire farm boy. All through it come opal splashes of lustrous poetry like this:

'This is the hidden place that hiders know;
This is where hiders go.
Step soft, the snowfall here is different snow.
The rain has a different sting.
Let your eyes be sealed
With two blue muscadines
Stolen from secret vines
Or you will never find in the lost field
The table spread, the signs of the hidden feast.'

"Through the years walks John Brown's body. He strides in front of the armies. A straggler meets him going along to Manassas with his gun on his shoulder, his phantom sons at heel, his eyes like misty coals. A dead man sees him at Seven Pines, the bullets whistling through him like a torn flag. A madman beholds him whetting a sword on a Bible, a cloud above Malvern Hill.

"Humble and highborn lovers walk in and out of the grim episodes, enchanting lyrics and Negro jubilees break into the clash of battle, until in the Appomattox meadow the arms are stacked. A few bronzed, tattered, gray men, weeping or silent, tear some riddled bits of cloth from color staffs and try to hide them under their uniforms. So John Brown's body lies a-mouldering in the grave. Spread over it the bloodstained flag of his song for the sun to bleach and the snow to cover with a pure fleece until there is nothing there that ever knew a master or a slave. Bury with it the purple dream of that America we have not been, a tragic America seeking the warm sea, the last foray of aristocracy. Bury this destiny unmanifest, the system broken underneath the test. Bury it all beside John Brown.

"What I am attempting to convey to this revered assembly is the fact that the absolute poetry of this Iliad of Lincoln, Lee and the big and little men of the sixties is the greatest piece of art of this generation. It is untrammeled, free, fierce, Olympian, American."

[17] Stephen Vincent Benét, "John Brown's Body," Doubleday, Doran & Co. 377 pp. $2.50.

SCHOOL AND SOCIETY

EDITED BY J. McKEEN CATTELL

WITH WHICH IS COMBINED THE

EDUCATIONAL REVIEW

EDITED BY WILLIAM McANDREW

Volume XXVIII | Saturday, November 10, 1928 | Number 724

CURRICULUM RESEARCH[1]

By Professor EDWARD L. THORNDIKE

TEACHERS COLLEGE, COLUMBIA UNIVERSITY

I AM commissioned to describe and discuss scientific researches concerning the curriculum. But first let me say a few words in recognition of the merits and importance of four other sorts of study of the curriculum. Teachers in the course of their work observe certain facts about the results which certain courses of study have upon certain pupils and make up their minds that this, that and the other features of the course of study have such and such advantages or weaknesses. They then proceed to change the curriculum in so far as they have the zeal and power to do so. Many improvements have had such an origin, for example, the change in certain schools for Negroes from a predominantly literary to a predominantly realistic and industrial curriculum. The zero difficulties in arithmetic were appreciated by sagacious observers and the curriculum was modified to provide fuller attention to them years before Coffman, Stone, Courtis and others began their more scientific observations.

Committees or other groups of wise educators appointed to plan or criticize courses of study may collect, combine and evaluate such observations and opinions with profit, tempering their extravagances, eliminating their eccentricities and presenting a digest of the general drift of fact and opinion.

Bureaus, called bureaus of research, and combining research and service, may carry on this work of collecting fact and opinion still more elaborately and continuously. They may utilize various statistical techniques to determine what the best present practices are in the opinion of those qualified to judge. They may also, of course, make strictly scientific observations and experiments. Whether they do or do not, their labors may be very useful. They are, at least they should be, impartial; and they do not need to make compromises as committees so often do.

Men or women of genius may suggest changes in the curriculum, as, for example, Stanley Hall and John Dewey have done in this country. The suggestions of such always deserve attention. Prudence as well as decent modesty should make all scientific workers listen to the notions, even the vagaries, of creative thinkers. When a mind of broad scope and keen insight also takes pains to possess all the relevant facts about learners, learning and the things to be learned, it will often be able to solve a problem about the curriculum nearly as well in a hundred hours of thought and

[1] Address at the Convocation of the University of the State of New York, Albany, October 18, 1928.

study as could be done by thousands of hours of special research.

Scientific research does not oppose or seek to supplant the observation and reflection of teachers or the combined wisdom of committees or the investigations of bureaus or the insights and theories of genius. It merely seeks to extend and improve the observations, to discover more facts and better methods for committees and bureaus to use and to check and test the theories.

The scope of scientific study of the curriculum is very wide, including, substantially, everything about what is to be learned, everything about what use the learners are to make of it and everything about how they learn it.

Research concerning What is to be Learned

As a new branch of science appears and grows, we need to know about it and what it may do for the curriculum. For example, we need to study anthropology to ascertain whether it has material better suited for the education of youth than parts of the history now in the curriculum. As a new fact within some branch of science is discovered, we need to decide what to do with it in the curriculum. For example, how shall we revise the customary treatment of electric currents to fit the facts of electrons? The most exciting fact of government to Americans to-day is prohibition. What, if anything, should be said and done about prohibition in the curriculum?

Since we are concerned with any existing or proposed content of the curriculum as something to be learned, we need to know how hard it is to learn, and what, if anything, must have been already learned as a basis or propaedeutic. It is the answers to these questions which will largely determine, for example, our treatment of the electron for pupils in grade 9. A knowledge of the difficulty (for specified learners) of learning each of the things to be possibly learned is a primary consideration in selecting the elements of a curriculum and in arranging them to fit the increase in ability to learn which goes with the years from five to fifteen, and probably to twenty or later.

So students of the science of education have been busy in efforts to determine the difficulty of learning that $4+9=13$ compared with that of learning that $4+2=6$, of learning to spell each of the three or four thousand most needed words, and the like. The task is by no means easy. It is not hard to find out how imperfect learning has been, that is, how many pupils make errors at each of these tasks. Thus, if at the end of grade four ten thousand representative pupils make sixty errors with $9+2$ and a hundred errors with $9+7$, we know that the latter has been less well learned. Some students of the curriculum have assumed that such a status proves that the latter is harder to learn, and measures its greater difficulty. But this would be true only if equal time and attention had been devoted to learning each and if each had received an equal balance of benefit and harm from other acts of learning. If *radish* and *could* were equally often misspelled by pupils in grades three, four, five, six, seven and eight, I would still dare to predict that in an experiment with equal conditions, it would be harder to learn to spell *could* than *radish*. Experiments with equality of conditions to determine the difficulty of learning various items of knowledge, skill and attitude will, as a matter of fact, require much ingenuity and an enormous expense of time and devotion.

The interest or attractiveness or appeal of any given experience or act of learning to specified groups of learners is a second fact which curriculum-makers need to know about each of the elements of content from which they have to choose. Here, too, scientific workers have been busy accumulating facts and testing the opinions of practitioners and theorists. Limits of time forbid any summary of their findings, but I will quote one sample, partly because it will amuse you and lighten this somewhat heavy recital, and partly because it is a good concrete illustration of experimental studies of curriculum problems. Abbott and Trabue had pupils from grade five up through the graduate schools of universities read various beautiful poems and also three mutilations of each. In one, the "sentimental," they falsified the emotion "by introducing silly, gushy, affected or otherwise insincere feelings." In another, the "prosaic," they reduced "the poet's imagery to a more pedestrian and commonplace level." In the third, they rendered "the movement either entirely awkward or less fine and subtle than the original."

For example, the pupil read Amy Lowell's "Sea Shell" and these three mutilations of it. He made a record of which of the four he liked most and which he liked least.

Read the poems A, B, C, D, trying to think how they would sound if read aloud. Write "Best" on the dotted line above the one you like best as poetry. Write "Worst" above the one you like least.

TO A SEA SHELL

The good version: A(....................)

Sea Shell, Sea Shell,
Sing me a song, Oh please!
A song of ships and sailor men,
Of parrots and tropical trees.
Of islands lost in the Spanish Main
Which no man may ever find again,
Of fishes and coral under the waves,
And sea-horses stabled in great green caves—
Sea Shell, Sea Shell,
Sing me a song, O please!

The sentimental version: B(....................)

Tender, tender Sea Shell,
Wilt thou sing me, please,
Of thy happy, happy home
'Neath the tropic trees?
Ah, the coral islands!
Ah, the wondrous fish!
For such a song I'd give thee, dear,
Whate'er a Shell could wish.

The prosaic version: C(....................)

Sea Shell, please sing me a song
Of ships and sailor men;
Of strange kinds of birds and trees
On the Spanish Main:
Of fish and seaweed in the sea,
And whatever creature there may be,—
Sea Shell, please sing me a song!

The version without meter: D(....................)

Sea Shell, I ask you will
You sing a song, please.
All about the ships and sailors
And the parrots in their tropical trees.
The islands I have read about on the Spanish Main
That no one will see again,
The fish and coral under the wave,
Sea Horses that have their stables in caves;
Sea Shell, I ask you will
You sing a song, please.

It appears that pupils in grades five to eight are substantially without any liking or esteem for superiority in poetry. So far as we can judge they would, with the exception of a very few children specially gifted or specially trained, like the following as well as Miss Lowell's "Sea Shell."

Tender, loving Sea Shell!
Please sing a song
About fish silver and gold
And the trees new and old.
In the geography books she reads.
Oh, the lovely coral beads!
Oh, the happy sailors will bring
Them to us on a long string,
If we are tender and true
And do our duty as well as you.

Furthermore, the low results for the pupils in grades five to eight are not a mixture of some pupils who have good taste to a considerable degree and others whose taste is so definitely bad as to counterbalance the former. On the contrary, the valuation from one to eight right out of thirteen is almost entirely due to chance. The pupils in grades five to eight who have eight right in one test of thirteen sets of four versions are no more likely to have eight right in a second test with thirteen different sets than the pupils who had only one or more right in the first test. The correlation between score with Series X and score with Series Y for grades five to eight is substantially zero ($-.037 \pm .09$).

Excellence in respect of literary form has, then, almost zero appeal to elementary school children in general. This is amply confirmed in the case of children in the first three grades by Dr. Dunn's very careful investigation.

A primary factor in evaluating any curriculum or any features thereof is the changes which are actually produced in pupils by it. Educational bookkeeping used to be very one-sided. We kept an account of the money spent on plant and personnel and the time spent by pupils in school, but almost no account of what came of it all. Standard educational tests are causing a most beneficial change in this respect. Palmer and Franzen and their colleagues in the Child Health Organization, for example, are measuring changes in physique and health. Any school system can learn just how well its children can read or write or compute and how much they gain per year. The Carnegie Foundation's study of college education in Pennsylvania includes a comprehensive test of achievement in which a college senior spends twelve hours in displaying what he knows and can do.

A volume could be written concerning the use of such tests and measurements in the discovery of individual differences, in diagnosis, in placement, in measurements of the comparative value of certain selections of subject-matter or methods of instruction and in other ways. I will report only one small matter, the measurement of what we may call the minimum or guaranteed product of a curriculum. If a thousand pupils such as are admitted to senior high school in City A take its course in chemistry for a year, what will they all know about chemistry, what will even the least able or interested be able to do in chemistry, what will that course of study achieve with any and every pupil whose previous ability and interests cause him to be enrolled in it? The answer in this case is that he will know that water is H_2O and other facts of similar scope and difficulty. The answer for a nine months' course in algebra is that he will succeed with tasks like:

$4r + 3r + 2r = ?$ 3 times $7y = ?$ $\frac{12n}{4} = ?$ if $2x = 4$, what does x equal? If $3x + 3 = 9$, what does x equal? If one coat costs x dollars, what will 3 coats cost?

To find questions which 95 per cent. of college seniors, most of whom have had four years of English in high school and a year or more in college, can answer, we have to resort to such as these:

Is Portia a character in the "Merchant of Venice" or in "Twelfth Night" or in "All's Well that Ends Well" or in "Othello"?

Did Pepys write a diary or "Rasselas," or "Nydia" or "Friar Banzay" or the "Old Wives' Tale"?

Are Poe's tales escapes from every-day life into the realm of the imagination or realistic stories of contemporary American life or historical narratives or detective stories grouped around a famous sleuth?

These are answered correctly by about nineteen out of twenty of those who attempt them. A tenth or more will not attempt to answer them.

The educational product which any given curriculum will surely produce at the lower margin of interest and ability among those subjected to it seems to approximate zero.

Facts like these, though wholesome, may be somewhat distressing to you, and I will not give others. They are not necessarily distressing. I myself do not consider them as proof of inefficiency or negligence on the part of schools and colleges but as evidence that educational products depend more largely on the individual learner than has been thought. Apparently you can lead certain minds to the springs of knowledge and power but you can not make them drink.

Let us then turn to the studies of the use to which the acquisitions of the curriculum will be put.

RESEARCHES CONCERNING THE USES OF VARIOUS ELEMENTS OF THE CURRICULUM

What words will our pupils need to read and to spell? What arithmetical operations will they use? What geographical and historical items will they need to know? Our ignorance concerning the facts in the case was, and in most cases still is, pitiable. Take the simple case of word knowledge. Max Müller once said, or was reputed to have said, that the English peasant got along with a vocabulary of about three hundred words, and this fantastic estimate was quoted for years without challenge. Until a very few years ago we all taught reading with no clear idea of whether we were, in grades one to eight, to teach four thousand words or eight thousand or twelve thousand or sixteen thousand or twenty thousand. Nobody knew how many words eighth-grade pupils did know, or should know, much less which words they should be.

We still know far too little, but we at least know that the Max Müller estimate needs to be multiplied by ten or more, and that the early estimates of Bonser need to be divided by three or more. We also know the approximate order of importance for use in reading of the most important ten thousand words. We are in a position to prevent in the future such educational absurdities as having a total vocabulary of 9,500 words in the ten most widely used text-books in reading for grade three, with less than seven hundred words occurring in all the ten.

In the case of words to be spelled, our situation, thanks to the labors of O'Shea, Ayres, Horn, Anderson and others, has been improved, even more, with one curious exception. In counting the occurrences of words in correspondence, in order to find how often each is used, these workers paid no heed to what was written on the outside of the envelopes or to names of persons and places written inside. Yet a misspelling of the name of the destination of the letter is obviously of especial importance, since it may prevent the letter's being received at all. And misspellings of proper names are, other things being equal, of greater importance than misspellings of common nouns, since the things meant by them are less easily determined from the context.

These and other investigations of the uses of learning in the world have some defects and many limitations. We, who have made them, understand this perhaps even more fully than our critics. We do not think that the curriculum in reading should be based on the "Thorndike Word List" alone or the curriculum in spelling on the Horn list alone. They are imperfect measures of what the world does use; moreover, the step from what it does use to what it should is often a long one and at times in a different direction. But when they are applied with a reasonable allowance for other considerations the results upon the curriculum are demonstrably beneficial.

The same is true of the studies of the uses of arithmetic, history, geography, pharmacy, etc., made by Wilson, Mitchell, Rugg, Washburn, Charters and others. It would be unwise to frame a curriculum with no other criteria than their findings, but it would be a far greater folly to frame one without using their findings at all. And the remedy for their deficiencies consists precisely in more varied and more rigorous and more ingenious studies of the same sort.

Researches concerning Learners

In its actual day-by-day details, at least, the content of the curriculum is dependent upon our ideas of children's minds. Learning and the learner cannot usefully be divorced. The particular steps by which we attain a certain ultimate aim of the curriculum will vary enormously according to our psychology.

Indeed, the changes wrought in the actual details of the curriculum during the last generation have been in very large measure due to the psychological researches on mental discipline and on individual differences. Thirty years ago when the values of studies as general training for the mind were put very high, if not preeminent, much of the curriculum was indiscriminate. Learning to spell any word was supposed to train the pupil's memory. Learning to compute cube roots trained his reasoning. Any form of military drill inculcated general obedience. It is significant that our scientific studies of the actual uses of items of the curriculum were not begun until the psychologist had shown the impossibility of any general, formal, mental training irrespective of the particular habits and ideas and attitudes acquired and the restricted nature of transferred abilities.

The psychologist's researches concerning the transfer of training have been beneficial in reducing the undeserved bonuses which were attached to certain subjects, such as Latin. But they have been even more beneficial in forcing curriculum makers in all subjects to provide content that is of intrinsic value. For example, they warn present-day devotees of the project method and of learning by problem-solving that projects and problems must deal with essentially valuable facts and habits. Indiscriminate problem-solving for problem-solving's sake should not be tolerated, no matter what guise it puts on.

Psychological researches showing the wide range of individual differences have led to the specialization of the curriculum in multifarious ways, for the dull and for the gifted, for the sturdy and for the frail, for the matter-of-fact and for the artistic. A thousand (1,023) pupils taken at random in grade ten in a certain city showed 703 different programs of courses taken during the year. Five hundred and twenty-nine pupils in grade ten in another city showed 436 different programs for the year.

Researches concerning individual differences have also exposed the fallacies of judging curricula by their products without allowances for the selection of human material upon which the curriculum worked. For example, the Institute of Educational Research of Teachers College measured the gains in intellect, as measured by stock tests of intelligence, made by some 12,000 pupils in high schools during a year and then compared the gains of pupils who had taken various studies during the year. The differences in gain due to taking English, history, mathematics and Latin rather than English, history, typewriting and cooking is less than the difference in the gains made by very intellectual pupils, say the top two per cent., and average pupils taking identical programs, and is less than the difference in the gains made by white pupils and colored pupils taking identical programs. No thinker competent in educational science would now dare to use the achievement of graduates of Oxford and Cambridge as evidence of the superiority in the curricula of Oxford and Cambridge. Unfortunately, some of our writers about education are not competent in educational science.

Researches concerning the psychology of reading, arithmetic, algebra, spelling, handwriting and drawing are modifying the teaching of these subjects, often in fundamental ways. The modifications are largely in what may be called methods of teaching rather than the content of the curriculum. But such a division into methods and content is largely artificial. A curriculum in operation is determined by methods as truly as by content. When, for example, the psychologist makes arithmetic largely experimental and inductive and verifying instead of dogmatic, deductive and ritualistic, the curriculum is changed fundamentally. If further researches confirm my hypothesis that the learning of spelling takes place largely in the course of ordinary reading, the curriculum in spelling ceases to be primarily the memorizing of letter sequences and becomes primarily the formation of habits which will enable the experiences of ordinary reading to provide more useful knowledge of spelling.

Besides these special studies of school learning the psychologists are year by year discovering facts concerning all sorts of learning.

The more general and fundamental our researches concerning learning are, the more productive they will be in the end for the curriculum. For example, experiments on learning in the lower animals have probably contributed more to knowledge of education, per hour or per unit of intellect spent, than experiments on children. Experiments to determine just what repetition does to a mental connection or habit, just how rewards and punishments act to favor and hinder the states of affairs or responses to which they are attached and just what physiological action corresponds to the formation of habits and the acquisition of ideas should produce in the end important consequences in the betterment of learning and teaching.

What the exact nature of these consequences will be cannot be foretold, but they may be illustrated by two recent bits of work, one by Dunlap and one by myself. Dunlap found that in certain habits, notably such bad nervous habits as biting the nails, deliberate voluntary scheduled repetition weakened the habit, even to the point of cure. His prescription for nail-biting would be enforced nibbling say four times daily just after meals and just before going to bed. These observations are of value, not only intrinsically, but especially because they inspire us to discover why it is that repetition usually strengthens mental connections, but in Dunlap's sorts of learning (and in others that might be cited) does not. That discovery should help to explain many failures of drill in school and to improve many forms and features of drill.

I experimented with cases when a situation (call it S) is repeated, say a hundred times, with varying responses, say A, B, C, D and E, of which one, say A, is much more frequent than any of the others. It has been an attractive doctrine in psychology that in such cases the frequent connection will grow stronger at the expense of the less frequent, so that if A occurs in the first hundred say forty times to twenty each for B and C and ten each for D and E, A will occur more than forty times in a second hundred, and so on increasingly until perhaps it becomes the sole response to S. The educational implication of the doctrine would be that if we could establish a tendency to a certain relative strength, compared with other tendencies, mere time and repetition would take care of it thereafter. A good start would be half the battle.

No such waxing of the more frequent at the expense of the less frequent was found. If a pupil spells reason, "reason" twelve times out of twenty, "reson" five times, and "resun" three times, we can not expect that mere repetition thereafter will increase the relative frequency of the correct spelling one jot or tittle. So far as its effect is concerned the sixty per cent. for "reason" will be no larger and the fifteen per cent. for "resun" will be no smaller after ten thousand spellings. The selective force of mere repetition of a situation is zero.

These two sets of experiments, one showing repetition doing something unexpected and the other showing repetition failing to fulfil a certain expectation, exemplify also the incompleteness and superficiality of existing knowledge of learning. Education, politics, government, business, social work and all other branches of human engineering are being held back by the gaps and inadequacies in the fundamental sciences of human nature. In the case of the curriculum we have shifted from one practice to another without adequate understanding of either. Parts of what we discard may well be better than parts of what we cherish. With the progress of research into the fundamental facts of learning, our analyses will be more perfect and our practice safer and surer and more truly progressive.

On the whole, we may properly be very optimistic concerning the use of the scientific spirit and scientific methods in the study of the curriculum. In the few years of their operation they have already done useful service. They have so proved their worth to responsible authorities that expenses for such studies are a recognized part of the educational budgets of progressive states and cities and a recognized feature in the grants of our great philanthropic foundations. More money has been allotted specifically for scientific studies of education in the past ten years than in the previous ten thousand. Their results are made use of widely in the training of teachers and the construction of text-books and other instruments of instruction. They are earning the respect of workers in the older and more established branches of science and letters. The learned world has called on scientific students of education for help more in the past five years than in the previous five hundred. They are attracting the interest of young men and women of intellect and idealism who will gladly make educational research their life's work if they can be shown a reasonable prospect of a living wage thereat.

Less and less every year the curriculum will be based on the traditions of the multitude or the personal prestige of some reformer. More and more it will be the product of our laboratories and experimental schools, certified by experts.

A GRADUATE STUDENT CRITICISM OF THE COLLEGE OF EDUCATION

By G. R. PEASE
COLLEGE OF THE PACIFIC

In this age of universal questioning, the educational system has had its full share of criticism. Most of it has been directed, however, against the outworks of the system. The heart of the citadel is the college of education; from it emanate the principles which in their application have raised the storms of criticism. Therefore, inasmuch as every one else is taking a shot at some part of the system, from the soap-box senate at the cross-roads to the professor of English who suggested a few months ago that we begin a reform by killing off the professors of education, why not include a criticism from within the whirling, grinding wheels of the machine itself? Why not give the grist an opportunity to criticize the mill?

Of course it is not done! It is perfectly plain to a graduate student why no such criticism has heretofore come to publication. But the questioning, the weighing, the acrid scorn of many parts of the system are found in most student groups, and I, for one, am disgusted with a type of criticism that hides itself from the light of day. If it is worth anything, let's have it in the open. If it is worthless, let us find its fallacies, and try a new track. I introduce myself, then, as a self-appointed spokesman for the graduate student group in the colleges of education—a spokesman who realizes fully that fools step in where angels fear to tread.

Both the matter and the method of the college of education are under the domination of the men who hold the professorships. The graduate student is on the way to attach a Ph.D. degree to his name; incidentally the shadow of a coming degree falls a long way ahead of its reality. No matter how loudly the average graduate student may voice his ideas of the system in student groups, he is very careful to make it "sotto voce" as he draws near to his examinations. He has a very profound respect for the weight of the steamroller.

The man who has newly donned the hood is looking for a position. The power of recommendation for desirable positions lies in the hands of the men who sat on his committee, or at least helped pour into him the mystic brew which makes a man eligible for the doctorate. This is no time for a newly fledged doctor of philosophy to speak his mind in criticism of the machine! He might voice his criticism—but he also knows that when the dust has settled he may find himself the superintendent of a rural consolidated school.

By the time a man has so established himself in the university world that he may speak his mind without fear or favor, he has no mind to speak—in respect to criticism, of course. He is so immersed in his own research and writing that he has forgotten that he ever had a student-criticism of the system. Occasionally he overhears a disturbing remark from a student group as he passes through the halls, but his momentary uneasiness is soon lost in the joy of leading a new class through the intricacies of his latest research, or in expounding his pet philosophy.

I have listened to graduate-student criticism in two of the outstanding universities of the nation, one in the élite East, the other in the corn-fed Middle West. The only appreciable differences were in the inflection of the voices. I am venturing to pass on the heart of such student criticism. Incidentally, I may confide in you that I am in an ideal position to undertake the task. Only one short week ago the hood was dropped over my head, so I have not yet had time to forget what I have heard students say about the work of the graduate school. Also, I have a position, with a properly signed contract insuring the same to me, except I commit murder or run away with some other man's wife.

Student criticism can well be summed up under two broad heads: (1) poor teaching, and (2) poor organization of the courses and materials.

As I see it, the poor teaching is but a hardy weed grown from the rich soil of research. Research has become for university men both a Mecca and a mania. From sophomore to president, it is the *summum bonum* of the academic cosmos. It is the sesame that opens the door to the inner and upper circles, to preferment, to position. It is the talisman that gives one a hearing in professional journals or in learned convocations. Far be it from me to question the worth of research. I only rise to remark that many graduate students wonder why there is not more good teaching than they have been able to locate.

Some one asks, "Is there really such poor teaching in the graduate college?" And some one else growls, "What do you want, a kindergarten?" The most common remark in a group of graduate students leaving the classroom is: "If I had a high-school teacher that did as poor a job of teaching as that, I would fire her at the end of the first week."

Some one else asks, "Why should one expect good teaching in a graduate course?" I do not know that one should expect it, except that if poor teaching will put the material over, any real graduate student could get it without a teacher. Most of the time spent in the classroom seems to us to be sheer waste anyway. We are perfectly willing to take the assignments and meet for discussion once a week, or once a month. But the cast-iron system demands a certain number of hours or majors of class attendance, so we go on enduring dry, dead lectures over material we could get in half the time for ourselves.

To spread the indictment clearer, let me point out that from graduate assistants up to heads of departments, men are picked not on the basis of successful teaching experience, but on the fact of research completed, in hand, or in prospect. Although it apparently has never dawned on the deans of colleges of education, men have the same sort of individual differences that are so boldly pointed out to the embryo teachers in order that they may understand how to handle public-school pupils. One man is fitted by nature and training for research. Another man is, by reason of his personality and inclinations, an inspirational teacher. The research man freely admits that he detests his teaching work. The other man enjoys the give-and-take of the classroom far more than research. But the system demands that the researcher teach, and the teacher research. One of the few real teachers I have known, recently advised me not to take a certain course of his as he was so overloaded by direction of research that he could no longer put over a lecture period with his old-time enthusiasm and inspiration.

I would suggest as an original problem in research, that some one carry on an investigation to find if the "continuous tub" in common use in psychopathic hospitals would lower the research mania enough so that common-sense could put the race horses on the track, and the draft horses on the plow instead of mismatching them in the academic harness.

The second general student criticism bears upon the organization (or lack of organization) of the courses offered. The first undergraduate course in the field of professional education is usually considered quite interesting. With the second course one begins to find large overlapping of material. If a student is carrying principles of education and educational psychology he will often find that the same collateral readings do for both courses. Soon the undergraduate begins to consider the work in education a soft snap, the prevalent student sentiment, by the way.

The farther one goes the worse the overlapping becomes until after a few courses have been covered the work becomes a bugbear to the average student. My own experience is still quite vivid, so may well serve as an example of what the student finds as he progresses in his graduate work.

A course labeled secondary education was very largely a study of curriculum construction. It interested me very much, and as I wished to learn more of the subject I registered for a course entitled curriculum construction. To my surprise, I found that I had covered all the worth while material in the former course. A course in junior high school turned out to be about two thirds a recovering of the subject of curriculum construction. My next experience was with a course catalogued as secondary school administration. Most of the course was taken up with the subject of curriculum construction. In desperation, I tackled a course in educational sociology only to find in a few days that I was again face to face with my old friend, curriculum construction. By this time I was about full of curriculum construction, so I changed my major to psychology. I am really sorry now that, for the glory of research, I did not continue my work in the field of secondary education until I had found just exactly how many differently labeled courses were concerned, in whole or in part, with the construction of a curriculum.

After a series of experiences like the above, one begins to wonder if any professor has a suspicion of a hint of an idea what the other professors are teaching in their courses. I firmly believe that if the available material were spread on the table and carefully organized into courses with some sort of sequence and direction, our two or three hundred courses in education offered by an outstanding university would shrink to something like a fifth of that number. I am not trying to lay the blame for such condition at any one's door—I am merely passing on the prevalent student criticism that the whole material of education needs some common-sense organization and needs it badly.

I have a suggestion for a way out of this Tower of Babel which goes by the name of the college of education. The suggestion seems so simple, however, that there surely must be something wrong about it or some one would have followed it out long ago. At least, I will make an effort at laying the plan before you for your criticism.

As I see the field of professional education, there are three broad divisions that are both logical and pedagogical in nature. I freely admit that my viewpoint may not be a very exalted one due to a bit of myopia; but others who are farther from their graduate student days than I must also have eye trouble or the lack of organization would have been remedied long ago. The suggested departments under which courses in education would be organized are as follows: a history-philosophy department, a department of educational psychology, and a department of administration. If these departments need subdivisions to cover the elementary and secondary fields, that could be easily arranged.

The work in history of education is very intimately tied up with educational sociology and the philosophy of education. There is perhaps no greater need to-day than that the student of education get such a view of past and present educational objectives, methods and results as shall enable him to work out a philosophy of education which will meet the needs of the present age. Our administration shows its lack of a sound philosophy by its erratic fad-following surges hither and yon. Give us such an organization of the materials of the field, and such a sequence of courses as shall make it possible for the student to build a scientific philosophy of education—an organization that will be possible only when such kindred subjects are handled under a common departmental direction.

To be perfectly honest, the larger portion of professional training in education is really applied psychology. Then why not put all such courses under the direction of a department of educational psychology, so that the material can be presented in the most economical and practical way, instead of parading it under a half dozen departments as at present? The psychology of the child and adolescent should fall to this department as well as courses pertaining to child guidance and mental hygiene. Courses in the psychology of teaching and learning would naturally be listed here. Courses in general and special methods ought to be considered largely as applied psychology courses for, after all, they are at their best, just that. Given the philosophy of education by the first named department, and the organization of a curriculum or curricula to meet the objectives of such a philosophy, all that is left in the way of training in methods of teaching, discipline, etc., is applied psychology. Then why turn to the English department for methods in English, to the mathematics department for methods in algebra, geometry, etc.? Let the educational psychologist work out the problem for the various fields as has already been so well begun in the field of algebra by such men as Rugg, Clark, Thorndike and others.

The department of administration would organize courses along the lines of administration, teacher personnel, curriculum construction, school costs, etc. Such departmental control would insure some sort of organization in these courses—a thing that is not in evidence at present, to any large degree.

And what should we gain by this procedure? We could easily eliminate half the courses at present offered without in the least detracting from the actual materials of instruction. Such careful organization of materials and courses would give the student far better training for his task, and at the same time eliminate the waste motion incident to repeated covering of the same material. Farther, it would release many of the most useful research men from the classroom so that they could make their best possible contributions to the cause of education without in the least increasing the costs of the college of education in the average university. Finally, such scientific organization of the courses and departments would give to professional education the respect it now lacks in many circles. The world waits to see the physician heal himself. Why should thinking men take much stock in a college of education as a trainer of teachers when it fails to properly organize and carry on its own work according to the principles it tries to impress upon its students?

EDUCATIONAL EVENTS

THE SIZE OF CLASSES IN ENGLISH SCHOOLS

Lord Eustace Percy, president of the British Board of Education, delivered the opening address at a conference of the Reading District Teachers Association held recently at Reading University. He is reported by the London *Times* to have said:

Last year, 1927–28, the number of classes with over 50 children on the books was reduced by rather more than 3,500. In the last four years the number of these classes has been reduced from nearly 25,000 to about 16,700, *i.e.*, by one third. Progress has been particularly satisfactory in the case of the junior classes. You will remember that a year ago I had to draw attention to the fact that the number of large classes in the junior schools was actually increasing, owing to the high birthrate after the war. Last year we more than wiped out this increase, reducing the number of these classes by over 2,300, in spite of the fact that the number of children under 11 increased by 60,000. If this result be compared with the record of the year 1924–25, when the number of children under 11 fell by 24,000, while the number of large classes containing such children was reduced by less than 1,100, it will be seen how substantial have been the results of the work of new school building and reorganization which we have been carrying out. Last year, too, there was a further reduction of nearly 1,000 in the number of classes of over 40 in the senior schools.

A legend has grown up that the number of big classes in our schools increased during the Geddes period and that their reduction dates from 1924. In justice to Mr. Fisher and Lord Irwin, this legend ought to be exploded. In the three years, 1920–23, there was a steady fall in the number of these classes, totaling 7,000. In the one year, 1923–24, there was an apparent fall of more than 6,000, but this is partly accounted for by a slight change made at that time in the basis of the statistics. What is true is that the fall during this earlier period was largely automatic; for in the four years, 1920 to 1924, there was a fall of no fewer than 320,000 in the number of children on the books of the schools. This fall continued until 1925, but since then we have had to deal with a stationary or slightly rising school population. On March 31 last our school population was almost exactly the same as in March, 1925, and only about 30,000 less than in March, 1924; so that we can fairly claim that our progress during these four years has been the result of our deliberate efforts, not of favorable circumstances. Of course, classes of 49 or 50 are too large, but the public should realize that what we are doing by applying this maximum standard for children on the books is to ensure that even at the time of year (the end of March) when the schools are usually most crowded there shall be no class in which the normal attendance exceeds 45. In fact, as you know, 85 per cent. of the classes in rural areas and nearly 50 per cent. in urban areas have a normal attendance of less than 40.

RURAL EDUCATION

The U. S. Bureau of Education, through its division of rural education, has recently compiled in tabular form some basic statistics concerning rural education. These statistics are presented under four major heads, namely, personnel of instruction, schools, enrolments and finances. Comparable urban statistics are given to facilitate comparisons, and sufficient explanatory material accompanies the table to show how the data were derived and how similar items may be computed for the individual states. The publication is available from the U. S. Bureau of Education as Rural School Circular No. 27.

The figures given in this publication for rural schools are, in the nature of things, derived rather than absolute, but, according to W. H. Gaumnitz, associate specialist in rural secondary education, who compiled them, they probably constitute the most usable data in this field for the nation as a whole now obtainable. The Bureau of Education emphasizes the need of more accurate and complete rural school statistics.

Progress and improvement, it believes, can only be expected when the actual conditions obtaining in all our schools become thoroughly known and when comparisons between favorable and unfavorable school conditions are readily made. The inferior status of the average rural school has, in a general way, been known, but only seldom has this status been established numerically. This has been the chief object of the study under consideration. The large number of facts revealed and the technique suggested will undoubtedly be helpful in solving rural school problems and in bringing the educational opportunities of the rural child into closer parity with his urban cousin. Some of the most interesting facts brought out in the table are the following.

Ninety per cent. of all the schools of America are found in localities 2,500 or less in population; urban schools enjoy the services of 83 principals and supervisors per 100 schools, whereas the rural schools must be content with the guidance and leadership of only 6.2 of these functionaries per 100 schools; city schools are in session an average of 183 days annually, whereas in rural schools this number is 156; the average per capita cost in urban schools is $129.82; in rural schools it is $75.01; the average value of school property per pupil enrolled is $299 in the cities and $99 in the country, and teachers' salaries are found to average $1,787 per school year in urban communities as against $855 in rural, with an average salary of $748 being paid in one-teacher schools.

With respect to secondary education, it was found that 22.7 per cent. of the urban as against 8.3 per cent. of the rural public school children are enrolled in high school; that urban high schools show an average of 26.3 teachers per school, while in the average rural high school the entire secondary program is dependent upon 4.3 teachers; and that 47.2 per cent. of the urban high schools have reorganized on a junior high school basis, whereas only 11.9 per cent. of the rural high schools have so reorganized.

EDUCATIONAL MOTION PICTURES

ACCORDING to the Bureau of Education, about fifteen thousand educational institutions of all types in this country are equipped for motion-picture projection.

Many state universities maintain film libraries in their extension departments and systematically supply films to school and community organizations in their own respective states. Yale University has participated in the preparation of a series of films on American history, and Harvard is cooperating with film producers in making pictures bearing on science. Cleveland, Ohio, has installed projecting machines in all its city school buildings.

The stock of available films of excellent quality has greatly increased, the Bureau of Education says, but the number of text films—that is, those which may be used in direct connection with the daily teaching—is far from adequate. The portable type of projector seems to solve the problem of classroom use, safety films avoid fire risk, the improved devices make it possible for the teacher or an intelligent pupil to operate the machine with little training, and a narrow film reduces the cost materially.

A teacher may give her lesson, using an illustrative film to supplement verbal instruction, and leave an enduring impression upon the minds of her pupils.

Under the platoon plan of organization, where groups alternate in the classroom and at other work, the auditorium showings of films approach more nearly the character of class instruction. In the platoon schools of Detroit, Pittsburgh and other cities, one day in the week is given to motion pictures as a part of the auditorium exercises. The programs are arranged in advance, and care is taken to make the pictures coordinate with the classroom teaching.

Great effort has been made in recent years under private endowment to develop text films for classroom use. Satisfactory film has resulted. Twelve cities, from Newton, Massachusetts, in the east, to Oakland, California, in the west, and from Rochester, New York, in the north, to Atlanta, Georgia, in the south, were chosen for experiments involving twelve thousand children, half of whom received instruction without the use of films, and the other half with it as a supplement to the teacher and the text-book.

Thus instruction with and without motion pictures has been going on side by side. Results have been measured and a report of findings is almost ready. It will furnish the first conclusive evidence of the value or lack of it of the motion picture in education.

NEW YORK STATE CONFERENCE OF NORMAL SCHOOLS AND TEACHERS COLLEGE FACULTIES

THE third annual conference of normal schools and teachers college faculties was held in Syracuse on October 11 and 12.

The primary purpose of the meeting, as reported in the *Bulletin* of the University of the

State of New York, was to carry on the work begun two years ago in revising the present curriculums for the preparation of elementary teachers. The afternoon sessions were general in character. One speaker pleaded for the preparation of elementary teachers in terms of the work which will be required of them after graduation. Another urged that the teacher-training institutions should continuously experiment with the elementary program and that the graduates should be trained to teach in terms of what ought to be done in education rather than in terms of the present programs in public elementary education. Still another urged that training should be general and of cultural and disciplinary values. These three viewpoints deal with fundamental philosophies in teacher training and should stimulate discussion throughout the state.

Speakers at the general sessions and at the banquet which was held in the evening of October 11 were: Dr. Ernest C. Hartwell, superintendent of schools, Buffalo; Dr. Frank E. Baker, president of the State Teachers College, Milwaukee, Wisconsin; Wilbur H. Lynch, superintendent of schools, Amsterdam; Dr. Harlan H. Horner, field secretary of the New York State Teachers Association; Earl W. Anibal, principal of the Irvington High School; Dr. Frederick C. Ferry, president of Hamilton College.

A special feature of the meeting was the organization and management of the work by the students in each of the ten schools on Thursday, October 11. New York State is believed to be the first state in which the work has been carried on in all the teacher-training institutions by the students in the absence of the faculties. This arrangement resulted in worth-while educational values for the students. It afforded them an excellent opportunity to assume heavy responsibilities, to exercise their powers of initiative and to meet unusual problems resourcefully.

Nearly 400 of the faculty members were present. This represents 98 per cent. of the total faculty membership. The absence of the remaining 2 per cent. is accounted for by the fact that some were unable to attend because of illness or for other sufficient reasons. Three of the normal schools had 100 per cent. attendance. This record of attendance from all the institutions is a clear expression of the professional interest of the normal schools and teachers colleges, especially in view of the fact that each member attending pays his own expenses.

Dr. Percy I. Bugbee, principal of the State Normal School at Oneonta, and Florence Matteson, of the same school, were president and secretary of the association, respectively, during the past year. The association elected Dr. James G. Riggs, principal of the State Normal School at Oswego, as president for the ensuing year, and Katherine A. Hayes, of the Oswego school, as secretary.

COMMITTEE FOR THE INVESTIGATION OF PROPAGANDA IN THE PUBLIC SCHOOLS

Dr. Edwin C. Broome, superintendent of schools at Philadelphia, has been appointed by President Uel W. Lamkin, of the National Education Association, as chairman of a Committee of Ten to investigate the use in schools of materials provided by outside agencies or organizations. According to an announcement made by J. W. Crabtree, secretary of the National Education Association:

> The purpose of the committee will be to constructively study the question of how schools may bring themselves into closer touch with everyday life through proper use of the vast amount of material which various organizations and agencies now have available for school use. The committee will also state the principles which should guide school officials and teachers in using such material so that children may be protected from one-sided viewpoints and from exploitation for commercial advertising purposes. The committee will study the question as it concerns all schools and all business and educational organizations, rather than confining itself to particular institutions or organizations.

Dr. Broome rendered outstanding service to the Department of Superintendence of the National Education Association by serving for four years as chairman of the Department's Commission on the Curriculum. This commission, which completed its work last February, was responsible for the publication of four yearbooks on curriculum study and its study has resulted in the present nationwide interest in the development of better courses of study for the public schools.

The committee was authorized by the association's board of directors at Minneapolis last July, in the following resolution:

Resolved, That the Board of Directors condemn the policy and efforts of agencies to put propaganda into the schools, and hereby authorize the president of the association to appoint a committee of ten to prepare a report for the meeting of the association in 1929 on the following points: (1) What principles of school administration should guide school authorities, and what principles of school procedure should guide teachers in handling material which might be classed as propaganda; and (2) what machinery, if any, needs to be set up on a local, state or national basis to serve as a protection to individual school officers and teachers.

The complete membership of the committee is as follows:

Edwin C. Broome, superintendent of Philadelphia public schools, Philadelphia, *chairman;* Frank W. Ballou, superintendent of schools, Washington, D. C.; Miss Cornelia S. Adair, Richmond, Virginia, former president of the National Education Association; Miss Eva J. Pinkston, Dallas, Texas, president of the National Education Association's Department of Elementary School Principals; J. Stevens Kadesch, Medford, Massachusetts, president of the Association's Department of Secondary School Principals; C. E. Partch, dean of the school of education, Rutgers University, New Brunswick, New Jersey; L. A. Pittenger, president Ball Teachers College, Muncie, Indiana; A. T. Allen, state superintendent of public instruction for North Carolina, Raleigh; David A. Ward, superintendent of schools, Wilmington, Delaware, and Paul C. Stetson, superintendent of schools, Dayton, Ohio.

APPROPRIATIONS FOR RESEARCH AT CORNELL UNIVERSITY

THE Heckscher Foundation for Research at Cornell University, on recommendation of its council and the approval of the University Board of Trustees has appropriated $70,294 for forty-two separate research projects to be conducted this year, according to an announcement made by Professor R. A. Emerson, secretary of the council.

This year's use of the income of the fund which Mr. August Heckscher established at Cornell in 1920 marks a departure from the previous policy. While providing for research in the physical and biological sciences as well as the humanities, the major portion of this year's funds will be devoted to researches in the natural sciences with particular emphasis on physics and chemistry. As a result of a careful examination of many suggested researches, involving numerous conferences with men in the fields of physics and chemistry and related biological fields, it was decided to undertake a somewhat coordinated attack on problems in the general field of radiation.

Some of the researches thus provided for are purely physical studies of the nature of radiation, some make use of radiations of various kinds in studies of the structure of matter, and some deal with the effects of radiation on chemical reactions and on certain biological phenomena. Many of the studies of the various forms of radiant energy are under way and already give promise of interesting results. The investigations which were announced last July involve almost the entire range of wave-lengths, from X-rays on one extreme, through the ultra-violet, the visible spectrum, and the infra-red, to the shorter radio waves at the other extreme.

In addition to the previously announced researches in the field of radiation, the following grants have been made to members of the Cornell faculty for the current year:

Professor J. Papish. The occurrence, distribution and association of the rarer chemical elements.

Professor A. C. Gill for a petrographic investigation of the Tully limestone.

Professor J. B. Sumner for materials and assistance in connection with a study of the preparation and properties of crystalline urease.

Professor J. A. Dye for materials and assistance in a study of tissue respiration and endocrine functions.

Professor G. C. Embody to aid him in his studies of the rate of growth of wild trout in streams.

Professor Cornelius Betten for aid in the preparation of a manuscript dealing with the Trichoptera.

Dr. Grace H. Griswold for assistance in the preparation of a manuscript on chalcidoid parasites of aphids.

Professor L. H. MacDaniels for assistance in a histological study of the phloem tissue of woody plants.

Professor Allan Nevins for assistance in a study of the history of American railways.

Professor J. F. Mountford for aid in the publication of his "Thesaurus Servianus necnon Donatianus."

Professor J. C. Needham for assistance in his study of the Ephemeridae and other Neuropteroid insects.

Professor G. E. G. Catlin for the study of the specific nature of certain social problems and the appropriate legislation for dealing with them.

Professor O. A. Johannsen for the study of the development and biology of Diptera.

Professor O. F. Curtis for the study of the movement of materials within a plant.

Professor H. Ries for an investigation of the moulding sand resources of the United States.

Dr. G. H. Maughan for a study of the effect of radiant energy on the development of certain glands of chickens.

Professor H. S. Liddell for assistance in his study of conditioned reflexes in the sheep and goat.

Professor C. K. Burdick for a comparative study of restatements of torts and agency and conflicts of laws.

Professor Harry Caplin for the publication of a manuscript: the "De Imaginatione" of Gianfrancesco Pico della Mirandola: text, commentary, introduction, and translation.

THE PROPOSED ENDOWMENT FOR WOMEN'S COLLEGES

THOMAS W. LAMONT was the principal speaker at a dinner given in Philadelphia on November 2, under the auspices of the Alumnae Committee of Seven Colleges, in Philadelphia, before 1,000 alumnae of Smith, Vassar, Wellesley, Mount Holyoke, Radcliffe, Barnard and Bryn Mawr. The function was given in honor of the seven presidents of the colleges, and the purpose was to call attention to the need of increased endowment for these institutions.

Mr. Lamont is reported to have said in part:

We are here to-night, as I take it, not to pass the hat or raise money, but discuss the present crisis which the women's colleges are facing. This plight is not common alone to the seven colleges under whose auspices this meeting has been arranged. I believe it applies to all of them. But these seven institutions have been wise enough to see the situation early and to make common cause in order to meet it. I congratulate them most heartily upon this cooperation which they are undertaking.

As for the present case of women's colleges, no better statement could be made than that which appeared in the *Atlantic Monthly* for November, 1927, from the heads of the seven colleges who are working together in this matter. Dean Gildersleeve, of Barnard, in her annual report for 1928 again presents the situation clearly. To these statements I can add little. At this point, however, I wish to give figures in round numbers, showing the contrast in endowment between seven of the large men's colleges and these seven women's colleges, warning you beforehand that these figures in themselves by no means tell the whole story.

Harvard	$ 82,000,000
Columbia	63,000,000
Yale	49,000,000
Chicago University	39,000,000
Mass. Ins. Technology	29,000,000
Leland Stanford	29,000,000
Duke	27,500,000
Total	$318,500,000
Vassar	$ 6,500,000
Bryn Mawr	6,300,000
Wellesley	5,800,000
Smith	5,000,000
Radcliffe	4,300,000
Barnard	4,100,000
Mount Holyoke	4,000,000
Total	$ 36,000,000

A total of more than $318,500,000 for the seven men's colleges, as against approximately $36,000,000 for the women's. This vast discrepancy is not, however, to be wondered at. Most of the men's colleges have been founded for generations, some of them for centuries; while the women's colleges date in their foundations only sixty or seventy years back. The reason I mention these figures is to point out how adequately we have been attempting to provide proper intellectual training for our men and *per contra* how inadequately—even considering the smaller number of students at the women's colleges—we have as yet provided for the training of our young women.

THE NEW BUILDING FOR THE COLLEGE OF EDUCATION OF THE UNIVERSITY OF CALIFORNIA AT LOS ANGELES

To house the College of Education on the new site of the University of California at Los Angeles, the regents of the university have decided to erect at once a building to cost approximately $525,000. Arrangements for the financing of the building have been made by the finance committee of the regents, and the location and plans are in the hands of the committee on grounds and buildings.

When the regents at their September meeting decided to move the Teachers' College to Westwood site next summer, there had been no arrangements made for its housing, as previously it had been voted to move only the College of Letters and Science. With the decision to take the Teachers' College to the new site, the problem of providing space for it became acute, for the buildings under construction were not designed to meet this need.

Funds for the new structure have been provided through an arrangement with Los Angeles financiers, who are purchasing property owned by the regents, adjoining the present site on Vermont avenue, under an agreement to resell it to the university at the purchase price at any time.

The building planned will be principally for classrooms; and as no expensive equipment is required, it is believed that $525,000 will provide an entirely adequate structure. There are under construction at the present time four buildings, provided by the 1926 bond issue. All the buildings, including the one now projected, will be ready for occupancy next summer, when the move to the new campus is made.

EDUCATIONAL NOTES AND NEWS

WILLIAM MCANDREW, editor of EDUCATIONAL REVIEW and recently superintendent of the Chicago schools, expects to sail next week for Europe, where he will make a prolonged stay. During his absence he will continue to edit the section of SCHOOL AND SOCIETY in which the EDUCATIONAL REVIEW is continued. This section will be included in the first issue of each month. Communications for Mr. McAndrew addressed to 3939 Grand Central Terminal, New York, will be forwarded to him.

DR. HOMER H. SEERLEY has retired from the presidency of the Iowa State Teachers College at Cedar Falls, Iowa, on reaching the age of eighty years. Dr. Seerley, who has been head of the college for forty-two years, now becomes president emeritus. At a celebration in his honor held this week the speakers include Dr. Albert E. Winship, editor of the *Journal of Education,* who is three years older than President Seerley and has been his friend for nearly half a century. President Uel W. Lamkin, of the National Education Association and president of the Northwest Missouri State Teachers College, is also taking part in the celebration.

DR. FRANK PARKER DAY, who is lecturing on advanced English at Swarthmore College, was elected president of Union College, Schenectady, N. Y., at a recent meeting of the board of trustees of the college in this city. He succeeds President Charles Alexander Richmond, who, as reported last week in SCHOOL AND SOCIETY, retires after holding the office for twenty years. Dr. Day was born in Nova Scotia in 1881. As a Rhodes scholar he earned the degree of Master of Arts at Christ Church College, Oxford, in 1907. For some years he was professor of English at the University of New Brunswick and later at the Carnegie Institute of Technology.

WITH representatives from over thirty colleges and universities attending, Dr. Earl Alan Roadman was installed as the tenth president of Dakota Wesleyan University on October 26. President John L. Seaton, of Albion College, delivered the charge to the president, whose inaugural address was entitled "The Community from which Students Come and to which Graduates Go." The ceremony was part of a two-day celebration at the university, the annual home-coming day being on the twenty-seventh. On the morning of the twenty-sixth the presidents of the state and independent colleges of South Dakota convened in an educational conference. President Seaton, who was professor of psychology and Bible at Dakota Wesleyan from 1904 to 1914, was given the degree of doctor of laws at the inaugural exercises.

DR. WILLIAM S. THAYER, professor emeritus of medicine at the Johns Hopkins University, has received the degree of doctor *honoris causa* from the University of Paris.

SIR WILFRED GRENFELL, known for his work as a missionary in Labrador, has been elected lord rector of St. Andrews University, succeeding Dr. Fridtjof Nansen.

DR. HERMAN SCHNEIDER, acting president of the University of Cincinnati, has been made an honorary member of the Cincinnati Academy of Medicine.

THE new Welch Medical Library of the Johns Hopkins University, named for Dr. William H. Welch, who returned recently from Europe, will be opened in a few weeks. President Goodnow has announced the appointment of Lieutenant-Colonel Fielding H. Garrison, of the library of the Surgeon-General's office in Washington, as consulting librarian. William G. Shules is named assistant librarian.

IN recognition of Professor Edward L. Rice's thirtieth year as a member of the faculty of Ohio Wesleyan University, thirty of his students in the field of botanical and zoological sciences have created an Edward L. Rice scholarship fund. A presentation of the fund to the university was made by Dr. Dwight M. DeLong, professor of zoology and entomology at the Ohio State University, at the chapel service on October 27, as a feature of the annual homecoming celebration. The fund will provide a scholarship each year for at least one advanced student, enabling him to do graduate summer-school laboratory work at one of the biological stations. Professor Rice went to Ohio Wesleyan as the head of the department of zoology in 1898. He is the son of Dr. William North Rice, three times acting president and now professor emeritus of geology at Wesleyan University.

PROFESSOR THOMAS C. ESTEY, since 1922 dean of Amherst College, has sent his resignation to President Arthur S. Pease. He will take a year's sabbatical leave and will then return to the college as professor of mathematics, a position he formerly held. He is a graduate of Amherst in the class of 1893 and has been connected with the faculty since 1905.

SUPERINTENDENT FRANK G. PICKELL, of Montclair, New Jersey, was recently elected to honorary membership in the National Council of Education.

T. J. MCCORMACK completed his twenty-fifth year as principal of the La Salle-Peru Township High School and his fourth year as director of the La Salle-Peru-Oglesby Junior College last June. An alumni subscription made possible the presentation of his portrait to the institutions over which he presides. The portrait, which is painted by Paul Trebilcock, will be exhibited at the Chicago Galleries Association and later in New York City.

A RECEPTION and tea was tendered to Miss Theresa G. Keenan at Public School 88, Manhattan, on October 10, in honor of her recent promotion to the principalship of Public School 31, Manhattan. Miss Keenan was presented with a platinum brooch set with diamonds and sapphires.

MICHAEL H. LUCEY, principal of the Julia Richman High School and president-elect of the New York Society for the Experimental Study of Education, delivered his inaugural address at the dinner of that society on October 20.

DR. JACOB S. ORLEANS, formerly research associate in the educational measurements bureau, New York State Department of Education, has accepted a position on the editorial staff of the World Book Company. He is associated with Dr. Arthur S. Otis.

DR. DONALD A. LAIRD, director of the Colgate University Psychological Laboratory, has been appointed chairman of the central New York section of the Taylor Society. Richard Pass, of the Onondaga Pottery Company, is vice-chairman, and R. S. Gardner, of the L. C. Smith-Corona Company, is secretary-treasurer.

PROFESSOR RALPH S. HOSMER, who is head of the department of forestry at the New York State College of Agriculture, is serving on the City Planning Board of Ithaca.

WALLACE B. DONHAM, dean of the Harvard Graduate School of Business Administration, has been elected a director and chairman of the finance committee of the Royal Baking Powder Company.

DONALD M. CAMPBELL, who graduated from the Sheffield Scientific School of Yale University last June, has been appointed assistant to the president of Lake Forest College. He will be in charge of new student work and undergraduate activities, including athletics.

DR. ALFRED D. SIMPSON, for the last eleven years a member of the Connecticut State Board of Education, has been appointed assistant commissioner for finance in the New York State Education Department. He succeeded Clark W. Halliday, who recently retired. While on the staff of the Connecticut board he was engaged from 1917 to 1923 in state supervision, special inquiry and school surveys. In 1923 with the establishment of a division of research and survey, he became the first director of that division. When a division of teacher preparation was established in 1927 he was appointed director of that division.

THE new principal of the University High School at Oakland, California, is Dr. George A. Rice, who was formerly professor of education in the University of California.

DR. BOYD EDWARDS has assumed the headmastership of Mercersburg Academy, Pennsylvania, the formal inauguration being omitted at his special request. On Alumni Day, October 13, memorial exercises were held for the late head master, William Mann Irvine.

PERCY ANGROVE, of Lansing, known for his work in vocational education, has been appointed assistant superintendent of Wayne County Training School, in Detroit, Michigan.

PROFESSORS J. B. EDMONSON and Raleigh Schorling, members of the building committee of the University of Michigan School of Education, have been in the east visiting schools in Boston and New York. They were accompanied by Mr. Fish, who has been named by the Board of Regents as adviser to the committee, and by Mr. Balle, of Detroit, who has been retained as the architect.

DR. FRANCIS MARTIN GARVER, professor of education in the University of Pennsylvania, has been appointed head of a commission to investigate the school system of New Jersey.

SPEAKERS at the annual two-day convention of the western district of the New York State Teachers Association, that opened in Buffalo on November 2, included Dr. E. C. Hartwell, superintendent of schools in Buffalo; Dr. Frank Boynton, of Ithaca, president of the department of superintendence, National Education Association; Dr. Lotus D. Coffman, president of the University of Minnesota; W. Howard Pillsbury, superintendent of schools in Pelham, and Dr. Augustus O. Thomas, commissioner of education for the State of Maine and president of the World Federation of Educational Associations.

PROFESSOR THOMAS A. LARREMORE, now on leave of absence from the University of Kansas to the University of Pennsylvania, and one of the founders of the Missouri Valley Intercollegiate Glee Club, was elected honorary president of the organization at a recent meeting. He was its president for the first three years, and was director of the University of Kansas men's glee club. Other officers elected were: *President,* E. B. Connant, Washington University, St. Louis; *vice-president,* Marchell F. Bryant, University of Missouri, Columbia; *secretary,* R. H. Richards, University of Missouri; *treasurer,* Eugene Christy, University of Kansas, Lawrence. The contest number to be sung by the association this year will be "Songs My Mother Taught Me," by Dvorak-Smith.

MEMBERS of the academic council of the Department of Education of the State of New York have been appointed by the regents as follows: George L. Bennett, principal of Charles E. Gorton High School, Yonkers, for a term of four years, to succeed Charles W. Lewis, formerly of Kingston; Ernest M. Robinson, principal of Troy High School, for a term of five years, to succeed A. B. Davis, Mount Vernon; T. A. Zornow, principal of Madison Junior High School, Rochester, for a term of two years.

DR. ROBERT A. LAMBERT, director of the School of Tropical Medicine in San Juan, Porto Rico, which is under the auspices of Columbia University, has resigned to accept a post as associate director of medical education with the Rockefeller Foundation. Dr. Earl B. McKinley, formerly a member of the staff of the International Health Division of the Rockefeller Foundation, has been appointed professor of bacteriology in the College of Physicians and Surgeons, Columbia University, and succeeds Dr. Lambert as director of the School of Tropical Medicine.

PROFESSOR WILLIAM JOHNSTON BERRY has been appointed head of the department of mathematics of the Polytechnic Institute of Brooklyn, to succeed Professor J. B. Chittenden, who died last April.

DR. WAYLAND F. VAUGHAN has been promoted from instructor to assistant professor of philosophy in the college of liberal arts of Boston University.

RECENT additions to the liberal arts faculty of the University of Arizona are Assistant Professor Sidney Barlow Brown and Associate Professor Melvin T. Solve. Dr. Brown was formerly head of the French department of Bates College, Maine, and Dr. Solve was formerly of the University of Michigan.

EDWARD T. INGLE succeeds O. K. Armstrong as assistant professor of journalism at the University of Florida.

DR. CARL C. HARVEY, of Middletown, Connecticut, has been appointed acting medical director of Wesleyan University in the absence of Dr. Edgar Fauver, head of the department of physical education and college physician, who will be on leave of absence.

DR. FLORENCE BASCOM, professor of geology at Bryn Mawr College, having reached the age of retirement, will continue her work at the U. S. Geological Survey, Washington, D. C.

DR. ALFRED ATKINSON, after a year of research work and travel in Europe and in this country, has reassumed his duties as president of Montana State College, Bozeman. It was Dr. Atkinson's second sabbatical leave in the twenty-one years that he has been connected with the college.

J. J. MALLON, warden of the Toynbee Hall of the Universities' Settlements in East London, an authority on social and industrial questions, spoke at the Northwestern University convocation, on November 5, on "The International Regulation of Industry." Mr. Mallon was commissioner of industrial unrest in 1917, was a member of the National Industrial Conference appointed by Lloyd George in 1921 and has served on many reconstruction committees.

DR. C. A. BUCKNER, professor of secondary education at the University of Pittsburgh, will lecture before the junior-high-school teachers of Los Angeles during the school week beginning on December 17.

PROFESSOR FRANCHINI, director of the Institute for Tropical Diseases at the University of Bologna, delivered recently an illustrated lecture in English on Marcello Malpighi to the students of the De Witt Clinton High School, New York City.

THE laboratory recently established at the Massachusetts Institute of Technology for research in inorganic chemistry has been named the Henry Paul Talbot Laboratory in honor of the late Professor Talbot. A portrait presented by Mrs. Talbot, who was present at the ceremony, was unveiled when the new laboratory was named. Dr. F. K. Keyes, director of the laboratory and in charge of the department of chemistry, presided, and Professor H. M. Smith, in charge of the division of inorganic chemistry, made an address describing Dr. Talbot's long and distinguished association with the institute and particularly his services in the teaching of chemistry. Dr. Talbot was professor in the department of chemistry from 1892 to 1927.

DR. CHARLES F. WHEELOCK, formerly assistant state school commissioner of New York, died after a long illness on November 4. He was eighty years old.

DR. ELIZA M. MOSHER died, as the result of a fall, on October 16 at the age of eighty-two years. After graduation at the University of Michigan she practised as a physician and later occupied several institutional positions. In 1886 Dr. Mosher became the first dean of women at the University of Michigan. She retired in 1902 to resume private practise in

Brooklyn, New York, in which she continued until her accident last March.

FREDERICK WILLIAM BALL, member of the Board of Education of Newark, New Jersey, a former president of the board, died on October 14 of heart disease at Maitland Bridge, Nova Scotia, while hunting in the woods. Mr. Ball was forty-nine years of age.

THE death is announced of Miss Jessie Claire McDonald, for fifteen years principal of the National Cathedral School for Girls, Washington, D. C.

DR. J. W. CRABTREE, secretary of the National Education Association, in urging present members of the association to become life members, writes: "In 1918 there were 8,000 active members. We now have 190,000 with '200,000 by Christmas' as our slogan. We now have 1,900 life members. Why not 2,000 by Christmas? Some predict that within five years the enrolment of life members will be equal to the entire enrolment of active members in 1918. The results of this year will determine whether the 8,000 goal is possible by 1933."

THE National Council of State Superintendents and Commissioners of Education will hold a meeting in Washington, D. C., on December 11 and 12 to confer with federal authorities on questions vital to the council. Three main topics have been selected for discussion with government officers. They are: Educational statistics, uniform reports, and how the United States Bureau of Education can best serve as a clearinghouse for state departments of education.

THE fourth annual convention of the Pacific Coast Association of Collegiate Registrars, which is interrelated with the American Association of Collegiate Registrars, will be held at Riverside and Pomona, California, on November 19 and 20. Registrar J. P. Mitchell, of Stanford University, and Registrar Ernest L. Rea, of Riverside Junior College, respectively president and secretary of the Pacific Coast Association, will be in charge of the meetings. The general theme will be "The Development of the Junior College." The Pacific Coast Association has a membership of about one hundred institutions of higher education. The last convention was held in November, 1927, at the Oregon State College, Corvallis, and the University of Oregon, Eugene.

THE Association of Deans and Advisers of Men will meet at Washington, D. C., under the auspices of George Washington University, on April 11, 12 and 13, 1929. Dean George B. Culver, of Stanford University, is president; Dean Henry Grattan Doyle, of George Washington University, is vice-president, and Dean F. M. Dawson, of the University of Kansas, is secretary of the association. Dean Doyle will be in charge of local arrangements for the meeting. The program for the sessions will be announced later.

OVER thirty-five universities and colleges were represented when the Eastern College Personnel Officers Association held its fall meeting at Yale University on November 9. The program included a luncheon to be held that day in Memorial Hall, at which President James Rowland Angell spoke. Discussion groups met during the afternoon to consider such problems as selection for admission, organization of bureaus of personnel, vocational counseling, senior placement, graduate placement, term-time student employment and administration of financial assistance. Business transacted by the association consisted of the election of officers, reports of committees and reports on the findings of the discussion groups. A dinner was held in Memorial Hall. Addresses were given by Dean Herbert E. Hawkes, of Columbia College, who spoke on "Recent Developments in College Personnel Work," and by Ralph Delano Paine, a senior in Yale College, whose subject was "The Activities of a Bureau of Personnel Study from the Student's Viewpoint." Members of the association who remained over Saturday attended the Maryland-Yale football game as the guests of Albert B. Crawford, director of the Yale Department of Personnel Study and Bureau of Appointments. The officers for the meeting were: Dean Paul Nixon, Bowdoin, *president;* Miss Florence Jackson, Wellesley, *first vice-president;* N. M. McKnight, Columbia University, *second vice-president;* Walker H. Daly, Harvard University, *third vice-president;*

Norman H. Abbott, Boston University, *secretary;* N. Aborn Pennell, Massachusetts Institute of Technology, *treasurer,* and the *Executive Committee,* composed of Albert B. Crawford, Yale, *chairman;* Francis J. A. Neef, Dartmouth; and Miss Agnes B. Leahy, Connecticut College for Women.

THE Boston Museum of Fine Arts, under the will of George Nixon Black, of Boston, is given $150,000 and the residue of the estate, which is estimated at $5,000,000, after various bequests have been made. These include Massachusetts General Hospital, St. Luke's Home for Convalescents and the Perkins Institution for the Blind, $10,000 each; Society for the Prevention of Cruelty to Children, Society for Prevention of Cruelty to Animals and the Society for the Employment of Bible Readers, $5,000 each.

WITH the aid of the $100,000 gift by David Schapiro, publisher of *The Day,* a New York Yiddish newspaper, a chair for Yiddish is to be established in the Institute of Jewish Studies, of the Hebrew University in Jerusalem. The curatorium of the institute has indorsed the proposal and accepted the gift.

WESLEYAN UNIVERSITY has announced the establishment of ten scholarships, each of $500, to be awarded beginning in 1929–30, to seniors of high standing who need financial help to complete their college course. These scholarships will be known as the Denison Scholarships and are made possible by the gift of $5,000 from Mr. and Mrs. Charles L. Denison, of New York City. Mr. Denison is a member of the Board of Trustees.

DISCUSSION

EDUCATIONAL WASTE

EDUCATION, as carried on in our public schools, is wasteful in that it is largely useless to those who partake of it. The schools are enormously expensive. The most the elementary school does is to teach children to read. This mothers could easily do, while the children are growing up in the home, as a part of the children's play, and at no expense at all. That children should be taught to read at public expense is a disgrace to every parent that makes it necessary.

Our education is what might properly be called "shot-gun" education, in that we teach a multitude of things, hoping that sometime, somewhere, a few of them may prove useful.

No one has any very clear idea as to what a particular subject, as geography, history, algebra or geometry, does to or for a person. The country is full of testers who worry the helpless children by measuring their respective amounts of progress in the various studies. If a study is worthless, it makes little difference whether a child's progress in it is fast or slow. And if a study is of great value, it is of little consequence that it takes one child a week longer to master it than is required by another. The important thing to know is whether a branch of study is worth while.

A child in school should have experiences that profoundly modify his life in a practical way. He should, on the one hand, be studying and mastering the everyday machines and tools and situations that are fairly common to everybody. Everything in or about a home should be mastered as to principle and mechanism or practical operation: stoves, lights, furnaces, door-bells, water faucets, meters, sewers and sewerage, food, cooking, the mechanical, chemical and physiological aspects of the human body, health and disease, radio, telephone. In a word, children should, through coming to understand and use the parts of the world which lie closest to them, *master* them. This mastery should come—in fact it must come—from studying and manipulating the things themselves and not from reading books about them.

On the other hand, children should be receiving in school experiences that lay the foundation for a life of enjoyment and appreciation in art, music, literature and nature.

When we say that education should be practical, we do not mean that it should always have a money value. We mean that education should always contribute either to our ability to make a living or to our ability to enjoy living. As now conducted, our schools fail as much in one of these directions as in the other. The courses in literature, for example, quite often entirely fail to give students a knowledge or a love of literature. Although English has a larger place in our high school curriculum than any other study, the courses often develop a hatred of literature.

For another example of waste, let us take physics. Boys often enter high school courses in physics with great expectations of learning the mechanisms of all the machines and appliances in their immediate world, presently to discover that the course is a technical one, largely mathematical and quite out of their range of interests. What a disappointment!

Our curricula in the elementary and high schools should be stripped of their useless rubbish. What is left should be taught with the greatest thoroughness and made to become a real and active part of the pupils' lives. At present, children too often take their education lightly. The knowledge acquired is vague and faraway. It is too often really of another world. It is not found to be necessary to life. It is only necessary to *examinations*. When they are over, the knowledge quickly falls into a blessed oblivion. The things taught to a child should be *so necessary* to him that he *could not* forget them, but must live them.

The public schools have made but little contribution to the moral development of the children. This is partly because they have not tried to do much, but also partly because they have not done properly even the little attempted. About all the schools know to do for a child is to give him a book. And so, when moral training is taken up, the child is given a book. Now the only way to build up the moral life of a child is to help him to form proper habits. The schools have scarcely ever made any systematic attempt at such a procedure. They have required the child to learn the ten commandments and the golden rule and to *pass an examination upon them as bits of knowledge.*

In our great cities, the cost of education is so enormous that it is difficult to raise sufficient taxes to meet it. What is the return? These same great cities are jungles full of robbers, murderers, thieves. On every hand are graft and corruption. One would think that there ought to be some return in the form of good citizenship. The fact is, the public school does not function practically, except in a very small degree. The school has our children nearly all day, ten months of the year for twelve years. If that time were properly used, every child would be equipped to know and understand the world; to make a living; to enjoy music and art, and be able to express himself in some form of each. He would know Nature in her various aspects, and most of all, would be a good citizen. There would be some exceptions, of course, but they would be taken care of in such a way that they would not be a menace to society.

Briefly: The schools are wasteful in that they teach so many useless things. The valuable things taught are not taught in such a way as to become effective in the lives of the children.

The way to eliminate waste is to teach only things that are of vital importance to human life, either in a practical and economic way, or in a way that will bring joy and happiness to the possessor.

A great part of the stuff taught under the names of history, geography, mathematics, grammar and even science, is worthless rubbish as far as becoming effective in the children's lives is concerned. In so far as it is ineffective, it is a waste of time and money to teach it. Any one who forms useless habits or acquires useless knowledge is wasting his time. Life is so short that we should not waste any of it. If we would eliminate all waste in education, there would be time enough and money enough to do all the *right things* to make life whole and complete. There is no value in going to school or in learning unless the going to school and the learning lead to results beneficial to life.

W. H. PYLE

TEACHERS COLLEGE,
DETROIT, MICHIGAN

EFFICIENT TEACHING AND A RETIREMENT SYSTEM

BETTER efficiency in our schools is the strongest argument teachers have to give the tax-paying public for teacher retirement systems.

Our schools are made better because our teachers are made better by retirementt legislation. The children and the community are the direct beneficiaries. The fact that twenty-two states and the District of Columbia now have state-wide laws, with eleven more states having laws that apply to certain cities only and the other sixteen states working diligently toward state-wide retirement legislation, shows that, nationally, the public and the teaching profession recognize the value of teachers' retirement to the teaching profession.

We believe in a retirement system that is actuarially sound, built up by both the public and the teacher.

We believe in a retirement system that is absolutely fair to the teacher and to the public. Such a system will safeguard the interests of the teacher in case of early retirement, death, disability or removal to another state.

When all states have a sound system a reciprocal relation—relation to years in service—can be arranged for teachers moving from one state to another.

A sound teacher retirement law attracts and holds capable young people to the teaching profession. It gives a better guarantee of promotion within the profession because of the retirement of teachers at retirement age.

The efficiency of the teachers is increased by a retirement system because it lengthens the period of teaching efficiency by relieving the teacher's mind of a fear of destitute old age and again by making it possible for a teacher to invest in study and training and travel without endangering the provision made for his later years.

The support of sound teacher retirement legislation on the part of all teachers is a professional duty.

Sound teacher retirement legislation can entail no hardship upon any teacher. If after being a member of a retirement system for a number of years he chooses to withdraw from the profession, the deposits made toward building up his annuity fund are returned to him. Joining a retirement system, therefore, means no personal sacrifice, even though a teacher may not continue in the profession until the age for normal retirement. On the other hand, the failure of a small group of teachers to support retirement legislation may make such legislation difficult or impossible of enactment and result in harm both to teachers and children. Every teacher should give his support to the enactment of a sound teacher retirement system, if for no other reason than his interest in the advancement of the profession.

E. Ruth Pyrtle

Lincoln, Nebraska

QUOTATIONS

THE EDUCATIONAL REVIEW AND WILLIAM McANDREW

For twenty-nine years Dr. Nicholas Murray Butler, with all his other occupations, edited the *Educational Review,* a monthly periodical devoted to raising the intellectual standards of the teaching profession. It immediately took and held the foremost place among educational journals in that it gathered into its columns "the most sober and constructive contributions to educational thought." But the increasing pressure of other obligations compelled him to give over its editorial direction to other hands. Dr. Frank Pierrepont Graves carried it forward on the same high plane for a few years, when he also had to relinquish the editorship. Then that able and ebullient educator, Dr. William McAndrew, who a little later became through the assistance of Mayor Thompson an international figure, undertook with his left hand to edit it while with his right hand he guided the affairs of the Chicago schools. This month it appears as a "combined" part of School and Society—the excellent weekly which, itself the result of a merger of two older journals established in the 70s, has under the competent editorship of Dr. J. McKeen Cattell become a trustworthy source of educational news and authoritative comment.

Dr. McAndrew brings to it fresh observations from the field and presents them in a way to arrest the attention of every one who opens its pages. His comments in the first joint number are devoted especially to teachers' meetings, "institutes" they are usually called, which sorely need revising. Incidentally, he gives sound advice as to meetings in general—advice to hearers for which public speakers will thank him. It relates first of all to filling the front seats. "The back-seat habit is discreditable to the service." Speakers should include in their agreement to talk a promise from the local committee or conductor "to dispose your audience so that they will sit with no empty seats in front of them." The bare bench is "stupid, unethical, rude, inhospitable and unprofessional." It is a good rule for one attending any meeting at which there are addresses not to take a seat behind an empty seat.

Another mission on which Dr. McAndrew has sent his pen is in protest against representations by the press in editorials or cartoons of an alleged dislike of school and teacher by the pupil. Those who carry on the tradition suggested by Shakespeare's schoolboy, "creeping like snail unwillingly to school," do not know the modern school. They should take advantage of the invitations which are now pressed upon parents and taxpayers to see the schools. American teachers, Dr. McAndrew assures us, "have made the schoolhouse the favorite resort of children."

Chicago has lost much in parting with Dr. McAndrew, but it is worth while to have such a man at large in the country.—*The New York Times.*

REPORTS

REFORM OF THE ITALIAN SCHOOL SYSTEM

THE full text of the statement translated by the Bureau of Education from various issues of "Bollettino Ufficiale" and "Revista de Pedagogia" for September, printed in the *U. S. Daily,* follows.

Among other recent pronouncements on education by Premier Mussolini, he has expressed himself with respect to Italian culture abroad and to the fostering of syndicalism in Italian schools, that is, organizing each trade into a separate guild such as existed in the middle ages.

In an address before the Italian Senate made by Il Duce on June 5, 1928, he said:

The government has recently created an institution for the diffusion of Italian culture in foreign countries, an activity whose importance has often been emphasized. Both in Italy and in foreign countries a number of institutions have been organized for this purpose but these institutions, organized by both private and public initiative, have only too often duplicated work with wholly inadequate means. The new committee will study ways of coordinating the various activities, and a permanent central office will be organized for this special purpose. In the meantime, the General Directorate of Italian Schools abroad has continued its work and we have had the satisfaction of seeing new schools established for elementary instruction in many countries of Europe and South America.

The increase in the duties of the Ministry of Public Instruction was approved after an investigation of the progress of the schools under the Gentile Reform, at the meeting of the Grand Council of the Fascist Party in November, 1927.

Two of the twelve articles approved by the Grand Council for use by the Minister of Justice in preparing the text of a law which should transform the Chamber of Deputies into an elective body representing the corporations, are given here in full:

2. The syndicalistic organizations, which have been recently organized are as yet insufficiently prepared to take the place of the Fascist Party in the political action of the Regime, and stand alone in the field of national representation. They can only be granted a first step in this direction.

* * *

7. The right to vote is not conferred on all citizens according to the old democratic system of universal suffrage but only on those who, by paying their syndicalist dues show they are active elements in the life of the nation, in addition to other categories, not specifically mentioned in the law on collective labor contracts, but which nevertheless are useful to the national collectivity.

It has been announced that the present Chamber of Deputies will remain in function until 1929, and will, with the Senate, pass on the law which is to have such a far-reaching effect on Italy.

The transfer to the Ministry of Public Instruction of the schools that were under the direction of the Ministry of National Economy until late in July, 1928, approved by the Grand

Council as already stated, was made the subject of an order signed by Premier Mussolini in person and reading as follows:

In harmony with and as a vindication of the general reform of the school made by the Fascist Government on the recommendation of Senator Gentile while Minister of Public Instruction—a reform that will be even more effective after the reorganization that will have to take place in that department as the result of the transfer of the schools which have been administered by the Ministry of National Economy—Minister Belluzo will develop his activities on the following lines:

I. He will give the Italian elementary school a text-book that is unique for the purpose of educating the adolescent in the new atmosphere created by Fascism and developing keen consciousness concerning:

(a) What the Italian people have been and claim to have been in history. (b) Their contribution in discoveries, in inventions, and in the patrimony of knowledge, art and civilization, to all peoples. (c) The beauty and revitalization of Italy. (d) The part played by Italians scattered over the earth in the productive activity of the various nations.

II. He will coordinate and strengthen the professional instruction that forms an end in itself, training the workers for the office and the field as directors and managers, and preparing technical men for agriculture, industry, and commerce, and stimulating initiatives of a syndical character in the field of instruction of the worker and the farmer.

To this end he will unify the continuation school programs and give them a special professional-artistic, industrial, agricultural or commercial character, depending on the predominant activity in the province or municipality where located. He will gradually transform the sections of the present technical institutes into professional-industrial, agricultural or commercial schools of the corresponding grade where such do not already exist, and will suppress the sections of the technical schools where the professional schools do exist already.

III. In the middle school that prepares youth for the university, the institutes, or the higher schools, he will unify, strengthen, and develop the combinations of indispensable foundation studies, introducing only into the later years special instruction for those whose foundation must be laid on classical knowledge and for those who seek a scientific-technical career.

IV. He will take up for reconsideration the problem of the government university and higher schools of various types with respect to their needs in relation to the activities of each locality, with a view to reducing the activities of those that have only a few students and do not appear to respond to local requirements, and, on the other hand, he will develop the activities of those faculties that respond to the needs of science, production, and the liberal professions.

The constitution of the Higher Council of Public Instruction will be amended to meet the requirements of the transfer to that department of the higher institutes formerly under the jurisdiction of the Ministry of National Economy.

V. He will give a special trend to the scientific laboratories connected with the universities and higher schools, in accordance with the program of the investigating committee, and fix the status, economically and legally, of the regular workers in such laboratories.

VI. He will restore many special subjects now taught in new chairs in the universities and higher schools, to the foundational courses of instruction, though extended and strengthened.

VII. He will amend the laws covering archeological discoveries, giving adequate encouragement to investigators and rewarding discoverers, but covering underground researches from an archeological standpoint by permanent legislation.

VIII. He will complete the fascistization of all schools, not only that of the programs but of the individuals themselves.

The so-called "earthquake in the school" of five years ago thus vindicated by Premier Mussolini was pushed through and put into effect by Senator Giovannia Gentile, then Minister of Public Instruction, under authority of an act of Parliament passed December 3, 1922. Among other changes, the reform included the restoration of the teaching of the Roman Catholic religion in the schools, the redistricting of the Kingdom, for school purposes, on the basis of the 19 former kingdoms and the "redeemed provinces" instead of the 75 provinces, the reorganization and reduction of "Minerva," the central education office at Rome, the establishment of government examinations for entrance to the secondary schools and further promotion, and the division of the elementary schools with respect to their maintenance, into classified, provisional and subsidized schools. Under the reform, schools with 40 pupils or more are entitled to be in the classified list and are under immediate official supervision; those of less than 40 pupils but having more than 15, are provisional schools and are not under the immediate direction of the government, and schools of fewer pupils are subsidized and are carried on by non-government organizations and individuals with government inspection.

Among the changes which the reform made in the secondary schools was the abolition of the "scuola technica," an excellent school with a course of three years based on elementary school training of from four to six years. The work formerly done by this school was divided between the three year complementary school which requires an examination for entrance and fits for immediate work in offices, and the technical school of four years which leads to the 4-year technical institute. Under this new order of Premier Mussolini, these technical institutes will be replaced, where possible, by the professional schools transferred from the Department of National Economy. These include:

(a) Industrial institutes, mining schools, trade schools, industrial preparatory schools, laboratory schools, women's industrial schools.

(b) Commercial institutes and schools and higher institutes.

(c) Higher agrarian institutes, higher institutes of veterinary medicine, secondary agrarian schools, and practical schools of agricultural associations.

SOCIETIES AND MEETINGS

THE SIXTH INTERNATIONAL CONGRESS ON ART EDUCATION

AT Prague, Czechoslovakia, from July 28 to August 4, was held the Sixth International Congress on Art Education, Drawing and Art Applied to Industry. Mr. Huger Elliott, director of educational work, and the writer attended as delegates of The Metropolitan Museum of Art.

The general subject, toward which all discussion seemed to lead, might be stated: New methods of developing self-expression in art instruction; though more adequately suggested in the cliché—more learning and less teaching. Thus, methodology and regularity of fixed school curriculum were set against creative stimulation of sense and aptitude by constructive manipulation of actual material. This resolves itself into a glorification of craftsmanship, interpreted both in the original sense of unique production and in the contemporary sense of a craftsman attitude toward multiple manufacture. It emphasizes the *Werkstätte* and, finally, gives to design, which has the objective of products to be sold, its rightful place as an economic consideration not to be ignored even by general schools, as contrasted with drawing, hitherto so studiously fostered as an end in itself.

More narrowly, topics such as the following were assigned to upward of one hundred speakers, often followed by discussion from the floor, in which as many as twelve others participated: "Cultural Importance of Art Education from an Economic Standpoint"; Artistic Education and Teaching Methods"; "Professional Training of Art Teachers"; "Psychologic Research in the Appreciation of Beauty"; "Training of Gifted Pupils"; "Art Instruction and the Growth of Style"; "Instruction in Technical and Art Schools," various locally developed methods and results being presented by directors of schools and others. At a morning session the writer was given an opportunity to present the subject "Art in Industry: an Educational Responsibility and an Economic Necessity."

All addresses were presented wholly or in part in four languages: Czechoslovak, English, French and German, so that each was rendered complete in one language and in briefer form in three others. The best addresses were those of the Germans, whose general teaching methods seem to have been carried farther than those of any other country and who certainly have more local or individual experiments in art teaching under way. The American addresses numbered not over twelve, the total in English not over twenty-five, including discussion. The American presentation was far from convincing on the platform, though reinforced by drawings exhibited in the same building. A most interesting sidelight on the whole undertaking was the fact that but one speaker, other than the undersigned, mentioned museums of art as important educational factors or as useful collaterally in art teaching.

Sessions were held twice daily, 8 A. M. to noon and 2 to 5 P. M., in two large halls simultaneously, one at the city's Exposition Grounds and the other in the Masaryk School. The delegates were received officially at the Hradcin, now occupied by President Masaryk, and also by the minister of public instruction, Dr. Milan Hodza, of the Czechoslovak Republic, by the Mayor of Prague and by Mr. Lewis Einstein, the American Minister.

The attendance was 2,982, of whom close to one thousand were Americans. There was a special evening dinner session of the American contingent, at which Mr. Elliott spoke with reference to procedure regarding the next congress, which has been scheduled for Vienna and will be held in 1932. Figures for earlier meetings might be of interest in this connection:

	Delegates	Members	Countries
Paris, 1900	30	516	15
Berne, 1904	172	823	21
London, 1908	299	1819	38
Dresden, 1912	345	2201	38
Paris, 1925	187	1600	21
Prague, 1928	217	2982	22

As a concomitant of the meetings and continuing a week longer, an exhibition was arranged showing the work of various countries, cities, schools and even of individual instructors, filling two large exhibition buildings. The more important exhibits were: United States, Great Britain, Sweden, Japan, Canada, Poland, Austria, Latvia, Hamburg, Paris, Vienna, Dessau, Dresden, Professor Cizek. All these together occupied as much space as the very impressive exhibit of Czechoslovakia alone.

Among the American exhibitors were: The Metropolitan Museum of Art, Massachusetts School of Art, Cleveland School of Art, Cleveland Museum of Art, Teachers College, Columbia University, Los Angeles public schools, Ohio State University, Syracuse University, Seattle public schools, Washington Irving High School (New York), George Washington High School (New York). The ten mounts, each with captions and text in English, French and German, prepared by The Metropolitan Museum, were displayed to advantage and occupied a central position on a wall space about thirty feet wide. The Cleveland Museum exhibit contained six posters, a large number of drawings made in the galleries mounted in seven volumes and two painted diagrams in aerial perspective to show Cleveland Museum as the cultural center of the city and gifted children from numerous institutions going to the museum for study. There were numerous commercial booths advertising drawing materials, etc.

The congress has been described as a sublimated training school for teachers of art, as the stamping ground for pet theories, as the best opportunity for broadcast restatement of accepted method or the reassertion of truths that are foregone conclusions in even the weakest school. All these may be, in fact, probably are, correct descriptions, but they represent conditions which would obtain to some degree in the best managed meeting of the kind. In any case, they are incomplete unless we place with them and ahead of them the better description of the congress on art education as the best available opportunity for art teachers and all others occupied in educational work in art to discover their own weaknesses, to assure themselves of tendencies taking shape in their own field, to observe at first hand not only methods tested elsewhere and found good but also new methods that hold promise for art-educational progress.

According to available information, this is the first of these congresses in which a museum of art was officially represented, the first to carry in its title the words "art applied to industry" or any similar words; the first to include in its program or discussion any phase, other than that of teaching method, of the subject art in industry; the first to emphasize the economic significance of industrial art teaching.

Present prospects would seem to be that industrial art will appear regularly in future congresses and that museums of art will be counted upon in the study of tendencies in the development of art teaching.

RICHARD F. BACH
METROPOLITAN MUSEUM OF ART,
NEW YORK, N. Y.

EDUCATIONAL RESEARCH AND STATISTICS

INTELLIGENCE OF ONE THOUSAND STUDENTS OF FOREIGN LANGUAGES

IF the layman were to give full credence to all the reports citing lack of intelligence[1] as a primary cause of failure in the foreign languages, he would find it difficult, in view of the high rate of mortality in this field,[2] to conceive the students of these subjects as other than a hopelessly imbecile group. That such an assumption is not substantiated in fact, and, incidentally, that something must be quite wrong with teachers' diagnoses of failures, is evident from the following study of the intelligence[3] of 1,002 students, distributed through eight semesters of Spanish in eighteen junior and senior high schools of San Diego and Los Angeles.[4]

The measures of central tendency and variability for the total sampling of cases are summarized separately by sex in Table I. From a study of these and of their graphical representations in the accompanying charts, it is evident that the personnel of Spanish classes is distinctly select. For the girls, the mean shows a deviation of nearly eight points from the normal; the median, one of approximately seven

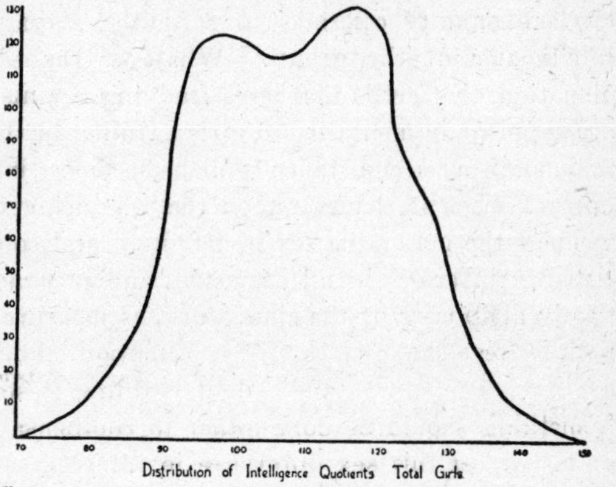

Distribution of Intelligence Quotients Total Girls

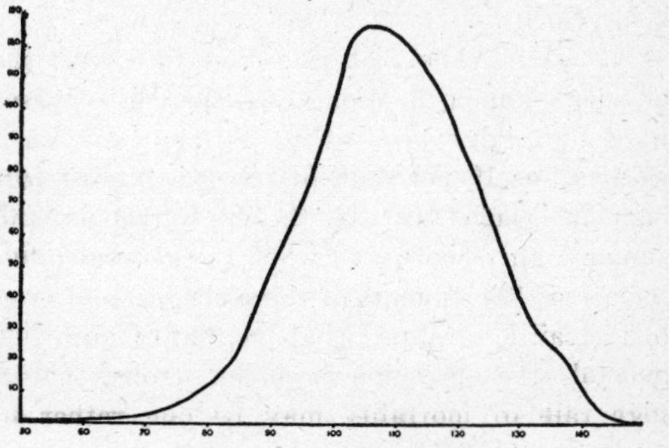

Distribution of Intelligence Quotients Total Boys

points, and the first quartile, one of less than two points from the theoretical average of a typically normal distribution. Among the boys, selection is even more conspicuous, though relatively less evident from the higher mean and

TABLE I

MEASURES OF CENTRAL TENDENCY AND VARIABILITY FOR THE INTELLIGENCE QUOTIENTS OF 1,002 JUNIOR AND SENIOR HIGH SCHOOL STUDENTS IN SPANISH

Measures	Girls	Boys
Number of cases	568	434
Range	78	61
Mean	107.590	108.917
P.E. of M.	± .354	± .429
Pearson C. of V.	11.618	12.156
Percentile 10	91.584	91.763
Quartile 1	98.400	100.276
Median	106.893	108.661
Quartile 3	116.541	118.043
Percentile 90	125.158	126.984
10–90 Range	33.574	35.221
Quartile deviation	9.071	8.884
Standard deviation	12.500	13.240

[1] See, for example: Committee Report, "Foreign Languages in the Junior High Schools," *California Quarterly of Secondary Education*, 2: 366–368, 1927.

[2] Ralph L. John, "High School Failures," *California Quarterly of Secondary Education*, 3: 186–194, 1928.

[3] I.Q.'s as derived from the Terman Group Test of Mental Ability.

[4] The writer acknowledges with gratitude his indebtedness to Dr. George W. H. Shield, director of foreign languages, Los Angeles, California, for cooperation in securing data from the junior and senior high schools of his city.

median than from the superior ability of pupils in the first and third quartiles. As a whole the boys outrank the girls in all levels of mental ability.

This superiority of the male group is of more than incidental significance in that it seems to imply a sex difference in language interest or inclination. It must be that languages do not make as wide an appeal to masculine as to feminine taste, and that in consequence only boys of superior ability elect Spanish and continue the study after beginning it; or it may be that Spanish is more difficult for boys, in which case a higher percentage of elimination in the lower levels of ability operates to raise the average intelligence of the group. Whatever the explanation, the fact is that boys studying Spanish are superior in mentality to girls enrolled in the language—a circumstance which becomes important when it is understood that the achievement of the masculine sex is definitely and consistently inferior[5] in all semesters and in practically all phases of the class work, as measured both by teachers' grades and scores upon standardized vocabulary and silent reading tests. Something should be done either to compensate or to correct this sex difference in interest and achievement.

Something should also be done to correct the obvious standardization of Spanish courses upon too high a level of mental ability. When as many as 19 per cent. of the students of foreign language fail[6] in the high schools and junior high schools, and when the general intelligence of the students of these classes, and even of the failing groups,[7] is above that of pupils in general, the suspicion becomes strong that a high rate of mortality may be due rather to faults in the teaching and organization of the courses than to deficiencies in the students themselves. There is no conclusive evidence to prove that Spanish or any foreign language is so intrinsically difficult as to necessitate more intelligence than the average pupils possess. The fact that a higher level of mentality is required at present mere indicates that *the courses as now offered are not adequately adjusted to the abilities, interests and capacities of the large majority of high-school students.*

To a large extent the blame can be traced directly to current methods of foreign language teaching. The still prevalent custom of relying upon formal grammar as the predominant medium of instruction, as evidenced by the content of widely used Spanish text-books and contemporary teaching practice,[8] would seem sufficient in itself to stifle interest and to discourage pupils from continuing foreign language work; and when this method of instruction is placed in the hands of teachers—generally specialists in languages, with only a minimum amount of training in education, and practically no preparation in the science of linguistic method or the psychological foundations of pedagogy—who are most apt because of the nature of their subjects and the general absence of directors of foreign language to be poorly supervised, the situation in Spanish classes is far from ideal.

Grammar as a medium of learning language is not a natural method of acquiring speech. It is far from nature's way of teaching man. It is logical and artificial where natural learning is *psychological* and spontaneous. It is deductive and formal where natural learning is *inductive* and informal. In a word, grammar is the approach of the scholar trained in syntactical technique, rather than of the uninitiated beginner. Thus a relatively high and predominantly *abstract* form of intelligence, possessed only by students in the upper levels of mental ability, is prerequisite to its most facile comprehension and ultimate mastery. For this reason it seems that *only by means of a thorough reorganization both of the methods and materials of instruction, together with a more homogeneous ability grouping of pupils, can the prevalent high rate of student mortality be reduced.* Until this reorganization is accomplished, let not the teachers of foreign language

[5] Walter Kaulfers, "Prognostic Value of the I.Q. in Spanish," Stanford University Thesis, chapters 4 and 5, 1928.

[6] *Op. cit.*, Ralph L. John.

[7] *Op. cit.*, Walter Kaulfers, chapter 6.

[8] George A. Rice, "An Analysis of the Classroom Practices of 210 Teachers of Modern Foreign Language," *California Quarterly of Secondary Education*, 2: 283–289, 1927. See also parenthetical note, page 18, to Belle E. Bickford, "Some Important Problems in the Modern Language Program," *The Modern Languages Forum*, 13: 17–19, 1928.

continue to seize upon the intelligence of their pupils—nor upon that other alibi, equally fallacious,[9] "lack of linguistic aptitude"—as the convenient excuse for their own poor teaching.

Walter Kaulfers

Stanford University

MORE ABOUT SEX DIFFERENCES

The data serving as the basis for the following comparisons were obtained in a survey of intelligence and achievement in the schools of a small city with a total enrolment of about three thousand. The National intelligence test and the Stanford achievement test were given to the fifth-grade pupils, about two hundred in number. The McCall multi-mental scale was given to all the children from the third grade up to and inclusive of the high-school grades.

Intelligence

The following is a table of mean scores obtained on the McCall intelligence test by the children, classified according to age and sex. Only the ages from nine to fourteen are included because the other ages were not considered to be represented by sufficient numbers. The scores are expressed in terms of mental age, *i.e.*, in years and months:

Comment: There seems to be a consistent difference shown in favor of the girls. What are we going to conclude? That the girls are brighter or that the McCall scale favors the girls? Whatever we may decide upon, it seems pretty clearly indicated that the McCall multi-mental scale makes apparent a difference (whether of testing technique or of real developmental difference between the sexes) that many other tests do not show. The National intelligence test, for instance, shows no difference between the boys and the girls in total score. When the I.Q.'s of the fifth-grade boys and girls, obtained on the N.I.T., were compared, it was found that they were, respectively, 100.3 and 100.0. Thus the median I.Q.'s of the N.I.T. favored neither sex. But when these same fifth-grade boys and girls had their median I.Q. calculated from the results on the McCall test, it was found that the girls enjoyed a median I.Q. of 99.1 and the boys a median I.Q. of only 94.4. This difference of six points in favor of the girls would lead us naturally to believe that the McCall test makes apparent a difference that the National does not show.

Age		9	10	11	12	13	14
Mean	Boys	10–3.0	10–5.9	11–2.0	11–6.6	12–4.1	13– 4.9
	Girls	10–6.0	10–8.4	11–4.2	12–1.1	13–1.8	13–11.8
Difference		3.0	2.5	2.2	6.5	9.7	6.9
P. E. of difference (roughly)		1.3	1.1	1.5	1.9	2.5	2.8
No. of cases	Boys	92	105	94	102	97	70
	Girls	98	119	98	101	84	70

Are girls brighter than boys of the same age? Lincoln, in his book, "Sex Differences in School Children," suggests that they are, at least up to fourteen or fifteen, because of the advanced maturity of the girls, as indicated by most anatomical and physiological tests. But most intelligence tests do not show this. The reason for this, according to Lincoln, is that most intelligence tests are weighted in favor of the boys, and hence do not show a difference where they should. It may be, then, that because of the character of the test items the N.I.T. would show no difference between the boys and girls, although one may really exist. The McCall test seems to support Lincoln in his contention, since, as indicated from the results reported here, this scale shows the girls to be more mature intellectually from the ages of nine to fourteen than the boys—provided, of course, that the McCall test is a valid measure of intelligence.

Achievement

The following is a table of scores obtained from measuring the achievement of eighty-five boys and ninety girls, enrolled in the fifth grade. The Stanford achievement test was the instrument used, and the scores are expressed in points:

[9] John W. Todd, "Is there a Language Talent?" *The Modern Languages Forum*, 13: 7–10, 1928.

Sub-test		Arith.	Read.	N. S.	H. & L.	Lang.	Dic.	A. Q.
Median	Boys	153.7	129.4	34.8	20.4	15.0	87.8	101.2
	Girls	147.7	134.6	29.1	16.7	19.2	98.7	100.0
Difference		6.0	5.2	5.7	3.7	4.2	10.9	1.2
P.E. of diff. (roughly)		2.8	2.9	1.1	1.0	1.1	2.1	1.1

Comment: All the differences, with the exception of that existing between A.Q.'s, seem to be reliable. The boys are superior to the girls in arithmetic, nature study, history and literature. The girls surpass the boys in reading, language usage and dictation. These results seem to be in line with those reviewed by Lincoln.

Variability

The following is a table of standard deviations obtained from the Stanford achievement data, the results of testing eighty-five boys and ninety girls:

Sub-test		Arith.	Read.	N. S.	H. & L.	Lang.	Dict.	A. Q.
Standard Deviation	Boys	33.2	34.6	13.7	12.1	14.5	24.1	13.8
	Girls	28.1	26.3	7.4	10.5	9.32	23.4	11.3

In all cases, the boys show greater variability than the girls. The same trend is apparent from the data obtained with the McCall test.

With the exception of the eleventh year, the boys show themselves to be more variable than the girls.

Age		9	10	11	12	13	14
Standard Deviation	Boys	15.5	16.6	17.2	23.8	30.9	30.2
	Girls	14.0	14.2	20.9	22.0	25.6	30.1

Comment: In reviewing the data accumulated on the relative variability of the sexes, Lincoln does not find any consistent difference in favor of the boys. "Thus we may say that sex differences in variability are conditioned by the particular trait considered, the age of the children measured, their social condition and the community in which the data are obtained. There are indications that the most potent factor is that of maturity, for there appears a tendency for the girls to exceed the boys in variability at the ages from about ten to fourteen more than in any other years."

Because of the fact that, when physiological development is considered, there does not seem to be any greater variability present in the male sex than in the female, we may perhaps be allowed to conclude that those traits in which greater male variability is shown are more affected by environmental and accidental circumstances. That is, the greater male variability may be an acquired rather than an innate thing, and this may be due to differences in traditional upbringing and education. Thus the boys show greater variability in such abilities as are measured by the Stanford achievement test, because the home and the school and the whole social situation would allow more leeway to the interests and whims of the growing boy. The girls might be expected to conform more closely to social standards, in scholastic abilities as well as in morals, while the boys would be expected to be more free-lancing in following their inclinations and interests. Such an attitude would create greater variability among boys than among girls in the acquired traits.

Can the same thing be said of the differences appearing in intelligence test results? Probably, if we remember that the test situation is really a social one after all. We measure what is innate only through what has been acquired, and this would be further qualified by the amount of effort put forth and by the child's reaction to the test-situation.

W. D. Commins

St. Louis University

SCHOOL AND SOCIETY

EDITED BY J. McKEEN CATTELL

WITH WHICH IS COMBINED THE

EDUCATIONAL REVIEW

EDITED BY WILLIAM McANDREW

Volume XXVIII | Saturday, November 17, 1928 | Number 725

EDUCATION IN THE REPUBLIC OF TURKEY

By LUCY L. W. WILSON

SOUTH PHILADELPHIA HIGH SCHOOL

Before the Great War, public education in Turkey was almost entirely religious. From the mosques radiated out elementary schools, where little children were taught the language but not the meaning of the Koran, and little else. Higher education was provided for in the "medressehs," practically ecclesiastical seminaries.

In the sixties came a few secular schools. In Constantinople the Galata Serai, originally a palace in which were trained the royal pages, became a lycée with high academic standards. Here were educated Turkish boys of the upper classes. French was the language used in all classrooms. In consequence, rather universally, Turkish gentlemen spoke French fluently and with distinction. There were four other schools of similar quality, Mulkie, Dar-Ushaffaca and two colleges in Stamboul. Later, the Sultan founded a normal school to prepare teachers for private schools, probably with the idea of stemming the tide that was carrying the younger generation westward to seek their education. The so-called University of Stamboul, organized in 1845, reorganized in 1901, was made up of two schools only, one teaching law, the other, medicine.

Not until the Young Turks came into power (1908) was any attention given to the education of women. In 1913 they were granted a high and a normal school, both excellent.

In addition, there were good military schools, legitimate successors to the remarkable residential colleges where were educated the famous janissaries until their final extermination.

Except for the military academies, native schools with high scholastic standards were inadequate in number to the need. Fortunately for the Turks, however, they were reinforced by excellent secondary schools and colleges under foreign control—French, American, British, German. These brought with them Western culture and education along Western lines. In addition, the *millets* (Greek, Armenian, Bulgarian, Catholic, Jewish groups, with communal autonomy based on religious rather than political differences) each had its private schools, thus preserving its own language and its own culture.

This educational patchwork, strange mixture of the East and the West, of the old and the new, had been functioning nearly three generations, yet the Republic found the mass of Turkish people still illiterate.

The revolution of 1920–22 inaugurated drastic changes with lightning-like rapidity. Immediately the Sultan, the Sultanate and the Ottoman government were swept aside. The Caliphate followed; then the

Moslem schools and the dervish orders, their properties confiscate to the State. All foreign concessions, including the capitulations with their economic privileges and the *millets* were abolished. The veil of the women and the seclusion of which it was a sign disappeared. The fez, old forms of salutation, many commonly used Arabic and Persian words and phrases, Turkish time including both clock and calendar, the harem, the eunuch system, polygamy, easy divorce—all have vanished. Soon the Arabic alphabet will be displaced by Latin characters, and the Moslem Friday, keeping its own name however, will be synchronized with the Christian Sunday. New manners and customs grow apace. Education is being reformed and developed with amazing enthusiasm and intelligence. Like the other new republics, Turkey recognizes its supreme creative and unifying power, and so they have made it a fundamental concern of the nation, an important function of the government. The new schools already are influencing the economic and social development of the whole country.

The Influence of John Dewey

Every Turkish teacher knows something about John Dewey. Many of them can discuss intelligently his educational philosophy. Few of them realize that he was a gratefully accepted gift to the government from Charles R. Crane, our former minister to Turkey. Indeed the current comment is "But why did he stay so short a time? It must have cost our government so much to bring him here."

Avni Bey, one of the four ministerial specialists, in answer to a question as to why Dewey had been chosen, answered, "Well, I was not then in the ministry, but of course we knew that he was the greatest educational philosopher in the world, and I dare say that his long and successful experience in China made us feel that he would understand our problems, too."

Dewey's contributions were two: first, a survey which showed the fundamental weakness of much-divided responsibility; and second, his insistence that knowledge of the world around them and of human relationships should motivate the curriculum. "What you call civics, of which formerly we knew nothing," naïvely explained one of the teachers.

Dr. Dewey spent about six weeks in Turkey (1924), constantly at the service of the government in conference, writing, lecturing to teachers through an interpreter. Both in Turkey and in China he has made a deep impression on the rank and file—those who in this country know him not. One wonders why. Are the oriental people more philosophically minded, or is it able interpretation?

Dewey's "School and Society" has been translated into Turkish and has been read and is understood by every progressive teacher in Turkey. "Democracy and Education," too, has been translated. It is used as a text in the university and has been read quite generally by ambitious school inspectors (superintendents). Both these translations were made by Avni Bey whose command of English, self-acquired, is remarkably wide and exact.

In answer to the question, "What do you wish me to cite as the most important forward step that you have taken in education?" Nedjati Bey, the minister of education, said, "The reorganization of the elementary schools on the plan Dr. Dewey outlined when here."

The Elementary Schools

Stimulated by Dewey's philosophy, helped quite definitely and concretely by German text-books, formulating *Lebens-Kunde* (life knowledge) by means of *Gesammt Unterricht* (our project, the Russian Complex), the specialists in the Ministry of Education wrote a course of study for the elementary schools. This course was first tried out in a few selected schools in 1925–26; then, revised in accordance with their findings, it was put into the hands of all of the teachers in 1926–27. Now, finally, it has become mandatory.

There is a separate course for urban and rural communities. In addition, a large sheet helps to point the way to method. In the first column, under the caption "Life Knowledge," the project is outlined. Successive columns, labeled "Language," "Mathematics" (translated for me as "Geometry and Calculus!"), "Handicraft and Drawing," "Music," and "Games," suggest initial or correlated activities.

The projects are excellently analyzed and synthesized. Nowhere, however, is the teacher given the first aid that surely she needs to enable her gradually to throw more and more responsibility upon the children, educating them to freedom by releasing their creative abilities. Instead, always the words are "tell," "explain," "show."

It is true in Turkey, as it would be anywhere, that large numbers of teachers do not understand even yet the real meaning of the course. Perhaps therefore its writers deliberately have used academic phraseology, thinking that subject matter must be mastered before methods are indicated.

By the laws of 1926, the five years of primary education are compulsory and free. In practice, a fee of seventy-five cents per month is fairly usual. In spite of much building and great increases in the number of normal-school graduates, primary education is not even yet universal.

In the much larger area of the Ottoman Empire there were in 1913–14 only 2,632 primary schools, with 8,165 teachers and 254,990 children. There are now (1927–28) 5,883 primary schools, with 11,766 teachers and 385,455 pupils, including 7,677 in kindergartens as well as 3,347 in elementary boarding (free) schools—two expensive types formerly non-existent. In other words the Republic, much smaller in area and in population, is caring for nearly 52 per cent. more children of elementary grade, with 44 per cent. more teachers, in nearly 124 per cent. more buildings. Moreover, these increases in schools, pupilage and teachers have been made in the last half-dozen years.

But what of the quality of teaching? Many Turks complain bitterly that in the effort to get enough teachers the former standards have been lowered. The large foreign population of Constantinople is quite ready to ask, "but what do they learn in the Turkish schools?" On the other hand Dr. Eleanor I. Burns, dean of the American Woman's College of Constantinople, told me that the improvement in the quality of preparation in the last few years was nothing short of miraculous; that the Turkish girls who formerly came to the college knew nothing except Turkish; that they had scarcely heard of the four fundamental arithmetical operations, for example. Not only is this *ex parte* testimony, but one must take into consideration the fact that the comparison is made between the now relatively large numbers of Moslem Turkish students and the very few of the older groups. It will be remembered how difficult it was for Halideh Edib Hanoun to continue until finally she was graduated, the first woman to receive an A.B. Probably relatively few of the present-day numerous Turkish students have a tithe of her mental ability.

In the Turkish Republic all elementary schools are coeducational. The so-called Schools of the Ghazi, in Angora, were originally intended one for girls and the other for boys. Now both are coeducational! In both schools the teaching is just as modern as the teachers know how to make it. Music is an integral part of the instruction, with foods and clothing for the girls, agriculture for the boys and well-planned excursions for both every Monday afternoon. As in all Turkish elementary schools, however, the project reigns for three years and then subject teaching rules the last two. Religion is minimized, an hour a week each for the Koran and the life of Mahomet, both taught from the historical point of view.

Secondary Education

The pupils from elementary schools feed into continuation schools (404 pupils), into industrial schools (1,536 pupils), commercial schools (530 pupils), or else, if they show promise of scholarship, into the middle schools (10,040 pupils). The middle schools are equivalent to our junior high schools. They are now coeducational. Ultimately they will be universal and free. Religious teaching is prohibited by law in all the higher schools. The graduates of the middle schools who do not wish to enter a lycée soon will be offered a wide choice in vocational ("professional") schools. Much time and effort and money will be devoted (1928–29) to the greater development of these needed schools. Two years ago a German educator was called into consultation. This year, the planning for their present and future development has been put into the hands of a Belgian, M. Buysée, the founder of the Labor College of Charleroi, later director of technical education in Brussels.

In this respect, the Turkish policy resembles that of Japan. They do not hesitate to employ foreign teachers, but they have no idea of continuing to be dependent upon them. For 1928–29 they are sending eighty carefully selected students to technical schools in France, Germany, Belgium, Czecho-Slovakia, Sweden. It must not be forgotten that Turkey is a country with large, numerous, varied and undeveloped resources.

The middle schools feed the lycées. Originally the French language, French ideals, French methods and standards dominated the higher schools of the Ottoman Empire. During the war the German influence expressed itself not only in German schools but also in administrational methods. The reaction was equally strong, however. The present attitude is intensely nationalistic.

One of the old lycées, that of Galata Serai in Constantinople, of deservedly glorious memory, continues to teach in French even in its preparatory department three hours out of five. Most of its advanced work is entirely conducted in French. In general, French prevails in the morning, Turkish in the afternoon.

Some of the lycées are coeducational—Adana, Angora, Smyrna—but usually there are separate schools for boys and girls. Only a third of the pupilage (7,002) is feminine.

Formerly Latin and Greek were optionally taught, but these have given way to Persian and Arabic. One foreign language is obligatory. In the last year they may elect between science and letters.

The lycée leads directly to the university or else to one of the higher professional schools—Fine Arts, Public Service or the Institutes of Geography or Anthropology.

The Universities

That only the State may found a university was a decision that caused the resignation of Dr. Mary Patrick from the American Woman's College. The dream of her life had come true. A real medical school, its fine building planned by the architects of the Harvard Medical, a memorial to his wife given by William Bingham, of Ohio, had had one year of existence and was about to be dedicated. This law closed its doors. There were compensations. The fine medical school of the University of Stamboul was opened to women.

In Angora, a school of law was inaugurated in November, 1925, shortly after the substitution of the new codes for Moslem law. These codes are based on the best available—the civil code on the Swiss, the criminal on the Italian and the commercial on the German. Probably to the school of law will be added other schools as the need arises, until finally Turkey will have another full-fledged university.

In the meantime, the University of Stamboul marches on. Its evolution from a mere school to a real university is one of the big landmarks in the advance of education in the Republic.

The medical school is now at Haidar Pasha, one of the two conspicuous buildings to be seen in any view of Constantinople that embraces the Seraglio end of old Stamboul together with the Asiatic shore. The main building of the university occupies the old War Ministry, a new vision, let us hope, of the old prophecy, "their swords shall be beaten into ploughshares."

TEACHER TRAINING

There are now 25 normal schools in the Republic of Turkey with more in process of construction. Some of these are for men, some for women, one for kindergarteners, another for teachers of music. In Angora, a million-dollar normal school is now being built, to be opened in September, 1929. It will be used by men and women, to train both elementary and secondary teachers.

The normal schools for rural teachers are located in rural districts. There is one in Cesarea which the railroad has just reached. Another is at Desmida, fairly near Smyrna. The course is three years. They will graduate their first class in June, 1929.

The distinguishing feature of the rural normal schools is a science course, with much practical field work, in charge of a graduate of an agricultural college. Like other normal schools, they are free boarding schools, with an additional small allowance for clothing, books and other necessary expenses. In return the students promise to serve the State eight years as teachers in rural schools or else to return the cost of their education to the State.

The normal school for kindergarten teachers and that for teachers of music, also, will graduate their first classes in June, 1929. The course for kindergarteners lasts two years, while five are required from the music teachers. The first class of music graduates numbers about twenty-five. The director of the school, Zeki Bey, is also the leader of the orchestra and a fine musician. Under his direction, much research work has been done on the folk music of Anatolia, which else might easily have been lost in the new passion for occidental music.

The normal school in Constantinople was counted excellent in the old days. It is still good but entirely inadequate from the point of view of the numbers of teachers required.

Selim Sirri Bey, the very able director of physical training in the Constantinople Normal School, spent his ten weeks' vacation (1928) at the Amsterdam Olympiade and in Germany. He came back full of enthusiasm for the new ideals and accomplishments of German leaders in physical education. He believes thoroughly in the emancipation from the military motive and the denial of the Jahn idea that muscle is king. He believes, too, that before fortifying the muscles all articulations must be made supple, in whole body movements, and, above all, in perfect harmony between the mind and the body. Such is his ability and authority, such the intelligence and power of the Ministry of Education, that one can not help believing that in a very few years there will be in Turkey, as there is in Germany, a new type of normal school, a higher secondary school of physical training, accepting only graduates from the lycées as students. From such a school, says Selim Sirri Bey, may be sent to the remotest regions of Anatolia, as well as to large urban communities, understanding teachers of the new physical training. In the meantime, interest in games and sports in Turkey is intense and wide-spread. To see children enthusiastically playing football, often encouraged by their fathers, both in the larger cities and in smaller villages, is amazing to those who knew old Turkey. Perhaps the compulsory adoption of European dress has contributed something to this change.

The output for the normal schools has been steadily increasing—35 per cent. more graduates in 1927–28 than in 1926–27—in its turn 21 per cent. greater than the number graduated in 1925–26. But the numbers do not keep pace with the demand. For this reason every summer courses are offered, usually in normal schools, which means free lodging with low costs for food to which graduates of secondary schools are eligible. These courses are intended to prepare them for teachers' examinations. Those who are successful receive appointments as assistant teachers. A second vacation course whose content is pedagogy and psychology will give a permanent certificate to those who are successful in the classroom as well as in passing examinations. In 1927, 2,383 would-be teachers were taking these courses in the various centers at which they were offered. Vacation courses are offered to teachers in service at low cost in the same centers. In 1927, 770 availed themselves of these opportunities. Successful teachers who are also successful in this work are in line for promotion to primary inspectorships.

And then there are the much sought after foreign scholarships. The recipients are selected by a very stiff competitive examination. This year, in addition to the sixty already mentioned sent to prepare themselves for teaching in the so-called professional schools, eighty others were sent for academic study. The examinations for the twenty-six vacancies allotted to Constantinople took place in early August and lasted twelve consecutive hours. No one was allowed to leave the room even to eat. A frugal and silent meal was served the candidates, however. In mathematics and physics a third of the candidates were women. In natural science less than a quarter were women. In geography and history, none, and in foreign languages, all were women.

The Financial Situation

Turkey has at last balanced her budget. In 1928, nearly half the national income was spent for defense and toward the public debt. Only three and one third per cent. ($3,500,000) was allotted to education. To this, the local budgets added 16,000,000 Turkish pounds ($8,000,000), more than was given to anything else. Next came roads, then health, then agriculture. The percentage given to education varies in the different communities. It averages 40 per cent.

School buildings are constructed out of a national fund created by the return to Angora of ten per cent. of the local tax each year for five years. Next year, however, the Assembly will be asked to authorize long-term bonds for these and other permanent improvements.

Salaries are very low. However, they compare fairly favorably with the low salaries in other occupations. Elementary teachers receive 50 Turkish pounds ($25) per month with an increase of 4 pounds per month every two years for 24 years. At the end of 25 years a pension is promised.

Private Schools

In addition to 47 Turkish private schools, there are now 128 schools for the minorities and 81 foreign schools. In the old days there were not far from 1,300 non-Turkish schools, about 500 each, French and American, the rest largely German and British. The astonishing decrease in numbers is largely due to territorial losses, notably Syria and Palestine, as well as to government closings. It is against the law to teach any religion, even the Mohammedan, in secondary schools. The law is especially drastic in reference to the discussion of religious problems with minors in school or out. Their religion is presumably that of their parents—and that's the end of it. Of course when one parent is an Armenian Christian and the other a Moslem the enforcement of the law is a bit complicated. This is a part of the basis of a second appeal against the closing of the American School in Brussa. Its teachers were sentenced to a small fine ($13.00) and a very brief imprisonment on their own grounds.

In all foreign and minority schools Turkish language, literature, geography, history and art must be taught each year for five hours weekly (ten hours in the last year of a lycée) by government-appointed Turkish teachers. There has been much complaint among the students of the time wasted. A recent graduate, a Turk, told me that the methods used in his class were archaic, that the whole group of 30 to 40 waited while each individual went in turn to whisper in the ear of the seated master. I understood his statements better after looking at a picture in the last art exhibition in Constantinople called "An Old Time Turkish School." At his desk sat a turbaned howja with closed eyes listening to a single student. Two of the class were trying to write, but all the others were in more or less wild disorder. The spectator—though not the master!—could almost hear the noise!

This year the secondary schools of Jewish children were given permission to increase the number of hours devoted to French, but without diminishing the number assigned to Turkish. In the normal school of Constantinople ten places yearly are reserved for Jewish high-school graduates who wish to become teachers. They are externes only and released from the obligation of the internes to serve the State for eight years after graduation.

Adult Education

No one knows, apparently, just how many illiterates there are in Turkey. This summer the Ghazi spoke of the 10 per cent. literates and in the next sentence of the 80 per cent. illiterates. Every one knows, however, how eager all now are to learn to read. One of the arguments advanced in favor of the use of Latin rather than Arabic characters was that the written language would be much easier for the illiterate to learn. Last winter, 1927–28, there were a hundred centers in session every evening, 67,895 adults in attendance. Usually two courses were demanded and given, one for those absolutely unable to read or write and another for those who had already acquired some facilities in the use of these tools.

Quite considerable work in the liquidation of illiteracy has already been accomplished in the army. This, however, is not under the direction of the ministry. For the most part the army teachers are the former army chaplains.

In addition to the usual tools for adult education common to all civilized countries, namely, clubs, concerts, art exhibitions, museums, libraries, not all of them well developed even in Constantinople, the indigenous *ojaks* (hearths or foyers) deserve special mention. They were born in the medical school twenty years ago but very speedily developed into discussion groups on more general topics. Even before the revolution they concerned themselves with the liberation of women and the release of the people from the stagnation of oriental thought and life. Of course they did little but talk. Before the war some twenty-eight such groups were organized. They were the first to admit women to their conferences, to put them on their committees.

Now there are nearly three hundred groups with more than 40,000 members. They organize conferences and expositions and give courses in foreign languages, in music, in Turkish history and in the history of revolutions. They open libraries and reading rooms, in addition to carrying on much social work, especially with children of school age. They organize excursions at regular intervals. They publish an important monthly review. The foyers in Angora, for example, undertook the sanitation of some forty villages, seeing that they received necessary medical attention, distributing medicine to the villages and instructive posters to the schools.

The government gives the *ojaks* some money but most of their income comes from dues.

Every year delegates from the local groups meet in Angora. The congress of 1927 was asked by Persia to develop similar institutions there. They decided that while the Persians were at liberty to study their methods and to use any or all of their devices, their own heads and hands were too full with Turkey to be free to think out details for any other country!

Mustapha Kemal: Teacher

And then, last, there is the Ghazi using the same methods to free his people from their various inhibitions that he used on the field of battle to free them from the domination of the Allies. His constant success is amazing. But so is that of every other successful teacher. Why do the children obey him, following his lead, often contrary to their own strong desires?

An example illustrating the pedagogical methods of the Ghazi is the story of the campaign for the substitution of the Latin alphabet for the much-modified Arabic script in use for many centuries.

The Education Bill of 1926 prescribed the Latinization of the alphabet, making a government commission responsible for the details. This commission is made up of officials from the Ministry of Education together with several deputies. They have been studying carefully not only English, French, German and Italian alphabets, but also the unit sounds in the Turkish language that needs must be represented. In the Arabic script, for example, there are only four vowel symbols. But in the beautiful spoken language there are many more vowel sounds. While awaiting a report from the commission, there has been much discussion of the contemplated change, both *pro* and *con,* sometimes *ad nauseam,* not only in the newspapers, in the *ojaks,* at other meetings, on the streets, in families, but also in booklets and in books.

The tentative alphabet was finally published last summer (1928). Instead of the 482 characters now actually in use, there have been substituted 29 others of Latin form, called by the Ghazi "the new Turkish characters." Three vowels have been added to our *a, e, i, o, u,* namely, an undotted *ı*, umlauted *o* and *u*. Soft *c* and *s* are indicated by adding a cedilla; the soft *g* by topping it with the breve; *w* and *x* are omitted.

The commission is now working quietly and steadily on the new dictionary.

In his beautiful palace on the Bosphorus, the Ghazi began early to practice writing with the new alphabet. Then he organized a little private class including his adopted daughters and palace officials. From this class some were able to graduate in a few days, others required a week or more. Shortly after the initiation of the class, at a dinner given in his honor by the Party of the People, the Ghazi was observed making a few notes. He used Turkish characters, but the young man to whom he gave them to read aloud hesitated for a moment. Thereupon the Ghazi substituted a brief note in the new characters. This was glibly read to the assembled multitude by one of the deputies of the commission seated at the same table. Then the Ghazi addressed them directly. "Citizens, comrades," said he, "it is time to set to work. I am sure that neither you nor I need to talk much. Instead we need rather to march forward, to march on and on. Much has been accomplished. But to-day there is something new to be done. It is not the last task, but it is now the most necessary. We must quickly learn the new Turkish characters, and we must teach them to every citizen—to men, women, people of leisure and workers of all kinds. Let us do this as a nationalistic and patriotic duty. . . . A little later, perhaps in a year or two, every Turk will know the new characters, and our nation will show in its writing, by its culture, that it is on the same level as the other nations of the civilized world."

Later in the evening, or rather at 3 A. M., he arrived at a ball given by the Red Crescent. Here he dictated a few sentences to the leader of the orchestra asking him to use the Latin alphabet. This exercise he corrected with his own hand and the leader actually felt honored! In the meantime words and sentences using the new alphabet in his own handwriting were reproduced in the daily papers. In passing it may be noted that his writing steadily improved. A favorite sentence was, "The new Turkey crowns the revolution that she has made during recent years by adopting Latin characters."

The Ghazi, excellent teacher that he is, knows that it will be impossible to change the language of a country in a single summer. The plan of campaign is (1) continuance of popular discussion, (2) drafting a law by the National Assembly making the change finally obligatory January, 1931, and (3) doing everything possible to prepare the whole nation for the change. Already banks and other business houses have taken the initiative in forming classes for their officials and employees; shops, streets and tramways are latinizing their signs. Most significant of all, the opening of State schools was postponed to give the teachers the opportunity to master the new characters before meeting their pupils.

It is interesting to note that the Turks of Azerbaijan have been using a Latin alphabet for at least two years. The Soviet government called a congress of *savants* interested in the civilization and languages of the Turkish people at Baku, July, 1926. There were twenty-seven delegates present, among them Pavlovitch, the head of the University of Oriental Studies, and Oldenburg, secretary of the Academy of Science, Leningrad. There were also distinguished representatives from Hungary and Germany. In view of the fact that fifty-seven different varieties of alphabets were employed in writing the numerous Turkish dialects, the Congress recommended that all Turkish people should adopt a single alphabet, namely, the Latin, already in use by the press of Azerbaijan. Oddly enough, this example was never quoted in Turkey, even by those who favored the change, although much use was made of the adoption of Latin characters by *Berliner Tageblatt!*

Mustapha Kemal used the same methods to substitute the hat for the fez. This was an extremely difficult reform because the fez is a religious symbol and, moreover, almost a necessity to those who pray daily, even if only once, instead of the five times commanded by the Koran. At the name of Allah prostration is universal. This involves touching the forehead to the ground again and again.

Against the advice of his friends, the Ghazi initiated the preliminary campaign against the fez by appearing in full European costume, including a silk hat, before an audience in a small, deeply religious and very conservative village. Raising his hand to his head he said, "This is called a hat. It is the head covering used in all European countries. We are a civilized nation and we do not want either in form or in spirit to differ from other, western nations. Therefore we shall wear the hat."

There was not a single protest, and this district was one of the first voluntarily to reject the fez.

Of course everywhere there was much discussion and objection, particularly from the *howjas,* but the substitution was almost universally accomplished before it became a law, with a last day named and prison for those who did not comply. One of the deputies, a former *howja,* a poet, could not drive himself to conform. It was suggested that he go into voluntary exile in Egypt. There he now is translating the Koran into Turkish at the expense of the Turkish government!

Mustapha Kemal has not been equally successful in changing the head-gear of the women, although as far as skirt length and silken hose are concerned the Turkish women quite hold their own with the women of the Occident. Most of them have unveiled, but not all; many of them have abandoned the *tcharchaf,* but relatively few of them have adopted the hat. Instead they wrap a bit of georgette or gauze about the head, quite bewitchingly. They urge its superior economy and convenience. Clever teacher that he is, the Ghazi is using other methods than the law to induce them to uncover. Never has he made an ultimatum with a date. Always it has been a request. Recently, at a ball, he asked two individual women to remove the gauze, saying with a gay and compelling smile how beautiful was the uncovered hair. After they had complied with his request, each was invited to dance with him and each felt flattered!

On the whole, the educational outlook in the Republic of Turkey is hopeful. Its greatest needs are more buildings, more teachers, better salaries. The highest light is its comprehensive forward-looking program, adapted to the needs and temperament of the Turkish people. Perhaps even more valuable are the understanding, the devotion and the enthusiasm of its educational leaders.

THE EDUCATIONAL EXPERT AND THE COLLEGE TEACHER OF MODERN LANGUAGES

By COLLEY F. SPARKMAN

UNIVERSITY OF WYOMING, LARAMIE, WYOMING

NOT so many years ago the so-called educational experts were, with a very few outstanding exceptions, a negligible group of pseudoscientists who were groping futilely towards an apparently hopeless goal. That hazy new science of education had no well-defined objectives, no well-organized texts and no body of trustworthy data.

Fellow-departmental heads, jealous of the "expert's" having reached their level with lesser effort than they, were predisposed to see no good whatsoever in the outcome of his endeavors. The poor professor of education sensed this tension and smarted under it. Down in his heart he felt a bit apologetic. He realized that his subject was hardly worthy of the name of a science. He knew its principles were not unified and coordinated. No authoritative background could be cited. Conflicting theories vied with each other for supremacy. Each pedagogue had to be a law unto himself.

Under such circumstances it is not strange that blunders were made. Something was expected of the incumbent of this newly created department. Hiding his inferiority complex under a show of bravado, he insisted on showing his colleagues how to teach their college subjects. No more fatal error could have been committed. Hadn't these smug professors been doing this very thing for a number of years?

How could a new upstart, with no tradition behind him, with only a smattering of their subject, dare to suggest to them improved methods of technique?

The war continued, and the disdained professor of education took his wares where they were more appreciated. He began to work with the younger and more plastic material who, for various reasons, had drifted into his classes. Some of these were prospective teachers who came with no preconceived notions of technique. They were eager to learn anything that might help them to be more efficient teachers. The professor of education, awake to the importance of the occasion, called up his past experiences and endeavored to coordinate them with the scrappy bits of educational psychology and the principles of education he had acquired. In a very short time he came to feel that he had something of importance to offer. Enthusiastic teachers, alive to the helpful nature of his instruction, helped to build his prestige. Superintendents, quick to perceive the results of pedagogical courses, soon demanded a certain number of hours as a part of the qualification of new teachers.

This progressively improving procedure has been going on for a number of years. It would be astonishing indeed if this formerly half-baked science of education had not developed into a well-rounded science. Experiments have been carried out, results have been tabulated, and a creditable body of literature on the subject has grown up. Specialists have developed, devoting themselves to one single phase of the problem.

Chairs of education in our colleges are now occupied by men who are unquestionably on a par with their colleagues. Having had to fight for their rights, professors of education are unusually dynamic and aggressive. Being human, they have not forgotten the time when they as a class were snubbed and rebuffed. They are now in a position to take a mild revenge. One could hardly expect them to have a marked love for modern languages, because we modern language teachers were once their most relentless enemies. We believed that a knowledge of foreign languages presupposed *ipso facto* an inherent knowledge of the technique of instruction.

Having the whip hand, the educationists now take pride in pointing out our obvious defects: our unattainable objectives; our failure to have a proper perspective; our unscientific approach to our problems; our failure to analyze the various phases of the difficulties that confront us, and, lastly, our woeful lack of results in keeping with the expenditure of time. Instead of offering their help, they now advise the restriction or elimination of foreign language courses. Superintendents and curriculum-making bodies depend upon them as professional advisers. The far-reaching prestige of the once-downtrodden professor of education is easily seen if one scans the prescribed requirements that govern high schools accredited by the North Central Association of Colleges and Secondary Schools. Modern languages figure here only as casually suggested electives.

The result is that students, in greater numbers each year, enter college with no credits in modern languages. Fortunately, the professional pedagogue's influence has not yet been sufficiently strong to control the college curriculum, and most colleges still prescribe as a minimum two years of a modern language. With this ever-increasing throng of students who take modern languages solely in order to fulfil requirements, college instructors find themselves facing a serious situation. The average college freshman is keenly alive to the value of his time. He wants to master, in the shortest time possible and with a minimum of effort on his part, enough of the new language to make a passing grade. If he can bluff his way through, he is willing to do so, but he soon learns that bluff is of little avail in elementary language courses. Facing a real problem, he reacts in a natural way in demanding that his time be not wasted. Since the college professor is no longer a venerable hero, due to his exalted position, but instead a salesman of his subject, students will openly show their dissatisfaction if he does not use the methods employed by a high-powered, live-wire salesman of a commercial line.

This dissatisfaction soon grows into a widespread antipathy to the study of modern languages. Two results are noticeable: the administration senses the aversion to modern languages and advises curtailment of requirements, and the majority of students, having learned by experience that the efforts are not in keeping with the results, refuse, after requirements are fulfilled, to elect any more courses in modern languages.

We can not change the conditions that confront us. The only solution seems to be to improve our technique. The worst feature of the matter is that the training usually acquired by the average college instructor of modern languages did not include anything that might be used to this end.

It would not be fair to say that modern language teachers have accomplished nothing along the line of improved technique of instruction, but what has been done has usually had to do with teaching devices and methods in the narrower sense. The fundamental problems have been scarcely touched. In reality these problems belong to the educational expert. They touch the larger field of education proper, the laws of which apply, in a modified way, to all subjects of the curriculum. The educational expert has been trained to see such problems in their totality, while the modern language teacher must view them from a more restricted angle. The former, unprejudiced by time-honored methods, could coolly and scientifically evaluate each step in the teaching act. Accustomed to appraising objectives in allied fields, he could show us what was really possible and what was merely visionary. Knowing the laws of mental processes, he could evolve a psychological technique that would insure the accomplishment of desirable objectives.

In addition to being able to evaluate and solve the many problems quite obviously related to similar problems in allied fields, the educational expert is in a position to experiment on those special problems that more particularly concern special phases of modern language teaching. He has had training in the technique of experiment. He can so arrange and control conditions that results will be of value. He can effectively measure results. He has procurable data of similar experiments in closely related fields.

Obviously, experienced language teachers can not qualify in meeting all the conditions listed above, any more than can the educational expert lay claim to an adequate teaching knowledge of foreign languages. We must humble ourselves to call in his aid. It need not be humiliating to call in expert aid. The business man does not hesitate to make use of all kinds of experts to perfect his business organization.

Below are some of the unsolved problems that confront us—problems whose solution would undoubtedly revolutionize the teaching of foreign languages.

Basic Principles

(1) Analysis of the function of language in general, showing wherein the learning of a foreign language is similar to that of learning the vernacular and wherein it is radically different.

(2) How native language interference might be reduced to a minimum and possibly used as an ally rather than an impediment to progress.

(3) What takes place in the learner's mind as he progressively masters the foreign language.

(4) What are the specific problems involved in learning each of the three major phases of language use: reading, writing and speaking.

(5) The most economical technique in the widely different aspects of the teaching act destined for: (a) acquirement of grammatical facts; (b) skill in interpretation of reading content; (c) skill in the active use of the language, and (d) literary appreciation of masterpieces.

(6) What relation exists between a passive and an active vocabulary? Which should be prior? What are the problems of learning each, and the principles underlying the transference of a passive vocabulary into an active one?

Objectives

(1) Analysis of established objectives and the relation of the length of the course to their respective attainment.

(2) Experimental investigation to determine what objectives may be accomplished in courses covering one, two, three and four years, respectively.

(3) Determination of the most economical order of admittedly established objectives, judged from the principles of education, collected data and controlled experiments.

METHODS

(1) Appraisal and evaluation of current methods with reference to pupil age, length of course and other qualifying conditions.

(2) Scientific evaluation of a technique of instruction that will meet the needs of each separate fundamental problem in desirable objectives.

(3) Preparing, in cooperation with actual language teachers, suitable texts in conformity with basic principles, objectives and methods scientifically determined as suggested above.

Admittedly, the foregoing is a large order, and no one pedagogue can expect to fill it, but trained experts, accustomed to dealing with the machinery of education, could be of incalculable assistance in throwing light on the many dark areas that now so hopelessly baffle us. We must not let the professional educator shoulder alone all our burdens; he needs our help at every turn. In reality, there are some features of our work that he had best not meddle with at all. He is not in a position even to advise us as to content of courses. He can give very little helpful advice as to values to be attained. He can act only as a corrective agent in limiting and curtailing objectives. But concerning underlying principles, fundamental problems and the machinery of education, his cooperation is indispensable.

EDUCATIONAL EVENTS

LIMITATION OF THE NUMBER OF STUDENTS IN THE SCOTTISH TRAINING COLLEGES

THE London *Times Educational Supplement* reports that last May the central executive of the national committee, in view of the surplus of outgoing students who had not found employment, intimated a resolution to limit the number of entrants during the session 1928–29 to 1,200 in all. The imminence of the opening of the session calls for a further statement on the details of the policy as they affect applicants for admission. By way of preface, the limitation of numbers is described as an emergency measure, designed to meet special conditions which may prove to be temporary. No ground is mentioned for entertaining a hope that this may be so, but a gradual reduction in the size of classes or an addition, voluntary or statutory, to the average age of leaving school might involve an addition to staffs of which there is no present indication.

The central executive, after careful scrutiny of all aspets of the question was finally drawn to the conclusion, foreshadowed in May, that there was no alternative but to accord preference to applicants who were graduates. Conscious as the executive is that not every graduate may prove a successful teacher, it has established an efficiency bar at the end of the first term of training. If the graduate student fails at that point to obtain an adequate mark both in the art of teaching and in the other subjects of study, his or her selection will be liable to cancellation. Of the 1,200 places no fewer than 960 are being reserved for graduates. The exact number can not be ascertained until the results of the autumn degree examinations have all been issued. But the conclusion meantime pointed to is that four out of every five accepted students will have satisfied the university of their qualifications to receive an M.A. degree. The remaining 240 vacancies have been duly assigned to non-graduate women, the selection having been made on the results of the leaving certificate and the promise of teaching ability. In order to maintain the supply of Gaelic-speaking teachers all candidates have been admitted who have made a satisfactory appearance in the language at the leaving certificate examination.

It is said that the chief hardship will fall on the limited number of applicants who may be kept hanging on in hope of vacancies through the failure of graduates to complete their degree examinations within the next week or two. A reserve list will, if necessary, be drawn up, and efforts will be made to reduce to a minimum the inconvenience arising from delay in the commencement of the course by these students. It is considered better to make sure at the outset that there will be employment for those trained than to allow more to go on than the schools can absorb. That would merely be to aggravate the evil which restriction is designed to cure and to prevent from recurring. No exception will be made in favor of students from outside Scotland, save in the case of the Craiglockhart (Edinburgh) Roman Catholic College, which will be allowed to accept students from without until session 1933–34 or such shorter period as may serve to bring up the teachers of the denomination to the full strength required for Scottish schools.

HIGH SCHOOLS OF CITY AND COUNTRY

FROM facts compiled by the federal Bureau of Education it appears that there are to-day in the United States 21,700 high schools. Reports have been received from 17,711 of these, of which 3,960, or 22.4 per cent., are urban high schools; that is, they are located in centers of 2,500 or more population; 13,751, or 77.6 per cent., are rural—located in centers of 2,500 or less in population.

In the 13,751 rural high schools in the United States there are only 1,079,086 children, or 28.8 per cent., of the total high-school enrolment; in the 3,960 urban high schools there are 2,662,364 children, or 71.2 per cent., of the total enrolment.

Rural communities are making heroic efforts to provide high schools for their children, but thus far their achievements in this direction have been less successful than those of urban centers. In point of numbers, more than three out of every four high schools are located in rural areas; in attendance these schools reach fewer than three out of every ten children now receiving a high-school education in the public schools. These figures become startling when it is considered that while 52.8 per cent., or more than half, of all the children between 15 and 18 years of age live in rural territory, only 25.7 per cent. of them are enrolled in the rural high schools; whereas 71.1 per cent. of the children of this age-group living in urban centers are enrolled in urban high schools. It is clear that rural high schools are either inaccessible or that they do not offer opportunities sufficient to attract a high percentage of rural children of high-school age.

Generally speaking, the school term is much shorter in rural than in urban schools. While 10.9 per cent. of the pupils who attend rural high schools are limited to a school term of 160 days or less, only 0.3 per cent. of urban pupils attend such short-term schools. Of all high-school pupils enrolled in schools having a term over 180 days in length, 92.4 per cent. attend urban schools; only 7.6 per cent. of them enjoy so long a term in rural schools.

It is estimated that more than 18 of every 100 children 15 to 18 years of age in urban areas continue their education beyond the high school, while only 7.2 of every 100 children of the same age-group in rural areas seek further education preparation.

To differentiate its curriculum to fit the needs of its pupils is one of the great problems of the rural high school. The cost of differentiation comparable to that obtaining in the larger high schools would be prohibitive. This is a natural consequence owing to the small attendance in the rural high school.

As a public secondary education has developed and is now functioning, the urban high-school child has a much better chance to go to high school, and when he does go he enjoys an educational opportunity much better adjusted to life's needs than that now available in the rural schools.

THE WORK OF BEREA COLLEGE

EDUCATIONAL progress in the southern mountains is described in a report issued by President William J. Hutchins, of Berea College and allied schools, which for nearly seventy-five years has provided a Christian education for tens of thousands of mountain young people.

President Hutchins characterizes the 2,554 young men and women at Berea in the past year as "ranging all the way from the student 30 years of age in the seventh grade, to the student 25 years of age graduating from college with a degree acceptable in any university in the country."

Poverty, economic and educational, is the rule among the student body, he states. "The 829 students in our elementary departments are retarded from one to twenty-four years, four being the medium. This implies not lack of intelligence but of opportunity. These students come from sections where 86 per cent. of the roads can scarcely be called roads at all, and from homes ranging up to fifty-two miles and averaging six miles from a railroad."

Nearly half the students are entirely dependent on themselves for their support in school. Through the Berea labor program, whereby every student is provided with remunerative work, the earnings of all students in the past year, totalling nearly $150,000, averaged 76 per cent. of the individual school expense, which is under $150. More than one fifth of the students met their entire school costs through campus labor alone.

Among evidences of educational results are the increased demand for Berea graduates in teaching positions throughout the country and the winning of a national college essay contest by a Berea student.

President Hutchins notes that the bakery, besides providing the college needs, filled orders from New York City and several other large centers, and furnished 40,000 hours of remunerative labor to a regular force of fifty-eight boys and girls. The dairy produced 38,542 gallons of milk. The 600 laying hens of the poultry farm produced better than 185 eggs per bird. Thirty varieties of vegetables were produced in the garden. The woodwork department handled 3,248 jobs, its student payroll amounting to $15,210. The fireside industries employed more than 400 young women in the making of hand-woven fabrics and also furnished work to 160 women in mountain homes. The broom factory produced 8,500 dozen house brooms. The College Press continued to edit and print the town newspaper and produce the printed matter of the institution.

A RESIDENTIAL HALL FOR HARVARD UNIVERSITY

ANNOUNCEMENT of an anonymous gift of $3,000,000 to build and endow a "House" or group of dormitories, dining halls and common rooms for 200 or 300 students within Harvard College has just been made at Cambridge in a statement by Dr. A. Lawrence Lowell, president of Harvard University.

The establishment of such houses was suggested three years ago in a report presented by an undergraduate "committee on education," appointed by the student council. The new project is described by President Lowell as the "capping stone" to the tutorial system which has been built up at Harvard during the last fifteen years.

Further details of the new house are contained in the following statement by President Lowell:

For a generation there has been much discussion of the policy of breaking up our large colleges into smaller social units in order to secure at the same time the advantages of the large and small institutions. Many men here have felt that this must come if we are to confer the greatest benefit upon our undergraduates. The very thoughtful Report of the Student Council Committee on Education, published in 1926, advocated strongly such a plan, and may be taken to express the opinion of undergraduates who have given grave consideration to the problems of life in the college. To the officers of the faculty the method of approach has seemed to lie in the creation of a residential group or house of students capable of strong scholarly interest and achievement associated with members of the instructing staff, including their tutors, and if possible with research fellows in different lines of work.

An effort had been made to obtain the funds required for such a house, but the plan had remained a long-cherished aspiration until last week when a benefactor, who prefers to remain unknown, but who desires to carry into effect the policy of smaller social units, and who is convinced that our mode of attacking the question is feasible, offered to give the three million dollars needed to build and endow the proposed house.

The plan involves no change in the method of teaching; and in fact our tutorial system lends itself to it perfectly. The men will attend the college courses like other students, but the tutoring will normally be done in the house. Nor does the plan affect the functions of Harvard College and the faculty of arts and sciences in education, as the great undergraduate center and the authority for granting degrees and determining the qualifications therefor. The students in the house are not to be selected from those concentrating in particular subjects. On the contrary, it is of the essence of the plan that they should be interested, and really interested, in different things, that the life and talk may be broadly stimulating. Moreover they are not to be isolated from their fellow students or cut off from outside activities or clubs, for the object is a larger and more vigorous life, deeper contacts inside the walls, without loss outside.

While we may derive much that is valuable from the example of Oxford and Cambridge, where a similar system has proved successful, mere imitation would be fatal. American conditions and traditions are not the same as those of the English universities, and to urge that we should do anything because it is done in a college there is futile. The general plan is good, and seems capable of adaptation to our needs, with a wisdom that grasps the object to be sought and perceives the means that will promote it here. Of course it will be misunderstood and discussed as something that it is not. Of course, as in the case of the general examination and the tutorial system, time and experience will be needed to perfect it. Rightly considered it is, indeed, a logical step in the progress of that system, a capping stone in the structure we have been striving to build. It is also a natural development from the idea of the freshman halls.

When the general examination was proposed for a single division of the faculty the objection was made that if successful it would have to be adopted by the others. That has proved true, but not an objection. A first step in a path that turns out well is not to be criticized because it leads to others not less good. Such a house seems an experiment with prospects of great usefulness.

THE JULIUS ROSENWALD FUND

EXTENSION of the activities of the Julius Rosenwald Fund, heretofore chiefly concerned with building negro rural schools, to include support of medical services to people of moderate means, is the basis of an announcement made by Edwin R. Embree, president of the fund.

Michael M. Davis has been appointed to the executive staff of the fund as director for medical services. Dr. Davis is known as an authority on hospitals and clinics and as a writer on public-health subjects. His recent book "Clinics, Hospitals and Health Centers" is the standard work in that field. As executive officer of the Committee on Dispensary Development he was responsible for the organization of the Pay Clinic in New York City of the Cornell University Medical College. During the past few years he has been engaged in studies of hospital problems for the Rockefeller Foundation and in private work as consultant to various organizations. Dr. Davis will direct the program which the fund is planning to undertake in cooperation with the medical profession to improve the organized facilities for medical service to the average man. In these activities special attention will be given to pay clinics.

William B. Harrell, now assistant auditor of the University of Chicago, has been appointed secretary and comptroller of the Julius Rosenwald Fund. Born and educated in the South, Mr. Harrell has the degrees of B.A. and M.A. from the University of North Carolina. He has been an instructor in economics and a member of the business offices of the universities of North Carolina and Chicago.

Clark Foreman, a graduate of the University of Georgia, who is now with the Phelps-Stokes Fund of New York, has been appointed associate field agent of the Julius Rosenwald Fund for southern schools and colleges.

Franklin C. McLean, chief of the medical clinics of the University of Chicago, has been elected a trustee of the Julius Rosenwald Fund.

Commenting upon the new work which Dr. Davis is to direct, Mr. Embree, president of the fund, said:

Great loss in human welfare and happiness and in economic efficiency is caused by sickness, much of which can be cured or prevented by modern medicine. While the brilliant achievements of medical science are among the triumphs of the century, the full benefits of recent discoveries and present knowledge do not yet reach the average man. As Dr. William H. Welch, dean of American medicine, puts it: "The health field has a woefully ineffective distribution service as compared with its enormously effective production service." It is common knowledge that people of moderate means find it harder to get good modern facilities for diagnosis and treatment of illness than do the poor and indigent through charity services and free hospitals.

The Julius Rosenwald Fund is planning to study and from time to time to give practical aid to clinics and other organized medical services, including pay clinics.

THE AMERICAN FOUNDATION FOR MENTAL HYGIENE

THE establishment of the American Foundation for Mental Hygiene, Inc., was announced on November 8, at the nineteenth annual meeting of the National Committee for Mental Hygiene in New York City. The meeting was attended by several hundred physicians, psychologists, educators and social workers from various parts of the country.

According to the account in the New York *Times,* Dr. Arthur H. Ruggles, chairman of the executive committee of the National Committee, spoke of the project as "a permanent guarantee of the continuance of the work begun twenty years ago for better treatment of the insane and feebleminded, the reduction and prevention of mental and nervous disorders and defects and the promotion of mental health."

Discussing the plans of the foundation, Clifford W. Beers, founder of the mental hygiene movement and secretary of the National Committee, stated that it was the first foundation organized "for the exclusive purpose of financing and doing work that will enable men, women and children to live happier, healthier and more efficient lives through a better understanding and management of the processes of their minds and of the controlling forces in human behavior." The foundation comes into existence without an endowment of its own, Mr. Beers said, but with confident hope of obtaining funds to carry out its purposes. Pledges toward its first $1,000,000 endowment, he said, have so far reached $150,000.

"The American Foundation for Mental Hygiene should in the future be one of the greatest instruments for good," said Dr. Bernard Sachs, vice-president of the National Committee, who presided at the meeting. "Ultimately, physical health depends upon mental health; ultimately, social and industrial problems depend for their solution on mental health. As we visualize the future, the work of this foundation should appeal to very many interests, non-medical as well as medical, and thus its support in the future will be assured."

The officers of the foundation are: *Honorary President,* Dr. William H. Welch; *president,* Dr. Arthur H. Ruggles; *vice-presidents,* James R. Angell, the Right Reverend Dr. William Lawrence and Dr. William L. Russell; *treasurer,* Frederic W. Allen; *secretary,* Clifford W. Beers. The trustees of the foundation include, besides the officers named, the following laymen and physicians: Dr. C. Floyd Haviland, W. Curtis Bok, Dr. Charles P. Emerson, Charles A. Stone, Dr. William A. White, Dr. Frankwood E. Williams, Harry P. Robbins, Dr. Bernard Sachs, Dr. Clarence J. D'Alton, Lindley H. Hill and Dr. George L. Wallace.

Plans for the first International Congress on Mental Hygiene, to be held in Washington in May, 1930, were adopted at the meeting. Out of the congress is expected to come an international committee which will act as a clearing house for information on all phases of mental hygiene for the benefit of all countries.

Speakers at the meeting included also Dr. C.-E. A. Winslow, professor of public health, Yale University, and president of the Connecticut Society for Mental Hygiene, and Dr. Frankwood E. Williams, medical director of the National Committee. The following were elected officers of the National Committee for the ensuing year: Dr. Charles P. Emerson, *president;* Dr. James R. Angell, the Right Reverend Dr. William Lawrence, Dr. William L. Russell and Dr. Bernard Sachs, *vice-presidents;* Frederic W. Allen, *treasurer,* and Clifford W. Beers, *secretary.*

THE NEW ENGINEERING BUILDING OF PRINCETON UNIVERSITY

PRINCETON UNIVERSITY'S new building which will house the School of Engineering was formally dedicated on November 15. More than 100 representatives from colleges and engineering schools throughout the east attended the exercises.

The engineering building, which was erected at a cost of $500,000, was opened at the beginning of the present college year for classes, but the dedication was postponed until it was completed. Dr. Michael I. Pupin, of Columbia University, was the chief speaker at the laying of the corner-stone for the building in May, 1927. At the same time, building operations were started on a new chemistry laboratory, but as yet this has not been completed.

Both of these new additions to the Princeton campus are Collegiate Gothic style, in keeping with the new university chapel and McCosh Hall, across Washington Road. The engineering building is three stories in height, with a floor area of 50,000 square feet. There are three large laboratories, in addition to fourteen classrooms that will accommodate engineering students in the college and graduate school.

The equipment for experimental purposes includes steam, gas and refrigerating laboratories in the north wing, with a laboratory for hydraulics and electricity in the opposite wing. A research laboratory for faculty members and graduate students is provided on the second floor with a room for silograph work and photometer testing. A large oil-burning boiler has been installed in conjunction with the steam laboratory to provide steam for the engines and for testing purposes by the students.

Another feature of the modern equipment is a cooling tower 48 feet high, which will be used for experimentation and part of the refrigerating plant, gasoline and steam engines. The object of the laboratory work at Princeton, according to Dean Greene, is to supply the students with machines of sufficient size to get commercial results, yet not so large as to make the operating charges excessive. It is aimed to familiarize each student with the apparatus, let him become acquainted with its operation and finally make tests to determine its efficiency.

The first floor contains a well-furnished conference room and a large library opening on the foyer at the entrance to the building. The furniture was donated by the Princeton Engineering Association, graduates of the university. The offices of Dean Greene and other faculty members are also on this floor.

Next to the engineering building it is planned to erect a laboratory for testing materials. In this structure will be housed apparatus for tests for tension, compression, bending torsion, impact, friction, hardness, repeated stress measurements and other physical properties. In the engineering annex, which was formerly the chemical laboratory, industrial chemistry will be studied, while the metallographic work will be carried on in the new chemistry building.

Dean Greene became head of Princeton's Engineering School in 1922, and since that time its enrolment has more than doubled, so that it now numbers 180 students. The dedicatory program was held on the steps of the building, with John Grier Hibben, president, receiving the keys from Charles Z. Klauder, architect. Later in the day a luncheon was held at the Princeton Inn. Carlton S. Proctor, of New York, president of the Engineering Association; Dean Augustus Trowbridge, of the Princeton Graduate College, and Dean Dexter S. Kimball, of the Cornell Engineering College, were the speakers.

EDUCATIONAL NOTES AND NEWS

John Roscoe Turner will be installed as president of the University of West Virginia on November 28.

At the convocation ceremonies on September 20, at Beloit College, the degree of doctor of laws was conferred on Dr. Ernest Hatch Wilkins, president of Oberlin College, who delivered the convocation address.

At the annual Founders' Day exercises of Lafayette College on November 15 an honorary degree was conferred on Dr. Charles Ezra Beury, president of Temple University.

The degree of bachelor of laws was conferred by Carleton College upon Secretary of State Frank B. Kellogg on the occasion of the dedicatory exercises for Severance Hall, new dormitory for men. Secretary Kellogg delivered the address of dedication. Severance Hall, the final unit of the men's quadrangle, was named in honor of the late Cordenio A. Severance, former law partner of Mr. Kellogg. The late Mr. Severance was for two years a student at Carleton.

At the ceremony on the occasion of the opening of the term at the University of Paris, the degree of doctor *honoris causa* was conferred on Sir Charles Sherrington, Waynflete professor of physiology at the University of Oxford and president of the Royal Society. As was reported in School and Society last week, the honorary doctorate was also conferred on Dr. W. S. Thayer, of Baltimore, formerly professor of medicine in the Johns Hopkins University.

A bust of Dr. John Dewey, professor of philosophy in Columbia University, was unveiled in the Education Library of Teachers

College on November 9. Dr. Dewey attended the exercises and Dr. William Heard Kilpatrick was the principal speaker.

DR. CHARLES F. THWING, president emeritus of Western Reserve University, celebrated his seventy-fifth birthday on November 9.

KING GUSTAF V of Sweden has bestowed the Order of the North Star, with the rank of Knight, on Dr. Amandus Johnson, of Philadelphia, formerly assistant professor in Scandinavian languages at the University of Pennsylvania and now president and chief organizer of the American Sons and Daughters of Sweden.

DR. WILLFORD I. KING, professor of economics and statistics of the school of commerce, accounts and finance of New York University, was recently appointed a member of the advisory committee on the U. S. Census by the American Statistical Association.

DR. FREDERICK W. LEWIS, for ten years president of the College of Emporia, Kansas, has announced that he has resigned to become associate executive of the Biblical Seminary, New York City.

DR. HARLAN HINES has accepted an appointment as professor of education in the Eastern Montana Normal School, at Billings.

DR. EDWIN BARLOW EVANS, formerly lecturer on literature at New York University, has become professor and head of the department of English at the State Teachers College, Fairmont, West Virginia.

DR. SHIRLEY SMITH, after four years in Rockford College, Illinois, became in the fall of 1927 a professor of the classical languages in New Jersey College, Rutgers University.

ALFRED M. DAME has resigned as head of the department of Greek at Washington and Jefferson College to accept a similar post at Middlebury College, Vermont.

DR. FRED LEWIS PATTEE, one of the oldest members of the Pennsylvania State College faculty in point of service and an authority on American literature, has resigned his position. Professor Pattee was for many years head of the English department in the college and had been on the faculty for thirty-four years.

HARVEY C. EMERY, formerly assistant to the dean of students at the University of Michigan, has been appointed "counsellor of pre-medical students," at the request of Dean Hugh Cabot, of the Medical School. The office is a new one and has been created with the idea of aiding pre-medical students in the selection of courses and the solution of other special problems which confront them.

DR. JOSEPH MARR GWINN, superintendent of schools of San Francisco City and County, was elected president of the California Teachers Association, at the recent annual meeting.

WILLIAM R. JACK, Portland, Maine, was elected president of the New England Association of School Superintendents at the recent annual convention on November 11. Other officers elected were: *Vice-president,* Isaac O. Winslow, Providence; *secretary-treasurer,* S. Howard Chace, Beverly; *directors,* C. W. Bickford, Lewiston, Maine; William G. English, Lebanon, New Hampshire; Ernest A. Hamilton, Newport, Vermont.

HARRY W. LANGWORTHY, superintendent of schools at Gloversville, was elected president of the New York State Council of Superintendents at the annual meeting held from October 1 to 3 at the Lake Placid Club. Charles S. Wright, superintendent of schools at Lawrence, was elected vice-president and E. L. Ackley, superintendent of schools at Johnstown, was reelected secretary-treasurer.

ROBERT M. MACNAUGHT, of Windham, superintendent of schools of the second supervisory district of Greene County, was elected president of the New York State Association of District Superintendents at the seventeenth annual meeting, which was held from October 4 to 6. Other officers elected at the meeting were: *First vice-president,* P. B. Matthews, of the first supervisory district of Suffolk County; *Second vice-president,* Leon J. Coon, of the first supervisory district of Ontario County; *Secretary,* Mrs. Emma C. Chase, of the third supervisory district of Sullivan County; *Treasurer,* Orrin A. Kolb, of the second supervisory district of Niagara County.

Dr. Charles P. Emerson, professor of medicine and dean of the medical faculty of the University of Indiana, was elected president of the newly established American Foundation for Mental Hygiene, on November 8, at the annual meeting of the National Committee for Mental Hygiene held in New York City. It is proposed to raise $1,000,000 for the support of the foundation, of which amount the sum of $150,000 has already been subscribed. Plans for the first International Congress on Mental Hygiene, to be held at Washington in May, 1930, were also adopted at the meeting.

The Abraham Flexner lectureship at the Vanderbilt School of Medicine will be inaugurated by a series of five lectures on melistic structure by Dr. Heinrich Poll, director of the institute of anatomy at the University of Hamburg.

President Arthur E. Morgan, of Antioch College, will address the Babson Institute in Wellesley Hills on the morning of November 24.

A meeting in memory of Edgar Fahs Smith, formerly provost and Blanchard professor of chemistry in the University of Pennsylvania, will be held on December 4 at four o'clock in the Irvine Auditorium of the university. Addresses will be made by Dr. Francis X. Dercum (class of '87 medical), president of the American Philosophical Society; Dr. Marston Taylor Bogert, professor of organic chemistry at Columbia University, and by Dr. Josiah H. Penniman, provost of the university.

Dr. Victor Emanuel Emmel, professor of anatomy in the college of medicine of the University of Illinois at Chicago, died suddenly on November 8. Dr. Emmel was fifty years old.

Elbert W. Griffith, formerly for more than twenty-seven years superintendent of schools at Glens Falls, New York, and for more than fifty years engaged in school service, died on November 7 in the Lynn (Massachusetts) Hospital from injuries received when struck by an automobile the day before. Dr. Griffith was seventy-seven years old.

The Reverend Dr. Caesar Augustus Rodney Janvier, principal of Ewing Christian College at Allahabad, India, died on November 3 from injuries received in a fall. He was sixty-eight years old.

Edward Voorhies Walton, for nine years supervising principal of the Roselle public schools, New Jersey, died on November 5 at the age of sixty years. Mr. Walton was a member of the executive committee of the New Jersey State Teachers Association and a member of the National Council of Education.

The presentation of the new school of business administration and the inauguration of Alfred H. Upham as fourteenth president of the university were celebrated October 19 and 20 by Miami University, Oxford, Ohio, in connection with the annual alumni home-coming. Among the speakers were Dr. Julius Klein, of the Department of Commerce; George M. Verity, president of the American Rolling Mill Company; John R. Simpson, president of the Cuba Cane Sugar Company; Dr. W. O. Thompson, president-emeritus of the Ohio State University, and President Upham. Both the former president of Miami, Dr. R. M. Hughes, of Iowa State College, and the new president were students at Miami University during the presidency there of Dr. W. O. Thompson, 1891–1899. By recent agreement of the two boards of trustees Oxford College for Women has been merged with Miami University, which undertakes to affiliate the alumnae and to perpetuate the name of the college in connection with the main building, to be used as a residence hall for university women. Oxford College, one of the oldest colleges for women in America, traces its establishment to 1830.

The members of the American Educational Delegation to Russia were the guests of honor at a dinner given by the American Society for Cultural Relations with Russia on November 10. The speakers were Professor John Dewey, of Columbia University; Dr. Donald J. Cowling, president of Carleton College; Fola La Follette, of the City and Country School, and Waldemar G. Bogoras, of the faculty of the University of Leningrad. Dr. Stephen P. Duggan, director of the Institute of International Education, presided.

Plans to erect 1,500 modern rural schools have been approved by the Department of Education, Cuba. Many unsanitary old-fashioned schools will be replaced and several hundred new schools will be erected. Funds for the construction will be obtained from the $5,000,000 set aside from the $50,000,000 recently contracted for by the government in New York.

Richardson Hall, the new building of the Brooklyn Law School of St. Lawrence University, which was built at a cost of $1,000,000, was dedicated on November 10. Dean Roscoe Pound, of the Harvard Law School, was the principal speaker. Others on the program included Dr. Richard Eddy Sykes, president of the St. Lawrence University; Dean William Payson Richardson, of the law school, and John J. Meagher, president of the law school's alumni.

Lecturers at Cornell University on the Jacob H. Schiff Foundation for the Promotion of Studies in Human Civilization include Professor Pierre S. Porohovshikov, public attorney at the High Court in St. Petersburg before the Russian Revolution, who will speak on "Russian Drama" and on "Social Conditions and International Relations of Russia before the War"; and Professor Ernest R. Groves, research professor of sociology in the Institute of Research in Social Sciences at the University of North Carolina, on "Modern Marriage and its Problems," "Family Experience and Personality" and "The Social Significance of Childhood."

Dr. Paul L. Dengler, director of the American Institute in Vienna, who is visiting the United States, has announced that the Austrian government will offer six fellowships to American students for study at the University of Vienna during 1929. The fellowships will provide for board and lodging as well as for tuition.

A graduate summer session course in household economics will be given for American teachers under the auspices of Teachers College, Columbia University, in London, England, in July, 1929, by Professor Benjamin R. Andrews, of Teachers College. The plan is to study home and community living conditions at first-hand, particularly as regards housing and town planning, cooperative enterprises, public health, education and organizations for home-making, child-care, social insurance, various aspects of industry and other factors affecting the life of the average family. Those who may possibly be interested in the course are asked to communicate at once with Professor Andrews, Teachers College, Columbia University, New York City, as the course is offered subject to a minimum number of registrations.

Fourteen colleges were represented at the seventeenth meeting of the Association of Colleges in New England, which was held at the University of Vermont on October 24 and 25. The representatives reported were: Amherst—Arthur S. Pease, president; Thomas C. Esty, dean. Boston University—Daniel L. Marsh, president; William M. Warren, dean; Lyman C. Newell, professor of chemistry. Bowdoin—Kenneth C. M. Sills, president; Stanley P. Chase, professor of English literature. Brown—Roland G. D. Richardson, dean of the graduate department; Henry B. Huntington, professor of English. Clark—Homer P. Little, dean. Dartmouth—Craven Laycock, dean; James D. McCallum, professor of English. Harvard—A. Lawrence Lowell, president; Clifford H. Moore, dean of the faculty of arts and sciences; Alfred C. Hanford, dean of Harvard College. Middlebury—Llewellyn R. Perkins, professor of mathematics; Burt Hazletine, dean of the men's college. Trinity—Remsen B. Ogilby, president; Thurman L. Hood, dean. Tufts—George S. Miller, secretary of the faculty and assistant professor of government and history. University of Vermont—Guy W. Bailey, president; Elijah Swift, assistant dean of the college of arts and sciences Wesleyan—James L. McConaughy, president; Frank W. Nicolson, dean. Williams—Harry A. Garfield, president; George E. Howes, dean. Yale—Clarence W. Mendell, dean of Yale College; Charles H. Warren, dean of Sheffield Scientific School.

Applications for associate librarian, to fill a vacancy in the Bureau of Education, must be on file with the Civil Service Commission at Washington, D. C., not later than December 12. The entrance salary is $3,200 a year. Higher-salaried positions are filled through promotion. The work involves general administration and supervision of the library of about 125,000 volumes with a staff of seven persons; selecting books and periodicals for purchase; editing record and current educational publications, and supervising bibliographies of special educational subjects. Competitors will not be required to report for examination at any place, but will be rated on their education, experience and fitness, and a thesis or publication to be filed by the applicant. Men are desired for this position.

With complete returns not yet available, enough is known to assure the passage of the so-called anti-evolution bill voted on by the people of Arkansas at the election on November 6. The bill is short and simply prohibits the teaching in any state-supported school of any theory that man is descended from a lower order of animals. A vigorous fight against the bill was conducted by the president and faculty of the State University, the presidents of two or three church colleges, a few ministers and private citizens, and by some of the newspapers of the state.

Miss Agnes Birmingham has appealed to the New York State Commissioner of Education from the decision of the New York City Board of Examiners in denying her a license to enable her to assume the directorship of the Bureau for Speech Improvement. She has also appealed from the action of the Board of Education in appointing Mrs. Letitia Raubicheck as her successor. Miss Birmingham served seven years as acting director of the bureau, for which she received a satisfactory rating from the superintendent in charge.

Arrangements have been concluded between Rutgers University, the State University of New Jersey and the research department of the Training School at Vineland, New Jersey, whereby formal recognition of the graduate training in abnormal and clinical psychology offered at the Training School is now granted by Rutgers University through the department of education. Under this arrangement Rutgers grants extension credit for the following formal courses at the Training School: technique of Binet testing, intelligence and achievement tests, elementary psychological clinic, practicum in mental diagnosis, seminar in abnormal psychology, seminar in current literature, seminar in research. Recognition is also granted for major research as M.A. or Ph.D. dissertations. When combined with standard campus courses available for week end commutation it is now possible for research fellows at the Training School to meet the residence requirements for the M.A. degree.

The General Education Board will provide the department of zoology at the University of Texas with $135,000 to be used in the development of graduate instruction and research during the next eight years. Approximately one half of this sum will be given by the General Education Board; the rest will be raised by the university. The zoological staff plans to use a portion of this fund for technical assistance and for fellowships.

The Carnegie Foundation has made a grant of $100,000, distributed over a period of five years, to be used for the development of the fine arts at the University of Michigan.

Members of the commission appointed to investigate the relationship between the State of New Jersey and Rutgers University, meeting on November 9, had under advisement the question of an increased annual appropriation for the university. Edward D. Duffield, of Newark, chairman, said at the conclusion of the hearing at the state house that the difficulty which the commission is seeking to solve is whether the institution can be supplied with public funds while it remains under private control. Rutgers has been receiving state aid, but Dr. John M. Thomas, president, maintained that the appropriations are insufficient to permit the university to meet the scholastic demands made upon it. Supported by the alumni, Dr. Thomas advocated the imposition of a half-mill tax, which would supply approximately $3,000,000 a year and permit Rutgers to expand. He pointed out that the legislative support fluctuates annually while the enrolment of the university constantly increases. Mr. Duffield stated that the commission would render its report at the next legislature.

AN increase of $1,000 a year in the salaries of Williams College faculty members has been authorized by the board of trustees. Under the new scale the salaries will be: Professor $6,000, associate professor $5,000, assistant professor $4,000, instructor $3,000. The salaries will go into effect not later than 1930. The board states that the maximum salaries have hardly more than kept pace with the increased cost of living.

GROUND has been broken on the Columbia University campus for a new building to house the natural science department, which will be erected at a cost of $1,000,000. It will be situated in the southeast corner of the Grove on Amsterdam Avenue, facing 119th Street, and will be ten stories in height. Architecturally it will be almost identical to the Chandler Chemical Laboratories.

ON November 7 ground was broken for the erection of new buildings for the State Teachers College at Buffalo, when the mayor of the city inaugurated the work on the project. The president of the local board, Mr. Edward H. Butler, also participated and President H. W. Rockwell, of the State Teachers College, introduced the speakers. The new plant will include five buildings—a main college building, a vocational building, a school of practice and a gymnasium, arranged in quadrangular form, and a residence for the president near at hand. It will be built on a new campus of twenty acres recently taken over, situated opposite the old Pan-American Exposition grounds, and directly across Elmwood Avenue from the Albright Art Gallery and the new Art School. The Historical Building and the McKinley Vocational School in the immediate neighborhood will, with the new State Teachers College, form a striking educational center. The plans drawn by the state architect, William E. Haugaard, are of Georgian colonial type.

NATIONAL fellowships for research in child development are awarded upon the advice and recommendation of the committee on child development of the National Research Council, their purpose being to promote fundamental research in the several sciences basic to child development. Individuals of either sex, who are residents of the United States or Canada, and who possess the doctor's degree in one of the basic sciences or in medicine, are eligible. In addition, the candidate must present tangible evidence of research ability. Fellowships are open for study only in the United States or Canada, and carry a stipend of $1,800 a year and upward, varying with individual requirements. In addition to the basic stipend some provision is made for travel. Further information can be obtained from Mervin A. Durea, executive secretary, Committee on Child Development, National Research Council, B and 21st Streets, Washington, D. C.

THE seventeenth annual conference of British Educational Associations will be held at University College, London, from December 31, 1928, to January 5, 1929.

SPECIAL CORRESPONDENCE

RECASTING COURSES AND PERSONNEL WORK AT OREGON

THE University of Oregon opened this fall with a new threefold program that has already shown that each phase will work out successfully. Under this program, which was drawn up and adopted by the faculty under the direction of President Arnold Bennett Hall, are found an entirely new and very different plan of organization for lower division work (freshman and sophomore); a personnel bureau that is demonstrating that a close and helpful contact between student and faculty and administration is feasible, and a much more rigid scholarship requirement to remain in the university.

The most important single factor on this ambitious program is the new lower division plan. This operates chiefly in the college of literature, science and the arts, although it also affects students in the various professional schools during their first two years. With a single stroke the university abolished the former plan of "majoring" in special fields during the freshman and sophomore years, and instead students choose a field of interest from one of four special groups.

The entire lower division curricula has been apportioned among the four groups, which are called as follows: (1) Language and Literature, (2) Social Science, (3) Physical Science, (4) Biological Science. In each of these groups survey courses have been devised for the first year, and "option" courses for the second year. During the first two years each student takes either option or survey in three of the four groups, and the fourth course is also permissible. Thus the student will enter his junior year with a thorough background, and will be capable of choosing his major interest in which to specialize for his life work.

It is a recognized fact that a great many students come to universities without knowing definitely what they wish to take up for their life work. They may have an interest in chemistry, in mathematics or in other fields. It is obviously unfair to put them in the chemistry department, merely because they have a passive interest there. They may abandon this subject after a year or so, or worse yet, they may remain and graduate mediocre chemists. Under the system now in operation here, a student who showed an interest in chemistry would be assigned to the physical science group, in which he would take a survey course. At the same time, however, he would be taking courses in other fields, and should he find greater interest and fascination in one of these, he may make his choice of major field in this subject at the beginning of his junior year.

Thus the university solves at once two major problems, that of the student who comes to the university without definite ideas on what profession or vocation he wishes to follow, and that of the student whose interests change during the first two years.

Many other features of the new plan are also desirable. Under the survey and option system of classes the students are divided into sections for instruction, and into still smaller groups for conferences. The professors will thus act in the double capacity of adviser and instructor, and the freshman will be brought at once into contact with some of the outstanding members of the faculty at a time when the influence of such instructors will count the most in the training of the intellect and the moulding of character.

Students who come to the university with a professional career in view, such as medicine, law, journalism, architecture or education, enter immediately into their respective schools. This takes the place of one of the three required groups, thus leaving the student still with the opportunity to gain a broad background during the first two years before specialization becomes intense.

At the same time that the course of the first two years was reorganized, the line was drawn more sharply between upper and lower divisions. At the end of his first two years the student will be given a junior certificate, or if he prefers, a certificate of graduation from the lower division. Provided the student has maintained a high average in his work, he will be given a junior certificate with honors privileges and be entitled to enrol in honors courses.

The work from the beginning of the junior year to the receipt of the bachelor degree will be intensive and highly specialized. At least two thirds of the courses must be of advanced nature and designated as upper division work.

In small colleges contact between student and professor, and—what is of almost equal importance—contact between student and administration, is made easy simply because the institution functions almost like a family. Every one knows every one else, advice on student problems can be given because the instructors and even the president can know the student and his background and understand the case. In a large institution it is simply impossible for any group of faculty members to know more than a small portion of students, while members of the administrative staff often find themselves even further removed from the young men and women.

Student problems in a state university or other large institution naturally fall into two classes, general and individual. The general problems can be attacked through statistics, tables prepared from college or even high school records, and from examinations given periodically. For this purpose Dr. Hall has created a special "research bureau" which has three distinct branches, psychological, educational and statistical. This bureau cooperates directly with a research committee, and with the office of the registrar.

For the individual problems, which are held to be the most important, Dr. Hall has organized a "personnel council." This is composed of the dean of women, dean of men, psychology department, the placement or employment service, university health service, school of physical education, registrar and representatives of the university at large. The members of this council will deal directly with students.

Thus a definite plan is at hand to meet any student situation that may arise, general or individual. The research bureau can investigate the reasons for adding or dropping courses in the curriculum, while a student who is having difficulty with his studies can find a point of contact through the personnel council. Nor will it be necessary for students to seek the help of this council. Should one be found making poor grades he will be reported by the registrar. Immediately his psychological test record will be checked, his health record looked up, while the dean of men will call him in for a confidential, sympathetic conference. If his courses are not suited to his needs, or if he has interests in other studies, changes can be arranged. Every effort will be made to keep the student interested, aware of his responsibilities, and to give him the feeling that he is at the university to get the utmost good out of his studies.

The function of the entire system, although involving several persons and several departments, is simple and a definite check can be kept on all operations. Both the research bureau and the personnel council are composed of persons appointed by the president, to whom they are to report. Problems on student personnel originating at any point are referred to the council, which presents data to the research bureau when necessary. The research bureau has at hand the services of the research committee, a body of experts, and the registrar's department. After investigation, the bureau reports back its findings to the council, which in turn can pass on its decisions in the form of recommended legislation to the faculty. At all times the administration is kept in close touch through reports.

The plan has been carefully worked out, and represents the result of two years of work on the part of Dr. Hall and a committee of the faculty. Although it was adopted only at the close of last year, its advantages are already evident. Duplication of effort is avoided, the administration is kept in constant touch with general and specific conditions, while the advantage to the student, who has an understandable approach for his problems, is of utmost importance.

The plan of personal contact begins even before the student gets into the university, for the research bureau is to devote much time and effort to a study of high school records and problems, and the interest of the university will continue after graduation, for the system calls for a placement service, which will aid in employment and in vocational adjustment.

In line with the new plans the faculty has tightened up scholarship requirements. In the lower division students on probation for poor scholarship are required to carry and successfully pass twelve hours or be dropped from the university. The old rule called for but nine in many cases. In the upper division the status of probation (making between seven and ten hours) is entirely abolished, and the student failing to make ten hours will be dropped.

Both because a certificate of graduation can be obtained at the end of two years and because the student in the upper two years must face a rigorous program of intensive study, many students of average ability or below will find the end of the second year a convenient stopping place in their university careers. The prospect of obtaining at least the foundation of a liberal education in two years and securing the certificate of graduation in a shorter time will doubtless attract many who might regard a four-year course as too costly or too formidable.

It is pointed out that, in the long run, the new departures are not likely to make any material change in the number who receive instruction at the university. A rising standard of university achievement has always been a challenge to students of superior ability who come in increasing numbers, and the periods following the stiffening of scholarship requirements have been, at the University of Oregon, marked by material increases in enrolment.

GEORGE H. GODFREY

UNIVERSITY OF OREGON

DISCUSSION

THE SENIOR FELLOWSHIPS OF ST. JOHN'S COLLEGE

AT the first meeting of the two hundred and thirty-second year of the existence of St. John's College, Annapolis, since its beginning as King William's School, held on October 19, 1928, the board of visitors and governors unanimously passed the following resolution:

For the purpose of improving the scholarship and elevating the intellectual outlook of the student body of St. John's College, and for the further purpose of making clear by example the difference between academic freedom as a reality and academic freedom as a mere form of words, it is

Resolved: 1. That there are hereby established the senior fellowships of St. John's College.

2. That annually there shall be elected in June of each year, not more than three (3) members of the junior class of that year, to be senior fellows of St. John's College during the following year.

3. That election to the senior fellowship shall be made by the board of visitors and governors of the college, upon the nomination and recommendation of the president and faculty. In making nominations and recommendations for the senior fellowships the president and faculty shall take into consideration, and be guided by, not merely the academic grades attained by the students during the first three years of their course, though due weight shall be given to these grades; but also, and chiefly, by the interest in, devotion to, and promise of notable achievement in the intellectual life, as evidenced by the work and attitudes of the students during the first three years of their course.

4. That the sole requirement which shall be made of a senior fellow after his election shall be that he must be in residence at St. John's College during the academic year following his election. During the year of tenure of his fellowship the fellow shall not be required to attend classes, or to take examinations, or to pay any fees whatever to the college. At the end of the year of his fellowship the fellow shall be given his degree in course. During the tenure of his fellowship the fellow shall be given complete and absolute freedom to pursue the intellectual life in residence at St. John's College in whatever manner and direction he himself chooses, as the guest of the college.

5. That a senior fellowship can be terminated during the year of its tenure only because of the commission of a crime, as defined by the laws of the State of Maryland, by the fellow; or because the fellow becomes insane, as defined by the laws of the State of Maryland.

6. That this resolution shall become operative and go into effect immediately upon its passage, and that announcement of the existence of the senior fellowships of St. John's College, and the conditions of their award and tenure shall be made in all future catalogues of the college.

This resolution inaugurates an educational experiment of considerable interest. As result of a number of causes, which can not be detailed here for lack of space, there has been plainly observable for a long time past an increasing tendency to make American college and university education more and more Procrustean in its technique. Some years ago, in discussing the age of persons elected to the National Academy of Sciences, the following statement was made:[1]

It is at least possible, and I incline personally to think it probable, that the increasing organization, standardization, mechanization and constant striving for efficient mediocrity in all our college and university life, which every thoughtful person has seen going on during the past thirty years, and which some have deplored and vainly endeavored to stop, is showing as one of its most dreadful effects the curbing and fettering of the progress of the really brilliant student. That some such idea as this is forcing itself upon many minds is indicated by the National Research Council's study of the problem of the brilliant student, under the direction of Professor C. E. Seashore, and by Professor Wheeler's brilliant paper on "The Dry-Rot of our Academic Biology." Much ink has been spilled about the subject of academic freedom, but nearly always with reference to the freedom of the professors to do various things, sometimes obviously absurd or ridiculous. Is it not about time to consider seriously the subject of the freedom, within academic precincts, of the student to develop his intellectual powers in the way he personally wants to?

The schoolmaster-pupil attitude, which may or may not be a necessary and efficient pedagogical technique in secondary education, has been carried over, in ever-increasing degree, into college and university life. The student is beset by rules, classifications, standards, credit hours and the like. If any one were to suggest

[1] Pearl, R., *Proc. Nat. Acad. Sci.*, 11: 760, 1925.

to any intelligent undergraduate to-day that colleges and universities are traditionally places of intellectual freedom, where one had an opportunity freely to think and to cultivate ideas, he would be listened to with politeness, no doubt, but also, and chiefly, with complete incredulity.

But, on the other hand, probably no thoughtful person not himself a part of the system and profiting by its existence and continuance, could be found to maintain that the Procrustean rigidity of our undergraduate pedagogical technique has any intrinsic virtue as a means of developing the "genius, taste, judgment or normal capacity" of the individual on whom it is practiced. The schoolmaster-pupil relation finds its chief demonstrable value redounding to the benefit of the master, not the pupil. It is the easiest way to manage an aggregation of youths, some of whom are as turbulent mentally as others are physically.

There is, however, much to be said for the intrinsic virtues of freedom as a developer of intellectual powers. The prize fellowships of Trinity College, Cambridge, have a comprehensive intellectual and personal freedom as perhaps their chief element. Does any one question that this element has been of prime importance in producing the extraordinary record that the Trinity prize fellowship plan has achieved? If he does I suggest that he talk with any of the distinguished British men of science who have held these fellowships in the past.

The St. John's College senior fellowships simply push the Trinity plan back one year into undergraduate life. It seems likely, though it is a point which must be determined by experience, that the effect of the St. John's senior fellowships will not be confined to their holders. They will serve as a constant reminder to every undergraduate and every member of the faculty that St. John's College regards the free and untrammeled pursuit of the intellectual life as the highest good, an ideal which has somehow been mislaid or forgotten in many American institutions of learning. They will also suggest to the undergraduate that St. John's College is ready and willing to regard him as a responsible human being and not as a child. Finally to the student of outstanding ability they hold out the prospect of recognition, encouragement and reward of almost inestimable value, which may, and probably will, profoundly influence the course of his whole life.

Raymond Pearl
Institute for Biological Research,
The Johns Hopkins University

COMPULSORY CHAPEL AND AN EXPERIENCE-CENTERED CURRICULUM

There is so much criticism abroad in the land to-day respecting compulsory chapel that an institution which has this academic "survival of medievalism," as it is sometimes called, is under obligation to state clearly its position and the reasons therefor. This statement is not an attempt at rationalization nor an apologetic, but a description of practice covering nearly forty years.

In the beginning let it be said that we do not wish standards for institutions of higher learning in the United States which shall be universally applied. We need different types of institutions with the spirit of experimentation permeating each.

Under no circumstances would I recommend at this stage of the game a compulsory chapel service for a state university, because the people are so deeply set in their judgment with reference to the separation of church and state that there would be serious objection. However, when we have come to the point where we understand that the separation of church and state does not mean necessarily the separation of education and religion, we may properly find state institutions that would require compulsory chapel attendance for its curriculum value.

Independently endowed institutions are free to use their own best judgment in respect to this matter and many of them have recently fallen away from the idea of compulsory attendance on chapel, and the sad fact is that as a consequence only forty or fifty or sixty out of institutions numbering thousands will be found in attendance on the chapel services.

Some denominational colleges, too, trying always to compare themselves in matters of practice with tax-supported and independently endowed institutions, have discontinued the practice of compulsory attendance on chapel.

There is a false assumption in the conclusion of those who advocate free chapel attendance for denominational colleges, in that they assume that religious expression and religious instruction are separate things. There is no reason in the world why a class in any subject in the college curriculum may not be a genuine worship experience for pupil and instructor. That it is not more often the case is a reflection on the ability of the teachers rather than the lack of any specific requirement in a place set apart in free time for the worship experience.

In a great many instances classes in all subjects open with prayer, but this method does not necessarily ensure the worshipful attitude. It is the reverent approach to the problems and issues involved in any situation in any class that brings into consciousness the inherent moral and religious implications in any case.

In view of these general principles, it is just as proper for a denominational college to require attendance on its chapel services as it is to require attendance on classes in Bible or religious education or mathematics or chemistry.

Immediately it will be objected that the student has the privilege of election with reference to subjects of the curriculum. The answer to this objection is twofold:

1. No college permits absolutely free election of courses of study. A system of majors and minors has generally been worked out and faculty advisers help students in selecting their courses. There is an atmosphere of freedom and of the lack of compulsion, but every college administrator knows that it is largely atmosphere. So do the students. You can't deceive them.

2. The second answer, however, is the complete one—that there is only one universal interest and that interest is religion. On this point the church college must stand unequivocally, and for this reason, in the practice of the institution in which I have the honor to be president, we would feel that we had violated the fundamental purpose of our existence if we did not make it a requirement that every student should face the issue and problems involved in the religious life in a situation involving social solidarity, in which religion finds many of its highest values.

Our purpose at Elon is not to make people religious through our chapel services, but to teach them the elements of the religious life and to emphasize their place in a corporate way. Our chapel, therefore, consists of song, of prayer, of responsive and Scripture readings, and of a brief address enforcing some of the ideals of the Christian life, usually a single ideal. Often we bring in distinguished speakers and alumni to present any phase of life interest that is upon their minds or hearts, but in such a way as to emphasize the Christian implications and ideals involved.

Students, too, conduct our chapel services and we find that this makes for catholicity of outlook, of insight and of expression. Students and faculty together control the chapel services through a joint committee, who select the speaker for each service and assign the topic. In this way the vital problems of student and college life are presented with Christian emphasis.

No doubt, there are some of our students who are unable to worship at chapel, though, as I have said, our fundamental purpose is not worship, but instruction in a compulsory situation involving social solidarity. For those who can not thus worship we have provided abundant opportunities in the organization of the college for student voluntary religious activities.

It is our practice during Freshman Week of each year frankly to discuss with incoming freshmen the requirement for attendance on chapel and the underlying reasons. Also in group discussions at any time and in classes where this matter is injected in class discussions, we go over the subject fully with our students. There may be certain individuals who resent this requirement as they resent the major and minor requirements or any other requirement, such as the requirement which we make that they take physical exercises so many hours a week, but the great majority of students see the position of the institution and sympathetically fall in line with it.

There has been no propaganda from the outside touching this matter and it might be that the raising of the issue by some one who held decided convictions against compulsory chapel would change our entire atmosphere as respects this matter. Investigators who visit college campuses have a way of finding what they are looking for. This is because college students are highly suggestible.

The requirement of modern education that students be permitted to initiate, participate in and control educational processes in cooperation with faculty members is, we think, fully met in our arrangement for chapel. Our administrative practice, too, ensures that our chapel service shall be experience-centered, since the problems which come up before the faculty-student committee controlling the service include all the issues of the campus from the standpoint both of student and faculty, interpreted in terms of the highest values inherent in the moral, religious, spiritual view of personal life and of the universe.

W. A. HARPER

ELON COLLEGE,
NORTH CAROLINA

QUOTATIONS

WHY SO MANY STUDENTS FAIL

CRITICS of America's educational system have never been few, even among those engaged in the task of teaching the army of youth. Seldom, however, has there been such agreement among educators as now that too many youths who are attending the high schools are not fitted either by mental equipment or inclination to pursue academic courses and that more vocational schools should be organized to meet their need.

Several weeks ago Dr. Gilbert J. Raynor, principal of the Alexander Hamilton High School, in Brooklyn, set forth this point of view in the following words:

> In this school not more than 50 per cent. of our entering pupils are qualified to do successfully anything that can be honestly called high-school work. Many, probably most of them, are more or less manually minded and would enjoy and succeed in a vocational type of education. Our compulsory education law forces these pupils into our high schools, where they find little that interests them. . . . Their distaste for school leads many into truancy, and truancy is an early step to crime.

Dr. John L. Tildsley, district superintendent in charge of secondary education, in a report dealing primarily with science instruction, declares that one of the chief obstacles to effective science teaching is "the quality of many pupils entering high schools; . . . their lack of mastery of the fundamental processes of arithmetic, which results in a tendency to avoid subjects and processes which require sustained effort and thinking." Like Dr. Raynor, Dr. Tildsley suggests establishment of vocational schools, but he doubts this can be done in the near future.

Another witness in this self-inquiry by the high-school system is Dr. A. Mortimer Clark, principal of the James Madison High School, an institution which has been widely praised for its system of classifying bright, normal and dull students and modifying the curriculum to meet the abilities of each type. But the pupils in the dull section are not making much progress. In the words of Dr. Clark, the percentage of failure among them is "terrific," notwithstanding the fact that "the curriculum has been reduced to a minimum; that classes are small; that teachers especially sympathetic to this type of pupil have been chosen to teach them." Dr. Clark also advocates more vocational schools. In an address before the New York Society for the Experimental Study of Education he said:

> . . . we are in no way equipped to give these boys and girls the training they need. Their crying need is for vocational training. They can be given the type of education that will enable them to live happy, useful and successful lives. We are not giving them that training at all; we have not the means of doing it.

A poll taken among the high-school principals of the city would reveal an overwhelming agreement with the views of Messrs. Raynor, Tildsley and Clark. Why, then, not build more vocational schools at once? Why permit thousands of boys and girls to waste their time in a vain effort to assimilate an academic training?

It is true that the board of education is planning several more vocational schools, but far from enough to meet the need indicated in the remarks quoted herein. The board should not be condemned for apparent blindness to the situation, however. Assuming that half a dozen new, well-equipped vocational schools could be thrown open at the beginning of the next semester, where would the students come from? How many parents would be willing to take their children from academic or commercial high schools and transfer them to schools where they could learn a trade involving wearing of overalls and abandonment of the white collar?

The problem of the high schools—and the colleges—crowded with unwilling or incapable students can not be solved by educators alone. They can but point the way.—*The New York Sun.*

EDUCATIONAL RESEARCH AND STATISTICS

INTELLIGENCE TEST SCORES AND CHOICE OF MAJOR FIELD

The principal problem of this study might be stated as follows: Is there any relationship between the choice of college major and the mental ability of the teacher or prospective teacher as shown by his (or her) score on the Otis self-administering tests of mental ability? The subsidiary problems that are considered are: (1) Age in relation to intelligence test scores; (2) college year and intelligence test scores; (3) a comparison of the group studied with the norm for college students, and (4) an analysis of the variability of the scores for the various groups.

The data for this study were collected from a southern teachers' college supplemented by data on forty-one teachers doing summer school work in a southern liberal arts college. These data were collected by the instructor in charge of various classes in psychology and educational psychology, and all scoring of papers as well as tabulation of the data thereon were done by him. Complete data are available on 331 students, showing age, sex, year in college, major subject and score made on the Otis Self-Administering Tests of Mental Ability. The time limit used was twenty minutes and the scores given are in terms of this time limit. Table I shows the relationship between major subject and intelligence. In this table no consideration is given to age, sex or year in college.

TABLE I

Average Scores for the Various Groups of Major Fields

Group	Otis S.-A. Score	Coefficient of Variability
Psychol., sec. ed. and rel. ed.	49.20 ± .97	19.2
(Psychology alone)	55.5	
Modern and classical language	48.23 ± 1.35	17.5
Science, mathematics, chemistry and physics	46.11 ± 1.31	21.9
Phys. ed. and health	45.97 ± .90	16.4
Social science group	45.89 ± .92	15.8
English and lib. science	43.60 ± .91	22.9
Fine arts, dramatics and music	42.30 ± 1.32	17.26
Primary and elementary ed.	41.15 ± .78	21.65
Agr., home ec. and ind. arts	40.30 ± .86	20.63
Public health nursing	40.00 ± 1.73	20.25

The data are grouped according to the average scores made for the different years in college in Table II. The median score by college students on the Higher Examination with the twenty-minute time limit is forty-one points. With the exception of the first year and special students the mean of this group is above the median for college students. There are data available, however, for only twelve first year

TABLE II

Average Scores by College Year for 345 Subjects Taking the Otis Test

College year	Otis S.-A. Score	Coefficient of Variability
First	39.50 ± 1.86	24.1
Second	45.70 ± .61	15.5
Third	43.18 ± .59	20.6
Fourth	43.36 ± .71	22.8
Graduate students	48.70 ± .69	17.2
Special students	38.07 ± 1.03	14.45

students and thirteen special students. In averaging the scores of all the men and women separately we find that the men average 47.5 ± 6.4, while the women average 44 ± 6.06. However, a comparison of undergraduate men with undergraduate women reduces the difference in the average scores made to 1.1 in favor of the men. The average score for undergraduate students (including specials) is 43.39. This is 2.39 points above the median as given on the norms for college students. An ogive curve of the data shows the group to fall into a normal distribution, and further, the curve follows very closely the curve found from the results of 2,516 college students. Since the plotted curve is constantly above the curve for college students, there is an indication that there is a significant difference between this group and the average.

Certain cautions on the interpretation of these data are very necessary. Since the graduate students have the highest score and since there is a reliable difference between the graduate group and the other group, this factor must be taken into account. The group made up of psychology, education and religious education are in the main graduate students; therefore the scores from this group are not wholly comparable to the scores from the other groups. An analysis of the data at hand shows that this can not account for differences existing elsewhere in the different fields of work. The ten students of Table I in public health nursing comprise ten of the group of thirteen in Table II classified as specials; therefore these two groups comprise almost wholly the same subjects. Seventy-nine per cent. of the graduate students listed are men. The graduate students have a high average score, and this is a factor very important in interpreting the difference found between the average for men and that of the women.

The probable errors of the difference found between the different groups and the graduate group were as follows:

Graduate group with the first year group	1.98
Graduate group with the second year group	.92
Graduate group with the third year group	.91
Graduate group with the fourth year group	.96
Graduate group with specials	1.24

Book[1] makes the following conclusion from a state-wide survey of the seniors of the Indiana high schools: "If the sexes are combined and the groups selecting different favorite subjects are considered as units, foreign language, mathematics and science subjects are regularly preferred by the brightest seniors of the state. English and history occupy a position about midway between the language and science groups on the one hand and the vocation groups on the other." Discarding the psychology and education groups, which are made up mainly of graduate students, one notices a close similarity between the findings of this study and those of Book's. Further conclusions arrived at from this study are:

(1) The graduate group is superior to the other groups of students. The first year class appears inferior to the other classes.[2] There is no reliable difference between the other three classes.

(2) Age bears no reliable relation to mental ability in this study. (See Table III.)

TABLE III

AVERAGE OTIS SCORE BY AGES FOR 333 SUBJECTS

Age	Average score
18	48.38 ± 1.89
19	43.21 ± .98
20	41.23 ± .90
21	45.65 ± 1.04
22	43.20 ± .99
23	46.54 ± 1.23
24	46.56 ± 1.15
25–26	46.33 ± 1.71
27–29	41.13 ± 1.14
30–34	44.48 ± 1.18
35–39	44.27 ± .90
40–44	46.20 ± 1.81
45 and above	40.13 ± 1.20

(3) The undergraduate subjects of this investigation (teachers and prospective teachers) average a few points higher than the median

[1] W. F. Book, "Intelligence of High School Seniors," 1922, p. 146.

[2] One can not say with accuracy to what extent such factors as experience with tests, emotional control and college orientation enter in for the freshman class.

for college students. The graduate students average 7.7 points higher than the norm for college students.

(4) English shows the greatest variability, while social science shows the least.

(5) The variability by college year as shown in Table II shows the first year students the most variable, and the specials least.

K. C. Garrison

North Carolina State College

CORPORAL PUNISHMENT AND SUSPENSION

In connection with the much-discussed trend from government by force or elimination to government by sundry more refined and modern methods, the following objective data from a large city are interesting.

The printed proceedings of the Board of Education of the City of St. Louis have carried for many years quarterly reports of the superintendent of instruction covering the number of cases of corporal punishment and suspension. A compilation of such data at intervals of five years beginning with 1881–82 is shown in Table 1 below.

TABLE 1

Number of Cases of Corporal Punishment and of Suspension, by Five-Year Intervals, 1881–82 to 1924–25

Year	Corporal Punishment	Suspension
1881–1882	4981	353
1886–1887	2975	351
1891–1892	1749	308
1896–1897	1849	342
1901–1902	666	206
1906–1907	719	309
1911–1912	561	272
1916–1917	153	185
1921–1922	82	123
1924–1925	124	145

It will be observed that there was only one case of corporal punishment in 1924–25 to 40 in 1881–82 and there were less than half as many suspensions.

This decrease has taken place in spite of a large gain in enrolment; so in order to show its true proportions a computation is made on the basis of cases per thousand pupils in average daily attendance, and the results set forth in Table 2.

TABLE 2

Cases of Corporal Punishment and of Suspension per Thousand Pupils, by Five-Year Intervals, 1881–82 to 1924–25

Year	Corporal Punishment	Suspension
1881–1882	141.1	10.0
1886–1887	79.6	9.4
1891–1892	40.9	7.2
1896–1897	34.8	6.4
1901–1902	11.4	3.5
1906–1907	11.5	5.3
1911–1912	9.0	4.3
1916–1917	2.1	2.6
1921–1922	1.1	1.7
1924–1925	1.7	2.0

The trend is pronounced through the period, with only two minor interruptions, one between 1901–02 and 1906–07, and the other at the end of the period, and certainly indicates a profound change in method of administration.

Since the data were furnished by quarters, it seemed worth while to consider any possible seasonal variation in iniquity or the control thereof; so the totals by quarters were made and are found in Table 3.

TABLE 3

Total Cases of Corporal Punishment and Suspension by Quarters for the Years Included in Tables 1 and 2

	Quarter 1	Quarter 2	Quarter 3	Quarter 4
Corporal punishment	3970	3577	3588	2727
Suspension	654	769	680	491

It seems that the first quarter is the time of heaviest punishment and the last quarter of the lightest, and that the peak for suspensions comes in the second quarter. The lag in peak of suspensions behind corporal punishment may be due to a tendency to try whipping first, and then suspend if the whipping fails.

H. H. Davis

Ohio State University

SCHOOL AND SOCIETY

EDITED BY J. McKEEN CATTELL

WITH WHICH IS COMBINED THE

EDUCATIONAL REVIEW

EDITED BY WILLIAM McANDREW

Volume XXVIII SATURDAY, NOVEMBER 24, 1928 Number 726

THE UNIVERSITY IN PROSPECT[1]

By Dr. FREDERICK JAMES KELLY

It would be pleasant on this happy occasion to dwell upon the cherished honor which goes along with election to the office of president of the University of Idaho. I deeply appreciate this distinction. This occasion calls, however, rather for a canvass of the heavy responsibilities which likewise go with the office. There has been no time in the history of the American state university when the responsibilities of the president were greater than now. Society is passing through a stage which does not permit state-supported higher institutions to run along serenely, basking in universal public confidence. Higher education has come, in recent years, to face a new challenge and that challenge is adding greatly to the burden of responsibility which the president must assume, who represents on the one hand the faculty and student body, and who represents on the other hand the board of regents and the people whose institution they manage.

Few things in all human history have been more sublime than the faith in public education which has grown up in the American public mind. This faith is still the dominant quality in the great majority of our people. Not only is this faith shown in the unprecedented growth in attendance in all the schools and colleges in the last decades but in the more significant fact that, in ever-increasing numbers, America's children carry their education on through high school and into college. While the increase in the number of children attending elementary schools in this country scarcely kept pace with the growth of population from 1890 to 1926, the increase in high-school enrolments during the same period was more than tenfold, and the increase in college and university enrolments was more than fivefold. In 1890 the average school life of a child was 770 days, whereas in 1926 it was 1,246 days. Even since 1910, the attendance in high schools has more than trebled, while the attendance in colleges and universities has nearly trebled.

Not only has this faith manifested itself in attendance but in the extent of public support as well. From the people's taxes there was paid in 1916 for the education of each child in average daily attendance in the public schools less than forty-five dollars, but by 1926, ten years later, this amount had increased to more than one hundred dollars. The amount spent per child in average daily attendance has increased even faster than the value of the dollar has decreased since 1914. It should not be forgotten, however, that national wealth has increased approximately as fast as school expenditures. Nevertheless, we have so completely staked our faith on edu-

[1] Address delivered on the occasion of the installation of the president of the University of Idaho.

cation that we are willing to strain our resources in order that public schools and colleges should have every chance to solve our perplexing social problems. Perhaps it should be said in passing that possibly we are not straining ourselves to meet educational costs as much as we allow ourselves to think. Not until we spend as much for schools as we do for tobacco will I believe the strain is over severe.

Those who live in intimate touch with college life like to look neither to increasing attendance nor to increasing support for the most compelling evidences of faith in education. We like to look rather to those students who plead for a chance to go to college and to those parents who make truly heroic sacrifices that their children may go to college. To be sure, we have on college campuses, as in every other group of young people, those whom college students themselves have appropriately dubbed lounge lizards and tea hounds, but no one acquainted with the typical American college will gainsay the fact that the bone and sinew of the college group is to be found in students who are as serious to-day as students ever have been and who are living, in many cases, most pathetically in order that they may avail themselves of the opportunities of college study. Letters inquiring about opportunities for self-support which come from students themselves and from their widowed mothers, who in many cases are mortgaging their homes, would indeed touch any heart. One of the most serious handicaps of the University of Idaho to-day is the meagerness of opportunity which its environs afford for self-supporting students. If I were asked to name the way in which a good philanthropist could aid the University of Idaho most I would not urge the gift of a great building nor the gift of a great library, even though the urgency of that need is pressing, but I would suggest instead that the philanthropist might combine his philanthropy with business acumen and establish at Moscow or at Pocatella a great industrial enterprise in which the labor could be performed by students, each job being available to a pair of students, four hours for one and four hours for another. Probably the largest educational loss being sustained by the state of Idaho to-day comes from the inability of a considerable fraction of her young people to secure work to enable them to attend the University.

But this sublime faith of the American people in education is of late years being subjected to severe tests. People are looking about them and seeing that in this nation, which of all the nations of the world is spending by far the most on education and in which more years of attendance are obtained by far larger proportions of her children, we still have the greatest disrespect for law; we still have amazing corruption among our politicians; we still have a larger proportion of the wealth of the country being concentrated in the hands of a smaller and smaller proportion of our people; we still have more crime and less efficient criminal court procedure than in other countries; we still have an increasing proportion of our families breaking down in divorce. These evidences of the failure in this country to bring about the essentials of successful democratic life are giving pause to people who have rested confidently in the assumption that if we but gave education a sufficient chance we could not fail to solve our social problems.

We are entering into a period of the most searching criticism of education, and particularly of higher education, which we have had in this country from its beginning. For one to assume the presidency of a tax-supported institution at this period is a somewhat different responsibility than it was formerly. The university to-day must face a slump in public confidence, a slump due to criticisms not from enemies of education but from the friends of education, who in many cases are saying, "I want to have my faith in education renewed, but as I look about me I find it difficult to defend it on the basis of its present product."

We have sometimes undertaken to console ourselves somewhat with the thought that all these evidences of social instability may be attributed merely to the times through which we are passing and that education can scarcely be charged with responsibility for them. We can not avoid the disquieting realization, however, that education is the agency for which society is paying a tremendous price, in the belief that it will guide social evolution rather than merely reflect what is current in the social mind. Education must build public opinion, not be moulded by it. Education must bring about correction of social ills rather than be content to perpetuate conditions as they are. With this disquieting consciousness I can not close my ears to the barrage of current criticisms of higher education.

In assuming the duties of president of the University of Idaho, then, I feel called upon to examine, with the cooperation of the faculty, the basic philosophy of American higher education. I feel compelled to turn the spotlight of rigid inquiry upon all the traditions and current practices of higher education, no matter how sacred and revered they may be. "Follow the truth" is as valid for educational administration as for the laboratory sciences.

When I undertake to analyze the most thoughtful criticisms of higher education, they appear to fall into three categories. To begin with they seem to me to raise the fundamental question of why the state supports higher education anyway. We have so long taken state support for granted out in this section of the country that perhaps nothing more useful can be done in this address than to bring back to mind those fundamental reasons why in America, in the newer states particularly, higher education has been regarded as a state function, and why, accordingly, these states have created state universities controlled by the state and supported by the people's taxes.

Idaho, in common with a few other states, incorporated in her constitution provisions under which tuition in the state university should for all time be free. The constitution does permit of tuition fees in certain professional schools of the university, but the general purpose of the provision is to make higher education free to the young people of Idaho. This attitude on the part of Idaho's pioneers was but a reflection of their general belief in democracy as a mode of life. Persons were to them persons, born free and equal. They should have a government which would assure them equality of opportunity. They had sought homes in this state as their forefathers had for the most part sought homes on this side of the Atlantic, in order that they might have the benefits of democracy as a mode of life. The countries from which their forefathers came were good countries, but in them children had to choose, or their parents for them, whether they should attend an elementary school at state expense, which would predestine them to a life among the industrial classes, or whether they should attend, at their own expense, a secondary school which would offer them a chance for admission into the universities, and thence into the learned professions or into political or military careers. But in America the same educational system was to be available for all children. Since some needed to go on through the university, then the university should be available to all without any regard to whether the individuals or their families had money to pay for the privilege. The state needed educated people and therefore it was in the state's interest that the children should be educated—and therefore the state should pay the cost.

It must not be forgotten, however, that in America our traditions are not unmixed. Before the time when we had states which recognized the necessity for an educated citizenship for their preservation and development, we had people who harked back to the mother country for their educational traditions. Colleges were established before public schools—colleges patterned essentially after the English colleges, colleges in which boys should pay the major cost of their education. This tradition of privately owned and endowed colleges and universities has persisted during all the time that state-supported universities have had their remarkable growth. It will no doubt be something of a surprise to many of you to know that during the year 1926–27, while the amount of money which was raised in this country from taxation by city, state and federal governments for the support of all universities and colleges was $116,000,000, the amount accruing from private gifts for the support of colleges and universities was $168,000,000, 45 per cent. more. Indeed, the amount raised from taxation was not as great as the amount which students paid in tuition fees in colleges and universities in this country. Furthermore, for every ten youths enrolled in tax-supported universities and colleges, there were eighteen in privately controlled ones. The rate of increase in the amount of money raised from private gifts has been greater in the last half dozen years than has the rate of increase in the amount of money raised from taxation for the support of higher education. It must not be forgotten, therefore, that in this country we are not entirely committed to state-supported higher education as our means of providing educational opportunity for our young people. In fact, the question is being raised more persistently from year to year whether it is not a mistake for the state to maintain institutions which are essentially like the institutions being supported on private foundations. It is said, for example, that if New York state can have the advantage of Columbia University in the city of New York with its upwards of $75,000,000 of endowment, why should it support a state university? If the income from the endowment at Columbia University will pay even half the cost of education, is it not better, say these questioners, for the state of New York to provide scholarships at Columbia to pay the other half of the cost of education for such young people as she thinks it is appropriate for the state to assist in educating?

To bring the question home to people of Idaho, let us suppose that some good philanthropist should create a university, say, at Boise, and endow it with $20,000,000, which would thus provide an income of $1,000,000 per year, enough to pay half the cost of higher education of all the students in the University of Idaho. The State of Idaho would then face this question: "Shall we join with this privately controlled university at Boise and provide scholarships which will pay half the cost while the endowment pays the other half, or shall we maintain the state university which the state controls and appropriate funds for practically the full cost?"

I like to see the question stated in this rather pointed way because until it is so stated we are not likely to get the full force of the issue involved. If education is a state function, maintained for the benefit of the state, not of the individual, then the state can not yield up its control. Just as I do not believe that the state can safely turn over to any agency the education of its children in the grades and high school, in the same way I believe that the state must maintain the control of its higher education.

It is difficult to enter upon a discussion of this question without being accused of casting unmeant and unwarranted aspersions upon the lofty purposes which have actuated donors in making gifts to privately endowed institutions. I have no wish to cast any such aspersions. On the contrary, I believe that gifts have been made in practically all cases with the idea that through higher education money can do more to secure social progress than it can through any other channel. Nothing but the highest motives has actuated donors in the building of great educational endowments. If, however, by these generous gifts we are to be blinded to the fact that for its perpetuation democracy must keep the control of the institutions which determine its philosophies, we may one day find ourselves in the same position as he who of old was charged with selling his soul for a mess of pottage.

In examining such questions we have to keep in mind the inevitable tendencies to disintegration in a democracy. It seems to be man's nature to think of himself as superior to some other group, whether that group differs in color of skin, religion, political faith, economic status or even in the mere accident of place of birth. Class distinctions seem to develop in human consciousness as soon as the need passes for the heroism of pioneering. For the rich to grow richer and the poor to grow poorer, for the ins to stay in and the outs to stay out, for the Republicans to stay Republicans and the Democrats to stay Democrats, is such a powerful tendency in human life that it is necessary to use all available agencies to keep ourselves democratic. Justice is no objective thing which may be defined accurately in a way acceptable to all, but justice is a quality so tinged with a background of human experiences, ideals, loves, hates, fears and ambitions, that what seems just to one seems unjust to another. If the end of democracy is the greatest happiness of the largest number, then anything which removes from the people themselves the control of those agencies, such as universities, which determine those ideals, loves, hates, fears and ambitions, takes away from the people the means of guiding their own destiny.

This must not be understood to imply that teachers in privately endowed universities or the trustees of these endowed universities have any sinister purpose in mind. It merely means that their mind-set, their attitudes toward human equality, liberty and justice, toward democratic modes of life, are the result of their training and environment. The same is of course true of the teachers and the boards of regents in state-supported institutions. The question is merely whether the ideals in these two types of institutions inevitably tend to grow apart; whether the private universities will tend to cater to one class, while the state universities cater to another, thus tending to break down the humanity-wide sympathy and understanding which is the foundation of democratic life; in short, whether democracy will be as safe if it entrusts the training of its future leaders to an institution which is not beholden to the people at large for the educational ideals which it fosters.

It should be said in passing that the experience of state-controlled universities offers many discouraging illustrations of how far we yet have to go before the machinery of government provides for the wishes of the people in the management of the university. Public interest and political interest have been found too often divergent, and it is little wonder that as yet many thoughtful parents prefer to entrust their children, and philanthropists their money, to these stable, adequately supported, privately controlled universities than to the unstable, less well-supported, state-controlled universities which have been so often subjected to the caprice of small-minded politicians.

Without regard to the basic issue between privately endowed universities and state-supported universities, there are two phases of the situation concerning which I have come to have a clear conviction. In the first place, state-supported universities may not safely adopt a lower standard of excellence than that attained in privately endowed universities. If the people of Idaho come to look to privately endowed institutions for excellent training and are content with mediocre training for their sons and daughters who attend the state university the reason for the continuance of the state university will presently vanish. If we accept the principle that excellence of educational opportunity depends upon one's ability to pay for it rather than upon the value to the state in having those young people excellently trained who can return the greatest good to the state in return for that training, we immediately fasten upon future generations a class distinction based upon economic status which will ultimately spell the doom of our cherished democracy.

It is equally clear to me that the state may not safely adopt an educational régime in its state university suited to students of mediocre ability and leave to the privately endowed institutions the educational régime suited to students of superior ability. There is a marked tendency for institutions to group themselves on this basis. One distinguished president of a great endowed institution said not long ago that he believed the universities of the country should classify themselves on the basis of native ability of the students admitted to them and that the privately endowed institutions should serve those of superior ability, leaving to the state institutions the training of those of lesser ability.

Here again the issue is far-reaching. If the state university sets its standards at such a level that students of superior ability will be served less effectively than they will be served in privately endowed institutions then again we place a handicap upon the youth of superior ability who happens not to have financial resources which allow for his attendance at privately endowed institutions. If the time ever comes when society will tend to stratify on the basis of intellectual sheep and goats, one group attending institutions supported by the state and the other group attending institutions supported by private endowment, there again we may foresee the disintegration of democracy.

All this discussion assumes that we in America are still interested in giving democracy a real trial. If, as a matter of fact, we have already concluded that government of the people, for the people and by the people is but a dream and that we may as well recognize social stratification in the interest of those of greater wealth or greater intellectual gifts or greater physical power or greater something else, and that those with lesser gifts are destined to serve the other class in American society then naturally we shall be perfectly willing to see this stratification fostered by such a division in our educational system. For the present it is my own firm conviction that privately endowed institutions and state-supported institutions should be engaged in a common task on a common level for a common group of students. If any other theory ultimately prevails it would seem to me that a state would be compelled by the logic of the situation to close its state university and pay the tuition charge for its students at the privately endowed institutions where they might have the benefit of private endowments.

A second question which is being more and more persistently raised with reference to higher education is frequently put in this fashion, "Are we not educating too many students in college?" Of course there is no categorical answer to such a question. No one knows what proportion of the rising generation should be educated in college. There are certain criteria to determine fairly accurately the number who should be prepared for the law, for medicine, for dentistry, for pharmacy, and the like, but how many should devote the college years to a broadening of their conception of their civic and social obligations, to preparing themselves to enjoy more keenly the delights available for the ever-increasing hours of leisure, to raising the standards of political and industrial life, no one can yet say. How much society can afford to pay for this lengthening effort at liberalizing the mind of youth it is impossible accurately to determine. The test is perhaps actually an educational one. There must be found a way of ascertaining when, in the case of each student, we reach the point of diminishing returns —a place where it should be possible to say that further training of the individual at state expense is economically unsound.

Educational opinion is crystallizing rapidly these days, with reference to this question. With the recent growth and expansion of high schools we now find that much of the work formerly done in college is now done in high school. At the same time the college has maintained itself on a four-year basis above the high school. There is no essential difference in purpose and method between the work done by the high school in languages, sciences, history, and the like, and the work done by the college in the elementary courses in these same fields. Great economies could be effected and the continuity of purpose established if the high school and the college would cooperate more intimately in devising a course of study which unified the work of these two divisions of our educational system. It is becoming common educational opinion that, with such unification, the point of diminishing returns for a considerable number of students would be reached at the end of the first two years of college and that therefore that point should be made a terminal point in college organization. If the junior college is properly dovetailed with the high school, and if the high school and the junior college agree upon the common purpose to be achieved throughout both these units, a considerable fraction of students should be able to acquire the essentials of a liberal training by the end of the junior college period. Even at present scarcely more than 50 per cent. of students who enter college go beyond the sophomore year. But under the present régime they leave the institution thinking of themselves as failures. The course should be so planned that those who are earnest and have the capacity to profit by this amount of general study should leave the institution at the close of two years not as failures but as successes. They should feel charged with the responsibility of carrying forward the idealism and the intellectualism for which the institution stands. The junior college should be for them a finishing institution rather than an institution of beginnings. When it is so regarded, one step will have been taken in answering the question, whether or not too many students are going to college. Only those who are capable of and interested in an entirely different type of intellectual effort would be expected to go forward to those aspects of university work which follow the junior college. When the standards can be so fixed that the university above the junior college will appeal only to those who can profit by an intensive and highly specialized type of study there is no danger that too many students will continue their attendance.

But from this conclusion I would not be understood as believing that too many students are attending college. I am more interested in a certain type of youth who should be in college but who is not than I am in the earlier elimination of those who ultimately prove incapable. There are many young people to-day who, by all the tests known to educational doctors, show every evidence of marked ability. They should be in college, but they are not. The devices for interesting them in college and the means of making their attendance possible mean far more to society than the elimination of the poor college students. Educational guidance, discovering abilities and aptitudes in young people, helping them to fit themselves into the proper niche in life—this is the educational movement of the day with the promise of greatest dividends. With its development we hope to take the next step in answering the question whether too many students are attending college.

A third question put by the friendly critics of the university comes usually in some such form as this: "Are not the superficial things in college crowding out the fundamentals?" Put in other words, are we not in the colleges too tolerant of the loafer, the butterfly, the student interested mainly in the social or athletic activities of the institution; are we not adopting regulations, using artificial incentives and even devising courses suited only to students not interested in the fundamentals of an education?

A perusal of biographies, especially autobiographies, of men who were in college 50 to 75 years ago helps us to realize that youth has been youth for a long time. Evidences are not wanting that college students in days gone by exhibited many frivolous tendencies. There is, however, one difference between the situation as it appears to exist to-day. At that time the university or college limited itself to educational fundamentals. Whatever frivolity and excess of youthful exuberance there were constituted a part of the student life outside of college or university sanction. At present the universities have incorporated within their own jurisdiction practically all the activities of the students. Furthermore, they have reduced many of them to a basis of credits and now enter into a bargain with students to buy their interest in these activities. They have assumed responsibility for student life. Education in the mind of the typical college student is a matter of grades, credits, honor points, and the like. His chief interest is in the click of the cash register which records his educational accomplishments. He is not averse to handing in a spurious coin now and then just so long as it will get by with the cashier. In short, the college to-day operates in such a way as to encourage intellectual frivolity if not actual dishonesty. I have never known youth as a class to fail to respond to high motives, and I am not willing to believe that the resort to artificial and unworthy incentives which characterizes our high-school and college practices to-day is made necessary by the intellectual immaturity of our students.

The loafer and the butterfly types will soon disappear from our colleges if we take the academic side of college life seriously enough ourselves to make it a challenge to the worthiest impulses of youth.

One other phase of the question of fundamentals in college seems to me of utmost importance, although I think it is not so often in the minds of our friendly critics. Undergraduate students are devoting their time to highly differentiated aspects of subjects at the expense of a broad understanding of those studies fundamental to the proper appreciation of our common life and to our continuous intellectual growth. This tendency to spread college courses over the whole field covered by a given department is the result of a conception of education which I think is unsound. Without critical examination of the point involved, we have just fallen into the way of thinking that the school and college years complete one's education. Whatever we believe an educated person should know we suppose must be taught him in school or college.

A moment's reflection will of course serve to dispel that notion. Education is, instead, a life-long process. How well any one of us becomes educated does not depend essentially on how much he comes to know in his school and college years but rather upon how effectively he has come to be imbued with the spirit of study in his school and college years so as to assure his remaining a student throughout life. It is amazing how general the notion seems to be that we study only when we have teachers who require it. Learning is the result of study! Teaching is not a substitute for learning but is only a stimulus to it. Teaching, then, should be confined to those fundamentals which serve best as a basis for subsequent learning. College days should not be wasted upon those highly differentiated aspects of subjects, the mastery of which will naturally follow if genuine intellectual interests are created or stimulated during college years.

This theory seems to me to hold quite as surely in professional curricula as in liberal studies. We may not devote college years to the training of an electrical engineer with the idea that his education is completed when he graduates and that he is accordingly a full-fledged electrical engineer. There must be years of a sort of apprenticeship in enterprises having to do with electrical engineering before the graduate of the college can be safely entrusted with large responsibilities in electrical engineering. All highly differentiated aspects of electrical engineering will be met with in these apprenticeship years, and the real test of whether the successful electrical engineer is in the making in this college graduate is to be found in whether his bases of mathematics and physics and chemistry and those subjects which develop his humanitarian interests and impulses have been so thoroughly mastered that this graduate will continue to grow intellectually and professionally in the midst of these electrical engineering problems. The danger is that he will settle back into some routine phase of electrical engineering which requires but little initiative and intellectual effort on his part.

My answer, therefore, to this third criticism is to acknowledge that colleges have in my judgment departed from their most fundamental purpose in their attempt to finish the job of educating youth. In the University of Idaho this has a very practical significance in that with the relatively small student body the university is called upon, under the plan of extensive differentiation of courses, to offer a large number of subjects each of which is wanted by only a few students. If my contention is correct, it should provide a method whereby, by confining our curricula to the more common and fundamental needs of students, we can avoid somewhat the high cost which inevitably attaches to the former policy. I would not, however, advocate this change on the basis of lower costs if I were not convinced that the change is sound educationally without any regard to the financial question involved.

During this brief address I have raised three questions and have undertaken to make the following answers: First, that the state-supported and state-controlled university is a necessary aspect of the maintenance of our democratic mode of life. While private endowments should be welcomed to aid in this higher educational undertaking it would be disastrous if it turned out that higher institutions under private endowment and higher institutions under state support classified themselves on any basis such as would accentuate the ever-present tendency toward stratification in social life. Second, because our educational system has grown up in several independent units there is at present inadequate coordination among these units and therefore a considerable loss of time. Probably the college should be divided more definitely into lower and upper divisions, the first of which, dovetailing with the high school, should constitute the finishing point for a considerable proportion of students who now enter college and for many who do not now enter. The senior division should be organized with distinctly different purposes and methods and should appeal essentially to those young people with sufficient intellectual gifts to profit by specialization and a large measure of independent study. Third, college practices have shifted the responsibility from the student to the teacher, the emphasis from learning to teaching, with the result that development of fundamental strengths of purpose or of lasting habits of study is rare. Genuine educational motives and worthy incentives must be reestablished. Furthermore, college curricula have developed in practically all lines into very highly differentiated aspects. The undergraduate years of college students have come to be devoted too largely to these at the sacrifice of the more fundamental phases of college work. College is a place to learn how to educate oneself rather than a place in which to be educated.

A SPELLING-BOOK OF THE SIXTEENTH CENTURY

By Professor H. G. GOOD

OHIO STATE UNIVERSITY, COLUMBUS, OHIO

WHEREVER the Renaissance penetrated it stimulated the study of the modern national languages; and when it came into England our vernacular spelling-books began to make their appearance together with the earliest English dictionaries. In the growing elementary schools these became necessary tools and the schoolmasters became active in preparing them; but that Richard Mulcaster (1531–1611) prepared an English spelling-book and strongly urged the preparation of an English dictionary seems to be matter for surprise since he was not the teacher of an elementary school but a classical scholar who owed to his scholarship his appointment as the first headmaster of Merchant Taylor's and later his appointment to the headmastership of the famous St. Paul's School, an institution with which the names of Colet and Lily and the great Erasmus are also connected. Mulcaster's book is entitled "The First Part of the Elementarie which entreateth chefelie of the right writing of our English tung set furth by Richard Mulcaster." It was published "in London by Thomas Vautroullier dwelling in blak-friers by Lud-gate 1582," and dedicated to that "Robert Dudlie, Earle of Leicester," in whose household the poet Spenser had a place. This famous but hitherto inaccessible book has recently been reissued in what is substantially a facsimile of the original; and it seems to deserve far more study by philologists and by historians of literature and of education than it has yet received.[1]

Mulcaster was a writer on education whose vision extended far beyond the book

[1] E. T. Campagnac [Editor], "Mulcaster's Elementarie," Oxford University Press, 1925. The introduction states that there were two printings in 1582, and none since until the present one. The present reissue was printed from a photograph of the Bodleian copy. The editor, Professor Campagnac, of the University of Liverpool, is one of the coeditors of Sadoleto (Oxford, 1916). For a study of Mulcaster's views on education see also R. H. Quick [Editor], "Positions: by Richard Mulcaster," London, 1888. This is a reprint of the edition of 1581.

and the birch. He was able to keep his attention fixed upon the school and the nation at the same time; to interpret his technical knowledge of schoolmastering into the terms of public welfare and policy. He was a patriot as well as a teacher; and he was an Elizabethan writer and scholar. He lived in an expansive age which indeed he helped to bring in, for he was the teacher of Edmund Spenser. His close connection with both humanism and modernism in language and literature is quite clear. His position as a teacher was based upon his scholarship in Greek, Latin and Hebrew. His familiarity with Quintilian and Cicero and the whole tradition for which these names stand appears upon many of his pages. But, in the second place, Mulcaster was an Englishman and was connected with a movement of European extent for the development of native languages and national cultures. He was identified with the forces which were building up a great English nation and a worthy language for the expression of that nation's mind. We will briefly exhibit these two tendencies.

The plan of the "Elementarie" itself may have been influenced by that of the "Institutes of Oratory." Quintilian wrote his book in three parts: one, a treatment of education-at-large; two, a technical treatise on rhetoric and oratory, and three, a work of literary criticism in which he calls the magnificent roll of the great writers of Greece and Rome. Finally, he adds an eloquent concluding section which is filled with general observations upon the work of the orator. The "Elementarie" likewise falls into three divisions and they are strangely parallel to those of Quintilian. The first treats of elementary education in general; the second, of the English language and of the technical rules for the guidance of writers, and the third division is a general table of English words. Finally, corresponding to the section on the work of the orator which concludes the "Institutes" Mulcaster provides a peroration, "wherein manie things are handled, concerning learning in generall, the natur of the English and foren tungs. . . ." Whatever one may think of this parallel, the "Elementarie" on page after page contains the clear evidence that its author was profoundly influenced by the Ciceronian tradition which the rediscovery (1416) of the complete text of Quintilian did so much to foster. Of all ancient writers only Plato is more often directly cited in its pages than is the great Roman teacher whom Mulcaster calls "a Rhetorick master among the Romanes and of no lesse account in his cuntrie than he was of cunning and so estemed of among us."[2]

And he was an enthusiastic worshiper of the English tongue who had at the same time at least some familiarity with French, Italian and German. It would be a strange discovery to find that Mulcaster taught modern foreign languages in his sixteenth-century classical school; but it is certain that Edmund Spenser learned them while he was a student there because in his last year at Merchant Taylor's or immediately afterwards he translated from the French of Du Bellay into English verse; and these poems were published and are included in his "Works."[3] That Mulcaster taught the

[2] "Elementarie," Campagnac edition. *Vide* pp. 9, 10, 14, 18, 20, 23, 25, 45, 188, 251–254, 264 for references to Plato; and pp. 10, 17, 23, 41, 56, 70, 104, 105 for notices of Quintilian.

[3] For two divergent views upon the faithfulness of Spenser's early translations see A. H. Upham, "The French Influence in English Literature," New York, 1908, p. 44; and R. W. Church, "Spenser," New York, 1902, p. 13. Spenser's versions are apparently paraphrases but the decision either way will not much affect the argument in regard to Mulcaster. Dean Church unaccountably says: "It is a curious illustration of the fashionableness of Italian [*sic*] literature in the days of Elizabeth, that a school-boy just leaving

native tongue at Merchant Taylor's rests upon his own affirmation which no one questions;[4] but doubtless he taught it or had it taught mainly to the boys in the preparatory classes and before they entered upon the study of the classical languages. Yet his statement seems to indicate that those upper-form pupils whose English was defective were given opportunity to supplement their inadequate preparation in the mother tongue. Perhaps then it is not after all surprising that he should have busied himself in the preparation of a spelling-book.[5]

For the enrichment of the English language, Mulcaster supported the practice of borrowing from the ancient and modern tongues without, however, relinquishing the right of the borrowers to Anglicize the new words. "For mine own words and the terms that I use," he wrote, "theie be generallie English. And if anie be either an incorporate stranger [= borrowed word], or otherwise translated [= used in an unusual sense], or quite coind a new, I have shaped it as fit for the place, where I use it, as my cunning will give me."[6] He held that both ancient precedent and the judgment of the best modern writers gave Englishmen full warrant "to be bold . . . for either enfranchising the foren [words] or translating our own . . . or else to invent new [ones]" at need.[7] Whether learned from Mulcaster or not Spenser followed this dictum by reviving the archaic words of Chaucer and Langland, introducing foreign terms and incorporating into the "Shepheard's Calendar" the rustic speech of the north of England which was the native region of both Spenser and Mulcaster. Of this practice Ben Jonson complained saying that Spenser "in affecting the Ancients writ no Language."[8] At all events, Mulcaster saw that the English was a growing language, responsive to the needs of his day and people; and this can not be controverted by quoting, as is sometimes done, a single passage, torn from its context, in which he seems to say that the speech of England had reached its acme.[9]

The first fifth of the "Elementarie" deals with the education of children before the age of twelve; the remaining four fifths treat of "the right writing of our English tung," that is, its spelling. "But the ortografie calls me," he says at page 68; and at page 187, just before he introduces the "generall table" of English words, he declares: "It were a thing verie praiseworthie in my opinion, and no lesse profitable then praise worthie, if some one well learned and as laborious a man, wold gather all the words which we use in our English tung, whether naturall or incorporate, out of all professions, as well learned as not, into one dictionarie, and besides the right writing . . . wold open unto us therein, both their naturall force and their proper use; that by his honest travell [labor] we might be as able to judge of our own tung, which we have by rote, as we ar of others, which we learn by rule." Other men also, as we have seen, had felt the same needs and had

Merchant Taylor's should have been so much interested in it." Spenser's later works, of course, disclose a wide knowledge of both Italian and French poetry. W. L. Renwick, "Edmund Spenser, An Essay on Renaissance Poetry," London, 1925, presents the case, perhaps somewhat too strongly, for the influence of Mulcaster upon Spenser's English.

4 "Elementarie," p. 255.

5 *Ibid.*, p. 186. Mulcaster realized that he was out of his proper field ("Mine own course doth carie me quite another waie . . ."), but he tries to justify these efforts in a new department of scholarship.

6 "Elementarie," p. 287.

7 *Ibid.*, p. 287.

8 "Discoveries," edited by G. B. Harrison, London, 1923, p. 70. In the Gifford edition of Jonson's "Works" (1875) the passage is found at IX, p. 194.

9 "Elementarie," pp. 178, 179. This much-quoted passage clearly recognizes the changes taking place in English; and for the rest, it merely expresses Mulcaster's patriotism.

begun to supply them. Mulcaster's book was one of a number that were now appearing.

Our English spelling-books and dictionaries grew out of the glossaries and word-lists of the Middle Ages. These were in the first instances Latin and Greek word collections made by scholars and monastery-teachers for their pupils. The oldest of these collected glosses that contain anything that might be called English (Old English) date from the seventh century. They are the Epinal and Erfurt Glossaries commonly known as EE. The Epinal Glossary is an alphabetic vocabulary of approximately three thousand Latin words and the meanings of these are given in easy Latin or in the English of that time. Bi-lingual glossaries of this sort have been discovered in great numbers and furnish the means of recovering the early history of the English dictionary and other aids to the study of the language. With the Renaissance a great impetus was given to language study; and as already indicated spelling-books and dictionaries now followed each other in rapid succession. A few of each may here be named. Sir Thomas Smith in 1568 issued his "De recta et emendata linguae Anglicae scriptione"; and the following year John Hart wrote "An Orthographie." In 1580 appeared W. Bullokar's "Booke at Large for the Amendment of Orthographie for English Speech"; in 1582, Mulcaster's "Elementarie"; in 1596 Edmund Coote's "The English Scholemaister, teaching . . . distinct readinge and true writinge our English tonge. . . ." This last in three decades went through seventeen editions[10] and yet it has now so completely vanished that copies can hardly be found. Thus we reach the end of the sixteenth century. We may venture further quotations from the title-pages of a very few of the much larger number of seventeenth century spelling-books. Richard Hodges (London, 1649) endeavored to give "the plainest directions for the true-writing of English"; Richard Lloyd (London, 1654) meant to aid the schoolmaster and his pupils "to read and write English dexterously" and Tobias Ellis (London, 1680) announced a practice and a principle which have been much stressed in recent times when he issued "The English School: Containing a Catalogue of all the words in the Bible . . . Together with a brief and compleat table of the most usual and common English words." The practice just mentioned is that of making an exhaustive list of all the words in a book or other body of writing; and the principle is the very simple one that "the most usual and common words" are of wider usefulness than the unusual ones. Indeed this must always have been self-evident to any one who took the pains to think about it. At any rate it was stated by Mulcaster and as far as he was able he followed it. His application lacked precision, for he did not, apparently, count frequencies. It will be noted further that the books which have been listed are of two kinds: those propounding a theory of spelling and those merely providing for its practice and teaching; books of real or attempted scholarship and pedagogical books. Mulcaster's "Elementarie" traverses both of these fields as we shall see in a moment.

The first English dictionary containing only English words also appeared within Mulcaster's lifetime. This seems to have been Robert Cawdrey's "A Table Alphabeticall, conteyning and teaching the true writing, and understanding of hard usual English wordes . . . with the interpretation thereof by plaine English words, gathered for the benefit and helpe of ladies, gentlewomen, or any other unskilfull persons . . . At London, printed by I. R. for Edmund Weaver and are to be sold at his shop at the great north doore of Paules

[10] Otto Jespersen, "A Modern English Grammar on Historical Principles," Heidelberg, 1909, p. 7.

Church: 1604." The gentlewomen and other unskilful persons for whom he wrote must have been very unskilful indeed, for he directs: "If thou be desirous (gentle reader) rightly and readily to understand, and profit by this table and such like, then thou must learn the alphabet, to wit, the order of the letters as they stand, perfectly without book, and where every letter standeth; as (b) neere the beginning, (n) about the middest, and (t) toward the end."[11]

Bi-lingual and tri-lingual dictionaries containing some English are much older than Cawdrey or Mulcaster, going back as we have seen to the seventh century. In the fifteenth century they multiply, for we have remaining a number including the "Promptorium" (c. 1440) and the "Catholicon" (1483). These are extensive collections. And in the sixteenth century there is a flood of such books, Latin-English, French-English, English and Welsh. In the preparation of purely English dictionaries Cawdrey was followed by Bullokar (1616), Cockeram (1623), Blount (1656) and many others from those days to the present. Mulcaster's advice in 1582 was prophetic.

With such scanty philological knowledge or opinion as was available three centuries before Franz Bopp (1791–1867) wrote on comparative grammar, Mulcaster tried to organize English spelling, to provide a body of principles which should guide it,[12] and to supply a list of words to which students and writers might refer. The "Generall Table" consists of rather more than 8,000 English words, arranged alphabetically, with occasional notes and alternate spellings.[13] His aim was to collect the words most frequently used and those which were typical of considerable groups of the common vocabulary.[14] This he succeeded in doing.[15] In the work of a pioneer we must not expect perfection. It is not strange that his own practice does not always square with his table. So he writes "unpossible" in the "Elementarie" (p. 91) but in the table "impossible"; "heall" (p. 95), but in the table "heal." A longer list of similar variations from his own practice might easily be collected. In the "Elementarie," also, he uses a great many words which do not appear in his table: "nedefull" (p. 72); "aspectable" (p. 73); "randon"[16] (p. 91) and "encumbred" (p. 172), for examples. The student may extend and broaden the examination at pleasure.

Such a study as this may suggest the close connection between classical humanism and the modern humanism which expresses itself in our national languages and literatures. With the development of the English Renaissance came a great interest in the English language, in the study of

[11] This title and quotation are taken from Gilbert M. Tucker's "Our Common Speech," New York, 1895; but Cawdrey's work is mentioned in many accounts of the origin of the English dictionary.

[12] "Elementarie," pp. 68–189. Mulcaster says that spelling should be guided by sound, custom, reason and art. He opposes the current efforts among contemporary grammarians to make English phonetic. The principles of his orthography do not differ much from the practice which was used in books or by the educated classes. And as English spelling has varied but little since the sixteenth century most of his forms are similar to those now in use or even identical with them. See also R. E. Zachrisson, "Pronunciation of English Vowels, 1400–1700," Göteborg, 1913, pp. 170 ff; and C. Benndorf, "Die englische Pädagogik im 16ten Jahrhundert," Vienna, 1905, pp. 31–59 and 81–84.

[13] A few variants are: childeren, children, childern; clark, clerk; elephant, elefant, substituting "f" for the Greek "ph"; furnace, furness; perfect, perfit; yet, yit. He generally uses "ie" for final "y." But any extensive study of his spelling would require a long paper.

[14] "Elementarie," pp. 183–185.

[15] See *Educational Research Bulletin*, 8: 273–275, Oct. 3, 1928.

[16] "Randon" is not a printer's error. The Oxford Dictionary has "1591. Shaks. 1. Hen. VI, v, iii, 84, He talks at randon; sure the man is mad."

English in schools and hence in the preparation of English spelling-books and dictionaries. Richard Mulcaster, intelligent conservative, was schooled in the older traditions of more experienced peoples, the French, the Italian and fundamentally the Latin and the Greek. And due to such factors his "Elementarie," now after three and one half centuries reissued, shows that he hewed very close to the direct line of future progress. As a result his list of words is intelligible to the educated man of the twentieth century; and what he says, about language and about general education as well, is worth far more attention than it has yet received, even from students. For those who will pay the price there is information and inspiration in it.

EDUCATIONAL EVENTS

EXAMINATIONS IN ENGLAND

THE British departmental committee on examinations for part-time students was appointed in 1927 "to inquire and report as to the arrangements for the examination of students attending part-time schools under the regulations for further education, with particular reference to the place and value of examinations as an element in training for industrial, commercial and professional activity." Its report has now been published and, according to the journal *Nature,* contains chapters—notably those on the purpose of examinations and the planning and conduct of examinations—which should be read by all teachers. It is said to be of special interest to teachers in technical institutions, since they particularly will be affected by its recommendations.

Briefly, the report recommends a compromise. For some years now there has been a sharp division between supporters of the purely external and of the purely internal systems of examination. Indeed, the controversy which the report is expected to settle may be traced back to 1911, when the Board of Education's Circular 776 withdrew the old science and art examinations and gave freedom to institutions to organize internal examinations, the final certificate of which would be endorsed by the board. But it appears that the scheme has not been widely used, and the weakness would appear to have lain in the fact that many part-time classes are taught by part-time teachers who are sometimes not expert in setting and marking papers. But this was not the only cause of the failure of purely internal examinations. Most part-time students take courses in order to benefit vocationally. They therefore need a certificate of which employers all over Great Britain will recognize the value. The certificate granted by a school as a result of an internal examination does not yet fulfil that condition.

Many teachers have naturally desired to retain the principles of Circular 776, which they regarded as a charter of freedom, and the time will doubtless come when those sound principles will be found generally practicable. In the meantime, the present report sees the value, particularly in their possibilities of counting such important things as laboratory and home work, of internal examinations. But it also sees their present defects, and has decided upon a compromise in the form of modified external examinations. It envisages a system in which they are conducted by unions of local education authorities throughout Great Britain.

THE SCHOOL-LEAVING AGE IN WALES

THE Cardiganshire, Wales, Education Committee has, according to a report in the London *Times Educational Supplement,* agreed that children who have no job in view shall be compelled to stay in school until the age of fifteen years, though they are to be allowed to leave as soon as they obtain work. This leaves an open door which may be used for the exemption of children under fifteen years of age; but it is considered better than nothing, and the acceptance of the principle that children should be kept in school until they reach the age of fifteen years is a considerable advance. The correspondent of the *Supplement* writes:

The next step is to determine the type of education proper for these children. A committee has been considering how far the county can be reorganized on the lines suggested by the Hadow Report. But little has been done. A beginning has been made with the Central School at Lampeter. The chief difficulty, however, as in most rural areas, is the reorganization of the church schools. Cardiganshire, in spite of its past educational record, needs reorganization, and needs also much more expenditure on its educational services than is now granted to it. The new proposals for rural education which are about to be thrown upon the educational market will need expenditure and a much more generous outlook than has hitherto been customary.

Before this can come much patient spade work is necessary even in Cardiganshire. The health of the children in the county is an index to the health of the parents. Yet the death-rate in Cardiganshire can not bear comparison with that in other counties. Much strain is also put upon the children. A high percentage of them have to walk two and three miles to school each day and to remain at school with no more substantial food for dinner than bread and butter with tea to wash it down. The schools also are not generally well maintained. In far too many there is no water supply, in many also the lighting and heating are of the most primitive type. Yet, with these conditions prevalent, physical training does not receive the attention in the county which it should, though the authority has at its doors opportunities of using the staff responsible for physical training at the University College, Aberystwyth. Nor is the provision for the medical inspection of schools very satisfactory. The board of education has recently written to point out that the medical inspection of the children is not complete, even in the routine age groups, that visual defects when discovered have often to wait for a year before treatment is provided, and, what is perhaps even more serious, that there is no adequate scheme of dental treatment in the county. The authority has referred the matter to its finance committee—a committee not usually associated with any desire to spend money on new schemes.

AGRICULTURAL EXTENSION WORKERS UNDER THE CAPPER-KETCHAM ACT

According to an announcement made by C. W. Warburton, director of extension, of the United States Department of Agriculture, during the first four months in which funds under the new Capper-Ketcham Act have been available, 197 new extension workers in agriculture and home economics have been appointed in the 39 states reporting to date.

Thirty-four of these new workers are county agricultural agents in new counties, 43 are assistant county agricultural agents, two are negro county agents, 62 are county home demonstration agents, nine assistants, six negro home agents, 22 men county club agents, 18 women county club agents, and one a state girls' club agent.

The Capper-Ketcham Act, passed at the last session of the Congress, provided $20,000 for each state and the Territory of Hawaii, available on July 1, 1928, for immediate use. It also authorizes a similar sum and an additional $500,000 appropriation to be divided among the states and the Territory of Hawaii each fiscal year following, to be in addition to the extension funds available under the Smith-Lever Cooperative Extension Act of May 8, 1914. In both acts the additional funds provided are to be allotted to the states and Hawaii Territory in the proportion which the rural population of each bears to the total rural population of the United States, provided that each makes a like amount available from state or other sources to be used for the same purposes as the federal funds.

At the time the Capper-Ketcham Act was passed a staff of approximately 5,000 technically trained men and women, including county workers, specialists and administrative workers, were engaged in cooperative extension work. The extension system as contemplated, that is, with a man and a woman agent in each agricultural county, was about half completed, with the agricultural work much in advance of other phases. With the provision in the Capper-Ketcham Act that 80 per cent. of the money appropriated shall be used for the payment of salaries of extension agents in counties and that these agents shall be men and women "in fair and just proportions," it was felt that work with farm boys and girls and farm women would be greatly stimulated, a hope which is apparently to be realized.

Director Warburton believes that "marked progress will unquestionably be made, toward rendering the information of the state agricultural colleges and the department available to every farm man, woman, boy and girl who may desire it."

VISIT TO EUROPE OF THE NATIONAL HIGH-SCHOOL ORCHESTRA

JOSEPH E. MADDY, of the University of Michigan School of Music, chairman of the instrumental affairs committee of the Music Supervisors National Conference, and moving spirit behind the National High-school Orchestra, is engaged in working out the details of a plan whereby an all-American orchestra of possibly one hundred and fifty of the most talented boy and girl musicians in the United States high schools will visit Europe during July or August of 1929. The immediate object of the orchestra's European trip will be to play before the delegates to the World Conference on Education at Geneva and the Anglo-American Music Conference at Lausanne, but it is expected that while the juvenile orchestra is abroad it will also give public concerts in London, Berlin and other large centers.

The invitation to Mr. Maddy to bring the National High-school Orchestra to life again for the international meetings of educators was extended jointly by Percy A. Scholes, of London, and Paul V. Weaver, of the University of North Carolina, respectively the chairmen of the British and American committees in charge of the programs for the Lausanne meeting. Mr. Scholes was in America last spring and heard the National High-school Orchestra play before the Music Supervisors National Conference convention in Chicago and reported that in his opinion it was the finest juvenile orchestra in the world. The coming of the American school orchestra to Europe, he said, would be an event of importance, and he expressed confidence that it would be very warmly received in England and on the continent.

The plan to take the group of American school musicians abroad has the enthusiastic support of Dr. P. P. Claxton, formerly U. S. commissioner of education; Superintendent Randall J. Condon, of Cincinnati, past-president of the Department of Superintendence of the National Education Association; Dr. Howard Hanson, of the Eastman School of Music; George H. Gartlan, director of music of the City of New York; Mabelle Glenn, president of the Music Supervisors National Conference, and many others in the fields of music and education.

The personnel of the orchestra will be between 100 and 150. Within it will be the material for a band and chorus.

In 1926 at Detroit the first National High-school Orchestra of over 200 players gave several concerts under the batons of Mr. Maddy and Ossip Gabrilowitsch, conductor of the Detroit Symphony Orchestra. Similar orchestras of school players from all over the country played in Dallas in 1927 and in Chicago last spring. However, it was felt that more would be accomplished if members of these orchestras could have a longer period of training than was possible by assembling the orchestra for specific occasions. This led to the founding last year of the National High-school Orchestra Summer Camp at Interlochen, Michigan, where 300 of America's most gifted school musicians each year are given the opportunity of eight weeks of intensive training under competent instructors and conductors. Mr. Maddy is the musical director of this camp.

THE ORIGINS OF BUSINESS LEADERS

AN inquiry into the social and economic origins of American business leaders has just been undertaken by Professor F. W. Taussig and C. S. Joslyn, of the Department of Economics at Harvard University. Questionnaires are being sent out this week to 15,000 leading business men throughout the country, in an attempt to secure first-hand information regarding the social classes from which business leaders are recruited, the extent of their education and training, and the circumstances surrounding the early stages in their business careers. The research is being carried out under a grant from the Milton Fund, a foundation which this year is supporting thirty-seven research projects undertaken by various members of the Harvard faculty.

The questionnaire is addressed to the officers, owners and directors of the leading business organizations of the United States. The list of names used in the inquiry has been selected from those given in the recently published Poor's "Register of Directors," the most comprehensive and authoritative source of its kind at present available. The undertaking is being sponsored by an advisory committee composed of Julius H. Barnes, president of the American Chamber of Commerce, James Bell, president of the Washburn-Crosby Company, Walter S. Gifford, president of the American Telephone and Telegraph Company, Alexander Legge, president of the International Harvester Company, Paul M. Warburg, president of the American and Continental Corporation, Clarence Woolley, chairman of the Board of the American Radiator Company, and Owen D. Young, chairman of the Board of the General Electric Company.

The authors of the inquiry, Professor Taussig and Mr. Joslyn, describe it as the first systematic attempt on a large scale to collect data which will have important bearings on the problem of social stratification. They say:

> Every business man has ideas of his own as to why some of his fellows succeed in attaining to high positions in the business world, while others are less fortunate in their achievements, or even fail utterly. Every business man also has opinions as to the relative importance of superior native ability and of superior advantages—such as social position, command of capital, influential connections and higher education—in determining achievement of this kind. And every person, whether in business or out of it, has more or less decided ideas as to the relative importance of heredity and environment, or nature and nurture, in determining social inequalities and in causing the persistence of these inequalities from one generation to another.

From the results of the inquiry the authors hope to be able to speak with greater authority than has hitherto been possible on such disputed questions as the comparative opportunities for advancement in business accorded to members of the various social classes, and whether the tendency in modern business is toward a wider diffusion or a closer restriction of such opportunities. If the investigation now under way proves successful, it will be followed by a supplementary study of similar nature for the professions.

REPORT OF THE TREASURER OF YALE UNIVERSITY

THE annual report of the treasurer of Yale University is devoted in large part to statistics in regard to gifts and pledges made to The Yale Endowment Fund, the campaign for which was completed during the fiscal year ending June 30, 1928. Official and revised figures of this show that a total of $20,993,918.56 was subscribed by over 22,000 contributors, including the alumni, undergraduates and other friends of Yale University. Unique features in regard to the raising of the fund as emphasized in the report are that it was oversubscribed to the extent of almost $1,000,000 within the period originally set for its completion and that, in addition to the subscriptions for endowment made by himself and others, Edward S. Harkness, '97, gave $500,000 to cover the expenses of the campaign which was carried on for two years in every state of the United States and in many foreign countries.

Tables show that of the total pledged for new endowment $4,524,822.94 is in the form of gifts for various schools and departments of the university, $2,105,684.50 in the form of restricted gifts for scholarship, fellowship and research funds and for other special purposes, and $14,363,411.12 for the university's general endowment. Income which will be available from this for each of the schools and departments at the end of the five year period covering subscriptions is indicated in other tables.

In another section, dealing with the work of the Yale Alumni University Fund Association, satisfaction is expressed that the Yale Alumni Fund, "Yale's greatest asset" as it is called, appears to have been strengthened rather than weakened as a result of the two years' campaign for the endowment fund. Figures given in regard to the Alumni Fund show that during the university year 1927–1928, over 7,000 graduates contributed: enabling the Alumni Fund Association to give the university $218,902.34 as income to balance its budget for the year, while at the same time adding $391,114.82 to the principal of the Alumni Fund.

As a result of additions to Yale's endowment funds received during the year, and chiefly in the campaigns mentioned, the total endowment of the university and all its schools has risen from $49,144,159.96 on June 30, 1927, to $58,024,459.36 on June 30, 1928. Of this amount, $32,554,468.47 represents General Endowment, $10,294,476.40 professorship and lectureship funds: and $5,750,811.53 funds for fellowships, scholarships and prizes.

In its investment of these funds the university holds bonds valued at $24,720,503.79, 42.6 per cent. of the total: $7,609,686.25 real estate mortgages, representing 13 per cent.: and holds stocks bought for $16,270,322.95 constituting 28 per cent. of its assets.

Not included in the assets of the university are notes given by students and former students for money borrowed by them to help in meeting the expenses of their college course. The total amount of these outstanding at the end of the year was over $390,000, of which only about $21,000 was overdue. From the Teachers Emergency Loan Fund for the benefit of members of the faculty loans aggregating $243,712.29 have been made to 395 borrowers since the establishment of the fund in 1910.

THE GEORGE WASHINGTON SCHOOL OF GOVERNMENT

THE first formal convocation of the foreign service branch of The George Washington University School of Government will be held Saturday afternoon, November 24. The Assistant Secretary of State, Mr. Nelson T. Johnson, will be the speaker of the occasion, taking as his topic, "The Meaning of Foreign Service."

The convocation is coincident with the annual convention in Washington of the National League of Masonic Clubs, which body, as part of its comprehensive educational program, has undertaken the establishment in The George Washington University of two chairs in foreign service. The convocation will be attended by the delegates to the league conventions as well as by officials of the university and members of the faculty of the School of Government.

Preceding the convocation, a conference of members of the league and university officials will be held. A short history of the development of the foreign service project will be given by DeWitt C. Croissant. Professor Charles E. Hill will give an analysis of the curriculum for foreign service work. C. Walter Young, of the political science department of the university, will tell of the objectives in the teaching of international relations and Richard Norman Owens, professor of accounting and business administration, will speak on "Business Training in its Relationship to Foreign Service."

In selecting The George Washington University as the school in which to establish its foreign service chairs, the National League of Masonic Clubs stated that "The choice is peculiarly appropriate in that the university serves a national purpose, in that it is for the benefit of all the people in the country, and in that it is along the lines indicated by Washington himself, in his last will and testament."

The George Washington University School of Government was established last year through the one million dollar endowment of the supreme Council of the Scottish Rite Masons of the Southern Jurisdiction, as a memorial to "George Washington, the Mason." The resolutions drawn up by the council to accompany the gift called attention to the efforts of George Washington to provide for the maintenance in the national capital of a national institution to aid youth in acquiring knowledge in the theory and fundamentals of politics and government, and stated that after a careful survey of the conditions surrounding The George Washington University, the supreme council had reached the conclusion that it could best promote his ideals and thus hasten the fruition of the desire of George Washington. One million dollars was therefore appropriated out of the funds of the treasury for the establishment of the school.

Students from nineteen states and from the District of Columbia are registered in the School of Government, which opened this autumn.

CHANGES IN THE DEPARTMENT OF EDUCATION OF THE OHIO STATE UNIVERSITY

DR. W. W. CHARTERS, professor of education of the University of Chicago, has become head of the Bureau of Educational Research of the

Ohio State University. Dr. Charters succeeds Dr. B. R. Buckingham, who has accepted a position with Messrs. Ginn and Company and who is lecturing in the graduate school of education at Harvard University. In the department of school administration the following members have been added to the staff: Dr. W. J. Osburn, director of the division of tests and measurements in the Wisconsin State Department of Education; Dr. H. H. Davis, of the division of records and reports in the public school system of St. Louis and Mr. F. L. Simmons, of the Collinwood High School, Cleveland. Dr. Oscar Williams, of the department of school administration of DePauw University, will serve for four consecutive quarters in the position vacated for the year by Dr. C. C. McCracken. Three additions have been made in the department of the principles of education. These are Professors Amy Bronsky, Laura Zirbes and H. F. Seely. Miss Bronsky leaves a professorship at the State Teachers College at Superior, Wis., and Dr. Zirbes has taught at Teachers College, Columbia University, George Washington University, the University of Chicago, the University of Cincinnati and George Peabody Teachers College. Both Miss Bronsky and Dr. Zirbes are specialists in elementary education. Dr. Zirbes has arranged to devote half of her time to the Ohio State Department of Public Instruction. Professor Seely comes to the university from the John Burroughs School, St. Louis. He has for the past five summers offered graduate courses in the teaching of English, Teachers College, Columbia University. At Ohio State University he will direct the supervision of student teachers in English.

EDUCATIONAL NOTES AND NEWS

DR. FRANKLIN WINSLOW JOHNSON, professor of education at Teachers College, Columbia University, has accepted an invitation to succeed the late Dr. Arthur J. Roberts as president of Colby College.

THE RIGHT REVEREND DR. JAMES HUGH RYAN was last week installed as rector of the Catholic University of America. In connection with the ceremonies at the inauguration the doctorate of laws was conferred on President Coolidge.

PRESIDENT EZRA SQUIER TIPPLE, of Drew University, has presented his resignation to take effect upon the election of his successor. While resigning from the presidency, he stated that he had no thought of severing his connection with the institution.

AN Associated Press dispatch reports that George Stuart Gordon, Merton professor of English literature at the University of Oxford since 1922, has been elected president of Magdalen College, Oxford.

DR. FREDERICK C. HICKS, president emeritus of the University of Cincinnati, was elected president of the Association of Urban Universities at the last session of the three-day annual convention held last week at Columbia University. Dr. Hicks succeeds President Frederick B. Robinson, of the College of the City of New York.

DR. M. G. NEALE, dean of the school of education of the University of Missouri, has been elected president of the State Education Association.

ON the occasion of Dean Frederick E. Bolton's retirement from active service as dean of the school of education of the University of Washington, Phi Delta Kappa and Pi Lambda Theta, honorary education societies, gave a joint banquet in his honor and presented him with a testimonial. He still retains his professorship and has been given the title of dean emeritus. Dr. Bolton will continue his teaching and outside lecturing as before.

DR. TORALD SOLLMANN, professor of pharmacology at Western Reserve University, has been appointed dean of the school of medicine. He succeeds Dr. Carl A. Hamann, whose request that he be permitted to resign was regretfully acceded to by the trustees.

NOBEL prizes have been awarded in chemistry for 1927 to Dr. Heinrich Wieland, professor of chemistry in the University of Munich, for his investigations of gall acids, and to Dr. Adolf

Windaus, professor of chemistry in the University of Göttingen, for his study of vitamines. The 1927 prize for literature has been awarded to M. Henri Bergson, the philosopher, and for 1928 to Mme. Sigrid Undset, the Norwegian authoress. As we have already announced, the prize in medicine was awarded to Dr. Charles Nicolle, head of the Pasteur Institute in Tunis, known for his work on typhus fever.

THE Third Order of the Sacred Treasure has been conferred by the Emperor of Japan on Dr. D. W. Larned, for more than fifty years a professor at Doshisha University in Kyoto, in recognition of his meritorious service in the field of education.

PROFESSOR WILLIAM A. NITZE, head of the department of Romance languages of the University of Chicago, has been decorated by France as Chevalier of the Legion of Honor.

DR. MARVIN F. BEESON, formerly director of education in the State Teachers College, San Diego, California, has been appointed associate professor of educational psychology and education at the College of William and Mary in Williamsburg, Virginia.

MISS MARION L. HORTON, principal of the library school of the Los Angeles Public Library for the last ten years, has been appointed supervising instructor of home-study courses in the school of library service, Columbia University.

PROFESSOR GEORGE D. STRAYER and Professor N. L. Engelhardt are acting as educational consultants to State Superintendent R. E. Tidwell and Governor Graves, of Alabama, on the extension of teacher training in that state. In this capacity, they have studied existing institutions and are submitting a report covering the proposed expansion of the work.

DR. EDWARD LEROY SCHAUB, head of the department of philosophy at Northwestern University, will leave in December for India, where he will tour the country and lecture at the universities of Dacca, Calcutta and Lucknow. Later he will study in a European university, returning to his work at the university next September.

FELIX ROTHSCHILD, director of the demonstration schools of the Missouri State Teachers College at Kirksville, has been given nine months' leave of absence which he is spending in study at Teachers College, Columbia University.

PROFESSOR EMIT DUNCAN GRIZZELL is on leave of absence from the University of Pennsylvania and is spending the year in studying English and Continental secondary schools.

DR. HARL R. DOUGLASS, of the University of Oregon, is spending a year's leave of absence as visiting lecturer in secondary education at the University of Pennsylvania.

MISS MARJORIE LOGAN, head of the department of art of Milwaukee-Downer College, has returned to the college from Harvard University, where she has been during the past summer, working as an American Institute of Architects fellow.

PROFESSOR MARY SCOTT SKINKER, of the department of biology of the Pennsylvania College for Women, Pittsburgh, Pennsylvania, is on leave of absence for study during the winter of 1928–1929. During her absence Dr. Anna R. Whiting will substitute as head of the department and professor of biology.

THE trustees of Holderness School, Concord, New Hampshire, have announced that the Reverend Alban Richey, Jr., has been appointed rector, effective on December 1. Dr. Richey is at present rector of St. James's Church, Hyde Park, New York.

WINSLOW S. ANDERSON has been appointed dean of men of Rollins College, and will be associated with President Hamilton Holt in developing the Rollins Conference Plan of Instruction. During the past two years Dean Anderson has visited over two hundred colleges and universities in the United States studying undergraduate problems.

DR. EDWIN R. EMBREE, president of the Julius Rosenwald Fund, announces that the activities of the fund, heretofore chiefly concerned with building negro rural schools, will be extended to include support of medical services for people of moderate means. Dr. Michael M. Davis has been appointed to the executive staff of the fund as director for medical services. As executive officer of the Committee on Dispensary

Development, Dr. Davis was responsible for the organization of the pay clinic of the Cornell University Medical College. In the last few years he has been studying hospital problems for the Rockefeller Foundation. William B. Harrell, now assistant auditor of the University of Chicago, has been appointed secretary and controller, and Clark Foreman, a graduate of the University of Georgia, now with the Phelps-Stokes Fund of New York, has been appointed associate field agent for southern schools and colleges.

THE council of Amherst College held its annual meeting on November 17. Charles E. Kelsey, '84, of Newton Center, was chosen president for the coming year, and the following were elected vice-presidents: James H. Tufts, '84, Chicago, Ill.; Cornelius J. Sullivan, '92, New York City; Sir Herbert B. Ames, '85, Montreal; Frederick A. Allis, '93, was reelected secretary and treasurer. The meeting was addressed by President James Rowland Angell, of Yale University; President Arthur S. Pease, of the college, and Edward T. Estey, '97, Worcester, who completes this year his tenth year of service as alumni trustee.

DR. WALDO G. LELAND, of the department of historical research of the Carnegie Institution of Washington, lectured on November 20 before the institution on "French Sources of American History."

DR. LOUIS I. DUBLIN, of the Metropolitan Life Insurance Company, gave on November 10 a lecture on "Health and Wealth" before the New York Association of Biology Teachers.

ALBERT E. WIGGAM, author of "The New Decalogue of Science" and other books, and E. A. Filene, president of William Filene Sons Company, of Boston, recently gave lectures at the University of Wisconsin.

DR. TRUMAN LEE KELLEY, professor of education at Stanford University, will deliver on December 3 and following days a course of lectures, under the auspices of the graduate school and the department of psychology of the Ohio State University. The subjects of the lectures are as follows: "The Inter-relationship between Method of Research and Field of Investigation," "The Rôle of Judgment in 'Objective Measurement,'" "In What Units shall we Measure Intelligence and Achievement?" "Mental Structure and its Bearing upon Problems of Inheritance and Education," "The Mental Traits of Men of Science."

THE cornerstone of the twelve-story building for Temple University, Philadelphia, was laid on November 14. The ceremonies were opened by Dr. Charles E. Beury, president, and the orator of the day was Dr. Kenneth G. Matheson, president of Drexel Institute. The cornerstone was laid by Dr. Laura H. Carnell, associate president.

DR. THOMAS C. CHAMBERLIN, emeritus professor of geology at the University of Chicago and an original member of the faculty, died on November 15 at the age of eighty-five years.

WILLIAM NORTH RICE, professor emeritus of geology in Wesleyan University, died on November 13, at the age of eighty-three years. Dr. Rice had been three times acting president of the university.

DR. ALEXANDER ZIWET, professor of mathematics, for thirty-seven years a member of the faculty of the University of Michigan, died on November 18, at the age of seventy-five years.

PROFESSOR ALEXANDER W. MAIR, a leading authority on Greek and professor at Edinburgh University, was burned to death in his study at Edinburgh on November 14.

THE REVEREND THOMAS DAVIS ANDERSON, D.D., fellow of Brown University since 1890, and secretary of the Brown Corporation for thirty-four years, died in Providence on November 11, aged seventy-six years.

PROVIDED satisfactory arrangements can be concluded, the annual conference of the American Library Association will be held in Washington, D. C., during the week of May 13, 1929.

THE National Association of Deans and Advisers of Men will meet in Washington under the auspices of George Washington University on April 11, 12, 13, 1929.

To assist in the collection of a fund of $2,-000,000 for the Clarke School for the Deaf at Northampton, Massachusetts, a luncheon was given in Washington, D. C., on November 16. After the luncheon and meeting, Mrs. Coolidge, who was formerly a teacher in the school, entertained the sponsors of the program at the White House. Gifts amounting to $1,000,000 were announced at the luncheon. These include: William Boyce Thompson and family, $135,000; Clarence W. Barron, Earle P. Charlton, Henry L. Doherty and Fred M. Kirby, each $110,000; Andrew W. Mellon, $100,000; Cyrus H. K. Curtis, Edward S. Harkness, William A. Paine, Frank Phillips and John J. Raskob, each $50,000; Clarence Dillon and Arthur Curtiss James, each $25,000; Edwin C. Jameson, George D. Pratt and Herbert L. Pratt, each $20,000; Mr. and Mrs. George F. Fuller, $11,000; Joseph S. Frelinghuysen, Mr. and Mrs. Ernest H. Graham, Robert L. Studley and Albert H. Wiggin, each $10,000; Mrs. Francis A. Kinnicutt and Frank H. Metcalf, each $7,500; Howard Clark Davis, Jeremiah Milbank, the Horace A. Moses Foundation, George F. Naphen and Adolph S. Ochs, each $5,000.

THE dedicatory exercises for the new physics building at the University of Minnesota will be held on Friday, November 30, in conjunction with the November meeting of the American Physical Society. The program opens with an address by Professor Hermann Weyl, of the University of Zürich, on the "Law of Conservation and Rules of Intensity in Quantum Theory." This is followed by a symposium on "Electron Impact Phenomena," in which K. T. Compton will speak on "Electron Scattering"; E. U. Condon and J. R. Oppenheimer on "Quantum Theory of Aperiodic Effects"; F. L. Mohler on "Experiments on Photoionization and Recombination," and Irving Langmuir and Lewi Tonks on "Motion of Positive Ions in Ionized Gases." Following the symposium, members of the Physical Society will be guests of the university at a dinner, and at the dedicatory exercises. The dedicatory address will be given by Dr. John Zeleny, of Yale University, on "The Place of Physics in the Modern World."

SENIORS in the School of Architecture of Cornell University have been housed in the former home of Ezra Cornell, "Forest Park," enabling those men in their last year in architecture to live together in home-like surroundings and in close association with some of their faculty members, thus strengthening the *esprit de corps*. On the ground floor are the common rooms for general daily use, weekly teas and occasional parties. One room is reserved as a guest room for college visitors and out-of-town lecturers. Two faculty members have a suite; there is a single room for another faculty member and a room for the graduate fellow. The second floor includes rooms for about twenty students. These are for the most part very large and many of them have fireplaces. There are also two sleeping porches on this floor. The third floor is given up to a dormitory and a room for two working students. The house is surrounded by a five-acre park and shaded by magnificent trees.

THE Ellen C. Sabin Hall, the science building of Milwaukee-Downer College, which was dedicated last June, is being occupied this fall. The building cost approximately $283,000 and houses the departments of bacteriology, geography, botany, zoology, chemistry, physics and geology; it will have a laboratory of psychology, a crafts shop and some rooms for home economics.

JULIUS ROSENWALD has pledged a contribution not to exceed $5,000 for a period of five years for the purchase of books, periodicals and other scientific publications for the medical library at the University of Chicago, the yearly contribution to match whatever sums are contributed from other sources up to the amount of the pledge.

THE Institute of Mathematics and Applied Mathematics of the University of Paris, dedicated to the memory of Henri Poincaré, was opened on November 1, with ceremonies presided over by Premier Poincaré. The money for building the new institute was provided by Baron Edmond de Rothschild and the International Education Board, which also subscribed $18,000 for the founding of a chair of applied mathematics. The new building contains two lecture halls capable of seating 200, and also 100 students' offices and studies on the ground floor, a library on the second floor and display rooms for astronomical and geometrical models on the third floor.

SPECIAL CORRESPONDENCE

THE NEW PEDAGOGIC INSTITUTE IN PERU

The month of December marks the close of the first year of existence of the National Boys' Pedagogic Institute, formed, by the executive decree of July 2, 1927, from the former Boys' Normal School at Lima, which had previously been functioning for some twenty-three years. The work done this year in the institute is being watched with special interest, for, if it is a success, it is expected that next year the Girls' Normal School of Lima will be transformed into a National Girls' Pedagogic Institute, to be run on similar lines.

The special feature of the new institute is its higher normal section for the preparation of well-equipped teachers for the *colegios* (secondary schools) of the nation. To enter this higher normal section the student must be graduated from the full secondary-school course, requiring five years of study, and must pass an entrance examination.

The four-year course of this section contains two years of general cultural and professional studies, offering the following subjects: Spanish, mathematics, biology, hygiene, anatomy and physiology, physics, chemistry, geography, history, languages (English, French, German or Italian can be selected), psychology, education and general teaching methods, history of education, school and social hygiene, national and comparative school legislation, administration and supervision, and school organization and statistics. During the last two years of work the student specializes in either arts or sciences, according to the subjects he expects to teach, and takes courses in special teaching methods in many of these subjects. According to provisions of the law, primary and secondary training schools, as well as laboratories for child-psychology and a class of sub-normal children, are to be connected with the institute for experimental and practice work.

Besides this advanced section, which grants a diploma of secondary-school teacher of arts or sciences, there are lower and upper grade normal sections training elementary school teachers for the lower and upper grade schools, while upper grade school teachers of special subjects, such as manual training and agriculture, are trained in a one-year special normal course.

As is usually the case in Latin-America, the government is very generous in granting scholarships, and twenty each (one for each province) are provided for the higher normal section and the lower grade normal section, and one hundred scholarships for the upper grade normal section and the special section. These scholarships are given to boarding students at the school, and it is expected that the recipients upon graduation will teach at least several years in the public schools of the nation.

This first year only the following courses are open: The section for upper grade teachers, the primary practice school and the first-year courses of the lower grade normal section and the higher normal section. The institute has now about thirty teachers and one hundred and sixty students, but it is expected that the enrolment will increase next year and that in a few years the full course in each of the sections will be given.

R. S.

Division of Education,
Pan-American Union

DISCUSSION

USING WHAT WE HAVE

It is time to take an inventory of our stock of educational literature. There will be found an abundant supply of unconsumed goods, for there has been extensive production and excessive repetition. Utilization does not keep pace with the issuing of original and worthy writings, to say nothing of the numerous disregarded productions. There is considerable wildcat experimentation written up in bulky and uninviting fashion and frequently without clear or valid conclusions. Something should be done to safeguard the young science of education from the orgies of publication speculation, for the furious zeal of the stock exchange seems to be prevalent among the ambitious authors and the get-famous-quick faddists who fill up the shelves of our educational libraries.

And yet, overproduction is not the most pressing problem relating to educational literature. It is well known that in certain industries—notably coal, copper, petroleum and rubber—there is an occasional disastrous condition of overproduction, but with all the premature and superfluous presentation of studies, dissertations, tracts, articles, bulletins and books, the chief difficulty is not excess subject-matter but indifference and neglect of the most commendable materials. Our mediocre practice of teaching indicates an urgent need for counsel from those in authority, but too little attention is accorded those writings that seem to possess the highest guidance value. There is, however, an enormous capacity in immature and aspiring instructors for consuming attractive, effectively presented educational publications. There is a thirst in young teachers for vicarious professional experience that will transfer in some degree to improved instruction, and there will always be a prominent place for educational writings of superior quality.

Our problem is to see that the candidates for teaching success read the right things and make practical application of the recommendations found in our finest professional publications. It would be easy to be concrete here if space allowed. Either the literature has not been read, or, having been dutifully read, is not in any way linked to the daily life of the school. Our problem, then, seems to be underconsumption or an unintelligent interpretation of the material covered. In certain instances it may be a lack of initiative on the part of the teachers or an absence of opportunity and encouragement by supervisory officers.

There should be no slackening up of genuine research, but there should certainly be a higher standard and a more severe criterion for those who present their material for publication. Our system of education should make it possible and desirable to use what we have and to profit by all the advice of the experts; but too few receive the counsel of those who are truly experts. Individual teachers most in need of solid substance seldom see the very things they need most to study, whereas they are exposed to the lesser compositions that have nothing constructive to offer. Many schools are provided with current journals and the files of the leading educational magazines, but in many known cases these have received only superficial inspection. If the contents of our circulars, journals and books are worth the paper on which they are printed, they are worth a good, thorough reading. There is too seldom any recall or after-reflection with adaptation to personal needs in mind. There is too seldom any stimulating discussion dealing with adoption for school uses. Principals, supervisors and older teachers frequently fail to point out and recommend the better books and most helpful articles. Considerable contact with summer-session students, teachers enrolled in extension and correspondence courses and even the experienced members of seminar groups has revealed a surprising ignorance concerning the educational writings accepted as standard. Unfamiliarity with our foremost source materials, scientific monographs, association yearbooks and government bulletins is all too common. It is equally true that these students respond enthusiastically to suggestions concerning good books to own and the best articles to read. And right here is where our hope resides, especially since beginning teachers are even more susceptible to suggestion and eager to become acquainted with the more reliable writers. When the uninitiated discover the opportunities and privileges they possess to grow through continuous professional study, we shall have less need for shut-in production of educational literature, except that we shall always be compelled to keep raising the publication standards for would-be authors.

Let those who are in positions of authority induce students of education to use what we have to best advantage and to cultivate a taste for only the truly scientific and constructive. Help is needed to differentiate between the writings of quality and the weak work of those who seek chiefly to satisfy their personal desires to break into print. Let us recommend and urge the study of some of the classic authors and the more seasoned books, which have as much value to-day as they had ten or fifteen years ago. We should encourage the conservative adoption of new formulas, doctrines and devices and we should disillusion the neophytes concerning panaceas and pedagogical patent medicines. We should persuade young teachers to practice what they preach on rapid silent reading and the employment of the effective single-reading method, and we should help them to conserve their time and energies for the reflective rereading of the more substantial contributions of the professional press. We need pioneering and exploration on the part of the specialists and experimenters, but selfish exploitation of hobbies and personal passions is not desirable. Writings that are both more scholarly and better composed, both better organized and more effectively edited, will result in a more profitable market; and better judgment in individual and group reading activities will accomplish a needed improvement in the quality of the output. Numerous bibliographies are now of great assistance, some of them annotated and exhaustive. Digests in magazines and in card-index form are helping tremendously—also the book reviews of critically minded men—to raise the level of appreciation and to modify favorably the public demand for professional literature. Every superintendent and building principal should work out for his groups of teachers a program of required and optional reading and make easily accessible the very best publications. To hold teachers to some degree of accountability and to make possible the application of principles and procedures discussed in current journals and text-books in the schools of the country would do much to secure a more complete consumption of our educational goods.

We want no pauses in research and publication, but we do need a speeding up of consumption. More reading and better selection will keep high the quality of our scholarship. There must be a spurt in utilization in order to keep pace with the rapid production, and the practical art of instruction must never lag far in the rear of theory and science. We should diminish the influx and excess of poor material by rejecting everything inferior and unworthy. Teachers are no longer the gullible creatures of fifty years ago. They are older, more scientifically trained, better informed, more widely experienced, and they are not so easily sold and deceived. They seek truth and serviceable advice, and they are learning to discriminate between column-crowding filler and writing with a message. Let us help to encourage a natural demand in the educational market for new supplies of the raw material of professional study. The profession of education will receive a greater degree of respect from the general public if we can succeed in bridging the gap between literary production and schoolroom practice, between the publication of scientific and theoretical studies and the actual and universal practice of legitimate instructional principles. We need assimilation and appreciation of what we have, else the research experts will push their pedagogical pens too far out on the frontier to be of any material assistance to the general run of public-school teachers. Now that we have the technique for scientific experimentation in education, let us not abuse it or treat it as a toy. Now that we have complete press facilities, let us not rush into print every time we think we have made a discovery. Certainly we should not crave the laurel of authorship until we have created something quite exceptional or worked out a technique of supreme importance to the profession. If our progress is to be sure and lasting, we should make haste more slowly; if we are to rise to a truly professional level, we must avoid vain repetitions and empty prattle.

We can illustrate in a fairly virgin field. A large number of experiments have been carried on and scientific studies published in the last few years dealing with the problems of college teaching, and within the last year some excellent bibliographies have appeared. This is an indication that leaders in this field of investigation mean to keep their accounts posted and their books balanced. They mean to get a hearing for their offerings and to seek continuous achievement. They intend to avoid duplication and wasteful enterprise. But this is far from enough. The presence of bibliographies and specially dedicated yearbooks is no proof or promise of improved college teaching. There must be administrative leadership and professional cooperation of the highest sort to place the bibliographies and bulletins in the hands of those who need the counsel. There must be demonstrations of superior instruction in every institution of higher learning, and there will have to be favorable attitudes generated on the part of those who have long remained skeptical concerning acquiring a technique of teaching. The consumption and utilization of the literature on college teaching will have to be widespread if we are to make a genuine contribution to educational progress. The test of educational literature should be: Does it get across? Does it touch the classroom? Does it improve practice? Does it win supporters? Is it widely accepted? Has the circulation phase failed to keep up with the production end? Are we neglecting to use what we have? If so, then here is a feature of our educational program that will require some attention.

CARROLL D. CHAMPLIN
PENNSYLVANIA STATE COLLEGE,
STATE COLLEGE, PENNSYLVANIA

QUOTATIONS

THE HARVARD RESIDENCE HALL

THREE million dollars could not be better spent than for the work to which President Lowell now proposes to use this fund. Harvard has become a vast university full of educational opportunities unknown in Cambridge a century ago. And yet, with all the rich gains of growth, inevitably there has occurred a certain loss. Values which Harvard men of thirty and more years ago highly treasured have become less and less easily accessible to the undergraduate body. The intimacy of relationship possible in a college having only a few hundred students becomes in many ways impossible in a college having an enrolment numbered in thousands. Now President Lowell would provide means to recover some of the earlier values, while losing nothing of the new. He would build up one "house" at Harvard where not more than 250 or 300 men from the sophomore, junior and senior classes may live together during three consecutive years. Thus, within the university, they would find themselves members of a group reduced to comfortably human scale, in which there may well arise universal acquaintance among all members, and where the contacts which support friendship will not be broken each year by enforced changes of residence from one part of the campus to another.

In all this it is clear, however, that President Lowell is more moved by an educational ideal than by any purely social purpose. He conceives of the new "residential group or house" as a place where "students capable of strong scholarly interest and achievement" may be "associated with members of the instructing staff, including their tutors, and if possible with research fellows in different lines of work." Surely there is need in our colleges to-day to make special arrangements which will promote, in every way possible, the interest of the most serious-minded members of the undergraduate body, and to advance their possibilities of scholarly attainment. The existence of this need is a direct result of the vast increase of enrolments which our colleges have experienced since the war. Where once the young Americans who "went to college" were a comparatively homogeneous group, to-day the entrants into our colleges are of extremely varied types, coming from all sorts and types of homes, with differing cultural backgrounds.

But the outstanding merit of President Lowell's new experiment is that it seems so planned that whatever good it may accomplish will be pure gain, without an accompanying loss. No one can say that the proposed new "house" will in any way operate to the damage of Harvard University as now constituted. A complete reorganization of Harvard upon this new residential plan inevitably would have done violence to many existing values and merits. But the development of the single "house" will work no harm, and has the promise of large good.—*The Boston Transcript.*

CAN the great American university regain the benefits of close social contacts enjoyed by the small college and at the same time retain the advantages of its own superior facilities? A $3,000,000 experiment is being undertaken by Harvard University to answer this question. It involves perhaps the nearest approach to the English college system yet undertaken in the United States. As explained by A. Lawrence Lowell, president of Harvard, the plan, which is financed by an anonymous gift, contemplates the establishment of a "hall" or "house" accommodating from 200 to 300 students. Much more than a dormitory, such a unit will provide a dining hall and clubroom and living quarters for its own dean and staff of tutors.

While constituting, in one sense, a college within a college, the proposed house will be only the center, not the circumference, of its members' associations. They will attend university lectures, retain membership in clubs, and participate in athletics and other student activities. Moreover, they will be drawn from all strata of the student body; such mixing of varied interests is expected to prove one of the plan's major benefits. Already, by relaxation of rules enforcing attendance at lectures and by development of its tutorial system, Harvard has gone a long way toward helping the student to recognize a responsibility he must in any case ultimately accept—that of educating himself. This experiment, it is hoped, will be the capstone of that program.

Increasingly recognition is being given to the fact that the mechanics of education can be overemphasized. Providing fine equipment and talented instructors does not suffice if the student refuses to make full use of them. Some current educational efforts are assigning a larger rôle to the human factor. President Garfield is credited with saying that a log with a teacher on one end and a pupil on the other might be a university.

Any one who has watched the Oxford or Cambridge system in operation will hope that more than one such unit will be tried before judgment is rendered. In England, rivalry between colleges within the university, both in sports and studies, adds greatly to the value of the system. As Dr. Lowell recognizes, much will depend on the wisdom with which the Harvard venture is conducted. It might be unwise to make an undergraduate in the United States pay a fine for being outside the college walls after 10 p. m., or to print the rules governing his conduct in Latin.

But if a genuine community of scholarship can be built up, if the power known as "college spirit" in its better manifestations can be developed, if the sense of mutual responsibility which puts a moral compulsion on the slacker student can be attained, if pupils can discover that tutors are also worthy opponents at tennis and fine hosts at breakfast, if athletics can find that esthetics sometimes makes good friends, if there can be high talk in friends' rooms after dinner of politics, religion and literature—if those things can be, the "house" will prove an intellectual and social home—a veritable alma mater—and the experiment a success.—*The Christian Science Monitor*.

REPORTS

DEBATING IN OUR HIGH SCHOOLS

DURING the early summer a questionnaire was mailed to the extension division or some other agency in all the states of the union. This was designed to study the organization, popularity and results of debating in the high schools. Detailed replies—in many cases accompanied by other documentary evidence—have been received from Arkansas, Colorado, Georgia, Kansas, Kentucky, Louisiana, Michigan, Minnesota, Nebraska, New Jersey, North Carolina, North Dakota, Ohio, Oklahoma, Rhode Island, South Dakota, Tennessee, Texas, Utah, Virginia, Vermont, Washington, West Virginia and Wisconsin. Several other states are known to have no formal organization fostering high-school debating. The results obtained, coming from states in all parts of the union, may therefore be said to be fairly inclusive of the chief methods used in high-school debating. Three or four of the questions of the original list have been eliminated as being of no great public interest. For the sake of clearness, the others have been repeated in brief form, followed in each case by a statement of the results, with some additional comment when this seems significant or typical of all. In a few instances there is some overlapping, as in question two, where the results show that no single type of question is favored, but two or three are mentioned in a certain reply. Each is counted in the results.

(1) "What organization fosters high-school debating in your state?" Extension divisions in thirteen states organize the high schools into various groups or districts, in five cases with the assistance of some state organization of teachers; in five states independent societies or

institutions manage the debates; in four states the English or speech departments; in two states no general organization exists. Most have a high-school debate league or association, with headquarters at the state university, and with officers chosen in part from the high schools participating.

(2) "What types of questions have proved most suitable for debates?" Seven mention political topics; four, those "of national interest"; five, economic; three, social; and only two, topics of local or distinctly state interest. Four complain that subjects are often chosen that are too technical or difficult for high-school students.

(3) "Are the propositions for debate chosen by a single person, a committee, or by vote of the participating schools?" Seven report that the committee of officers chooses the propositions for debate; four, a committee of high-school teachers; eight report a referendum by the participating schools; two report action by an individual. In four cases the schools submit the subjects, and the committee chooses from the entire group so collected; in eight instances the committee submits the subjects, and the schools, by majority vote, pick from that list sent them.

(4) "How is the championship of the state determined?" In eighteen states there is some type of elimination contest by districts, counties or conferences, and then the winners proceed to some central point, usually to the state university, for a final championship tournament. One state has a tournament open to all high schools; one arranges for district championships only; one has both district and "conference" contests; one allows any team that wins both sides to appear in the final tournament at some central point.

(5) "What special methods have been used to increase the interest in debating among high-school students themselves?" In eight different states rewards in the nature of prizes, wall plaques or debate certificates are offered; in six, unusual newspaper publicity tends to attract debaters, and one reply mentions that debating attracts interest similar to that in athletic contests; two states send intercollegiate debaters out to talk before high-school audiences; five emphasize radio talks by the secretary of the state league; and four mention enlisting the sympathy and cooperation of school officials. Four recall the difficulties in gaining the financial support of school boards.

(6) "What was the approximate size of the audiences at the championship contests last year?" Of the specific replies to this query, the numbers mentioned are given in order: 200, 4,000 (in Michigan for 1928, increased by 500 over the 1927 audience), 300–500, 300, 1,000, 600, 200, 400, 300, 400, 100, 400. These figures tend to show that debating still draws fair-sized crowds. Inasmuch as most of the championship teams appeared before audiences away from home, it seems that a considerable number of the persons who heard debates were attracted not by friendship for the speakers, but by interest in the debates as contests or in the subjects discussed. Four replies mention that public interest in debate is small, but seven note a gradual increase from year to year.

(7) "Was admission charged for the championship contests?" Negative replies, thirteen; affirmative, five; occasionally, three; not specified, three.

(8) "From what class, group or occupation do you select judges most often?" Professional men in general are mentioned the greatest number of times, eight; more definitely, teachers are named five times; debate coaches, three; college professors, five; lawyers, six; student intercollegiate debaters, three; and clergymen, two. Two replies specify that judges are usually chosen from among those who have had collegiate experience in debating.

(9) "Do you use the single, critic judge in any debates?" Yes, fourteen, including four that use no other type; no, three; will change to single-judge plan, three; use single-judge seldom, one; indefinite replies, four. Despite the apparent trend toward the use of one judge who is known to be well qualified by experience, the greater majority of states still use most often the three-judge plan of decision.

(10) "Comment on any notable successes or failures in the judging systems that you have been using." Five mention that their plans are working well, but seven express general or specific dissatisfaction with some form or all forms of judging; four use only expert judges in state contests; North Dakota has, for two

years, used successfully seven judges in the championship debate. No special comment is found in six replies. Some difficulties are found in getting judges to travel long distances, especially in cold weather; in getting school boards to finance debating or pay the travel expenses of judges; in getting persons comparatively free from bias. Some of the unfavorable comments are here quoted.

Any debate brings discussion as to the merits and demerits of judges. 'Tis hard to lose, you know.

People are willing to judge and want to judge honestly but they can not.

Under three-judge system, the home team won too often.

Any of the systems causes trouble.

Judges often don't know what debating is. Wouldn't recognize it if they saw it.

Fails in that no one can be sure that students present original material in the main speeches.

Failures are due to the use of prominent men who do not know debating.

We had some trouble with certain persons interested in one valley or section rather than in the best debaters.

(11) "If anything except the most simple rules are given to guide the judges, will they carry out the directions faithfully?" Only fourteen replies were received to this question. Seven said in effect that judges will not follow rules carefully; one stated that they will try to do so; one said that they will observe directions sometimes; two thought the judging satisfactory; three criticized some form of judging. No reply advocated more than very simple rules for judges. Some of the comments further elucidate the opinions of the authors of the replies to the questionnaire. The most significant ones are quoted.

No. Squabbles result if detailed instructions are given.

I believe in no rules. Judges are intelligent enough to vote fairly and honestly.

Next year we hope to place a copy of the State League Constitution in the hands of the judges at least five days before a debate.

General regulations are given judges, but the decision is based largely on their private opinions.

If they are competent judges, they do not need rules; if they are incompetent, they can not understand rules.

One may not be wholly justified in generalizing from the replies to these questions. They seem to show the trend, however, in several directions. Subjects seem to be chosen from among broad, national topics of the times rather than from local or sectional ones. More than half the states of the Union have definitely organized debating in the high schools, and in nearly every instance there is provision for a state tournament or some similar means of determining the best school debate in a given season. Judging still is a sore point in more than one state, with the tendency in favor of having one or a few expert judges. Finally, so far as public interest goes, most of the states seem to be holding their own. Whether the high-school debaters are making much of an impression on their home communities can hardly be determined. Yet, out of the hundreds of debates on the McNary-Haugen Bill or on the Curtis-Reed Bill or some other national education measure, undoubtedly there has been no little sublimation of popular opinion.

H. Adelbert White
University of Nebraska

EDUCATIONAL RESEARCH AND STATISTICS

THE PROGNOSTIC VALUE OF GENERAL LANGUAGE

Reported observation and practical experience, though always valuable, are never as convincing as impersonal proof. From the scientific standpoint, the recent literature on the prognostic value of general language has been founded far too much on subjective opinion, and entirely too little on objective fact. It is largely to furnish a more scientific basis for intelligent discussion that the following comparative study of the relationship between pupil achievement in general language and foreign language is presented.

The data of the investigation are the final grades earned in general language by 186 pupils of the Woodrow Wilson Junior High School,[1] San Diego, California, during the fall term, 1927, and the end-semester marks received by the same students in the first half year of Spanish, French and Latin during the spring term, 1928. For the purpose of correlation, all grades were translated into point-score equivalents on the basis of their standard deviation distances on the linear scale of the normal frequency curve.[2]

The measures of central tendency and dispersion for the grades in general language are summarized in Table 1. It is worthy of note

TABLE 1

MEASURES OF CENTRAL TENDENCY AND VARIABILITY FOR GRADES IN GENERAL LANGUAGE

Measures	Boys	Girls	Total
Number of Cases	78	108	186
Range	7	7	7
Mean	7.782	8.148	8.160
P. E. of Mean	±.014	±.096	±.101
Pearson C. of V.	23.618	18.232	24.963
Percentile 10	4.867	6.253	6.100
Quartile 1	6.420	6.940	6.570
Median	8.172	8.333	8.263
Quartile 3	8.840	8.860	8.840
Percentile 90	11.480	11.460	11.450
10–90 Range	6.613	5.207	5.350
Quartile Deviation	1.210	.960	1.135
Standard Deviation	1.838	1.486	2.037

that the girls slightly excel the boys in achievement. Judged from the larger values of the measures of spread, the work of the masculine sex is somewhat more irregular than that of the feminine. This circumstance possibly indicates that interest in foreign languages is relatively more variable among boys than among girls.

TABLE 2

MEASURES OF CENTRAL TENDENCY AND VARIABILITY FOR GRADES IN FOREIGN LANGUAGE; VIZ., FRENCH, LATIN, SPANISH

Measures	Boys	Girls	Total
Number of Cases	78	108	186
Range	10	10	10
Mean	6.731	7.037	6.673
P. E. of Mean	±.191	±.158	±.139
Pearson C. of V.	37.218	34.645	41.931
Percentile 10	1.700	4.810	3.250
Quartile 1	4.300	4.810	4.560
Median	6.250	6.607	6.488
Quartile 3	8.470	8.750	8.610
Percentile 90	11.290	11.230	11.119
10–90 Range	9.590	6.420	7.869
Quartile Deviation	2.085	1.970	2.025
Standard Deviation	2.505	2.438	2.798

Practically the same situation is revealed by the distribution of foreign language grades in Table 2. Attention, however, should here be called to the fact that the boys in the ninetieth percentile not only equal, but even surpass the girls. To the extent to which this difference is reliable, the data tend to show that the better male students occasionally excel even the best pupils of the opposite sex.

Of greater significance is the appreciably

TABLE 3

MEASURES OF RELATIONSHIP AND LACK OF RELATIONSHIP BETWEEN GENERAL LANGUAGE AND FOREIGN LANGUAGE GRADES

Measures	Boys	Girls	Total
Number of Cases	78	108	186
Pearson r	.486	.369	.442
P. E. of r	±.058	±.056	±.0399
Coefficient of Alienation	.874	.928	.897

higher correlation reported in Table 3 for the masculine than for the feminine group. If the comparison had been between intelligence quotients and grade-point averages rather than between two independent distributions of teachers' marks, this difference might easily mean that the boys work up to capacity more than the girls. In the present case, the explanation ob-

[1] For a description of the general language course offered for two years to nearly 1,400 pupils in the seventh and eighth grades of the Woodrow Wilson Junior High School see W. Kaulfers, "Observations on the Question of General Language," *School Review,* 36: 275–283. 1928.

[2] A detailed account of this method has been given by the writer in his discussion, "Prognostic Value of the I.Q. in Spanish," chapter II, Stanford University thesis, 1928.

viously can not hold. Substantial correlations are just as apt to be registered by pupils doing consistently poor work as by students performing uniformly good work. A coefficient of correlation does not in itself indicate whether lack of perfect agreement is attributable to superior or to inferior achievement in one subject as compared with another. Some indication of the general trend of discrepancy is necessary before a satisfactory explanation can be given.

TABLE 4

Comparison of Grades in General Language with Grades of the Same Pupils in First Semester Foreign Language

Comparison	Boys		Girls		Total	
	Number	Per cent.	Number	Per cent.	Number	Per cent.
Grades same in both cases	20	25.7	29	26.8	49	26.3
Grades higher in general language	48	61.5	61	56.5	109	58.6
Grades lower in general language	10	12.8	18	16.7	28	15.1
Total	78	100.0	108	100.0	186	100.0

A practical solution is offered in Table 4. The number of boys earning the same marks in general language as in French, Latin or Spanish is apparently only 1.1 per cent. less than for the girls. The proportion receiving lower grades in foreign language than in general language, however, is 5.0 per cent. greater, and the number receiving higher grades is 3.9 per cent. lower, than the corresponding ratios for the feminine sex. Thus it seems that *the girls do better in the regular courses than in the exploratory-tryout classes, and that the boys in general do worse.* The less substantial correlation obtained for the girls is apparently attributable to the fact that the group as a whole tends to improve, while the male students either continue as before or achieve on a lower level. The lack of high correlation for the total distribution is primarily due to the tendency among the great majority of the students to fare better in the tryout courses than in the regular language classes. These trends are of more than incidental significance, since it is always important in making predictions from past performance to know whether a pupil is likely to achieve on a higher or lower level in his prospective work than in his previous occupation.

From the standpoint of predictive validity, the correlations are none too substantial. Prognoses of probable success from the coefficients would not be over 7.2 per cent. better than random guesses for the girls, and scarcely 12.6 per cent. better for the boys. This degree of accuracy is certainly too low to warrant the unqualified employment of the measures in pupil guidance. At best they can be used with safety only in classifying pupils into roughly homogeneous groups. It is indeed doubtful if a particular student should ever be directed with respect to the choice or avoidance of foreign language work on the basis of his grade in general language alone. For a girl, the probabilities are that she will do better; for a boy, that he will do worse; but in no case is the correlation sufficiently high to ensure accurate prognosis.

Compared with the findings for a large number of students reported by the writer in another connection,[3] the correlations indicate that *teachers' marks in general language are no more certain predictive measures for foreign language than ordinary intelligence quotients, and appreciably less accurate than simple grades in English.* Thus the general language work can scarcely be justified on its exploratory-guidance merits. Indeed, the very theory of the course, in so far as it assumes the existence of a so-called "language talent" or "linguistic aptitude," seems, in the light of recent investigations,[4] to rest upon an exceedingly precarious foundation. It is partly for these reasons and partly because the course did not yield generally satisfactory results, even after a fair trial of more than two years under very favorable conditions, that the work was recently discontinued in the Woodrow Wilson Junior High School and throughout the city schools of San Diego.

Walter Kaulfers

Stanford University

[3] *Ibid.*, chapters X and XI.

[4] See John W. Todd, "Is there a Language Talent?" *The Modern Languages Forum*, 13: 7–10. 1928.

SCHOOL AND SOCIETY

EDITED BY J. McKEEN CATTELL
WITH WHICH IS COMBINED THE

EDUCATIONAL REVIEW

EDITED BY WILLIAM McANDREW

Volume XXVIII | SATURDAY, DECEMBER 1, 1928 | Number 727

POLITICAL EDUCATION IN RUSSIA

By Professor THOMAS WOODY
UNIVERSITY OF PENNSYLVANIA

A COMPARATIVE study convinces that so far as educational principle and practice in political education is concerned, Soviet Russia offers no great contrast to Prussia (before the war), Italy and other more or less autocratic states of the west, of past and present time. The difference lies in the content of the teaching; and the Workers' Republic is being more systematic than others. She follows, nevertheless, a precedent long established, and as the less autocratic states grow more autocratic the divergence between them and Soviet Russia decreases. A close and perhaps in some respects a closer parallel exists between the Soviet system of political preparation and the catechumenal stages—*audientes, genuflectentes* and *electi*—whereby early devotees of Christianity became full-fledged members of the church. The purposes of both were and are to form belief, impress the need for loyalty, establish habits and give a certain amount of information about the work and purpose their members are to do and serve.

The *raison d'être* of strict and thorough indoctrination in the field of social science is found in these facts: a new régime has replaced the old, not by gradual transition and evolution, but by revolution; any new régime, and especially a quite radical one, is for the time being, at least, on the defensive; besides, the new régime professes motives, holds notions, that were long suppressed and which it hopes to make permanent. Indoctrination is at once its defense, building strong the walls against the well-known old foes within and those without; little support can be expected from aged disciples, but the young are ready, pliant, strong. The way is clear, the means well known, and every "advanced" nation uses them to-day, whether avowedly or not.

"School must be life" is a dictum accepted generally by educational leaders in Russia; and political life can not be separated from the rest of it and excluded from school. "Our task in the school world," said Lenin, "is to overthrow the bourgeoisie and we declare openly that the school apart from life, apart from politics, is a lie and a hypocrisy."[1] In other countries, he pointed out, cultural education apart from political life had been an ideal, but one which, he averred, was not honestly adhered to. This idea of non-political or neutral education is but a hypocrisy of the bourgeoisie—a means of duping the masses. "In all the bourgeois states, the bonds which unite politics to education are very slender; but if bourgeois society does not recognize it, it does, nevertheless, educate the masses by means of the church and by means of all the organizations which rest on private property."

Lunacharsky, Shatsky, Pistrak, Krupskaya—in fact, all leading educators of Rus-

[1] First Educational Congress, August 25, 1918.

sia—believe in the necessity of political education. Of more import than that is the fact that it is practiced everywhere in Russia to-day. It begins in earliest youth for those who go to school or preschool institutions and is likewise provided for adults whose education has been neglected. "The entire work [in the pre-school institutions] is carried on in the mother tongue and has as its purpose the development of a materialistic conception of the world, creative activity and collectivistic habits of life." A similar purpose, though stated variously, is found in all Russian schools. The Unified Labor School aims at "the education of children in the ideas of collectivism, that they may be accustomed to live, learn and work collectively."

This purposeful political and social education upon which the Soviet Union has so frankly embarked is to be classified generally under three heads: first, mass educational institutions, such as the multifarious clubs, "red corners," village reading rooms, libraries, correspondence courses and circles for self-instruction; second, schools and courses for adult workers; and third, the political and social education of the regular schools. But in addition to regular instruction in these institutions, a work that is perhaps even more important is carried on in the organizations of the *Octabrists,* young *Pioneers* and *Komsomols.* To the foundations laid in the lives of Octabrists and Pioneers we shall give attention later.

The simplest and, according to my observation, the most usual form of club is the "red corner"—a Lenin shrine. Books, pamphlets, posters, decorations in red, mottoes and a bust of Lenin constitute the usual layout. In one Revolutionary museum the "red corner" was a reproduction of Lenin's tomb. These "red corners" are found everywhere, in factories, schools, libraries, museums, nurseries. Clubs of more elaborate nature pursue a variety of activities through "circles" organized to meet the special interests of individuals. As a rule about half of the "circles" are concerned with dramatics, art, music, chess, radio and the like; 19 per cent. are political, 8 per cent. vocational, 5 per cent. are concerned with workers' correspondence, 6 per cent. with scientific and about 8 per cent. with anti-religious interests. But if interests seem varied, the political end is never lost sight of. The clubs seek always to unite satisfaction of individual demands for entertainment and refreshment with political education. Figures given by the Commissariat of Education show 3,861 clubs operating in cities in 1927–28. Typical activities of clubs are shown by the average of one hundred clubs reported for the month of December in 1925: six evenings devoted to vocations, twenty-eight devoted to questions and discussions, 791 to cinemas, 261 to theatricals, 108 to concerts, 304 to lectures, eighty-seven to the "living newspaper," five to entertainments, thirty-four to representations of justice and forty to excursions.

In the country villages and towns the chief cultural and social center is the village reading room; but here, too, may be found more elaborate clubs and the simple "red corner." In 1926–27, there were 20,049 red corners, 1,275 clubs and 14,229 reading rooms in the villages. The reading room generally has a wall newspaper, and organizes clubs with scientific, political and agricultural interests besides its regular work as library. The purpose is to acquaint properly the peasants and small villages with the principles of Communism and the work of the Soviet government, bringing them to cooperate in socialistic upbuilding by raising the level of their political and general education. Specifically, this means, among other things, liquidation of illiteracy, aid in self-education, study and explanation of current events abroad and in the U. S. S. R., carrying on propaganda for the improvement of local agriculture and sanitation and warfare against superstitious practices and beliefs. Their work is at all times linked carefully with practical everyday needs of the local peasantry.

Apart from libraries connected with clubs and village reading rooms there is a large number of independent libraries which play a leading part in the political and social education of the locality by recommending worth-while books, organizing study circles, giving information, and so on. Some of these have reading rooms, others not. Some are stationary; others, because of the desire to use to the fullest the available supply of books, are migratory, securing their supply of books from the larger centers. There were, in 1926, 13,263 stationary and, in the country alone, 25,579 moving libraries, the latter sort having doubled in number each year of the preceding three. Stationary libraries had 34,507,065 titles and an average of 286 readers. Comparative figures on the kinds of books read before the revolution and since show a marked increase in the fields of history, sociology, mathematics, natural science and applied sciences; while there is a decline of interest in philosophy and *belles lettres*.

Very recently there has been an enormous increase in correspondence courses and self-instruction circles in connection with libraries, reading rooms and clubs, which play an important part both in general and vocational education of the citizen of New Russia. In 1926 there were 7,250 self-instruction circles, with 120,000 members. The number enrolled in correspondence courses alone, in 1927, was given as 27,100, and in February, 1928, had risen to 57,450.

The second group of agencies for political education includes schools for the education of illiterates, half-literates, adult schools of the second grade, evening courses for workers, courses for peasants, workers' universities and party schools and universities.

The liquidation of illiteracy is considered of first importance by Soviet officials; and to the end that it may be accomplished by 1933–34, liquidation centers have been established throughout the Soviet Union. The campaign has been waged steadily since the beginning of the new régime. In 1920–21, the number of schools for this purpose was stated to be 39,834, with 1,124,849 pupils. During the hungry years 1921–23, activity suffered a decline to 2,503 schools and 78,961 pupils. Since then, there has been a steady increase, there being, in 1926–27, 29,591 schools and 898,255 students. Notwithstanding these impressive figures, the most difficult part of the task, according to educational authorities, is still ahead: liquidation of illiteracy among the masses of peasants. According to the figures of 1926, there were, in the European part of Soviet Russia, 541 to the thousand (both sexes) who could read and write. In city districts those who could read and write numbered 690 per thousand, but in rural sections the average was only 392.

Instruction in liquidation centers is expected to go much beyond reading and writing, including writing and reading of many-place figures, addition and subtraction of three-place figures and an understanding of the most generally used metric weights and measures. Observation shows, however, that actual practice does not measure up to this standard. The content of reading and writing is related to the everyday life of the worker and political material is gradually introduced. In schools for half-literates which aim to bring students to full understanding of reading, writing and arithmetic, so that they can use newspapers, books and reference works, instruction usually covers a period of six months, six hours a week, depending on the ability and advancement of the student.

The adult schools of the second grade aim to raise the general cultural level of the workers, furthering their political development, so as to make active and creative participators in the upbuilding of a Communistic society. There are generally three types: some with agricultural, others with industrial leanings and still others which combine agricultural and industrial interests. The purpose of each determines the selection of material, emphasis being placed on the practical application of science to the problems of each field. Students of at least seventeen years are received who have a mastery of the four fundamental operations, decimal and metric systems, and are given instruction for three years. The range of work corresponds approximately to that of the regular schools of the second grade. Instruction is grounded on practical work in laboratory, library, workshop and factory, the prime consideration being that all material of instruction be taken from life itself. As the students have their domestic, social and vocational duties to perform, instruction in the schools of the second class is generally limited to three or five times a week and not more than twenty hours.

Workers' evening courses are established and may be attended by students over eighteen years of age who can read, write and do the four fundamental operations of arithmetic. The courses are generally for one year, three times a week, and at least a total of twelve hours weekly. While they have a general educational purpose, special subjects may be offered, such as drawing, modeling, etc., if demanded by the workers.

Special courses are established for peasants similar to those for workers in the cities. They last a year, or sometimes two, where conditions permit, giving instruction three times a week and two to four hours per session. Students eighteen years of age are admitted. Instruction, which is closely related to everyday life, and where possible by the project method, covers the following fields: political life, with special attention to Soviet law relating to villages and agricultural questions, mathematics, Russian language, natural science, agronomy, agriculture and social science.

A significant addition to the facilities for social and political education of workers is the workers' evening universities, of which in 1926–27 there were twenty-seven, with 6,900 students. These institutions offer two-year or sometimes three-year courses. The work is divided into two classes: required and special studies. To the former belong courses in Leninism, history of the class struggle, economics, natural science; the latter category contains special groups of courses, such as electrotechnics, chemistry, mechanics, in the natural science and technical division, and, in the department of social science, courses in public economy and management of corporations and cooperatives, and so on, the student being free to elect those suited to his needs. Through these courses the government hopes, first, to strengthen the Communistic point of view in the workers; second, help him to extend his general education; and third, raise his vocational efficiency by scientific education and thus fit him for more effective cooperative social life.

Under the head of political education must also be mentioned the Soviet and party schools and Communist universities. These are the most specialized of all and are intended for members of the Communist party. In 1926–27, there were 7,743 schools and courses with more than 190,000 attending; 213 Soviet and party schools with nearly 20,000 enrolled, and 13 Communist universities with almost 6,000 students.

It is impossible, in the scope of this article, to cover political education in all its ramifications as it exists in Russia to-day. We shall keep chiefly to the foundations of it which are laid in the education of young children and adolescents. The foregoing has indicated the purpose of it, the determination which is behind it, the institutional means of accomplishing it; but it is possible to get a more intimate glimpse of its spirit and content from the literature of the *Octabrists, Pioneers* and *Komsomols,* the plans for social science study in schools and the text-books used, as also the pamphlet guides to party education for adult workers.

Some of the books of the youth organizations lie before me: Krupsky's "Paths of the Pioneer Movement," (1927); Smirnov's "Octabrist Relief to Pioneers" (1926); the "Pioneer's Companion" (1925); "Always Ready," a general view of the attainments of the Pioneers (1928), by Maryamov; Edwin Gernle's "Communistic Children's Groups," translated from the German (1924), which shows youth on a brilliant background blowing taps: *Be Ready;* "Work for Pioneer Divisions in the Winter" (1927); "Theory and Practice of the Children's Communist Movement" (1928); Makarov and Leaman's "Agricultural Work for Young Pioneers in the Country" (1927); "Party, Komsomol and Children's Movement, a Collection" (1928); "International Children's Communist Movement" (1927); "Questions of the Pioneer Movement" (1928), and a host of others which sketch the outlines of the whole political education of children from the earliest years to manhood and womanhood, when they can become candidates for the Communist party. Let us glance at the contents of a few.

All the nations of the West, almost all in the world, we have said, recognize to-day the need of enlisting the belief of children in themselves as a necessary step to securing their support. This belief on the part of children is first bid for by appealing to their love of heroic and magnificent figures before they are yet able to grasp the abstractions and principles for which the nation or party may stand. Such a place, occupied in the life of German children by the emperor before the war, the position of high esteem held by Washington and Lincoln in the minds of our own sons and daughters, is accorded to Lenin by Russian youth. Reverence of him is not as old, but it is deeply founded, assiduously cultivated and is becoming stronger. Lenin appeals to them not just because he was a heroic figure in a time of storm and stress, but because they are told he loved children; that there was once a time when he played with them, ran races, or told them stories about the life of workers and the struggle with the bourgeoisie; that not only Ukrainian and Russian children know him but Chinese, Indian, German and those of many other lands as well. Why should they not venerate such a heroic, widely known, yet friendly playmate? Why should not "the man who saw Lenin" become in time truly famous? Moreover, Lenin himself recognized the value of children as makers and preservers of the revolution. As early as 1913 he said, to one who argued it were better for workers not to have children, that "Children are our future," and continued,

> We lead a life filled with innocent oppression and suffering. For our generation it is more difficult than for our fathers. But in one respect we are vastly more fortunate than our fathers—we have learned, and quickly learned, to struggle—not to struggle alone as did they but better than they; our children will struggle more successfully than we and will be victorious. Already we are walling up the foundations of the new structure; our children will complete it.[2]

Just as the revolution released forces which had sought to create a universal edu-

[2] Krupskaya: *O rabotye VLKSM. sredi dyetee,* 3.

cational system before the war, it also opened the way to organization of the youth movement—not an entirely free youth movement, certainly, for it is used for a purpose in Russia as elsewhere. It is still young but counts 1,681,983 Pioneers in 1928, a slight decrease of the number previously reported.[3]

Smirnov makes a clever appeal to the youngster's desire for activity, and especially to his love for group association.

> Vanya is lonesome; there is no one to play with him, so he mopes at the window. On the other side of the street he sees a group of Pioneers and wishes he could be with them. Are there many children thus inactive and unhappy like Vanya? Many indeed! In order not to be so, they must organize. Workers are strong because organized. . . . Children will live happily, interestingly, fully, when they are organized. . . . Youth have wanted to organize for a long time, and they have begun. In 1923, the Red *Zernishki*, made up of children seven to ten years old, appeared at Odessa; elsewhere *Red Poppies* sprang up; and, in 1924, groups of Octabrists suddenly began to be organized everywhere—in Ukraine, Crimea, Siberia and Russia proper. . . . Many children want to be Octabrists. Their rapidly swelling ranks constitute the present children's army. By 1926 the Octabrists numbered about 450,000 children in all Russia. Their work is not lost. Their organization renders relief to older comrades.

Lenin had no children of his own, the Octabrist is informed, but just the same hundreds of thousands call themselves his grandchildren and are filled with the thought and wish to do as he bade them. They follow his footsteps with the others—the Pioneers, Komsomols, Communists and all workers—as they sing:

> Join link to link; let chain join chain
> While songs resound full valiantly;
> Let every step and every glance
> Turn towards his mausoleum.
>
> And if the call to arms comes,
> To escape a peace in chains,
> Let every heart within our breast,
> Beat its reply, "We're ready, Lenin."

[3] *Nasha Smena*, 8.

What injunctions did Lenin give to young Octabrists? "First, and most important, constantly help the workers and peasants in their struggle; second, study; third, and last, make strong your own organization." These injunctions of Lenin the young Octabrists will honestly fulfil. They receive knowledge, indispensable for the revolution; they will build their school, extend their ranks; and every one will keep in step with the life and struggle of the workers.

Children grow up quickly, go to school, join Octabrist groups and become good Octabrists. Well, what can they hope to do beyond that? The young Octabrist, without hesitation, answers, "I want to become a regular Pioneer." On their banner it is written: "We are Octabrists—future Pioneers." Komsomols and young Pioneers help the children enter the ranks of the Pioneers' army. Octabrists often work with the latter; indeed, the Octabrists are a school in which Pioneers are educated. Of the Octabrists it is often said: "They are the third guard," and truly, for "they are the youngest generation of Bolsheviks."

Every Octabrist must remember the laws and customary duties which he must render everywhere and in every place: "*First,* the Octabrist helps Pioneers, Komsomols, Communists, workers and peasants; *second,* Octabrists strive to become young Pioneers; *third,* they are bound to keep body and clothing clean; and *finally,* it is their duty to love work."

Suggestions are made to guide in organization of Octabrist groups, explaining how they may work, and play and sing at home and at school and how they may keep healthy. "Let me write the songs of a people and I shall write their history," is an old thought. The period of the revolution has brought forth a new flood of children's literature, but nothing is more important than these songs which, in the minds and hearts of Octabrist, Pioneer and

Komsomol, prepare defenders of the workers' revolution. "Red Army," "Demonstration," "Sickle and Hammer," "Octabrists," the "International," are favorites in school, on street and on country marches where I frequently saw them. . . . They're getting off the train now and marching down the platform at Obneensky as they sing "A March of the Young Pioneers:"

We Pioneers
Are children of workers.
There comes the dawn
Of a brighter day—
Hark, the Pioneers' cry:
Always be ready!

With youthful strength
A happy throng
We shall be ready
For labor or battle
We shall be first
In labor and strife—
Hark, the Pioneers' cry:
Always be ready!

With joyous step
And blithesome song
We join the ranks
Of the Komsomols.
There comes the dawn
. . .
Hark, the Pioneers' cry:
Always be ready.

Who are these Pioneers who sing? They are, says the "Companion," "the organized advance guard of the children of the proletariat. Their labors are directed to the end of preparing worthy, valuable relief to the present soldiers of the revolution—the Bolsheviki."

Fundamentals of Pioneer life, with some of the specific things they must learn and the services they are to perform, are set forth under the following heads in the "Pioneer's Companion:" Laws of the Pioneers, habits, Pioneers at school, Who are the Pioneers?, our brothers, links (groups), camps, songs, games, physical education and sanitation, first aid, metric measures, what Pioneers should read, calendar of holidays for the Pioneer, calendar of the seasons and what to read in physics and other sciences.

The Pioneer must be loyal to the affairs of the working class, as Lenin commanded. This is the first law. What does it mean? "It means that one must know how all workers live and struggle not only in the Soviet Republic but in all the world—know how rich capitalists oppress millions of white, yellow and black people—it is necessary to aid the oppressed and hate the rich."

"A Pioneer is the younger brother and assistant of the Komsomol and Communist." According to this, the second law, it is clear that he is preparing for great things. One who prepares to become a Komsomol must know the history of the workers' struggle and Communistic society; must promote and participate in collective labor; must aid collectively the R. L. K. C. M. (Russian Lenin Communist Society of Youth); must carry through meetings, club evenings, exercises and other work; must, especially, actively assist Komsomols in work in the country; must strive in every way to be exemplary so as to become a member of the above society; and in all undertakings and at every call of the Communist Party and Komsomols, Pioneers must be able to answer: "Always Ready."

The Pioneers must observe a third law; namely, that they are

> Comrades of children of workers and peasants throughout the world, who in their struggle look hopefully to the Pioneers of the Soviet Republic. Hundreds of thousands of Pioneers—children of Western workers and peasants—strive with the Komsomols against wealthy capitalists, who put them in prisons, banish their organizations, and in general in every way harm our comrades in labor. It is necessary to organize regular correspondence, make collections, establish lotteries and sales of literature, for the benefit of children of Western workers; and observe their life attentively, sharing our experience in our work. . .

Pioneers organize circles of children and participate with them in group life. The Pioneer is an example to all children.

He will not avoid those who stand apart but go to them, try to draw them into his work and acquaint them with the organization, for this is the fourth law. In school the Pioneer must actively share in school life, support discipline and draw other children into club activities, circles and games; arrange meetings and explain the tasks and purposes of Pioneers—and especially the commands of our leader and teacher, comrade Lenin.

Finally, the Pioneer must "strive for knowledge—knowledge and skill—strength in the struggle of labor." Nothing would be more humorous than a Pioneer who could not read and write; if he were going along the street he could not find the address of his own comrades; he could not write to suffering comrades in the West; could not hold up his head if he heard the words of Lenin: "Learn! learn! learn!"

Numerous other duties are laid upon the loyal Pioneers, but they are all in accord with these laws. Whatever they do individually, though it be but to follow the injunctions as to how they may secure and preserve good health, they are admonished that it is not for their own beauty or perfection for their own sake, but to prepare themselves for the "strenuous life of labor"; and whatever they do collectively is for those above, below or around them, or for those who labor beyond the seas. These ideals they continue to serve as they become Komsomols and eventually candidates for party membership; advanced years bring heavier, more serious, tasks but do not alter the conceptions of duty with respect to the government of workers and its enemies that have grown strong within them.

More than two thousand years ago a certain wise man, having explained how the ideal state was to be organized, directed and maintained, was faced by the problem of first establishing belief in the new system. He recognized clearly human dislike of innovation; therefore there must be careful preparation for its acceptance. His solution, like those of many others who have proposed what they considered "perfect" or "nearly perfect" systems for the benefit of their fellows, was a resort, to "a single spirited fiction [whereby] we may bring even the rulers themselves, if possible, to believe it, or if not them, the rest of the city." A skeptical listener, seeing difficulties in this solution, queried, "Can you suggest any device by which we can make them believe this fiction?" and received the candid reply: "None at all by which we could persuade the men with whom we begin our new state, but I think that their sons and the next generation and all subsequent generations might be taught to believe it."

The problem of social control was faced frankly. Systematic indoctrination of youth was to accomplish the firm establishment of the new social order. Modern statesmen, though oft inclined to ridicule the ideas of mere philosophers, have nevertheless succumbed to them, whether for good or evil. Thus Western nations began to regiment the thinking of their nationals in more or less vigorous fashion through organized schools. This development was earlier and more vigorous in some lands than others. In purely autocratic states and dictatorships the purpose of indoctrination was much more frankly avowed, clearly stated, effectively performed. Prussia became leader and teacher of her sister German states, of Europe and America as well. Czarist Russia copied western tactics. "The aim of the government in the education of students," as one ancient set of instructions declared, "is the training up of faithful sons of the Orthodox Church, loyal subjects of the Czar, good and useful servants of the Fatherland. . . . The soul of education and the supreme virtue of the citizens is humility. . . ." Our friends and neighbors in Soviet Russia have plenty of good (or bad) precedents to guide their practice.

IS THE AMERICAN COLLEGE STILL NEEDED?

By Professor N. E. BYERS
BLUFFTON COLLEGE

WE are witnessing to-day the strange paradox of a rapidly increasing college attendance with a decreasing confidence in real college education. Never did so many go to college. But what are they studying? In the early years many are trying to learn to use English, taking courses in elementary algebra and geometry, beginning the study of Latin, French, Spanish or German. These we formerly classed as secondary subjects. In the later years some specialize in liberal arts subjects; many take vocational subjects such as education, commerce, engineering, journalism, home economics, agriculture; and others are given leave of absence during one or two years to begin medical, theological or law courses. Are not all of these university courses?

This obvious fact has been the basis for the suggestion that since the first half of the college course is largely secondary in character and the second half university, the four-year course should be divided and the first two years be added to the high school and called a junior college, and the last two be taken over as an integral part of the graduate and professional work of the university. Obviously that would entirely eliminate the American college as a distinctive institution.

This threatened danger of the college is no doubt due to several causes. The college imported from England was an aristocratic institution. It educated an intellectual, well-to-do class in the arts of leisure. As life became more democratic and complex this type of learning did not satisfy many of those desiring higher education. Since many had not been well trained in the high schools the demand for secondary education was met by introducing high-school subjects. Some were kept interested by substituting vocational training, since that seemed to them to be of real value for life. Some of the professors, in the meantime, trained in German universities and later in American graduate schools, became interested in highly specialized, technical scholarship and, forgetting the function of the college, introduced university courses. A few students could be interested in some one of the specialized departments, but no student could be interested, as a specialist would be, in all his required courses. As a result there was no one inclusive, challenging objective that united the students and faculty in a way to call forth loyalty and enthusiastic work. College morale could be maintained only through the various activities that the students introduced.

The American college will live only if it has a distinctive function to perform not supplied by either the secondary school or the university. Its objectives must be consciously held by united faculties, and such as will appeal to the college youth of modern America. In order that the college may be free to do her own task we must insist that the high school complete the task of secondary education. This, I take it, is to introduce the pupil to the life of the effective cultured citizen of to-day and at the same time provide all the tools needed for his college work. With the improved secondary school of six years, professionally trained supervisors and teachers should be able, after all these years of progress, to do all the things needed to prepare the pupils for real college work, while, at the same time, preparing them for successful living as good citizens.

Six years of high-school English should enable them to use the English language so that freshman composition may be omitted. Such elementary algebra, geometry and trigonometry as are needed to understand the natural and social sciences for cultural purposes should be taught in the high school and not prescribed in college. Such foreign languages as are desired for studying the cultural resources of other nations and other times should be mastered before coming to college.

With this preparation the freshman at the age of eighteen should be able to take up seriously and with real interest the essential work of the liberal arts college. This I take to be the understanding of all phases of our common life for the purpose of living life at its best and of interpreting and criticizing it with the view of becoming leaders in real social progress. Having provided for all the social arts and tools of learning in the secondary school and postponing all vocational and professional training for the university, we must further distinguish between the cultural education of the college and the secondary school on the one hand, and the college and the specialized scholarship of the university on the other. Illustrating in the field of the natural sciences I would say that in the secondary school the pupil should learn enough in this field to live with intelligent appreciation and success in the world of nature and applied sciences; the college student should be able not only to adjust himself to the conditions of modern life but to so understand it as to use his methods of thinking and his rational insight to become a critic of our present life and be a leader in social progress, while the university specialist becomes a master of one field of science and makes some contribution to our knowledge of that field. The school prepares for life, the college for improving life and the university adds to our knowledge.

In order to accomplish this aim the college student should be introduced to the four phases of our environment, *viz.*, the world of the natural sciences, our institutional life, the esthetic creations of man in literature and the arts and the moral and religious life. Orientation courses in these four fields could be given during the first year. This should enable the student to see life on the whole, appreciate its values, understand its problems and give a basis of information for building a personal philosophy of life.

Having found some special interests and some challenging problems he could select during the second year certain limited fields of study and in special courses and by independent study, under the guidance of tutors, try his hand at the solution of some life problems. He would study chemistry not because of his interest in the subject or to become a chemist but because of its aid in improving life. The same problem might call for knowledge of economics, psychology and Christian ethics. During the third year while bringing to a conclusion the study of life in some of its special phases the chief interest would center in gathering together all the insights gained and integrating them into a satisfactory philosophy of life.

I would, therefore, set aside three years, for those well-prepared and having serious intellectual interests in life, in order that they may be trained to become leaders in social progress. I do not believe that this can be well done in connection with vocational or professional interests or in a university atmosphere. Vocational interests are too absorbing and limiting to leave the mind free for the larger life problems. Nor can the junior college, dominated by the high-school standards and the influence of the average home life, in two years nurture much independent thinking on serious life problems. The junior college may be needed for pre-vocational or pre-university training, but it is not adapted for liberal arts education. The independent small college, the typical American institution, or a group of colleges, such as is being established at Pomona, or the college within the university, as at Wisconsin, it seems to me, will be the type of institution that can function as true liberal arts colleges. A small group in close personal association, with the student activities supplementing the curriculum requirements, students and faculty living together in a real community life—there only can we center all interest on learning how to live and how to improve life. This should not be regarded as preparatory work for any higher institution. The courses would not serve for premedical or preengineering work. Not all physicians or engineers are interested in the general community life. Not all candidates for the Ph.D. degree would some this way, for alas! what do many of them care for life at its best?

For some callings, however, this cultural education would be essential. All those professions that aim directly at improving life should be prepared for in this fundamental way. Teacher, ministers, librarians, editors, authors, legislators, public officials should certainly be trained first of all to understand life. But the influential, public-spirited, leading citizens will not be limited to any profession. In a democracy much depends on leaders, but they may be found in any vocation or any class of society. The American college should be able to train such leaders.

By eliminating all secondary and vocational training and centering all work definitely on our liberal arts objectives I believe that three years is all that we need for this purpose. The demands for professional training are such that students can not afford more than this and vocational interests can not be longer postponed. On the other hand, if the definite task set for the college is well done the student should continue his cultural interests and be able to help himself in taking his place in the cultural life of his community while taking up his vocational preparation. With a true philosophy of life he will subordinate his vocation to his life interests and make it a real part of his life as a true citizen and cultured member of society.

Scholarship gives us more knowledge but we need wisdom to use it to the best advantage of humanity. Vocational training will help us make a better living provided we have the appreciation of what good living is. To-day in America we lack the wisdom and appreciation needed to utilize all the resources of our civilization. If we ever needed education to understand and improve life it is to-day when we are in the midst of a reconstruction period. We need leaders of prophetic insight and vision to enable us to use our resources wisely. We need them in every vocation and in every community to guide us in the solution of all our problems that affect our community life. No institution aims to do this specific and most important task except the American college.

EDUCATIONAL EVENTS

GOVERNMENT GRANTS FOR JEWISH SCHOOLS IN PALESTINE

THE government of Palestine, according to a report in *The Christian Science Monitor*, has given notice of its intention to reorganize the system of public education, and has published a draft education ordinance which foreshadows important and far-reaching changes.

The latest annual report of the Education Department of Palestine shows that in 1927 there were 315 public elementary schools, with 20,079 pupils, as against 171 schools, with 10,662 pupils, in 1920. Special attention has been given to the educational requirements of the rural areas, for which little or nothing was done by the Turks.

At the government schools the language of instruction is Arabic. They do not, therefore, provide for the Jews, whose vernacular is Hebrew, and who form about 17 per cent. of a total population of about 900,000. Accordingly, an important part in the educational system is played by the Jewish voluntary schools.

In 1927 it was recognized that, since the Jews obtained no benefit from the government schools and had built up an educational system of their own, they were entitled to more substantial assistance from public funds. It was accordingly agreed that, in return for submitting to a certain measure of government supervision, the Zionist organization should receive a block-grant for the schools under its control at the rate of £20,000 a year.

The new ordinance also provides for the partial decentralization of the educational system through the establishment of local education authorities. These are to be identical with the municipal councils in the 21 towns in which such bodies exist. Outside the municipal areas the powers of a local educational authority are to be exercised by such village or local councils as the High Commissioner may designate.

Special arrangements are made for the maintenance and management of what are described as "community schools," *i.e.*, schools belonging to the constituted authorities of one of the recognized communities in Palestine. All community schools coming within the scheme are to be under the control of a committee of management of four members, of whom three are to be nominated by the community owning the school, while the fourth is to be nominated by the local educational authorities, but it is also, whenever possible, to be a member of the community.

These provisions, however, do not entirely meet the case of the Hebrew schools at present controlled by the Zionist organization. These are, of course, Jewish schools, but they do not belong to the local Jewish community within the meaning of the ordinance, so they can not be treated as community schools in the technical sense of the term.

THE TRAINING OF TEACHERS OF FRENCH

ACCORDING to an article by Professor B. Cognet, of the Lycée de Chartres, published in the *Revue de l'Enseignement Secondaire des Jeunes Filles* and translated by the Bureau of Education, Department of the Interior, more calls than can be filled come from abroad for teachers of French prepared by the École de Préparation des Professeurs de Français à l'Étranger (School for the Preparation of Teachers of the French Language in Other Countries).

This school is in the wing of the Sorbonne that faces Saint Jacques Street in Paris, and was founded eight years ago by M. Ferdinand Brunot, at that time dean of the faculty of letters in the University of Paris. One of the professors of that faculty, M. Huguet, became the director of the new school, and M. Sudre was made the secretary general, according to an article published by Professor B. Cognet, of the Lycée de Chartres, in the *Revue de l'Enseignement Secondaire des Jeunes Filles,* Paris, issue for October 15, 1928.

Professor Cognet says that the opportunities offered teachers of French vary in different countries, but that the best are found in the United States. Since American schools prefer to know their teachers before making a permanent engagement, candidates for posts in this country are sent on a scholarship for a year's probational teaching.

About thirty of these candidates have been sent by the École de Préparation to the United States. The entrance salary has been $2,000. To obtain such positions a good knowledge of English is necessary.

On the other hand, not a single graduate of the École de Préparation is teaching in England, not even in the French Lycée in London. However, some students of this school, the École de Préparation, act as assistants in British schools while perfecting their knowledge of English.

On returning from England or America, many French students, and others, try for the certificates indicating advanced education in foreign language and literature which are awarded by the University of Paris. Certain examinations and attendance for a semester are required to win each such certificate.

Secondary school graduation in France, or its equivalent officially recognized, allows the applicant to obtain four of the advanced certificates and four are necessary to succeed in obtaining the desired "licence des lettres." No conditions are attached to the gaining of three of the university certificates except the requirements as to attendance and scholarship.

Countries other than England which train their own teachers of French include Italy and Poland. Italy has French institutes at Rome, Naples and Florence, which furnish good teachers, and Poland trains nearly all the teachers of French that she needs.

LAKE COUNTY, MINNESOTA, ORGANIZED AS ONE SCHOOL DISTRICT

THE last Minnesota Legislature passed a law known as Chapter 82 of the Session Laws of 1927 permitting a county to organize under certain conditions as one school district with a County Board of Education.

The question of consolidation under this law was submitted to the voters of Lake County at the last general election on November 6 and was carried with a comfortable majority. It not only passed with a majority in the city of Two Harbors, but also passed in the rural districts.

On July 1, 1929, this law will go into effect in Lake County and thereafter it will be known as County District of Lake. It will have a County Board of Education consisting of six members which will organize in the same manner and at the same time as boards of independent districts. This board will have all the powers and will be subject to the same laws and regulations as school boards of ten or more townships and independent consolidated districts in Minnesota. The salaries of the secretary and treasurer will be fixed by the County Board of Education. Other members will receive a per diem of six dollars while attending any regular or special meeting of the board, but not more than seventy-two dollars in any one year and shall receive four cents per mile in going to and from their places of residence to the place of meeting by the usual route of travel.

The county board will employ a superintendent of schools who will have charge of all the schools of Lake County, and on January 1, 1930, said superintendent will perform all the duties of the county superintendent of schools, and the office of the county superintendent of schools in said county as an elective office will cease to exist.

This is a new departure for Minnesota and will, no doubt, be watched with considerable interest by legislators and educators.

CONFERENCE OF RURAL SCHOOL SUPERVISORS

THE United States Department of the Interior, Bureau of Education, announces a conference of rural school supervisors of the southern states to be held in the Hotel Roosevelt, New Orleans, on December 17 and 18.

Participants will come from 14 states: Alabama, Arkansas, Florida, Georgia, Kentucky, Louisiana, Mississippi, North Carolina, Oklahoma, South Carolina, Tennessee, Texas, Virginia and West Virginia. They will include state and assistant state supervisors of rural schools and other members of state departments of education, county supervisors, county superintendents, professors of education in teacher training institutions, officers of state education associations, the superintendent of a state school and colony for mental defectives and the president of the National Congress of Parents and Teachers.

The topics to be considered include problems involved in the supervision of larger rural schools; greater unification of preservice and inservice training of teachers; equalizing educational opportunity for and essential characteristics of the type of education best adapted to the needs of exceptional children in rural school systems; extension of information relating to the value of rural school supervision, and reports of studies of the organization and programs of teachers' meetings and of procedures helpful in raising their standards of achievement.

The forthcoming conference is the fourth regional supervisory conference sponsored by the United States Bureau of Education. Two preceding conferences in each of which the southern states were represented were held in 1925 and 1926. In the third conference, held in New York City last April, eleven of the northeastern states were represented.

It is expected that the December, 1928, conference will contribute materially to coordinating the efforts of persons employed in various types of educational work; to assisting supervisory officials to attack certain problems more intelligently; and to clarifying the ideas of rural education officials as to the true function of supervision and the significance of various supervisory agencies.

THE TEACHING OF EVOLUTION IN ARKANSAS

THE anti-evolution act approved by the voters of Arkansas at the last election becomes effective on December 6. The bill provides "that it shall be unlawful for any teacher or other instructor in any university, college, normal, public school or other institution of the state which is supported in whole or in part from public funds derived by state or local taxation to teach the theory or doctrine that mankind ascended or descended from a lower order of animals, and also it shall be unlawful for any teacher, textbook commission or other authority exercising the power to select text-books for above-mentioned institutions to adopt or use in any such institution a text-book that teaches the doctrine or theory that mankind descended or ascended from a lower order of animals." A fine of $500 and dismissal from state service is provided as the penalty for violation of the law.

The correspondent of the New York *Times* reports that it is not believed that the heads of any state institutions will question the validity of the act or attempt to secure an interpretation of it from a higher court. J. P. Womack, state superintendent of schools, says that the law will not affect the common schools because no state-adopted text-books for use there ever have contained any matter that comes within the new law. The State Text-book Commission adopts books for the first eight grades only and has no control over texts used by high schools and higher institutions.

Another problem that confronts Arkansas teachers is what is to be done with the courses now in progress in various state institutions and what methods may be employed in complying with the law by eliminating unlawful text-books with the least possible inconvenience and expense to students. Books in numerous schools are selected by the president on recommendation of the members of the faculty.

But while the teaching force of the state is preparing to go ahead with complete compliance with the law, various groups of professional men are intimating that they will contest its validity on numerous grounds. They feel that there are absurd features in the act which the voting public did not appreciate. It is contended that the language of the act prohibits only the teaching that "mankind ascended or descended from a lower order of animals," and that this does not prohibit the academic discussion of such a theory in the classroom provided teachers or text-books do not seek to present the theory as a fact.

CANDIDATES FOR HONORS AT HARVARD COLLEGE

More Harvard undergraduates are candidates for honors than ever before. The report shows the relative number of undergraduates in the various fields of concentration and gives the percentage of "approved candidates for honors" in each of these various fields. Only those undergraduates who have shown by their work in courses that they have a fair chance of receiving the degree with honors are included in the approved list.

The number of candidates for honors this year is 830, out of a total of 2,370 concentrators, or 35 per cent. of all concentrators. This is an increase of 3.7 per cent. over last year and 6.7 per cent. over the year before. Mathematics shows the highest percentage of candidates for honors, with 55.3 per cent. of its students enrolled as seeking the degree with honors. History and literature is second with 48 per cent. of its students seeking honors, and government, third, with 42 per cent. These figures apply only to the ten largest fields. Astronomy, for instance, the smallest of all 25 fields, has all four of its concentrators candidates for honors.

Because of the practice among members of the sophomore and junior classes of changing their fields, probably the most interesting figures are those for the senior class. Of those seniors concentrating in mathematics, 68 per cent. are candidates for honors, and 66.7 per cent. of the seniors in the department of history and literature are candidates for honors.

The combined field of history, government and economics is by far the largest in the college, with 775 members of the three upper classes enrolled. It has shown a gradual, but steady gain since 1926. One of its departments, that of economics, has been the largest single field in the college, displacing English, which until this year was in first place. Economics now counts 417 members, as against 394 for English. History ranks as the third largest field, with 233 concentrators. The combined field of modern languages, containing the Romance languages, German and English, numbers 634 concentrators, which is a considerable decrease over its 1926 total when it numbered 776, but far larger than any other combined field except history, government and economics.

Among other large fields which show gain over the previous year, the departments of history and literature, of the fine arts and of biochemical sciences, are outstanding. Fine arts has risen from the tenth to the sixth largest field in two years. Government, mathematics, philosophy, psychology and the Romance languages all show losses.

THE NEW PHYSICS BUILDING AT THE UNIVERSITY OF MINNESOTA

Leading American scientific men in the field of physics gathered at the University of Minnesota on November 30 and December 1 for the sessions of the American Physical Society as guests of the university at dedicatory exercises for the new physics building. The actual dedication took place at 8:15 P. M., Friday, November 30.

Dr. John Zeleny, of Yale University, formerly of the Minnesota faculty, delivered the dedicatory address on "The Place of Physics in the Modern World."

At sessions of the Physical Society on Friday afternoon Professor Karl T. Compton, of Princeton University, read a paper on "Scattering of Electrons," and Professor E. U. Condon, also of Princeton, one on "Quantum Theory of Aperiodic Effects." Dr. F. L. Mohler, of the United States Bureau of Standards, discussed "Photo-ionization and Recombination," and Irving Langmuir, of the General Electric Company, spoke on "Electron Impact Phenomena in Gases."

Members of the society and visiting speakers were guests of the University of Minnesota on Friday night at a dinner in the Minnesota Union. President L. D. Coffman welcomed the guests, Professor Compton responding. Short addresses were delivered by Professor S. C. Lind, head of the school of chemistry at Minnesota, and by Professor W. F. G. Swann, of the Franklin Institute, Philadelphia, formerly a member of the faculty of the University of Minnesota.

From the dinner the physicists went to the new building, where, with President Coffman presiding, the keys were delivered by Fred B. Snyder, of the board of regents, to Dean John B. Johnston, of the College of Science, Literature and the Arts.

Addresses of acceptance by Dean Johnston and Professor Henry A. Erikson, of the department of physics, were followed by Professor Zeleny's dedicatory address.

The meeting of the American Physical Society continued on Saturday morning, December 1, followed by a drive around the Minneapolis boulevard system and luncheon at the Minikahda Club.

Dr. Zeleny, of Yale University, the principal speaker, is a brother of Professor Anthony Zeleny, of the University of Minnesota. The new physics building stands on the University Mall, facing the library. It was completed early last spring.

BEQUESTS OF THE LATE PAYNE WHITNEY

The appraisal of the estate of the late Payne Whitney was made public on November 22. The value of the whole amounts to $194,328,514. Among the public beneficiaries, New York Hospital, of which Mr. Whitney was vice-president, receives the largest gift of the total of nearly $60,000,000 left to charities, institutions and organizations. In the last two years before his death Mr. Whitney gave the hospital $1,367,056, while in his will he left it thirty-three parts of the residuary estate, which has been divided into 300 parts, the bequest amounting to $18,632,176.

New York Hospital will benefit further under the clause of the will giving forty-six parts of the residue, or $25,972,134, to the trustees, to apply the principal or income "for the furtherance or development of such charitable, benevolent, hospital, infirmary, public educational, scientific, literary, library or research purposes as said trustees shall in their absolute discretion determine to be in the public interest." The testator, however, suggested that "it would be agreeable" to him if the trustees used the fund "for aid or development of such of the above enumerated purposes as I have been interested in during my lifetime."

The trustees submitted to Deputy Commissioner Stephenson a statement of their decision as to this fund, in which they said they had "carefully considered" the best means of disposing of the forty-six parts in order to carry out Mr. Whitney's intentions as expressed in his will. "After full consideration of the matter," said the trustees, "we have decided that the capital shall be distributed among the New York Hospital, Cornell University, for the maintenance and support of Cornell Medical College, the New York Public Library, the Groton School, Yale University and the Nassau Hospital."

The shares left under the will to these organizations, other than New York Hospital, were appraised as follows: New York Public Library, $6,210,725; Cornell University, $2,823,657; Yale University, $2,823,657; Groton School, $1,129,272 and Nassau Hospital, which got only one share, $564,611.

EDUCATIONAL NOTES AND NEWS

Dr. Paul Monroe, director of the International Institute of Teachers College, Columbia University, sailed on November 23 for China to attend a meeting of the Boxer Indemnity Board in December. The board has $20,000,000 at its disposal over a period of years with which to subsidize the Chinese school system.

Dean Anson Marston, of the Iowa State College, was elected president of the Association of Land-Grant Colleges at the concluding session of the Washington meeting held on November 23.

Honors from foreign governments have been conferred on three University of Chicago scholars. Professor William A. Craigie, of the department of English, who is compiling the "Historical Dictionary of American English," was knighted in June by King George of England for his work in bringing the monumental "Oxford Historical Dictionary" to completion. Professor William A. Nitze, chairman of the university's department of Romance languages, was created Chevalier of the French Legion of Honor on November 13 by President Doumergue for his service in the spreading of French culture. On November 19, Professor James C. M. Hanson was made knight and commander of the Order of St. Olav by commission from King Haakon VII of Norway, and was called "the father of modern library science."

The Royal Society, London, has awarded its Royal Medals to Professor A. S. Eddington, Plumian professor of astronomy in the University of Cambridge, for his contributions to astrophysics, and to Dr. Robert Broom, professor of geology and zoology at Victoria College, Stellenbosch, South Africa, for his work on the origin of mammals.

On his twenty-fifth anniversary as dean of the college of engineering at the University of Wisconsin a banquet will be given on December 11 in honor of Professor Frederick E. Turneaure, who since 1903 has guided the technical training of Wisconsin students of engineering. Professor E. R. Maurer, a Wisconsin graduate and head of the department of mechanics, will preside at the dinner and Professor D. W. Mead, head of the department of hydraulic engineering, will be the principal speaker.

At the close of the fortieth anniversary conference in New York City of the Child Study Association a dinner was given on November 20 in honor of Mrs. Howard S. Gans, president of the association. Dr. John Lovejoy Elliott presided and the speakers included Dr. Edward L. Thorndike, Dean William F. Russell, Mrs. Henry L. Moskowitz, Dr. Bernard Glueck and Professor Patty Smith Hill.

An award of $5,000 in recognition of her twenty-six years' labor on behalf of the southern children was presented on November 21 to Miss Martha Berry, founder of the Berry Schools at Mount Berry, Georgia, by *The Pictorial Review*. The presentation was made by William P. Ahnelt, publisher of the magazine, at a luncheon in New York City. In accepting the award Miss Berry said: "To-day is one of the crowning days of my life. I shall invest the money in the boys and girls of the South who need the help of our schools. I can use the money most splendidly and I am profoundly grateful that my work for them has resulted in so generous a response."

President Mordecai W. Johnson, of Howard University, has announced a grant by the Julius Rosenwald Fund of $80,000 to be expended over a period of five years. The purpose of the gift is to make possible the continuation of the research of Dr. Ernest E. Just, professor of zoology since 1912, and to build up a department offering instruction to graduate students who may take positions in other Negro colleges.

Arthur W. Loasby, president of the Equitable Trust Company of New York City, has been elected a trustee of Syracuse University to succeed Horace Wilkinson, of Greenwich, Connecticut, who has resigned.

Dr. Frederick W. Lewis, president of the College of Emporia, Kansas, has been elected vice-president of the New York Biblical Seminary.

DR. ALBERT S. HURST, dean of Teachers College, Syracuse University, for eight years, has presented his resignation, to become effective at the end of the present scholastic year. He will resume his former post of professor of history and education in the college.

DR. CHARLES G. CROOKS, dean of Centre College and professor of mathematics for twenty-seven years, has retired, and Dr. Frank L. Rainey, professor of biology, has been selected as dean.

THE Ohio State University has initiated a new Department of Parental Education, which is in charge of Mrs. J. A. Charters, who will cooperate with the Ohio State branch of the National Congress of Parents and Teachers, and with other state and local organizations for the education of parents.

PROFESSOR HERMANN T. VULTE, organizer of the department of household chemistry of Teachers College, Columbia University, has retired from active service and is spending the winter in California.

THE REVEREND DR. G. CAMPBELL MORGAN, formerly pastor of Westminster Congregational Chapel, Buckingham Gate, London, and for many years preacher in the Fifth Avenue Presbyterian Church, New York City, has resigned from the faculty of the Los Angeles Bible Institute, because the Reverend Dr. John Murdoch MacInnis, dean of the institution, has placed his resignation in the hands of the board, following charges concerning a book entitled "Peter, the Fisherman Philosopher."

WILLIAM MOYLES, desk editor of the New York *Times,* has been given three months' leave of absence to accept an appointment as special lecturer during the winter quarter in the school of journalism of the University of Washington at Seattle. Mr. Moyles was formerly on the editorial staff of the *Philadelphia Public Ledger,* the *Springfield Republican,* the *Manchester Guardian,* the *Nashua Telegram* and the Associated Press. He will teach courses in newswriting, copyreading and specialized reporting. During the spring quarter his place will be taken by Sidney I. Snow, feature writer for the *Philadelphia Public Ledger.*

DR. FRANK M. QUANCE has been appointed dean and professor of education in the College of Education, which was established last year in the University of Saskatchewan, Saskatoon, Canada.

APPOINTMENTS to the faculty of the State Teachers College at Harrisonburg, Virginia, for the present session include Dr. H. G. Pickett, professor of physics and general science; Mr. Raus M. Hanson, associate professor of geography; Miss Grace Palmer, associate professor of fine arts; Miss Julia Robertson, associate professor of home economics and Mrs. Adele Raymond Blackwell, associate professor of home economics. Miss Katherine M. Anthony, director of the training school, has resumed her position after a year's leave of absence for graduate study at the University of Chicago under a fellowship offered by the General Education Board, and Miss Margaret V. Hoffman has returned to the English department after a year's graduate work at the University of Pennsylvania.

HENRY TYLER, formerly a member of the staff of the department of psychology of Teachers College, Columbia University, has been appointed to the faculty of the Teachers College of Indianapolis.

D. L. BAILEY, formerly superintendent of schools at Harbor Springs, Michigan, has accepted the position of director of rural education at the Western Illinois Teachers College.

GEORGE H. CHATFIELD has been nominated to the post of director of attendance by the Board of Superintendents of New York City, at a salary of $12,500 a year.

DR. BEN GRAHAM, first assistant superintendent at Pittsburgh, Pa., has been relieved of his assignment to supervision of the elementary schools, and given charge of the department of junior and senior high schools. Dr. J. Freeman Guy, superintendent of the Bellevue schools, has been made associate superintendent, at a salary of $7,500. He succeeds Dr. Graham in the supervision of the elementary schools.

J. F. WADDELL, of South Milwaukee, Wisconsin, has become supervisor of high schools in the Wisconsin state education department.

MARION J. WESLEY, who has been elementary supervisor of the Lynn, Massachusetts, public schools for the past three years, has been appointed assistant superintendent and director of elementary education in the public schools of Luzerne County, Pennsylvania.

DR. JOHN R. CLARK, formerly of the faculty of the Lincoln School, Teachers College, and last year a member of the faculty of New York University, has returned to the Lincoln School as principal of the high-school division.

DR. HOMER L. DODGE, dean of the graduate school and professor of physics at the University of Oklahoma, will spend his sabbatical leave of absence in England. He and his family sail on December 13 for London, where they will reside for several months. Dr. Dodge will study educational conditions in England, with particular reference to the adaptation of graduate study to social and economic needs.

DR. W. B. FORD, professor of mathematics in the University of Michigan, has been granted leave of absence for the current academic year and will travel in Europe. Representing the Carnegie Endowment for International Peace, he will lecture at the Universities of Leiden and Utrecht, the University of Brussels, the Universities of Lille and Grenoble, and the University of Pisa.

THROUGH the French government, Centre College has arranged an exchange professorship in the Romance language department. By its terms, Professor J. Tourret, of Aix-en-Provence, is teaching this year in Centre College and Professor J. McCurdy is teaching in France.

AFTER a survey of the educational systems in Latin America, Miss Heloise Brainerd, chief of the section of education of the Pan-American Union, has arrived in Panama on her return to the United States. Miss Brainerd will also visit the educational institutions of Panama and the Canal Zone.

THE first public presentation of the findings and recommendations of the Florida survey will be made before the Florida Education Association on November 30 and December 1 by Professors Strayer, Engelhardt, Bagley, Hillegas and Mort, of Teachers College, Columbia University, and by Professor Knight, of the University of North Carolina.

DR. THOMAS WOODY, professor of the history of education in the University of Pennsylvania, who has returned from a three months' investigation of education in Russia, will lecture during the coming summer at the University of California at Los Angeles, giving courses in "History of American Education" and "Comparative Education in Europe at the Present Time."

DR. GEORGE E. VINCENT, of the Rockefeller Foundation, will be the next commencement speaker at Smith College.

DR. FOWLER D. BROOKS, associate professor of education at the Johns Hopkins University, lectured recently at the Eastern Division of the Illinois State Teachers Association at Charleston, Illinois, on "Individualizing Instruction in Reading" and "The Place of Literature in Developing Personality during Childhood and Adolescence."

DISCUSSION

GROUP INSURANCE FOR TEACHERS

IN addition to the pay check received by modern industrial workers, many receive substantial bonuses of stock or dividends or cash. The encouragement to long tenure and small turnover of labor is further enhanced by the provision for indemnifying the employee through group insurance. This insurance is taken by the management of business concerns, and is either paid for by the employer, or partly so. It has recently been estimated that the number of wage earners thus indemnified runs to about three million. Not only are the employees of private concerns thus protected. Many municipalities have their office holders covered by group insurance. Group insurance holds at least two advantages for teachers. First, the advantages of protection are thus extended to all. Under the non-compulsory present plan, many teachers are entirely unprotected against sickness, accident and their accompanying train of bills to be paid. The late

Dr. Searson, of Kansas State University, used to say that, "if it were not for the possibility of visiting friends and relatives, eighty-five per cent. of teachers would have to beg or work for a living during their vacations." Under the group plan, all teachers would have at least a modicum of indemnity in the form of insurance. Then, too, group insurance is cheaper than individually subscribed forms. The very fact that so many teachers have no means left for support during the vacation months reveals their need of cheap protection. The average income of teachers further demonstrates the need of low rate insurance. While the average income of all persons gainfully occupied in 1926 was $2,010, the income of teachers and administrators in public schools was $1,275.[1] It is revealing to note that the average income of trade union members for that year was $2,502, and United States Government employees received an average income of $1,809. Aside from these two rather tenable arguments which urge the advisability of working out a system of group insurance for public school employees, one could make a case in its favor on the ground that such a policy would tend to decrease turnover in the teaching staffs and encourage more men of families to remain in the service of education. It is quite generally recognized by thoughtful speakers and writers that school teachers are consciously more than mere wage earners. They, taken by and large, realize that they owe society a double duty. It is theirs to transmit the priceless heritage of the past, in knowledge, science and ideals. It is also the teacher's task to encourage the open-mindedness necessary for invention and progress in all things which make for a more abundant life individually and collectively. Full devotion can not be expected of teachers who are not protected either by salary or insurance from the stern visitations of misfortune to which man is still heir. A higher type of service could confidently be counted on from teachers whose incomes were adequately protected against accident, sickness and death losses. From the standpoint, then, of public welfare, a policy of group insurance for teachers would be a statesmanlike policy.

[1] *Journal of the National Education Association*, December, 1927, p. 290.

Why not have group insurance for public school employees?

BURTON ELSWORTH DAVIS

LEADERS—BORN OR MADE?

WILLIAMS, I think it is, in his cartoons in the daily papers, seems to hold the conviction that "heroes are made, not born." It is true, naturally, that heroes must be born, but I do not think it true that they are born to be heroes, and I have much the same conviction in regard to leaders. The desire to be a leader is inherent in all of us. But whether we become leaders depends in part on early environment and the personalities with which we come in contact. The desire for leadership may be repressed by lack of understanding on the part of parents and teachers. Other factors may tend to develop emotional conflicts which make leadership impossible. However, the normal boy has a strong inclination for leadership; he wishes naturally to excel in some field of endeavor, whether it be sports, scholarship or manual dexterity. Repeated failure will of course turn him to other unhealthier means of obtaining the recognition he desires, as, for example, disorderly conduct in school or truancy. It is obvious that it is better for the boy, for the school and for the community to see that this yearning for leadership is fostered along desirable lines.

Leadership and responsibility go hand in hand. A leader without responsibility is a figurehead; a leader without a sense of responsibility soon loses his followers. To develop leadership we must encourage responsibility, and this can only be done by putting trust and faith in the boys. If we are afraid to trust them, they assume no obligations, and any leadership developed will be leadership along lines of their own choosing; and it frequently happens that this leadership is contrary to our desires and to their best interests. Boys thrive on responsibility allied with trust, but without trust their attitude is passive or antagonistic.

The schools have endeavored to some extent to foster leadership by monitor systems and student governments. To a large extent these have been failures, so far as the development of leadership is concerned, however successful they may be in lessening discipline troubles. This failure is due, I believe, to two definite causes:

First, that the positions of leadership have carried no responsibility—the monitor or student officer initiated no policies, he carried out nothing along lines of his own devising, he was a liaison officer between the school authorities and the pupils; second, an effort has always been made to see that a student of the "right sort" was elected. In other words, while teaching democratic principles, we have "fixed" the elections if we could. In the language of the day, we have not been objective in our plans for leadership; somehow we have acquired the idea that leadership had something to do with discipline and honor systems. We have endeavored to "kid" the students, and they haven't fallen for the plan. In the effort to lighten the burden of our jobs we have missed a glorious plan for leadership development.

The failures of the past should, however, spur us to new and greater efforts. Our attempts, although often seemingly futile, have met with some small degree of success. One of the paramount needs of the present age is that of responsible, trustworthy leaders. Psychology, indeed, teaches us that the individual is going to acquire those habits or attitudes that give him satisfaction; and it is for us, as educators, to see that the kind of leadership we wish to develop is a means of satisfaction to the pupil. If John can get as much satisfaction and can meet with as much success in doing those things which help to make for a better school, as he now gets in being a leader in mischief, he will abandon his asocial behavior, and we will then have him on the road to becoming a useful member of the community. He is determined to express himself, to be a leader in some way. We can not balk him, but we can direct him and help him to develop the abilities and attitudes that society needs.

KENNETH R. LAVOY

NOTTINGHAM HIGH SCHOOL,
SYRACUSE, NEW YORK

BUST OF PROFESSOR DEWEY

WHAT may prove to be one more step in the progress of education had its beginning recently in Teachers College, Columbia University. A special reading room has been opened for students in the philosophy of education where they are permitted free access to books on required reading lists. Heretofore they have had to ask at the loan desk for books on reserve and have been limited in time and in the number of books permitted them at one time. Now, under the new ruling, students may come in and help themselves at the shelves without any restrictions. In the words of one student, "It is fine, when we have only a minute between classes, to know we can come in and take down a book without the delay we have always had." It is hoped by the new plan to bring about a more intimate contact between students and their reading matter and to be the means of closer cooperation between prescribed courses in education and library facilities.

A pleasing ceremony took place soon after the opening of the new room when a bust of John Dewey, the work of Epstein, was placed in one end of the room. The occasion was a quiet one, marked with no display or ostentation. The thing most worthy of notice was the eager manner in which the students crowded into the room to see the man who figures so prominently in the educational world, for John Dewey himself was present.

The work is a culmination of the efforts of a group of friends and admirers of Mr. Dewey who collected a sum of money and when Epstein was in this country had him do the bust, whereupon they presented the work to Mr. Dewey as a token of their esteem and friendship. Pleased as he was, in Mr. Dewey's words it was somewhat of a "white elephant" because he had as yet found no suitable place in which to exhibit the work.

When Dr. Kilpatrick approached him with the idea of the new philosophy of education reading room and how much they would appreciate having the bust placed in the room for all his students and followers to see, Dr. Dewey gave his consent.

As library assistant in the special reading room in the afternoons, it has been my privilege to watch reactions on the part of the students. Hardly a day goes by that some one does not come in and say, with a smile, "I just wanted to see the bust of John Dewey," or else, there for some other purpose, they pause long enough to go and look upon the face of one who is outstanding in the field of modern education. There for all time one can see the kindliness and the philosophical yearning of this man whose books are the inspiration and guidance of all who come under their influence.

Florence Corya

SPECIAL CORRESPONDENCE

OPPORTUNITIES TO STUDY FOR A DOCTORATE AT OXFORD

Just after the war, when Oxford had yielded to the pressure brought to bear upon the Convocation to grant the graduate degree of Doctor of Philosophy so necessary to attract mature foreign students, the D.Phil. (as it is stubbornly called) was something of an *x* in an equation whose variables had still to be established by precedents. From the beginning it was clear that the university had no intention of awarding the degree to industrious clerks for what is known in some American universities as "research." The research had to be done, but in the presentation of the results and their interpretation the faculties of Oxford uniformly insisted upon some distinction of style and thought. Naturally the mortality among the first candidates permitted to come up for the degree was shocking. The chagrin of many candidates entirely worthy of Ph.D.'s in the approved American tradition was only equaled by the mortal terror that their fate inspired in those who had not yet come up for the examinations, which include a written general examination, the scrutiny of the thesis and the public *viva voce*.

It became evident that many foreign students, chiefly Americans, were being admitted to advanced standing and allowed to read for the degree who did not possess the critical maturity to work almost unaided upon a major research problem. Accustomed to the careful shepherding of courses and seminars, the American students were quite lost, as a rule, when confronted with the necessity of saving their own souls, aided only by what was often the very casual advice of a supervisor and by the bewildering wealth of lectures and libraries in which they might browse at will.

The university turned, therefore, after some pressure from the Society of Post-Graduate Students, to the expedient of not admitting to candidacy for the degree without an extra-legal probationary period of a term or two of reading in the field of research with a tutor. The student who came heavily fortified with previous graduate work, with recommendations and with a clear-cut formulation of an acceptable problem might hope to escape this testing. Admission to candidacy for all others, even though they were burdened with M.A.'s and Phi Beta Kappa keys, depended then, and I believe still does, upon the tutor's willingness, at the end of the probationary period, to vouch for the candidate's maturity and ability to do independent research. The results have been to make the mortality far less heavy. Often the blow is further softened by giving the Bachelor of Literature degree as a sort of consolation prize.

The Oxford doctorate of philosophy is, however, something of a gamble still, in which one has to be willing to back his ability to produce a book worthy of publication *in extenso* and on the judgment of difficult critics. He must be willing to derive such help as falls to him from the supervisors appointed to aid him, and that differs enormously with individuals and even with faculties. Generally, if he is a competent student, he can hope to get the supervisor whom he desires. In any case, if he be willing to work pretty much alone for the necessary minimum of six or seven Oxford terms (the smaller number for high honors men who have done the Oxford B.A.) he may enjoy an opportunity that no American university affords for absorbing, unhindered, the cream of a rich tradition of scholarship. Of course this freedom has the defects of its virtues, but its virtues are very real; even though preparation for teaching, in the routine fashion, is not one of them. The D.Phil. is primarily a research and not a professional degree.

We bewail in the United States the falling off of historians who can write, of scholars who are something more than specialists. Yet our graduate study, perhaps because of the nature of our undergraduate study, assumes the character of a rigidity and inflexibility in the program both of special and general studies equaled only by medieval scholasticism. We turn out increasing numbers of men acquainted with a large field, well-grounded in a special field, and unable to think or write with any depth of distinction about either. In their graduate study they have been led by the hand too long. The words of a great president of one of our greatest universities come to me, as he commented on a doctor's thesis: "Exhaustive, uninspired, uncritical, dull—thoroughly worthy of our Ph.D. degree!"

The blight of the Ph.D.—there is such a thing—has not as yet descended upon the Oxford degree. For the very reason that its administration is still flexible, that its award is made dependent upon results, not on formulae for fulfilling certain requirements—an independent graduate student may find it very heaven. For research in philosophy, history, literature, politics, law, the humanities, this is particularly true. It is not, I fear, equally true in economics or in psychology or in some of the physical sciences where the guidance of great scholars is more difficult to be had just now at Oxford. In the other fields, whose opportunities have already been presented as subjects of study in this series of papers, I can say from experience and observation that the student need not want for guidance or advice, if he does not require that he be personally conducted to the degree. The libraries and the lectures at Oxford are adapted to special students as well as to undergraduates. The freedom of travel and vacations affords an entry into the whole storehouse of European scholarship.

What, after all, do we expect of graduate study? For those who hope merely for a teaching degree, Oxford is not the place. But for those who desire to study a problem under a master, and within reach of a wealth of tools, Oxford offers unique opportunities. The degree has not yet been "organized" to uniformity of standards. It is still a little exotic to Oxford life. But the candidate who can work in that rich atmosphere of a fellowship of scholars that is an Oxford college at its best, will grow instead of being forced. He will have only himself to blame if he lacks intellectual stimulus or if he fails to gain the rare perspective of a wisdom that lives on intimate terms with classic antiquity, its own medieval past, and the contemporary problems of a great empire.

W. Y. Elliott

Harvard University

QUOTATIONS

INTELLIGENCE TESTS FOR VOTERS

Professor Munro, of Harvard, has urged that other states follow the example of New York in requiring intelligence tests for first voters, so that "no one gets on the voters' list unless his intelligence is at least equal to that of a 10-year-old child." Nineteen states have so-called "literacy" tests, but they are applied by registrars of voters or election officials and are usually perfunctory. In this state, however, the test is made to discover whether the would-be voter can use the English language "intelligently." The examination set by the State Education Department is a reading-writing test.

We have in the United States reached the "uttermost limits" in the expansion of suffrage. This experiment in intelligence testing, which has been in successful operation for at least five years, is hailed as the "next step in the evolution of the American electorate." The results of the tests are interesting. There is not likely to be again the property qualification exacted in the earlier days of the Republic, and it is certain that the franchise given women will never be withdrawn. But it is probable, as Professor Munro has predicted, that such slight restriction as now obtains in this state will become general. Universal suffrage will be "trimmed at the edges" by the elimination of the least intelligent, using the best-equipped agencies of the state for making the decision. This might be considered undemocratic if the state did not at the same time make it possible for every man and woman, even of low intelligence, to receive without cost at least an elementary education. Evening schools are maintained especially for those who, having come as adults to this country from lands of other than English speech, wish to qualify as voters. It is now virtually prescribed in this state that all must pass through the schoolhouse to the ballot box.

This year the demands upon the principals, teachers and others conducting the tests given uniformly, through the state, were especially heavy. The number of applicants was about three times as great as in 1927. Of these, 66,461 (46,809 men and 19,652 women) passed the tests, while 8,347 failed (7,184 men and 1,163 women). This is a considerably better showing than in previous years, for in them the percentage of failures has been much higher. But it is still large enough to prove that such a test is worth while, for, though very elementary, it discovered nearly ten thousand persons not qualified on these minimum terms to vote, who, under the old system, would probably have been admitted without question. Moreover, most of these 66,461 would not, except for this requirement, have taken the pains to prepare themselves by attending night schools or receiving other instruction. The school authorities and teachers deserve praise for this patriotic service.—*New York Times.*

SOCIETIES AND MEETINGS

THE 1928 ANNUAL MEETING OF THE COLLEGE ENTRANCE EXAMINATION BOARD

The establishment of an examination in English for foreign students, to be given in foreign countries, was authorized by the College Entrance Examination Board at its annual meeting held on November 1 at Columbia University. Action was taken by the board in response to numerous appeals from individuals, institutions and associations, culminating in an urgent request from the American Association of Collegiate Registrars.

The present problem grows out of the immigration law, which demands that, for admission to the United States, foreign students must have been accepted in advance by some reputable American college or university. There have been not a few attempts at "bootlegging" of non-quota foreigners under the guise of students. Partly to meet this aspect but chiefly to provide that foreign youths shall be adequately prepared to profit by study here, various institutions and associations advocated an English examination before the students leave their own lands. As the College Entrance Examination Board regularly holds its June examinations in various foreign countries it seemed the logical body to conduct this additional examination.

The report of the commission which investigated the problem was presented to the board at the November 1 meeting by Professor Adam Leroy Jones, of Columbia University, as chairman. The commission set forth the purpose of the projected examination as being "to test the candidate's ability to understand written English, to read English, to understand spoken English, and to express his thoughts intelligibly in spoken English." To accomplish this there will be need for an aural test—which is not provided for in the ordinary examinations of the college board. The expense of examining is to be borne by the candidate on the regular cost basis of the board. It is understood that, for advanced students capable of research, the speaking test is to be less rigorous than for younger foreigners who propose to mingle with American undergraduates.

Members of the commission which investigated and recommended the new examination are: Professor Jones; Dr. Claude M. Fuess, of Phillips Andover Academy; J. Wilson Hobbs, of the Public Latin School, Boston; Ralph S. Minor, university examiner, University of California; Professor Kenneth B. Murdock, Harvard University; Dr. David A. Robertson, assistant director, American Council on Education; Ira M. Smith, registrar, University of Michigan, and Edwin B. Stevens, registrar, University of Washington.

That the commission on the scholastic aptitude test is making satisfactory progress in its development of valid items for the annual test was reported by the chairman, Professor Carl C. Brigham, of Princeton University. Professor Brigham said that "the problem is to get a sufficient stock in trade of test items to take care of tests in the future. When we have approximately 1,500 valid items we can stop." The board voted to appropriate $25,000 for the work of the commission and for conducting the scholastic aptitude test in June, 1929. Last June this test was taken by 8,349 candidates, including 529 boys and girls not expecting to enter college until 1929.

The total number of candidates examined by the board in various subjects last June at 351 examination centers throughout the United States and abroad was 22,720, according to the twenty-eighth annual report presented by Secretary Thomas S. Fiske. The 15,817 boys and 6,903 girls examined were representatives of 1,873 secondary schools. Of these 1,099 were public schools, which sent up 5,141 boys and 2,436 girls, and 774 were private schools, which sent up 9,959 boys and 4,276 girls. "In regard to 908 of the 22,720 candidates the board's records do not indicate whether they were from public or private schools." A table giving a general classification showed that the candidates had attended schools and were going to colleges largely in New England and the Middle Atlantic states.

In paying a ten-dollar examination fee, candidates paid less than the expenses of the board per candidate, according to the report of Professor Fiske as treasurer. The total expense per candidate was $10.74, of which the largest item, $2.88, was salaries of readers, with other items including the following: expenses of readers, $1.18; supervisors, $1.02; printing and supplies, $1.02; executive salaries, $1.27; extra clerical assistance, $1.10; scholastic aptitude test, $1.07.

The deficit in examination fees was offset by income from the sales of publications by the board and the annual dues of members of the board. "I am happy to announce," said Professor Fiske, "that receipts for the year exceeded disbursements by $21,578." His report gave total receipts as $265,621 and total disbursements as $244,042.

The board voted to authorize the secretary, under the direction of the executive committee, to expend $223,500 for the conduct of his office and the conduct of the 1929 examinations. For the preparation and scoring of the scholastic aptitude tests of 1929 an additional authorization of $25,000 was made.

Reporting for a special committee on the finances of the board, Professor H. W. Tyler, of the Massachusetts Institute of Technology, advised that some of the accumulated surplus of the board should be invested, as such investment would bring a considerable increase in the board's revenue. Professor Tyler recommended also, for another committee, changes in the constitution and by-laws "in the interests of simplicity and brevity."

The new definition of the English requirement framed by the national conference on uniform requirements in English was adopted by the board as its examination requirement, this upon recommendation of the committee on review, presented by Professor R. N. Corwin, of Yale. This committee "has referred to appropriate associations for advice on certain recommendations for changes in the board's definitions of European history, American history and French." The board voted to ask the Mathematical Association of America to make a recommendation as to a school course combining plane geometry and solid geometry as a substitute for the present plane geometry course.

Chairman Henry Pennypacker, of Harvard, reported for the executive committee that, at the examinations next June, candidates will not write their names and the names of their schools on their answer books, so that their identity will not be known to readers of their answers.

Dr. Wilson Farrand, of Newark Academy, reported for the committee on examination ratings that the six hundred readers did "a most satisfactory job last June. The surprising thing was the uniformity of their grading, the fewness of their mistakes and the speed of the returns." Dr. Farrand told of a study begun by the readers in English to improve the board's comprehensive examination in English.

The board passed a resolution expressing its sense of the service to the board and to education rendered by the late Dr. William Mann Irvine, headmaster of the Mercersburg Academy.

Officers for 1928–29 were elected as follows:

Chairman: Henry Pennypacker, Harvard University.

Vice-Chairman: Professor Harry W. Tyler, Massachusetts Institute of Technology.

Executive Committee: Henry Pennypacker, Harvard University; Professor Robert N. Corwin, Yale University; Radcliffe Herrmance, Princeton University; Vice-provost G. W. McClelland, University of Pennsylvania; Islay F. McCormick, Albany, N. Y.; President Ellen F. Pendleton, Wellesley College; Dr. Alfred E. Stearns, Andover, Mass.; Professor Harry W. Tyler, Massachusetts Institute of Technology; President Marion E. Park, Bryn Mawr College.

Custodians: Professor A. L. Jones, Columbia University; President Mary E. Woolley, Mount Holyoke College; Dr. Wilson Farrand, Newark, N. J.

Secretary and Treasurer: Professor Thomas S. Fiske, Columbia University.

RAYMOND WALTERS

SWARTHMORE COLLEGE

EDUCATIONAL RESEARCH AND STATISTICS

PREDICTING SUCCESS IN FIRST SEMESTER COLLEGE SOCIAL SCIENCE

THE data which form the basis for this report were obtained from the records of the State Teachers College of San Diego. Five measures for purposes of prediction were used, in addition to the measure of success in the study of first semester college social science, average grade points per semester unit of credit earned. These five measures were (1) average grade points per year (unit) of credit in social science in high school, (2) number of years of study (units) of study of social science in high school, (3) total scores on the Thorndike Intelligence Examination, Series of 1925–1929, (4) decile ranks on the reading section (Part III) of the Thorndike Intelligence Examination, and (5) decile ranks on the trade information section (Part II, section 5) of the Thorndike Intelligence Examination. Decile ranks were used because they allow ready comparisons of any one student with the group of which he is a part. The attempt in this investigation has been to determine which of these five measures, if any, is valuable in predicting what the high-school graduate will achieve in his first semester of study in college social sciences.

Table I presents the measures of central tendency, of unreliability and of variability for the several series of measures just named.

Table I may be readily interpreted, as follows: The average grade points per unit of social science completed by all first semester students in the State Teachers College of San Diego was 1.51.[1] The middle 68 per cent. (two times the standard deviation, taken plus and minus the mean) is included in 1.72 grade

TABLE I

Measure	Mean	P.E. (Mean)	Standard deviation	C. of V. (Pearson)
Average grade points per unit in college	1.51	.036	.861	57.01
Average grade points in high school	2.16	.027	.644	29.81
Number units in high school	3.06	.038	.908	29.66
Thorndike score	63.78	.556	13.28	20.82
Thorndike reading decile rank	6.46	.113	2.71	41.90
Thorndike trade decile rank	4.71	.119	2.85	60.57

Number of cases, 259.

Note: Courses in history, economics, sociology and civics were counted as social science courses both in high school and in college.

[1] The interpretation of the grade point in the college is as follows:

Excellent	3 grade points.
Good	2 grade points.
Average	1 grade point.
Poor (passing)	0 grade points.
Failure	−1 grade point.

points. The chances are even that the true mean lies between 1.474 and 1.546. The relative spread of average grade points is roughly twice that of average grade points per unit of credit in high school, etc.

There are at least two points deserving further comment. Fifty-four per cent. (approximately) of this group of 259 students reached or exceeded the mean score for the college on the Thorndike Intelligence Examination (61.8, 1,233 cases). It suggests that the investigator should determine whether this is a significant difference, or one that is likely to occur from the chance sampling of similar materials. The difference divided by the standard error of the difference was found to be 2.12. The chances, then, are about 92 in 100 that the true difference between the measures (the difference between the true measures) is greater than zero. The finding (2.12) is about 71 per cent. of what it should be to insure always a difference greater than zero.

It was interesting to find that marks in high school were much higher on the average than marks in college. The distributions are shown in Fig. 1. Not only are marks in high school

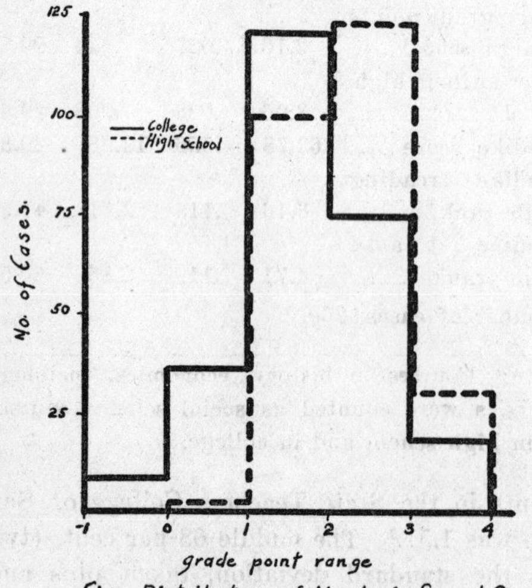

Fig. 1. Distribution of Marks in Social Science in College and High School in Terms of grade points.

higher on the average, but marking in high school is characterized by greater homogeneity than marking in college, since the middle 68 per cent. of marks in high school are included in 1.288 grade points, while in college the middle 68 per cent. are included in 1.722 grade points.

Table II presents the measures of relationship, of unreliability of these measures and of lack of relationship.

TABLE II

Measures compared with average grade points per unit of college social science	r (Pearson)	P.E.$_r$	k
Average grade points per unit of high-school social science	.207	.040	.978
Number of units in high school	.112	.041	.993
Thorndike total scale	.230	.040	.973
Thorndike reading decile rank	.266	.039	.964
Thorndike trade decile rank	.089	.041	.996
Number of cases, 259.			

All the coefficients of correlation are low. They are so low, in fact, that they are but little better than a chance guess for purposes of exact prediction. For this reason it seems necessary to make certain that the reader will not jump to conclusions too hastily and condemn the practices of educational guidance in college. For practical purposes, we do not greatly need tests which will predict achievement throughout the entire range of the scale which is the criterion. The departmental adviser is chiefly concerned with knowing whether the pupil concerned will be able to do satisfactory (passing) work in college social science. For this purpose he needs a critical measure indicating the probability that the pupil will do such work. Exact prediction is of relatively minor importance. It would appear that a carefully standardized test of mental ability designed to secure a critical measure of the ability of high-school graduates to do college work will supply this needed data (see Fig. 1) even though the scores obtained do not correlate point for point with subsequent achievement.

M. Eustace Broom,
Guy F. Fox
State Teachers College,
San Diego, Calif.

EDUCATIONAL REVIEW

Edited by WILLIAM McANDREW

MATTERS OF MOMENT

Public-school Flying.—You need not be so very old to be able to remember when Paul Hanus and others accused high schools of being too much up in the air. The course, they said, resists all attempts to adjust it to the life of the present century. What a thrill one might enjoy to see those dear old academic headmasters taken through the public high schools of Galt, California. This institution combines a high school and junior college service in a progressive town. Galt is in the Sacramento Valley, twenty-five miles from Stockton and an equal distance from the state capital. The board of education is elected by the voters of the consolidated district. The curriculum is the usual standard one to which are added for those who elect them courses in aeronautical science and practice. The college announcement presents aviation as an attractive career for young men who have a good education, sound health and keen spirits. Air-mail service is demanding more and more pilots; the army and navy need them; commercial air service is on the rapid increase. To meet these demands the Galt Union High School and Junior College gives two years of instruction in aeroplane building, rigging, engineering, meteorology, navigation, air-commerce regulations, repairing, flying and military tactics. At the end of the course the successful students are given the test for junior aeroplane pilot, United States Army.

William Rutherford, principal and president, tells me that boys in the second year of the high school elect the flying course and carry on for four years. They are taken up by experienced pilots and soon get "air wise." Lieutenant LeRoy Gregg is chief pilot. Mr. Rutherford himself teaches aerodynamics and navigation. The course has been in operation only a few years but it has resulted in over six hundred applications for admission this year, of which, owing to the crowded condition of the school and college, only seventy-five were accepted. The enrolment shows students from Alaska, Pennsylvania, New York, Minnesota, Montana, Ohio, Louisiana, Georgia, Kansas, Illinois, Colorado, Nevada, Arizona, Nebraska, New Jersey and California. The Galt community gives this instruction free as its contribution to the progress of science.

Routine and Responsibility.—I remember hearing Charles Hanson Towne tell how his employer, the proprietor of a monthly magazine, argued that the subscribers pay for the publication and ought to decide what it prints. He sent Towne on a tour through central New York equipped with a list of subscribers. Towne was instructed to call upon these good people and to find out what they wanted. They didn't know. Again and again the young assistant editor tried to get some one to tell him what the magazine ought to be. Nobody cared. They subscribed because the newsdealer suggested it. They perused it for amusement and instruction, and by force of habit. The magazine was theirs. They paid for it. But reading it was routine. Routine is easy and agreeable. It puts responsibility to sleep.

Of course you recognize what effect routine has on community projects. This is our government. We, the people, established it. We pay for it. By the great Overturn of '76 it was thought that the grand privilege of government would be so valued that every one would be active in thinking of civic issues. Discussion would determine selection of our representatives. Their acts would be scrutinized by their constituents. Reelection or rejection would be an act of the popular will. In a multitude of schools this excellent theory is taught as though it were actually working. Lincoln's brilliant maxim—a government of, for and by the people—is taught as though we had such a government. I do not know that in any city where a political machine is in power, any public school teaches the fact that its community is getting a government of the bosses, for the bosses, by the bosses. Most of the people whom I know are like the subscribers to Towne's magazine. Their government is a routine. They do not think about it. They take part in it only when urged to do so.

Routine and Education.—Similarly, the public schools belong to the people. The people pay the bills. With almost no exception they let the schoolmasters determine what the schools teach, as they let the governmental policies be determined by the office holders. The comfort of routine satisfies the people's educational representatives: the school board. The routine superintendent, as Dr. Winship reminds us, lasts longer, on the average, than any other. In view of which, Dr. Eliot and Dr. Charters characterized the schoolmaster as being many years behind in doing what he knew should be done. Two generations ago Emerson had put upon education the charge of still abiding in antiquity.

Education and the Revolution.—Yet every perusal of the history of the American public school brings out the fact that it was instituted as a feature of our political organization and for civic, not scholastic purposes. Not for culture, nor for personal ornament or distinction, not for increasing earning power, not for leadership, not for acquaintance with the intellectual inheritance of the race, not for leisure, not for worthy home membership, not for the predominant educational purposes formulated by schoolmasters, was education taken from parents and made a part of government, but for community benefit, for civic, for political ends. We have had abundant utterance of this American educational purpose from Washington, from Franklin, from Jefferson, from Madison, from Monroe, from both Websters, Daniel and Noah, from Rush, from Clinton, from Mann, from Lincoln, from Roosevelt, from Coolidge—none of them schoolmasters, all of them speaking from the standpoint of statesmen. We have it from our last national commissioner of education: "the school system is an institution of the people, by the people, for the people, conceived by the founders of this government to guarantee our democracy in a republic, to establish freedom, equality, and justice."

Slowness of Schoolmasters.—A circumstance that impresses our critics is the slowness with which we schoolmasters (all of whom were constituted governmental officers for the political service specified) adjust the old educational process which was devised for other and more ancient ends.

With answers prepared for them by educators, many prominent Americans, some in politics, have subscribed to the cultural and scholastic aim of school as all important. Members of the Supreme Court have so far differed from the expressed purpose of those who founded the nation and proposed education for its maintenance, as to designate schooling a personal and family affair. But when a statesman begins his thinking of education from the national origin, and not from the scholastic beginning, he, as Roosevelt or Wilson or Senator Ferris, concludes that the public school is the citizen's safeguard, not the scholar's instrument, and is for national ideals, not for cultural propaganda. A canvass made by the *World's Work* touching a hundred editors trained by experience to think public-mindedly showed their almost unanimous conviction that the purpose of education at public expense is identical with the purpose expressed in the preamble of the National Constitution. If it were possible to induce all citizens to think upon the origin of American educational legislation, to review the arguments made for the taxing of all persons in support of the schools, and to consider the proposals of those who founded this republic, these owners of the educational system would, it seems likely, modify the practices of schoolmasters to a large degree.

What the Layman Thinks.—This magazine has sought to present in every issue the layman's view as corrective of the routine and complacency to which an organized and established service is peculiarly prone.

An example of the kind of citizen whose thinking upon the large problems of school goes beneath the surface is William Smith, M.D., whose comments radiating from Kernville in California have illuminated me. I have just had a talk with him. Will you join in the conversation?

Cogitatio Medici.—Said the Doctor, "Your magazine keeps hammering away on the theme that educational progress ought not to be so slow and is too much tied up to supplementary things, evading the large purposes which the original makers of the nation had in mind when they took over school from parents and made it a civic service for the realization of political ideals. Are the school people entrusted with this mission big enough to realize it?"

"Alas! No, they are not."

"Why?"

"That's a long story. You reviled the pedagogue for thousands of years. You let the teachers of the American Colonies be recruited from the almshouses and jails of Europe. You paid such low wages that multitudes of men who could command more money doing something else refused to teach. You left your children in charge of girls who earned pin money while waiting for husbands. You put a stigma on the majority of teachers and on elderly maidenhood by making marriage a cause for dismissal. To the manager of a school system for a work that needs long planning and careful nursing you give a term so short he can no more than get his feet into the stirrups. You give him no assurance that good management and good schools will protect him, as wit, Messrs. Finegan, Suzzallo, Engleman, Corson, Van Sickle, West, Ettinger, Bush and a roster of some of the best superintendents in the country. You haven't big teachers because you, the employers, are so small in your treatment."

"Exactly," said the Doctor, "and because public education is so poor and because it is the main hope of the progress of the world it appeals to unusual men of wealth as a large philanthropy. John Harvard, Elihu Yale, Stephen Girard recognized it; Charles Pratt and John D. Rockefeller put oil money in; Carnegie and Phipps invested the earnings of iron; the Booths have just planted newspaper profits in a school. Next will come the motor millionaires."

"Henry Ford has no use for schooling."

"Oh, yes, he has. Not the kind now prevalent. No more than Edison has. But no one has shown them that the kind of education the propounders of the American public school system expected ought to be tried. Keep in mind that this motor industry in one branch under the financial tutelage of the Du Ponts and the captaincy of Raskob has produced eighty millionaires in the last ten years. Bear in mind that when Henry Ford gets back in the lead of the cheap car market he will command the greatest aggregation of fluid costs in the history of the world. Consider that a Chrysler has engineered a combination with the Dodge interest that commands a third stupendous aggregation of fluid money. Out of these three combinations in the next twenty years can come a thousand million dollars for educational purposes if there can be awakened in the right quarters an interest in the real American plan of public education. Who'll strike that rock for a gushing fountain of hope for the common people? Talk about your foundations! If a thousand million of dollars or a fraction thereof could be lined up for the real intent of the public school founders the names of the donors would go ringing down the ages."

"We've had ringing enough. We want realization."

"You can't get it without realizers—men who will cause the schools to be devoted primarily to the purpose of the best-known words of the Gettysburg speech, 'that this government by the people shall not perish from the earth.' 'That this prayer of the bravest heart America has produced shall be answered as he hoped depends on the corollary that our educational system shall produce' a school of the best of the present, by the best talent living to-day, for the best people, whom we have taught to read, write, and cipher—little else."

"And," said I, "according to Learned, Bagley and Snedden we have not taught them to do that as well as it is done elsewhere."

"There's no use," said the Doctor, "comparing our rudiments with those elsewhere. Get after the big things and the fundamentals will take care of themselves. School boards point to buildings and equipment and boast of success. It's what goes on in the buildings that counts. It's the old saying that even a log is equipment enough if Mark Hopkins is sitting on it beside a pupil. We must stop harping on the glorious achievements of our schools—which I truly believe are the best accomplishments we have made. We must concentrate on their known short-comings and failures. I may be able to put only in feeble words what I see they have failed to do."

"Well, try it."

The Best Training for the Best People by the Best Teachers.—"Take my own two universities: California and Chicago, with Rush thrown in for specialization. They can stand for the best varieties of higher education for the manner of our youth. They turn out about five thousand 'graduates' a year. These young men and women have been fed the best American educational viands obtainable. From such meat the red blood of youth should strive for idealism in American life as the best and most profitable policy, if for no other reason. When you multiply this army of graduates up to the hundred thousand turned out by all our schools of higher learning each year, and consider what they do, you begin to realize the failure of the system."

"The alumni root for the football team."

"They do not consciously form a living nucleus for the American ideal. The great multitude of college-bred should by now, had they been taught and led, have set in motion the evangelism that the founders saw in their vision and that every real educator is devoted to promote. That graduate horde has not done this thing. There is no indication, save in sporadic instances, that the word 'higher' belongs in our system. Our educated thousands are not numerously going higher. Like the educated Indian, they step out from the higher institutions and go back to the blanket."

"Alas, too many of them do."

"What do I mean by the evangelism of education? I don't exhort to extending pure science. We have more than we can use in the next hundred years. I don't cry for more accommodations for the increased body of students in the same sort of college we have now. The college-bred army is still short of weapons and ammunition in its war on materialism."

"What then?"

"We want in the daily life of our hungering and thirsting American society a use of the mind towards those ends that have been lost sight of in the rush of material speed and mobility which science has let loose among us."

"Woodrow Wilson tried your idealism in Princeton. See what Princeton did to him."

"I do see. I see the spirit of idealism left by the wayside while youth marches past. There is standing at the fork of the road an angel with a flaming sword pointing to a better and grander national life. Few have seen his face. Few have followed the pointing sword. A new evangelism must put practiced idealism back where it was predestined by the founders of our scheme."

"How, then, thou Californian visioner, notice I do not say visionary, how shall American idealism be realized?"

"I may seem mixed in metaphor and flaming in speech. Fire gets up steam. Here is the practical and specific. Motorization is the greatest problem of our national life. It is blamed for the rapid loosening of the old close family ties. But you can not reverse. We must go ahead though we perish. But do we need to perish?"

"I hope not."

Time for an Educational Revolution.—"Haven't we brains enough to adjust ourselves to the rush? Yea, verily. Not only to keep up but to lead."

"How, then?"

"By a well-financed unit of education worked into a new leadership. What's wrong with the present leading? The failure to correct the graduate's notion that he is educated and can go out and cash in. It is a failure of persuading youth that it has only the bare tools of an education and that it must educate itself in the larger leadership of the world toward destiny. The splendid, eager, young army of boundless possibilities for remaking the world goes back to the blanket of its tribe or its group."

"Well, Doctor, my university was a dispensing concern offering various knowledges. I got little or no reminder that the state had educated me for serving and advancing it. No member of the faculty told me I had a civic mission or a political duty. I suppose they assumed I ought to have known that, myself. There was little idealism visible in my college. The student aspiration was sporty and cheap. If the faculty was organized to guide student sentiment the fact was not evident."

"It was the same in mine," continued the other William. "Now, you may be sure that what happened with Girard's shipping money, Stanford's railway cash, the iron and oil funds, is going to be the course of the motor wealth. Interest the lords of the automobile in carrying to a logical conclusion the spiritual obligation of the material thing they have let loose among us. The aeroplane is the next speed unit that will become safe in the next few years. The present masters of motors will be lords of the air and of its income. Get them to see the fundamental difference between education as it is and education as the best minds know it ought to be. List your Mark Hopkinses, teachers, not recitation-hearers, trainers of men. Get your Mark Hopkinses there in person. That will be the fundamental difference between your school and all others even with their extension and mail departments. Make no mistake. The world is hungering for real manhood-culture. On twenty-four hours' notice, when the town knows you have a real Mark Hopkins ready to train men and women, you will find a class ready, anywhere.''

''Very good, my Helvetius, but where are the Mark Hopkinses to be found?''

''Sir, where were the men of '76, of '87, of '61 to be found? Where were those geniuses who mobilized the national resources ten years ago to be discovered? Let these new masters of the industrial world put their endorsement on teaching; let them offer a salary indicative of their faith in this type of training so that a man will not have to do something else to give his wife and children a chance; get this endorsement and investment; take it to any Herbert Hoover, Newton Baker, Walter Lippman, Geoffrey Parsons, Brand Whitlock, Abraham Flexner, or any one you please, and see what he says.''

''I'd pick you, Doctor, for one of the first in the faculty. Sitting here surrounded by your pure-clad peaks in God's great classroom, I'd give you the chair of Educational Polity and Replenisher of the Exchequer.''

A REVIEW OF BETTER BOOKS

HOI BIBLIOLOGOI

Eighteen book-talkers were present in the Rosegarden for the thirtieth conclave of this club devoted to speaking our minds regarding professional literature for teachers. A sharp stimulus in the outside air sent indoors more pinkness of cheeks than usual and caused to be hung on the ingenious folding racks made by the Stevedore more wraps than usual—yellow, red, blue for the women, black and blue for the men. The snapping fire in the Roses' grate waved a warm welcome to the guests. On the side table a pile of new books engaged the members, each selecting what he thought he ought or would like to read before the old year passes.

The principalship grows.—Said Martin the traveler:

"Arthur Gist[1] is well and favorably known to us of Chicago because of his intelligent and generous work editing four successive year-books of the National Department of Elementary School Principals. He holds, with me, that the efficiency of American education rests more with the master of the common school than with the teacher or superintendent. His year-books have done yeoman service in showing why this must be so; his new book affords effective aid to realizing the proposition. The book is, I should say, indispensable in the case of one preparing for a principalship and during the first experience of a new occupant, but, if I were the czar of all the schools, I'd make even the ancient and honorable schoolmasters study it, for their numbers contain the largest amount of slow-moving traffic in our profession. He lives up to his name—this author—for he has given the gist, the essential, the substance, the backbone and spirit of school management: school ideals, aims, contacts, routine, extension into the community, managing the teachers, noting varying emotional temperaments, the way to get the most good out of superintendents, and an interesting array of matters such as an observant worker who thinks and takes notes might be expected to collect.

"He stresses the sometimes forgotten fact that the real work of the school is where and when the teacher and the learner are in contact. The one who ought to guard against waste of this vital time is the principal. Often he is an impediment to efficiency because of his interruption of the teaching process by his circulation of notices and by his unproductive class visits. He's a business executive. His main work is maintenance of efficient instruction. He should organize and deputize for everything

[1] Arthur S. Gist, ''The Administration of an Elementary School,'' Charles Scribner's Sons, New York. 308 pp. $1.80.

other than direct inspection, appraisal, encouragement and follow-up. He can't read every paper that the pupils write, but he can sample those of every class and find the typical excellences and faults prevailing in his school. He can keep informed of the plan-books and use of them by all the teachers. He can see that foresight and concentration on essentials become the habit of every teacher. He can see that stock is taken of the accomplishments of every pupil in every study. He should outline his work by term, month, week and day. The time has passed when the schoolmaster can be content with dropping in to cheer the teacher on her way. The modern school woman despises a mere jollier. She wants an expert opinion on the work she's doing just as an art student is so desirous of criticism as to be willing to pay good money for it. The principal must set definite goals for the abilities to be cultivated, he must make them decidedly clear to the teacher who is training them. He must prepare tests to ascertain, for her, his own and the community's benefit, whether the abilities are secured or not. Why to do all these things, how they are best being done, is the theme of this excellent book. It closes with a superior account of the traits of a good principal with, next, a list of his personal qualities, then with an objective schedule based on the condition of the school. There are specimens of blanks for rating a principal. There is a summary of points as an estimation blank devised for the principal to make it his basis of self-appraisal. That is good so far as it goes. But better than self-estimation is the scheme to call a teachers' meeting, to seat the participants so that they can not see the work of one another, to pass out a printed list of the personal qualities with the grades: very strong, strong, weak, very weak, after each quality, and to desire the teachers by means of a pencil check-mark, so that their authorships may not be known, to analyze the principal's professional virtues and vices."

"Absurd!" sniffed Anna the argumentative.

"It ought to be done early in the week when they're feeling more at peace with the world," said the Signpost.

"For most of the rates it would be a hope rather than a belief," said the General.

"It would be as stupid as for a husband to seek anonymous ratings from his wife, children, mother, father, brothers and sisters," said the General.

"Stupid, absurd, vicious, unnatural, subversive, silly, foolish, worthless and idle as is the whole system of rating the teachers," concluded Anna.

"As I seem to have thrown an apple of discord into this harmonious company," said Martin, "I withdraw the apple. In fairness to Brother Gist, I remind you that the scheme was mine, not his."

Preaching to Boys.—"It is common for us schoolmasters," said the General, "to desire that there should permeate the program an ethical spirit, making for character. When I was a schoolboy we had an assembly called chapel. The principal read from the Bible; he applied the texts to what we should do; he closed the exercise with a prayer beseeching God to help us be good boys and girls, himself to be a good man. To-day, we have assemblies full of interest, information, spice and pep. There is dancing sometimes in costumes only seen in old days in what was advertised as the naughty can-can in shows for men only. The law forbids us to read the Bible or to offer prayer in Illinois schools. To my mind this is the utter absurdity of an itching for legislation. I don't believe one one hundredth of one per cent. of the religious exercises in public schools were sectarian or offended the religious beliefs of anybody. But the crank, the unreligious bigot, the man who wants to be noticed, works himself into an excitement and, while the rest of us are asleep, gets his anti-Bible legislation adopted. The result, in my opinion, is that ethical teaching is more observed in other than the public schools. I so judge from reading 'The Education of the Modern Boy,' a book by six masters of New England boarding schools and from this little work[2] by the Senior Master of Groton School. Here are twenty short sermons which he preached, alternating with the head master in the chapel on Sundays. Here is a man plain-spoken without truculence, gentle without weakness, religious without narrowness, a New Englander with a world-wide view. Hear him

[2] Sherrard Billings, "Talks to Boys," Houghton, Mifflin Co., Boston, 176 pp. $1.75.

tell the truth about the forefathers: 'The serious trouble with our Puritan ancestors was they made religion too easy. It is not hard to hang witches and expel heretics and set up a commonwealth apart from the world. Puritan means separate. If not anti-social it is anti-universal. We inherit their tendencies to apartness.' Dr. Billings' talks to these selected young Americans on their duty in a republic is blood-warming. The American idea means team work—people serving together. They are not uniform personalities. But they have a strong sense of common interests. They should differ as individuals, not as classes. In a republic, sympathy is a peculiar duty. The greatest danger confronting us is classes, groups who do not understand one another. Interest can be cultivated. It is our duty. We are less cursed with caste than any other people on earth. We have greater possibilities for good than any other nation in the world. But every one of us must work for the fellowship on which a real republic is based. Take care. The number of men who are working public-spiritedly to-day is so great that many who want to be idle can easily live on what has been done by others. These talks are virile. Duty, courage, work, ambition, heroism, purpose, unselfishness, the sterner virtues of manhood, are preached directly to the boys as Arnold used to aim his sermons in old Rugby. You'll profit by the book. It is a good antidote for the prevailing tendency to look on our social and political life as an amusing joke. When the master speaks to the school let him realize that his children instinctively desire to get from him ideas of high import, worth remembering. Let him not disappoint them.

"Forty years afterward, I recall with honor and respect two masters who did this in my school days and one whom I now despise as a zero. He couldn't preach for he was a hypocrite and crooked. Children find such things out. But if a schoolmaster makes a program for assembly talks with intent to lead his flock to pure-mindedness, honesty, courage and devotion to the public good, he thereby does much to train himself toward that completeness which is our only respectable goal. This book is a real help toward such a program."

Research is well under way.—This is the offering of Dr. Batwell.

"Everybody here remembers that we heard about research when we were in college. My professor made me write an essay on euphuisms in Shakespeare. I had to count the instances. No one but he and I read my composition. I am not sure that he did. Since then, research has come with a bang. Our own Monroe—W. S. Monroe of the University of Illinois—tells us a lot of it is padding with technical terms establishing nothing. Much of it consists of elaborate articles telling how the researcher proceeded, what kind of pencil and paper he used, and how he found out that the differences between school children are quite different. Such stuff has appeared galore in the educational journals and in the theses of candidates for the doctorate. Claude Crawford's work[3] is in refreshing contrast. It has none of the old unsubstantiated assertion in it. Prove all things; hold fast to that which is good, seems to be its motto. Science, says our book, has gone through a long history of blasting popular superstitions. Copernicus knocked one; Columbus, another, yet in Zion City and in Bloemfontein they still teach the earth as flat and the sun going round it. Education is full of old wives' tales: that teaching is unhappiness, that we are social outcasts. Research is counting facts and telling the truth quantitatively. I know a conscientious lady principal, here, who writes the superintendent periodically to tell him that the teachers are unhappy. If she were a researcher she would tell him, out of forty-eight teachers, two say they are unhappy; out of fifty-two farmers examined, eighteen appear to be unhappy; out of twelve doctors, three; of sixteen stenographers, six. Conclusion: Forty-eight teachers are happier than the farmers, doctors and stenographers studied. The trouble is, says our Crawford, people do not take the pains to decide what they are distressed about. They are like animals that are uneasy from hunger, thirst, cold or pain; they fuss around until by hit or miss they find relief. Research is a contrast to this blind and aimless conduct of beings who do not think. Make a study of

[3] Claude C. Crawford, "The Technique of Research in Education," University of Southern California Press, Los Angeles, 306 pp.

the situation; analyze it; consider correct procedures to correct it; try the most likely ones; keep trying until a remedy is found; perfect it; report it. That is research. That is what Ford does, the Wright brothers, Edison, Goodrich, Bell, Pasteur, Carrel, the authentic workers in the world. Research is intelligent hunting. The absence of it suggests laziness, complaint, whining, waste of life. This book is written to persuade us that we are getting in line with the promoters of progress and may make our lives count if we seek truth and follow it, especially when others, by intelligent investigation, have found it and report it. The errors of so-called research seem simple enough as here demonstrated. To avoid them and use the methods of investigation found reliable gives us a technique. What the best technique at present is fills the body of this volume. There is research by case study, by survey, by job analysis, by interview, by questionnaire, by observation, by measurement, by statistics, by reading the works of researchers. Each and others are covered with due recognition of the value and risks of all. To start with a conviction and to gather facts to prove it, common as it is with superintendents and board members, is the very nightmare of unintelligent procedure. A hobby is the insecurity which makes science impossible. Cold accuracy is indispensable. Every quantitative statement must be absolutely correct. Check it sedulously. One error may do more harm than all the other real truths do good. An observer of teaching—say a principal in a classroom—should create an atmosphere such that things go on when he is there as though he were not. Let him manifest no approval or disapproval lest he cause a change in the procedure or create an undesirable state of mind. Let him make the teacher come to regard his presence as a natural, everyday situation. Let him not tell the teachers how others do what she is trying. Let him not make his written notes in her presence. Let him never tell tales about the teacher observed even though they are true."

"I don't agree to all this," said Anna, the Arguer. "A principal who says to me each day, 'that's a fine piece of work,' gets more out of me than your wooden Indian who never opens his head."

"Sure!" said the Signpost. "And your superintendent who tells the teachers they are the finest in the world and who never bothers them with statistics to show that their children can't add, subtract, multiply nor divide, is the chap who wins popularity, gets presents of watches, cuff-buttons and loving cups. What are facts among friends?"

"Suburbanitas ad absurdum," sniffed Anna.

"Time!" said Papa Rose, "what's next?"

Teachers need to read professionally.—"Carter Good is next," said the doctor. "We've had him here in print before. He is the type Dr. Crawford tells us education needs—the sort of director the Champaign Duke of Buckingham says is most desirable among our 'inspirational' educators, because such a one tells when, how much, and exactly what. The Good book[4] might properly be entitled, 'How to keep your head' or 'Things they ought to tell in normal schools' or 'Antidotes to inherited ills.' Dr. Good seems to me a living proof that an education may be formal, critical, meticulously exact, and at the same time interesting from first to last. You can't read this book without enthusiasm. You have the delight of following a guide who knows where he is going, who guesses not at all, who has studied the authorities that have written about the trip, and who tells you exactly what they said and on what page they said it. You have confidence in him as a careful, accurate, informative author with no desire to make you admire him, who has a sound knowledge of what you need and an unpersonal, professional mode of stating it. 'What is the worth of research?' he asks, at the outset. His answer is his own and those of a representative few researchers, school superintendents and professors of education. There follows a sober, searching chapter on our reading. We don't know our educational authorities, our school periodicals, nor our professional books so well as the dentists, pharmacists, engineers and lawyers know theirs. Dr. Good does not work himself into sarcastic contempt over this. He gives the facts. He tells us the advantage of bracing up. We must learn the exact vocabulary of our profession.

[4] Carter V. Good, ''How to do Research in Education,'' Warwick and York, Baltimore, 298 pp.; $2.60.

It's different from what it was when we began our service. Then come his definite principles and procedures by which, with our growing seriousness, we may become professionally sound and thereby more useful, more respected, more indispensable to civic progress. 'The Techniques of Research' gives the kinds, the data, the procedures, the obstacles, the false paths, the main researches already made and the books and monographs describing them. We have come farther into knowing what we are about in the last twenty years than in the two hundred and fifty before. I, myself, am saying this. Dr. Good—and he is right—wouldn't deliver a generality like this. He would list and evaluate the conclusions of the two hundred and fifty years. He would do the same for the twenty-five years. He would let you count the gains. I wish the Bibliologoi could get him to one of our meetings with note-book and pencil and then to tell us where we should amend our ways. He has some observations on educational-book reviewing which ought to make us all resolved henceforth to lead better lives. Eight educational journals, he says, have bona fide critical estimates of new books. Those eight have reviews by recognized authorities. On the other hand there are the uncritical, informal, gushing book chats. Sakes alive! I'm not an authority on anything, and here I am reviewing a book of one who seems to me to be an expert of the experts. And, as for gush, I think our recorder who sends our proceedings to SCHOOL AND SOCIETY AND THE EDUCATIONAL REVIEW, ought, in addition to his kindly service of correcting the grammar of our informal speech, to lead us to leave out our enthusiasms, compliments and praise."

"Question of privilege," said Anna the Different. "Did not we hear just now that the author of this book discloses that the school workers do not read enough in their profession? Was it not the purpose of this book club of ours to make professional reading attractive? Does not Professor Good say that eight journals provide the critical estimates in book reviews which enable the selective students of education to know the poor books and to abstain from buying them? Has not the editor told us that readers of the journal write in that they like our style? Have not their epistolatory bouquets perfumed our meetings? Have not publishers increased their requests from about six a month to over twenty that we review their books? Has not the number of professional works published shown an increase by leaps and bounds since we encouraged their reading?"

"Who desires to answer these questions?" asked the Paterfamilias.

"I move we're on the right track and every day in every way, we're getting better and better," said the Signpost, "and I also second the motion. It is unanimous."

"Wherefore," resumed the reviewer, "I conclude by advising you that what you all need is the steadying influence of a book like this: scholarly, pertinent, important, dignified, solid, satisfying, delivered at your door by a genuine carter of the goods."

Some Watson wallops.—"I have paid my respects to Dr. John Watson in this company heretofore," continued the doctor. "Let me now discuss a new volume[5] by the same vigorous and profitable experimenter, philosopher and friend of babes and men. Dr. Watson, apostle of behaviorism, has made a moving book on mental hygiene of the very young with by-products of high value in the form of slaps on mama's wrist. Mothers resent advice on their treatment of children. You find resistance in the homes of college professors, you find it even with 'advanced' mothers. Dr. John sees that with the slow permeability of parents to discoveries in this line, finer and happier children would be given the world if they were taken away from their mothers as soon as possible. Failures in health, in mental adjustment, in happiness, are due to bringing up. Such failures with the knowledge we now have are avoidable. No woman should bear a child unless it can have a room of its own during the first two years. We don't need more babies. We need better-reared ones. There are altogether too many people in the world already: crippled personalities tied up with infantile defects and leading unhappy lives.

[5] John B. Watson, "Psychological Care of Infant and Child," W. W. Norton & Co., 70 Fifth Avenue, New York. 195 pp., $2.00.

"So here comes a run of pages and pictures illustrating what the maternity wards of hospitals, the orphan asylums and private homes have been able to teach the observers. Children have but two natural fears: loud noise and removal of support. All the rest of the terrors of life: dark, animals, masks, strangers, lightning, are made by suggestion. Read the chapter upon too much mother-love. Especially you who have been bolstering your opposition to the introduction of the platoon schools on the ground that the child can not be mothered enough in school unless he has one woman teacher all day long and every day. Read the lively treatment of rage and temper tantrums. The chapter on sex instruction is so comfortably free of all the old namby-pamby, downcast-eyes manner that it reads without shock. He concludes with 'the behaviorist's apologia,' the gist of which is that the kind of child he wants to develop is the problem-solver, free of sensitivities and independent of the family situation."

A remarkable conference.—The doctor continued: "While we are on the subject of research may I mention another Chicago book[6] of remarkable timeliness and value? It is a series of talks secured at a conference by the Chicago Association for Child Study and Parent Education. W. W. Charters, Ira Wile, Patty Hill, William Burnham, Margaret Blanton, John Anderson, Mary Murphy, Carleton Washburne, Sidonie Gruenberg, Rochelle Yarros, Henry Neumann, Ernest Horn and Walter Dearborn are some of the participants. Its purpose is to give to parents and teachers by means of workable projects the best of the conclusions that research and experimentation have reached in the laboratory. The changing family, the healthy mind, sunlight, weariness, ignorant well-to-do mothers, important happenings before the school age, sex-teaching that is making good in the common-school program, adolescence, adjustments, character training and citizenship are covered here with a freshness and frankness that is decidedly gratifying. There isn't any wild and glad emotionalism anywhere in the whole series. Ernest Horn's remarks are typical. He will not give way to the sentimentalists who are telling us to cater to the transient interests and purposes of children. We don't need any more nondescript initiative and self-expression. Our era wants responsibility. Indirect teaching of reading, spelling and arithmetic has been tried. It failed. Indirect instruction in moral and civic education will follow the same fate. Whoever says that morals are too indefinite to be taught directly has not gone about the job with energy or sympathy. Dr. Horn's elaboration of the direct method will do you good. So will the book as a whole."

Less philosophical mystery, more scientific sureness.—"Still they come," said Carolina, when the pater indicated her, "These conduct and behavior[7] books. Professor Hunter has become convinced that to approach the problems of human nature in terms of consciousness does not bring us very far into dependable truth. There's too much assumption of mysterious elements which can not be verified by science—the nature of mental activity has been tied up with philosophical speculation. Science is badly handicapped when it has to use words that lead to philosophical controversy. The chief concern of science is observable facts. We are divorcing the study of behavior from entangling alliances with philosophical assumptions. In the present work behavior means the muscular and glandular activity of the organism, such, for example, as is present in speaking, in walking, in fear. Educational theory, in so far as it is scientific and not philosophic, turns to biology and to anthroponomy (the study of facts and laws of human behavior), for its fundamental conceptions. The book considers the place of man in the world, his earliest types, social and political, situations and activities, unlearned behavior, habit and thinking. Without language thinking is impossible. Thinking can in no sense be called an instinct. It is not inherited. It is learned. Thinking is efficient to the extent that it adjusts with the least expenditure of effort the organism to its environment in the best way. There is no better field for demonstrating efficient thinking than by the

[6] "Intelligent Parenthood." Twenty-five papers. University of Chicago Press, 326 pp. $2.

[7] Walter S. Hunter, "Human Behavior." Published by University of Chicago Press, 353 pp., $2.10.

study of cause and effect in science. The stimulus to science is this, that all phenomena have causes which can be discovered sooner or later by scientific thinking. Only in recent years has man undertaken to regulate his individual and social acts by science, by proved thought. He has the handicap of inheriting a multitude of customs, replete with maladaptations and superstitions. No profession, probably, is more hindered by these unscientific emotional beliefs, prejudices and fears than ours. We are not yet scientists, but we are nearer than we were."

The teacher's responsibility for conduct control.—"Professor Symonds,[8] Teachers College, Columbia University, also will have us liberated from superstition and mystery in the mental field. He begins by some illuminating paragraphs clearing out of your minds the foggy conception of conduct, putting there exactly what he means. Psychology is wallowing among words that are saturated with bewildering implications gathered during ages when it was more fashionable to spin out theories from the armchair than to go out and study facts. There is a review of physiology as it exists in 1928. This is so different a body of knowledge from what we were given in school that it seems a new story. Then come the main divisions of conduct and a remarkable collection of conduct codes. Dr. Symonds is strong in the use of everyday, familiar situations used to illustrate the subject he considers. You will be assisted by his treatment of maxims, helps to the student, schoolroom problems and personal ones. I like his definite studies of courage, loyalty, kindness, obedience and thrift. Polly, here, ought to read this book, for it goes into political conduct, too. The General, who has given us reviews of treatises on religious training, will find his subject covered. Climate, crime, character, manners, etiquette, health and the laws of conduct-formation are topics which are treated with brilliant common sense and put on a scientific basis. The prevailing spirit of the book is that no form of control has a greater possibility for influencing the well-being of society than the control of conduct. We are suspicious of a traditional system that fosters war, persecution and intolerance; that taboos an examination of the relations of men and women. We want to see the problems of conduct brought out into the open. It is especially the concern of teachers. We timidly try to influence the conduct of our charges. What do we know about it? Unproved maxims made by some old antediluvian who never tried them out! Home has lost much of its control. School is trying to shoulder character development. Books like this, in which a cool-headed yet optimistic student with a singularly graphic power of presentation gathers the latest discoveries for us, will have to be studied by our school practitioners."

Who are "the progressives"?—The next reporter was our Anna, nicknamed The Argumentative.

"I have read and annotated all my books," she said. "You can boil down my reports as suits your space. I read Mr. Stanwood Cobb[9] first. He's quite carried away by what he calls progressive education, which I guess is a composite of what Ethel Dummer, Flora Cook, Angelo Patri, Otis Caldwell, Frank Slutz, Marietta Johnson, Euphrosyne Langley, and, in all, about a hundred untrammeled souls mentioned by the author preach as a new gospel. The book radiates a wealth of enthusiasm. Variety is the spice of life. To cast the minds of all children into one mould is to turn this delightfully diverse world into a monotony of boredom. The progress of humanity, says Comrade Cobb, consists in variation forward, not in repetition of a type. Those who insist on uniformity are cutting at the very roots of a new race evolving itself. The ideal school will encourage differences of personality and furnish a rich environment in which the native ability of each child will blossom and fructify.

"I like the book immensely and find much that I doubt. For instance, 'the lack of respect which the teaching profession receives from the general public is perhaps as much the fault of the teaching profession and of the system of education as it is of the parent and laity.' I

[8] Percival M. Symonds, "The Nature of Conduct," The Macmillan Co., New York, 346 pp. $2.

[9] Stanwood Cobb, "The New Leaven," The John Day Co., New York. 340 pp., $2.50.

don't know where Mr. Cobb has been or what he has read to justify a statement like that. The American parent and laity can have just as respectable teachers as they want if they will respect teachers and put their respect into measurable form. From a despised and degraded caste recruited from almshouses, prisons and social derelicts, the teachers of America have in two hundred years raised their reputation to whatever grade it now has by the efforts of the profession in the face of obstacles set by the people through their school boards. Find any community in which political grip and its corresponding degradation have been removed from schools and you will find it has been done by teachers. Mr. Cobb is not bothered much by the inroads which, through the development of scientific measurement, have been made upon wild educational statement, otherwise he would scarcely have the face to say that if we wish to see where the art of teaching is most effectively and most happily used we have only to turn to the field of adult education where voluntary attendance enforces methods that enlist interest and cooperation. I find, in these days of Missouri readers, a sad lack of proof, volume and page, supporting much of the delightful author's assertions.

"For instance, 'The soul is not bounded by earth-years. The difference of a few earth-turns around the sun does not mean that the soul of the child is necessarily younger than that of the adult. That the soul at birth is in a helpless body does not prove a paucity of spiritual life within. In the world of ideas the child is as much at home as the adult and as unlimited.' Maybe so! maybe so! But it sounds like what any impromptu speaker before the parents' club might say and get applause if he put emotion enough into his manner.

"I presume this book was not written for students of education. The progress that has been made and is making in public-school teaching gets such scanty recognition that I wonder how much and how lately the author has been in a public school. I wonder where he gets the foundation for saying that 'classes which have always been considered homogeneous are now seen to be most heterogeneous.' Who sees them as most heterogeneous? Not the intelligence testers and achievement measurers. They find differences in children of the same classroom but not so many differences as likenesses. Children pretty generally agree as to liking a teacher, narrations, drawing, music, looking at pictures. They eat the same food, are subject to the same hurts and benefits to a large degree. That they are different in various things teachers have always known and have acted accordingly. To assert that the children of a classroom graded with the usual care are most heterogeneous, a superlative difference, seems to me a wild statement. A common lesson in arithmetic, geography, any school subject, with such individual administration as an ordinary teacher makes, seems to me a logical and effective piece of work. I think it gains, by the effect of group participation, what no system of individual tutoring ever secured. But there, I'm guessing! just as this author does. I am bewildered by statements like this: 'Our college youths seem babes in the woods as compared with European intellectuals.' I recall that the Mosely commission was sent to study our education because Mr. Mosely said he noticed the American college men were better able to solve real problems than were the European. Mr. Cobb might well have avoided saying that a defect of our secondary school system is the uncultured and uninspiring quality of teacher so common in it, as well as its narrow-minded and dogmatic instruction. Where does he find this? New England says, 'It is not in me.' The west says, 'I have it not.' Surely there is a vein for this brass where they find it. This is cheap stuff, unworthy a serious writer on education. In these twenty years I have known schools here and in Pennsylvania and in Iowa but have not found these things nor the drudgery on which he harps, nor the distaste for knowledge he says is formed in the mind of the child. He seems to be seeing things, but he does not tell where. It is an old game to set up a man of straw, name it 'public-school,' and cudgel it to pieces. But that is not the mode among educators, now. It is back-number stuff. How one could call himself a progressive educator and fail to tell where, when and how much puzzles an ordinary public-school teacher like me.

"I have to raise my brows at this, 'The secondary schools retort that they regret the necessity for drill.' Dear me! Here the experimenters and psychologists have been showing us how habit, mastery, skill, ability surely come by intelligent and adapted drill. Here is every athletic coach, dramatic director, choir master, violin teacher, all around us in our high schools, unblushingly getting his progress through drill and unashamed of it. Really I believe I could by drill improve Mr. Cobb's reasoning processes and his English so that he wouldn't say, 'The teachers mark in ways unknown to *each other.*' The book seems to me to have been written to please parents who wish to send their children to private schools. All the loose criticism assailing the public schools can be swallowed without thought by this class of readers. Progressive education is a good title. But why limit it to the fine work done by the Cobbs, the Caldwells, the Johnsons *et al.?* The public school in which I work is progressive. So are many hundreds such high schools all over. Otherwise one would hardly see an increase of over 600 per cent. membership in the past ten years. If Mr. Cobb had been less positive in putting the claim-brand of his own and of his selected educators on the progressive ideas now common in schools and increasing daily, if he had cited place and time as we have been taught we nowadays must do in serious educational writing, he would have done a better piece of work, for he has the propulsive spirit of the crusader in him. His advocacy of the standard achievement test is logically defended. He does fine service in arguing for creative teachers for the young children. His condemnation of requiring foreign language for boys with no taste for it is superb. His plea to the colleges to center their entrance requirements on living qualities rather than upon dead and meaningless memory affairs is splendid. So is his urge for comradery between teacher and child. His fling at poor teaching in the national Naval Academy loses force for any one who has been personally acquainted with any graduate of that institution. My brother may have sacrificed some of his childish freedom for the efficient training gotten at Annapolis. But neither he nor I can join Mr. Cobb in his regrets at the tyranny of that instruction. I like Mr. Cobb for his movable seats, for elimination of strain, for abundant handwork and for interesting projects. We have them in the public schools. I admire his frank admission that some children are not fit for freedom and democracy. The private school dismisses them. We can't. We don't want to. Our mission is to all the children of all the people, the good and the bad. And yet we are progressive. Mr. Coolidge, Mr. Hoover, Mr. Tigert and Professor Judd have all recently said we are. More of us are opposed to the anti-social uses to which marks and prizes have been put than the proportion of opposers in private schools. Mr. Cobb's treatment of this is decidedly excellent, as is also his condemnation of giving mediocre treatment to superior children. His praise of handwork merits the highest compliment. 'It is the glory of America,' he says, 'to have achieved the first civilization in the history of the world founded upon universal work.' I read the whole book, every word of it, with intense interest. I recommend it heartily. A man who has so clear a vision of the possibilities of education will not long let the old mist of tradition becloud his judgment as to public schools. They are not all 'progressive,' but the proportion of progressives in them is as great as in the schools with which good Mr. Cobb is more familiar."

Thus ended the stated meeting. But the Signpost and Anna, with others joining, continued an informal discussion of the value of the Cobbs, Johnsons and Deweys to public school education. By socratic fencing, her antagonists drove the belligerent lady into a corner from which she flung her final shot that progressive educators who accuse their brothers and sisters who are in the public service reduce the benefit of progressive education by approximately ninety-two and fifty-seven hundredths per cent.

There was plain Swedish bread with curds, there was a sweet Swedish baking of the nature of a crisp cake. There were Swedish sandwiches of quaint flavors, Swedish confections of delicious variety, Swedish hot drinks and cold, all under the auspices of the Abjornson lady. There were bravos for her in Swedish which the recorder does not know how to spell. Then the break-up and home goings.

SCHOOL AND SOCIETY

EDITED BY J. McKEEN CATTELL

WITH WHICH IS COMBINED THE

EDUCATIONAL REVIEW

EDITED BY WILLIAM McANDREW

Volume XXVIII | Saturday, December 8, 1928 | Number 728

ADMINISTRATIVE RELATIONS IN COLLEGES[1]

By FRANK L. McVEY

PRESIDENT OF THE UNIVERSITY OF KENTUCKY

BEHIND this hard and pedantic title is a great sea of romance on which have sailed the barks of learned men in the quest of knowledge for youth. The story of colleges and their government goes back many centuries and parallels the history of government, business and religion. This story in its details would cover many pages, much controversy, a large number of failures and numerous successful enterprises, and it would at the same time show the effort to throw off the trammels of tradition and the struggle to push aside the heavy hand of privilege.

Under its hard and pedantic title this paper tries to cover three phases of one problem in administration adjustments. The first has to do with the place of a board of trustees in the American college; the second, in contrast with it, concerns the functions of a college faculty; and the third, the relationship of administrative officers to boards and faculties. The contention which is upheld in these pages is very brief. It is likely, in fact, to pass unnoticed. To formulate it is to accept it, though in practice this theory is by no means the prevailing one in the government of American colleges.

The theme can be stated in the following form: Boards of trustees and faculties are cooperating factors in American education and administrative officers are their executive agents. The boards of trustees are in fact the directors of business affairs, the guardians of money, the planners of building enterprises and the protectors of the legal rights of the institution, its staff, alumni and student body. The faculty has its function in the formulation of courses of study, the making of by-laws and the establishment of the legislation for the government of students. The administrative officer by virtue of his office and his relations to the board and the faculty is an executive agent for both. In this triple relationship none assumes arbitrary powers but all work together, each in his respective field. That such understanding of functions works toward progress has been seen again and again in America in contrast to the failure of institutions to hold and develop the spirit of learning under an arbitrary and despotic college government.

The theory being stated, there may be some value in attempting to outline the history of university and college development. No adequate presentation can be made in a few pages, but the drift of institutional government can be brought out clearly.

[1] Address delivered at the inauguration of H. L. Donovan, as president of the Eastern Kentucky Teachers College, on October 26, 1928.

The university in Europe had two beginnings; one a student origin, the other founded by the masters. In neither was there a board of trustees. Students gathered in some city and there set up their own institution with the courses, texts and rules worked out by them. The lecturers were employed by the students and subjected to student regulations in the matter of hours, tardiness and the manner of instruction. Great numbers of students found their way to the university towns to an extent that parallels the attendance at the largest institutions in America to-day. The University of Bologna was a university of scholars; the University of Paris an institution founded by masters. The student guilds later selected their own rector and made the governing regulations. In the passage of time student autonomy and student control broke down and bodies of governors were appointed by the state. The church was interested in this educational movement and with its power the university came under ecclesiastical control here and there. Thus the colleges ceased to be a voluntary organization of scholars and drifted into a representative and a new teaching type of government.

Harvard College was founded in 1637 with the title of fellows and tutors for the governing board. It was a resident government but in the controversy over ecclesiastical matters the resident government was taken from the teaching group and placed in the hands of an absentee government. Since 1800 no teacher has been elected a member of the board of fellows. In 1693 William and Mary College, a body corporate, had a government designated as president and masters. Yale in 1701 was under an ecclesiastical board when ten clergymen were given the authority to establish a college. It was a new provision of the Princeton charter in 1746 that authorized a company of non-scholars with full power to organize a college. The beginning of Harvard College was in line with European experience. The group of teachers were their own governors. Because of difficulties of ecclesiastical import the lay board, often meeting away from the college town, came into existence. The absentee government required a representative in the person of a president who should have more authority than the presiding officer of a body of scholars. As the absentee lay boards could not know the problems in a personal way the members kept in touch through the key man, the president. It was natural as this system spread through the educational institutions, both old and new, that there should be a marked difference of function for the lay board and the faculty. The American type of college president associated with the lay board was soon engaged in administrative duties and enmeshed in details. The faculty was subordinated to teaching duties, and the board of trustees, as this system of government got into swing, came into possession of all authority and so determined by virtue of that power the educational, financial and administrative policy of the institution.

In the course of two centuries of educational history in America the management of higher education moved a long way from the European system. Certain advantages arose from the government of educational institutions employed in America. There was a unity of purpose in the conduct of the institution that rested upon the centralization of policy and administration. In a large measure this accounts for the rapid growth of colleges in numbers, support and material equipment. The interest of lay members of boards was enlisted and larger financial support ensued as a consequence. But there is a disadvantage in the subordination of educational policy to financial and administrative interests which weighs heavily at times upon the ambitions and hopes of faculties. In our American system the place and authority of the teaching group are reduced to a much lower place in influence and standing than that occupied by the staffs of European universities.

As in everything else, the college faculty has passed through many changes in its development. In the early history of educational institutions in this country it was both a debating society and an administrative body. Its members discussed educational problems, adjusted student courses and determined the nature and extent of disciplinary matters when students came before the group for disobeying the rules of the institution. As time went on, student bodies increased in size and the faculty found it difficult to act as an administrative body and at the same time deal with the individual cases that arose from time to time in the student body. It therefore moved more and more in the direction of a legislative group, establishing principles and creating rules and regulations for the conduct of courses of study and the administration of student matters. With this development the administrative officer came to be a representative of the faculty group and its executive agent in carrying out legislative enactments.

Where a faculty has an indefinite and hazy place in institutional organization there results a wobbly type of legislative organization, and when the acts of the faculty can be vetoed by the president or the board of trustees, this body falls to a low estate with no power and very little interest in the general problems of the institution. Thus the written constitution of an educational institution should set forth clearly the rights, power and authority of the different governing groups in the organization. The faculty should be something more than a traditional body engaged in routine educational matters. It should in fact be the group that determines educational policy. When this is done the faculty has a self-respect and a larger interest in the affairs of the institution, in that the creation of courses of study not only involves money, but the staff, its personnel and the general purpose of the institution. Consequently the faculty possessing such an important rôle in institutional organization should have a definite place with prescribed duties, and its position, integrity and rights should be fully recognized in a constitutional provision. In the larger institutions the faculty remains a college organization and the legislative affairs of the institution are considered in a senate which is composed of representative membership. This senate has some control over the colleges in their courses of study and general policy. It also passes the regulations applicable to the institution as a whole and its purpose is to develop unity of action and to define the objectives of the institution. As an organization the senate is wholly legislative. It is not an administrative body and in consequence the administrative officer comes into the possession of great authority and executive power.

One of the important problems which confronts every institution is the establishment and organization of a budget system. A budget is an orderly presentation of the financial affairs of an institution and has for its purpose the planning of income and expenditures. In its creation the heads of departments, deans, president and the board of trustees have a part. The senate, as such, does not possess authority or power of budget making. This, however, is an anomaly and the senate as the representative body of the teaching group ought to have something to say through a committee or by group action in the important matter of budget making. There are many difficulties in carrying out such a democratic move. Disagreements are sure to arise on the allotments that are made to different departments and to the various objectives of the institution. A resultant disruption of good feeling is likely to ensue and in the present status of organization of institutions it is a question whether the institution should not preserve its essential unity rather than adhere to a principle that might for the time being work havoc in its progress.

At present, and for that matter for some years past, the organization of colleges and universities has followed very closely the corporation development in industry. That is, a board of directors selected for various reasons and representing different groups determines the policy and works out the general line of development that the institution has before it. In such a system, with absentee members of the board constituting the controlling government, the executive officer is entrusted with large authority and his colleagues are bound to take the necessary steps to carry out the policies, whatever they may be, of the board. The staff of the institution is employed upon the recommendation of the administrative officer and its functions and its work are likewise determined by the executive. Where this system is used in its simplest form and applied to educational problems the institution which follows it becomes a one-man institution and the faculty has only an incidental part in its conduct. Without doubt the American system of college administration has led to concrete results, but very much of it has been accomplished at the expense of the spirit of democracy. If the educational purpose should be emphasized over the financial and building program, the faculty instead of being subordinated would be looked upon as a body of experts engaged in the development of educational processes and attempting to provide courses of study that would meet the changing requirements of modern life. The faculty would in fact become the agency in the institution through which the educational policy is determined and administered.

When the view is taken that the administrative officer is a representative of a board of trustees whose members are living in various parts of the country then that officer is likely to place his emphasis on the business side of the institution and neglect its educational purposes. But if the view is accepted that the executive officer is to carry out the purposes of the two groups, board and faculty, then a different place is given to the educational functions of the institution. The president in the second instance administers finance and business as well as educational policy. If he regards the board of trustees and the faculty as the formulators of policy then he ceases to be an arbitrary officer, acting as a kind of educational despot, but becomes instead advisory and administrative in his relationship to these groups. In fact, his position parallels more and more that of the cabinet officer under a parliamentary government who is subject to the rule of opinion.

Unquestionably the functions of boards of trustees are being materially modified in these days and there are many instances where the view set forth in this discussion has been accepted and the educational policy of the institution determined by the teaching staff. In fact there is now a movement away from the earlier attitude and some return to the European viewpoint. In the process of building and fund collection there is great need for the lay board. But in the modification of education processes the faculty importance steadily increases and the distinction between the business and financial policies of the institution and those of education steadily emphasizes the difference of functions in the two groups. Under the European system both functions are carried on by one group, the faculty, but we have not yet reached in this country a condition which makes that possible. It is quite essential that the two groups whose relationship and attitude materially affect the life of the institution should be brought together. The secrecy of board meetings is passing and copies of the minutes are now distributed to the members of the faculty in many institutions. Other groups are being represented on the board of trustees, such as the alumni. The time will come when members of the faculty and possibly representatives of the student body will be found on the membership of the institutional board. Meantime there might very well be joint committees and joint assemblies of board and faculty for the purpose of bringing together the two groups. Certainly a board of trustees can not administer the affairs of an institution without knowing rather clearly its educational ambitions. And, on the other hand, a faculty can not understand the difficulties attendant upon financial matters unless their attention is called to them in a vital way. Undoubtedly, in this country we are entering upon a new stage in education. That stage is placing the larger and more important emphasis upon educational principles. With this shift in view, the president becomes an advisory officer with executive functions. He is particularly charged with the development of mutual esteem and respect between the board of trustees and the faculty group. The European university lacked the advice of men of affairs; the American college has too often failed to have the recommendations of the educational groups associated with it. Neither is a happy situation. The combination of the two with the recognition of the rights and abilities of both is more productive of results that are sound and far reaching. When this is done, in times of stress and difficulty as well as in the days when all goes nicely, the American college can progress in the true spirit of learning. The college must recognize the unity of purpose, the demand of the democratic spirit and the cooperative character of education in its government as it has in its teaching.

COOPERATIVE COURSES IN COLLEGES

By W. H. TIMBIE

PROFESSOR OF ELECTRICAL ENGINEERING AND INDUSTRIAL PRACTICE, MASSACHUSETTS INSTITUTE OF TECHNOLOGY

WHEN this paper is finished it will probably look like a patchwork quilt, for I am going to include a little history, a few statistics, a short discussion of fundamental educational principles, try to correct some of the false ideas concerning cooperative courses in general and tell how the cooperative courses in electrical engineering at the Massachusetts Institute of Technology are conducted. If it does look like a patchwork quilt, at least the patches will be small.

The cooperative plan of education in engineering was introduced into America in 1906 by Dean Schneider at the University of Cincinnati. At first it was limited to the engineering school, but the idea has steadily spread until now practically the whole University of Cincinnati, with upward of four thousand pupils, is on the cooperative schedule. Nineteen other colleges scattered throughout the country are operating cooperative courses in engineering, and two of the largest engineering schools in the country are planning to put in cooperative courses next June. At least two colleges are offering even students of liberal arts the advantages of this plan. A recent report in the *Journal of Engineering Education* shows that cooperative schedules are offered in fourteen different curricula, including the regular branches of engineering, architecture, commerce, administration, arts, textiles, mining, etc.; in fact, the statement can be truly made that at the present time a student in the United States may have the advantage of the cooperative plan in practically any college course which he may wish to take, providing, of course, he picks out the right educational institution. At present, between five and six thousand engineering students alone are receiving their training by the cooperative method.

In spite of this rapid spread of the cooperative idea among the various colleges in the country, there is a deep-rooted misconception concerning the underlying educational principles and concerning the various details of operation. In the first place, it should be definitely stated that the cooperative plan is not a makeshift introduced into the schools in the place of some more desirable plan which the school finds itself unable to carry on. The cooperative plan has, in general, been adopted because the educational authorities in these schools believe it to possess educational values and opportunities which are superior to the educational values and opportunities of the old-line methods of instruction. The plan has been adopted because it is based on recognized educational foundations and does a better job of education. The student graduating from a cooperative course is not only acquainted with the practical conditions in the business world, but he also knows his theory better. All during the time he has been studying the theories and principles in the classroom he has been acquiring a knowledge of their application. This knowledge throws light upon the theories, makes them alive, interesting and shows their utility. In other words, the student no longer just memorizes theories and methods in school, but actually in the plants he lives theories and methods. They become not only a part of his information, but a part of his experience, a part of his life, a part of himself. Thus, a big by-product of the practical experience is a more thorough understanding and a surer grounding in the studies which the student pursues at school. This is of the utmost importance, although it is more or less a by-product.

It has been said that that college graduate is successful who is able to match up his practical experience with his theoretical instruction. Yet this matching up by the old method was left more or less to chance. Too many times a student, by the old-line method, would be unable to obtain the necessary practical experience until long after he had forgotten his theoretical instruction. The cooperative scheme matches theory and practice bit by bit as both are acquired. In a properly laid-out course very little of this matching is left to chance. It is all carefully planned and supervised. Do not infer from this that there should be a day-to-day or even a week-to-week correlation between the classroom work and the practical experience. This is undesirable, even if it were possible. The correlation consists rather in so planning the schedule that when the student is at work he is engaged on tasks the theory of which he has studied the previous term at school. As a result of this parallel working and learning comes, I believe, one of the principal benefits of the cooperative scheme—there is little or no demotion when the student graduates from school and enters industry. One of the most unsatisfactory things about the old-line educational plan is that the college student has been training and exercising his mental abilities to the maximum degree right up to commencement day. Upon his graduation, he is trained mentally above many of the tasks which will be his at the start of his industrial life. If he is to become thoroughly familiar with industry, he must go through the various subordinate positions, doing menial tasks and routine work. For a week or two this probably requires a certain amount of mental exertion, and the young man is fairly contented. Soon, however, the work becomes more and more mechanical and routine, requiring little mental exertion. The young man begins to feel much like a highly-trained athlete who is compelled to remain inactive for several weeks. He misses the mental exercise and mental stimulus, and naturally so. This mental exercise is something that he needs in order to keep himself mentally fit and growing in efficiency and capacity for work. It is a common sight to see college graduates drifting around for a year or two trying to find themselves and wondering what the matter is, whether the trouble lies with the world in general, with themselves or with their education. And the truth is that during their four or five years in college they may have dropped behind in the industrial race, as far as being able to fit into industrial life is concerned. Until they can catch up they are bound to be discontented and to question the wisdom of having spent these four years in study.

The picture of the cooperative graduate is different. While he is yet an undergraduate, and while he is still acquiring his fundamental scientific and theoretical knowledge, which is later going to be of so much use to him, at this early stage he is doing the menial tasks in industry, carrying out his routine work and going through the various subordinate positions. In other words, he is carrying on his industrial training in parallel with his theoretical training. When he graduates from college he also graduates from a large amount of the more or less undesirable details in business. He is able to take a position of greater responsibility—a position that requires more mental exertion and which tends to keep him mentally active and in good spirits. He suffers little, if any, demotion. Often, graduation from college is accompanied by a promotion in the company with which he has taken his practical training.

While these facts are only more or less known to the staff of the educational institutions, they are a matter of common knowledge to the personnel staff of the industry of the country. The members of the personnel staff in any company can tell you how difficult it is to fit the ordinary college graduate into the organization, and with how much greater ease the graduate of the cooperative course enters the industrial world. If the cooperative method of education did nothing but this one thing of lessening the demotion of the college man upon graduation, it has proved its worth.

Another false idea prevalent concerning the cooperative plan is that it is suited only for the training of operators and so-called practical men. The cooperative course in electrical engineering at M. I. T. was started mainly to train particularly high-grade engineers for creative design and original research, tasks demanding the utmost theoretical knowledge. Already, graduates of this class are holding successfully positions as creative designers, where it is necessary to know the latest facts and theories of science and to be able to adapt them to the design and development of modern electrical and mechanical machinery.

This audience is made up of educators, a group that would naturally be interested in the educational bases of cooperative courses, and I am going to discuss these for a few minutes. In the first place, it should be laid down as fundamental that the cooperative course is not an abridgement of any regular course. Every study that is in the regular course should be in the cooperative course. Valuable as the practical experience is, it can not take the place of the subjects taught in school. A young man or woman goes to college in order to obtain the mental training and education which school offers. When practical experience is substituted for some of the school work, the pupil is robbed of just so much of that for which he entered the educational institution. A cooperative course, therefore, which is conducted on the right lines, contains in its curriculum everything that the curriculum of the old-line plan contained.

Secondly, not only should a cooperative course present all the subject-material of the non-cooperative course, but it should present this material in the same form and in the same extent. There should be no abbreviated or condensed subjects. The cooperative student should not carry a bit heavier schedule at school than the non-cooperative student. It is axiomatic that if it is most desirable to give a certain subject to non-cooperative students a certain number of times a week and a certain number of weeks a year, it is just as desirable to present the subject at the same rate to cooperative students. The utmost care should be taken to see that the cooperative students and the non-cooperative students receive their instruction in any given subject at precisely the same rate. What is best for one is certainly best for the other. Put in another way: the scholastic requirements for graduation from a cooperative course should be the same as those of a non-cooperative course, both as to quantity and quality of subject-matter and instruction. When this policy is pursued, the superiority of the cooperative method is apparent, because if the two courses have exactly the same subject-material, taught in exactly the same way, then all the benefits derived from the practical experience obtained in the industry will be a clear gain over and above the advantages of the non-cooperative course, with the additional advantages which are derived from the coordination.

Thirdly, in order to make the time spent in practical experience of the greatest educational value, the practical experience should be laid out into a definite course. The student should not be given just a series of jobs, but should be put through a carefully-planned and supervised course of experience. The basis for laying out this course should not be primarily the plant convenience of the cooperating company, but the educational value of each operation, the test question in each case being, "Does this job offer at this time the greatest educational opportunity to the student?" The term "educational opportunity" includes two features. The job should show how the various operations are planned and carried out in that particular part of the industrial field in which the student wants to engage after graduation. The job also may have a certain vocational-guidance value; that is, it may acquaint a student with some part of the field other than the one in which he is at present particularly interested, so that he may more intelligently choose his life's work. A course in practical experience, properly laid out, will so arrange the tasks that each job is scheduled shortly after the time when the fundamental principles upon which it is based have been studied at school. The length of time which he may spend on the particular job should be determined entirely by the educational value of each day spent upon it. When the student would benefit educationally by a transfer to the next job, he should be transferred immediately. His progress through the company should be one of increasing responsibility and greater demand upon his mental training and ability, so that upon graduation he is ready to step into a job the requirements of which, in responsibility and mental training, are commensurate with his scholastic attainments. In order to produce this result the student must be a real producer during his cooperative periods, not a mere observer. He must learn to do by doing, not by just observing.

The length of the cooperative periods varies in different colleges from two weeks to a semester of practically nineteen weeks, the length of the technology period being nineteen weeks for the fall and spring terms and sixteen weeks for the summer term. We believe that there is a decided advantage in the student remaining at the institute one full term at a time, in order to complete the regular units of study without interruption, and in order to be able to enter the usual campus life and student activities of the institute. From an educator's standpoint the first reason is probably the more potent of the two, but I fear the students have much regard for the second. At any rate, the cooperative students at M. I. T. have taken full advantage of this opportunity and have been represented in practically every student activity, including varsity athletics. A period of full-term length not only allows the student to complete regular units of study at the institute, but it also provides opportunity for organized instruction in institute subjects while the students are at the plants of the cooperating companies. As a matter of fact, two regular institute studies are carried on by the students while they are away from Cambridge. Class sessions are held two evenings a week, one session in engineering and the other in a so-called humanistic or cultural subject. To carry on this instruction, members of the institute instructing staff are located permanently at Pittsfield, Massachusetts; Schenectady, New York, and at New York City, in addition to the regular staff at Cambridge. These classes prevent any hiatus in the student's study-habits, and offset any real or imagined coarsening or materialistic tendency, which some have supposed is prevalent in the modern industrial world. Whether or not credit can be given to these humanistic studies, nearly nine years' experience has shown that contact with industry has not coarsened the cooperative men nor has it made them noticeably materialistic. It should be stated in this connection that the work done by students in these classes at the works is on the whole better than the work done by these same students in their classes at the institute. This is probably due to the fact that the student concentrates upon two subjects only while at the plant, and can naturally do better than when his attention is divided among several subjects, as it necessarily is when he is at the institute. One by-product of these classes has been the development in young engineers of the habit of studying several evenings a week when they are employed during the day. The employers of the graduates of this course report that this habit is as hard to break as it is to form and that the men continue with their evening study after graduation. This result alone, in my opinion, makes it worth while to maintain this feature of cooperative work. The success of the young graduate depends as much upon keeping up his habits of study as it does upon how well he carries on his daily tasks. The student who closes his text-books upon graduation is very likely at the same time to close his mind to effort and his eyes to opportunity.

Another result of these after-hours classes is to maintain the student's fitness during the practice period, so that there is little lost motion in changing from plant to school life again.

Another operating principle of the M. I. T. course is that any one student should receive his practical experience entirely with one company. Since there are five cooperating companies, each representing a particular branch of the electrical industry, there is an opportunity for a student to apply to that company which offers the kind of experience he desires. These five companies are the General Electric Company, the Edison Electric Illuminating Company of Boston, Boston Elevated Railway, Stone and Webster, Inc., and the Bell Telephone System, each of which is comprehensive enough to make it well worth a student's spending eighteen months in its various departments.

The scientific and theoretical training which the student receives at the institute is the same, regardless of the company with which he takes his practical work. His school work lays a general scientific foundation, the practical work and experience more or less specialize his engineering in one particular field. The fundamental reason for scheduling the practical work of a student with one company is in order that he may get a unified conception of the company's policy, and become imbued with the spirit of loyalty, which is so much needed in business organizations of the present day. The growth and stability of modern business depends fully as much upon the loyalty and team-work of the engineers and executives as it does upon their individual attainments and brilliancy. The school training should develop to the highest degree the mental and personal qualities of each student. The company-training should add to this the important virtues of loyalty and cooperation. His intimate contact with one company during his school years should teach a student that loyalty and enthusiasm are prime requisites for his advancement and ultimate success.

A third requirement of the M. I. T. course is that the student should finish his foundation work in physics, mathematics and chemistry before he starts his practical work. In other words, the student starts his professional and engineering studies and his practical experience at the same time. For this reason, the first two years of the technology course are non-cooperative and are identical with the first two years of the regular courses. The cooperative periods start with the third year and continue throughout the junior, senior and graduate years, the student spending alternate terms, including the summers, at the works and at the institute. An average of five weeks each year is allowed for vacation.

The M. I. T. course is not only an undergraduate course; it is also a graduate course, for the successful completion of which the student receives a degree of master of science, in addition to that of bachelor of science. Thus, it takes no longer for a man to receive his master's degree by the cooperative method than it ordinarily does by the non-cooperative method, the time being usually five years in both cases, the fifth year of the cooperative students' course consisting entirely of individual graduate work.

A recent study of the positions and salaries of graduates of this cooperative course indicates that it is unusually successful. The average salary of the median graduate of this course is increasing at a rate 55 per cent. faster than the average salary of the median graduate of the engineering schools of America, as reported by the society for the promotion of engineering education. Until recently, two departments only, the chemistry and the electrical, offered cooperative courses. Last June the civil engineering department started a cooperative course in railroad operation, the practical experience being obtained with the Boston and Maine Railroad.

The Massachusetts Institute of Technology offers a good example of a school located in a distinctly industrial center operating particularly successful cooperative courses. Antioch College and others demonstrate how schools located at some distance from large industrial plants can operate upon this plan with success. The truth is that the cooperative plan of education possesses such great flexibility that it readily can be adapted to the local conditions of practically any community, and to the ideals, standards and traditions of any educational institution. It is just as well adapted to prepare in a particularly successful manner the keenest intellects for a successful career in theoretical research and creative design, as it is to train the man of slower mentality for the more practical and equally important tasks of constructing and maintaining the mechanical equipment necessary to turn the wheels of modern industry.

The ultimate possibilities of the cooperative method of education are so great that they are only just beginning to be sensed by the colleges and the industries.

THE INFERIORITY COMPLEX AND THE RURAL TEACHER

By I. D. WEEKS

NORTHERN STATE TEACHERS COLLEGE, ABERDEEN, SOUTH DAKOTA

During the past few years much has been said about the "inferiority complex." People have come to look upon it as a great monster, a "Frankenstein." It has been discussed frequently at educational meetings, in classes of education and psychology. It has even found its way into the programs of women's clubs and parent-teacher associations. The term is almost as common as "static" and "X-ray."

It is the purpose of this article to point out the relation of this complex to teachers of rural schools. An instructor in rural education in one of the teachers' colleges of the northwest said to a group of prospective rural teachers, "It is important that you develop a superiority complex rather than one of inferiority."

Has the country teacher an inferiority complex? If the responses of teachers are any indication it would seem so. Some of these responses are exemplified in the following illustrations: A visiting-teacher, as she was being introduced to various teachers of the county, casually asked where they were teaching. One little teacher replied in a weak and timid voice, "in District Fifty-six." Another representing about the same amount of training replied in a cheerful, optimistic manner, "in Franklin." What is the difference in these two situation positions? District Fifty-six is located in the open country, while Franklin is a little village of some four hundred souls. It would seem that the average person does not think of the village as being rural, though rural sociologists are generally agreed that towns and villages having a population of less than twenty-five hundred are distinctly rural.

The teacher of the rural school has tended to be ashamed of her job. She has felt that it was a stamp of inferiority. A student said to the author the other day, "I do hope that I can get a position in a town school next year. I do not want to teach in the country."

There are other reasons for this feeling of dissatisfaction and inferiority on the part of those teaching boys and girls in the open country. For instance, the rapid turnover of teachers in the one hundred sixty thousand rural schools of the United States indicates that these people are looking for greener pastures, which they hope to find in the schools of the towns and villages.

A comparatively small number of students in the teacher-training institutions of the nation are electing courses in rural education, in spite of the fact that a large proportion of these folk will spend their first years of teaching in the rural school. Few students in the teachers' colleges and normal schools are specializing in rural education. These factors seem to point out an unwillingness on the part of young teachers to cast their lot with agrarian life.

The question that arises in the minds of the readers is: What is the reason for this attitude? There are probably a number of things contributing to the present condition.

Some one says it is the low salaries. The teacher in the country receives such meager remuneration that she can not be expected to be proud of her position. Taking the United States as a whole there is no doubt some truth in this statement. However, there are many teachers in the rural schools of the northwest, who are receiving salaries on a par with or above those paid in the towns and villages. A goodly number of rural teaching positions in South Dakota are paying as much as one hundred and fifty dollars per month. On the other hand, there are so-called urban positions that are paying considerably less than one hundred fifty dollars per month. Inadequate salaries may account in part for the present attitude but it is not the only factor.

Some one says the reason that teachers wish to leave the open country is because of the adverse living conditions. As one drives about and observes the great distances that teachers are compelled to travel from the nearest suitable farm home to the schoolhouse and as one studies the varied settlements, whose customs and ways of life are so different from those of the average teacher, one is prone to agree that the living conditions of the rural teacher present a significant problem.

The writer hears still another group who say it is not salaries or living conditions that breed discontent, but it is rather the lack of wholesome social life. In some communities this may be the case. However, the reader will recall the splendid social times in parties, clubs and the Literary Club. While this form of social life is passing, another is taking its place. Community clubs, parent-teacher associations and Grange organizations are springing up throughout the rural areas of the United States. These societies afford a fine opportunity for self-expression, education and wholesome recreation that compares favorably with the dance, the movie and the bridge party of urban centers. "When the artist wishes to paint a picture that reveals the true values of a nation he goes out into open country."

In the judgment of the writer there is still another reason for the too frequent inferiority complex of the rural teacher. It is the social stigma that has been attached to those who till the soil or engage in related activities. The roots of this attitude are discovered on the pages of human history. It was the slaves of Rome who tilled the soil. It is the peasant of Europe who lives on the land. Theoretically, this is not the case in America. God forbid that it may ever be so! Nevertheless, such expressions as "the clodhopper," "the countryjake" and "the hayseed" are not unknown in this fair land. There has been a subconscious feeling that people farm because they are not able to do anything better. Perhaps the farmer is partially to blame for this situation. Too often has he said to his son, "Get an education so you will not have to work as I have," the inference being that an education should equip one so that he can do something on a higher social and economic level than that of agriculture.

This attitude is found in the following illustration. James went to the state agricultural college after he was graduated from the village high school. The folk at home looked upon such procedure with misgivings. They did not believe that an education was necessary if one wished to become a farmer. However, after studying at the college for some time, James obtained a position as an assistant to a man who was testing cattle for tuberculosis. James was receiving the magnificent salary of one hundred fifty dollars per month. The people at home thought this was fine and they pointed to James with a great deal of pride. It was not long, however, until he began to feel the call of the farm. He therefore gave up his position, went back to the farm, and began raising purebred livestock. The attitude of the people at home changed. They no longer pointed to James with pride but rather as an example of failure, a failure because he was a farmer. The general-store philosophers of the village, in discussing the youth of the community, remark with admiration about the boys who have gone forth to the city and are now lawyers, bankers, or street-car conductors.

The foregoing paragraphs will give the reader an idea as to why the rural teacher may have an inferiority complex. It is true that agriculture has suffered many economic depressions. It is also true that there have been many "hick" farmers, but have there not been "quack" doctors and incompetent business men?

Agriculture is the largest single industry in the country. More than ten millions of people are engaged in it. It employs more people than do the railroads, the textile, or the machine industry. Chance farming governed by the moon has passed into oblivion. The new agriculture is carried on by educated, intelligent men and women. By scientific methods two blades of grass have been induced to grow where one grew before. By the same token will the efficiency of marketing be raised to a higher plane. The farmer uses hydro-electric power. He rides in a high-powered automobile and sends his children to college.

In lieu of the new agriculture it seems evident that a new country teacher must enter the rural drama. It has often been said, "the salvation of rural America depends upon education." Is there any reason why those people who teach the youth of those engaged in America's greatest industry should feel inferior?

Rural teaching is a great challenge. It is likewise a great opportunity. It should appeal to the highest type of manhood and womanhood. The rural school is located in the wonderful laboratory of nature. It is out there where one "can thrill with Spring's first flutes and drums." The teacher of the country school is free from a lockstep system.

The principal work of the school does not have to be sidetracked by an undue amount of emphasis on extra-curricular activity. Boys and girls have a greater opportunity to develop and display initiative, resourcefulness and individuality than do their city cousins. A teacher has more opportunity to play a significant part in the lives of youth than is possible with mass education in the urban centers.

In the mind of the author there is no valid reason for a teacher of a rural school having an inferiority complex. Nevertheless, the reader must not be led to believe that there are no problems in connection with rural teaching.

R. L. Bunting, of Sam Houston State Teachers College, and Verne McGuffy, of Jamaica Training School for Teachers, in the May issue of the *Teachers' College Record,* point out the need for rural-teacher training. They suggest that it is the business of the teacher-training institutions to prepare teachers for the situations in which they will teach. Along with better training must come closer supervision and a more lucrative emolument. Moreover, teachers' colleges and normal schools, especially in the agricultural regions of the United States, should realize that there is a problem of rural-teacher training. When this challenge is accepted and departments of rural education are established with dignity and support the inferiority of the rural teacher will disappear.

EDUCATIONAL EVENTS

THE NEW LONDON UNIVERSITY

SIR WILLIAM BEVERIDGE, a former vice-chancellor of the University of London, gave a lecture on November 16 to the London Society in the hall of the Royal Society of Arts, on "The Physical Relations of a University to a City." Lord Chelmsford, chairman of the college committee of the University of London, presided.

Sir William Beveridge, as reported in the London *Times,* spoke of the purchase of the site on the Bedford estate by the University of London, and outlined the scheme by which the university will erect on this site its administrative offices, a university library, specialized research institutes, such as the Institute of Historical Studies, and a university hall for ceremonies, with smaller halls for examinations and public lectures. It was recorded in bluebooks that the University of London had about 14,000 students, 1,100 appointed and recognized teachers and many other teachers, but these students and teachers could not be found by visiting what was called the University of London, in the Imperial Institute building at South Kensington. They could only be found in the colleges, particularly the great college in the central area of London, King's, the School of Economics, Bedford, Birkbeck and the medical schools.

Hitherto, while the bulk of the university was in the center of London, it had no center of its own. A year and a half ago the university, with the help of a gift from the Rockefeller Foundation, bought its own site on the Bedford estate. During the past year it had obtained powers to close all the roads across the site so as to make an island area of ten acres. This area lay next to the British Museum, between the central colleges, near the center of gravity of the university. The possession of this site would not mean the uprooting of any of the colleges. It was primarily for the central purposes of the university. It was hoped that arrangements would be made for social and residential facilities, including a faculty club for teachers and administrators, and a university students' union, or day house, bringing together students of the many colleges. While London University could never become predominantly a residential university, like Oxford and Cambridge, much could be done to give to that half of the London students who did not live at home a chance of living, whether in halls of residence or in approved lodgings, in an academic quarter close to the colleges, and of giving the same chance to teachers.

To use the site the university would need gifts on a scale not dreamed of before; these gifts would go, not to some temporary undistinguished purpose, but to benefit the lives of generations of students. The buildings erected on this site would, it was hoped, be the outcome of creative imagination in architecture. Whatever the design, two things were certain. Nothing would be built on the Bloomsbury site that was not beautiful, and nothing would be built that would not be characteristic of London and of this age.

Lord Chelmsford said that London did not realize that it had a university. When it did realize the existence of the University of London and the progress it had made, he felt sure that London, with its great wealth, would make this scheme for the centralization of the university possible.

EDUCATIONAL FACILITIES IN MEXICO

DURING the last five years a gradual and systematic increase in budget appropriations for educational purposes has taken place in Mexico and it is the intention of the administration to continue this expansion until full educational facilities are granted to every child in the republic, according to a statement on the progress of education in Mexico issued by the embassy in Washington. The statement reads in part:

This result, it is admitted, requires time, money and the gradual training of an army of teachers, but the results already achieved fully justify brighter expectations for the future.

A very interesting feature of the present educational movement in Mexico is its practical character, teaching the children the use of local natural resources, raw materials and natural products, and winding up in rural and grammar schools with the elements of mechanical trades, farming, dairy industries and poultry raising.

Special attention has been given to the rural schools. The great mass of the population in Mexico lives in the country and it is very important that the children derive all possible benefit from the elementary education they obtain before joining their parents at the farm.

With this end in view a typical method has been devised and eight "cultural missions" of professors and specialists in practical farming, cattle raising, farm industries, horticulture, aviculture, apiculture, sericulture, sanitation, cooking, hygiene, floriculture, tanning, small industries, physical culture, etc., visit all rural schools in rotation, raising extra attendance from parents and children to the lectures and demonstrations and going through a brief course in all the subjects enumerated, to supplement and increase the regular teachings.

In order to encourage the Indians to cooperate in the educational movement special Indian schools have been established, where illiterates are given an education and a trade, to go back home and show others the practical advantages obtained in school.

THE NOBEL PRIZES

FOR the twenty-eighth consecutive year the Nobel prizes have been awarded by the Swedish Academy, the Academy of Science and the Academy of Medicine. This year Norway received one prize in literature, France one in literature and one in medicine and Germany two in chemistry. The prize in physics was held over.

According to a statement in the New York *Herald Tribune* on December 10 each Nobel prize winner will this year receive about $42,-060, as compared to $32,478 in 1927. Originally each prize was worth $40,511, but the value shrank to $30,802 in 1923, the lowest so far. In 1926 the prizes were worth $31,094 each. The increase in value this year is due partly to the remission of some of the Swedish taxes and partly because of improved business conditions.

Since 1901, the first year when the prizes were distributed, 140 persons have been awarded prizes aggregating about $3,975,000. Twenty-six of the prizes were awarded in medicine, 33 in physics, 25 in chemistry, 28 in literature and 28 for peace work.

A survey of the nationality of the winners shows that 31 of the prizes have gone to Germany, 21 to France, 20 to the British Empire, 9 each to Sweden and the United States, 7 each to Switzerland, Denmark and Holland, 5 each to Norway, Austria and Italy, 4 to Belgium, 2 to Poland and 1 to Russia.

Four Americans have won the peace prize—Theodore Roosevelt (1906), Elihu Root (1912), Woodrow Wilson (1918) and Charles G. Dawes (1926). The other American winners are A. A. Michelson (physics, 1907), A. Carrel (medicine, 1912), T. W. Richards (chemistry, 1914), R. A. Millikan (physics, 1923) and Arthur Compton, sharing the 1927 prize in physics with Professor C. T. R. Wilson, of England.

Six women have been prize winners, and of these Mme. Curie, Paris, got half a prize in physics and later one in chemistry. The others were Baroness von Suttner, Austria (peace); Selma Lagerlof, Sweden, Signora Grazie Deledda, Italy, and Sigrid Undset, Norway (literature).

STUDENT LOAN FUNDS

A BULLETIN recently issued by the U. S. Bureau of Education contains the results of a questionnaire in regard to student loan funds sent out by Mr. Walter J. Greenleaf, associate specialist in higher education. He reports that students who desire to finance their college education on the instalment plan have many opportunities to borrow money, go to college, graduate and afterwards repay their loans in a business-like manner. We are living in what appears to be the "instalment age," where people make large purchases by paying so much down and so much per month. Higher education is no exception to the rule and, as an investment, yields a high rate of interest with the passing years. Ambitious students are assisted in financing their education by the colleges and universities themselves and by many independent organizations.

In 282 colleges and universities, funds amounting to nearly $4,000,000 are loaned annually to students of character and ability for the purpose of completing their college education. Although these funds are administered by the several institutions, there is no uniformity as to the manner in which they are handled. Various conditions are imposed according to the policy of the institution—the need of the student and ability of his parents, locality, restrictions imposed by donors and other factors. In some cases no interest whatever is charged, while in others the rates run as high as 8 per cent., but 6 per cent. is the usual requirement.

Individual loans average $100 to $150 and many are twice as large. Repayment generally begins at a stated period after graduation. Applications for these institutional loans should be made directly to the dean of the college in question, who will provide proper blanks and specific information.

As soon as a student decides upon the institution to be attended, he should find out by correspondence what loan funds and scholarships are available and what self-help opportunities may later be open to him.

Besides these institutional resources, there are many educational loan funds maintained by independent agencies to aid boys and girls in college. These funds are administered by their respective organizations and some are restricted to students attending specified or affiliated colleges. Some of the funds, established years ago by subscription or collection, have been administered in such a way that the original amounts have been increased many times over. Some, new within the year, are not yet organized to aid the number of students they will eventually serve.

The questionnaire was sent to over 100 agencies and foundations which were presumed to aid students.

THE FINANCES OF WESLEYAN UNIVERSITY

THE total property of Wesleyan University increased by $745,901 during the fiscal year ending June 30, 1928, according to the recently published report of the treasurer, Clinton D. Burdick, and the income from the general investments has been distributed at the rate of 6.01 per cent., .22 per cent. greater than the 5.79 per cent. rate for 1926–27.

The budget for 1927–28 totaled $508,780; it was met, due principally to the Alumni Fund gift of $10,680. The budget for 1928–29 contemplates an increase of about $35,000.

The cost of the university buildings, grounds and equipment on June 30 amounted to $3,394,755, an increase of $765,259. The cost to date of the Olin Memorial Library amounts to $722,476 and of the Shanklin Laboratory of Biology $178,330.

The Hall Laboratory of Chemistry has been completed, $12,992 having been spent upon it for construction and $1,648 for equipment. The Shanklin Laboratory of Biology has been completed, $178,330 having been spent upon it for construction and $868 for apparatus and equipment. Also the Harriman Dormitory has been completed and is being occupied by students; the amount expended for construction to date is $233,268. The steam distributing system of the heating plant has been extended at a cost of $21,565.

The following approximate figures on income and expenditures are obtained by using the average active attendance of undergraduates for the year, *i.e.,* 600; in the income from students the figures for room rent, board, infirmary, etc., are included:

INCOME

	Total	Proportion of total	Amount per student
Students	$205,784	40%	$342
Investments	224,885	45%	375
Miscellaneous	52,853	10%	88
Gifts	25,010	5%	40

EXPENDITURES

Instruction and Library	$338,641	67%	$564
Administration	52,359	10%	86
General	31,569	6%	52
Plant	86,209	17%	143

THE INTERNATIONAL HALL OF PHILOSOPHY OF THE UNIVERSITY OF SOUTHERN CALIFORNIA

As a memorial to Seeley W. Mudd, mining engineer of Los Angeles, a new hall is being erected which is to house the department and the Hoose Library of Philosophy of the University of Southern California. The new hall, in the North Italian Renaissance tradition, will contain offices for the philosophical faculty, a number of classrooms and seminar rooms, a large lecture hall to be known as the International Hall of Philosophy and a spacious library and reading room and a special room for the growing collection of rare books. In the 140-foot clock tower that surmounts the building will be a number of individual study rooms for the use of advanced students in philosophy. The building, which is to cost $265,000, is being erected on the university campus, facing Exposition Park. It is proposed that there shall be built up about the department a center of general philosophic culture, wherein public lectures, discussions and library and reading-room facilities shall be available to those who can use them to advantage.

To carry out this program the department seeks to bring to the university each year some outstanding visiting professor in philosophy, who shall be representative of his school of thought. During 1926–27 Dr. F. C. S. Schiller, of the University of Oxford, was the guest teacher. Last year Dr. J. H. Muirhead, English authority, lectured on contemporary philosophy, and this year the guest professor is Dr. Joseph Alexander Leighton, head of the department of philosophy at Ohio State University. To supplement these influences the university proposes to invite each year a representative of Oriental thought to lecture at Southern California. In this way it is proposed that the best thought of the East and West may find at this university a common meeting-place, and that in time a philosophical rapprochement between the Orient and the Occident may be established.

Provision is to be made in the new hall for a library that will ultimately number 200,000 volumes. The departmental library, which has been described as the best collection of books on philosophy on the Pacific coast, has been made possible by the generosity, first of Colonel Mudd, and latterly of other friends. It contains at the present time more than 8,000 volumes, including a number of incunabula and other well-nigh priceless volumes. To care for these a special room with fire-proof shelves and provision against theft is being included in the new hall.

As a supplement to this library the advanced students in the department are privileged to use the Henry E. Huntington Library at San Marino, which is about an hour's drive from the university. In this library, one of the finest private libraries in existence, are more than 4,000 incunabula and a vast store of precious material, much of which is still unexplored by modern scholars.

SERVICE TO NORMAL SCHOOLS AND TEACHERS COLLEGES AT NEW YORK UNIVERSITY

DURING the past year the School of Education, New York University, has reorganized its service so as to provide courses on the undergraduate and on the graduate levels, on the campus and in the Institute of Education at extra-mural centers, for present and prospective officers and teachers in the following types of positions: (a) Administrative officers of teachers colleges, normal schools and university schools and colleges of education and of college departments of education. (b) Professors and teachers in the several departments of instruction in teacher-training institutions. (c) Directors and principals of laboratory schools (experimental and demonstration schools, participation centers and cooperating training schools for "apprentice" or "practice" teaching) connected with teacher-training institutions. (d) Supervising "critics" or supervisors of training in campus laboratory schools and in cooperating public-school systems where "apprentice" or "practice" teaching is done. (e) "Training," "critic," "apprentice," or "practice" teachers (elementary and secondary). (f) "Demonstration" teachers (elementary and secondary). (g) Teachers in experimental schools (elementary and secondary). (h) "Helping" teachers and supervisors of beginning teachers (elementary and secondary).

A considerable number of the departments of the School of Education contribute courses for administrative and supervisory officers in the Normal Schools and Teachers Colleges of the country and every department contributes a number of courses of specific interest to present and prospective instructional officers in such institutions. Nearly all the courses offered for persons who classify in groups (a), (b) and (c) above are graduate courses and those courses offered for laboratory school staff members. The (d) to (h) above, though open to students of the undergraduate group as well, are intended primarily for teachers. Nearly all courses are organized in such units as will permit of their completion in a single semester or during a summer term. Hereafter it is planned to have a full program of courses which will begin at the middle of the summer term. This plan will offer special advantages to those summer school teachers in normal schools and teachers colleges who are not free to go to New York till about August 1. The attendance in all courses offered in this division has shown an increase during the past year and especially during the summer term of 1928.

FINANCES OF THE CHICAGO SCHOOLS

AN Associated Press dispatch reported, under date of November 27, that the schools of Chicago face a deficit approximating $12,000,000, caused by financial troubles "inherited from previous administrations, coupled with tremendous loss in revenue this year from uncollectable taxes."

Some extra-legal means of maintaining current expenses must be found until more tax money becomes available about February 15. It is reported that private funds from public-spirited citizens will be called upon if necessary.

Already 75 per cent., the legal limit, of this year's tax levy for educational purposes has been borrowed and spent, and as a result the public-school system faces a deficit of about $12,000,000 before borrowing can be started on next year's funds.

A civic body named by Mayor Thompson when he took office, to cooperate in school matters, considered one of two alternatives to keep the schools from being closed before more funds are available. One was to find some "good angel" who would lend money beyond the legal limit for the payment of bills and the other was for school employees, including all the teachers, to go unpaid until funds are available.

All declared that the schools would be kept in operation, but most city officials said that school employees could not be induced to work without pay for three months. Either method of relief, all admitted, would be only temporary, for the figures also showed that it has cost about $4,000,000 more a year to send Chicago's 500,000 boys and girls to school than has been provided in tax levies.

The only ultimate way out of the situation is an increased tax rate for school purposes or increased valuations. As the limit of borrowing has been reached, credit has been exhausted, and some other method is necessary to keep the schools going. The budget for this year was set at more than $47,000,000 for current expenses, and the expected revenue was anticipated as more than $45,250,000, but slow tax payments and objections because of tax inequalities have left the collections several millions short of anticipations, while expenses have risen about to the budget expectations.

According to the latest information, the financial dilemma of the schools has been solved with the signing of $2,500,000 worth of tax anticipation warrants by H. W. Caldwell, president of the school board, and Charles S. Peterson, city treasurer. As a result, teachers and school-board employees who might have faced the Christmas holiday without their pay checks will be paid as usual and the deficit will be wiped out by the sale of the warrants, which carry a maximum of five per cent. interest. The city treasurer announced he would ask the city council to confirm his action, and said he hoped late collections of 1928 taxes would provide further funds.

THE OHIO STATE EDUCATIONAL CONFERENCE

APRIL 4, 5 and 6 are the dates of the Ninth Annual Ohio State Educational Conference at Columbus. "Evaluating education" will be the keynote of this three-day meeting conducted by the College of Education at the Ohio State University. Each year the attendance materially increases. Last year's gain of 335 pushed the number who took part in the three general and 38 sectional meetings to more than 4,800. Since 1923 the attendance has practically doubled.

To extend the "conference" idea, allowing group interests to have even wider consideration, Friday and Saturday forenoons and Friday afternoon will be given over to sectional group meetings. General sessions will be held on Thursday and Friday nights only. The customary Saturday morning general session will give way to sectional meetings.

Groups admitted to the conference for the first time will be represented this year by sections concerned with adult education, higher education, and attendance supervisors, school nurses and visiting teachers. In addition to the three new groups mentioned, one or more sectional meetings will be given to problems of groups interested in biological science, city superintendents, clinical psychology, commercial education, county superintendents, educational and intelligence tests, elementary principals, elementary teachers, English, geography, high-school principals, history, home economics, industrial and vocational education, journalism, junior high-school principals, kindergarten and primary teachers, Latin, mathematics, modern language, music, non-biological science, parent-teacher association, physical education, religious education, school business officials, school librarians, special education, teacher training and village and consolidated school superintendents.

EDUCATIONAL NOTES AND NEWS

THE American Association for the Advancement of Science and the associated scientific societies will hold one of the larger convocation meetings in New York City, beginning on Wednesday, December 27. The addresses of the retiring chairmen of the sections of education and psychology will probably be given at a dinner on Saturday evening, at which Professor Arthur I. Gates, of Teachers College, Columbia University, will speak on "New Movements in the Field of Educational Psychology," and Professor Knight Dunlap, of the Johns Hopkins University, on "The Outlook of Psychology."

G. CARL ALVERSON, superintendent of schools at Syracuse, was elected president of the New York State Teachers Association at the recent Buffalo meeting to succeed Ernest C. Hartwell, superintendent of the Buffalo schools.

Dr. J. L. Jarman, president of Farmville Teachers College, was elected president of the Cooperative Education Association of Virginia at the recent Richmond meeting.

President A. O. Thomas is expecting to go to Geneva during the present month to make final arrangements for the third biennial conference of the World Federation of Education Associations which will be held at Geneva from July 25 to August 3, 1929.

The three teachers' organizations of Chicago gave on December 7 a testimonial banquet to Superintendent William J. Bogan.

Owen D. Young, of the General Electric Company and of the Radio Corporation of America, has been elected a trustee of Teachers College, Columbia University. M. Gordon Neale, since 1923 dean of the school of education of the University of Missouri, has been elected an alumni trustee.

Dr. Charles R. Thwing, chancellor emeritus of Western Reserve University, celebrated his seventy-fifth birthday on November 9.

Edmund H. Wuerple, director of the school of fine arts of Washington University, has been critically injured in an automobile accident.

Dr. R. Tait McKenzie, professor of physical education at the University of Pennsylvania and sculptor of the Scottish war memorial presented last year to the city of Edinburgh by American citizens, was the recipient of a special gold medal of the St. Andrew's Society of Philadelphia on the occasion of its one hundred and seventy-ninth anniversary.

James C. M. Hanson, professor of library science in the University of Chicago, was created Knight and Commander of St. Olav by special commission of King Haakon VII of Norway in a ceremony at the University Club. Following a dinner in his honor, Professor Hanson received diploma, star and ribbon from Olaf Bernts, Norwegian consul, for distinguished service as "the father of modern library science." Professor Hanson, who was chief of the cataloguing division of the Library of Congress for fourteen years, devised the card and catalogue systems which are now standard throughout the world. Having spent four years bringing modern methods to the library of the University of Wisconsin, he became associated with the Newberry Library in Chicago in its early years. He came to the University of Chicago in 1910 as associate director of libraries.

The students of St. Andrews University have elected Sir Wilfred Grenfell as lord rector by a majority of 157 votes, the defeated candidate being Lord Melchett. The rectorial election at St. Andrews is non-political.

Professor A. Fraenkel, of Kiel, has been invited to become head of the mathematical institute of the Hebrew University, Jerusalem.

Dr. John Harold Clapham, fellow of King's College, Cambridge, has been elected to the newly established professorship of economic history in the university.

The Reverend E. Graham, rector of Boyton with Sherrington, has been appointed principal of Cuddesdon College, Oxford, in the place of Canon J. B. Seaton, recently appointed Bishop of Wakefield.

Dr. William F. Butler, of University College, Cork, for many years assistant commissioner of education, has been appointed principal officer of the secondary branch of the Irish Free State Ministry of Education.

Dr. Walter Bradford Cannon, George Higginson professor of physiology in the Harvard Medical School, has been appointed exchange professor to France for 1929–30. His term will fall in the second half year.

Professor N. J. Aiken is acting head of the school of business administration of the Washington State College. Dr. Fred R. Yoder has been appointed head of the department of sociology, and Dr. C. O. Johnson, formerly of the University of Chattanooga, is the new head of the department of history and political science.

Miss Margaret J. McCooey, sister of John H. McCooey, the Democratic leader of Brooklyn, N. Y., has been elected by the New York Board of Education to serve as an associate superintendent of schools for a second six-year term. The salary of the position is $12,500 a year. When Miss McCooey was elected six years ago a precedent was set in that she was the first elementary school principal to be advanced over the district superintendents to an associate superintendency.

THE annual winter meeting of the Harvard chapter of Phi Beta Kappa for the reception of new members and for dinner was held at the Harvard Union on December 4. It was expected that Dr. William S. Thayer, president of the chapter, would preside; President A. Lawrence Lowell was among the speakers announced.

THE Christmas week lectures on the James Mapes Dodge Foundation of the Franklin Institute, Philadelphia, will be given at 3 P. M. on Wednesday, Thursday and Friday, December 26, 27 and 28, in the hall of the institute. The lecturer this year will be Professor A. S. Eve, head of the department of physics, McGill University, and his subject will be "Things that Spin; Things that Swing; Things that Wave."

PROFESSOR EARLE R. HEDRICK, of the University of California, delivered an address on "Approximation Processes in Mathematics and in Science" at the Ohio State University on November 27, and on December 3, at the same university, Professor George D. Birkhoff, of Harvard University, lectured on "Mathematics and Art." These addresses are intended for the intellectual and scientific public rather than for professional mathematicians.

DR. STANTON COIT, president of the Ethical Church, England, lectured on "A Foundation for Moral Leadership" at Cornell University on November 22.

AT the inauguration of Dr. Harvey Nathaniel Davis, former professor of mechanical engineering at Harvard University, as third president of the Stevens Institute of Technology, Hoboken, New Jersey, a bronze tablet was unveiled of Dr. Alexander Crombie Humphreys, second president of the institute. Arthur G. Glasgow, of London, an alumnus of the institute, has offered $25,000 for the Humphreys Memorial professorship in the economics of engineering if the alumni raise a like amount by January 1.

FIELDSTON, the new school of the Ethical Culture Society at 238th Street and Riverdale Avenue, New York City, was dedicated on November 28, following the annual dinner and meeting of the society. Dr. Felix Adler, founder of the society, made the dedication address. Professor B. H. Bode, professor of education at the Ohio State University, was among the speakers.

THE *Journal of Education* reports that the Henry Barnard Club of Rhode Island celebrated its fiftieth anniversary on November 1 with a dinner and program. A portrait of Dr. Barnard was presented to the Rhode Island College of Education by Irving C. Mitchell. The history of the club was given by Dr. Herbert W. Lull, and other addresses were by Drs. John L. Alger and Walter E. Ranger, President W. H. P. Faunce, Isaac O. Winslow and Dr. Arthur C. Boyden.

IN memory of the first woman graduated from Massachusetts Institute of Technology, a bas-relief of Mrs. Ellen H. Richards, who for more than 30 years was an instructor in sanitary chemistry at the institute, was unveiled on the afternoon of December 3. Mrs. Richards was the wife of Robert H. Richards, professor emeritus, formerly head of the department of mining and metallurgy, and it was he who unveiled the memorial in the presence of a large gathering of her former students and colleagues on the faculty. The bronze is the work of Miss Bashka Paeff and is the gift of the alumni.

DR. FRANK C. WAGNER, president of the Rose Polytechnic Institute, was killed on November 21 when his automobile was struck by an Indianapolis train. Dr. Wagner had been a member of the engineering department since 1896 and became president of the institute in 1923.

DR. WILLIAM DAWSON JOHNSTON, European representative of the Library of Congress and a well-known bibliographer, died on November 19. He was fifty-seven years old. Dr. Johnston was librarian of the U. S. Bureau of Education from 1907 to 1909, of Columbia University from 1909 to 1914, of the Public Library of St. Paul, Minnesota, from 1914 to 1921, and of the American Library at Paris from 1921 to 1925.

COLIN V. DYMENT, who was at one time dean of the school of journalism at the University of Washington, died recently in California, where he owned a newspaper in Hayward. He was also on the faculty of the University of Oregon for some years.

MILTON WYLIE HUMPHREYS, said to be the last surviving member of the original faculties of the University of Texas and of Vanderbilt University and for twenty-five years professor of Greek at the University of Virginia, died on November 21, at Charlottesville, Virginia. He was eighty-four years old.

PROFESSOR A. W. KNEELAND, member of the first faculty of Macdonald College until he retired a few years ago, has died at Quebec in his seventy-fifth year. He was an authority on Canadian history.

MISS MARY A. GALLAGHER, who has been a public school teacher for forty years, was killed by an automobile on November 23.

THE fourth session of the Institute of International Relations will be held at Riverside Mission Inn and the University of Southern California from December 9 to 14, according to an announcement made by Chancellor R. B. von KleinSmid. The 1928 institute, consisting of morning, afternoon and evening sessions for six days, will provide for the Pacific coast similar opportunities for discussion of world affairs as are provided through the Institute of Politics at Williamstown, Mass., and the Institute of Pacific Relations at Honolulu. Dr. Karl C. Leebrick, professor of political science at the University of Hawaii, is director of the institute, and Dr. Charles E. Martin, dean of the faculty of social sciences at the University of Washington, Seattle, is chairman of the executive committee.

THE education department of the Buffalo Museum of Science, which occupies a new structure in Humboldt Park, was formally opened on September 22. Representatives of leading educational institutions of the city took part in the program dedicating the department. The services which the Buffalo Museum has outlined were explained by Chauncey J. Hamlin, president of the Buffalo Society of Natural Sciences. Among other services he mentioned a children's story hour, visits of school pupils to the museum under the guidance of expert instructors, the loan of manuscript lectures and slides, library facilities, lectures by distinguished scientists and radio talks on scientific subjects. Other speakers were Dr. Samuel P. Capen, chancellor of the University of Buffalo; Reverend P. F. Cusick, president of Canisius College; Dr. Harry W. Rockwell, president of the State Teachers College; Dr. Ernest C. Hartwell, superintendent of schools at Buffalo, and Mayor Frank X. Schwab.

THE second "Floating University" sailed on *The President Wilson* from Jersey City on November 8 and will probably reach New York on the return journey on June 11, 1929. The members of the student body include both men and women of university age. They are under the leadership of Sydney Greenhie in general charge of the group and of Dr. E. A. Ross, of the University of Wisconsin, head of the educational work. Dr. Henry D. Gray, of Stanford University, is dean of men and Mrs. Greenhie the dean of women. It was planned to pass through the Panama Canal, sailing up the west coast as far as San Francisco and in December to visit Japan and China, sailing from there to India. The last two months of the trip will be spent in Europe. Classes will be held at the places visited as well as on the ship.

THE American Council on Education has authorized a letter to President Coolidge, urging that the office of the commissioner of education be kept out of politics. The letter is signed by Dr. C. R. Mann, director of the council; Dr. Frederick B. Robinson, president of the College of the City of New York, and Dr. Samuel P. Capen, chancellor of the University of Buffalo. The letter expresses the opinion that the commissionership is one of the most influential educational posts in the country and that it calls for a highly trained expert, and that only in such a person will the educational profession have confidence. It continues further: "The office is not in any sense political, and it should have no relation to party politics. The tenure of its incumbent should be unaffected by changes of national administration. Only once in the last forty years has it been treated as political spoils. The educational profession is convinced that this general tradition of the political inviolability of the commissionership must be sustained."

THE John C. Green School of Science, a three-story stone structure and one of the oldest buildings of Princeton University, was destroyed by fire on November 27. The loss is estimated at $200,000. The building had been occupied until two weeks ago by the School of Engineering, which moved to a new building. Since then it housed the offices of the departments of economics, politics and social institutions. It was erected in 1873 and its early abandonment had been planned.

BOWLES HALL, made possible by a gift of $350,000 from Mrs. Philip E. Bowles, the first dormitory to be owned by the University of California, is practically completed, and will be opened for men students in January. The dormitory will accommodate approximately 105 men. There will be 46 suites of two bedrooms and study, two suites of bedroom and study and 11 single rooms. The rates for the new dormitory have not been announced, but they will include both board and room.

JULIUS ROSENWALD has offered the sum of $500,000 to the Hebrew Union College in Cincinnati. Mr. Rosenwald attached a provision to his pledge requiring that the college endowment fund must contain $3,500,000 besides his $500,000 by July 1, 1929, and that $3,000,000 of the $4,000,000 shall be available in cash or in pledges of not more than 10 annual instalments. He also stipulated that $3,000,000 must be used entirely within 25 to 33 years or be removed from the endowment trust into an available surplus and reserve fund. The $3,000,000 shall be donated, he said, with an understanding that in addition to the annual interest, from 3 to 5 per cent. of the capital shall be set aside anuually by the trustees to be used for current expenses or placed in a surplus or reserve fund, to be drawn upon for budget or other requirements. Mr. Ochs and Henry Morgenthau, formerly United States Ambassador to Turkey, have volunteered to tour the United States in an effort to complete the endowment fund and meet the provisions of Mr. Rosenwald's offer.

KALAMAZOO COLLEGE has received a bequest of $350,000 for a library by the will of the late Mary Senter Mandelle, of Detroit.

EUGENE P. STOVE, a trustee of Colorado College since 1912, has given $250,000 to the college to erect a chapel on the campus as a memorial to his "clergymen ancestors." In making this gift Mr. Stove requested the trustees to undertake to increase the endowment of the college by a minimum of $300,000 by June 1, 1930.

ACCORDING to the will of Mrs. Sally Stalker Smith, the Iowa State College has come into possession of a house to be used as a residence for male foreign students of the college and as headquarters for the Cosmopolitan Club. The house is a fine residence, formerly the home of the president of the college, and is in exceptionally beautiful grounds. The formal opening of this international house took place on December 1.

A GIFT of $100,000 has been made to Dartmouth College from Mrs. William Pierce Johnson, of San Francisco.

YALE UNIVERSITY will receive $60,000 as residuary legatee of the estate of the late Mrs. Jessie L. Ward.

DURING the past six months New York University has received gifts amounting to $277,292. They ranged from less than $100 from anonymous donors to $50,000 from the estate of the late Elbert H. Gary. One anonymous donor gave $40,000 toward the expenses of alterations at the Washington Square center of the university which will begin soon. The Altman Foundation contributed $30,000 for the department of fine arts during 1927–28. Other gifts include the sum of $14,066 for the purchase of busts and toward the expense of unveilings in the Hall of Fame, for which the university is trustee.

CYRUS S. EATON, of Cleveland, O., has given $60,000 to build, equip and endow a model rural school in his native district of Pugwash Junction, N. S.

A COMMUNITY CENTER on which $2,000,000 will be expended has been given by Mr. Milton S. Hershey, chocolate manufacturer, to the town of Hershey, near Harrisburg, Pennsylvania. Work of demolition of buildings to make room for the structure that will house a theater, an added auditorium, a hospital, a library and other conveniences for the people of the village founded by Mr. Hershey, has begun. Active building will be started next spring. This is the second large gift of Mr. Hershey in recent months. Early in the fall he started the construction of two golf courses. One of these is in the park surrounding his own residence, which will be turned into a country club for the townspeople. The other is near the public park maintained by Mr. Hershey, the chief attraction of which is a 3,000 capacity auditorium where have appeared the country's best singers and musical organizations. The golf courses and the Hershey residence are valued at $2,000,000. The new building will be similar to the high school, donated in memory of Mr. Hershey's mother, which is equipped with laboratories and appliances beyond those usually found in large city schools.

MORE than $100,000,000 will be asked by the New York State Department of Education to defray the expenses of operating schools in the state during 1929 and 1930. Officials who are now working out the budget for the coming year have been told that $101,962,000 will be needed for educational purposes. This amount is $6,000,000 more than the entire state budget of ten years ago.

WILLIAM J. BOGAN, superintendent of the Chicago schools, has appealed to parents to cooperate with police and school authorities to report all evidence of speakeasies in the vicinity of schools and Police Commissioner Russell has ordered the police to close all establishments found selling liquor or operating slot machines. Teachers and students are said to be divided in their reactions to the intensive campaign. Some admitted the existence of drinking and gambling among both boys and girls. Some, however, termed the investigation an "outrage" and a reflection on the conduct of the city's 80,000 high-school students.

THE Associated Press reports from Riverside, California, that charges of gross inefficiency and cruelty on the part of superintendents of Indian schools and recommendations that the government withdraw and let each state supervise its own Indian problems were made on November 24 by an Omaha tribesman and a former Indian school principal. They testified at a hearing of the United States Senate Committee on Indian Affairs, composed of Senators J. Lynn Frazier, of North Dakota, and W. B. Pine, of Oklahoma. The committee is examining conditions in California.

AN a ppeal has been made by the president of the Porto Rico Teachers Association for contributions to rehabilitate those schools of Porto Rico which were devastated by a cyclone on September 13. Subscriptions may be sent to the treasurer of Porto Rico, San Juan, P. R. Nearly fifty per cent. of the population is homeless and the agricultural products of the island are almost totally destroyed. The government is using its resources to overcome such evils as hunger, sickness, lack of shelter, etc. It is feared that it will be unable to grant sufficient funds to maintain the school system, especially since a large proportion of the buildings were destroyed.

IN compromise settlement of its suit against the Texan oil corporations, involving excess charges for gathering oil from wells upon land owned by the University of Texas in Reagan County, that institution has received a refund of $1,000,000. The money was deposited to the credit of the permanent fund, increasing it to approximately $11,000,000. This amount, with the exception of the $1,000,000, was received as royalties on oil production upon university lands. Payments are still being received at the rate of more than $150,000 a month.

A NATIONAL Child Welfare Congress will be held in Havana in December. The subjects discussed will include: hygiene, medicine, psychology, education, sociology, legislation, abnormality and delinquency. All who are engaged in the study, protection or education of children, or who represent institutions or groups working on the behalf of children, are eligible to attend the congress.

IN "Rural Education in England and the Punjab" (*Occasional Report* No. 15 of the Bureau of Education, India), according to *Nature*, two members of the Indian Educational Service describe impressions received in the course of a three-months' tour throughout the length and breadth of England, and make instructive comparisons with conditions in the Punjab, and suggestions for creating a genuinely "rural atmosphere" in village schools in that province. The "rural bias" question which has been so much in evidence of late in conferences on education in England is a hundredfold more important in India, owing to the immense preponderance of agricultural as compared with urban occupations, the much deeper cleavage between village and urban life, and the hitherto almost exclusively urban bias of the teacher-training institutions and inspectorate. Attempts, begun more than forty years ago, to popularize and vitalize the town-made teaching in the country districts of the Punjab, proved ineffectual until, soon after the war, school farms were introduced. Of the reforms recommended in the present report, the most important have to do with the training of village teachers. In selection of candidates, more consideration should be given to health, physique, caste and domicile, and the duration of the course should be increased from 9 months to 18 or 24 months.

SPECIAL CORRESPONDENCE

THE RURAL COMMUNITY CENTER ON A CHANGING FRONTIER

MOST people probably think of community centers as urban institutions. There are more than a hundred community halls in Montana, however, which are decidedly rural in character and around which are evolving strong rural organizations with fine programs of social improvement.

To understand the function of these community centers, it is necessary to know something of their geographical setting. For one who has always lived in thickly settled sections, it is difficult to appreciate the vastness of many Montana areas which technically must be classed as communities. It is true that the state has a number of highly productive valleys where intensive farming is practiced, where the average ranch is small and where the population is comparatively dense. But a larger state agricultural area is devoted to "dry farming" and grazing, with the ranches large, the population sparse and the towns, even small ones, far apart. Some conception of this condition may be gained by considering the fact that Beaverhead County is more than four times as large as the entire state of New Jersey, yet the county has an estimated present population of only 5,800, as compared with New Jersey's 3,749,000. In fact, forty-eight of Montana's fifty-six counties are larger than New Jersey, thirty-two are larger than Delaware and six are larger than Connecticut. To visualize such areas, with a total population of only five or ten thousand people, will give one a proper setting for a consideration of the Montana rural community center.

One might think that no community social life would be found in such areas, but that a state of individualism would obtain. Such is not the case, however, for distance is not a barrier to social contacts in the west. So long as the "flivver" will run and the roads are passable, western people think nothing of driving from twenty-five to a hundred miles for business or pleasure.

The rural people in the west are keenly awake to the value of effective community organization as a means of achieving wholesome social life. Their most difficult problem has not been the lack of desire for community contacts, nor the size of communities, but rather the finding of a suitable place to meet. In the open country, the only public building is the schoolhouse, usually a small structure erected to accommodate from six to a dozen pupils. In the villages, the only public buildings are the schoolhouses and the churches. The schoolhouse usually has no gymnasium-auditorium, and the buildings of home-mission churches are usually inadequate for general community meetings.

In more than a hundred rural communities of Montana the need for a community center has been met by the erection of a special building usually called the "Community Hall." Some of them are situated in a village, where they serve both the villagers and the farmers, and are also used as gymnasiums by the school pupils; more are located in the country, many of them ten, twenty-five and even fifty miles from any town or village of consequence.

In most cases these halls were erected by the people of the community as a whole, although in some instances by a community organization of limited membership, such as a fraternal lodge. Where the entire community is responsible for their erection, sometimes a building corporation is formed, while at other times there is no organization. It has been found the more successful practice, however, to incorporate rather than to exist as a loose organization. Money is raised by the sale of shares of stock in the corporation, subscriptions from local persons unable to buy shares of stock and more especially from business men in surrounding towns and by entertainments of various kinds. Much of the material and the labor necessary for the hall is contributed by the farmers and ranchers in the community. Many of the halls are one- or two-room structures, sometimes made of logs, costing between three and five thousand dollars, while a few are relatively more pretentious buildings, costing between thirty and forty thousand dollars. Frequently the smaller buildings are twenty by forty or thirty by sixty feet, while larger ones are forty by one hundred or fifty by one hundred and twenty-five feet in size. A few have only one room, while some of the larger have as many as nine rooms, the average number being three. The prosperity of the community and the probable demands on the building are the factors determining the size and cost. Practically every hall is equipped with a stage, piano, chairs or benches, and kitchen utensils, while some have a phonograph, radio, motion picture machine, athletic supplies and a community library.

A few communities have been successful in erecting halls but unsuccessful in maintaining them. The most satisfactory means of assuring their success seems to be for the corporation to have a board of directors or trustees to determine general policies of management and to employ a custodian to be directly in charge of the center. In most cases the funds for the upkeep of the building are obtained from renting the halls, subscriptions from people in the community and dues from members of the corporation or organization owning the building. The budgets for maintaining the centers vary from two hundred dollars to four thousand dollars per year, the average being around eight hundred dollars.

The organizations using the buildings include farm bureaus, home demonstration clubs, 4-H clubs, rural Boy Scouts, American Legions, religious organizations, lodges and various other social and business groups. In many of the communities individuals are allowed to use the halls for private entertainments upon payment of nominal rental fees. Around these halls are centered community development programs along the lines of education, recreation, religion, health, beautification and home-making. School and home-talent programs, lectures on various subjects, religious meetings, dances, banquets, community fairs and athletic contests are but a few of the many types of meetings regularly held in these community centers.

That these halls are not a passing fancy is shown by the fact that a few were erected between 1900 and 1910, the largest number of them between 1910 and 1920, and a large number between 1920 and the present date; furthermore, during 1927 six communities began erection of halls. The leaders in the majority of the communities maintaining these centers state that the halls are being used a great deal more than they were when first erected, that practically all of them have had a decidedly beneficial effect on community spirit, that the organizations centering around them are becoming stronger and that people are more and more considering them indispensable social institutions.

In short, these rural community centers have had a far-reaching effect in changing the rural social life in Montana communities from the "Wild West" individualistic frontier type depicted in the story book and on the motion picture screen, to one of laudable and progressive modern cooperative social action.

J. WHEELER BARGER
MONTANA AGRICULTURAL
EXPERIMENT STATION

DISCUSSION

SUPERVISION IS TEACHING

THAT'S what it is for me. I didn't reach that conclusion until rather recently, but since I have reached it I know that I am right—for me. For several years I have been reading about supervision in long chapters and even whole books devoted to the subject. None of this reading gave me just the thing that I could carry away with me to supply a satisfying comprehension of the purpose and method of my work as I went about among the teachers I was trying to supervise. I couldn't keep the long explanations in my mind; I lacked some central thought that was sufficiently inclusive and yet reliable. But since I have learned that supervision is teaching (for me) I get along much better. I have with me on my round of supervisory duties a guide, subjective but helpful and faithful.

Some one may say that if supervision is teaching it must be a special kind of teaching. Of course I recognize the different types of teaching. There are the special methods for different subjects. There are also the various teaching techniques for the basic types of learning, such as motor-learning, memory-associations, habit-formation, reflection, etc. But I can't see that supervision differs from these other types of teaching any more than they differ from each other. Through them all there runs a common set of principles—common to all forms of teaching.

Some one else may say, "But teachers are *adults.*" To this I would answer that they are no more adults than most college students, and the latter are still being taught, we trust. I am reminded, too, that the great majority of teachers are very young. Many if not most of them have not passed through the rear gate of adolescence. Then, too, I have been fortunate enough to do most of my supervising in smaller systems where most of the youngest teachers are (and, by the way, where most of the boys and girls of the land go to school). Therefore, any even well-substantiated argument in favor of different methods for teaching adults is not so applicable to the kind of teachers I supervise for the most part. I recall, furthermore, that some very good authorities maintain that the method of learning for adults is not essentially different from that of children. None of these considerations, then, causes me any misgivings about my proposition that supervision is teaching.

Another source of inspiration to me for my proposition is a comparison of the principles I use in supervision with the accepted principles of good teaching. I find that I must use motivation, for instance, in my work as supervisor, as I did when I was a classroom teacher. I have to find out, too, what the teacher knows and what she does not know as a basis for my efforts to improve her teaching, just as I used to diagnose the needs of my pupils as a basis for instruction. I find also that if I get my teachers working upon problems in the profession they become more interested, as my pupils formerly did. Then there are the projects in curriculum revision, establishing time-allotment schedules, devising library lists, etc., that enlist the interest and effort of the teachers, just as classroom projects prove effective in teaching children. I find that teachers, like pupils, learn through self-activity rather than by being preached to. I find that the matter of passing judgment upon their work is quite as delicate as assigning marks was for the pupils I used to teach. I find that teachers respond to cheer and to promotion and to just and kindly treatment much as my pupils in the classroom did. In fact, in my effort to think of some good teaching method (or bad one) that will not apply in supervision I have failed. This further confirms my conviction that supervision is teaching.

Again, I note that authorities on supervision say that it is characterized by certain devices, such as conferences between teacher and supervisor, demonstration teaching, teachers' meetings, school exhibits, and the like. But I know that good teachers use these same devices with pupils. They have individual conferences with them to go over difficult matters. They provide demonstrations in connection with the mastering of classroom material, either by doing the demonstrating themselves or by having it done by apt pupils. They have meetings of their pupils even in addition to the natural classroom congregation for the purpose of presenting programs and giving opportunity for imparting ideals and arousing enthusiasm. They have their rooms equipped with facilities for exhibiting the work of the pupils so that one can see what the others are doing, and they sometimes hold larger exhibits for similar purposes. I am unable to think of any essential device that I use as a supervisor or that other supervisors use that is not also used by good classroom teachers. This adds more weight to my theory.

When I come to appreciate this close relationship between supervision technique and good teaching—approaching identity as I see it—I regret that I did not get this point of view earlier. I had mastered to a reasonable degree the principles of teaching before I became a supervisor. I could have carried these principles over into my supervisory work much more directly and promptly had I recognized the close connection. But I thought supervision was quite different from teaching. I thought teaching was only what I was to supervise and not also the method I was to use. My notion of the function of supervision and of its method were both vague. I had no central idea to tie to. I don't think the first teachers I tried to supervise liked my method very well; I acted too much like an overseer. I didn't have the democratic attitude and the humility that a true teacher has, so admirably exemplified in the earthly life of the Great Teacher.

I have come to perceive another advantage in looking upon my supervision as teaching. I have to take some of my own medicine in curing my own shortcomings. I used to preach to the teachers that they should not preach to their pupils. I shot clear through the roof of the auditorium in institute, telling young teachers that they should not shoot over the heads of their pupils. In short, I used strictly unpedagogical methods in trying to induce my teachers to adopt the ways of good pedagogy. But now since I have decided that I am still a teacher myself I am forced to apply the principles of teaching I advocate to my own procedure as a supervisor. Since I have begun to do this in earnest I feel an increase in real power. I sense a better response from the teachers I try to supervise. They liked all their good teachers when they were pupils and they like me in so far as I act the part of a good teacher to them now. I do not mean that they necessarily think of me as a teacher, but they instinctively respond to those things that I do in my professional relationship with them which are in keeping with sound principles of teaching and learning.

I don't enjoy thinking of myself as a supervisor; that prefix, "super," is distasteful. But I like to try to be a teacher—a true teacher—because such a one brings real help and promotes growth and development and is always liked and respected.

R. V. HUNKINS
LEAD, SOUTH DAKOTA

FREEDOM IN PROGRESSIVE EDUCATION

IN the modern vocabulary, "freedom" is a term particularly subject to confusion and murkiness of thought. Its several connotations are quite different to various minds. Freedom is not easy to define.

Every American recognizes, however, that freedom is among the most cherished traditions of our republic. Ideally the individual under the law should have maximum freedom to attain true happiness. Freedom is both a means and a goal. It is ethereal ichor, the blood which flows in the veins of the gods. It is a state of mind, and also a condition of society. The history of humanity reveals little freedom; it lies in the future, not in the past.

The root-meaning of "free," from the old North-European tongue, implies love and affection, as distinguishing the members of a family in contrast to slaves and serfs. Freedom is exemption or release from slavery, imprisonment or restraint. It connotes readiness, ease, facility and boldness and vigor of conception or performance. This root-meaning obviously has important educational implications.

In the modern school, the pupil's freedom to develop naturally is an essential principle. The environment and program of the pupil are so constructed and controlled as to stimulate him to govern *his own* conduct, according to the social needs of his community. The old school method was to domineer him by arbitrary laws superimposed from above.

Freedom, on the other hand, emphatically does not mean mushy or fatuous license; rather, a rigorous activity program of self-education. Strong character, like the rose on the cheek, best comes from within.

The modern school endeavors to provide, as fully as possible, opportunity to each pupil for personal initiative and constructive self-expression. The school environment is rich in interesting educational materials of many kinds, and readily available for the free use of every pupil.

An amusing parody on the misuse of "freedom" is the apocryphal story of the Alameda County teacher, who said one day to her class:

"Now, children, each one is to write a short composition. Don't write anything you've ever heard or seen before. Write just what's in you."

In due time Johnny marched forward with the following "creative" essay—

"Inside of me there's a heart, a liver, two lungs, and a stomach. Inside my stomach is some chocolate, mush, stewed prunes, toast," etc.

Many laughable tales might be told concerning the mistakes of excessive zeal in giving children "freedom." These peccadillos are negligible, however, when one considers the harsh tyranny and cruel, pitiful repression with which dyspeptic and sour-visaged teachers once ruled with sadistic "hickory stick" and "birch rod."

By "natural development" is meant the unfolding and growth of normal personality. Of course, the feeble-minded may develop "naturally"; but the modern school thinks in terms of typical, wholesome, non-pathological children. Extroverts and introverts require special régimes. The atypical should be segregated and given specialized training, definitely adapted to meet their peculiar requirements.

"Freedom to develop" means the full and complete expression of personality, in many forms of creative activity and in many realms of human endeavor. The progressive school places emphasis upon the vast resources of latent aptitudes, talents and abilities, rather than upon the shortcomings and deficiencies of children. Old-fashioned methods of marking and grading put a fictitious emphasis upon failure; progressive education stresses success.

The progressive teacher fits the tasks to the child's ability, instead of racking him upon the inquisitorial torture-apparatus of Gargantuan lessons beyond his hope of achievement. The new note of freedom in the modern schools is one of the most inspiring evidences of the present glorious renaissance of education.

The Italians have a proverb, *Giudicar l'arbor ad' frutti maturi*, "Judge a tree by its ripened fruit." Much of the fruit upon the trees of progressive education is still immature; another decade or two will be necessary before judgment can be passed.

In general, however, the new educational technique is immensely successful. People would no more go back in education to the methods of medievalism than they would return, in mechanics, to the stone hatchets of our Paleolithic ancestors.

The door upon the crudities of the past is closed.

VAUGHAN MACCAUGHEY
SAN FRANCISCO, CALIF.

QUOTATIONS

ENGLISH SCHOOL BOOKS

ON another page this morning is printed a summary of the report to the Board of Education by its Consultative Committee on the nature and the supply of books in elementary schools. Briefly the committee are by no means satisfied that the books used in these schools are good enough, or that there are enough of them, and they make various recommendations by which both quality and quantity may be improved. The schools, it appears, are still hampered by the survival of a tradition originating in very different times from the present, when schooling meant primarily instruction in reading without much regard for the matter read, and when reading was almost entirely confined to the classroom. Since those primitive days the world has become deluged with printed matter; books and newspapers are everywhere, and mere ability to read leads nowhere unless with its acquisition the foundations are laid of good taste, discernment and a critical attitude towards what appears in print. From this state of affairs several consequences flow. Nothing can be too good for children to read, either in class or out of it; the love of good books must be encouraged in school and at home; children must be familiarized with the appearance of bookshelves and led to make use of libraries and to take a proprietary interest in books. Books, the committee admit, are not everything in education, but they deserve the most careful choosing in consequence of the spread of the reading habit. That children should be "masters of the printed word, not its slaves or dupes," is the ideal.

The committee are particularly concerned to see that children are introduced to the best of a great literary inheritance, and they are far from confining their recommendations to what has to be read in school. But in school they suggest that valuable opportunities are often lost. They have been told by witnesses that recent generations of children show less and less acquaintance with the traditional and illustrative commonplaces of English literature. Knowledge of the language and the contents of the Bible is declining, and this weakens the adult's power to understand the great English classics and impoverishes imagination and feeling. That is partly because the Bible is too often unsuitably printed for children's use, and better printed editions of separate books are accordingly recommended, as is also a good Bible anthology, but there should be no attempt to water down the Bible story in other words. Similarly the committee find that school anthologies of poetry too often ignore many old favorites of tradition. This impression will be shared by those who have studied the numerous anthologies now in currency. It is not that the less known or newer verse in these books is poor in itself, but that it is not famous enough; it seems rather as if anthologists grew tired of repeating the classics, forgetting that the children have a right to be given them in preference to the neatest work of modern poets. For famous books and poems are not only works of art; they are often also historical events of inexhaustible effect—though compilers of selections for school use sometimes forget this aspect of literature. It is a mistake which was never made by those who pursued the old classical curriculum, however faulty it may have been in other ways. The remedy lies in no compulsory uniformity of school books—that is the last thing the committee wish to bring about—but in a more deliberate pursuit of excellence by teachers who in the last resort must choose the books, and by compilers and publishers of books, and in the more careful machinery of selection and supervision which the committee suggest should be set up.—*The London Times.*

REPORTS

QUANTITY, QUALITY AND ECONOMY IN EDUCATION[1]

One of the most perplexing problems confronting the American educational system arises from the simultaneous impact upon the school of three popular demands—that pupils be accommodated in greater numbers, that training of better quality be offered and that there be greater economy in all public expenditures.

The American people want educational opportunities to be widely extended. Our nation was founded upon the assumption that all men are created free and equal and we have come to believe that all should have an equal chance. We desire no leader to be selected on account of his wealth alone, no child to be bound by the accidents of birth; and we hope that the time may soon come when the race of life will be run from an even start with a free field. Franklin and Lincoln are our heroes. "Onward and upward" is a favorite motto. The most gratifying spectacle to most of us is that of the poor boy rising to the gilded heights. The humble origins of Smith and Hoover are political capital. This is the explanation of the growth of our school system and forms the underlying cause of the extraordinary expansion of all its parts. The public school is dear to the hearts of the American people. Through it they hope to realize their fondest desires, and they will not rest content until every boy and every girl is given opportunity commensurate with ability, regardless of birth, wealth or health. Americans want more education.

At the same time they want better quality of education. They are not satisfied with the schools as they are. Returning travelers receive thoughtful attention when they pronounce American education inferior to European. Merchants and manufacturers complain of the deficiencies of the graduates of our schools. Famous critics perceive a lack of thoroughness, they detect a certain softness in our teaching,

[1] Part of the annual report of William F. Russell, dean of Teachers College, Columbia University.

and they plead for the production of true scholars and a return to scholarly ideals. Legislatures enact laws requiring higher standards and better teachers. School authorities advance admission requirements and restrict attendance. Certain colleges practically elect to membership a favored few. Waiting lists are long. Institutions secure popular support by announcing as their aim education of fine quality, and they point with pride to small classes, individual instruction and education by conference under a tutorial system.

The American people want quantity and quality, and at the same time display a solicitude concerning all public expenditures. The economy program of the national administration, which has had wide public appeal, has been reflected in states and localities by the appointment of budget directors, the adoption of economy policies, the rigid scrutiny of all payments and the reduction of taxes. Some experts assert that the United States can not afford to support its present educational program. This seems absurd, but one may well pause when he looks into the future. If the American people proceed with a policy of extending education widely and at the same time increase expenditures in order to work for quality, the time may be not far distant when we shall be forced to consider whether we, as a nation, can afford to pay for all that we want. It is to be hoped that our economists will address themselves to this problem. A portion of the people by their own labors are able to support the balance who are not at work—the young, the aged, the ill, the unemployed and those who are in school. The ratio of the productive to the unproductive depends upon a variety of factors, among them being wealth of natural resources, geographical location, climatic conditions, length of the working day, week and year, degree of productivity, economy and thrift, amount of unemployment, age of retirement, birth and death rates, ratio of children to adults, general health conditions and the effect of the educational system upon such of these as are modifiable. Thus the early age of retirement in France, the low productivity of China, the frequent holidays of Spain and the extravagance of the United States, considered by themselves alone, would be conditions tending to limit the educational program; while, on the other hand, the thrift of Holland, the long hours of labor of Germany and the high degree of productivity of the United States, considered by themselves alone, would have the opposite effect. From the weighing and interlocking of these factors will come in time the answer to the question of how good and how extended an educational system a country can have. It seems reasonable to believe that in general we can pay for our present program—and with a more equitable distribution of the burden we can probably afford a more extended one; but the time will surely come when the economic limit will be reached and beyond that we dare not go.

The problem is as difficult as it is important. Those who favor quantity are extending educational facilities and welcoming the hordes of students who flock to the doors of our schools and colleges. Those who think first of quality are restricting attendance in order to do their best for small numbers. If it were possible to give a satisfactory education to large numbers in big institutions under conditions of reasonable economy, the results would be of utmost importance. After all, it is a question of the possibility of quantity production of quality in education.

We are apt to forget that there is nothing new in this idea. Long ago the leading countries of the world embarked upon such a program. Once the typical educational relationship was a teacher and one pupil at a time, and even in the present day, when one considers the teachers in the old-style schools in Confucian, Buddhist and Mahometan countries, masters with apprentices, and the adults who are the teachers among primitive peoples, it is probable that there are more teachers in the world teaching one pupil at a time than there are teachers teaching more than one. Until relatively recent times, the educational process was looked upon much as we view tutoring. In the days when the mass of the people received no schooling, when a few were chosen to receive the rudiments of knowledge, and only the children of the nobility were to be educated, it was possible to find and support tutors in quantity sufficient for the task. It was only when the people demanded that all should go to school, that individual instruction had to be abandoned and the need became apparent for some sort of quantity production. Various experiments were made. Individuals otherwise employed were pressed into service, assuming teaching in addition to other occupations by which they made their living. Thus priests and pastors, dames and housewives were placed in charge of schools. Bell and Lancaster devised plans whereby one could teach hundreds, but the class in a school under the direction of a person whose prime function it was to teach proved to be the most successful and economical solution to this problem and as such has persisted to the present day. Group instruction is an effort toward quantity production.

Class work has often been criticized adversely. There has been much discussion concerning proper limits of effectiveness, upper and lower extremes and the optimum size of the group to be taught. Recent research is giving encouragement to the adherents of the tutorial system. Careful studies of the exact way in which children learn to read, to spell, to add and subtract reveal that much of it is an individual matter. Class exercises, they say, may serve to help the teacher to diagnose difficulties, to test results and to give directions; but the learning process is more economical when the individual works alone. This has not forced the abandonment of class work; rather it has called for a new technique of teaching. Educators have found ways so to vary the procedures of class management that individual instruction can be given under school conditions without greatly increased cost. The plan resembles a correspondence course given in residence. Undoubtedly the American genius for administration when turned to this problem will find in the future more perfect methods of supplementing the individual contacts of teacher and pupils so that better results will ensue. It is said that Mark Hopkins on one end of a log and a student on the other would make a university. One wonders why so obvious a statement should be handed down from generation to generation. Naturally it would be a fine institution and the annual tuition charges per student would be exactly the salary of a distinguished man like President Hopkins. The real problem is so to arrange the logs like the spokes of a wheel that a Mark Hopkins may sit at the hub and pupils and students on the rim in numbers sufficient to carry the cost with economy. Our public schools are progressing toward a solution.

Once when the colleges were small there were intimate relations between students and faculty. Students were few. Famous teachers surrounded by their books gave individual attention to a small group. Research was attacked together; interpretation was made incidentally; great scholars were the inspiration; great scholars were the result. As a general thing these times are past. Now the colleges have thousands of students, huge buildings, multiplicity of offerings and a variety of departments. Professors mourn the days that are gone, and the temptation is to try to bring back former conditions. But the commitments are here. Students make their demands. Sheer numbers force a change. In occasional subjects, such as anthropology and astronomy, the old methods are still possible, but for most subjects they are out of the question. The conference becomes a lecture course. What was formerly personal advice is now a printed syllabus. Some of the research guidance is given in a class, and the library, formerly the workroom, the meeting room, the research laboratory and the classroom, tends to become a collection of books, housed in a separate building, upon the campus to be sure, but in no sense holding the intimate and integral relation to the life of the institution that once it held. The colleges are not remaining static. Despite the fact that some are strictly limiting attendance, there are many that are trying to improve their methods the better to adjust themselves for numbers. There is no part of our educational system in which so many changes are being made and so many new ideas being introduced.

Thus the school and the college as we find them are already making efforts toward quantity production in response to the demand that many be educated. They are modifying their procedures so that many may be educated better. By giving quality in quantity they are serving the interests of economy; but the persistent demands for extended facilities, the criticism of American standards, and the call for reduced expenditures indicate that the problem is not yet solved and that much remains to be done.

EDUCATIONAL RESEARCH AND STATISTICS

DO COLLEGE STUDENTS KNOW AND UNDERSTAND THE LORD'S PRAYER?

THE school law of Tennessee requires the teacher to read at least ten verses of the Bible each day. The reading is generally followed by a repetition of the Lord's Prayer by the entire school. The child also goes to church, and there he often repeats the same prayer, until finally it becomes a habit as many other duties of the school. It seems that the ability to repeat the Lord's Prayer is one of the essentials for teaching, based on the amount of repetition and the different occasions upon which it is used. The teacher repeats this prayer not only while she is out in the field at work, but also when she comes to the teachers' college. We are safe in saying that the college student who comes to the teachers' college has been well drilled in learning the Master's prayer. According to the law of repetition there should be no question as to whether the average college student should know the Lord's Prayer from memory.

This problem was suggested to the writer by a previous study made by Matthews,[1] who studied the papers collected from the seventh, eighth and ninth grades in the public schools and compared these results with those of academy students. He found that approximately four out of five of the students in the junior high school and academy could not repeat the Lord's Prayer, and about 67 per cent. of the students comprehended what they were able to repeat.

DO COLLEGE STUDENTS KNOW THE LORD'S PRAYER?

The writer made the following experiment. He gave to each student of the East Tennessee State Teachers College, during the spring of 1928, a blank sheet of paper, and instructed the entire group to write out the Lord's Prayer from memory. The papers were collected, graded carefully and also checked. All words misspelled or left out were counted as wrong. Table I shows the number of cases used in the study.

[1] M. Taylor Matthews, "A Written Reproduction Test for The Lord's Prayer," SCHOOL AND SOCIETY, 26: 242.

TABLE I

Class	Men	Women	Total
Freshmen	47	286	333
Sophomores	35	78	113
Juniors	16	35	51
Seniors	17	26	43
Total	115	425	540

The percentages of the different classes in spelling and repeating the Lord's Prayer correctly are as follows:

TABLE II

Class	Per cent. Correct
Freshmen	95
Sophomores	95
Juniors	96
Seniors	97
Total average	96

The results indicate that the students can repeat with a fair degree of accuracy this masterpiece, but there is a slight difference between the different classes. We found that there was no material sex difference in either repetition or comprehension and for this reason all of the data have been thrown together.

CAN COLLEGE STUDENTS INTERPRET THE LORD'S PRAYER?

In order to answer this question we had first to divide the Lord's Prayer into fifteen different thought units as shown in Table III. The students were given a copy of the thought units, and a blank space was left after each unit to be filled out by the student. The papers were collected and later scored and checked. A copy of the thought units of the Lord's Prayer was sent also to each of the ten ministers in the city, representing five different denominations, to be filled out as they thought best from the light of their study. A score card was constructed, based upon the interpretation of the ministers, which was used to score the students' papers on the meaning of each thought unit. All the different ideas of the ministers were included in the score card. If the student included one of the thought units which was in the score card under the meaning of a certain passage in the prayer it was counted correct. This was done throughout the fifteen different units of the Lord's Prayer and the percentage correct was computed, the results being shown in Table III. The writer realizes that there is a great deal of subjective material, but maintains that it gives a general trend of the group as measured by the interpretations of the ministers who might be classified as experts in this field. Table III shows the percentage of correct answers to the thought units of the Lord's Prayer by the different classes.

TABLE III

Thought Units	Years in College I	II	III	IV	Approximate average
Our Father	42	39	50	43	44
Which art in heaven	44	49	58	50	50
Hallowed be thy name	77	86	81	71	79
Thy kingdom come	38	43	54	36	43
Thy will be done	69	64	63	86	71
On earth as it is in Heaven	65	57	58	82	66
Give us this day	59	48	56	57	55
Our daily bread	60	55	64	57	59
And forgive our debts (or trespasses)	84	81	92	89	87
As we forgive our debtors	76	75	77	86	79
And lead us not into temptation	76	87	87	79	82
But deliver us from evil	76	81	67	86	78
For thine is the kingdom	56	58	64	61	60
And the power	76	81	79	82	80
And the glory, for ever, Amen	41	46	67	39	48
Total average	63	63	68	67	65

The above table seems to indicate that there is quite a variation in difficulty in the different thought units. For example, the easiest passages were—"and forgive our debts" and "lead us not into temptation"; while the most difficult passages are "Thy kingdom come" and "Our Father." There seems to be very little difference between the classes in their total average of the entire prayer. It is clear that according to our standards of meaning the college students do not understand what they have repeated over and over many times. The average student who will be going out to teach children and who will continue to repeat this famous classic, understands roughly only about two thirds of what he will repeat almost daily in the schoolroom. There is also a general trend toward a better understanding on the part of the upperclassmen, but the difference is very small, as is shown in Table III. We also compared the interpretations of the different denominations which were represented in the college, and the following results are shown:

Denomination	Per cent. Correct
Baptist	61
Christian (Progressive and Non-progressive)	62
Presbyterian	63
Methodist	65
Average	63

There were a number who gave no denomination and the other denominations were so few that the results were thrown out on account of the small number of cases. There seems to be a slight difference between the different denominations which might indicate a general trend, but the difference is so small that no definite conclusions could be safely drawn.

This study has shown that a much larger percentage of the students know and can repeat the Lord's Prayer than can interpret or understand the meaning. It also indicates that the school and church are failing in teaching the student the wider and more subtle meaning of this well-known passage. If these students who are prospective teachers do not know the meaning, there is not much hope of their teaching the Lord's Prayer to the children whom they will teach. If college students understand only about two thirds of the prayer the ignorance of the average child will probably be more appalling than this study indicates. This study also emphasizes the fact that mere repetition in the church and in the school is not enough. We must apply other laws of learning and not assume that the child or the college student understands what he is able to repeat from memory.

LESTER R. WHEELER
EAST TENNESSEE STATE TEACHERS COLLEGE,
JOHNSON CITY, TENNESSEE

SCHOOL AND SOCIETY

EDITED BY J. McKEEN CATTELL

WITH WHICH IS COMBINED THE

EDUCATIONAL REVIEW

EDITED BY WILLIAM McANDREW

Volume XXVIII | SATURDAY, DECEMBER 15, 1928 | Number 729

STATISTICS OF REGISTRATION IN AMERICAN UNIVERSITIES AND COLLEGES, 1928

By Dean RAYMOND WALTERS

SWARTHMORE COLLEGE

AN advance of two per cent. in full-time students—the smallest annual increase since the war—is shown in reports just received from 216 colleges and universities of the United States and Canada which are on the approved list of the Association of American Universities. As compared with figures of a year ago, 115 institutions report increases and 101 report decreases. A tabulation as to size groups follows:

1928 AND 1927 GROUP COMPARISONS

Size of Group	No. Reporting Increases	No. Reporting Decreases
3,000 and up	27	18
1,000 to 3,000	34	22
500 to 1,000	30	31
Up to 500	24	30
TOTALS	115	101

An analysis by states shows that in twenty-six states there are more full-time students enrolled in approved colleges and universities of those states than in 1927, and in twenty-two states there are fewer such students. As to the causes of decrease in enrolment various explanations have been suggested, such as agricultural and industrial conditions, the development of junior colleges, a trend, in certain areas, away from the small colleges to the state universities, and deliberate limitation of enrolment. An institutional tabulation by states is given below.

Based on November 1 reckoning, the 1928 full-time enrolments of 216 institutions on this list total 417,526, which, compared with 1927 figures, is an increase of a little more than two per cent. The five-year increase of these institutions, 1922–1927, had totaled 25 per cent.

The figures in the next half dozen years must be awaited to determine whether a definite break has come in the rate of increase of collegiate enrolment. In this connection there is significance in facts as to the American birth-rate cited recently by Frank M. Phillips, chief of the division of statistics of the U. S. Bureau of Education. He pointed out that, applying the birth-rate and the infant mortality rate for each year, "22.5 children per thousand of the population reached the age of one year in 1916 and less than 20 per thousand in 1926." Restricted immigration likewise is a factor. If these conditions continue, both school enrolments and college enrolments will soon reach stationary periods.

ANALYSIS OF INSTITUTIONS BY STATES

State	No. of Increases	No. of Decreases	Enrolment 1928	1927
Ala.	1	2	3,617	4,280
Arizona	1	0	1,719	1,537
Ark.	1	0	1,615	1,420
Calif.	5	4	25,439	25,689
Col.	2	0	3,565	3,470
Conn.	0	4	6,419	6,471
Del.	0	1	690	698
D. C.	2	1	3,790	3,785
Fla.	2	0	3,713	3,411
Ga.	0	2	1,533	1,574
Hawaii	1	0	713	588
Idaho	1	0	1,786	1,778
Ill.	10	5	27,841	27,570
Ind.	5	4	13,834	13,421
Ia.	3	5	13,735	14,093
Kan.	2	2	5,091	5,119
Ky.	1	0	2,410	2,339
La.	0	1	2,351	2,359
Me.	3	1	3,193	3,149
Md.	1	2	5,069	5,404
Mass.	11	5	34,859	32,046
Mich.	1	2	11,720	10,471
Minn.	4	2	14,304	13,589
Miss.	1	0	1,109	1,072
Mo.	2	4	9,379	9,692
Mont.	1	0	1,410	1,313
Neb.	0	2	6,458	6,470
Nev.	0	1	812	823
N. H.	0	2	3,428	3,836
N. J.	2	2	6,071	6,671
N. Y.	17	6	66,203	62,563
N. C.	1	2	4,828	4,811
N. D.	1	0	1,579	1,573
Ohio	10	7	32,429	31,345
Okla.	0	1	4,604	4,738
Ore.	2	2	7,270	7,244
Pa.	9	9	28,476	30,195
R. I.	0	1	1,903	2,158
S. C.	1	2	3,707	3,848
S. D.	0	1	896	929
Tenn.	2	2	5,121	4,667
Tex.	1	2	7,262	7,103
Utah	1	1	3,667	3,761
Vt.	0	2	1,936	2,008
Va.	3	4	6,343	6,231
Wash.	0	2	7,830	7,910
W. Va.	0	1	2,449	2,504
Wis.	3	2	11,352	11,012
Wyo.	1	0	1,079	982

It may well be added that the present collegiate period, if it is a plateau, is nevertheless a plateau 25 per cent. higher than it was five years ago and very markedly higher proportionately than any similar popular level reached in other countries.

Table I gives figures in detail of universities which have been included for some years in statistical articles in *Science* and later in SCHOOL AND SOCIETY. Table III supplies a less detailed report upon students and teachers of additional institutions, with the aim of making the study broader. A few of the statistics for teachers and administrative staff are for 1927. The institutions asked to furnish statistics were those on the list approved by the Association of American Universities, as given in the association's most recent printed report.

Following the differentiation introduced in this series in 1920, Tables I, II and III are arranged to bring out clearly the enrolment of full-time and of part-time undergraduates. The full-time regular student is defined for this series as a student who has completed a four-year high-school course and is devoting his full time (twelve hours a week or more) to study during the collegiate year. The student whose main time and attention are given to some other employment and who takes college and university courses in late afternoon, evening and Saturday classes is listed as a part-time student. The grand total figures for 1928 include full-time regular students, part-time students and summer-school students of 1928 but do not include extension and correspondence students, who are, however, recorded in Table I.

The foregoing definitions of these terms, as used in the SCHOOL AND SOCIETY series, were endorsed by the American Association of Collegiate Registrars at its 1922 meeting, and all the undergraduate enrolments are now reported on this basis.

Table II gives a list of the twenty-five largest institutions of those considered in this series.

The ten largest liberal arts colleges or departments are in the following institutions: University of California (including the division at Los Angeles), 9,783; Wisconsin, 6,121; Michigan, 5,519; New York University, 5,381; Minnesota, 4,654; College of the City of New York, 4,498; Illinois, 3,997; Texas, 3,424; Columbia, 3,381; Harvard, 3,233.

The enrolment of men undergraduates in the five largest liberal arts colleges or departments is as follows: College of the City of New York, 4,498; California, 4,091; New York University, 3,943; Wisconsin, 3,447; Michigan, 3,329.

As to women undergraduates, the size order of enrolment in coeducational universities for the five largest is as follows: California, 5,692; Wisconsin, 2,674; Michigan, 2,190; Illinois, 2,127; Minnesota, 1,912.

The ten largest exclusively women's colleges on the approved list are: Hunter, with 4,918 students; Smith, 2,022; Wellesley, 1,592; Florida State College for Women, 1,550; Vassar, 1,156; Mount Holyoke, 1,006; Goucher, 979; Radcliffe, 907; Randolph-Macon Woman's College, 795; Elmira, 588.

The five technical schools or departments reporting the largest engineering enrolments are: Massachusetts Institute of Technology, 2,868; Purdue, 2,366; Minnesota, 1,762; Illinois, 1,573; Ohio State, 1,548.

Among law schools the five largest on this list are: New York University, 1,785; Harvard, 1,589; Fordham, 1,465; Columbia, 638; Michigan, 557.

The five largest medical schools in the United States are: Michigan, 668; Minnesota, 636; Pennsylvania, 557; Harvard, 515; Chicago, 501.

The five largest non-professional graduate schools in American universities are as follows: Columbia, 2,497; California, 1,631; Chicago, 1,426; Minnesota, 1,024; Harvard, 908.

An increase in enrolment of agricultural students is general among the institutions on this list, which does not, however, include all of the leading schools of agriculture. Ohio State is first in numbers, having 793, or two more than Minnesota.

The five largest registrations of students in commerce and finance are reported as follows: Boston University, 3,683; Pennsylvania, 2,255; Ohio State, 1,827; Illinois, 1,822; New York University, 1,050.

Among dental schools, Pennsylvania has taken the numerical lead with 430 students. The six next largest are: Northwestern, 396; Michigan, 357; Pittsburgh, 340; Minnesota, 277; California and Columbia, each 250.

Teachers College of Columbia University has 4,681 students. Second in size is Teachers College, University of California at Los Angeles, where there are 2,009 students, to which 555 additional university students in education are added. Ohio State reports 1,716 students in education; Indiana has 1,479, and Minnesota has 1,446.

Chicago has the largest divinity school, with 298 students. The forestry school at Syracuse University, with 414 students, is largest in this field. The largest school of journalism is that of the University of Missouri, which reports 298 students. Among university schools of music, that of Northwestern leads with 265 students. The Columbia registration of 681 students is the largest pharmacy enrolment.

The extent to which the urban universities are making collegiate work available

TABLE I

	California	Chicago	Cincinnati	Columbia	Cornell	Harvard	Illinois	Indiana	Iowa	Johns Hopkins	Kansas	Michigan	Minnesota
College men	4091	1593	489	2298	1238	3233	1870	1430	1564	331	1312	3329	2742
College women	5692	1276	544	1083	663	...	2127	1037	1245	...	958	2190	1912
Engineering	1171	...	1519	207	1107	270	1573	...	329	287	556	1421	1762
Law	341	437	143	638	189	1589	436	118	225	...	143	557	270
Medicine	266	501	269	423	257	515	503	432	472	282	301	668	636
Non-Prof. Graduate	1631	1426	226	2497	602	908	895	248	283	354	238	953	1024
Agriculture	398	...	...	...	625	...	642	...	...	...	...	...	791
Architecture	...	...	...	95	190	80	254	...	...	...	...	312	...
Art	151	...	328	...	11	...	...	66	*	...	326	...	*
Commerce	899	240	*	382	...	868	1822	173	269	66	131	166	301
Dentistry	250	...	...	250	...	114	207	176	192	...	...	357	277
Divinity	...	298	...	...	...	110	...	...	...	...	...	...	...
Education	2564	66	594	4681	562	290	899	1479	...	...	120	793	1446
Forestry	65	...	...	...	100	18	...	...	...	...	...	30	*
Journalism	...	...	...	152	...	...	51	169	...	...	*	...	*
Music	48	...	...	...	...	...	125	92	109	...	*	...	*
Pharmacy	316	...	...	681	...	...	656	...	119	...	78	89	148
Other courses	401	142	185	433	616	115	103	188	354	92	...	242	665
Deduct duplicates	947	351	...	129	845	...	13	1441	114	...	125	153	159
Total	17337	5628	4297	13691	5315	8110	12150	4167	5047	1412	4038	10954	11815
Part-time	...	2523	4721	7058	...	...	...	66	705	3056	...	...	...
Summer session	10228	6338	1310	14007	2150	3149	2270	1984	3263	1107	1102	3486	6041
Deduct duplicates	1003	1827	...	2720	...	466	860	765	989	750	...	1550	...
Gd. tot., Nov. 1, '28	26562	12662	10328	32036	7465	10793	13010	5452	8026	5575	5140	12890	17856
Gd. tot., Nov. 1, '23	23139	12191	5710	28861	7090	8925	10557	5262	6701	3900	4561	11162	12322
Gd. tot., Nov. 1, '18	10471	7241	2731	9910	5783	4891	6096	3010	4116	1659	3916	...	5860
Exten. courses	14213	6510	1252	10706	...	1050	127	7171	1740	...	1550	...	6843
Teaching staff	957	765	433	2075	918	1244	1135	299	533	570	274	768	770
Administrative staff	60	75	18	71	13	197	71	31	118	13	6	73	10

* Included elsewhere.

for secondary school teachers and others who take late afternoon, evening or Saturday classes is shown in Table I under part-time enrolment.

The five largest summer schools for the 1928 summer session were: Columbia, 14,007; California, 10,228; Chicago, 6,338; Minnesota, 6,041; Wisconsin, 5,065. In general, summer-school attendance in 1928 showed no great increase over the 1927 figures.

The following paragraphs explain statistics presented in Table I and give additional information:

The University of California returns include the "University of California at Los Angeles," as it is now called, the designation Southern Branch being discontinued. There are 5,860 students at Los Angeles, of whom 3,832 are in the College of Letters and Science and 2,009 in the Teachers College. The teaching staff at Los Angeles comprises 220 persons. The 401 students listed in Table I under other courses are distributed as follows: Training School for Nurses, 160; agriculture non-degree, 230; dental hygienists, 11. The summer-school figures include 2,104 intersession students

TABLE I—(*Concluded*)

Missouri	Nebraska	Northwestern	Ohio State	Pennsylvania	Pittsburgh	Princeton	Stanford	Syracuse	Texas	Tulane	University of Washington	Virginia	Washington University	Western Reserve	Wisconsin	Yale
1134	1090	1188	1755	1389	1611	2051	2959	1012	1878	549	...	1135	693	753	3447	1630
586	771	1328	674	...	496	...	500	864	1546	438	...	7	744	714	2674	...
421	671	248	1548	138	493	175	219	346	1111	211	...	156	411	...	1080	669
146	162	321	297	484	275	...	204	140	349	97	...	284	182	289	341	318
75	307	521	330	557	261	...	177	182	284	436	...	240	300	245	291	208
164	343	330	844	157	859	228	366	166	167	122	...	163	226	48	959	614
274	549	...	793	...	...	...	...	66	...	...	...	8	...	...	555	...
...	...	...	...	327	...	...	...	...	...	68	...	...	111	...	...	100
112	460	...	...	36	...	...	16	706	*	156	...	60	137	...	...	149
187	652	414	1827	2255	774	...	68	953	226	153	...	138	183	...	224	...
...	92	396	245	430	340	...	...	...	...	...	...	...	195	174	...	...
...	...	...	...	...	...	...	...	...	...	...	...	...	...	...	...	217
371	1414	175	1716	761	731	...	99	115	95	*	...	101	...	389	*	63
...	...	...	...	...	...	...	...	414	...	...	...	1	...	...	...	39
298	177	70	*	...	...	...	37	*	*	*	...	...	...	...	119	...
...	*	265	*	30	...	...	...	*	...	42	...	119	...	...	157	115
...	112	...	188	...	433	...	...	...	75	23	...	...	...	114	81	...
...	102	301	254	147	22	...	...	457	67	193	...	...	262	630	115	1038
...	667	...	...	...	...	...	1186	233	4	137	...	326	40	...	1001	170
3667	6235	5557	10293	6711	6235	2454	3459	5188	5794	2351	7282	2086	3404	3356	9042	4990
274	249	5027	119	5862	3641	...	...	233	420	620	...	12	303	5493	...	753
1861	3320	2052	3504	2271	2798	139	1345	1679	3158	1133	3057	2792	948	1983	5065	87
474	907	600	1254	...	...	139	461	218	1113	...	...	579	297	...	1168	...
5328	8897	12036	12662	14844	12674	2454	4343	6882	8259	4104	10339	4311	4358	10832	12939	5830
4767	8220	8229	9725	14632	8553	2226	2778	5486	7511	3746	6627	4399	4774	4372	11088	4970
...	3955	5272	4888	4938	3402	1113	1864	3747	3785	2356	...	2140	1367	2654	5944	2554
3325	2485	...	...	2074	1087	...	...	829	3112	...	1781	470	10162	...	18261	...
284	360	615	883	1362	851	272	506	583	410	412	370	166	371	658	594	602
25	28	8	8	44	57	28	60	35	29	24	70	19	22	25	39	46

at Berkeley, 5,272 summer session at Berkeley and 3,658 summer session at Los Angeles.

At the University of Chicago there are increases over last year in the number of students in law, non-professional graduate courses and divinity, with decreases in medicine, business and education. Decreases exceed increases by ninety as compared with 1927. The figures 142 under other courses in Table I include 132 in social service administration and ten in the Graduate School of Library Science.

The University of Cincinnati report reveals an increase of 756 in the full-time enrolment and of 640 in the grand-total figures. Of the 328 students of applied arts listed under art in Table I, 193 are men and 135 are women. The 185 listed under other courses include ninety-eight in household administration and eighty-seven taking nursing and health courses.

Columbia's tremendous enrolment continues at substantially the 1927 height. With the addition of the Seth Low Junior College in Brooklyn and of St. Stephen's College at Annandale, the number of undergraduates is 13.5 per cent. greater than a year ago. The total of graduate non-professional and professional students is

TABLE II

University	Regular Students Full-Time	Rank	All Resident Students	Rank
California	17,337	1	26,562	3
Columbia	13,691	2	32,036	1
Illinois	12,150	3	13,010	7
Minnesota	11,815	4	17,856	5
Michigan	10,954	5	12,890	9
New York U.	10,711	6	26,303	4
Ohio State	10,293	7	12,662	11
Wisconsin	9,042	8	12,939	8
Boston U.	8,520	9	12,234	13
Harvard	8,110	10	10,793	16
U. of Wash.	7,282	11	10,339	17
Pennsylvania	6,711	12	14,844	6
Pittsburgh	6,235	13	12,674	10
Nebraska	6,235	14	8,897	19
Texas	5,794	15	8,259	20
Chicago	5,628	16	12,662	12
Northwestern	5,559	17	12,038	14
Cornell	5,315	18	7,465	23
Syracuse	5,188	19	6,882	24
Iowa	5,047	20	8,026	21
Yale	4,990	21	5,743	.....
C. C. of N. Y.	4,929	22	28,287	2
Oklahoma	4,604	23	6,664	25
Cincinnati	4,297	24	10,328	18
Fordham	4,175	25	7,859	22
Western Reserve	3,356	.....	10,832	15

twenty-two less than 1927—a decrease of .2 per cent. With the 1928 summer session registration of 14,007, with 7,058 part-time students and with 10,706 in university extension (7,519 home study, 2,336 extramural and 851 in special courses) the "super grand total" of all students receiving instruction of Columbia University is 42,742. This breaks all records at Columbia and elsewhere.

Forty fewer students than last year are indicated in the 1928 Cornell figures. There are no pronounced decreases in any departments. A supplementary statement shows a total of 1,299 women students at Cornell, of whom 663 are in the College of Arts and Sciences, 350 are taking home economics, 123 are doing non-professional graduate study and 89 are in agricultural courses. Under the term other courses in Table I are included 131 students in Cornell's new course in hotel management, 134 in veterinary work and 351 in home economics.

Due to an increase of 123 students in the Graduate School of Business Administration and to small increases in four other departments which offset decreases in four other departments, the Harvard figures for 1928 are somewhat higher than those for 1927. The full-time total is eighty larger. The grand total is eighty-one less, inasmuch as the 1928 summer school was smaller by 131 than that of 1927.

Slight decreases in the undergraduate enrolment at the University of Illinois are counterbalanced by increases in the professional and non-professional graduate schools, so that the total of full-time students is 117 larger than in 1927. The engineering figures in Table I include 1,219 in engineering, 222 in architectural engineering and 132 in chemical engineering. The 103 listed under other courses are students in library work.

With the single exception of dentistry, all departments of Indiana University report small increases over last year. The 1928 summer session was somewhat larger than that of 1927. In the extension enrolment of 7,171 there are included 769 correspondence students. The 188 listed under other courses in Table I are students taking nurse's training.

There are 354 students in nursing at the State University of Iowa who are included in Table I under other courses. Of the 705 part-time students recorded in this table, 382 are graduate students, 313 are liberal arts students and 10 are commerce students.

The full-time enrolment at Johns Hopkins is reported as 284 smaller and the grand total as 1,486 larger than in 1927. The latter is explained by the increase in part-time students living in and around Baltimore, of whom there are 3,056. Under other courses in Table I are included 91 in the School of Hygiene and Public Health.

The 1928 attendance at the University of Kansas remains practically at the 1927 level, with a few more in full-time enrolment and a few less in the grand total. The 326 students listed in Table I under art "include students in fine arts and in music."

Registrar Ira M. Smith writes that there is a reduction in the number of students in residence at the University of Michigan for the current year, but that an increase of 664 extramural students produces a total increase. "All of our extramural students are taking work in regular academic subjects and no courses are offered by the home study or correspondence study method."

The University of Minnesota has 508 more students than a year ago. The law school reports a decrease of twenty-six; every other department reports gains. The 1928 summer session was 597 larger than that of 1927. In Table I the figures for engineering include 274 in chemistry and 118 in mines. Under other courses are embraced 614 in nursing and 51 in dental hygiene. The total for agriculture includes students in forestry and home economics.

Small decreases in most of the departments of the University of Missouri aggregate a decrease of 283 in the full-time enrolment, which is now 3,667. A gain of over 200 in the 1928 summer school brings the grand total up to nearly the 1927 figures.

Numerical increases in medicine, nonprofessional graduate, agriculture, journalism and pharmacy students at the University of Nebraska make up for decreases in seven other groups. The full-time enrolment is four less and the grand total enrolment is forty-four larger than in 1927. Students in music are included under the art figures in Table I. The 102 listed under other courses are students in nursing.

Northwestern University's report discloses a gain of 138 full-time students over 1927 and a gain of 738 in grand totals. The increases are due to small advances in most of the departments, with 528 more part-time students. The 301 persons listed under other courses in Table I are students in speech.

At Ohio State University, increases in liberal arts men, in medicine, in non-professional graduate enrolment, in agriculture, in commerce and in education bring the full-time registration to 10,293, or 258 more than in 1927. Students in journalism are included in the School of Commerce and Administration. The total for other courses in Table I is made up as follows: veterinary medicine, 110; arts-law, arts-medicine, science-medicine, etc., 83; school of nursing, 31; applied optics, 30. The 1928 summer session had nearly 500 students more than that of 1927.

Under its new policy of limiting attendance in certain schools, the University of Pennsylvania full-time enrolment is now 6,711, or 854 less than a year ago. The decrease is principally in the Wharton School of Finance and Commerce and in the liberal arts college. The engineering total in Table I includes 33 in chemistry and chemical engineering. Under other courses are embraced 85 students in veterinary medicine, 47 in biology and 15 in landscape architecture. Beyond the 157 men and women devoting full time to nonprofessional graduate study, there are 1,353 others doing part-time work. The College Courses for Teachers have 138 students, mostly young women, with 776 others listed as "partial students for certificates." In

TABLE III

Institution	Students Full-time	Students All residents	Teaching Staff
Agnes Scott	452	460	53
Albion	766	778	45
Alfred	494	588	39
Allegheny	614	698	40
Amherst	725	732	66
Baker	398	461	33
Bates	633	882	38
Beloit	473	479	43
Birmingham-South..	875	2,391	57
Boston C.	1,508	2,472	104
Boston U.	8,520	12,234	411
Brooklyn Poly. ...	444	597	42
Bowdoin	558	558	50
Brown	1,903	2,199	175
Bryn Mawr	484	484	86
Bucknell	1,090	1,348	...
California I. of T..	606	614	109
Carleton	793	805	68
Carnegie Tech. ...	2,450	3,358	286
Carthage	232	297	28
Case	640	682	69
Catholic U.	892	1,634	115
Central	676	950	41
Clark	324	541	38
Coe	809	929	68
Colby	623	627	35
Colgate	990	990	75
C. City of N. Y. ...	4,929	28,287	650
C. of New Rochelle.	732	762	48
C. of the Pacific ..	613	846	64
C. of St. Catherine.	415	540	40
C. of St. Elizabeth.	267	327	35
C. of St. Theresa ..	380	756	39
C. of Wooster	867	930	56
Colorado C.	575	613	63
Columbia	13,691	32,036	2,075
Conn. C. for W. ...	538	548	55
Converse	432	438	40
Cornell C. (Ia.) ..	504	538	47
Cornell	5,315	7,465	918
Dartmouth	2,273	2,273	231
Davidson	602	693	42
Denison	866	1,047	81
De Pauw	1,589	1,615	86
Dickinson	554	554	30
Doane	223	230	25
Dominican	185	348	56
Drake	1,311	2,183	96
Drury	441	461	34
Duke	1,722	3,044	107
Earlham	392	404	38
Elmira	588	588	51
Emory U.	1,081	1,705	227
Eureka	230	230	23
Fla. S. C. for W...	1,550	2,146	130
Fordham	4,175	7,859	212
Franklin	287	291	26
Franklin and M. ..	680	683	42
Georgetown U. ...	2,504	2,504	363
Gettysburg	642	830	47
Goucher	979	979	84
Grinnell	693	738	58
Hamilton	438	438	43
Hamline	378	378	44
Harvard	8,110	10,793	1,244
Haverford	295	295	36
Heidelberg	399	495	41
Hobart	307	307	35
Holy Cross C.	1,090	1,090	67
Howard C.	741	1,836	45
Hunter	4,918	6,202	608
Illinois College ...	418	418	25
Illinois Wesleyan .	663	663	48
Ill. Women's C. ...	343	351	41
Indiana	4,167	5,452	299
Ia. State A. & M...	3,982	4,930	400
Johns Hopkins ...	1,412	5,575	570
Kenyon	262	264	27
Knox	598	598	41
Lafayette	1,076	1,076	90
Lake Forest	343	353	22
Lawrence	1,034	1,054	61
Lehigh	1,475	1,635	150
Macalester	523	484	39
Marietta	376	393	31
Mass. Ag. C.	885	1,015	100
Mass. Inst. Tech. .	2,868	3,343	487
McGill	2,555	3,068	473
Miami U.	1,822	2,538	125
Middlebury	626	1,127	53
Mills	548	595	71
Milwaukee-Downer .	383	400	45
Monmouth	474	696	37
Morningside C. ...	744	1,003	47
Mount Holyoke ...	1,006	1,028	108
Muhlenberg	440	1,398	31
New York U.	10,711	26,303	1,383
N. Y. State T. Coll.	1,149	1,803	70
North Central	517	572	40
Northwestern U. ..	5,557	12,036	615
Oberlin	1,614	1,717	161
Occidental	621	654	61
Ohio State	10,293	12,662	883
Ohio U.	2,084	2,177	200
Ohio Wesleyan ...	1,803	1,803	163
Oregon S. Agr. ...	3,433	4,172	268
Otterbein	380	382	32
Our Lady of the Lake	168	867	27

the School of Education there are 617 part-time candidates for degrees and 181 partial students for certificates. Extension students include 985 in accounts and finance and 1,089 listed as teachers. Counting all taught in University of Pennsylvania classes, the total is 15,741.

The grand total of the University of Pittsburgh is slightly above that of 1927. In the full-time figures there is a falling off, the decreases in four departments being larger than the increases in six departments. The 22 students listed under other courses in Table I are in retail training research. Counting 1,087 extension students, the number receiving instruction totals 13,761.

The Princeton figure of 2,454 includes an increase of 35 students in the engineering school of 175, an increase of 14 in the graduate school of 228, and an increase of 199 in the total enrolment of the university.

Stanford University continues to restrict its enrolment of women students to exactly 500, with freshmen chosen from a large number of candidates. The total of men students is forty-seven more than a year

TABLE III—(*Concluded*)

Institution	Students Full-time	Students All residents	Teaching Staff
Park	492	500	36
Penn. State	3,754	6,582	375
Pomona	764	1,102	72
Princeton	2,454	2,454	272
Purdue	3,765	4,221	303
Radcliffe	907	1,109	150
R'dolph-Macon M.	220	220	28
R'dolph-Macon W.	795	816	66
Redlands	542	575	43
Reed	326	343	30
Rensselaer Poly. I.	1,412	1,412	115
Rice Inst.	1,300	1,300	86
Ripon	420	464	26
Rockford	411	526	44
Rosary	275	557	30
Rose Poly.	257	257	22
Rutgers	2,875	3,955	256
Simmons	1,431	1,699	134
Simpson	645	742	41
Smith	2,022	2,022	227
Stanford	3,459	4,343	506
St. Lawrence U.	3,825	3,993	103
State U. of Iowa	5,047	8,026	533
Stevens Inst. of T.	475	489	43
Swarthmore	540	540	70
Sweet Briar	445	445	39
Syracuse	5,188	6,882	583
Trinity (Conn.)	270	276	34
Trinity (D. C.)	394	408	48
Tufts	2,037	2,037	400
Tulane	2,351	4,104	412
Union	823	913	76
Utah Agr. C.	1,006	1,496	73
U. S. Mil. Acad.	1,266	1,266	168
U. of Akron	1,026	1,589	78
U. of Alabama	3,001	4,617	136
U. of Arizona	1,719	2,270	165
U. of Arkansas	1,615	2,375	150
U. of Buffalo	1,420	3,206	383
U. of California	17,337	26,562	1,387
U. of Chattanooga	348	387	23
U. of Chicago	5,628	12,662	765
U. of Cincinnati	4,297	10,328	433
U. of Colorado	2,990	6,426	276
U. of Delaware	690	988	73
U. of Florida	2,163	3,853	194
U. of Hawaii	713	1,167	69
U. of Idaho	1,786	2,410	148
U. of Illinois	12,150	13,010	1,135
U. of Kansas	4,038	5,140	274
U. of Kentucky	2,410	3,318	230
U. of Maine	1,379	1,652	135
U. of Maryland	2,678	3,681	450
U. of Michigan	10,954	12,890	768
U. of Minnesota	11,815	17,856	770
U. of Mississippi	1,109	1,431	55
U. of Missouri	3,667	5,328	284
U. of Montana	1,410	1,850	97
U. of Nebraska	6,235	8,897	360
U. of N. Hampshire.	1,155	1,495	124
U. of Nevada	812	942	68
U. of N. Carolina	2,504	4,221	210
U. of N. Dakota	1,579	1,868	116
U. of Notre Dame	2,975	3,737	160
U. of Oklahoma	4,604	6,664	270
U. of Oregon	3,019	4,307	283
U. of Penna.	6,711	14,844	1,362
U. of Pittsburgh	6,235	12,674	851
U. of Richmond	542	650	
U. of Rochester	995	3,311	105
U. of the South	323	337	35
U. of S. Carolina	1,513	2,088	88
U. of S. Dakota	896	1,195	92
U. of Tennessee	3,064	4,487	328
U. of Texas	5,794	8,259	410
U. of Utah	2,661	3,420	179
U. of Vermont	1,310	2,222	198
U. of Virginia	2,086	4,311	166
U. of Washington	7,282	10,339	370
U. of Wisconsin	9,042	12,939	594
U. of Wyoming	1,079	2,020	95
Vanderbilt	1,385	1,385	223
Vassar	1,156	1,244	143
Wabash	402	402	29
Washburn	655	947	69
Wash. & Jefferson.	500	742	41
Washington & Lee.	910	910	58
Washington U.	3,404	4,358	371
Wellesley	1,592	1,597	164
Wells	237	237	37
Wesleyan	621	621	56
Westminster (Mo.)	283	283	17
West Virginia	2,449	3,251	...
West. C. Women	397	397	32
Western Reserve	3,356	10,832	658
Westminster (Pa.)	492	528	29
Wheaton	450	450	46
Whitman	548	548	40
Willamette U.	491	575	..
William & Mary	1,345	2,145	68
William Jewell	416	420	19
Williams	807	807	75
Wilson	444	454	41
Winthrop	1,762	3,337	103
Wittenberg	1,081	1,960	88
Worcester Poly.	575	601	67
Yale	4,990	5,743	602
TOTALS	417,526	650,951	...

ago. In education there is an increase of twenty-three students.

Larger enrolments in every department except law bring the full-time total at Syracuse to 5,188, or 176 more than on November 1, 1927. The 1927 summer school had 234 students more than in 1926, its registration being 1,679.

An increase of 258 over the 1927 full-time enrolment is shown in the report of the University of Texas. There are small gains in nearly all departments. The 1928 summer session was slightly under the 1927 attendance. In Table I the engineering figures include 676 students in engineering and 435 in mines. The 67 students noted under other courses are taking nursing. A supplementary statement discloses that 1,810 students are taking education courses of the university.

Departmental increases and decreases at the Tulane University of Louisiana are about equal for the full-time enrolment. Due to a larger summer school (a gain of about 100), the grand total registration is higher for 1928 than for 1927. Of the 211 listed as engineering in Table I, 44 are chemistry students. Beyond the 436 medical students indicated in the table there are 178 registered in the Graduate School of Medicine, primarily physicians taking review courses.

The report from Seattle shows that the 1928 full-time enrolment of the University of Washington is 7,282, as compared with 7,354 on November 1, 1927; and 10,339 for grand total enrolment, compared with 10,603 a year ago. There are 1,781 extension students, or 381 more than last year. Detailed statistics were not received in time for printing in Table I.

A somewhat larger summer session, 2,792 students, accounts for the grand total gain at the University of Virginia over the 1927 figure. In the full-time classification there is a decrease of forty-nine, due chiefly to a lessened engineering attendance.

The 1928 registration of Washington University remains practically at the 1927 level for full-time students (20 higher), and the grand total is 104 larger than that of a year ago. The 262 students noted under other courses are in nurse's training.

Outstanding in the report of Western Reserve University is the enrolment of 389 students in education, which is 230 more than last year. There were general departmental increases bringing the full-time total to 3,356, or 433 higher than last year—a 14 per cent. gain. Under other courses in Table I are included 207 students in the School of Applied Social Sciences, 184 who take nursing, 158 in the Cleveland College and 81 taking library science.

Somewhat lower figures at Wisconsin for men and women in liberal arts are met by higher registrations in law, medicine, non-professional graduate and commerce courses. The present full-time enrolment of 9,042 is precisely 100 more than last year. The total of 115 students under other courses is made up of 74 in graduate nursing and 41 in library work. The "super-grand total" of all students receiving instruction under the university's auspices is 31,200.

Every state and territory and some thirty foreign countries are represented in the student body of 4,990 at Yale. The figures under other courses in Table I include 890 students in the freshman year who will later enter either Yale College or Sheffield Scientific School, 78 taking the course in drama and 70 who take the course in nursing. The 602 listed in the teaching staff include 144 part-time teachers.

The statistics in Table II afford opportunities for comparing attendance in colleges and universities of similar character.

POSSIBILITIES OF VOCATIONAL EDUCATION

By K. E. EVANS

"To know what ought to be known," wrote a Japanese sage, "and to do what ought to be done, that is enough. There is no time for anything else."

Obviously, the statement does not get us very far. The question, "Just what ought to be known or done?" still faces us. Nor would most of us fully endorse its seeming ban on recreation both mental and physical—unless, of course, its author would grant freely that one "ought to take recreation." None the less, the statement does give emphasis to the truth that some things, some tasks, some studies are more essential than other tasks and studies, some fields of learning more important, some activities more vital, and that a sound education is acquired, not just by collecting miscellaneous information, but by becoming acquainted with those realms of knowledge which surround our daily life and labors. "Why did you take that course in athletic psychology?" a father asked of a student in a western university. "Because, Dad, I needed just two credits more to graduate in mid-year." Possibly in this case the selection was justified. Yet, needless to say, a degree picked up in this fashion, two credits here, four there, without regard to the relative value and personal utility of the courses, would not prove one a well-educated man. Indeed, despite Ludwig Lewisohn's strictures in "Up-stream," the young fellows who went to Ohio State to learn how to become better undertakers and accountants were perhaps more truly educated than was Horace Walpole's famous uncle, who "knew a little of everything except how to hold his tongue and how to apply his knowledge."

And this the more because it is increasingly difficult to know even a little of almost everything. Three, perhaps two, generations ago that was relatively possible. A real all-around education was not a mere polite figure of speech. Since then, however, not only have many new fields of knowledge been opened, but it has become harder and harder to keep up with the fresh and frequently revolutionary discoveries made in old and new fields alike. Even history, where once a few courses in college plus a first-class memory sufficed, is no longer an exception. Has not the history of the World War, indeed, already been rewritten several times? With this tremendous increase of possible knowledge some narrowing of each man's domain becomes inevitable. Despite, or thanks to the encyclopaedias, specialization is in order. One must major willy-nilly in some things and not even minor in others. But major in what, select his studies on what principle? In our American universities the answer is found more and more in the student's future profession or avocation. The young man plans to become a lawyer or an engineer, and his courses are arranged accordingly. But what of the great mass who never reach the university, never get beyond the high school, if indeed, even through it? Granting that there are certain common studies indispensable to every one, simple English, for example, and elementary arithmetic, and some acquaintance with American history, still, in our secondary schools, should not the pupil's curriculum be equally governed or shaped by, or perhaps centered around, the work he will probably do when he goes out into the world?

To this an increasing number are answering, if somewhat hesitantly, "Yes." Despite the protests and laments of both classicists and theoretical democrats, vocational courses indeed (the commercial, the domestic science course) are no longer a novelty in our high schools, while industrial and vocational schools have arisen in our larger cities. Unfortunately, however, these vocational schools are still too often regarded as poor relatives of the others—which some of them are—as finishing schools for the stupid, detention camps for the mischievous. Nor have educators as yet fully realized the possibilities of vocational education. It has been too largely a substitute for a training supposedly better; has lacked unity of purpose; has, in practice, meant the elimination of some subjects rather than the regrouping of studies around some new center of interest. We have grown so used to fitting or attempting to fit the pupils into our conventional curriculum that we can not quite make up our minds to reorganize our curriculum to fit the needs of future bricklayers or carpenters.

And of course there are practical difficulties in the way. For one thing—who are to be the future carpenters? At nineteen or twenty the average young man has often a hazy idea of what he wants to be or do. His special capacities, his dominant interests have developed. At fourteen or fifteen, however, this is not so often the case. Indeed, many a boy, then, is less sure of himself and his goal than he was five years earlier, when to be an aviator or perhaps a policeman was his pet ambition. Yet some boys at fifteen do show a definite trend; others, it is reasonably certain, could be easily guided in some definite direction, instead of being left to wander aimlessly along, at last, untrained, to stumble into the wrong job. If only, in dawning adolescence, their personal interest be aroused, the human possibilities and social utility of some occupation shown them, their lives and future labors taken as seriously as their Latin, and carpentry made as attractive as chemistry. "But this is unfair to the boy who, left to himself might eventually become a—Congressman." Is it? He can still run for Congress later on if he wishes to or sell cabbages or vacuum cleaners. While, if one says solemnly—"This is not the task for the educator; education means the training of the mind"—the reply is obvious. Assuredly the mind does not develop in a vacuum. It is the mind of John Smith in a living world. Why not link his mental training with some form of activity that will help him to earn his living?

And this the more since, whatever the vocation—carpentry, house-painting, tool-making—John's thorough preparation for it is no holiday task, but a job for a life-sized teacher. Here, indeed, some college-bred educators fail to sense the facts. They think of the crafts as just hand-crafts and nothing more, of vocational education in such cases as just manual training plus, of course, some arithmetic, English and civics. The truth is, in the words of a high official in a large western factory, "We have no mere hand-workers in our plant. The men in the shops work just as much with their heads as the men in the office." He might have put it even more strongly. To be a first-class mechanic very possibly requires greater intelligence than to be a first-class stenographer; while to master thoroughly the technique of cloth-making or steel construction would tax the brain of many a dentist or lawyer. That some men get by in these trades without overmuch intelligence or knowledge does not invalidate this statement. So, too, some get by in dentistry or at their bar examinations. Did not a Wisconsin school superintendent assert that he knew of a high-grade moron who was a teacher in his own city schools? Granted that many of our craftsmen—the painters and paper-hangers, for instance, are inadequately trained—this but emphasizes the need of a better, fuller industrial or vocational education begun in our secondary or elementary schools under the leadership of men and women who realize that the house-painter, no less than the portrait painter, must mix his paint "with brains."

So much for the technical side where mathematics and physics and chemistry have often their share in or their bearing on a full training for this craft or that. Yet this is not all. Would the average boy take more interest in geometry were its problems worked out less on the blackboard than on the carpenter's bench or in the pasture? Would the laws of physics be more easily remembered if he had to apply them in the shop—perhaps learned them there? But almost equally economics forms naturally a part of his industrial curriculum. It is important for him to know how his craft fits into the industrial life of the world, how his product will be valued and his wages determined. To understand this more fully he needs the aid of history, and to appreciate the significance of his craft more fully he needs the help of literature and art as well.

In other words, a complete vocational education, thorough and well rounded, is by no means a narrow one. The craft, the industry forms a base for it, a core, if you please, or a starting-point. It does not wall it in nor set a limit. "How much may it include?" That depends, no doubt, on the pupil. Enough here that the so-called culture studies have naturally some part in it. Only now they are approached from a new angle, seen in a new light, and because of that fact may often awaken far more interest than they did before. Take history, for example. The story of every trade is woven into the history of the world. Nor less does the history of the world have its influence on the development of every trade. "Why did the masons build castles nine centuries ago? But five centuries later rear chateaux instead? And now erect factory chimneys?"—Go find the full answers to those questions, my young builder, you have grasped not a little of the history of civilization. Or again—"Why does the Lord Chancellor of England sit upon a wool-sack, my youthful farmer or weaver?" Ah, if you are to know your business thoroughly you must learn that it includes not only raising sheep and weaving cloth but also raising kings and weaving empires.

So, too, with literature as it reflects the varied life of man—its poetry, its drama, its fiction have special messages for those of every calling. Indeed, even Latin literature, probably in translations, might have some interest for the embryo craftsman. Ordinarily a boy finds it dull. After straggling along behind Caesar's weary legions and dozing beneath Cicero's eloquence, he has no heart to put to sea with Vergil. But what occurs when there are no "college requirements" to be satisfied? In the opening chapter of "The Real Log Cabin" Chilson Aldrich tells his own experience. He had become completely disgusted with Latin until one rare day he ran across a gentleman named Horace who actually found pleasure in the life of the farm and the fields. Perhaps there are others like Aldrich who would not find Latin literature or even the Latin text so wearisome, if only they were introduced to authors who were not trying, it would seem, to write texts for the grammarians, but to picture the common life of their time made uncommon by their pens. Be this as it may, however, the literature of Europe, of England, of America with her Whitman, offers the future craftsman no meager fare. So much there is in each that recalls the great yesterdays of his chosen art, revives its traditions! So much that may kindle his fresh enthusiasm! So much that can clothe his coming task with beauty and with meaning! Can its master-artists do more than that—stimulate his mind, develop his powers of self-expression, widen his vision of life, help him to sense how the whole universe presses around the workshop and the farm. One sets no limits to their powers, but first of all, wisely selected, they can help him, dramatists and poets and story tellers, to find himself in his work.

Is this aiming too high, expecting too much of a vocational course? No doubt in the schoolroom, as elsewhere, the response will vary, and some boys and girls will get more, and some less. Suffice it to show that, though based on a special trade or group of trades, a vocational educational need not therefore be, should not be either narrow or deadening. It can reach out into the world and up. Science and history and literature can have a part in it; art can lend its inspiration. Without lessening the technical demands, each coming craftsman can be helped to realize that his craft has a culture of its own, and withal a share in the larger life and thought of civilization which he can cultivate if he will.

But helped by whom? Will it take a rare breed of teachers gifted of hand as well as of brain, of brain as well as of hand, and with a spirit that enlightens both? Ay, must we reorganize our Normal Schools to train more of such teachers, have schools such as William Morris might have founded?

If so, let us have them soon.

EDUCATIONAL EVENTS

THE ELECTION OF AMERICAN RHODES SCHOLARS

THE results of the annual election of American Rhodes scholars are announced by Dr. Frank Aydelotte, president of Swarthmore College and American secretary to the Rhodes trustees. Elections were held in thirty-two states of the Union. In order to qualify, the Rhodes scholar must either be a resident of the state or have received at least two years of his college education in one of the colleges in that state.

Rhodes scholars are appointed in the first instance for two years, with the option of remaining for a third year, and with an annual stipend of £400 (about $2,000). Nearly all the scholars-elect hold American university degrees and some have already begun post-graduate work. The choice is based upon intellectual attainments, combined with qualities of character and leadership and interest in outdoor sports.

The present year marks the beginning of a new basis of tenure for the Rhodes scholarships. Rhodes scholars were formerly appointed for three years, but because of the fact that it is now possible for an American graduate to take a degree at Oxford in two years, the Rhodes trustees have authorized appointments for only two years in the first instance, with a possibility of each scholar remaining for a third year, providing his record justifies it, and providing he presents a satisfactory plan of study. Still further changes in the regulation of Rhodes scholarships are contemplated in a bill which has been introduced in the present session of the British Parliament. This bill, if passed, will make it possible to carry out a proposal made some years ago by the American Rhodes scholars and endorsed by the leading educational authorities in the United States, changing the basis of appointments from states to districts.

The Rhodes scholars just elected will begin their work at Oxford in October, 1929. For the thirty-two scholarships open this year there were 398 candidates. Each candidate had previously been selected to represent his college or university in the competition. The list of Rhodes scholars-elect, subject to confirmation by the Rhodes trustees with the institution from which accredited, is as follows:

Arizona—Edwin R. Casady, Jr., Cornell.
Connecticut—George T. Washington, Yale.
Delaware—Richard K. Irons, Worcester Polytechnic.
Florida—Albert A. Murphree, Florida.
Idaho—Farnsworth Jennings, Idaho.
Illinois—Robert Z. Hickman, Illinois.
Indiana—Richmond Lattimore, Dartmouth.
Kentucky—Aubrey M. Cates, Louisville.
Louisiana—Cleanth Brooks, Jr., Tulane.
Maine—Dana Merrill Swan, Bowdoin.
Maryland—Manasses Jacob Grove, Yale.
Massachusetts—Malcolm A. MacIntyre, Yale.
Montana—Matt Pakala, Montana State.
Nevada—Frederick M. Anderson, Nevada.
New Hampshire—Carl Bernhardt Spaeth, Dartmouth.
New Jersey—William Winters McQuilkin, Princeton.
New Mexico—Richard D. Mallery, New York Univ.
New York—George A. Lincoln, U. S. Mil. Acad.
North Carolina—Daniel E. Huggins, Jr., North Carolina.
North Dakota—Frederick L. Hovde, Minnesota.
Ohio—Royal C. Bryant, Western Reserve.
Oklahoma—Savoie Lottinville, Oklahoma.
Pennsylvania—R. Max Goepp, Jr., Lehigh.
Rhode Island—Albert Cornsweet, Brown.
South Carolina—Robert Emmett Houston, Jr., Yale.
South Dakota—John King Fairbank, Harvard.
Tennessee—Robert Earle McGee, Southwestern.
Utah—Paul D. Schettler, Univ. of Utah.
Vermont—Charles F. Malam, Middlebury.
Virginia—Armistead Lloyd Boothe, Virginia.
West Virginia—S. Roger Tyler, Jr., Marshall.
Wyoming—Robert E. Burns, Wyoming.

WORK OF THE BUREAU OF EDUCATION

THE Secretary of the Interior, in his annual report, calls attention to the outline made by the Bureau of Education of what it terms "important movements in the field of education," and its summary of the operations of the bureau. Educational surveys constitute an important function of the Bureau of Education. Two of these are cited.

In March, 1927, the bureau undertook a resurvey of Negro colleges and universities in the United States. The report has been completed and is now in process of publication. The survey shows the remarkable gains made in the development of institutions of higher learning for Negroes in the past ten years, and the need for ever greater development of colleges and universities, that the needs of the race may be fully met.

The work of the survey of the land-grant colleges was begun in July, 1927, when the funds appropriated by Congress became available. Rapid progress has been made. Large numbers of persons are actively participating in this survey as members of local committees and of the field staff. Many of the questionnaires have been prepared and distributed to the colleges for final filling out. The bureau's field staffs to handle four of the questionnaires have been organized and their members have commenced to make visits to the institutions.

The bureau emphasizes the increasing need of research in the field of education on a comprehensive basis such as no other agency aside from the Bureau of Education is in a position to perform. Perhaps this purpose may be served, it holds, by the organization of a number of successive studies national in scope, with definite objectives and limited in time, for which specific appropriations may be asked. It has in mind a series of studies similar to the survey of the land-grant colleges and universities, which is now in progress.

The Bureau of Education has asked for $50,000 to begin a study of secondary education, to be followed in successive years by appropriations of $75,000 and $100,000, respectively. This, it holds, would be a small outlay for a comprehensive study in the field of secondary education, with a view to bringing about some order in this chaotic section of education. The National Education Association and numerous regional associations have passed resolutions that such a study be made.

The Bureau of Indian Affairs has asked the Bureau of Education to make a study of Indian schools and to suggest methods for their improvement. This study has been approved by the Secretary of the Interior, and a preliminary visit made to a number of Indian schools with a view to setting up this investigation. Using the report of the Institute for Government Research as a basis, a very valuable service can now be rendered through the Bureau of Education to the Indian schools.

The state superintendents of public instruction and commissioners of education have decided to hold a two-day conference in Washington in December with the Federal Commissioner of Education. One of the problems which they propose to discuss is the support and financing of schools. In view of the fact that the costs of public schools have more than doubled in the last few years, it seems that such a study would be highly serviceable to the cause of education; measures might be formulated in the interest of economy that would prove most efficacious.

This whole field is relatively unexplored. Every conceivable form of taxation is used in the effort to support schools. No one has attempted to show the most satisfactory ways of raising funds for school purposes. A sound and economic program for expenditures is equally as important as a proper system of revenue. These and other studies, the bureau believes, ought to be made as quickly as funds are available.

THE CASE METHOD OF LEGAL EDUCATION

The case method of legal education, developed at Harvard Law School and subsequently adopted by the leading schools of the country, has been found unsuited to the demands of modern life, according to a statement made by Dean Young B. Smith, of Columbia Law School, in his annual report. It will be abolished at Columbia.

Law has developed so fast during recent years and the field has become so vast and complex that the case method is no longer adequate. The new method which will be worked out gradually will begin with the proposition that law is a form of social control, and from there seek to enunciate the basic principles, the "energizing forces," behind the laws themselves.

The new policy, which Dean Smith warns must be developed through a slow and arduous readjustment, had its beginnings in the 1923 report of Supreme Court Justice Stone, then dean of the Columbia Law School. The matter has been the object of study since then, and at present certain changes in courses which are regarded as the beginning of the actual change to the new policy actually have been put into effect.

In enunciating the new aims, Dean Smith's report says:

> For a number of years after the inauguration of the case method law teachers were so engrossed in preparing case books and perfecting the technique of this pedagogical device that, except for a limited amount of research in legal history, little thought was given to other aspects of legal education.
>
> During this same period the law was expanding rapidly in every direction to meet the exigencies of modern life. In time its content became so enormous and complicated that it became impossible for any one man to master the intricacies of common law doctrine, to say nothing of legislation, except within very limited areas.
>
> In their efforts to keep abreast with the courts, legal scholars tended to become specialists in the legal doctrine which had developed in particular fields, without first acquiring an adequate knowledge of the changes in the social structure which had caused the expansion of the law.
>
> Undue emphasis was placed upon the rules of law developed by the cases, and too little consideration was given to the economic, political and other social problems which had brought the rules into being. As a result there was a tendency to disregard the relationship of one branch of the law to another and to lose sight of the function of law in society.

REPORT OF THE COMPTROLLER OF CORNELL UNIVERSITY

The annual report of the comptroller of Cornell University for the fiscal year ending June 30 shows that the cost of conducting the endowed colleges at Ithaca during the year exceeded the available income by $12,896.70, thereby increasing the accumulated deficit, which was $411,545.63, to $424,442.33. To apply on this deficit the trustees appropriated $98,241.60 from profits received on securities sold during the year, thus reducing the deficit to $326,200.73. Of this deficit approximately $136,000 resulted from the purchase of land bordering on the campus and needed by the university to supplement or protect its existing holdings; $78,000 was for the equipment of new buildings, and the balance of about $112,000 came from ordinary running expenses. In addition there are being carried in a special account the Franklin C. Cornell property, $200,000; the Bool Mill at Forest Home, $9,000; additions to the Women's Residential Halls site, $64,974.18, and land in Fall Creek for future water-power developments, $75,170.20. This brings the total indebtedness of the university up to $675,345.11.

In the Medical College in New York the cash deficit for the year was $51,951.52, which increased the accumulated deficit to $263,444.90. This was reduced by the receipt of $85,000 from the estate of the late Payne Whitney and of $67,531 transferred from the Medical Increment Fund, thus reducing the accumulated deficit to $110,913.90.

The year's work in the Veterinary College showed a deficit of $1,509.54. But there was a surplus a year ago of $17,438.51, which offsets this and leaves a balance of $14,928.97.

Likewise the deficit of $12,671.28 in the College of Agriculture is met by the surplus of $56,949.45, which leaves a balance of $26,298.25.

The College of Home Economics showed a surplus of $4,937.54, which added to the previous surplus swells it to $21,989.82.

The Geneva Experiment Station showed a deficit of $888.66, which is met by a surplus of $2,023.38, making a balance of $1,134.72.

The income-bearing funds were increased during the year by about $500,000 to $19,909,108.38, of which $15,472,931.59 is for the benefit of the University at Ithaca and $4,436,176.79 is for the Medical College in New York. The average return on investments was 5.459 per cent. The market value of the securities held on April 1 exceeded the book value by over $1,100,000. During the year the university realized somewhat over $335,000 of profits from the sale of securities.

The Semi-Centennial Endowment Fund campaign netted subscriptions amounting to $6,652,044.43. From this amount there has been charged off as uncollectible $187,776.26. Of the amount remaining, $6,464,268.17, $2,427,390 is still unpaid.

Gifts received during the year and recorded in the comptroller's office amounted to $4,043,559.05.

Through the Cornellian Council there was received during the year $532,008.25. The total amount paid in through the Cornellian Council since 1913, inclusive, is $2,059,098.81.

The total income was $8,973,318; the total expenses were $7,262,171.99. The total value of the property has increased by $2,913,619.19 and now amounts to $37,783,515.33.

REPORT OF THE PRESIDENT OF THE CARNEGIE FOUNDATION

NEW grants of $2,000,000 and payments on previous grants totaling $4,000,000 were made by the Carnegie Corporation during the fiscal year ended September 30, according to the annual report of the president, Dr. Frederick P. Keppel.

The Carnegie Endowment for International Peace received $150,000 for its program in the United States. The Institute of International Education, used by foreign students studying in the United States and Americans studying abroad, also received a large grant.

One third of the total sum voted was given for the support of educational studies, scientific research and publications, the president's report shows. The California Institute of Technology received $200,000 for research in physics and chemistry conducted by Professor R. A. Millikan. The President's Conference on Unemployment received $75,000 for a study of economic changes by the National Bureau of Economic Research. The Carnegie Foundation for the Advancement of Teaching received the sum of $50,000 for the study of education in Pennsylvania.

Amounts ranging from $5,000 to $50,000 were given for studies in land economics, pyorrhea, economics of medicine, non-college technical education, cooperative education in Africa and traveling fellowships.

Adult education was emphasized, $102,000 going for this purpose. Library schools were given $140,000. Grants totaling $110,000 were made to the American Federation of Arts for administrative development over a five-year period. Art endowment grants of $50,000 each were made to Milwaukee-Downer College, the

University of Rochester, Vassar College and Wesleyan University.

Mr. Keppel's report gives particular attention to the uses made of the income of a fund of $10,000,000 for study in Canada and the British colonies. From this source the corporation embarked on a five-year program in British Africa. Responsible organizations in Africa are to administer funds for the selection and oversight of scientific research, including a major scientific research in what is known in South Africa as the "Poor White" problem; assistance was given to the fine arts departments of Natal Technical College, the University of Witwatersrand and the University of Cape Town; publication of a work on Bushmen cave paintings was provided for, and an exchange of African leaders arranged. Funds were voted for additional support of the Jeanes Schools, which represent the adaptation of the fruits of our American experience with the southern Negroes to the education of the native African. Two librarians of international reputation, Mr. S. A. Pitt, of the Mitchell Library, Glasgow, Scotland, and Milton J. Ferguson, state librarian of California, were sent to Africa to make a special study of library conditions and opportunities. Also, during the year, Dean Emeritus James E. Russell was sent to Australia and New Zealand as well as to South Africa in behalf of the corporation to make a study of educational opportunities.

The report of Mr. Keppel includes statements of progress of large enterprises supported by corporation grants made in previous years, such as the Institute of Economics, Food Research Institute, the American Law Institute and the Graduate Library School of the University of Chicago.

THE COMMITTEE ON STATE HISTORIES OF EDUCATION

President F. C. Ensign, of the National Society of College Teachers of Education, has appointed a committee to examine and evaluate current state histories of education. A first duty of the committee will be to discover whether each and every state in the union has, in available form, a comprehensive, scholarly and up-to-date history of its educational development. In case the committee in its report to the February meeting of the society makes the disclosure that certain states have defective, or otherwise inadequate histories, a second duty will be to devise ways and means for securing the publication, whatever needed, of properly-prepared historical treatises.

Each of the state histories of education at present in circulation will be critically examined by some member of the committee to determine whether it provides a thorough, accurate and readable account. The committee has adopted a uniform set of criteria for evaluating the state histories.

The following professors of education, as members of the committee, assisted by a number of their colleagues in various institutions, will contribute to the report: Dr. Edward H. Reisner, Teachers College, Columbia University; Dr. Thomas Woody, University of Pennsylvania; Dean W. J. Gifford, State Normal College, Harrisonburg, Virginia; Dr. Edgar W. Knight, University of North Carolina; Dr. Frederick Eby, University of Texas; Dr. Harry Good, Ohio State University; Dr. George J. Jackson, University of Michigan; Dr. R. F. Seyboldt, University of Illinois; President Sheldon E. Davis, State Normal College, Dillon, Montana; Dean H. D. Sheldon, University of Oregon; Dr. John C. Almack, Stanford University; Dr. Zora Klain, Rutgers University; Stuart G. Noble, chairman, Tulane University.

TESTIMONIAL TO PRESIDENT ALDERMAN

Alumni of the University of Virginia plan to raise a fund towards the purchase of a gift for Dr. Edwin Anderson Alderman in commemoration of his quarter century of service as the university's first president.

Dr. Alderman assumed the duties of president of the University of Virginia on September 15, 1904, after having served as the administrative head of the University of North Carolina and of Tulane University. He will end his twenty-fifth academic year at the University of Virginia with the close of the final exercises on June 11, 1929.

The board of managers of the Alumni Association of the University voted at its November meeting, several weeks ago, to make a gift to

President Alderman next June and the first notice to the thousands of Virginia alumni was mailed on December 9.

The proposal for this testimonial was first made by McLane Tilton, alumni secretary. Expenses for carrying out the plan for solicitation of alumni have been underwritten by a gift from Gordon M. Buck, of New York City, a former president of the Alumni Association.

The letter being sent to all alumni reads:

The year 1929 marks the completion by Dr. E. A. Alderman of twenty-five years of continuous service as the university's first and only president.

It seems proper that such an event should be recognized by Virginia's alumni in the form of a substantial and fitting testimonial of appreciation of his devoted, distinguished and effective services to our Alma Mater.

While the board is certain that this movement, undertaken by them at the suggestion of numerous alumni, will meet with hearty and generous approval and support, they also feel that such a gift will carry to Dr. Alderman a deeper and broader expression of alumni affection for him rather than a large subscription from a few. The board has, therefore, decided to ask each alumnus to subscribe to the fund. Every dollar received will be applied to the gift as the alumni office is handling the matter and has already received a subscription made for the purpose of defraying all necessary expenses.

The form of the gift will depend upon the contributions received, but you may be assured that it will be one well becoming the occasion as well as of a character acceptable to Dr. Alderman.

EDUCATIONAL NOTES AND NEWS

DR. HERVIN U. ROOP, head of the department of psychology at Wheaton College, has been elected president of Lincoln Memorial University.

THE REVEREND G. MORRIS SMITH was installed as president of Susquehanna University, Selinsgrove, Penna., on November 23. Dr. Smith has served pastorates in Mt. Vernon, N. Y., and Buffalo, N. Y., and at one time was teacher in Blair Academy in New Jersey.

MISS E. ADELAIDE HAHN, of Hunter College, New York City, was elected president of the New York State Phi Beta Kappa Association at the recent meeting held in Buffalo. Other officers elected were Dean Edward Fitch, of Hamilton College, *vice-president;* H. B. Smart, of Cornell University, *treasurer,* and the Reverend Charles D. Broughton, *secretary.*

AFTER thirty-four years of service as a member of the Pennsylvania State College faculty, Dr. Fred Lewis Pattee, an authority on the history of American literature, has severed his connection with the college. He will spend the winter in Florida, writing and lecturing at Rollins College. In appreciation of the service of Dr. Pattee and as a token of their esteem, students on December 9 presented him with a gold watch and chain, suitably engraved. Having served for thirty-one years as superintendent of St. Paul's Methodist Episcopal Sunday-school of State College, Dr. Pattee also received an engrossed parchment from the school expressing its appreciation.

BISHOP FRANCIS J. MCCONNELL, of New York City, is chairman, and Dr. John Dewey, of Columbia University, first vice-chairman, of a committee of seventy organized to prevent propaganda in American schools on behalf of "special interests, groups and causes."

WARREN W. KNOX has been appointed to succeed Clarence E. Baer as New York State supervisor of science.

DR. RUTH WHEELER, professor of physiology and nutrition at Vassar College, has been appointed director of the Summer Institute of Euthenics at Vassar to succeed Professor Annie MacLeod, now dean of the college of home economics at Syracuse University.

IN the school of education of the North Dakota State College, Dr. Jesse A. Tanner takes the place of P. J. Iverson, professor of secondary education, who is on leave of absence. Dr. Tanner will supervise the work of the training school. In the department of physical education, C. C. Finnegan succeeds Ion Cortright as director.

AT the University of Texas, Professor H. J. Ettlinger has been appointed director of intercollegiate athletics for the year beginning December 1, 1928. The appointment is temporary, to meet an emergency. He will continue full work as professor of mathematics.

PAUL E. BARR has been appointed associate professor and acting head of the department of art in the school of education of the University of North Dakota.

ADRIAN O. MORSE, dean of men in the University of New Hampshire, has received a three-month appointment as secretary to Secretary of Agriculture W. M. Jardine. During his absence Dr. George N. Bauer, officer in charge of freshmen and a member of the faculty of the college of liberal arts, will serve as acting dean.

DR. W. L. CRUM, professor of statistics in the graduate school of business of Stanford University, has been elected editor of the *Review of Economic Statistics*, published by the Harvard Economic Society.

DR. H. H. TURNER, Savilian professor of astronomy at the University of Oxford, accompanied by Mrs. Turner, is coming to the United States in order to represent the British Association at the New York meeting of the American Association for the Advancement of Science. Dr. Turner will give a lecture on "The Scientific Retrospect."

PROFESSOR J. W. GARNER, of the University of Illinois, and Professor E. M. Patterson, of the University of Pennsylvania, have joined the faculty of the Institut Universitaire des Hautes Etudes Internationales at Geneva. Professor Garner is at the university at present, lecturing on American foreign policy and conducting a seminar class on "Nationality." Professor Patterson will take up his work at the beginning of the spring term. Both will remain for the summer session of 1929.

PROFESSOR GEORGE D. STRAYER and Professor N. L. Engelhardt, of Teachers College, Columbia University, assisted by several graduate students, have recently made reports of school surveys in Rye, N. Y., Greenville and Edgemont in Westchester County, N. Y., and Paducah, Ky.

PROFESSOR ALZADA COMSTOCK, of Mount Holyoke College, has been granted a semester's leave for the first half of 1928–29 for a study of land reform laws, which she will begin in Estonia.

IT is reported that Mrs. Yayoi Yoshioka, principal of the Woman's Medical College, Tokyo, who visited the United States after the close of the Pacific Women's Conference in Hawaii in August, has returned to Tokyo.

GEORGE MCANENY, president of the Municipal Art Society, Tony Sarg and Richard F. Bach, of the Metropolitan Museum, were the principal speakers at the eighteenth annual meeting of the School Art League, which was held in the Hotel Plaza on December 8. Dr. J. Herbert Low, principal of Erasmus Hall High School, acted as chairman. The alumni meeting followed a luncheon for three hundred guests in the grand ballroom of the Plaza.

THE REVEREND S. PARKES CADMAN will be the Selden Memorial Foundation speaker at the Connecticut College for Women, New London, next April.

DR. TRUMAN LEE KELLEY, professor of education and psychology at Stanford University, gave a course of public lectures, under the auspices of the graduate school and the department of psychology of the Ohio State University, beginning on December 3. The titles of the lectures were: "The Inter-relationship between Method of Research and Field of Investigation," "The Rôle of Judgment in 'Objective Measurement,'" "In What Units shall we Measure Intelligence and Achievement?", "Mental Structure and its Bearing upon Problems of Inheritance and Education," "The Mental Traits of Men of Science."

A MEMORIAL, probably in the form of an endowment for scholarships, will be established with funds from the estate of the late James A. O'Donnell, who, at the time of his death last summer, was principal of the Isaac Remesne Junior High School, New York City.

PRESIDENT ADA L. COMSTOCK, of Radcliffe College, on learning of the death of Alice M. Longfellow, daughter of the poet, Henry Wadsworth Longfellow, said: "Miss Longfellow was not only a leader in the small group of men and women who founded Radcliffe College; she was also one of those who have brought it to maturity. For fifty years Radcliffe has had the benefit of her judgment, her interest and her generous sympathy. To lose her is a staggering blow; but the realization of her faith and her devotion will stay with us as a precious heritage."

DR. BASHFORD DEAN, honorary professor of zoology at Columbia University and of fine arts at New York University, honorary curator of fishes in the American Museum of Natural History, honorary curator of arms and armor in the Metropolitan Museum of Art and trustee of the museum, died suddenly in the Battle Creek Sanitarium on December 6, at the age of sixty-one years.

PROFESSOR GUSTAV GRUENER, of Yale University, a distinguished German scholar and one of the oldest members of the Yale faculty, died on December 5, at the age of sixty-five years.

PROFESSOR ROBERT MCLEAN CUMNOCK, founder of the school of speech at Northwestern University, died on November 28. In addition to teaching at Northwestern, Dr. Cumnock was also a professor at Garrett Biblical Institute, gave private lessons, and found time to give public readings two or three times a week.

CHARLES FRANCIS WHEELOCK, from 1910 to 1923 assistant commissioner of secondary education of New York State, died on November 4, in his eightieth year.

DR. ELBERT W. GRIFFITH, superintendent of schools in Glens Falls, New York, for twenty-seven years, has died from injuries received when he was struck by an automobile.

WILLIAM GRANT EGBERT, founder and for many years president of the Ithaca, New York, Conservatory of Music, has died at the age of fifty-nine years.

DR. ALEXANDER MAXIMOW, professor of anatomy in the University of Chicago, prior to the Russian revolution professor in St. Petersburg, died suddenly on December 3, at the age of fifty-four years.

THE Chicago board of education failed to meet its bi-weekly pay roll of $3,500,000 for 13,000 teachers on December 4. Neither was there any issuance of promissory notes or script or any assurance of when the salaries would be paid. As reported here last week, school authorities had expected to raise money for the pay roll by the sale of tax anticipation warrants. Leading bankers, however, declared that the collection of taxes was so uncertain this year they did not care to buy the tax anticipation warrants despite the high interest these short-time securities pay. When the bankers declined the securities nobody else cared to purchase them.

THE New Education Fellowship will hold an international conference at Elsinore, near Copenhagen, from August 8 to 21, 1929. The subject of discussion will be "The New Psychology and the Curriculum." The Castle of Kronborg, overlooking the sea (the scene of Shakespeare's "Hamlet") will be the headquarters of the conference, the speakers at which will include the following: Professor Cizek, of Vienna; Dr. W. Boyd, lecturer in education, University of Glasgow; Dr. Decroly, of Brussels; Dr. Adolphe Ferrière, of Geneva; Dr. P. Dengler, of Vienna; Dr. C. W. Kimmins, Dr. Percy Nunn, Miss Helen Parkhurst, Professor J. Piaget, Dr. O. Pfister, Dr. Harold Rugg, Mrs. Beatrice Ensor, Dr. Elizabeth Rotten, Rabindranath Tagore. Details can be had from the secretary, Miss D. Matthews, 11 Tavistock-square, London, W. C.

A CONFERENCE of rural school supervisors of the southern states will be held in the Hotel Roosevelt, New Orleans, on December 17 and 18. Participants will come from fourteen states: Alabama, Arkansas, Florida, Georgia, Kentucky, Louisiana, Mississippi, North Carolina, Oklahoma, South Carolina, Tennessee, Texas, Virginia and West Virginia. They will include state and assistant state supervisors of rural schools and other members of state departments of education, county supervisors, county superintendents, professors of education in teacher-training institutions, officers of state education associations and the president of the National Congress of Parents and Teachers.

THE first building of the Yeshiva College in New York City was opened and dedicated on December 9. The ceremonies, at which Mayor

Walker was one of the speakers, were attended by 20,000 persons. The new building, erected at a cost of $2,500,000, will be ready for occupancy in January and will house the college until its building program is completed. The buildings will eventually occupy three blocks. Dr. Harry Fischel is acting president of the college, which is the outgrowth of a merger between the Rabbi Isaac Elchanan Theological Seminary and the Yeshiva College. In addition to Mayor Walker, the speakers included Judge Otto A. Rosalsky, Dr. Bernard Revel, president of the faculty; Dr. Frederick B. Robinson, president of the College of the City of New York; Samuel Levy, chairman of the college campaign committee which raised funds for the building, and Rabbi Simon Shkop, dean of the Talmudical Academy of Grodno.

CYRUS H. K. CURTIS has made a gift of ground valued at $250,000 to the Drexel Institute of Philadelphia.

THE University of Buffalo has received a gift of $100,000 for general endowment from Mr. and Mrs. Walter P. Cooke. The gift was made public simultaneously with the announcement of the beginning of a campaign by the university for a $5,000,000 fund, $1,500,000 to be used for buildings and $3,500,000 for endowment.

CORNELL COLLEGE, Mt. Vernon, Iowa, has raised $1,016,000 in its campaign for $1,100,000.

Two anonymous alumni have contributed $25,000 to Lafayette College. One gift is for the endowment of the college infirmary, the other is the first contribution to the project for new dormitories. In addition to these gifts there have been received in the last two wteks $40,000 from three givers for a new college heating plant.

AN appropriation by the Carnegie Corporation of New York of $200,000 to be applied toward the construction of an office building to cost $1,000,000, for the use of the Pan-American Union, was announced on December 5, at the meeting of the governing board of the union, composed of the diplomatic representatives of the Latin-American republics at Washington and the Secretary of State. The new structure will be situated on a triangular plot of ground in the rear of the present Pan-American Union building.

THE Imperial University Library in Tokyo built by a gift of four million yen from Mr. John D. Rockefeller, Jr., has been formally dedicated, the American and British ambassadors and the minister of education participating. The building replaces that destroyed in the 1923 earthquake. It contains 600,000 volumes, largely gifts from America and Great Britain.

THE University of Cambridge has been offered £50,000 by the British Exchequer and a further £50,000 from the Empire Marketing Board toward the sum required to enable the university to accept the conditional grant of £700,000 from the Rockefeller Foundation, to provide new facilities for the study of agriculture, biology and physics, and to build a new university library.

DEAN PAUL CLOKE, of the College of Technology of the University of Maine, announces that honors groups are to be started in the departments of civil engineering and electrical engineering. Only exceptional students, selected on the basis of scholarship and promise of achievement, will be admitted to the groups. The establishment of honors groups was suggested about a year ago by Professor Embert H. Sprague, of the department of civil engineering, and follows a conference recently held at Swarthmore College by President Harold S. Boardman and Dean Paul Cloke with President Frank Aydelotte. It is expected that honors groups will be organized in other departments of the university.

IT is reported from Washington that the Civil Service Commission is perfecting an arrangement for personal contact with colleges and universities to meet the competition of private industry for the services of new graduates from technical and scientific courses. Many of the larger private employers send their agents to educational institutions each year to recruit new workers from the graduating classes. Under the plan of the Civil Service Commission such recruiting for the government will be undertaken by employees of the technical and scientific bureaus who find it necessary to visit the educational institutions from time to time for conference and research. The federal civil service employs nearly 3,500 engineers of various kinds, more than 1,000 chemists and large numbers of other technical and scientific workers. The junior technical and professional workers enter the government service at $2,000 a year. The highest salary paid is $9,000.

SPECIAL CORRESPONDENCE

THE NEW TURKISH ALPHABET

ONE of the most daring and far-reaching reforms in recent educational history was written into the law books of Turkey when the Grand National Assembly, as one of its first acts after reassembling, gave formal approval to the adoption of the "New Turkish Alphabet." This is no less than the adoption of a phonetic system of writing, with letters of Latin origin, for the Turkish language, which for centuries has been written in the flowing Arabic letters. Omitting three of the English letters, "q," "w" and "x," and adding a few diacritical marks, familiar to Europeans, such as the cedilla, which is added to both "c" and "s," the new alphabet is able phonetically to express all the sounds in the attractive Turkish language. Indeed, it is a much more adequate system than the now discarded Arabic, for Turkish contains several sounds not used in Arabic, so that one Arabic letter was called on to express two or more Turkish sounds.

The new reform has its foundations in the freer spirit of the early twentieth century when savants discussed the possibility of adopting Latin characters, just as similar proposals have from time to time been put forward for the writing of Japanese and other oriental languages in Latin letters. With the coming of the Nationalist movement, with its frank adoption of many Western ideas and ideals, the agitation was renewed, and at length a government commission was appointed to study the matter. But this commission might have come to naught as so many commissions east and west have often done, had it not been for the energy and the enthusiasm of that remarkable leader of modern Turkey, Mustafa Kemal Pasha, the president, known generally as "the Ghazi," the victorious one. He threw the weight of his tremendous personal and official prestige in favor of the reform, with the result that months before the National Assembly could meet and pass the law, it was officially approved and plans made for its early introduction. In June the western form of the numerals, which, strangely enough, were always written left to right as in the West, came into force. Next officials began generally to write their signatures in the new letters. Busy committees drew up rules and regulations, busy presses poured out text-books, teachers in all the government schools were advised to learn the new system and had to pass examinations before they could resume their work, and throughout the country the date for opening schools was delayed to allow all to be ready. With the fall term of 1928, all education was to be in the new characters. In the summer papers began to appear with some parts printed in the new form, though the bulk of the material continued to appear in the Arabic.

By the new law the new forms are fully approved and correspondence written thus is to be given full credence. After December 1, all newspapers, magazines, etc., are to be printed only in the new letters, as are the titles of cinemas, handbills, etc. By January all the government departments are to do writing in the new alphabet, save only the courts and the military, which are allowed till June 1, 1929, to complete the change.

The educational possibilities of this reform are most important. It is estimated that the time required for children to learn to read and write will be greatly reduced. But more important than this is the determination of the government, by means of popular courses throughout the entire country, arranged at the slack times in each district, to teach every one to read and write. The president and other leaders are urging the learning, and on those who know it, the teaching, of the new alphabet as a national duty.

Another important by-product of the present change is the help it is giving toward the simplification of the Turkish language. Owing to the influence of Arabic and Persian culture, many Arabic and Persian words have been taken into Turkish, and even where equivalent Turkish words were available, the Arabic and Persian forms were regarded as more elegant, and were used by the educated and cultured classes to such an extent that persons perfectly familiar with ordinary conversational Turkish found themselves lost in reading official communications or listening to formal addresses. The new government is strengthening the movement for a simplification along two lines: one the elimination wherever possible of the foreign words in favor of the simpler Turkish words, and where this is inconvenient, the Turkification of the foreign forms, so that their declension and conjugation will follow Turkish rather than the less familiar foreign forms.

The reform has already attained a surprising success. Everybody who knew how to read and write in Arabic characters has set himself to learn the new forms, while many illiterates have been encouraged to learn to read and write. With the early appearance of newspapers, books and correspondence generally in the new letters, a great impetus will be given, to the extent of making its use compulsory.

CASS ARTHUR REED
INTERNATIONAL COLLEGE,
SMYRNA, TURKEY, Nov. 10, 1928

DISCUSSION

THE RELATIONSHIP BETWEEN STUDENTS' MARKS AND STUDENT ATTITUDE TOWARD INSTRUCTORS.

Do college marks form any sort of index to the attitudes of the recipients of these marks toward the instructor? Do students tend to like an instructor from whom they receive good marks and to dislike the one from whom they receive poor marks? Are there any measurable individual differences among instructors in this regard, *i.e.,* do some instructors tend to be liked or disliked in relation to the kind of marks they give, while others do not?

These questions, apart from mere curiosity which most instructors would have with reference to answers to them, have, of course, definitely practical bearings upon the student-instructor relationship and therefore upon the classroom teaching situation and its results. Should it be true that the average student tends to have his attitudes toward instructors influenced by the marks he receives, this would constitute an important psychological fact to be kept in mind by the instructor and possibly also by the student.

Answers to these questions of the opinion variety are easily available. Without any quantitative data to submit in support of this observation, it is my judgment that most instructors believe that students do tend to regard teachers as either better or worse teachers, depending upon the marks assigned to the students, other things being at all equal. The issue is, however, important enough to warrant a more careful and analytical approach to the problem, and it was therefore decided to investigate it by means of an instrument[1] available for the purpose. For the purpose of the present study it will be sufficient to state that the student rates the instructor—anonymously—by means of a graphic rating scale on the following ten traits:

(1) Interest in Subject.
(2) Sympathetic Attitude toward Students.
(3) Fairness in Grading.
(4) Liberal and Progressive Attitude.
(5) Presentation of Subject-Matter.
(6) Sense of Proportion and Humor.
(7) Self-reliance and Confidence.
(8) Personal Peculiarities.
(9) Personal Appearance.
(10) Stimulating Intellectual Curiosity.

Ratings of eleven instructors—seven Purdue University seniors who had just completed their practice teaching in local high schools and four college instructors—were obtained from 409 students in seventeen different classes. Seven

[1] The Purdue Rating Scale for Instructors. The Lafayette Printing Company, Lafayette, Ind. For a description and experimental data concerning the scale see G. C. Brandenburg and H. H. Remmers, "A Rating Scale for Instructors," *Educ. Admin. and Superv.*, September, 1927, and H. H. Remmers and G. C. Brandenburg, "Experimental Data on the Purdue Rating Scale for Instructors," *ibid.*, November, 1927.

of these classes were composed of high-school pupils and ten were students at Purdue University. Thus 409 judgments were obtained on each trait, making a total of 4,090 judgments.

In order to make possible a study of the relationship between students' marks and their ratings of instructors, the students who were above the average of the class relative to marks were asked to mark a cross on their papers, their names being read off by the instructor immediately after the ratings were completed. This procedure retained the anonymity of the ratings and avoided invalidation of the ratings which might have resulted from any foreknowledge of the purpose of the ratings. So far as the students were aware, they were simply rating the instructor under ordinary conditions.

The results, when tabulated and statistically treated, provide answers to the questions propounded at the beginning of this paper. It will be sufficient here, without going into the technical details of the statistical treatment, to give the interpretations made of the results.

It appears, first, that there is no noticeable tendency for students to vary their ratings of an instructor with the kind of marks which they receive from the instructor. The average correlation between ratings and marks for all traits is .070—practically zero. The rather prevalent notion that students tend to like the instructors from whom they receive high marks and to dislike those from whom they receive low marks is not substantiated in so far as the average ratings on the Purdue Rating Scale for Instructors give a measure of such likes and dislikes for these students and instructors, who are typical students and instructors of the kind described.

There do appear to be, secondly, tendencies toward individual differences among instructors. While for the average instructor the correlation between marks and students' ratings is practically negligible as determined from 187 correlations (one for each of the ten traits for seventeen different classes and one for each averaged rating) some instructors show a positive correlation for all or most of the ten traits while *others yielded consistently negative correlations.* These latter apparently have the happy faculty of "flunking them and making them like it." The highest positive correlation for any single trait was +.890; the highest negative correlation, −.860. When all the traits were averaged for each instructor, the highest positive correlation for a given instructor was +.317, the highest negative correlation, −.142.

Thirdly, there is no appreciable tendency for students to vary their ratings for any single trait for *all* instructors. The extreme variations of average correlations here are represented by "Presentation of Subject-Matter" (−.066) and "Liberal and Progressive Attitude" (+.144). It has been shown elsewhere[2] that there is very little tendency for students to take a "generalized" attitude toward their instructors. They do discriminate among the various traits for a given instructor, as shown by the relative absence of intercorrelation among the ten traits of the Purdue Rating Scale for Instructors. These facts taken together would seem to indicate that in the students' judgment each individual trait adds something to the total picture of the instructor and no one particular trait bears any more significant relationship to scholastic performance than any other. It is, of course, quite possible and certainly consonant with "common sense" that an instructor may be so outstanding in some desirable traits that deficiencies in others are adequately compensated for. The main point, however, is that on the average there is no appreciable relation between marks and ratings.

H. H. REMMERS

PURDUE UNIVERSITY

DO CHILDREN APPRECIATE EYE STRAIN?

IT is a well-nigh universal recommendation that children should read at fourteen inches or the metrical equivalent of thirty-five centimeters, as it appears in European books. The school law of Massachusetts directs the teacher to send "notice card" when a child shows symptoms of defective eyes, including the holding of his book at less than twelve inches. For decades writers have gone on putting this recommendation into their books, apparently thinking that most chil-

[2] J. M. Stalnaker and H. H. Remmers, "Can Students Discriminate Traits Associated with Success in Teaching?" to be published in an early number of the *Journal of Applied Psychology.*

dren read at fourteen inches or can by suggestion be brought to read at that distance.

In actual practice children read at much less than fourteen inches. I have found that when children start in school they hold their books at the same distance as they hold other objects for close examination. This distance is short, obviously because the child is small. As he grows he holds objects, including his book, farther away until at adolescence he reaches mature size, and his reading distance remains stationary.

When a six-year-old child reads at his normal distance of seven or eight inches he is using more of his accommodation than a sixteen-year-old child uses when he reads at his normal distance of approximately fourteen inches, because the six-year-old child has very little more accommodation than the sixteen-year-old child. I have already offered evidence on this point in SCHOOL AND SOCIETY of April 7, 1928, page 428, and consider it one argument that children are not very sensitive to tensions of accommodation and convergence.

A second argument involves the question of whether hyperopic children read at the same distance as normal children. From what I can gather from the literature, it is a rather common belief that hyperopic children make some allowance for their hyperopia by holding their books farther than normal from their eyes. This view can be questioned on the ground that the normal reading distance of children has apparently not previously been known. The average reading distance of children varies so definitely with age, or some factor closely correlated with age, such as physical growth, that a table such as the following would be needed before it could be said that hyperopic children make any allowance in their reading distance for their hyperopia. The following table is typical and shows how reading distance increases with age. It represents three hundred cases distributed quite evenly over the different ages. These children were measured away from school, each child by himself. Under such circumstances children seem to hold their books a trifle nearer than in the day's work at school. Several measurements were taken of each child.

I have had the opportunity of measuring the reading distance of a few children of different

Years	Inches
6	6.8
7	7.5
8	8.5
9	8.8
10	9.6
11	10.2
12	11.0
13	11.6

degrees of hyperopia, and though the cases are too few for generalization, they show no tendency to hold the book farther than the average for their respective ages. An observation made by an English doctor while conducting a school examination has a possible bearing on this point. In his report in *Lancet*,[1] he says:

It was noticed that three children, about eight years of age, were sitting at a desk. . . . These children were stooping over their books writing, their eyes two and one half inches or so from the books. One of these children I found to be suffering from a high degree of myopia; the other two children were probably unconsciously copying the example of the elder myopic child.

If children would thus use all their accommodation apparently in imitating another child, it seems not improbable that hyperopic children would use most of their accommodation, if necessary, to imitate the postures of their classmates.

From my study of reading distance, I have come to the conclusion that the reading distance of children is determined more by imitation than by any other factor. Another factor of lesser influence seems to be the amount of mental effort the child is putting forth. If it should be found that hyperopic children read at the same average distance as children with normal refraction, it would be more evidence that imitation or physical growth determines reading distance. At any rate, the old standard of fourteen inches is fictitious when applied to children, and in its stead might as well be substituted the fact that children have normal age standards. As to whether children should use a greater distance and thereby use less accommodation is another matter.

E. B. NOTSON

SMITHTON, MO.

[1] September 19, 1908, p. 903.

QUOTATIONS

THE RHODES FELLOWSHIPS

OFTEN throughout the year the people of the United States are reminded of the Rhodes fellowships at Oxford by events in the news. At this season particularly, when Dr. Aydelotte, American secretary to the Rhodes trustees, announces the names of American youths who are going to Oxford under the plan, the subject holds much interest. Almost as many candidates as last year competed in the trials, and now thirty-two fellows from as many states are to continue the contact which Cecil Rhodes hoped would produce an English-speaking imperial leader of unprecedented equipment and training.

Rhodes was an enthusiast who believed that Great Britain, the United States and the British colonies and possessions would eventually make common cause, and it was unquestionably his belief that the fellowship idea would help to evolve leaders for his dream. He was inclined, late in his life, to admit the Teutons—the Latins never—as worthy partners in the sodality of nations—a fraternal impulse which the World War temporarily set aside. Too practical to be certain of, and yet visionary enough to expect, the development at Oxford of a super-Amero-Anglian, the Rhodes exchange plan has been in force for over twenty years without the appearance of any prodigy of statecraft. Because of his continued absence, there has occasionally arisen some criticism of the Rhodes "scholar" system. In our own country it has now and then been remarked that no Rhodes man has turned up very often in the light of dazzling fame or with the credit of distinguished achievement. In England the comment has been heard that the students, who in 1904 were too often "moral" leaders in such movements as anti-rum and anti-cigarette clubs, are now too consistently recruited from the ranks of athletes who have harmed Oxford athletics by exhibiting skill which keeps the English undergraduates from trying for track team or crew. In more remote circles in both countries it has occasionally been said that the Rhodesians at Oxford from America were inclined to "colonize" themselves and did not move enough among the English student groups.

The answer to the charge that Rhodes men remain as a group obscure in American life seems conclusive; the oldest of them are barely 40 and just entering their zone of high achievement, while those who have made important progress have turned to the cloistered occupations of scholarship, economics, government service and the law. Their percentage of emergence in the trade which familiarizes names only a little less easily than public life—creative fiction—is high, with Christopher Morley and Elmer Davis springing quickly to mind. The accusation that the students too often are athletes need hardly be answered. In fact the most ponderable criticism of the workings of the plan is questioning the requirement that the students be chosen by states, as if they were senators, with New York, for example, being entitled to no more places than Arizona. Now parliament is being asked to change the selective arrangement and divide this country into districts. That may improve the quality of the educational exiles. But even as things stand they are making their mark in this country, and their turn toward public life is not yet overdue. —*New York Times.*

THE EDUCATIONAL DAWN IN THE EAST

LET those who think they live in the most progressive nations in the West stop for a moment and pay respects to reawakening nations in the East. It is a fact that the United States gives more time and money to schooling than any other country. One third of its entire population is giving full time to the business of education. England continues to be such a seat of learning that scholars from every point of the earth make pilgrimages thereto in increasing number. But there is honor in the East. China, with something like 90 per cent. of its 365,000,000 people illiterate, has set out to teach a simplified Chinese language to every one, young and old, rich and poor, and in an exceedingly short space of time. China's greatest revolution is her educational revolution.

India with her noble cultures undimmed through thousands of years moves on an extensive scale to adapt these cultures to modern requirements. Turkey boldly sets aside her written language, centuries old, and adopts overnight the plain A B C—throughout the whole gamut of her social and economic life. Japan, which until a few decades ago took note of little beyond her own borders, has not only undertaken to educate herself with a zeal unexcelled by any other land, but has applied wholesale, yet intelligently, a new educational method which the United States has little more than begun to put into practice.

China's political revolutions are only instrumental or incidental to the remarkable educational movement now spreading rapidly over the country. For the present it is almost altogether a matter of language. Countless dialects which have caused the Chinese to be foreigners within their own land, if they but went so far as fifty miles from their own home community, are being systematically displaced by that dialect which is already spoken by the greatest number.

One national tongue is the goal. Instead of allowing a written language of thousands of cumbersome characters to persist, a courageous reduction has been accomplished. And in order that Chinese anywhere in China proper may write to one another, and be understood, a dictionary of 1,000 words has been published. Every man, woman and child is asked to learn this vocabulary. Everybody is at it. Regular schools, special schools, lecturers, stereopticon lessons, all possible means are used. Every one who writes for the press, the magazines or books is requested to keep within the 1,000-word vocabulary. The greatest business of all, according to Dr. William Hung, visiting professor at Harvard University, is to find the kind of ideas to put into all this printed material that will help the Chinese people to begin to think along those lines which will propel them toward civic and spiritual growth, as individuals and as a nation.—*The Christian Science Monitor.*

BOOKS AND LITERATURE

School and Society in Chicago, by George S. Counts, Professor of Education in Teachers College of Columbia University. Harcourt, Brace & Company. 1928. 367 pp.

From the standpoint of the popular appeal of its subject-matter or its charm of style, a school survey or the conventional book on education affords little ground for a place among such best sellers as lively stories of philosophy or microbe hunters. It is true that the author of a recent work on education advanced the claim that his book differed from all other educational books in that it was interesting. The present reader would reserve this place for "School and Society in Chicago."

The battle of the history books under the standard of 100 per cent. Americanism did not have the international significance attached to it by many of the subjects of King George, but it has great significance for all who are interested in the integrity of American schools. It is the purpose of the book to penetrate the "smoke screen" so artfully raised by the belligerent Mayor Thompson and to reveal the conflicting groups and interests that were engaged in a real battle for the control of the schools of Chicago.

The first chapter, "The Triumph of the Politicians," opens with the suspension of Superintendent McAndrew, and describes the progress of the mock trial. King George was not the real issue. Educational policies are seldom considered solely on their merits. The Chicago spectacle is studied from the point of view of a survey of the social medium in which the schools of our great cities must function.

In "The Growth of a City" is pictured the aggregation of groups of nationalities, religious and other conflicting interests, with the schools, offering an irresistible temptation to all types of profiteers and patrioteers. It is proposed to discuss, first, the conflict of interests within the school organization, and second, the outside forces which condition school administration.

Neither the earlier school laws nor the later provisions of 1917 succeeded in divorcing the schools from politics or in defining the limits of authority. "Responsibility is shared by the state legislature, the mayor, the city council, the board of education, the superintendent of schools, the business manager, the attorney and the teaching staff. So the law makes fairly certain that clash of authority which perpetually attends the administration of public education in Chicago." Between the board and the superintendent and teachers there has been constant strife and suspicion. The relations between the superintendent and teachers are largely determined by teachers' organizations and the attitude of the superintendent towards them. The Teachers' Federation, under the leadership of Miss Margaret Haley, had successfully appealed to the legislature on pensions, salaries and tenure of office, and had made itself a factor in school policy. This and other teachers' organizations became antagonistic to Superintendent McAndrew when their attempts to participate in the formulation of the new program were rejected, and this antagonism became pronounced when the Teachers' Council was abolished. The council had been fostered and utilized by Mrs. Ella Flagg Young and other superintendents, and had been given legal status by the Board of Education. It is no light matter for a superintendent to ignore the influence of his predecessors and the attitude of his teachers. The teachers supported Mayor Thompson on account of their own grievances, not on account of the tyranny of King George.

In addition to the internal conflicts the educational system "is perpetually pushed and pulled and molded by a vast array of external forces." Of these, the most powerful are selected for description as typical of the interests of finance, labor, women, churches, the press and politics.

The Association of Commerce antagonized labor through its advocacy of the Cooley bill, which aimed at establishing a separate system of vocational schools. It has sponsored in the schools a plan of vocational guidance, safety education, "sound" civics, efficiency in the "three R's," industrial art and civic-industrial clubs in high schools. It has consistently cooperated with other "best elements" to influence educational policies and programs. Superintendent McAndrew's close relation with the Association of Commerce and his request for them to make an "appraisal of schools" led to strong opposition from other quarters.

The Federation of Labor opposed the Cooley bill as an attempt to bring in a caste system of education. It joined issue with Superintendent McAndrew on the junior high school, the platoon system and the intelligence test. It regarded the superintendent as the tool of the vested interests.

The educational program of the women's clubs is extensive, and their accomplishments enviable. Their projects include kindergartens, compulsory education, vacation schools, social centers, penny lunches and the merit system. Their attitude toward the policies of Superintendent McAndrew was generally favorable.

As to the churches—"One comes away from a study of the influence of the religious factor in the conduct of the public schools of Chicago with a certain feeling of despair," and yet, "That any religious group in Chicago has far-reaching designs on the educational system of that city is highly improbable."

The influence of politics in the Chicago school system has been notorious. The power of city hall was challenged by Superintendent McAndrew upon his arrival in Chicago. By appointments and removals, frequently illegal, successive mayors had directly dictated the policy of the Board of Education. During the two earlier terms of Mayor Thompson there is a picture of two contending boards, of a superintendent illegally locked out of his office, of board members serving jail sentences, of an orgy of graft connected with school sites and supplies. The scandal aroused general indignation and resulted in the election of Mayor Dever. But the public has a short memory. The schools that had been rescued from corruption were now to be rescued from King George. Labor and teachers were already in opposition to the superintendent, and various other groups were about to be won over by lurid appeals to racial and national prejudices.

The concluding chapter, "The Riddle of Control," discusses the conflicting interests involved and various proposals for solution. The separation of the schools from city hall by the election of board members at large, the enlarging of the power of the superintendent, might to some extent simplify the problem, but would not eliminate the conflicting play of social forces. Politics, in the broader sense, can not be kept out of the schools. "Therefore, rather than seek refuge in the cautious course of removing the school from politics, we should move forward under the assumption that the real business of politics is to provide the channels through which the living energies of society may flow into new forms and patterns." Boards of education may be more truly representative by the direct recognition of various groups. Some form of organization of the entire body of teachers is necessary for the due evolution of policies and programs and professional responsibility.

The value of this survey of school and society in Chicago lies not in offering a program, but in demonstrating the fact that in the formulation of school policy more attention must be paid to the social influences by which it may be aided or wrecked. In addition to a survey of plant and equipment, of organization and efficiency, there will be surveys of how the schools have functioned in the community and of the attitudes of the teaching staff and the various social groups.

JOHN F. REIGART

YONKERS, NEW YORK

EDUCATIONAL RESEARCH AND STATISTICS

A PROJECT IN STUDENT PERSONNEL SERVICE AT THE COLLEGE LEVEL

THE purpose of this paper is to present the results of a project in student personnel service in a small college. In brief, the theory underlying the project is this: *Each student should achieve at the level of his ability.* In practice this theory turns the attention of the administrator to the *student as achieving,* or failing to achieve, rather than to the *grades which are achieved.* It gives the grades, on any unit scale, meaning in relationship to the individual student as well as in relationship to a definite standard of scholarship. Grades, having this dual reference, furnish a basis for expert advisement.

It is proposed as a just and defensible thesis that every student who enters college should be there with a serious purpose; that he may be expected to achieve up to the level of his ability; that to expect more is to require the impossible of the student, and to permit less is to brand the administration as myopic and inefficient.

Believing in this thesis, and with the cooperation of students and faculty at Graceland College, the writer has reduced it from hypothesis to practice. The project was possible only with the heartiest support of the entire institution, of which the writer was serving his fourth year as dean of student personnel. Graceland College is a junior college, located at Lamoni, Iowa. Its enrolment is about two hundred and fifty students per year. The same project undertaken in a large college or university would meet the complexities of administration incident to the larger institution.[1]

In the fall of 1927, the faculty of the college was called together two days in advance of freshman registration for committee meetings and round table discussions. In all, four discussion periods were held. The topics discussed were: (1) The responsibility of the college to the students and their homes; (2) the personnel bureau and its services; (3) the aims, tasks, personality and technique of the teacher; (4) objective testing and grade computation.

As an outgrowth of these pre-registration meetings, the faculty took as its slogan "Help each student achieve at the level of his ability." In order to remove this slogan from the realm of sentimental well-wishing and blind strivings the two variables of the slogan were defined. The "level of ability" of each student was determined by his T-Score upon a composite raw score of seven tests given to the freshmen during the early weeks of the school year. The tests used were:

1. Iowa Placement Examination: Mathematics Aptitude, Series M. A. 1 Revised, A.
2. Iowa Placement Examination: Mathematics Training, Series M. T. 1 Revised, A.
3. Iowa Placement Examination: English Aptitude, Series E. A. 1 Revised, A.
4. Iowa Placement Examination: English Training, Series E. T. 1 Revised, A.
5. Iowa Comprehension Test, Series D-1.

[1] The writer is indebted to Dean C. E. Seashore and Professor George D. Stoddard, of the State University of Iowa, both of whom had an active interest in the project.

6. Iowa High School Content Examination.
7. American Council of Education Psychological Examination, 1927 edition.

These seven tests contained a total of 841 items, requiring five hours and eighteen minutes of working time. They are diagnostic of the basic abilities which contribute to college success. They test the student's aptitude and previous training in two of the fundamental courses in college—English and mathematics. They test a fundamental tool subject of the student—his ability to read. They test the educational foundation for college work—knowledge of high-school subjects. Finally, they test the prime requisite for scholastic success—mental ability. One hundred twelve freshmen took these tests. Table I summarizes the data covering the significant group tendencies.

TABLE I

	M.A. 1	M.T. 1	E.A. 1	E.T. 1	D-1	H.S.C.	Psy.	Comp.
Mean	18.11	23.19	36.65	88.32	19.8	109.37	106.5	400
S. D.	10.44	10.68	9.69	35.91	7.86	35.46	41.8	123.2
P. E.	7.94	7.20	6.52	24.22	5.3	23.90	28.23	83.0
Range	1–56	4–48	12–61	8–171	6–38	34–209	25–228	135–776

The raw scores for each student on both the composite and separate tests were converted into a type of "T-Scores" by using this formula: $T\text{-}Score = 50 + \frac{10(X\text{-}M)}{P.\,E.}$. X represents any raw score on a test; *M*, the mean for that test; *P. E.*, the probable error; *10*, an arbitrary constant to eliminate decimals, and *50*, an arbitrary number to place all the means at 50. This formula reduced all the scores to a comparable scale with the mean for each at 50 and with five probable error deviations each way from the mean. With the scores thus reduced to a comparable scale a diagnostic chart was devised and each student's scores were graphed on an individual chart. This level of ability as determined by the composite score on the seven tests was called the student's "expectancy" level.

The student's "achievement" was defined as his grade point average on the quarterly and semester grade reports from his classes. These scores were also converted to T-Scores and scaled in a column opposite the expectancy level. Each quarter as the grades came in they were converted to T-Scores and scaled on the student's diagnostic chart. The students were then classified in five groups representative of their achievement in ratio to expectancy:

A: Those achieving at 2½ P.E.'s or more above expectancy.
B: Those achieving from 1 to 2½ P.E.'s above expectancy.
C: Those achieving within 1 P.E. of expectancy.
D: Those achieving from 1 to 2½ P.E.'s below expectancy.
E: Those achieving more than 2½ P.E.'s below expectancy.

Students in Class C were considered as doing satisfactory work—all that could be justly required. Students in Classes A and B were considered unusually successful—doing more than expected. Students in Classes D and E were considered unsuccessful—not doing as much as could be justly expected. Remedial procedures concentrated upon the two latter groups, in an attempt to bring them up to expectancy, while constructive personnel measures were used with all to keep them achieving at their levels of ability.

No small part of the project undertaken at Graceland College lies in its personnel service bureau. Graceland is a small college. The student personnel service bureau here outlined was devised to meet its needs. The organization is simple, the functions diversified. Responsibility was both centralized and distributed. The writer was responsible for organizing the bureau, inaugurating the personnel program and for many of the technical phases such as the testing program, personal interviews, counseling, correspondence with parents, teaching the class on study methods, diagnosing difficulties, prescribing remedies and ironing out most of the serious difficulties of the students. Different members of the faculty, many of them experts in the field, coordinating their work with that of the central office, were responsible for student employment, literary societies, intramural contests, music, athletics, dramatics, religion, budgeting of time and supervision of health.

The following list outlines briefly the essential personnel services developed at Graceland:

(1) *Faculty cooperation:* Student personnel service is at its best when, and only when, it enlists the hearty, unstinted and intelligent cooperation of all the faculty. At Graceland College a high degree of cooperation has been reached. The administrators, the faculty, the students and the parents have so interwoven their efforts that a school spirit both joyous and efficient has been developed.

(2) *Freshman days:* At the opening of the school year a program of freshman days was arranged, which brought the freshmen to the campus two days in advance of the upperclassmen. During these two days the students were registered; had their entrance examinations and physical examinations, and were inducted into the ideals and spirit of the school, all under the guidance of and in contact with the faculty and the officers of the student organizations.

(3) *A Class in Methods for Freshman Students:* This class, entitled "The Business of Being a College Student," was conducted by the writer and attended by all freshmen. It met one hour each week and dealt with the essential problems incident to student success in college. "Methods of Study," by C. C. Crawford, was used as a text.

(4) *Letters to Parents:* To enlist the support of the parents a program of correspondence was carried out. Personal letters were sent to the parents of each student at the following times: immediately following his enrolment; at the end of the first nine weeks, enclosing grades and commenting upon the student's success; at the end of the first semester, and on occasion in accordance with special needs of individuals.

(5) *Student Interviews:* To establish close cooperation with and an understanding of each student, a series of personal interviews was held. These consisted of a "get-acquainted" interview with each freshman at the beginning of the school year; interviews with students scholastically below their expectancy level, and interviews of a special nature dealing with moral problems, philosophical disturbances and general problems of individual adjustment.

(6) *Time Budgets:* During freshman week, in the class for freshmen and in personal interviews, methods of budgeting time were discussed. A large percentage of the students developed the habit of scheduling and conserving their time, and at one time or another during the year each student made out a written schedule for his time.

(7) *Class Attendance and Absences:* Daily records of class attendance were filed in the writer's office. Negligence in class attendance was quickly detected and remedial means provided. "Being there" is one of the best methods of making a good record in a given class.

(8) *Rooming Quarters:* Practically all the students roomed in dormitories under college supervision or in their own homes in town. Quiet hours for study and rest were scheduled and well observed. The rooming quarters were supervised by resident members of the faculty in most instances. An atmosphere of homelikeness and studiousness prevailed in these quarters.

(9) *Health Supervision:* All students were given a physical examination during freshman days; courses in physical training were required, and an active program of intramural contests was sponsored. All these contributed constructively to the health of the students. A resident nurse and a college physician were maintained to detect and care for those who were sick.

(10) *Extra-curricular Activities:* A rich program of literary, religious, athletic, musical, dramatic and forensic activities was provided through the student organizations and the varsity activities. Every student participated in some form of extra-curricular activity.

(11) *Student Difficulties:* Student difficulties are multiform and numerous. These were adjusted through the central personnel office, relying largely upon the diagnostic chart and the personal interviews, and using the available

channels of college activities for remedying them.

The above outline is too sketchy to give an adequate picture of the personnel services but indicates briefly the many avenues through which the student is known and provisions made for his growth.

The results of the project show many advantages to both students and administrators. Some of the most important ones are listed below:

(1) From 77 per cent. to 81 per cent. of the students achieved at or above their level of expectancy throughout the year as measured by the standard adopted for this project. Table II shows the numerical, quantitative results in-

TABLE II

SHOWING THE NUMBER OF STUDENTS FALLING IN EACH OF THE FIVE CLASSES FOR EACH OF THE FOUR QUARTERS OF THE COLLEGE YEAR 1927–28. FRESHMAN CLASS OF 112 STUDENTS

Quarter	Class A	Class B	Class C	Class D	Class E	Total
1st	1	31	58	17	5	112
2nd	2	22	61	21	2	108
3rd	1	26	50	22	4	103
4th	3	23	50	21	2	99

dependent of the qualitative ranking of the student.

(2) Sixty per cent. of the students below the level required for graduation were achieving at or above their levels of expectancy. By use of the diagnostic chart, the advisers' time, ordinarily given indiscriminately to students low scholastically, could be given more helpfully to the forty per cent. whose expectancy level indicated that they should have been above the graduation dead line, but were not. Table III summarizes these facts.

(3) The 60 per cent. of the advisers' time ordinarily misdirected was applied to students who ordinarily are neglected, since their grades are above the academic danger line, but who are actually far below their own level of expectancy. An analysis of individual charts showed eight individuals for each of the first three quarters and five for the fourth who had grades above the *average* of the freshman class, yet far enough below their own expectancies to

TABLE III

SHOWING THE NUMBER OF STUDENTS BELOW GRADUATION LEVEL; THE NUMBER AND PERCENTAGE OF THESE IN CLASS C; ABOVE CLASS C; AND BELOW CLASS C; FOR EACH OF THE FOUR QUARTERS OF THE YEAR

Quarter	Number below graduation level	In Class C		Above Class C		Below Class C	
		No.	Per cent.	No.	Per cent.	No.	Per cent.
1st	30	18	60	0	0	12	40
2nd	24	13	54	2	8	9	38
3rd	25	12	48	3	12	10	40
4th	13	7	54	0	0	6	46

be classed D and E. These received counsel and assistance and profited by it.

(4) Students below expectancy for a given quarter showed marked gains in the succeeding quarters. Ability to detect those who were below their levels of ability gave directness to remedial procedures with fruitful gains. Sixteen students counseled at the end of the first quarter showed an average improvement of seven points on the T-Scale of achievement.

(5) Where gains were not registered in the succeeding quarters and students remained below expectancy, the reasons were ascertained. In some of these cases the causes could not be removed. They consisted of such factors as being required to work long hours for room and board, illness or the lack of the power of self-direction. This latter factor requires several semesters of practice to show improvement.

(6) The methods used in carrying out the project created a general interest in scholarship, on the part of students, comparable to their interest in other supervised activities. It gave each student a goal as stimulating as those of athletics, music or forensics.

(7) It enabled the administration to deal with the problem student more wisely and with a greater degree of accuracy and expertness.

(8) It focused the attention of the faculty and administration upon the *student as an individual* rather than upon the *average tendencies of students as a mass.*

LONZO JONES

THE STATE UNIVERSITY OF IOWA

SCHOOL AND SOCIETY

EDITED BY J. McKEEN CATTELL

WITH WHICH IS COMBINED THE

EDUCATIONAL REVIEW

EDITED BY WILLIAM McANDREW

Volume XXVIII — SATURDAY, DECEMBER 22, 1928 — Number 730

THE ART OF TEACHING[1]

By A. H. UPHAM

PRESIDENT OF MIAMI UNIVERSITY

THE history of Miami University through her century and more of achievement is a record of great teachers. All her thirteen presidents also have themselves conducted classes, most of them combining this experience with their administrative duties. The roster of these scholarly and sympathetic men is more impressive than financial budgets or rapidly mounting enrolment figures, perhaps even than the accumulated achievements of a hundred graduating classes. For these teachers of Miami men have awakened the youthful interest and quickened the young hearts of many generations of students who in turn have passed on the inspiration to countless others.

President Robert H. Bishop and his son, one mighty in philosophy and the other in Latin; William Holmes McGuffey, who composed his famous readers while a professor of the classics; John W. Scott, who instituted science teaching at Miami, and Orange Nash Stoddard, who continued the tradition; David Swing, developing among his lads of the preparatory school the love of humanity which enriched the message of a great preacher; Charles Elliott, not always absorbed in his Greek; Robert White McFarland, whose boys followed him from the mathematics classroom to the battlefield; Andrew D. Hepburn, so long the kindly object of student veneration; W. O. Thompson, an inspiring teacher as he has always been a vigorous leader; Raymond M. Hughes, reluctantly closing the door of his laboratory to undertake administrative tasks; Bruce Fink, honored by a long line of distinguished botanists who have profited by his instruction; these and many others have written the Miami record and established her position among colleges.

Confronting such a list, one seeks naturally for the common factors of their greatness. There ought to be some pervasive characteristic in them all, some distinctive Miami method which we can all cultivate and apply. But the search is at first disheartening. Their practices have little in common but the primitive simplicity forced upon them by circumstances. One at least, we are told, was delightfully absent-minded. Others never appeared so. Some were severe. Others were suspected of being very easy. Some quizzed regularly in Socratic fashion. Others could always be beguiled into lecturing.

Indeed the records indicate that Miami has always been a rather simple-minded,

[1] Inaugural address delivered at the exercises at Miami University, Oxford, Ohio, October 20, 1928.

conservative institution. At first she was quite content to be the "Yale of the West," transplanting a New England curriculum into the Ohio Valley for the rugged sons of the pioneers. Upon marked innovations both faculty and trustees have looked askance. A law school was projected in 1827 and promptly given up. A medical school, considered in 1830, never came into being. The decade of the fifties saw the institution of a normal course for teachers, a department of physical education and a course in engineering, no one of which aroused much interest or survived beyond the Civil War. Miami's unique contribution, the successful coordination of a new normal college with a very old college of liberal arts, was practically forced upon her by the legislature in 1902. As there has been no uniform procedure in instruction, so there appears to have been no epoch-marking discovery as to purpose or organization. Ohio did not officially realize until 1885 that Miami was a state university. Yet it is generally recognized in American scholarship that the service of Miami University to higher education has been eminently valuable and far-reaching.

Perhaps there has been a Miami system operating unobserved. Classes, for example, have always been small. For many years there were not students enough to provide any other kind. When larger numbers came additional instructors were found for them, and the old order continued. There has been intimate personal acquaintance between faculty and students. This, too, has been happily inevitable. Encouraged by the faculty, students of Miami have continually devoted themselves to self-education, with a notable display of initiative and independence. As early as 1827 some of these students purchased a printing press, installed it in the old Main Building and began publishing a monthly magazine. The literary societies provided abundant drill in debate and oratory and often challenged faculty authority instead of following it. Moreover, the battles of wits in their halls encouraged no small amount of original research in history, economics and political science. Students turned to books on their own initiative.

But the outstanding fact of the system seems to have been the personalities of the teachers and the success with which they imparted ideals of culture and a love of learning to their young associates. They were men of high and noble character. They were deeply religious men, devout and God-fearing. Philosophy in its literal sense was the guiding spirit of their lives, as our friends of Phi Beta Kappa would have it. Around the subjects of their thought and research played the creative fire of their own imaginations, and they were able somehow to bring their students into the circle of this radiance. They knew and loved their boys. They were conscious of them sometimes as an audience for which they performed impromptu histrionic tricks to catch and hold their attention, sometimes as colleagues in age and interest with whom they shared their theories and enthusiasms.

The contagion worked, as such contagion always does. With such apparently hopeless media of communication as Greek roots and Latin inflections and the higher mathematics, these lads caught unexpected visions and sometimes readjusted their entire lives. A manufacturer of international repute has noted as the greatest influence in his young manhood the drill-work in Latin syntax in a Miami classroom. A graduate once noted for his numerous college escapades built up a rare and valuable collection of Roman coins, which he finally presented to the university. They were not routine-worshiping pedants, these Miami professors; they were teachers of men. Theirs was the *art* of teaching, the re-creation of subject-matter in a crucible of living fire.

At any other time than this I should apologize for these constant references to Miami and her history, for the conditions I have described are by no means unique. They have been duplicated more or less in many of the earlier American colleges and universities, in which other devoted teachers, lacking a standardized method, unaccustomed to think of education as a science, practiced it successfully as a fine art.

I have no thought of attempting to discredit the marvelous developments of recent years in our knowledge of educational methods and technique, the measurement of results and the application of scientific knowledge and procedure to our problems. Such an attempt would be as ungracious as it would be futile. Miami University is thoroughly committed to the modern conceptions in education and is undertaking her full share of responsibility for experiment and practice in advancing these still further. Neither would I reflect adversely upon any of the plans, ideas or discoveries promulgated rather freely of late in both secondary and higher education. They seem natural enough in the restless, well-ripened, almost surfeited civilization in which we live. Comparable, one might imagine, was the Athens of the first century, in which Saint Paul found that "all the Athenians, and strangers which were there, spent their time in nothing else, but either to tell or to hear some new thing."

Some of these new things are new. All of them are excellent and are destined for success when operated by sympathetic or even evangelistic partisans. I am only insisting that really effective education consists of method plus something else or formula plus something else; that, however much it may be a science, it is still blest of the Almighty because it is an art. Shakespeare once had Hamlet remark: "There are more things in heaven and earth, Horatio, than are dreamt of in your philosophy"; and there is reason to believe that he meant "natural philosophy," as they then called one phase of science. At about the same time a very real English physician, Sir Thomas Browne, declared: "I love to lose myself in a mystery, to pursue my reason to an O altitudo!"

When the alumni of our colleges endeavor to interpret the greatness of professors they once had, and grow incoherent in the process, it is highly probable that they are still captivated by some indefinable and unconscious classroom artistry or some soaring of the spirit that caught them up to the heights.

Some of us have known master teachers who combined in a remarkable degree an accurate, detailed, impersonal sense of fact with the rare humor and contagious enthusiasm that made them almost objects of reverence. Sometimes they themselves have not realized wherein their greatness lay. More frequently their young disciples, unable or unwilling to grasp the full significance of the experience they were enjoying, have gone out to practice the mysteries of the master only to find the wand broken and the charm lost. For they have imitated the mechanism of method, the meticulous accuracy of detail, and have forgotten the spirit back of the process.

Impressed by the unparalleled advances in scientific knowledge in the past generation, we have all been intrigued by its accuracy and strict methodology. Subjects of study which once made little or no pretense to such distinction we have sought to reclassify as sciences and to reorganize in terms of scientific method. In exactness, we have said, lies real virtue. Then closing our eyes to the many-sidedness of this great master spirit of the age, we have set about converting all things to its obvious mechanism. Creation and appreciation in literature almost gave place to the more teachable scientific philology. Psychology set up as a science; then sociology and pedagogy. Recently there have been demands that even art itself should adopt more scientific methods.

Accuracy in detail and a rigid structure of fact are excellent things. But an ex-professor of English does not need to remind you that these are not all of science. "A great empire and little minds," said Edmund Burke, "go ill together." The vast empire of the sciences requires a breadth of vision and a range of faculties in those who are at home in it that might well discourage the best of us. A well-known author was recently described facetiously as "a Methodist in a laboratory apron." Again reverting to original meanings one might express a caution lest laboratory aprons clothe too many who are methodists and little else.

For youth certainly and perhaps for most of us much of the contagion of the sciences lies on what we may call their art side. We are challenged by the mysteries into which they venture, by the imaginative flights which anticipate discoveries, by the courage that ventures even life itself for the good of mankind. For the sake of recognition among the sciences, our subjects of scholarly interest can ill afford to neglect the very factors which make science itself a vital, human thing. As always, scholarship is a narrow, devious path between the wilderness of dilettantism and the morass of pedantry.

Perhaps by now we have arrived at the secret of Miami University, seen prophetically by its founders and handed down for a century. The great tradition of Old Miami seems to be the tradition of culture and liberal learning, sympathetically interpreted by men of character, scholarship and genial humanity. I tried to say this publicly once before. Promptly I was interpreted as saying that the only work in Miami worth while was that of the liberal arts college and all things else should give way to it. Which only goes to show how we are enslaved in our thinking by formulas and categories. Let us think rather of the *spirit* of liberal culture, which is loath to be bound by the confines of schools or so-called departments of instruction. It is a changing, illusory element, and our attempts to harness it have changed much through the years. Perhaps it is just an interest in life as well as living, a longing to relate our routine experiences to the scheme of things here and hereafter.

When Miami University first undertook, under her charter, to cultivate "the liberal arts and sciences," she did so with a fixed curriculum consisting of four years of Latin, four years of Greek, a year and a half of Hebrew, two and a half of mathematics. There was a year of history and a year of philosophy, but only a half year each of chemistry, physics and political economy. She cherishes the liberal spirit now with a wide variety of sciences and modern languages, with economics, sociology and politics, and with Shakespeare's portion of "a little Latin and less Greek."

This is not all the story. Twenty-five years ago Miami entered upon what observers considered the hazardous enterprise of maintaining a professional school for teachers alongside and cooperating with the traditional college of liberal arts. Hazardous it was, for these were at first elementary teachers, and the course was of only two years' duration. This project brought girls to the campus in unheard-of numbers; also summer sessions and a practice school. It was an interesting experiment and the patient nearly died. But the leaven of the great tradition began to work, and actual, understanding cooperation became first a theory, then a welcome fact. The school of education, eagerly seeking after constant advancement in spirit as in method, now speaks with the arts faculty a common language of scholarly ideals and the appreciation of the arts. The professional spirit is tempered by the liberal, even as the liberal spirit is quickened into greater vitality and effectiveness by the presence of a professional objective.

Another quarter century sees us at the threshold of another similar experiment. We have assembled here this week in honor of the institution of another academic division of Miami University. This, too, is a professional training-school, the school of business administration. It recognizes the unprecedented trend of our young manhood in recent years to business pursuits, the elevation of business itself to be a thing of scholarship, ethical ideals, sound practices and a mission of unselfish service —in the best sense a profession. Here in the midst of a crowded industrial region, in a land teeming with schools and colleges of business, one naturally questions what particular function shall be assumed by the Miami School of Business Administration that it may render most valuable service to its public.

The answer, I am sure, is found once more in the Miami tradition. It was anticipated in the birth of this school out of the very heart of the liberal arts college; anticipated too in the years of conference and planning with which President Hughes prepared the way so carefully for this new development. This is to be a liberal college of business administration, building its more technical subject-matter on a firm, well-laid foundation of language and literature, history and government. Again there appears the time-honored ideal of technique plus something else.

Even for the immediate future the circle does not seem complete. A century of recognition of esthetic and spiritual values seems to point directly at a school of fine arts, where appreciation and creation may both be encouraged. It would indeed be another bridging of the gap, a harmonizing of extremes. Until recently art schools and conservatories have deplored time wasted on scholastic studies, and colleges have considered only art history and the theory of music really educational. There have been concessions here and there. Music students were encouraged to acquire a little French and Italian; they might need it in singing. Courses in play-production and the writing of poetry found their way into academic curricula because they were sponsored by the old and reliable department of English. Students confused the issue still more by asking credits for band-practice and sign-painting. Now we stand face to face with a situation where young people desire to cultivate a talent they think they have and reinforce it with a college education. Perhaps the day is also at hand when our colleges of liberal arts will find comfort in the fine arts against the invasions of the practical arts. Imagination, a fine sense of the exquisite or the beautiful, the creative impulse cultivated or admired—these are the quickening factors in all our teaching and our scholarship that is not mere routine drudgery. In the fine arts these qualities all come into their own.

After all, Miami appears to have something of the unique about her, being considerably given to paradoxes. She is new in that she admits being old and frankly relies upon an ancient tradition. She seeks distinction not in novelty or extreme, but in attempting a golden mean, a harmonizing of the time-honored ideals of culture and the humanities with the most modern technique of certain of the professions. Being a state university dedicated at public expense to public service, she has no ambition in the direction of technological instruction or the multiplicity of courses of any sort. Most state universities began that way, but pressure to prepare for one thing and another has complicated them beyond measure as their enrolment has mounted far beyond anticipation. Being a state university Miami is still comfortably small, as modern colleges go, with a genuine community life, centered upon the campus. Sequestered in a country village in which education is the chief industry, Miami lies within an hour and a half of perhaps a million people representing an enormous variety of industries.

Miami is not *the* state university; she is *a* state university, which only of late has entered upon the real significance of her name. Ohio alone, among the states, accepted as her wards two institutions of learning which came with the acquisition of great tracts of private lands, and has acknowledged and performed faithfully her obligation of guardianship and support. Other states in considerable number maintain both state university and agricultural college, and are often at a loss to differentiate their scope and function. Ohio, in addition to a great central state university of which the agricultural college is a part, provides Ohio and Miami universities, both still keeping their trust as associations of colleges with closely-related objectives and united in loyalty to the humanities. As publicly supported junior colleges spring like mushrooms from the fertile soil of local pride and ambition, and state normal schools advance themselves to four-year, degree-granting colleges with expanded curricula, it becomes more apparent every year that the State of Ohio in her leaner decades constructed a comprehensive and effective system of higher education for the time of her prosperity.

It has come to me, as to few other men, to know intimately the great teachers who have made and kept the Miami tradition. A few I have known in person; most of them through the records of their impress and the testimony of young admirers in whom age did not dim the glory of these memories. Perhaps this is why I am irresistibly drawn to look backward on this occasion for the inspiration to look forward. Our real task is with the Miami of to-morrow, with her constantly renewed problems of adjustment to new conditions and the anticipation of others yet to come. In the primitive middle west of a century ago Miami University was a leader of pioneers. In a riper, more luxurious civilization Miami must still nurture and send forth the young pioneers of thought and discovery, with the prayer that their measure of service may be as large and reputable as that of their forebears. In assuming my humble part in the evolving human force we call Miami University it is my conviction that a century of history has taught us that our prime responsibility here is that of teaching in the love of it students who may catch the contagion of scholarship from our lips as they learn the dignity of character from our lives.

THE AMERICAN FIELD SERVICE FELLOWSHIPS

By ARCHIE M. PALMER

ASSISTANT DIRECTOR OF THE INSTITUTE OF INTERNATIONAL EDUCATION

Ever since the days when Benjamin Franklin and Thomas Jefferson were exerting themselves in the interest of an *entente cordiale* between France and the struggling young American Republic, there has been gradually evolving a strong intellectual sympathy between the two countries. The late World War has contributed to a greater extent than any other single event in arousing and bringing the American people to a full realization of the wealth of intellectual and inspirational opportunities available in France for Americans.

With the cultural background provided by the outstanding contributions of her many great masters in all fields of thought, it is not at all surprising that France should attract American scholars. The mere enumeration of the great names of those savants who have developed and passed on this tradition of learning and culture would resolve itself into a catalogue of the French intellectual leaders who have in many fields—in literature, in science and in art—set standards not only for France but for the entire world.

These great men were usually skilful teachers as well as creators and discoverers, and they had many worthy disciples, capable young scholars who spread abroad the ideas and vision of their masters, thereby prolonging and extending their influence by supplying the needed interpretations and elaborations. In many fields these young scholars set the pace of intellectual progress in Europe.

It was in order to develop a more complete realization and consideration of the immeasurable contribution to science and learning made through the ages by these great minds that an organization known as the American Field Service Fellowships for French Universities was established shortly after the World War. It was also "in order to provide an enduring memorial to the one hundred and twenty-seven Field Service men who gave their lives to the cause and to perpetuate among future generations the mutual understanding and fraternity of spirit which marked their relations during the war that the organization has continued its activities.

Each year awards are made of a series of fellowships for advanced study in France to qualified candidates selected from among the graduates of American colleges and universities and from the technical and industrial field. A limited number of these fellowships are available for the year 1929–30. Each will carry a stipend of $1,200 and will be tenable for one year. A fellowship may be renewed for a second year upon application provided circumstances warrant it.

In general, these fellowships are offered in the following fields of study: agriculture, anthropology, archeology and history of art, architecture, astronomy, biology, botany, chemistry, classical languages and literature, criminology, economics, education, English language and literature, geology, geography, history, law, mathematics, medicine and surgery, oriental languages and literature, philosophy, political science and international law, psychology, religion, Romance languages and literature, Semitic languages and literature, Slavic languages and literature, sociology and zoology. A candidate may choose the field of study he prefers but usually the fellowships will be granted only for the pursuit of advanced study in the field in which the candidate has shown proficiency.

The fellowships are offered for study in the universities and faculties and other institutions of higher learning in Paris and in the sixteen provincial universities. The candidate may designate his choice of the institution in which to pursue his work, but the desirability of a period of residence in a provincial university is strongly recommended.

The fellowships are open at present only to men. A candidate must be a citizen of the United States or of one of its possessions. He must at the time of making application be a graduate of a college of recognized standing or of a professional school requiring three years of study for a degree; or, if not qualified in either of these ways, must be twenty-four years of age and must have spent five years in work requiring high technical skill. He must be of good moral character and intellectual ability, of suitable personal qualities, and must have a practical ability to use French books both in general subjects and in his own field, and be able to speak French and understand lectures delivered in French.

Applicants who accept the award of a fellowship are expected to sail for France on or about July 1, or preferably earlier, in the year in which the award is made. Unless already so proficient in the language as to be exempt from this requirement they are required to devote the first summer to the study and practice of oral French. It is strongly recommended that in such cases the first few months be spent in the provinces, where experience indicates that the most rapid progress can be made in learning the language.

Rich opportunities in every field of study and research are afforded in the universities of France to American students. The graduate of an American college who desires to proceed to an advanced degree will find that a French university degree equivalent in standing to the Ph.D. of an American university of recognized standing and declared by the French university authorities to have the same scientific and academic value as the state doctorate (*doctorat d'état*) can now be obtained in all of the faculties of the University of Paris and at all of the other sixteen French universities, while opportunities for study in the specialized national and independent institutions are also available to him.

Applications must be filed not later than January 1 of the year in which the award is to be made. Full information and application blanks may be obtained by addressing Archie M. Palmer, the Assistant Director of the Institute of International Education, 2 West 45th Street, New York, N. Y.

The tremendous increase in recent years of interest in the study of Romance languages, and particularly of French, has caused many an American student to cast a longing eye on the possibilities of study in France. Teachers of French can benefit greatly from a period of study in France where they can observe and learn at first hand the spirit and culture and institutions of the country whose literature they interpret to their own students in the classroom and from the lecture platform. Not merely do the teachers themselves profit from this experience but they carry back to their own people an intelligent and sympathetic understanding and appreciation of their subject-matter.

It is not always possible for the ambitious young teacher who is devoting himself to a life of service in the field of education to provide from his meager earnings the necessary funds for a trip abroad, much as he may recognize and cherish its value to him personally and to the enhancement of his professional advancement. Opportunity for such deserving scholars to enjoy the advantages of foreign study is made possible through the American Field Service Fellowships and a number of other fine fellowships and scholarships established by far-sighted individuals, foundations, colleges and universities, and other institutions.

The fundamental idea behind practically all these foreign study opportunities is the desire to make it possible for America to broaden her horizon and to promote international goodwill through a better mutual understanding between the United States and foreign countries. That the furtherance of this ideal is being realized is clearly manifest in the activities of those who have returned after an enjoyment of these opportunities and the increasing breadth of vision and of interest in international affairs on the part of our people generally and of our youth particularly.

Although a great deal of interest in the American Field Service Fellowships is manifested by the graduates of American colleges and universities the selection of candidates is accomplished through a very effective refining process which results in the final consideration of only those candidates having the highest qualifications. Out of the several hundred applications submitted for the American Field Service Fellowships available for study in France for 1928–29, only ninety-one were taken into final consideration. According to the addresses given on their applications these candidates hailed from thirty states in the Union and from three foreign countries. They were well distributed, many of them coming from states west of the Mississippi. About one third expressed the intention of pursuing their advanced study in France in the field of Romance languages and literature. Preferences for work in history, especially French history, in political science and international law, in philosophy and in the physical sciences were expressed by a large number.

The fellowships for the year 1928–29 have been awarded to the following persons:

William T. Bandy, Jr., assistant in French at the University of Illinois; B.A., M.A. Vanderbilt University, also studied at the University of Paris; will work in the field of Romance languages and literature under the direction of Professor Baldensperger at the University of Paris for doctorat de l'Université de Paris on *L'Evolution de la Critique Baudelairienne.*

Albert E. Blumberg, graduate student at Yale University; A.B. Johns Hopkins University; will continue work begun at Yale University on the history and philosophy of science.

William G. Crane, instructor in English at the University of Cincinnati; B.A., M.A. State University of Iowa; will study English literature of the Renaissance and its continental background under Professor Feuillerat at the University of Rennes.

Grayson L. Kirk, assistant in political science at the University of Wisconsin; A.B. Miami University, A.M. Clark University; will make a study of French colonial and domestic administration at the École Libre des Sciences Politiques in Paris.

George S. Lane, American-Scandinavian Foundation fellow at the University of Iceland; B.A., M.A. State University of Iowa; will study comparative philology under Professor Meillet and will work in Sanskrit and Celtic.

Milton Lowenstein, graduate student at New York University; A.B. Columbia University, also studied at the University of Paris and the Fontainebleau School of Fine Arts; will complete a treatise on monastic Romanesque architecture of the twelfth and thirteenth centuries.

Cornwell B. Rogers, graduate student and instructor in history at Yale University; A.B. Princeton University, M.A. Columbia University, also studied at Harvard University and the University of Grenoble; will do historical research in the period of the French Revolution.

Clifford N. Wall, instructor in physics at the University of Illinois; B.A., M.S., Ph.D. University of Illinois, also studied at Northwestern College and Carnegie Institute of Technology; will work at Strasbourg and Paris in an attempt to construct a theory which will quantitatively account for the magnetic properties of ferromagnetic crystals such as pyrhotite, magnetite, iron crystals, hematite, etc.

Herbert C. Youtie, graduate student at Columbia University; B.A. University of Cincinnati; will study Greek paleography at the École Pratique des Hautes Études of the University of Paris.

The fellowships have been renewed for the second year for the following who spent the academic year 1927–28 in France as American Field Service fellows:

William L. Crain, instructor in Romance languages at Lehigh University; B.A. University of North Dakota, M.A. University of Chicago; is working on Balzac and plans to bring out a critical edition of *Sur Catherine de Médicis.*

Don L. Demorest, assistant professor of Romanic languages at Miami University; B.A., M.A. Ohio State University, Diplôme de l'École de Preparation de Professeurs de Français à l'Étranger; is working in Paris on the imagery in Flaubert's works.

Robert Lee Humber, student at the University of Paris; B.A., LL.B. Wake Forest College, M.A. Harvard University, B.Litt. Oxford; is working on a thesis on Calhoun's political ideas.

Some years ago at a meeting of international societies the late Andrew Carnegie remarked that in time there would be no place in the world for the peace societies which he had founded, but that there would always be need for organizations which would bring different countries together in points of intellectual contact.

Whether one is a foe or a friend of internationalism, whether one believes in a society of nations or thinks that the human race will prosper best when parceled into small, assertive nationalities, one must admit that in the future, as in the past, nations will be stimulated by the contact of one civilization with another. The understanding and appreciation of one's neighbors can be best realized through a comprehension of their culture, of their social life and of their psychology. In what more effective way can this end be attained than through the interchange of students and teachers, thereby effecting the interpretation through the observing eyes of critical youth?

The American Field Service Fellowships are now approaching the completion of a decade during which one hundred and fifty-nine of these fellowships have been awarded to the American Field Service fellows. The positions which they have assumed since their return to the United States are an indication of the high type of candidate, both academic and professional, which has been selected to enjoy these opportunities. A study of the records and subsequent accomplishments of the returned fellows is contemplated during the current year which will serve as an attempt to survey the results of the initial ten years of this movement to develop a more complete realization and consideration of the contributions made to science and learning by the great minds of France.

REMARKS AT THE UNVEILING OF DR. DEWEY'S BUST[1]

By Professor WILLIAM H. KILPATRICK

TEACHERS COLLEGE, COLUMBIA UNIVERSITY

A few of your friends, Professor Dewey, are here gathered to perform an act of friendship. We who are present are but a few of the many who participate with us. And these conscious friends are but a minute fraction of that larger number who profit from the contribution you have made to the world.

It is an act of friendship, I say. We do not claim that we are here to honor you. We should like to do so, but it is not for us to honor you, not at any rate by gift or ceremonial. Possibly by living out your teachings and extending them it might be done, but we do not come making any such claim. It is as friends, appreciative of what you have done for us, that we come to let you and others know somewhat of our debt of gratitude and our admiration.

I am permitted to speak for the others. They in their letters to the committee approving the plan use such expressions as:

"Great pleasure," "happy to have part," "tremendously interested," "very happy," "very great pleasure," "great satisfaction," "glad to have the opportunity," "the privilege of sharing," "delighted," "greatly pleased," "it is a rare opportunity," "I am filled with pleasure to have the opportunity," "Anything in connection with John Dewey arouses my enthusiasm," "I am delighted to join with the rest of you in paying a

[1] The bust of Professor Dewey was presented to him by his former students and others who wished to express in some measure their indebtedness to him. It stands for the time being, by the kindness of Professor Dewey, in the philosophy of education reading room at Teachers College, Columbia University.

tribute of affection and admiration to John Dewey.''

Our Lady of Mercy: ''It gives me great pleasure indeed to be allowed to join in this tribute of affectionate regard to a great man whom I am proud to look upon as my friend.''

. . . homage to America's foremost thinker.

No financial contribution, however great, could indicate the extent to which all of us at Columbia are indebted to John Dewey, not merely as scholar and teacher, but as leader and friend.

From the standpoint of the ages John Dewey is *the* great man of our age.

Rarely do we meet a teacher whose influence is so lasting as that of John Dewey.

. . . easily the first and greatest of all our philosophers of education.

. . . not only a great admiration. . . . He is one of the best men I have ever known.

Within the span of his own lifetime, Dr. Dewey's influence has been immeasurable.

My contact with him, as a student, has been among the outstanding experiences of my life; it has left a profound impress and exerted an influence upon my ideals, mind and character that has been continuous and invaluable. I love and revere him as one of the few truly great men whom it has been my good fortune to know. My gratitude to him is boundless.

My profound appreciation of the service which Dr. Dewey has rendered to the thinking of our time and therefore to future civilization. For multitudes of us he has made a new world. I recall with increasing gratitude the three years of graduate work which I had chiefly with him in the University of Chicago. It is an honor and a privilege to have a small part in giving permanent recognition to his profound and lasting services to humanity.

But not all in writing to the committee have expressed themselves in the same strain. There were other and variant voices.

A more inappropriate gift could hardly have been chosen.

. . . a pleasure for me to serve on the Advisory Committee. . . . I like to give advice . . . in this case I have two headings for the advice:

First, tell Dewey, when he sits, not to look so damn benign, gentle and easy: it is not entirely natural and it is an obstacle for those of his friends who try to put his principles at work in a world of people who like a statue or a picture of a seer to look a little fierce or scrappy. Tell Dewey to think of ———, or university administration, or Governor Fuller.

My advice to Epstein is not to fall for that benign expression. Tell him to aestheticize the intellectual-barroom strain in Dewey's ensemble. Make him read Dewey's crucifixion of ——— and catch the spirit of that. . . .

I have some more advice . . . a sculptor or a painter, when he does a real star, expects to be paid less than for an ordinary commission. Good business men, and many painters and sculptors are that, know that the advertising value of their preserving celebrities for the future, is of the first rank. I think you could take a chance with Epstein by pleading that reason and reinforce it by a hard-luck story accompanied by tears.

And now I wish to direct my remarks not to Professor Dewey, but to the others here gathered. I shall be pardoned, I hope, if I say a word or two of my own opinion regarding our friend.

Any right that I have to speak for his place in philosophy may be questioned, but I think he has made the greatest contribution to thought yet made by an American, and that he must be included among the great thinkers of all time to now. Certainly these things are true of his contribution to education. No school child in this country but feels the effect of his teaching, and no teacher or school official. And his influence grows not only here but elsewhere; many foreign countries feel it. He is the widest known American educator. Where the influence of his ideas is not yet felt, there is (to my judgment) evident want of it.

As we look to the ancient days for comparisons I see in Professor Dewey the modest sincerity of Socrates, the radical constructive thinking of Plato, the balanced outlook of Aristotle. Like Socrates he too has brought philosophy down from the clouds to dwell among men. Like Plato he has married philosophy and education with like fertile results. Like Aristotle he has mediated conflicts, but less often by finding a "mean" between contending elements than by showing the unreality of conflict and shifting the problem to more fruitful lines.

If we look for analogous comparisons to the history of British thought, we see in Professor Dewey the same common sense approach to experience which characterized John Locke, but with a penetration more like Hume's. Unlike Hume, however, he leaves us with a positive program.

As we come to the time in which Professor Dewey has lived, I hesitate to speak, especially in Professor Dewey's presence. It is difficult to choose from the many lines of contribution he has made. To me his contributions lie principally (1) in the conception of experience to which he directs us and the extraordinarily penetrating analyses he has made of it, thus changing our conception of philosophy and delivering us from so many old puzzles; (2) in his biological psychology so fertile in its functional control; (3) allied to both the foregoing, in his conception of intelligence as primarily instrumental, which through his *How We Think* is revolutionizing teaching on all sides; (4) in his demarking of the significance of the social factor in experience.

These and more are so conceived as to constitute the most thoroughgoing grasp yet achieved of how civilization is to be placed on a functional and dynamic basis.

More personally, to those of us who know him, the modesty of the man, his kindliness, his generosity, his friendliness, are possibly the characteristics that most make us love him; while his marvelous penetration, his alertness to new and hitherto unnoted significances—in a word his creative ability—win our profoundest admiration.

This is "our friend, a man as we may say, the best of all his time that we have known, and moreover the most wise and the most just."

To you, Professor Dewey, whom we thus cherish, in behalf of all who have participated with us, I now present this bust. As enduring as may be its bronze, more lasting will be your influence for good among men.

EDUCATIONAL EVENTS

AMERICAN GIFT TO THE UNIVERSITY AT HEIDELBERG

According to a wireless dispatch to the New York *Times*, Ambassador Jacob Gould Schurman on December 17 turned over to Heidelberg University, where he was a student fifty years ago, a donation from Americans of more than $500,000 for the construction of a new auditorium. The ambassador was made an honorary citizen and after festivities in connection with these acts a torchlight procession was held in his honor. Dr. Schurman had been called upon to make four speeches, which he delivered in German.

The streets and buildings of this beautiful city on the Neckar were decorated with the Stars and Stripes side by side with the German national flag and the university colors. The students were dressed in the uniforms of their corps and further color was added by the picturesque dress of the natives. Paul Loebe, president of the Reichstag, and several government officials attended the ceremonies.

Last spring when an honorary degree was conferred on Ambassador Schurman by the university he learned that there was need of a new structure for lecture rooms for the increasing student body. He consulted a number of his friends and former students of Heidelberg with regard to raising a fund of $300,000, which it was estimated was required. John D. Rockefeller, Jr., promised half the entire amount and the remainder was contributed by W. A. Harriman, P. Chrysler, Clarence L. Dillon, George F. Baker, William Fox, Mortimer L. Schiff, James Speyer, Charles P. Taft, Paul and Felix Warburg and others. Later realizing that this estimate was inadequate, the Ambassador asked for another $200,000, which was quickly oversubscribed.

After recalling incidents of his student days at Heidelberg Dr. Schurman made this Christmas present "in recognition of high and helpful service to American students for over a century."

Immediately afterward, Dr. Walz, mayor of Heidelberg and a fellow-student with Dr. Schurman at the university, conferred on him honorary citizenship. Regarding the proposed building Dr. Schurman said:

I can not but think of this building and of the former service of the university to America as a manifestation of genuine friendship which exists between our two peoples. We have much in common—blood to no inconsiderable extent, but also social and commercial relations, culture, science, political institutions and international ideals, and devotion to peace and the highest progress of mankind. May the new hall be an abiding token of our friendship and of the high objects for which both nations stand.

THE CHILDREN'S BUREAU OF THE U. S. DEPARTMENT OF LABOR

CITING as one of the outstanding achievements of the year in the field of child welfare the saving of thousands of infant lives, making the infant mortality rate for 1927 the lowest in the history of the United States, Miss Grace Abbott, chief of the children's bureau of the U. S. Department of Labor, in her annual report made public on December 11 describes the activities carried on throughout the country on behalf of children, and indicates also that some progress is being made toward reducing the maternal mortality rate.

Pointing out that there were 65 infant deaths per 1,000 live births in the birth-registration area in 1927 as compared with 73 for the area in 1926, Miss Abbott's report shows that 21 States had an even lower rate than 65 during the year.

"Though these rates reflect great progress," she states, "no State has as yet reached the low level of New Zealand, where the rate was 39 in 1927. Idaho, Oregon and Washington, however, have rates sufficiently low to lead to the hope that if the present resources and facilities are continued and developed it may yet be said that there are some States in which it is as safe to be a baby as in New Zealand."

Oregon, with an infant death rate of 48 per 1,000 live births, holds the place of honor, and Idaho ties with Washington for second place with a rate of 50. Other States with low rates are: Nebraska, 51; Minnesota, 52; Utah, 54; Iowa and Kansas, 55, and New York, Wisconsin, Indiana, Connecticut, all of which had a rate of 59.

A study of the causes of death among American babies, Miss Abbott says, shows that in the expanding birth-registration area since 1920 there has been a marked decrease in mortality rates for gastro-intestinal diseases and a slight decrease in rates for natal and prenatal causes. For the former the average annual rate of decline from 1920 to 1926 was 6.9 per cent., and for the latter 1.2 per cent.

The decreases, the report declares, "are unquestionably associated with the general improvement in public health, the establishment of child-health conferences, the development of prenatal clinics, the distribution of literature, and public education regarding the importance of breast feeding."

Pointing out that "it is too much to expect that the death rate among women in childbirth will show so general and substantial a reduction as does the infant death rate," the report shows that in 16 of the 34 States for which Census Bureau figures were available at the time of writing, the maternal death rate had declined, and had remained stationary in two States only. A comparison of maternal mortality prior to operation of the maternity and infancy act with maternal mortality during the period of operation of the act in States in the birth-registration area and cooperating under the act for a specified period shows percentage declines ranging from 0.9 to 31.8 during the period of cooperation.

The maternity and infancy act, under which 45 states and the Territory of Hawaii are now cooperating to promote the health of mothers and babies, comes to an end June 30, 1929. "This act," Miss Abbott says, "has served its purpose in demonstrating the usefulness of Federal, State and local cooperation in the promotion of the health of children. In some States the work will go forward, although less rapidly, should the Federal Government adhere to the policy of complete withdrawal; but in a larger number the time and resources available have not been adequate to make more than a beginning in the initiation of a State-wide program, so that the health of mothers and babies is certain to suffer if such a policy is followed."

INSTITUTE OF WOMEN'S PROFESSIONAL RELATIONS

A NEW research organization, the Institute of Women's Professional Relations, has recently been established with headquarters at the North

Carolina College for Women, at Greensboro. It is under the direction of a board sponsored by the American Association of University Women, but financed by a group of private individuals.

The institute has a five-year program of research looking toward the coordination of business and professional requirements with women's education, the cultivation of greater interest in pre-professional courses and the profitable entrance of women into various fields such as merchandising, finance and specialized professional service.

In addition to its research the institute will act as a national clearing house covering the activities of the college guidance bureaus and of research and other agencies interested in the work and education of women. No placement work is to be done.

The object of research is to provide specific facts on occupations open to college women, the aptitudes and training required and the opportunities in various fields, including cooperation with business and the professional organizations in working out programs of training, the development of plans for functional education and a study of the better adjustment of the home and women's professional and business interests.

The members of the board of directors of the institute are Mrs. Catherine Filene Dodd, Washington, D. C., *chairman;* Miss Helen Bennett, Woman's World Fair, Chicago; Mr. Walter Dubois Brookings, U. S. Chamber of Commerce; Dr. Alice M. Baldwin, dean, Duke University; Dr. Julius I. Foust, president, North Carolina College for Women; Mr. A. Lincoln Filene, Boston, Mass.; Dr. Lillian M. Gilbreth, Montclair, N. J.; Professor Harry D. Kitson, Columbia University; Dr. C. R. Mann, American Council on Education; Mrs. William Brown Meloney, New York *Herald Tribune;* Professor Howard Odum, University of North Carolina; Dr. Iva L. Peters, dean and director of personnel, Syracuse University.

Ex-officio members of the board are the following officers of the American Association of University Women: President Mary E. Woolley, *president;* Mrs. A. Ross Hill, *treasurer;* President Ada Comstock, *chairman* Educational Policies Committee.

NEW DORMITORIES FOR THE UNIVERSITY OF CHICAGO

Acting President Frederic Woodward, of the University of Chicago, announces the university's program for the construction of residence halls to cost five million dollars. Incidentally, he said that the announcement should put an end to the rumor, utterly without foundation, that the undergraduate colleges are to be abolished.

Construction of dormitories for about 400 men and 380 women, at a cost of about three million dollars, will be begun as early in the spring as possible. It is probable that most, if not all, the units will be erected south of the Midway on ground already owned by the university. The Board of Trustees is prepared to build additional units, but definite authorization of further construction has not yet been given.

The financing of the plan was made possible by the generous cooperation of Mr. Julius Rosenwald with the Board of Trustees of the university. Mr. Rosenwald is a member of the board. The university had in hand funds which are available for investment in dormitories, and Mr. Rosenwald, by agreeing to contribute up to forty per cent. of the construction costs, has made feasible the comprehensive plans of the board.

Acting President Woodward, in making the announcement, called attention to the fact that the present dormitories, north of the Midway, house about 320 men and 290 women, so that when the units now authorized are complete approximately 1,400 students will be provided for. In the near future the total may be raised to 2,000. Although there will undoubtedly be some overlapping, the plan contemplates the housing of graduate students, so far as may be practicable, on the north side of the Midway, and of undergraduates on the south side.

"The implications of this program of dormitory construction and its meaning to the future of the University of Chicago are far-reaching, and will be gratifying to the alumni and friends of the university," said Mr. Woodward. "At present, only a small minority of our students live in university dormitories. Many live at home, a considerable number of men live in fraternity houses, but too many of our students are widely scattered over the Hyde Park and Woodlawn districts. Though the university, through its housing bureau, has tried to secure at reasonable rents comfortable quarters for all, this has year by year become more difficult. The new dormitories will not only in large measure solve the housing problem, but will make it possible to provide for a large proportion of the student body, those stimulating associations and wholesome influences outside the class-room which are essential to a well-rounded educational program."

One of the important features of the dormitory project will be ample provision for recreation grounds for intramural sports immediately adjacent to the new halls. The halls will be of the entry type, each entry serving a group of perhaps 35 or 40 students, and will be arranged in quadrangles. Plans are now being considered and it is expected that a design will soon be accepted.

A PROPOSED SCHOOL OF FOREIGN SERVICE

THE creation of a foreign service school, modeled somewhat after West Point and Annapolis, was recommended in a bill introduced in the Senate on December 14 by Senator Thomas, of Oklahoma, who favors dividing the course of instruction into two branches, one to prepare applicants for the consular service, the other for the diplomatic service.

He would establish a "board of foreign affairs" in the State Department to supervise the school and advise with the President and Secretary of State regarding foreign relations. The board would collect information, and "if not incompatible with the public interest," report to the Congress such information about foreign relations as it considers necessary.

The board would include in its membership the Secretary of State, the Under Secretary of State, the Solicitor of the State Department, the Secretary of Commerce, the Director of the Bureau of Foreign and Domestic Commerce and the chairman and ranking minority members of the Senate Foreign Relations and House Foreign Affairs Committees. It would have power to employ and fix the salaries and number of professors and instructors in the foreign service school and prescribe the course of instruction. Each member of the Congress would have the power to name one person to the school. Applicants must be between seventeen and thirty-one years of age and pass physical and mental examinations.

Senator Thomas said:

> The suggested personnel of this board is intended to afford the President and Secretary of State the best assistance and cooperation in formulating and carrying on our foreign relations activities.
>
> The great powers with whom we are forced to deal have rulers with life-time or long tenure of office and, in addition, have foreign offices made up of men especially trained and of long experience. In our government the President and Secretary of State change or may change every four years.
>
> The bill is intended to create a permanent and efficient board of foreign affairs so that all administrations, new and otherwise, may have the best possible information and advice in formulating and putting into force the policies of our government. The continued progress of this country depends on peaceful relations with the world. Creation of the school and board are steps toward that end.

THE UNITED STATES MILITARY ACADEMY

CONSTRUCTION involving more than $4,000,000 in appropriations for the United States Military Academy at West Point was forecast by a committee of Congress that visited the academy on December 8. The committee completed an investigation of buildings, curriculum and general conditions of the academy.

According to a statement in the New York *Evening Post,* erection of cadet barracks costing nearly $1,000,000 will soon be started. Enlargement of the gymnasium, doubling its capacity and costing $500,000, will be approved. Officers' apartments will cost $600,000 and enlisted men's quarters will run to another $500,000.

Announcement was made by the committee that a new set of buildings, including a post exchange to house all warehouse commissaries, agencies and concessions under direction of the post exchange, will be erected. The new World War Memorial Building, estimated at $2,000,000, was not mentioned.

This is the first time in six years that the Board of Visitors has actually visited West Point, due to the restraining effect of the old law which forbade committees being appointed to come here except while the Congress was in session. The committee consisted of Congressmen Morin, Pennsylvania; Wainwright, New York; Hughes, West Virginia; Fisher, Tennessee; Chapman, Kentucky, and Hoffman, New Jersey.

A building program covering twelve years of constant construction was outlined by members of the visiting body. Congressman Morin said that the buildings at West Point would then be among the finest in the country and added that money already had been authorized to raze the old cadet mess hall, on the site of which new cadet barracks will be built. The work, he said, probably would begin next July. Building of officers' quarters has been begun and the money will be forthcoming to complete this work without delay.

Representative Wainwright spoke of the need of new quarters for enlisted men and their families. Mr. Wainwright stressed the conditions under which the enlisted personnel of the academy now live and added that though they should be a model for the rest of the army they were undoubtedly the worst in the country at present. Mr. Wainwright scored the attitude of ignoring the enlisted men at West Point, who, he said, were the means of helping to train the future officers of the army.

The committee investigated the matter of favoritism in entrance of cadets to West Point, such as might be employed in gaining entrance for certain football players or political friends. They found that no favoritism existed under the West Point system.

SCHOOL BUILDINGS FOR NEW YORK CITY

THE Board of Education of New York City on December 12 adopted a building program for 1929 which will cost $57,224,000 and will provide for fifty-three new school buildings and additions to twenty-one old structures. This is an increase of $15,557,000 over the amount spent last year, which was $41,445,000.

The 1929 program calls for one addition only to a school in Manhattan, to enlarge the building of P. S. 43, at 509 West 129th Street. The largest number of new buildings and additions will go to Queens, with twenty-two scheduled, while Brooklyn will get sixteen, the Bronx thirteen and Richmond three.

The total number of new elementary schools or additions will be fifty-five, at a cost of $26,450,000. There will be thirteen new high and vocational schools and additions to old buildings costing $26,574,000. The rest will be devoted to the improvement of athletic fields, $1,500,000; awards for sites, $2,000,000, and $700,000 for salaries of draftsmen and assistants in the bureau of buildings.

The most costly single building will be the new Brooklyn Technical High School, which it is estimated will cost $5,900,000. Other new high schools planned are for Ridgewood, Gravesend Avenue section of Brooklyn, South Jamaica, and Walton, in the Bronx. There will

TABLE I

High Schools	
Brooklyn—Brooklyn Technical	$5,900,000
Bronx—Morris (addition)	900,000
Brooklyn—Manual Training (addition)	200,000
Queens—Ridgewood	2,000,000
Brooklyn—Gravesend Avenue	2,400,000
Queens—South Jamaica	2,400,000
Richmond—Curtis (girls' gym)	200,000
Brooklyn—Erasmus Hall (elevator)	12,000
Brooklyn—Bushwick (elevator)	12,000
Brooklyn—Bay Ridge (addition)	300,000
Bronx—Walton	2,000,000
Total for high schools	$16,324,000
Vocational and Continuation Schools	
Bronx—Girls' Vocational	$1,500,000
Bronx—Boys' Vocational	1,125,000
Brooklyn—Boys' Vocational	1,125,000
Brooklyn—Williamsburg Continuation	1,125,000
Richmond—Staten Island Continuation and Vocational	1,125,000
Queens—Jamaica Training	2,000,000
Queens—Jamaica Continuation	1,125,000
Bronx—Bronx Continuation	1,125,000
Total	$10,250,000

be three new continuation schools in the Bronx, two in Brooklyn, two in Queens and one in Richmond.

William J. Webber, chairman of the building committee of the board, said in presenting the report that when all these structures were completed it was hoped that the problem of part time would be wiped out at last.

The schedule for new buildings for high schools and vocational schools and the estimated cost in each case will be found in Table I.

Since this budget was adopted two more buildings, estimated to cost $1,185,000, have been added to the program. This brings the total estimated cost for next year up to $58,409,000.

EDUCATIONAL NOTES AND NEWS

THE annual dinner of the New York Alumni Association of Union College was held in the Hotel Astor on December 13 in honor of Dr. Charles Alexander Richmond, who is retiring after twenty years as president. Dr. James R. Angell, president of Yale University, was one of the speakers.

A MEMORIAL tablet was unveiled on November 27 at the Carnegie Institute of Technology, Pittsburgh, Pennsylvania, of Arthur Arton Hamerschlag, first president (1903 to 1922) of the institute. Dr. Frederick P. Keppel, president of the Carnegie Foundation, made the address. The memorial, designed by a former instructor of sculpture, Berthold Nebel, has been placed in the corridor of the Administration Hall.

As has already been reported, Dr. Allen E. Miller, of the editorial division of the U. S. Bureau of Education, has been retired from active service, having reached the age of seventy years. Dr. Miller was with the bureau for forty-one years. The *School Board Journal* calls attention to the fact that Dr. Miller was one of four men who entered the service of the bureau at the same time in 1887, among these L. A. Kalbach, chief clerk and present acting commissioner, James C. Boykin, chief of the editorial division, and Henry R. Evans, assistant to Mr. Boykin. These men were appointed to the bureau during the incumbency of Mr. Nathaniel H. R. Dawson and have been in the service of the bureau during the terms of William T. Harris, Elmer E. Brown, P. P. Claxton, and John J. Tigert.

ATANASIO MONTOYA, of Albuquerque, has been elected state superintendent of education of New Mexico.

ACCORDING to a press report Ira Insco Cammack, for fifteen years superintendent of schools in Kansas City, has retired. Mr. Cammack plans to make his home in California.

R. L. COOLEY, of Milwaukee, was elected president of the American Vocational Education Association at the close of the recent annual meeting in Philadelphia. The convention in 1929 will be in New Orleans.

PROFESSOR WILLIAM A. HEIDEL, professor of Greek at Wesleyan University, has been named research associate of the American Council of Learned Societies to enable him to complete and publish the results of studies of early Greek thought and the bearing of this philosophy upon modern ideas. The appointment carries an appropriation from the Carnegie Corporation of New York and will also be aided by the Carnegie Institution of Washington. The work will require ten years.

ULRICH B. PHILLIPS, professor of American history at the University of Michigan, has been awarded the prize of $2,500, in addition to book royalties, for the best unpublished work on American history, offered by Little, Brown and Company. The judges in this contest, which closed on October 1, were James Truslow Adams, of Brooklyn, author of "The Founding of New England"; Worthington C. Ford, of Boston, editor of the Massachusetts Historical Society, and Allan Nevins, professor of history at Columbia University.

PROFESSOR FLORIAN CAJORI, of the department of mathematics of the University of California, has been elected one of a committee of eleven scholars representing the world as an International Commission on the History of

Science. The commission was formed at a congress recently held at Oslo, Norway. Six of the leading nations of the world are represented on the commission: France, England, Germany, Austria, Italy and the United States. The chairman is Professor A. Mieli, of Paris.

A Boston Society of Friends of the Hebrew University in Palestine has been formed, with Dr. Milton J. Rosenau, professor of preventive medicine and hygiene at Harvard Medical School, as chairman. Members of the committee include Professor Kirsoop Lake, Professor Nathan Isaacs, Professor David G. Lyon and Professor George F. Moore, also of Harvard University.

Dean Leroy Allen, of Southwestern College, Kansas, has been elected a member of the National Institute of Social Science in recognition of his contribution to the field of social science in founding Pi Gamma Mu and the magazine *Social Science*.

Professor William J. Cunningham, of Harvard University, succeeds C. H. Emery, of the American Express Company, as president of the Traffic Club of New England.

Professor H. T. Manuel, of the department of educational psychology in the University of Texas, is in charge of research on the education of Mexican children, the cost of which is defrayed by the Laura Spelman Rockefeller Fund.

Professor A. D. Lindsay, of Baliol College, Oxford, is reported to be visiting the United States to confer with Harvard officials on the new "college" idea which Harvard is now entertaining in connection with the anonymous gift of $3,000,000.

George Stuart Gordon, professor of English literature at the University of Oxford, has been elected president of St. Mary Magdalen College.

Edwin A. Esper, associate professor of psychology at the University of Washington, has been invited by Yale University to deliver a series of lectures at the language institute to be held there next summer. His topic will be "The Psychology of Language."

Dr. Walter B. Ford, professor of mathematics at the University of Michigan, has been granted leave of absence for the current academic year and is traveling in Europe as a representative of the Carnegie Endowment for International Peace. He will lecture at the Universities of Leiden and Utrecht, the University of Brussels, the Universities of Lille and Grenoble, and the University of Pisa.

Dr. Ernest M. Patterson, professor of economics at the Wharton School, University of Pennsylvania, has been granted a leave of absence for the second half of the year 1928–29. During that time he will lecture on international economics at the Institut Universitaire des Hautes Etudes Internationales, Geneva, Switzerland.

Dr. Howard H. Preston, professor of business administration at the University of Washington, has been granted a leave of absence for 1928–29 and is teaching at Dartmouth College. Dr. Preston taught during the summer session at the University of Michigan.

Professor Harry E. Miller, of Brown University, will offer a series of lectures on current problems in finance at Clark University under the auspices of the Carroll D. Wright fund established in honor of the first president of Clark College.

Dr. Alfred Atkinson, after a year of research work and travel, has resumed his work as president of Montana State College, with which he has been connected for the past twenty-one years.

Dr. H. M. Woodward, professor of philosophy of education at Brigham Young University, is on leave of absence for the year 1928–29. He is spending the year on a trip around the world as a member of the faculty of the Floating University.

Professor John O. Creager, now dean of the school of education of the University of Arkansas, will be in charge of a program in college education dealing with the problems of administration and teaching in colleges in the summer school of New York University.

Herbert Spencer, associate principal of the Frick Training School in Pittsburgh and since 1922 a part-time member of the staff of the University of Pittsburgh in charge of practice teaching in vocational education, has been appointed assistant professor of secondary education and director of teacher training in secondary education at the university.

CHARLES A. WALKER, superintendent of the schools of Chelmsford, Massachusetts, was recently elected superintendent of the Maynard schools.

THE *School Board Journal* reports that A. M. Cartright, of Middletown, New York, enjoys the distinction of succeeding his father as superintendent of schools of the third district of Orange County, New York. His father, the late Sanford A. Cartright, had served as superintendent for seventeen years.

WILSON HAWKINS, for many years superintendent of the schools of Canton, Ohio, has presented his resignation.

FLOYD R. MECHEM, professor of law at the University of Chicago since 1903, an international authority on the law of agency, sales and public officers, died on December 12 following a brief illness, at the age of seventy years. Professor Mechem came to the University of Chicago Law School the year following its organization from the University of Michigan, where he had been Tappan professor of law for eleven years.

MISS MARY GRACE CALDWELL, for thirty years head of the Latin department of Dana Hall School, Wellesley, has died.

AS a memorial to the late Frank Wagnalls, of the Funk and Wagnalls Publishing Company, his daughter, Mrs. Mabel Wagnalls Jones, of Northport, Long Island, has given $40,000 toward the erection of a $100,000 high school at Lithopolis, Ohio, where Mr. Wagnalls was born.

MR. SAINSBURY, of the National Union of Teachers in England and delegate of the World Federation, expects to spend considerable time in Geneva supervising the many necessary steps in the organization of the Congress, which will be held from July 25 to August 4. An exposition of teaching material, books, etc., will be opened at the same time, but will doubtless last till the end of September. The Congress at Geneva will be immediately followed by that of the International League for New Education at Copenhagen.

THE British Conference of Educational Associations will be held during the early days of January, 1929, at University College, London. The North of England Education Conference will be held at Newcastle-upon-Tyne, on January 3, 4 and 5.

THE Progressive Education Association will hold a regional conference in Richmond, Virginia, January 17, 18 and 19. A program of practical talks has been prepared on the principles of progressive education, and various leaders in the South will report on the work done there. January 19 will be devoted to an excursion to Jamestown, Yorktown and Williamsburg, under the auspices of the College of William and Mary.

AN Institute of International Relations for the promotion of better world relations met at Riverside Mission Inn and the University of Southern California from December 9 to 14. The program included the names of Frederick M. Davenport, United States Congressman from the state of New York and professor of law and politics at Hamilton College; A. H. Robertson, Rear Admiral, U. S. Navy, Commandant Eleventh Naval District; Contessa Maria A. Loschi, of Rome, Italy; Colonel Jason Joy, director of industrial relations, Association of Motion Picture Producers, Hollywood; Karl C. Leebrick, professor of international relations, Syracuse University; Roy Hidenichi Akagi, general secretary of the Japanese Students' Christian Association in North America; Chester H. Rowell, editor and publicist; Charles K. Edmunds, president of Pomona College; Thomas J. Orbinson, M.D., former chief of the Latvian Section of the Baltic Mission of the American Relief Administration; Tully C. Knoles, president of the College of the Pacific; Mrs. Thomas Winter, past president of the Federation of Women's Clubs, and Allen Blaisdell, director of the International House, University of California. Included in the program was a celebration of the signing of the pact of Paris, and the formal opening of the Los Angeles University of International Relations, offering specialized training in consular, diplomatic and foreign service.

CHILD Labor Day will be observed on January 26, 27 and 28 in Sunday schools, churches, schools and clubs. The National Child Labor Committee looks to these groups to serve as interpreters of its findings to an ever-increasing circle of the nation's citizens. When public opinion demands the abolition of child labor, then and only then will the United States slough off this crime against her children. This year the legislatures of forty-three states meet, giving to the people in these states another chance to bring their child labor laws up to standard. The National Child Labor Committee, 215 Fourth Avenue, New York City, will send free of charge to any interested individual or group an analysis of the law of his state, together with program, leaflets, posters and other material to be used in the observance of Child Labor Day.

A GIFT of $500,000 has been made to Temple University by Cyrus H. K. Curtis, the publisher. The money will be applied toward erection of the third or twenty-three-story skyscraper unit in the "Greater Temple" building project now under way.

A GIFT of $250,000 toward the endowment fund of $2,000,000 from Edward Harkness, of New York City, to the Albany Medical College for advancement of its graduate work has been announced by the medical department of Union University. Income from the endowment fund will help to support courses designed to give village and county physicians opportunities for continued progress. Half the fund is needed adequately to endow the training of good general practitioners.

Two unconditional gifts, amounting to $200,000, were recently received by the semi-centennial committee of the University of Southern California from Edward L. Doheny, Jr. Mr. Doheny is an alumnus of the university of the class of 1916 and was the first president of the Greater Alumni Association.

ARRANGEMENTS have been completed with the General Education Board whereby the department of zoology at the University of Texas will have $135,000 to be used in the development of graduate instruction and research during the next eight years. Approximately one half of this sum will be given by the General Education Board; the rest will be raised by the university. The zoological staff plans to use a portion of this fund for technical assistance and for fellowships.

RADCLIFFE COLLEGE receives $50,000 by the will of the late Miss Alice Longfellow. Other bequests are made as follows: $1,000 to the Holy Ghost Hospital, Cambridge; $2,000 to the Judge Baker Foundation; $2,000, Tuskegee Institute; $4,000, Hampton Normal and Agricultural College; $5,000, Boston Museum of Fine Arts; $15,000, Harvard University, as a memorial to her father for the purchase of foreign literature; $25,000 in trust for the care, treatment and training of crippled persons, and $10,000 for the care of crippled persons in Massachusetts.

PERMISSION to establish a chapter of Phi Beta Kappa was recently granted to the State College of Washington. A preliminary organization has been effected and the preparation of a constitution and by-laws is under way. This chapter is one of the first to be established in a land grant college.

MORRIS HARVEY COLLEGE, Barboursville, West Virginia, has opened a building program which is designed to remake in large measure the campus when completed, some time between 1935–38. Early American Colonial architecture is being employed. McDonald Hall, the gift of Bruce McDonald, of Logan, West Virginia, was opened for occupancy by men at the beginning of the fall quarter. The building is fireproof and cost about $100,000. Rosa Harvey Hall, for women, is expected to be opened about January 1, and will cost $150,000. A college cafeteria will be on the ground floor. It commemorates the memory of the wife of Morris Harvey, donor of the school, funds from whose estate have been used for its erection. It replaces a frame building by the same name, which has been in use more than twenty-five years. Immediately upon completion of this building it is planned to start work on the Hallanan Building, which is to be the gift of Walter S. Hallanan, an alumnus of the school. This structure will house the administrative offices of the school, special class rooms and the library of the department of Bible and religious education. Other buildings already designed include a new administration building, science hall, library, music building and chapel. Only one of the buildings now on the campus will not be replaced by this program, this being the present administration building.

COOPERATION of the Commonwealth Fund of New York and the University of Kansas extension division in providing a cooperative school health service is announced by H. G. Ingham, director of university extension. Miss Maud A. Brown, with seven years' experience in foundation work, is the consultant in charge. She recently completed a five-year program for the Commonwealth fund in North Dakota and when commissioned to carry on a school health program selected Kansas because of the already developed "public health consciousness" and the facilities offered through the extension division of the university. The service will include personal conferences attended by Miss Brown and her assistants in planning and supervising classroom health work, and the use of a large collection of teaching material, including films, slides, models, charts and books of reference. It is planned to establish contacts in not more than a dozen communities of Kansas, for the first year, and it is desired that these contacts represent various types of schools, from the one-room rural school, to the ward school of the city of the first class. Applications for the service will be filed soon after the first of the year, and the points to be served will be selected in April or May. The extension division of the university now has six bureaus in its community service program, including the bureau of general information, of visual instruction, of lectures and lecture courses, of school service and research, and the municipal reference bureau.

IN an effort to end the social discrimination charged against Princeton University's system of upper class clubs, which has been in vogue since 1879, a recommendation has just been made by the undergraduate council that a university club be established. This would provide a center for the 150 or more upper classmen, who, for social or financial reasons, are not included in the membership of any of the 18 regular clubs. Each year about 79 per cent. of the members of the upper classes are elected to membership in these clubs, leaving from 150 to 200 students unaffiliated.

To meet a demand for graduates equipped for the teaching of more than one subject, the vocational education department of Iowa State College, which has heretofore offered courses only in agricultural education and in agricultural and manual training, has arranged a course in agriculture and science. This will include a major in agriculture and two minors selected from the fields of bacteriology, biological science, botany, economic science, English, geology, economic history, journalism, manual arts, mathematics, physical education, physics, sociological science and zoology. One of the minors may also be taken in the departments of animal husbandry, farm crops and soils, horticulture or dairy industry. The course is expected to provide for men desiring to work in rural consolidated schools or in other schools attended by relatively large numbers of rural pupils.

SPECIAL CORRESPONDENCE

A RUSSIAN EXPERIMENT IN CRIMINOLOGY

THE problem of dealing with the youthful criminal to-day looms large in every country and is dealt with according to various theories of criminology. Accepting the axiom that criminal tendencies need correction rather than punishment Soviet Russia has established communities called "Labor Communes" for young criminals between the ages of sixteen and twenty-two years. The pioneer group of this nature, the Labor Commune of the G. P. U., is located a short distance from Moscow. The letters G. P. U. stand for a long Russian name, which freely translated means Government Political Society, or perhaps the word police should be substituted for political. It is really neither a police nor a political organization, but a combination of both, if such a thing is possible. It is the successor of the famous or rather notorious "tcheka," that infamous secret police department which terrorized the people during the tzars' régime. The title "Labor Commune" describes the institution admirably because the one fundamental requirement is that every member must work.

The revolution and later the dreadful famine left in Russia great hordes of homeless children. The newspapers have published from time to time pictures of the "wild boys of Moscow," the Bezprizorni. Some of these children were really victims of the revolution, others were only incorrigible children who ran away from home to live with the "strays." Regardless of where they started, it is easy to see how a large number of youthful criminals would develop among this group. The labor commune was not organized to care for the so-called "strays" but for actually convicted criminals. The work was started in 1924 by Derjinsky, of the tcheka, as an experiment, when a number of boys, all under eighteen years old, were taken from various prisons to become members of the camp. To-day the group numbers 170 boys and 15 girls and whether the experiment has justified itself must be decided by future results.

There is nothing in the appearance of the commune to indicate that it is a penal institution. The casual visitor could spend hours wandering about the grounds, in and out of the buildings, and leave without knowing that he had seen a criminal camp. There are no bars or guards and there is no attempt made to keep the members within the bounds. Quite the contrary, if a boy runs away, no effort is made to find him and have him readmitted. It is difficult for the average person to accept the line of reasoning employed by the directors concerning the problem of escape. The argument used is as follows: It is not anti-social to allow these criminals to escape and be at large in the community, because they are not skilled workers and, being unable to earn a living, they must return to their life of crime, where they will eventually be caught again. Since the aim of the experiment is to redirect talent and energy along useful channels, there is no need felt for confinement.

In view of the fact that this is a corrective rather than a penal institution, it is conducted in the belief that there must be freedom for young people. This policy of freedom is adhered to consistently. When the working week is over at noon on Saturday each boy's time is his own until Monday morning. He does not even have to stay on the grounds of the camp, but may go to the city if he wishes. The boys who go away for the week-end are expected to return on Sunday night. In spite of the ease with which any one can escape, only four boys ran away last year. The spring of the year is the season when these roving spirits answer the call of the road, and in some cases the first cold days of fall see them back asking for readmission. The decision in regard to these readmissions rests with the members of the camp, as a vote upon the question is taken at the regular weekly assembly.

The members of the commune, all convicted criminals between the ages of sixteen and twenty-two years, are for the most part children of workers, and represent every type of crime. It could not be definitely determined whether there were any murderers among them. They are selected by a committee on membership, consisting of the boys themselves, from three groups: first, from those recommended by the members of the commune; second, from those who apply for admission when they are convicted and sent to prison; and third, from those recommended by the administrations of regular prisons. The admission of new applicants must be passed upon by a committee consisting of and elected by the boys themselves. A boy's physical condition plays no part in his admission; if medical care is required, it is given. The first three months serve as a probation period, and although the same freedom is allowed, permission to leave the ground must be obtained during this period.

The one requirement which must be observed by every member is that he must work and learn a trade. For this purpose there are four factories in the camp. These represent four industries, shoe manufacturing, metal work, wood work and knitting. They manufacture sports goods, sport shoes, skates, sleds and sweaters. The regulation eight-hour day is enforced and the boys receive union wages which average from 60 to 120 rubles a month. From these each boy must pay his living expenses, about 35 rubles a month. When the camp was started, true to communistic principles all expenses were paid out of a common fund, all profits went into this, and each boy received an allowance. This was not successful and it was found advisable to go back to the old system of paying regular wages and allowing every one to keep his own extra savings. More spending money, better clothes, etc., have proven a great stimulus for better work. Since the factories need more workers than the commune can house, free workers from the neighborhood are employed. No distinction is made between the free workers and the inmates in regard to wages, amount of work or privileges granted.

After the working day is over the time is spent in cultural pursuits. Although a regular school session is maintained during the winter months, it is not compulsory except for the illiterate, who must attend until they can read and write. The boys are not anxious to go to school but prefer the dramatic clubs, the radio clubs and the movies which are shown three times a week. Just as in every institution in Russia, political training plays an important part in the general plan of the commune and a circle of young communists has been organized. Here the doctrines of communism are taught and from these circles members of the party are recruited. This privilege is still allowed the boys, although they may not serve in the Red Army.

The staff in charge of the commune functions in an advisory capacity only. The boys are the owners and the managers of the camp, and the members of the staff are expected to be guides and advisers, not guards. The entire student body participates in the weekly meetings to govern the commune. At these meetings committees are elected to take charge of such matters as household, welfare, amusements, punishments and admissions. The teachers have no vote but are always ready to guide with mature advice, and there has been established among the boys a feeling of confidence in this advice.

The committee on punishments holds the most important place in the scheme of self-government. The reason for this is not difficult to see when it is understood that even here the director has no power and can mete out no punishment for any infringement of the rules. The chief evils with which the committee on punishments has to cope are intoxication and the use of cocaine. Unfortunately, many boys come to the commune confirmed drug addicts and a constant watch must be kept against this evil. Public opinion in the commune has abolished the use of drugs and now if a new member takes drugs he is looked upon with such contempt by his fellows that he soon discontinues his vicious habit. Intoxication has been more difficult to combat, as drinking intoxicating liquor has always been a part of Russian life. It is forbidden to bring intoxicants into the commune, but when the boys go to Moscow over Saturday and Sunday they can not be so easily controlled. It is the duty of every member of the commune to report a fellow member seen drunk in the city. These offenders are dealt with according to their past records; a first offender will fare better than one who regularly appears before the committee. The most effective punishment is a fine, which sometimes is as high as 50 rubles. For minor offenses the loss of privileges suffices as punishment.

The length of term depends upon the sentence received upon conviction. When the term expires the boys are discharged. Last year forty boys received their liberty; however in many cases discharged members have applied for readmission. These boys may leave at any time they wish. As the housing conditions in Moscow made it difficult to return to the city, some of the discharged boys now live in the adjoining village and work in the commune factories.

Last year, for the first time, fifteen girls were admitted. More dormitories are being built in order to increase the membership of both boys and girls. In spite of adverse predictions, the work with girls has so far proven successful. In the camp two of the boys are married to two of the girls.

The government is trying to extend this work and similar communes have been started at Ovel, Rostov and several other cities. It is not unusual for reliable members from the Moscow center to be sent to other places to assist in the establishment of new and similar communes.

EMILY A. STEIN

DISCUSSION

WHAT IS INTELLIGENCE?

DURING the last two decades a great many definitions of intelligence have been attempted, but there is more or less conflict between them, and none seems entirely satisfactory. Otis[1] refers to intelligence as "brightness," but McCall[2] speaks of "brightness" in certain subjects. It seems obvious that brightness in a particular subject might be increased by education, but presumably education does not increase intelligence. The "brightness" conception is inconsistent with the generally accepted theory that intelligence is inherited, and furthermore an explanation or definition of one trait given in terms of another is usually inadequate.

According to Stern,[3] "Intelligence is a general capacity of an individual consciously to adjust his thinking to new requirements." He also speaks of it as the ability to adjust to new situations. But why only to new requirements or new situations? It seems that the ability to meet successfully recurrent old situations would also to a great extent involve the matter of intelligence. The changing seasons, annual taxes, periodical political campaigns, and the like, would serve as examples. However, it is very likely that no one ever encountered an entirely new or an entirely old situation. Every situation is a mixture of both the old and the new. Furthermore, if the ability to meet new situations is the sole criterion for determining intelligence some of the lower animals are superior to man. Young animals that hibernate or migrate at the approach of winter may be said to meet new situations even more successfully than man, in some respects at least. However, we are not willing to admit that they are more intelligent than man.

Colvin says, "An individual possesses intelligence in so far as he can learn to adjust himself to his environment." This conception is also inadequate, for again referring to the lower animals many of them are perhaps better adapted to their environment than man. Besides, psychiatrists have reported instances of children that were poorly adjusted because of superior intelligence. Ideals and attitudes also would interfere in many cases. Imagine Lincoln adjusting himself to the environment of a group of opium smugglers! Men like Longfellow and Shakespeare probably never could have successfully adjusted themselves to the environment of a meat-packing house.

To attempt to define intelligence as the ability to meet new situations successfully or to adjust to one's environment seems rather superficial and short-sighted. In terms of their own interests, the martyrs of old failed in the matter of adjustment to environment. With the idea of meeting new situations and adjusting to environment, what may be said of the intelligence of Socrates, of Columbus in his later days and of Galileo? From a personal standpoint does a far-seeing statesman who sacrifices his own comfort, his own financial interests and his own social or political welfare for the good of his country meet situations successfully? What may be said of the great producers of music, art and literature? Some failed utterly to adjust. Some adjusted to the present, but others did more than that: they went far beyond the present and produced for generations to come.

Thorndike maintains that there are different types of intelligence or mental ability: social intelligence, or the ability to get along well with people; mechanical intelligence; and the ability to think in terms of abstract ideas or symbols. Such a classification has its merits, but it is quite obvious that there is much overlapping between these types.

[1] A. S. Otis, "Statistical Method in Educational Measurement," Chapter 13. World Book Company, 1925.

[2] William A. McCall, "Tables for the TGBF Scale System for all Standard Tests and Teachers' Examinations." Bureau of Publications, Teachers College, Columbia University, 1925.

[3] W. Stern, "The Psychological Methods of Testing Intelligence." Warwick and York, Baltimore.

Social affairs of various kinds relate themselves to the mechanical, and certainly to the abstract as well. As a matter of fact, it is in our social life that abstract ideas function in greatest abundance and to the greatest extent. Also, the mechanical has its social aspects, and furthermore has associated with it many abstract ideas, such as smoothness, friction, power, velocity, revolutions, leverage, temperature, compactness, durability and so on. Besides, some individuals succeed in dealing with mathematical symbols, some with word or language symbols, and some succeed much better in one language than in another.

Spearman[4] has advanced the two-factor theory of intelligence: general and specific. He maintains that all intellectual activity depends upon the same general fund of mental energy, and that ability in a particular kind of performance depends upon specific capacity for that performance. His idea of a "fund of mental energy" is by no means clear, and neither is the matter of "specific capacity," for he seems to use "ability" and "capacity" synonymously, when capacity should be considered only as potential ability. It may be correct to use intellect, intelligence and capacity in somewhat the same sense, but ability, like knowledge and skill, depends upon experience and training. Specific ability would, therefore, depend upon more or less specific training.

Freeman[5] refers to intelligence as a composite of mental abilities. He says, "Our tests are most successful as measures of the composite of mental abilities which is sometimes called intelligence." Such mental abilities would be due to training, and the response to training depends upon mental capacity. Moreover, intelligence is not a composite, but is that which makes a more or less composite response possible.

Henmon[6] says that intelligence is intellect plus knowledge. If this is true, intelligence can be improved. He apparently fails to make a distinction between intellect and capacity and between intelligence and ability.

[4] C. Spearman, "The Theory of Two Factors," *Psy. Review*, 21: 101–115. 1914.

[5] Frank N. Freeman, "Mental Tests," p. 5. Houghton Mifflin Company, 1926.

[6] Henmon, *Journal of Educational Psychology*, 1921.

Two very good definitions of intelligence have been given by Peterson[7] and Burt,[8] respectively. (1) "Intelligence seems to be a biological mechanism by which the effects of a complexity of stimuli are brought together and given a somewhat unified effect in behavior." (2) "Higher intelligence seems to mean high capacity for continually systematizing mental behavior by forming new psycho-physical coordinations, older coordinations being retained, so that newer coordinations bring with them increased complexity and incessant change."

Peterson refers to biological mechanisms and complexity. Burt refers to capacity, complexity and coordination. It seems that in these concepts lies the true definition of intelligence, and with these in mind the author offers the following definition. Intelligence is the ability to see things in their various relationships, to think complexly and coordinately in such a way as to produce a composite, or more or less unified reaction. It has its basis in neural capacity and may be defined as the coordinate functioning of related reaction groups. The degree or amount of one's intelligence is determined by his native capacity or neural complexity. It is inseparable from depth or breadth of comprehension, and it was for the purpose of determining to what depth or degree of complexity an individual was able to think that the first and presumably all the subsequent mental tests were devised.

ROBERT P. CARROLL
TEACHERS COLLEGE,
SYRACUSE UNIVERSITY

"ME" OR "I"

"No, that requisition does not come to I," was actually said to me last Thursday morning at ten thirty by an assistant dean in a college office where there seems to be a great effort made to do things nicely. The person who said it had been in college for four years, and, what is more, had majored in English, which only goes to show that a study of the language had not brought perfection or cleared up a powerful early training.

[7] Peterson, *Journal of Educational Psychology*, 22: 195. 1921.

[8] C. Burt, "Experimental Tests of General Intelligence," *British Jr. of Psychology*, 2: 94–177. 1909–1910.

The evening of that same day an economics instructor came bounding up my front steps to say, "Won't you come for a ride with my wife and I?"

The trouble with these two educated people, I have been cogitating, is that they had too much pedantic education or too much of the little learning which is a dangerous thing. At any rate untrained folks would not have made the mistakes they did. I often wonder if the mistakes of the educated are not as great as those of others. These people in their young school days had so much emphasis put on the awkward forms of the pronouns that they have spoken ever since under the impression that "I" is more elegant than "me" and is to be used on careful occasions.

The cause is not strange; they had been corrected many times or had heard others corrected and the corrections had always been made when they said "me" when they should have said "I." To see the source of the trouble I went through some grade school grammars in which I found lesson after lesson, drill after drill on

It is I
It is he
It is she
It is they

and I did not find corresponding drills on pronouns after prepositions and verbs such as

Give it to me
Tell it to her
Tell it to Minerva and her
Please help them
Please help the workers and them

In the exercises in which the blanks are to be filled by "I" or "me," "he" or "him," "she" or "her," "they" or "them" the trick is to use the nominative case and to realize how wrong it is to use the accusative case. I am afraid it is almost time to write new grammars with the drills on the accusative case. That would bring us back to the position we should have been in without any drills at all.

The reason for the drills in the grammars is apparent: the writers of the books, not considering whether we need the expressions or should use them if we knew them, acquired some time ago the habit of putting the emphasis on the forms which often are not correctly used. That emphasis has become a distortion.

I grant that during a life there are a few times when we need to write "it is I, he, she, or they," but there are not many times when we need to say it. A few days ago when I telephoned to a twelve-year-old friend of mine to ask him to go on a picnic I said, "Is Jimmie Jackson there?" The answer came, "This is he." "The poor little fellow," I thought, "what a beginning for a picnic! Why didn't he say 'This is Jimmie' or almost anything else?" Some teacher spoiled him. I have noticed many times when particular people are talking that they have to go a long way around to be purely correct. In nearly every case I think there is a more natural and easy expression, and a more concrete and vivid one.

Therefore, I conclude that this hullabaloo about the correct pronouns has done more harm than good; not only has it made people self-conscious, but it has unnecessarily trained them in the way of awkwardness without even teaching them the fundamental grammatical principle which underlies the use of pronouns. No teaching at all would have kept them clearer of errors, and, if there must be teaching on the subject, I should say it might be a simple explanation with examples better balanced. Anyway "me" is all right, has its own place and is as good as "I" any day.

HELEN RAND
ENGLISH DEPARTMENT,
THE UNIVERSITY OF ILLINOIS

QUOTATIONS

A CHAPTER ON CHICAGO'S SCHOOL ADMINISTRATION

A NEW YORK professor found the school turmoil of Chicago of sufficient interest to prompt him to write a book about it. And then he found much to write. The story embodies about all the evils that could possibly creep into the government of a school system.

The troubles which may arise when a board of education becomes subservient to a mayor and a city council are graphically told, the battles which a school superintendent encounters when he strives to govern the schools and ignores the politicians are described, and the downfall of the schoolmaster stricken by the hand of gang rule is chronicled. The book tells too how the bane of race and religious prejudice may enter into the administrative labors of a school system.

The appearance of this somewhat remarkable book on school administration may lead to the *thought* that the Chicago school situation is but an index of what prevails in other American cities. The author, however, makes it clear that while "no community in the nation, large or small, escapes altogether the action of organized groups, such action seems to proceed more openly in Chicago than elsewhere."

The truth of the matter is that no American city has behind it a school administration history as vexatious and deplorable as that presented by Chicago. Certain weaknesses and minor irregularities may be found in every school system, but on the whole the average community in the United States has an honest and capable system of school administration.

It would be deplorable, indeed, if the Chicago situation were even approximately indicative of the evils that prevailed elsewhere. The turmoil which has existed more or less in the management of the Chicago school system for the past two decades stands singular and alone in the field of school administration.

The larger American cities are distinguished for the efficient and high-minded boards of education they maintain and the excellent educational forces they employ. Look for a moment at the great cities in the east, including New York, Boston, Springfield, Philadelphia, Baltimore and Pittsburgh. Come to the mid-west and examine the school systems of Detroit, Cleveland, Cincinnati and Dayton; turn to the far west and measure up the school interests of Denver, Oakland, San Francisco, Los Angeles, Seattle and Portland. The boards of education of these cities are composed of splendid citizens, the superintendent in every instance is an educational leader of unquestioned ability, the school machinery is of the most modern type, and the service rendered measures up with the best achievements of the day.

It is well to know how far a community may sink into a deplorable situation in the management of its schools, but let no one get the impression that because one city has been derelict all other cities are equally guilty. America's system of popular education is being directed by the best minds, who have a proper conception of the sacred task that is theirs. They are able, honest, and loyal in the performance of that task.—*School Board Journal.*

THE SCHOOLS AS AN INDEX OF PROSPERITY

MORE than 28,000,000 students are enrolled in the schools and colleges of the United States, according to the latest report of the Federal Bureau of Education. A figure so vast as this is likely to be dismissed without much consideration by the casual reader. The significance of the report is apparent only when it is reflected that, counting every man, woman and child in the nation, one in every four is receiving formal instruction of some kind.

The statistics of the bureau of education are for the year 1926. They show the enrolment thus divided among the various types of educational institutions:

ELEMENTARY SCHOOLS[1]	
Public	20,984,000
Private	2,143,000
SECONDARY SCHOOLS	
Public	3,786,000
Private	346,000
TEACHER-TRAINING SCHOOLS	
Public	252,000
Private	17,200
COLLEGES	
Public	280,000
Private	486,000

[1] Kindergartens included.

To instruct this multitude of students an army of 970,000 teachers is necessary. The cost for the entire enterprise is not given in the summaries of the report now available, but its magnitude may be judged from the fact that the maintenance of the public elementary and high schools alone was $2,026,308,000 for the year 1926.

More significant even than the total figures is the trend of high-school enrolment. This has doubled since 1920. In the cities, it is estimated, 70 per cent. of the children of high-school age are in attendance at such institutions; in the rural districts the proportion is but 25 per cent., while for the nation as a whole it is estimated at more than 50 per cent. In other words, the chances are more than even that a boy or girl between the ages of 15 and 18 is attending a school above the elementary grade. By contrast, the official report points out, the opportunities for a high-school education in 1900 were but one in seven for a youth of similar age.

There is, perhaps, no better index of the widespread prosperity in the nation than this increase in enrolment above the traditional grade school. The normal parent is always anxious to improve the opportunities of his children; when economic conditions permit him to do so he keeps them at school as long as they seem to benefit by the instruction—and often a great deal longer.—*The New York Sun.*

REPORTS

CONDITIONS AT BROWN UNIVERSITY[1]

THE scholars who have joined our faculty in the last few years are bringing many new suggestions as to methods of teaching, and we welcome experimentation. Smaller classes, closer personal contacts, laboratory methods, responsibility of the student for his own education—these are some of the things that we now especially emphasize. I have seen at a western university 1,500 students listening to a single lecturer, who of course did not know and did not care to know his auditors. But a teacher who is discussing some problem with 10 students in his office is pursuing a wholly different method with a wholly different result. We are realizing that the old custom of playing with "hours" and marks and grades and percentages is a childish game. Fifteen "semester hours" does not constitute a liberal education, and a student with the grade of *B* or *C* may possess such initiative and energy as to make him a far more valuable citizen than the student with a sponge-like mind who gains an *A*. We are seeking to allow greater self-direction to the individual student. Teaching is not telling; it is causing another to know. The chief duty of the student is not to recite, but to use, what he knows. Democracy in education does not mean the equal treatment of unequals, but the treatment of each separate student so as to enable him to attain the utmost development of his powers. Quantitative standards may defeat our object. Too much specification regarding majors and minors and grades may turn a registrar's office into an adding machine, or may force us to admit that a bachelor's degree is given to men not on the ground of alert and disciplined intelligence and wide horizon, but on the completion of 120 semester hours. Are we forgetting that the student is an integer, a personality, and focussing our attention on the course, the subject, the quiz, the regurgitation of facts?

Great changes are obvious in the daily life of our students on the campus and in the city. In recent years we have made definite provision for the better housing and more adequate direction of the so-called "student activities." These activities may be a mere drain on a student's time and strength, or they may be, when rightly developed, an admirable preparation for life. Since the opening of our new athletic field and the erection of our new gymnasium our student games and athletic sports are admirably provided for. But the other student activities, musical, dramatic, literary, social, fraternal, have outgrown all their accommodation and equipment. The excellent dramatic presentations of our students deserve and demand a "little theater." The students' dramatic society has turned its back on the paltry shows often to be found in the theaters of the city, and its list of recent offerings includes "Oedipus Rex," "Androcles and the Lion," "Measure for Measure," "Ghosts," "The Tempest," "Widowers' House," and several other classics, ancient and modern. Such a program deserves the encour-

[1] From the annual report of President W. H. P. Faunce.

agement which only a true theater, of modest size, could give. No other small building is now so deeply needed. Such a theater could be used also by the musical clubs and for intimate lectures by visiting scholars. The various student publications are usually characterized by good taste and dignity—in marked contrast to some of the gladly-forgotten publications of fifty years ago. But if we stigmatize as professional the student who receives money for playing baseball, what should be our attitude toward the students who receive compensation as editors of a college paper or publishers of a college "annual" or a college song-book?

One of the most important acts of the corporation during the year has been the appointment of a committee on survey of organization of the university. All the trustees and fellows feel the need of a fresh appraisal of the powers and duties of all the officers appointed by the corporation, in order to promote efficiency, avoid either interference or duplication, and determine what should be the functions of each officer and each office in years to come. The modern university has grown so rapidly as to make "ancient good uncouth." In some cases there is overlapping, waste effort, and needless routine. We who are on the inside of the university often fail to see our work in its true perspective and because a certain procedure was needed twenty years ago we may imagine that it is needed forever. The committee has engaged expert advice from sources entirely outside the university, that we may compare our procedure with that of other institutions and may decide what our history, our location, and our ideals demand in the years to come. Large results are expected from the survey of the committee, which is constituted as follows: Albert L. Scott, Clarence A. Barbour, Hermon C. Bumpus, Fred T. Field, Norman S. Tager, and R. G. D. Richardson.

The changes in modern knowledge are not yet adequately reflected in our venerable "departments" of study. The dividing lines between some departments have become almost invisible, yet still the old divisions continue, sometimes with little basis in reality. Artificial separation of departments may mean not only actual competition, but limited vision, divided effort, piecemeal progress. In what "department," for example, should we place the study of the "Emancipation Proclamation"—in history, or political science, or English, or psychology? Should a study of Milton's "Paradise Lost" be confined to the department of English, or must it be included in any study of English puritanism, or modern astronomy, or Christian faith? Political science is in some universities combined with history, in others with social science. The partition wall between chemistry and physics has clearly become attenuated. Why, then, do we hesitate to visit one another's classes? No surgeon would decline to operate before his competent fellow surgeons. Why should not a teacher be glad to show his fellow teachers how he creates enthusiasm for the poet Horace, or how he interests young Americans in the origin and growth of the American Constitution?

EDUCATIONAL RESEARCH AND STATISTICS

AN EXPERIMENT IN REMEDIAL READING EXERCISES AT THE COLLEGE LEVEL

A. Summary of Previous Investigations

STONE[1] reports the results of an experiment to improve the reading ability of college students in fifteen classes, two of which served as control groups. The Monroe Standardized Silent Reading Test and Stone's extension of it were used to determine the initial reading ability of the students. Several motives for improvement were developed. Definite practice assignments were given. Each student was encouraged and aided in the diagnosis of his own difficulties, and every effort was made to secure persistence in practice. At the end of three weeks the students were again tested. The results showed clearly the superiority of the practice groups.

[1] C. W. Stone, "Improving the Reading Ability of College Students," *Journal of Educational Method*, 2: 8–23. 1922.

Stone and Colvin[2] arranged for twenty hours of controlled practice in reading for forty-five students in educational psychology in addition to critical examinations of their own study habits and systematic study of the psychology of silent reading. "As measured by the Monroe Silent Reading Test with Stone's Extensions, their average rate score after practice and study was 74 per cent. gain over that of average scores before practice and study"; their average improvement in comprehension was 84 per cent. The students with the lowest initial scores made the greatest gains, indicating that many poor readers among college students are making use of habits which can be improved through the use of appropriate methods.

Book[3] reports an investigation in which he found a definite relationship between the ability of college students to read and academic success. The reading ability was measured by the Whipple Reading Test for College Students, and also by a special test on the mastery of the ordinary assignment. Academic success was measured by credit points. The subjects were 900 freshmen and 214 sophomores and juniors, all of Indiana University.

Book also reports in the same article an experiment carried out with fifty-four students on improvement in reading ability. Lectures on how to study, conferences on individual difficulties, and definite practice periods in reading were given. The group showed definite and marked improvement in speed of reading, after four weeks and at the end of the semester.

A similar procedure was followed out by Book with 112 students in educational psychology classes. A control of 109 students in other educational psychology classes was maintained. The control group was slightly higher in intelligence. Six regular class periods in the experimental group were devoted to lectures upon improvement in study habits, and in particular to reading. Conferences were held outside of class. At the end of six weeks the experimental groups scored on a reading test 69.5 in comparison to the 59.2 of the control.

Averill and Mueller,[4] using sixteen adult women as subjects, employed a variety of motives along with practice periods in an effort to improve their reading ability. There were three forty-minute practice periods per week, given for three months. A gain in speed of approximately 100 per cent. was obtained, with a slight decrease in comprehension. Emphasis throughout their study was placed upon speed rather than comprehension.

B. THE PROBLEM

A previous investigation at Purdue University revealed, among other things, a rather startling deficiency in reading rate and comprehension for an experimental group[5]—the average achievement on a standardized reading test being approximately that of eighth-grade pupils. Individual students ranged as low as fifth-grade reading ability.

It was found, moreover, that there was considerable negative correlation between the number of eye-movements in reading and scholastic achievement[6] −.646 and −.614 respectively for two different kinds of material.

In an unpublished study on forty-four seventh- and eighth-grade children carried out by H. O. Bennett under the direction of Remmers the correlation between school marks and eye movements was found to be −.638.

When it is recalled that both the number of eye movements and school marks are not particularly high in reliability—errors of measurement are fairly large—the correlations just cited become even more significant. School marks may be safely estimated to have a reliability not in excess of +.80. Independent measurements of eye movements by two untrained students, V. L. Brink and H. D. Black, for

[2] C. W. Stone and Carl Colvin, "How to Study (as a Source of Motive in Educational Psychology)," *Journal of Educational Psychology*, 11: 348–54. 1920.

[3] W. F. Book, "How Well College Students Can Read," SCHOOL AND SOCIETY, 26: 242–48.

[4] L. A. Averill and A. D. Mueller, "The Effect of Practice on the Improvement of Silent Reading in Adults," *Journal of Educational Research*, 17: 125–29. 1928.

[5] H. H. Remmers, "A Diagnostic and Remedial Study of Potentially and Actually Failing Students at Purdue University," pp. 35–37, Figure 6a and Table 12, pp. 113 and 115.

[6] *Ibid.*, p. 36.

twenty-two individuals—sophomores in one of Remmers' classes in elementary psychology—gave a reliability of +.66 for the reading of a paragraph of fifteen lines.

Correcting the correlation between eye movements and school marks for attenuation on the basis of these figures gives a "true" correlation[7] between these two factors of .882—an unusual amount of relationship for two factors which on *a priori* grounds would hardly be expected to be so closely associated.

The populations involved in these correlations are, of course, too small to warrant broad generalization, but they are sufficiently significant to warrant further investigation. The writers accordingly planned an experiment to obtain a tentative answer to the question, "For a given type of material can the reading rate and comprehension of students in the lower fourth of entering freshmen relative to psychological examination scores be improved by remedial exercises?"

If the above question were found to be answered in the affirmative it would, of course, not *necessarily* follow that there should be a corresponding increase in the scholastic achievement of the students involved in the experiment. The established facts concerning the transfer of training would indicate, indeed, that such increase would be contrary to expectations. It is quite possible that it might be necessary to give such remedial drill for the various types of reading content encountered by the student. The problem of transfer remains for future investigations.

C. PROCEDURE

The experiment here reported was designed primarily to gain some insight into, and mastery of, a justifiable and sound technique, in the hope that a broader and more comprehensive future experiment might be carried out. There were developed, accordingly, two forms of the Purdue Reading Test,[8] to serve as measures of comprehension external to the reading content of the experimental material itself. These two forms contain various types of reading material taken from college text-books and are practically identical in difficulty.

The students in the lower fourth of freshman men on the American Council on Education Psychological Examination (1927 edition) were called together for the purpose of explaining to them the results of the previous year's investigations of reading difficulties, and the implications of these results for possible remedial work. The students were told that volunteers were desired for such remedial instruction, the cost of which to each of them would be a two-dollar book. Ten volunteers were obtained, but of these only eight participated in the experiment at all, and of these one dropped out after the first two weeks of the experiment. The number obtained, however, was sufficient for our purposes.

The experiment was begun on March 13 and was discontinued May 2, the subjects meeting four evenings a week for ten to forty minutes for remedial drill and measurement of progress. The first and last meetings were devoted to the administration of the two forms of the Purdue Reading Test.

At the first meeting the subjects were also told in more detail of the experimental results on reading. The various factors influencing reading rate and comprehension were discussed in elementary fashion, and the demonstrated improvability of these was emphasized. The need for urging oneself beyond one's accustomed rate was especially stressed, with the reminder that one must, of course, understand and remember the material read. This injunction was repeated several times during the experiment.

Each student kept a graphic record of his progress in terms of the average number of lines read per minute. A comprehension score was also kept in terms of the percentage of correct answers on an objective test (matching and true-false items), so that each student was able to assess his progress in terms of both rate and comprehension.

The book used for the remedial exercises was C. C. Crawford's "The Technique of Study," Houghton Mifflin Company, 1928. This book lends itself admirably to such an experiment as this in that (1) the content would presumably be useful for the student's self-management; (2)

[7] T. L. Kelley, "Statistical Method," p. 204.

[8] Published by the Lafayette Printing Company, Lafayette, Indiana.

the difficulty appears to be well within the range of the ability of our students, and (3) objectively scored tests are appended to each chapter.

At the beginning each chapter was broken up into approximately three equal parts, one evening being devoted to each part. Later this was increased to half a chapter and finally to a whole chapter. The students were all started reading at a given signal, and as each one finished, the time was read from a stop watch and recorded in his book. As soon as each man had plotted his achievement for the evening on his individual graph, he left his book in the custody of the experimenter, so that the student had access to his book only during the time spent in speed drill. A total of eight chapters containing 184 pages was covered in the experiment.

D. Results

Table 1 gives the data for the composite achievement of the group in speed. It will be observed that there is a rather steady increase in the average number of lines read per minute. The end period represents a gain of 24.6 per cent. over the initial period. This is a rather surprising gain when it is noted that the total actual reading time was only three hours.

TABLE 1

The Average Number of Lines Read Per Minute, the Average Time in Minutes, and the Total Number of Lines Read

Practice Period	1	2	3	4	5	6	7	8	9	10	11	12	13
Av. No. lines read per minute	20.7	22.3	22.8	22.2	24.6	26.8	25.3	25.5	26.8	26.9	25.3	24.8	25.8
Av. time in minutes	8.8	8.3	9.9	13.2	10.9	10.9	11.6	11.9	11.5	19.3	18.8	30.4	24.3
Total No. lines read	177	190	226	281	263	284	284	291	300	487	458	753	595

TABLE 2

Comprehension Scores in Terms of Per Cent. Correct on Successive True-False Tests

Test No.	1	2	3	4	5	6
Per cent. correct	60.6	62.9	87.1	77.6	71.5	81.3

Gain in speed alone, however, is in itself of no consequence. If there is not a corresponding gain or at least no drop in comprehension, there would be no cause for satisfaction. Table 2 was made to throw light on this question. It is obvious that there is a decided tendency for the comprehension scores to parallel the speed scores.

It is pertinent here to state the assumptions involved in this study. It is assumed: (1) that the reading difficulty of the material is approximately constant throughout the book; and (2) that the consecutive tests are approximately equivalent in difficulty.

It was not feasible to test these assumptions experimentally, but this might be done in a future more comprehensive experiment.

A comparison of the scores on the two forms of the Purdue Reading Test showed practically no change in average score. The average scores were 61.6 and 62.0 respectively before and after the experiment.

E. Summary

An experiment with seven students was carried out to study the gain in speed and comprehension of motivated remedial speed drills. The results indicate that for approximately three hours of actual reading time spread over a period of nearly two months the increase in both these functions approximates twenty-five per cent. for the material read. It is not known to what extent if any this gain transferred to other types of reading situations.

H. H. Remmers
J. M. Stalnaker
Purdue University

SCHOOL AND SOCIETY

EDITED BY J. McKEEN CATTELL
WITH WHICH IS COMBINED THE
EDUCATIONAL REVIEW
EDITED BY WILLIAM McANDREW

Volume XXVIII   SATURDAY, DECEMBER 29, 1928   Number 731

EDUCATIONAL BOOKS OF 1928

By JOSEPH L. WHEELER
ENOCH PRATT FREE LIBRARY, BALTIMORE, MD.

In preparation for the Annual Selected List of Sixty Educational Books which will appear in the *Journal* of the National Education Association, probably for March, careful search has been made for all publications of 1928 on teaching, school administration and educational research. The following list is the result.

The list is similar in plan, and also in length (over four hundred titles) to that prepared a year ago. Approximately the same proportions are kept between regular trade books in bound form, and the theses and studies issued by various organizations and institutions. The list contains no foreign books, and only those English books that have been imported and are for sale in this country. It does not include courses of study from various cities and states or books on religious education.

As last year, the list is divided under subject headings, although any such arrangement can hardly satisfy all, either as to choice of subjects or the assigning of titles under the various headings. To find a given book, the headings should first be run through.

A preliminary copy of the list was sent on October 24 to all publishers for revision, and for news of any additional 1928 titles that would appear before December 30. Any missing data as to pages, prices, etc., are due to lack of response from publishers. Copies of the preliminary list were sent to over two hundred specialists whose comments and scorings are used as the basis for the selection of the sixty outstanding books of the year.

While the total number of titles is about the same as last year, it is interesting to note the changing proportion of titles devoted to the various subjects. If a record were made from year to year, such changes would be a good barometer of the ebb and flow of national interest in each phase of education, for though the extensive "trade" books usually reflect and incorporate developments only after several months, often a year or two, the theses and bulletins from research centers are the very essence of progress and new ideas, freshly distilled. Space permits only mention of the decrease in titles on school health and physical education from thirty-two to twenty-six, suggesting that what some consider an over-emphasis on this phase is being retarded. Unfortunately, the small number of studies on rural education has dropped from thirteen to six, all these being small institutional and governmental studies, without a single well-planned or comprehensive book for the rural school worker as such. Titles on higher education, on the other hand, have increased from twenty-two to twenty-nine.

The chief value of the following list is, we hope, its attempted completeness and its convenience as a key to even smaller publications on special topics.

LIST OF EDUCATIONAL BOOKS

Purposes, Principles and Philosophy of Education (*General*)

Bell, Bernard I. Common Sense in Education. 321 p. 1928. Morrow. $2.50.

Bruce, Gustav M. Luther as an Educator. 318 p. Augsburg Pub. House. $2.00.

Clem, Orlie M. A Work Book Syllabus in Principles of Education. 170 p. 1928. Warwick & York. $2.00.

Cobb, Stanwood. The New Leaven: Progressive Education and Its Effect upon the Child and Society. 340 p. 1928. John Day. $2.50.

Duvall, Sylvanus M. The Methodist Episcopal Church and Education up to 1869. (Cont. to Educ. No. 284.) 127 p. 1928. Teachers College, Columbia. $1.50.

Finney, Ross L. A Sociological Philosophy of Education. 563 p. 1928. Macmillan. $2.50.

Fisher, T. Ernest. Democracy and Mission Education in Korea. (Cont. to Educ. No. 306.) 188 p. 1928. Teachers College, Columbia. $1.75.

Grizzell, Emit D. Education: Principles and Practices. 428 p. 1928. Macmillan. $2.40.

Harris, Pickens E. Changing Conceptions of School Discipline. 384 p. 1928. Macmillan. $2.00.

Indiana University School of Education. The Economic Effects of Education as Shown by Statements of Economists. 39 p. 1928. Univ. Book Store. $.50.

Kandel, I. L., *ed.* (Fourth) Educational Year Book of the International Institute of Teachers College, Columbia University. 618 p. 1928. Teachers College, Columbia. $3.50.

Kellermann, Fritz. The Effect of the World War on European Education. (Harvard Bulletins in Educ. No. 13.) 89 p. 1928. Harvard Univ. Press. $1.00.

Kelly, F. J., and Capen, S. P. The Influence of Standardizing Agencies in Education. 23 p. 1928. Univ. of Minn.

Klain, Zora. Educational Activities of New England Quakers: A Source Book. 241 p. 1928. Westbrook Pub. Co. $3.50.

Leighton, Joseph A. Individuality and Education. 204 p. 1928. Appleton. $2.00.

Mary Rosalita, Sister. Education in Detroit Prior to 1850. 364 p. 1928. Michigan Historical Commission.

Milton, John. (Ainsworth, Oliver M., *ed.*) Milton on Education. (Cornell Studies in English No. 12.) 369 p. 1928. Yale Univ. Press. $2.75.

National Education Association. Proceedings of the Sixty-sixth Annual Meeting. 1205 p. 1928. The Association. $2.00.

National Society for the Study of Educational Sociology. Bibliographies on Educational Sociology; First Yearbook. 154 p. 1928. The Society, New York Univ., N. Y. $1.50.

Naumberg, Margaret. The Child and the World: Dialogues in Modern Education. 328 p. 1928. Harcourt, Brace. $3.50.

Payne, E. George. Principles of Educational Sociology: An Outline. Rev. ed. 169 p. 1928. New York Univ. Press Book Store. $1.50.

Rozanov, Mikhail G. (N. Ognyov, *pseud.*) The Diary of a Communist Schoolboy. Tr. by Alexander Werth. 288 p. 1928. Payson & Clarke. $2.50.

Rusk, Robert R. The Philosophical Bases of Education. 205 p. 1928. Houghton Mifflin. $2.00.

Smith, Walter R. Principles of Educational Sociology. 773 p. 1928. Houghton Mifflin. $3.00.

Snedden, David. Educational Sociology for Beginners. 636 p. 1928. Macmillan. $3.50.

Walsh, Mrs. Louise, and Walsh, M. J. History and Organization of Education in Pennsylvania. 276 p. 1928. M. J. Walsh. $2.00.

Washburne, Carleton, and Stearns, M. M. Better Schools. 342 p. 1928. John Day. $2.50.

Whitridge, Arnold. Dr. Arnold of Rugby. 243 p. 1928. Holt. $5.00.

Wilson, Mrs. Lucy L. The New Schools of New Russia. 230 p. 1928. Vanguard Press. $.50.

Wynne, John P. Principles of Educational Method. 285 p. 1928. Globe Book Co. $2.00.

Zimmern, Alfred. Learning and Leadership: A Study of the Needs and Possibilities of International Intellectual Cooperation. 112 p. 1928. Oxford Univ. Press. $2.00.

Administration and Supervision
(*See also Teachers and Teaching Methods*)

Allen, Ira M. The Teacher's Contractual Status as Revealed by an Analysis of American Court Decisions. (Cont. to Educ. No. 304.) 147 p. 1928. Teachers College, Columbia. $1.50.

American School and University. Yearbook on School Buildings and Equipment for Schools and Colleges, 1928–1929. 383 p. American School Pub. Corp. $5.00.

Ayer, F. C., and Barr, A. S. The Organization of Supervision. 397 p. 1928. Appleton. $2.25.

The Chicago Principals' Club. Third Yearbook (The Second Cooperative Report of the Studies of Curriculum and of Supervision.) 196 p. 1928. Chicago Principals' Club. $.90.

Counts, George S. School and Society in Chicago. 367 p. 1928. Harcourt, Brace. $2.50.

Engelhardt, Fred, Hegel, N. H., and Womrath, G. F. Selecting Sites for School Buildings. 20 p. 1928. Univ. of Minn. Press. $.50.

Foster, Herbert H. High School Administration. 665 p. 1928. Century. $2.75.

Gist, Arthur S. The Administration of an Elementary School. 308 p. 1928. Scribner's. $1.80.

Irvin, Oscar W. State Budget Control of State Institutions of Higher Education. (Cont. to Educ. No. 271.) 122 p. 1928. Teachers College, Columbia. $1.50.

Keesecker, Ward W. Laws Relating to Compulsory Education. (Bulletin No. 20.) 1928. U. S. Bureau of Education.

Lindsay, E. E. Problems in School Administration. 544 p. 1928. Macmillan. $2.50.

Linscheid, Adolph. In-service Improvement of the State Teachers College Faculty. (Cont. to Educ. No. 309.) 100 p. 1928. Teachers College, Columbia. $1.50.

Mangun, Vernon L. The American Normal School: Its Rise and Development in Massachusetts. 442 p. 1928. Warwick & York. $3.50.

Marberry, James O. The Administration of Public Education in Centralized and Coordinated Schools. (Bulletin No. 2810.) 123 p. 1928. Univ. of Texas. $.50.

Mort, Paul R. The Individual Pupil in the Management of Class and School. 383 p. 1928. American Book Co. $1.60.

National Conference on Educational Method. First Yearbook. Educational Supervision: A Report of Current Views, Investigations and Practices. 270 p. 1928. Teachers College, Columbia. $1.50.

National Education Association. Department of Elementary School Principals. Seventh Yearbook. The Elementary School Principalship. 639 p. 1928. The Association. $2.00.

Neulen, Lester N. State Aid for Educational Projects in the Public Schools. (Cont. to Educ. No. 308.) 84 p. 1928. Teachers College, Columbia. $1.50.

Nutt, Hubert W. Current Problems in the Supervision of Instruction. 538 p. 1928. Johnson Pub. Co. $2.00.

Pierce, Anna E. Deans and Advisers of Women and Girls. 636 p. 1928. Professional & Technical Press. $4.00.

Reeves, C. E., and Ganders, H. S. School Building Management: the Operation and Care of School Plants. 395 p. 1928. Teachers College, Columbia. $3.75.

Schroeder, H. H. Legal Opinion on the Public School as a State Institution. 81 p. 1928. Public School Pub. Co. $.75.

Sears, Jesse B. Classroom Organization and Control. Rev. ed. 400 p. 1928. Houghton Mifflin. $2.15.

Sturtevant, S. M., and Strang, Ruth. A Personnel Study of the Work of Deans of Women in Teachers Colleges and Normal Schools. (Cont. to Educ. No. 319.) 95 p. 1928. Teachers College, Columbia. $1.50.

Thomas, Minor W. Public School Plumbing Equipment. (Cont. to Educ. No. 282.) 128 p. 1928. Teachers College, Columbia. $1.50.

Tidwell, Clyde J. State Control of Textbooks with Special Reference to Florida. (Cont. to Educ. No. 299.) 78 p. 1928. Teachers College, Columbia. $1.50.

Tiegs, Ernest W. An Evaluation of Some Techniques of Teacher Selection. 108 p. 1928. Public School Pub. Co. $1.50.

University of the State of New York. Education Law as Amended to July 1, 1928. (Bulletin 910.) 338 p. Univ. of the State of N. Y. 1928. $.50.

University of the State of New York. Law Pamphlet 7. Election of District Superintendents. (Bulletin 905.) 17 p. 1928. Univ. of the State of N. Y. $.05.

University of the State of New York. Proceedings of the Sixty-third Convocation of the University of the State of New York. (Bulletin No. 899.) 80 p. 1928. Univ. of the State of N. Y. $.50.

University of the State of New York. Regulations and Directions Governing the Issuance of Certificates of Literacy and Conduct of New York State Regents Literacy Test. (Bulletin 911.) 16 p. 1928. Univ. of the State of N. Y. $.05.

Young, Dale. Control of Available Public School Income; with Special Reference to Cities of New York State. (Cont. to Educ. No. 305.) 111 p. 1928. Teachers College, Columbia. $1.50.

Ziegler, Carl W. School Attendance as a Factor in School Progress. (Cont. to Educ. No. 297.) 63 p. 1928. Teachers College, Columbia. $1.50.

General Surveys and Statistics

(For Surveys of Special Phases see other Headings)

Abel, James F. Major Trends of Education in Other Countries: Advance Sheets from Biennial Survey, 1924–26. (Bulletin No. 13.) 48 p. 1928. U. S. Bureau of Education. $.10.

Blose, David T. Statistics Concerning Education of the Negro Race. (Bulletin No. 19.) 1928. U. S. Bureau of Education.

Educational Press Association of America. Fourth Handbook. 23 p. 1928. The Association.

Engelhardt, Fred, and Melby, E. O. The Supervisory Organization and the Instructional Program, Albert Lea, Minnesota. (Univ. of Minnesota Educational Monograph No. 17.) 72 p. 1928. Univ. of Minn. $.50.

Foster, Emery M. Items of Statistics for Public School Systems. (Bulletin No. 14.) 14 p. 1928. U. S. Bureau of Education. $.05.

Holzinger, Karl T. Statistical Methods for Students in Education. 372 p. 1928. Ginn. $3.60.

Huffaker, C. L. A Mental Survey of the Intermediate Grades of the Public Schools of Eugene, Oregon. (Univ. of Oregon Education Series Vol. 1, No. 5.) pp. 222–238. 1928. University Press.

Hull, O. R., and Ford, W. S. Santa Ana School Housing Survey. 88 p. 1928. Univ. of S. Cal. $1.00.

Hull, O. R., and Ford, W. S. Survey of the Alhambra Public Schools. 107 p. 1928. Univ. of S. Cal. $1.25.

Klein, A. J., Deffenbaugh, W. S., Covert, Timon, and Lathrop, E. A. Educational Surveys. (Bulletin No. 11.) 67 p. 1928. U. S. Bureau of Education. $.15.

Meader, J. J. Normal School Education in Connecticut. (Cont. to Educ. No. 307.) 96 p. 1928. Teachers College, Columbia. $1.50.

Mousaw, C. J. A Study of Educational Need and Opportunity in the Town of Crown Point, Essex County, N. Y. (Bulletin 907.) 29 p. 1928. Univ. of the State of N. Y. $.10.

O'Shea, M. V. Report to the Educational Commission of Virginia of a Survey of the Public Educational System of the State. 669 p. 1928. The Commission, Richmond, Va.

Phillips, Frank McG. A Graphic View of Education in Our States. 63 p. 1928. Houghton Mifflin. Gratis.

Phillips, Frank McG. Statistical Survey of Education. 1925–1926. (Bulletin No. 12.) 13 p. 1928. U. S. Bureau of Education. $.05.

Strayer, G. D., and Engelhardt, N. L. The Junior High School Proposed for Oradell, N. J. 24 p. 1928. Teachers College, Columbia.

Strayer, G. D., Engelhardt, N. L., and others. The Need for Further School Accommodations in Districts Number 2 and Number 3, Rye, N. Y. 65 p. 1928. Teachers College, Columbia. $.50.

Strayer, G. D., and Engelhardt, N. L. The Need of Further School Accommodations in Pleasantville, N. Y. 24 p. 1928. Teachers College, Columbia. $.50.

Strayer, G. D., Engelhardt, N. L., and others. Report of the Survey of the Schools of Closter, N. J. 138 p. 1928. Board of Educ., Closter, N. J. $.50.

Strayer, G. D., and Engelhardt, N. L. School Building Program for District Number 6, Town of Greenburgh, N. Y. 20 p. 1928. Teachers College, Columbia. $.50.

Strayer, G. D., and Engelhardt, N. L. A School Building Program for the City of Paducah, Ky. 87 p. 1928. Teachers College, Columbia, $.50.

U. S. Bureau of Education. Educational Directory: 1928. (Bulletin No. 1.) 144 p. 1928. The Bureau. $.20.

U. S. Bureau of Education. Statistics of Nurse Training Schools. 1926–27. 57 p. (Bulletin No. 2.) 1928. The Bureau. $.10.

Wilson, Florence. Near East Educational Survey: Report of a Survey Made during the Months of April, May, and June, 1927. 108 p. 1928. European Centre of the Carnegie Endowment for International Peace.

Curriculum

Harap, Henry. The Technique of Curriculum Making. 315 p. 1928. Macmillan. $1.80.

Maryland School Bulletin. Curriculum Making in Problems of American Democracy as Applied to the Unit—Public Opinion. (Bulletin Vol. X, No. 2.) 46 p. 1928. State Dept. of Educ.

Monroe, W. S., and Herriott, M. E. Reconstruction of the Secondary School Curriculum: Its Meaning and Trends. (Bulletin No. 41.) 120 p. 1928. Univ. of Ill. $.50.

Monroe, W. S., Hindman, D. A., and Lundin, R. S. Two Illustrations of Curriculum Construction. (Univ. of Illinois Bulletin. No. 39.) 53 p. 1928. Univ. of Ill. $.50.

National Education Association. Dept. of Superintendence. Sixth Yearbook. The Development of the High School Curriculum. 584 p. 1928. The Association. $2.00.

Rugg, Earle U. Curriculum Studies in Social Sciences and Citizenship. 214 p. 1928. Colorado State Teachers College. $2.00.

Williams, L. A. The Making of High-School Curricula. 233 p. 1928. Ginn. $1.76.

CONDUCT AND CHARACTER FORMATION

Boston High School Head Masters' Association Report. Character Education in Secondary Schools. 156 p. 1928. Boston Public Schools.

Chicago Association for Child Study and Parent Education. Building Character: Proceedings of the Midwest Conference on Parent Education, Feb. 1928. 351 p. 1928. $1.00.

Edwards, R. H., and Hilgard, E. R. Student Counseling. (Bulletin 7.) 64 p. 1928. National Council on Religion in Higher Education. Barnes Hall, Ithaca, N. Y. Free on request.

Fanshawe, John E. J. Education for Tolerance. 30 p. 1928. Independent Education. $.60.

Fishback, Elvin H. Character Education in the Junior High School. 190 p. 1928. Heath. $1.24.

Gregg, F. M. Character Education: Supplementary Bulletin. 28 p. 1928. Nebraska Dept. of Public Instruction.

Hartshorne, Hugh, and May, M. A. Studies in Deceit. (Columbia Univ. Teachers College Studies in the Nature of Character, vol. 1.) 720 p. 1928. Macmillan. $4.50.

Manry, James C. World Citizenship. Studies in Character, vol. 1, no. 1. 1928. Univ. of Iowa Institute of Character Research.

Robbins, Charles L. The Will to Work: a Study in Character Education. 221 p. 1928. Row, Peterson. $1.60.

Shuttleworth, F. K. The Measurement of the Character and Environmental Factors Involved in Scholastic Success. 1928. Univ. of Iowa. $1.00.

Slaght, W. E. Untruthfulness in Children: Its Conditioning Factors Involved in Scholastic Success. 1928. Univ. of Iowa. $1.00.

Symonds, Percival M. The Nature of Conduct. 346 p. 1928. Macmillan. $1.90.

EDUCATIONAL PSYCHOLOGY

Arlitt, Ada H. Psychology of Infancy and Early Childhood. 228 p. 1928. McGraw-Hill. $2.00.

Averill, Lawrence A. The Hygiene of Instruction. 386 p. 1928. Houghton Mifflin. $2.00.

Blanchard, Phyllis M. The Child and Society: an Introduction to the Social Psychology of the Child. 369 p. 1928. Longmans, Green. $2.25.

Boston Public Schools. Training the Emotions: Controlling Fear. (School Doc. No. 2.) 127 p. 1928. Boston Public Schools.

Cooper, Mabel L. Seven Psychological Portraits: a Handbook for Parents and Teachers. 181 p. 1928. Morehouse. $2.00.

Ellis, Robert S. The Psychology of Individual Differences. 533 p. 1928. Appleton. $3.50.

Erleigh, Viscountess, *ed.* The Mind of the Growing Child. 230 p. 1928. Oxford Univ. Press. $1.75.

Garrison, Karl C. An Analytic Study of Rational Learning. (Cont. to Educ. No. 44.) 52 p. 1928. George Peabody College for Teachers.

Hollingworth, Harry L. Psychology; Its Facts and Principles: A New Contribution to Theoretical Psychology. 539 p. 1928. Appleton. $3.00.

Hollingworth, Leta S. The Psychology of the Adolescent. 259 p. 1928. Appleton. $2.00.

Jordan, Arthur M. Educational Psychology. 474 p. 1928. Henry Holt. $2.50.

Kelley, Truman L. Crossroads in the Mind of Man. 238 p. 1928. Stanford Univ. Press. $4.00.

Morgan, John J. B. The Psychology of Abnormal People with Educational Applications. 627 p. 1928. Longmans, Green. $3.75.

Muse, Maude B. A Study Outline in Educational Psychology. 140 p. 1928. W. B. Saunders.

Myers, Gary C. Schoolroom Hazards to the Mental Health of Children. 7 p. 1928. Nat'l Committee for Mental Hygiene.

Orata, Pedro T. The Theory of Identical Elements. 204 p. 1928. Ohio State Univ. Press.

Piaget, Jean, and others. Judgment and Reasoning in the Child. Tr. by Marjorie Marden. 260 p. 1928. Harcourt, Brace. $3.75.

Pyle, William H. The Psychology of Learning. Rev. ed. 441 p. 1928. Warwick & York. $2.32.

Sandiford, Peter. Educational Psychology: An Objective Study. 406 p. 1928. Longmans, Green. $3.50.

Thom, Douglas A. The Mental Health of the Child. 46 p. 1928. Harvard Univ. Press. $1.00.

Tonks, Helen L. Psychological Foundations of Teaching. 212 p. 1927. (Omitted in 1927 List.) Globe Book Co. $1.67.

Weill, Blanche C. The Behavior of Young Children of the Same Family. 220 p. 1928. Harvard Univ. Press. $3.00.

Wickman, E. K. Children's Behavior and Teachers' Attitudes. 247 p. 1928. Commonwealth Fund.

INTELLIGENCE TESTS AND MEASUREMENTS

(*For Special Subject Tests see other Headings*)

Dearborn, Walter F. Intelligence Tests. 336 p. 1928. Houghton Mifflin. $2.50.

Dougherty, Mary L. A Comparative Study of Nine Group Tests of Intelligence for Primary

Grades. 112 p. 1928. Johns Hopkins Press. $1.75.

Ellis, Robert S. Standardizing Teachers' Examinations and the Distribution of Class Marks. 170 p. 1928. Public School Pub. Co. $.75.

Fenton, Norman, and Worcester, D. A. An Introduction to Educational Measurements. 149 p. 1928. Ginn. $1.40.

Goodenough, Florence L. The Kuhlman-Binet Tests for Children of Pre-School Age. 146 p. 1928. Univ. of Minn. $2.00.

Greene, Harry A. Work-Book in Educational Measurements. 156 p. 1928. Longmans, Green. $1.80.

Hammond, H. P., and Stoddard, G. D. A Study of Placement Examinations. 64 p. 1928. Univ. of Iowa. $1.00.

Hollingshead, Arthur D. An Evaluation of the Use of Certain Educational and Mental Measurements for Purposes of Classification. (Cont. to Educ. No. 302.) 64 p. 1928. Teachers College, Columbia. $1.50.

Hull, Clark L. Aptitude Testing. 536 p. 1928. World Book Co. $2.68.

Jensen, Milton B. Objective Differentiation Between Three Groups in Education: Teachers, Research Workers and Administrators. (Genetic Psychology Monographs, Vol. III, No. 5.) pp. 333–454. 1928. Clark Univ. Press. $2.00.

Jensen, Milton B. Stanford Educational Aptitudes Test. 1928. Stanford Univ. Press.

Keys, Noel. The Improvement of Measurement Through Cumulative Testing. (Cont. to Educ. No. 321.) 81 p. 1928. Teachers College, Columbia. $1.50.

Laws, Gertrude. Analysis of Parent-Child Relationships. 1928. Teachers College, Columbia. $.05.

Levine, A. J., and Marks, Louis. Testing Intelligence and Achievement. 399 p. 1928. Macmillan. $2.00.

Odell, Charles W. Traditional Examinations and New Type Tests. 469 p. 1928. Century. $2.50.

Orleans, Jacob S. An Experiment in the Local Construction and Uses of Objective Tests in Several School Systems of New York State. (Bulletin 906.) 43 p. 1928. Univ. of the State of N. Y. $.15.

Orleans, Jacob S. Manual of Instruction in Objective Tests for Use at Teachers' Conferences. (Bulletin 902.) 36 p. 1928. Univ. of the State of N. Y. $.10.

Orleans, J. S., and Sealy, G. A. Objective Tests. 374 p. 1928. World Book Co. $2.20.

Sims, Verner M. The Measurement of Socio-Economic Status. 33 p. 1928. Public School Pub. Co. $.50.

Smith, H. L., and Wright, W. W. Tests and Measurements. 540 p. 1928. Silver, Burdett. $3.00.

Snedden, Donald S. A Study of Disguised Intelligence Tests. (Cont. to Educ. No. 291.) 48 p. 1928. Teachers College, Columbia. $1.50.

Uhrbrock, Richard S. An Analysis of the Downey Will-Temperament Tests. (Cont. to Educ. No. 296.) 78 p. 1928. Teachers College, Columbia. $1.50.

Van Wagenen, Marvin J. A Teachers' Manual in the Use of the Educational Scales. 276 p. 1928. Public School Pub. Co. $1.50.

Wilson, G. M., and Hoke, K. J. How to Measure. Rev. ed. 597 p. 1928. Macmillan. $2.00.

EXCEPTIONAL CHILDREN

Day, Herbert, Fusfel, Irving, and Pintner, Rudolf. A Survey of American Schools for the Deaf, 1924–25. 296 p. 1928. National Research Council.

Fletcher, John M. The Problem of Stuttering. 362 p. 1928. Longmans, Green. $2.25.

Goddard, Henry H. School Training of Gifted Children. 226 p. 1928. World Book Co. $2.00.

McDowell, Elizabeth D. Educational and Emotional Adjustment of Stuttering Children. (Cont. to Educ. No. 314.) 57 p. 1928. Teachers College, Columbia. $1.50.

Richardson, Frank H. The Nervous Child and His Parents. 400 p. 1928. Putnam. $2.50.

Sayles, Mary B. The Problem Child at Home: A Study of Parent-Child Relationships. 342 p. 1928. Commonwealth Fund. $1.50.

Stowell, Agnes, Samuelson, E. E., and Lehman, Ann. Lip Reading for the Deafened Child. 186 p. 1928. Macmillan. $1.25.

U. S. Bureau of Education. Industrial Schools for Delinquents, 1926–27. (Bulletin No. 10.) 22 p. 1928. The Bureau. $.05.

U. S. Bureau of Education. Schools and Classes for Feeble-Minded and Subnormal Children, 1926–27. (Bulletin No. 5.) 21 p. 1928. The Bureau. $.05.

U. S. Bureau of Education. Schools for the Deaf, 1926–27. (Bulletin No. 8.) 17 p. 1928. The Bureau. $.05.

Wilson, F. T. Learning of Bright and Dull Children. (Cont. to Educ. No. 292.) 56 p. 1928. Teachers College, Columbia. $1.50.

Educational Research

Bixler, Harold H. Check Lists for Educational Research. 118 p. 1928. Teachers College, Columbia. $1.50.

Brouillette, J. W., and others. A Comparative Study of the School Progress of Foreign-Speaking Children and English-Speaking Children in the Elementary Grades. 64 p. 1928. Scott, Foresman. (Information not verified by publisher.)

Chapman, Harold B. Organized Research in Education. 221 p. 1927. Ohio State Univ. Press. $1.50. (Too late for 1927 list.)

Crawford, Claude C. The Technique of Research in Education. 320 p. 1928. Univ. of S. Cal. $2.50.

Good, Carter V. How to Do Research in Education. 298 p. 1928. Warwick & York. $2.50.

Koos, Leonard V. The Questionnaire in Education. 178 p. 1928. Macmillan. $1.25.

Monroe, W. S., and Engelhart, M. D. The Techniques of Educational Research. (Univ. of Illinois Bureau of Educational Research Bulletin No. 38.) 84 p. 1928. Univ. of Ill. $.50.

Monroe, W. S., Odell, C. W., Herriott, M. E., Englehart, M. D., Hull, M. R. Ten Years of Educational Research. 1918–1927. (Univ. of Illinois Bureau of Educational Research Bulletin No. 42.) 367 p. 1928. Univ. of Ill. $1.00.

National Society for the Study of Education. Twenty-Seventh Yearbook: Nature and Nurture. Pt. I, 465 p. Pt. II, 393 p. 1928. Public School Pub. Co. $1.75 each.

Odell, Charles W. Glossary of Three Hundred Terms Used in Educational Measurement and Research. (Univ. of Illinois Bureau of Educational Research Bulletin No. 40.) 68 p. 1928. Univ. of Ill. $.50.

Osburn, W. J. Overlappings and Omissions in Our Courses of Study. 167 p. 1928. Public School Pub. Co. $1.50.

U. S. Bureau of Education. Bibliography of Current Research Studies in Education. 80 p. 1928. The Bureau.

Voegelein, L. Belle, *comp.* List of Educational Subject Headings. 337 p. 1928. Ohio State Univ. Press. $5.00.

Wright, E. A., and Phillips, M. S. Bulletins of the Bureau of Education, 1906–27. (Bulletin No. 17.) 1928. U. S. Bureau of Education.

Teachers and Teaching Methods

(*See also Administration, Special Subjects and Age Groups*)

Almack, J. C., and Lang, A. R. The Beginning Teacher. 478 p. 1928. Houghton Mifflin. $2.40.

Armentrout, Winfield D. Conduct of Student Teaching in State Teachers Colleges, 1923. 2nd. ed. 198 p. 1922. Colorado State Teachers College. $2.00.

Bell, J. C., and Suhrie, A. L., *ed.* Contributions to Education. Vol. 2. (New York Society for the Experimental Study of Education.) 425 p. 1928. World Book Co. $2.20.

Brouillette, J. W., and others. How to Teach Foreign-Speaking Beginners to Speak and to Read English. 42 p. 1928. Scott, Foresman. $.25. (Information not verified by publisher.)

Butterworth, Julian E. The Parent-Teacher Association and Its Work. 149 p. 1928. Macmillan. $1.25.

Clarke, Clarence L. Tenure of Teachers in the Profession with Special Reference to Wisconsin. 144 p. 1928. Alumni Press, Univ. of Mich. $1.25.

Crawford, Claude C. The Technique of Study. 353 p. 1928. Houghton Mifflin. $2.00.

Dorris, Anna V. Visual Instruction in the Public Schools. 481 p. 1928. Ginn. $2.64.

Drum, Warren N. A Preview of Teaching. 338 p. 1928. Ginn. $1.80.

Elsbree, Willard S. Teacher Turnover in the Cities and Villages of New York State. (Cont. to Educ. No. 300.) 88 p. 1928. Teachers College, Columbia. $1.50.

Ferrière, Adolph. The Activity School. Tr. by F. D. Moore and F. C. Wooton. 339 p. 1928. John Day. $4.00.

Jacobs, Charles L. The Relation of the Teacher's Education to Her Effectiveness. (Cont. to Educ. No. 277.) 97 p. 1928. Teachers College, Columbia. $1.50.

Lippmann, Walter. American Inquisitors. 120 p. 1928. Macmillan. $1.25.

McCall, W. A., and Bixler, H. H. How to Classify Pupils. 83 p. 1928. Teachers College, Columbia. $1.25.

Maguire, Edward R. The Group-Study Plan. 203 p. 1928. Scribner's. $1.80.

Marie Paula, Sister. Shibboleths—Tests in Teaching Efficiency. 160 p. 1928. Benziger. $1.75.

Marsh, J. Frank. The Teacher Outside the School. 234 p. 1928. World Book Co. $1.80.

Mary Esther, Sister. The Christian Teacher. 113 p. 1928. Bruce Pub. Co. $1.00.

Mason, Martha S., *ed.* Parents and Teachers: A Survey of Organized Cooperation of Home, School and Community. Prepared under the auspices of the National Congress of Parents and Teachers. 317 p. 1928. Ginn. $2.00.

Mersereau, E. B. Observation Assignments for Practice Teachers in High School. 38 p. 1928. Baylor Univ. Press. $.60.

National Education Association. Dept. of Classroom Teachers. Third Yearbook—Problems and Opportunities in Teaching. 112 p. 1928. The Association. $.50.

Park, Maxwell G. A Problem-Outline in Fundamental Principles of Teaching and Learning. 122 p. 1928. Century. $1.25.

Park, Maxwell G. A Problem-Outline in Introduction to Teaching. 84 p. 1928. Century. $1.00.

Paulu, E. M. Differentiated Assignments in Classroom Management. 1928. Heath. $2.36.

Pryor, Hugh C. A Manual for Student Teachers. 173 p. 1928. Macmillan. $.75.

Reese, Webster P. Personality and Success in Teaching. 145 p. 1928. Badger. $1.75.

Rugg, H. O., and Shumaker, Ann. The Child Centered School. 359 p. World Book Co. $2.40.

Snyder, Agnes. The Value of Certain Measurements in the Training of Teachers. 146 p. 1928. Johns Hopkins Press. $2.50.

Stillman, Bessie. Training Children to Study. 247 p. 1928. Heath. $1.60.

Strickler, Fred. The Training and Experience of 480 Industrial Arts Teachers. 121 p. 1928. Teachers College, Columbia. $1.00.

Thayer, V. T. The Passing of the Recitation. 331 p. 1928. Heath. $2.00.

Vaughn, James. Positive Versus Negative Instruction. 172 p. 1928. National Bureau of Casualty and Surety Underwriters. $1.75.

Weber, Joseph J. Picture Values in Education. 156 pp. 1928. Educational Screen, Inc. $2.00.

Wright, Charles B. The Making of Note-Books. 100 p. 1928. Middlebury College Press. $2.00.

Pre-school, Kindergarten and Elementary Schools

(*See also Special Subjects and Teaching*)

Alport, Augusta. The Solving of Problem-Situations by Preschool Children. (Cont. to Educ. No. 323.) 69 p. 1928. Teachers College, Columbia. $1.50.

Andrus, Ruth. An Inventory of the Habits of Children from Two to Five Years of Age. 51 p. 1928. Teachers College, Columbia. $.50.

Carmichael, Max A. Moral Situations of Six Year Old Children as a Basis for Curriculum Construction. 104 p. 1928. Univ. of Iowa. $1.00.

Collings, Ellsworth. Project Teaching in Elementary Schools. 571 p. 1928. Century. $3.00.

Davis, Mary D. Primer of Information about Kindergarten Education. (City School Leaflet No. 30.) 11 p. 1928. U. S. Bureau of Education. $.05.

Gambrill, B. L., and Farwell, Louise. An Analytical List of Kindergarten-Primary Tests of Intelligence and Achievement. 35 p. 1928. Whitlock's Book Store, New Haven, Conn.

Gesell, Arnold. Infancy and Human Growth. 418 p. 1928. Macmillan. $3.50.

Henderson, Joseph L. Materials and Methods in the Middle Grades. 375 p. 1928. Ginn. $2.00.

Holley, Charles E. Modern Principles and the Elementary Teacher's Technique. 431 p. 1928. Century. $2.00.

Howes, Ethel P., and Beach, Dorothea. The Cooperative Nursery School. 74 p. 1928. Institute for the Coordination of Women's Interests, Smith College. $.75.

Howes, Ethel P., *ed.* The Nursery School as a Social Experiment. 38 p. 1928. Institute for the Coordination of Women's Interests, Smith College. $.25.

Hsia, Jui-Ching. A Study of Sociability of Elementary School Children. (Cont. to Educ. No. 322.) 65 p. 1928. Teachers College, Columbia. $1.50.

Illinois State Teachers Association. Efficiency Committee of the Central Division. Stenographic Reports of 18 Lessons in the Elementary School. 96 p. 1928. Public School Pub. Co. $.40.

Institute of Child Welfare, University of Minnesota. Child Care and Training. 180 p. 1928. Univ. of Minn. $1.00.

Johnson, Harriet M. Children in the Nursery School. 325 p. 1928. John Day. $3.00.

Lewis, Mary H. An Adventure with Children. 250 p. 1928. Macmillan. $1.75.

MacLatchy, Josephine H. Attendance at Kindergarten and Progress in the Primary Grades. 144 p. 1928. Ohio State Univ. Press. $1.25.

Macmillan, Margaret. Life of Rachel Macmillan: A Biography of the Founder of the Nursery School Movement. 214 p. 1928. Morrow. $2.50.

Raleigh Elementary Education Council. A Suggested List of Activities for Grades 1 to 6. 66 p. 1928. Raleigh, N. C., Public Schools. $.50.

Reed, Mary M. An Investigation of Practices in First Grade Admission and Promotion. (Cont. to Educ. No. 290.) 136 p. 1928. Teachers College, Columbia. $1.50.

Reynolds, Martha M. Negativism of Pre-School Children. (Cont. to Educ. No. 288.) 126 p. 1928. Teachers College, Columbia. $1.50.

Shea, Patrick F. Accident Prevention through Education in the Elementary Schools: A Manual for Teachers and Pupils. 86 p. 1928. Heath. $.68.

Smith, Nora A. The Home-Made Kindergarten. Rev. ed. 150 p. 1928. Houghton Mifflin. $1.50.

Stetson, F. L., and Huffaker, C. L. Pupil Counseling in Grades Seven to Twelve. (Univ. of Oregon Education Series, Vol. 1, No. 6.) p. 243–264. 1928. Univ. of Ore. Press.

Stormzand, M. J., and McKee, J. W. The Progressive Primary Teacher. 352 p. 1928. Houghton Mifflin. $2.40.

Stott, L. V. Eight Year Old Merchants. 158 p. 1928. Greenberg. $2.00.

Watson, John B. Psychological Care of Infant and Child. 195 p. 1928. Norton. $2.00.

Wiecking, Anna M. Education through Manual Activities. 351 p. 1928. Ginn. $1.80.

JUNIOR HIGH SCHOOL

(*See also Teaching, Administration, etc.*)

Fritz, Ralph A. An Evaluation of Two Special Purposes of Junior High Schools: Economy of Time and Bridging the Gap. 80 p. 1928. Univ. of Iowa. $.75.

Holbrook, H. L., and McGregor, A. L. Our Junior High School. 211 p. 1928. Allyn & Bacon. $1.20.

Wiley, G. M., and Van Cott, H. H. The Junior High School in New York State. 283 p. 1928. Univ. of the State of N. Y. $.70.

SECONDARY EDUCATION

(*See also Curriculum, Teaching, etc.*)

Cole, Robert D. Private Secondary Education for Boys in the United States. 353 p. 1928. Univ. of Pa. $1.75.

Crofts, J. M., and Jones, J. D. Secondary School Examination Statistics. 88 p. 1928. Longmans, Green. $1.00.

Drewry, Raymond G. Pupil Participation in High School Control. 220 p. 1928. Harcourt, Brace. $1.75.

Fontaine, E. Clarke. Ways to Better Teaching in the Secondary School. 271 p. 1928. Ginn. $1.60.

Griffin, Orwin B. The Evolution of the Connecticut State School System with Special Reference to the Emergence of the High School. (Cont. to Educ. No. 293.) 261 p. 1928. Teachers College, Columbia. $2.50.

Jessen, Carl A. Requirements for High-School Graduation. (Bulletin No. 21.) 1928. U. S. Bureau of Education.

Judd, Charles H. The Unique Character of American Secondary Education. 63 p. 1928. Harvard Univ. Press. $1.00.

Little, William F. Why Go to High School? 281 p. 1928. Bobbs, Merrill. $1.50.

Monroe, W. S., and Weber, O. F. The High School. 511 p. 1928. Doubleday Doran. $2.50.

Mueller, A. D. Teaching in Secondary Schools. 452 p. 1928. Century. $2.25.

Roemer, Joseph. Secondary Schools of the Southern Association. (Bulletin No. 16.) 1928. U. S. Bureau of Education.

Troxell, Oliver L. State Control of Secondary Education. 232 p. 1928. Warwick & York. $2.50.

University of Illinois. High School Visitor's Office. Proceedings of the High School Conference of November 17, 18, 19, 1927. 336 p. 1928. Univ. of Ill.

University of the State of New York. Report on Secondary Education in the State of New York for the School Year Ending July 31, 1927. 93 p. 1928. Univ. of the State of N. Y.

Waples, Douglas, and others. Problem Exercises for High School Teachers. 99 p. 1928. Univ. of Chicago Press. $1.00.

READING, WRITING, LANGUAGES AND LITERATURE

Anderson, Charles J. The Development of a Supervisory Program in Reading. 48 p. 1928. Laurel Book Co. $.50.

Briggs, LeBaron R. To College Teachers of English Composition. 50 p. 1928. Houghton Mifflin. $.80.

Burch, Mary C. Determination of the Content of the Course in Literature of a Suitable Difficulty for Junior and Senior High School Students. (Genetic Psychology Monographs, Vol. 4.) p. 163–332. 1928. Clark Univ. Press. $3.00.

Cavins, Lorimer V. Standardization of American Poetry for School Purposes. 134 p. 1928. Univ. of Chicago Press. $1.50.

Cox, Sidney. The Teaching of English. 172 p. 1928. Harper. $1.50.

Detroit Teachers College. Syllabus for a Course in Literature for Children. 138 p. 1928. Detroit Teachers College.

Field, Walter T. A Guide to Literature for Children. 287 p. 1928. Ginn. $1.72.

Gates, Arthur I. New Methods in Primary Reading. 236 p. 1928. Teachers College, Columbia. $2.25.

Gray, William S. Summary of Reading Investigations (July 1, 1926, to June 30, 1927.) 48 p. 1928. Univ. of Chicago Press. $.20.

Hagboldt, Peter. Building the German Vocabulary. 72 p. 1928. Univ. of Chicago Press. $.50.

Hanes, Ernest, and McCoy, M. J. Manual to Readings in Contemporary Literature. 117 p. 1928. Macmillan. $.68.

Hitchcock, Alfred M. Bread Loaf Talks on Teaching Literature. 119 p. 1928. Holt. $1.00.

Huber, Miriam B. The Influence of Intelligence upon Children's Reading Interests. (Cont. to Educ. No. 312.) 39 p. 1928. Teachers College, Columbia. $1.50.

La Brant, Lou L. Diagnostic Tests and Remedial Measures for the Teaching of English in the High School. (Univ. of Kansas Studies in Education. Bulletin No. 10.) 22 p. 1928. Univ. of Kansas.

Mackaness, George. Inspirational Teaching. 225 p. 1928. Dutton. $2.70.

Masters, H. V. A Study of Spelling Errors. 80 p. 1928. Univ. of Iowa. $.75.

Meader, Emma G. Teaching Speech in the Elementary School: a Comparative Study of Speech Education in the Elementary Schools of England and of the United States. (Cont. to Educ. No. 317.) 129 p. 1928. Teachers College, Columbia. $1.50.

Meadows, Leon R. A Study of the Teaching of English in Teachers Colleges in the United States. (Cont. to Educ. No. 311.) 95 p. 1928. Teachers College, Columbia. $1.50.

Monroe, Marion. Methods for Diagnosis and Treatment of Cases of Reading Disability. (Genetic Psychology Monographs, Vol. 4, Nos. 4 and 5.) 1928. Clark Univ. Press. $3.00.

Morgan, B. Q., *ed.* German Frequency Word Book. 87 p. 1928. Macmillan. $.60.

Opdycke, John B. In the Service of Youth: on the Teaching of English in Junior and Senior High Schools. 404 p. 1928. Pitman. $3.00.

Orleans, J. S., and Thompson, H. G. A Survey of Achievement in First Half Year Latin in New York State. (Bulletin No. 892.) 48 p. 1928. Univ. of the State of N. Y.

Orleans, J. S., and Thompson, H. G. A Survey of Achievement in the Second Half of First Year Latin in New York State. (Bulletin 897.) 24 p. 1928. Univ. of the State of N. Y. $.10.

Pavey, Mary C. Lesson Aids for Our First English. 118 p. 1928. Scribner's. $1.00.

Phillips, Barbara E. The Use of Modern Literature in High Schools. 113 p. 1928. Badger. $1.75.

Starbuck, E. D., and Shuttleworth, F. K. A Guide to Literature for Character Training. Vol. 1. 389 p. 1928. Macmillan. $2.00.

Stephens, Stephen D. Individual Instruction in English Composition. 150 p. 1928. Harvard Univ. Press. $2.50.

Ullman, B. L., and Smalley, A. W. Progress Tests in Latin. 178 p. 1928. Macmillan. $.84.

University of the State of New York. State Dept. of Education. A Tentative Syllabus in Ancient Languages. Rev. ed. 94 p. 1928. Univ. of the State of N. Y.

Wheeler, C. A., *comp.*, and others. Enrollment in the Foreign Languages in Secondary Schools and Colleges of the United States. 453 p. 1928. Macmillan. $2.00.

Wiley, James A. Practice Exercises in Silent Reading and Study. 368 p. 1928. State Teachers College. $2.00.

Willing, Matthew H. Practice Exercises in the Mechanics of Written English for the High School and Teacher's Manual. 76 p. 1928. Teachers College, Lincoln School. $1.25.

Wohlfarth, J. H., and Bermejo, F. V. Method of Teaching English in First and Second Grades. 147 p. 1928. World Book Co. $.88.

Yoakam, Gerald A. Reading and Study. 502 p. 1928. Macmillan. $2.00.

Zirbes, Laura. Comparative Studies of Current Practice in Reading; with Technique for the Improvement of Teaching. (Cont. to Educ. No. 316.) 229 p. 1928. Teachers College, Columbia. $2.25.

School Libraries

American Library Association. Education Committee. School Library Yearbook No. 2. 189 p. 1928. The Association. $1.55.

Brown, Zaidee, *ed.* Standard Catalog for High School Libraries, Supplement 1926–1927. 182 p. 1928. H. W. Wilson.

Collins, Agnes, *comp.* A Catholic High School Library List. (Education Bulletin No. 1.) 208 p. 1928. National Catholic Welfare Conference, Bureau of Education. $1.00.

Hutchins, Margaret, Johnson, G. S., and Williams, M. S. Guide to the Use of Libraries. 78 p. 1928. H. W. Wilson. $.50.

Logasa, Hannah. The High School Library. 283 p. 1928. Appleton. $1.75.

Maryland School Bulletin. Library List for High School Teachers of Science and Mathematics. (Vol. 10, No. 5.) 72 p. 1928. State Dept. of Educ.

Nason, W. C. Rural Libraries. (U. S. Dept. Agr. Farmers' Bull. 1559.) 50 p. 1928. The Department.

Webb, Hanor A. The High-School Science Library for 1928. (Reprint from the Peabody Journal of Education, Vol. 5, No. 5) pp. 278–290. 1928. The Journal, Nashville.

Wilson, L. R., and others. High School Library Standards. 77 p. 1928. Univ. of N. C. $.50.

MATHEMATICS AND SCIENCE

Blackhurst, James H. Principles and Methods of Junior High School Mathematics. 355 p. 1928. Century. $2.50.

Brownell, William A. The Development of Children's Number Ideas in the Primary Grades. (Bulletin No. 35.) 241 p. 1928. Univ. of Chicago Press. $1.50.

Cajori, Florian. Mathematics in Liberal Education. 169 p. 1928. Christopher Pub. House. $1.50.

Everett, John P. The Fundamental Skills of Algebra. (Cont. to Educ. No. 324.) 1928. Teachers College, Columbia. $1.50.

Horton, Ralph E. Measurable Outcomes of Individual Laboratory Work in Chemistry. (Cont. to Educ. No. 303.) 103 p. 1928. Teachers College, Columbia. $1.50.

Hoyt, F. S., and Peet, H. E. Success in Teaching Arithmetic. 320 p. 1928. Houghton Mifflin. $.92.

Knight, Frederic B., and Behrens, Minnie S. The Learning of the One Hundred Addition Combinations and the One Hundred Subtraction Combinations. 82 p. 1928. Longmans, Green. $1.00.

National Council of Teachers of Mathematics. Selected Topics in the Teaching of Mathematics —Third Yearbook. 276 p. 1928. Teachers College, Columbia. $1.75.

Shaaf, William L. A Course for Teachers of Junior High School Mathematics. (Cont. to Educ. No. 313.) 160 p. 1928. Teachers College, Columbia. $1.75.

University of the State of New York. State Department of Education. Tentative Syllabus in Elementary Algebra. 12 p. 1928. Univ. of the State of N. Y. $.05.

University of the State of New York. Tentative Syllabus in Junior High School Mathematics. 77 p. 1928. Univ. of the State of N. Y.

University of the State of New York. State Department of Education. Tentative Syllabus in Solid Geometry. 13 p. 1928. Univ. of the State of N. Y. $.05.

Woodring, Maxie N., and Sanford, Vera. Enriched Teaching of Mathematics in the High School. 128 p. 1928. Teachers College, Columbia. $1.50.

SOCIAL STUDIES, ARTS AND MUSIC

Andrews, George G. Aids for History Teachers: XI The Study of Original Sources. (Extension Bulletin.) 16 p. 1928. Univ. of Iowa. $.10.

Beck, Walter. Self-development in Drawing, as Interpreted by the Genius of Romano Dazzi and Other Children. 295 p. 1928. Putnam. $5.00.

Birge, Edward B. History of Public School Music in the United States. 296 p. 1928. Ditson. $2.00.

Branom, Mendel E. A Teacher's Geography. 252 p. 1928. Macmillan. $2.40.

Carr, William C. Education for World Citizenship. 225 p. 1928. Stanford Univ. Press. $2.50.

Duffus, Robert L. The American Renaissance. 321 p. 1928. Knopf. $3.50.

Farnum, Royal B. Education through Pictures. 94 p. 1928. Art Extension Society.

Glenn, Mabelle, and Lowry, Margaret. Music Appreciation for the Junior High School. Teacher's Manual. 32 p. 1928. Silver, Burdett. $.48.

Kelty, Mary G. Teaching American History in the Middle Grades of the Elementary School. 748 p. 1928. Ginn. $2.40.

Kimmel, W. G. Map Study and the Use of Outline Maps in Teaching the Social Studies. 8 p. Univ. of the State of N. Y. 1928. $.05.

Macdonald, A. F. Elements of Political Science Research Sources and Methods. 94 p. 1928. Prentice-Hall. $.90.

McKinley, A. E., Howland, A. C., and Dann, M. L. Teachers' Manual to Accompany World History in the Making and World History Today. 110 p. 1928. American Book Co. $.60.

Mahan, Thomas J. An Analysis of the Characteristics of Citizenship. (Cont. to Educ. No. 315.) 44 p. 1928. Teachers College, Columbia. $1.50.

Mary Bartholomew, Sister. The Teaching of History. (Educational Handbook No. 2.) 129 p. 1928. Marquette Univ. $.25.

Maryland State Dept. of Education. Tentative Goals in Geography and History, Grs. I–III and Tentative Goals in Geography, Grs. IV–VII. 186 p. 1928. State Dept. of Educ. $.60.

Nesle, Oscar W. Picture Study in the Grades: Manual for Students and Teachers. 456 p. 1928. C. N. Caspar. $3.00.

Ridgley, Douglas C. A Study of Children's Learning about Places. 142 p. 1928. Clark Univ. Press. $.80.

Rugg, Earle U. The Social Studies in Teachers Colleges and Normal Schools. 162 p. 1928. Colorado State Teachers College. $1.50.

University of the State of New York. State Depart. of Education. Syllabus for Elementary Schools—Geography, Grades 5 and 6. 98 p. 1928. Univ. of the State of N. Y. $.10.

University of the State of New York. State Depart. of Education. Tentative Syllabus for History in the Elementary Schools, Grades 4–8. 113 p. 1928. Univ. of the State of N. Y. $.15.

Winslow, Leon L. Organization and Teaching of Art. Rev. ed. 243 p. 1928. Warwick & York. $2.30.

VOCATIONAL

American Management Association. Committee on Relations with Colleges. Education in Labor Problems and Training in Labor Administration in Engineering Colleges. 7 p. 1928. The Association. Gratis.

Bennett, G. Vernon. Vocational Education of Junior College Grade. 239 p. 1928. Warwick & York. $2.75.

Bevier, Isabel. Home Economics in Education. 2nd ed. 226 p. 1928. Lippincott. $2.00.

Blackstone, E. G. Research Studies in Commercial Education. II. (Univ. of Iowa Monographs on Education.) 127 p. 1928. Univ. of Iowa. $.50.

Brown, C. M. T., and Haley, A. H. The Teaching of Home Economics. 395 p. 1928. Houghton Mifflin. $2.00.

Carnegie Institute of Technology. College Training in Printing. 64 p. 1928. Dept. of Printing. Gratis.

Dyer, Annie R. The Administration of Home Economics in City Schools: a Study of Present and Desired Practice in the Organization of the Home Economics Program. (Cont. to Educ. No. 318.) 143 p. 1928. Teachers College, Columbia, $1.50.

Eastern Commercial Teachers Association. First Yearbook. Foundations of Commercial Education. 423 p. 1928. The Association. $2.50.

Henig, Max S. Safety Education in the Vocational School. The Reconstruction of a Curriculum for Accident Prevention. 110 p. 1928. National Bureau of Casualty and Surety Underwriters. $1.40.

Lomax, Paul S. Commercial Teaching Problems. 200 p. 1928. Prentice-Hall. $1.25.

Malott, J. O. Commercial Education in 1924–1926. (Bulletin No. 4.) 33 p. 1928. U. S. Bureau of Education. $.10.

Nebraska State Board for Vocational Education. Report of the Annual State Conference for Vocational Agriculture Teachers. 58 p. 1928. The Board.

Nebraska State Board for Vocational Education. Vocational Education in Smith-Hughes Schools in Nebraska. (Bulletin No. 17.) 26 p. 1928. The Board.

Nebraska State Board for Vocational Education. Vocational Education. The Choice of a Life Work. (Bulletin No. 6.) 46 p. 1928. The Board.

Proffitt, Maris M. Private and Endowed Schools Offering Trade and Industrial Courses. (Bulletin No. 18.) 50 p. 1928. U. S. Bureau of Education. $.10.

Schmidt, G. A. Efficiency in Vocational Education in Agriculture. 314 p. 1928. Century. $2.25.

Slay, Ronald J. The Development of the Teaching of Agriculture in Mississippi, with Special Emphasis on Agriculture as a Part of School Curricula. (Cont. to Educ. No. 310.) 194 p. 1928. Teachers College, Columbia. $2.00.

Smith, Homer J. Teaching Aids for the Asking. (Free Material for Manual Art Teaching.) 60 p. 1928. Univ. of Minn. $.50.

Teeter, Verl A. A Syllabus on Vocational Guidance. 217 p. 1928. Macmillan. $1.00.

U. S. Federal Board for Vocational Education. Cooperative Part-Time Education: The Present Status of Cooperative Schools and Classes in the United States. (Bulletin No. 130. Trade and Industrial Series No. 34.) 35 p. 1928. The Board. $.10.

U. S. Federal Board for Vocational Education. A Course in Farm Shop Work for Teachers of Vocational Agriculture. (Monograph No. 5.) 10 p. 1928. The Board. $.05.

U. S. Federal Board for Vocational Education. Foreman Training in the United States. Bulletin No. 131. Trade and Industrial Series No. 37.) 28 p. 1928. The Board. $.10.

U. S. Federal Board for Vocational Education. Plant and Equipment for Vocational Classes in Home Economics for Use of Those Responsible for Determining Plant and Equipment for Vocational Schools and Classes. 123 p. 1928. The Board. $.40.

U. S. Federal Board for Vocational Education. Progress in Foreman Training: A Study of the Results of Eleven Leader-Training Conferences. (Bulletin No. 127. Trade and Industrial Series No. 34.) 27 p. 1928. The Board. $.10.

U. S. Federal Board for Vocational Education. The Training of Teachers for Agriculture Evening Class Work. (Bulletin No. 129. Agricultural Series No. 34.) 69 p. 1928. The Board. $.15.

Warner, W. E. Policies in Industrial Arts Education. 90 p. 1928. Ohio State Univ. Press. $1.00.

HEALTH AND PHYSICAL EDUCATION

American Child Health Association and Metropolitan Life Insurance Company. Health Programs from Many Lands. A Report of the Health Section of the World Federation of Education Associations, Toronto, August 8–12, 1927.

209 p. 1928. American Child Health Association. $.50.

Bennett, Henry E. School Posture and Seating. 323 p. 1928. Ginn. $2.00.

Brownell, Clifford L. A Scale for Measuring the Antero-posterior Posture of Ninth Grade Boys. (Cont. to Educ. No. 325.) 60 p. 1928. Teachers College, Columbia. $1.50.

Cattell, Psyche. Dentition as a Measure of Maturity. (Harvard Monographs in Education No. 9.) 91 p. 1928. Harvard Univ. Press. $1.00.

Chapin, Henry D. Heredity and Child Culture. Rev. ed. 278 p. 1928. Dutton. $2.50.

Griffith, Coleman R. Psychology and Athletics. 281 p. 1928. Scribner's. $2.00.

Lowman, C. L., Colestock, Claire, and Cooper, Hazel. Corrective Physical Education for Groups. 521 p. 1928. A. S. Barnes. $4.50.

McCormick, Mary G. Suggestions to the Rural Teachers on the Selection of Their Own Diet. 7 p. 1928. Univ. of the State of N. Y. $.05.

Maroney, Frederick W. Physical Education Teaching Manual. 397 p. Lyons & Carnahan. $2.00.

Morrison, W. R., and Chenoweth, L. B. Normal and Elementary Physical Diagnosis. 384 p. 1928. Lea & Febiger. $4.00.

Myers, A. F., and Bird, O. C. Health and Physical Education. 342 p. 1928. Doubleday Doran. About $1.50.

Panzer, Henry. A Teacher's Manual of Physical Education: General Gymnastics for Boys. 237 p. 1928. A. S. Barnes. $2.00.

Rodgers, Martin. A Handbook of Stunts. 515 p. 1928. Macmillan. $3.00.

Rogers, J. F. Ten Steps in the Promotion of Health in Rural Schools. (U. S. Bureau of Education, School Health Studies No. 14.) 8 p. 1928. The Bureau. $.05.

Smith, H. N., and Coops, H. L. Play Days: Their Organization and Correlation with a Program of Physical Education and Health. 45 p. 1928. A. S. Barnes. $.75.

Stafford, George T. Preventive and Corrective Physical Education. 328 p. 1928. A. S. Barnes. $3.00.

Sterling, E. B. 1. Health Studies of Negro Children. 2. Physical Status of the Urban Negro School Children in Atlanta, Georgia. (Public Health Reports, Vol. 43, No. 42.) 1928. U. S. Public Health Service. $.05.

U. S. Bureau of Education. Professional Training in Physical Education. (Physical Education Series No. 9.) 45 p. 1928. The Bureau. $.05.

University of Michigan. Dept. of Physical Education. Physical Education Activities for High School Girls. 322 p. 1928. Lea & Febiger. $3.50.

University of the State of New York. The Administration of the Medical Inspection Law. Health Bulletin 1. (Bulletin 912.) 38 p. 1928. Univ. of the State of N. Y. $.10.

Wayman, Agnes R. Education through Physical Education. Rev. ed. 378 p. 1928. Lea & Febiger. $4.00.

Wood, Thomas D. Conserving the Sight of School Children: A Program for Public Schools. Rev. ed. 56 p. 1928. National Society for the Prevention of Blindness. $.35.

Wood, Thomas D., and Lerrigo, Marion O. Fresh Air in the School Room. 8 p. 1928. Public School Pub. Co. $.05.

Wood, Thomas D., and Lerrigo, Marion O. The Health Behavior Supplement. 32 p. 1928. Public School Pub. Co. $.25.

Wood, Thomas D., and Lerrigo, Marion O. Teaching How to Get and Use Human Energy. (Book I of the Series Teachers' Problems in Health Education.) 1928. Public School Pub. Co. About $.75.

EXTRACURRICULAR ACTIVITIES

Abbott, Mary A. Motion Pictures for Different School Grades. 42 p. 1928. Teachers College, Columbia. $.40.

Blackburn, Lura. Our High School Clubs. 253 p. 1928. Macmillan. $1.25.

Deam, T. M., and Bear, O. M. Socializing the Pupil through Extra-Curricular Activities. 324 p. 1928. Sanborn.

Jordan, Riverda H. Extra-Classroom Activities in Elementary and Secondary Schools. 302 p. 1928. Crowell. $2.50.

Martin, Mrs. Ida (Shaw). The Sorority Handbook. Rev. ed. 169 p. 1928. Ida S. Martin. $2.25.

Roberts, A. C., and Draper, E. M. Extra Class and Intramural Activities in High Schools. 529 p. 1928. Heath. $2.40.

RURAL EDUCATION

Covert, Timon. Educational Achievements of One-Teacher and Larger Rural Schools. (Bulletin No. 15.) 1928. U. S. Bureau of Education.

Gaumnitz, W. H. Comparative Status of Secondary Education in Rural and Urban Communities. (Rural School Leaflet No. 44.) 14 p. 1928. U. S. Bureau of Education. $.05.

Holloway, William J. Participation in Curriculum Making as a Means of Supervision of Rural

Schools. (Cont. to Educ. No. 301.) 1928. Teachers College, Columbia. $1.50.

Samuelson, Agnes, and Parker, J. M. Standardization of Rural Schools. 27 p. 1928. Iowa Depart. of Public Instruction.

Tennessee Department of Education. Building Plans for Rural School Houses. 56 p. 1928. The Department.

U. S. Bureau of Education. Professional Preparation of Teachers for Rural Schools. (Bulletin No. 6.) 71 p. 1928. The Bureau. $.15.

Higher Education

Angell, Robert C. The Campus. 239 p. 1928. Appleton. $2.50.

Arnett, Trevor. Teachers' Salaries in Certain Endowed and State-Supported Colleges and Universities in the United States, with Special Reference to Colleges of Arts, Literature and Science, 1926–27. (Occasional Papers No. 8.) 84 p. 1928. General Education Board.

Benn, John A. Columbus-Undergraduate. 149 p. 1928. Lippincott. $2.00.

Chittenden, Russell H. History of the Sheffield Scientific School of Yale University. 1846–1922. 2 vol. 660 p. 1928. Yale Univ. Press. $10.00.

Coulter, Ellis M. College Life in the Old South. 381 p. 1928. Macmillan. $2.25.

Crawford, Nelson A. A Man of Learning. 272 p. 1928. Little Brown. $2.50.

Edwards, R. H., Artman, J. M., and Fisher, G. M. Undergraduates: A Study of Morale in Twenty-three American Colleges and Universities. 376 p. 1928. Doubleday Doran. $4.00.

Goodspeed, Thomas W. William Rainey Harper. 241 p. 1928. Univ. of Chicago Press. $3.00.

Greenleaf, Walter J. The Land-Grant Colleges and Universities, 1927. (Bulletin No. 14.) 77 p. 1928. U. S. Bureau of Education. $.15.

Guandolo, Joseph, *ed.* Centennial McKendree College with St. Clair County History. 643 p. 1928. McKendree College. $10.00.

Halle, Rita S. Which College? 268 p. 1928. Macmillan. $1.50.

Ho, Ching-Ju. Personnel Studies of Scientists in the United States. (Cont. to Educ. No. 298.) 59 p. 1928. Teachers College, Columbia. $1.50.

Hudelson, Earl. Class Size at the College Level. 299 p. 1928. Univ. of Minn. $3.00.

Hudelson, Earl, *ed.* Problems of College Education. 449 p. 1928. Univ. of Minn. Press. $3.00.

Kelly, Robert L., *ed.*, and others. The Effective College. 302 p. 1928. Association of American Colleges. $2.00.

McConn, Max. College or Kindergarten? 275 p. 1928. New Republic. $1.00.

Meyer, Jacob G. Small Colleges and Teacher Training. 162 p. 1928. Public School Pub. Co. $1.00.

National Catholic Welfare Conference Bureau of Education. 1928 Directory of Catholic Colleges and Schools. 591 p. 1928. N. C. W. C. Bureau of Educ. $4.50.

National Education Association Research Division. The College of Tomorrow: Its Relation to the High School and to Life. 24 p. 1928. The Association. $.10.

Ogg, Frederic A. Research in the Humanistic and Social Sciences. 454 p. 1928. Century. $2.50.

Quiller-Couch, Sir Arthur T. A Lecture on Lectures. 60 p. 1928. Harcourt, Brace. $1.00.

Rammelkamp, Charles H. Illinois College: A Centennial History. 600 p. 1928. Yale Univ. Press. $7.50.

Remmers, H. H. A Diagnostic and Remedial Study of Potentially and Actually Failing Students at Purdue University. (Purdue Univ. Studies in Higher Education No. 9.) 164 p. 1928. Purdue Univ. $.75.

Robertson, David A., *ed.* American Universities and Colleges. 884 p. 1928. Scribner's. $2.50.

Shaw, J. H., and Whitney, F. L. The Junior College Movement. 48 p. 1928. Colorado State Teachers College. Gratis.

Shultz, Irving T. A Descriptive and Predictive Study of a Class in a School of Education. 131 p. 1928. Univ. of Pa.

Thwing, Charles F. The American and the German University. 238 p. 1928. Macmillan. $2.25.

U. S. Bureau of Education. Accredited Higher Institutions. (Bulletin No. 41.) 40 p. 1928. The Bureau. $.10.

U. S. Bureau of Education. Survey of Negro Colleges and Universities. 1928. The Bureau. (Fourteen sections published by state. Not yet completed.)

University of the State of New York. Report on Higher Education in the State of New York for the School Year Ending July 13, 1926. (Bulletin No. 395.) 80 p. 1928. Univ. of the State of N. Y.

Whitney, Frederick L. Junior College in America. 300 p. 1928. Colorado State Teachers College. $2.75.

ADULT EDUCATION

Alderman, L. R. College and University Extension: Helps in Adult Education. (Bulletin No. 3.) 35 p. 1928. U. S. Bureau of Education. $.10.

American Association for Adult Education. Annual Report of the Executive Director in Behalf of the Executive Board for the Year 1927–1928. 23 p. 1928. American Association for Adult Education.

American Association for Adult Education. Digest of the Proceedings of the Third Annual Meeting, Swarthmore, Pa., May 14–16, 1928. New York. Bulletin of the American Association for Adult Education. 161 p. 1928.

American Federation of Teachers. The Place of Workers' Education in the Labor Movement; Proceedings of the Fifth Annual Conference of Teachers in Workers' Education, 1928. 74 p. 1928. American Federation of Teachers. Brookwood, Katonah, N. Y.

Association of Urban Universities. Summary of Proceedings of the Association at the Carnegie Institute of Technology, Pittsburgh, 1927. 160 p. 1928. The Association, Pittsburgh.

Beglinger, Nina J. Methods in Adult Elementary Education. Rev. ed. 185 p. 1928. Scribner's. $1.00.

Campbell, Olive D. The Danish Folk School, Its Influence in the Life of Denmark and the North. 359 p. 1928. Macmillan. $2.00.

Cleveland Conference for Educational Cooperation. Report of the Committee on Adult Education. 70 p. 1928. The Conference, Cleveland.

Elliott, Harrison S. The Process of Group Thinking. 229 p. 1928. Association Press. $3.00.

Fernandes, Grace. A Critical Study of Periodical Reading in Farm Homes. (Oklahoma Agr. Exp. Sta. Bulletin 176.) 16 p. 1928. Okla. A. & M. College, Stillwater, Okla.

Noffsinger, John S., *comp.* Home Study Blue Book: A Directory of Approved Correspondence Courses. 21 p. 1928. National Home Study Council.

Thorndike, E. L., Bregman, E. O., Tilton, J. W., and Woodyard, E. Adult Learning. 335 p. 1928. Macmillan. $2.25.

University of the State of New York. Certification and Training of Adult Immigrant Education Teachers. 7 p. 1928. Univ. of the State of N. Y. $.10.

EDUCATIONAL EVENTS

SCHOOLS IN ICELAND

AN Icelandic correspondent of the International Bureau of Education *Bulletin* sends a letter on the present conditions in public education in his country, in which he says:

Do the children in the public schools of Iceland reach the same level as the Danish children? Mr. Magnus Helgason, director of the Normal School, made a trip to Denmark to decide this question. Mr. Helgason thinks that the children of Reykjavick, Akureyri and Isafjödur are just as far advanced as their Danish comrades, except perhaps in gymnastics and singing. But in these cities the school year lasts nearly eight months. What about the pupils of the itinerant schools of the rest of Iceland, where most of the children only go to school eight to twelve weeks a year? Obviously they can not learn much at school. However, the teachers in the city secondary schools think that these children as a rule do better in the secondary schools than their city brothers. Although possessing less knowledge, they are more developed and thoughtful. This is due partly to their quiet life, but also to the history of the language and literature of Iceland. This country has a magnificent literary heritage, almost as old as the race itself. Iceland was already inhabited in the year 930, and writing was known in the 11th century. In the 12th and 13th centuries the Eddas and the legends telling the history of the origin of Norway and Iceland were composed. The Icelandic language has hardly changed since that time, so that all Icelanders can read these masterpieces, and many of them know them by heart.

The northern winter is long; night comes early, and the people have leisure to read and think. Their dwellings are very far from each other, and each must be sufficient unto itself. Books become friends. In the evening the family gathers together to work while some one reads aloud, then they discuss what has been read. Thus the young people acquire a very sure literary taste, and absorb much general culture. Intellectual curiosity is developed, and those who can not afford to go to the secondary school continue to learn by reading at home.

Unfortunately, many of the country people are moving into the cities, so that the remaining farmers must work harder and have less leisure for reading. At the present time, the transformation of secondary education is being discussed in Iceland, with a view to increasing the number of schools and improving the program.

CONFERENCE OF ENGLISH HEADMASTERS

According to a wireless to the New York *Times,* boys in British "public" schools will henceforth receive Old Testament instruction only when they reach the higher grades. The headmasters decided this at a recent conference. In its place, to the youngest children will be taught a "Christian View of God" from the Gospels, and their Old Testament knowledge will be concerned chiefly with the great stories which it contains.

"There is a very real danger," the headmasters said in their report, "that what may be called the 'Old Testament view of God' should be accepted by the young as the normal, indeed, the orthodox view, slightly modified by the New Testament. We are, therefore, anxious to see the truer view laid from the first.

"At the earliest stage, for children starting at three and a half years, we wish to see the Gospels studied not so much from the viewpoint of a criticized text as on the broad lines of Christian belief and Christian practice, so that the boys and girls may realize that the only Christian view of God is that which Christ held."

The later years of the child's religious education, in the opinion of the headmasters, should be devoted to the Old Testament.

"Every boy and girl," their report declared, "should be taught to recognize that the main importance of the Jewish contribution to the world lies in the prophets and the psalms."

For the third and last stage of the child's religious education the headmasters recommended studying the growth of the early Christian Church.

The headmasters appeared deeply concerned by the revelation that young medical students, boys and girls together, were carrying on experiments in medical laboratories, beginning at sixteen years old.

"It is a terrible thing," said H. Craddock-Watson, headmaster of the Merchant Tailors School, "that in the medical profession young people should be thrust into the chartered freedom of the universities at the age of sixteen to embark on studies which in some phases are rather coarsening. It is difficult to think of boys and girls, who are flung at that age into mixed classes in the dissecting room, developing into the intimate, confidential family friend that the doctor often becomes."

The conference decided to "use pressure" on the universities to have these conditions remedied.

APPROPRIATIONS FOR THE UNIVERSITY OF MINNESOTA

Including its support and equipment appropriations, its building fund and its special appropriations for agricultural extension, iron ore investigations and medical research, the University of Minnesota received $4,637,902 from the state of Minnesota by state appropriation and millage tax in the year 1927–28, for which the annual report of the comptroller, W. T. Middlebrook, has been issued.

The building appropriation of $560,000 grew to $595,505 as a result of interest on certificates of deposit; appropriations for special purposes came to $223,775, and state support for maintenance and equipment amounted to $3,818,621, of which $426,121 came from the 23-100ths millage tax, $3,275,000 from the maintenance appropriations, $100,000 for hospital support and the remainder as special support for outlying divisions.

The university also received $293,633 in federal grants of many kinds, $142,513 from the permanent university fund, which was once thought sufficient to support higher education, and $75,328 from the swamp land fund. Student fees added $1,045,348 to receipts, and a series of items called university income added $423,670.

Service enterprises and revolving funds, whereby the university conducts its cafeterias, dormitories and the like, produced income of $1,784,756, most of which was balanced by approximately corresponding outlay. Intercollegiate athletics brought in $386,705, after other teams had been granted their share of the receipts. Trust funds, including gifts of principal, interest and money received from securities maturing for reinvestment, yielded $737,443, making the grand total $9,527,303.

Outlay, including payment of $615,729 for the Field House, partly from money obtained the year before by sale of certificates of indebtedness, amounted to $10,504,673, including the investment of $642,918 of trust funds in various securities.

Chief items making up the university's outlay were: Administration, $184,925; general expense, $421,782; instructional salaries, supplies and expenses, $4,728,149; physical plant on all campuses, including cost of the field house, $2,079,574; dormitories and dining halls, $390,418; stores, $335,660; student service enterprises, $164,995; general service enterprises, $681,352; revolving funds, $164,450; intercollegiate athletics, $249,448; trust funds investments, $642,918; bond redemptions, (1) from building fund for payment on Northern Pacific track removal, $336,000; (2) for retirement of field house certificates, $125,000; grand total, $10,504,673.

Among individual colleges, agriculture, forestry and home economics cost most, with $822,520, and science, literature and the arts next most, with $793,897. The University Hospital cost $336,777, exclusive of physical plant and construction costs. General extension cost $196,076 and agricultural extensions, $285,522. Physical plant costs amounted to $1,880,918 on the main campus, including construction costs, and $295,311 at University Farm.

Under "detail of student enrolment" Mr. Middlebrook's report shows that there were registered during the year 15,851 students of college ranking, including summer sessions registrants. There were 1,451 in sub-collegiate courses, including the schools of agriculture and university high school; 1,622 in various short courses on the agricultural campus; 8,975 students in the General Extension Division, made up of 2,470 taking correspondence work, 6,023 in evening courses and 482 in short courses. The total registration for the entire year in all branches came to 25,895 after the subtraction of 2,004 duplicate registrations between the regular year, summer sessions and extension courses.

THE FINANCES OF NEW YORK UNIVERSITY

A TOTAL of $5,675,596.08 was spent by New York University during the past year for the operating expenses of the eleven degree and six non-degree schools and divisions of the university, according to the annual report of William M. Kingsley, president of the United States Trust Company of New York and treasurer of the university.

The report showed a $105,939 deficit for the year, which is more than $100,000 less than the deficit for the preceding year. Nearly half the total expenditure for the twelve months, $2,753,793.23, was spent on salaries for the faculty members in all centers of the university. The payroll of the employees of the university other than faculty amounted to $431,494.08.

Gifts and bequests to the university amounted to $942,343. Gifts toward university capital totaled $730,532, while those for immediate use amounted to $211,810.

The report showed that $674,444 was added to the productive endowment of the university, the total endowment now amounting to $4,256,767. The interest from endowment accounted for $197,467 of the total income of the university, while tuition collections amounted to almost $5,000,000.

One item of expense in the report indicated the development of night instruction, which is a growing characteristic of all great urban educational institutions. New York University spent $68,000 to illuminate classrooms and laboratories during the year. Most of the university buildings are open for instruction purposes six nights a week. Approximately 10,000 students attended night classes during the last academic year. Telephone charges amounted to $31,000.

During the year 1927–28 New York University provided for scholarships and fellowships for 701 worthy students. Of the total amount of more than $75,000 set aside for scholarship help, $25,910.40 was derived from special endowments given for that purpose.

COMMERCIAL OCCUPATION SURVEYS

COMMERCIAL occupation surveys and researches contributed more than all other factors to the progress of commercial education during the years 1924–26. The facts obtained from the surveys have resulted in a better understanding of the needs of those who are preparing for business occupations.

According to Bureau of Education *Bulletin,* 1928, No. 4, those investigations have given direction not only to the program of commercial education and training, but to the programs of guidance, placement, follow-up and extension education. These studies have been encouraged by the Bureau of Education and other agencies.

One of the most valuable reports issued during 1924–26 was a survey of 8,200 women in clerical and secretarial positions in 191 business establishments in Minneapolis. A unique feature of the study is that it was sponsored by a group of civic, professional, educational and commercial organizations. It revealed that there is a very general indifference on the part of employers regarding experience in many types of office work. More than 58 per cent. did not require experience, 31.8 per cent. indicated some experience was required, and the remainder required certain minimum amounts of experience. The survey also revealed the small amount of effort that is put forth by the public schools to find employment for the drop-outs and graduates. Less than 11 per cent. of the commercial workers in that city were placed by the public schools and more than 30 per cent. were placed by commercial employment agencies.

Two studies were conducted by the division of research of the Board of Education, at Cleveland, Ohio, and by Mr. J. T. Giles, state high school supervisor, of Madison, Wisconsin. The latter study of 4,918 graduates from commercial departments of 108 Wisconsin high schools, 1921–1925, indicates that the commercial curricula in Wisconsin high schools are better adapted to the needs of the girls than of the boys. Seventy-three per cent. of the graduates from these curricula are girls. Thirty-eight per cent. of the girl graduates hold positions requiring a knowledge of stenography and only 13 per cent. of the boys hold such positions. Forty-five per cent. of the graduates of the larger high schools hold positions calling for stenography, while in the smaller schools only 16 per cent. of the graduates hold such positions.

Many other surveys have been made and additional ones are in progress. Occupational studies are reported in progress in Elizabeth, New Jersey, Huntington, West Virginia, Grand Rapids, Michigan, Madison, Wisconsin, and Allentown, Pennsylvania, and state-wide studies in Connecticut, Minnesota and Wyoming. More than 1,500 business firms cooperated in the office equipment survey in Philadelphia.

THE NATIONAL LEAGUE OF NURSING EDUCATION

The National League of Nursing Education, New York City, asks the cooperation of the library profession in its program for the wider dissemination of information on nursing.

The league will supply on request: (1) A list of recommended books on nursing. (2) Material on the subject of nursing as a profession to be added to the other material on vocational guidance in libraries, *viz.,* a booklet entitled "Opportunities in the Field of Nursing."

The close physical relationship of the three national nursing organizations, including the editorial offices of the *American Journal of Nursing* and *The Public Health Nurse,* the recent addition of the committee on the grading of nursing schools, the National Health Library and the various health organizations, provide at headquarters ample machinery for source and exchange of information.

The list of information available includes material on (1) Ratio of nurses to patients; (2) how to establish the eight-hour day; (3) how to establish a hospital nursing school; (4) how to organize a university nursing school; (5) how to organize a central school; (6) what resources are needed in a community for organizing a nursing school; (7) method of establishing affiliations; (8) courses for graduate nurses both in hospitals and universities; (9) staff education; (10) supervision; (11) ward teaching; (12) case study; (13) new type examination questions; (14) libraries, organization and conduct; (15) bibliographies; (16) endowments; (17) loan funds; (18) scholarships; (19) health programs and how to introduce them in a school; (20) salary schedules; (21) budgets; (22) comparative cost to the hospital of a graduate nurse staff and maintaining a school; (23) records; (24) personnel classification; (25) commencement exercises; (26) ward equipment and classroom equipment; (27) duties of nurses' examining boards; (28) preparation and opportunities of male nurses; (29) preparation and opportunities for trained attendants, etc.

The league is now making an Index of Nursing Periodical Literature, in connection with the Library Index of The National Health Council at 370 Seventh Avenue, New York City.

THE PHI BETA KAPPA SENATE

JOHN W. DAVIS, former ambassador to Great Britain, and Dr. Frank Pierrepont Graves, N. Y. state commissioner of education, newly elected members of the Phi Beta Kappa Senate, attended a meeting on December 21 in New York City, and were installed in their new offices. Dwight W. Morrow, ambassador to Mexico; Owen D. Young and Dr. Raymond B. Fosdick, also elected to the Senate, were unable to be present and were formally declared seated.

It was decided that seven new charters be established at the following institutions: Emory University, Atlanta, Ga.; University of Richmond, Richmond, Va.; Ohio University, Athens, Ohio; Rice Institute, Houston, Texas; University of Southern California, Los Angeles; Mills College, Oakland, Cal., and the State College of Washington, Pullman, Washington.

It was decided that plans for encouraging scholarships, under the charter received by the Board of Regents of the University of the State of New York, would be formulated in cooperation with the Classical League and similar organizations, in celebration of the Virgil bimillennium celebration. An endowment was recently raised for these scholarships.

The following were among the members of the Phi Beta Kappa Senate present at the meeting: Dr. John Grier Hibben, president of Princeton University; Dr. Darwin P. Kingsley, president of New York Life Insurance Company; Dr. Charles F. Thwing, president emeritus of Western Reserve University; Mary Emma Woolley, president of Mount Holyoke College, and Ellen Fitz Pendleton, president of Wellesley College. Dr. Clark S. Northup, professor of English, Cornell University, and president of the United Chapter of the Phi Beta Kappa, presided.

EDUCATIONAL NOTES AND NEWS

DR. GEORGE REEVES THROOP, professor of Greek and acting chancellor of Washington University, St. Louis, has been elected chancellor by the governing board to succeed the late Herbert Hadley.

DR. JAMES M. KIERAN, dean of the faculty of education and acting president of Hunter College, has been elected president to succeed Dr. George S. Davis, now on leave of absence, who retires on February 1.

MRS. SUSAN M. DORSEY, after thirty-two years of service in the schools of Los Angeles, resigned as superintendent of schools at the meeting of the Board of Education on December 6. Frank A. Bouelle, assistant superintendent, was named as her successor and W. W. Tritt, principal of Belmont High School, was nominated to fill the latter vacancy. Mrs. Dorsey's resignation becomes effective on January 31, on the eve of her seventy-second birthday and at the close of the first year of her third four-year contract. Following the reading of her letter to the board, President John B. Beman thanked Mrs. Dorsey for the great service she had rendered in upbuilding the school system of Los Angeles, saying, "I feel that we are losing the services of the best superintendent that this or any other city could have. I am not able to express the deep appreciation and admiration that we as members of this board feel for Mrs. Dorsey."

A. B. DAVIS, who recently retired as principal of the Mount Vernon, N. Y., high school after a service of thirty-five years, has been named principal emeritus of the school. In honor of Mr. Davis and the work which he did as principal of the school, the board has recommended that the next new high school be named the A. B. Davis High School.

IN appreciation of his thirty-eight years' service to the University of California and of his contributions to science in the field of geology, the regents at their regular November meeting unanimously passed a commendatory resolution in honor of Professor Emeritus A. C. Lawson, who retired from active service at Berkeley this year. The resolution concluded: "The regents, the president and all those professors who have had the privilege of knowing Professor Lawson place a very high value upon the services he has rendered to human society under the auspices of the university, and they regret to learn that it was necessary to comply with the request of Professor Lawson for relief from active duty; but they find deep satisfaction in his decision to remain in Berkeley as a member of the university community, with definite purpose, as stated by himself, to serve further 'the purposes of the university for a few years, by setting down in writing some of the results of observation and study that have accumulated in the course of a fairly active life.' "

Dr. George S. Counts, associate director of the International Institute and professor of education at Teachers College, Columbia University, will deliver the Inglis lecture for 1929 at the graduate school of education of Harvard University. His subject will be "Secondary Education and Industrialism."

Dr. George J. Fisher, deputy chief scout executive of the Boy Scouts of America and president of the American Posture League, has been awarded the Luther Halsey Gulick award of the New York Physical Education Society for distinguished service in the field of physical education this year. Formal presentation of the medal will take place at a dinner to be held in May.

The Belgian Academy of Sciences, Letters and Fine Arts has elected Professor James T. Shotwell an associate in the section of history and letters. As director of the division of economics and history of the Carnegie Endowment for International Peace, Professor Shotwell is engaged in editing the "Economic and Social History of the World War," a work which will comprise 200 volumes when completed. 103 volumes have already been published.

Hermann Diederichs, John E. Sweet memorial professor of engineering at Cornell University, has been elected faculty representative on the board of trustees.

Dr. LeRoy A. King, professor of educational administration of the University of Pennsylvania, has been appointed by Governor Fisher member of the State Council of Education. Professor King has made studies of the problems of educational finance in the state.

Professor Henry B. Hall, of Boston, has accepted appointment as head of the department of history at Colby College for the remainder of the year, to replace Professor George L. Ridgeway, who has been forced to resign because of illness.

Dr. Fred L. Pattee, for many years professor of American literature at Pennsylvania State College, has resigned his position and has accepted a similar office on the faculty of Rollins College. His course in American literature will begin on January 2. The title of professor emeritus has been conferred on Dr. Pattee by the Pennsylvania State College.

Francis K. W. Drury, assistant professor of library science and assistant librarian at Brown University, has resigned to become executive assistant to the board of the library and adult education of the American Library Association, with his headquarters in the John Crerar Library Building, Chicago.

Governor-elect Roosevelt, of New York State, is reported to have decided to appoint Miss Frances Perkins as state industrial commissioner at the head of the Department of Labor, to succeed Dr. James A. Hamilton. Miss Perkins is now chairman of the State Industrial Board.

Dr. Louise Stanley, chief of the bureau of home economics of the U. S. Department of Agriculture, known for her scientific investigations in nutrition, has been appointed as official representative of the department of Agriculture on the American Standards Association.

Because of the pressure of his work as educational director of the Commonwealth Fund, Professor Edward Bliss Reed has resigned from his position as an editor of *The Yale Review*, which he has held since 1911.

Miss Edna Gerkin, director of public education in the Durfee High School, Fall River, Massachusetts, and a former student in the department of biology and public health at Massachusetts Institute of Technology, has been appointed to assist in establishing a health program for school children in the Philippine Islands.

GEORGE R. RAY, superintendent of schools at Darlington, Wisconsin, has purchased the controlling interest in the Parker Teachers Agency and will take over the management on January 1, 1929.

THE Institute of Economics, now part of the Brookings Institution, is conducting an economic and social survey of Porto Rico under the directorship of Dr. Victor S. Clark, until recently editor of *The Living Age*. Dr. Clark will be assisted by Mr. Hugh J. Reber, recently a member of the American financial mission in Persia, who holds a research fellowship from the Brookings Institution, and by Professor Erich W. Zimmermann, who is on a leave of absence from the University of North Carolina.

DR. CASIMIR D. ZDANOWICZ, chairman of the Romance language department of the University of Wisconsin, is on a year's leave of absence studying seventeenth century literature at the Bibliothèque Nationale in Paris.

PROFESSOR FREDERICK A. BUSHEE, University of Colorado, acting dean of the school of business administration and head of the department of economics and sociology, has been granted a sabbatical leave of absence for the academic year of 1928–29, and is spending the time in travel and study in Europe.

DR. HOMER P. LITTLE, dean of Clark University, leaves New York on February 14 to spend a year's leave of absence in Europe.

DR. E. R. HEDRICK, professor of mathematics at the University of California at Los Angeles and president-elect of the American Mathematical Society, undertook in November and December a lecture tour, during which he visited the following universities: Missouri, Ohio State, Cincinnati, Kentucky, Oberlin, Michigan, Wisconsin, Northwestern, Indiana, Pittsburgh, Carnegie Institute, West Virginia and Pennsylvania.

PROFESSOR CHARLES HALL GRANDGENT will become acting dean of the faculty of arts and sciences of Harvard University during the second half of the college year, 1928–29, taking the place of Dean Clifford H. Moore, who will be on leave of absence. Professor Grandgent has been for thirty-two years professor of Romance languages.

HARVEY H. DAVIS, director of the division of records and statistics of the St. Louis, Missouri, schools, has become assistant professor in the department of school administration at the Ohio State University. Mr. Davis will work under Professor W. James Osborn, who has recently become professor in the department of school administration.

PAUL G. EDWARDS, a teacher of chemistry at the Lane and Crance Technical high schools, Chicago, has been made supervisor of science in the Chicago public schools.

A. F. STAUFFER has been appointed assistant superintendent of schools at Jersey City, N. J. He is a graduate of the Pennsylvania State Normal School and Lafayette College and holds degrees given by Lafayette College and Columbia University.

HENRY SMITH, of Antigo, Wis., has been elected superintendent of schools at South Milwaukee, Wisconsin. Mr. Smith is succeeded by Mr. R. E. Balliette, of Madison.

SIR WILLIAM BEVERIDGE, director of the London School of Economics, has been appointed to deliver the Sidney Ball lecture at the University of Oxford in Michaelmas term next year.

WALDO G. LELAND, of the department of historical research of the Carnegie Institution of Washington, gave a lecture at the institution on November 20, entitled "French Sources of American History."

DR. DANIEL L. MARSH, president of Boston University, was the principal speaker at the regular meeting of the Massachusetts Schoolmasters' Club on December 15. Dr. Marsh spoke on "Natural Tendencies as Related to Programs of Education."

JOHN MERLE COULTER, the distinguished botanist, died on December 23 in his seventy-eighth year. Dr. Coulter was professor in the University of Chicago from 1896 to 1925 and had previously been president of the University of Indiana and of Lake Forest College. Since his retirement in 1925 from the directorship of the department of botany at the University of Chicago he has been botanical adviser of the Boyce Thompson Institute at Yonkers, New York.

HENRY B. FINE, professor of mathematics and dean of the departments of science at Princeton University, died on December 21 at the age of seventy years. Professor Fine suffered injuries from an automobile while riding a bicycle.

FRANK SARGENT HOFFMAN, Archibald Spencer professor emeritus of philosophy at Union College, where for thirty-three years he was a professor, has died, aged seventy-six years.

DR. LEVI SEELEY, from 1895 to his retirement in 1924 professor of pedagogy in the State Normal School of Trenton, New Jersey, died on December 23, aged eighty-one years.

THE joint session of the International Federation and the health section of the World Federation of Education Associations, which is to be held at the Geneva convention in 1929, will discuss the subject of "The Health of the Child in Home, School and Community." Dr. Thomas D. Wood, of Columbia University, health chairman of the International Federation, will preside at this session.

THE eighteenth annual meeting of the Council of Church Boards of Education will be held at Chattanooga, Tennessee, on January 7, 8 and 10, in conjunction with the fifteenth annual meeting of the Association of American Colleges which will be held on January 10 and 12.

MORE than 200 educators, including supervisors, superintendents, school administrators, critic teachers, members of faculties of education in colleges and normal schools, attended the three-day conference of the Indiana State Conference of Student Teaching at Ball Teachers College, Muncie, Indiana, on December 6, 7 and 8. Dr. W. H. Burton, of the University of Chicago, was the principal speaker. The general theme of the conference was "The Critic Teacher Holds the Strategic Position in the Improvement of Student Teaching." Ten of the thirteen members of the Indiana state board of education took part in the conference.

THE eighteenth annual meeting of the College Art Association of America is holding a three-days meeting which began on December 27 at the Metropolitan Museum of Art. Delegates from all over the United States and Europe are in attendance. The College Art Association was founded in 1912 by a group of university professors from different sections of America but has in recent years become international in scope. The officers of the association are: John Shapley, *president;* Alfred V. Churchill, *vice-president;* James B. Munn, *secretary;* J. Donald Young, *treasurer.*

THE ninth annual convention of the Progressive Education Association will be held at St. Louis, Missouri, on February 21, 22 and 23. It is planned to make the occasion of international importance, with notable speakers from this country and abroad. Special railroad rates with stop-over privileges for the convention of the National Education Association at Cleveland, Ohio, February 23–28, 1929, will be offered. The association will conduct next summer at State College, Pennsylvania, the first institute of instruction under its auspices. A three weeks' course will be offered, three courses in the principles and practices of Progressive Education, one week each, from July 1–19, 1929. College credits for those taking the courses will be granted by State College. A faculty of teachers has been organized who are experienced in their respective fields.

MORE than seven hundred American sociologists and educators are meeting in Chicago from December 26 to 29 for the twenty-third annual session of the American Sociological Society. The majority of meetings are at the Hotel Congress, and are directed by Dr. John M. Gillette, president of the society and professor of sociology at the University of North Dakota. Problems of the American rural community are the main topic of discussion, although attention is being paid to problems of the American family, the community, and educational sociology. The delegates expected to be welcomed by William J. Bogan, superintendent of the Chicago schools.

THE American Historical Association planned to hold its forty-third annual meeting at Indianapolis on December 28, 29 and 31. The following affiliated societies meet at the same time: Mississippi Valley Historical Association, Conference of Historical Societies, Agricultural History Society, American Catholic Historical Association, American Oriental Society—Middle West Branch, and the Bibliographical Society of America. The opening meeting is a joint one, in which the American Association and the Mississippi Valley group participate. The following topics are among those which have been selected for discussion: English history, history and other social studies in the schools, modern European history, medieval history, the West Indies, the American revolution, United States history, the south, the college and research, public archives, colonial and revolutionary history, American pre-history, the far east, Hispanic America, ancient history, modern European history and the problem of freshman history instruction.

THE appropriations committee reported to the House on December 13 a bill which carries $1,070,940 for the Bureau of Education. An item of $50,000 is included for starting an investigation of secondary education. This would occupy three years at a total cost of $225,000. For administration of Indian affairs, $16,267,803 is provided, an increase of $1,973,294; for the national park service, $7,340,940, an increase of $2,681,240, and for the reclamation service, $6,449,000, a little more than half of the current appropriation for this branch.

MYRON C. TAYLOR, of New York, chairman of the finance committee of the United States Steel Corporation, has given to Cornell University, of which he is an alumnus, the sum of $1,500,000 for a new building for the school of law.

GIFTS amounting to $2,500,000 to Phillips Exeter Academy in New Hampshire during the last year were announced by Dr. Lewis Perry, principal, at the forty-seventh annual dinner of the school's New York Alumni Association. The chief item in the list of gifts was a fund of $1,600,000 for the purpose of increasing salaries of teachers and possibly adding to the faculty. Edward S. Harkness gave $320,000 of this amount on condition that the remainder be raised and Dr. Perry reported completion of the fund. The dinner was in honor of Colonel William Boyce Thompson. Besides contributing to the fund, Mr. Thompson gave $350,000 for a new natural science and administration building at the academy and $163,000 for a baseball cage. He had previously given a gymnasium.

IT is reported that of 47,760 pupils enrolled in evening elementary schools in New York City during the school year, 1926–27, about 80 per cent., or 38,149, were of European birth. In all 28 nationalities or racial groups were represented, exclusive of the United States, which contributed only 5,438 pupils. More than half of the pupils, 19,226, were born in Central Europe. Germany headed the list with 9,336 pupils, Russia was next with 6,040, Italy sent 5,889, and 5,385 were from Poland.

DISCUSSION

THE NEW TYPE OF COLLEGE FRESHMAN

TEN years ago the college freshman was initiated to campus life by one grand brawl. He was treated like a savage by savages and came to the natural conclusion that a freshman at college was the least desirable of mankind. Arriving in the college town, he was greeted in a far less hospitable manner than was Columbus. Through the chasms between the mountains of trunks he heard the wild cries of the taxi drivers. He had no place to pitch his tent, no guide to help him. The process of registration was discouraging. It was nearly impossible to find any one who would accept his tuition money. Homesick, he signed his name and the name of his home town nearly fifty times during registration and longed for that home town each time he wrote its name upon the card. As he was shunted from the gymnasium to the recorder's office, from the athletic office to the classification committee, the sophomores turned his coat inside out, fastened his garters around his neck, rolled up his trousers and made life altogether miserable.

Now much if not all of this has changed. There has appeared something new under the sun—a new type of college freshman. This has come about largely on account of what is known as freshman week.

Though still a lusty infant of only five years, the idea of freshman week, which first saw the light of day at the University of Maine, has rapidly been adopted by more than a hundred colleges and universities throughout the land.

In most colleges where the plan is being tried the freshmen are invited to make their appearance a few days before the opening of the fall term. The freshmen have the entire campus to themselves. Only a few selected upper classmen are on hand and make it their business to supplement the activities of the administration in relieving the incoming freshmen of the most severe trials of the campus. The freshmen are given a royal welcome and made to feel at home at once. In fact the freshmen are treated as the most popular persons at the university. They are welcomed by the president and the deans, the churches make them feel at home and the fraternities prize their friendship.

Before leaving their homes each freshman has received a freshman week bulletin, giving in detail the program of activities. Having been met at the train, he soon finds himself in the college chapel for his first general assembly. Here he gets acquainted with the faculty members who have freshman week in charge and with the various group leaders. He quickly discovers that the purpose of freshman week is to help initiate him into the life of the university and to acquaint him with his various duties and privileges.

In a remarkably short time, and without a great deal of fuss, he finds that he has passed through a physical examination, the usual routine of registration, a series of library lectures, and has made the acquaintance of several faculty members in the process. In the general assemblies he begins to learn the college songs and yells, and unconsciously acquires the school spirit.

He soon gets acquainted with the deans, who lecture to him on the general rules, regulations, customs, traditions, and so on, of the institution. Through the Y. M. C. A. and Y. W. C. A. "mixers," "pep" and song festivals, picnics and moving picture shows he gets well acquainted with the other entering freshmen.

The freshmen, by this time, are becoming quite class-conscious. Arrangements are made to hold the first meeting of the freshman class for purposes of organization. At this meeting they choose their officers. Class spirit begins to blossom. This being an appropriate time, the freshmen are photographed, and their photographs are filed in the personnel office for use by the administration.

Having arrived early, the new freshman finds it easier than he had imagined to bridge the gap between high school and college. He is kept so busy that he finds little time for the usual fit of homesickness. He comes in closer contact with the faculty and students, and acquires, in a short period of time, a larger insight into the university life which is to be his. He has a much better opportunity to choose the proper course of study and to locate his rooming and boarding place. He has lost his verdant hue. He is already enrolled in the university, and has all the advantages of a few days of experience as a college student by the time the larger proportion of upper classmen arrive.

This new type of college freshman is in a much more receptive frame of mind than was the freshman of ten years ago. Instead of carrying a bruise in his heart he has thankfulness toward his newly made home; instead of being made to perform for the others' amusement, he is made a prince in a strange principality.

EARL K. HILLBRAND

THE GRADUATE SCHOOL,
MUNICIPAL UNIVERSITY OF WICHITA

HIGHER STANDARDS FOR ELEMENTARY SCHOOL TEACHERS

IT has been generally conceded that the high-school teacher should have a college education, because of the advanced character of the subject-matter to be taught, but the feeling still persists in some quarters that any one can teach in the elementary school. As a matter of fact the high-school teacher is required to teach a very limited field and is dealing with a group of children who have passed that most trying age when they want to know the last detail of everything in which they happen to have an interest. Given the proper text-books and reading assignments, the high-school student must depend but comparatively little upon the general knowledge of the teacher.

The foregoing is not true of the elementary school, where the teacher continues to be the final court of appeal on questions involving almost every field of human knowledge. Logically, then, the elementary-school teacher should have a broader and more general fund of informational knowledge than is required of the high-school teacher. It is a notorious fact that in most of the American commonwealths one may secure a certificate to teach in the common schools with very little training above high-school graduation, and in some instances, with even less than that.

Few of the institutions for the training of teachers for elementary-school work are providing for or requiring more than two years of work above high-school graduation—most of this consisting of abstract theories of technique in the hundred and one divisions and subdivisions into which the art of teaching has been artificially divided. In the past the teacher-training institutions of Colorado have been granting life elementary certificates or diplomas upon the completion of a two-year course of study above high-school graduation.

At a recent meeting of the presidents of the three state-supported institutions for the training of teachers, State Teachers College at Greeley, Western State College at Gunnison and the Adams State Normal School at Alamosa, an agreement was reached whereby the life diploma will not be granted upon the completion of the two-year course to any who matriculates after the close of the 1928 summer session. The course leading to the life diploma will henceforth be of four years' duration and carry the A.B. degree in addition to the diploma.

In the Adams State Normal School, with which the writer is affiliated, this course will carry a goodly content of orientation courses in the various fields of general knowledge and, instead of the customary methods courses, the student will be required to present from sixteen to thirty-two quarter hours as a "student in training." This time is spent in solving the every-day problems of actual school situations in the various classrooms of the city system, which constitutes the laboratory for the teacher-training institution, under the direction of trained supervisors with whom all problems of whatever kind are discussed and solved. The student is virtually an assistant teacher in the room.

The institutions will continue to grant teaching certificates at the end of the second year. However, they will be valid for only a limited period but will be convertible into the life certificates upon evidence of two years' successful teaching under same and completion of an additional year of prescribed or acceptable work in the institution. The life diploma at the end of two years' work has been nothing less than a "ball and chain" fettered to the right foot of educational progress. The new ruling should certainly be acclaimed as a step in the right direction.

C. E. HAGIE

ADAMS STATE NORMAL SCHOOL,
ALAMOSA, COLORADO

QUOTATIONS

EDUCATION IN THE NEAR EAST

THE Near East of former days is passing away. In its place there emerges a new social order. Unaccompanied by any blaring of trumpets, this geographical center of the ancient world is entering a new era in history. Many conditions and circumstances have tended to stimulate this process of change. The theme of nationalism has captivated the peoples of Syria, Turkey, Bulgaria and Greece. Reconstruction of political, social and economic systems always follows in the wake of an aroused sense of national destiny. Industrialism, too, has brought the countries bordering on the northern and eastern Mediterranean into a totally new world, not only among themselves, but in their relations with other nations.

To education, however, belongs the major credit for the making of the new Near East. The contribution which the West has made to the Near East in the realm of education has proved to be an unmixed blessing. The six American colleges in that territory have rendered a high service both to native populations and to the world at large. These educational institutions have served as channels for the expression of the idealism of the United States among Near East peoples. In turn they have raised the cultural and ethical standards of the multitudes to whom they have ministered. Robert College of Constantinople, the University of Beirut, Syria, the Constantinople Woman's College, the International College of Smyrna, the American College of Sofia and Athens College are the six schools that have so indelibly stamped their influence upon the corporate thinking of the Near East.

The international character of these six schools may best be appreciated by glancing at the national background of a typical student body. The total number of students registered at Robert College last year was 747. Of this number 373 were Turks, 111 were Greeks, 94 were Armenians, 62 were Bulgarians, 35 were Jews, 22 were Russians, 11 were Albanians and 9 were Persians. Other nationalities included American, Arabs, English, Syrians and Germans. Of the 91 members of the teaching staff, 34 were Americans, 22 were Turks, 9 were Armenians, 8 were Greeks, with the remainder of the faculty representing seven other nationalities. Greeks are contributing to the education of Bulgarian youth. The Bulgarian government is cooperating in every possible way in adding to the effectiveness of the American College at Sofia.

The Armenian Educational Foundation makes an annual appropriation to the American University at Beirut to help defray the tuition expenses of a number of students. The government of Turkey has sent twenty-four of its own nationals to study engineering at Robert College. The government of Irak supports twenty-seven students at the American University at Beirut, the Palestinian government seven, Ethiopia six, and the Sudan five. Graduates of this university are now being employed by many of the governments of the Near East for the reorganization of their respective secondary schools.

In this very practical way the forces of education are at work building bridges of understanding between the United States and the new Near East.—*The Christian Science Monitor.*

REPORTS

REPORT OF THE UNITED STATES COMMISSIONER OF EDUCATION

The United States commissioner of education, in his report to the secretary of the interior for the fiscal year ended June 30, 1928, gives a brief outline of important movements in the field of public education during the year under consideration, and presents the following statistics, based on data collected by the Bureau of Education for 1926: In the year 1926 there were 20,984,002 pupils enrolled in public, and 2,143,100 in private elementary schools including kindergartens; 3,786,071 in public, and 346,054 in private secondary schools; 252,907 in public, and 17,209 in private teacher-training institutions; 280,437 in public, and 486,704 in private colleges and universities excluding preparatory students. This made a total of 28,296,484 pupils in such schools in the United States. The total number of teachers employed in all types of schools is 977,291. The total cost of maintaining and operating these schools is reported as $2,744,979,689, and the total value of school property is $8,125,085,472, which amount includes endowments valued at $1,061,589,042.

The total cost of public elementary and high schools in 1903 was $251,457,625; by 1913 this amount had doubled, being $521,546,375; by 1920 it had doubled again, $1,036,151,209, and in 1926 again doubled to $2,026,308,190. This doubling process promises not to continue indefinitely since the increase in expenditures has been slowing down during the past two or three years. The cost per pupil in average daily attendance was $95.17 in 1924, $98.45 in 1925, and $102.05 in 1926. Expenditures per capita of population for these years are $16.25, $17.15 and $17.50.

Although the latest available statistics show a larger increase in the number of pupils enrolled in small high schools than ever before, these increases are as yet not keeping pace with the increases in enrolments in the urban high schools. Either because of inaccessibility or because of the failure of the objectives, materials or methods of instruction now obtaining in these high schools to meet satisfactorily the needs of rural life, these schools are reaching a relatively small proportion of the rural children. Only 25.7 per cent. of the children 15–18 years of age dwelling in rural communities are enrolled in rural high schools; whereas 71.1 per cent. of the children of the same age group in urban communities are found in urban high schools. Thus nearly three times as large a proportion of city children go to high school as rural children. Rural dwellers can not hope to compete advantageously with urban dwellers so long as their educational equipment is so generally inferior.

The junior high school as the immediate unit of centralization, and the senior high school and junior college as a second or third unit are showing growth. The junior high-school reorganization as such has not, however, made the rapid progress in rural communities that the advantages offered by it seemed to promise. Thus far only 12 per cent. of the rural high schools have reorganized upon this basis, whereas 47.2 per cent. of the urban high-school systems have organized on the junior high school plan.

The consolidation movement in rural schools progressed normally during the year. It is estimated that there were more than 3,000,000 children enrolled in approximately 17,000 consolidated schools in the United States during the school year 1927–28. These statistics do not include many rural high schools which transport pupils, and are, therefore, essentially of the consolidated type.

The growth of secondary education, which has been one of the outstanding developments in recent years, continues at almost undiminished rate. At the present time more than one half of the population of high-school age is in actual high-school attendance. The figures for urban as distinct from rural enrolments reveal greater opportunities of high-school attendance offered to city than to rural youth. It is better than an even chance that the city boy of 14–17 is in high school; by contrast the probabilities were seven to one against his father having had opportunities for a high-school education in 1900.

High-school enrolments have more than doubled since 1920. The extension of secondary education to include in its junior high school some of the grades formerly assigned to elementary schools accounts in some measure for this growth. The larger city school systems are expeditiously placing more and more of their pupils into junior high schools, while the smaller systems are less rapidly but quite consistently also adopting the junior high-school organization. In cities of over 10,000 population between 75,000 and 100,000 pupils are being transferred from elementary schools into junior high schools every year.

One of the significant movements in education during the past few years has been the rapid growth of the platoon or work-study-play plan of school organization in the cities of the country. In 1922, only 33 cities had platoon schools, while in 1928 there are 146 cities in 38 states which have one or more of their schools organized upon the plan, or an increase at the rate of 18 cities a year. Recent reports show that there are over 800 platoon schools in these cities.

SOCIETIES AND MEETINGS

THE ASSOCIATION OF COLLEGES AND SECONDARY SCHOOLS OF THE MIDDLE STATES AND MARYLAND

ABOUT five hundred representatives of public and private schools and of colleges and universities attended the forty-second annual convention of the Association of Colleges and Secondary Schools of the Middle States and Maryland, November 30 and December 1 at Atlantic City. The program included two main sessions of the association and the annual dinner on

November 30 and meetings of affiliated associations on the morning of December 1.

"Religion in School and College To-day" was the topic of papers read by Professor Rufus M. Jones, of Haverford College, and Dean Herbert E. Hawkes, of Columbia College, at the opening session. Principal Henry P. Miller, of the Atlantic City high school, gave the address of welcome. A response was made by Head Master Arthur F. Warren, of the Collegiate School, president of the association.

At the afternoon session the general topic was the survey of education in Pennsylvania recently made by the Carnegie Foundation for the Advancement of Teaching in cooperation with the Joint Commission of the Association of Pennsylvania College Presidents and the State Department of Education. Deputy Commissioner James N. Rule, of the state department, reported on the test given last May to forty thousand seniors in Pennsylvania high schools. The results as to scores in the general test of educational achievement taken in May by four thousand four hundred seniors in forty-nine colleges of Pennsylvania were presented by Dr. William S. Learned, of the Carnegie Foundation, and by Dr. Ben D. Wood, of Columbia University.

The business of the session included reports on colleges and schools accepted for the approved lists of the association, submitted respectively by Professor Adam Leroy Jones, of Columbia University, chairman of the Commission on Higher Institutions, and by Professor Arthur J. Jones, of the University of Pennsylvania, chairman of the Commission of Secondary Schools.

Speakers at the dinner, which was attended by more than three hundred, were President William Mather Lewis, of Lafayette College, Dean Helen Taft Manning, of Bryn Mawr College, and Head Master Boyd Edwards, of Mercersburg Academy. Head Master Warren served as toastmaster.

At the round table conference for colleges and school administrators on the morning of December 1, answers to the question, "How can we promote genuine scholarship in college preparation?" were given by Head Master Wilson Farrand, of Newark Academy, Dean Radcliffe Heermance, of Princeton University, and Head Master C. C. Tillinghast, of the Horace Mann School.

Meetings were held of the Association of History Teachers of the Middle States and Maryland, the Association of Modern Language Teachers of the Middle States and Maryland, College Conference on English in the Central Atlantic States, Association of Teachers of Mathematics of the Middle States and Maryland, and Association of Science Teachers of the Middle States and Maryland.

Officers of the association for 1928–29 were elected as follows:

President: Provost Josiah H. Penniman, University of Pennsylvania.

Vice-Presidents: New York—President Murray Bartlett, Hobart College; New Jersey—Superintendent Frank G. Pickell, Montclair, N. J.; Pennsylvania—Head Master H. A. Nomer, Shady Side Academy, Pittsburgh; Maryland—President Paul E. Titsworth, Washington College; Delaware, District of Columbia—Rector James H. Ryan, Catholic University of America.

Secretary: Vice-Provost George Wm. McClelland, University of Pennsylvania.

Treasurer: Principal Stanley R. Yarnall, Germantown Friends' School.

Executive Committee: Head Master Arthur F. Warren, Collegiate School, New York; Dean Mabel Douglass, New Jersey College for Women; District Superintendent John H. Tildsley, New York City Public School System; Head Master Burton P. Fowler, Tower Hill School, Wilmington, Del.

New Members Commission on Higher Institutions (term of three years): Professor Adam Leroy Jones, Columbia University; Dr. Augustus S. Downing, Albany, N. Y.; Head Master Wilson Farrand, Newark Academy; Registrar R. N. Dempster, Johns Hopkins University.

New Members Commission on Secondary Schools (for three years): Assistant Commissioner George M. Wiley, New York State Department of Education; Head Mistress Miriam Bytel, Cathedral School of St. Mary; Principal William A. Wetzel, Trenton High School.

R. W.

EDUCATIONAL RESEARCH AND STATISTICS

WHY "HONOR" ENGINEERING STUDENTS THINK THEY SUCCEED IN COLLEGE[1]

SCHOLASTIC success and failure are subjects of much current educational discussion and investigation. Many schemes have been evolved for the purpose of encouraging the one and preventing the other. At the University of Illinois, a system of honors has been developed by means of which "public official recognition is given to such students as attain a high grade of scholarship." The "honors" group is composed of those "students in the upper 10 per cent. of each class"—freshman, sophomore, junior and senior. It occurred to the writer that it might be well worth while to inquire of such "honor" students as to the reasons they assign for their success. For the purpose of securing this and other information, the honor students enrolled in the college of engineering during the first semester of 1926–27 were asked to meet the writer in group and individual conferences. Forty-eight students responded.

In the personal interview of about twenty-five minutes, the principal question considered was, "Why do you think you have succeeded?" This question was amplified and talked about, notes being made as significant points were brought out. Every effort was made to put the students at ease and also to make them feel that they were contributing to a worth-while investigation. Sometime during the interview, the question was turned around and made less personal by being stated, "Why do you think students fail, or have difficulty in making passing grades?" This served to put a different angle on the matter and usually brought out points not thought of previously. Almost invariably a student regarded as causes of failure characteristics diametrically opposed to those that he conceived to be reasons for his own success. It should be emphasized that the investigator did not approach the interview with any preconceived notions about reasons for success which he imposed upon the students. In fact, he conscientiously limited himself to asking, clarifying and amplifying the question. Table I makes it apparent that without any suggestions before them, most students thought of only a few reasons for success (seldom more than three and usually only one); whereas, with a list of suggestions, each student found that several applied to him.

After twenty-five students had been interviewed, their reasons for success were listed. This list of twenty-two reasons, with one added by the investigator, was presented to each of the remaining twenty-three students after the interview had proceeded as just outlined. Each student was instructed to indicate those reasons that he considered potent in producing his own success and those that he felt had no bearing on his success. In addition, since each student evinced a desire to indicate the two or three reasons that he thought were especially important, these also were marked.

Table I presents a tabulation of the results. This table is of interest, first, because it contains the reasons that a group of markedly successful students in a professional school assign for their scholastic success; second, because of the character of these reasons. Two types of reasons are outstanding: (a) study habits and (b) attitudes toward school work. Furthermore, certain generally recognized malpractices, such as cramming, are given small significance as compared with accepted good practices, such as purposing to get the content of courses and allowing grades to come as a natural consequence.

Careful scrutiny of this list of reasons for success helps to confirm one in the conviction that in a study of the problems of scholastic success and failure it is well worth while to direct the inquiry toward those students who are distinctly successful. Of course students representative of the whole range of success and failure must be studied, but some types of investigation are better suited to certain groups of students than to others. For instance, it is probably much more profitable to ask "honor" students why they succeed than to ask failing students either why they fail or why they do not succeed. It is fairly obvious that "honor" students are likely to have a more favorable attitude and to be able to make a more helpful analysis. Probably, however, the most signifi-

[1] The writer wishes to acknowledge his indebtedness to Professor Walter S. Monroe, director of the Bureau of Educational Research, and Dean Milo S. Ketchum and Assistant Dean H. H. Jordan, of the College of Engineering, for their advice and cooperation.

TABLE I. REASONS ASSIGNED BY FORTY-EIGHT "HONOR" STUDENTS FOR THEIR SUCCESS[2]

Reason	Mention by first 25		Rating by 23 other students: Potent		Especially important		Lacking	
	f	r	f	r	f	r	f	r
1. Interest in engineering and engineering subjects	10	1.5	21	1	3	10	0	2.5
2. Regularity of class attendance—few or no cuts	2	12	20	3	5	5	2	10.5
3. Concentrated effort when studying	7	5	20	3	6	3	0	2.5
4. Close attention to what is done in class	2	12	20	3	4	7.5	0	2.5
5. Punctuality in handing in work	5	7.5	19	5	2	13	1	6.5
6. Good study conditions, including physical conditions, influence of roommates, general atmosphere, and the like	8	3.5	18	6.5	5	5	2	10.5
7. Purposing to get content of courses—grades will come	1	19	18	6.5	1	17.5	0	2.5
8. Regularity of daily preparation, including persistent effort and "hard work"	10	1.5	17	8.5	8	1	1	6.5
9. Thoroughness in all work	5	7.5	17	8.5	4	7.5	2	10.5
10. "Mastery" of the first part of each course	1	19	16	10	3	10	1	6.5
11. Native ability, *i.e.*, intelligence			14	11	7	2	2	10.5
12. Proper evaluation of different phases of courses, giving greater attention and emphasis to the important phases	2	12	12	12	3	10	1	6.5
13. Anticipation of what will be asked on quizzes	1	19	11	13	2	13	3	13.5
14. School work and success in it valued above other phases of college life	2	12	9	15	1	17.5	3	13.5
15. Practical experience closely related to the work in the College of Engineering	6	6	9	15	2	13	8	17.5
16. Always easy to get school work	1	19	9	15	5	5	8	17.5
17. Maturity	1	19	8	17	0	22	9	20
18. Purposing to get high grades	2	12	6	18.5	1	17.5	7	15
19. High-school work had much in common with the work in the College of Engineering	8	3.5	6	18.5	1	17.5	8	17.5
20. Successful cramming	2	12	5	20	0	22	12	23
21. Necessity—can not afford not to get high grades	1	19	4	21	1	17.5	8	17.5
22. Study lessons at first opportunity after being assigned	1	19	3	22.5	1	17.5	10	21
23. Keep ahead of the class in so far as possible	2	12	3	22.5	0	22	11	22

[2] This table should be read as follows: "Interest in engineering and engineering subjects" was mentioned by ten of the first twenty-five "honor" students as a major factor of their scholastic success; twenty-one of the twenty-three students in the second group checked it as a potent factor; three checked it as especially important; and none checked it as lacking. This factor had a rank in each of the four lists of 1.5, 1, 10 and 2.5, respectively. The remainder of the table should be read in similar manner. Attention should be called to the fact that the ranking of items in each of the four respects is on the basis of frequency of mention with reference to significance as factors of scholastic success. Thus, the greater the frequency of mention, the higher the rank in the first three columns; but in the fourth or "lacking" column, the ranks and frequencies bear a reversed relation to each other.

cant feature of such an approach is that it is from a positive rather than from a negative point of view. It results directly in a list of characteristics to be possessed rather than in a list of prohibitions. For a solution of the problems of scholastic failure, the scholastically successful students are worthy of careful study.

M. E. Herriott

Bureau of Educational Research,
University of Illinois